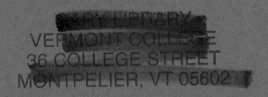

SEVENTH EDITION

The Practice of Social Work:

Applications of Generalist and Advanced Content

SEVENTH EDITION

The Practice of Social Work:

Applications of Generalist and Advanced Content

Charles H. Zastrow
University of Wisconsin—Whitewater

THOMSON
BROOKS/COLE

Australia • Canada • Mexico • Singapore • Spain • United Kingdom • United States

THOMSON
BROOKS/COLE™

Executive Editor: *Lisa Gebo*
Assistant Editor: *Alma Dea Michelena*
Editorial Assistant: *Sheila Walsh*
Marketing Manager: *Caroline Concilla*
Marketing Assistant: *Mary Ho*
Production Coordinator: *Mary Vezilich*
Production Service: *Luana Richards*
Permissions Editor: *Elizabeth Zuber*
Copy Editor: *Luana Richards*
Cover Designer: *Patrick Devine*
Cover Art: *Jose Ortega/SIS*
Compositor: *Thompson Type*
Print Buyer: *Kristine Waller*
Printing & Binding: *Transcontinental—Louiseville*

Printed in Canada
1 2 3 4 5 6 7 06 05 04 03 02

Library of Congress Control Number: 2002106134

ISBN 0-534-60030-1

Brooks/Cole—Thomson Learning
511 Forest Lodge Road
Pacific Grove, CA 93950
USA

Asia
Thomson Learning
5 Shenton Way #01-01
UIC Building
Singapore 068808

Australia
Nelson Thomson Learning
102 Dodds Street
South Melbourne, Victoria 3205
Australia

Canada
Nelson Thomson Learning
1120 Birchmount Road
Toronto, Ontario M1K 5G4
Canada

Europe/Middle East/Africa
Thomson Learning
High Holborn House
50/51 Bedford Row
London WC1R 4LR
United Kingdom

Latin America
Thomson Learning
Seneca, 53
Colonia Polanco
11560 Mexico D.F.
Mexico

Spain
Paraninfo Thomson Learning
Calle/Magallanes, 25
28015 Madrid, Spain

To Kathy
My wife and confidant

CONTRIBUTING AUTHORS

Wallace J. Gingerich, MSW, Ph.D.
Professor, Mandel School of Applied Social Sciences
Case Western Reserve University
Cleveland, OH

Grafton H. Hull, Jr., MSW, Ed.D.
Director and Professor
BSW Program
University of Utah
Salt Lake City, Utah

Karen K. Kirst-Ashman, MSW, Ph.D.
Professor, Social Work Department
University of Wisconsin—Whitewater
Whitewater, WI

Donald Nolan, MSSW, BCD, ICSW
Clinical Social Worker
Regent Mental Health Center
Madison, WI

Heidi J. Pendleton, MSW
Social Worker
Juneau County Department of Human Services
Mauston, WI

Lloyd G. Sinclair, MSSW, ACSW
Certified Sex Educator, Sex Therapist, and
Sex Therapist Supervisor
Midwest Center for Psychotherapy and Sex Therapy
Madison, WI

Carolyn Wells, MSW, Ph.D.
Professor, Social Work Department
University of Wisconsin—Oshkosh
Oshkosh, WI

James P. Winship, MSW, DPA
Associate Professor, Social Work Department
University of Wisconsin—Whitewater
Whitewater, WI

ABOUT THE AUTHOR

Dr. Zastrow is a full professor and former chairman in the Social Work Department at the University of Wisconsin—Whitewater. He received his MSSW degree in 1966 and his Ph.D. in Social Welfare in 1971 from the University of Wisconsin—Madison. He is the author of nine books, of which four are social work textbooks. He has also authored more than 35 articles in professional journals. Dr. Zastrow has been a member of CSWE accreditation site teams visiting 23 colleges and universities; he has chaired 13 of these site visits. He is a member of the Commission on Accreditation of CSWE. Dr. Zastrow is certified as an Independent Clinical Social Worker in the State of Wisconsin. His other social work texts are *Introduction to Social Work and Social Welfare, Social Work with Groups,* and he is co-author of *Understanding Human Behavior and the Social Environment.*

CONTENTS

PART 1 Introduction 1

CHAPTER 1 Overview of Social Work Practice 2

CHAPTER 2 Social Work Values 33

PART 2 Social Work Practice 57

CHAPTER 3 Assessment 58

CHAPTER 4 Social Work with Individuals: Interviewing 82

CHAPTER 5 Social Work with Individuals: Counseling 94

CHAPTER 6 Social Work with Groups: Types of Groups and Guidelines for Leading Them 116

CHAPTER 7 Social Work with Groups: Concepts and Skills 143

CHAPTER 11 *Evaluating Social Work Practice* 253

CHAPTER 12 *Social Work Practice with Diverse Groups* 275

CHAPTER 13 *Spirituality and Religion in Social Work Practice* 309

PART 3
Taking Care of Self 323

CHAPTER 14 *Surviving and Enjoying Social Work* 324

Counseling Theories Resource Manual (CTRM) 351

MODULE 1 Psychoanalysis 353

MODULE 2 Client-Centered Therapy 364

MODULE 3 Transactional Analysis 371

MODULE 4 Behavior Therapy 385

MODULE 8 *Neuro-Linguistic Programming* 454

MODULE 9 *Prominent Specific Treatment Techniques* 464

MODULE 10 *Sex Counseling and Therapy* 491

MODULE 11 *Analysis of Therapy Approaches* 511

PREFACE

The Council on Social Work Education (CSWE) is the national organization in the United States that accreditates baccalaureate and master's degree programs in social work education. In 2001 CSWE adopted EPAS (Educational Policy and Accreditation Standards) for baccalaureate and master's degree programs. A major thrust of *The Practice of Social Work; Applications of Generalist and Advanced Content* is to present material that is consistent with the following mandated content on social work practice in EPAS.

> Social work practice content is anchored in the purposes of the social work profession and focuses on strengths, capacities, and resources of client systems in relation to their broader environments. Students learn practice content that encompasses knowledge and skills to work with individuals, families, groups, organizations, and communities. This content includes engaging clients in an appropriate working relationship, identifying issues, problems, needs, resources, and assets; collecting and assessing information; and planning for service delivery. It includes using communication skills, supervision, and consultation. Practice content also includes identifying, analyzing, and implementing empirically based interventions designed to achieve client goals; applying empirical knowledge and technological advances; evaluating program outcomes and practice effectiveness; developing, analyzing, advocating, and providing leadership for policies and services; and promoting social and economic justice.

Also, consistent with the EPAS requirements, content is presented on social work values and ethics, diversity, and populations-at-risk and the promotion of social and economic justice.

This text provides the theoretical and practical knowledge needed for entry levels of practice in social work. Material is presented covering generalist practice, social work values, confidentiality, principles of interviewing, contemporary theories of counseling, sexual therapy, social work with individuals, social work with groups, social work with families, social work with organizations, social work community practice, assessment, evaluation, general systems theory, cross-cultural social work, working within a bureaucratic system, burnout, and the frustrations and satisfactions of being a social worker. A number of case examples are included to illustrate the theory that is presented.

The Practice of Social Work is designed for use in practice courses in social work at both the undergraduate and graduate levels. Social work practitioners will also find the text valuable as it describes a variety of approaches to social work practice, including sexual treatment techniques, hypnosis, biofeedback, relaxation approaches, mediation, neuro-linguistic programming, milieu therapy, task-centered practice, systematic desensitization, family counseling concepts, feminist intervention, transactional analysis, reality therapy, rational therapy, and behavior therapy. An eclectic approach is used in presenting these diverse types of therapies. After each therapy approach is described, a critical review of the theory is presented to help the reader assess its merits and shortcomings.

This book is unique in that it combines the key components of existing practice texts, both traditional and contemporary, into one text. As much as possible, jargon-free language is used so the reader can more readily grasp the theory. Exercises for students are presented at the end of each chapter to illustrate key concepts and to help students learn how to apply the theoretical material to social work practice.

In this seventh edition material has been added on Educational Policy and Accreditation Standards of CSWE; outcome-based practice; privacy and confidentiality in the era of modern computer technology; computer-assisted assessment forms; three models of community practice (locality development, social planning, and social action); the constructivist approach to family therapy; a focus on assets in working with communities; Internet and online services related to social work practice; working with hostile clients; information about Temporary Assistance for Needy Families; the emerging limited partnership between social work and religion in the provision of social services; revised information on the devolution revolution; and the social worker's ethical and legal responsibilities on the issue of partner notification of a client who tests HIV-positive.

Plan of the Book

Part 1 is an introductory section with two chapters. The first chapter conceptualizes social work practice. It describes what social workers do, explains how social work is distinct from other professions, and summarizes the knowledge, values, and skills needed for beginning-level social work practice. This chapter also describes the goals of social work practice, gives a brief history of social work, indicates that social work is a multiskilled profession, and summarizes professional activities performed by social workers, including casework, case management, group work, group therapy, family counseling, and community organization. Various role models of social work practice are defined, including that of an enabler, broker, advocate, and activist. Generalist practice in social work is also defined and described.

The second chapter summarizes social work values. Values described include self-determination, individualization, confidentiality, belief in the institutional approach for the delivery of services, focus on family, advocacy for those being discriminated against, and accountability.

Part 2 has several chapters that describe generalist social work practice. Social work with individuals, social work with groups, social work with families, social work with organizations, and social work community practice are covered in depth. Techniques for interviewing and counseling clients are given considerable attention. Eight stages of a problem-solving approach to counseling clients are presented. Guidelines are also provided on how to begin and end interviews, how to phrase interview questions, and how to take notes while interviewing. Chapters are also included on assessment, and on evaluating social work practice. Material is summarized on computer applications in social work practice, and on systems analysis. This part covers material on changing the delivery system to serve clients better, cross-cultural social work (for example, white workers and Native American clients), spirituality and social work practice.

Part 3 focuses on taking care of oneself. To be of help to others, social workers must first take care of themselves. Suggestions are presented for resolving common concerns of students receiving professional training in social work. Techniques to manage stress and prevent burnout are described. Safety guidelines for social workers are described. This part concludes with a discussion of the importance for social workers (as well as other people) of developing a positive identity and provides guidelines on how to develop a positive sense of self.

The final part of the book is a Counseling Theories Resource Manual (CTRM). To highlight the uniqueness of the CTRM, material is presented in modules, rather than chapters. This CTRM presents and critiques the prominent theories of counseling that are widely used by social workers, including: client-centered therapy, feminist intervention, reality therapy, rational therapy, behavior therapy, psychoanalysis, transactional analysis, neuro-linguistic programming, and sex counseling and sex therapy. Specific treatment techniques are also described, including assertiveness training, token economies, systematic desensitization, aversive techniques, milieu therapy, psychodrama, crisis intervention, parent effectiveness training, mediation, muscle relaxation approaches, deep-breathing relaxation, imagery relaxation, meditation, hypnosis, biofeedback task-centered practice, and solution-focused therapy. The final module is devoted to an analysis and comparison of prominent theories of counseling.

One of the reviewers of this text remarked that this book is an "encyclopedia of social work interventions." The comprehensiveness of the text perhaps approaches that of an encyclopedia; however, it is not necessary for the instructor to cover all the theories of intervention presented in this text. Rather, it is suggested that he or she (with the consultation of other faculty in the program) decide which of the intervention theories described in the CTRM are most important for students to learn to best serve clients in the school's geographic area.

Counseling as a Component of Generalist Practice

A small minority of social work educators assert that counseling is not a component of generalist social work practice. This author strongly asserts that counseling is a key component of generalist practice. A generalist practitioner uses the problem-solving approach to bring about positive changes when working with individuals, families, groups, organizations, and communities. Much of social work practice with individuals, treatment groups, and families requires the social worker to utilize counseling principles and theories extensively. Competence in counseling is as essential for generalist-practice social workers to have as are competencies in other areas (such as brokering, policy making, lobbying, and planning). The vast majority of baccalaureate degree and master's degree social workers are engaged primarily in providing direct services to individuals, treatment groups, and families—with the provision of counseling services being a major component of the direct services provided.

When a social worker identifies himself or herself as being a clinical social worker or a psychotherapist, it does not mean that the person is uninvolved in other areas of generalist practice. In fact, every clinical social worker (at times) works with changing organizations and communities to benefit clients.

Because counseling is a key component of generalist social work practice, this text has a unique Counseling Theories Resource Manual, which presents contemporary theories of counseling that are useful in working with individuals, treatment groups, and families.

From one point of view, the first 14 chapters of this text (Parts I, II, and III) focus on generalist practice, while the CTRM focuses exclusively on counseling. However, the reader will note that in describing social work practice with individuals, families, and groups it is essential to discuss aspects of counseling. In fact, most of the "generalist chapters" (the first 14 chapters) describe some aspects of counseling, as the following indicates.

Chapter 1 (Overview of Social Work Practice) links the social work goal "Enhance people's problem solving, coping, and developmental capacities" with counseling. It also describes how counseling is an integral component of "social casework," "group therapy," and "family therapy."

Chapter 2 (Social Work Values) describes a number of values that relate to counseling—such as confidentiality, privileged communication, whether to inform partners of clients in counseling that a client is HIV-positive, and establishing professional boundaries with clients.

Chapter 3 (Assessment) discusses strategies and approaches to assessing the issues of clients in counseling, and has counseling case examples.

Chapter 4 (Social Work with Individuals: Interviewing) focuses on interviewing, which is directly related to counseling.

Chapter 5 (Social Work with Individuals: Counseling) focuses exclusively on counseling.

Chapter 6 (Social Work with Groups: Types of Groups and Guidelines for Leading Them) has considerable content on therapy groups.

Chapter 7 (Social Work with Groups: Concepts and Skills) has several pages on "starting, leading, and ending therapy groups."

Chapter 8 (Social Work with Families) describes family therapy, and has a lengthy family therapy case example.

Chapter 9 (Social Work with Organizations) examines various models of organizational behavior and gives guidelines for surviving in a bureaucracy.

Chapter 10 (Social Work Community Practice) describes three models of community practice and key knowledge that makes one's work with the community more effective.

Chapter 11 (Evaluating Social Work Practice) primarily focuses on describing evaluation approaches to assess the effectiveness of counseling and other direct practice services. It also has content on counseling services provided on the Internet.

Chapter 12 (Social Work Practice with Diverse Groups) has considerable content on cultural competence for social workers who provide ethnic sensitive services to clients who receive counseling and other services.

Chapter 13 (Spirituality in Social Work Practice) describes the importance of assessing the religious and spiritual aspects of clients, including clients receiving counseling. Also described are religious and spiritual interventions with clients receiving counseling.

Chapter 14 (Surviving and Enjoying Social Work) has content on common concerns of social work students who are preparing to provide services to clients, including clients receiving counseling.

Acknowledgments

I wish to express my deep appreciation to the following people who made this book possible: the contributing authors; and Vicki Vogel, Ralph Navarre, and Diane Sonsthagen, who assisted in conceptualizing various chapters and helped in a number of ways with the writing of this text. My thanks also go to the reviewers of this edition: Mary Yu Danico, California State University, Pomona; Robin Lake, Austin Community College; Ester Langston, University of Nevada—Las Vegas; Evelyn Mercer, Southwest Baptist University; and Loretta Rivers, New Orleans Baptist Theological Seminary.

I especially want to thank Lisa Gebo (Social Work Editor at Brooks/Cole), who helped substantially in conceptualizing this revision and who is a pleasure to work with. I also wish to thank the copy editor, Luana Richards, for her creativity and dedication. A final thank you to the staff at Brooks/Cole for their support and highly professional assistance with the texts I have authored.

Charles H. Zastrow

PART 1

Introduction

CHAPTER 1

Overview of Social Work Practice

The Practice of Social Work, Seventh Edition, is intended for use in social work practice courses. The focus of this book is on the theoretical and practical knowledge students need to perform the tasks of workers in entry-level positions that require either a bachelor's (B.S.W.) or master's (M.S.W.) degree in social work. This book is designed to be read by students preparing for, or already in, field placement.

The Purpose of This Chapter

What do social workers do? How is social work different from psychology, psychiatry, guidance and counseling, and other helping professions? What is the relationship between social work and social welfare? What knowledge, skills, and values do social workers need to be effective? Hundreds of intervention techniques are available, but which ones should social workers learn? This chapter will address these questions. A number of other efforts have addressed these same issues. (See Baer & Federico, 1978; Bartless, 1970; "Conceptual Frameworks II," 1981; Council on Social Work Education, 1982, 1992a, 1992b, 2001; Germain & Gitterman, 1980; Loewenberg & Dolgoff, 1971; National Association of Social Workers, 1973, 1976, 1981, 1982; Pincus & Minahan, 1973; "Special Issue on Conceptual Frameworks," 1977.) This chapter is largely an effort to integrate these prior conceptualizations and to describe social work as a profession, thereby assisting social workers and other interested persons in understanding and articulating what social work is and what is unique about the social work profession. We will begin with a brief look at the history of social work.

The History of Social Work

Social work as a profession is of relatively recent origin. The first social welfare agencies appeared in urban areas in the early 1800s. These agencies, or services, were private and were developed primarily at the initiation of the clergy and religious groups. Until the early 1900s, these services were provided exclusively by the clergy and affluent "do-gooders" who had no formal training and little understanding of human behavior or of how to help people. The focus of these private services was on meeting such basic physical needs as food and shelter and on attempting to cure emotional and personal difficulties with religious admonitions.

An illustration of an early social welfare organization was the Society for the Prevention of Pauperism, founded by John Griscom in 1820 (Bemner, 1962, p. 13). This society investigated the habits and circumstances of the poor, suggested plans by which the poor could help themselves, and encouraged the poor to save and economize. One of the remedies used was house-to-house visitation (a very elementary type of social work).

By the latter half of the 1800s, a fairly large number of private relief agencies had been established in large cities to help the unemployed, the poor, the ill, persons with physical or mental disabilities, and orphans. Their programs were uncoordinated and sometimes overlapping, and so an English invention—the Charity Organization Society (COS)—soon caught the interest of a number of American cities (Cohen, 1958). Starting in Buffalo, New York, in 1877, COS was rapidly adopted in many cities. In charity organization societies, private agencies joined together (1) to provide direct services to individuals and families—in this respect, they were the forerunners of social casework and of family counseling approaches—and (2) to plan and coordinate the efforts of private agencies to meet pressing urban social problems—in this respect, they were the precursors of community organization and social planning approaches. Charity organizations conducted a detailed investigation of each applicant for services and financial help, maintained a central client registration system to avoid duplication, and used volunteer *friendly visitors* extensively to work with those in difficulty. The friendly visitors were primarily "doers of good works," as they generally gave sympathy rather than money and encouraged the poor to save and to seek employment. Poverty was viewed as a personal shortcoming. Most of the friendly visitors were women.

Concurrent with the COS movement was the establishment of settlement houses in the late 1800s. Toynbee Hall was the first settlement house, established in 1884 in London; many others were soon formed in larger U.S. cities. Many of the early settlement house workers were the daughters of ministers. The workers, who were from the middle and upper classes, would live in a poor neighborhood to experience the harsh realities of poverty. Simultaneously, in cooperation with neighborhood residents, they sought to develop ways to improve living conditions. In contrast to friendly visitors, they lived in impoverished neighborhoods and used the missionary approach of teaching residents how to live moral lives and improve their circumstances. They sought to improve housing, health, and living conditions; find jobs; teach English, hygiene, and occupational skills; and change environmental surroundings through cooperative efforts. Settlement houses used change techniques that are now called social group work, social action, and community organization.

Settlement houses emphasized "environmental reform" while "they continued to struggle to teach the poor the prevailing middle-class values of work, thrift, and abstinence as the keys to success" (Becker, 1968, p. 85). In addition to dealing with local problems by local action, settlement houses played important roles in drafting legislation and in organizing to influence social policy and legislation. The most noted leader in the settlement house movement was Jane Addams of Hull House in Chicago, who summarized settlement houses as follows:

> The Settlement, then, is an experimental effort to aid in the solution of the social and industrial problems which are engendered by the modern conditions of life in a great city. (Addams, 1959, pp. 125–126)

Settlement house leaders believed that by changing neighborhoods they would improve communities, and through altering communities they would develop a better society.

The first paid social workers were executive secretaries of charity organization societies in the late 1800s (Dolgoff & Feldstein, 1980, pp. 233–234). In the late 1800s charity organization societies received some contracts from the cities in which they were located to administer relief funds. In administering these programs, COS hired people as executive secretaries to organize and train the friendly visitors and to establish accounting procedures to show accountability for the funds received. To improve the services of friendly visitors, the executive secretaries established standards and training courses. In 1898 a training course was first offered by the New York Charity Organization Society. By 1904 the New York School of Philanthropy offered a one-year program. Soon after, colleges and universities began offering training programs in social work. Initially, social work education focused on environmental reform approaches to meet social problems. (Such approaches focus on changing the system to better meet people's needs. The enactment in 1935 of the Social Security

Act to meet the needs of the poor and the unemployed is an example of an environmental reform approach.)

Richard Cabot introduced medical social work into Massachusetts General Hospital in 1905 (Dolgoff & Feldstein, 1980, pp. 233–234). Gradually, social workers were employed in schools, courts, child guidance clinics, and other settings.

In 1917 Mary Richmond published *Social Diagnosis,* a text that presented for the first time a theory and methodology for social work. The book focused on how the worker should intervene with individuals. The process is still used today and involves study (collecting information), diagnosis (stating what is wrong), prognosis, and treatment planning (stating what should be done to help clients improve). This book was important as it formulated a common body of knowledge for casework.

In the 1920s Freud's theories of personality development and therapy became popular. The concepts and explanations of psychiatrists appeared particularly appropriate for social workers, who also worked in one-to-one relationships with clients. The psychiatric approach emphasized intrapsychic processes and focused on enabling clients to adapt and adjust to their social situations. For the next three decades, social workers switched their emphasis from reform to therapy. In the 1960s, however, social workers expressed a renewed interest in sociological approaches, or reform. Several reasons account for this change. Questions arose about the relevance and appropriateness of talking approaches with low-income clients who have urgent social and economic pressures. Furthermore, the effectiveness of many psychotherapeutic approaches was questioned (Eysenck, 1961). Other reasons for the renewed interest included the increase in status of sociology and the mood of the 1960s, which raised questions about the relevancy of social institutions in meeting the needs of the population. Social work at the present time embraces both reform and therapy approaches.[1]

Not until the end of World War I did social work begin to be recognized as a distinct profession. The Depression of the 1930s and enactment of the Social Security Act in 1935 brought about an extensive expansion of public social services and job opportunities for social workers. Since 1900 there has been a growing awareness by social agency boards and the public that professionally trained social workers are needed to provide social services competently. In 1955 the National Association of Social Workers was formed to represent the social work profession in this country. Its purpose is to improve social conditions and to promote high quality and effective social work practice.

In recent years considerable energy has been expended to develop a system of registration or licensing of social workers. Such a system helps assure the public that qualified personnel are providing social work services and also advances the recognition of social work as a profession. All states now have passed legislation to license or certify the practice of social work.

Social work is one of the most important professions in our society in terms of the number of people affected, the human misery treated, and the amount of money spent.

A Definition of Social Work

The National Association of Social Workers (NASW) has defined social work as follows:

> Social work is the professional activity of helping individuals, groups, or communities to enhance or restore their capacity for social functioning and to create societal conditions favorable to their goals.
>
> Social work practice consists of the professional application of social work values, principles, and techniques to one or more of the following ends: helping people obtain tangible services; providing counseling and psychotherapy for individuals, families, and groups; helping communities or groups provide or improve social and health services; and participating in relevant legislative processes.
>
> The practice of social work requires knowledge of human development and behavior; of social, economic, and cultural institutions; and of the interaction of all these factors. (Barker, 1999, p. 455)

The term *social worker* is generally applied to graduates of educational programs (either with bachelor's or master's degrees) in social work who are employed in the field of social welfare. A social worker is a *change agent,* a helper who is specifically employed for the purpose of creating planned change (Pincus & Minahan, 1973, p. 54). As a change agent a social worker is expected to be skilled at working with individuals, groups, families, and organizations, and in bringing about community changes. Barker (1999) adds:

> Social workers help people increase their capacities for problem solving and coping, and they help them obtain needed resources, facilitate interactions between indi-

[1]The author believes there is little difference between the terms *psychotherapy* and *counseling* (for emotional and behavioral problems); therefore, these terms will be used interchangeably in this text.

> viduals and between people and their environments, make organizations responsible to people, and influence social policies. (p. 456)

The Relationship Between Social Work and Social Welfare

The goal of social welfare is to fulfill the social, financial, health, and recreational requirements of all individuals in a society. Social welfare seeks to enhance the social functioning of all age groups, both rich and poor. When other institutions in our society (such as the market economy and the family) fail at times to meet the basic needs of individuals or groups of people, social services are needed and demanded. Barker (1999) defined social welfare as follows:

> A nation's system of programs, benefits, and services that help people meet those social, economic, educational, and health needs that are fundamental to the maintenance of society. (p. 455)

Examples of social welfare programs and services are foster care, adoption, day care, Head Start, probation and parole, public assistance programs, public health nursing, sex therapy, suicide counseling, recreational services (Boy Scouts and YWCA programs), services to minority groups and veterans, school social services, medical and legal services to the poor, family planning services, Meals on Wheels, nursing home services, shelters for battered spouses, services to persons with acquired immune deficiency syndrome (AIDS), protective services for victims of child abuse and neglect, assertiveness training, public housing projects, family counseling, Alcoholics Anonymous, runaway services, services to people with developmental disabilities, and rehabilitation services.

Almost all social workers are employed in the social welfare field. There are, however, many other professional and occupational groups working in the field, as illustrated in Figure 1.1.

What Is the Profession of Social Work?

The National Association of Social Workers defines the social work profession as follows:

> The social work profession exists to provide humane and effective social services to individuals, families, groups, communities, and society so that social functioning may be enhanced and the quality of life improved. . . .
>
> The profession of social work, by both traditional and practical definition, is the profession that provides the formal knowledge base, theoretical concepts, specific functional skills, and essential social values which are used to implement society's mandate to provide safe, effective, and constructive social services.[2]

Social work is thus distinct from other professions (such as psychology and psychiatry) because it has the responsibility and mandate to provide social services.

A social worker needs training and expertise in a wide range of areas to effectively handle problems faced by individuals, groups, families, organizations, and the larger community. Although most professions are increasingly becoming more specialized (for example, most medical doctors now specialize in one or two areas), social work continues to emphasize a generic (broad-based) approach. The practice of social work is analogous to the old general practice of medicine. A general (or family) practitioner has professional education to handle a wide range of common medical problems; a social worker has professional education to handle a wide range of common social and personal problems. The case example involving a rape on page 8 highlights some of the skills needed by social workers.

Generalist Social Work Practice

There used to be an erroneous belief that a social worker was either a caseworker, a group worker, or a community organizer. Practicing social workers know that such a belief is faulty because every social worker is a change agent working with individuals, groups, families, organizations, and the larger community. The amount of time spent at these levels varies from worker to worker, but every worker will, at times, work at each of these levels and therefore needs training in all of them.

The Council on Social Work Education (the national accrediting entity for baccalaureate and master's programs in social work) requires that all bachelor's and master's level programs train their students in generalist

[2]Published 1982, National Association of Social Workers, Inc. Reprinted with permission, from *Standards for the Classification of Social Work Practice,* Policy Statement 4, p. 5. Copyright National Association of Social Workers, Inc.

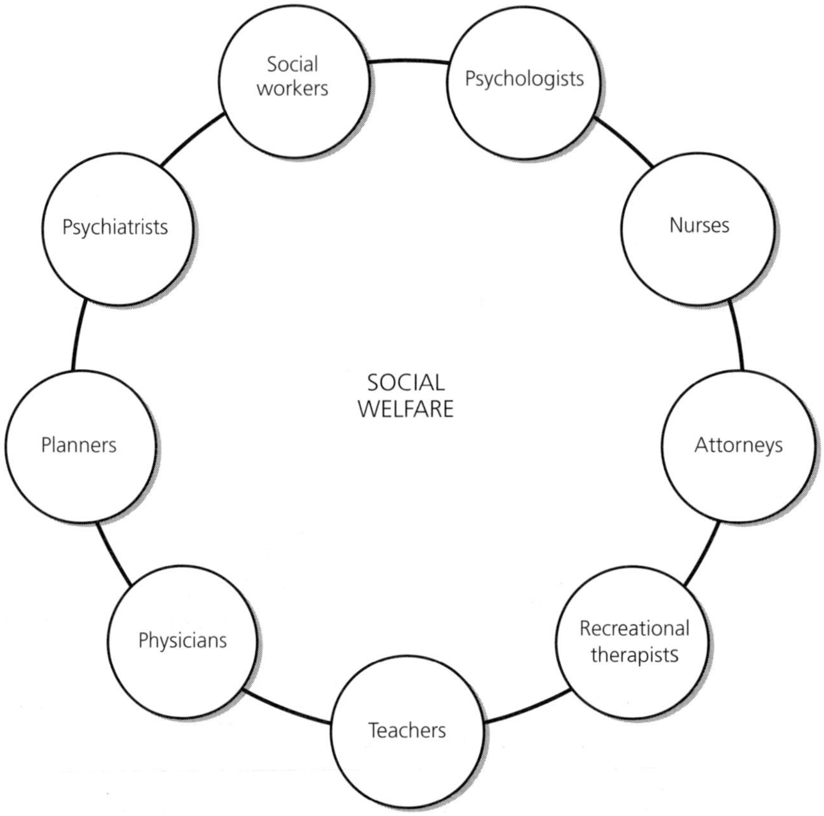

FIGURE 1.1 Examples of professional groups within the field of social welfare include attorneys providing legal services to the poor; urban planners in social planning agencies; physicians in public health agencies; teachers in residential treatment facilities for the emotionally disturbed; psychologists, nurses, and recreational therapists in mental hospitals; and psychiatrists in mental health clinics.

social work practice. (M.S.W. programs, in addition, usually require their students to select and study in an area of concentration. They generally offer several choices, such as family therapy, administration, corrections, or clinical social work.)

A generalist social worker is trained to use the problem-solving process to assess and intervene in the problems confronting individuals, families, groups, organizations, and communities. Anderson (1981) identified three characteristics of a generalist social worker: (1) the generalist is often the first professional to see clients as they enter the social welfare system; (2) the worker must therefore be competent to assess their needs and to identify their stress points and problems; and (3) the worker must draw on a variety of skills and methods in serving clients.

Brieland, Costin, and Atherton (1985) defined and described generalist practice as follows:

> The generalist social worker, the equivalent of the general practitioner in medicine, is characterized by a wide repertoire of skills to deal with basic conditions, backed up by specialists to whom referrals are made. This role is a fitting one for the entry-level social worker.
>
> The generalist model involves identifying and analyzing the interventive behaviors appropriate to social work. The worker must perform a wide range of tasks related to the provision and management of direct service, the development of social policy, and the facilitation of social change. The generalist should be well grounded in systems theory that emphasizes interaction and independence. The major system that will be used is the local network of services. . . .

The public welfare worker in a small county may be a classic example of the generalist. He or she knows the resources of the county, is acquainted with the key people, and may have considerable influence to accomplish service goals, including obtaining jobs, different housing, or emergency food and clothing. The activities of the urban generalist are more complex, and more effort must be expended to use the array of resources. (pp. 120–121)

Hull (1990) defined generalist practice as follows:

The basic principle of generalist practice is that baccalaureate social workers are able to utilize the problem solving process to intervene with various size systems including individuals, families, groups, organizations, and communities. The generalist operates within a systems and person-in-the-environment framework (sometimes referred to as an ecological model). The generalist expects that many problems will require intervention with more than one system (e.g., individual work with [a] delinquent adolescent plus work with the family or school) and that single explanations of problem situations are frequently unhelpful. The generalist may play several roles simultaneously or sequentially depending upon the needs of the client (e.g., facilitator, advocate, educator, broker, enabler, case manager, and/or mediator). They may serve as leaders/facilitators of task groups, socialization groups, information groups, and self-help groups. They are capable of conducting needs assessments and evaluating their own practice and the programs with which they are associated. They make referrals when client problems so dictate and know when to utilize supervision from more experienced staff. Generalists operate within the ethical guidelines prescribed by the NASW Code of Ethics and must be able to work with clients, co-workers and colleagues from different ethnic, cultural, and professional orientations. The knowledge and skills of the generalist are transferable from one setting to another and from one problem to another. (p. 7)

The crux of generalist practice involves a view of the situation in terms of the person-in-environment conceptualization (described in an upcoming section of this chapter) and the capacity and willingness to intervene at several different levels, if necessary, while assuming any number of roles. The case example on page 10 illustrates how social workers respond at several different levels in a variety of roles.

Barker (1999) defines a generalist social worker as:

A social work practitioner whose knowledge and skills encompass a broad spectrum and who assesses problems and their solutions comprehensively. The generalist often coordinates the efforts of specialists by facilitating communication between them, thereby fostering *continuity of care*. (p. 190)

This text teaches the generalist-practice approach in social work by describing a variety of assessment and intervention strategies. Once you have learned these strategies, you can then select those approaches that hold the most promise in facilitating positive changes in clients.

In working with individuals, families, groups, organizations, and communities, social workers use a problem-solving approach. The problem-solving process can be described in a variety of ways but would include these steps:

1. Identify as precisely as possible the problem or problems.
2. Generate possible alternative solutions.
3. Evaluate the alternative solutions.
4. Select a solution or solutions to be used and set goals.
5. Implement the solution.
6. Follow up to evaluate how the solution worked.

Another conceptualization of the problem-solving approach is the change process of social work practice, which is described next.

The Change Process

A social worker uses a *change process* in working with clients. (Clients include individuals, groups, families, organizations, and communities.) The Council on Social Work Education (2001) in EPAS (Educational Policy and Accreditation Standards) identifies ten skills that are needed for social work practice:

1. Engaging clients in an appropriate working relationship.
2. Identifying issues, problems, needs, resources, and assets.
3. Collecting and assessing information.
4. Planning for service delivery.
5. Using communication skills, supervision, and consultation.
6. Identifying, analyzing, and implementing empirically based interventions designed to achieve client goals.
7. Applying empirical knowledge and technological advances.
8. Evaluating program outcomes and practice effectiveness.

CASE EXAMPLE

Rape

Dr. Richard Carr referred Kay Barber to Lakeside Counseling Center (a mental health center). Kay is 17 years old and a senior at West High School. The previous evening she had been raped by four males in a parking lot near West High. The rape had occurred after Kay left a school dance, about 1:00 A.M. The intake worker assigned the case to Karen Bowman, a social worker who had in the recent past counseled most of the agency's sexual assault cases. Ms. Bowman immediately met with Kay.

In tears, badly bruised, and still shaking from terror, Kay was angry, confused, and deeply hurt emotionally. In the next 50 minutes, she briefly described the details of the assault and some of her feelings. She was getting into her dad's car, alone, when she was grabbed by two youths and pulled into some bushes. Behind the bushes were two other youths, one of whom she recognized as the son of a college professor in the community. Following the assault, the youths warned her there would be serious trouble if she informed anyone. Hurt (emotionally and physically) and terrified, she returned home. Her mother was awake when she returned and immediately recognized that something had happened. Kay informed her parents. Kay's mother was horrified and angry but attempted to comfort Kay. Kay indicated that her father was even more upset, and even today was talking about shooting the rapists if he could find out who they were. (Kay had not as yet informed him that she knew one of the attackers for fear of what her father might do.)

Kay indicated that on hearing of the assault her parents took her to the police station. There she was questioned by two male police officers. Kay indicated that she revealed only sketchy details of the rape to the police officers as she was in tears, still terrified, and on the defensive because she felt many of the officers' questions suggested she contributed to the rape. She also felt that the officers did not believe she was assaulted.

Earlier this morning her parents took her to the family doctor, Richard Carr, who provided medical attention and then referred the case to the counseling center.

Kay was especially confused about a number of issues. Should she inform the police that she knows one of the youths who assaulted her? If she reveals his identity, would she have to appear in court? If she appears in court, what effect might this have on her reputation? If she doesn't inform the police of the identity of one of her assailants, might not these youths rape others, or perhaps even her again, in the future? In either case, how would she face the other students in school who she felt would hear, one way or the other, about the attack? Why did the police officers doubt her story about being raped, and why did the officers imply she may have contributed to the assault? What were her chances of getting pregnant? If she were pregnant, what would she do then? (Ms. Bowman indicated that the medical services she received might well have prevented her from now being pregnant—and this could be checked with Dr. Carr.) Should she inform her father that she knew one of the assailants? If she did, what might be the consequences? How could she ever learn to deal with the terror she experienced? She also indicated that she felt she would never go out in the evening, alone or with anyone else, in the future, unless she went with a member of her family. And, she wondered why this had to happen to her.

Ms. Bowman listened attentively and conveyed warmth, empathy, support, and a sincere sense of caring. After Kay had ventilated her concerns, Ms. Bowman expressed her understanding that Kay had been deeply hurt and was now feeling overwhelmed by this situation. Ms. Bowman gradually informed Kay that something could be done about all of her present concerns. The way to proceed would be to take her concerns, one by one, and work on resolving them. Ms. Bowman asked Kay to indicate her most urgent concerns. Kay thought awhile and said they were whether to inform her parents that she knew one of the attackers and how to react to schoolmates who might make cruel remarks related to the rape.

Kay was then asked to elaborate her concerns in each of these two areas. Her concerns about telling her parents centered around what her father might do. With regard to cruel remarks from others, Ms. Bowman suggested to Kay that they role-play how she might respond to such remarks. Ms. Bowman first played Kay's role to model a few assertive strategies to respond to cruel remarks. The roles were then reversed, with Ms. Bowman role-playing someone giving a crude remark, and Kay practicing responding to it.

After this initial hour and 40-minute meeting, Kay became a little more relaxed. Kay mentioned that she was really worried about what her father might do. Ms. Bowman suggested that her parents (who were in the waiting room) might be brought in to discuss their concerns. Kay agreed. A rather lengthy meeting was then held with the Barbers. They began by ventilating a great deal of anger, wanting to find out who did this. Mr. Barber indicated he was going to shoot whoever did this. Ms. Bowman mentioned that Kay was partially upset, now, by what her father might do if he found out, and she asked Mr. Barber if he was aware of this. Following a lengthy discussion of the negative consequences of taking the law into one's own hands, Mr. Barber cried and acknowledged that he would not carry out his threats and that he was only making the threats because he felt so helpless. After Mr. Barber gave full assurance that he would not do anything illegal, he was informed that Kay thought she knew one of the attackers. Another meeting was arranged with the Barbers for the next day to talk further about their concerns. Time was also set aside for Kay and Ms. Bowman to meet the next day to continue to discuss her concerns.

As indicated earlier, this case was only one of several sexual assault cases that Ms. Bowman was handling. These cases led her to conclude that the area she was living in (320,000 population) needed a well-publicized rape crisis center. She began by gathering data on the incidence of sexual assault in the community—from the police department (many cases go unreported) and from other social service agencies in the community. She then convinced the director of the counseling center to form a committee of representatives from other interested social service agencies in the community and from certain women's organizations in the community. After formation of the committee (of which Ms. Bowman was a member), a questionnaire to obtain further information on the incidence of sexual assault was constructed. Committee members distributed the questionnaire to women shoppers at a large shopping center (respondents in this way remained entirely anonymous). The results suggested less than one rape in ten was being reported to the police, which further documented the need for a rape crisis center that would be well publicized so that victims would know where help was available. Another proposed service of the center would be to provide speakers to schools and other organizations on how to avoid becoming a victim and on what to do if an assault occurred. The center would also work with the police department and the court system to "humanize" the reporting and processing of sexual assault cases. The committee then wrote a grant proposal. After 11 months of searching for funding, the proposal was funded for a three-year test period by the city and the United Way. Because of her capacities in this area, Karen Bowman was appointed assistant director of this rape crisis center.

Counseling Skills at Work in Generalist Practice

This case illustration documents the wide range of generalist practice skills displayed by Ms. Bowman: interviewing skills, ability to effectively counsel individuals with families during a crisis, ability to work effectively with other agencies, research and grant-writing skills, public speaking capacities, program development and fund-raising skills, and knowledge of how to handle ethical/legal issues that arise.

Perhaps the most basic skill a social worker needs is to be able to counsel clients effectively. If an individual is not able to do this, he or she should probably not be in social work, certainly not in direct service. Another key skill is to be able to interact effectively with other groups and professionals in the area. Social workers need to learn a wide range of skills and intervention techniques that will enable them to intervene effectively with (1) the client's common personal and emotional problems and (2) the common social problems faced by groups, organizations, and the larger community.

CASE EXAMPLE

Generalist Practice Involves Options Planning

Jack Dawson is a social worker at a high school in a midwestern state. Four teenagers have been expelled (consistent with school board policy) for drinking alcoholic beverages at the school during school hours. Mr. Dawson assesses the situation and identifies the following potential courses of action. He can serve as an advocate for the youths by urging the school board and the administration to reinstate the youths. Mr. Dawson is aware that the expulsions are upsetting not only to the youths and their parents but also to the police department and the business community (because expelled youths tend to spend the day on city streets). He can involve the four teenagers in one-to-one counseling about their expulsion and their drinking patterns. He can involve these youths (along with others having drinking problems) in group counseling at the school. He can function as a broker to have the youths receive individual or group counseling from a counseling center outside the school system. He can ascertain the willingness of the parents to become involved in family therapy and serve as a broker to link the interested families with a counseling center that offers family therapy. He can raise the issue (to parents, to the business community, to the police department, to the school administration, and to the school board) of whether expulsion from school for drinking alcoholic beverages is a desirable policy. (Perhaps a better school system policy, in cases like this, is to place the youths on "in-school suspension," where they are required to stay in a study room for a few days.) Expulsion is a drastic measure that may adversely affect the futures of these youths. Mr. Dawson can serve as an organizer and a catalyst to encourage interested parents and school staff to use the incident as a rationale for incorporating educational material on alcohol and other drugs into the curriculum. (The selected courses of action will depend on a variety of factors, including a cost-benefit analysis of each course.)

9. Developing, analyzing, advocating, and providing leadership for policies and services.
10. Promoting social and economic justice.

The first eight of these skills, interestingly, provide an excellent framework for conceptualizing the change process in social work.

Phase 1: Engaging Clients in an Appropriate Working Relationship

Let's examine the change process in the case example entitled "Generalist Practice Involves Options Planning." Recall that four teenagers were expelled for drinking beer at school during school hours. The first step in the change process is to identify all potential clients. The second step is to engage them in an appropriate relationship.

In this case example, there are a number of "potential clients." Clients are the people who sanction or ask for the worker's services, those who are the expected beneficiaries of the service, and those who have a working agreement or contract with the worker. Using this definition, the four teenagers who were expelled from school (and their parents) are potential clients as they are the expected beneficiaries of the services. The high school is a client as it has a contractual agreement with the worker, Mr. Dawson. (The high school is also a client here because it asks Mr. Dawson for assistance with this situation.) The other students in the school (and their parents) are also potential clients as they are expected beneficiaries of his services.

In order to be effective, it is essential that a worker seek to form appropriate, professional relationships with all potential clients. A working relationship is facilitated when the worker reflects empathy, warmth, and sincerity. (Chapter 5 contains additional information on forming and maintaining professional relationships with clients.)

Phase 2: Identifying Issues, Problems, Needs, Resources, and Assets

The first step in phase 2 is to identify issues, problems, and needs. Only then can the available resources and assets be determined.

The school social worker, Jack Dawson, identifies a variety of issues (questions/concerns/problems), including the following: Do the youths have a drinking problem? Were the youths, disenchanted with the school system, displaying their discontent by breaking school rules? What short-term and long-term adverse effects may the expulsions have on the youths? Will the expulsions have an adverse effect by marking these youths as "trouble makers," and thereby leading them into further delinquent behavior? How will the parents of these youths react to the drinking and to the expulsions? What effects will the expulsions have on other students at the school? (A possible positive effect: The expulsions may be a deterrent to other students who consider violating school rules. A possible negative consequence: The expulsions may encourage other students to violate school rules in order to be expelled and relieved of the obligation to attend school.) Will the expulsions create problems for merchants in the community if the expelled youths spend their days on the street? Is the school policy of expelling youths for drinking on school grounds constructive or destructive? Does the school system have a responsibility to add a drug-education component to the curriculum? Do certain aspects of the school system encourage youths to rebel? If so, should these aspects be changed?

Based on the initial identification of issues, problems, and needs, the social worker must then determine what resources and assets are available to confront the situation. This comprehensive list will serve as a guide during the next phase (collecting and assessing information). (The Pincus-Minahan systems approach described in Chapter 3 is a good framework to use here.)

Mr. Dawson is aware that the high school has a number of resources and assets to confront these issues. A number of professionals (teachers, psychologists, other social workers, nurses, and guidance counselors) are available to provide services, including assistance in developing and implementing new programs to address the identified problems, needs, and issues. If need be, the school has funds to hire one or more consultants who are experts in alcohol and drug issues. The school also has an established bureaucracy (including a school board) that has procedures and policies for establishing new programs. State and federal grant money may be available for initiating drug prevention programs.

Phase 3: Collecting and Assessing Information

In this phase an in-depth collection and analysis of data are undertaken to provide the social worker with answers to the issues and problems raised in Phase 1. On some of the issues, useful information can be obtained directly from the clients (including the youths in this example). Thus, the question of whether the youths have a drinking problem can be answered by meeting with them individually, forming a trusting relationship, and then inquiring how often the youth drinks, how much the youth consumes when drinking, and what problems the youth has encountered while drinking. For the remaining issues raised in Phase 1, information must be collected from other sources. For example, the issue of short- and long-term adverse effects of the expulsion on the youths may be answered by researching the literature on this topic.

Assessment is the process of analyzing the data to make sense of it. The processes of collecting data and arriving at valid assessments are described in Chapter 3.

Phase 4: Planning for Service Delivery

After information is collected and assessed, Mr. Dawson and other decision makers in the school system need to decide whether the school system should provide services in this situation. (Often such a decision involves an assessment as to whether the prospective clients meet the eligibility requirements of the agency.) The decision to provide services in this case is easy to make, as the school system has an obligation to provide services to all enrolled students. The next decision—which services to provide—is dealt with in phases 5–7.

Phase 5: Using Communication Skills, Supervision, and Consultation

Effectiveness as a social worker is highly dependent on the worker's communication skills—both oral and writing skills. (Many agency directors assert that writing skills are as important as interviewing and counseling skills—as workers need to document assessment and treatment plans, as well as write court reports and the other reports required by the agency.) Also important are the worker's capacities to give presentations; be a witness in court; and communicate effectively with clients, staff, and professionals at other agencies.

Every agency administrator wants social workers who are "team players," and who respond to supervision in a positive manner—that is, who do not become defensive when critical comments and suggestions are given. (In this case example, Mr. Dawson has frequent meetings with his supervisor, Dr. Maria Garcia, Director of Pupil Services at the high school, about what courses of action he should take.)

Workers also need to know when consultation may be beneficial, and then be willing to utilize such consultation. Thus, after contacting the state's Department of

Public Instruction, Mr. Dawson finds that a department consultant, Dr. Raul Alvarez, has considerable expertise in nationwide alcohol and drug prevention and treatment programs. Dr. Alvarez is available to the school at no direct charge. The two arrange to meet and discuss pertinent issues in Mr. Dawson's community and which programs Dr. Alvarez feels may fit well with this situation.

Phase 6: Identifying, Analyzing, and Implementing Empirically Based Interventions Designed to Achieve Client Goals

The case example summarizes a variety of interventions that are valid and consistent with the common purposes, values, and ethics of the social work profession. There are several potential interventions for this case. Mr. Dawson can seek to involve the four youths in one-to-one counseling about their drinking patterns and their expulsions. He can offer group counseling at the school for the four youths and for other students having drinking problems. Or, he can seek to have the four youths receive individual or group counseling from a counseling center outside the school system. Mr. Dawson could also seek to have the youths and their parents receive family therapy from a counseling center outside the school system. Yet another intervention strategy is to raise the issue (with parents, the business community, the police department, the school administration, and the school board) as to whether expulsion from school for drinking alcoholic beverages is a desirable policy—perhaps "in-school suspension" would be a better policy. An additional intervention strategy is to incorporate educational material on alcohol and other drugs into the curriculum.

Mr. Dawson discusses these strategies with Dr. Alvarez and obtains his thoughts (based on the results of interventions in other communities) as to which will be most cost effective. (Cost-benefit analysis compares resources used to potential benefits.) Only rarely are social workers able to pursue *all* worthy interventions, because of time and resource limitations.

Mr. Dawson selects the preventive approach as one intervention—that is, he will work to expand the health curriculum to include material on alcohol and other drugs. Numerous questions related to this intervention now arise for Mr. Dawson. What specific material should be covered in a drug-education program? Which drugs should be included? (Mr. Dawson knows that describing certain drugs, such as LSD, may cause some parents to ask whether educational material about seldom-used drugs might encourage some youths to experiment.) *Where* should the drug-education component be added to the curriculum—in large assemblies with all students required to attend? In health classes? In social science classes? Will the school administration, teachers, school board, students, and parents support a proposal to add this component to the curriculum? What strategy will be most effective in gaining the support of these various groups?

As a first step in this phase, Mr. Dawson meets with his immediate supervisor, Dr. Garcia, to discuss these issues and to generate a list of alternative strategies. Three strategies are discussed:

1. An anonymous survey could be conducted in the high school to discover the extent of alcohol and other drug use among students. Such survey results could document the need for drug education.
2. A committee of professional staff in the Pupil Services Department could develop a drug-education program.
3. The Pupil Services Department could ask the school administration and the school board to appoint a committee representing the school board, the administration, the teachers, the students, the parents, and the Pupil Services Department. This committee would explore the need for, and feasibility of, a drug-education program.

Mr. Dawson and Dr. Garcia decide that the best way to obtain broad support for the drug-education program is to pursue the third option. Dr. Garcia meets with the high school principal, Mary Powell, who after some contemplation agrees to explore the need for such a program. Ms. Powell asks the school board to support the formation of a committee. The school board agrees, a committee is formed, and it begins holding meetings. Mr. Dawson is appointed by Dr. Garcia to be the Pupil Services' representative to this committee.

Mr. Dawson also decides to pursue the following additional interventions: (1) seek to involve the four youths in one-to-one counseling about their drinking patterns and their expulsions—however, only one youth comes to see him on a regular basis; the other three have a pattern of making excuses for not coming, and (2) seek to change the policy of expelling students from school for drinking alcoholic beverages on school grounds to an in-school suspension policy. For conciseness, this text will focus on the preventive approach—that is, adding educational material on alcohol and other drugs to the curriculum. (Identifying and implementing alternative interventions is described in further detail in Chapters 5, 7, 8, and 10.)

Phase 7: Applying Empirical Knowledge and Technology

One of the first questions raised by committee members during initial deliberations is, "If a drug-education program is developed, what specific drugs should it include?" Some committee members, as expected, are concerned that providing information about drugs not currently in use among young people in the community may encourage the use of such drugs. As a result, the Pupil Services Department is asked to conduct a student survey to identify the mind-altering drugs currently in use, and to discover the extent of such use.

A second related issue arising in the committee is the broader question of whether a drug-education program has preventive value, or whether such a program might promote illegal drug use. Mr. Dawson responds by suggesting that Dr. Alvarez meet with the committee to discuss this issue. Dr. Alvarez then shares information on the preventive value of a variety of drug-education programs across the nation.

After fourteen months of planning and deliberation, the committee presents its proposal for drug education to the school board. Their program is designed to be part of the health curriculum in the district's middle schools and high schools.

The drug-education program contains the latest research-based knowledge on drugs commonly used by young people in the community and includes the following: mind-altering effects, characteristics of physical and psychological dependency, and withdrawal and long-term health effects. The curriculum also contains research-based information on the most effective treatment approaches, ways a family can cope with a drug-abusing member, how to confront a friend or relative who is abusing, the dangers of driving under the influence of drugs, associations between drug use and sexually transmitted diseases (including AIDS), suggestions for people concerned about their own drug use, and practical ways to say "no" to drugs.

Helpful technologies in this program include computer databases that contain effective drug-education programs in other school systems, software for processing surveys of student drug use and attitudes in the district, and current films and videotapes that offer age-appropriate drug-education material. (Additional information on research in social work practice is described in Chapters 5, 7, and 11.)

Phase 8: Evaluating Program Outcomes and Practice Effectiveness

To evaluate this preventive approach, the Pupil Services Department decides to conduct an annual survey of a random sample of students to assess the extent of drug use/abuse and to elicit students' thoughts about the merits and shortcomings of the drug-education program. The Pupil Services Department also decides to survey parents to elicit their thoughts on the merits and shortcomings of the program, and to obtain their suggestions for improvement. Such surveys provide a way to monitor and evaluate the program's outcomes.

The final phase of any intervention is termination. The committee that developed the drug-education program has its final meeting after the school board approves the proposal. Most members experience mixed emotions at this meeting. They are delighted that their task is successfully completed, but they feel some sadness because this group, which has become an important and meaningful part of their lives, is now ending. (With any committee, if a close working relationship has formed among members, termination is often a painful process. As issues were addressed, some dependency may have developed, and as a result members may experience a sense of loss when termination occurs.) (Chapters 5–8, 10, and 11 describe termination and evaluation in greater detail.)

A Variety of Roles

In working with individuals, groups, families, organizations, and communities, a social worker is expected to be knowledgeable and skillful in filling a variety of roles. Particular roles should (ideally) be determined by what will be most effective, given the circumstances. The following material identifies some, but certainly not all, of the roles assumed by social workers.

ENABLER. In this role a worker *helps* individuals or groups articulate their needs, clarify and identify their problems, explore resolution strategies, select and apply a strategy, and develop their capacities to deal with their own problems more effectively. The enabler is perhaps the most frequently used role in counseling individuals, groups, and families. The model is also used in community practice, primarily when the objective is to help people organize to help themselves.

(This definition of the term *enabler* is very different from the definition used with chemical dependency. There the term refers to a family member or friend who facilitates the substance abuser in continuing to use and abuse the drug of his or her choice.)

BROKER. A broker links individuals and groups who need help (and do not know where to obtain it) with community services. For example, a wife who is frequently physically abused by her husband might be referred to a shelter for battered women. Nowadays even moderate-sized communities have 200 or 300 social service agencies/organizations providing community services. Even human services professionals are often only partially aware of the total service network in their community.

ADVOCATE. This role is borrowed from the law profession. It is an active directive role; that is, the social worker advocates for a client or for a citizen's group. When a client or a citizen's group is in need of help and existing institutions are uninterested (and sometimes openly negative and hostile) in providing services, the advocate's role may be appropriate. The advocate provides leadership for collecting information, arguing the correctness of the client's need and request, and challenging the institution's decision not to provide services. The object is not to ridicule or censure a particular institution but to modify or change one or more of its service policies. In this role the social worker is a partisan who serves the interests of a client or of a citizen's group exclusively.

EMPOWERER. A key goal of social work practice is empowerment, which is the process of helping individuals, families, groups, organizations, and communities increase their personal, interpersonal, socioeconomic, and political strength and influence by improving their circumstances. Social workers who engage in empowerment-focused practice seek to develop the capacity of clients to understand their environment, make choices, take responsibility for their choices, and influence their life situations through organization and advocacy. Empowerment-focused social workers also seek to gain a more equitable distribution of resources and power among different groups in society. This focus on equity and social justice is a hallmark of the social work profession, as evidenced through the early settlement workers such as Jane Addams.

ACTIVIST. An activist seeks basic institutional change; often the objective involves a shift in power and resources to a disadvantaged group. An activist is concerned about social injustice, inequity, and deprivation. Tactics involve conflict, confrontation, and negotiation. Social action is concerned with changing the social environment to better meet the recognized needs of individuals. The methods used are assertive and action oriented (for example, organizing welfare recipients to work toward improvements in services and increases in money payments). Activities of social action include fact finding, analysis of community needs, research, dissemination and interpretation of information, organization of activities with people, and other efforts to mobilize public understanding and support on behalf of some existing or proposed social program. Social action activity can be geared toward a problem that is local, statewide, or national in scope.

MEDIATOR. Mediators intervene in disputes between parties to help them find compromises, reconcile differences, or reach mutually satisfactory agreements. Social workers have used their value orientations and unique skills in many forms of mediation between opposing parties (for example, divorcing spouses, neighbors in conflict, landlord-tenant disputes, labor-management disputes, and child custody disputes). A mediator remains neutral, not siding with either party in the dispute. Mediators make sure they understand the positions of both parties. They clarify positions, recognize miscommunication, and help the parties present their cases clearly.

NEGOTIATOR. A negotiator brings together those who are in conflict over one or more issues, then helps them bargain and compromise to arrive at mutually acceptable agreements. Somewhat like mediation, negotiation involves finding a middle ground that all sides can live with. However, unlike a mediator (which is a neutral role), a negotiator usually is allied with one of the sides involved.

EDUCATOR. Educators give information to clients and teach them adaptive skills. To be an effective educator, the worker must first be knowledgeable. Additionally, the worker must be a good communicator so that information is conveyed clearly and is readily understood by the receiver. Examples include teaching parenting skills to young parents, instructing teenagers in job-hunting strategies, and teaching anger-control techniques to individuals with difficulties in these areas.

INITIATOR. An initiator calls attention to a problem, or to a potential problem. A problem does not have to exist before attention can be called to it. For example, a proposal to renovate a low-income neighborhood by building middle-income housing units may dispossess the current residents, because they cannot afford the cost of the new units. Because calling attention to problems usually does not resolve them, the initiator role must often be followed by other kinds of work.

COORDINATOR. In this role the worker brings components together in an organized manner. For example, in the case of a multiproblem family, several agencies often work together to meet the complicated financial, emotional, legal, health, social, educational, recreational, and interactional needs of the family members. Frequently, one social worker assumes the role of case manager and coordinates services from the different agencies to avoid duplication of services and conflicting objectives.

RESEARCHER. At times, every worker is a researcher. Research in social work practice includes researching the literature on topics of interest, evaluating the outcomes of one's practice, assessing the merits and shortcomings of programs, and studying community needs.

GROUP FACILITATOR. A group facilitator is a leader for some group experience. The group may be a therapy group, an educational group, a self-help group, a sensitivity group, a family therapy group, or a group with some other focus.

PUBLIC SPEAKER. Social workers occasionally talk to a variety of groups (for example, high school classes, public service organizations such as Kiwanis, police officers, staff at other agencies) to inform them of available services or to advocate developing new services for clients whose needs are not being met. In recent years a variety of new services have been identified as being needed (for example, family preservation programs, and services for persons with AIDS). Social workers who have public speaking skills are better able to interpret services to groups of potential clients and are also apt to be rewarded (including financially) by their employers for their public speaking services.

A Systems Perspective

Social workers are trained to have a systems perspective in their work with individuals, groups, families, organizations, and communities. A systems perspective emphasizes looking beyond the presenting problems of the client to assess the complexities and interrelationships of problems. Based on systems theory, key concepts include wholeness, relationship, and homeostasis.

The concept of *wholeness* means that the objects or elements within a system produce an entity that is greater than the sum of the parts. Systems theory is antireductionistic; it asserts that no system can be adequately understood or totally explained once it has been broken down into its component parts. (For example, the central nervous system carries out thought processes that would not occur if only parts were used.)

The concept of *relationship* asserts that the patterning and structuring among the elements in a system are as important as the elements themselves. For example, Masters and Johnson (1970) found that sexual dysfunctions occur primarily because of the nature of the husband-wife relationship rather than the psychological makeup of each partner.

Systems theory opposes simple cause-and-effect explanations. For instance, whether a child will be abused in a family is determined by a variety of variables and the patterning of these variables: the parents' capacity to control their anger, relationships between the child and the parents, relationships between the parents, degree of psychological stress, characteristics of the child, and opportunities for socially acceptable ways for parents to ventilate anger.

The concept of *homeostasis* suggests that most living systems endeavor to maintain and preserve the current system. Jackson (1965), for example, noted that families tend to establish a behavior balance or stability and to resist any change from that predetermined level of stability. Thus, a state of imbalance is typically driven back toward the previous state of balance *or* driven forward to a new balance. If one child is abused in a family, that abuse often serves a function in the family as indicated by the fact that if that child is removed a second child is often selected to be abused. Or, if one family member improves through counseling, the improvement often upsets the balance within the family; other family members will have to change (which may be adaptive or maladaptive) to adjust to the new behavior of the improved family member.

Ecological theory is a subcategory of systems theory. Ecological theory has emerged as a prominent force in social work practice, as discussed in the next section.

Counseling as a Component of Generalist Practice

A small minority of social work educators assert that counseling and clinical social work are not components of generalist social work practice. For instance, in

Understanding Generalist Practice, Kirst-Ashman and Hull (1999) do not use the terms *counseling* and *clinical social work,* nor do they describe contemporary theories of counseling (such as rational therapy, reality therapy, and behavior therapy). In *Social Work Practice: A Generalist Approach,* Johnson (1986) does not use the terms *counseling* and *clinical social work* either, although she does give a half-page introduction to each of the contemporary theories of counseling.

I believe that counseling and clinical social work are key components in generalist practice. A generalist practitioner uses the problem-solving approach to bring about positive changes when working with individuals, families, groups, organizations, and communities. Much of social work practice with individuals, treatment groups, and families involves counseling and what has been called clinical social work. Barker (1999) has defined clinical social work as:

> The professional application of social work theory and methods to the treatment and prevention of psychosocial dysfunction, disability, or impairment, including emotional and mental disorders. Some professional social workers use the term as a synonym for *social casework* or *psychiatric social work,* although others believe that each of these terms has a somewhat different meaning. Most professional social workers agree that clinical social work practice includes emphasis on the *person-in-environment perspective.* (p. 82)

Every social worker who provides services to individuals, treatment groups, and families uses counseling principles and theories extensively. Competence in counseling is as essential for generalist-practice social workers to have as are competencies in other areas (such as brokering, policy making, lobbying, and planning). The vast majority of baccalaureate degree and master's degree social workers are engaged primarily in providing direct services to individuals, treatment groups, and families—with counseling services a major component of the direct services provided (Hopps & Collins, 1995). More social workers are psychotherapists in the United States than psychologists or psychiatrists are psychotherapists (Cutler, 1995). For many social workers, the term *clinical social worker* is synonymous with *social work psychotherapist.*

When a social worker identifies himself or herself as being a clinical social worker or a psychotherapist, it does not mean that the person is uninvolved in other areas of generalist practice. In fact, in providing quality services to individuals, treatment groups, and families, every clinical social worker at times works with changing organizations and communities to benefit clients. One example would be advocating that social service agencies in the community change their eligibility guidelines for services so that clients (and individuals with similar needs in the community) can receive services to meet their health, welfare, and recreational needs.

Because counseling is a key component of generalist social work practice, in this text I emphasize principles and guidelines for counseling and present contemporary theories of counseling that are useful in working with individuals, treatment groups, and families.

Modules 1–11 in the Counseling Theories Resource Manual in this text present and critique the prominent theories of counseling that are widely used by social workers, including client-centered therapy, feminist intervention, reality therapy, rational therapy, behavior therapy, psychoanalysis, transactional analysis, neuro-linguistic programming, and sex counseling and sex therapy. A number of specific treatment techniques are also described, including assertiveness training, token economies, systematic desensitization, aversive techniques, milieu therapy, psychodrama, crisis intervention, parent effectiveness training, meditation, muscle relaxation approaches, deep-breathing relaxation, imagery relaxation, meditation, hypnosis, biofeedback task-centered practice, and solution-focused therapy.

The Medical Model versus the Ecological Model of Human Behavior

The Medical Model

From the 1920s to the 1960s, most social workers used a medical model to assessing and changing human behavior. This model, initiated primarily by Sigmund Freud, views clients as *patients.* The service provider first diagnoses the causes of a patient's problems and then provides treatment. The patient's problems are viewed as being inside the patient.

The medical model conceptualizes emotional and behavioral problems as *mental illnesses.* People with emotional or behavioral problems are then given medical labels, such as schizophrenia, paranoia, psychosis, and insanity. Adherents of the medical approach believe the disturbed person's mind is affected by some generally unknown, internal condition. That unknown, internal condition is thought to result from a variety of possible causative factors: genetic endowment, metabolic disorders, infectious diseases, internal conflicts, unconscious uses of defense mechanisms, and traumatic early experiences that cause emotional fixations and prevent future psychological growth.

The medical model has a lengthy classification of mental disorders that are defined by the American Psychiatric Association. The major categories of mental disorders are listed in Module 1 in the Counseling Theories Resource Manual at the end of this book. The *DSM-IV-TR* (American Psychiatric Association, 2000) defines numerous mental disorders. Several specific mental disorders are discussed briefly here.

SCHIZOPHRENIA. This malady encompasses a large group of disorders, usually of psychotic proportion, manifested by characteristic disturbances of language and communication, thought, perception, affect, and behavior and lasting longer than six months.

DELUSIONAL DISORDER. The essential feature is the presence of one or more delusions that persist for at least one month. A delusion is something that is falsely believed or propagated. An example is the persecutory type, in which an individual erroneously believes that he or she is being conspired against, cheated, spied on, followed, poisoned or drugged, maliciously maligned, harassed, or obstructed in the pursuit of long-term goals.

HYPOCHONDRIASIS. This is a chronic maladaptive style of relating to the environment through preoccupation with shifting somatic concerns and symptoms, a fear or conviction that one has a serious physical illness, the search for medical treatment, inability to accept reassurance, and either hostile or dependent relationships with caregivers and family.

BIPOLAR DISORDER. This is a major affective disorder characterized by episodes of both mania and depression; it was formerly called manic-depressive psychosis. Bipolar disorder may be subdivided into manic, depressed, or mixed types on the basis of currently presenting symptoms.

PHOBIA. A phobia is characterized by an obsessive, persistent, unrealistic, intense fear of an object or situation. Common phobias include *acrophobia* (fear of heights), *algophobia* (fear of pain), *claustrophobia* (fear of closed spaces), and *erythrophobia* (fear of blushing).

PERSONALITY DISORDERS. Some of the most common personality disorders and their characteristics are as follows:

- *Paranoid.* A pattern of distrust and suspicion such that others' motives are interpreted as malevolent.
- *Schizoid.* A pattern of detachment from social relationships and a restricted range of emotional expression.
- *Schizotypal.* A pattern of acute discomfort in close relationships, cognitive or perceptual distortions, and eccentricities of behavior.
- *Antisocial.* A pattern of disregard for, and violation of, the rights of others.
- *Borderline.* A pattern of instability in interpersonal relationships, self-image, and affect; also characterized by marked impulsivity.
- *Histrionic.* A pattern of excessive emotionality and attention seeking.
- *Narcissistic.* A pattern of grandiosity, need for admiration, and lack of empathy.
- *Avoidant.* A pattern of social inhibition, feelings of inadequacy, and hypersensitivity to negative evaluation.
- *Dependent.* A pattern of submissive and clinging behavior related to an excessive need to be taken care of.
- *Obsessive-compulsive.* A pattern of preoccupation with orderliness, perfectionism, and control.

The medical model arose in reaction to the historical notion that the emotionally disturbed were possessed by demons, were mad, and were to be blamed for their disturbances. These people were "treated" by being beaten, locked up, or killed. The medical model viewed the disturbed as in need of help, stimulated research into the nature of emotional problems, and promoted the development of therapeutic approaches.

The major evidence for the validity of the medical model comes from studies that suggest that some mental disorders, such as schizophrenia, may be influenced by genetics (heredity). The bulk of the evidence on the case for heredity comes from studies of twins. For example, in some studies identical twins have been found to have a concordance rate (that is, if one has it, both have it) for schizophrenia of about 50 percent (Rosenhan & Seligman, 1995, p. 54). Keep in mind that the rate of schizophrenia in the general population is about 1 percent (p. 54). When one identical twin is schizophrenic, the other is 50 times more likely than the average to be schizophrenic. This suggests a causal influence of genes, but not genetic determination, as concordance for identical twins is only 50 percent, not 100 percent.

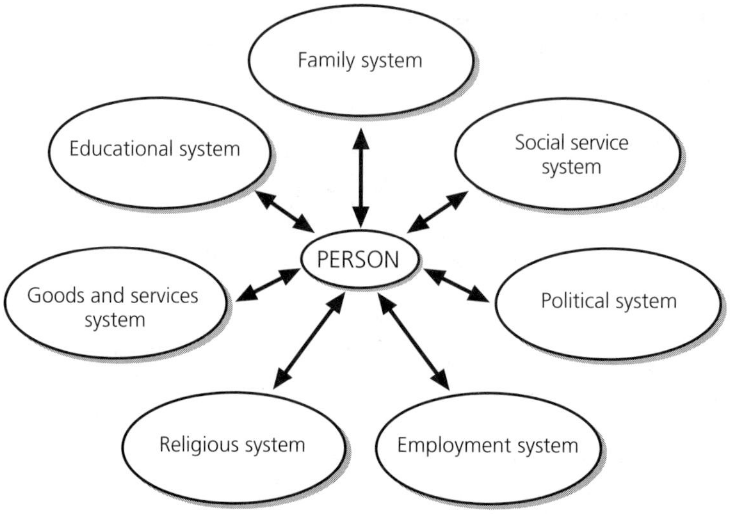

FIGURE 1.2 Person-in-environment conceptualization

The Ecological Model

In the 1960s some social work scholars began to question the usefulness of the medical model. Environmental factors were shown to be at least as important as internal factors in causing a client's problems. Research was also demonstrating that psychoanalysis was probably ineffective in treating clients' problems (Stuart, 1970).

In the 1960s social work shifted at least some of its emphasis to a *reform approach,* which seeks to change systems to benefit clients. Enactment of antipoverty programs (such as Head Start) is an example of an effort to change systems to benefit clients.

In the past several years, social work has increasingly focused on an *ecological model.* This model integrates both treatment and reform by conceptualizing and emphasizing the dysfunctional transactions between people and their physical and social environments. Human beings are viewed as developing and adapting through transactions with all elements of their environments. An ecological model gives attention to both internal and external factors. It does not view people as passive reactors to their environments but rather as being involved in dynamic and reciprocal interactions with them.

This model tries to improve the coping patterns of people and their environments so that a better match can be attained between an individual's needs and the characteristics of his or her environment. One emphasis of the model is on the person-in-environment. The person-in-environment conceptualization is depicted in Figure 1.2.

As is evident in the figure, people interact with many systems. With this conceptualization, social work can focus on three separate areas. First, it can focus on the person and seek to develop his or her problem-solving, coping, and developmental capacities. Second, it can focus on the relationship between a person and the systems he or she interacts with and link the person with needed resources, services, and opportunities. Third, it can focus on the systems and seek to reform them to meet the needs of the individual more effectively.

The ecological model views individuals, families, and small groups as having transitional problems and needs as they move from one life stage to another. Individuals face many transitional changes as they grow older, like learning to walk, entering first grade, adjusting to puberty, graduating from school, finding a job, getting married, having children, having children leave home, and retiring.

Families also have a life cycle. Here are only a few of the events that require adjustment: engagement, marriage, birth of children, parenting, children going to school, children leaving home, and loss of a parent (perhaps through death or divorce).

Small groups have transitional phases of development as well. Members of small groups spend time getting acquainted, gradually learn to trust one another, begin to self-disclose more, learn to work together on tasks, develop approaches to handle interpersonal conflict, and face adjustments to the group eventually terminating or some members leaving.

The model's central concern is to articulate the transitional problems and needs of individuals, families, and small groups. Once these problems and needs are identified, intervention approaches are then selected and applied to help individuals, families, and small groups resolve the transitional problems and meet their needs.

An ecological model can also focus on maladaptive interpersonal problems and needs in families and groups, including communication processes and dysfunctional relationship patterns. These difficulties cover an array of areas, including interpersonal conflicts, power struggles, double binds, distortions in communicating, scapegoating, and discrimination. The consequences of such difficulties are usually maladaptive for some members. An ecological model seeks to identify such interpersonal obstacles and then apply appropriate intervention strategies. For example, parents may set the price for honesty too high for their children. In such families children gradually learn to hide certain behaviors and thoughts, and even learn to lie. If the parents discover such dishonesty, an uproar usually occurs. An appropriate intervention is to open up communication patterns and help the parents understand that, if they really want honesty from their children, they need to learn to be more accepting of their children's thoughts and actions.

Two centuries ago people interacted primarily within the family system. Families were nearly self-sufficient. In those days, the person-in-family was a way of conceptualizing the main system that individuals interacted with. Our society has become much more complex. Today, a person's life and quality of life are interwoven with and interdependent on many systems, as shown in Figure 1.2.

Goals of Social Work Practice

The National Association of Social Workers (1982) has conceptualized social work practice as having four major goals.

Goal 1: Enhance People's Problem-Solving, Coping, and Developmental Capacities

Using the person-in-environment concept, social work practice at this level focuses on the "person." With this focus, a social worker serves primarily as an *enabler.* In this role the worker may take on the activities of a counselor, teacher, caregiver (providing supportive services to those who cannot fully solve their problems and meet their own needs), and behavior changer (that is, changing specific parts of a client's behavior).

Goal 2: Link People with Systems That Provide Them with Resources, Services, and Opportunities

Using the person-in-environment concept, social work practice at this level focuses on the relationships between individuals and the systems they interact with. In this situation a social worker serves primarily as a *broker.*

Goal 3: Promote the Effective and Humane Operation of Systems That Provide People with Resources and Services

Using the person-in-environment concept, the focus of social work practice at this level is on the systems people interact with. One role a worker may fill at this level is an *advocate.* Additional roles include:

Program developer: The worker seeks to promote or design programs or technologies to meet social needs.

Supervisor: The worker seeks to increase the effectiveness and efficiency of the delivery of services through supervising other staff.

Coordinator: The worker seeks to improve a delivery system by increasing communications and coordination between human service resources.

Consultant: The worker seeks to provide guidance to agencies and organizations by suggesting ways to increase the effectiveness and efficiency of services.

Goal 4: Develop and Improve Social Policy

Similar to goal 3, social work practice at this level focuses on the systems people interact with. The distinction between goal 3 and goal 4 is that the focus of goal 3 is on the available resources for serving people. Goal 4 works on the statutes and broader social policies that underlie such resources. The major roles at this level are *planner* and *policy developer.* In these roles workers develop and seek adoption of new statutes or policies and propose elimination of ineffective or inappropriate ones. In these planning and policy development processes, social workers may take on an advocate role and, in some instances, an activist role.

The Council on Social Work Education (CSWE) is the national accreditating body for social work education in the United States. It defines the purpose of social work as follows:

> The social work profession receives its sanction from public and private auspices and is the primary profession in the development, provision, and evaluation of social services. Professional social workers are leaders in a variety of organizational settings and service delivery systems within a global context.
>
> The profession of social work is based on the values of service, social and economic justice, dignity and worth of the person, importance of human relationships, and integrity and competence in practice. With these values as defining principles, the purposes of social work are:
>
> - To enhance human well-being and alleviate poverty, oppression, and other forms of social injustice.
> - To enhance the social functioning and interactions of individuals, families, groups, organizations, and communities by involving them in accomplishing goals, developing resources, and preventing and alleviating distress.
> - To formulate and implement social policies, services, and programs that meet basic human needs and support the development of human capacities.
> - To pursue policies, services, and resources through advocacy and social or political actions that promote social and economic justice.
> - To develop and use research, knowledge, and skills that advance social work practice.
> - To develop and apply practice in the context of diverse cultures.[3]

This definition of the purpose of social work is consistent with the four goals of social work mentioned above. However, it adds four additional goals of social work, as follows.

Goal 5: Enhance Human Well-Being and Alleviate Poverty, Oppression, and Other Forms of Social Injustice

The social work profession is committed to enhancing the well-being of all human beings. It is particularly committed to alleviating poverty, oppression, and other forms of social injustice. About 15 percent of the U.S. population has an income below the poverty line. Social work has always advocated for developing programs to alleviate poverty, and many practitioners focus on providing services to the poor.

Poverty is global, as every society has members who are poor. In some societies, as many as 95 percent of the population lives in poverty. Social workers are committed to alleviating poverty not only in the United States, but also worldwide. Alleviating poverty is obviously complex and difficult. Social work professionals work with a variety of systems to make progress in alleviating poverty, including educational systems, health care systems, political systems, business and employment systems, religious systems, and human services systems.

Oppression is the unjust or cruel exercise of authority or power. In our society a number of groups have been oppressed—including African Americans, Latinos, Chinese Americans, Native Americans, women, persons with disabilities, gays and lesbians, various religious groups, and people living in poverty. (The listing of these groups is only illustrative, and certainly not exhaustive.) Social injustice occurs when some members of a society have less protection, fewer basic rights and opportunities, or fewer social benefits than other members of that society. Social work is a profession that is committed not only to alleviating poverty but also to combating oppression and other forms of social injustice.

Goal 6: Pursue Policies, Services, and Resources Through Advocacy and Social or Political Actions That Promote Social and Economic Justice

Social justice is an ideal condition in which all members of a society have the same basic rights, protection, opportunities, obligations, and social benefits. Economic justice is also an ideal condition in which all members of a society have the same opportunities to attain material goods, income, and wealth. Social workers have an obligation to help groups at risk increase their personal, interpersonal, socioeconomic, and political strength and influence through improving their circumstances. Empowerment-focused social workers seek a more equitable distribution of resources and power among the various groups in society. Diverse groups that may be at risk include those distinguished by age, class, color, disability, ethnicity, family structure, gender, marital status, national origin, race, religion, sex, and sexual orientation.

Goal 7: Develop and Use Research, Knowledge, and Skills That Advance Social Work Practice

Social workers are expected to contribute to the knowledge and skill base of social work practice. Included in this expectation is the responsibility of social workers

[3]Reprinted from Educational Policy and Accreditation Standards (EPAS). (Alexandria, VA: Council on Social Work Education, 2001).

to objectively assess their own practice, and to assess the programs and services they provide.

Goal 8: Develop and Apply Practice in the Context of Diverse Cultures

Our society is changing rapidly. By the middle of the 21st century nearly half of the U.S. population will be people of color. Because of demographic changes and other social trends, human service practitioners and organizations will increasingly deal with people who are more diverse, politically more active, better informed, and more aware of their rights. These trends will demand significant changes in the nature, structure, and quality of human service organizations, and also changes in the sensitivity, knowledge, and skills of social service providers. There is thus a need for ongoing efforts to develop new approaches to preparing culturally competent social workers. In order to become culturally competent, a social worker needs to (1) become aware of culture and its pervasive influence; (2) learn about her or his own culture; (3) recognize her or his own ethnocentricity; (4) learn about other cultures; (5) acquire cultural knowledge about the clients she or he is working with; and (6) adapt social work skills and intervention approaches to the needs and styles of the cultures of these clients.

Micro, Mezzo, and Macro Practice

Social workers practice at three levels: (1) *micro*—working on a one-to-one basis with an individual, (2) *mezzo*—working with families and other small groups, and (3) *macro*—working with organizations and communities or seeking changes in statutes and social policies.

The specific activities performed by workers include, but are not limited to, the following categories.

Social Casework

Aimed at helping individuals on a one-to-one basis to meet personal and social problems, casework may be geared to helping the client adjust to his or her environment or to changing certain social and economic pressures that adversely affect an individual. Social casework services are provided by nearly every social welfare agency that provides direct services to people. *Social casework* encompasses a wide variety of activities, such as counseling runaway youths; helping unemployed people secure training or employment; counseling someone who is suicidal; placing a homeless child in an adoptive or foster home; providing protective services to abused children and their families; finding nursing homes for stroke victims who no longer need to be hospitalized; counseling individuals with sexual dysfunctions; helping alcoholics acknowledge they have a drinking problem; counseling those with a terminal illness; being a probation and parole officer; providing services to single parents; and working in medical and mental hospitals as a member of a rehabilitation team.

Case Management

Recently a number of social service agencies have labeled their social workers *case managers*. The tasks performed by case managers are similar to those of caseworkers. The job descriptions of case managers vary from service area to service area. For example, case managers in a juvenile probation setting supervise clients, provide some counseling, monitor clients to make certain they are following the rules of probation, link clients and their families with needed services, prepare court reports, and testify in court. Case managers at a sheltered workshop are apt to provide job training and counseling, arrange transportation, discipline clients for unacceptable behavior, act as an advocate, and act as liaison with the people who supervise clients during their nonwork hours (which may be at a group home, foster home, residential treatment facility, or their parents' home). Hepworth and Larsen (1986) described the role of a case manager this way:

> Case managers link clients to needed resources that exist in complex service delivery networks and orchestrate the delivery of services in a timely fashion. Case managers function as brokers, facilitators, linkers, mediators, and advocates. A case manager must have extensive knowledge of community resources, rights of clients, and policies and procedures of various agencies and must be skillful in mediation and advocacy. (p. 563)

Barker (1999) defined case management as follows:

> A procedure to plan, seek, and monitor services from different social agencies and staff on behalf of a client. Usually one agency takes primary responsibility for the client and assigns a case manager, who coordinates services, advocates for the client, and sometimes controls resources and purchases services for the client. The procedure makes it possible for many social workers in the agency, or different agencies, to coordinate their efforts to serve a given client through professional teamwork, thus expanding the range of needed services offered. Case management may involve monitoring the progress of a client whose needs require the services of

> many different professionals, agencies, health care facilities, and human services programs. (p. 62)

Group Work

The intellectual, emotional, and social development of individuals may be furthered through group activities. In contrast to casework or group therapy, *group work* is not primarily therapeutic, except in a broad sense. Different groups have different objectives, such as socialization, information exchange, curbing delinquency, recreation, changing socially unacceptable values, and helping achieve better relations between cultural and racial groups. For example, through group activities a group worker at a neighborhood center may seek to curb delinquency patterns and change socially unacceptable values, or a worker at an adoption agency may meet with a group of applicants to explain adoption procedures and help applicants prepare for becoming adoptive parents. Activities and focuses of groups vary: arts and crafts, dancing, games, dramatics, music, photography, sports, nature study, woodwork, first aid, home management, information exchange, and discussion of such topics as politics, sex, marriage, religion, and selecting a career.

Group Therapy

Group therapy is aimed at facilitating the social, behavioral, and emotional adjustment of individuals through the group process. Participants in group therapy usually have emotional, interactional, or behavioral difficulties. Group therapy has several advantages over one-to-one counseling, such as the operation of the helper therapy principle, which maintains it is therapeutic for the helper (who can be any member of a group) to feel he or she has been helpful to others. In contrast to one-to-one counseling, group pressure is often more effective in changing individuals' maladaptive behavior, and group therapy is a time saver as it enables the therapist to treat several people simultaneously. For example, group therapy might be used for individuals who are severely depressed, have drinking problems, are rape victims, are psychologically addicted to drugs, have a relative who is terminally ill, are single and pregnant, are recently divorced, or have an eating disorder.

Family Therapy

A type of group therapy aimed at helping families with interactional, behavioral, and emotional problems, *family therapy* can be used with parent-child interaction problems, marital conflicts, and conflicts with grandparents. A wide variety of problems are dealt with in family therapy or family counseling, such as communication problems and disagreements between parents and youths on choice of friends, drinking and other drug use, domestic tasks, curfew hours, sexual values and behavior, study habits and grades received, and choice of dates.

Community Organization

The aim of *community organization* is stimulating and assisting the local community to evaluate, plan, and coordinate efforts to provide for the community's health, welfare, and recreation needs. Although it is not possible to define precisely the activities of a community organizer, they often include encouraging and fostering citizen participation, coordinating efforts between agencies or groups, public relations and public education, research, planning, and being a resource person. A community organizer acts as a catalyst in stimulating and encouraging community action. Such specialists are apt to be employed in community welfare councils, social planning agencies, health planning councils, and community action agencies. The term *community organization* is now being replaced in some settings by *planning, social planning, program development, policy development,* and *macro practice.*

Barker (1995) defined community organization as:

> An intervention process used by social workers and other professionals to help individuals, groups, and collectives of people with common interests or from the same geographic areas to deal with social problems and to enhance social well-being through planned collective action. Methods include identifying problem areas, analyzing causes, formulating plans, developing strategies, mobilizing necessary resources, identifying and recruiting community leaders, and encouraging interrelationships between them to facilitate their efforts. (pp. 90–91)

Policy Analysis

Policy analysis involves systematic evaluation of a policy and the process by which it was formulated. Those who conduct such an analysis consider whether the process and result were clear, equitable, legal, rational, compatible with social values, superior to other alternatives, cost-effective, and explicit. Such an analysis frequently identifies shortcomings in the policy. Those conducting the policy analysis then usually recommend modifications in the policy that are designed to alleviate these shortcomings.

Administration

Administration involves directing the overall program of a social service agency. Administrative functions include setting agency program objectives; analyzing social conditions in the community; making decisions about what services will be provided; employing and supervising staff members; setting up an organizational structure; administering financial affairs; and securing funds for the agency's operations. Administration also involves setting organizational goals; coordinating activities to achieve the selected goals; and monitoring and making necessary changes in processes and structure to improve the effectiveness and efficiency of processes that contribute to transforming social policy into social services. In social work, the term *administration* is often used synonymously with *management*. In a small agency, administrative functions may be carried out by one person, whereas several people may be involved in administrative affairs in a larger agency.

Other areas of professional activity in social work include research, consulting, supervising, planning, program development, policy development, and teaching (primarily at the college level). Social casework, case management, group work, group therapy, family therapy, and community organization constitute the primary professional activities that beginning-level social workers are apt to provide. All of these activities require social workers to have counseling skills. (Counseling involves helping individuals or groups resolve social and personal problems through the process of developing a relationship, exploring the problems in depth, and exploring alternative solutions—this process is described in Chapter 5.) Caseworkers, case managers, group workers, group therapists, and family therapists obviously need a high level of counseling skills to work with individuals and groups. Community organizers need to be perceptive, and they need skills in relating to other people in assessing problems and developing resolution strategies—skills that parallel or are analogous to counseling skills. Therefore, a major emphasis of this text will be on counseling.

Counseling skills, however, are not the only skills social workers need. For example, caseworkers also need to be able to construct social histories and to link clients with other human services. Some agencies require skills in public speaking, preparing and presenting reports to courts and to other agencies, and teaching parents better parenting techniques. Research capacities to evaluate one's own practice and other programs are also important. The essential skills needed for social work practice are further described in the next section. As you will see, generalist social workers are expected to have an extensive knowledge base and numerous skills and to adhere to a well-defined set of professional social work values.

The Knowledge, Skills, and Values Needed for Social Work Practice

Knowledge

The NASW has identified the knowledge needed for effective social work practice as follows:

Knowledge of casework and group work theory and techniques.

Knowledge of community resources and services.

Knowledge of basic federal and state social service programs and their purposes.

Knowledge of community organization theory and the development of health and welfare services.

Knowledge of basic socioeconomic and political theory.

Knowledge of racial, ethnic, and other cultural groups in society—their values and lifestyles and the resultant issues in contemporary life.

Knowledge of sources of professional and scientific research appropriate to practice.

Knowledge of the concepts and techniques of social planning.

Knowledge of the theories and concepts of supervision and the professional supervision of social worker practice.

Knowledge of theories and concepts of personnel management.

Knowledge of common social and psychological statistical and other research methods and techniques.

Knowledge of the theories and concepts of social welfare administration.

Knowledge of social and environmental factors affecting clients to be served.

Knowledge of the theories and methods of psychosocial assessment and intervention and of differential diagnosis.

Knowledge of the theory and behavior of organizational and social systems and of methods for encouraging change.

Knowledge of community organization theory and techniques.

Knowledge of the theories of human growth and development and of family and social interaction.
Knowledge of small-group theory and behavioral dynamics.
Knowledge of the theories of group interaction and therapeutic intervention.
Knowledge of crisis intervention theories and techniques.
Knowledge of advocacy theory and techniques.
Knowledge of the ethical standards and practices of professional social work.
Knowledge of teaching and instructional theories and techniques.
Knowledge of social welfare trends and policies.
Knowledge of local, state, and federal laws and regulations affecting social and health services.[4]

In regard to the knowledge base of social work, this text summarizes a number of intervention approaches at the micro, mezzo, and macro levels of practice.

In their EPAS (Education Policy and Accreditation Standards), the Council on Social Work Education (2001) has categorized the following fundamental knowledge that accredited baccalaureate and master's degree programs must provide to social work students:

A. Values and Ethics
Social work education programs integrate content about values and principles of ethical decision making as presented in the National Association of Social Workers Code of Ethics. The educational experience provides students with the opportunity to be aware of personal values; develop, demonstrate, and promote the values of the profession; and analyze ethical dilemmas and the ways in which these affect practice, services, and clients.

B. Diversity
Social work programs integrate content that promotes understanding, affirmation, and respect for people from diverse backgrounds. The content emphasizes the interlocking and complex nature of culture and personal identity. It ensures that social services meet the needs of groups served and are culturally relevant. Programs educate students to recognize diversity within and between groups that may influence assessment, planning, intervention, and research. Students learn how to define, design, and implement strategies for effective practice with persons from diverse backgrounds.

C. Populations-at-Risk and Social and Economic Justice
Social work education programs integrate content on populations-at-risk, examining the factors that contribute to and constitute being at risk. Programs educate students to identify how group membership influences access to resources and present content on the dynamics of such risk factors and responsive and productive strategies to redress them.

Programs integrate social and economic justice content grounded in an understanding of distributive justice, human and civil rights, and the global interconnections of oppression. Programs provide content related to implementing strategies to combat discrimination, oppression, and economic deprivation and to promote social and economic justice. Programs prepare students to advocate for nondiscriminatory social and economic systems.

D. Human Behavior and the Social Environment
Social work education programs provide content on the reciprocal relationships between human behavior and social environments. Content includes empirically based theories and knowledge that focus on the interactions between and among individuals, groups, societies, and economic systems. It includes theories and knowledge of biological, sociological, cultural, psychological, and spiritual development across the life span; the range of social systems in which people live (individual, family, group, organizational, and community); and the ways in which social systems promote or deter people in maintaining or achieving health and well-being.

E. Social Welfare Policy and Services
Programs provide content about the history of social work, the history and current structures of social welfare services, and the role of policy in service delivery, social work practice, and attainment of individual and social well-being. Course content provides students with knowledge and skills to understand major policies that form the foundation of social welfare; analyze organizational, local, state, national, and international issues in social welfare policy and social service delivery; analyze and apply the results of policy research relevant to social service delivery; understand and demonstrate policy practice skills in regard to economic, political, and organizational systems, and use them to influence,

[4]Published in 1982, National Association of Social Workers, Inc. Reprinted with permission, from *Standards for the Classification of Social Work Practice,* Policy Statement 4, p. 17. Copyright National Association of Social Workers, Inc.

formulate, and advocate for policy consistent with social work values; and identify financial, organizational, administrative, and planning processes required to deliver social services.

F. Social Work Practice
Social work practice content is anchored in the purposes of the social work profession and focuses on strengths, capacities, and resources of client systems in relation to their broader environments. Students learn practice content that encompasses knowledge and skills to work with individuals, families, groups, organizations, and communities. This content includes engaging clients in an appropriate working relationship, identifying issues, problems, needs, resources, and assets; collecting and assessing information; and planning for service delivery. It includes using communication skills, supervision, and consultation. Practice content also includes identifying, analyzing, and implementing empirically based interventions designed to achieve client goals; applying empirical knowledge and technological advances; evaluating program outcomes and practice effectiveness; developing, analyzing, advocating, and providing leadership for policies and services; and promoting social and economic justice.

G. Research
Qualitative and quantitative research content provides understanding of a scientific, analytic, and ethical approach to building knowledge for practice. The content prepares students to develop, use, and effectively communicate empirically based knowledge, including evidence-based interventions. Research knowledge is used by students to provide high-quality services; to initiate change; to improve practice, policy, and social service delivery; and to evaluate their own practice.

H. Field Education
Field education is an integral component of social work education anchored in the mission, goals, and educational level of the program. It occurs in settings that reinforce students' identification with the purposes, values, and ethics of the profession, fosters the integration of empirical and practice-based knowledge, and promotes the development of professional competence. Field education is systematically designed, supervised, coordinated, and evaluated on the basis of criteria by which students demonstrate the achievement of program objectives.[5]

[5]Reprinted from Educational Policy and Accreditation Standards (EPAS). (Alexandria, VA: Council on Social Work Education, 2001).

As indicated, baccalaureate and master's degree programs are mandated to provide this foundation curriculum content. In addition, master's programs provide "advanced curriculum content," which the Council on Social Work Education (2001) in EPAS describes as follows:

> The master's curriculum prepares graduates for advanced social work practice in an area of concentration. Using a conceptual framework to identify advanced knowledge and skills, programs build an advanced curriculum from the foundation content. In the advanced curriculum, the foundation content areas . . . are addressed in greater depth, breadth, and specificity and support the program's conception of advanced practice.

Master's programs offer "concentrations," from which students can choose their specialization. A concentration component should build knowledge, values, and skills for advanced practice in an identifiable area. Areas frequently offered by master's programs include fields of practice, problem areas, populations-at-risk, and intervention methods or roles.

This text provides material primarily in the social work practice content area. It also includes material on social work values and ethics, diversity and populations-at-risk, and promotion of social and economic justice.

Core Practice Skills

A number of efforts have been made to articulate the essential skills for entry-level social work practice positions. A few of these conceptualizations are presented here to indicate contemporary thinking about core practice skills. Numerous similarities exist among these conceptualizations, but as yet there is not full agreement on these core skills.

Federico (1973, pp. 146–147) indirectly described social work skills by outlining roles and activities:

1. *Outreach worker*—reaching out into the community to identify need and follow up referrals to service contexts.
2. *Broker*—knowing services available and making sure those in need reach the appropriate services.
3. *Advocate*—helping specific clients obtain services when they might otherwise be rejected, and helping to expand services to cover more needy persons.
4. *Evaluator*—evaluating needs and resources, generating alternatives for meeting needs, and making decisions between alternatives.

5. *Teacher*—teaching facts and skills.
6. *Mobilizer*—helping to develop new services.
7. *Behavior changer*—changing specific parts of a client's behavior.
8. *Consultant*—working with other professionals to help them be more effective in providing services.
9. *Community planner*—helping community groups plan effectively for the community's social welfare needs.
10. *Care giver*—providing supportive services to those who cannot fully solve their problems and meet their own needs.
11. *Data manager*—collecting and analyzing data for decision-making purposes.
12. *Administrator*—performing the activities necessary to plan and implement a program of services.

Baer (1979, p. 106) identified the following ten competencies as being essential for successfully performing the responsibilities of entry-level positions:

1. Identify and assess situations in which the relationship between people and social institutions needs to be initiated, enhanced, restored, protected, or terminated.
2. Develop and implement a plan for improving the well-being of people, based on problem assessment and the exploration of obtainable goals and available options.
3. Enhance the problem-solving, coping, and developmental capacities of people.
4. Link people with systems that provide them with resources, services, and opportunities.
5. Intervene effectively on behalf of populations most vulnerable and discriminated against.
6. Promote the effective and humane operation of the systems that provide people with services, resources, and opportunities.
7. Actively participate with others in creating new, modified, or improved service, resource, or opportunity systems that are more equitable, just, and responsive to consumers of services; work with others to eliminate unjust systems.
8. Evaluate the extent to which the objects of the intervention plan were achieved.
9. Continually evaluate one's professional growth and development through assessment of practice behaviors and skills.
10. Contribute to the improvement of service delivery by adding to the knowledge base of the profession as appropriate and supporting and upholding the standards and ethics of the profession.

These ten competencies were originally developed by Baer and Federico (1978).

The National Association of Social Workers has identified the following skills as being essential for social work practice:

Skill in listening to others with understanding and purpose.
Skill in eliciting information and in assembling relevant facts to prepare a social history, assessment, and report.
Skill in creating and maintaining professional helping relationships and in using oneself in relationships.
Skill in observing and interpreting verbal and nonverbal behavior and in using a knowledge of personality theory and diagnostic methods.
Skill in engaging clients in efforts to resolve their own problems and in gaining trust.
Skill in discussing sensitive emotional subjects in a nonthreatening supportive manner.
Skill in creating innovative solutions to clients' needs.
Skill in determining the need to end therapeutic relationships and how to do so.
Skill in interpreting the findings of research studies and professional literature.
Skill in mediating and negotiating between conflicting parties.
Skill in providing interorganizational liaison services.
Skill in interpreting or communicating social needs to funding sources, the public, or legislators.[6]

NASW has identified the following abilities, which are closely related to conceptualizing essential skills, as being needed for social work practice:

Ability to speak and write clearly.
Ability to teach others.
Ability to respond supportively in emotion-laden or crisis situations.
Ability to serve as a role model in a professional relationship.
Ability to interpret complex psychosocial phenomena.
Ability to organize a workload to meet designated responsibilities.

[6]Published 1982, National Association of Social Workers, Inc. Reprinted with permission, from *Standards for the Classification of Social Work Practice,* Policy Statement 4, pp. 17–18. Copyright National Association of Social Workers, Inc.

Ability to identify and obtain resources needed to assist others.
Ability to assess one's performance and feelings, and to use help or consultation.
Ability to participate in and lead group activities.
Ability to function under stress.
Ability to deal with conflict situations or contentious personalities.
Ability to relate social and psychological theory to practice situations.
Ability to identify the information necessary to solve a problem.
Ability to conduct research studies of agency services or one's practice.[7]

In EPAS, the Council on Social Work Education (2001) mandates that accredited baccalaureate and master's programs in social work programs must provide content on the following ten skills, which we discussed in detail earlier in the chapter:

1. Engaging clients in an appropriate working relationship.
2. Identifying issues, problems, needs, resources, and assets.
3. Collecting and assessing information.
4. Planning for service delivery.
5. Using communication skills, supervision, and consultation.
6. Identifying, analyzing, and implementing empirically based interventions designed to achieve client goals.
7. Applying empirical knowledge and technological advances.
8. Evaluating program outcomes and practice effectiveness.
9. Developing, analyzing, advocating, and providing leadership for policies and services.
10. Promoting social and economic justice.

The acquisition of social work skills depends partly on innate ability and partly on learning experiences. Social work education programs facilitate the learning of these skills by presenting theoretical material to students (such as material on how to interview), by monitoring and critiquing students who are practicing applying these skills (for example, videotaping students in simulated counseling situations), and by extensively supervising students in practicum courses.

[7]Published 1982, National Association of Social Workers, Inc. Reprinted with permission, from *Standards for the Classification of Social Work Practice*, Policy Statement 4, p. 18. Copyright National Association of Social Workers, Inc.

Values

Should the primary objective of imprisonment be rehabilitation or punishment? Should a father committing incest be prosecuted given that the ensuing publicity may lead to family breakup, or should an effort first be made, through counseling, to stop the incest and keep the family intact? Should a wife who is occasionally abused by her husband be encouraged to remain with him? Should an abortion be suggested as one alternative for resolving the problems of someone who is single and pregnant? Should youths who are claimed to be uncontrollable by their parents be placed in correctional schools? If a client threatens serious harm to some third person, what should the social worker do? If a client indicates he or she is HIV-positive and continues to persist in behavior that places a partner in danger of contracting the disease and refuses to warn the partner of the peril, what should the social worker do? All of these questions involve making value-based decisions. Much of social work practice depends on making such decisions.

The National Association of Social Workers has identified the following broad-based values as necessary for social work practice:

Commitment to the primary importance of the individual in society.
Respect for the confidentiality of relationships with clients.
Commitment to social change to meet socially recognized needs.
Willingness to keep personal feelings and needs separate from professional relationships.
Willingness to transmit knowledge and skills to others.
Respect and appreciation for individual and group differences.
Commitment to developing clients' ability to help themselves.
Willingness to persist in efforts on behalf of clients despite frustration.
Commitment to social justice and the economic, physical, and mental well-being of all in society.

Commitment to a high standard of personal and professional conduct.[8]

The Council on Social Work Education (2001) in EPAS states, "The profession of social work is based on the values of service, social and economic justice, dignity and worth of the person, importance of human relationships, and integrity and competence in practice."

Because values play a key role in social work practice, it is essential that social work and education programs (1) help students clarify their values and (2) foster the development of values that are consistent with professional social work practice. Social work values will be discussed further in Chapter 2.

Goals of Social Work Education

The Council on Social Work Education (2001) in EPAS identifies the purposes and goals of social work education as follows:

> The purposes of social work education are to prepare competent and effective professionals, to develop social work knowledge, and to provide leadership in the development of service delivery systems. Social work education is grounded in the profession's history, purposes, and philosophy and is based on a body of knowledge, values, and skills. Social work education enables students to integrate the knowledge, values, and skills of the social work profession for competent practice.
>
> Among its programs, which vary in design, structure, and objectives, social work education achieves these purposes through such means as:
>
> - Providing curricula and teaching practices at the forefront of the new and changing knowledge base of social work and related disciplines.
> - Providing curricula that build on a liberal arts perspective to promote breadth of knowledge, critical thinking, and communication skills.
> - Developing knowledge.
> - Developing and applying instructional and practice-relevant technology.
> - Maintaining reciprocal relationships with social work practitioners, groups, organizations, an communities.
> - Promoting continual professional development of students, faculty, and practitioners.
> - Promoting interprofessional and interdisciplinary collaboration.
> - Preparing social workers to engage in prevention activities that promote well-being.
> - Preparing social workers to practice with individuals, families, groups, organizations, and communities.
> - Preparing social workers to evaluate the processes and effectiveness of practice.
> - Preparing social workers to practice without discrimination, with respect, and with knowledge and skills related to clients' age, class, color, culture, disability, ethnicity, family structure, gender, marital status, national origin, race, religion, sex, and sexual orientation.
> - Preparing social workers to alleviate poverty, oppression, and other forms of social injustice.
> - Preparing social workers to recognize the global context of social work practice.
> - Preparing social workers to formulate and influence social policies and social work services in diverse political contexts.[9]

Objectives of Social Work Education

The Council on Social Work Education (2001) in EPAS has specified the foundation program objectives for both baccalaureate and master's degree programs. These objectives, which follow, highlight much of the knowledge, values, and skills needed for social work practice. (The symbols "B6" and "M6" apply, respectively, to baccalaureate programs and master's degree programs.) Graduates of baccalaureate and master's degree programs in the United States are expected to demonstrate the ability to:

1. Apply critical thinking skills within the context of professional social work practice.
2. Understand the value base of the profession and its ethical standards and principles, and practice accordingly.
3. Practice without discrimination and with respect, knowledge, and skills related to clients' age, class, color, culture, disability, ethnicity, family structure, gender, marital status, national origin, race, religion, sex, and sexual orientation.
4. Understand the forms and mechanisms of oppression and discrimination and apply strategies of advocacy and social change that advance social and economic justice.

[8]Published 1982, National Association of Social Workers, Inc. Reprinted with permission, from *Standards for the Classification of Social Work Practice,* Policy Statement 4, p. 18. Copyright National Association of Social Workers, Inc.

[9]Reprinted from Educational Policy and Accreditation Standards (EPAS), (Alexandria, VA: Council on Social Work Education, 2001).

5. Understand and interpret the history of the social work profession and its contemporary structures and issues.

B6. Apply the knowledge and skills of generalist social work practice with systems of all sizes.

M6. Apply the knowledge and skills of a generalist social work perspective to practice with systems of all sizes.

7. Use theoretical frameworks supported by empirical evidence to understand individual development and behavior across the life span and the interactions among individuals and between individuals and families, groups, organizations, and communities.
8. Analyze, formulate, and influence social policies.
9. Evaluate research studies, apply research findings to practice, and evaluate their own practice interventions.
10. Use communication skills differentially across client populations, colleagues, and communities.
11. Use supervision and consultation appropriate to social work practice.
12. Function within the structure of organizations and service delivery systems and seek necessary organizational change.[10]

In stating these objectives, the Council on Social Work Education (2001) notes: "A program may develop additional objectives to cover the required content in relation to its particular mission, goals, and educational level."

Graduates of master's degree programs are also required by the Council on Social Work Education (2001) to meet the objectives of the concentration that they specialize in, as specified in the following statement:

> Graduates of a master's social work program are advanced practitioners who apply the knowledge and skills of advanced social work practice in an area of concentration. They analyze, intervene, and evaluate in ways that are highly differentiated, discriminating, and self-critical. Graduates synthesize and apply a broad range of knowledge and practice with a high degree of autonomy and skill. They refine and advance the quality of their practice and that of the larger social work profession.[11]

[10]Reprinted from Educational Policy and Accreditation Standards (EPAS), (Alexandria, VA: Council on Social Work Education, 2001).
[11]Reprinted from Educational Policy and Accreditation Standards (EPAS), (Alexandria, VA: Council on Social Work Education, 2001).

A Greater Focus on Outcomes

The Council on Social Work Education is a specialized accreditation entity. A number of specialized accreditation entities exist, such as the American Bar Association, which accredits law programs throughout the United States. The fairly large number of higher-education accreditation entities in the United States are accountable to the Council for Higher Education Accreditation (CHEA). CHEA is thus the association that accredits higher-education accreditation entities in the United States. (Membership on CHEA is primarily composed of representatives from chancellors and presidents of U.S. colleges and universities.)

In recent years CHEA has mandated that the higher-education accreditation entities that it accredits must have a greater focus on outcomes. As a result, the Council on Social Work Education now requires that accredited baccalaureate and master's programs in social work must demonstrate that students in social work programs are in fact attaining the stated objectives of those programs. Thus, faculty now strongly focus on students attaining these objectives, and they also measure the extent to which students attain these objectives.

Key Objectives

This text uses an integrative approach to present prominent methods in social work practice. Thus, the key objectives of this text are as follows:

- Provide content on social work practice, social work values and ethics, diversity and populations-at-risk, and promotion of social and economic justice that is consistent with EPAS.
- Prepare students for generalist social work practice by informing them of contemporary assessment and intervention strategies.
- Develop students' interviewing and counseling skills and capacities so they can intervene effectively with individuals, families, and groups.
- Develop students' macro practice skills and capacities in intervening with organizations and communities.
- Help students develop a philosophical value orientation that is consistent with social work practice.
- Develop students' capacities to function effectively in a variety of social work roles, including enabler, empowerer, broker, advocate, activist, mediator,

EXHIBIT 1.1

Partial list of intervention therapies at the micro and mezzo levels

Task-centered therapy
Psychoanalysis
Client-centered therapy
Transactional analysis
Feminist intervention
Rational-emotive therapy
Reality therapy
Crisis intervention
Behavior modification
Provocative therapy
Radical therapy
Adlerian therapy
Analytical therapy
Existential therapy
Encounter therapies
Ego psychology approaches
Cognitive approaches
General systems approaches
Role theory approaches
Time management
Biofeedback
Marathon groups
Alcoholics Anonymous
Weight Watchers
Psychodrama
Solution-focused therapy
Gestalt therapy
Assertiveness training
Token economies
Contingency contracting
Systematic desensitization
In vivo desensitization
Implosive therapy
Covert sensitization
Aversive techniques
Thought-stopping
Sex therapy
Milieu therapy
Play therapy
Parent effectiveness training
Muscle relaxation
Deep breathing relaxation
Imagery relaxation
Meditation
Hypnosis
Self-hypnosis
Encounter groups
Sensitivity groups
Parents Anonymous
Neuro-linguistic programming

negotiator, educator, initiator, coordinator, researcher, and group facilitator.

- Foster in students an awareness, understanding, and appreciation of how to intervene effectively with people of diverse racial, ethnic, cultural, social, and class backgrounds.
- Expand students' capacities to evaluate and modify human service programs and systems to make human services more equitable, humane, and responsive to consumers.
- Foster philosophical conceptual skills so that graduates can critically evaluate and further develop their own practice capacities throughout life.
- Help students develop a positive sense of self and an awareness and appreciation of the importance of continuing to evaluate their professional skills and professional growth.

Which Intervention Strategies Should Social Workers Learn?

Literally hundreds of intervention approaches have been developed at the micro, mezzo, and macro levels of practice. A partial list of available techniques that can be used at the micro and mezzo levels of practice appears in Exhibit 1.1.

It is impossible for social workers to have an effective working knowledge of all of these intervention approaches. What social workers can do, however, is continue to learn additional approaches throughout their careers and also learn to apply the approaches they already use more effectively. Social work agencies encourage this continual learning by offering in-service training and workshops, sending workers to conferences, and encouraging workers to take additional college courses in the helping professions.

Workers should continue to learn a wide variety of intervention approaches so they can select from their "bag of tricks" the approach that is apt to be most effective (given each client's unique set of problems and circumstances). Workers soon become aware that their own personalities also partially determine which intervention approaches they are more comfortable with and effective in applying.

Because there are so many intervention techniques (as suggested in Exhibit 1.1), students may be bewildered about which intervention approaches to learn. It is therefore crucial that faculty guide students by (1) making carefully thought-out decisions, as a group, regarding the intervention theories that are most useful for students in their geographic area to learn; (2) giving an overview so that students are familiar with a wide number of theories; and (3) conveying material on each theory's merits and shortcomings. Future chapters in this text summarize most of the intervention approaches listed in Exhibit 1.1. The instructor of this course, along with the other social work faculty members, should decide which intervention approaches to cover in this class.

Once you graduate and obtain employment, your work setting will be a deciding factor in which intervention approaches you should use. If you are working with shy or aggressive people, assertiveness training may be appropriate. Alcoholics Anonymous may be appropriate for people with drinking problems, rational therapy for people who are depressed, in vivo desensitization for people who have phobias, and so on.

A competent social worker generally has a working knowledge of a variety of intervention approaches.

In working with clients, the worker should focus on selecting effective intervention approaches that help clients solve their problems rather than trying to redefine the problems in terms of the worker's favorite intervention approach.

Summary

Social work is the professional activity of helping individuals, families, groups, organizations, and communities enhance or restore their capacity for social functioning and create societal conditions favorable to their goals. The term *social worker* is generally applied to graduates of either bachelor's- or master's-level social work programs who are employed in the field of social welfare. A social worker is a change agent who is skilled at working with individuals, groups, families, organizations, and communities. Almost all social workers are employed in the field of social welfare.

The profession of social work is distinct from other helping professions because it has the responsibility and mandate to provide social services and it uses the person-in-environment concept. Social work has a number of goals, including to (1) enhance the problem-solving, coping, and developmental capacities of people; (2) link people with systems that provide them with resources, services, and opportunities; (3) to promote the effectiveness and humane operation of systems that provide people with resources and services; (4) develop and improve social policy; (5) enhance human well-being and alleviate poverty, oppression, and other forms of social injustice; (6) pursue policies, services, and resources through advocacy and social or political actions that promote social and economic justice; (7) develop and use research, knowledge, and skills that advance social work practice; and (8) develop and apply practice in the context of diverse cultures.

A social worker needs training and expertise in a wide range of areas to effectively handle problems faced by individuals, groups, families, organizations, and the larger community. Most professions are becoming increasingly more specialized, but social work continues to emphasize a generalist (broad-based) approach.

Social work uses a problem-solving approach. Social workers practice at three levels: micro, mezzo, and macro. Specific activities include social casework, case management, group work, group therapy, family counseling and family therapy, community organization, policy analysis, planning, program development, policy development, research, consulting, supervision, and administration. The knowledge, skills, and values needed for social work practice were summarized.

Literally hundreds of intervention approaches have been developed for social work practice. It is impossible for any social worker to have an effective working knowledge of all of these theories. Educational programs have an obligation to provide social work students with an overview of the commonly used theories and to convey information on the merits and shortcomings of these approaches. Social workers have an obligation to continue throughout their careers to learn a variety of intervention approaches. In working with clients, a worker should focus on selecting the most effective intervention approaches for solving clients' problems rather than redefining clients' problems to fit the worker's favorite intervention approach.

EXERCISES

1. *BREAKING THE ICE*

Goal: To get acquainted and to reduce anxiety.

Step 1: Starting a new class can be both exciting and anxiety producing for students and instructor. Brainstorm about what you would like to know about other members of the class. Examples might include marital status, hometown, work or volunteer experience in social work, and most unforgettable experience. List these questions on the blackboard.

Step 2: Answer the questions developed in Step 1.

Step 3: Ask your instructor questions you may have about her or his educational background and professional experiences.

(continued)

EXERCISES
(continued)

Step 4: (Optional) In groups of two, share an experience that has had a profound effect on your life. Listeners should be encouraged to ask questions to seek clarification. After each person has had a chance to speak, class re-forms to report on what students have learned about their partners.

2. SEARCHING FOR DESCRIPTORS

Goal: To facilitate student interaction and to establish a positive class atmosphere.

Step 1: A list of descriptors is distributed to the class. (A descriptor is a word or phrase that identifies an item.) Some possibilities are listed below. Each student finds one student (or two or three students in larger classes) who says "yes" to having specific descriptors. (Each student can be listed only once on the sheet by each "searcher.") After several minutes the instructor indicates time is up. The instructor then reads each descriptor and asks for the names of those who were listed by at least one "searcher." The instructor ends the exercise by finding out who has the largest list, and then giving a small prize (such as candy) to the winner.

Sample Descriptors:

Plays golf
Likes classical music
Is a fan of the Dallas Cowboys
Has had a paid or volunteer job in social work
Was born west of the Mississippi River
Has traveled in Mexico
Has traveled in Europe
Is married
Likes to jog
Has never flown in an airplane
Has meditated
Has water-skied
Likes the psychoanalytic approach to therapy
Has been hypnotized
Has been to a gay pride festival
Has traveled in Canada
Has gone deer hunting
Enjoys fishing
Attends church regularly
Has received a speeding ticket
Has visited, or lived on, a reservation

C H A P T E R 2

Social Work Values

Value Dilemmas

Let's assume that you are a social worker and are assigned the following case. What would you do to help this family?

Mrs. Kehl is two months pregnant. She works part-time in a shoe factory and is paid at the minimum wage. Her husband is a janitor in a business office and earns only slightly more. They already have seven children and are living in substandard poverty conditions. They do not wish to have additional children; this pregnancy resulted from a failure of the birth control method they were using. The family is Catholic and attends church regularly. On one hand, they want to have an abortion; they feel their family is already being hurt because of a lack of money. On the other hand, they believe having an abortion is immoral.

This case raises a number of questions about values. As a social worker, how would you help this family weigh their views about abortion against their desire to limit their family size to improve their living conditions?

This case is not unique. Most situations that clients face involve, at least partially, value dilemmas. Here are a few more examples.

Mr. Ritter is 82 years old and has terminal cancer. He has lived a full life but now is in severe pain. He is rather depressed and is seriously considering taking his own life. Should he be allowed to?

Mr. and Mrs. Sinclair have a 2-year-old child who has a profound cognitive disability, and who also needs extensive medical care. They have three older children. The family's emotional and physical resources are being severely drained, and family relationships are increasingly tense. Yet the family feels the child will develop at a faster pace in their home than in an institution or in a group home. What should they do?

Mr. and Mrs. Fedders have been married for six years and have two children. Their love for each other has been practically nonexistent for the past three years. Mr. Fedders recently discovered his wife has been having an affair. They both hold religious beliefs against divorce, but they are seriously considering terminating their marriage. How should a social worker help them?

Mr. Franzene is on probation for two years for theft. For the past 18 months he has stayed out of trouble. He inadvertently reveals to his probation officer that he took two pens from a discount store. Should his probation officer make a report on this?

LaVonne Hall recently left a mental hospital and was helped by her aftercare worker to obtain a filing job. While intoxicated and angry, Ms. Hall calls her worker and says that she has been fired. She then says that she is going to shoot her former employer and hangs up. What should the worker do?

Mr. Townsend's neighbors occasionally hear cries of anguish from Mr. Townsend's two children. The neighbors report this to protective services because they suspect abuse. A protective service worker investigates, and Mr. Townsend and the children state the cries are the result of spankings. How does the worker decide when harsh spanking should be considered abuse?

Mr. and Mrs. Stonek's only child was taken away two years ago and placed in a foster home because of neglect. The father drank excessively, and the mother was very depressed. Over the past two years, the Stoneks have occasionally made efforts to improve their lives but have always "slid back." For the past two months, Mr. Stonek has been involved in Alcoholics Anonymous and has only occasionally gotten drunk. Mrs. Stonek presently seems less depressed and feels having her son back would make her life more meaningful. The Stoneks ask to have their child returned. Should the child be returned? How would you as the worker arrive at a decision?

Mrs. Barta seeks counseling at a comprehensive mental health center. She states her husband is having intercourse with their 11-year-old daughter. The counselor arranges a joint meeting with the Bartas. Mr. Barta first denies the accusation, but then admits it after being confronted with what his wife has seen and heard. How should the worker attempt to help this family?

Mrs. Johnson is a caseworker at a public welfare agency in a rural county. She observes and collects evidence that the director makes a range of decisions that deny migrant workers in the area (most of whom are Mexican Americans) public assistance benefits for which they are eligible. If she confronts the director with this evidence, Mrs. Johnson believes she will be fired, or at least denied merit increases and promotions at work. What should she do?

Mrs. Gordon seeks counseling from a sex therapist. She indicates she is fairly content with her marriage and has an enjoyable sex life with her husband. Yet she feels substantial guilt about her desire and following through on her desire to masturbate. How can the therapist help her?

A community worker in an inner city is working with residents to organize a rent strike against a landlord who neglects making essential repairs. The building does not have adequate heat and is infested with rats and roaches. The organizer wonders whether she should fully inform the residents of the risks involved in a rent strike (such as being evicted). She fears that if she fully informs the tenants of the risks, they probably will decide not to strike, and essential improvements in living conditions will not be made. What should she do?

These examples highlight the fact that much of social work practice involves value dilemmas. Social work is both an art and a science. Because social work is partly an art, a worker must frequently make decisions based on values rather than on knowledge. It also means that the change techniques workers use are often based on theory and value assumptions rather than on proven intervention techniques.

One value assumption that is frequently useful in helping clients resolve value dilemmas is the principle of self-determination. This principle asserts that clients have the right to hold and express their own opinions and to act on them, as long as in so doing they do not infringe on the rights of others. When clients face a dilemma, a worker can often proceed effectively by helping the clients first define their problems precisely and then examine fully the merits and shortcomings of the various alternatives to resolving the problem. After this is done, clients are then given the responsibility to decide which course of action they desire to pursue. This problem-solving format might be useful for many of the situations listed above. For example, the Kehls might list all their reasons for and against having an abortion, and then make a decision. This same approach might also be useful in helping the Sinclairs decide whether to place their child with the profound cognitive disability in an institution or a group home, and in helping the Fedders decide whether to terminate their marriage.

Although this self-determination principle can be useful, *there are no absolutes in social work practice.* Guidelines are simply guidelines. What works in one situation may not resolve problems in others. Suppose, for example, that Mr. Ritter makes a list of the reasons for and against taking his life and decides that there is no rational reason for him to endure further pain. Such a decision raises a value dilemma for the social worker regarding whether the worker should attempt to stop Mr. Ritter from taking his life. Or, suppose the Bartas decide they do not want further counseling on the incestuous relationship between Mr. Barta and his daughter because they both conclude that delving into it further will break up their marriage and their family. What should the worker do then?

Much of social work practice depends on the worker's professional judgment. Directors of social welfare agencies frequently tell me that their best workers are those who have common sense and who are able to "trust their guts" (that is, trust their feelings, intuition, and perceptions). This chapter will spell out value assumptions and principles of social work practice. These guidelines (and all other guidelines presented in this text) are not to be applied as absolutes but simply as concepts that may be useful in working with people. An effective worker understands and uses these guidelines to make a professional judgment on whether a guideline is, or is not, appropriate when working with particular people.

Knowledge and Values

It is important for workers to be able to distinguish between values and knowledge and to be aware of the role each plays in social work practice.

Pincus and Minahan (1973) concisely defined the difference between values and knowledge:

> Values are beliefs, preferences, or assumptions about what is desirable or good for man [humans]. An example is the belief that society has an obligation to help each individual realize his fullest potential. They are not assertions about how the world is and what we know about it, but how it *should* be. As such, value statements cannot be subjected to scientific investigation; they must be accepted on faith. Thus we can speak of a value as being right or wrong only in relation to the particular belief system or ethical code being used as a standard.
>
> What we will refer to as knowledge statements, on the other hand, are observations about the world and man [humans] which have been verified or are capable of verification. An example is that black people have a shorter life expectancy than white people in the United States. When we speak of a knowledge statement as being right or wrong, we are referring to the extent to which the assertion has been confirmed through objective empirical investigation. (p. 38)

The distinction between values and knowledge can be illustrated in some of the cases described earlier. First, let's look at the abortion question. Suppose a person questions the abortion procedure because she feels it is immoral. The person believes it means killing an unborn baby. Implicit in this value statement is the belief that life begins at or shortly after conception. Deciding whether life does in fact begin at conception is a belief that is not verifiable.

However, if a person has qualms about an abortion because she fears the risks of the medical procedure or fears there is a high probability of feeling remorseful after the abortion, then informational questions are raised. Knowledge, or empirical evidence, can be presented in these situations showing that the health risks of having an abortion are less than those of carrying the child to full term, and evidence can be presented showing that only a small percentage of women who have an abortion have severe remorse (Hyde & DeLamater, 1997).

Mrs. Gordon's guilt over masturbating is also a useful illustration. If she feels guilty because she believes masturbating is immoral and sinful, then she obviously has a belief system that asserts it is wrong to masturbate. For her to resolve this value dilemma involves having her either change her belief system or stop masturbating. However, if she feels guilty because she fears she is hurting herself physiologically or hindering her sex life with her husband, she could be shown that both of these beliefs are erroneous by pointing out that most married men and women masturbate, masturbation is highly recommended by sex therapists, and masturbation usually fosters rather than hinders a sexual relationship (Hyde & DeLamater, 1997).

As these case examples suggest, it is much easier to change a client's belief if it conflicts with current knowledge. Changing a belief that is based on a value is much more difficult because the "rightness" or "wrongness" of the belief cannot be determined with empirical evidence.

Value Dilemmas of Clients versus Workers

It is important for social workers to distinguish just who has the value dilemma. (This will be discussed in more detail later.) An important guideline in social work practice is not to become overly emotionally involved in a client's case. (If you find yourself frequently taking clients' problems home with you so that your dwelling on their problems interferes with your life, then you are overly involved.) If a client faces a dilemma about whether to obtain a divorce, or have an abortion, or place a member of the family in an institution, it is important for you to be aware that it is the *client's* dilemma and not yours. By being aware that it is not your dilemma, you will best be able to remain objective and thereby be most helpful to a client.

However, if you feel strongly that a client is doing something immoral (for example, if you believe abortions are unethical), then *you* face a value dilemma. In such situations it will be very difficult for you to remain objective.

When you face a dilemma about a client's actions or plans, the following guidelines are sometimes helpful.

1. The first step in resolving such a question is to recognize its existence. Such self-awareness is often difficult to attain. Ethical questions are often ambiguous and make us feel uncomfortable. Therefore, we like to avoid them.

2. Self-awareness is not enough unless it is put to use with clients. Kelman (1965) recommended that workers should "label" their values for the client and allow the client to "talk back" in a sort of mutual influence situation. Such an approach *may* be useful in working with clients who are involved with drugs, or having extramarital affairs, or have been arrested for stealing, and so forth. However, there is a danger to this approach. The worker's values may not be in the client's best interest. When the workers share their values, they are influencing (and perhaps also manipulating) the client. For example, if a worker is morally opposed to abortions, sharing those values with a young unmarried and pregnant woman probably will influence her not to have an abortion, which may or may not be in this woman's best interest. In deciding whether to share values, that worker has to make a professional judgment as to what will be most constructive and helpful for the client.

3. When a worker's personal values conflict with the values of the social work profession (for example, in the area of sexual orientation), it is generally advisable for the worker to adhere to the values of the profession when providing services to clients. The Code of Ethics of the National Association of Social Workers is a useful guide to the values of the social work profession. (A copy of this code appears at www.naswdc.org.)

4. Clients should be encouraged to explore their own values and to relate alternative actions to their own value systems. Clients need protection against manipulation that would encroach on their freedom of choice. For example, if a worker is morally opposed to abortions, clients might well be encouraged to see (and referral arrangements be made to see) someone who views abortions as a viable alternative.

5. A useful moral code advanced by Glasser (1965) allows clients to fulfill their needs and to do what they want to do, as long as by doing so they do not deprive others of the ability to fulfill their needs. I have found this code very useful in counseling people considering abortions, and in a wide variety of other situations—counseling gays and lesbians, people involved in premarital relationships, and so forth. The code is also useful in working with adults involved in child abuse, incest, and extramarital affairs because those involved need to examine the effects of their actions on others. There is no one right moral code—what works for one person may not work for another due to differences in lifestyles, life goals, and personal values.

6. Loewenberg and Dolgoff (1988) have developed a rank order of ethical priorities. They suggest that social work practitioners can use these prioritized values when making ethical decisions. In the event that two values are competing, the social worker should abide by the one higher in the order. For instance, if the worker is debating between value 1 (protection of life) and value 2 (maintenance of autonomy, independence, and freedom), the worker should act in accordance with value 1. Likewise, value 2 should take precedence over values 3–7, and so on.

Loewenberg and Dolgoff's (1988, p. 122) prioritized values are as follows:

1. Protect life (basic survival needs of individuals and/or society).
2. Maintain autonomy, independence, and freedom.
3. Foster equality of opportunity and equality of access.
4. Promote a better quality of life.
5. Strengthen every person's right to privacy/confidentiality.
6. Speak the truth and fully disclose all relevant information.
7. Practice in accord with rules and regulations voluntarily accepted.

To illustrate the application of these prioritized values, let's consider an example. A social worker encounters a group of African Americans in a heated conflict over a race-related issue with members of the Ku Klux Klan. There is imminent danger of physical violence. The worker's first objective in this collision of values is to protect the lives of everyone involved—perhaps by calling the police for immediate intervention. At some later date, values lower on the list can be confronted—such as the value of fostering equality of opportunity for the African Americans involved in this dispute.

Respect for the Dignity and Uniqueness of the Individual

Every human being is unique in a variety of ways—value system, personality, life goals, financial resources, emotional and physical strengths, personal concerns, past experiences, peer pressures, emotional reactions, self-identity, family relationships, and deviant behavioral patterns. In working with a client, a social worker needs to perceive and respect the uniqueness of the client's situation. *Individualization* is the ethical value in social work and other helping professions of viewing, and relating to, the client as a person or group rather than as one whose characteristics are simply typical of a class.

Individualization is relatively easy for a social worker to achieve when the worker is assisting clients who have values, goals, behavioral patterns, and personal characteristics similar to the worker's. Individualization is harder to achieve when a worker is assigned clients who have values or behavioral patterns that the worker views as disgusting. For example, a worker may have difficulty viewing a client with respect when that client has raped a young girl, or is involved in an incestuous relationship, or has killed a member of his family, or has severely abused a child. A general guideline in such situations is that the worker should accept and respect the client but not accept the deviant behavior that needs to be changed. If a worker is unable to convey acceptance of the client, a helping relationship will not be established. If such a relationship is not established, the worker will have practically no opportunity to help the client change deviant behaviors. A second guideline is that if a worker views a client as being disgusting and is unable to establish a working relationship, then the worker should transfer the case to another worker. There should be no disgrace or embarrassment in having to transfer a case for such reasons; it is irrational for a worker to expect to like every client, or for every client to like the worker (Ellis & Harper, 1977).

Social workers occasionally encounter "raw" situations. For a while I worked in a mental hospital for the criminally insane and had a variety of clients who had committed a wide range of asocial and bizarre acts, including incest, rape, decapitation of a girlfriend, sodomy, sexual exhibitionism, and removing corpses from graves. I've worked in a variety of other settings and encountered other raw situations. Achieving an attitude of respect for people who commit bizarre actions is difficult at times, but rehabilitation will not occur unless it is achieved.

Social psychologists have firmly established the theoretical principle that people's images of themselves develop largely out of their interactions and communications with others. A long time ago Charles Cooley (1902) called this process the *looking glass self-concept*. The looking glass says that people develop their self-concept in terms of how other people relate to them, as if others were a looking glass or mirror. For example, if a person receives respect from others and is praised for positive qualities, he or she is apt to feel good about himself or herself, will gradually develop a positive sense of worth, will be happier, and will seek responsible and socially acceptable ways to maintain the respect of others.

Conversely, if a person commits a deviant act and *then* is shunned by others, viewed as different, and treated with disrespect, that person will develop a *failure identity*. According to Glasser (1972), people with failure identities either withdraw from society, become emotionally disturbed, or express their discontent in delinquent and deviant actions.

For example, if a neighborhood identifies a youth as being a troublemaker (a delinquent), the neighbors are apt to relate to the youth as if she were not to be trusted, may erroneously accuse her of delinquent acts, and will label her semidelinquent and aggressive behavior as being delinquent. In the absence of objective ways to gauge whether she is, in fact, a delinquent, she will rely on the subjective evaluations of others. Thus, gradually, as she is related to as being a delinquent, she is apt to perceive herself in that way and will begin to enact the delinquent role.

Compton and Galaway (1975) expanded on the importance of social workers' attending carefully to their communications with clients:

> Social workers and other professionals intervening in the lives of people are well advised to be constantly sensitive to the message they are extending to others about their worth. Do we, in the little things we do, communicate to the other person that he is a unique individual to be highly prized? What, for example, is the message communicated when we safeguard time and provide a

client with a specific time to be seen as opposed to a catch-me-on-a-catch-as-catch-can basis for visits? Do appointments in advance communicate to the client a higher sense of respect than unannounced visits or hurriedly arranged telephone appointments? And, speaking of telephoning, how about the all too frequently overlooked return call? What message does the client get from the worker in terms of the client's worth when the worker does not have the courtesy or good sense to return telephone calls promptly? How about the ability to listen to clients, to secure from them their own account of their situation, and to avoid prejudgments? And does not privacy, both in terms of how the social worker conducts the interviews and how he treats the material gained from interviews, communicate something to clients about the esteem in which they are held? A worker attempting to operationalize the premise of individual uniqueness and dignity may find it useful to repeatedly inquire of himself, "What does this action on my part communicate to the client about my perception of his personhood?" (pp. 106–107)

The principle of individualization also plays a key role in social work treatment. Various problems, needs, goals, and values of clients involve different patterns of relationships with clients and different methods of helping. For example, consider the needs of a teenaged male who is placed in a group home for being beyond parental control. At times he may need an understanding but firm counselor who sets and enforces strict limits. At times he may need encouragement and guidance in how to perform better at school. If conflicts develop between the youth and other boys at the group home, the counselor may need to play a mediating role. If the youth is shy, counseling on how to be more assertive may be needed. If his parents are fairly ineffective in their parenting role, the counselor may seek to have the parents enroll in a parent effectiveness training program (Gordon, 1970). If the youth is being treated unfairly at school or by the juvenile court, the counselor may play an advocate role and attempt to change the system. If the youth has behavior problems, the reasons need to be explored and an intervention program developed.

A thorny problem facing social workers involves striking an effective balance between classification and individualization. There is a need in all human service areas to generalize beyond individuals and to organize data on the basis of common characteristics. Classification is essential to make sense out of a mass of data and is an essential part of developing theories. The danger of putting people into a particular category is that such a classification may lead social workers to respond to people as objects rather than as individuals. Compton and Galaway (1975) commented about the labeling process:

> The pitfalls of this process are being documented in a growing body of literature from sociologists studying deviance from a labeling perspective. Not only does labeling or classification lead to a distortion of individual differences, but, as labeling theorists and their supporting research are noting, a person labeled deviant, those doing the labeling, and the surrounding audience frequently respond to the deviant on the basis of the label rather than on the basis of individual characteristics. This creates conditions for the development of a self-fulfilling prophecy in which the person becomes what he has been labeled. (p. 107)

In the same vein, Toch (1970) noted:

> Playing the classification game in the abstract, as is done in universities, is a joyful, exhilarating experience, harmless and inconsequential. Classifying people in life is a grim business which channelizes destinies and determines fate. A man becomes a category, he is processed as a category, plays his assigned role, lives up to the implications. Labeled irrational, he acts crazy; catalogued dangerous, he becomes dangerous or he stays behind bars. (p. 55)

This labeling process, most simply stated, occurs due to Cooley's *looking glass self* in which people define who and what they are in terms of how others relate to them. A person labeled as mentally ill, or a delinquent, or an ex-con, or a welfare mother is then apt to define himself or herself in terms of these labels and unfortunately begin playing these roles.

Social workers have to continue to be alert to the dangers of labeling and should interact with each client (or judge, attorney, professor, and so forth) as a person rather than a label.

The Client's Right to Self-Determination

As indicated earlier, social workers believe that clients have the right to express their own opinions and to act upon them, as long as by so doing clients do not infringe on the rights of others. This principle is in sharp contrast to the layperson's views that a social worker seeks to "remold" clients into a pattern chosen by the worker. Instead, the workers' efforts are geared to enhancing clients' abilities to help themselves. Client self-determination derives logically from belief in the inherent dignity of each person. If people have dignity, then it follows that they should be permitted to determine their own lifestyles as far as possible.

Social workers believe that making all decisions and doing everything for a client is self-defeating, because it leads to increased dependence rather than greater self-reliance and self-sufficiency. For people to grow, to mature, to become responsible, they need to make their own decisions and take responsibility for the consequences. Mistakes and emotional pain will occur. But that is part of life. We learn by our mistakes and by trial and error. Respect for the clients' ability to make their own decisions is associated with the principle that social work is a cooperative endeavor between clients and workers (client participation). Social work is done *with,* not *to,* a client. Plans imposed on people without their active involvement have a way of not turning out well.

Four points should be made in operationalizing the principle of *client self-determination.* First, self-determination implies that clients should be made aware that there are alternatives for resolving the personal or social problems they face. Self-determination involves having clients make decisions—that is, making a choice selected from several courses of action. If there is only one course of action, there is no choice and therefore clients would not have the right of self-determination. As will be expanded on in later chapters, the role of a social worker in helping clients involves (1) building a helping relationship, (2) exploring problems in depth with clients, and (3) exploring alternative solutions with clients, then choosing a course of action. This third step is the implementation of the principle of self-determination.

Second, self-determination means that the client, not the worker, is the chief problem solver. Workers need to recognize that the client *owns* the problem and therefore has the chief responsibility to resolve the problem. This is an area in which social work differs markedly from other professions. Most professionals, such as physicians and attorneys, advise clients in terms of what they believe clients ought to do. Doctors, lawyers, and dentists are experts in advising clients. The client's decision making after receiving the expert's advice in such situations is generally limited to the choice of whether to accept the professional's advice.

In sharp contrast, social workers should not seek to establish an expert-inferior relationship but a relationship between equals. The worker's expertise does *not* lie in knowing or recommending what is best for the client. Rather, the expertise lies in assisting clients to define their problems, develop and examine the alternatives for resolving the problems, maximize their capacities and opportunities to make decisions for themselves, and implement the decisions they make. In conjunction with this principle, Dumont (1968) noted:

> The most destructive thing in psychotherapy is a "rescue fantasy" in the therapist—a feeling that the therapist is the divinely sent agent to pull a tormented soul from the pit of suffering and adversity and put him back on the road to happiness and glory. A major reason this fantasy is so destructive is that it carries the conviction that the patient will be saved only through and by the therapist. When such a conviction is communicated to the patient, verbally or otherwise, he has no choice other than to rebel and leave or become more helpless, dependent, and sick. (p. 60)

Third, self-determination does not prohibit or restrict social workers from offering an opinion or making a suggestion. In fact, social workers have an obligation to share their viewpoints with their clients. Compton and Galaway (1975) noted:

> Workers have the obligations of sharing with clients their own thinking, perhaps their own experiences, not as a way of directing the clients' lives but rather as an additional source of information and input for the clients to consider in their own decision making. It is imperative, however, that the social workers' input be recognized as information to be considered and not an edict to be followed. (p. 111)

The key to implementing this principle is for the social worker to phrase the alternative as a suggestion rather than as advice. For example, if a client is worried about how her elderly mother, who is living alone and whose physical and mental capacities are deteriorating, will be able to have her physical, emotional, and social needs met, the social worker should not advise: "The best thing for you to do is to place her in a nursing home." Instead the worker should offer a suggestion for the client to consider: "Have you thought about placing your mother in a nursing home?"

Fourth, client self-determination is possible and should be encouraged even in areas in which the social worker has the additional function to protect society. Three areas in social work for which the worker has this additional function are in protective services, in prisons, and in probation and parole. Compton and Galaway (1975) noted:

> A probation agency, for example, may enforce the legal requirement that the probationer must report to the probation officer; this is not a matter for client self-determination. But the sensitive officer can allow for considerable client self-determination in the frequency of reporting, the length of the interviews, the time of reporting, and the content to be discussed during the interviews. (p. 112)

Actually, probationers can also be informed that they even have a choice in reporting to the probation officer. In working with involuntary clients who are angry with the legal authority held by the social worker, it is often helpful for the worker to inform the clients that they do have a choice regarding whether they are willing to meet the minimum legal requirements. The consequences of not cooperating (such as being sent to prison, or having their children taken away in the case of abusive parents) are also made clear to them. This approach appears to be useful because it reduces the clients' inclination to view the social worker as a parent or a cop. Instead of playing the game of how much they can get away with, this approach puts the responsibility for their future squarely on the clients. They are faced with the decision of reporting or suffering the consequences of not reporting; of deciding whether to stop abusing their children or of suffering the consequences of making no effort to refrain from abusing their children. In this connection O'Connor (1972) noted:

> The recognition of man's [a person's] right to free choice guarantees that he may choose to run his life as he sees fit. This choice may run counter to society's welfare and even his own, yet essentially it is his choice and his prerogative. Society may censure, but it cannot take from him his right; nor would society strip him of his dignity by a censure. The criminal then has a right to say "crime is my choice and I am willing to pay the price. If you send me to prison, I am paying my debt to society and refuse to submit to your attempts to reform me." The principle of self-determination makes it incumbent upon society to honor such a plea. (pp. 485–486)

In working with involuntary clients whose actions have adversely affected other people in the past (for example, abusive parents), the worker's obligation is to outline the minimum legal requirements (for example, no further incidents of abuse) and specify the consequences if these clients decide not to meet these requirements. Even in such situations, clients have a choice in deciding whether they will meet the requirements. If they are not met by a client, the worker must follow through and implement the consequences to maintain credibility with the client. Often the consequences have therapeutic shock value as clients learn they can no longer manipulate the system and are responsible for the consequences they suffer.

Confidentiality

Confidentiality is the implicit or explicit agreement between a professional and a client that the professional will maintain the private nature of information about the client. An *absolute* implementation of this principle means that the professional will not share client disclosures with anyone else, except when authorized by the client in writing or required by law. Because of the principle of confidentiality, professionals can be sued if they disclose information that the client is able to document has a damaging effect on him or her.

One of the reasons confidentiality is important is that clients may not share their hidden secrets, personal concerns, and asocial thoughts and actions with a professional if they believe the information will be revealed to others. A basic principle of counseling is that clients must feel comfortable in fully revealing themselves to the professional without fear that their secret revelations will be used against them.

Confidentiality is absolute when information revealed to a professional is *never* passed on to anyone in any form. Such information would never be shared with other agency staff, fed into a computer, or written in a case record. A student or beginning practitioner tends to think in absolutes and may even naively promise clients *absolute confidentiality*.

Absolute confidentiality is seldom achieved. Social workers today generally function as part of a larger agency. Much of the communication is written into case records and shared orally with other staff in the system as part of the service-delivery process. Social workers share details with supervisors, and many work in teams and are expected to share information. Therefore, instead of absolute confidentiality, it is more precise to indicate that a system of *relative confidentiality* is being used in social work practice (Wilson, 1978, p. 3).

Confidentiality is a legal matter, and there is a fair amount of uncertainty as to what is an unlawful violation. In addition, there have been few test cases in court to determine this issue. Let me provide a brief summary of how agencies are now handling issues related to confidentiality.

Practically all agencies allow (and in fact encourage) their workers to discuss a client's circumstances with other professionals employed at the same agency. At many agencies (such as a mental hospital) the input of many professionals (psychiatrist, psychologist, social workers, nurses, physical therapist, and so forth) is used in assessing a client and developing a treatment plan.

Many agencies feel it is inappropriate to share or discuss a client's case with a secretary. (Yet, the secretary does the typing and usually knows as much about each client as the professional staff does.)

Most agencies believe it is inappropriate to discuss a client's case with professionals at another agency unless the client first signs a release-of-information form (see Figure 2.1). (Yet, informally, professionals employed by different agencies do at times share information about a client without the client's authorization.)

Nearly all agencies share case information with social work interns. (Whether it is legally permissible to share information with student interns has not been determined.)

It is certainly permissible to discuss a case with others for educational purposes if no identifying information about the client is given. Yet this is another gray area, because the person talking about the case will not be able to determine precisely when identifying information is being given. Let me give you an example.

Some years ago I was employed at a maximum security hospital for the criminally insane and had on my caseload a young male who had decapitated his 17-year-old girlfriend. Such a criminal offense is indeed shocking and rare. People in the client's local area will never forget the offense. If I were to discuss this case in a class at a university (which I occasionally do), I would never be fully assured that no one would be able to identify the offender. There is always the chance that one of the students may have lived in the client's home community and would recognize the offender.

A question that is sometimes raised in relation to confidentiality is whether clients have a right to see the agency's records on them. The 1974 Federal Privacy Act legislated that any agency receiving federal funds must allow clients to see their records. Furthermore, if a client requests a copy of the record, the agency must provide one. If the client is a minor, both the child and the child's parents have the right of access to the client's records. (For children who are 18 years old or older, or who attend postsecondary institutions, the access to educational records and the consent required before access by others resides with them rather than their parents.)

It is probably a good idea not to put anything into a client's record that you do not want the client to see. A number of voluntary agencies also now have policies to allow clients access to their records.

Another problematic area is the thorny question of when a professional should violate confidence and inform others. Again, many gray areas surround this question (Wilson, 1978).

Most state statutes permit or require the professional to inform the appropriate people when a client admits to a past or intended *serious* criminal act. Yet, the question of how serious a crime must be before there is an obligation to report it has not been resolved. On the extreme end of the severity continuum, it has been established that a professional *must* inform the appropriate people.

A precedent-setting case occurred in *Tarasoff v. Regents of the University of California, 1974* (*University of Pittsburgh Law Review,* 1975). In this case a university student informed his psychiatrist that he was going to shoot his girlfriend. The psychiatrist informed the campus police of this threat but did not inform the intended victim or her parents. Campus security picked up and questioned the student and soon released him, concluding that he "appeared rational." Shortly afterward he murdered his girlfriend. Her parents sued the psychiatrist, and the Supreme Court ruled:

> When a doctor or a psychiatrist, in the exercise of his professional skills and knowledge, determines, or shall determine that a warning is essential to avert danger arising from a medical or psychological condition of his patient, he incurs a legal obligation to give that warning. (*University of Pittsburgh Law Review,* 1975, p. 159)

The court also concluded:

> The public policy favoring protection of the confidential character of patient-psychotherapist communication must yield in instances in which disclosure is essential to avert danger to others. The protective privilege ends where the public peril begins. (p. 161)

Thus, the court set a precedent holding that a professional is liable for failure to warn the intended victim. This precedent has continued to be upheld in court decisions involving a helping professional's obligation to inform the intended victim (Schwartz, 1989, pp. 225–226).

For what intended crimes must a helping professional inform the police and the intended victim?

Lakeside Counseling Center
Consent for Release of Confidential Information

__________________ at Lakeside Counseling Center requests permission from __________________
(Name of social worker)

__________ to release confidential information about __________. This information will be released to:
(Name of client) (Name of client)

Name: ____________________ Address: ____________________

Position: ____________________ ____________________

Agency: ____________________

Material to be released: ____________________

Reason for this disclosure: ____________________

____________________ must abide by the following limitations in their
(Name of person and the agency receiving the information)

use of the information received: ____________________

My signature verifies that I know what information is being disclosed and have had the opportunity to correct the data to make certain it is accurate. I am aware that this consent can be revoked (in writing) at any time. I am also aware of the consequences that might occur as a result of signing this form or of my refusal to do so.

My signature means that I have read this form and/or have had it read and explained to me in language I can understand. I have checked this form, and upon signing it will receive a copy.

This consent form expires on __________ unless revoked by me in writing prior to that date.
(Date)

__________________ __________ __________
(Client's signature or "X") (Date signed) (Witness)

__________________ __________ __________
(Client's guardian—if applicable) (Date signed) (Witness)

__________________ __________
(Lakeside Counseling Center representative) (Date signed)

FIGURE 2.1 Release-of-information form (sample copy of a suggested format).

Source: One of the sources from which this release-of-information form was adapted is Suanna J. Wilson, *Confidentiality in Social Work: Issues and Principles* (New York: Free Press, 1978).

Do such crimes include embezzlement, pornography, and larceny? Apparently not. Schoener (2000) has reviewed court decisions in this area, and concludes helping professionals are only obligated to inform the intended victim (along with the police) when a client threatens serious physical violence to a specific person.

Student interns or beginning practitioners are advised to ask their supervisors when questions in this area arise.

Several years ago I was the faculty supervisor for a student in a field placement at a public assistance agency. The student intern had an unmarried mother on his caseload. A trusting, working relationship between the intern and the mother was developed. The mother then informed the student she was dating a person who was sometimes abusive to her when he was drunk. The mother further indicated there was a warrant for the boyfriend's arrest in another state for an armed robbery charge. The student intern contacted me inquiring whether it was his obligation to inform the police, thereby violating confidentiality. My response was that he should discuss this with his agency supervisor to find out the agency's policy in regard to this question.

Wilson (1978) further concluded:

> In summary, a professional whose client confesses an intended or past crime can find himself in a very delicate position, both legally and ethically. There are enough conflicting beliefs on how this should be handled, so that clear guidelines are lacking. Social workers who receive a communication about a serious criminal act by a client would be wise to consult an attorney for a detailed research of appropriate state statutes and a review of recent court rulings that might help determine the desired course of action. (p. 121)

In a number of other areas a professional is permitted, expected, or required to violate confidentiality.[1] These areas include:

When a client formally (usually in writing) authorizes the professional to release information.

When a professional is called to testify in a criminal case (state statutes vary regarding guidelines on what information may be kept confidential in such criminal proceedings, and therefore practitioners must research their own particular state statutes in this area).

When a client files a lawsuit against a professional (for example, for malpractice).

When a client threatens suicide and a professional may be forced to violate confidentiality to save the client's life. (The treating professional is encouraged to violate confidentiality in such circumstances, but there is not necessarily a legal requirement to do so.)

When a client threatens to harm his or her therapist.

When a professional becomes aware that a minor has committed a crime, when a minor is used by adults as an accessory in a crime, or when a minor is a victim of criminal actions. In such situations most states require that counselors inform the legal authorities. Again, the question arises of how serious the crime must be before it is reported.

When there is evidence of child abuse or neglect. Most states require professionals to report the evidence to the designated child-protection agency.

When a client's emotional or physical condition makes his or her employment a clear danger to self or others (for example, when a counselor discovers that a client who is an airplane pilot has a serious drinking problem).

In all these areas, professional judgment must be used in deciding when the circumstances justify violating confidentiality.

Privacy and Confidentiality in the Era of Modern Computer Technology

Protecting the confidentiality of files and records in human service organizations is becoming much more difficult as the technology of compiling, storing, and receiving information on clients expands exponentially. With modern technology, vast amounts of data can be gathered, recorded, stored, and processed quickly, easily, and inexpensively. Dickson (1998) notes:

> At one time, a patient's or client's record might have consisted of some basic information on a single file card, or a number of pages of personal data, process notes, and observations. Today, such a record might consist of hundreds of pages of text along with still or moving visual images and recorded sound, all stored on tape, disk, hard drive, or CD-ROM as electronic/magnetic impulses. The record might be copied into a central database of case records, and could be linked with or contain cross-references to other databases containing other records for the same individual, family, or condition. The records could be accessed, sorted, merged, compiled, and transmitted. They could be downloaded and printed, instantly copied, and transmitted by fax or computer modem to numerous other locations, anywhere in the country or internationally. And with the appropriate linkages, the record could be accessed by other computers or other data systems near and

[1] An extended discussion of these areas is contained in Suanna J. Wilson, *Confidentiality in Social Work: Issues and Principles* (New York: Free Press, 1978), and in Donald T. Dickson, *Confidentiality and Privacy in Social Work* (New York: Free Press, 1998).

> far. Along with all this, the expansion of federal and state government and private third-party insurers in monitoring and reimbursing service delivery has greatly increased the potential for broad access to and dispersion of recorded information. (pp. 124–125)

With technology, it is now possible (although some legislative acts prevent certain linkages) to link or combine a client's health, mental health, social service, juvenile court, adult court, education, and law enforcement records. At times, individuals have had inaccuracies in their records entered into computerized databases, which has severely and adversely affected them—for example, inaccuracies in credit ratings have prevented a number of people from obtaining a loan.

Preserving privacy and confidentiality in the electronic era poses crucial issues in social work. Confidentiality can now be violated in ways that didn't exist a decade ago. Faxed or computer-transmitted records and emails can be intercepted by a third party, for example. Confidential information about someone can be posted on the Internet, and then seen and copied by millions of people—anywhere around the world.

Even the destruction of records is no longer as simple as it once was. Records can be shredded, torn up, or erased from a computer file, but with modern information technologies, a record that was assumed to be destroyed or erased may exist in another location, or under another name or identification number. Therefore, it is now important for human service agencies to keep a log of what client information has been transmitted and also when, to where, and in what form it was transmitted.

Because of the potential for violations of privacy and confidentiality with modern technology, it is crucial that social workers have an in-depth understanding of privacy rights and confidentiality rights of individuals and families. Also, what information to gather, store, replicate, transmit, and who has access and for what purposes, have become crucial issues in social work.

Privileged Communication

Privileged communication is closely related to confidentiality but is narrower in scope. *Privileged communication* refers only to the legal right that protects clients, under certain circumstances, from having their communication with a professional revealed in court without their permission. Bernstein (1975) defined privileged communication as follows:

> In states where certain professional groups are granted privileged communication, the client or his attorney has the privilege of preventing the professional from answering questions about their communication when called as a witness in court. (p. 521)

Privileged communication is a legal term dealing with the admission of evidence in a court, whereas confidentiality refers to the laws or rules of professional ethics that regulate the disclosure of information by a client to a professional.

In addition, privileged communication protects the client, and the right to exercise this privilege belongs to the client, not to the professional. Four fundamental conditions are necessary to establish privilege against disclosure:

1. Communications must originate in the confidence that they will not be disclosed;
2. The element of confidentiality must be essential to the maintenance of the relationship between the parties;
3. The relation is one which in the opinion of the community ought to be fostered;
4. The injury that would inure to the relationship as a result of disclosure must be greater than the benefit gained in regard to the correct disposal of litigation. (Wigmore, 1961, p. 52)

These conditions represent the foundation for the determination of privileged communication by the judiciary. Every case that raises the issue of privileged communication is evaluated in terms of whether it meets these conditions.

Many state statutes contain exceptions to privileged communication whereby the professional must testify in court. A list of these exceptions is contained in Wilson (1978). Examples of such exceptions include:

- The client waives privilege.
- The client introduces privileged material into litigation.
- A communication does not meet Wigmore's four criteria.
- The social worker is called to testify in a criminal case.
- A client sues his or her counselor.
- A client commits or threatens a criminal act.
- A patient threatens suicide.
- A client threatens to harm his or her therapist.
- Physicians must report certain medical conditions and treatments.
- A minor is involved in criminal activity.

- Child abuse or neglect is suspected.
- A client is using certain types of drugs.
- A client's condition makes his or her employment hazardous to others.
- The court orders a professional examination.
- Involuntary hospitalization is needed for someone's protection.
- The client dies.
- A treating professional needs to collect fees for services rendered.
- Information is learned outside the professional treatment relationship.
- Information is shared in the presence of a third person.
- The federal government needs certain information.
- The right of privileged communication is not transferable from one state to another.
- Emergency action is needed to save a client's life.
- Legal action is needed for protection of a minor.
- A client engages in treasonous activities.
- A presentence investigation report is prepared.

In the past few decades, social workers have been successful in most states in attaining passage of state legislation that recognizes social worker–client privileged communication to avoid forced disclosures of confidential information in court. In states in which social workers are not granted privileged communication, they can be subpoenaed by any party to a court action, and thereby forced to testify in court fully and under oath all that transpired between the client and the social worker. If they fail to testify, they can be found in contempt of court by the judge and either fined, sent to jail, or both. Such court appearances can be detrimental to the client–worker relationship, and to future work with the client.

Social workers in recent years have been successful in all states in securing passage of legislation that licenses (or certifies) social workers. A section of such legislation usually contains a provision that recognizes social worker–client privileged communication. In various states a number of other professionals have been licensed and have secured recognition of privileged communication with clients. These professionals include attorneys, accountants, physicians, the clergy, guidance counselors, marriage counselors, nurses, psychiatrists, and psychologists.

Explaining Confidentiality to Clients

Given all the above material on confidentiality, how should a worker respond to clients' questions about confidentiality? Clients often wonder when they seek services how the information they reveal will be used. Clients need to be assured that the information they divulge will be kept confidential; otherwise they are unlikely to share their secret concerns. Compare the following two explanations involving a question asked by a husband who is seeking marriage counseling for himself and his wife:

First response:

Husband: Will what we say here be told to others?

Worker: Our agency operates on a system of relative confidentiality. This means I may discuss certain aspects of your case with other staff members at this agency, but I will not discuss your case with anyone else outside the agency. There is one exception to this: if I am subpoenaed (which might happen if you decide to get a divorce and the divorce is contested), then I would have to reveal what we talked about. I guess there might be one additional exception. Should the need arise for me to talk with professionals at other agencies (for example, your doctor), then I would first ask you to sign a release-of-information form allowing me to discuss your case.

Second response:

Husband: Will what we say here be told to others?

Worker: No, what you say here will be kept within this agency. I know when clients first come to an agency they often wonder how the information they reveal will be used. I assure you that what we talk about will be kept confidential.

The second response is probably the most desirable at agencies when the chances of subpoenas are unlikely. The first response, while more thorough, is apt to suggest to clients that there is a moderate chance that information they reveal will be used against them at some future time, which will inhibit them from sharing their "secret" concerns.

However, if a worker is providing services in an area with a moderate or high chance of court action, then clients should be informed about the limits of confidentiality. For example, a probation and parole officer should inform clients (early in the supervision period) about his or her obligations to the court if a client reveals a violation of the conditions of probation (for example, by committing another offense), as illustrated in this excerpt from an interview:

Probation Officer: I'm here to help you in any way I can. If you have personal concerns and want to talk to someone, I'd be happy to talk with you. If you choose to talk with someone else, that's certainly okay with me. The important thing is that when you have personal concerns, you get them worked out. We all have personal concerns at times. If you choose to talk to me, it will be kept confidential. The only information that will not be kept confidential is a violation by you of the conditions of probation, which we have discussed and which you have a copy of. If you violate the conditions of probation, and I find out, either by your telling me, or in some other way, I am required to make a report to the court of the violation. Do you have questions about this?

Probationee: No.

Probation Officer: All right, if you have some concern, now, or in the future, I'll be happy to talk with you.

Probationee: There is one concern I have. My girlfriend's parents as yet don't know I've been arrested and placed on probation. He's a minister, and his wife is a schoolteacher. I don't know what they will say when they find out I'm in trouble. How do you think I should handle this? [The interview continues—and a trusting, helping relationship begins to develop.]

Ethical Dilemmas About AIDS

The major social concerns and controversies encompassing AIDS are far too numerous to be addressed here, so the focus will be on a select few. The intent is to provide a perspective for how massive and complicated the issues are.

A core concern and one that has many offshoots is confidentiality. Once a person has been positively diagnosed as having antibodies to HIV and therefore is capable of transmitting the virus to others, who else should have access to this information? Do social workers have an obligation to help protect the public health that outweighs their clients' interests? Is it ethically permissible for social workers to notify identifiable partners who are in danger of contracting the AIDS virus, if their clients refuse to change high-risk behaviors or to warn their partners? Where does a social worker's obligation to preserve client confidentiality end and duty to protect or warn another person begin?

Clients who are HIV-positive may be reluctant to inform their sexual partners for a variety of reasons. They may be concerned about the possibility of being abandoned. They may be angry that their partners may, in fact, have infected them. They may fear that their partners might tell others that they are HIV-positive.

The NASW's policy statement (Landers, 1993) on HIV/AIDS concerning whether there is a duty to inform is as follows:

> Practitioners and agencies may perceive a responsibility to warn third parties of their potential for infection if their spouses, other sexual partners, or partners in intravenous drug use are HIV-infected and the partners refuse to warn them. (p. 3)

In this HIV/AIDS policy statement, NASW refers to the "duty to warn" principle, which was established by the 1974 case *Tarasoff v. Regents of the University of California* (*University of Pittsburgh Law Review,* 1975). In this precedent-setting case, the California Supreme Court ruled that psychotherapists have a duty to warn a potential victim when the professional believes there is a clear danger, even if this means breaching confidentiality. The court concluded: "The protective privilege ends where the public peril begins." Whether *Tarasoff* applies to AIDS cases has not been tested. All *Tarasoff* cases tested in court have involved threats with weapons or arson, not sexually transmitted diseases.

In regard to the thorny issue of partner notification, Dickson (1998) states:

> For social workers—and other professionals—disclosure of a patient's or client's HIV/AIDS status to others presents significant ethical and perhaps legal problems. Ethically, a strong argument can be made that if the patient or client refuses to tell a spouse, sexual partner, or other who is in danger of exposure, the social worker should take steps to protect that individual. . . . However, there is often a conflicting state confidentiality statute, with penalties for unauthorized disclosure of HIV or AIDS. Until the case and statutory law are better harmonized, the best course for the social worker is to work with the patient or client to get him or her to notify those at risk or, failing that, to gain an informed consent for notification. If this is unsuccessful, a court-ordered release of the confidential information is possible. As always, consultation and careful documentation are called for. (p. 212)

Another issue related to confidentiality is mandatory testing for antibodies to the AIDS virus. Who should be tested and what should be done with the results? For example, there is a danger that HIV-positive health care workers may transmit the AIDS virus to some of their patients. This danger raises the question "Should all health care workers (such as doctors, dentists, and nurses) be required to be tested for the AIDS virus?" Should all persons who apply for a marriage license be required to have an AIDS antibody test?

AIDS testing of prisoners is now standard policy in federal and many state prisons. However, knowing or having established that a prisoner is HIV-positive then raises several complex issues—including who should be informed of the results, how to safeguard the privacy rights of those who are found to be HIV-positive so that they are not discriminated against because of their HIV status, and how to prevent the transmission of the virus to staff and to other prisoners.

There are many ramifications to testing. People have lost jobs, been thrown out of residences and schools, and been denied services they desperately needed. For instance, some physicians and other health care professions have refused to serve people with AIDS. Morticians have refused to prepare the bodies for burial. People with AIDS need to have their rights protected, including their right of free choice. Mandated testing does not guarantee protection from discrimination.

In regard to mandatory testing for the AIDS virus, Dickson (1998) advises:

> Whatever benefits might accrue from knowing an individual's HIV-positive status, they must be balanced against the real costs. First, as many newspaper articles and much litigation has shown, keeping this information confidential is extremely difficult. If the information becomes known, a legal action for invasion of privacy is possible. Second, if an agency knows that a client is HIV-positive or if an employer or supervisor knows that a worker is HIV-positive, actions taken by the agency or employer may become suspect and scrutinized as potentially discriminatory. For known HIV-positive patients or clients, a denial of benefits or changes in or termination of service may be harder to defend or justify. For known HIV-positive employees, changes in working conditions, a failure to promote or reward, transfers or firing all become suspect as being based on the medical condition and not workplace performance. (p. 205)

An important issue is the distinction between confidential testing (also called "name-associated testing") and anonymous testing. In *confidential testing,* the identity of the person being tested is recorded, although supposedly not made public. Questions have been raised regarding who has (or should have) access to a person's positive results—those having access may include secretaries in testing sites, the state's communicable disease center, the person's physician, and even insurance companies. With confidential testing, there is a danger that those who have access to the test result may then discriminate against the person who tested positive; for example, an insurance company may find an excuse to cancel a health or life insurance policy. *Anonymous testing* involves no identification. An individual goes in for testing, uses a code word or number, and returns approximately two weeks later to receive the results. Names are neither mentioned nor recorded. One drawback is that the state's communicable disease center is not informed of a positive test result and therefore is unable to contact and encourage the person's past and present sexual partners to also be tested.

A body of law is beginning to be established that extends the legal protection against discrimination (already available to those with a physical disability) to people with AIDS. For example, AIDS is now legally recognized as a disability under the Americans with Disabilities Act.

Yet another issue concerning health care directly involves the providers of such care. A number of people in the health care professions either refuse to treat people with AIDS or treat them very differently from their other patients. For example, one medical attendant would talk to a person with AIDS only when wearing surgical clothing including gown, gloves, and mask. Under no circumstances would he touch or shake hands with a person having AIDS. How would such behavior make a person with AIDS feel? Such a person may already be feeling isolated and scourged. Such differential treatment could make anyone feel much like a leper must have felt in Biblical times.

Other health care issues involve nursing homes. Some homes refuse to admit people with AIDS. Is this fair or right? What other alternatives are available to people with AIDS when their health is seriously fading and they need extensive care?

Solutions to the last two problems must involve educating people about AIDS and preparing them to work with people who have it. Health care professionals need to learn what is safe and what is not. They need to work on their own fears and personal conflicts. It is unlikely that making new laws and mandating to people how they must behave will be enough. Would you like to have a physician remove a cancerous brain tumor from your skull when she was forced to do the surgery totally against her will?

In 1991 the American public was shocked when it was revealed that Kimberly Bergalis had apparently contracted the AIDS virus from her dentist while receiving dental services. An extensive investigation concluded that four other dental patients had also contracted the AIDS virus from this same dentist. Exactly how these patients became infected is unknown. Nationwide, very few people have contracted the AIDS virus from health care workers, such as dentists, physicians, and nurses. Therefore, because so many patients are believed to have contracted the AIDS virus from the Florida dentist (who died of AIDS), some authorities have questioned whether he intentionally engaged in dental procedures that put his patients at risk (Findlay, 1991). The risk of contracting the AIDS virus from infected health care workers is minimal. Findlay (1991) noted:

> Even if the doctor is infected, most procedures, such as a routine checkup or blood-pressure reading, put patients at no risk. . . . Even in surgery, risk is minimal. Odds are between 1 in 42,000 and 1 in 417,000 of your picking up the virus from an infected surgeon who uses proper precautions, says the CDC [Centers for Disease Control]. In contrast, your chance of dying in a car accident this year is 1 in 5,300. . . . The CDC puts your chance of contracting HIV from an infected dentist at between 1 in 263,000 and 1 in 2,632,000. (p. 66)

The danger of patients becoming infected by health care workers has led the American Medical Association, the American Dental Association, and the Centers for Disease Control to recommend that HIV-infected health care workers (who know they are infected) stop performing certain at-risk procedures. The only time for concern is when a health care procedure exposes some of the patient's blood to the blood of the infected health care worker.

Actually, health care workers are at a greater risk of contracting the AIDS virus from infected patients than vice versa. (Drawing blood, for example, from an infected patient can result in an accidental needle prick, perhaps transmitting the AIDS virus.) Substantially more health care workers have contracted the AIDS virus from infected patients than the other way around (Lloyd, 1995). The risk of transmission of the virus, however, has raised numerous complex questions. When (perhaps for what health care procedures) should patients be told that one of their health care providers has the AIDS virus? Are there circumstances or medical conditions that would warrant informing health care workers that their patient is HIV-positive? Most patients and health care workers who are HIV-positive are unaware they are infected. Are there circumstances or medical conditions for which HIV testing of either patients or health care workers should be mandated?

Many other issues have not even been mentioned here. There are opposing views regarding the conditions under which children with AIDS can go to school. Likewise, there are opposing views over whether free needles should be distributed to intravenous drug users. Will this procedure prevent them from sharing needles and thereby contracting AIDS, or will it only encourage their antisocial drug-abusing behavior? Another controversial issue is whether free condoms should be distributed to adolescents at school. Proponents say it helps prevent the spread of AIDS; opponents claim it promotes sexual promiscuity.

All of these matters merit serious attention and consideration, because people who contract this deadly disease deserve attention and compassion.

Other Values

Additional values and principles of social work practice will briefly be summarized in this section. You should also study the Code of Ethics of the National Association of Social Workers, and the Canadian Association of Social Workers' Code of Ethics, which summarize important practice ethics for social workers. The NASW is the largest professional association representing the social work profession in the United States, and the Canadian Association of Social Workers is the largest professional association representing the social work profession in Canada. (The NASW Code of Ethics appears at www.naswdc.org.)

The Institutional Orientation

Currently there are two conflicting views of the role of social welfare in our society (Wilensky & Lebeaux, 1965). One view, which has been termed *residual,* promotes a gap-filling or first-aid role. This view holds that social welfare services should be provided only when an individual's needs are not properly met through other societal institutions, primarily the family and the market economy. Social services and financial aid should not be provided until all measures or efforts have failed (other efforts include the exhaustion of the individual's or the family's resources). In addition, this view asserts that funds and services should be provided on a short-term basis (primarily during emergencies) and withdrawn when the individual or the family again becomes self-sufficient.

The residual view has been characterized as being "charity for unfortunates" (Wilensky & Lebeaux, 1965, p. 14). Funds and services are seen not as a right (something to which one is entitled) but as a gift, with the receiver having certain obligations (for example, to receive financial aid the recipient may be required to perform certain low-grade work assignments). An associated belief holds that the causes of recipients' difficulties are rooted in their own malfunctioning (that is, recipients are brought to their predicament through their own fault, because of some personal inadequacy, or ill-advised activity, or sin).

Under the residual view, there is usually a stigma attached to receiving services or funds. The prevalence of the residual stigma can be shown by your asking yourself, "Have I ever in the past felt a reluctance to seek counseling for a personal or emotional situation that I faced because I was wary of what others might think of me?" For almost everyone the answer is yes, and the reluctance to seek help is due to the residual stigma.

The opposing point of view, which has been called the *institutional view,* holds that social welfare programs are to be "accepted as a proper, legitimate function of modern industrial society in helping individuals achieve self-fulfillment" (Wilensky & Lebeaux, 1965, p. 14). Under this view, there is no stigma attached to receiving funds or services; recipients are entitled to such help. Associated with this view is the belief that individuals' difficulties result from causes largely beyond their control (for example, a person is unemployed because of a lack of employment opportunities).

The residual approach characterized social welfare programs from our early history to the Depression of the 1930s. Since the Great Depression, both approaches have been applied to social welfare programs, with some programs being largely residual in nature while others are more institutional in design and implementation. Social workers generally believe in the institutional approach and strive to develop and provide programs with this orientation.

At the present time a "devolution revolution" is occurring with regard to the provision of human services in our society. *Devolution revolution* refers to the fact that decisions about provision of key social welfare programs are being transferred from the federal government to the state level. One of the major programs that was affected by the devolution revolution was Aid to Families with Dependent Children (AFDC).

From 1935 to the middle 1990s, the federal government required all states to provide the AFDC program to eligible families. (The program was created by the 1935 Social Security Act.) This public assistance program provided monthly checks primarily to low-income mothers with children under age 18. The precise parameters of eligibility for AFDC varied from state to state. Payments were made for both the parent (or parents) and the children in eligible families. Financing and administration of the AFDC program was shared by federal and state governments. In many states, counties also participated in financing and administration. In 1996, federal legislation was enacted that dismantled the AFDC program. The entire concept that poor families are entitled to basic human and health services has now been questioned. As Chapter 13 indicates, many policymakers now believe that private charities can respond more cheaply to local social problems than public services can. The 1996 Welfare Reform Act (the Personal Responsibility and Work Opportunity Reconciliation Act) calls for the following: (1) Each state sets its own eligibility rules and amounts for financial assistance. The federal government provides block grants to states to assist in financing the programs that are developed. (2) Recipients of financial benefits receive no more than two years of assistance without working, and there is a five-year lifetime limit of benefits for adults.

In 1935, when the AFDC program was enacted, it was thought best for single mothers to stay at home to raise their children. The 1996 welfare reform legislation asserts that such single mothers (and fathers) have an obligation to work for a living. The safety net for poor families with young children now has some major holes. Clearly, the legislation marks a shift by our society to the residual approach. The profession of social work is being challenged to confront the devolution revolution and to respond to the needs of those who are falling through the holes in the safety net.

Establishing Professional Boundaries with Clients

Is it appropriate for a social worker to have lunch or dinner with a client? Is it appropriate to attend a party (where alcoholic drinks are being served) where clients may be present? Is it appropriate to hug a client who is experiencing emotional distress? These are examples of boundary questions that arise in interactions with clients.

As the years have passed, I have seen a variety of boundary problems. A well-meaning male psychotherapist was charged by a female client for unethical conduct because he occasionally gave her hugs and because he overstepped (according to her) the boundaries of a professional relationship by giving her his room air-conditioner after he had central air installed in his home. In another case, a man charged a female psychotherapist with alienation of affection after the psychotherapist and the man's wife, who was a client of the female therapist, had dinner a few times and the wife became attracted to the therapist. Some social work faculty members have dated social work students, and now universities across the country are questioning the propriety of such relationships. (A power differential exists between students and faculty, and many campuses now view such dating relationships as evidence that the involved students could use to prove sexual harassment.) A female social work intern at a group home for adolescent males was confronted by her agency supervisor because she sought to become friends with the residents. She frequently played pool with them and occasionally shared some of her "partying" stories, and one of the residents became infatuated with her. A male intern at a shelter for runaway youths occasionally related jokes that had some sexual connotations; one of the female residents charged that such behavior was evidence that the intern was making romantic advances toward her. A female intern was terminated at her field placement at a halfway house for chemically addicted correctional residents after she began dating one of the residents. A male intern at a shelter for battered women was confronted by his agency supervisor about the "provocative and revealing" clothes he tended to wear, which was a factor in some of the residents becoming infatuated with him.

Social workers have an obligation to establish appropriate boundaries in professional relationships with clients. The Canadian Association of Social Workers' Code of Ethics (1994) contains the following statements on these boundary issues:

A social worker shall not exploit the relationship with a client for personal benefit, gain or gratification.

A social worker shall not become involved in a client's personal affairs that are not relevant to the service being provided.

The social worker shall distinguish between actions and statements made as a private citizen and actions and statements made as a social worker.

The social worker shall not have a sexual relationship with a client.

The social worker shall not have a business relationship with a client, borrow money from a client, or loan money to a client.

The NASW Code of Ethics (1996) contains these statements on boundary issues:

> Social workers should not take unfair advantage of any professional relationship or exploit others to further their personal, religious, political, or business interests.
>
> Social workers should not engage in dual or multiple relationships with clients or former clients in which there is a risk of exploitation or potential harm to the client. In instances when dual or multiple relationships are unavoidable, social workers should take steps to protect clients and are responsible for setting clear, appropriate, and culturally sensitive boundaries. (Dual or multiple relationships occur when social workers relate to clients in more than one relationship, whether professional, social, or business. Dual or multiple relationships can occur simultaneously or consecutively.)
>
> Social workers should under no circumstances engage in sexual activities or sexual contact with current clients, whether such contact is consensual or forced.
>
> Social workers should not engage in activities or sexual contact with clients' relatives or other individuals with whom clients maintain a close, personal relationship where there is a risk of exploitation or potential harm to the client. Sexual activity or sexual contact with clients' relatives or other individuals with whom clients maintain a personal relationship has the potential to be harmful to the client and may make it difficult for the social worker and client to maintain appropriate professional boundaries. Social workers—not their clients, their clients' relatives, or other individuals with whom the client maintains a professional relationship—assume the full burden for setting clear, appropriate, and culturally sensitive boundaries.
>
> Social workers should not engage in sexual activities or sexual contact with former clients because of the potential for harm to the client.
>
> Social workers should not provide clinical services to individuals with whom they have had a prior sexual relationship.
>
> Social workers should not engage in physical contact with clients where there is a possibility of psychological harm to the client as a result of the contact (such as cradling or caressing clients). Social workers who engage in appropriate physical contact with clients are responsible for setting clear, appropriate, and cultur-

ally sensitive boundaries that govern such physical contact.

(The NASW Code of Ethics appears at www.naswdc.org.)

It is impossible to develop guidelines that answer all the questions that can arise when social workers set boundaries with clients, but the following guidelines may be useful in resolving some boundary dilemmas:

- In your professional *and* personal life, try to be a role model for the values and principles of the social work profession.
- In relationships with clients, try to gain their respect and to exemplify the values and principles of the social work profession, rather than establish a friend-to-friend relationship.
- Never try to meet your personal needs or wants in relationships with clients.
- Try to increase your awareness of your own needs, feelings, values, and limitations so you become increasingly aware of how such factors may affect client relationships.
- When questions arise about the appropriateness of certain interactions with a client (such as whether to go to lunch), try to arrive at an answer by gauging whether the interaction will have a constructive impact on the client and your relationship. If a concrete beneficial impact cannot be objectively specified, do not engage in the interaction.
- Constructive professional relationships with clients require a certain amount of distance. If you have questions about whether contemplated social interactions will interfere with the boundaries of a professional relationship, consult your supervisor or a respected colleague.
- In your professional social work role with clients, be aware of any inappropriate behavior, verbal communications, and dress on your part. For example, sharing details of your "wild" parties with teenage clients is unprofessional.

Promoting Social and Economic Justice

Social workers have an obligation to promote social and economic justice for those who are oppressed or victimized by discrimination. The Council on Social Work Education has identified populations-at-risk (that is, populations in the United States with a history of subjection to discrimination, economic deprivation, and oppression) to include, but not be limited to, people of color, women, gay and lesbian individuals, and those populations who are oppressed due to their ethnicity, culture, age, class, religion, or physical or mental ability.

The social work profession holds that society has a responsibility to all of its members to provide security, acceptance, and satisfaction of basic cultural, social, and biological needs. Only when individuals' basic needs are met is it possible for them to develop their maximum potentials. Therefore, social workers have a special responsibility to protect and secure civil rights based on democratic principles and a moral responsibility to work toward eradicating discrimination for any reason. Clients' civil rights need to be protected to preserve human dignity and self-respect.

In promoting social and economic justice for oppressed populations, social workers are expected to have an understanding of (1) the consequences and dynamics of social and economic injustice, including the forms of human oppression and discrimination, and (2) the impact of economic deprivation, discrimination, and oppression on populations-at-risk. Social workers have an ethical obligation to understand and appreciate human diversity. They are expected to have and use skills to promote social change that furthers the achievement of individual and collective social and economic justice.

Focus on Family

The focus of social work services is often on the family. A family is seen as an interacting independent system. The problems faced by any person are usually influenced by the dynamics within a family, as illustrated in the following example.

A schoolteacher became concerned when one of her pupils was consistently failing, and she referred the child for psychological testing. Testing revealed a normal IQ, but failure was found to be due to a low self-concept (the girl was reluctant to do her academic work because she saw herself as being incapable of doing it). A school social worker met with the family and observed that the low self-concept was primarily a result of the parents' ridiculing and criticizing the child and seldom giving emotional support, encouragement, or compliments.

A family is an interacting system, and change in one member affects others. For example, with some abusive families, the abused child is a scapegoat on which the parents vent their anger and hostility. If the abused child is removed from the home, another child within the family is at times selected to be the scapegoat (Leavitt, 1974).

Another reason for the focus on the family rather than on the individual is that the other family members are often needed in the treatment process. For example, other family members can put pressure on an alcoholic to have him or her acknowledge that a problem exists. The family members may also need counseling to help them cope with the person when he or she is drinking, and these family members may play important roles in providing emotional support for the alcoholic's efforts to stop drinking.

Accountability

Increasingly, federal and state governmental units and private funding sources are requiring that the effectiveness of service programs be measured. Gradually, programs found to be ineffective are being phased out. Although some social workers view accountability with trepidation and claim the paperwork involved interferes with serving clients, members of the social work profession have an obligation to funding sources to provide the highest quality services. Two hundred years ago, bloodletting was thought to be an effective treatment technique. Only a few decades ago, lobotomies were erroneously thought to be effective. Now the value of electroshock therapy, psychoanalysis, and some other therapy techniques is being questioned. Program outcome studies have also demonstrated that: orphanages are not the best place to serve homeless children; long-term hospitalization is not the best way to help those who are emotionally disturbed; probation generally has higher rehabilitative value than long-term confinement in prison; the Job Corps program of the 1960s was too expensive for the outcomes achieved; children with a cognitive disability can be better served in their home communities through local programs than by confinement in an institution; and so on.

Social workers need to become skilled at evaluating the extent to which they are being effective in providing services. A wide variety of evaluation techniques are now available to assess effectiveness of current services and to identify unmet needs and service gaps. One of the most useful approaches is management by objectives (MBO). This technique involves specifying the objectives of a program, stating in measurable terms how and when these objectives are to be met, and then periodically measuring the extent to which the objectives are being met.

Management by objectives is also one of the most useful approaches that social workers can use to assess their effectiveness in providing services. Many agencies now require their workers, with the involvement of their clients, to: (1) identify and specify what the goals will be for each client—generally this is done together with clients during the initial interviews; (2) write down in detail what the client and the worker will do to accomplish the goals—deadlines for accomplishing these tasks are also set; and (3) assess, when treatment is terminated (and perhaps periodically during the treatment process), the extent to which the goals have been achieved.

If goals are generally not being achieved, the worker needs to identify and examine the underlying reasons. Perhaps unrealistic goals are being set. Perhaps the program or the treatment techniques are ineffective. Perhaps certain components of the treatment program are having an adverse effect. Perhaps other reasons account for the low success rate. Appropriate changes then need to be made.

Conversely, if the goals are generally being met, workers can use this information to document to funding sources and to supervisors that high-quality services are being provided.

Summary

Several values underlying social work practice and their implications for practice were presented. Social work is both an art and a science. Because social work is partly an art, a worker frequently must make decisions based on values rather than on knowledge. Change techniques used by workers are often based on theory and value assumptions rather than on proven therapy techniques.

Values were distinguished from knowledge. Values are beliefs, preferences, or assumptions about what is desirable or good for people. Knowledge statements are observations about the world and people that have been verified or are capable of verification. It is much easier to change a client's belief that conflicts with current knowledge than it is to change a belief based on values. Guidelines were presented for how a worker should handle a value conflict between the worker and the client.

An important value of social work is respect for the dignity and uniqueness of the individual. The importance of individualizing each client was discussed, and guidelines were presented on how to relate to clients whose behavior is viewed as disgusting by the worker. Involved in individualization is the ability to accept clients but not the deviant behavior to be changed, careful attendance to clients' communications, and the discreet use of labeling.

Self-determination is the clients' right to express their own opinions and to act on them, as long as clients do not infringe on the rights of others. Clients should be made aware that there are alternatives for resolving the personal and social problems they face. Self-determination means that the client, not the worker, is the chief problem solver, although the worker has an obligation to offer suggestions of resolution approaches that the client may not be aware of.

Confidentiality is the implicit or explicit agreement between a professional and a client to maintain the private nature of information about the client. In professional practice a system of relative confidentiality currently exists, rather than a system of absolute confidentiality. Numerous unresolved questions surrounding confidentiality were raised, and some guidelines on how beginning practitioners should handle these questions were presented. At times, circumstances arise in which a professional is permitted, expected, or required to violate confidentiality, and a number of these circumstances were listed—for example, when a client admits to a past or intended serious criminal act. Protecting the confidentiality of clients' files and records in human service organizations is becoming much more difficult as information technology expands exponentially.

Other values of social work practice were summarized: belief in the institutional approach for the delivery of social services rather than the residual approach; establishment of professional boundaries with clients; promotion of social and economic justice for those being oppressed or discriminated against; focus on family instead of the individual in provision of services; and accountability.

In presenting guidelines for social work practice, you were advised that such guidelines are not to be applied as absolutes but simply as concepts that *may* be useful in working with people.

EXERCISES

1. CONFIDENTIALITY

Goal: To get a feel for when to uphold, and when to violate, confidentiality.

Step 1: Divide into groups of about five students. Each group then answers questions raised in the following vignettes.

a. You're a social worker at a public school and have been working with a family that has multiple problems. Two of the children are in special education programs for the emotionally disturbed. The mother has occasionally been hospitalized for emotional problems. The father has been investigated by protective services for child abuse in the past. Mother and father are having marital problems and are presently separated. The father comes to your office and demands to see the school's records on his children and his family. As a social worker, would you show him these records?

b. You're a social worker at a mental health center and are working with a client who appears to be emotionally upset. He states he has heard that his girlfriend is seeing someone else. While saying this, he becomes enraged and says he intends to shoot her. He asks you not to tell anyone what he has said. As you endeavor to discuss his threat, he becomes more upset and walks out, stating, "I'll make sure she doesn't cheat on me." Should you violate confidentiality and inform someone? If so, who would you inform?

c. You're a social worker at a drug abuse treatment center and you're working with a 23-year-old female. You establish a good working relationship with her. She says something has been bothering her for a long time, but she states she won't discuss it unless you agree not to tell anyone. You

(continued)

EXERCISES
(continued)

assure her that what she reveals will be kept confidential. She then reveals that in the past she had an incestuous relationship with her stepfather that started when she was 14 and lasted nearly three years. She believes her unresolved feeling about this experience is one of the reasons she sometimes drinks too much. In a staff meeting on this client, would you reveal to the other staff what she has said?

Step 2: The groups share their answers with the class. The instructor then summarizes the text's answers to these questions, which involve (a) the 1974 Federal Privacy Act, (b) the 1974 *Tarasoff v. Regents of the University of California* decision, and (c) guidelines about sharing information with other staff.

Step 3: Class discussion about how social work practice uses a system of relative, rather than absolute, confidentiality. Class review of chapter guidelines on when to uphold and when to violate confidentiality.

2. *CLARIFYING VALUES*

Goal: To clarify values on a number of prominent issues in social work.

Step 1: Class discussion of why social workers need to be aware of their personal values and aware of professional values, when workers should take a nonjudgmental position with clients, and when they should seek to sell to clients (or enforce to clients) a particular set of values.

In groups of three, develop answers, and reasons for your answers, to the following ten questions.

a. You are a protective service worker and you have evidence that a father is committing incest with his 10-year-old daughter. Would you seek to end the incest by (1) providing counseling services to all family members to keep the family intact, (2) bringing legal charges against the father, or (3) seeking to do both at the same time?

b. Do you support a constitutional amendment to make abortions illegal?

c. Does a social worker have an obligation to preserve confidentiality if an HIV-infected client refuses to inform their sexual partner of the infection (while persisting in behavior that places the partner at risk), or does the social worker have an obligation to warn the partner about the peril?

d. Do you support affirmative action programs that assert that certain minority groups and women should be given preference in hiring over white males?

e. If an elderly person who is terminally ill and in intense pain wants to end their life, should physicians be allowed to provide assistance in helping this person end their life?

f. Do you believe the United States should support an extensive program to develop the capacity to clone human beings?

g. Do you believe in capital punishment for certain crimes?

h. Do you think a gay or lesbian teacher should be allowed to teach in elementary and secondary schools?

i. Do you think women in military service should fight in combat?

j. Should condoms and other birth control contraceptives be provided to requesting students through health care clinics located in middle schools and high schools?

Step 2: Groups present and discuss their answers. Each question is taken one at a time. (*Note:* the purpose of this exercise is to help you clarify your values and not to sell any particular value system.)

Step 3: Discuss how you felt when others in class expressed views that you strongly disagree with.

3. NEW FRONTIER TO RINGS OF FIRE

Goal: To help you clarify your values about humanity.

Step 1: Form groups of about five. Your instructor reads the following vignette to the students:

The United States has recently completed building a remarkable spaceship, named *New Frontier,* that is capable of carrying 7 people to planets in other galaxies. *New Frontier* uses nuclear power and is guided by a new computer system that does not require a pilot to fly the spaceship.

Our government has recently discovered a new planet in a faraway galaxy that is very similar to our Earth's atmosphere and appears capable of supporting life. This planet has been named Rings of Fire as it has a red hue and several rings around it similar to those of Saturn.

Your group has been chosen by the president of the United States to select the 7 people who will take the first flight. *New Frontier* is presently located on a remote Samoan island.

Suddenly a nuclear war breaks out in the Middle East, and the superpowers quickly enter the conflict. The bombs and the radioactive fallout will destroy civilization as we know it. The chief scientist frantically calls your group. She indicates your group has 15 minutes to select the 7 people to go on *New Frontier* to Rings of Fire. A country we are fighting in this war has sent a nuclear missile to this Samoan island to destroy *New Frontier.* There are 13 people close enough to board *New Frontier.* The chief scientist wants your group to select the 7 people so that these 13 people do not begin fighting among themselves. If your group does not select 7 people in 15 minutes, there is a danger the human race will cease to exist. The 7 people selected may well be the only hope for continuing the human race. Your group has only the following information about the 13 people.

1. Chief scientist, 57 years old, has a husband and three children who live in Beaumont, Texas.
2. Male Korean medical student, 24 years old.
3. White male rabbi, 28 years old.
4. Female Samoan prostitute who has herpes, 35 years old.
5. White male professional baseball player, 26 years old and gay.
6. Protestant male child, 8 years old.
7. White female who has a cognitive disability from not having enough oxygen at birth, 10 years old.
8. White Catholic male who is unemployed and has cerebral palsy, 27 years old.
9. White male truck driver who has a history of not getting along with people and of getting into numerous fights, 34 years old.
10. Samoan farmer who has had a vasectomy, 22 years old.
11. Female Japanese stockbroker, 27 years old.
12. White female who is depressed and has a long history of being hospitalized for emotional problems, 35 years old.

(continued)

E X E R C I S E S
(continued)

13. White female who is a millionaire via inheritance and detests working, 26 years old.

Step 2: Distribute copies of this list to each group. Each group has 15 minutes to complete the task; your instructor will announce when 10, 5, 3, and 1 minute remain.

Step 3: Group presentation of its choices and the reasons for its selections. Class discussion of (a) the values underlying the selections and (b) the merits and shortcomings of this exercise.

P A R T **2**

Social Work Practice

CHAPTER 3

Assessment

A simplified paradigm of the problem-solving process in social work is: assessment→intervention→termination and evaluation. In this chapter, we discuss the first element, assessment.

Assessment is a critical process in social work practice. The selection of goals and interventions depends largely on the assessment. An inaccurate or incomplete assessment can lead to inappropriate goals and inappropriate interventions. When an inaccurate or incomplete assessment is made, positive changes are unlikely to occur.

Hepworth and Larsen (1986) defined assessment as follows:

> Assessment is the process of gathering, analyzing, and synthesizing salient data into a formulation that encompasses the following vital dimensions: (1) the nature of clients' problems, including special attention to the roles that clients and significant others play in the difficulties; (2) the functioning (strengths, limitations, personality assets, and deficiencies) of clients and significant others; (3) motivation of clients to work on the problems; (4) relevant environmental factors that contribute to the problems; and (5) resources that are available or are needed to ameliorate the clients' difficulties. (p. 165)

In a closely related definition, Barker (1999) defines assessment as:

> The process of determining the nature, cause, progression, and prognosis of a problem and the personalities and situations involved therein; the social work function of acquiring an understanding of a problem, what causes, it, and what can be changed to minimize or resolve it. (p. 32)

Assessment has sometimes been referred to as *psychosocial diagnosis* (Hollis, 1972). But the term *diagnosis* focuses on what is wrong with the client, family, or group being diagnosed—such as having a disease, dysfunction, or mental problem. Because diagnosis has a negative connotation, many other social work educators, myself included, prefer the term *assessment*. Assessment includes not only what is wrong with the client[1] but also the resources, strengths, motivations, functional components, and other positive factors that can be used to resolve difficulties, to enhance func-

[1]The term *client* in this chapter will often be used in a generic sense to refer to an individual, family, group, organization, or community that a practitioner is working with.

tioning, and to promote growth. In fact, assessment in its broadest sense is the base for the development of an intervention plan.

The *nature* of the assessment task varies significantly with the setting in which the social worker practices, but the *process* is similar in all settings. A social worker in a nursing home who is assessing an applicant for potential placement will look at variables that are radically different from those examined by a social worker in a protective service setting who is assessing an allegation of child abuse.

In some settings (as in many protective services programs), the social worker makes an independent assessment. With independent assessments, the social worker may consult with colleagues or professionals in other disciplines on complicated cases. In other settings (for example, mental health clinics, schools, and medical hospitals), the social worker will likely be a member of a clinical team that makes an assessment. Other team members may include a psychologist, psychiatrist, nurse, and perhaps professionals from other disciplines. Team members have specific roles in the assessment process, which is based on their special professional expertise. The psychologist, for example, focuses primarily on psychological functioning and would probably administer a variety of psychological tests (including personality and intelligence tests). The social worker compiles a social history to assess family background, marital dynamics, environmental factors, and employment and educational background. In settings in which the social worker is the primary assessor, the assessment is generally completed in one to three sessions. With a clinical team approach, the case is usually more complicated, and assessment by the various professionals may take a few weeks.

Assessment is sometimes a product and sometimes an ongoing process. As a product, an assessment is a formulation at a point in time regarding the nature of a client's difficulties and resources. An example is a mental status assessment at a psychiatric hospital. Such an assessment is first focused on determining whether the client is sane or psychotic. If the client is assessed as psychotic, a psychiatric label is assigned and a recommended treatment approach is then stated. Product assessments usually have to be updated and revised months or sometimes years later. Such an assessment is, in essence, a working hypothesis of a client's difficulties and resources based on current data. As time passes, the client may change and so will environmental factors. Such changes require the assessment to be periodically updated and revised.

Assessment can also be an ongoing process, from the initial interview to the termination of the case. The length of time a client receives services may be weeks, months, or even years. During this time, the professionals working with the case are continually receiving and analyzing new information. In the early stages of client contact, the focus is primarily on gathering information to assess the client's problems and resources. Once these are tentatively specified, problem solving is emphasized, as resolution strategies are suggested, analyzed, and then one or more strategies selected and implemented. But even in the problem-solving phase, new information related to the client's difficulties and resources is apt to emerge, necessitating a revision of the assessment. In fact, as contact between the professional and client continues, the client may disclose additional problems that need to be assessed and then resolved. It is common in initial contact for a client to withhold vital information for fear of condemnation. For example, a parent who is abusing a child may initially deny that the abuse is occurring. As time passes, if the parent comes to trust the worker, the parent may disclose that she at times loses control and then hits the child. As new information is provided, the initial assessment needs to be revised.

Hepworth and Larsen (1986) noted that assessment continues to occur even during the termination phase:

> The process of assessment continues even during the terminal phase of service. During the final interviews, the practitioner carefully evaluates the client's readiness to terminate, assesses the presence of residual difficulties that may cause future difficulties, and identifies possible emotional reactions to termination. The practitioner also considers possible strategies to assist the client to maintain improved functioning or to achieve additional progress after formal social work service is concluded. (p. 166)

The Strengths Perspective

For most of the past several decades, social work and the other helping professions focused primarily on diagnosing the pathology, shortcomings, and dysfunctions of clients. One reason may be that Freudian psychology was the primary theory used in analyzing human behavior. (Freud's theories of personality development and psychopathology are summarized in Module 1.) Freudian psychology is based on a medical model and its concepts are therefore geared to identify illness or pathology. It has very few concepts for identifying strengths. As described in Chapter 1, social work is now shifting to a systems model in assessing human behavior. This model focuses on identifying both strengths and weaknesses.

It is essential that social workers include clients' strengths in the assessment process. Today social workers routinely focus on the strengths and resources of clients to help them resolve their difficulties. However, to utilize client's strengths effectively, social workers must first identify those strengths.

Unfortunately, Maluccio (1979) found that many social workers focus too much on clients' perceived weaknesses and underestimate or are blind to their strengths. Maluccio concluded:

> There is a need to shift the focus on social work education and practice from problems or pathology to strengths, resources, and potentialities in human beings and their environments. (p. 401)

A primary focus on weaknesses can impair a worker's capacity to identify the clients' growth potential. Social workers strongly believe that clients have the right (and should be encouraged) to develop their potential fully. Focusing on pathology often undermines this commitment.

Another reason for attending to clients' strengths is that many clients need help in enhancing their self-esteem. Many have feelings of worthlessness, feelings of inadequacy, a sense of being a failure, and a lack of self-confidence and self-respect. Glasser (1972) noted that low self-esteem often leads to emotional difficulties, withdrawal, or criminal activity. To help clients view themselves more positively, social workers must first view their clients as having considerable strengths and competencies. Berwick (1980) underscored this point in working with neglectful parents of children who fail to thrive:

> Self-esteem is already at a low ebb in many of the parents of these children, and the success of the hospital in nourishing a child when the mother has failed only serves to accentuate the pain of failure. . . . Even in the few cases that require foster care, the health care team's task is to seek strengths and to develop a sense of competence in both the parents and the child that will permit a synchronous nurturant relationship to emerge. (p. 270)

The strengths perspective is closely related to the concept of empowerment. *Empowerment* has been defined by Barker (1995) as "the process of helping individuals, families, groups, and communities to increase their personal, interpersonal, socioeconomic, and political strength and to develop influence toward improving their circumstances" (p. 20). The strengths perspective seeks to identify, use, build, and reinforce the strengths and abilities people already have. This is in contrast to the pathological perspective, which focuses on their deficiencies and inabilities. The strengths perspective is useful across the life cycle and throughout all stages of the helping process—assessment, intervention, and evaluation. It emphasizes people's abilities, values, "interests, beliefs, resources, accomplishments, and aspirations" (Weick, Rapp, Sullivan, & Kisthardt, 1989).

According to Saleebey (1997, pp. 12–15), five principles underlie the guiding assumptions of the strengths perspective:

1. *Every individual, group, family, and community has strengths.* The strengths perspective is about discerning these resources. Saleebey notes:

> In the end, clients want to know that you actually care about them, that how they fare makes a difference to you, that you will listen to them, that you will respect them no matter what their history, and that you believe that they can build something of value with the resources within and around them. But most of all, clients want to know that you believe they can surmount adversity and begin the climb toward transformation and growth. (p. 12)

2. *Trauma, abuse, illness, and struggle can be injurious, but they can also be sources of challenge and opportunity.* Clients who have been victimized are seen as active and developing individuals who, through their traumas, learn skills and develop personal attributes that help them cope with future struggles. There is dignity to be found in having prevailed over obstacles. We often grow more from crises in which we find ways to handle situations effectively than from periods in our lives when we are content and comfortable.

3. *Assume that you do not know the upper limits of the capacity to grow and change, and take individual, group, and community aspirations seriously.* This principle means workers need to hold high expectations of

clients and to form alliances with their visions, hopes, and values. Individuals, families, and communities have the capacity for restoration and rebounding. When workers connect with the hopes and dreams of clients, clients are apt to have greater faith in themselves. Then they are able to put forth the effort needed for their hopes and dreams to become self-fulfilling prophecies.

4. *We best serve clients by collaborating with them.* A worker is more effective when seen by the client as a collaborator or consultant rather than as an expert or a professional. A collaborative stance by a worker makes her or him less vulnerable to many of the adverse effects of an expert-inferior relationship, including paternalism, victim-blaming, and preemption of client views.

5. *Every environment is full of resources.* In every environment (no matter how harsh) there are individuals, groups, associations, and institutions with something to give, and with something that others may desperately need. The strengths perspective seeks to identify these resources and make them available to benefit individuals, families, and groups in a community.

Sources of Information

Information used in making an assessment comes from a variety of sources. The following are the primary sources.

The Client's Verbal Report

A client's verbal report is often the primary source and in some cases the only source of information. (For example, social workers in private practice sometimes obtain information only from the client.) A variety of information can be obtained in this way: description of the problems; feelings about the problems; views of his or her personal resources to combat the problems; motivations to make efforts to resolve the problems; the history of the problems; views of the causes; a description of what has already been done in attempting to resolve the problems; and so on.

Although clients are often fairly accurate in describing their difficulties and resources, workers should be aware that verbal reports are sometimes distorted by embarrassment, bias, distorted perceptions, and strong emotions. For example, a married woman whose husband has left her for someone else may be so immersed in her emotional reactions that she cannot be objective about the role she played in the breakup of her marriage. In some settings, clients deliberately try to conceal, or even distort, information. Abusive parents, for example, may deny they have abused their children. Alcoholics, because of the nature of the addictive process, are apt to deny they have a drinking problem. Correctional clients may try to conceal some of their illegal activities.

Client's verbal reports should be respected as valid until additional information indicates otherwise. In some settings, as in protective services, it is often necessary to verify a client's denial that a problem exists by checking with other sources, such as neighbors, relatives, and school personnel.

Assessment Forms

Many agencies, before or after the first interview, ask clients to supply such information as name, address, telephone number, employer, years of school completed, marital status, description of problem, names of family members, and so on. Such information is most efficiently collected by having the client fill out a form.

Self-report forms can also be used in the assessment process. Some clients, particularly adolescents, may be more relaxed and more truthful if they can answer questions on a form, while being assured that only helping professionals at the agency will see the answers. Examples of self-report forms for children and adolescents are the Piers-Harris Children's Self-Concept Scale (Piers & Harris, 1969), and the Personal Problems Checklist for Adolescents (Schinka, 1985). Both of these instruments repeat questions in different ways so that the examiner can get a sense of reliability—that is, the extent to which the respondent answers the same question in the same way. These instruments also have validity indexes. There are also self-report instruments for adults, such as the Forty-Eight Item Counseling Evaluation Test: Revised (McMahon, 1971).

If a worker chooses to use a self-report instrument, he or she should be knowledgeable about the instrument and guidelines for its use. Research on its reliability and validity should be carefully studied to evaluate its usefulness. Also, the worker needs to use common sense in interpreting the results. Like so many other parts of the assessment process, a test result is a starting point, not an end product. Corcoran and Fischer (1987) provide a comprehensive review of a number of instruments that can be used to assess various aspects of client's functioning.

Computer-Assisted Assessment Forms

Nurius and Hudson (1993) have developed a computer-based evaluation tool that includes the Walmyr Assessment Scales. These scales were developed by Hudson (1992) and include scales that measure self-esteem, depression, anxiety, clinical stress, peer relations, homophobia, sexual attitudes, alcohol involvement, marital satisfaction, sexual satisfaction, physical abuse of partner, nonphysical abuse of partner, parental attitude toward children, children's attitudes toward father and mother, family relations, sibling relations, children's behavior, and a general screening inventory. Depending on clients' preferences, they can complete the scales manually, or on a personal computer.

Computer programs accommodate different types of scales, including self-anchored, single-item, multiple-item, checklists, multidimensional rating scales, and others. Hepworth, Rooney, and Larsen (1997) note:

> Computer-aided assessment deserves the attention of practitioners. Clients reportedly respond well to this technology. The greatest potential for use of this tool derives from the computer's ability to process, integrate, and synthesize data from expanded sources of information. The computer's objectivity also reduces evaluative errors caused by subjective interpretations of data by practitioners. (p. 202)

Collateral Sources

Information is sometimes collected from collateral sources: friends, relatives, neighbors, physicians, other social agencies, teachers, and others who may be able to provide relevant information. In some cases, clients have received social services from a number of other agencies. Summary information about such clients is often obtained from these agencies.

Some workers overlook collateral sources; as a result, potentially valuable information is not collected. Less frequently, workers spend too much time gathering collateral information. In social work practice, a practitioner needs to exercise prudence in deciding what information is needed. In many circumstances, it is essential to get the client's verbal consent and have the client sign release-of-information forms before contacting collateral sources. (See Chapter 2 for a description of confidentiality and release-of-information forms.)

Psychological Tests

There are a variety of personality and intelligence tests. Most psychological tests are designed to be administered by psychologists. An exception, however, are the tests, described earlier, that Hudson (1992) has developed for clinical social workers.

Caution should be used with psychological tests, because most tests are not designed to be administered or interpreted by social workers. Such administration and interpretation is the responsibility of psychologists. In addition, most personality tests have low validity and reliability and should be used with extreme caution, if at all.

Nonverbal Behavior

Clients' nonverbal behavior provides a valuable source of information. As practitioners become more experienced, they give greater attention to, and become more competent in, identifying and interpreting nonverbal cues. These cues are invaluable in identifying what clients are actually thinking and feeling. Nonverbal cues include gestures, posture, breathing patterns, tension in facial and neck muscles, facial color, eye movements, choice of clothes, physical appearance, eye contact, and tone of voice. Such cues give information about stress levels, kinds of feelings being experienced, and whether the client is telling the truth. For example, a client who folds his arms over his chest and frowns every time a worker brings up a particular topic is conveying valuable information about his feelings related to that topic.

Interactions with Significant Others and Home Visits

Observing a client interacting with people who are important in her life reveals a lot of information. These significant others include family members, other close relatives, peers, friends, and neighbors. The way a client presents herself in an office may differ dramatically from the way she interacts at home. In an office setting, a client may present an image that is atypical for her. A home visit provides information not only about how a client interacts with significant others but also about environmental factors. For example, a home visit investigating a charge that a single mother is neglecting her children will reveal information about home cleanliness, available food and diet, presence of animals (including pets and rats), presence of cockroaches and insects, available clothing, possible drug abuse by the parent, home interactions between mother and children, interactions between the mother and neighbors, type of neighborhood, and financial circumstances.

Social work emphasizes the importance of assessing the person-in-environment. Home visits are an integral part of assessing the environmental factors that affect a client.

Remember that an office setting is an unnatural arena for family interaction. In an unnatural setting, families are less apt to interact as they do at home. As with any source of information, conclusions drawn from observed interaction can be erroneous. For example, the way a family interacts while being observed may be atypical of how they interact when they know they are not being observed.

Additionally, clients will often feel some discomfort if the worker is better educated and has a higher societal status. Most people are more relaxed in their own home, and a home visit can help such clients feel more accepted and less anxious.

Worker's Conclusions from Direct Interactions

Clients often manifest similar interactional patterns in their social relationships. The way clients interact with a worker therefore provides clues to their difficulties or successes in interactions with others. Some of the many ways in which a worker may experience clients include their being nonassertive, passive, submissive, aggressive, withdrawn, passive-aggressive, personable, caring, manipulative, highly motivated, insecure, or dependent. Such observations can provide valuable information about a client's problematic behavior. For example, I once counseled a 22-year-old college coed who complained that her roommates used her as a "doormat." They frequently borrowed her car, failed to pay for gas, wore her clothes without asking, and ate the food she bought without asking. In the interview she came across as nonassertive (with her verbal and nonverbal communication) and as making extraordinary efforts to please me. I pointed out these specific behaviors to her and asked whether she might be inadvertently communicating through these behaviors that she would not object to her roommates "using her things." She thought about it for a while and acknowledged that my assessment was probably accurate. She was then instructed in how to express her concerns assertively to her roommates. With role playing, she gradually acquired the confidence to confront her roommates about these concerns.

There are cautions and limitations to using your personal conclusions to assess a client's interactions with others. A client may interact atypically with a social worker because he wants to convey an atypical image. Just as some people change their patterns when interacting with a police officer, some clients seek to convey an atypical image when interacting with a worker.

Also, the worker's personality may lead clients to interact atypically. For example, if a worker comes across as aggressive and highly confrontive, two reactions are common: The client becomes either passive and submissive or aggressive. Therefore, to use observations effectively in assessing clients' behaviors, the worker must have substantial awareness of self and an awareness of how he or she tends to affect others during interactions. The worker must also convey a nonjudgmental attitude. For lasting change to occur, most clients need to feel competent. To feel competent, most clients need to value and believe in themselves.

Knowledge Used in Making an Assessment

An extensive knowledge of human behavior and the social environment is needed for a high degree of accuracy when assessing the problems of a client system. Hepworth and Larsen (1986) noted:

> To assess the problems of a client system (individual, couple, or family) . . . requires extensive knowledge about that system as well as careful consideration of the multifarious systems (e.g., economic, legal, educational, medical, religious, social, interpersonal) that impinge upon the client system. Moreover, to assess the functioning of an individual entails evaluating various aspects of that person's functioning. For example, one must consider dynamic interactions among the biophysical, cognitive, emotional, cultural, behavioral, and motivational subsystems and the relationships of those interactions to problematic situations. (p. 172)

As identified by Hepworth and Larsen, conducting an assessment may require a broad array of knowledge about

- Multifarious systems
- Biophysical factors
- Cognitive factors
- Emotional factors
- Cultural factors
- Behavioral factors
- Motivational factors
- Family systems
- Environmental factors

At first glance, learning about all these factors seems overwhelming, but such knowledge is obtained in college from a variety of social work courses. A key course in most social work programs is thus a course in human behavior and the social environment. Practice and policy courses also cover some of these areas. Other disciplines that provide background information are sociology, psychology, anthropology, biology, political science, women's studies, ethnic studies, history, communication, philosophy, religious studies, and economics.

In addition, the overall purpose of an assessment gives considerable focus to what knowledge is needed. For example, a social worker assessing an elderly applicant for placement in a nursing home would first need to know the nursing home's criteria for accepting applicants. Such criteria may include financial resources, medical conditions, physical strengths and impairments, emotional and behavioral patterns, special needs, level of cognitive functioning, and degree of willingness to enter a nursing home. Based on the nursing home's criteria, the social worker would then obtain information from the client, family members, physicians, and other relevant sources to determine the extent to which the client meets the criteria.

A careful assessment sharpens the focus on what factors should be examined. For example, for a fourth-grade child who is performing considerably below his grade level in schoolwork, the following variables might be examined: Does he have a learning disability? What is his IQ? Is he having emotional difficulties? Does he have low self-esteem? Is this contributing to his low level of performance? Does he have a visual or hearing impairment or other medical problems? Are there factors in his home and family life that are influencing his school performance? What specific educational subjects and tasks is he doing fairly well at, and which is he having the most trouble with? How does he interact with peers and with teachers? Has he experienced significant traumas in the past that may still be affecting him? Is he involved in using and perhaps abusing drugs? Is he motivated to do his best in school? How does he feel about his school performance?[2]

The theory or theories a practitioner uses have a major influence on what is examined during an assessment. For example, Freudian psychology focuses on pathology, or unconscious processes, on fixations during a child's development, on sexuality, and on traumatic experiences during childhood. In contrast, rational therapy asserts that thinking patterns determine emotions and actions, and therefore the focus is on identifying client self-talk that leads to unwanted emotions and dysfunctional behaviors. (Module 6 summarizes rational therapy.) What workers look for in their analysis has a big effect on the outcome. For example, practically everyone has traumatic early childhood experiences—so it is not surprising that an adherent of Freudian psychology doing an assessment would identify some traumatic early childhood experiences and then hypothesize them as causes of the client's current problems. Similarly, all individuals talk to themselves in negative ways at times, so it is not surprising that a rational therapist would find evidence to support his theory in an assessment.

The worker's favorite theories of assessment and intervention can have enormous consequences for the client. For example, adherents of Freudian psychology are much more apt to assess a person as psychotic (because they believe mental illness exists) than are adherents of reality therapy, who believe that mental illness is a myth. (Modules 1 and 5 examine, respectively, Freudian psychoanalysis and reality therapy.)

Most theories of human behavior have not been proven. Many practitioners make the mistake of assuming that their favorite theory or theories are factual. When an assessment is based on a theory of human behavior, the practitioner should be aware that the results of the assessment rest on the accuracy of

[2]Additional material elsewhere in this text may be valuable in conducting an assessment: Chapter 4, how to write a social history; Chapters 4 and 5, interviewing and counseling (helpful when gathering information from clients and from collateral resources); Chapters 6 and 7, group dynamics; Chapter 8, family functioning and family systems (useful in assessing families); Chapter 9, how to analyze social welfare organizations; Chapter 10, how to assess community needs and how to conduct a community needs assessment; Chapter 12, diversity and populations-at-risk; Chapter 13, spirituality; Modules 1–3, 5, and 6, contemporary theories of personality development and psychopathology; Module 4, summary of learning theory approaches to conceptualizing behavioral dysfunctions; Module 7, gender-role stereotyping and the feminist perspective; Module 8, a communications model that has useful concepts in assessing human behavior; Module 10, assessing sexual dysfunctions.

the theory (and many theories have not yet been proven). Practitioners need to realize that their assessment of someone is not "gospel" but only a hypothesis.

Environmental Systems Emphasis

As described in Chapter 1, social work is increasingly using an ecological perspective in assessing human behavior. The ecological perspective involves considering the adaptive fit of human beings and their environments—that is, the ecology of people in their "life space," which includes all the components of the social and physical environments that have an impact on them. An ecological perspective stresses the importance of assessing the person in the environment. Such an assessment therefore focuses not only on the person but also on the environmental systems that have an impact on him or her.

When assessing environment, the worker should limit his or her attention to those elements that are affecting (positively or negatively) the problem situation. In some cases the elements may be obvious (for example, substandard housing and serious financial problems). In other cases the elements may be subtle (for instance, having aloof parents who give little encouragement).

Although the assessment of environmental factors should be limited to those that affect the client's problematic situations, a number of basic environmental needs are universal. A partial list of these includes:

- Adequate housing
- Safety from hazards and safety from air, noise, and water pollution
- Opportunities for a quality education
- Adequate social support systems (for example, family and relatives, neighbors, friends, and organized groups)
- Access to quality health care
- Access to recreational facilities
- Adequate police and fire protection
- Adequate financial resources to purchase essential items for an acceptable standard of living
- Sufficient food and opportunities for a nutritional diet
- Adequate clothing
- Emotional support from significant others
- Support from significant others to be drug free

Some students majoring in social work have the misconception that social workers sit in offices and counsel clients. True, counseling is a function, but workers have many more responsibilities. They work with families, of course, but they also work with organizations and a variety of other groups to assess community needs and to meet unmet needs. For most social workers, in-office counseling is only a small fraction of the total services provided. A major part of their work involves assessing environmental systems and then endeavoring to change those systems that have a negative impact on clients. To change the environment, a worker may use a variety of skills, such as brokering, advocacy, program development, mediation, research, enabling, and case management. Here are a few examples:

- A protective service worker removes a child from a family in which she is being sexually abused and places her in a foster home.
- A worker arranges for visiting nurses and Meals on Wheels (home-delivered hot meals for homebound persons) to serve an elderly couple so they can continue to live independently.
- A worker arranges for homemaker services for a single mother with three young children; such services involve shopping, cleaning, budgeting, preparing balanced meals, doing the laundry, and teaching these same skills to the mother.
- A worker works with a women's group to develop a shelter for battered women and their children in the community.
- A worker helps a community develop local chapters of needed self-help groups, such as Alcoholics Anonymous, Narcotics Anonymous, and Parents Anonymous.
- A worker refers a family with a terminally ill member to a hospice program.
- A practitioner works with parents of children with special needs to establish closer collaboration with schoolteachers to enhance the children's functioning in school.
- A worker joins with other health professionals in seeking to raise the state's licensing standards for residential treatment centers, nursing homes, or day-care centers.

Assessing Problems

As indicated earlier, assessments focus on evaluating the clients' needs and problems. In assessing needs and problems, it is helpful to use the concept *problem system*. Hepworth and Larsen (1986) have defined a problem system:

> The configuration of the client(s), other people, and elements of the environment that interact to produce the problematic situation are designated as the problem system. The problem system revolves around the client's concerns and is limited to those persons and factors directly involved in the client's ecological context. (p. 174)

The following 15 questions are useful guides for assessing problem systems.

1. WHAT SPECIFICALLY ARE THE PROBLEMS? Many problems have several dimensions. It is crucial in an assessment to articulate the subproblems and dimensions of the problem as specifically and accurately as possible. For example, a 27-year-old wife with two children whose husband is killed in a traffic accident caused by a drunk driver may have a variety of needs and problems. She will probably undergo several emotional reactions to the death, including denial of the tragedy, depression, anger at the drunk driver, possible guilt over unresolved conflicts she had with her husband, anger that the husband has left her with two children to raise alone, and nightmares. Because intensive grieving is highly stressful, she may come down with one or more stress-related illnesses (such as skin rashes, ulcers, or hypertension). She may seek to escape her problems by using drugs. She is apt to have financial difficulties caused by loss of her husband's income. She will need companionship and emotional support. Her children may have a variety of emotional reactions to the death, which they will need help in handling. She may need help in learning to take on the child care responsibilities that were previously performed by her husband. She may face a sharp reduction in her standard of living with the loss of her husband's income. She may be forced to seek a job (if she is not working) or to seek a higher-paying job. She may be forced to apply for public assistance benefits and have to cope with the embarrassment she may feel about being on welfare. She may need legal help in receiving any death benefits she is entitled to. At some point in the future, she may have to decide whether to begin dating again. For the social worker to do an accurate assessment, he or she must identify, prioritize, and specify these problems and subproblems. Those subproblems that are not identified in an assessment will not be combated in the problem-solving phase.

2. HOW DOES THE CLIENT VIEW THE PROBLEMS? The meanings that clients assign to negative events in their lives are often as important, or more important, than the events themselves. For example, a woman may end a relationship with a man she has been engaged to for over a year. The man's view of the breakup will largely determine the problems he faces. Let's assume he tells himself the following: "Life is not worth living. My life is ruined forever. I might just as well end it right now." Such a person is very depressed and perhaps suicidal. These are the problems he then needs help with.

In contrast, let's assume he tells himself the following: "I'll miss her somewhat, but it's probably best we end it now. The last three or four months we apparently grew in different directions. I'm somewhat relieved she broke up with me, as I was thinking about ending the relationship myself. It's easier with both of us wanting out of the relationship. I'll soon find someone else to date." In this case the man will probably be somewhat sad but also relieved that the relationship is over. With such views he may have little need for social services.

3. WHO IS INVOLVED IN THE PROBLEM SYSTEM? The problem system includes all the people who are involved in producing the problematic situation. In the example where the husband was killed in a traffic accident, the problem system would definitely include the surviving wife and her two children. The problem system may also include others who are highly involved with this family, such as in-laws, other relatives, neighbors, friends, or employers. Such people may need help for the grief they are experiencing, and some may also be part of the intervention process by becoming a social support system for the wife and her children. Another problem system that may or may not be identified is the drunk driver and his close family members. The drunk driver and his family may need help for the guilt and remorse they are experiencing, and the driver is probably also in need of help for his or her drinking problem.

4. HOW ARE THE PARTICIPANTS INVOLVED? Here the focus is on identifying the roles that each person plays in the problem system. Some systems become very complex, and a multiproblem family will require considerable analysis to determine the roles played by each member. All the problems need to be identified, and for each problem, each family member may be playing one or more roles. Detailed information is needed about how each person affects, and is affected by, others and about consequences of events that perpetuate the problematic behavior.

5. WHAT ARE THE CAUSES OF THE PROBLEMS? Frequently, identifying the causes of problems will suggest ways to intervene. If husband abuses his wife when he is angry, then helping him learn alternative ways to vent his anger (such as jogging or expressing his feelings in an assertive rather than an aggressive manner) may be constructive. If he abuses his wife when under stress, then instructing him in stress management techniques (such as relaxation techniques) may be useful. If he abuses his wife only when intoxicated, he may benefit from an alcohol treatment program.

In making an assessment, remember that all human behavior is purposeful. A powerful way of analyzing human behavior is in terms of

Antecedents→Thought Processes→

Behavior→Consequences

The following is an example:

Antecedent: Jim Schroeder, age 20, is raised in a family and peer culture that glorifies sexual conquests. He is on his second date with a woman and is alone with her late in the evening in her apartment.

Thought Processes: "She is really sexy. Since I've wined and dined her twice, it's time for her to show her appreciation. She wants it as much as I do. I'll show her what a great lover I am. She may protest a little, but I can overcome that. Once we get involved sexually, she'll be emotionally committed to me."

Behavior: Date rape.

Consequences: The woman is traumatized. She calls the police after Mr. Schroeder leaves. He is arrested and charged with first-degree sexual assault. The police also immediately refer the victim to a rape crisis center, and she receives medical services and extensive counseling.

Why did Mr. Schroeder commit date rape? Analyzing behavior in terms of this model identifies the antecedents and the thought processes that led to the date rape. Once these antecedents and thought processes have been identified, interventions can be made to prevent and deter such victimization in the future. For example, Mr. Schroeder might have benefited from educational programs in middle school and high school that emphasize (a) communication about sexual interest between people who are dating rather than aggressive behavior, (b) the rights of women in our society, and (c) the consequences of date rape and the long-term effects on victims. Current interventions for Mr. Schroeder may include (a) individual counseling, (b) correctional time for having committed a serious offense, (c) probation, (d) community service, and (e) group therapy for sexual offenders—perhaps with a component that has victims of sexual assaults describe the long-term adverse effects that they experience. The only way to prevent Mr. Schoeder from committing sexual assaults in the future is to change his thought processes.

6. WHERE DOES THE PROBLEMATIC BEHAVIOR OCCUR? Problematic behavior tends to occur in certain locations and not in others. A child may throw temper tantrums at home but not at school or when visiting relatives. Perhaps the child has learned that having a tantrum at home manipulates his parents into giving him what he wants; perhaps he has also learned that throwing a tantrum elsewhere results in ridicule instead of getting what he wants. Identifying where problematic behavior does *not* occur is as important as identifying where it does occur—both may provide clues to factors that trigger the behavior and factors that prevent it from occurring. For example, a married couple may get into heated arguments when they visit the wife's parents but not when they visit the husband's parents. Perhaps certain factors lead to increased tension when the couple visits the wife's parents—such as the husband's feeling he is being "put down" and not accepted by the wife's parents. An excellent way to determine why arguments occur at the wife's parents' home is to ask each spouse what the arguments were about and why they occurred.

7. WHEN DOES THE PROBLEMATIC BEHAVIOR OCCUR? Closely related to *where* the problematic behavior occurs is the question of *when* it occurs. The process of identifying when problematic behavior occurs and when it does not occur frequently reveals valuable clues to factors that trigger the behavior. If a client frequently becomes depressed at a certain time of the year, she may be grieving about a serious loss that occurred at that time some years ago—such as the death of a loved one or a divorce—or she may be suffering from seasonal affective disorder (SAD). Identifying when serious arguments occur for a married couple may suggest factors that trigger the conflict: one or both drinking at a party, one having contact with someone she or he dated in the past, one spouse participating in activities that the other is excluded from, or a misbehaving child (the parents disagree about discipline). A child may feign a headache or throw a temper tantrum when she has to go someplace she does not want to go, or when she is told to do something (such as studying her spelling words) that she views as unpleasant. A male in a romantic relationship may start talking about taking his life whenever his woman friend suggests they stop dating. A person with a drinking problem may drink to excess whenever she has intense unwanted emotions, such as anger, frustration, depression, and feelings of insecurity. Once the antecedents that trigger the problematic behavior are identified, the intervention phase can then focus on making the kinds of changes that will reduce the frequency of the behavior.

8. WHAT IS THE FREQUENCY, INTENSITY, AND DURATION OF THE PROBLEMATIC BEHAVIOR? Someone who becomes intoxicated once or twice a year may not have a drinking problem, whereas someone who becomes intoxicated once or twice a week probably does. Someone who becomes depressed for a day or two every three months probably does not have a serious problem with depression, but someone who is depressed daily certainly does.

Closely related to the frequency of the problematic behavior is its intensity. Someone who is mildly depressed is much more functional than someone who is so severely depressed that he sleeps 15 hours a day, cries frequently during his waking hours, and cannot think rationally. Many other problematic behaviors have varying degrees of intensity, such as extent of intoxication, extent of violent behavior when angry, intensity of family arguments, and extent of overeating.

The duration of the behavior is also an important assessment variable. For example, when someone is intoxicated, how long does she continue to drink to maintain the intoxication? Or, if he is angry or depressed or under high stress, what is the typical duration of the problem behavior? A marital disagreement that lasts three weeks is obviously much more serious than one that lasts 20 minutes.

An assessment of the frequency, intensity, and duration of the behavior helps specify its severity and clarify its impact on the client and members of the family.

9. WHAT IS THE HISTORY OF THE PROBLEMATIC BEHAVIOR? Examining the history of a problem often identifies the events that triggered the dysfunctional behavior. For example, if an eighth-grade child develops a school phobia, looking into the history of the problem would first seek to identify when the phobia began to occur. Then what was happening in the child's life at this time could be identified—what made her fear going to school? Perhaps she was not getting the grades she desired. Perhaps her classmates were making her life miserable. Perhaps her parents were having severe marital conflict, and she erroneously believed that by staying home she could help ease the marital conflict. Perhaps it is part of a larger anxiety-related problem that has been developing for years. Identifying the antecedents or triggers will help in designing an intervention plan to reduce the frequency and severity of the behavior.

However, identifying the antecedents that initially caused the dysfunctional behavior may not fully isolate the current factors that are maintaining the behavior. For example, a child developed a school phobia because two of his classmates were "bullying" him, but they have now moved to another city. Therefore, other factors are probably causing the child to want to stay home, such as being able to watch television or play all day long, and not having any schoolwork to do.

For voluntary clients, it is also often revealing to seek out the *precipitating events* that led them to seek help. Often, their problems have existed for months, even years, and identifying the precipitating events yields valuable information. For example, a person who has been bulimic for 2½ years seeks help after she notices blood in her vomit. She believes she might have internal bleeding; she is referred to a physician who finds that her esophagus is severely damaged. A married couple who have been arguing periodically for three years seek counseling after they have their first serious physical fight; both are fearful their feuding has entered a new phase that could potentially be life-threatening to both. Precipitating events can usually be identified by the practitioner's asking (and probing) clients to identify the reasons for seeking help at this time.

Involuntary clients usually have a crisis, or a series of crises, that results in their being seen by a practitioner. A practitioner needs to obtain as much information about these crises as possible (often from collateral sources) to determine why an involuntary client is being referred and what his problems are. Such information is also useful in confronting the involuntary client. (Involuntary clients frequently deny they have a problem.)

10. WHAT DOES THE CLIENT WANT? A key social work value is to start where the client is. In an initial interview with a client, whether voluntary or involuntary, it is crucial to address any problems that the client identifies. Failure to do so may leave the client feeling helpless or annoyed, both of which interfere with the eventual intervention effort. Additionally, too often assessment is made from the practitioner's perspective rather than the client's. An adult services worker for a public welfare department was assigned the following case. A 78-year-old man was living alone in a house on a farm where he had been born and raised. The house was a shambles; it was filthy and had no running water or toilet facilities. Dishes were washed (when they were washed) in rainwater. A small wood-burning stove in the kitchen was used to heat the house. The elderly man was mentally alert but suffered from a variety of minor medical problems: he was overweight and had gout and hypertension. The man drank to excess and also rolled and smoked his own cigarettes, which was a potential fire hazard especially when he was intoxicated. The worker decided it was best for the man to be placed in a nursing home where adequate care could be given. To the worker's surprise, the man refused and bluntly stated, "I was born and raised here, and I'm going to die here. If you would get a court order to place me in a nursing home, which I don't believe you will be able to get, I'll give up the will to live, and die quickly there." The worker was shocked. She discussed the case with her supervisor, and her supervisor pointed out that she may have been viewing the situation from what she wanted rather than what the client wanted. The worker agreed.

This example points out that what a worker views as being a problem may not be viewed as a problem by a client. If the client chooses to live in a substandard living situation, that is *his* choice—and he has a right to do so, *as long as he is not hurting anyone else in the process*. If, however, young children were living with this elderly man, then child neglect would need to be considered. Should that be the case, changes in living conditions would need to be made, or the children might need to be removed from the home.

In any assessment it is crucial to accurately obtain the client's view of the problem and what the client wants. If the client's desires are realistic and obtainable, satisfying them should generally be a major goal of the helping process. If what the client wants is not realistic, the reasons that her desires cannot be fulfilled need to be tactfully explained to her.

11. HOW HAS THE CLIENT ATTEMPTED TO HANDLE THE PROBLEM? The ways in which clients have attempted to cope with their problems provide valuable information during an assessment. Clients may have tried ways of resolving their problems that did not work. Those strategies can be then eliminated from consideration in the problem-solving phase.

Suppose the clients have tried strategies that were partially successful. Perhaps with increased effort or some modifications, they will work. For example, a client suffering from a high level of stress learned to relax using imagery relaxation. However, she did not think to use the technique when she was highly anxious or frustrated. She was then instructed to set aside 15 minutes every morning before going to work and 15 minutes in the evening to practice the technique. (See Module 9 for a description of imagery relaxation.) Structuring imagery relaxation into daily activities proved to be a useful way of helping her combat the stress.

Examining the strategies that clients have used to try to resolve their problems can reveal valuable information about their coping and problem-solving skills. If clients have marked deficits in problem solving, it may be helpful to instruct them in the no-lose problem-solving approach (see Module 9 for a description of this approach).

Some clients respond to interpersonal difficulties by becoming passive or nonassertive. Others become aggressive. If either is the case, it may be desirable to instruct clients in using assertiveness to handle interpersonal conflict (see Module 4 for a description of assertiveness training).

Often, clients have good problem-solving and interpersonal skills in some situations but not in others. For example, a schoolteacher was able to handle disruptive students in his classroom but was ineffective in dealing with his own children. A closer examination revealed that he was divorced and was fearful that if he disciplined his children they would want to live with his ex-wife. Through counseling he came to realize that his children would respect him more if he more clearly specified and enforced behavioral limits. Once this was accomplished, he was able to use the same child management skills he used in the classroom with his own children.

12. WHAT SKILLS DOES THE CLIENT NEED TO COMBAT THE PROBLEM? An assessment of a problematic situation should also identify the skills that clients need to resolve their difficulties. If a parent is having difficulties with a child, needed skills may include listening, negotiating, setting limits, following through on consequences, and nurturing. If a couple is having marital conflicts, they may need problem-solving, communication, listening, and conflict management skills. (Sometimes helping a couple learn these skills is more productive in the long run than helping them resolve their present conflicts.) If a client frequently loses considerable sums of money while gambling, he may need to learn how to say no assertively when his friends ask him to play poker or go to the racetrack. If a client is depressed, she may need to learn what she can do to counter the depression (see Modules 6 and 11 for some strategies).

13. WHAT EXTERNAL RESOURCES ARE NEEDED TO COMBAT THE PROBLEM? An assessment should identify not only the skills that clients need to combat their problems, but also the external resources they need. A single mother on public assistance may need day-care services, transportation, and job training to help her become employable. Someone addicted to gambling may need a self-help group, such as gamblers anonymous, to give him the emotional support and guidance he needs to combat his addiction. A bulimic may need medical attention to assess and treat physical damage from binging and purging, one-to-one counseling to stop the binge-purge cycle, support from a self-help eating disorders group, and instruction in what is a nutritious and well-balanced diet. Once an assessment is made, a social worker often acts as a broker or case manager in connecting clients with needed services and resources. Frequently, some or all of the needed services are not provided by the practitioner's agency, and arrangements need to be made for the services to be provided by other agencies, organizations, self-help groups, and natural support systems (such as neighbors, family members, fellow workers, church groups, and social groups).

14. WHAT ARE THE CLIENT'S RESOURCES, SKILLS, AND STRENGTHS? As mentioned earlier in this chapter, a quality assessment also identifies the resources, strengths, and skills that clients already possess to combat their problems. The importance of identifying such strengths has been described. Sometimes problems are resolved by empowering clients to use resources and skills they already have to mitigate their problematic behavior. Clients who have frequent stress-related illnesses may learn, through counseling, that applying the following techniques will help them relax and reduce their high stress levels: positive thinking, problem solving rather than "awfulizing" about their problems, using social support systems, and being more assertive with significant others in expressing their feelings and concerns. A couple who has marital problems may find their relationship improving when they treat each other with the same kind of respect that they give to strangers and acquaintances; many spouses use tact in communicating with acquaintances but not in communicating with each other. A person who is grieving about the death of a loved one may find that discussing her grief with friends and relatives not only helps ventilate her grief, but also helps her develop a social support system for putting her life back together.

15. WHAT ARE THE RECOMMENDED COURSES OF ACTION? The recommended courses of action are also called the *treatment plan* and the *intervention plan*. Once a client's difficulties and strengths have been assessed, the next step is to set goals and arrive at a course of action to accomplish the goals. Some authorities conceptualize goal setting and specifying recommended courses of action as a process that follows an assessment. However, in social work practice most assessments contain a recommended course of action; therefore, this process is discussed briefly here.

The goals should be jointly agreed to by the client and the worker and should be realistic and obtainable. The goals should be geared to resolving the identified problems and should be stated in such a way that they are operational and measurable. An *operational goal* can be directly translated into a course of action so the goal can be accomplished. For example, for a nonassertive client, an operational goal might be to learn to be assertive with significant others with assertiveness training being the course of action to accomplish this goal. A *measurable goal* can be measured in its contribution to achieving the goal. One way to measure whether a client is making progress in becoming more assertive is for the client to record for two weeks the number of times he is assertive and nonassertive in interactions with significant others. The client is then given training in being assertive. Afterward, he keeps records for another two weeks. If the number of assertive behaviors after treatment is higher, measurable progress has occurred.

The stated courses of action should be realistic and obtainable. They also should usually be agreed to by the client; if the client disagrees with these courses of action, she is unlikely to carry them out. (With some involuntary clients, there are exceptions to this guideline. For example, a parolee may not agree with the parole officer's assessment that her violation of the rules of parole warrants a recommendation to the court for a return to prison.)

The stated courses of action should usually be selected through the following process. After a goal is set, the client and the worker generate a list of feasible courses of action to accomplish the goal. The strengths and shortcomings of each alternative should be considered. Then, the client and the worker together select the course of action.

In some settings the worker or the clinical team selects the recommended courses of action, with minimal input from the client. For example, when an assessment is done for an elderly person's admission application for a nursing home, the recommendation will usually be based on the extent to which the elderly person's characteristics meet the nursing home's criteria for admission.

A Systems Perspective: The Pincus-Minahan Model[3]

A systems perspective emphasizes looking beyond a client's presenting problems to assess the complexities and interrelationships of the problems. Through a systems analysis of a case, the most effective intervention targets and strategies can usually be identified. A system is a regularly interacting or interdependent group of items that forms a unified whole. A social service system is comprised of groups of social workers, supervisors, clients, advisory and oversight groups (for example, county boards), and others who regularly interact to address social welfare concerns in the community. Many models are available to help workers understand how to use systems theory and systems analysis. The most publicized systems model in social work literature is the Pincus-Minahan (1973) approach.

In 1973 Allen Pincus and Anne Minahan wrote *Social Work Practice: Model and Method,* which to many has become the primary way of applying systems analysis to social work practice. Their basic premise is that a *common core* of skills and concepts is essential to the practice of social work (Pincus & Minahan, 1973, p. xi). That this premise even needed to be formally stated shows the lack of professional image of social work at that time. Assessment skills are part of the common core of skills needed by social work practitioners.

Pincus and Minahan theorized that there are four basic systems in social work practice: a change agent system, a client system, a target system, and an action system. The *change agent* system is composed of professionals who are employed specifically for the purpose of creating planned change. The employing organizations of the change agents (Pincus & Minahan, 1973, p. 54) are also part of this system. The term *employing organization* is important, because Pincus and Minahan viewed only *paid* individuals as change agents. A change agent, then, is a professional who is employed specifically for the purpose of creating planned change. Social workers are thus seen as change agents—professionals who work with individuals, groups, families, organizations, and communities to facilitate positive changes. Of course, we know that volunteers in groups such as Big Brothers/Big Sisters also help others make positive changes. The change agent terminology employed here simply relates to professional "territory," and certainly is not meant to imply that volunteers or parents (or others) cannot be powerful helpers who facilitate positive changes.

The *client system* is composed of the people who sanction or *ask* for the change agent's services, who are the expected beneficiaries of the service, *and* who have a working agreement or contract with the change agent (Pincus & Minahan, 1973, p. 56). *Client* is used here in a more limited sense than is often used by social workers, precluding the possibility of "doing things" for people or organizations without their knowledge or agreement.

The *target system* is composed of the people, agencies, and/or organizational practices that the worker wishes to change in some measurable way to reach the goals of the change agent (Pincus & Minahan, 1973, p. 59). By analyzing the changes of the target system, the worker can measure effectiveness and provide a mechanism for accountability.

The last defined system is the *action system.* This term is used to describe those with whom the social worker works to accomplish the tasks and achieve the goals of the change effort (Pincus & Minahan, 1973, p. 61). The worker may need to involve numerous different action systems in different aspects of a planned change effort to accomplish all the different goals of the change agent. The concepts of strategies and outcome

[3]The material on a systems perspective was especially written for this text by Donald Nolan, M.S.S.W., BCD (Board Certified Diplomate in Clinical Social Work). Mr. Nolan is a clinical social worker in private practice.

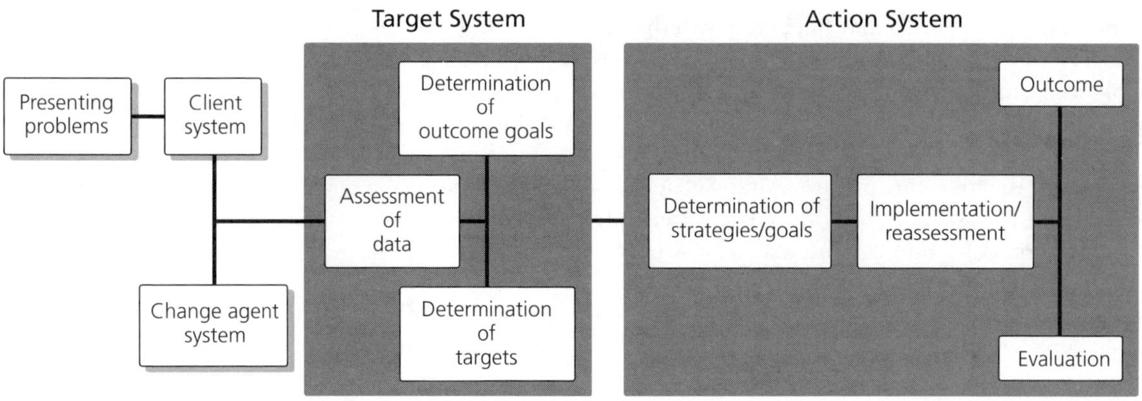

FIGURE 3.1 The basic conceptualizations of the Pincus-Minahan model.

goals are also used to further differentiate how action systems and target systems are developed and utilized. Figure 3.1 displays the basic conceptualizations of the Pincus-Minahan model.

Although data assessment is presented in this model as occurring within the target system, assessment also occurs within the client and change agent systems. Specifying the problem and its causes is, of course, one step in assessment, which also involves analyzing the client's perception of the problem and assessing who and how others are involved in the client system. In developing a target system, the practitioner must consider the history of the behavior as well as where and when it occurs. Assessing the frequency and intensity of the behavior and past attempts to solve the problem are also important in developing goals within a target system. In addition, the systems approach helps a practitioner develop targets for change; it presents a framework for analyzing client needs and wants and the external resources that may have to be developed or modified. The changes a client needs to make also become targets in the comprehensive assessment. The information thus acquired is then put into an action plan through which recommended courses of action are developed. Ongoing assessment continues to occur in the implementation and evaluation phases.

The four systems presented in Figure 3.1 are not mutually exclusive but can and do overlap in many cases. Such overlap is illustrated in Figure 3.2. The John Hecht case example shows how the Pincus-Minahan model could be used in a school setting.

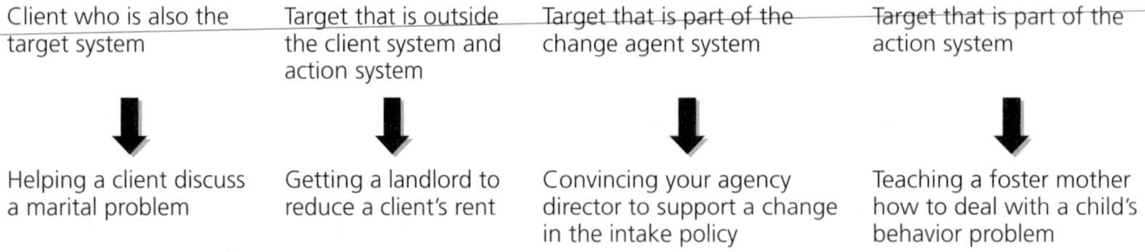

FIGURE 3.2 Examples of the association and overlap between various systems in the Pincus-Minahan model.

CASE EXAMPLE

Involving John Hecht in a School Setting

Richard Thomas, a social worker in a school setting, receives a referral from a teacher, Mr. Phillips. Mr. Phillips states that one of his students, John Hecht, a third-grade boy, is not behaving well in class (not complying with teacher directions, not listening, and not completing assignments). The teacher asks Mr. Thomas to counsel the student to improve his attitude—a simple enough referral, and one in which the problem may be one of motivation or attitude. Counseling sessions could be beneficial; and given time limitations, this is often the way social workers would intervene in this case. The implicit assumption is that there is an identified problem (the student), and to solve this problem the student must change. However, by not analyzing the problem more fully, the worker may miss a number of other problems.

In using systems analysis to assess the problem, Mr. Thomas would first list the presenting problems and then decide who his client is in this situation. Using the prior definition of what determines a client, only the teacher and in some sense the school can be defined as clients at this point. John or his parents may be potential clients in the future (see Figure 3.3).

The next phase is to establish clear targets. Going back to Figure 3.1, this part of the analysis involves a more thorough investigation and assessment of the data and then development of long-range or outcome goals as targets are identified. Exhibit 3.1 shows the beginning step in this assessment.

During the data assessment phase, outcome goals need to be developed. Then targets can be established to accomplish these goals. This continuing process of assessment is diagrammed in Exhibit 3.2.

At this point, goals and targets have been identified, and it is now necessary to develop an action system. The first part of this process, as seen in Figure 3.1, is to determine strategies. (Determination of strategies is a later part of the assessment process.) These strategies must be linked to the targets and must be individualized to meet the needs of the target population. Systems analysis requires that intervention strategies be based not on the worker's favorite techniques but on the worker's objective professional judgments about which strategies will most effectively meet the clients' needs. For example, a worker may prefer to use the small-group intervention skills at which she is particularly adept, but she should choose this strategy only when systems analysis suggests such an approach is the best way to change a target and ultimately accomplish the goal. Exhibit 3.3 shows that determining strategies is the first step in developing an action system.

Now that consistent outcome goals, targets, and strategies have been developed, the next step is to plan the *implementation* of the action system (see Figure 3.1). Often the social worker must decide what is practical and feasible at the time. Additionally, the worker prioritizes needs according to the most immediate and pressing needs of the client. Of course, the worker must also be prepared to reassess the strategies as intervention progresses, by observing the extent to which the desired *outcomes* are occurring. There may also be changes in client and change agent systems along the way as assessment continues. In this case the change agent system now includes not only the school social worker but also the school principal, the referring teacher as he alters his teaching style, the school guidance counselor, and social workers from the County Social Services Department in the areas of financial assistance, child management training, and protective services. In addition, some potential clients (such as John and his mother) may also become actual clients during the implementation phase of the action system.

In forming action systems that involve other agencies and other professionals, a key social work goal is to keep the process moving. The referring social worker should serve as an advocate of both the client and the outcome goals. It is often necessary to restate these goals to others and to find ways to encourage other change agents to continue to provide services when "roadblocks" are encountered. In fact, monitoring progress should be expected; a systems analysis approach implies that there will be a group of people working together and thus there will be a need for coordination and direction.

(continued)

CASE EXAMPLE
John Hecht
(continued)

It is also imperative to *evaluate* and stabilize the change effort after a prescribed amount of time. This evaluation (another part of overall assessment) should measure the extent to which the initial outcome goals of the target system are being accomplished.

This case did in fact exist, and assessment and strategy were developed as described. Note that many, and perhaps most, social work cases are as complicated as this one. As such, systems analysis can help the worker understand the complexities of the case and serve to organize and drive assessment. Systems analysis can be applied by virtually all social workers.

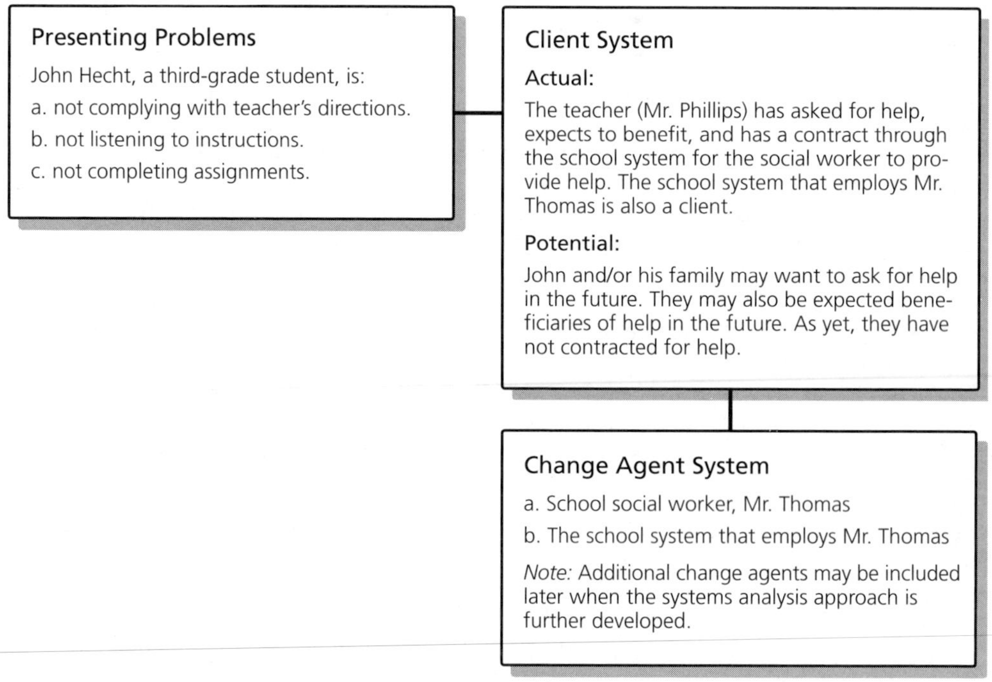

Presenting Problems
John Hecht, a third-grade student, is:
a. not complying with teacher's directions.
b. not listening to instructions.
c. not completing assignments.
Client System
Actual:
The teacher (Mr. Phillips) has asked for help, expects to benefit, and has a contract through the school system for the social worker to provide help. The school system that employs Mr. Thomas is also a client.
Potential:
John and/or his family may want to ask for help in the future. They may also be expected beneficiaries of help in the future. As yet, they have not contracted for help.
Change Agent System
a. School social worker, Mr. Thomas
b. The school system that employs Mr. Thomas
Note: Additional change agents may be included later when the systems analysis approach is further developed.

FIGURE 3.3 The first steps of the systems analysis approach in the John Hecht case.

The Jane Angell case example on page 77 demonstrates how systems analysis can be applied in a clinical setting. Psychiatric social work has long been seen as different or distinct from other types of social work practice: Its roots are more clinical and psychoanalytic than those of generalist social work practice. Also, some authorities view a clinical approach as more limited in scope than a generalistic-practice approach (for example, social action and macropractice approaches are seldom used in clinical practice). The assessment process is similar in all settings, although the comprehensiveness and the specifics may differ. In the Jane Angell case example the major focus is on analyzing the client's presenting problem. This analysis is done by a social worker who has extensive training in systems analysis and considerable experience in using the approach. This example demonstrates that after a practitioner gains experience with the approach she can do much of the analysis "in her head," rather than diagramming the components, as was done in the John Hecht example. Systems analysis at this level becomes more of a conceptual and cognitive exercise.

EXHIBIT 3.1

Data assessment in the John Hecht case

The social worker, Mr. Thomas, seeks to develop a target system. He begins by collecting the following data:

A. The student's behavior in class is more complicated than originally reported. The student is often belittled by the teacher and frequently ignored when he asks for help. Additional in-class observations show that many other students also demonstrate inappropriate behavior. The teacher, Mr. Phillips, appears to have difficulty with classroom control. Also, conversations with him reveal that he has a pattern of negative comments toward low-income students.

B. The student's attendance is a matter of concern. Over the past two years, John has averaged approximately 25 percent nonattendance. He also is not completing much of his schoolwork, is not following directions, and is being disruptive. Further assessment shows that John is not relating very well to his peers.

C. On talking with John's mother, a single parent, Mr. Thomas finds a pattern of school absences by the other two children in the family and a home situation reflecting economic problems, family arguments, and questionable parenting skills. In discussions with other teachers John has had, and other school faculty who "know of" the family, the social worker finds concerns about parental supervision at home, including the suspicion that John's mother has problems with alcohol abuse and is often not home.

EXHIBIT 3.2

Determination of outcome goals and of targets in the John Hecht case

Determination of Outcome Goals	*Determination of Targets*
(These goals represent the goals that were set in John Hecht's case, and relate to the three sets of problems identified in the beginning data assessment stage in Exhibit 3.1.)	(These targets identify the focuses of the change effort.)
A. Improve the teacher's classroom control and attitude toward students.	A. Target: Mr. Phillips, the teacher 1. Attitudes toward low-income students. 2. Shortcomings in classroom control. 3. Using an asset approach.
B. Improve John's behavior, attendance, and peer relationships in school.	B. Target: John Hecht 1. Inappropriate attitudes and behaviors in school. 2. Inadequate peer relationships. 3. Frequent absences from school.
C. Bring more stability to John's home situation.	C. Target: The Hecht family 1. Financial difficulties. 2. Mrs. Hecht's lack of management skills and inadequate supervision of children. 3. The possibility of alcohol abuse by Mrs. Hecht.

EXHIBIT 3.3

Determination of strategies in the John Hecht case

A. Target: Mr. Phillips, a third-grade teacher.

1. Discuss concerns about Mr. Phillips' attitudes toward low-income students with the school principal and ask that the principal help by providing educational supervision in this area—that is, by arranging an in-service training session for teachers on (a) the societal conditions that contribute to the financial and family change problems that are occurring in the area; (b) the destructive effects on low-income students of teachers' negative attitudes; and (c) the benefits for low-income students of a nonjudgmental attitude by teachers. Ask the principal to help Mr. Phillips individualize more of his assignments for students so he can better recognize individual differences and can give students academic work that is at their individual grade level.

2. Discuss the issues of classroom management with Mr. Phillips and provide material on behavioral strategies of positive and negative reinforcement. Explore with Mr. Phillips the benefits of developing some type of student charting system so that John (and potentially other students) can work toward goals on a daily basis. Finally, consult with Mr. Phillips periodically about problematic behavior in his classroom, problem-solve these situations, and suggest more effective techniques for controlling disruptive student behavior.

3. Discuss an asset development approach with Mr. Phillips, such as the one formulated by the Search Institute.[4] An asset approach is a way to identify what initially appear to be only small resources or assets (such as Mr. Phillips assuming more of a mentor role to John). Such resources or assets can, over time, have a powerful effect on a client. It is possible, for example, that Mr. Phillips is frustrated by what he perceives to be the lack of success in his students, and therefore he needs to see that his efforts in his classroom can make a difference.

B. Target: John Hecht.

1. Provide counseling to John to help him find more constructive ways to confront others, to develop goals as a learner, and to take responsibility for his actions. The need for counseling is evident in order to develop rapport with John, to help him develop more effective problem-solving skills, and to demonstrate a positive adult role model.

2. Talk to the school guidance counselor about the possibility of John's joining one of the small groups the counselor is currently leading, or joining one in the future. This could help John improve his relationships with other students. Additionally, discuss with the counselor the need for developing a classroom guidance program, perhaps for the entire school, directed toward improving human relations.

3. Refer the problem of frequent absences to the Protective Services Unit of the County Social Services Department, as a case of unexcused absences or truancy. This referral will bring to the change effort the resources of another agency to help with the overall family difficulties. This referral also provides the County Social Services Department with an access point to the family, not primarily as a monitoring role, but as an agency that can offer resources (such as in-home assistants, respite care services, and access to health care).

C. Target: The Hecht family.

1. Inform Protective Services of the family's economic difficulties and ask them to investigate whether the family is receiving all the financial assistance they are eligible for, and whether financial counseling is needed to better budget the family's resources.

2. After assessing the seriousness of the home management difficulties, refer this matter to the County Social Services Department. Realistically, this difficulty will involve the same Protective Services worker (at least as a case manager) who received the referral for truancy and financial assistance. The Protective Services worker may well ask other workers to provide certain services to this family, such as involving the mother in a Parent Effectiveness Training class (see Module 9). It is important that timing the involvement of several workers not overwhelm the family. Together with Mrs. Hecht and the social workers from the County Social Services Department, develop a treatment plan to help Mrs. Hecht improve her child development and parenting/behavioral practices. This plan may involve individual counseling, participation in a parenting group, or demonstrating behavioral practices through modeling.

3. Investigate the alleged alcohol abuse further and then decide whether to refer Mrs. Hecht for alcohol and other drug abuse assessment, which is provided by the County Social Services Department. Since Mrs. Hecht also appears somewhat depressed and lacking in energy, an adult psychiatric referral may also be considered in the future. Additionally, since alcohol problems are not unidimensional, suggest that the County Social Services Department assist Mrs. Hecht in finding employment or in receiving job training. Also, it is likely that Mrs. Hecht will need some support (either through group or individual counseling) to help her meet the demands of being a single parent.

[4]Roehlkepartain, J., & N. Leffert, 1999. *What Young Children Need To Succeed.* Minneapolis, MN: Search Institute; Benson, P., J. Gailbraith, & P. Espeland, 1998. *What Kids Need to Succeed.* Minneapolis, MN: Free Spirit.

CASE EXAMPLE

Involving Jane Angell in a Clinical Setting

Jane Angell comes to a private mental health facility with vague concerns of unhappiness. She is referred by a friend. The psychiatric social worker explains that a thorough assessment needs to occur before a treatment plan can be developed. Ms. Angell is the client system at this point. Terra Montana (a social worker) and the clinic where she practices, are the initial change agent system. Because several of Ms. Angell's complaints suggest depression, Ms. Montana needs to identify and examine Ms. Angell's symptoms as part of the assessment. Some types of depression are now viewed as having contributing factors that are medical in nature. Depression is an affective disorder with a number of distinguishing symptoms. Some research suggests that depression is partly caused by chemical imbalances within the brain and central nervous system (Coryell et al., 1988; Rasmussen & Tsuang, 1986). Imbalances in chemicals called neurotransmitters that transmit messages from one nerve cell to another appear to cause problems with dysphoria (marked and persistent unhappiness, often without specific cause) as well as difficulties with concentration and often worry and guilt.[5] Environmental stressors also play a role and are often seen as "triggers" that can eventually lead to neurotransmitter imbalance in susceptible individuals. Ms. Montana, in assessing mental health issues in the client, needs to find out the following:

1. What is the client's current perception of her problems? What is the history of the apparent depression, including history of past treatment, successful or not?
2. Are there disturbances of sleep, including nightmares or night terrors, sudden awakening, early morning awakenings, insomnia, or excessive sleep? What is the overall quality and history of sleep behaviors?
3. Are there disturbances of appetite, including loss or lack of appetite, periods of binging or purging of food, or specific *avoidance* of certain foods?
4. Is there a history of headaches? If so, specifically when and how often do these headaches occur? Do the headaches cause accompanying nausea, fatigue, or difficulty going outside because of light sensitivity? Do they cluster together? Is there history of sinus trouble and, if so, has this been medically assessed?
5. Is there a history of stomachaches or other gastrointestinal difficulties, such as chronic constipation or diarrhea? Did these difficulties also occur in childhood?
6. Is there a history of somatic or physical complaints, such as backaches, joint or knee pains, a general feeling of malaise or not feeling well? Has the individual sought medical care? If so, is there history of "doctor hopping," perhaps because physicians cannot find medically diagnosable conditions?
7. Is there a history of anxiety or worry? How dysfunctional is this? Are there specific phobias that interfere in the person's lifestyle? Is there history of panic behaviors; that is, a sudden feeling of intense anxiety and uneasiness often accompanied by rapid heartbeat, difficulties in breathing, intense perspiring, and at times fear?
8. How does the client perceive what are normally pleasant times, such as birthdays and holidays?
9. Is there any seasonal nature to the unhappiness? For example, does the client have a history of more symptoms of depression in the late fall and winter? A condition called seasonal affective disorder seems to coincide with winter seasons and the corresponding low amounts of daylight. It is relatively rare for depressed individuals to only experience seasonal changes in symptoms. More often, symptoms get worse during times of high stress.
10. Are there difficulties in sexual functioning or desire? If there are, how does the client interpret these? Is there past history of rape or incest?

[5]Two excellent resources discuss depression comprehensively: Nancy Andreasen, *The Broken Brain* (New York: Harper & Row, 1985), and Donald Klein and Paul Wender, *Understanding Depression* (DuPage County, IL: National Alliance for the Mentally Ill, 1993). Additionally, specific diagnostic criteria for depression are found in the American Psychiatric Association's *The Diagnostic and Statistical Manual of Mental Disorders* (4th ed. Revision) (Washington, DC: American Psychiatric Association, 2000).

(continued)

CASE EXAMPLE
Jane Angell
(continued)

11. What is the client's prevalent mood? Is there history of fearfulness and crying, ruminating, worry, feelings of worthlessness, or thoughts of death or suicide? Has her mood generally been stable and predictable, or are there substantial variations sometimes associated with excess energy or manic feelings?

12. Does the client have difficulty concentrating and remembering things?

13. How is the client functioning at home, at her job, and within her social context? Is she chronically tired? Does she feel "slowed down"? What are her family or friends telling her about her actions or moods? If married, what is the status of the marital relationship? If there are children in the family, how is the client relating to them?

14. Is there a history of obsessive unwanted thoughts or compulsive actions, such as pacing or hand wringing?

15. Is there current alcohol or drug abuse, including abuse of prescription medications (such as Valium or other minor tranquilizers)? Is the client in denial of these problems? Is there any past history of treatment?

16. What is the client's history as a child and teenager, and how does she view her parents? Does she view her parents as contributing to, or helping with, past or current problems? Are there dysfunctional ways of thinking that were developed in childhood (for example, the client viewing herself as a "bad child" as a result of being an adult child of an alcoholic)?

17. How did the client function in school, including history of past learning problems or disabilities, social interactions, patterns of dealing with school stresses and pressures, and possible past feelings of failure?

18. What is the client's personal medical history, including relevant illnesses, exposure to toxins, medications used, allergies, and accidents? Has specialized medical care or previous psychiatric consultation occurred? How does the client view medical practitioners? If female and previously pregnant, were there problems associated with postpartum depression or possible termination of pregnancies? Does the client have any history of premenstrual syndrome (PMS)?

19. What is the client's genetic history? Certain types of depression are often seen as biologically or genetically influenced, so a very careful and thorough history is essential.

Although this type of assessment is time-consuming, it is necessary in psychiatrically oriented social work practice. In developing change agent, client, target, and action systems for this case, information related to these areas is used in combination with information about environmental stressors and client strengths to develop a treatment plan. In this example, Ms. Angell is assessed as having many of the physical and emotional symptoms of depression. Because she has not seen her personal physician in some time, she needs a comprehensive physical (action system). She will then need a psychiatric consultation to confirm a diagnosis of depression and to determine whether any medications may help in an overall treatment plan (action system).

Because current research indicates that some depression may be related to neurochemical imbalances, antidepressant medication may be necessary to restore the balance (action system). Ms. Angell, who is married and has two young children, is also assessed as having difficulties in these family relationships. Family therapy will become part of the action system, with targets of the relationships between family members. Mr. Angell does not understand his wife's difficulties with depression. He is often angry with her and blames her for being depressed. He needs to understand why she is depressed and to be aware of what he and the children can do so they do not make the depression worse. The children (target system) have behavioral problems at home, and therefore he and his wife need to develop (together with the therapist) an agreed-on discipline plan. The couple (target system) also needs to increase their capacities to listen and to communicate with each other.

Ms. Angell also has past feelings of worthlessness, derived in part from feeling that her parents viewed her as a failure. She (target system) needs individual therapy (action system) to counter and change her negative views of herself (see Module 6) and to improve her capacities to be assertive with her husband and her parents (see Module 4). Job stress also appears to trigger problems with depression. Ms. Angell may need to reconsider her job (target system) demands or her vocation itself; she may even need career counseling (action system).

Thus, a presenting problem of generalized unhappiness becomes a system of interrelating difficulties and numerous targets. As targets and action strategies are developed, client and change systems are also more fully developed. The overall change effort with this case involves the development of a treatment plan that evolves from a systems analysis of Ms. Angell's problems and life circumstances. People's lives are complex, and it is a disservice to them to treat only the presenting problem without assessing all facets of their lives.

Summary

Assessment is a critical process in social work practice. The selection of goals and interventions largely depends on the assessment. An assessment should include not only what is wrong with a client but also the client's resources, skills, and strengths that can be used in resolving difficulties and promoting growth. Too often in the past, assessments have focused only on clients' shortcomings and pathology.

The nature of the assessment process varies significantly with the type of setting in which the social worker practices. In some settings the social worker makes an independent assessment, and in other settings the social worker is a member of a clinical team that makes an assessment. An assessment is, in essence, a working hypothesis of a client's difficulties and resources based on current data. As time passes, assessments have to be revised and updated as changes occur in the client and in his or her environment.

Data used in making an assessment are derived from various sources: the client's verbal report, assessment forms, computer-assisted assessment forms, collateral sources, psychological tests, the client's nonverbal behavior, home visits, observation of client interacting with significant others, and the worker's intuition after interacting with the client.

To do a quality assessment, a worker needs an extensive knowledge of human behavior and the social environment. An assessment may require knowledge about multifarious systems, biophysical factors, behavioral factors, motivational factors, family systems, and environmental factors. Such knowledge is obtained from a variety of courses that social work majors typically take in college. The purpose of an assessment is to give focus to the kinds of factors that are examined.

The theory or theories of human behavior that a practitioner subscribes to will have a major influence on what is examined during the assessment. What a worker examines in conducting an assessment has a large effect on the outcome. Most theories of human behavior have not been proven; therefore practitioners need to be aware that their assessment of someone is only a hypothesis that is based on unproven theories.

Social work is increasingly using an ecological perspective to assess human behavior. An ecological perspective asserts that it is important to assess the person-in-environment. This chapter presented 15 questions that serve as guides for what to examine in conducting an assessment.

Systems theory is one way of organizing data so as to conceptualize problems and form action/treatment plans. Through systems analysis of a situation, the social worker can attempt to understand the relative importance of the many influences in the client's life. The social worker can conceptualize issues in terms of client, change agent, target, and action systems to determine goals and strategies in a planned change effort. A systems perspective highlights the importance of looking beyond the client's presenting problems to assess the complexities of his or her life. A dynamic balance exists between individuals and their environments. Assessment, using a systems analysis approach, seeks to understand this balance so that compensating changes can improve the client's life within the environment of systems included in the change effort.

EXERCISES

1. WRITING AN ASSESSMENT

Goal: To give you experience in writing an assessment.

Step 1: Your instructor explains the purpose of the exercise and then summarizes the 15 key questions for writing assessments. (Alternatively you can read these questions in the text.)

Step 2: A volunteer constructs a *contrived* problem prior to the next class period. At the next class period, your instructor interviews the volunteer about the contrived problem. The other students in the class then independently write up an assessment that covers the following topics:

a. Specific problems.
b. Client's views of problems.
c. People involved in the problem system.
d. Roles of participants in problem system.
e. Causes of problems.
f. Where the problematic behavior occurs.
g. When the behavior occurs.
h. Frequency, intensity, and duration of the behavior.
i. History of the behavior.
j. Client's goals regarding this behavior.
k. Strategies client has used to handle the problem.
l. Skills client needs to resolve the problem.
m. External resources needed to combat the problem.
n. Client's resources, skills, and strengths.
o. Recommended courses of action.

During the interview your instructor will ask questions that provide you with the data for topics a–n. A significant percentage (40 percent) of your grade will be based on the quality of your response to "Recommended courses of action."

Step 3: Write up your assessment and turn it in on the designated date. Before returning the graded papers, your instructor will read one or two high-quality recommended courses of action.

Step 4: Student discussion of the merits and shortcomings of this assignment.

2. IDENTIFYING CLIENT AND CHANGE AGENT SYSTEMS[6]

Goal: To give you practice in determining client and change agent systems.

Step 1: Class review of the definitions of client and change agent systems.

Step 2: In the following situations, list who is part of the client system and of the change agent system. Identify actual and potential categories in each system.

a. A mother and her son come to a social services agency seeking food and shelter.

[6]Exercises 2 and 3 were specially written for this text by Donald Nolan, M.S.S.W., BCD (Board Certified Diplomate in Clinical Social Work). Mr. Nolan is a clinical social worker in private practice.

b. A social worker employed by a public mental health center asks a psychiatrist for a consultation regarding whether a young woman the social worker has seen is clinically depressed.

c. A social worker in a hospital setting is asked by a nurse to talk with a single mother who has just given birth to her first child. The young woman's parents may also have some concerns and are presently visiting her.

d. A high school student is taken by his parents to a social worker in private practice because the parents are concerned with their son's violence and destructive behavior.

Step 3: Class discussion of student answers.

3. *FORMING TARGET AND ACTION SYSTEMS*

Goal: To give you practice in developing target and action systems.

Step 1: Class review of Figure 3.1, writing comments on a blackboard if possible.

Step 2: Using the following situation, devise outcome goals, targets, and strategies. Remember that there should be some logical consistency between each outcome goal, the targets for that goal, and strategies for achieving that goal (see Exhibits 3.2 and 3.3).

You are a social worker employed by a family services agency. Through your involvement with the juvenile court on a number of delinquency cases, a judge refers a group of teenagers who are required to attend weekly court-ordered counseling sessions to you. In your data-gathering/assessment process, you find out that these teenagers all come from the same large public housing complex in a low-income section of the city. This part of the city is considered a problem area by the police department because of high rates of crime and high unemployment among adults. Numerous social service and volunteer organizations are involved with this part of the community, but there seems to be no coordination among them. There is a neighborhood organization, but few people attend its meetings. The school is concerned about a high truancy rate and a high dropout rate. You have heard that the managers of the public housing complex in the area have generally discouraged the tenant organizations, and there are serious problems in the maintenance of the apartments. As a result, there is a high rate of mobility in and out of the complex.

Step 3: Identify the client systems and change agent systems in this situation.

CHAPTER 4

Social Work with Individuals: Interviewing

Social work practice with individuals is aimed at helping them on a one-to-one basis to meet personal and social problems. Perhaps the two most essential skills social workers need in working with individuals are interviewing and counseling skills. This chapter presents material on how to interview; the next chapter focuses on how to counsel. This chapter covers types of social work interviews, how to begin and close interviews, how to phrase questions, note taking, and use of audiotapes and videotapes. Workers spend a great deal of time interviewing, and much of what they are responsible for depends on what they learn from these interviews.

Three Types of Social Work Interviews

Most social work interviews can be classified as either informational (to obtain data for a social study or for a social history), assessment (to arrive at an appraisal), or therapeutic (to help clients change). Often, the three types overlap. For example, a protective services worker in the initial interview with a couple suspected of child abuse will often obtain background information about the family members and seek to arrive at an appraisal of whether child abuse has occurred. If abuse is occurring, the worker may also begin helping the family make changes to end further abuse. In spite of overlap, the three types of interviews differ in the way they are structured and conducted.

Informational or Social History Interviews

Informational interviews are designed to obtain background or life history material related to the client's personal or social problem. The purpose is not to learn all there is to know about the person's background but to seek information that will enable the worker (or agency) to better understand the client so that decisions can be made regarding the kinds of services that should be provided. Such information includes both objective facts and subjective feelings and attitudes. In addition to the client, others interviewed or contacted may include parents, friends, other relatives, employers, and other agencies having contact with the client (such as social service agencies, police departments, and schools). The specific information desired in a social history varies somewhat from agency to agency. An adoption agency, for example, is interested in information about the child-rearing philosophies of potential adoptive parents, whereas a sheltered workshop is interested in the specific work capacities of potential clients. As the social history example in Exhibit 4.1 shows, a social history usually has fact sheet information (name, age, occupation, and so on), plus information about the presenting question or problem, early childhood experiences and development, family background, school performance, dating and marital history, employment history, contact with other agencies, and general impressions. The desired objectives and format of social histories vary greatly from agency to agency.

Here are a few examples of informational interviews. A social worker at a mental hospital seeks background information to better understand the problems and social functioning of an inpatient. A probation officer conducts a social investigation to guide the court in dealing with someone charged with a felony. A worker for a community welfare council interviews people in a multiproblem neighborhood to identify what they view as their most urgent unmet needs. A worker at a nursing home does a social history on a new resident to obtain information on current social and personal problems and on special interests, which will help determine the kinds of services and activities that are needed to meet the resident's needs and interests.

Assessment Interviews

Assessment or decision-making interviews are more focused in purpose than informational interviews. The questions asked in assessment interviews are aimed at making *specific* decisions involving human services. For example, a protective service worker investigates a child abuse complaint to determine whether abuse is occurring. A public assistance worker interviews an unmarried woman who is pregnant to determine eligibility for financial assistance. A vocational rehabilitation counselor interviews a client with a developmental disability to determine eligibility for a range of services including financial assistance, vocational training, and sheltered workshop participation. A social worker at a residential facility for persons with developmental disabilities interviews the parents of a child with a severe cognitive disability to obtain information that will be used by the admissions committee to determine whether the child should be admitted. A director of a group home for adolescent boys interviews a youth on juvenile probation who is having severe conflict with his parents to determine whether he would benefit from the group home, or whether a correctional school is more appropriate.

Therapeutic Interviews

The purpose of therapeutic interviews is to help clients make changes, or to change the social environment to help clients function better, or both. A shy parent is counseled on how to be more assertive. A depressed, lonely, or suicidal client is counseled on how to handle such problems better. A client on probation is counseled on how to apply for and find a job. A couple having marital problems are counseled on how to communicate and handle their problems better. A newly married couple distressed by the husband's premature ejaculation are counseled on how to resolve such a dysfunction (Hyde, 1994). A couple with problems disciplining their children might be given instructional sessions in Parent Effectiveness Training techniques (Gordon, 1970). These are all examples of helping clients make changes.

Other therapeutic interviews are geared to changing the social environment to facilitate a client's social functioning. The spouse of a client with a drinking problem is counseled on how to help the spouse stop drinking and develop a meaningful life separate from alcohol. Kadushin (1972) gave other examples:

> Interviews may have a therapeutic purpose but the person for whom the therapeutic change is sought may not be present. These include interviews with persons important in the client's life, where the social worker acts as a broker or advocate in the client's behalf. The social worker engaged in brokerage or advocacy may interview people in strategic positions in an attempt to influence them on behalf of the client. The purpose of the interview is to change the balance of forces in the social environment in the client's favor. The school social worker may interview a teacher in order to influence her to show more accepting understanding of a client. The social worker at the neighborhood service center may interview a worker at the housing authority or at the local department of public welfare in order to obtain for his client full entitlement to housing rights or to assistance. Or a social worker may accompany an inarticulate client to an employment interview in an effort to influence the decision in the client's favor. In each instance the scheduled interview has a definite, and in these cases, therapeutic purpose on behalf of the client. (p. 19)[1]

[1]Alfred Kadushin, *The Social Work Interview.* Copyright © 1972, Columbia University Press, New York. This and all other quotations from the same source are used with permission.

EXHIBIT 4.1

Example of a social history

WISCONSIN STATE HOSPITAL
SOCIAL HISTORY

Donald Cooper*

Birth date: June 30, 1974
Occupation: Accountant
Race: White
Religion: Unaffiliated
Marital status: Divorced, and currently engaged

Height: 5'10"
Weight: 180
Home Address: 2030 Lincoln Drive
Milwaukee, Wisconsin
Phone: (414) 726-4567

PRESENTING PROBLEMS: Mr. Cooper was committed to this hospital by Judge Cherwenka of Washington County for a 60-day observation period. Mr. Cooper was arrested on August 1 on the charge of sexually molesting a minor earlier in the day. The reported victim was an 8-year-old girl whom Mr. Cooper reportedly enticed into his car at the girl's school, and then fondled her genitals after driving to a secluded area.

Mr. Cooper has been arrested on three previous occasions for fondling young girls; each time the charges were dropped after Mr. Cooper consented to receiving psychiatric care. Besides minor traffic violations, he has no other arrest record.

FAMILY BACKGROUND AND EARLY HISTORY: Mr. Cooper's father, Dave Cooper, has been a dairy farmer near Stevens Point all his life. His income has been marginal through the years. Dave Cooper gives the impression of being a meek, submissive person who reportedly has a drinking problem. Dave Cooper indicated he has no idea why his son would become involved in his current difficulties.

Dave Cooper's wife died when Donald was 8 years old, after being ill with cancer for a relatively short time. Dave Cooper mentioned this was a substantial blow to the children and to himself. He added that he has not as yet fully adjusted to his wife's death.

Donald has one sibling, Mary, who is one year older. She is currently married to a serviceman, and they are now stationed in San Diego.

Dave Cooper reported his son's developmental milestones were normal, except he sometimes was enuretic until age 5. Dave Cooper reported Donald had a very close relationship with his mother but seemed to adjust satisfactorily to her death. Dave Cooper continued to provide and care for the two children after his wife died.

SCHOOL PERFORMANCE: Mr. Cooper received slightly above average grades in elementary and high school and received a two-year associate degree in accounting from Portage County Vocational School. Mr. Cooper reported he neither disliked nor liked school and that he was somewhat of a loner during his school years.

GENERAL HEALTH: Mr. Cooper reports his health has been good. He had a hernia operation at age 20 with no lingering complications.

MARITAL HISTORY: Mr. Cooper was married at age 19 to Nancy Riehle, whom he met in high school. It was a forced marriage and ended after one year because of "incompatibility." His ex-wife was interviewed and had no explana-

*Name and other identifying information have been changed in this social history.

Therapeutic interviews are the most common in social work, and therefore this text will focus mainly on this type.

The Place of the Interview

Social work interviews can take place anywhere—in the office, in the client's home, on street corners, in restaurants, and in institutions. Office interviews permit control of the physical setting, usually make the interviewer comfortable, and can usually be arranged to assure privacy. Office interviews also reduce the worker's travel time between interviews.

Home visits have an advantage in helping the interviewer better understand the living conditions of the interviewee. Family interactions can also be observed. Some clients, such as those with severe disabilities,

tion for his involvement in his current difficulties. She is currently receiving $360 per month in child support, and is currently a typist and caring for their 10-year-old daughter. The daughter has not been informed of her father's current confinement; she seldom has contact with her father. The ex-wife appeared to be very dominating and overly critical of Donald, whom she views as "morally immature."

Mr. Cooper is currently engaged to Mary Gautier, and the marriage was planned for December 2 of this year. Miss Gautier indicated she is now reconsidering the upcoming marriage. She is a charming, attractive, petite person currently employed at Jones High School as a secretary. She mentioned she was shocked on being informed of her fiancé's arrest, and had not previously known about his prior arrests. She mentioned she still loves Donald, but feels that unless his reported involvement with young girls is discontinued, it would be better for them to break their engagement. She mentioned she has had sexual relations with Mr. Cooper about twice a week for the past six months, which she described as "satisfying" for her, and she also thought for her fiancé.

EMPLOYMENT HISTORY: Mr. Cooper has been employed as an accountant at Paul Realty Company for the past five years. His supervisor, John Namman, reported his work is reliable, that he associates well with other employees, but is sometimes "moody." Mr. Cooper reported he likes his current job and hopes he can return after his confinement.

Prior to this position, Mr. Cooper worked as an accountant for two other firms where his work was also reported as acceptable. While in high school and in vocational school, he helped his father on the farm.

PRIOR CONTACT WITH SOCIAL AGENCIES: Since Mr. Cooper's first arrest for fondling young girls six years ago, he has been seeing Dr. Timmer at Midwest Psychiatric Center occasionally.

Dr. Timmer reported Mr. Cooper's difficulty is due to the following past history. (Mr. Cooper also related these events in an interview.)

Mr. Cooper mentioned his family life was fairly normal until his mother died when he was 8 years old. His father then began drinking. When sober, his father was considerate, quiet, and an adequate family provider. However, when intoxicated, he was verbally, and sometimes physically, abusive to the children. The children became terrified when they knew their father was drinking. Therefore, when they heard him coming home, they learned to hide by crawling under a blanket. While under the blanket, in fear, they began fondling each other, which seemed to make them feel better. Now, Mr. Cooper mentioned when he feels "moody" or depressed, he seeks young girls to fondle, hoping to feel better again.

In treating Mr. Cooper, Dr. Timmer has been using a modified psychoanalytic approach, but he admits the therapy has apparently not yet curbed Mr. Cooper's involvement with young girls.

GENERAL IMPRESSIONS: In the interviews, Mr. Cooper appeared to be very concerned about his fondling behaviors with young girls and displayed motivation to curb the deviant behavior. He appears to have traditional middle-class values. He is fairly attractive, and has a pleasant personality.

Mr. Cooper, however, has had repeated incidents of involvement with young girls, even while under psychiatric care. The latest incident occurred at a time when Mr. Cooper is engaged; and as he reported, when he is having satisfying relations with his fiancée. His deviant behavior is apparently deeply entrenched. Sexual activities such as Mr. Cooper's are difficult to change. Perhaps covert sensitization, a form of behavior therapy, might be attempted.† Or, rational therapy might be used to teach him other ways of handling his emotions of depression and moodiness, instead of through seeking to fondle young girls.‡ Also, an arrangement might be made with the local mental health center to have Mr. Cooper call and receive immediate counseling (perhaps staying overnight at the center) whenever he has a strong urge to fondle young girls.

†See Module 4.
‡See Module 6.

find it difficult or impossible to travel to an office; therefore, home visits are common in social work. Other clients find an office "foreign" to them and, therefore, are more comfortable in their home or in other settings.

The home visit also offers opportunities for the worker to enter the life of the interviewee as a participant—opening a stuck door, moving furniture, holding a crying baby. However, there is also the chance that the interviewer may have to respond to conflict between family members if it occurs, and some clients may feel that a home visit suggests that the worker is spying on them. Distractions are also more apt to occur—for example, telephone calls, TV programs that other family members want to watch, friends dropping by to visit.

In practice I have found that although the physical setting may have an effect on the start of an interview, these effects can almost always be handled by a skillful interviewer. For example, on a home visit where a number of other people are present, the worker can suggest to the client that they go to a restaurant where they can have a soda and talk without interruptions from other family members. The interviewer's skills are almost always more important than the setting in determining the productivity of an interview.

Opening the First Interview

When Interviewee-Initiated

If someone has asked to see a social worker and has come, it is best to let that person state just what he or she is concerned about. The counselor should, of course, greet the client with something like "Hi, I'm Jane Bernes, and I'm a counselor at this agency." After the client has been seated, the client often begins indicating his or her concerns. If this does not happen, the worker should say something brief and neutral (not to sidetrack the client) to help the client get started, such as: "You came in here to see me about something today."

Openings that are *not* as desirable include the following: (1) "I'm glad you came in this afternoon"—the client may know that you are being superficial and may not in fact be glad to hear what he or she has to say. (2) "In what way can I help you?" The worker should not erroneously convey that he or she is the chief problem solver—the client owns the problem and is the primary problem solver. (3) "You have a problem?" The word *problem* in a counseling situation may suggest to the client that the worker is viewing the client as a psychiatric case.

Benjamin (1974) recommended the following about small talk at the beginning of an interview:

> Sometimes at the outset there is room or need for small talk on the interviewer's part, something to help the interviewee get started. But we should attempt this only when we truly feel that it will be helpful. Brief statements such as the following may break the ice: "With traffic the way it is around here, you must have found it hard to get a parking place" or "It's nice to have a sunny day after all that rain, isn't it?" (p. 13)[2]

[2]Alfred Benjamin, *The Helping Interview,* 2nd ed. Copyright © 1974, by Houghton Mifflin Company. This and all other quotations from the same source are used with permission.

Kadushin (1972) gave these suggestions on how to start an interview:

> It is helpful if the interviewer can greet the interviewee by name. She invites her in, goes through the familiar social amenities—taking her coat, offering her a chair, and demonstrating her concern that she is reasonably comfortable. The interviewer gives the interviewee a chance to get settled—to compose herself, to absorb first impressions, to get her bearings, to catch her breath. She needs a little time to get used to the room and the interviewer. . . .
>
> It is helpful, particularly at the beginning and the end of the contact, to make general conversation rather than engage in an interview. . . . The preliminary chit-chat may be about the weather, parking problems, cooking, baseball, or the high cost of living.
>
> This socializing is not a waste of time. It eases the client's transition from the familiar mode of conversational interaction into a new and unfamiliar role which demands responses for which he has little experience. The conversation has the additional and very important advantage of permitting the interviewee to become acquainted with and size up the interviewer as a person. (pp. 130–131)

When Interviewer-Initiated

Whether talking to a client, or to a client's relative, or to professionals at other agencies, the worker should indicate his or her role or position at the agency and then state the purpose of the interview. Thus, a school counselor may say to a student who is receiving failing grades, "Hi, John. I'm Mr. Roberts, a social worker at this school. I asked that you see me today because I was looking at your grade report. It looks as if you are having difficulty in some of your courses. Perhaps we can talk about the reasons." A protective services worker might say, "Hi, I'm Mary Seely, a protective services worker with Rock County Social Services. Information that raises questions about the care your child is receiving has come to our attention. I realize there are always two sides to any such report, and therefore I would like to talk with you about this."

Closing an Interview

Closing is not always easy. Ideally, both the interviewer and the interviewee should accept the fact that the interview is ending, and the subjects being discussed should not be left hanging. Saying something like, "Well, you really have serious problems, but I've got to catch my ride. When can we talk further?" is too abrupt and unprofessional. Such abrupt endings are apt to be perceived by the interviewee as being discourteous and uncaring.

There are some useful guidelines on how to terminate an interview. Kadushin (1972) recommended:

> Preparation for termination begins with the very beginning of the interview. The interviewee should be informed explicitly at the beginning that a definite period of time has been allotted for the interview, that she is free to use some, or all, of this time but that going beyond the time limit is clearly discouraged. Unless an unusual situation develops, it is understood that the interview will terminate at the end of the allotted time. (p. 207)

When the allotted time is nearly up, the interviewer may inform the interviewee by saying something like: "Well, our time is just about up. Is there anything you'd like to add before we look at where we have arrived, and where we now go from here?" It is often helpful to summarize what was discussed at the end of the interview. If the interview focused only on exploring the client's problems, another interview should be set up for fuller exploration and to begin looking at alternatives.

I have found it helpful to give clients "homework" assignments between interviews. A couple who is having trouble communicating with each other, for example, might be encouraged to set aside a certain amount of time each evening to discuss their personal thoughts with each other. At the next interview this "homework" assignment is then reviewed.

Reid and Shyne (1969) have found that if an agency establishes a set, limited period for contact with the client (including both the number of interviews and the length of each interview), both the worker and client make more productive use of the time as they mobilize their efforts to accomplish the tasks within the designated time.

Ideally, the interviewee should be emotionally at ease when the interview ends; therefore, the interviewer should not introduce emotionally charged content at the end but should seek a reduction in intensity of emotion.

If an interviewee displays a reluctance to end the interview, it is sometimes helpful to confront this directly by saying, "It appears to me that you wish we had more time." The reasons for the interviewee's reluctance can then be discussed, and perhaps another appointment made.

Just as it is sometimes advisable to begin an interview with small talk, a short social conversation at the end can be useful as it provides a transition out of the interview. There are many styles of closing. The style used will depend on the interviewer, the interviewee, and what was said during the interview.

At times an interview can be closed with a restatement of the way both the interviewer and interviewee agreed to proceed; for example, "I'm glad you have decided to have the pregnancy test. If it's positive, give me a call so we can arrange another time to further discuss the options we briefly talked about here."

At times the interviewer may make a more explicit summation of what was discussed, what decisions were arrived at, what questions remain to be resolved, and what actions will be taken. A somewhat different approach is to ask the interviewee to summarize the decisions he arrived at during the interview and what actions he now intends to take.

Sometimes in closing an interview, concerns that were alluded to but not fully discussed might be mentioned as topics that will be discussed at the next interview. I have found some clients will first reveal their most serious concerns at the end of the interview, perhaps because they need time to become comfortable and to gain confidence that the interviewer is a competent person who may have some useful suggestions. In such instances, the interviewer has to decide whether to extend the interview beyond the allotted time or to set up another appointment to discuss these concerns.

Benjamin (1974) observed:

> Closing is especially important because what occurs during this last stage is likely to determine the interviewee's impression of the interview as a whole. We must make certain that we have given him full opportunity to express himself, or, alternatively, we must set a mutually convenient time for this purpose. We should leave enough time for closing so that we are not rushed, since this might create the impression that we are evicting the interviewee. (p. 32)

Questioning

Questions are asked for a variety of purposes: to obtain information, to help clients tell their stories, to build a relationship, to help clients look at alternative strategies, and to help clients select solutions.

The tone in which the question is asked is often as important as the question itself. For a client who is depressed, an appropriate tone should indicate caring and understanding. For someone who is angry, the tone should imply recognition of the anger and a willingness to examine the anger. For someone who is anxious, the tone should convey reassurance.

In exploring clients' problems and alternative solutions, a series of questions with an increasingly specific focus is usually advisable. Kadushin (1972) expanded on this point.

> The successive questions should act as a funnel, moving from general to more specific aspects of the content being discussed. As discussion of one area is completed at the more specific end of the funnel, the new content area introduced for discussion should start with another general, open-ended question. (p. 149)

"How do you feel about that?" is a common question that I find useful for a variety of situations; for example, when a client is pregnant or is involved in a failing romance. Another common question that I ask when a client has a problem that involves someone else is "Could you describe what kind of a person *(name)* is?" Such questions facilitate getting a rapid impression of the client's thoughts and feelings about the other person.

Probing questions are used by skilled interviewers to help clients elaborate on the specific details of their concerns and to help clients look in greater detail at the merits, shortcomings, and consequences of possible resolution strategies. Probing questions with a client who feels her husband drinks too much might include the following: "How much does he drink?" "How often does he drink?" "How does he act when intoxicated?" "What concerns you most about his drinking?" The concerns she mentions also need to be explored in depth, using probing questions such as: "Given his drinking, how do you now feel about him?" "Does he recognize that he has a drinking problem?" "Do you think he would be willing to come in to talk about these concerns?" Probes should not be used in a cross-examination fashion but in a manner that gradually permits the interviewer and the interviewee to see the situations more clearly.

A variety of errors should generally be avoided in phrasing questions. A number of these are shown in Exhibit 4.2. The questions classified as "errors" should not be used unless a worker has a *specific, constructive* purpose for phrasing the question in that fashion.

Note Taking

Note taking is an integral part of counseling. Workers need notes to refresh their memory of past interviews, to record the contracts made with clients, to record information for social histories, to share important facts with colleagues, and to record what has been done or left undone.

Benjamin (1974) observed:

> In our culture, when note taking is discriminately handled, it is not resented. On the contrary, its absence may be looked upon as negligence or lack of respect. Usually no explanation of our recording practice is required. However, should an explanation be requisite because of the needs of either or both partners in the interview, it can be easily provided. (p. 58)

Note taking should be subordinate to interviewing. Don't let note taking interfere with the flow of the interview; for example, avoid saying or conveying, "I wish you would talk slower, I can't write that fast." Don't turn note taking into cross-examination; for example, "Let's see if I got it right, you state you sometimes think about getting a divorce because you find marriage confining." Convey that you are relaxed and comfortable with note taking; don't be secretive about taking notes; this may cause the client to become suspicious or anxious.

Note taking presents a possible distraction to interview interaction. When a worker breaks eye contact to make notes, the focus may shift from what *is being* said to what *has been* said. Ideally, workers should acquire the capacity to take notes unobtrusively without seeming to shift their attention from the client to what is being written.

At times it is important for a worker to record certain kinds of information to demonstrate an interest in the client; such expected information includes certain addresses, names, telephone numbers, contract goals, and tasks.

Kadushin (1972) advised:

> The effect of note taking needs to be assessed periodically during the interview. If at any point the interviewee appears to be upset or made hesitant by note taking, this should be raised for explicit discussion. If, despite the interviewee's stated assent, note taking appears to be a disruptive tactic, one might best forget it. (p. 206)

EXHIBIT 4.2

Phrasing questions

Errors in Phrasing Questions	*A Desirable Neutral Formulation*
THE LOADED QUESTION: This question assumes an unknown action is occurring.	
"When did you last hit your wife?"	"Have you ever hit your wife?"
"What are you going to do when John breaks up with you?"	"Do you think John is considering breaking up with you?"
THE SUGGESTIVE, OR LEADING, QUESTION: The interviewer suggests a "desired" answer.	
"Don't you think it's high time you stop drinking and shape up?"	"Do you think you have a drinking problem?"
"You're really making good progress—aren't you?"	"What progress do you think you're making?"
YES-NO QUESTION: Such questions do not encourage elaboration.	
"Do you ever do anything together with your husband?"	"What kinds of things do you and your husband do together?"
"You really don't like Mary—do you?"	"How do you feel toward Mary?"
EITHER-OR QUESTION: The interviewee might prefer both or neither or a third.	
"Would you like to talk about your marriage or your job this morning?"	"What would you like to talk about this morning?"
"Have you and Tim decided to get married or to have an abortion?"	"What alternatives have you and Tim talked about?"
BOMBARDING: The interviewer asks two or more questions at the same time.	
"How are you feeling today, and did you and your husband get a chance to further discuss what we talked about last week?"	Such questions should be asked separately.
"What were your parents' reactions when you told them you were pregnant? Did they suggest getting an abortion? How do you feel about having an abortion?"	
"Since graduating from high school have you found a job, a place to live, and are you still dating the same person?"	
GARBLED QUESTION: Such questions usually occur when the interviewer is unclear about what he or she wants to ask.	
"You've been considering, uh, what was it, oh yeah, something about what we talked about last time—now how do you feel about that?"	Interviewers need to be clear about what they want to ask before speaking. Pauses are better than asking garbled questions.
"Have you thought about—no, that wouldn't work, another possible thing you could do is—I don't know. What were we talking about?"	

Note taking generally decreases in quantity as a worker gains experience. In recording, don't emphasize the importance of note taking by, for example, sitting with a pen and paper between you and the client, or by recording most of what clients say. Most experienced interviewers find they often don't need to make notes during the interview. Frequently, writing down a few key phrases and points afterward enables the worker to recall important points. Benjamin (1974) stressed honesty in taking notes:

> I am certain of one thing: we must be honest. If the notes taken are to be used for the purpose of research, we should state this at the outset. In the event that the information gathered cannot be kept confidential, we should frankly indicate this, too. Above all, we should not promise confidentiality if we are not certain that we can provide it. (p. 60)

Tape Recording and Videotaping

Audio and video recording of interviews are increasingly being used. Both have advantages over note taking because they provide a full record of what was said. However, a worker cannot refer to tapes as readily as to written notes. Tapes can be transcribed, but this is expensive.

Tape recordings and note taking are generally used for different purposes. Tape recordings are used as a mirror to reflect either to interviewer or interviewee exactly what was said and how. As such they have a *self-confrontation* or *sensitivity* value, because they reflect how a person interacts with others. Playing back tapes can show clients where they have interactional problems (for example, shyness). For interviewers, the tapes can improve counseling and interviewing skills.

An initial concern of interviewers in deciding whether to use tape recordings is how the interviewee will react to being taped. I have used both audiotaping and videotaping extensively for the past several years and have found that clients soon forget the interview is being taped. A number of other authorities agree. Benjamin (1974), for example, said:

> I am firmly convinced that after the first few minutes he will not react to it at all for he will no longer notice it. It is my belief that, as a matter of ethics, the fact that the interview is being taped should not be concealed. If I tell him that it is my custom to record interviews to learn from them afterwards and that the tape will be kept confidential, he will usually not object. He will not be uneasy unless he feels that I am. If I can say that he, too, may listen to the tapes to learn, so much the better. If after all this the interviewee still objects, it is probably best to respect his feelings. Some people are simply afraid or suspicious. In areas or cultures in which the tape recorder is seldom used or seen, for the interviewer to insist might prove harmful indeed. When one finds he is working with suspicious people, the wise thing to do is to get at the suspiciousness and leave the tape recorder alone for the time being. (p. 62)

Some counselors now routinely videotape interviews so clients can more fully grasp what was said and also gain valuable feedback on how they interact. Videotaping allows both the interviewer and the interviewee to study their verbal and nonverbal communication simultaneously.

Videotaping for Training Purposes

Most educational programs in social work and counseling now use videotaping of simulated counseling situations to help students develop and assess their interviewing and counseling skills. Our program (similar to a growing number of other programs) also uses videotaping as one approach to assess students' aptitude for social work.

It is our belief that an essential capacity of social work is the ability to counsel and relate to people. We believe this capacity is necessary in social work practice with individuals, groups, families, organizations, and communities, and for performing competently in micro, mezzo, and macro practice.

In the first practice course of our program, students have to demonstrate a level of counseling and interviewing skills that will give field placement agencies substantial assurance that they will be able to counsel clients. Students demonstrate their interviewing and counseling capacities via videotaped role playing. Each student in the class is videotaped in the role of a counselor while counseling someone else in the class about a contrived problem. This videotape is later reviewed jointly by student and instructor. Students are graded on a pass/fail basis on this videotaped role-play. They are permitted to videotape a role-playing situation as many times as they want. If they fail to make an acceptable tape, they are not allowed to pass the course and are encouraged to transfer to another major. This course, therefore, serves as a first step in "screening out" students from the program. The emphasis of this requirement, however, is not on culling students from the program but on helping them develop their interviewing and counseling techniques. If the student feels the instructor's review of the tape is unfair, an appeal process is available in which the student can take the tape to other social work faculty members for their review.

When we studied the effectiveness of videotapes as a training tool, we found (Zastrow & Navarre, 1979) that students are initially apprehensive about the videotaped role playing. This apprehensiveness is partially reduced by lecture material and class discussions on "how to counsel," and by role-playing counseling situations in class (generally two students counseling two other students about a contrived problem). Following the videotaped role playing, most students express considerable increased confidence in their capacities to counsel and a substantial reduction in their apprehensiveness about being videotaped in the future.

These student responses of how videotaping is helpful are typical (Zastrow & Navarre, 1979):

> It helped make me comfortable in a counseling situation. I was able to test out different ways in helping a client and when reviewing the tape I saw what things I did well, and what I need to work on to become a better counselor.
>
> I became aware of my own voice, posture, and gestures and the importance they play in counseling.
>
> I was able to see an actual picture of myself, not what I thought I looked like, and was able to see where I made my mistakes and could have done something different.
>
> I feel that the best way to learn something is to actually do it, instead of just talking about it. I also thought it was useful to watch the tape and look for your mistakes. This is the best way to correct them.
>
> I became aware of exactly how I came across to the client and I noticed that I was suggesting things to him—which I didn't even realize before reviewing the tape.
>
> Made me more aware of my self-presence (mannerisms). Gave me the opportunity early in my academic career to have a slight taste of what counseling is about and what I might be in store for!
>
> I was not confident in my counseling skills at first. But after seeing the videotape I saw that I could do it. Videotaping is a good confidence builder. (pp. 201–202)

The benefits of using videotaped role playing to assess and develop counseling skills include:

1. Students report it is a valuable tool in learning how to counsel.
2. Difficulties that students have in counseling and relating to people can be identified and shown to the student; then efforts can be made to make improvements.
3. Students whose capacities lie elsewhere can be identified early in their college career and counseled into some other major.
4. Videotaping links theory with practice and thereby makes the course more meaningful and relevant.
5. Students report videotaping provides considerable feedback on themselves and on how they relate to others.
6. Students report videotaping builds their confidence for counseling "real" clients in the future and gives them an opportunity to test their skills and interpersonal behaviors in a safe setting.
7. This laboratory approach helps students make the transition from theory to real practice.
8. The approach provides assurance to field placement agencies that student interns will have an acceptable level of counseling capacities.

We also found that almost all students are able (sometimes after three or four attempts) to develop their interviewing and counseling skills to an acceptable level. It is interesting that the few students who have been identified with this approach as not having the aptitude for social work have, for the most part, voluntarily decided to switch to another major. They also concluded after viewing their videotapes that they didn't have the capabilities to be a social worker.

Summary

Most social work interviews are informational (to obtain data for a social study or for writing a social history), assessment (to arrive at an appraisal), or therapeutic (to help clients change). Often, the three types overlap. Therapeutic interviews are the most common in social work. Their purpose is either to help clients make changes or to change the social environment to help clients function better, or both.

Social work interviews can take place anywhere. Most commonly, they occur either in the interviewer's office or the client's home. Although location does affect an interview, the interviewer's skills are almost always more important in obtaining a productive interview.

Material on how to begin and how to end interviews was presented. In interviewee-initiated interviews, the initial focus is on helping clients become comfortable and start relating their concerns. In interviewer-initiated interviews, the initial focus, after the introductions, is for the interviewer to state the purpose concisely and then begin the dialogue. There are a variety of ways to close interviews. The style used depends on the interviewer, the interviewee, and what was said during the interview. Ideally, both the interviewer and the interviewee should accept the fact that the interview is ending, and topics being discussed should not be left hanging. Most interviews end with either the interviewer or the interviewee summarizing what was said or what course of action is now planned.

Questions in interviews are used for a variety of purposes—to gather information, to help clients tell their stories, to help them look at alternative solutions, and to help them select a strategy. The tone in which a question is asked is often as important as the question itself. Probing questions are common in social work practice. However, several types of questions should usually be avoided: loaded questions, suggestive questions, yes-no questions, either-or questions, clustered questions (bombarding), and garbled questions.

Note taking is an integral part of counseling and should be unobtrusive so it does not interfere with the flow of the interview.

Audiotape and videotape recordings are increasingly used to provide a full recording of what was said. They are generally used for different purposes than note taking. For clients, reviewing tapes helps them grasp more fully what was said and gives them valuable feedback on how they interact. For counselors, reviewing tapes is particularly valuable in helping them assess and further develop their interviewing skills.

EXERCISE

WRITING A SOCIAL HISTORY

Goal: The purpose of this exercise is to give students practice in writing a social history.

Step 1: At an earlier class session, the instructor informs the class there will be an exercise in a future session designed to teach them how to write a social history. Students read the material contained in this chapter on how to write a social history. The instructor informs the students they may either use the format and subheadings contained in the example of a social history in this chapter (see Exhibit 4.1) or an adaptation of it. The instructor asks for a volunteer to develop a contrived story of (1) some unusual incident that has led him or her to become a client of an agency and (2) background information covering the following material:

Birth date	Education*	
Religion	Kindergarten	*Places, grades,
Occupation	Grade school	relationships to
Marital status	Junior high	other students,
Height	High school	and attitudes
Weight	College	about these schools
Address	Employment history	
Home phone	Where worked	
Why referred	How long	
By whom	Health	
Early developmental history	Family life	
Toilet trained (what age)	Dating	
First walked (what age)	Courtship	
First talked (what age)	Prior contact with other social agencies	
Relationship to parents, brothers, sisters		

The instructor informs the class that at a future session she/he will interview the "client" and that each student will have to write a social history based on this interview. (The volunteer may be excused from having to write the social history.) The instructor informs the students that a significant part of their grade for this project will depend on their *realistic* recommendations on how to intervene effectively to help this "client." The instructor indicates that bringing tape recorders to the interview for the write-ups is acceptable.

Step 2: The instructor interviews the "client" at a future class session, covering the information contained in step 1. In this interview the instructor explores problems, but ends the interview before the client chooses specific courses of action to resolve the situation. A major focus of this exercise is to give students practice in arriving at recommendations for how to intervene. (The instructor sets a deadline for when students are to hand in their social histories.) After grading them, the instructor reads to the class one or two (without naming the writers) that were particularly well done.

CHAPTER 5

Social Work with Individuals: Counseling

Counseling someone with personal problems is neither magical nor mystical.[1] Although training and experience in counseling is beneficial, everyone has the potential of helping others by listening and talking through their difficulties. Counseling with a beneficial outcome can be done by a friend, neighbor, relative, the local barber, hairdresser, banker, and bartender, as well as by social workers, psychiatrists, psychologists, guidance counselors, and the clergy. This is not to say that everyone is effective at counseling. Professional people, because of their training and experience, have a higher probability of being effective, but competence and rapport, rather than degrees or certificates, are the keys to desirable outcomes. The focus of this chapter is on how professional counseling should be done. All of us at one time or another counsel others; the closer that counseling (including friend-to-friend counseling) approaches professional counseling, the higher the probability of a successful outcome.

Counseling from the Worker's Perspective

Simply stated, counseling consists of three phases: (1) building a relationship, (2) exploring problems in depth, and (3) exploring alternative solutions with the client and selecting a course of action. (These phases are components of the problem-solving approach, described in Chapter 1.) Successful counseling gradually proceeds from one phase to the next, with some overlap. While exploring problems, the relationship between counselor and client continues to develop in many cases, and problems are generally being examined in greater depth even as alternative solutions/strategies are explored. At the end of a series of counseling interviews, there is often the fourth phase of termination and evaluation. (Guidelines on the counselor's role in each of these phases are presented in the next section.)

[1]This chapter is adapted from three other chapters written by this author: (1) "How to Counsel," in *The Personal Problem Solver,* edited by Charles Zastrow and Dae H. Chang, © 1977, pp. 267–274. Adapted by permission of Prentice-Hall, Inc., Englewood Cliffs, New Jersey; (2) "Self-Talk in Counseling," in *Talk to Yourself: Using the Power of Self-Talk,* © 1979, pp. 266–279. Adapted by permission of Prentice-Hall, Inc., Englewood Cliffs, New Jersey; (3) "The Counseling Process," in *Introduction to Social Work and Social Welfare,* 7th ed. (Pacific Grove: Brooks/Cole, 2000), pp. 185–189.

Many times before the initial interview a counselor is unaware of the concerns (or problems) new clients have. What should be the counselor's objective in the first interview? Simply put, to build a helping relationship and to begin exploring the client's problems. The third phase—examining alternative solutions—may or may not be arrived at in the initial interview. Every interview has a goal or an objective, and the counselor should use this goal to give focus to the interview.

On many occasions the first problem that clients present may not be the one that they are most concerned about. Clients sometimes initially present problems that they believe are more socially acceptable to test how objective, accepting, and helpful the counselor will be. I once had a client who mentioned six "presenting" problems before sharing the one she was most concerned about, which was the guilt she experienced over masturbating.

Counseling from the Client's Perspective

The counseling process can also be conceptualized from the client's point of view. For counseling to be successful, clients must arrive at a progressive series of "self-talk" statements (that is, clients must arrive at having certain thoughts and beliefs). These self-talk stages are:

Stage I *Problem awareness:* "I have a problem."
Stage II *Relationship to counselor:* "I think this counselor has what it takes to help me."
Stage III *Motivation:* "I want to improve my situation and am willing to put forth the effort to do so."
Stage IV *Conceptualizing the problem:* "My problem is not overwhelming but has specific components that can be changed."
Stage V *Exploration of resolution strategies:* "I see there are several courses of action that I might try in order to do something about my situation."
Stage VI *Selection of a strategy:* "I think this approach might help, and I am willing to try it."
Stage VII *Implementation:* "This approach is helping me."
Stage VIII *Evaluation:* "Although this approach takes a lot of my time and effort, it's worth it."

The advantage of this conceptualization of the counseling process is that it presents a framework for assessing and improving the effectiveness of counseling. When counseling is not producing positive changes in clients, this framework helps identify the reasons for the lack of progress. Once these reasons are identified, changes can be made.

Stage I: Problem Awareness

At this initial stage, clients must say to themselves, "I have a problem—I need to do something about my situation." If clients refuse to acknowledge that they have problems, they will not be motivated to change. In some areas of counseling (for example, working with problem drinkers), people have difficulty acknowledging that they have a problem. Involuntary clients (those forced to seek counseling) frequently deny that a problem exists. Social workers encounter involuntary clients in a variety of settings: protective services, corrections, certain public school settings, group homes, mental health facilities, nursing homes, and hospitals.

For people in denial, constructive changes are not apt to occur unless counselors find a way to convince them that there is a problem. Counselors focus on the denial by exploring why clients believe the problem doesn't exist and by gathering evidence to document the existence of the problem. Clients then need to be confronted (in a tactful manner) with this evidence. If after such a confrontation they are still in denial, counselors must accept that the client *owns* the problem, and there is little more that counselors can do constructively at this time, except perhaps to indicate they will be available in the future if the client wants to talk. (For additional strategies on how to work with hostile, involuntary clients, see Exhibit 5.1.)

At times people who acknowledge their problem may prefer to try to resolve it without help from others. They "own" their problem, and therefore have a right to decide how they want to handle it. If they decide to work on it alone, counselors should respect this decision but also indicate that they will be available in the future by saying something like, "If you do decide later that you'd like to talk about it, my door is always open."

Stage II: Relationship to Counselor

The client/counselor relationship is operative in every stage in the counseling process. For counseling to be effective, clients must arrive at the point where their self-talk is, "I think this counselor has what it takes to help me." If clients think, "This counselor can't help

EXHIBIT 5.1

Strategies for working with hostile, involuntary clients

A significant number of involuntary clients are openly hostile in initial (and sometimes later) contacts with their assigned worker. What strategies can workers use to develop rapport with such clients, and to motivate them to make positive changes? A number of strategies are summarized here.

1. Treat such clients with respect. Workers need to understand that such clients probably do not want to discuss their situation with the worker. Modeling respect can help calm clients, and may then lead clients to show respect for the worker.
2. Allow clients to vent their unhappiness over being forced to see the worker. In many cases, it is useful to indicate, "It is understandable that you are upset about having to be here—if the tables were turned and I was in your situation, I wouldn't want to be here either. It may help you begin if you start with your concerns about being forced to be here." Venting their concerns can have a calming effect.
3. Allowing clients to vent concerns may also generate goals that the worker can help clients work toward. For example, if a client is seeing a child welfare worker because he physically abused his son while disciplining him, the worker can say, "I know you disciplined your child because you want the best for him—however, hurting a child is not acceptable. I wonder if we could explore some alternatives, like timeouts for Timmy and anger management techniques?" *A key ingredient in working with involuntary clients is establishing goals that are personally meaningful to them.* Workers should seek to limit involuntary goals to legal mandates, and then seek to add realistic goals that clients desire. The strategy here is to search for common ground between the legal mandates and clients' personal goals. Often, redefining the problem in a way that adequately addresses the concerns of both client and referral source reduces the client's resistance and makes a workable agreement possible.
4. Utilize the "disarming technique" (described in greater detail in Chapter 7), which involves finding some truth in what involuntary clients are saying, even when workers believe they are largely wrong, irrational, unfair, or unreasonable. There is always a grain of truth to be found, even if it sounds insulting or obnoxious. When workers disarm clients with this technique, clients may recognize that workers are offering respect; this may make them more cooperative. This technique also facilitates open (rather than defensive) communication.
5. Do not subject yourself to extensive verbal abuse. If hostile clients become overly verbally abusive, postpone the contact with something like, "Sir, I'm treating you with respect, and in exchange I also have a right to be treated with respect. I see we presently are not getting anywhere. I will contact you tomorrow—by that time we will hopefully be better able to more calmly discuss this."
6. If clients continue to be verbally abusive in subsequent meetings, workers should meet with their immediate supervisor to discuss available options—such as referring the involuntary client back to the original referral source, or transferring the case to another worker.

---

me. I don't need a head shrinker. I just don't trust this counselor," counseling will fail unless a more positive relationship is established. Throughout counseling, and especially in the initial meetings, counselors must be aware of and give attention to the kind of relationship that is developing with their client.

Eriksen (1979) emphasized the importance of a helping relationship being formed with clients:

> The relationship that develops between worker and client is the very cornerstone of helping. Through the helping relationship, the client and worker come together to unblock communication that is preventing problem solving. . . .
>
> Through the vehicle of the helping relationship, the client can communicate to the worker what she thinks, knows and feels about her problem. This kind of in-depth communication, when reinforced by effective responses by her worker, will strengthen the helping relationship itself and will soon open the door to problem solving. (p. 54)

The following guidelines can help build a constructive relationship.

1. Try to establish a nonthreatening, comfortable atmosphere where clients feel safe to communicate fully their troubles while feeling accepted as a person.

2. In initial contacts with clients, you need to "sell" yourself, not arrogantly, but as a knowledgeable, understanding person who may be able to help and who wants to try.

3. Be calm, do not laugh or express shock when clients begin to open up about their problems. Even subtle responses can lead clients to believe that you are not going to understand their difficulties, and they will usually stop discussing them. Remaining calm is not always easy. I remember one interview with a client

who had brutally murdered his estranged partner by decapitating her. It took 45 minutes for the client to explain his reasons for killing her and to recount how he had planned and carried out this murder. The details were shocking, but I had to continue to take a professional approach, to remain calm, and to continue to maintain a nonthreatening atmosphere so that he would feel free to relate what occurred.

4. Be nonjudgmental, not moralistic. Show respect for clients' values and do not try to sell your own. Values that work for you may not be best for someone else in a different situation. For example, if a single client is pregnant, do not attempt to force your values on adoption or abortion on her. Let her decide on the course of action after a full examination of the problem and an exploration of alternative solutions.

5. View clients as equals. "Rookie" counselors sometimes make the mistake of thinking that because clients are sharing intimate secrets the counselor must be very important, and they end up constructing a superior-inferior relationship. If clients feel they are being treated as inferiors, they will be less motivated to reveal and discuss personal difficulties.

6. Use a shared vocabulary. This does not mean using the same slang words and the same accent as clients. If clients see counselors as artificial in their use of slang or accent, they may be seriously offended. Use words that clients understand and that are not offensive.

7. Your tone of voice should convey that you empathetically understand and care about the client's feelings.

8. Keep what clients say confidential. People unfortunately have nearly irresistible urges to share "juicy secrets." If clients discover that their confidentiality has been violated, a working relationship can be quickly destroyed.(See the material on confidentiality in Chapter 2.)

9. If you counsel a relative or a friend, you are probably emotionally involved, and you may get upset or begin to argue. If that happens, it is almost always best to drop the subject immediately, as tactfully as possible. Perhaps after tempers cool the subject can be brought up again, or perhaps you should refer the individual to someone else. When you find yourself becoming upset, further discussion will not be productive. Many professional counselors refuse to counsel friends or relatives because of the emotional involvement. A calm, detached perspective is needed to help clients objectively explore problems and alternative solutions.

Stage III: Motivation

For counseling to be effective, clients must (sooner or later) conclude, "I want to improve my situation and am willing to put forth the effort to do so." Unless clients become motivated to change, constructive changes are not apt to occur. In counseling, the key variable in determining whether clients will improve their circumstances is their motivation to want to improve and put forth the necessary effort (Losoncy, 1977).

Counselors can best motivate discouraged or apathetic people by being an encouraging person. According to Losoncy (1977), encouraging people have the following characteristics:

1. Complete acceptance of the discouraged person, but not of the dysfunctional behavior that has to be changed. Convey "I accept you exactly as you are, with no conditions attached."

2. A nonblaming attitude, so the discouraged person no longer feels a need to lie, pretend, or wear a mask.

3. Empathy. Be aware of and to some extent feel what the discouraged person is feeling. Empathy occurs, as described by Kadushin (1972), when a counselor

> *feels* with the client rather than for him. Feeling *for* the client would be a sympathetic rather than an empathic response. Somebody once said that if you have a capacity for empathy you feel squat when you see a squat vase and feel tall when you look at a tall vase. Empathy is entering imaginatively into the inner life of someone else. It is not enough simply to be empathically understanding; one needs to communicate to the client that one accurately perceives and feels his situation. (p. 52)

4. Genuine interest in the client's progress; convey that the client is an important, worthwhile person.

5. Confidence in the capacity of the discouraged person to improve.

6. Sincere enthusiasm about the discouraged person's interests, ideas, and risk-taking actions. Discouraged people need to believe in themselves, and they also need an encouraging person who conveys that they are important, worthwhile persons.

7. Nonjudgmental listening, so the discouraged person's real thoughts and feelings can be expressed freely, without fear of censure.

8. The ability to notice (reward) every small instance of progress (particularly during the beginning of the relationship), and to notice (reward) positives about the client. Even small compliments about something

unrelated to the counseling goals go a long way toward motivating clients.

9. The ability to motivate. Motivating a discouraged person takes a long, long time. Discouraged people often have a long history of failures. Reversing this trend requires time. Listen and understand this person as fully as possible.

10. A sincere belief in the discouraged person's ability to find a purpose in life.

11. The ability to allow the person to take risks without passing judgment.

12. The ability to reinforce the person's *efforts*. The important thing is that people try, not that they necessarily succeed. By making efforts to improve, there is hope.

13. The ability to help the discouraged person see the falsehood and negative consequences of self-defeating statments (such as "I'm a failure"). Every person has skills and deficiencies, and every person should be encouraged to improve both strengths and weaknesses.

14. The capacity to recognize that all that you can do is give your best effort in trying to motivate the person. Success is not guaranteed. A counselor with no hope of motivating is no longer effective.

15. The skill to look for the client's uniquenesses and strengths. These should be communicated so that clients begin to realize they are special and worthwhile. This process leads to a sense of improved self-worth and gives them courage to take risks and change.

16. Awareness of the negative consequences of overdependency. As clients begin to take risks and make constructive changes, counselors should start to help the client develop self-encouragement, in which they are encouraged to make and trust their own decisions and to take more risks.

(*Note:* These guidelines on motivating clients are also useful in building counseling relationships with them.)

Stage IV: Conceptualizing the Problem

For counseling to be effective, clients need to recognize, "My problem is not overwhelming, but has specific components that can be changed." Many clients view their situation as so complex that they become highly anxious and emotional, and thereby cannot see that their problem is solvable. Several years ago I counseled a teenager who had missed her menstrual period for three months and was so overwhelmingly afraid of being pregnant that she was unable to figure out on her own that the first step was to have a pregnancy test. (When she finally took the test, the results showed she was not pregnant.) To help clients conceptualize their problems, counselors need to explore the problems together in depth with clients. The following guidelines focus on how to explore problems in depth:

1. Many rookie counselors suggest solutions as soon as a problem is identified, without exploring the problem area in depth. For example, an advocate of abortions may advise this solution as soon as a single female reveals that she is pregnant, without taking the time to discover whether she is strongly opposed to abortions, really wants a baby, or intends to marry soon.

2. In exploring problems in depth, counselor and client need to examine the severity of the problem, how long the problem has existed, its causes, how the client feels about the problem, and the client's physical and mental coping capacities and strengths, before exploring alternative solutions. For example, the counselor and a single pregnant client need to explore the following: How does she feel about being pregnant? Has she seen a doctor? About how long has she been pregnant? Do her parents know? What are their feelings and concerns if they know? Has she informed her sexual partner? What are his feelings and concerns if he knows? What does she feel is the most urgent situation to deal with first? Answers to such questions will determine the future direction of counseling.

3. Once a problem area is identified, usually a number of subproblems can be identified. Explore all of them; for example, deciding how to tell the father, obtaining medical care, obtaining funds for medical expenses, deciding where to live, deciding whether to leave school or stop working during the pregnancy, deciding whether to terminate the pregnancy, making plans for after the child is delivered or the pregnancy is terminated.

4. In a multiproblem situation, the best way to decide which problem to handle first is to ask clients which problem they perceive as most pressing. If that problem can be solved, explore it in depth and together develop a solution strategy. Problem-solving success will increase clients' confidence in the counselor, and thereby further solidify the relationship.

5. Convey empathy, not sympathy. Empathy is the capacity to show that you are aware of and can to some extent feel what the client is saying. Sympathy is also a sharing of feelings, but it offers pity. The difference is subtle; empathy facilitates problem-solving but sympa-

thy is often problem-prolonging. Giving sympathy usually causes clients to dwell on their emotions without taking action to improve the situation.

Benjamin (1974) further described how to be empathic:

> The empathic interviewer tries as much as he possibly can to feel his way into the internal frame of reference of the interviewee and to see the world through the latter's eyes as if that world were his own world. The words "as if" are crucial for although the interviewer is empathic, he never loses sight of the fact that he remains his own self. Knowing all the time that he is distinct from the interviewee, he tries to feel his way about in the internal world of thought and feeling of the other in order to come as close to him as possible, to understand with him as much as possible. (p. 47)[2]

The difference between sympathy and empathy shows in responses to the following statement by a client whose male friend recently ended their three-year relationship, "How could he do this to me, after all I've done for him? He's hurt me so much."

Sympathetic response: "He's such a schnook! I don't see how you can ever face the world. You're probably going to be miserable for a long, long time."

Empathic response: "I know ending this relationship hurts deeply. Part of your emotional pain appears to be related to your confusion as to why he wants to end the relationship. Have you discussed this with him?"

Keith-Lucas (1972) gave a cogent example separating sympathy, pity, and empathy:

> Consider three reactions to someone who has told us that he strongly dislikes his wife. The sympathetic person would say, "Oh, I know exactly how you feel. I can't bear mine, either." The two of them would comfort each other but nothing would come of it. The pitying person would commiserate but add that he himself was most happily married. Why doesn't the other come to dinner sometime and see what married life could be like? This, in most cases, would only increase the frustration of the unhappy husband and help him to put his problem further outside himself, on to his wife or his lack of good fortune. The empathetic person might say something like, "That must be terribly difficult for you. What do you think might possibly help?" and only the empathetic person, of the three, would have said anything that would lead to some change in the situation. (pp. 80–81)

[2]Alfred Benjamin, *The Helping Interview,* 2nd ed. Copyright © 1974, by Houghton Mifflin Company, used by permission.

6. "Trust your guts." The most important tool counselors have is their feelings and perceptions. Counselors should continually strive to place themselves in their client's situation (with the client's values and pressures). To use the earlier example, if the client is 17 years old, single, and pregnant, and has parents who are very critical of the situation and who want her to have an abortion, a competent counselor will continually strive to feel what she is feeling and to perceive the world from her perspective, with her goals, difficulties, pressures, and values. We are never 100 percent accurate in placing ourselves in our client's situation, but 70–80 percent is usually sufficient to gain an awareness of the client's pressures, problems, and perspectives. This information is very useful in determining what additional areas need to be explored, what she should say to her parents, and what might be possible solutions. Stated somewhat differently, counselors should wonder "What is this person trying to tell me, and how can I make it clear that I understand not only intellectually but empathically?"

7. When you believe that the client has touched on an important area of concern, further communication can be encouraged in the following ways:

- Show interest nonverbally.
- Pause. Rookie counselors usually become anxious when there is a pause and hasten to say something, anything, to have conversation continue. This is usually a mistake, especially when it leads to a change in an important topic. Pauses give clients time to think about the important area of concern, so they can explore it thoughtfully.
- Probe neutrally. "Could you tell me more about it?" "How do you feel about that?" "I'm not sure I understand what you have in mind."
- Summarize what the client is saying. "During this past hour you made a number of critical comments about your spouse; it sounds as if some things about your marriage are making you unhappy."
- Reflect feelings. "You seem angry" or "You appear to be depressed about that."

8. Approach socially unacceptable topics tactfully. Tact is an essential quality of competent counselors. Try not to ask a question in such a way that the answer puts the respondent in an embarrassing position. Suppose you have good relationship with a teenaged client and you have reason to suspect that this person has concerns about masturbating. How would you tactfully bring up the subject? One possible approach is "When I was your age, I had a number of concerns about masturbating.

That was unfortunate. Most teenagers masturbate, and many have strong feelings of guilt or shame about it. Although masturbation has been stigmatized, it is a natural outlet for sexual feelings and is not harmful. In fact, most sex therapists recommend masturbating as a way to release sexual tensions. I'm wondering if you have some questions or concerns about masturbation that would be helpful for us to discuss?" Informing the youth that you also had concerns about this subject personalizes it and informs the teenager that you successfully dealt with similar concerns to those he or she is currently facing. This self-disclosing process fosters communication and relationship building.

A question occasionally arises as to when counselors should self-disclose by sharing past experiences. When such experiences are shared, clients may come to view the counselor as needing counseling. (The client is particularly apt to reach this conclusion if counselors reveal, by nonverbal and verbal communication, that they still have unresolved issues surrounding these experiences.) Also, when working in certain settings (for example, drug treatment centers), a statement that the counselor continues to engage in behaviors that the client needs to change (such as getting drunk or smoking pot) may be used as an excuse for the client to continue problematic behaviors. A good rule to follow in deciding whether to self-disclose is to first ask, "If I share these personal experiences, are they apt to have a constructive effect?" If you are unable to objectively specify a likely beneficial effect, you should not self-disclose the experience.

9. When pointing out a client's limitation, mention and compliment them on their assets. Mentioning a limitation causes clients to feel that something is being laid bare or taken away. A compliment in another area gives something back.

10. Watch for nonverbal cues. Competent counselors generally use such cues to identify when a sensitive subject is being touched on, as clients display their anxiety by changes in tone of voice, fidgeting, tightening facial or neck muscles, yawning, assuming a stiff posture, or flushing. Some counselors even claim they can tell when clients become anxious by observing when their pupils dilate.

11. Be honest. An untruth always runs the risk of being discovered. If that happens, your client's confidence will be seriously damaged, and your relationship may be seriously jeopardized. If a client asks an important question that you cannot answer, it is usually best to say, "Unfortunately I don't know the answer, but let me check into it and I'll let you know by __________ (a specified time)." Being honest goes beyond not telling lies. Counselors should always tactfully inform clients of shortcomings that they really need to attend to. For example, if an individual is being fired from jobs because of poor grooming habits, this fact needs to be brought to their attention. Or, if a trainee's relationship skills and intervention capacities are not suited for the helping profession, that person needs to be "counseled out" in the interest of clients and in the trainee's own best interests.

12. Listen attentively. View clients' words from their perspective, not from yours. Unfortunately, some counselors, caught up in their own interests and concerns, don't always tune out these personal thoughts while clients are speaking. This guideline seems simple, but it is not always easy to follow. Kadushin (1972) expanded on why listening attentively is difficult.

> The nature of spoken communication presents a special hazard, seducing the interviewer into an easy nonlistening. The hazard lies in the great discrepancy between the number of words that are normally spoken in one minute and the number of words that can be absorbed in that time. Thought is much more rapid than speech. The average rate of spoken speech is about 125 words per minute. We can read and understand an average of 300–500 words per minute. There is, then, a considerable amount of dead time in spoken communication, during which the listener's mind can easily become distracted. The listener starts talking internally to take up the slack in time. Listening to the internal monologue may go on side by side with listening to the external dialogue. More often, however, it goes on at the expense of listening to the external dialogue. The interviewer becomes lost in some private reverie—planning, musing, dreaming. (p. 188)[3]

Kadushin (1972) gave the following suggestions on how to listen effectively:

> Rather than becoming preoccupied as a consequence of the availability of the spare time between the slow spoken words, the good interviewer exploits this time in the service of more effective listening. The listener keeps focused on the interviewee but uses the time made available to the mind by slowness of speech to move rapidly back and forth along the path of the interview, testing, connecting, questioning: How does what I am hearing now relate to what I heard before? How does it modify what I heard before? How does it conflict with

[3]Alfred Kadushin. *The Social Work Interview.* Copyright © 1972 Columbia University Press, New York. Reprinted by permission.

it, support it, make it more understandable? What can I anticipate hearing next? What do I miss hearing that needs asking about? What is he trying to tell me? What other meanings can the message have? What are his motives in telling me this? (p. 190)[4]

Stage V: Exploration of Resolution Strategies

After (or sometimes while) a problem is explored in depth, the next step is to consider alternative solutions. In exploring solutions, it is almost always best for counselors to begin by asking something like "Have you thought about ways to resolve this?" Clients generally have been aware for some time that they have a problem. In most cases, they have already tried to resolve the problem. Therefore, this question often elicits alternatives that the client has tried but which have not worked. They can then be discarded. In addition, this question can also elicit high-quality alternatives from the client that the counselor has not thought of and that may well work for the client. Merits, shortcomings, and consequences of the client's alternatives should be tactfully and thoroughly examined. Counselors should then mention other potential solutions, and their merits and shortcomings should also be examined.

Each client is unique, and so are his or her problems. What works for one client may not work for another. An abortion, for example, may be compatible with one client's values and circumstances but undesirable for another client. If counseling is going to be effective, the client needs to say, "I see there are several courses of action that I might try to do something about my situation." Unless clients realize that resolution strategies exist, counseling is apt to fail.

Stage VI: Selection of a Strategy

After counselor and client discuss the probable effects and consequences of possible resolution strategies, it is essential that the client conclude, "I think this approach might help me, and I am willing to try it." If a client is indecisive or refuses to commit to a course of action, constructive change will not occur. For example, if a client says, "I know I have a drinking problem, but I am unwilling to take any action to cut down on my drinking," counseling will probably not be successful.

Clients usually have the right to self-determination—that is, to choose the course of action they want to take. The counselor's role is to help clients clarify and understand the likely consequences of each alternative. It is generally not the counselor's role to give advice or choose the alternative. If the counselor selects the alternative, there are two possible outcomes: (1) The alternative may prove to be undesirable, in which case the client will blame the counselor for the advice and the future relationship will be seriously hampered, and (2) the alternative may prove to be beneficial. This immediate outcome is desirable, but clients will not "own" the result—*they* didn't make the outcome happen, the counselor did. The client will then become overly dependent on the counselor, seeking his or her advice far too often and becoming reluctant to make decisions on their own. In practice, most courses of action have both desirable and undesirable consequences. An unmarried mother who keeps her child may receive considerable gratification from being with and raising the child, but she may also blame the counselor for her long-term financial hardship and isolated social life.

Not giving advice does not mean that counselors should not suggest alternatives. On the contrary, it is the counselor's responsibility to suggest and explore all viable alternatives with their clients. A good rule to follow is that when you believe a client should take a certain course of action, phrase it as a suggestion, "Have you thought about . . . ?" not as advice, "I think you should . . ."

Clients' rights to self-determination should be taken away only if the selected course of action will seriously hurt others or themselves. For example, if it is highly probable that a parent will continue to abuse a child, or if the client attempts to take her own life, counselor intervention is suggested. For most situations, however, clients have the right to select their resolution, even when counselors believe that another alternative is a better course of action. Frequently, clients are in a better position to know what is best for their situation, and if it doesn't work out, they should not be deprived of the opportunity to learn from the mistake.

Stage VII: Implementation

Counseling will be successful only if clients follow through on their commitment to try a resolution approach and then conclude "This approach is beginning to help me." If clients follow through on the commitment, but instead conclude "I don't believe this approach is helping me," counseling is again failing. If this occurs, counselor and client need to examine the

[4]Ibid.

EXHIBIT 5.2

Guidelines on formulating a contract

Contracts in social work practice specify goals and the tasks to be performed to accomplish them. In addition, contracts set deadlines for completing tasks and identify rewards for successful task completion. Contracts also specify consequences for unsuccessful completion of tasks. A contract is, therefore, an agreement between a social worker and one or more clients in their joint efforts to achieve specified outcomes. Formulating an explicit contract is directly related to a positive outcome for clients (Hepworth & Larsen, 1993, p. 365).

A contract, in outline format, should contain the following components:

1. Goals to be accomplished (ranked in order of priority).
2. Tasks to be accomplished by the client and by the worker. (These tasks must be directly related to accomplishing the goals, so that accomplishing the tasks results in successfully meeting the goals.)
3. Time frame for completing the tasks.
4. Means of monitoring progress in task completion and goal accomplishment.
5. Rewards for the client if the terms of the contract are met.
6. Adverse consequences to the client upon nonfulfillment of the terms of the contract.

Some workers prefer written contracts, and others prefer verbal contracts. A written contract has the advantage of emphasizing the commitment to the contract by both worker and client, and it also minimizes the risks of misunderstandings. A verbal contract avoids the sterility of a written contract. Research comparing the effectiveness of written versus verbal contracts shows that verbal contracts are generally as effective as written contracts with regard to meeting goals (Hepworth & Larsen, 1993, p. 381). If workers use a verbal contract, they should still record the essential elements of the contract in their notes for future reference.

The most difficult element in an effective contract is formulating goals. Goals specify what the client wishes to accomplish and should directly relate to the needs, wants, or problems being encountered by the client. Goals serve the following important functions:

1. Goals ensure that workers and clients are in agreement about the objectives to be accomplished.
2. Goals provide direction to the helping process and thereby reduce needless wandering.
3. Goals guide selection of appropriate tasks (and interventions) to achieve the objectives.
4. Goals serve as outcome criteria in evaluating the extent to which the tasks (and interventions) are succeeding.

Useful guidelines when setting goals include:

1. *Goals must relate to the desired end results sought by the client.* Clients must believe that accomplishing the selected goals will enhance their well-being. Therefore, workers need to integrally involve clients in selecting and specifying the goals.

2. *Goals should be stated in specific and measurable terms.* Nebulous goals (such as "Client gaining increased control over his emotions") are not sufficient and often lead the client to "drift" or wander in the helping process. A specific goal (such as "The client will express his angry feelings with his mother in an assertive rather than an aggressive manner when they are having conflicts") is more effective. In addition, it is also measurable, whereas a nebulous goal is not. The client's mother (and others) can monitor the number of times, over a specified period, that the client expresses his angry feelings assertively rather than aggressively. Clients tend to define goals more nebulously, so it is important for workers to help clients state goals that are both specific and measurable.

3. *Goals should be feasible.* Unachievable goals set clients up for failure, which then leads to disappointment, disillusionment, and a sense of defeat. It is vital that the goals chosen can be accomplished. For clients with grandiose tendencies, it is important for workers to assist them (tactfully) in lowering their expectations to what can reasonably be attained.

When arriving at feasible goal statements with clients, workers should agree only to assist them in working toward goals for which the workers have the requisite skills and

---

reasons for no gain, and perhaps try another strategy. Here are some guidelines on how to implement a resolution approach:

1. Attempt to form an explicit, realistic "contract" with clients. When clients do select an alternative, they should clearly understand the goals, what tasks need to be carried out, how to do the tasks, and who will carry out each task. Frequently, it is desirable to write a "contract" for future reference, with a time limit set for accomplishing each task. For example, if an unmarried mother decides to keep her child and now needs to make long-range financial plans, this goal should be understood and specific courses of action decided on—seeking public assistance, seeking support from the alleged father, securing an apartment within her budget, and so on. Furthermore, who will do what task within a set time limit should be specified.

Negotiating a contract (and perhaps renegotiating it in future interviews) brings a focus to the interview. Client and counselor are less likely to get sidetracked

knowledge. If the goal is beyond the worker's competence (for example, assisting the client in overcoming a complex sexual dysfunction), the worker should refer the client to a more appropriate resource.

Once clients settle on their goals, the final step in negotiating goal statements is to assign priorities to the goals. This ensures that the initial change efforts are directed to the goal that is most important to the client.

The following scenario provides an example. First, background information: Ray and Klareen Norwood have been married for three years. They seek counseling because Klareen is increasingly afraid of Ray's angry outbursts. Ray is physically and verbally abusive to her when he is angry. He has not hit Klareen yet, but she is afraid that Ray's escalating aggressiveness will lead to her being battered. Klareen is seriously considering separating from Ray. She has already contacted an attorney to discuss divorce proceedings. Both partners, however, state that they want to maintain the marriage. At the end of the second meeting with the Norwoods, this contract is prepared.

Goals: (a) Ray will cease being physically abusive to Klareen and will reduce by at least two-thirds his verbal abuse incidents over the next 30 days. (This goal is rated number one.)

(b) The Norwoods will begin discussing, at some future date, raising a family. (This goal is rated number two.) The Norwoods both agree to put off further discussion at this time because Klareen says she first needs to decide whether she wants to remain in the marriage.

Tasks of the participants: Worker: the social worker will instruct Ray in the following anger control techniques: (1) Expressing his angry feelings to Klareen in an assertive rather than aggressive manner (see Module 4). (2) Reducing the intensity and frequency of his outbursts by countering his negative and irrational self-talk with rational and positive self-talk (Module 6). (3) Countering his feelings of anger with deep-breathing relaxation (Module 9). And (4) learning to blow off steam nondestructively through such physical activities as jogging or hitting a pillow (Module 4).

Mr. Norwood: Ray will attend weekly counseling sessions to learn and practice anger control techniques. His main task is to use these techniques to cease his physical abuse of Klareen and to substantially reduce his verbal abuse of Klareen. After 30 days, if Ray succeeds, a renegotiation of the terms of the contract will occur.

Mrs. Norwood: Klareen will attend weekly counseling sessions with Ray. In addition, she will seek to calmly discuss issues she has with Ray (in and outside the counseling sessions) to avoid provoking Ray's anger. Klareen also has the responsibility to record any incidents in which Ray is physically or verbally abusive to her in the next 30 days.

Duration of contract: 30 days

Means of monitoring progress: Klareen will record incidents where Ray expresses his anger toward her in assertive or nondestructive ways. (This measures the positive ways in which Ray is learning to express his anger.) Klareen will also record any incidents in which Ray is verbally or physically abusive to her.

Rewards for Ray and Klareen if contract is met: They will continue their marriage, which is what both partners want.

Consequences for Ray and Klareen if contract is not met: If Ray hits Klareen one time in the next 30 days, she will separate. If Ray does not reduce by two-thirds the number of times he is verbally abusive in the next month, she will separate. (To get baseline information, Klareen is asked to identify in the past week—taking each day at a time—the number of times Ray was verbally abusive. Nine incidents are identified. As a result, Ray agrees he will, at most, be verbally aggressive to Klareen no more than 12 times in the next 28 days. If he exceeds this limit, it is agreed that Klareen will move in with her parents.)

by extraneous issues, and the interview's productivity can be sustained.

If the client and the counselor differ in their expectations of desired goals, or in their expectations of who will do what tasks, the contract negotiation process forces client and counselor to discuss and hopefully resolve their differences. For additional material on contracts, see Exhibit 5.2.

2. Counseling is done *with* clients, not *to* or *for* them. Clients should have the responsibility of doing many of the tasks necessary to improve the situation. A good rule to follow is that clients should take responsibility for those tasks that they can carry out, while counselors should attempt to do only those that are beyond the clients' capacities. Doing things *for* clients, similar to giving advice, risks creating a dependency relationship. Furthermore, succeeding at tasks leads to personal growth and prepares clients for future responsibilities.

3. Role-play certain tasks that clients lack confidence, or experience, in carrying out. For example, if a pregnant single woman wants help in telling her male friend about the pregnancy, role-playing will assist her

in selecting words and the strategy for informing him. The counselor can first play the woman's role and model an approach, with the woman playing the male role. Then the roles are reversed so the woman can practice telling her male friend.

Stage VIII: Evaluation

If constructive change is to be long lasting or permanent, clients must conclude, "Although this approach takes a lot of my time and effort, it's worth it." If they conclude, "This approach has helped a little, but it's really not worth what I'm sacrificing for it," then an alternative course of action needs to be developed and implemented.

When clients meet commitments, reward them verbally or in other ways. Rewarding clients increases their self-esteem and self-respect and motivates them to continue working to improve their circumstances.

One of the biggest reality shocks of new trainees entering the helping professions is that many clients, even after making commitments to improve their situations, do not carry out the steps outlined.

If clients fail to meet the terms of the contract, effective workers generally do not punish. Punishment usually increases hostility without producing positive lasting changes. Also, don't accept excuses when commitments are not met. Excuses let people off the hook; they provide temporary relief, but they eventually lead to more failure and to a failure identity. Simply ask, "Do you still wish to try to fulfill your commitment?" If clients answer affirmatively, another time deadline acceptable to the client should be set.

Whether or not clients reach all their goals, careful attention should be given to terminating the relationship. If clients still have unresolved problems, a referral should be made to an appropriate agency or professional. Care should be taken in terminating the contact so that clients do not erroneously conclude that the counselor is rejecting them. Also, clients should be asked whether there are additional concerns that they would like help with. If there are none, clients should be informed that the counselor's "door will be open" if help is needed in the future.

At the final interview, or a few weeks after termination, it is usually beneficial to ask clients (verbally or with a brief questionnaire) the following questions:

- Did the counseling help you? If "yes," how? If "no," why did it not help?
- What did the counselor do well?
- What were the shortcomings of the counseling that was received?
- What suggestions do you have for improving counseling services at this agency?
- Do you have some concerns for which you desire additional counseling?

This information is very useful in improving the counseling process and in determining whether the client needs additional help.

These guidelines on counseling should not be followed dogmatically, as they will probably work only 70–80 percent of the time. The most important tools counselors have are their feelings, perceptions, relationship capacities, and interviewing skills.

One final important guideline—counselors should refer their client to someone else, or at least discuss the case with another professional counselor for any of the following situations: (1) if counselors are unable to empathize with the client, (2) if they feel the client is choosing unethical alternatives (such as seeking an abortion) that conflict with their basic value system, (3) if they feel the problem is of such a nature that they will not be able to help, or (4) if a working relationship is not established. Competent and secure counselors know that it is possible to work with and help some people, but not all, and that it is in the client's and the counselor's best interests to refer clients they cannot help to others who may be able to provide the counseling needed.

Counseling Skills at Work in Generalist Practice

As you read Mrs. H's case example on the facing page, note that, the social work intern used the following roles that, as described in Chapter 1, are components of generalist social work practice: brokering Mrs. H to enroll in a work-training program; facilitating Mrs. H to receive employment; educating Mrs. H to understand she needed to seek employment; brokering Mrs. H to receive dental care; helping Mrs. H to problem-solve; and being an encouraging role model.

Clients' Reactions to Having a Personal Problem

In counseling clients, a crucial area that counselors need to be aware of and learn to handle effectively is clients' emotional reactions to having a personal problem. Lee Askew's example underscores the importance

CASE EXAMPLE

Counseling Mrs. H: Principles in Action

Our social work program (similar to social work programs at other universities) places students in social service agencies for internships. As social work interns, students observe, and soon begin to do, the kind of work that social workers do. A frequent "reality shock" reported by interns is that many clients are apathetic, discouraged, and simply not motivated to improve. Often, the result is that clients do not "follow through" on commitments made during counseling sessions to improve their circumstances.

Last year at a county social services agency, I was supervising an intern who was surprised and frustrated when clients failed to follow through on commitments. The intern was working with a small caseload of TANF mothers (Temporary Assistance to Needy Families program). The intern commented, "The case examples discussed in textbooks are always successes, and I have not yet seen improvement in my cases." I reassured her that she was not at fault and that lack of improvement is more often the rule than the exception. I added that textbooks are very selective in that they usually present success cases, rather than typical cases, to illustrate theory. Yet, I cautioned that if she became discouraged and gave up being an "encouraging person," she had *no* hope of being effective. After further discussion she developed an approach in which she used the counseling principles presented in this chapter. At the end of her internship, not all of the TANF mothers she was working with showed substantial improvement. Yet she had formed a respected working relationship with each client, and some were making significant efforts to improve their circumstances. At the end of the semester, she wrote the following summary about her contacts with one client:

I was assigned the case of Mrs. H. She was 33 years of age and had three children, ages 15, 11, and 7. She had been receiving TANF assistance for the past six years, ever since her husband deserted her. During the past four years, the agency had made several efforts to get her a job, without success. The records showed Mrs. H did not want a full-time job, because she felt she was too busy taking care of her children. She applied for several part-time jobs but was not hired. Mrs. H felt she did not have any marketable skills, as she had never worked outside of her home.

I was assigned Mrs. H's case when she requested a social worker's help with a problem she was having with her 15-year-old son. Mrs. H had found some "pot" in her son's clothes drawer and didn't know how to handle the situation. I met with Mrs. H. Her home had a general unclean appearance. Mrs. H's physical appearance gave the impression she had been through a war. Her clothes were wrinkled and had what appeared to be food stains on several places. Her hair was greasy, she was quite obese, and she had few teeth left in her mouth. Dark circles were under her eyes, suggesting a great deal of fatigue and stress.

We met for about an hour and a half, and Mrs. H related much of her life history. She had never held a full-time job and had a "forced marriage" (due to becoming pregnant) shortly after she graduated from high school. Her husband had been a road construction worker and had a drinking problem. She had not heard from him in the previous year. She felt if he did come back, she would not even want to see him. She had heard also that when he left he moved to a distant state with another woman.

My aim in the first interview was to build a working relationship, obtain Mrs. H's trust, and help her explore what she saw as her problems. Her immediate problem appeared to be what to do about her discovery of "pot." We discussed to some extent the legalities of smoking marijuana and the effects and consequences of the drug. I also said I could bring over some brief reading material on the drug the next day, and she responded by saying she would very much appreciate receiving such material.

We then role-played how she might bring up the subject of smoking marijuana with her son. First I played her role to model a possible approach, and she played her son. Then we reversed roles to give her practice in trying out an approach. Before discussing the subject with her son, she mentioned she wanted to look at the reading material I had promised her. I dropped off this material the next day. We also set another meeting for the following week.

(continued)

CASE EXAMPLE
Counseling Mrs. H
(continued)

At our next appointment, Mrs. H indicated she had discussed smoking marijuana with her son. Her son responded first with some surprise and some displeasure that Mrs. H had gone through his clothes drawer. The son, Jerry, indicated he had tried smoking marijuana only twice and was not that interested in smoking in the future. Mrs. H added that another related concern she had about Jerry was his interest in occasionally drinking beer with some of his friends. She indicated that she and Jerry had had some moderate disagreements in this area, and they are working on it.

I asked if she felt she needed help from our agency for this issue. She responded, "No, not at this time." I then asked if she needed any other additional help from our agency. She thanked me for the help I had given and said she was not aware of other areas where she needed help. I could have left, but I thought that as I had a good relationship established with her and had been of some prior help this might be an opportunity to have her take a look at her future.

I began by asking her what she would like to see herself doing ten years from now. She responded by saying, "I haven't given that much thought. I probably will be doing what I'm doing now." I asked if she was satisfied with her current life. She rather firmly said no, and went on at length about how difficult it is to live on an inadequate TANF budget and to raise three children by herself. She was also critical of her husband, who placed her in this situation by deserting her.

I conveyed an understanding of her concerns and mentioned that it was certainly true that past events had led to her current circumstances. But I added that what she wanted for the present and the future was largely up to her. She asked what I meant.

I said, "Take your financial situation, for example. You have a choice between staying home or seeking a job. Now, I know at the present time that working would not improve your finances very much. But if you don't begin learning an employable skill now, and gradually working your way up in a job, what's going to happen when, in a year, your TANF benefits expire? I explained to her that under the TANF program current (and future) single parents can only receive financial assistance for a maximum of two years. During that two-year period, they need to prepare themselves for holding a job, and then find a job. I added, "There are also other areas that we could work on; for example, dental care. But the choice is totally up to you. If you want to work on some of these areas, I'm very interested in working with you. If you aren't interested at the present time, there's little I can do."

Mrs. H responded by indicating she was aware that her teeth needed attention, but added she didn't have the money to pay a dentist. I indicated the expenses were covered under her medical card (Medicaid program). She expressed surprise and indicated she would make an appointment with a dentist. She thanked me for the information, and I noted her face showed a spark of interest.

I then asked if she had thought about obtaining a job. She mentioned that would be nice, but then started citing a number of reasons she thought that it would not be possible. Many of these appeared to me to be "self-defeating self-talk." The material on page 107 contains a summary of her negative self-talk, along with a more positive view for each reason that I suggested to her.

At this point I asked her to think over what we had talked about and indicated that I would ask Mrs. S to contact her.

A week later I stopped by to see Mrs. H. She mentioned that she had had an "inspirational" talk with Mrs. S. At that point she asked to be enrolled in our work-training program. I praised her decision. Within three months she had obtained a receptionist job for a new car dealer. Equally important, she appeared to have a renewed interest in living and had improved her personal appearance with increased grooming attention, some new clothes, and a set of dentures. For me, as a student social work intern, this turned out to be a deeply rewarding, gratifying person to work with.

Mrs. H's Reasons for Not Seeking a Job	*A More Positive View*
1. "I've tried finding a job several times in the past and was not able to obtain one."	1. "Having tried in the past and failed does not mean you can't obtain a job at this time. We could provide you with work training in an area that you are interested in, and also help you obtain a job after the training. You need to start thinking about your future, because in a year you will no longer be eligible for TANF assistance. Having a job now will help you prepare for the future. Also, there are other benefits in working, such as the opportunity to get to know other people."
2. "I'm really not skilled at any job. Frankly, it is very embarrassing to be turned down when I apply."	2. "Nothing ventured, nothing gained. As far as not having a skill, we can enroll you in a work-training program. We can also help you find a job. You are not alone in being turned down for a job. I have a friend who applied to 67 teaching positions before being hired. This person was becoming quite discouraged but kept on trying. She finally found one and really liked it. The key is to keep on trying and hoping."
3. "I won't be able to work and also take care of my home and family."	3. "A working mother does have a lot to do and limited time to get it all done. However, many mothers are able to do both." (At this point I asked if she would be interested in discussing this area with a friend of mine, Mrs. S. Mrs. S has four children and used to receive financial assistance, but now works full-time as a secretary. Mrs. S is an "encouraging" person. She got her job by first having work training, then volunteering at an agency to do clerical work. By volunteering she developed her typing skills, and after a year the agency hired her. Mrs. H indicated she would be interested in talking with Mrs. S.)
4. "Frankly, my personal appearance is such that I don't think that anyone would hire me."	4. "You're selling yourself short. Our agency can help you with dental care and in getting some new clothes. When you meet with Mrs. S, you will see she probably will not win a beauty contest but has an inner beauty (personality) that helped her get a job. I think with a more positive attitude, people would note an inner beauty on your part."
5. "I wouldn't, if I worked, be able to watch some of my favorite game shows and soap operas during the day. My present daily routine would be greatly altered."	5. "This is true. But you would be able to meet more people if you worked, and perhaps grow more as a person. Also, wouldn't your children be prouder of you if you worked? Are you really satisfied and contented with your present circumstances and current daily routine?"
6. "I don't own a car, and therefore don't have a way to get to a job even if I did get one."	6. "We can help you here by paying the cost of transportation and by helping you arrange for transportation. For example, we have volunteer drivers who would be able to provide transportation when you go for job interviews."

of this area. Mr. Askew has been an alcoholic for many years, and for most of these years he has been in denial. Why? First seen in counseling nearly three years ago, Mr. Askew has experienced a variety of problems related to his drinking. The following is a summary of of Mr. Askew's social history:

> Lee Askew is 43 years old and has been drinking heavily since he was 16 years of age. For the past several years, he has drunk an average of a quart of vodka each day. His second marriage is in trouble because his wife, Callie, claims their money is spent on alcohol rather than on paying bills. Also, his wife has informed him she can no longer tolerate his drunken behavior—nearly every evening he is in a drunken stupor and rambles on, repeating himself until he finally falls asleep, often by passing out. Mr. Askew's first wife divorced him because of his drinking. When he is sober, he is friendly and enjoyable to be with. But as the day moves along, he increasingly becomes intoxicated, and his behavior becomes intolerable. Five years ago he had a serious automobile accident while intoxicated and was nearly killed. Three and one-half years ago he was again arrested for drunken driving. In the past ten years he has held a variety of sales jobs and has been fired from three of these jobs for being intoxicated. Last night Mr. Askew physically abused his wife for the first time. This morning Mrs. Askew informed Lee that he must either seek help for his drinking or she will leave. Mr. Askew apologized for hitting his wife, claming he had had a bad day at work. Lee, however, refuses to acknowledge he has a drinking problem.

Mr. Askew's denial of his drinking problem is not unique. Clients display a variety of emotional reactions when confronted with evidence of a personal problem. The effectiveness of counseling frequently depends on counselors understanding such emotional reactions so they can help clients recognize that they do have a personal problem and need certain services.

In spite of the importance of understanding clients' emotional reactions, there is a paucity of literature in this area. An important contribution, however, has been made by Elizabeth Kübler-Ross. In *On Death and Dying,* Kübler-Ross (1969) presents the five stages of dying that terminally ill people typically experience. These stages are not absolute, and not everyone goes through each one. But helping professionals who counsel the terminally ill have found this paradigm, when used in a flexible, insight-producing way, to be valuable in explaining why patients behave the way they do. The five stages also typify individual's reactions when confronted with serious personal problems.

Kübler-Ross's Five Stages of Dying

Mauksch (1975, p. 10) provided a concise summary of Kübler-Ross's five stages of dying:

1. *Denial:* "No, not me." This is a typical reaction when patients learn that they are terminally ill. Denial, says Dr. Ross, is important and necessary. It helps cushion the impact of the patient's awareness that death is inevitable.

2. *Rage and anger:* "Why me?" Patients resent the fact that others will remain healthy and alive while they die. God is a special target for anger, since He is regarded as imposing, arbitrarily, the death sentence.

3. *Bargaining:* "Yes, me, but . . ." Patients accept the fact of death but strike bargains for more time. Mostly they bargain with God—"even among people who never talked with God before." They promise to be good or to do something in exchange for another week or month or year of life. Notes Dr. Ross: "What they promise is totally irrelevant, because they don't keep their promises anyway."

4. *Depression:* "Yes, me." First, people mourn past losses, things not done, wrongs committed. But then they enter a state of "preparatory grief," getting ready for the arrival of death. Patients grow quiet and don't want visitors. "A dying patient who doesn't want to see you anymore," says Dr. Ross, "is signaling he has finished his unfinished business with you, and it is a blessing. He can now let go peacefully."

5. *Acceptance:* "My time is very close now and it's all right." Dr. Ross describes this final stage as "not a happy stage, but neither is it unhappy. It's devoid of feelings but it's not resignation, it's really a victory."

In presenting these five stages, Kübler-Ross (1969) warns it is a mistake to expect that all terminally ill patients methodically pass through all five stages. Some never reach the fifth stage of acceptance. Others display reactions from two stages at the same time—for example, anger and denial. Still others waver between stages—reaching the depressed stage, and then returning to an earlier stage of denial or anger.

Kübler-Ross's Five Stages as Emotional Reactions

Kübler-Ross's five stages also typify clients' emotional reactions when they are confronted with evidence of their personal problem. Denial, rage and anger, bargaining, depression, and acceptance are, in my experience, common reactions in numerous situations: A husband is informed his wife is having an affair; a single teenager is informed she is pregnant; an employee is fired for incompetence; a woman is informed she has a malignant tumor in her breast; a woman informs her fiancé she is ending their engagement. This list could be expanded infinitely, because we are all likely to have these emotional reactions. When clients recognize they have a personal problem, they experience a sense of loss and Kübler-Ross's five stages are emotional reactions to loss. Lee Askew's case illustrates each stage.

STAGE 1: DENIAL ("NOT ME."). Admitting the existence of a problem is difficult because clients often then (erroneously) perceive themselves as weak, sinful, or irresponsible. Also, recognition brings with it an acknowledgment that change is inevitable. Clients often mourn the loss of that which must be changed. Alcoholics thus mourn the loss of their drinking because their social activities are centered around it. Unless clients already have an openness or reaching-out pattern with others, it can be very difficult for them to share a new problem openly. Denial helps cushion the impact of the client's awareness that change is inevitable.

Constructive changes are not apt to occur for people in denial, unless counselors find a way to convince them that the problem exists. Counselors therefore need to focus on the denial and explore why the person believes there is no problem. They should gather evidence to document the existence of the problem. Clients can then be confronted with this evidence in a tactful manner.

For more than 20 years, Mr. Askew has denied that he has a drinking problem. He believes that he needs alcohol to get through each day. He feels such a strong need for alcohol that he allowed his drinking to end his first marriage, and he will not face the fact that drinking is ruining his second marriage. He will not acknowledge that he nearly lost his life while driving when intoxicated, nor will he acknowledge that he has lost several jobs because of his drinking.

Mrs. Askew gave her husband an ultimatum—either he sees a counselor or she is leaving now. Mr. Askew reluctantly chose to see a counselor. In counseling, Mr. Askew denied he had a drinking problem. He had excuses for everything: His car accident resulted from slippery roads. He was fired because his employers didn't like his suggestions for increasing sales. He ended his first marriage because his wife was a "nag." He denied having more than a couple of drinks a day.

STAGE 2: RAGE AND ANGER ("WHY ME?"). Clients resent the fact that they have to change while others do not. Old friends, relatives, or society at large are doing the things that the clients must change. Anyone can be the target for their anger. Sometimes the anger is used to avoid discussing the issue at hand. At other times the anger is directed at the counselor for confronting the client with reality.

The underlying reasons for this anger need to be remembered here. Certain therapeutic techniques are especially helpful during this stage. Allowing clients to vent their anger reduces its intensity; once this happens, they are better able to examine their difficulties realistically. Conveying empathy and emotional support creates an atmosphere in which clients feel more comfortable examining their difficulties. Clients often feel overwhelmed by their problems, which is a factor in their intensely felt "Why me?" They need to see that their problems are not overwhelming but can be broken down into subproblems that are resolvable in a step-by-step fashion. During this stage it is helpful for counselors to realize that clients angrily attacking them should not be taken personally. Reacting personally or angrily to clients' anger will only prolong their hostile behavior.

Lee Askew at times displayed anger while in counseling with Paul Decker. As indicated earlier, Mr. Askew at first denied he had a drinking problem. He had excuses for all the problems that were being caused by drinking. Mr. Decker knew counseling would not be productive unless this denial was broken through. Mr. Decker suggested that at the next session the Askews meet jointly to get both their perceptions of their marital problems. Mr. Askew reacted angrily to this suggestion, castigating his wife for making up stories about him, particularly his drinking. The counselor allowed Mr. Askew to vent his anger, and then asked, "Are you fearful of what your wife might say?" Mr. Askew stated "No," and agreed to a joint meeting.

Several joint meetings were held with the Askews. Mr. Askew continued to deny his drinking problem. These denials were countered by Mr. Decker asking him questions that served to confront Mr. Askew with his problem, including how much he drank each day, how he acted while drunk, how Mrs. Askew felt about seeing her husband intoxicated, whether his drinking has gotten him in trouble at work and with the police. Mr. Askew used anger to avoid confronting his alcoholism. Mr. Decker let Mr. Askew "spit fire" and vent. On a few occasions after Mr. Askew calmed down, Mr. Decker asked, "I wonder why you are reacting angrily to what is being said?" or "It appears we are touching a sensitive chord with you." Such questions were designed to help Mr. Askew understand why he was reacting angrily.

At other times, Mr. Askew would go into a tirade about how many of his friends drank and had a good time. He fumed about his wife pressuring him to stop drinking. He was clearly going through the "Why me?" stage. After allowing Mr. Askew to vent, Mr. Decker pointed out that unlike social drinkers, his drinking controlled him; he was not in control of his drinking. Specific incidents were tactfully mentioned.

On one occasion Mr. Askew, with his wife present, castigated Mr. Decker for meddling in his family affairs. The counselor calmly listened, and then replied, "Are you feeling angry at me because I'm forcing you to see that you face a choice between giving up drinking or losing your wife?" Mr. Askew at first reacted angrily to this but later acknowledged the statement was true.

STAGE 3: BARGAINING ("YES, ME, BUT . . ."). During this stage, clients are beginning to accept the problem but will bargain for "just one more time." They promise to be good or to do something in exchange for another week or month before they embrace change. During this stage counselors should confront clients with the reality of their circumstances and their bargaining efforts.

During the bargaining stage, clients usually try to change a few circumstances in their lives, and they generally believe that just a few changes will allow them to continue in their old ways. They tell themselves that "if such and such changes, I can still continue to . . ." Bargaining is a common reaction. People who are urged to lose weight bargain for "strawberry shortcake"; smokers who are urged to quit bargain to smoke when tense; some spouses seek to preserve a marriage that is in trouble via a pregnancy.

Mr. Askew tried several bargains. He asked if he continued in counseling whether he could continue to drink socially. Both the counselor and Mrs. Askew doubted that he could quit after a few drinks and expressed their misgivings. Social drinking was tried for a week, and Mr. Askew became intoxicated on three occasions. At the next session Mrs. Askew again stated her ultimatum, "Stop drinking, or I'm leaving." Efforts were then made to get Mr. Askew involved in Alcoholics Anonymous (AA) meetings. Initial results in AA were good. Then a wedding came up and Mr. Askew bargained with his wife (outside of counseling) that he would continue in AA if he could socially drink at special occasions such as the wedding. His wife struck the bargain on the condition that he quit after a few drinks. Mr. Askew became intoxicated at the wedding, and his actions (including wetting his pants) were intensely embarrassing to Mrs. Askew. At the next counseling session, Mrs. Askew again stated her ultimatum, "Stop drinking completely, or else I'm leaving." After other similar bargaining efforts, Mr. Askew was confronted by Mr. Decker with the statement that it appeared he was not committed to giving up drinking but was striking bargains to continue his drinking. Mr. Askew at first reacted angrily (back to the anger stage) but gradually acknowledged he was bargaining.

STAGE 4: DEPRESSION ("YES, ME."). Clients in the depression stage become very quiet. They have, by now, stopped denying their problem. Their anger has subsided and they no longer try to bargain. They have gained insight into their particular problem and realize they must change. Alternatives, however, are not yet perceived as viable solutions. They blame themselves in a "self-downing" manner for their problems and frequently mourn what they will have to give up. During this stage, counselors need to convey empathy and help clients see that their problems are not overwhelming. Clients need hope; frequently this can be accomplished by helping them develop resolution strategies.

Mr. Askew and his wife had been coming to weekly counseling for $3\frac{1}{2}$ months. During this time Mr. Askew made some efforts to give up drinking. At times he would go for a week or two without drinking, but always returned to the bottle. In counseling sessions he vacillated between making excuses for his drinking (denial) and displaying anger, or bargaining when confronted with the need to stop drinking. At the counseling session following a drinking episode, he would usually be depressed, acknowledging he was ruining his life. He would deprecate himself, and beg his wife to give him one more chance. When she did, a week or two later he would find an excuse to start drinking again.

Mr. Askew came into counseling one day a little hung over, and very depressed. He indicated he had gotten drunk the day before, and he and his wife had argued. He wasn't certain, but he thought he may have slapped her a few times. He added that afterward she packed a bag, indicated she was going to file for divorce, and left. Mr. Askew stated that life was not worth living without his wife. He fully acknowledged he had a drinking problem and had to abstain completely. The counselor and Mr. Askew discussed various alternatives. Mr. Askew stated with emotion that he would never take another drink, and that he would demonstrate this to his wife. He further decided to wait for two weeks before contacting her so that she could sort out her feelings and thoughts. Mr. Askew left the interview depressed, realizing that his drinking may have ruined his marriage forever.

STAGE 5: ACCEPTANCE ("I HAVE A PROBLEM, BUT IT'S ALL RIGHT." "I CAN."). Clients make a concentrated effort at this stage to work out alternatives, not only those suggested earlier in treatment but also some of their own. Their attitude is now one of "I can do it." There is hope. A plan for rehabilitation can be presented if one was lacking or dismissed in the earlier stages. Fear is still present but very much reduced.

After two weeks Mr. Askew called his wife. They talked, and she agreed to attend the next counseling session. At this session, Mrs. Askew indicated she was ambivalent about ending her marriage, but she had totally had it with her husband's drunken behavior. They agreed to live apart for the next four months. If Lee participated in AA meetings and did not drink at all, then they would live together again, on the condition that he would never drink again.

That was over two years ago. Lee Askew has not had a drink, and he is active in AA helping other problem drinkers. He is also active in a speaker's bureau in which he talks to high school students and businesses and organizations about the dangers of alcohol and about treatment programs. After three months of separation, his wife returned, and both report their marriage and their careers are going well.

Summary

From the counselor's perspective, counseling can be divided into three phases: (1) Building a relationship; (2) exploring problems in depth; and (3) exploring alternative solutions, with the client then selecting a course of action. Successful counseling proceeds gradually from one phase to the next, with some overlap of these stages. At the end of a series of counseling interviews, there is often a fourth phase of "termination and evaluation."

From the client's perspective, for counseling to be successful, clients must give themselves a progressive series of "self-talk." (That is, they must arrive at having certain thoughts and beliefs.) These self-talk stages are:

Stage I *Problem awareness:* "I have a problem."
Stage II *Relationship to counselor:* "I think this counselor has what it takes to help me."
Stage III *Motivation:* "I want to improve my situation and am willing to put forth the effort to do so."
Stage IV *Conceptualizing the problem:* "My problem is not overwhelming but has specific components that can be changed."
Stage V *Exploration of resolution strategies:* "I see there are several courses of action that I might try to do something about my situation."
Stage VI *Selection of a strategy:* "I think this approach might help and I am willing to try it."
Stage VII *Implementation:* "This approach is helping me."
Stage VIII *Evaluation:* "Although this approach takes a lot of my time and effort, it's worth it."

This conceptualization presents a framework for improving the effectiveness of counseling. This framework indicates when counseling is not helpful; the reasons for lack of progress can be identified by examining clients' self-talk. Once these reasons are identified, changes can be made in the counseling process.

Counselors need to be aware of and learn to handle clients' emotional reactions to having a personal problem. Kübler-Ross's (1969) five stages of emotional reactions to loss are not unique to the terminally ill but are also typical reactions that clients display when confronted with evidence of a personal problem. Any time clients first recognize that they have a personal problem, a sense of loss occurs. Kübler-Ross's five stages are denial, rage and anger, bargaining. depression, and acceptance. Only when clients reach the fifth stage of acceptance are they ready to work effectively on alternatives for resolving their problems. With a better understanding of these emotional reactions, counselors will be more effective in selecting appropriate intervention strategies.

EXERCISES

1. UNDERSTANDING CLIENTS' REACTIONS TO HAVING A PERSONAL PROBLEM

Goal: This exercise is designed to help students understand clients' reactions to having a personal problem.

Step 1: The instructor explains the purpose of the exercise. The instructor indicates that when a person acknowledges he or she has a personal problem, almost always that person experiences a loss of some kind. The loss may involve giving up something one has had (such as an alcoholic giving up drinking). Or, the loss may involve recognition that a desired goal is not obtainable (for example, parents who have a child with a cognitive disability may feel the loss of not having a child of normal intelligence). When a loss is experienced, the person almost always has the emotional reactions described by Kübler-Ross. The instructor describes the following reactions to students: denial, anger and rage, bargaining, depression, and acceptance.

Step 2: The instructor asks students to volunteer to describe a loss they have had, and have them comment on whether they experienced the five reactions described by Kübler-Ross.

Step 3: The instructor explains that clients frequently are not ready emotionally to work on resolving a personal problem or a loss until they reach the fifth stage of acceptance. The instructor asks the students who describe a loss if in fact they had to reach the stage of accepting their loss before they were able to make a concentrated effort to work on alternatives for resolving the problems.

2. LEARNING HOW TO COUNSEL THROUGH ROLE PLAYING

Goal: The purpose of this exercise is to help students develop their counseling skills through role-playing counseling situations.

Step 1: The instructor describes the goal of the exercise. The instructor indicates that the counseling process from the counselor's view can be divided into five phases: (1) starting the interview; (2) building a relationship; (3) exploring problems in depth; (4) exploring alternative solutions with the client, then choosing one or more of the alternatives; and (5) ending the interview. (Material on these five phases is summarized in Chapters 4 and 5 of this text.) The instructor briefly summarizes guidelines on how a counselor should handle each of these phases.

Step 2: Two students volunteer to role-play being clients. The "clients" come up with their own contrived problems.

Examples of possible problems are:

a. Two college students are roommates. One believes the other has a drinking problem while the other refuses to acknowledge a problem exists.

b. Two siblings are concerned about their mother living alone. Her health is failing, and her husband has recently died. The siblings also believe they are unable to care for their mother as each is married and has a family, and the mother is not easy to live with.

c. A husband and wife both want children but the husband is infertile. The wife wants to become pregnant through artificial insemination. The husband objects to his wife getting pregnant using this means.

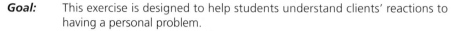

Step 3: The instructor counsels the two students who have contrived problems to demonstrate the five phases of counseling. After the counseling is completed, the class discusses the strengths and shortcomings of the counseling that was given.

Step 4: The instructor asks four more students to volunteer—two as clients having contrived problems and two as counselors for the two "clients." (It is useful to have two people, at this early stage, volunteer to be counselors to offset the potential of one counselor becoming "stuck" by not knowing what to say.) Role-play the interview.

Step 5: As an additional step, the instructor requires each student in the class to role-play as counselor and also as client (for some other student who role-plays being a counselor). Ideally each student should be videotaped in the role of the counselor, and this videotape should then be played back so students can assess the interview. (As described in Chapter 4, the videotaping may be used not only to help students develop their counseling skills but also as a screening device to counsel out students from the social work major if they are unable, after several tries, to make an acceptable videotape.)

Step 6: The instructor shows each videotape to the class. A brief class discussion is held after each tape is shown. This discussion should review the strengths and shortcomings of the counseling and also look at what else might be done. If each tape is shown to the class, it is helpful for each student to fill out the Interviewer Skills Rating Sheet on the following page, which is then given to the "counselor" for feedback purposes. (One advantage of showing each tape to the class is that students learn what should, and should not, be done in counseling.)

Note: Role-playing-contrived counseling situations (and also videotaping of such situations) can be structured in a variety of ways. This exercise presents some ideas, but the instructor of course has the autonomy to structure the role playing in ways that he or she believes will be most beneficial.

3. RESPONDING EFFECTIVELY TO CRITICAL STATEMENTS FROM CLIENTS

Goal: This exercise is designed to help students learn how to respond more effectively to highly emotional and complex statements made by clients.

Step 1: The instructor explains the purpose of the exercise. The instructor then reads to the class the first of the following client statements, and asks the class for their suggestions on the most effective way for a counselor to respond. There are a variety of effective responses. (One way of responding to each of these statements is presented in the Appendix.) A class discussion of the merits and shortcomings of some of the students' suggested responses is apt to be a productive learning experience.

Step 2: After the class responds to and discusses the first statement, the instructor should read the second statement and again seek responses and discussion from the students. This process continues with the remaining statements on page 115.

(continued)

EXERCISES
(continued)

INTERVIEWER SKILLS RATING SHEET

STUDENT ______________________________ DATE ______________

Skills	*Needs Improvement*	*Satisfactory*	*Excellent*
1. Opening remarks			
2. Explanation of counselor role			
3. Voice quality and volume			
4. Body posture			
5. Eye contact			
6. Behavioral congruence/facial expression (therapist's words match his/her outward appearance)			
7. Frequency of open-ended questions (not yes-no or multiple-choice questions)			
8. Amount of therapist's verbal activity			
9. Verbal following behavior (sequencing questions with client's answers preparing client for shift in subject matter)			
10. Clarity of questions			
11. Ability to confront client with inconsistencies			
12. Use of humor			
13. Warmth/ability to put client at ease			
14. Use of silence			
15. Ability to help client define problems			
16. Ability to have client specify goals			
17. Paraphrasing			
18. Reflection of client's feelings			
19. Summarization of client information			
20. Ability to answer client's questions—provide useful information			
21. Extent to which interviewer presented him/herself as a professional			
22. Extent to which necessary data about the problem was obtained			
23. Ending the interview/length of interview			
24. Completeness of interview			
25. Extent to which a helpful relationship was developed.			
26. Extent to which alternative solutions to the problem were begun to be explored			

Positive Comments About Strengths Demonstrated During the Interview:

____

____

Areas Needing Attention:

____

____

Client statements

1. *Male client* (fifth interview): "There's something that's been bothering me for the past few weeks (pause). I'm beginning to feel that you're not really interested in me as a person. I have the feeling that the only reason you're meeting with me is because you're getting paid to see me."

2. *Engaged female,* age 20: "I'm engaged to marry Kent. My uncle thinks he's terrific, but my parents are telling me I'm making the biggest mistake of my life to marry him. They dislike him and also think I'm too young to marry. I'm so confused about what I should do. Kent is putting a lot of pressure on me to elope."

3. *Juvenile probationee,* age 16—who is recognized as being a con artist—in required weekly visit with probation agent: "Your office is really cool. You've really got it made. I admire your taste in furnishing this office. You deserve what you've got in life. I admire you. Those are great photographs on the wall. Did you take them?" The probation officer is aware that students received their midterm grade reports this past week.

4. *Male client,* age 27 (fourth interview): "I'm feeling real tense today. I've got a lot on my mind (pause). I don't think we've made much progress in the last three meetings, although I am gradually coming to trust you (pause). I haven't been fully honest with you. You know the marital problems I've been having? Well, the main reason our marriage hasn't gone well, and Karen doesn't even know this, is because for the past few years I've been involved with someone else—who happens to be a male. Karen no longer turns me on because I guess I'm more attracted to males."

5. *African American client* from an inner city who has a white therapist: "You honkies don't know what life is really like for us who live in a ghetto. You say you want to help me, but I don't buy that jive. How can you possibly help me when you have no idea what it is like to be black and living in a ghetto?"

6. *Teenage male delinquent* caught with marijuana in his possession at a correctional institution: "Please don't report this. You know I've been doing really well here at school and have a clean record. If you report this, my stay will be extended. I was only holding the drugs for a friend here. I'm not using any of it myself. Give me a break—everyone needs one in life." The youth was involved with drugs when he committed the offenses for which he was sent to this correctional facility.

CHAPTER 6

Social Work with Groups: Types of Groups and Guidelines for Leading Them

The practice of social work in groups is not a new phenomenon.[1] The ideological roots of social group work can be traced most directly to the settlement houses, informal self-help recreational organizations (YMCA, YWCA), Jewish centers, and scouting, all of which developed during the first three decades of the twentieth century. During this period, many social workers found group-based methods of intervention effective and efficient for confronting a variety of personal and social problems. The last 70 years have witnessed a progressive interest in, and expansion of, group services in our society. The involvement of the social work profession in groups has broadened accordingly. Today it is not uncommon to find social workers as both group leaders and participants in a myriad of settings, helping solve or ameliorate human or social problems, and planning for and creating change. There are many reasons behind the attractiveness of groups for members and for practitioners. Johnson and Johnson (2000) define a group as

> two or more individuals in face-to-face interaction, each aware of his or her membership in the group, each aware of the others who belong to the group, and each aware of their positive interdependence as they strive to achieve mutual goals. (p. 20)

From this description we can see that the members of a group relate to one another within a context of sensing they form a distinct entity, that they share a common goal or purpose, and that they have confidence that together they can accomplish as much or more than would be possible were they to work separately. This commonality is characteristic of a wide variety of groups dealing with a multitude of societal problems. The beginning social worker is likely to be surprised at the diversity of groups in existence and excited by the challenge of practicing social work in groups. The period from 1960 to the present has witnessed an explosion in the number of groups and group-based techniques utilized by the social work profession.

[1]Material in this chapter is adapted from Charles Zastrow, "Social Work Practice with Groups," in *Social Work with Groups: Using the Class as a Group Leadership Laboratory*, 5th ed. (Pacific Grove, CA: Brooks/Cole, 2002).

Types of Groups

This section describes a significant sample of the types of groups in which social workers may become involved. This list is not exhaustive; only the creativity of the helping professional and the client group served will provide such limits. However, the groups discussed here are frequently encountered by social workers.

Recreation Groups

The objective of recreation groups is to provide activities for enjoyment and exercise. Often such activities are spontaneous, and the groups are practically leaderless. The group service agency (such as YMCA, YWCA, or neighborhood center) may offer little more than physical space and the use of some equipment. Spontaneous playground activities, informal athletic games, and an open game room are examples. Some group agencies providing such physical space claim that recreation and interaction with others helps build character and prevent delinquency among youth by providing an alternative to the street.

Recreation-Skill Groups

The objective of a recreation-skill group is to improve a set of skills while providing enjoyment. In contrast to recreational groups, this group has an adviser, coach, or instructor; also, there is more of a task orientation. Examples of activities include golf, basketball, needlework, arts and crafts, and swimming. Competitive team sports and leagues may emerge. Frequently such groups are led by professionals with recreational training rather than social work training. Social service agencies providing such services include YMCA, YWCA, Boy Scouts, Girl Scouts, neighborhood centers, and school recreation departments.

Educational Groups

The focus of educational groups is to help members acquire knowledge and learn more complex skills. The leader generally is a professional person with considerable training and expertise in the subject area. Examples of topics include child-rearing practices, assertiveness training, techniques for becoming a more effective parent, preparing to be an adoptive parent, and training volunteers to perform a specialized task for a social service agency. Educational group leaders often function in a more didactic manner and frequently are social workers. These groups may resemble a class, with considerable group interaction and discussion being encouraged. The case example shows how assertiveness training can be taught in an educational group.

Task Groups

Task groups are formed to achieve a specific set of tasks or objectives. Social workers are apt to interact with or become involved in a variety of task groups. A *board of directors* is an administrative group charged with responsibility for setting the policy governing agency programs. A *task force* is a group established for a special purpose and is usually disbanded after the task is completed. A *committee* of an agency or organization is a group formed to deal with specific tasks or matters. An *ad hoc committee,* like a task force, is set up for one purpose and usually ceases functioning after completion of its task.

Problem-Solving and Decision-Making Groups

Both providers and consumers of social services may become involved in groups concerned with problem solving and decision making. (There is considerable overlap between task groups and these groups; in fact, problem-solving and decision-making groups can be considered a subcategory of task groups.)

Providers of services use group meetings for such objectives as developing a treatment plan for a client or a group of clients, deciding how to best allocate scarce resources, deciding how to improve the delivery of services to clients, arriving at policy decisions for the agency, deciding how to improve coordination efforts with other agencies, and so on.

Potential consumers of services may form a group to study an unmet need in the community and to advocate the development of new programs to meet the need. Data on the need may be gathered, and the group may be used as a vehicle either to develop a program or to influence existing agencies to provide services. Social workers may function as stimulators and organizers

CASE EXAMPLE

Assertiveness Training—An Educational Group

Assertiveness training in a group is one kind of educational group. There are several advantages of group assertiveness training. A group provides a "laboratory" for testing or experimenting with new assertive behaviors. A group has a broader base for social modeling, as each person sees several others trying out a variety of assertive approaches. A wider variety of feedback is also offered. Furthermore, a group is generally understanding and supportive. Finally, group pressure and expectations motivate members to conscientiously develop and practice new assertive responses.

A typical format for an assertiveness training group is as follows: The size of such groups generally ranges from 5 to 20 members. The first session is devoted to a lecture presentation on the differences between assertive, nonassertive, and aggressive behavior. The specific steps in assertive training are then summarized. (These steps are presented in Module 4.) Several examples of typical situations are given to illustrate that assertive responses are generally more effective than aggressive or nonassertive responses.

In the following sessions specific situations involving assertive responses are then examined. At first it may be desirable to begin with situations that are not brought forth by members of the group (group members may at first be reluctant to reveal personal situations they face). Alberti and Emmons (1975, pp. 183–184) suggested the following situations be practiced:

1. Starting a conversation with a small group of strangers who are already engaged in conversation at a party.
2. Saying "no" assertively when a roommate or friend asks to borrow something that you do not want to lend to others.
3. Returning faulty or defective items to a store.
4. Asking someone next to you to extinguish a cigarette.
5. Asking someone to turn down a stereo that is too loud, or not talk so loudly in the library, theater, and so forth.
6. Asking for a date/refusing a date on the telephone and face-to-face.
7. Expressing positive feelings; "soft assertions."
8. Responding assertively to a date or spouse who is giving you "put-down" comments.
9. Assertively refusing to take an alcoholic beverage from a friend when you prefer not to drink.

For each situation the following steps are used: (1) Each member is asked to visualize (form a mental image of) his or her response. (2) One member is selected to role-play an assertive response. (3) The group briefly discusses the strategy after it is role-played. (4) If a more effective response is desired, a new assertive response is role-played by a member. And (5) the group then discusses the strategy.

Following this exercise, group members are encouraged to bring to the group real-life situations that are troubling them. These are often complex situations that involve close,

of such group efforts as well as participants (see Chapter 10 on social work community practice). One type of problem-solving group is the *nominal group*, which can be helpful in identifying problems. The case example on page 120 describes one such group.

In problem-solving and decision-making groups, each participant normally has some interest or stake in the process and may gain or lose, depending on the outcome. Usually, there is a formal leader of some sort, although other leaders sometimes emerge during the process. Three issues are of importance to problem-solving and decision-making groups: group versus individual decision making, groupthink, and decision by consensus versus decision by majority vote.

GROUP VERSUS INDIVIDUAL DECISION MAKING. Is group decision making superior to individual decision making? There is evidence that group decision

intimate relationships. Such situations may not have pat, simple resolutions. The following steps are recommended for group leaders in helping members become more assertive.

1. Help each group member identify the situations/interactions in which it would be to his or her benefit to be more assertive. Usually group members will bring up these situations themselves. Some members, however, may be reluctant to reveal problem interactions, or they may be unaware they could handle certain situations better by being more assertive. Considerable tact and skill by the leader is necessary in initiating problem areas of the latter type. (One approach that usually works is to have the members anonymously write the situations they want role-played on a note card.)

2. When a problem interaction is identified, each member of the group is asked to visualize a response silently. For complicated situations with no simple solutions, considerable discussion may arise about possible ways of resolving the matter.

3. A member (often someone other than the person with the problem situation) is asked to role-play an assertive response. The member with the problem may be asked to play the role of the person with whom he or she is having difficulty. The situation is then role-played.

4. The group briefly discusses the merits of the assertive strategy that was modeled in step 3.

If it is effective and the person with the problem is comfortable with it, that person is then asked to role-play the approach. If the group believes there may be a more effective approach, steps 3 and 4 are repeated. If the person with the problem is uncomfortable about using a strategy that is effective, the reasons for the discomfort are then explored. For example, for very shy people, certain attitudes, such as "don't make waves" or the "meek shall inherit the earth" may need to be dealt with.

5. The person with the problem is asked to rehearse an assertive strategy silently, thinking of what he or she will say and what the consequences may be.

6. The person with the problem is then asked to role-play an assertive strategy.

7. The group gives feedback about the merits of the strategy. Generally the person is praised for the effective aspects and coached on how to improve other aspects. This approach is practiced via role playing until it is perfected and the person has developed sufficient comfort and self-confidence for the "real event." For feedback purposes, if possible, the approach is recorded on audiotape or videotape.

8. The person tries out the new response pattern in an actual situation.

9. The person describes at the next group meeting how the real-life test went. The person is complimented on the degree of success attained, and assistance is given on aspects that could be improved.

making is usually superior to individual decision making (Johnson & Johnson, 2000). This conclusion applies even when the individual decision is made by an expert.

There appear to be several reasons why group decision making is generally superior. First, through group interaction the knowledge, abilities, and resources of each member are pooled. An individual acting alone often lacks some of the information, skills, or resources needed to arrive at the highest quality decision. Second, working in the presence of others motivates a person to put forth more effort, to be more careful, and to increase the quality of the work. Third, having more people working on a problem increases the probability that someone in the group will suggest the highest-quality solution. Fourth, through group interaction the members can build on one another's ideas and develop a high-quality decision that is based on this building block approach. Fifth, through group discussion there

CASE EXAMPLE

Nominal-Group Approach—A Problem Identification Technique for Problem-Solving Groups

The nominal-group approach was developed by Delbecq and Van de Ven (1971) as a problem identification technique in social program development efforts. The approach involves meeting with potential users of a service. A *nominal group* is defined as "a group in which individuals work in the presence of others but do not verbally interact" (Van de Ven & Delbecq, 1971, p. 205). This need-identification approach emphasizes the importance of understanding clearly the view of the population that the group is trying to serve, and asserts that potential consumers of new services should articulate their needs, problems, and goals. The main orientation is to respond to consumers' needs rather than independently develop programs for them. To accomplish this objective, the nominal-group approach is designed to receive input from all group members rather than just the more vocal or aggressive ones, as often happens in conventional group discussions. This technique has successfully been used in such applications as determining the housing difficulties of college students, reasons that have led delinquent youth into difficulty with police (Zastrow, 1973), and specific course topics wanted by students enrolling in social work courses (Zastrow & Navarre, 1977).

Research indicates that the nominal-group approach is superior to brainstorming and to other types of interacting groups in generating information relevant to a problem situation. Both quantity and quality of suggestions are enhanced with this technique (Van de Ven & Delbecq, 1971). Several features appear to be involved in leading to this superiority. The approach has a game mystique that stimulates the interest of participants. Creative tension is stimulated by the presence of others, which fosters individual commitment to the task. Evaluation of items is avoided, which substantially reduces the pressure against expressing minority opinions or conventional ideas. Conflicting, incompatible ideas are tolerated. Furthermore, the approach appears to be "a time-saving process since it can be activated and concluded with greater rapidity than interacting group processes" (Van de Ven & Delbecq, 1971, p. 210).

The mechanics of conducting a nominal group are as follows:

1. Gather together a group of participants, any size, ranging up to about 100, and explain the nature of the study. Emphasize the importance of their ideas related to this topic. Care should be taken to obtain a representative cross-section of the populations of interest.

---

is a greater chance of identifying the positive and negative consequences of each alternative. Therefore, the negative consequences of an inferior decision are more likely to be identified. Sixth, it is easier to identify other people's mistakes than it is to identify your own. Through group interaction we are more likely to identify the problem areas in the favorite alternatives of others, and others are more apt to identify the problem areas in our favorite alternative.

In general, the effectiveness of group decision making is enhanced when there is high involvement by all group members. High involvement increases the willingness of members to share their information and abilities in making a decision, increases their allegiance to the group, increases their commitment to implementing the decision, and increases their commitment to working for the group in the future. Most groups can become more effective by seeking to increase the involvement of all group members in making decisions.

There are only a few situations in which decisions might best be made by one or a few individuals: (1) when a decision has to be made so quickly it is not possible to have a meeting; (2) when the decision is relatively unimportant and the person making the decision follows precedents previously set by the group; and (3) when the decision is relatively unimportant, does not require committed action by most members of a group, and there is no reason to believe the group will object to the decision.

But there are also problems with group decision making. At times a subgroup will seek to "railroad" a decision that benefits them but is counterproductive for the whole group or for certain people outside the group. (Hitler, for example, used many tactics to sway groups he worked with to begin World War II and to exterminate 6 million Jews.) Railroading tactics include pressuring a group to make a quick decision without giving members time to analyze all the conse-

2. Randomly divide the participants into small groups ranging in size from 5 to 8. Seat each group around a separate table or in desks arranged in a circle.

3. Distribute to each participant a sheet of paper containing a question that must be answered. For example, the wording for determining desired course content might be

What specific subject topics do you want covered in this course?
PLEASE—NO TALKING

4. For 15–20 minutes, the participants privately list items they feel are in response to the question being asked; no talking is permitted during this period.

5. A round-robin listing technique is then used in which each individual in turn is given the opportunity to disclose one item at a time to the group. This listing is done separately for each group with one of the members acting as a recorder. Ideas may be recorded on flip-chart paper or on a chalkboard. This round-robin listing continues until all members indicate they have no further ideas to share. Until this point is reached, there is no discussion or evaluation of ideas presented.

6. Following the listing of all ideas, the flip-chart sheets are posted on the wall with masking tape. There is a brief, informal discussion of the items, which is focused on clarifying what the ideas mean. There are two different approaches to reviewing the items: (1) all items are made known to all participants, or (2) each group briefly reviews only the items recorded for their group. Both approaches appear to work. For smaller-sized groups, the first is usually used; with larger groups, in which the total number of listed items becomes very large, the second approach is generally used.

7. Once the participants are familiar with the items listed, each is asked to write privately on index cards the five items he or she feels are the most important.

8. These selections are then tabulated and posted. The highest ranked problems or topics represent those considered most important by the group members.

quences, withholding information that is adverse to the desired decision, buying votes with promises, and suggesting there may be negative consequences for members who do not vote for the desired decision.

Another problem in group decision making is that friendships and paybacks for past favors sometimes lead members to vote for "the person" rather than for a decision based on thorough analysis of the consequences of the alternatives. Republicans and Democrats in Congress, for example, largely vote along party lines.

Sometimes groups reach incorrect or ineffective decisions because of a phenomenon known as *groupthink*.

GROUPTHINK. Irving Janis (1971) identified groupthink as an unusual condition that prevents effective problem solving. Janis studied groups who advised presidents of the United States and found that powerful social pressures were often exerted whenever a dissident began to voice objections to what otherwise appeared to be a group consensus. Groupthink is a problem-solving process in which proposals are accepted without a critical, careful review of the pros and cons of the alternatives, and in which considerable social pressure is brought to bear against expressing opposing points of view. Groupthink occurs partially because the norms of the group hold that it is more important to bolster group morale than to evaluate all alternatives critically. Another group norm that increases groupthink is that members should remain loyal to the group by sticking with the policies to which the group has already committed itself, although those policies are not having the intended effects, or are even having disturbing unintended consequences.

Janis (1971) listed a number of factors that promote groupthink. They include:

- Members have an illusion of being invulnerable, which leads them to become overly optimistic about their selected courses of action, to take extraordinary risks, and to fail to respond to clear warnings of danger.

- Members have an unquestioning belief in the group's moral rightness, which leads them to ignore the ethical consequences of their decisions.
- The group applies social pressures of disapproval on any member who momentarily questions the basic policies or who raises questions about a policy alternative favored by the majority.
- The group constructs rationalizations to discount warnings and other forms of negative feedback that would, if taken seriously, lead the members to rethink basic assumptions about policies that are not working out well.
- Group members hold stereotyped views of the leaders of opposing groups. These leaders are viewed as either being so evil that it would be a mistake to try genuinely to negotiate differences, or they are viewed as so stupid or so weak that they will not be able to prevent the group from attaining its objectives.
- Members sometimes assume "mind guard" roles in which they attempt to protect their leader and the group from negative information that might lead them to question the morality and effectiveness of past decisions.
- Members keep quiet about their misgivings and even minimize to themselves the importance of these misgivings. Through self-censorship members avoid deviating from what appears to be group consensus.
- The members believe practically everyone in the group fully agrees on the policies and programs of the group.

Numerous poor decision-making practices result from groupthink. The group limits its discussion to only those courses of action that are consistent with past decisions and policies; as a result, more divergent strategies (some of which are viable) are not considered. The group fails to reexamine a selected course of action, even when they discover the risks, drawbacks, and unintended consequences that they had not previously considered. The group makes little effort to get cost-benefit information on possible strategies from experts who might be able to supply more accurate information. Members seek primarily to obtain facts and listen to opinions that support their preferred policy and tend to ignore facts and opinions that do not. The group fails to work out contingency plans to cope with foreseeable setbacks, and it spends little time considering how the chosen strategy might be sabotaged by political opponents or hampered by bureaucratic red tape.

CONSENSUS VERSUS MAJORITY VOTING. Decision making by consensus is usually the most effective approach for getting all members to support and work for the decision. Consensus means that everyone is willing to go along with the decision, at least temporarily. This approach is also the most time-consuming because the concerns of each member need to be dealt with. For many decisions, consensus is difficult to achieve because members are apt to have diverse opinions about what should be done.

To use consensus effectively, the group members need to have a certain mind-set, and the group has to have a trusting, cooperative atmosphere. For consensus to be arrived at, members need to feel free to present their views as clearly and logically as possible but to avoid blindly arguing their own individual views. They need to listen to and respect the views of other members. Members should *avoid* going along with the group if they believe the majority opinion is a mistake. It is a mistake to yield to the majority if the only reason is to avoid conflict and appear united. Members, however, might yield to the majority opinion if that position appears to have merit and is a position they believe has a fair chance of having positive outcomes.

To make consensus work effectively, differences of opinion are sought out and respectfully dealt with. Disagreements and divergent views are advantageous because they increase the chances that all crucial aspects will be reviewed, that members will build on the views of others, and that viable decisions will be made.

With consensus, the participation of all members is encouraged. The emphasis is on finding the best solution that everyone can agree on and support. If a group becomes stalemated between two possible alternatives, a vote is not taken to allow one subgroup to win while the other loses. Instead, a third alternative is sought to incorporate the major desires of both subgroups.

There are a number of benefits to consensus. Since consensus resolves controversies and conflicts, it increases the group's ability to make future high-quality decisions.

If group members feel they have participated in the decision and support it, they are more likely to contribute their resources to implement the decision. Consensus is useful in making important, serious, and complex decisions in which the success of the decision depends on the commitment of all members.

There are some disadvantages to consensus. It takes a great deal of time and psychological energy. The pressure for group consensus can lead to groupthink. In this situation members go along with what they believe is the majority opinion, even when they have evidence or information (which they fail to share for fear of making waves) that the probable decision will be unproductive or even destructive. In addition, consensus will not work in many groups for a variety of reasons. A high level of trust may not exist in the group, thereby not allowing candor, honesty, and directness. Some members may try to dominate or manipulate the group rather than listen and support one another as individuals. Some members may see the slow process required to arrive at consensus as painful, aggravating, and a waste of time.

Most groups make decisions by simple majority vote. With this approach, issues are discussed until they are clarified and a simple majority of the members have arrived at an alternative. A vote is then taken.

There are several advantages to this type of decision making. Decisions are arrived at much faster than with the consensus approach. Most decisions in a group are not so important that full support of all members is necessary to achieve the objectives of the decision. Also, majority vote does not require, to as great an extent, the characteristics that are essential for consensus (such as trust, open communication, and willingness to give up one's favorite position).

There are also shortcomings of the simple majority approach. Minority opinions are not always safeguarded. Racial groups, women, certain ethnic groups, gay men and lesbians, and people with disabilities are minority groups that in the past have suffered from adverse decisions made by simple majority voting. Majority voting frequently splits a group into winners and losers, with the losers often becoming angry, frustrated, and apathetic. Sometimes the group of losers is nearly as large as the winners (such as having 49 percent of the vote), but they end up feeling their concerns are ignored. A large-sized minority that feels it has been outvoted may not lend its resources to implement the decision and may even work to subvert or overturn it. If the final vote alienates a minority, the group's future effectiveness is diminished. The majority rule approach may be interpreted by the minority as being an unfair means of control and manipulation by the majority. Therefore, to maintain effective group functioning, groups that use majority voting should seek to create a climate in which members feel they have had their day in court and have an obligation to go along with the group decision.

A compromise between consensus and simple majority is a high-percentage majority vote (such as two-thirds or three-fourths). This approach requires more time to arrive at a decision than a simple majority as more votes are needed. But it takes less time than consensus as not everyone has to be convinced or persuaded. A strong minority (such as 45 percent) can block a decision it dislikes, but a small majority cannot force its views on a strong minority. However, a small minority may still feel it is being controlled and manipulated by a high-percentage majority vote. A high-percentage majority vote will generally draw stronger support from group members than the simple majority approach, but it will not generate as much support as the consensus approach.

Focus Groups

Closely related to task groups and problem-solving and decision-making groups are focus groups. Focus groups are formed for a variety of purposes: to identify needs or issues, to generate proposals to resolve an identified issue, to test reactions to alternative approaches to an issue, and so forth. A focus group is a specially assembled collection of people who respond through a semi-structured or structured discussion to the concerns and interests of the person, group, or organization that invited the participants. Members of the group are invited and encouraged to bring up their own ideas and views. A *representative group* is a version of the focus group. Its strength is that its members have been selected specifically to represent different perspectives and points of view in a community. At its best, a representative group is a focus group that reflects the diversity in the community and seeks to bring these diverse views to the table; at its worst, it is a front group manipulated by schemers to make the community think that it has been involved.

Self-Help Groups

Self-help groups are increasingly popular and are often successful in helping individuals with certain social or personal problems. Katz and Bender (1976) provided a comprehensive definition of self-help groups.

> Self-help groups are voluntary, small group structures for mutual aid and the accomplishment of a special purpose. They are usually formed by peers who have come together for mutual assistance in satisfying a common need, overcoming a common handicap or life-disrupting problem, and bringing about desired social, and/or personal change. The initiators and members of such groups perceive that their needs are not, or cannot be, met by or through existing social institutions. Self-help groups emphasize face-to-face social interactions and the

CASE EXAMPLE

Parents Anonymous—A Self-Help Group[2]

Parents Anonymous (PA) is a national self-help organization for parents who have abused or neglected their children. PA was originally established in 1970 by Jolly K in California, who was desperate to find help to meet her needs. For four years prior to this time, she struggled with an uncontrollable urge to severely punish her daughter. One afternoon she attempted to strangle her daughter. Desperate, she sought help from the local child-guidance clinic. She was placed in therapy. When asked by her therapist what she could do about this situation, she developed an idea; as she explained (Zauner, 1974, p. 247), "if alcoholics could stop drinking by getting together, and gamblers could stop gambling, maybe the same principle would work for abusers, too." With her therapist's encouragement, she formed "Mothers Anonymous" in 1970, and started a few local chapters in California. Nearly every major city in the United States and Canada now has a chapter, and the name has been changed to Parents Anonymous (since fathers who abuse their children are also eligible to join).

PA uses some of the basic therapeutic concepts of Alcoholics Anonymous. PA is a crisis intervention program that offers two main forms of help: (1) a weekly group meeting in which members share experiences and feelings and learn better control of their emotions, and (2) personal and telephone contact among members during periods of crisis, particularly when a member feels a nearly uncontrollable desire to take his or her anger or frustration out on a child. Parents may be referred to PA by a social agency (including protective services), or may be self-referrals of parents who are aware they need help.

Starkweather and Turner (1975) described why some parents who abuse their children would rather participate in a self-help group than receive professional counseling.

> It has been our experience that most (abusive) parents judge themselves more harshly than other more objective people tend to judge them. The fear of losing their children frequently diminishes with reassurance from other members that they are not the monsters they think they are.
>
> Generally speaking, PA members are so afraid they are going to be judged by others as harshly as they judge themselves that they are afraid to go out and seek help. Frequently our members express fears of dealing with a professional person, seeing differences in education, sex, or social status as basic differences that would prevent easy communication or mutual understanding.
>
> Members express feelings of gratification at finding that other parents are "in the same boat." They contrast this with their feelings about professionals who, they often assume, have not taken out the time from their training and current job responsibilities to raise families of their own. (p. 151)

PA emphasizes honesty and directness. In the outside world, parents who are prone to abuse their children learn to hide this problem because society finds it difficult to stomach. In contrast, the goal of PA is to help parents admit and accept the fact that they are abusive. The term abuse is used liberally at meetings. PA has found that this insistence on frankness has a healthy effect. Parents are relieved because they've finally found a group of people who are able to accept abusive parents for what they really are. Furthermore, only when they are able to admit they are abusive can they begin to find ways to cope with this problem.

During PA meetings parents are expected actually to say they are beating their child or engaging in other forms of abuse, and the members challenge each other to find ways to curb such activities. Members also share constructive approaches that each has found useful, and efforts are made to help one another develop specific plans for dealing with situations that have in the past resulted in abusive episodes. Members learn to recognize danger signs and to then take necessary action to curb the potential abuse.

Leadership in the group is provided by a group member selected by the parents themselves. The leader, called a chairperson, is normally assisted by a professional sponsor who serves as resource and backup person to the chair and the group members. The social worker who becomes the sponsor must be prepared to perform a variety of roles, including teacher-trainer, broker of community services needed by parents, advocate, consultant, and in some instances, behavior changer (Hull, 1978).

[2]This description of Parents Anonymous is adapted from Charles Zastrow, "Parents Anonymous," in *Social Work with Groups: Using the Class as a Group Leadership Laboratory*, 5th ed. (Pacific Grove, CA: Brooks/Cole, 2002), pp. 159–161.

assumption of personal responsibility by members. They often provide material assistance as well as emotional support; they are frequently cause-oriented, and promulgate an ideology or values through which members may attain an enhanced sense of personal identity. (p. 9)

To convey the varieties and focuses of self-help groups that now exist (see Exhibit 6.1), two different classifications of these groups are summarized in the following paragraphs. Katz and Bender (1976) classified self-help groups into the following five categories.

1. Groups that focus on self-fulfillment or personal growth. Examples include Alcoholics Anonymous, Recovery Inc. (for former mental patients), Gamblers Anonymous, and Weight Watchers.

2. Groups that focus on social advocacy. Examples include Welfare Rights Organizations, MADD (Mothers Against Drunken Drivers), and the Committee for the Rights of the Disabled. Katz and Bender (1976) noted that the advocacy "can be both on behalf of broad issues, such as legislation, the creation of new services, change in the policies of existing institutions and so on, or it can be on behalf of individuals, families, or other small groups" (p. 38).

3. Groups that focus on creating alternative patterns for living. Examples include Gay Liberation and certain religious cults such as the Moonies.

4. *Outcast haven* or *rock-bottom* groups. Katz and Bender (1976) defined this type as follows:

> These groups provide a refuge for the desperate, who are attempting to secure personal protection from the pressures of life and society, or to save themselves from mental or physical decline. This type of group usually involves a total commitment, a living-in arrangement or sheltered environment, with close supervision by peers or persons who have successfully grappled with similar problems of their own. (p. 38)

Examples include Synanon, at least in its early years, and many other ex–drug addict organizations.

5. Groups of mixed types that have characteristics of two or more categories. One such group is Parents Without Partners, which promotes personal growth, advocacy, and social events for its members.

Powell (1987) classified self-help groups into the following five categories:

1. *Habit disturbance organizations:* These organizations focus on a problem that is specific and concrete. Examples include Alcoholics Anonymous, Smokestoppers, Overeaters Anonymous, Gamblers Anonymous, Take Off Pounds Sensibly (TOPS), Women for Sobriety, Narcotics Anonymous, and Weight Watchers.

2. *General purpose organizations:* These organizations address a wide range of problems and predicaments. Examples are Parents Anonymous (for parents of abused children), Emotions Anonymous (for persons with emotional problems), the Compassionate Friends (for persons who have experienced a loss through death), and GROW, an organization that works to prevent hospitalization of mental patients through a comprehensive program of mutual aid. In contrast to habit disturbance organizations, general purpose organizations address a wider range of problems and predicaments.

3. *Lifestyle organizations:* These organizations seek to provide support for, and advocate for, the lifestyles of people whose members are viewed by society as being different (the dominant groups in society are generally indifferent or hostile to that difference). Examples of this category include Widow-to-Widow programs, Parents Without Partners; ALMA (Adoptees' Liberty Movement Association), Parents/FLAG (Parents and Friends of Lesbians and Gays), National Gay and Lesbian Task Force, and the Gray Panthers, an intergenerational group that advocates for the elderly.

4. *Physical handicap organizations:* These organizations focus on major chronic diseases and conditions. Some are for people with conditions that are relatively stable, some for conditions that are likely to get worse, and some for terminal illnesses. Examples of this category include Make Today Count (for the terminally ill and their families), Emphysema Anonymous, Lost Chord clubs (for those who have had laryngectomies), stroke clubs, Mended Hearts, the Spina Bifida Association, and Self-Help for Hard of Hearing People.

5. *Significant other organizations:* The members of these organizations are parents, spouses, and close relatives of troubled and troubling persons. Very often, members of significant other groups are last-resort caregivers. Significant others contend with dysfunctional behavior. Through sharing their feelings, they obtain a measure of relief. In the course of sharing, they may also learn about new resources or new approaches. Examples of such organizations include Al-Anon, Gam-Anon, Toughlove, and the National Alliance for the Mentally Ill.

Many self-help groups stress (1) a confession by members to the group that they have a problem, (2) a testimony by members to the group recounting their past experiences with the problem and their plans for

EXHIBIT 6.1

Examples of self-help groups

Organization	*Service Focus*
Abused Parents of America	For parents who are abused by their adult children
Adoptee's Liberty Movement Association	For adoptees searching for their natural parents
Alcoholics Anonymous	For adult alcoholics
American Diabetes Association	Clubs for diabetics, their families, and friends
American Sleep Apnea Association	For persons with sleep apnea and their families
Burns United Support Group	For burn victims
Candlelighters Childhood Cancer Foundation	For parents of young children with cancer
Conjoined Twins International	For families of conjoined twins
CROHNS	For persons with Crohns disease and their families
CUB (Concerned United Birthparents)	For adoption-affected people in coping with adoption, including assistance for locating family members
Concerned United Birthparents	For parents who have surrendered children for adoption
Depressed Anonymous	For depressed persons
Divorce Care	For divorced persons
Emotions Anonymous	For persons with emotional problems
Encephalitis Support Group	For those with encephalitis and their families
Families Anonymous	For relatives and friends of drug abusers
Fortune Society	For ex-offenders and their families
Gam-Anon	For families of gamblers
Gray Panthers	An intergenerational group
Herpes Anonymous	For persons with herpes and their families and friends
High Risk Moms, Inc.	For women experiencing a high-risk or problem pregnancy
Impotents World Association	For impotent men and their partners
Make Today Count	For persons with cancer and their families
Molesters Anonymous	For men who molest children
National Organization for Women	For women's rights
Overeaters Anonymous	For overweight persons
Parents Anonymous	For parents of abused children
Sexaholics Anonymous	For those with sexually self-destructive behavior
WINGS Foundation, Inc.	For men and women traumatized by incest

Note: Barbara White and Edward J. Madara in *The Self-Help Sourcebook,* 6th ed. (Denville, NJ: American Self-Help Clearinghouse, 1998) describe more than 800 self-help groups.

handling the problem in the future, and (3) support—that is, when a member feels an intense urge of a recurrence (such as to drink or to abuse a child), a member of the group is called, and that member comes over to stay with the person until the urge subsides.

There appear to be several other reasons that self-help groups are successful. The members have an internal understanding of the problems, which helps them help others. Having experienced the misery and consequences of the problem, they are highly motivated and dedicated to finding ways to help themselves and their fellow sufferers. The participants also benefit from the *helper therapy principle:* the helper gains psychological rewards by helping others (Riessman, 1965). Helping others makes a person feel good and worthwhile; it also enables the helpers to put their own problems into perspective as they see that others' problems may be as serious, or even more serious, than their own.

When people help each other in self-help groups, they tend to feel empowered as they are able to control important aspects of their lives. When help is given from the outside (from an expert or a professional), there is a danger that dependency may develop, which is the opposite effect of empowerment. Empowerment increases motivation, energy, personal growth, and an ability to help that goes beyond helping oneself or receiving help.

Some self-help groups advocate for the rights and lifestyles of people whose members are viewed by society as being different. One such group is the National Gay and Lesbian Task Force. Some self-help groups (such as the National Association for Retarded Citizens) raise funds and operate community programs. Many people with a personal problem use self-help groups in the same way others use social agencies. An additional advantage is that self-help groups generally are able to operate with a minimal budget. Hundreds of these groups are now in existence. Social workers often act as brokers in linking clients to appropriate self-help groups.

Riessman (1987, pp. ix–x) summarizes the distinctive characteristics of self-help groups as follows:

- A noncompetitive, cooperative orientation
- An anti-elite, antibureaucratic focus
- An emphasis on the indigenous—people who have the problem and know a lot about it from the inside, from experiencing it
- An attitude of do what you can, one day at a time (you can't solve everything at once)
- A shared, often revolving leadership
- An attitude of being helped through helping (the helper-therapy principle) . . .
- An understanding that helping is not a commodity to be bought and sold
- A strong optimism regarding the ability to change
- An understanding that although small may not necessarily be beautiful, it is a place to begin and the unit to build on
- A critical stance toward professionalism, which is often seen as pretentious, purist, distant, and mystifying. Self-helpers like simplicity and informality
- An emphasis on the consumer. . . . The consumer is a producer of help and services
- An understanding that helping is at the center—knowing how to receive help, give help, and help yourself . . .
- An emphasis on empowerment

Socialization Groups

The objective of socialization groups generally is to develop or change attitudes and behaviors of group members to become more socially acceptable. Developing social skills, increasing self-confidence, and planning for the future are other foci. Illustrations include working with a group of predelinquent youth in group activities to curb delinquency trends, a youth group of diverse racial backgrounds to reduce racial tensions, a group of pregnant young females at a maternity home to make plans for the future, a group of elderly residents at a nursing home to remotivate them and get them involved in various activities, and a group of boys at a correctional school to help them make plans for returning to their home community. Leadership of such groups requires considerable skill and knowledge in using the group to foster individual growth and change. These leadership roles are frequently filled by social workers.

Therapy Groups

Therapy groups are generally composed of members with rather severe emotional or personal problems. Leadership of such groups generally requires considerable skill, perceptiveness, knowledge of human behavior and group dynamics, group counseling capacities, and ability to use the group to bring about behavioral changes. Among other skills, the group leader needs to be highly perceptive regarding how each member is being affected by what is being communicated. Considerable competence is needed to develop and maintain a constructive atmosphere within the group. Similar to one-to-one counseling, the goal of therapy groups is generally to have members explore their problems in depth and then to develop one or more strategies for resolving them. The group therapist generally uses one or more therapy approaches as a guide for changing attitudes and behaviors; these approaches include psychoanalysis, reality therapy, learning theory, rational therapy, transactional analysis, client-centered therapy, and psychodrama.

Group therapy is being used increasingly in social work. It has several advantages over one-to-one therapy. The *helper therapy principle* (in which members interchange roles and sometimes become the helper for someone else's problems) is generally operative. In such roles, members receive psychological rewards for helping others. Groups also help members put their problems into perspective as they realize others have equally serious problems. Groups also help members who are having interaction problems test out new interaction approaches. Research has shown that it is generally easier to change the attitudes of an individual in a group than in one-on-one

CASE EXAMPLE

Socialization—A Group at a Runaway Center

New Horizons is a private, temporary-shelter care facility for runaways in a large midwestern city. It is located in a large house that was built over 80 years ago. Youth on the run can stay for up to two weeks. State law requires that parents must be contacted and parental permission received for New Horizons to provide shelter overnight. Services provided include temporary-shelter care, individual and family counseling, and a 24-hour hotline for youths in crisis. The facility is licensed to house up to eight youths. Since the average stay is nine days, the population is continually changing. During the stay, intensive counseling is provided the youths (and often their parents), focusing on reducing conflicts between the youths and their parents and on making future living plans. The maximum stay limit of two weeks conveys to youths and their families, beginning with day one, that they must work on the reasons for leaving home.

Every evening at 7 P.M. a group meeting is held. All the residents and the two or three staff members on duty are expected to attend. This group has four main objectives. One is to serve as a vehicle for residents to express their satisfactions and dissatisfactions with the facilities and programs at New Horizons. Sometimes the group meeting appears to be primarily a gripe session, but the staff make conscientious efforts to improve those aspects where the youths' concerns are legitimate. For example, the youths may indicate that the past few days have been boring, and staff and residents then jointly plan activities for the next few days.

Another objective is to handle interaction problems between residents, and between staff and residents. A wide range of problems arise: A resident may be preventing others from sleeping, some residents may refuse to do their fair share of domestic tasks, there may be squabbles about which TV program to watch, some residents may be overly aggressive, and so forth. Because most of the youths face a variety of crises associated with being on the run, many tend to be anxious and under stress. In such an emotional climate, interaction problems are apt to arise. Staff are sometimes intensely questioned by residents about their actions, decisions, and policies. For example, one of the policies at New Horizons is that each resident must agree not to use alcohol or illegal drugs while staying at this shelter, with the penalty being expulsion. Occasionally a few youths use drugs and are caught and expelled. Removing a youth from this facility has an immense impact on the other residents, and at the following group meeting staff are expected to clarify and explain such decisions.

A third objective of the group meeting is for staff to present material on topics requested by residents. Examples include sex; drugs; homosexuality; physical and sexual abuse (a fair number of residents are abused by family members); how to avoid being raped; AIDS; how to handle anger, depression, and other unwanted emotions; legal rights of youths on the run; how to be more assertive; how to explain running away to relatives and friends; and other human services available to youths in the community. During such presentations, considerable discussion with residents is encouraged and generally occurs.

The final objective of the group meeting is to convey information about planned daily activities and changes in the overall program at New Horizons.

counseling (Johnson & Johnson, 2000). Research on conformity has found that group pressure can have a substantial effect on changing attitudes and beliefs (Johnson & Johnson, 2000). Furthermore, group therapy permits the social worker to help more than one person at a time, with potential savings in the use of professional effort.

In essence a group therapist uses the principles of one-to-one counseling (discussed in Chapter 5) and of group dynamics (see Chapter 7) to work with clients to change dysfunctional attitudes and behavior. Generally the group leader also uses the principles of certain treatment techniques (such as reality therapy, rational therapy, Parent Effectiveness Training, and assertiveness training) to help clients resolve personal and emotional problems. The selection of the techniques to use should ideally be based on the nature of the problems presented.

CASE EXAMPLE

Therapy Group for Spouses of Adults with Cancer

Eight years ago Linda Sonsthagen's husband was diagnosed with cancer. Linda was a social worker, and her husband was a successful life insurance agent. They had two sons in grade school. Mr. Sonsthagen died 4½ years ago, after having gone through a variety of treatment programs and through considerable pain. He lost weight and his hair fell out. These years were extremely difficult for the Sonsthagens. Linda had to take a larger role in raising the children and was the primary caregiver to both her husband and the children. During these years, the Sonsthagens found that relatives and friends shied away from them—it took several months before they became aware that the reason was that friends and relatives saw cancer as something they didn't understand and wanted to avoid. Even more difficult was dealing emotionally with not knowing the course of the disorder, going through cycles of hope and then disappointment as different treatment approaches were tried. As her husband became more incapacitated, Linda found she had to assume more of his tasks—for example, home repairs, maintaining their two cars, disciplining the children, and other daily household tasks.

After her husband's death, Linda and the two children went through several months of mourning and grief. Linda also discovered it was somewhat awkward to go to social functions alone. Fortunately she had two single female friends with whom she increasingly socialized. These were very difficult years for Linda. She needed over two years after her husband's death to rebuild her life in such a way that she was again comfortable.

During these years she received some financial help from the local chapter of the American Cancer Society. She also met through this society another woman whose husband was dying of cancer. They gave each other emotional support and shared useful ideas for handling problems.

Eighteen months ago Linda proposed to the local chapter of the American Cancer Society that she was willing to volunteer her time to start a group for spouses of people with cancer, and for spouses adjusting to a recent cancer death. The Cancer Society gave their approval and endorsement.

Linda started with nine members. The objectives were to give emotional support, to help members handle the new responsibilities they had to take on, and to help them deal with their emotional reactions. Linda used primarily a combination of reality therapy and rational therapy (see Modules 5 and 6). Reality therapy helped the group members better understand and make decisions and plans for the problems they faced. For example, for the members whose spouses had cancer, one focus was how to inform and handle their friends' and relatives' reactions to illness. Survivors focused on rebuilding their lives. Rational therapy countered unwanted emotions. Common emotions included depression, guilt, anxiety, the feeling of being overwhelmed, and anger (particularly resulting from "Why does this have to happen to me?"). Members were instructed on how to do a Rational Self-Analysis (see Module 6) on their unwanted emotions, and members often shared and discussed their RSAs at group meetings.

Group members stated on several occasions that the group was very helpful. They mentioned that knowing others faced similar plights was beneficial in and of itself. Seeing how others handled difficult decisions inspired them and gave them useful ideas on how to handle crises they faced. When a member suffered a serious crisis (for example, a spouse hospitalized for a serious operation), other members were available for telephone contact and to lend physical assistance.

After eight months the local chapter of the American Cancer Society was so encouraged by the results that they offered Linda a full-time position to run additional groups and to be available for individual counseling for people with cancer and their relatives. Linda gave up her part-time job as a counselor at the YWCA and took this position. Her first effort was to divide her group, which was growing, into two groups. The definition of eligible membership was also expanded: One group was for adults who have a family member with cancer, and the other for survivors. At this time Linda is leading one group of the first type and two groups of the second type.

Encounter Groups

Encounter groups and sensitivity training groups (these terms are used somewhat synonymously) refer to a group experience in which people relate to each other in a close interpersonal manner, and self-disclosure is required. The goal is to improve interpersonal awareness. Barker (1999) states that an encounter group is

> designed to promote the personal growth of the participants. The emphasis is not on correcting disorders, but rather on increasing the emotional and sensory aspects of being and on increasing open communication and self-awareness. (p. 154)

Barker (1999) defines a sensitivity group as:

> A training and consciousness-raising group rather than one that meets to resolve psychosocial or mental disorders. Such groups typically consist of 10–20 members and a leader, called a trainer or facilitator. The members participate in discussions and experiential activities to demonstrate how groups function, to show how each member tends to affect others, and to help them become more aware of their own and other people's feelings and behaviors. (p. 434)

An encounter group may meet for a few hours or for as long a period as a few days. Once increased interpersonal awareness is achieved, it is anticipated that attitudes and behaviors will change. For these changes to occur, a three-phase process generally takes place: unfreezing, change, and refreezing.

Unfreezing occurs through a deliberate process of interacting in nontraditional ways. Our attitudes and behavior patterns have been developed through years of social experiences, experimentation, and refinement. Such patterns have now become nearly automatic. Our interpersonal style generally has considerable utility in our everyday interactions. Deep down, however, we may recognize a need for improvement but are reluctant to make the effort, partly because our present style is somewhat functional and partly because we are afraid to reveal things about ourselves. Unfreezing occurs when we decide certain patterns of our present behavior need to be changed, and we are psychologically ready to explore ways to make changes.

Tubbs and Baird (1976) described the unfreezing process in sensitivity groups:

> Unfreezing occurs when our expectations are violated. We become less sure of ourselves when traditional ways of doing things are not followed. In the encounter group, the leader usually does not act like a leader. He or she frequently starts with a brief statement encouraging the group members to participate, to be open and honest, and to expect things to be different. Group members may begin by taking off their shoes, sitting in a circle on the floor, and holding hands with their eyes closed. The leader then encourages them to feel intensely the sensations they are experiencing, the size and texture of the hands they are holding and so forth.
>
> Other structured exercises or experiences may be planned to help the group focus on the "here-and-now" experience. Pairs may go for "trust walks" in which each person alternatively is led around with his eyes closed. Sitting face-to-face and conducting a hand dialogue, or a silent facial mirroring often helps to break the initial barriers to change. Other techniques may involve the "pass around" in which a person in the center of a tight circle relaxes and is physically passed around the circle. Those who have trouble feeling a part of the group are encouraged to break into or out of the circle of people whose hands are tightly held. With these experiences, most participants begin to feel more open to conversation about what they have experienced. This sharing of experiences or self-disclosure about the here and now provides more data for the group to discuss. (p. 48)

The second phase of the process is *change*. In sensitivity groups change is facilitated by spontaneous reactions or feedback to how a person "comes across" to others. In everyday interaction we almost never get spontaneous feedback, and we tend to repeat ineffective interaction patterns because we lack knowledge of our effect on others. But in sensitivity groups, such feedback is strongly encouraged. The following set of interactions illustrates such feedback:

Carl: All right (in a sharp tone), let's get this trust walk over with, and stop dilly-dallying around. I'll lead the first person around—who wants to be blindfolded first?

Judy: Your statement makes me feel uncomfortable. I feel you're saying this group is a waste of your time. Also, it's the third time tonight you've ordered us around.

Jim: I feel the same way, like you're trying to tell us peons what to do. Even the tone of your voice sounds autocratic, and I get the message you're really down on this group.

Carl: I'm sorry, I didn't mean it to sound like that. I wonder if I do that outside the group too?

Such feedback provides us with new insights on how we affect others. Once problem interactions are identified, members are encouraged to try out new response patterns in the relative safety of the group.

The third and final phase is *refreezing*. Unfortunately this term is not the most descriptive because it implies rigidity with a new set of response patterns. The goal in this phase is to experiment with new sets of behaviors so that members become growing, continually changing people who increasingly become more effective in their interactions with others. In terminating a sensitivity group, the leader may alert the participants to be on guard, because former dysfunctional behavior patterns tend to creep back in.

Sensitivity groups usually generate an outpouring of emotions rarely found in other groups.

The goal of sensitivity groups provides an interesting contrast to that of most therapy groups (see Exhibit 6.2). In therapy, the goal is for all members to explore their personal or emotional problems, and then develop a strategy to resolve the problems. In comparison, sensitivity groups foster increased personal and interpersonal awareness, and then develop more effective interaction patterns. Sensitivity groups generally do not attempt to identify and change specific emotional or personal problems (such as drinking problems, feelings of depression, sexual dysfunctions, and so on). The philosophy behind sensitivity groups is that with increased personal and interpersonal awareness, people will be better able to avoid, cope with, and handle specific personal problems that arise.

Sensitivity groups are used for a wide variety of purposes: to train professional counselors to be more perceptive and effective in interpersonal interactions with clients and with other professionals, to train managers to be more effective in their business interactions, to help clients with overt relationship problems become more aware of how they affect others and to help them develop more effective interaction patterns, and to train interested citizens in becoming more aware and effective in their interactions.

Despite their popularity, sensitivity groups remain controversial. In some cases inadequately trained and incompetent individuals have become self-proclaimed leaders and have enticed people to join through sensational advertising. If handled poorly, the short duration of some groups can intensify personal problems—for example, when a person's defense mechanisms are stripped away without developing adaptive coping patterns. Many authorities on sensitivity training disclaim the use of encounter groups as a form of psychotherapy and discourage those with serious personal problems from joining such groups. Carl Rogers (1970), in reviewing his own extensive experience as leader/ participant, echoed these concerns:

> Frequently the behavior changes that occur, if any, are not lasting. In addition, the individual may become deeply involved in revealing himself and then be left with problems which are not worked through. Less common, but still noteworthy, there are also very occasional accounts of an individual having a psychotic episode during or immediately following an intensive group experience. We must keep in mind that not all people are suited for groups. (pp. 40–41)

In some cases the popularity of sensitivity groups has led individuals to enter harmful groups with incompetent leaders where normal ethical standards have been abused. Shostrom (1969, pp. 38–39) has identified means by which those interested in encounter groups can prevent exploitation: (1) Never participate in a group of fewer than a half-dozen members. The necessary and valuable candor generated by an effective group cannot be dissipated, shared, or examined by too small a group, and scapegoating or purely vicious ganging up can develop. (2) Never join an encounter group on impulse—as a fling, binge, or surrender to the unplanned. (3) Never stay with a group that has a behavioral ax to grind. (4) Never participate in a group that lacks formal connection with a professional on whom you can check.

After reviewing the research on the outcome of sensitivity groups, Lieberman, Yalom, and Miles (1973)

EXHIBIT 6.2

Contrasting goals of therapy and sensitivity groups

Therapy Groups

Step 1	*Step 2*
Examine problems in depth.	Develop and select from various resolution approaches a strategy to resolve the problem.

Sensitivity Groups

Step 1	*Step 2*
Help each person become more aware of self and how they affect others in interpersonal interactions.	Help person develop more effective interaction patterns.

provided an appropriate perspective for those interested in the intensive group experience:

> Encounter groups present a clear and evident danger if they are used for radical surgery to produce a new man [person]. The danger is even greater when the leader and the participants share this misconception. If we no longer expect groups to produce magical, lasting change and if we stop seeing them as panaceas, we can regard them as useful, socially sanctioned opportunities for human beings to explore and to express themselves. Then we can begin to work on ways to improve them so that they may make a meaningful contribution toward solving human problems. (p. 73)

How to Start, Lead, and Terminate Groups

In the remainder of this chapter we focus on guidelines for starting, running, and terminating groups. This section covers homework, session planning, relaxing before a meeting, cues on entering the meeting room, seating arrangements, introductions, role clarification, agenda, additional guidelines for leading a group, and terminating a group. Many students fear taking a leadership role in groups. They are uncertain about what leaders do, and they fear they do not have the qualities or traits to be a leader. Amazingly, the truth is that even the most fearful and anxious students have already taken leadership roles in many groups. Every student has in the past been a member of several groups and has performed some essential tasks for these groups. As we shall see in Chapter 7, performing an essential task is simultaneously an effective leadership action.

Homework

Extensive preparation is the key to a successful experience for group members (including yourself). Even experienced leaders prepare carefully for each group and for each meeting.

In planning a new group, the following questions need to be answered. What are the group's overall purpose and goals? What possible ways can these general goals be accomplished? What are the characteristics of the members? Do some members have unique, individual goals or needs? What resources do members need to accomplish the general goals? What should the agenda be for the first meeting? Group members should have considerable input in suggesting and deciding on the specific goals of the group—how can this best be accomplished? When the group first meets, should an icebreaker exercise be used—if so, what? Should refreshments be provided? How should the chairs be arranged? What type of group atmosphere will best help the group accomplish its tasks? What is the best available meeting place? Why have you been selected to lead the group? What do the members expect you to do?

As you plan for the first meeting, it is helpful to view the group as a new member would view it. Here are some questions and concerns that new member might have. What are the goals of this group? Why am I joining? Will my personal goals be met in this group? Will I feel comfortable in this group? Will I be accepted by other members? Will the other members be radically different in terms of backgrounds and interests? If I do not like this group, can I get out of attending meetings? Will other members respect what I have to say, or will they laugh and make fun of me? By considering such concerns, the leader can plan the first meeting in a way that helps members feel comfortable and will clarify their questions about the group's goals and activities.

It is *absolutely essential* for a group leader to identify needs and expectations before the first meeting. The quickest way to fail as a leader is to try to lead a group in a direction different from what the members want. For example, I once attended a workshop with other counselors titled "Grief, Death, and Dying." The counselors expected material on how to counsel clients who were grieving about the death of a loved one more effectively. The presenter instead gave a historical review of how present-day funeral rituals evolved since the Middle Ages. The audience was, of course, very disappointed because their expectations were unmet.

There are a variety of ways to identify what members want. Prior to the first meeting, try to ask at least some members about their expectations. If you are asked by someone to lead the group, it is essential to ask that person about the expectations for the group. At the first meeting ask members to give their views as to what they desire from the group. Another way (which needs to be done for preparatory reasons anyway) is to "scout" the following about the members:

1. How many members are expected?
2. What are their characteristics—ages, socioeconomic status, racial and ethnic backgrounds, sex mix, educational and professional backgrounds, and so on?

3. How knowledgeable and informed are members about the topics that will be dealt with?

4. What are likely personal goals and agendas of the various members?

5. How motivated are members to accomplish the group purposes? This can partly be determined by examining how voluntary the membership is. Groups composed of involuntary members (for example, one that is court ordered to attend because of conviction for driving while intoxicated) may have little motivation and may even be hostile because they are being forced to attend.

6. What are the underlying value systems of members? A group of teenagers on juvenile probation will differ significantly from a group of retired priests. (That said, take care to view the members as unique persons rather than in terms of stereotypes.)

In planning for the first meeting (and additional meetings), visualize in great detail how you, as leader, want the meeting to go. Here is an example:

> The members will arrive at various times. I will be there early to greet them, introduce myself, help them feel comfortable, and engage in small talk. Small talk likely to be of interest to these new members: _______, _______, and _______.
>
> I will begin the meeting by introducing myself and stating the overall purpose of the group. As an icebreaker exercise, I will ask the group to give me a list of four or five facts they would like to know about other members and then have members introduce themselves and give these facts about themselves. I will also briefly summarize my professional experience and encourage members to ask questions about me and the group.
>
> After the icebreaker exercise, I will again briefly state the group's overall purpose and ask if members have questions about this. Possible questions that may arise are _______. If such questions arise, my answers will be _______.
>
> We will then proceed to items on the agenda (which I previously mailed to the members). During the discussion of these items, the questions that may arise are _______. My answers to such questions, should they arise, are _______.
>
> The kind of group atmosphere I will seek to create is democratic. Such an atmosphere is best suited for encouraging all members to participate in formulating the group goals and then to contribute their time and resources toward accomplishing them. I will seek to do this by arranging the chairs in a circle, by drawing out through questions those who are silent, by using humor, and by making sure that I don't dominate the conversation.
>
> I will end the meeting by summarizing what has been covered and the decisions that have been made. We will set a time for the next meeting. Finally, I will ask if anyone has additional comments or questions. Throughout the meeting I will encourage a positive atmosphere, partly by complimenting the members on the contributions they make.

After a group has met for one or more times, the leader should review these questions. Have our overall goals been sufficiently clarified? If not, what needs to be done in this clarification process? Are we making adequate progress in accomplishing its goals? If not, what obstacles are slowing us down that we need to confront? Have we selected adequate courses of action to reach our goals, or are there more effective courses of action that we could consider? What items should be on the agenda for our next meeting? What activities should we plan? Will successful completion of these activities move us toward accomplishing our overall goals? If not, perhaps other activities need to be selected. Does each member seem sufficiently interested and motivated to help us accomplish its goals, or do some members appear to be disinterested? If so, why do they appear to be disinterested, and what could we try to stimulate their interests?

Session Planning

In planning a session, it is essential to be fully aware of the group's overall goals. It is also essential to identify specific goals for each session. Know *exactly* what you want to accomplish in each session and make sure that all the items on the agenda relate to these goals. Here are some suggestions.

1. *Select content that is relevant.* The material should be relevant not only to the specific goals for the session but also to the backgrounds and interests of participants. For example, in a time management presentation, the time-saver tips you give to college students probably will be quite different from those for business executives. An excellent way to evaluate the relevance of your material is to define precisely how it will be valuable to members. Ask yourself, "If a group member asks why should I know this, can I give a valid reason?" If you are unable to come up with more than a vague answer, consider discarding that material and selecting more relevant material.

2. *Use a number of examples.* Examples illustrate key concepts. They also stimulate interest. People

remember examples much more than statistics. Thus, in a presentation on spouse abuse, vivid real-life stories of the drastic effects of battering will stay with members much longer than statistics on spouse abuse.

3. *Present materials in a logical order.* It is generally a good idea to begin by summarizing the agenda for the session. Ideally, one topic will blend into the next. If group exercises are used, place them next to the related theoretical material.

4. *Plan the time.* Once you have the content of the session fairly well organized, estimate how long each segment will take. Accurate estimations will help you determine if you have too much or too little material planned for the allotted time. Plan what you will do if the content is covered faster or slower than what you are estimating. Always be prepared to cover extra material should the anticipated content be covered more quickly than you estimated. If you are showing a videotape or have a guest speaker, have appropriate substitute material in case something goes awry.

5. *Be flexible with your agenda.* A variety of events can make it desirable to change the agenda during a session. The material may be covered much faster than anticipated, or interpersonal conflict may erupt which may take considerable time to process. Some members may bring up subjects related to the group's overall purpose that are valuable for the group to focus on at the moment.

6. *Change pace occasionally.* People pay attention for longer periods if there is an occasional change of pace. Long, long lectures or discussions are boring. Change pace in a variety of ways: Use a group exercise, show a film, invite a guest speaker, take a break, have a debate, show slides, change topics, and so on. In group therapy sessions, change pace by switching from one member's problems to another's concerns. If you are presenting a lecture, you can increase attention in several ways:

- Speak extemporaneously rather than read the material.
- Occasionally walk around the room rather than stand or sit in one place.
- Draw out the participants by asking questions.

(An excellent way to learn how to give more stimulating presentations is to observe the nonverbal and verbal communication patterns of dynamic speakers.) Remember to use appropriate transitions so the topics blend into one another rather than becoming choppy and confusing. As you select methods, be aware that people remember information better if they receive it actively (such as through an exercise) than if they receive it passively (through listening).

Relaxing Before a Meeting

Before a meeting, you may be nervous about how it will go. Some anxiety is helpful; you will be mentally alert and you will attend more carefully to what is being communicated. Some leaders, however, have an excessively high level of anxiety that reduces their effectiveness. If your anxiety is too high, you can reduce it by engaging in relaxing activities. Relaxation techniques are highly recommended and are described at some length in Module 9. Other suggestions include taking a walk, jogging, listening to relaxing music, and finding a place where you can be alone to clear your mind. Effective group leaders learn they can reduce their level of anxiety by using one or more of these techniques. Practice in leading groups will also build your confidence.

Cues on Entering the Meeting Room

It is important for you, as leader, to be on time, and perhaps a little early. Being early allows you to see that everything is arranged as you planned. You'll be able to do what needs to be done—seeing that the refreshments are available, erasing the chalkboard, arranging the chairs, and so on.

It also allows you to observe the moods of the members. If you have not previously met the group, arriving early gives you an opportunity to gain information about the participants' interests by observing their age, gender, clothes and personal appearance, small talk, and the way they interact with one another. Effective leaders notice such cues and generally find ways to "join" the participants.

I was once asked to give a workshop on suicide prevention to a high school class. On arriving, I was informed by the teacher that a classmate had recently committed suicide. Instead of beginning with my planned presentation, I acknowledged that I had just been informed about their former classmate, and I asked each of them anonymously to jot down one or two concerns or questions. We then proceeded to have a lively discussion related to these. This discussion was no doubt more valuable than the formal presentation I planned to give because it zeroed in on their immediate concerns.

Seating Arrangements

Seating arrangements are important. They affect who talks to whom and influences who plays leadership roles. As a result, they can affect group cohesion and morale.

It is important in most groups for members to have eye contact with one another. It is even more important for the group leader to be able to make eye contact with everyone to obtain nonverbal feedback on what members are thinking and feeling.

A circle is ideal for generating discussion, for encouraging a sense of equal status, and for promoting openness and cohesion. The traditional classroom arrangement (with the leader in front, and everyone facing that person while sitting in rows) has the effect of placing the leader in a position of authority. It also tends to inhibit communication as members can only make eye contact with those closest to them.

Tables have advantages and disadvantages. They provide a place to write and to put work materials. Some members feel more comfortable at a table because it gives them something to lean on. However, tables also restrict movement and can serve as a barrier.

Carefully consider whether tables are desirable or undesirable for your group. If members are to sift through papers or are expected to take notes, tables are useful. In therapy groups, tables are seldom used because they act as a barrier.

In many settings, tables can often be arranged to best meet the goals of the meeting. For example, arranging small tables in a circle facilitates communication.

Tables influence how group members interact with each other. If the table is rectangular, it is customary for the leader to sit at one end, at the "head" of the table; this creates an "authority" dynamic wherein the "head" does more talking and has a greater influence on the discussion. If an egalitarian atmosphere is desired, use a round or square table. The "head of the table" effect can also be reduced by placing two rectangular tables together to make a square.

Tables also influence interactions by where people sit. People are most likely to talk to those sitting at right angles to them and then to those next to them. People sitting directly across receive less communication, and those sitting anywhere else are even less likely to be addressed.

When a group meets for the first time (and often later), members are most likely to sit next to friends. If it is important for everyone in the group to interact, it may be desirable to ask people to sit next to people they don't know to counteract potential cliquishness and to encourage members to get to know each other.

Introductions

During the introduction, summarize your credentials in such a way that members gain a sense of confidence that you as the leader can fulfill their expectations. If you are being introduced by someone else, a brief and concise summary of your credentials *for the expected role* is desirable. If you are introducing yourself, summarize your important credentials in a nonarrogant fashion. Deliver your summary in a way that creates the desired atmosphere—whether it is informal or formal, fun or serious, and so on. An excellent way to handle the introduction is to use an icebreaker exercise (described in Chapter 1).

In meeting with a group, it is highly desirable to learn members' names as quickly as possible. This requires extra attention on your part. Name tags facilitate this process for everyone. Members appreciate being called by name—it conveys that they have importance.

If the group is small, it is generally advantageous for members to introduce themselves—perhaps by using an icebreaker. This is also a good place for members to state their expectations for the group. This helps uncover hidden agendas. If a stated expectation is beyond the scope of the group, you should tactfully state and discuss it to prevent unrealistic expectations from becoming a source of frustration or dissatisfaction.

Role Clarification

As the leader of the group, you should be clear about your roles and responsibilities. If you are unclear, discuss with the group their expectations about the appropriate roles for the leader and members. One way of doing this is for the group to select goals and then decide which tasks and responsibilities each member will have in achieving those goals. In most situations it is clearly a mistake for the leader to do the majority of the work. Groups are most productive if all members make substantial contributions. The more members contribute to the group, the more they will feel a part of the group psychologically.

Even if you are fairly clear about what you would like your role to be, other members may be confused about your role, or may have different expectations of you. If there is a realistic chance that the other members are unclear about your role, explain carefully what you perceive your role to be. If members indicate they have different expectations, take time here to decide who will do what.

In explaining what you perceive your role to be, be humble about your skills and resources. You want to come across as a knowledgeable "human" rather than as an authority figure who has all the answers.

Always be prepared to explain the reasoning behind the things you do. If you are leading an exercise, inform the group about its goals or objectives. (If questions arise about whether its goals are consistent with the group's overall goals, be prepared to provide an explanation.)

The role that leaders assume in groups vary from situation to situation. For example, there are marked differences in responsibilities of the leader of a therapy group and those of a committee assessing the social service needs of a community.

Agenda

Most meetings have agendas. Ideally, all group members should have an opportunity to suggest items for the agenda. If possible, send the agenda to members several days before the meeting to give them an opportunity to prepare.

Agenda items should be briefly reviewed at the start of the meeting, before consideration of the first item. This review gives members a chance to suggest additions, deletions, or other changes. In some meetings it may be appropriate for the group to discuss, and perhaps vote on, the suggested changes in the agenda.

Additional Guidelines for Leading a Group

1. Remember that leadership is a shared responsibility. Every member at times will take on leadership roles. Designated leaders should not dominate a group, nor should they believe they are responsible for directing the group in all of its task functions and group maintenance functions. (These functions are described in Chapter 7.) In fact, productivity and group cohesion are substantially increased when everyone contributes.

2. Use decision-making procedures that are best suited for the issues facing the group. (The merits and shortcomings of decision making by consensus and by majority voting were discussed earlier in this chapter.)

3. Create a cooperative group atmosphere rather than a competitive one (see Chapter 7).

4. View controversy and conflict as natural and desirable for resolving issues and furthering discussion. In resolving conflicts and in handling the issues and problems facing the group, use a problem-solving approach rather than a win-lose approach (see Chapter 7).

5. Try to create an atmosphere of open and honest communication.

6. Give attention to how you end a session. A few minutes before the session is scheduled to end, or when it appears the group has exhausted a subject, conclude with a brief summary of the key points made in the meeting. Not only does this help members remember major points, it leaves them with a sense of achievement. Closing also helps members transition to the outside world.

Terminating a Group

Termination is about separating from the group and from group members. Separation typically involves mixed feelings that vary in intensity according to a number of factors, several of which are mentioned here. The greater a member's emotional closeness and investment in a group, the greater their feeling of loss. The greater the feeling of success in accomplishing group goals the greater the feeling of "sweetness and sorrow"—sweetness from feeling that they have grown and had success, and sorrow from separating from the group that has come to be an important and meaningful part of their lives. The more emotionally dependent members become on a group, the more they are apt to feel anger, rejection, and depression over termination. The more they have experienced difficulties in separating in the past from significant others, the more likely the group separation will be experienced as difficult, because the pattern is repeated.

There are several types of termination: (1) termination of a successful group, (2) termination of an unsuccessful group, (3) a member dropping out, (4) transfer of a member, and (5) departure of the leader.

TERMINATION OF A SUCCESSFUL GROUP. In a successful group members have generally accomplished their goals. Termination of such a group can generate the "sweetness and sorrow" reaction. They are delighted with their accomplishments, which are increasing their self-confidence and self-esteem. But they may also experience varying levels of loss because they are emotionally invested in the group. Such groups may decide to have dinner together or have some other ceremony to commemorate and recognize the group's accomplishments.

In terminating a successful group, it is essential that formal termination begin one or more meetings before the final one. Ideally, the date of the last meeting should be discussed and agreed on well in advance. (For some groups, the final meeting is scheduled even before the group begins to meet.) Sufficient time has to be allowed in terminating successful groups so that (1) group progress can be evaluated; (2) plans can be made for continued work; (3) work can be done on unresolved, last-minute issues; (4) emotional reactions to terminating can be handled; and (5) members can discuss whether they want to plan a special social event for the group's ending.

Good-byes are often sad, but negative feelings can be offset by emphasizing what members have given and received, the ways they have grown, the skills they have learned, and the accomplishments of the group. In some cases, an extra session is held to complete unfinished business items. The members may decide to have periodic "class reunions" or social get-togethers.

TERMINATION OF AN UNSUCCESSFUL GROUP. In an unsuccessful group most or all the group's goals are largely unmet. Members' reactions to the lack of progress will vary considerably: anger, frustration, disappointment, despair, guilt (for unproductive efforts or lack of effort), scapegoating, blaming, and apathy. In rare cases, it is possible for an unsuccessful group to be fairly pleased and accepting of its efforts. For example, a group formed to write a grant (when there was limited hope of funding from the federal government) may be pleased with its efforts and with the new relationships formed; members may be only mildly disappointed in the failure of the group's objective.

Terminating an unsuccessful group is as important as terminating a successful one. As with all groups, plans for termination should be made well in advance. The date of the last meeting should be discussed and agreed on by the members long before the final meeting. Sufficient time should be allowed so that (1) the reasons for the lack of progress of the group can be assessed and analyzed; (2) alternatives for achieving the goals can be discussed (these may involve changing the format of the present group, referral of members to other groups, and alternatives involving individual actions rather than group efforts); (3) emotional reactions to terminating and to the lack of progress can be handled; (4) members can work on unresolved, last-minute issues; and (5) members can discuss whether they want to plan for the group's ending.

At times ending an unsuccessful group is chaotic and abrupt. A group appointed to write a grant may be nearly finished when they are informed the funding organization has a financial shortfall and is therefore withdrawing its request for funding proposals. This group may end abruptly in despair. Or, in a group of involuntary members (such as at a prison or at an adolescent residential treatment facility), the leader may decide that continuing the group is counterproductive because members are continually goofing off and are not putting effort into achieving the group goals. In any case, the reasons for the group's ending should be fully explained and time given to handle members' reactions to the closing. If there is insufficient time at the last meeting to deal with these tasks, it is sometimes advisable either to have another session or for the leader to meet individually with members to discuss their reactions to the group's failure, alternatives for reaching goals, reactions to the group's ending, and unresolved concerns. When an unsuccessful group ends abruptly, some group members may be highly critical of the leader, of other members, or of group experiences. If the leader contracts members to learn their thoughts about the group, he or she should be prepared to respond to highly critical feedback. To prepare, the leader can "visualize" possible criticisms and then formulate positive and realistic responses.

DROPPING OUT. When a member drops out, that member terminates even though the group continues on. A member drops out for a variety of reasons. She becomes disenchanted with the group and feels that neither she nor the group will accomplish the goals. He disagrees with or dislikes another group member. She is a parent who must now provide child care at the time the group meets or has begun a new job whose work hours conflict with meeting times. There are numerous reasons.

When members drop out without informing the group of their reasons, you as leader should contact them to learn why they decided to terminate. In some instances, it is desirable for you to explain that leaving is a major decision that should not be made abruptly and that you would like the opportunity to explore the reasons that led to the decision. If the reason is conflict with another member, perhaps the conflict can be resolved. Perhaps other actions can be taken that will enable the member to return.

If the member decides not to return after being contacted and encouraged to return, the reasons for leaving should be attended to. The member may be raising legitimate concerns that need to be dealt with so that other members do not also become discouraged and leave. If a person drops out of a therapy group, sensitivity group, or an educational group and still has unresolved personal concerns, referral to another group or to one-to-one professional help may be advisable.

Whenever a member drops out, you need to inform them of their positive contributions to the group. Dropping out is often viewed as a personal failure, and therefore you need to thank the person for any positive contributions to help dispel their sense of personal failure.

Don't neglect remaining members; they too experience a variety of emotions. Some will feel they failed this person. Some will feel guilt for what they said or did—or failing to do or say what they believe would have led the member to stay. Some will feel relief or joy; perhaps they view the member as unworthy of the group or as an obstacle in the group's efforts to accomplish its goals. Others will feel sadness and be concerned that something tragic has happened to that member. Some will be angry, feeling the person is abandoning the group. Still others will feel personally rejected. Often rumors begin to circulate about the person's reasons for leaving. Therefore it is essential that the group be informed of the reasons. A member's leaving can be devastating to group morale. And if other members have also recently left, the group's survival can be jeopardized.

Ideally, the member leaving should inform the group of their reasons, either in person or in writing. If they do not, you or another member should contact them to ascertain their reasons for leaving, and inform the group.

TRANSFER OF A MEMBER. Transfer of a group member to another group or to some other type of professional services generally involves a planned arrangement between the group leader and the member. The transfer can occur for a variety of reasons. In a problem-solving group, the employing agency may decide that the member's talents and skills could be better used in another capacity. In a therapy group, the leader and person leaving may jointly decide that she will be served better by receiving more specialized services in another therapeutic format. A member may be transferred because of a conflict that cannot be resolved, especially when the conflict is severely interfering with group goals. (For example, a serious and insurmountable gap in mutual understanding and communication caused by differences in religious beliefs, values, or language may exist.)

When a transfer occurs, you as leader should do everything possible to keep it from being unexpected or abrupt. The member being transferred should clearly understand the reasons for their transfer and ideally should be accepting of it. Be sure to explain to the group why the person is transferring. Ideally, the member should explain their reasons to the group; this gives other members an opportunity to wish the person well and to gain a sense of "closure."

DEPARTURE OF THE LEADER. Sometimes you must terminate your work with a group. This termination is often difficult for both you and the members. Emotional reactions can be intense, and adequate time for working through them may not be available. Members who feel vulnerable and depend on you may be devastated. Some may erroneously personalize your leaving as resulting from something they said or did. Some may feel anger and betrayal; they made a commitment to the group, confided and trusted in you, and now feel rejected.

You may also experience intense emotions, including guilt, for not being able to follow through on your commitment to lead the group until its goals are accomplished.

When you leave, you should encourage members to express their feelings. You may want to initiate this expression by explaining fully why you are leaving, giving members positive comments about the group, and stating your feelings of sadness and guilt over leaving. Prior to leaving, you or the group should select a new leader. If the new leader is not a member of the group, you should inform the new leader (privately) about the goals, member characteristics, current tasks and difficulties in the group, and progress toward group goals. The new leader should be introduced to the group by you; your goal is a smooth transition shifting your responsibilities to the new leader.

Evaluating a Group

In the past few decades, accountability has become a major emphasis in social welfare. Funding sources demand research evidence that allocated funds are having a beneficial effect. An essential component of accountability is evaluation.

In broad terms, evaluation is designed to assess whether the services provided were effective and efficient. Services provided in which goals and objectives are unmet are definitely ineffective. In evaluating the services provided by a group, there are two dimensions of evaluation: process evaluation and outcome evaluation.

Process Evaluation

Process evaluation is an assessment, generally by group members, of the aspects of the group that were useful or detrimental. Feedback about techniques and incidents that blocked or enhanced process is of immense value to you as group leader. With this information, you can hone certain skills, eliminate materials, and give direction for approaches and materials to add. Positive feedback generally helps build your confidence. If feedback is highly critical, it can be humbling and even devastating. It is far better to make changes suggested by the evaluation than to reject and "deny" the feedback and repeat the same mistakes in future groups. You need to welcome criticism and be prepared to respond to it constructively, which is the way that social workers expect clients to take constructive criticism.

Process evaluation can be conducted orally by asking group members to discuss the aspects, techniques, materials, and incidents that were constructive and those that were counterproductive. An advantage of such an oral evaluation is that most members enjoy a verbal discussion. A disadvantage is that some members may not give constructive negative feedback verbally because of the social norm in such situations to focus on the positives.

Process evaluation can also be accomplished using a brief questionnaire in which members address these three key areas:

1. The group's strengths. (Cite specific materials and incidents. Also cite skills and techniques used by the leader.)
2. The group's shortcomings. (Cite specific materials and incidents. Also cite skills and techniques used by the leader.)
3. Specific suggestions for changes.

In process evaluations, group members typically cite positive factors more than negative ones (Hepworth & Larsen, 1986, p. 590). Such positive feedback not only has a "stroking value" but also enables leaders to be more aware of their strengths, so they are apt to increase the use of these strengths in the future.

Note, however, that negative feedback is as valuable as, and often more valuable than, positive feedback. It informs you of aspects that need improvement, which you can then attend to.

Another way of evaluating process is by *peer review*. Peer review is conducted by having one or more "peers" (usually other group leaders) periodically sit in on your group. (Some agencies have one-way mirrors so the group can be unobtrusively observed.) Before a peer review, the agency or organization should agree on a set of principles or criteria that reflect quality group leadership. A peer review is a review of a small portion of the total functioning of the group. That small portion may be typical, or atypical, of the total functioning of the group. (Many colleges and universities use a peer review process in which tenured faculty in a department sit in on classes of recently hired faculty.)

In a variation of the peer review process, meetings may be taped (either audio or video). The tape is played back and reviewed by you and a peer (or by your supervisor). Before taping a meeting, you should explain to the members the reasons for taping the meeting, indicate who will view the tape, and then ask members for their permission to tape the session.

Outcome Evaluation

Outcome evaluation involves assessing the extent to which the goals formulated when the group began have been accomplished. Specific approaches to measure goal attainment are single-subject design, task achievement scaling, and satisfaction questionnaire.

SINGLE-SUBJECT DESIGN. Single-subject design has become increasingly popular in the helping professions in the past several decades. There are more than a dozen variations of single-subject design, some of which are complex and rigorous. Fortunately, the simpler designs can be used by entry-level social workers in many situations. Single-subject design is described in considerable detail in Chapter 11.

TASK ACHIEVEMENT SCALING. The objective of this approach is to gauge the degree to which group members and the leader have completed agreed-on tasks. In this approach, work toward members and group goals is broken into many separate actions or

EXHIBIT 6.3

Group member satisfaction questionnaire

Thank you for taking a few minutes to evaluate your experiences in our group. Your answers to this brief questionnaire will help us improve future groups. Feel free to offer your comments. To assure anonymity, please do not sign your name.

1. Did you accomplish what you expected when you joined the group?
   ____ Yes, completely
   ____ Mostly
   ____ No real progress
   ____ Worse off now than before
   Comments ______________________________
2. Do you feel the group accomplished its goals?
   ____ Yes, completely
   ____ Mostly
   ____ No real progress
   ____ The group was an utter failure
   Comments ______________________________
3. How do you feel about the group leader?
   ____ Very satisfied
   ____ Satisfied
   ____ No feelings one way or another
   ____ Dissatisfied
   ____ Very dissatisfied
   Comments ______________________________
4. How do you feel about the other members in the group?
   ____ Satisfied with everyone
   ____ Satisfied with some, and dissatisfied with others
   ____ No feelings one way or another
   ____ Dissatisfied with most of the other members
   ____ Dissatisfied with all of the other members
   ____ Very dissatisfied with all of the other members
   Comments ______________________________

tasks. Tasks are selected by mutual agreement, and members are assigned or select specific tasks to reach their personal goal and the group's overall goal. Usually, a deadline is set for completing each task. *Task achievement scaling* rates the degree to which each agreed-on task has, in fact, been achieved.

Reid and Epstein (1972) used a 4-point scale to record progress on each task: 4 = completely achieved; 3 = substantially achieved, action is still necessary; 2 = partially achieved, considerable work remains to be done; and 1 = minimally achieved or not achieved. Where appropriate, they have a fifth rating, "no," for "no opportunity to work on task." With this approach, only results are rated—not effort, motivation, or good intentions. The appealing features of this approach are its simplicity and the fact that it can be used when more rigorous procedures are not feasible because of insufficient time or data, or difficulties in finding a suitable way to measure changes in the target behavior.

The approach has some limitations. For example, if the tasks are conceptualized as constructive in meeting group and member goals but are not constructive, then completing the tasks will have little effect on accomplishing the goals.

SATISFACTION QUESTIONNAIRE. Still another way to assess a group outcome is to have members fill out a questionnaire that measures satisfaction. An example is the Group Member Satisfaction Questionnaire shown in Exhibit 6.3.

Such questionnaires are a relatively simple and inexpensive way to measure members' satisfaction with the group. The questionnaire can be filled out at the last meeting or mailed to members some time later. Questions that evaluate process (described in this chapter) can also be included.

Satisfaction questionnaires have limitations, however. Responses are affected by the respondent's mood. In addition, dissatisfied members are less likely to fill out the questionnaire, particularly if it is administered by mail (Sheafor, Horejsi, & Horejsi, 1988, p. 390).

A few concluding comments are in order about the personal benefits you will receive in leading groups. Through learning how to lead effectively, you will grow as a person, become more self-confident, feel good about yourself, develop highly marketable skills, improve interpersonal relationships, and help yourself and other members accomplish important tasks. Leaders are not born. They are trained. We all have the potential to become effective group leaders. You can do it!

Summary

Social group work's historical roots are in the informal recreational organizations—the YWCA and YMCA, scouting, Jewish centers, settlement houses, and 4-H Clubs. Now almost every social service agency provides some group services. Most undergraduate and graduate social work programs provide practice courses to train students to lead groups, particularly socialization, educational, and therapeutic groups. Groups frequently encountered in social work practice include recreation, recreation-skill, educational, task, problem-solving and decision-making, focus, self-help, socialization, therapy, and encounter groups.

With problem-solving and decision-making groups, group decision making is usually superior to individual decision making. Problem-solving groups sometimes fall into groupthink, which can lead a group to make ineffective and even destructive decisions. Decisions made by consensus have the best chance of getting members to support and work for the decision. Decisions made by simple majority voting are arrived at much faster than those made by consensus. The decision-making technique you use will depend on many factors.

Socialization groups generally endeavor to develop or change attitudes and behaviors of group members in some socially accepted direction. Social skill development, increasing self-confidence, and planning for the future are other foci.

Therapy groups generally strive to help members explore personal or emotional problems and then develop strategies to resolve the problems. Group therapists use principles of one-to-one intervention and group dynamics to assist members in achieving positive changes in attitudes and behaviors. In contrast, sensitivity groups foster increased personal and interpersonal awareness and develop more effective interaction patterns.

The chapter concluded with guidelines on how to start, lead, and terminate groups. Aspects included homework, planning a session, relaxing before starting a meeting, cues on entering the meeting room, seating arrangements, introductions, clarifying roles, agenda, terminating a group, and evaluating a group.

EXERCISES

1. *ASSERTIVENESS TRAINING*

Goal: Demonstrate to the class how to run an educational group by illustrating how to run an assertiveness training group.

Step 1: The instructor indicates the purpose of this exercise. The instructor describes nonassertive, aggressive, and assertive behaviors (see Module 4 for descriptions).

Step 2: The instructor distributes a handout that describes the 12 steps of assertiveness training (contained in Module 4). The instructor summarizes these steps.

(continued)

EXERCISES
(continued)

Step 3: The instructor asks for volunteers (two for each situation) to role-play assertively the situations that the instructor gives them, such as:

a. asking someone who is smoking next to you to put out a cigarette.
b. asking for a date and refusing a date.
c. indicating to your objecting father that you want to live with the person you are dating.

After a situation is role-played, the class discusses the assertiveness strategy.

Step 4: Students write anonymously on a note card one or two situations involving assertiveness that they are struggling with and that they would like others in the class to role-play.

Step 5: The instructor collects these note cards and selects some situations for volunteers to role-play. After a situation is role-played, the class discusses the merits and shortcomings of the assertiveness strategy that was used.

2. *THE NOMINAL GROUP*

Goal: This exercise is designed to have the class learn how a nominal group is conducted.

Step 1: The steps of how to run a nominal group are described in this chapter. The instructor asks a question for the nominal group to consider, such as "What do you see as the shortcomings of our social work program (do not mention the names of faculty members)?" Then follow the steps for conducting a nominal group as described in this chapter.

3. *TRUST WALK*

Goal: This exercise is designed to demonstrate an approach—the trust walk—that is frequently used in sensitivity groups. A trust walk helps students get in touch with aspects of themselves that they are unaware of.

Step 1: The instructor informs the class of the purpose of the exercise. The students form groups of two. (If a member is without a partner, the instructor can be a partner.) A member of each subgroup closes his or her eyes and keeps them closed during the first part of this exercise. The "seeing" partner then is instructed to lead the "blind" partner down corridors, around the room, and perhaps outside. The "seeing" partner can lead the "blind" partner with verbal directions and by taking a hand. The "seeing" person has the responsibility to watch that the "blind" partner does not run into objects, fall, stumble, or get hurt in any way. (The instructor informs the students to be very careful going up and down stairs.)

Step 2: After 8 to 10 minutes, the partners reverse roles and continue the exercise for another 8 to 10 minutes.

Step 3: The students then discuss their feelings about doing this trust walk. The instructor asks questions such as the following. Did you occasionally open your eyes when you were the "non-seeing" partner? Did you have trust in your partner? Did you feel you would run into objects and hurt yourself? Were you afraid? If yes, how did you handle these fears? Did you become aware of feelings or thoughts about yourself that you previously were unaware of? If yes, what thoughts and feelings?

CHAPTER 7

Social Work with Groups: Concepts and Skills

In this chapter we look at key group dynamic concepts and guidelines for leading therapeutic groups.[1] We begin by reviewing ideas that are important in understanding group process: membership and reference groups, stages in group development, task and maintenance roles, leadership theory, and social power bases in groups.

Membership and Reference Groups

A membership group is any group we belong to. Membership in a group is clearly defined—either we belong or we don't. Membership is thus a boundary condition.

Some people are marginal members of a group. For example, Tim Kelly attends classes, works evenings, and doesn't live on campus. He likes his coworkers and knows very few students. He comes to campus only for classes and leaves immediately afterward. Tim is a marginal member of the student body.

Full psychological membership in a group occurs only when a person is positively attracted to being a member and is positively accepted as a member. Tim Kelly has limited psychological membership with the student body because he has only a slight identification with the campus. The more a person is attracted to a group, the greater that person's commitment to accomplishing the goals of the group.

Aspiring members include those who are seeking admission to a group but have not yet been admitted. They are not members but act as if they are. For example, students who want to join a fraternity or sorority will act like members to increase their chances of being admitted. Aspiring members psychologically identify with the group even though they are not as yet formally admitted.

There is also a difference between voluntary membership and involuntary membership. Individuals who deliberately choose to belong to a group, such as a fraternity or athletic team, are voluntary members. In many situations, people have little or no choice about becoming a group member. Social workers routinely work with groups whose membership is involuntary—

[1]Material in this chapter is adapted from Charles Zastrow, *Social Work with Groups: Using the Class as a Group Leadership Laboratory*, 5th ed. (Pacific Grove, CA: Brooks/Cole, 2001), pp. 13–22; 56–65; 81–85; 92–102 & 175–185. Grafton H. Hull, Jr., was a contributing author to this chapter.

for example, in prison settings, mental hospitals, and residential treatment facilities. Involuntary group members may initially be uninterested in participating and are sometimes hostile and disruptive.

Reference groups are groups whose influence we are willing to accept. We closely identify with these groups. Tim Kelly's work group is his reference group; the student body, for all practical purposes, is not.

Reference groups have two distinct functions. First, members' behavior, attitudes, and other characteristics become standards we use to judge and evaluate ourselves and others. Second, reference groups have a normative function in that we seek to conform to their standards.

In a given group only some members are referents for us. Referents are people who influence us and who we, in turn, seek to influence. In a large group we normally have only a small subgroup of referents. These referents make sense to us, or they are people we identify with, or they hold most of the power. We tend to "tune out" and interact less with other members.

Group Development

Groups change over time. Numerous models or frameworks describe group change; we examine a few here.

Garland, Jones, and Kolodny Model

The Garland, Jones, and Kolodny (1965) model identifies five stages of development in social work groups. This model describes problems that commonly arise as groups form and develop. Understanding these problems, it is theorized, enables leaders to anticipate and respond to member reactions more effectively. The conceptualization of Garland and his colleagues is particularly applicable to socialization groups, therapy groups, and encounter groups. To a lesser extent, the model also applies to self-help groups, problem-solving and decision-making groups, educational groups, recreation-skill groups, and task groups.

Closeness (how emotionally close members will allow themselves to become) is the central focus of this model. The question of closeness is reflected in *struggles* that occur at five stages of group growth: preaffiliation, power and control, intimacy, differentiation, and separation.

In the first stage, *preaffiliation,* members are ambivalent about joining the group. Interaction is guarded. Members test, often through approach and avoidance behavior, whether they really want to belong to the group. New situations are frightening, and members try to protect themselves from being hurt or taken advantage of. They attempt to maintain a certain amount of distance and to get what they can from the group without risking much. Individuals are aware that group involvement will make demands that may be frustrating or even painful. However, they are also attracted to the group because they have had satisfying experiences in other groups, and membership in this group offers similar rewards. In the first stage, the leader should seek to increase member's attractions to the group "by allowing and supporting distance, gently inviting trust, facilitating exploration of the physical and psychological milieu, and by providing activities if necessary and initiating group structure" (Garland & Frey, 1973, p. 3). The first stage gradually ends as members come to feel fairly safe and comfortable and view the rewards as worth a tentative emotional commitment.

The second stage, *power and control,* emerges as group characteristics begin to develop. Patterns of communication emerge, alliances and subgroups begin to appear, members take on certain roles and responsibilities, norms and methods for handling tasks develop, and membership questions arise. Such processes are necessary for the group to conduct its business. However, these processes lead to struggle as the members establish their places in the group. Each member seeks power, partly for self-protection and partly to gain greater control over the gratifications and rewards to be received from the group. In this struggle, the group leader is a major source of gratification. The leader is perceived as having the greatest power to influence the group's direction and to give or to withhold emotional and material rewards. At this point, members realize that the group is becoming important to them.

The second stage is a transitional stage wherein certain basic issues need to be resolved. Who has primary control over the group's affairs—the group or its leader? Limits of power for the leader and group are questioned.

This uncertainty results in anxiety among, and considerable testing by, members as they gauge the limits and seek to establish norms for power and authority. Rebellion is not uncommon, and dropout rates are often highest at this stage. During this struggle, leaders should (1) help members understand the nature of the power struggle, (2) give emotional support to weather the discomfort of uncertainty, and (3) help the group establish norms to resolve the uncertainty. It is very important that group members develop trust in the leader so that the leader can maintain a safe balance of shared power and control. When trust is achieved, members make a major commitment to become involved in the group.

In the third stage, *intimacy*, likes and dislikes are expressed. The group becomes a "family," with "sibling rivalry" arising between members and the leader sometimes even referred to as a parent. Feelings about the group at this stage are more openly expressed and discussed. The group is now viewed as a place where growth and change take place. Individuals examine and make efforts to change personal attitudes, concerns, and problems. Group tasks are worked on, and there is a feeling of "oneness" or cohesiveness. Struggle or turmoil during this stage leads members to explore and make changes in their personal lives, and to examine what the group is all about.

During the fourth stage, *differentiation*, members increasingly experiment with new and alternative behavior patterns. There is a recognition of individual rights and needs and a high level of communication among members. The group is able to organize itself more efficiently. Leadership is shared, and roles are more functional. Power problems are now minimal, and decisions are made and carried out with less emotion and on a more objective basis. Garland and Frey (1973) noted:

> This kind of individualized therapeutic cohesion has been achieved because the group experience has all along valued and nurtured individual integrity. . . .
>
> The worker assists in this stage by helping the group to run itself and by encouraging it to act as a unit with other groups or in the wider community. During this time the worker exploits opportunities for evaluation by the group of its activities, feelings, and behavior. (p. 5)

The differentiation stage is analogous to a high-functioning family in which the children have reached adulthood and are pursuing their own live successfully; relationships are between equals, members are mutually supportive, and members relate to each other in ways that are rational and objective.

The final stage is *separation*. The purposes of the group have been achieved, and members have learned new behavioral patterns that enable them to move on to other social experiences. Termination is not always easy. Members are sometimes reluctant to move on and may even display regressive behavior in an effort to prolong the safety of the group. They may also express anger over ending the group or even psychologically deny the end is near. Garland and Frey (1973) describe the leader's (or worker's) role in termination this way:

> To facilitate separation the worker must be willing to let go. Concentration upon group and individual mobility, evaluation of the experience, help with the expression of the ambivalence about termination and recognition of the progress which has been made are his major tasks. Acceptance of termination is facilitated by active guidance of members as individuals to other ongoing sources of support and assistance. (p. 6)

Tuckman Model

Tuckman (1965) reviewed more than 50 studies of therapy and sensitivity groups with limited duration and concluded that groups go through the following predictable stages:

1. *Forming:* Members become oriented toward each other, work on being accepted, and learn more about the group. A period of uncertainty ensues in which members try to determine their place in the group and the rules and procedures of the group.
2. *Storming:* Conflicts begin to arise as members resist the influence of the group and rebel against accomplishing the tasks. Members often confront their various differences, and management of conflict becomes the focus of attention.
3. *Norming:* The group establishes cohesiveness and commitment, and in the process group members discover new ways to work together. Norms are also set for appropriate behavior.
4. *Performing:* The group works as a unit to achieve the group's goals. The group develops proficiency in achieving its goals and becomes more flexible in its patterns of working together.
5. *Adjourning:* The group disbands. The feelings that members experience are similar to those in the "separation stage" of the Garland, Jones, and Kolodny model.

Bales Model

The Garland, Jones, and Kolodny model and the Tuckman model are sequential-stage models; that is, both models specify sequential stages of group development.

In contrast, Bales (1965) developed a recurring-phase model. He asserted that groups continue to seek an equilibrium between task-oriented work and emotional expressions to build better relationships among group members. (Task roles and social/emotional roles are described in the next section.) Bales asserts that groups tend to oscillate between these two concerns—sometimes focusing on identifying and performing work tasks that must be conducted to achieve goals and at other times focusing on building morale and improving the social/emotional atmosphere.

Note that the sequential-stage and recurring-phase perspectives are not necessarily contradictory. Both are useful for understanding group development. The sequential-stage perspective assumes that groups move through various stages while dealing with basic themes that surface as they become relevant to the group's work. The recurring-phase perspective assumes that the issues underlying the basic themes are never completely resolved and tend to recur.

It is common for leaders just beginning their work with groups to expect a smooth transition between stages and are often disappointed if this doesn't occur. Additionally, many new practitioners, lacking experience and trust in the group process, tend to prematurely force the group out of certain stages—that is, they rush the process of group development. Experience will demonstrate the futility of such efforts. Barring unforeseen circumstances, groups will move at their own pace and will eventually arrive at the same destination. Groups that skip stages or whose development is otherwise thwarted often return to a stage with "unfinished business." Good leaders recognize this and allow natural group processes to evolve. Although groups do sometimes get mired in one stage, this happens less often than feared.

Task and Maintenance Roles

All groups (whether organized for therapeutic reasons, for problem solving, or for other objectives) rely on members performing a variety of roles. Group needs require that both task roles and group-building roles be performed satisfactorily. Task roles are those needed to accomplish specific group goals; maintenance roles are those that strengthen social/emotional aspects of group life (Pfeiffer & Jones, 1976).

Johnson and Johnson (1975, p. 26) summarized these roles as follows:

Information and opinion giver: Offers facts, opinions, ideas, suggestions, and relevant information to help group discussion.

Information and opinion seeker: Asks for facts, information, opinions, ideas, and feelings from other members to help group discussion.

Starter: Proposes goals and tasks to initiate action within the group.

Direction giver: Develops plans on how to proceed and focuses attention on the task to be done.

Summarizer: Pulls together related ideas or suggestions and restates and summarizes major points discussed.

Coordinator: Shows relationships among various ideas by pulling them together and harmonizes activities of various subgroups and members.

Diagnoser: Figures out sources of difficulties the group has in working effectively and the blocks to progress in accomplishing the group's goals.

Energizer: Stimulates a higher quality of work from the group.

Reality tester: Examines the practicality and workability of ideas, evaluates alternative solutions, and applies them to real situations to see how they will work.

Evaluator: Compares group decisions and accomplishments with group standards and goals.

The Johnsons (1975, p. 27) also identified *group maintenance roles,* which strengthen social/emotional bonds within the group:

Encourager of participation: Warmly encourages everyone to participate, giving recognition for contributions, demonstrating acceptance and openness to ideas of others, is friendly and responsive to group members.

Harmonizer and compromiser: Persuades members to analyze constructively their differences in opinions, searches for common elements in conflicts, and tries to reconcile disagreements.

Tension reliever: Eases tensions and increases the enjoyment of group members by joking, suggesting breaks, and proposing fun approaches to group work.

Communication helper: Shows good communication skills and makes sure that each group member understands what other members are saying.

Evaluator of emotional climate: Asks members how they feel about the way in which the group is working and about each other, and shares own feelings about both.

Process observer: Watches the process by which the group is working and uses the observations to help examine group effectiveness.

Standard setter: Expresses group standards and goals to make members aware of the direction of the work and the progress being made toward the goal and to get open acceptance of group norms and procedures.

Active listener: Listens and serves as an interested audience for other members, is receptive to others' ideas, goes along with the group when not in disagreement.

Trust builder: Accepts and supports openness of other group members, reinforcing risk taking and encouraging individuality.

Interpersonal problem solver: Promotes open discussion of conflicts between group members to resolve conflicts and increase group togetherness.

Hersey and Blanchard (1977) developed a situational theory of leadership that serves as a guideline for when leaders should focus on task behaviors, on maintenance behaviors, or on both. In essence, the theory asserts that when members have low maturity in terms of accomplishing a specific task, leaders should engage in high-task and low-maintenance behaviors. Hersey and Blanchard refer to this situation as *telling,* because leader behaviors are most effective when they define members' roles and tell them how, when, and where to do needed tasks. The task maturity of members increases as their experience and understanding of the task increases. For moderately mature members, leaders should engage in high-task and high-maintenance behaviors. This combination of behaviors is referred to as *selling,* because leaders should not only provide clear direction as to role and task responsibilities but should also use maintenance behaviors to get members to "buy into" decisions.

Also, according to Hersey and Blanchard, when group members' commitment to the task increases, so does their maturity. When members are committed to accomplishing the task and have the ability and knowledge to complete the task, leaders should engage in low-task and high-maintenance behaviors, referred to as *participating.* Finally, for groups in which members are both willing and able to take responsibility for directing their own task behavior, leaders should engage in low-task and low-maintenance behaviors, referred to as *delegating.* Delegating allows members considerable autonomy.

Leadership Theory

There are at least four major approaches to leadership theory: trait, position, style, and distributed functions.

The Trait Approach

Aristotle observed, "From the hour of their birth some are marked for subjugation, and others for command" (Johnson & Johnson, 2000, p. 186). As implied by this comment, the trait approach to leadership has existed for millennia. This approach assumes that leaders have personal characteristics or traits that make them different from followers. It also implies that leaders are born, not made, and that leaders emerge naturally rather than being trained. The trait approach has also been called the *great person* theory of leadership.

Krech, Crutchfield, and Ballachey (1962) reviewed research studies on leadership traits. Their results suggested leaders need to be perceived as (1) being a member of the group they are attempting to lead, (2) embodying to a special degree the norms and values that are central to the group, (3) being the most qualified group member for the task at hand, and (4) fitting members' expectations about how the leader should behave and what functions he or she should serve.

Research on personality traits indicates that leaders, compared to followers, tend to be better adjusted, more dominant, more extroverted, and more assertive; they often have greater interpersonal sensitivity. Other traits, such as intelligence, enthusiasm, self-confidence, and equalitarianism, also frequently characterize leaders (Hare, 1962).

Although potential leaders tend to have more of all positive attributes than other members, they cannot be so extreme that they become deviates. In a classic study, for example, Davie and Hare (1956) found that B students were the campus leaders, whereas A students were sometimes treated as outcasts for being "curve wreckers." Also, people who do most of the talking often win most of the decisions and become leaders, unless they talk *too* much and antagonize the other members (March, 1956).

The following is a brief look at two leadership traits that have received considerable attention: charisma and Machiavellianism.

CHARISMA. Johnson and Johnson (2000, p. 189) defined charisma as "an extraordinary power, as of working miracles." Johnson and Johnson (1987) gave the following definition of a charismatic leader.

> A charismatic leader has (1) an extraordinary power or vision and is able to communicate it to others or (2) unusual powers of practical leadership that will enable him or her to achieve the goals that will alleviate followers' distress. The charismatic leader has a sense of mission, a belief in the social-change movement he or she leads, and confidence in himself or herself as the chosen instrument to lead the movement to its destination. The leader appears extremely self-confident in order to inspire others with the faith that the movement he or she leads will prevail and ultimately reduce their distress. (p. 190)

Some charismatic leaders inspire their followers to adore and be extraordinarily committed to them. Others offer members hope and promise of deliverance from distress.

Charisma has proven difficult to define precisely. Qualities and characteristics of charismatic leaders differ dramatically. Consider, for example, the characteristics of these charismatic leaders: Martin Luther King, Jr., General George Patton, Gandhi, and Hitler.

One difficulty with quantifying charismatic leadership is that charismatics express this quality in numerous ways. A second difficulty is that many leaders do very well without being charismatic.

MACHIAVELLIANISM. Niccolò Machiavelli (1469–1527) was an Italian statesman who advocated that rulers use cunning, craft, deceit, and duplicity to increase their power and control. (Machiavelli was not the originator of this approach; earlier theorists also conceptualized leadership in terms of manipulation for self-enhancement. However, the term *Machiavellianism* is now synonymous with the notion that politics is amoral and that unscrupulous means can therefore justifiably be used to achieve political power.) Machiavellian leadership is based on the concepts that followers (1) are basically fallible, gullible, untrustworthy, and weak; (2) are impersonal objects; and (3) should be manipulated for leaders to achieve their goals.

Christie and Geis (1970) concluded that Machiavellian leaders have four characteristics: (1) They have little emotional involvement in interpersonal relationships because it is easier emotionally to manipulate others if they are "impersonal objects." (2) They are not concerned with conventional morality and take a utilitarian (what they can get out of it) rather than a moral view of their interactions. (3) They have a fairly accurate perception of the needs of their followers, which facilitates their capacity to manipulate them. (4) They have a low degree of ideological commitment; they manipulate others for personal benefit rather than for achieving ideological goals.

Although some leaders have Machiavellian characteristics, the vast majority do not. Groups simply do not function effectively or efficiently with Machiavellian leaders.

In recent years the trait theory of leadership has declined in popularity, partly because research results raise questions about its validity. For example, different leadership positions often require different leadership traits. The characteristics of a good military leader differ markedly from those of a good group therapy leader. Moreover, traits found in leaders are also found in followers. Qualities such as intelligence and a well-adjusted personality have some correlation with strong leadership, but many intelligent, well-adjusted people never get top leadership positions. The best rule for selecting leaders involves choosing people with the necessary skills, qualities, and motivation to help a group accomplish its goals.

The Position Approach

Large organizations have several levels of leadership. The position approach defines leadership in terms of the authority of a particular position and focuses on the behavior of people in high-level positions. Training and personal background of leaders have also been examined.

Studies using the position approach, however, reveal little consistency in how people assume leadership positions. Obviously, individuals with little training become leaders; others spend years developing their skills. Also, individuals in different leadership positions display a variety of appropriate behaviors. Obviously, a drill sergeant is not expected to be empathetic, but a sensitivity group leader is. It is difficult to compile a list of leadership traits using this approach. Not surprisingly, the position approach has shown that what constitutes leadership behavior depends on the particular requirements of the position.

It is also difficult to define which behaviors are leadership behavior and which are not. Certainly not all the behavior of designated authority figures is leadership behavior. Also, leadership behavior among group members who are not designated leaders is often difficult to clarify. An experienced supervisor who joins a new firm, for example, may categorize her staff members according to guidelines set by her former employer. If the positions she uses are not interchangeable, communication problems may develop, and her leadership abilities or the ability of her staff will be questioned.

The Style Approach

Because research on the trait approach was turning out contradictory results, Lewin, Lippitt, and White (1939) focused on leadership *styles*. These researchers described three leadership styles: authoritarian, democratic, and laissez-faire.

Authoritarian leaders have more absolute power than democratic leaders. They alone set goals and policies, dictate the activities of members, and set major plans. They alone reward and punish, and they alone know the succession of future steps in the group's activities. In contrast, democratic leaders seek maximum involvement and participation of members in all decisions affecting the group. They spread responsibility rather than concentrate it.

Authoritarian leadership can be efficient and decisive. One hazard, however, is that group members often do what they are told out of necessity and not because of their commitment to group goals. The authoritarian leader who anticipates approval from subordinates for accomplishments achieved may be surprised to find backbiting and bickering common in the group. Unsuccessful authoritarian leadership generates factionalism, behind-the-scenes jockeying and maneuvering for position among members, and lead to a decline in morale.

Democratic leadership, in contrast, is slow in decision making and sometimes confusing but is frequently more effective because strong cooperation emerges when members participate in decision making. With democratic leadership, interpersonal hostilities between members, dissatisfactions with the leader, and concern for personal advancement are discussed and acted on. The danger is that the private, behind-the-scenes complaining that can happen in the authoritarian approach becomes public conflict in a democratic approach. However, once the public conflict is resolved, strong personal commitments develop that motivate members to implement group decisions rather than to subvert them. The potential for sabotage in authoritarian groups is high, and therein lies the advantage of the democratic style.

Democratic leaders know that mistakes are inevitable and that the group will suffer from them. Yet, such mistakes require that leaders stand by without interfering because to do otherwise harms the democratic process and impedes group progress.

In certain situations authoritarian leadership is most effective, whereas in others democratic leadership is most effective (Hare, 1962). As in any situation, groups are more effective when members' expectations about behavior are met. Where group members anticipate a democratic style, as they do in educational settings, classrooms, and discussion groups, the democratic style produces the most effective groups. When members anticipate forceful leadership, as in industry or military service, authoritarian leadership results in more effective groups.

In the *laissez-faire* style, there is very little participation by the leader. Group members function (or flounder) with little input by the designated leader. There are a few conditions where group members function best under laissez-faire style (when the members are committed to a course of action, have the resources to implement it, and need a minimum of designated leader influence to work effectively). Because different leadership styles are required in different situations (even with the same group), research interest in recent years has switched to the distributed functions approach.

The Distributed Functions Approach

In this approach, leadership is defined as the performance of acts that help the group reach its goals and maintain itself in good working order (Johnson & Johnson, 1975). Leadership functions include setting group goals, selecting and implementing tasks to achieve goals, and providing resources to accomplish goals. Leadership functions also include the group maintenance tasks of improving group cohesion and seeking to ensure that individual members are satisfied. This approach seeks to discover what tasks are essential to achieve group goals under various circumstances and how different group members should take part in these actions.

This approach stands in direct contrast to the great person theory of leadership. It asserts that any group member may at times be a leader by taking actions that serve group functions. Leadership is viewed as specific to a particular group in a particular situation. For example, telling a joke may relieve tension in some situations but may be counterproductive when members are revealing intense personal feelings in a therapy group.

The functional approach defines leadership as occurring whenever one member influences other members to help the group reach its goals. Because at times all group members influence other members, each member leads. However, being a designated leader and engaging in leadership behavior are different. A *designated leader* has responsibilities that continue for the duration of the group, whereas members who engage in leadership behaviors do so temporarily—this leadership role shifts from member to member.

The functional approach asserts that leadership is a learned set of skills that anyone with certain minimal requirements can acquire. Responsible membership is the same thing as responsible leadership; both involve doing what needs to be done to help the group maintain itself and accomplish its goals. This approach asserts that people can be taught the skills and behaviors that help the group accomplish its tasks and maintain good working relationships. The implication for a social work practice course is that practically everyone of you can learn to be an effective leader.

Like any member of the group, designated leaders may need to adopt one or more of the task specialist or maintenance specialist roles discussed earlier in this chapter. Indeed, leaders have a special obligation to be alert for such occasions and to assume or assist others to assume whichever roles are timely and appropriate. The leader's contribution to the group is not limited, however, by assuming specified roles. Leaders are responsible for functions that range from performing intake to planning for termination. The needs and developmental stage of a group will require a leader who can at different times assume the previously described roles and also these:

- Executive (the top coordinator of group activities).
- Policymaker (establishing group goals and policies).
- Planner (deciding the means by which the group will achieve its goals).
- Expert (source of readily available information and skills).
- External group representative (the official spokesperson for the group).
- Controller of internal relations (managing the structure as a way to control in-group relations).
- Purveyor of rewards and punishments (promotions, demotions, and pleasant and unpleasant tasks).
- Arbitrator and mediator (both judge and conciliator with the power to reduce or to increase factionalism within the group).
- Exemplar (shows what members should be and do).
- Ideologist (the source of the group's beliefs and values).
- Scapegoat (the target for members' frustrations and disappointments).

Social Power Bases in Groups

French and Raven (1968) developed a framework for understanding the extent to which group members have influence or power over each other. Five bases of power are identified: reward, coercive, legitimate, referent, and expert. This framework allows group leaders to analyze the source of their power and also suggest when, and when not, to use this power.

Power is often viewed negatively. But *all* our interactions involve power. In groups it is natural and generally desirable that every member seeks to influence other members—this is how personal goals and group goals are accomplished.

Reward power is based on the perception of B (one member) that A (another member, or the entire group) has the capacity to dispense rewards or remove negative consequences in response to B's behavior. A's power will be greater the more group members value the reward and the more they believe they cannot get the reward from anyone else. Rewards include such things as promotions, pay increases, days off, and praise. Group members often work hard for someone who has high reward power, will usually like the person, and will communicate effectively with him or her. But reward power can backfire if members feel they are being conned or bribed into going along, which can lead to dislike of the high-reward person. If A uses reward power in a conflict situation with B, B may feel he is being bribed and controlled.

Coercive power is based on B's perception that A can dispense adverse consequences or remove positive consequences. Coercive power stems from B's expectation that she will be punished by A if she fails to conform to A's wishes. The ability to fire workers if they fall below a given level of production is a common example of coercive power. The distinction between reward and coercive power is important. French and Raven noted that reward power tends to increase the attraction of B toward A, whereas coercive power decreases this attraction. If A uses coercive power to settle a conflict, it increases B's hostility, resentment, and anger. Threats often lead to aggression and counterthreats. Thus, coercive power can exacerbate the conflict by leading both A and B to distrust each other and to retaliate. Therefore, whenever possible, coercive power should not be used in a conflict situation. (Unfortunately, it often is, with the result that conflict is exacerbated. For example, military threats often increase conflict between rival countries.)

Legitimate power is based on B's perception that A has a legitimate right to prescribe behavior for him and that B has an obligation to accept this influence. Legitimate power is the most complex of the five power bases, and is based on some internalized value or norm. Cultural values constitute one common basis for legitimate power and include such things as intelligence, age, caste, and physical characteristics. For example, in some cultures the elderly are highly respected and granted the right to prescribe behavior for others. Acceptance of a social structure is another basis; legitimate power in a formal organization is largely a relationship between positions rather than between people (like the perceived right of supervisors to assign work.) A third basis is a legitimizing agent; the process of electing a group leader is a common way to legitimize a person's right to a position that has legitimate power associated with it.

The areas in which legitimate power may be used are generally specified (for example, in a job description). The attempted use of power outside the prescribed range decreases the legitimate power and attractiveness of the authority figure.

Referent power is based on B's identification with A. Identification in this context means either a feeling of oneness with A or a desire for such an identity. The stronger B's identification with A, the greater B's attraction to A and the greater A's referent power: "I am like A, and therefore I will believe or behave as A does," or "I want to be like A, and I will be more like A if I believe or behave as A does." In ambiguous situations, B will evaluate his thoughts, beliefs, and values in terms of what A thinks, believes, and values. In ambiguous situations, B is likely to adopt the thoughts, beliefs, and values of the individual or group with which he identifies. French and Raven noted that B is often not consciously aware of the referent power that A exerts.

Expert power is based on the perception that A has some special knowledge or expertise. Accepting a physician's advice in medical matters is a common example. Another would be accepting directions from a service station owner when in a strange city. For expert influence to occur, it is necessary for B to think that A has the right answer, and for B to trust that A is telling the truth. A client accepting a counselor's suggestion exemplifies expert power. Expert power is more limited than that of referent power, because the expert is seen as having superior knowledge or ability only in specific areas. French and Raven (1968) noted that the attempted exertion of expert power outside the perceived range of that power will reduce it; that is, an undermining of confidence takes place.

French and Raven (1968) theorized that for all five types, the stronger the basis of power, the greater the power. Referent power is thought to have the broadest range of power. Attempts to use power outside the prescribed range may reduce the power.

Personal Goals and Group Goals

A goal is an end toward which an individual or a group of people are working. It is an ideal or a desired end point that people value. A personal goal is one held by a member. A group goal is one held by enough members that the group can be said to be working toward its achievement.

All groups have goals, and every person who joins a group has personal goals. Groups have both short- and long-range goals. The short-range goals are stepping stones to reaching the long-range goals.

It is very important to set group goals. The effectiveness and efficiency of the group can be measured by the extent to which its goals are achieved. Goals give direction to groups and to their members. They direct the group's programs and efforts. Conflicts of opinions between members are often resolved by deciding which opinion is most helpful in achieving group goals. Group goals are a motivating force. Once members commit to achieving a certain goal, they feel an obligation to put forth their abilities, efforts, and resources to attain this end.

Members' motivation to work to accomplish group goals is increased by involving them in setting the goals. Through involvement, members (1) have a greater chance of having their personal goals for joining the group become a component of the group goals, (2) have an increased awareness of the importance of choosing these goals, and (3) feel a greater commitment to providing their resources to achieve the goals.

The more congruence there is between members' personal goals and the group's goals, the more attracted to the group the members will be and the more willing to provide their resources and energies to the group. Members' personal goals can be heterogeneous (different) or homogeneous (alike). The more homogeneous personal goals are, the more likely members will agree on group goals and work together to achieve them. They also tend to be happier with the group when personal goals are homogeneous.

When members have heterogeneous personal goals, hidden agendas can develop. A *hidden agenda* is a personal goal held by a member that is unknown to the other group members and that interferes with group goals. Hidden agendas can be very destructive. I have participated in groups where an individual observed the comments and actions of others to obtain evidence to bring legal harassment charges. Usually, however, hidden agendas are less destructive. For example, a lonely person who enjoys talking may slow a group down by monopolizing meetings with irrelevant small talk.

Because hidden agendas can severely hamper group processes, it is important that groups set goals that incorporate members' personal goals. With such a focus, hidden agendas are likely to be minimized.

Note, however, that *all* groups operate on two levels: the surface task and the hidden needs and motivations. Although hidden agendas siphon energy, they also reflect individual needs and may or may not be known to the person who holds them. All members join groups with the intention of meeting their personal needs. Sometimes after initial needs are met, other, less obvious ones surface. Such needs are normal and expected. The real issue is the effect these needs have on the group. The important question is whether meeting A's needs will prevent B (or the group) from satisfying needs. The goal is to find a means to legitimize individual needs in ways that allow for effective problem solving.

Managing hidden agendas requires that members and leaders be on the lookout for them and support members who try to bring hidden agendas to the surface. One such approach might involve saying "I wonder if we've said all that we feel about this idea. Perhaps we should go around the room once more and see whether anyone has anything to add." At the same time, leaders and members should be aware that some hidden agendas are best left hidden. Criticizing a member for a hidden agenda can create defensiveness and inhibit problem solving.

Conformity

Some classic studies have examined conforming behavior. Sherif (1936) examined the "autokinetic effect." In this experiment, subjects were placed in a darkened room and asked to judge how far a dot of light moves. Although the light appeared to move (the autokinetic effect), it actually did not. Each subject saw the dot of light and made a series of individual judgments about how far the light moved. The subjects were then brought together in groups of three to judge again how far the light moved. In this situation, their judgments tended to converge to a group standard. Later, when they again viewed the light alone, they often retained the group standard and gave that answer. The key finding this study and many after it is that when a situation is ambiguous and there is no objective way to determine the "right" answer, members rely on the group to define "reality." This means membership in a group determines for individuals many of the things they will see, learn, think about, and do.

Asch (1955) also examined conforming behavior. Asch investigated what happens when an individual's judgment conflicts with the judgments of other group members. The experiments were designed as follows. There were two sets of cards, as shown in Figure 7.1. Subjects were arranged in groups of seven to nine, seated at a table, and asked to state in turn which line was closest in length to the standard. In the control groups, practically all subjects chose line 2. Now, here is where things get interesting: In the experimental groups, all members, except for one subject, were accomplices of the experimenter. The subject was seated at or near the end of the line for giving his or her judgment. Accomplices all chose the same *incorrect* line. When it came to the subject's turn, he or she was then faced with relying on individual judgment or conforming to the group judgment. In a variety of similar studies, Asch found that more than one-third of the subjects conformed to the group judgment. Such a large percentage is amazing because there was no overt group pressure to conform, the situation was not ambiguous, and the subjects did not know each other. In addition, there were neither promises of future favor or advancement, nor threats of ostracism or punishment.

Conformity is the yielding to group pressure. For there to be conformity, there must be conflict—conflict between the influences exerted by the group and those forces in individuals that tend to lead them to value, believe, and act in some other way. For mem-

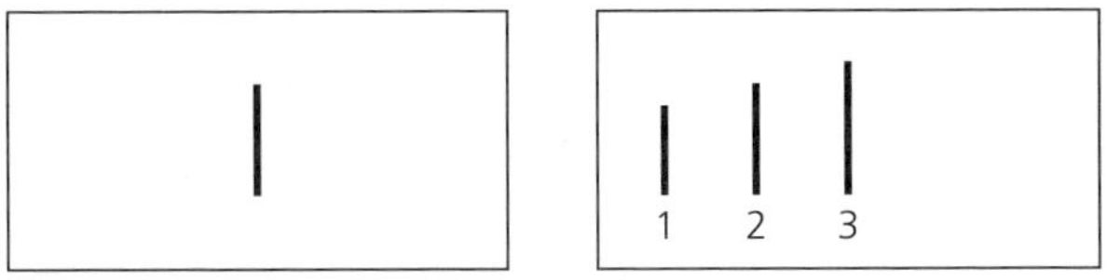

Standard Comparison lines

FIGURE 7.1 Cards in Asch conformity studies

bers experiencing such conflict, there are two available options: Announce an independent decision, or conform with the group's position. Conforming takes two forms: (1) The expedient conformer outwardly agrees but inwardly disagrees. (2) The true conformer both outwardly and inwardly comes to agree with the group.

A number of conclusions have arisen from conformity research (Krech, Crutchfield, & Ballachey, 1962, pp. 509–512).

1. Considerable amounts of yielding are produced by group pressure, even when the bogus group consensus is obviously wrong. In one study, 50 military officers were asked to indicate which of two figures, a star and a circle presented side by side, was larger in area. The circle was clearly about one-third larger, but under group pressure 46 percent of the men agreed with the bogus group consensus.

2. Many people can be pressured into yielding on attitude and opinion items, even those with significant personal implications. For example, 50 military officers were asked privately and under bogus group consensus to state their opinion on: "I doubt whether I would make a good leader." In private, none of the officers expressed agreement, but under unanimous group pressure, 37 percent expressed agreement.

3. Yielding is far greater on difficult, subjective items than on easy, objective ones.

4. Individual differences in yielding are extremely large. A few people yield on almost all items; a few yield on none; most people yield on some and not on others.

5. When people are retested individually and privately on the same items some time later, the yielding effect mostly disappears as they tend to revert to their own unchanged private judgment. But a small part of the yielding effect remains, indicating group pressure has a lasting effect on changing attitudes.

6. As a group increases in size, the pressure for yielding increases, and more yielding occurs. When a person is opposed by a single other person, there is very little yielding.

7. Yielding is markedly reduced when a person has the support of one other person (a partner) in the group. Apparently, a dissident opinion has a tremendous effect in strengthening the independence of like-minded people.

In a dramatic series of studies, Milgram (1963) demonstrated that subjects in an experimental situation would administer electric shocks of dangerous strength to another person when instructed to do so by the experimenter. (Unknown to the subject, the person did not actually receive the electrical shocks.) Most subjects complied with the experimenter's commands, even when instructed to give increasingly strong shocks to the victim, this in spite of the victim's protests and cries of anguish. These studies demonstrated that people will yield to "authoritative" commands even when the behavior is incompatible with their own moral, normal standards of conduct. Milgram suggested his studies help us understand why the German people complied with the unethical commands of Hitler. Group pressures, especially when viewed as authoritative, have a tremendous effect on our actions, attitudes, and beliefs.

Schachter (1959) developed a theory of social comparison. Schachter assumed that we all have a need to evaluate the "rightness" of our feelings, opinions, values, and attitudes. He also assumed that we all have a need to evaluate the extent of our abilities. Schachter then theorized and conducted studies to demonstrate that in the absence of objective, nonsocial means of evaluation, a person will rely on other people as comparison points of reference. To a large extent, the groups we belong to define social reality for us. For most of our opinions, values, beliefs, and abilities, there is no objective, nonsocial way to evaluate ourselves, so we rely on others.

Idiosyncratic Credits

Every member of a group gains credits (and status) by showing competence and by conforming to expectations at that time. Eventually these credits allow a person to break the group's norms and rules without being chastised. To some extent, after credits accumulate, nonconformity to general procedures or expectations serves as a confirming feature of one's status. Yet there is a limit on the number of earned idiosyncratic credits. Nonconformity beyond this limit results in a dramatic decrease in status and even rejection by other group members (Hollander, 1958).

Competitive and Cooperative Groups

Groups basically have either a cooperative or a competitive group atmosphere. In a cooperative group open and honest communication, trust, pooling of resources, and cohesion prevail. Research has found a number of positive consequences for a cooperative group atmosphere in problem-solving groups. Cooperation among members increases creativity, coordination of effort, division of labor, emotional involvement in group accomplishment, helping and sharing, interpersonal skills, cooperative attitudes and values, positive self-attitudes, liking among group members, positive attitudes toward the group and tasks, divergent thinking, acceptance of individual and cultural differences, and problem-solving skills (Johnson & Johnson, 1975, p. 88).

Cooperative group atmospheres result when members' personal goals are perceived as compatible, identical, or complementary. An example of a highly cooperative group is a successful basketball team in which the main goal of each member is to win, and the main goal of the team is to win. In a cooperative group, members seek to coordinate their efforts with those of other members to achieve the goals of the group. In establishing a cooperative atmosphere, rewards to members must be based on the quantity and quality of group performance rather than on individual performance.

In contrast, competitive atmospheres can be detrimental and destructive. Competitive atmospheres exist when members perceive their personal goals as incompatible, different, conflicting, or mutually exclusive. In highly competitive groups, a member achieves his or her goal only if other members fail to obtain their goals (Deutsch, 1949). An example is a job group interview held for several job applicants. The consequences of competition in problem-solving groups are numerous. Competition decreases creativity, coordination of effort, division of labor, helping and sharing, and cohesion. Competition promotes ineffective communication, suspicion and mistrust, high anxiety, competitive values and attitudes, negative self-attitudes, dislike among group members, and negative attitudes toward the group and its tasks. Competition encourages rejection of differences of opinion, divergent thinking, and cultural and individual differences. A competitive atmosphere leads to low effectiveness in solving complex problems (Johnson & Johnson, 1975, p. 97).

Kelly and Stahelski (1970) examined the question of what happens when a competitive person joins a group that has a cooperative atmosphere. Because cooperative groups are much more effective in problem solving than competitive groups, the question is significant. Three consequences were found to occur: (1) The competitive behavior of the new member leads other members to behave competitively; (2) the competitive person views the former cooperative members as having always been competitive; and (3) the former cooperative members are generally aware that their competitive behavior is largely a consequence of the new member's competitiveness. Thus, it appears that one competitive person can change a cooperative group into a competitive group. Why does a competitive person have such a strong, destructive effect? Apparently, the cooperative members realize the competitive person will, if given a chance, take advantage of their cooperativeness and use it to his or her own advantage. In many situations their only recourse to prevent exploitation is to also become competitive. If a cooperative group is to survive, it is important that new members have an orientation compatible with that of the other members.

Controversy and Creativity

Controversy is a debate, dispute, or discussion about differences in beliefs, information, opinions, ideas, or assumptions. Controversy in groups is natural. If handled constructively, controversy increases creativity, increases members' involvement, and leads to high-quality decisions. Emotional reactions to controversy can be positive (curiosity, affinity for other members, excitement, exhilaration, stimulation, involvement, commitment) or negative (frustration, disgust, anger, fear, resentment, rejection, distrust, apathy, paranoia), depending on how the group handles the controversy.

People react differently to controversy. Some people shy away from it. Others take a difference of opinion personally and become hurt or angered. Others find controversy stimulating and fun; they hope to find a little each day. Still others view controversy as a way for each side to express itself, vent concerns, and work out differences.

Controversy has much value for a group. Handled effectively, controversy encourages inquiry, stimulates interest and curiosity, sharpens analysis, and promotes objectivity. It also increases members' commitment to the group and improves the problem-solving process. Controversy stimulates members to search for new and better alternatives and to synthesize suggested alternatives into higher-quality decisions. Through controversy, members often reassess and clarify their values and beliefs and grow as people. Through learning how to resolve interpersonal conflicts, members may also learn how to become better managers of their internal conflicts.

However, some groups do not manage controversy well. Ineffective groups tend to suppress and withdraw from controversy. They have group norms that urge members to suppress conflicts and to agree outwardly even when some members believe the group is making a serious mistake. When controversy does arise in ineffective groups, the members often view the opposing positions in terms of "right versus wrong" or "we versus they."

The Win-Lose Approach versus the Problem-Solving Approach

Ineffective groups often view controversy as a *win-lose situation*. We live in a competitive society where in many fields (such as sports, business, and politics) individuals and teams are pitted against each other. Destructive controversies are often cast in the "win-lose" mold. Members interrupt each other to sell their positions without really listening to what others are saying. Power blocs form to support one position against proponents of another. The group's original goals and objectives fade into the background as victory at all costs becomes the driving issue.

In win-lose situations, each side denies the legitimacy of the other side's interests and concerns. Each side is concerned only about its own needs. Each side musters support and power for its position to defeat the other side.

In win-lose situations the group loses because it fails to achieve its objectives. The side that loses on an individual issue has little motivation to provide its resources to carry out the actions of the winning side. It resents the winner and may seek to reverse the decision or impede its implementation. Distrust increases, communication becomes limited and inaccurate, and cohesion or togetherness disappears. Often members create "gunnysacks" full of grievances that result in biased judgments and actions. In win-lose situations, members frequently refuse to vote for a good idea because they dislike the person who suggested it. Conflict in these situations leads to denial or distortion of unpleasant facts and information. It leads to blind spots in which members misinterpret the ideas and actions of members perceived as being opponents. Disagreement is interpreted as personal rejection. Decisions are of low quality and often incorrect.

A more effective approach for resolving conflicts is the *problem-solving approach*. Effective groups generally use this approach. The differences between a win-lose strategy and a problem-solving strategy are summarized in Exhibit 7.1.

In the problem-solving approach, members attempt to find a mutually satisfying course of action. Members listen to each other, recognize the legitimacy of one another's interests, and influence one another with rational arguments. The problem-solving approach functions in an atmosphere of cooperation. The steps in this approach can be summarized as follows:

1. The needs of each person or subgroup are identified and defined.
2. Alternative solutions are generated.
3. The alternative solutions are evaluated.
4. A highly evaluated solution that is acceptable to practically everyone is selected.
5. The solution is implemented.
6. There is follow-up to evaluate how well the selected solution is working.

The problem-solving strategy is based on two basic premises: (1) All members have the right to have their needs met, and (2) what is in conflict between the two sides is almost never their *needs* but their *solutions* to those needs.

The distinction between "needs" and "solutions" is important. For example, a student social work club is arguing over whether to fund a graduation party for seniors or a campus day-care center in danger of being closed. The club is arguing over solutions, not needs. The graduating seniors need to be honored, and the day-care center needs operating funds. However, there are a variety of ways to meet both needs. The club could spend its funds on a graduation party and hold a fund-raiser for the day-care center, or fund the center and hold a graduation party in which members donate food, refreshments, and a few dollars. Or, half of the club's funds could go to the center, and the remainder to a reduced-cost graduation party, and so on.

Adjusting win-lose situations so that the outcome is win-win is the goal of members and leaders committed to effective problem solving. It is difficult for any one

EXHIBIT 7.1

Win-lose versus problem-solving strategies

Win-Lose Strategy	*Problem-Solving Strategy*
The conflict is defined as a win-lose situation.	The conflict is viewed as a mutual problem.
Each side seeks solutions to meet only its needs.	Each person seeks solutions that meet the needs of all members.
Each side attempts to force the other side into submission.	Each person cooperates with others to find mutually acceptable compromises.
Each side increases its power by emphasizing its independence from the other, and the other's dependence upon itself.	Each person equalizes his or her power by emphasizing interdependence.
Each side inaccurately, deceitfully, and misleadingly communicates its goals, needs, and ideas; information inconsistent or harmful to one's position is not shared.	Each person honestly and openly communicates his or her goals, needs, and ideas.
No expression of empathy or understanding is made of the views, values, and opinions of the other side.	Efforts are made to convey empathy and understanding of the views, values, and opinions of others.
Threats are used to attempt to force the other side into submission.	Threats are avoided to reduce the defensiveness of others.
Rigid adherence to one's position is expressed.	A willingness to be flexible is expressed.
Changes in position are made very slowly in an effort to force concessions from the other side.	Positions are changed readily to help in problem solving.
No suggestions are sought from third parties as the focus is on forcing the other side to give in.	Third parties are sought to help in problem solving.

person to redirect a win-lose situation; usually a significant segment of the membership is needed to accomplish this goal. There are several ways to accomplish this. First it is important to have clear goals that all members understand and agree to. Issues that arise in a win-lose situation should be tested against goals to determine whether they really are relevant to the group's functioning. Being on the alert for win-lose situations is also important. When a member feels that he or she is being attacked by others or feels as if he or she is lining up support for a particular position, the likelihood is that a win-lose situation is developing.

Of course, active listening is often effective in these situations (see Module 9). The listener can be empathic, listen to the other's reasoning (and perhaps be persuaded), and at least understand the other's position. When responding to members' positions, it is better to suggest alternatives than to say, "This is the only intelligent way to do this." As you have seen in the preceding chapter, arriving at decisions through consensus rather than majority-minority voting tends to be more effective and reduces the win-lose nature of debate. Finally, it is important to test whether compromises or consensus agreements actually are accepted by all members. This is best done by polling all group members in turn, asking whether they would like to add anything to the discussion. The key to resolving win-lose situations is to try for a solution that is best for all members rather than attempting to get one's own way.

A cooperative, problem-solving atmosphere has a number of payoffs. It increases the chances of finding a high-quality solution. It increases the commitment of members to support and implement the group's decisions. It increases trust and reduces hostility. It increases communication and cohesion. It increases satisfaction with the group. It increases the chances of the group's achieving its long-range objectives. It leads members to interact together with fewer inhibitions. It sets up an atmosphere in which members can freely express and work out their frustrations and concerns. (If such frustrations are not expressed, they often fester, resulting in increased apathy and disengagement from the group.) The problem-solving approach keeps arguments focused on the present, as past conflicts have been worked out. It improves relationships with other members and leads to greater understanding of self and others.

A cooperative, problem-solving approach promotes creativity in groups. Creativity is the process of bringing something new into existence. Creativity results from productive controversy, as the problem is viewed from new perspectives, new alternatives are suggested, and a new synthesis of alternatives is formulated for resolving the problem.

Strategies for Conflict Resolution

Even though your group works toward consensus and uses a problem-solving approach, conflicts will still arise from time to time. A number of techniques have value in resolving conflicts. Role reversal, empathy, inquiry, I-messages, disarming, stroking, and mediation have all proven to be effective.

Role Reversal

A useful strategy in resolving both intragroup and intergroup conflict is role reversal. Here is the basic rule for role reversal: *Each person expresses his or her opinions or views only after restating the ideas and feelings of the opposing person.* These ideas and feelings should be restated in your own words rather than parroted or mimicked in the exact words of the other person. It is advisable to begin your restatement with "Your position is . . . ," "You seem to be saying . . . ," or "You apparently feel. . . ." Approval or disapproval, blaming, giving advice, interpreting, or persuading should be avoided.

In addition, nonverbal messages should be consistent with the verbal paraphrasing and convey interest, openness, and attentiveness to the opposition's ideas and feelings. Above all, role reversal should be the expression of a sincere interest in understanding the other person's feelings, ideas, and position.

Role reversal can result in a reevaluation and a change of attitude concerning the issue by both parties, for the group members involved are apt to be perceived as people who are understanding, willing to compromise, cooperative, and trustworthy. The approach has also been found to increase cooperative behavior between role reversers, to clarify misunderstandings, to change win-lose situations into problem-solving situations, and, most important, to allow the issue to be perceived from the opponent's frame of reference.

Empathy

A closely related technique to role reversal is the expression of empathy. Empathy involves putting yourself in the shoes of the person you are in conflict with and expressing your understanding of what the person is thinking and saying. Here are some phrases that help you get started:

"What you seem to be saying is . . ."
"I take it that you think . . ."
"I sense you feel ______ about this issue."

When expressing empathy, it is essential to mirror what was said in a nonjudgmental way and to grasp the essence of what the other person is thinking or feeling.

Similar to role reversal, the use of empathy facilitates open communication, assists in clarifying misunderstandings, increases cooperative behavior, and facilitates the process of no-lose problem solving.

Inquiry

If you are in conflict with someone and are confused about their thoughts and feelings, the inquiry technique is often useful. This technique involves using gentle, probing questions to learn more about what the other person is thinking and feeling. Tone of voice is crucial in this technique; asking a question sarcastically or defensively is apt to result in defensive responses.

I-Messages

Most of us are raised to respond to conflict with "you-messages." There are two types of you-messages: a *solution* message and a *put-down* message. A solution message orders, directs, commands, warns, threatens, preaches, moralizes, or advises. A put-down message blames, judges, criticizes, ridicules, or name-calls. Examples of you-messages include "You stop that," "Don't do that," "I hate you," and "You should know better." You-messages tend to inhibit open communication.

You-messages are generally counterproductive because people do not like to be ordered or criticized. You-messages frequently result in an ongoing struggle between the two people involved.

In contrast, I-messages foster open communication. They are nonblaming messages that communicate how the sender of the message believes the receiver is affecting the sender. I-messages do not provide solutions, and they do not criticize. It is possible to send an I-message without using the word *I*.

I-messages communicate much more honestly the effect of behavior, and they help the other person to assume responsibility for their behavior. An I-message conveys to the person you are in conflict with that you trust them to respect your needs and to handle the conflict constructively. I-messages are much less likely to provoke an argument. They facilitate honesty, openness, and more cordial relationships. (I-messages and you-messages are described in Module 9.)

Disarming

When you are in conflict with someone, the disarming technique is an effective way to move toward resolution. This technique involves finding some truth in what the other person (or side) is saying and then expressing this "agreement"—even if you feel that what the other person is saying is largely wrong, unreasonable, irrational, or unfair. There is always a grain of truth in what they are saying, even if it sounds obnoxious and insulting. When you disarm the other side with this technique, they will recognize that you respect them. As a result, they won't feel so dogmatic and will have less of an urge to insist that they are right and you are wrong. They are then apt to be more willing to examine the merits of your point of view. If you want respect, you have to give respect first. If you want to be listened to, this technique helps you listen to the other person first and avoids defensive communication. Friendly responses facilitate more open communication; hostile responses usually result in defensive communication.

In using the disarming technique, it is important that you be genuine in what you say, and express your agreement in a sincere way.

Stroking

Stroking is closely related to disarming. In this technique you say something genuinely positive to the person (or side) you are in conflict with, even in the heat of battle. Stroking tells the other side that you respect them, even though you may be angry with each other. During an argument or conflict, we have a tendency to reject the other person before we get rejected (so we can save face). Often we overreact, and differences of opinion blow out of proportion. To prevent this, let the other side know that although you are at odds you still think highly of them. This makes it easier for them to open up and to listen, as they feel less threatened.

Mediation

In the past several decades, mediation has increasingly been used to resolve conflicts. Mediation involves the intervention of an acceptable, impartial, and neutral, third party who has no decision-making power to assist contending parties in voluntarily reaching their own mutually acceptable settlement of issues in dispute. Mediation leaves decision-making power in the hands of the people in conflict. It is a voluntary process in that the participants must be willing to accept the assistance of the intervenor if the dispute is to be resolved. Mediation is usually initiated when the partners no longer believe they can handle the conflict on their own and when the only means of resolution appears to involve impartial third-party assistance. (Mediation is described more fully in Module 9.)

What If These Strategies Don't Work?

If used appropriately, these strategies will help resolve interpersonal conflicts in the vast majority of cases. When these strategies fail, you can probably correctly conclude that the person you are in conflict with does not want to resolve the conflict. Perhaps, for reasons beyond your control, they are very hostile and they want to generate conflicts to meet personal needs. Or, perhaps they really want to make your life uncomfortable!

What can you do when you realize that the other person really wants to sustain the conflict? Using the law of requisite variety is one option. This law states that if you continue to come up with creative new ways of responding to the daggers being thrown at you, that eventually the other person will tire of the turmoil and will finally decide to "bury the hatchet." Here is an example:

Janice and Pete Palmer were married about a year ago. Unknown to Janice, Pete was having lunch about once a month with a former partner (Paula) that he dated over a three-year period. Seven months ago Janice walked into a restaurant at noon and saw her husband with Paula. In a fit of rage, Janice stomped out. That evening she and Pete had a major blow up. Pete claimed Paula was just a friend, and that nothing romantic was occurring. Janice yelled and screamed. Pete indicated he would stop having lunch with Paula. But he didn't keep his promise. About once a month he continued to see Paula, and when Janice found out, they again had a major argument. Janice suggested a number of resolution options, including marriage counseling. Pete refused to go to counseling and also indicated (the win-lose approach) that he was going to continue having lunch with Paula. Then one day Janice ran into one or her former partners—Dave. Dave invited Janice for lunch or dinner. A light bulb went on for Janice—she accepted the invitation. Later she gleefully told Pete (Pete knew Dave had dated Janice in the past). Pete became jealous and tried to talk Janice out of the dinner. Janice of course said "No way." This threw Pete into fits of anguish. When Janice came home, Pete politely said he had called Paula that evening to inform her he was canceling their next scheduled lunch, and that he felt it was best that they no longer meet for lunch. Pete then asked Janice if she also would no longer get together with Dave—she indicated "Yes." Through this experience, Pete and Janice learned to respect and appreciate each other to a greater extent.

Handling Disruptive Behavior

There may be hostile or disruptive members in any group, even in groups whose members come voluntarily. However, they are more likely to be found in involuntary groups. Involuntary members often (at least at the initial meetings of the group) wish they were a thousand other places rather than in the group. They are often angry because they are forced to come and may believe that the group will be a "complete waste of time."

Social workers encounter involuntary clients in various settings: corrections, protective services, mental health facilities, certain public school settings, group homes, residential treatment facilities, nursing homes, and hospitals. In such settings, groups are often established that unwilling clients are required to attend and social workers are expected to lead. Disruptive behavior includes being aggressive, competing, fooling around, sympathy seeking, and failing to finish tasks on time. To more vividly describe these disruptive behaviors, we will ascribe "personalities" to the behaviors.

Bears openly express anger, rage, frustration, resentment, and hostility, They are unhappy as a member of the group or with what is happening in the group. They express discontent in a variety of ways: verbally, by attacking other members; nonverbally, by facial expressions; or physically, by aggressively pushing and shoving another member.

Bears who directly express unhappiness in an active fashion can also express unhappiness in passive-aggressive ways through indirect aggression. Bach and Wyden (1981) have called indirect aggression "crazy-making." Indirect aggressors maintain a front of kindness but find subtle, indirect ways to express their anger, rage, or frustrations. Bach and Wyden label direct aggression "clean fighting" because feelings are expressed openly and can be identified and resolved. "Dirty fighters" use indirect tricks and never clearly express their feelings, which often causes a great deal of pain and can destroy effective communication. Most disruptive behaviors involve an element of indirect aggression.

If you have a relationship with a "dirty fighter," he or she will identify what will "press your buttons." Dirty fighters will casually and subtly press these buttons to get you going.

Eager beavers volunteer to do crucial tasks but have little intention of completing them; they seduce other members into believing they are willing contributors. They may partially perform some of the tasks to show good faith but then will employ a variety of excuses to explain why the tasks can't be completed on time.

Clowns are disrupters who are rarely serious. They are always joking and clowning around, even when other members want to be serious. A clown inhibits other members from expressing their thoughts and feelings because they fear they will be ridiculed.

Psychoanalyzers continually analyze what other members do and say. They often use psychological terms and delight in analyzing what others really mean and what's wrong with them. The psychoanalyzer often slows a group by getting members to engage in mind-reading rather than task completion. Other members are inhibited from expressing their thoughts and feelings; they don't want to be analyzed.

Withholders have important information or resources that would help the group accomplish its task, but they intentionally withhold assistance. They are more interested in watching the group struggle and spin its wheels.

Beltliners are dirty fighters. Everyone has a psychological "beltline" under which lie subjects that we are extremely sensitive about. Beltline items include physical characteristics, intelligence, past behavior, past unhappy events, or personality characteristics. An overweight person, for example, may be highly sensitive about comments related to obesity. Beltliners make subtle negative comments about sensitive areas to threaten group cohesion and morale.

Guiltmakers attempt to control others by making them feel guilty. They trap the group into helping them with personal needs and goals, rather than working toward group goals. Guiltmakers use common expressions such as, "You never do anything for me" and "All I've done for you and this is the thanks I get," to trigger the guilt response.

Catastrophe criers, by exaggerating the seriousness of a problem, would have group members believe that consequences will be not minor but disastrous. Since "catastrophiers" focus only on examining the severity of the problem and not on developing and implementing problem-solving approaches, they exacerbate problems.

Subject changers do not want the group to deal with crucial issues or with controversy and conflict. When difficult situations arise, they change the subject. They prevent the group from dealing with crucial topics. There are a variety of reasons for seeking to change a subject; for example, changers may detest heated debates or may fear the debate will reveal something they wish to keep hidden.

Whiners continually complain about one thing or another without taking action to resolve the problem. Because they seek attention and sympathy, they slow group progress.

If a group is competing with another group, a betrayer, or **Benedict Arnold,** supplies confidential information to the other group. They encourage people outside the group to ridicule or disregard it or slyly have the group's funding cut back. Inside the group Benedict Arnolds attempt to prevent the group from accomplishing its goals.

Instead of honestly sharing concerns, frustrations, and discontent, **trivial tyrannizers** annoy the group with constant interruptions and digressions. They arrive late and leave early, fail to show up for crucial meetings, or bring up concerns the group has already acted on. Besides raising unnecessary questions about the wording of the minutes, for instance, trivial tyrannizers may yawn or read something when other members are speaking.

Shirkers are disruptive simply by failing to do anything for the group. When assigned certain tasks, shirkers will evade these responsibilities by using a variety of excuses.

Power grabbers attempt to become the group leader or the power behind the leader by convincing other members that they have more expertise than anyone else in the group or by buying the support of others with money, favors, or promises. Power grabbers create conflicts that make the leader look bad, and sabotage the efforts of the leader, even though they may not assume leadership power.

Because **paranoiacs** are excessively or irrationally suspicious and distrustful of others in the group, they always feel picked on. Much of their time is spent defending themselves and finding fault with other members. Paranoiac individuals often feel that other members must be discredited before they can amass enough evidence to discredit the paranoiacs.

Note that disrupters are often intentionally aware of the effects of their behavior. Most of the above examples are of this type. However, some disrupters act out of unconscious personal needs and may not be aware that their behavior is disruptive. The following suggestions for handling disruptive behavior apply whether disrupters are aware or unaware of the effects of their behavior.

There are three main ways leaders can handle hostile and disruptive behavior. The approach you choose should be based on your judgment as to which will be most helpful to the group.

1. *Allow the member to continue to express the disruptive behavior.* Such expression has a vent effect, so the member may become less disruptive as time goes on. It is often helpful to tactfully ask disruptive members to express their concerns.

Tactfully asking the member probing questions about his concerns, and modeling good listening skills while reflecting their feelings often helps defuse a disruptive situation. In certain instances there may be benefit in using a role reversal: Ask the disrupter to argue the alternate point of view while you take the disrupter's position. Whenever possible, disruption should be dealt with as a group issue, and the group may, in fact, decide to deal with at least some of the disrupter's concerns, especially those that are legitimate. Through resolution of some of these concerns, the disruptive member may become less unhappy and begin to see that the group has some payoffs.

2. *Assertively confront the member* about how their behavior is disrupting the group. This confrontation can take place with other group members present or leaders can meet privately with the person. (When confronting a disruptive member, it is helpful to seek to use one or more of the conflict resolution strategies described in the previous section.) Whether you confront

privately or publicly should be based on your judgment of which will be most beneficial. If other members are present, they may be able to help by elaborating on the ways in which the behavior is disruptive. Also, having others present emphasizes the seriousness of the problem. A disadvantage of confrontation when others are present is that hostile members may feel ganged up on and may be more inhibited in fully expressing what they are unhappy about. In some instances, simply indicating to the member in private that you are concerned about their behavior and are considering opening it up as a matter of discussion for the entire group will help them reconsider whether the disruptions are accomplishing the desired purpose.

3. *Have other members do the confronting.* Certain situations are best handled by someone other than the leader. Another member may have better rapport with the person, and the disruptive member may be more responsive if the confrontation comes from the neutral member.

Any of these approaches may prove fruitful. It is important to realize that conflict and differences in opinion are not uncommon or unnatural in groups, and may, in fact, be healthy.

Group Size

The size of a group affects members' satisfactions, interactions, and output. Smaller groups often rate more favorable in these aspects (Hare, 1962). Larger groups tend to create more stress, have more communication difficulties, and although successful in some tasks because of the greater number of skills available, are generally less efficient or productive. In larger groups each person has less opportunity to talk, and some people feel inhibited and reluctant to talk. In discussion groups it has been shown that as the size of the group increases, the most frequent contributor assumes an increasingly prominent role in the discussion. The bigger the group, the greater the gap in participation between the most frequent contributor and other members of a group.

Slater (1958) found in one classic study that groups of five persons were considered most satisfactory by members. Observations of the interactions of groups smaller than five indicated the members were inhibited from expressing their ideas through fear of alienating one another and thereby destroying the group. Above the size of five, members felt restrictions on participating.

Groups of two tend to avoid expressing disagreement and antagonism. This size also has high tension levels because each member is "on the spot," as each is forced to react to what the other says. In disputes deadlock often arises because there is no majority and the group then breaks up.

Groups of even size tend to have higher rates of disagreement and antagonism than odd-size groups; the "group of two" dynamic is apparently at work here.

Groups of three have majority-over-minority problems; that is, a two-to-one split leaves the minority feeling isolated.

To sum up, for any given task there is an optimal group size. The more complex the task, the larger the optimal size to ensure the greater number of needed abilities and skills.

Starting, Leading, and Ending Therapy Groups[2]

Extensive preparation is needed for leading therapeutic groups. Leaders should have considerable training in (1) assessing human behavior and human problems; (2) comprehensive therapeutic intervention approaches—such as reality therapy, behavior therapy, rational therapy, transactional analysis, and client-centered therapy (see Modules 3–6); (3) specialized therapeutic intervention techniques—such as assertiveness training and relaxation techniques (see Modules 4 and 9); (4) interviewing and counseling; and (5) principles of group dynamics—such as cohesion, task roles, social/emotional roles, and effects of authoritarian versus democratic styles of leadership. Baccalaureate and master's programs in social work generally provide considerable material on these areas. For any therapy group, leaders also need to study the literature on the causes of the problems that members are experiencing, the most effective intervention strategies, the prognosis for positive changes, and expectations as to the length of time intervention strategies need to be applied to induce positive changes.

In this section I summarize a number of guidelines for starting, leading, and ending therapy groups. Chapter 6 covered substantial material on preparation and

[2]Material in this section is adapted from Charles Zastrow, "Starting and Leading Therapy Groups: A Beginner's Guide," *Journal of Independent Social Work, 4,* no. 4, 1990, pp. 7–26. Adapted by permission of the Haworth Press.

homework, relaxing before starting a session, cues on entering the meeting room, seating arrangements, introductions, and clarifying roles. This material is directly applicable to therapy and will not be repeated here. (Students studying how to lead therapy groups should review this material.) In this section we focus on building rapport, exploring problems in depth, exploring alternative solutions, ending a session, and ending a group.

Building Rapport

In group therapy, as in individual therapy, there are two types of members: voluntary and involuntary. In voluntary groups, therapists can take a more casual, less directive approach to begin with. In such groups therapists may begin by involving members in small talk. This preliminary chitchat may be about the weather, parking problems, baseball, something currently in the news, and so on. Such casual conversation lets group members get acquainted with the therapist and other members. In involuntary groups, therapists often begin by introducing themselves and making a formal statement about the purpose of the group. Then members may be asked to introduce themselves. Generally, in involuntary groups, less is left up to the members themselves because they have less motivation for being there and less commitment to the group itself.

Sometimes, with both voluntary and involuntary clients, it is helpful (after introductions) to begin a session by providing some factual information. You as group leader can do this in a brief presentation or by showing a short film or videotape. For example, if your group is comprised of involuntary clients who have been convicted of driving while intoxicated, you might show a film that vividly demonstrates that as alcohol consumption increases, reaction times slow and the chances of serious accidents occurring dramatically increase. Factual information not only provides educational material but also triggers discussion. Sometimes after factual information is presented, it is useful to involve members in an exercise related to the material.

When members are forced to attend a group they do not want to attend, as is the case with involuntary clients, you may begin by saying something like, "I know most of you really don't want to be here, and I wouldn't either if I were forced to come. I wonder if we might begin by talking about your anger and unhappiness about being here." Then you can convey the purposes of the group, what is going to happen, and how the members can satisfy the minimal requirements of "passing." Mention that each member can (1) choose to participate actively and get as much out of the group as possible, (2) remain silent and listen to what others have to say, (3) vent their anger and unhappiness in disruptive ways (which will probably anger and alienate others in the group), or (4) refuse to come, which will have certain consequences. You can then indicate that you can in no way control their behavior, so the choice is up to them. Such an approach almost always leads involuntary clients to choose either the first or second alternative, perhaps because they conclude that you understand their anger. They then focus on fulfilling the requirements of their forced attendance in the least painful way.

If the group has met previously, you may choose to begin by bringing up for discussion a topic that was not fully discussed at the last meeting. Or, if homework assignments were given out, you may begin with "Jim, at the last meeting you indicated you were going to do (such and such). How did that work out?"

Try to establish a nonthreatening group atmosphere in which members feel accepted and safe enough to communicate their troubles fully. During the initial contacts, you need to "sell" yourself (but not arrogantly) as a knowledgeable, understanding person who may be able to help and who wants to try. Your tone of voice should convey the message that you understand and care about group members' feelings. Be calm and never laugh or express shock when members begin to open up about problems. Emotional outbursts, even if subtle, will lead group members to believe that you are not going to understand or accept their difficulties, and so they will usually stop discussing them.

View group members as equals. Inexperienced therapists sometimes make the mistake of thinking that because someone is sharing intimate secrets with them, they must be very important, and end up assuming a superior position vis-à-vis their clients. If members feel that they are being treated as inferiors, they will be less motivated to reveal and discuss personal issues.

Use a "shared vocabulary" with members. This does not mean that you should use the same slang and the same accent as group members. If clients perceive you are mimicking their speech patterns, they may be seriously offended. To communicate effectively, use words that members understand and do not find offensive.

You (and other members) need to keep what members say confidential. Unfortunately, many people have nearly irresistible urges to share "juicy secrets" with someone else. If a group member discovers that confidentiality has been violated, that member's trust in the group will be quickly destroyed. It is essential that you underscore the importance of "what is said in the group, remains in the group."

Exploring Problems in Depth

In exploring a member's problems in depth, you and group members need to examine such areas as the extent of the problem, how long the problem has existed, its causes, how the member feels about the problem, and what physical and mental capacities and strengths they have to cope with the difficulty, before exploring alternative solutions.

A problem area is often multidimensional; that is, numerous problems are usually involved. Explore all of these. A good way to decide which problem to handle first is to ask members which problems they feel are most pressing. If it can be solved, start by exploring that problem in depth and develop a solution together. Success in solving one problem will increase members' confidence in you, and thereby further solidify rapport.

Convey empathy, not sympathy, and encourage group members to do so, too. Empathy is the capacity to understand and to share in another person's feelings. Sympathy also involves sharing feelings, but it results in offering pity. The difference is subtle, but empathy encourages problem solving, whereas sympathy encourages members to dwell on their problems without taking action to improve the situation. For example, if you offer sympathy to a person who is frustrated and angry about someone ending a romantic relationship with him, that person will keep telling his sad story over and over, each time having an emotional outpouring reinforced by your sympathy, without taking any action to improve the situation. Telling the story over and over only reopens old wounds and prolongs the anger and frustration.

"Trust your guts." Your most important resources are your own feelings and perceptions. Continually strive to place yourself in members' shoes, understanding that their values and pressures may be different from your own. You will probably never be 100 percent on target in your appraisal of a client's pressures, problems, and perspectives, but 70–80 percent is usually sufficient to be helpful. Empathizing is very useful in helping you determine what additional areas need to be explored, what you should say, and what the possible solutions are.

When you believe that a client has touched on an important area of concern, further communication can be encouraged in a number of ways. Show interest nonverbally (by making and continuing eye contact, leaning forward, and raising eyebrows slightly); this encourages further sharing. Allow for pauses. Inexperienced therapists usually become anxious during pauses and hasten to say something—anything—to have conversation continue. This is usually a mistake, especially when it leads to a change in the topic. Although a pause may make members anxious, it gives them time to think about what areas of concern are most important and then usually motivates them to continue conversation in that area.

Neutral probes that do not control the direction of conversation but encourage further communication are helpful. For example, "Could you tell me more about it?" "Why do you feel that way?" and "I'm not sure I understand what you have in mind" all ask for further information, but just what kind is left up to the member. Reflecting feelings—for example, "You seem angry" or "You appear to be depressed about that"—works the same way. Summarizing what a group member is saying not only shows that you are listening but also that you have received the same message they sent. An example is, "During this past hour, you made a number of critical comments about your spouse; it sounds like you're fairly unhappy about certain aspects of your marriage."

Approach socially unacceptable topics tactfully. Tact is an essential quality of a competent therapist. Try not to ask a question in a way that the answer will put the respondent in an embarrassing position.

When pointing out a member's limitation, mention and compliment him or her on any assets. When a limitation is mentioned, they will literally feel naked, like something has been taken away. Therefore, compliment them in another area to give something back.

Watch for nonverbal cues and use them to identify sensitive subjects, as clients will generally display anxiety by a changing tone of voice, fidgeting, yawning, stiff posture, or a flushed face.

Be honest. An untruth always runs the risk of being discovered. If that happens, the group member's confidence in you will be damaged and the relationship seriously jeopardized. But being honest goes beyond not telling lies. Always point out shortcomings that are in the group member's best interest to correct. For example, if a father's negative comments to his son are a factor in the son developing a negative self-concept (which is partly responsible for the son receiving failing grades at school), bring this to the father's attention.

Exploring Alternative Solutions

After a problem is explored in depth, the next step is for you and group members to consider alternative solutions. Your role is generally to begin by asking something like, "Have you thought about ways to resolve this?" The merits, shortcomings, and consequences of the alternatives thought of by the member should then be tactfully and thoroughly examined. Next, involve other members by asking them if they are aware of other alternatives that might work for this situation. Those who suggest alternatives temporarily assume a "helper" role. In such a role, the helper therapy principle is operating as a member receives psychological rewards from helping others. If you have additional viable alternatives to suggest, mention them at this time. The merits, shortcomings, and consequences of the alternatives suggested by group members and by you should then be thoroughly explored.

Group members usually have the right to self-determination; that is, to choose a course of action among possible alternatives. Your role is to help each individual clarify and understand the likely consequences of each available alternative but generally not to give advice or choose the alternative. If *you* select the alternative, there are two possible outcomes: (1) The alternative may prove undesirable for the person, in which case he or she will probably blame you for the advice and your future relationship will be seriously hampered, or (2) the alternative may prove to be desirable for the person involved. This immediate outcome is advantageous, but the danger here is that the person will then become overly dependent on you, seeking your advice for nearly every decision in the future and generally being reluctant to make decisions on his or her own.

The guideline of not giving advice does *not* mean that you should not suggest alternatives that your client hasn't considered. On the contrary, it is your responsibility to suggest and explore all viable alternatives with a client. A good rule to follow is that when you believe a client should take a certain course of action phrase it as a suggestion, "Have you thought about . . . ?" rather than "I think you should . . ."

Group therapy is done *with* group members, not *to* or *for* them. Each member should have responsibility for doing many of the tasks necessary to improve a situation. A good rule to follow is that members should take responsibility for those tasks that they have the capacity to do. Doing things *for* group members, similar to giving advice, brings with it the risk of a dependent relationship. Furthermore, success leads to personal growth and better prepares clients to take on future responsibilities.

A group member's right to self-determination should be taken away only if the selected course of action has a high probability of seriously hurting the client or others. For example, if it is highly probable that a member will attempt to take his life, you must intervene (make arrangements for the member to receive inpatient psychiatric care) even if the intervention is a course of action that they object to. In most situations, however, members should have the right to select an alternative, even when you believe that another course of action is better. Frequently, clients are in a better position to know what is best for themselves, and if it doesn't turn out—well, they then get to learn from their mistake.

When members select an alternative, they should clearly understand the goals, what tasks need to be carried out, how to accomplish the tasks, and who will do them. Frequently, it is desirable to write a "contract" for future reference, with a time limit set for accomplishment of each task.

If a group member fails to meet the terms of a contract, do not criticize them or accept excuses. Excuses let people off the hook; they provide temporary relief, but they eventually lead to more failure and to a failure identity. Simply ask, "Do you still wish to try to fulfill your commitment?" If the person answers affirmatively, another time deadline acceptable to the member should be set.

Perhaps the biggest single factor in determining whether a member's situation will improve is their motivation to carry out essential tasks. Try to motivate apathetic members. One way to increase motivation is to clarify what will be gained by meeting a goal. When individuals meet commitments, reward them, verbally or in other ways. Never criticize members for failing. Criticism usually increases hostility and rarely leads to positive lasting change. It serves only as a temporary means of obtaining different behavior; when people no longer believe they are under surveillance, they usually return to their dysfunctional behavior.

If a group member lacks confidence or experience, role-play the task before they attempt it. For example, if a member wants help in telling his partner that he wants to end the relationship, role-playing the situation in the group will help him select words and an appropriate strategy. You or a group member can play his role and model an approach, letting him play his partner's role. Then, reverse the roles so that he can practice telling his partner.

Ending a Session

Ending is not easy. Ideally, you and the group members accept that the session is ending and that subjects being discussed should not be left hanging. Abrupt endings can be perceived as discourteous and rejecting.

There are some useful guidelines on how to terminate a therapy session. Preparation for ending the session should be initiated at the very beginning of the session. Members should be explicitly informed about when the session will end. Unless an unusual situation develops, assertively seek to terminate at the scheduled time.

When the allotted time is nearly up, inform members by saying something like "I see our time is just about up. Is there anything you'd like to add before we look at where we've arrived at and where we go from here?" At the end of the session, it is often helpful to summarize what was discussed. If this session focused only on exploring problems, another one should be set up for fuller exploration and to begin looking at alternatives for resolving the problems.

Give members "homework" assignments between sessions. A couple who is having trouble communicating with each other might be encouraged to set aside a certain amount of time each evening to discuss their personal thoughts with each other. At the next session this assignment is then reviewed.

Ideally, group members should be emotionally at ease when the session ends. Therefore, don't introduce emotionally charged content at the end but instead start to reduce the intensity of emotion. Just as it is sometimes advisable to begin a session with small talk, a short social conversation at the end can provide transition. If a member displays reluctance to end a session, it is sometimes helpful to confront this directly by saying, "It appears to me that you wished we had more time." The reasons for the person's reluctance can then be discussed.

At times a session can be ended by restating the way you and the group agreed to proceed. Or, you may undertake a more explicit summation of what was discussed, what decisions were arrived at, what questions remain to be resolved, and what actions will be taken.

A somewhat different approach is to ask each member to state one item that was discussed or learned from the session, and what they now plan to do. Some therapy groups end by having members state a "bad" feeling they now intend to get rid of, and then state a good feeling that will replace the bad one.

Sometimes concerns that were alluded to but not fully discussed are mentioned in closing as topics that will be taken up at the next session. Some members will reveal their most serious concerns for the first time at the end of a session, perhaps because they are ambivalent about whether they are ready to explore these concerns fully with the group. In these instances, you must make a professional judgment about whether to extend the session beyond the allotted time, to set up an appointment to discuss these concerns privately, or to wait until the next group session.

Sometimes it is helpful to end a group session by leading the group in a relaxation exercise. (Relaxation exercises are described in Module 9.) A relaxation exercise not only helps members relax but also reduces their level of stress so they can view their problems more objectively and work on resolving them after they leave.

Closing is especially important because what occurs during this last phase is likely to determine members' impressions of the session as a whole. Leave enough time for closing so the members don't feel rushed, which can create the impression that they are being "evicted."

Ending a Group

The ending phase of a group frequently offers the highest potential for powerful, important work. Group members often feel a sense of urgency as they realize there is little time left; this can lead them to reveal their most sensitive and personal concerns. Because the work remaining to be done is usually clearly identified at this point, members can focus on completing it. However, the relationship dynamics are also heightened in this phase as the members prepare to move away from each other, and the termination of the group can evoke powerful feelings.

If group members have grown emotionally close, the ending of the group will be viewed as a loss and will produce a variety of emotions. Kübler-Ross's (1969) stages of dying can also be used to describe other important losses, including the ending of a successful and cohesive group. Members may display denial (by ignoring the imminent end of the group), anger and rage, or sadness and depression. They may bargain for an extension of the group in various ways, such as urging that the group deal with additional problems. Ideally, members will vent and work through such feelings and gradually come to accept the ending of the group. (Kübler-Ross's stages are more fully described in Chapter 5.)

Other emotions may also be displayed. Some members may feel guilty because of adverse comments they made or because they believe they failed to take certain actions that would have benefited themselves or other members of the group. If a member left prematurely, some members may feel that the group let him or her down. Members may want to share their feelings about the support system they will lose when the group ends. If certain members want the group to continue, they may interpret the ending as a personal rejection. Conversely, members who feel that the group was very successful may want to have a celebration to give recognition to the successes and to say good-bye.

Concluding sessions are in many ways the most difficult. Strong emotions are often generated and should be worked through. It is painful to terminate a group when members have shared their most personal and important concerns and feelings. Our society has done little to train us to handle such separations; in fact, many of us adhere to the norm of being "strong" and not expressing feelings.

You can help members accept the ending of the group in a number of ways, and the process of terminating a group should, in fact, begin during the early stages of the group. This guideline is particularly relevant for time-limited groups. Attempt to prevent dependency between members and you. The goal is independence and better functioning; reiterate this whenever appropriate during group sessions.

Summarize the emotional reactions that people have to group endings, and an appropriate point for a discussion may occur when some members display denial, anger, guilt, bargaining, or sadness. When discussing these feelings, share your personal feelings and recollections, as the ending of the group has meaning for you as well. You, in effect, provide a model that can help members express their concerns about ending the group. Use a problem-solving approach to alleviate concerns; for example, if a member is apprehensive about future problems, suggest several other counseling resources.

The ending process should provide enough time for you and the members to sort out feelings and use the ending productively. A sudden ending cuts short necessary work and may not allow enough time to work through feelings and complete the remaining tasks. Sometimes, members indirectly express their anger by being late, appearing apathetic, being sarcastic, or battling over minor issues. In these situations, respond directly to the indirect cues by saying something like, "I wonder if your recent critical remarks are related to your anger that this group is ending? I know you have invested a lot in this group and may dislike the idea that our meetings are coming to an end." By helping members recognize and articulate their feelings, you can help them express and work through those feelings. Once such feelings are dealt with, members will be more productive during the remaining time.

At or near the end of some groups, members may test new skills and do things independently. They may report having tackled a tough problem or dealt with an issue by themselves. Acknowledge their independence and make positive remarks about the members' ability to "go it alone."

At times, you may be the person leaving the group, perhaps to take a job elsewhere. In these situations, try to create a smooth transition, and if appropriate, involve members in selecting the new leader. At times it is helpful for you and the new leader to be co-leaders for a brief period.

The ending of a group is always a transition to something else. The important element during the ending phase is to work with all members to help them develop a game plan so that the transition will enable them to work toward higher goals. The transition should not work to stifle members but to help them progress. Life is full of transitions and passages: from childhood to puberty, from school to the work world, from being single to being married, from working to retirement, and so on. In a transition phase we have the potential to control our future; the choices we make and the efforts we put forth will determine whether the transition will be constructive or destructive for us. Helping each member make productive, realistic plans for the future is a key goal of the ending phase.

During the process of terminating a group, obtain feedback on how to improve future groups by having members fill out a brief evaluation at the last (or next-to-last) session. This evaluation should be done anonymously. The following questions apply to a variety of therapy groups. For the first seven questions, use the following scale: (1) strongly disagree, (2) disagree, (3) neutral or uncertain, (4) agree, (5) strongly agree.

1. I am very satisfied with what this group accomplished.
   1 2 3 4 5
2. My personal goals in this group have been attained.
   1 2 3 4 5
3. I truly enjoyed being a member of this group.
   1 2 3 4 5
4. The therapist has done a superb job in leading the group.
   1 2 3 4 5
5. This has been one of the most rewarding groups I have participated in.
   1 2 3 4 5
6. I have grown extensively as a person through participating in this group.
   1 2 3 4 5
7. I have made substantial progress in resolving those personal problems that led me to join this group.
   1 2 3 4 5

The next three questions are open-ended.

8. The strengths of this group are . . .
9. The shortcomings of this group are . . .
10. My suggestions for changes in this group are . . .

At the final session it is also desirable for members to discuss what they got out of the group, the merits of the group, and suggestions for improving it. They should be given a chance to bring up unfinished business. In some cases an extra session may be held to complete unfinished business items.

You should refer an individual to another group or therapist, or at least discuss the case with another professional, if (1) you feel unable to empathize with that group member, (2) you have extreme personal difficulty in accepting the fact that a member is choosing alternatives (such as continuing to abuse his spouse) that you find disgusting, (3) the member's problems are of such a nature that you feel unable to provide therapeutic help, (4) a working relationship is not established with the member, or (5) the member is such a disruptive force in the group that he or she is preventing other members from constructively working on their problems. Competent therapists know that they can work with and help some people but not all, and that when the latter arises, it is in the client's and your best interests to refer the person to someone who can help.

Co-Facilitating Groups

Even though many settings do not have the resources for two leaders facilitating a single group, some programs do allow for this type of group facilitation. Also, many students in internships are given opportunities to co-facilitate groups with either their field instructor or some other professional at their agency. The co-facilitator approach has many advantages, including the following:

- Each facilitator can grow from working with, observing, and learning from the other.
- Group members can benefit from the different life experiences, insights, and perspectives of the two facilitators.
- The two facilitators can complement each other, with the group thereby benefiting.
- The two facilitators can provide valuable feedback to each other by discussing what happened in a session and how to approach a complex issue.
- The two facilitators can serve as models for the members with respect to how they relate and communicate to each other and to the group.
- If one of the leaders is female and the other is male, barriers that some members have involving gender can be effectively confronted, explored, and resolved.
- While one facilitator is working with a particular member, the other facilitator can scan the group to get a sense of how the other members are reacting.
- Co-leading offers a certain safety, especially when practitioners are leading a group for the first time. Beginning group facilitators often experience self-doubt and anxiety. Facing a group for the first time with a co-facilitator whom you respect and trust can make what initially seems a frightening task a delightful learning experience.

The major disadvantages of two facilitators leading a group occur when the facilitators fail to develop and maintain an effective working relationship. To develop a good working relationship, it is essential that they respect each other. Facilitators will have differences in leadership style and will not always agree or share the same perceptions and interpretations; this is normal and healthy. However, when there is mutual respect, they generally will be able to communicate and discuss these differences, trust each other, and work cooperatively instead of competitively. If trust and respect between the facilitators is lacking, the group is bound to sense the disharmony and be negatively affected. Power struggles between two incompatible co-facilitators can divide the group. Friction between facilitators can serve as a model for members to focus on negatives within the group and to subtly or overtly verbally hurt one another.

It is important for group facilitators to learn whom they can and cannot co-facilitate with. Even secure, competent, and experienced facilitators who respect one another don't always work effectively together. A facilitator who leads by giving suggestions aimed at providing quick answers for every problem will have trouble working with a facilitator who believes members grow by struggling and arriving at their own answers to their personal issues. If two facilitators discover that they can't work together effectively, it doesn't necessarily mean that one is right and the other wrong, or that one or both are incompetent. It simply means that their styles clash, and that each would be better off making arrangements to work with someone with a more compatible style.

It is important for co-facilitators to get together regularly (ideally shortly after the end of each session) to discuss where the group is and where it needs to go. Additional areas to discuss include how the facilitators view the group and individual members, how they feel about working with each other, and how to approach complex issues. They also need to make plans for the next session.

Legal Safeguards for Group Facilitators

Unfortunately, filing lawsuits has become a national pastime. The key way group facilitators can avoid malpractice suits (or provide a defense if one arises) is to maintain reasonable, ordinary, and prudent (wise and judicious) practices. The following are some guidelines that translate the terms *reasonable, ordinary,* and *prudent* into concrete actions.

- Screen candidates carefully for a group experience. Many potential problems can be avoided by effective screening practices. Select group members whose needs and goals are compatible with the goals of the group, who will not impede the group process, and whose well-being will not be jeopardized by the group experience.
- Adequately inform members about the group process. Entrance procedures, time parameters of the group experience, expectations of group participation, goals of the group, intervention methods that will be used, rights of members, responsibilities of members and facilitator, methods of payment (where appropriate), and termination procedures should be explained at the outset of the group.
- Obtain written parental consent for all minors who are attending a therapeutic group.
- Obtain written informed consent contracts at the outset of a group. Barker (1999) defines informed consent as:

> The granting of permission by the client to the social worker and agency or other professional person to use specific *intervention,* including diagnosis, treatment, follow-up, and research. This permission must be based on full disclosure of the facts needed to make the decision intelligently. Informed consent must be based on knowledge of the risks and alternatives. (p. 241)

- Have a clear rationale for the techniques and exercises you use in group sessions. Be prepared to concisely explain and defend the theoretical underpinnings of your techniques and exercises.
- Consult with your supervisor or an attorney on issues involving complex legal and ethical matters.
- Avoid becoming entangled in a social relationship with group participants.
- Be aware of those situations in which you legally are required to break confidentiality. (See the section on confidentiality in Chapter 2.)
- Carry malpractice insurance.
- Keep up with theoretical and research developments that apply to group therapy.
- Be knowledgeable of, and abide by, the codes of ethics for social workers. (In the United States refer to the NASW Code of Ethics (1996), and in Canada refer to the Canadian Association of Social Workers' Social Work Code of Ethics (1994).) (The NASW Code of Ethics appears at www.naswdc.org.)
- Be aware of when it is appropriate to refer a group member for another form of treatment, and also be aware when group therapy might be inadvisable.
- Instruct members in how to evaluate their progress toward their individual goals. Also, routinely assess the general progress of the group.
- Write and maintain adequate records on the needs and goals of each member and the progress (or lack thereof) made by each member in the group.
- Do not promise magical cures. Create reasonable expectations about what the group can and cannot achieve.

- Practice within the boundaries of your state and local laws.
- If you work for an agency, have a contract that specifies the agency's legal liability for your professional functioning.
- Abide by the policies of the agency that employs you. If you strongly disagree with agency policies and if they interfere with your ability to do your job, seek first to change these policies. If the policies cannot be changed, consider resigning.
- Define clearly to members what confidentiality means, why it is important, and that what the members disclose should be kept confidential—even though the members should be aware that confidentiality cannot be guaranteed as some members may intentionally or unintentionally breach confidentiality.

Summary

This chapter summarizes key group dynamic concepts and presents guidelines on how to lead therapy groups. A membership group is a group a person belongs to; a reference group is one whose influence a person is willing to accept.

Three models of group development over time were presented. The Garland, Jones, and Kolodny model hypothesizes five stages: preaffiliation, power and control, intimacy, differentiation, and separation. The Tuckman model conceptualizes groups as having the following stages: forming, storming, norming, performing, and adjourning. Bales developed a recurring-phase model in which he asserted that groups continue to seek an equilibrium between task-oriented work and emotional expressions to build better relationships among group members.

All groups have task roles and maintenance roles that need to be performed by members. Task roles are needed to accomplish the specific goals set by the group; maintenance roles strengthen the social or emotional aspects of group life.

The theory of leadership highlighted in this chapter is distributed functions. With this approach, leadership is defined as the performance of acts that help the group reach its goals and maintain itself in good working order. Leadership occurs when one member influences other members to help the group reach its goals. Because all group members at times influence other group members, each member in a group exerts leadership.

French and Raven (1968) identified the following five power bases in which group members influence each other: reward, coercive, legitimate, referent, and expert. Each power base has different effects on those being influenced.

Personal goals and group goals should be identified soon after a group is formed. The more congruent personal goals are with group goals, the more effective the group is apt to be. Conformity studies have found that a group has considerable influence on members' opinions and attitudes.

Groups are often more effective in cooperative group atmospheres than in competitive atmospheres. If handled constructively, conflict and controversy can have numerous beneficial effects on a group, including increasing creativity. The problem-solving approach is much more effective in resolving controversy than the win-lose approach. Additional strategies for resolving conflicts include role reversal, empathy, inquiry, I-messages, disarming, stroking, mediation, and the law of requisite variety. Hostile or disruptive members should generally be confronted by the leader or by other group members.

For any given task there is an optimal group size. The more complex the task, the larger the optimal size to ensure the greater number of needed abilities and skills.

This chapter concluded with guidelines on how to lead therapy groups. Aspects discussed included building rapport, exploring problems in depth, exploring alternative solutions, ending a session, and ending a group. Guidelines were also presented on how to cofacilitate therapy groups and on establishing legal safeguards for group facilitators.

EXERCISES

1. THE AUTOKINETIC EFFECT

Goal: To demonstrate that in ambiguous situations, people will usually rely on the group to help define reality.

Step 1: The instructor explains that this exercise is a study to measure students' capacities to judge how far a dot of light will move in the dark. The students sit in back of the classroom. The students need a pen and paper to record their answers. The instructor turns off all lights (the room has to have all lighting removed). The instructor places a small flashlight that will produce a dot of light in front of the room in a position where it can't move. The instructor turns the flashlight on for about 30 seconds, and then turns it off. Each student then records on a sheet of paper how far the light moved, without sharing this information with any other student. The instructor then repeats the turning on and off of the flashlight for 30 seconds for a second and third time. Each time the students record their answers as to how far the light moves. (The instructor does not let the students see that the flashlight is stationary.)

Step 2: The students form subgroups of about four, and continue to sit in back of the room. The instructor again turns the classroom lights off, and turns the flashlight on for 30 seconds and then off, for three more trials. After each time the flashlight is turned off, the subgroups discuss and record their answers about how far the light moved.

Step 3: The instructor indicates that for the final three trials the students will again have to record individually how far the dot of light has moved, without talking to each other. For the final three trials, the instructor turns the flashlight on again for 30 seconds and then off, and students record their answers.

Step 4: The instructor asks several volunteers to write their answers to the nine trials on the chalkboard. The class discusses whether the results are similar to previous studies that have found that the final three judgments tend to converge to the subgroup standard in trials four, five, and six.

Step 5: The instructor summarizes the results of conformity studies described in this chapter.

2. POWER BASES

Goals: To learn how to analyze influence efforts in terms of the bases of power identified by French and Raven (1968).

Step 1: The instructor informs the students of the purpose of this exercise. The instructor indicates that it is natural and desirable for group members to seek to influence each other. The instructor briefly describes the following five power bases: reward, coercive, legitimate, expert, and referent.

Step 2: The students form subgroups of five students each. Each subgroup has to answer the following questions.

a. What kinds of power does the instructor have in this class?
b. For each type of power that is identified, what are specific ways in which the instructor has sought to use this power?
c. How do the students feel about the instructor's use of each of these different power bases?

d. What power bases do students have in this class?

Step 3: The subgroups share with the class their answers to the four questions.

3. *TASK AND MAINTENANCE ROLES*

Goal: To identify task and maintenance roles.

Step 1: The instructor informs the students of the purpose of the exercise. The instructor describes task and maintenance roles, which are discussed in this chapter. The instructor indicates for the purposes of this exercise that the class can be assumed to be a group.

Step 2: The class forms subgroups of four or five students. The subgroups identify task functions and specific maintenance functions performed by the instructor and by students in this class.

Step 3: The subgroups share and discuss their conclusions.

4. *GROUP THERAPY IN ACTION*

Goal: To give class members an experiential awareness of being in a group therapy session.

Step 1: The instructor indicates that at the next class period a simulated group therapy session will be conducted. Each student is given the "homework" assignment of identifying one or two personal problems that a friend or relative currently has. Students are told that they should not reveal the identity of the person having the problem and that the personal problem should be that of a friend or relative (and not their own).

Step 2: At the next class period, the instructor begins by stating the following ground rules. "Today we will have a simulated group therapy session to give you an experiential awareness of being in group therapy. Because this is a class, I strongly request that you do not reveal any personal information about any dilemmas or difficulties you are experiencing. Instead, I ask you to describe one or two complicated personal dilemmas that a friend or relative is currently facing. For confidentiality reasons, please do not reveal the identity of the person whose problems you talk about. Remember, for reasons of confidentiality, what is said here, stays here. Are there any questions about what we are going to do, or about the ground rules?"

Step 3: The instructor asks students to begin sharing the concerns. If the class is reluctant, the instructor may initiate the process by asking a normally vocal student to begin. When a student is sharing, the instructor should encourage other students to probe with questions to explore the problem further and suggest realistic and creative courses of action to resolve the problem. (In group therapy sessions, each member at times takes on the role of a therapist.)

Step 4: After the dilemma revealed by one student is fully discussed and problem-solved, other students share the dilemmas they've brought. Continue until the end of the class period, or until no one has anything further to share. At the end of the exercise, the instructor asks students their thoughts about

(continued)

EXERCISES
(continued)

the benefits and shortcomings of the exercise and their suggestions for changes in the format of the exercise when it is again used.

Comment: During the exercise, one or more of the students may begin talking about a personal problem. At this point the instructor needs to make a judgment about whether to let the student continue. The instructor should not allow any students to divulge personal information that they are apt to regret later.

5. *FACILITATING AN INTERVENTION GROUP*

Goal: To develop skills at leading intervention groups.

Step 1: The instructor states the purpose of the exercise, and also indicates a component of most class sessions will be for the students to take turns in facilitating an intervention group. The instructor demonstrates an approach of how to do this. The instructor does this by sharing a personal issue that s/he is currently dealing with or has dealt with in the past. Possible topics are infinite: depression, grief management, ending a relationship, creative financing, stress management, assertiveness, resolving an interpersonal dispute, etc. The instructor then asks if anyone in the group has experienced a similar issue, and encourages volunteers to share. The instructor then asks the group for ideas (strategies) on how to seek to resolve dilemmas that have been raised. The merits and shortcomings of these strategies are then discussed. The instructor ends the exercise by summarizing important points that were made during the exercise.

Step 2: The instructor passes out a sign-up sheet where each student selects a date in class to lead the group in a similar fashion to the above example. Each student should take 15–20 minutes to lead the group. Each student is graded on a pass/fail basis by the instructor. Those students who do not "pass" at first are given additional opportunities to lead a group in later class sessions. The instructor should inform those students who have to "lead another session" of what they need to work on to improve. When students are facilitating such intervention groups it is advisable for the instructor to sit outside the circle of students, so that the students attend to the facilitator rather than to the instructor. When sitting outside the circle the instructor should evaluate the facilitator on such areas as: Facilitation strengths demonstrated, areas needing attention, and suggestions for changes. The instructor also notes to the facilitator whether s/he has "passed," or whether another session has to be led. If someone should continue to not receive a "pass" after several tries, the student and the instructor should meet privately to explore options of what to do. (Because of the importance of social work students being able to facilitate intervention groups, the instructor may choose to set the grading requirement that receiving a passing grade on this exercise is needed in order for students to receive a passing grade in the class.)

Note: During these intervention exercises, there are two ground rules that must be strictly followed:

1. Confidentiality—"What is said here stays here" and should not be revealed outside the class, and,
2. Emotional Safety—If someone begins to share and s/he feels his/her disclosure is becoming too personal, the student should say "this is becom-

ing too personal," and there should be no group pressure for that person to say more.

6. *RESOLVING INTERPERSONAL CONFLICTS*

Goal: To understand conflict resolution strategies and to become more skillful in resolving future interpersonal conflicts.

Step 1: Students write down on a sheet of paper a summary of a recent interpersonal conflict that they had—perhaps involving a friend, a relative, another student, or a faculty member. The summary should include who the conflict was with, what was at issue, and how it was resolved. (If the issue has not been resolved, the summary should contain a description of the current status of the conflict.)

Step 2: The instructor describes the following conflict resolution strategies: the win-lose approach, the problem-solving approach, role reversal, empathy, inquiry, being assertive, I-messages, disarming, stroking, mediation, and the law of requisite variety. (These strategies should be written on the chalkboard so students can refer to them later.)

Step 3: The class form groups of three students each. The subgroups share with each other the nature of the interpersonal conflict that they wrote on a sheet of paper. (Students have a right not to reveal what they wrote.) For each conflict that is shared in the subgroup, the students explore whether *needs* or *solutions* of the people involved in the conflict were primarily at issue. The subgroups identify whether any of these strategies were used (or would have been helpful to use) in resolving the conflict: the problem-solving approach, role reversal, empathy, inquiry, being assertive, I-messages, disarming, stroking, mediation, and the law of requisite variety.

Step 4: When the class re-forms, students have an opportunity to ask questions about conflict resolution. Some students may want to share a complicated unresolved conflict situation they are now experiencing to obtain feedback on how it may be effectively resolved.

CHAPTER 8

Social Work with Families

The focus of social work services is often the family, an interacting, interdependent system. The problems faced by people are usually influenced by the dynamics within the family, and dynamics within the family are, in turn, influenced by the wider social and cultural environment. Because a family is an interacting system, change in any member will affect all others. Tensions between a husband and wife, for example, will be felt by their children, who may then respond with disturbed behavior. Treating the children's behavior alone will not get to the root of the family problem (Compton & Galaway, 1999).

Another reason for the focus on the family rather than the individual is that other family members are often needed in the treatment process. They can help identify family patterns. In addition, the whole family, once members perceive the relationships among their various behaviors, can form a powerful team in reestablishing healthier patterns (Wells, 1998). For example, family members can pressure their alcoholic mother to acknowledge her problem. They may provide important emotional support for her efforts to stop drinking. They may also need counseling themselves (or support from a self-help group) to assist in coping with them when he or she is drinking.

Diversity of Family Forms

The family is a social institution that is found in every culture, and has been defined by Coleman and Cressey (1995, p. 124) as "a group of people related by marriage, ancestry, or adoption who live together in a common household." This definition does not cover a number of living arrangements whose members consider themselves a family, such as:

- A husband and wife raising two foster children who have been in the household for several years
- Two women, lesbians in a loving relationship, raising children born to one of the partners while in a heterosexual marriage that ended in divorce
- Grandparents raising grandchildren due to illness or addiction of the parents
- Where one spouse lives away from home—perhaps because of military service in a foreign country or because of incarceration
- Where one child who has a severe and profound cognitive disability lives in a residential treatment facility
- A man and a woman who have been living together for years in a loving relationship but who have never legally married

A wide diversity of family patterns exists in the world (see the case example on page 176). Families in different cultures take a variety of forms. In some societies, husband and wife live in separate buildings. In others, they live apart for several years after the birth of a child. In some societies, husbands are permitted to have more than one wife. In a few countries, wives are allowed to have more than one husband. Some cultures permit (and a few encourage) premarital and extramarital intercourse.

Some societies have large communes where adults and children live together. There are communes in which the children are raised separately from adults. In some cultures, surrogate parents (rather than the natural parents) raise the children. Some societies encourage certain types of homosexual relationships, and a few recognize homosexual as well as heterosexual marriages.

In many cultures, marriages are still arranged by the parents. In a few societies, an infant may be "married" before birth (if the baby is of the wrong sex, the marriage is dissolved). Some societies do not recognize romantic love. Some cultures expect older men to marry young girls. Others expect older women to marry young boys. Most societies prohibit the marriage of close relatives, but a few subcultures encourage marriage between brothers and sisters or between first cousins. Some expect a man to marry his father's brother's daughter, whereas others insist that he marry his mother's sister's daughter. In some societies, a man, on marrying, makes a substantial gift to the bride's father, whereas in others the bride's father gives a substantial gift to the new husband.

These are indeed substantial variations in family patterns. People in each of these societies feel strongly that their particular pattern is normal and proper, and many feel the pattern is divinely ordained. Suggested changes in their particular form are viewed with suspicion and defensiveness and are often sharply criticized as being unnatural, immoral, and a threat to the survival of the family.

In spite of these variations, sociologists note that most family systems can be classified into two basic forms: the extended family and the nuclear family. An *extended family* consists of a number of relatives living together, such as parents, children, grandparents, great-grandparents, aunts, uncles, in-laws, and cousins. The extended family is the predominant pattern in preindustrial societies. The members divide various agricultural, domestic, and other duties among themselves.

A *nuclear family* consists of a married couple and their children living together. The nuclear family type emerged from the extended family. Extended families tend to be more functional in agricultural societies where many "hands" are needed; the nuclear family is more suited to the demands of complex, industrialized societies, as its smaller size and potential geographic mobility enable it to adapt more easily to changing conditions—such as the need to relocate to obtain a better job.

Although the nuclear family is still the predominant family form in the United States, Canada, and many other industrialized countries, it is a serious mistake for social workers and other helping professionals to use the nuclear family as the ideal model that individuals in our society should strive to form. Many other family forms are functioning in our society, such as:

- A married couple without children who are the primary caregivers for the wife's mother, who has Alzheimer's disease and who resides with the couple
- Two gay men in a committed relationship, each of whom has joint custody of two children with his former wife
- A childless married couple who have decided not to conceive children
- A single parent with three young children
- A blended family in which the husband and wife have children in the current marriage, plus children from earlier marriages, all of whom live in the household
- An unmarried young couple living together in what amounts to a trial marriage

In the past few decades there has been a trend in the United States for greater diversity in marital arrangements and family forms. There are increasing numbers of transracial marriages, marriages between spouses of diverse ages and cultural backgrounds, transracial adoptions, single-parent families, and blended families. Although some social workers may personally judge a few of these types to be "wrong," it is essential that they not allow their personal beliefs to reduce the quality or quantity of professional services that are provided to these family units. It is also essential that social workers who work with families of diverse cultural backgrounds learn about those backgrounds and understand the customary norms for family functioning.

Some family forms have been discriminated against, such as a single-parent household, and a gay or lesbian couple with children. Recognizing this discrimination, the Council on Social Work in Educational Policy and Accreditation Standards (2001) identified "family structure" as a population-at-risk,

CASE EXAMPLE

Sex-Role Expectations Are Culturally Determined

In the classic study *Sex and Temperament in Three Primitive Societies,* Margaret Mead (1935) demonstrated that sex-role expectations are culturally rather than biologically determined. The study further showed that family socialization patterns are immensely influenced by the larger culture. The study was conducted with three tribes in New Guinea in the early 1930s. Mead found that many characteristics that Americans classify as typically feminine or masculine are classified differently in these tribes.

Both sexes among the Arapesh would seem feminine to us. Both men and women are gentle, nurturant, and compliant. The personalities of males and females in this society are not sharply differentiated by sex. Both girls and boys learn to be unaggressive, cooperative, and responsive to the needs and wants of others. Relations between husband and wife parallel the traditional mother-child relations in our society, with the Arapesh husband often seeing his role as providing training to his much younger wife.

In contrast, among the Mundugamors, both sexes would seem masculine to us. Both are headhunters and cannibals, are nonnurturant and aggressive, and actively initiate sexual involvement.

The most interesting society studied was the Tchambuli. This society virtually reverses our traditional sex-role expectations and stereotypes. The men spend much more time than the women in grooming and decorating themselves. Also, the men spend much of their time painting, carving, and practicing dance steps. In contrast, the women are efficient, impersonal, unadorned, managerial, and brisk. The women are the traders and have most of the economic power.

and thereby a group that social workers are obligated to work with to end discrimination.

Societal Functions of Families

Families in modern industrial societies perform the following essential functions that help maintain the continuity and stability of society:

1. *Replacement of the population.* Every society has some system for replacing its members. Practically all societies consider the family as the unit in which children are to be produced. Societies define the rights and responsibilities of the reproductive partners within the family unit. These rights and responsibilities help maintain the stability of society, although they are defined differently from one society to another.

2. *Care of the young.* Children require care and protection until at least the age of puberty. The family is a primary institution for the rearing of children. Modern societies have generally developed supportive institutions to help in caring for the young—for example, medical services, day-care centers, parent training programs, and residential treatment centers.

3. *Socialization of new members.* To become productive members of society, children have to be socialized into the culture. Children are expected to acquire a language, learn social values and mores, and dress and behave within the norms of society. The family plays a major role in this socialization process. In modern societies, a number of other groups and resources are involved in this socialization process. Schools, the mass media, peer groups, the police, movies, and books and other written material are important influences. (Sometimes these different influences clash by advocating opposing values and attitudes.)

4. *Regulation of sexual behavior.* Failure to regulate sexual behavior results in clashes between individuals due to jealousy and exploitation. Every society has rules that regulate sexual behavior within family units. Most societies, for example, have incest taboos, and most disapprove of extramarital sex.

5. *Source of affection.* Humans need affection, emotional support, and positive recognition from others (including approval, smiles, encouragement, and reinforcement for accomplishments). Without such affection and recognition, our emotional, intellectual, physical, and social growth would be stunted. The family is an important source for obtaining affection and recognition, because family members generally regard

EXHIBIT 8.1

A sampling of family problems

Divorce	Unemployment of wage earners
Alcohol or drug abuse	Money management difficulties
Unwanted pregnancy	Injury from serious automobile accident involving one or more members
Bankruptcy	A child with a severe cognitive disability
Poverty	Incarceration or institutionalization of one or more members
Terminal illness	Compulsive gambling by one or more members
Chronic illness	Victim of a crime
Death	Forced retirement of a wage earner
Desertion	Caregiver for an elderly relative
"Empty-shell" marriage	Involvement of a child in delinquent and criminal activities
Emotional problems of one or more members	Illness of a member who acquires AIDS
Behavioral problems of one or more members	A runaway teenager
Child abuse	Sexual dysfunctions of one or more members
Child neglect	Infidelity
Sexual abuse	Infertility
Spouse abuse	
Elder abuse	

each other as among the most important people in their lives and gain emotional and social satisfaction from family relationships.

Family Problems and the Nature of Social Work

An infinite number of problems occurs in families. Exhibit 8.1 lists a few of them.

When problems arise in a family, social services are often needed. The types and forms of services that social workers provide to troubled families are extremely varied. We can group them into two major categories: in-home services and out-of-home services.

In-home services are preventive. Although not all are offered literally within the home itself, they are specifically designed to help families stay together. They include financial aid; protective services (services to safeguard children or frail older adults from abuse and neglect); family preservation services (intensive crisis intervention within the home setting where children are so seriously at risk that removal to foster care would otherwise be required); family therapy (intensive counseling to improve family relationships); day-care (caretaking services for children or older adults to provide respite for caregivers who might otherwise be overwhelmed, or to permit them to work outside the home); homemaker services (for the same purpose); and family life education (classes, often offered at traditional family service agencies, that cover such topics as child development, parenting skills, communication issues, etc.). Obviously, not all of these services can be provided by social workers, but workers must know where to find them and how to help the family obtain them when needed (Suppes & Wells, 2000).

Out-of-home services, on the other hand, are those services that must be operationalized when the family can no longer remain intact. They are a manifestation that something has gone seriously wrong, since the breakup of any family amounts to a tragedy that will have ramifications beyond family boundaries. While family members usually receive the blame, the larger system (social environment, and the level of support it provides to troubled families) may be called into question. Out-of-home services include foster care, adoption, group homes, institutional care (for example, residential treatment centers), and the judicial system (which provides a different kind of institutional care, prison or jail, for family members who have run into difficulty with the law).

To perform these services, social workers engage in a variety of roles (for example, broker, educator, advocate, supporter, mediator). The following examples illustrate many common services and important roles.

- Mark Schwanke, age 32, has AIDS. Ms. Seely, a social worker with the AIDS Support Network in the community, serves as a case manager in providing a variety of services to Mark, his wife (who is HIV-positive), and their two children. These services include medical information and care, housing, counseling, emotional support services, and financial assistance. Because of frequent discrimination against persons with AIDS and persons with the AIDS virus, Ms. Seely often must advocate on the family's behalf to ensure that they receive the services they need.
- Beth Roessler, age 15, has been convicted of committing six burglaries. Steve Padek, a juvenile probation officer and social worker, is her juvenile probation officer. Mr. Padek provides the following services to Beth and her mother, who is divorced: He holds weekly supervision meetings with Beth to monitor her school performance and leisure activities, links Beth's mother with a Parents Without Partners group, and conducts several counseling sessions with Beth and her mother to mediate conflicts in their relationship.
- The aunt of Amy Sund, a 3-year-old child, has contacted Protective Services about Amy's mother (Pat) and her lover's physical abuse of Amy. Investigators confirm the abuse; Amy has bruises and rope burns on her body. Instead of referring the case to court, Protective Services refers the case to Family Preservation for services. Maria Gomez, social worker at Family Preservation, meets with Pat Sund and Amy a total of 37 times over the next 90 days. Pat Sund terminates her relationship with her abusive lover, is accepted into a financial assistance program through the Social Services Department for a two-year period, and enrolls in a job training program. Ms. Gomez arranges for child care for Amy when Ms. Sund is attending the job training program. Ms. Gomez also arranges for a temporary housekeeper who provides training in cleaning the apartment and in making meals. Ms. Gomez encourages Ms. Sund to join the local chapter of Parents Anonymous, which she does. (Parents Anonymous is described in Chapter 6.) Had family preservation services been unavailable or unsuccessful, Amy would have had to be placed in a foster home.
- Cindy Rogerson, age 27, has three young children. She is badly battered by her husband and contacts the House of Hope, a shelter for battered women and their children. Sue Frank, a social worker at the shelter, makes arrangements for shelter for Mrs. Rogerson and her children. The oldest child is attending school, so Ms. Frank arranges for him to continue attending school. Ms. Frank at the shelter provides one-to-one counseling to Mrs. Rogerson to help her explore her options and to inform her of potential resources that she may not be aware of. Ms. Frank also leads groups at the shelter for residents and nonresidents, which Mrs. Rogerson is required to attend while at the shelter. After 2½ weeks, Mrs. Rogerson decides she wants to return to her husband. Ms. Frank convinces Mrs. Rogerson to give her husband an ultimatum prior to returning—he must receive family counseling together with her from the Family Service agency in the community and must attend a group for batterers in the community. Mrs. Rogerson reluctantly agrees. Mrs. Rogerson, at the urging of Ms. Frank, only then returns to live with her husband, with the understanding that she will leave immediately if he hits her again or if he drops out of either family counseling or the group for batterers.
- Katy Hynek, age 76, has Alzheimer's disease. She has been living alone in her house since her husband died three years ago. Her physician contacts Adult Services of the Department of Social Services and requests that an assessment of living arrangements be conducted. Linda Sutton, social worker, does an assessment and determines that Katy Hynek can no longer live alone. Katy's son Mark and his wife Annette agree to have Katy move in with them. During the next 19 months, Ms. Sutton has periodic contact with the Hyneks. As is common with this disease, Katy Hynek's physical and mental condition continue to deteriorate. Ms. Sutton listens to Mark and Annette's concerns and seeks to answer their questions about the disease. She also provides suggestions to help them cope with the changes in Katy's condition. As Katy's condition deteriorates, Ms. Sutton makes arrangements for Katy to attend an adult day-care center during the daytime, partly for respite care for Mark and Annette. At the end of 19 months, Mark and Annette request a meeting with Ms. Sutton to discuss the possibility of placing Katy in a nursing home as her condition has so deteriorated that she now needs 24-hour care. (For example, she gets up in the middle of the night and gets lost in closets; she is also now incontinent.) The pros and cons of placing Katy in a nursing home are identified and discussed. Making the decision is exceedingly emotional and agonizing for Mark and Annette. With a

careful discussion of the entire situation with Ms. Sutton, Mark and Annette decide they have no choice but to seek a nursing home placement. Ms. Sutton gives them the names of three nursing homes, which they visit, and then proceed to select one.

Family Assessment

The two areas in family social work practice that have received the most attention are family assessment and family therapy. In this section we focus on family assessment.

There are a variety of ways to assess families. Conducting a social history of a family and its members is a widely used approach (see Chapter 4). With regard to family assessment, however, two techniques have received considerable discussion in recent years: eco-maps and genograms.

The Eco-Map

The eco-map (Figure 8.1) is a paper-and-pencil assessment tool used to assess specific troubles and plan interventions for clients. The eco-map, a drawing of the client family in its social environment, is usually drawn jointly by the social worker and the client. It helps both parties achieve a holistic or ecological view of the client's family life and the nature of the family's relationships with groups, associations, organizations, and other families and individuals. The eco-map has been used in a variety of situations, including marriage and family counseling and adoption and foster-care home studies. It has also been used to supplement traditional social histories and case records. The eco-map is a shorthand method for recording basic social information. The technique helps clients and workers gain insight into the clients' problems by providing a "snapshot view" of important interactions at a particular point in time. Ann Hartman (1978) is the primary developer of this tool.

A typical eco-map consists of a family diagram surrounded by a set of circles and lines used to describe the family within an environmental context. Eco-map users can create their own abbreviations and symbols, but the most commonly used symbols are shown in Figure 8.1.

First, a circle (representing the client's family) is drawn in the center of a large blank sheet of paper (see Figure 8.2). The composition of the family is indicated in the circle. Other circles are then drawn around the

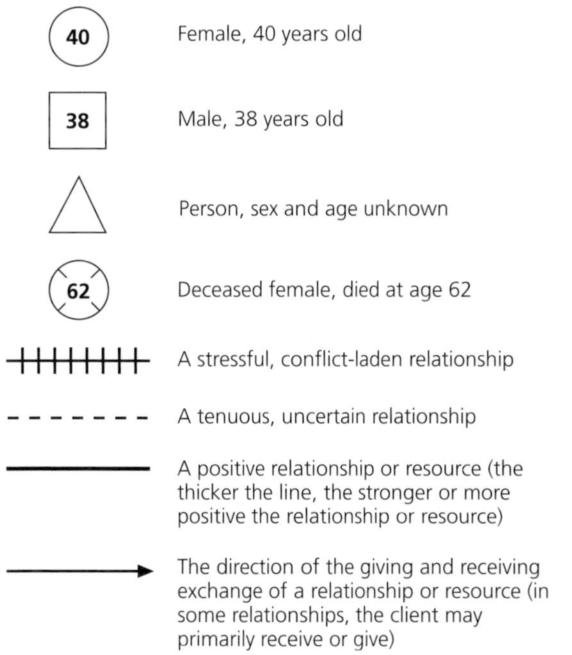
40
Female, 40 years old
38
Male, 38 years old
Person, sex and age unknown
62
Deceased female, died at age 62
A stressful, conflict-laden relationship
A tenuous, uncertain relationship
A positive relationship or resource (the thicker the line, the stronger or more positive the relationship or resource)
The direction of the giving and receiving exchange of a relationship or resource (in some relationships, the client may primarily receive or give)

FIGURE 8.1 Commonly used symbols in an eco-map

family circle. These circles represent other systems—that is, the groups, other families, individuals, and organizations—with which the family ordinarily interacts.

Lines are drawn to describe the relationships that members of the client family have with these systems. Arrows show the flow of energy (giving or receiving resources, and communication between family members and significant systems). Figure 8.3 on page 183 shows the eco-map for the Wilbur family case example.

A major value of an eco-map is that it helps both worker and client view the client's family from a systems and ecological perspective. Sometimes, as happened in the Wilbur case example, clients and workers gain greater insight into the social dynamics of a problematic situation.

In summary, eco-maps are useful to both workers and clients. For the worker, a completed eco-map graphically displays important interactions of a client family with other systems (that is, the groups, other families, individuals, and organizations) that the family ordinarily interacts with at a particular point in time. Such a diagram allows the worker to better understand the environmental factors impacting the family. It then helps the worker generate hypotheses of problematic dynamics in the family-environmental system, which the worker can then

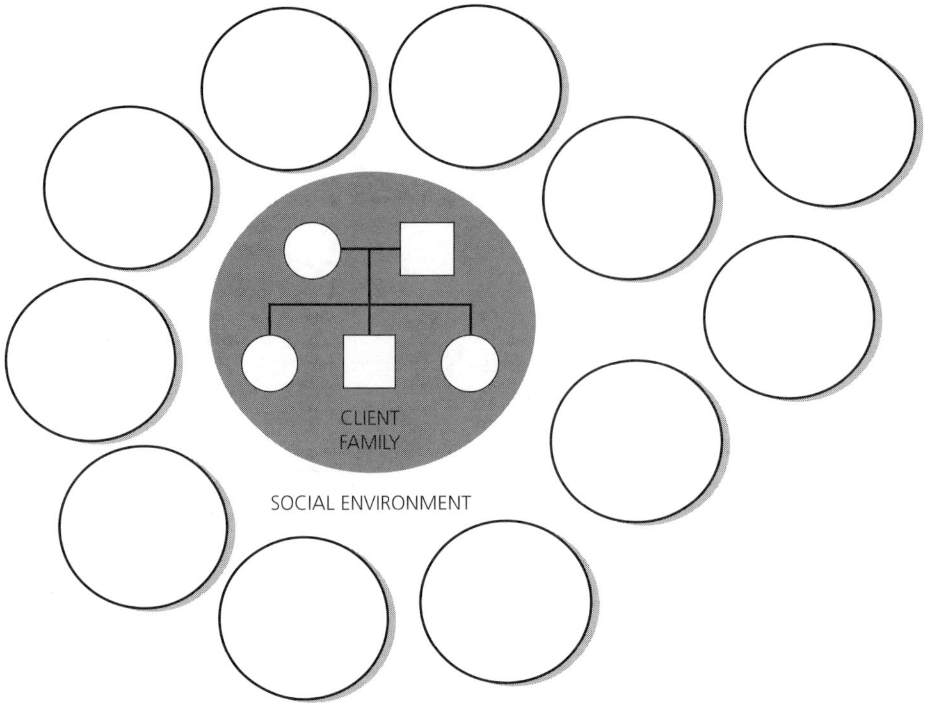

FIGURE 8.2 Setting up an eco-map

further explore by questioning the family members. Once problematic dynamics are identified, the worker can focus attention on helping family members generate strategies to resolve the problematic dynamics.

Similarly, for the client family members, an eco-map helps them identify and understand problematic dynamics in their family-environmental system. Once identified, family members are then in a position to generate strategies (together with their worker) to resolve the dynamics.

The Genogram

The genogram is a graphic way of investigating the origins of a client's or client family's presenting problem by diagramming the family over at least three generations. The client and worker usually jointly construct the family genogram, which is essentially a family tree. Murray Bowen is the primary developer of this technique (Kerr & Bowen, 1988). The genogram helps the worker and family members examine problematic emotional and behavioral patterns in an intergenerational context. Patterns tend to repeat themselves; what happens in one generation often occurs in the next. Genograms help family members identify and understand family relationship patterns.

Commonly used genogram symbols are shown in Figure 8.4 on page 184. Together, the symbols provide a visual picture of a family tree, for at least three generations, including the following: who the members are; their names, ages, and gender; marital status; sibling positions; and so on. When relevant, additional items of information are included, such as emotional difficulties, behavioral problems, religious affiliation, ethnic origins, geographic locations, occupations, socioeconomic status, and significant life events. The use of the genogram is illustrated in the Kull family case example on page 186.

In summary, genograms are useful to both worker and clients. For the worker, a completed genogram graphically points out intergenerational family dynamics. Such a diagram allows the worker to better understand the intergenerational patterns impacting a client family. It then helps the worker generate hypotheses of problematic patterns from prior generations, which the worker can further explore by questioning family members. Once problematic dynamics are identified, the worker can then focus attention on helping family members to generate strategies to resolve the patterns. A strengths perspective should also be used by workers—that is, they should also focus on helping family members identify intergenerational patterns that are *resources* that will help the family confront challenges. (Such resources include longevity, high educational achievement levels, valuing and practicing good health patterns, low rates of divorce, and high levels of constructive community participation.)

Similarly, for the client family, a genogram helps them identify and understand problematic intergenerational problem patterns and resources. Once such patterns are identified, family members can begin to generate strategies (together with their worker) to break these patterns.

The eco-map and the genogram have a number of similarities. With both techniques, users gain insight into family dynamics. Some of the symbols used in the two approaches are identical. There are differences, however. The eco-map focuses attention on the family's interactions with groups, resources, organizations, associations, other families, and other individuals. The genogram focuses attention on intergenerational patterns, particularly those that are problematic or dysfunctional.

Family Therapy in Systems Perspective

One of the many social services provided to families is family therapy (also called family counseling). A substantial amount of literature about family therapy has been developed in social work. The remainder of this chapter focuses on family therapy. Although social work with families involves many approaches and services in addition to family therapy, the importance of family therapy in social work practice necessitates an extended discussion of this approach.

Family therapy—what is it? Strictly speaking, it is a subset of the broader classification of group therapy that is aimed at helping families with whatever interactional, behavioral, and emotional problems arise in the course of everyday living. Problems include marital conflicts, parent-child interactional problems, and conflicts with grandparents or other relatives. A wide variety of problems are dealt with in family therapy: domestic violence, communication problems, disagreements between family members on drug use and abuse, curfew hours, school performance, money management, sexual values and behavior, performance of domestic tasks, and methods of disciplining the children.[1] Here is a typical scenario.

The Whitlock family walks into the therapist's office in an orderly fashion, the oldest son looking annoyed and bored, the younger children looking scared. Mrs. Whitlock introduces the group to the therapist immediately, saying that she is sure nothing is wrong with her family, yet the younger daughter Susan has been crying all the time lately and also doing very poorly in school of late; she was also obese. The mother says she is sure Susan will grow out of these problems, but the little girl's teacher called and said she was talking about suicide, so the mother decided to seek help for the girl. The only reason the rest of the family is here, she announces, is because the therapist requested that everyone be present at the first interview.

The father stands by the door while the mother talks, and no one sits down. The therapist notes that the older daughter stands close to the father, and the younger son looks at the floor. The older son moves to the window and looks out, whistling to himself. When the mother, holding Susan's hand, finishes her rapid-fire introductory speech, the therapist takes advantage of the pause to invite the family to be seated. She asks each person present to introduce themselves. She notes that the older daughter has difficulty with that request; she stutters badly and can't utter the first sound of her name. Let's leave the Whitlocks for a moment; we'll return to them later in the chapter.

Fortunately, not every family is seriously troubled. Some parents rear their children with minimum discomfort and maximum growth for all involved. Family therapy helps those other families who are hurting, overtly or covertly. Families enter into therapy because they hope to reduce their pain and increase their happiness, as individuals and as a group. Families that hurt internally are also likely to find their standing in the community diminished because one or more of the children exhibit embarrassing behavior in public, perhaps delinquent behavior. The family self-image of happiness and tranquility is likely to be shattered by angry, rebellious, or destructive behavior within the home. Crises precipitated by the children's behavior may precipitate flare-ups of old marital stresses and arguments

[1]The remainder of this chapter was especially written for this text by Carolyn Wells, Ph.D. Dr. Wells is Professor of Social Work at the University of Wisconsin-Oshkosh, and a practicing family therapist.

CASE EXAMPLE

Using an Eco-Map: The Wilbur Family

Barb and Dick Wilbur are contacted by Mary Timm, School Social Worker at East High School. The Wilburs' second-oldest son, Brian (age 16), had a knife in his jacket at school and liquor on his breath. The Wilburs are shocked. They agree to meet with Ms. Timm the next day to discuss these incidents. Brian will also be present.

At the meeting Ms. Timm asks Brian why he brought a knife to school. At first, he refuses to respond. Ms. Timm also notes that records show he used to receive mainly B's, but now his grades are primarily D's and F's. Mr. and Mrs. Wilbur also sternly ask Brian what is happening. They add that the school system has informed them that he apparently has been drinking during school hours. Gradually tears come to Brian's eyes. He says no one cares about him. He asserts his parents are too busy at work and too busy looking after his older brother, Steve, and his younger sister, Shannon.

At first, Mr. and Mrs. Wilbur are surprised. They indicate they love Brian very much. Gradually they disclose they have been so involved with the demands of their other two children that they may have been "shortchanging" Brian in recent months. Shannon, age 13, has Down's syndrome and requires considerable individual attention, especially with her coursework. (Shannon is enrolled in special education courses.)

Brian is asked where he obtained the knife. He hesitantly indicates his older brother, Steve, gave it to him for "protection." Brian adds that he sees nothing wrong with carrying a knife; Steve frequently carries a pistol. In addition, Brian says Steve urged him to take the knife to school, because some people who are unhappy with Steve have said they may come after Brian. Ms. Timm asks Mr. and Mrs. Wilbur if they know anything about this. Barb and Dick suggest it may be best if Brian is excused at this point. Ms. Timm sets up a later meeting with Brian, and he leaves.

Both Barb and Dick then become teary-eyed. They indicate they are nearing their wit's end. Both work full time, and in recent years Steve and Shannon have required so much of their attention that they now no longer are able to spend any time with their former friends. In addition, they have been arguing more and more. They feel that their family is disintegrating and that they are "failing" as parents. They also disclose that Steve is addicted to both alcohol and cocaine and has been for several years. He has been in for inpatient treatment three times but always goes back to using soon after leaving treatment. They don't know where Steve is getting the money for his cocaine habit. They fear he may be dealing. He hasn't been able to hold a full-time job. He is usually terminated because he shows up for work while under the influence. Currently, he is working part-time as a bartender.

Mr. and Mrs. Wilbur fear that unless something is done soon, Brian may follow in Steve's footsteps. They add they have contemplated asking Steve to leave but are reluctant to do so, because they feel it is their parental obligation to provide a house for their children as long as the children want to stay.

At this point Ms. Timm suggests it may be helpful to diagram their present dilemma. Together the Wilburs and Ms. Timm draw the eco-map shown in Figure 8.3.

While drawing the map, Ms. Timm asks whether providing housing for Steve is helping him or whether it may be a factor in enabling him to continue his drug use and his irresponsible behavior. The eco-map helps the Wilburs see that as a result of working full time and spending the remainder of their waking hours caring for Shannon, Steve, and Brian, they are gradually becoming too emotionally and physically exhausted to cope. During the past few years, they have stopped socializing. The Wilburs ask Ms. Timm to explain what she means by "enabling" Steve to continue his drug use and his irresponsible behavior. Ms. Timm explains enabling and indicates that a "tough love" approach may be an option. (In

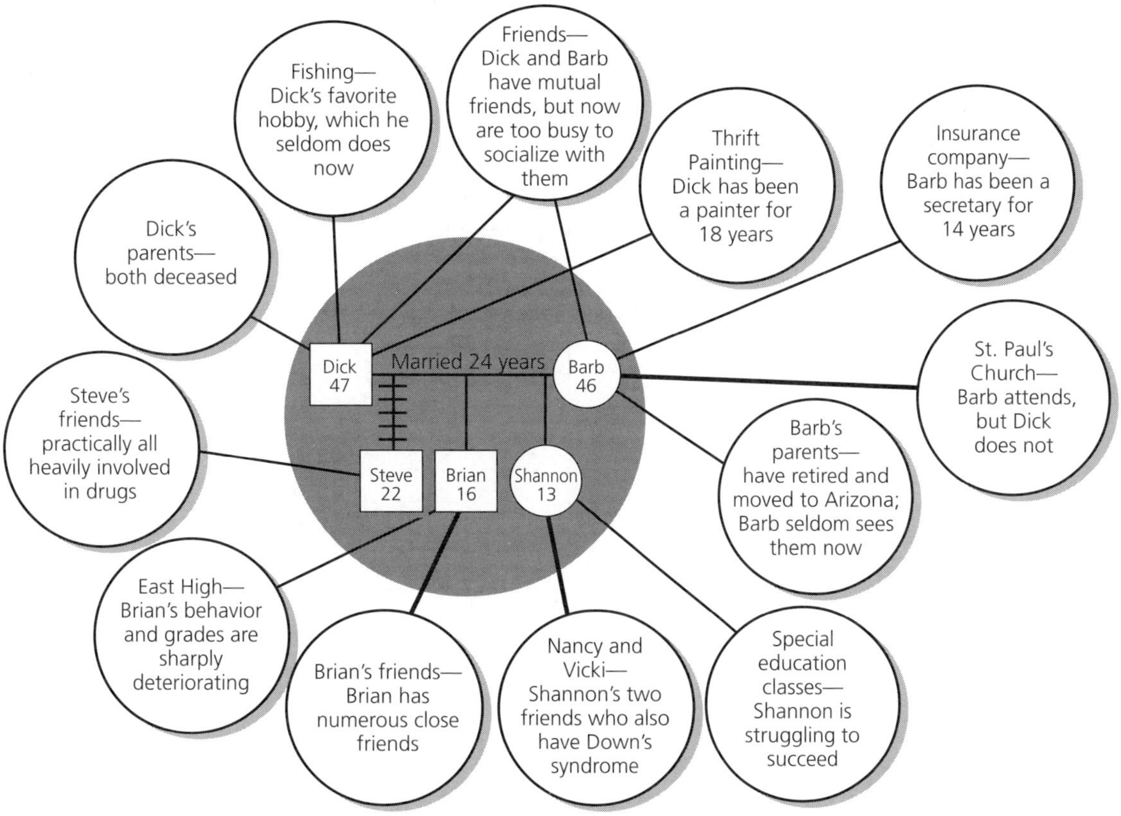

FIGURE 8.3 Sample eco-map: The Wilbur Family

this case, a tough love approach would involve the Wilburs' demanding that Steve live elsewhere if he continues to abuse alcohol and cocaine.) Ms. Timm also gives them pamphlets that describe enabling and tough love. They make an appointment for the next week.

For the next several weeks Ms. Timm continues to meet weekly with the Wilburs and individually with Brian. The Wilburs eventually decide to use a tough love approach with Steve. Steve leaves but continues to use alcohol and cocaine. However, living on his own does appear to be somewhat beneficial as he now works full-time at a maintenance job to pay his bills. With Steve out of the house, Barb and Dick Wilbur are able to spend more time with Brian and Shannon, and they begin to socialize again with some of their former friends.

Counseling Skills at Work in Generalist Practice

In the Wilbur case example, the social worker used the following roles that, as described in Chapter 1, are components of generalist social work practice: family counselor; educator (helping Mr. and Mrs. Wilbur realize they needed to use a tough love approach with Steve); broker (encouraging the Wilburs to again socialize with their friends); and problem-solver.

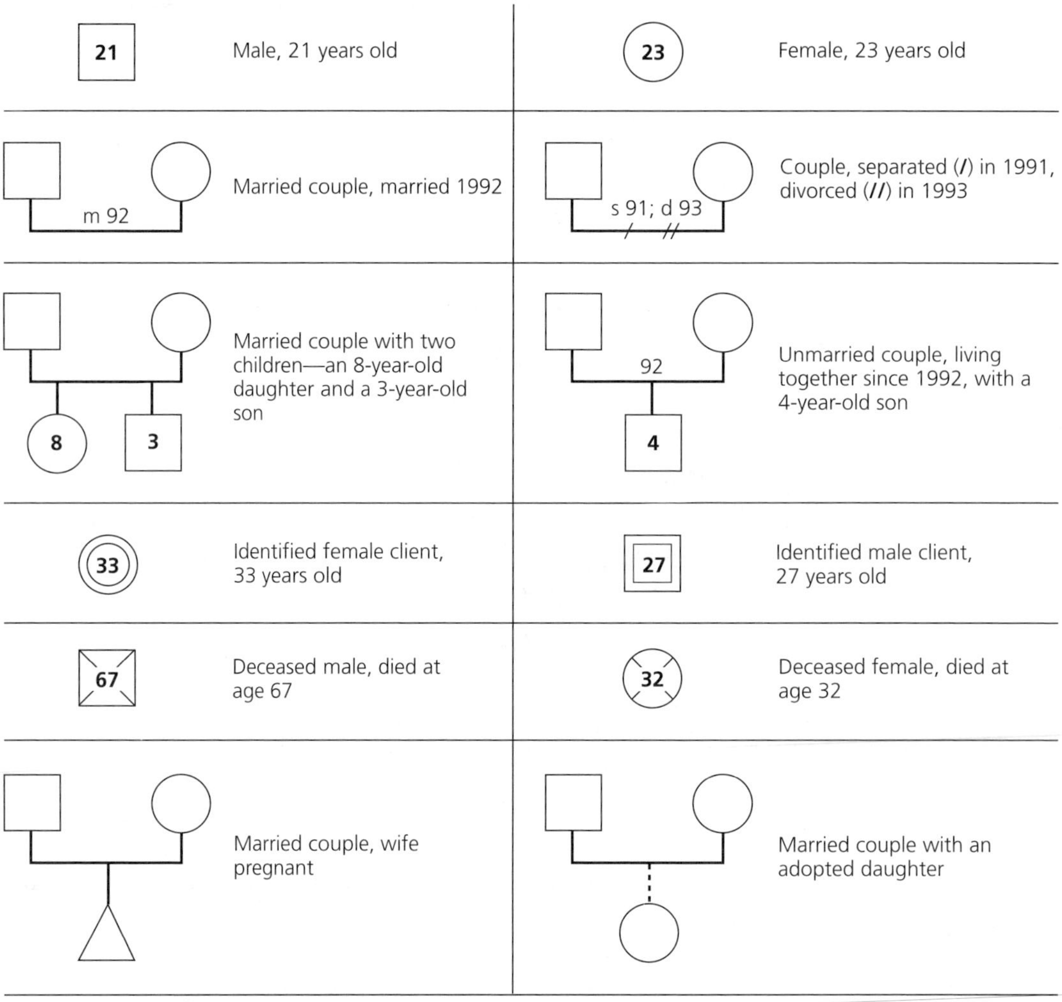

FIGURE 8.4 Commonly used genogram symbols

(see the case example on page 189). People suffer, and their self-esteem and personal growth are inhibited.

Virginia Satir, a noted social worker, worked with many troubled families. Satir (1972) believed that four factors differentiate troubled and untroubled families: level of felt self-worth, patterns of communication, type of family rules, and the way the family members relate to people and institutions outside the family (their pattern of linkage to society). She found that in troubled families self-worth is low; communication is indirect, vague, and dishonest; rules are rigid and non-negotiable; and the linkage to society vacillates between being fearful, placating, or blaming (Satir, 1972, pp. 3–4). By contrast, in nurturing families self-worth tends to be high; communication is clear, specific, and honest; rules are appropriate and flexible; and the linking to society is open.

Obviously, troubled and untroubled families stand at opposite ends of a continuum. Probably most families stand somewhere along the continuum. It takes a great deal of effort and energy to enter an activity like family therapy, and usually a family has to be far along the continuum toward the troubled end before it will seek help. Often the family is troubled for a long time before any effort is made to reach out for assistance. A particular event, such as the clash of a family member, often a child, with an outside authority (such as the school or the police), may precipitate seeking help.

Perhaps the sudden desertion of a spouse or a child's running away brings about a great enough crisis that the family will seek professional help. At any rate, members of middle-class American culture, who have been exhorted to solve their own problems and lift themselves up by their own bootstraps, tend to enter therapy well after external intervention would have been useful. Often the family member who finally reaches out is female, because males in our society are traditionally reared to believe that seeking help for individual and family problems is a sign of weakness. Unfortunately, seeking professional help for reasons of emotional adjustment will usually be perceived by the family as an admission of dependency and failure rather than as an assertive action in the direction of constructive problem solving.

When a family does consult a therapist for help in reducing their family pain, there is hope. The act of seeking help is itself a positive indication that the family is capable of at least one innovative act. However, the family often enters therapy using an identified client as a sort of "ticket for admission." In fact, the family may perceive that this identified client is their only problem. "If the therapist can only fix this person, the family will be just fine." Remember the Whitlock family? The younger daughter, obese and talking about suicide, is their identified client. In this first interview, family members don't appear to think anything else is wrong. They are merely tagging along (dutifully) so they can help the therapist "figure out what is wrong with the little girl." We will now leave the Whitlocks for a while, but keep the scenario of their first meeting in mind as you read on.

The family therapist will perceive the identified client as serving an important function in the family system. Like all systems, a family has an overall purpose; to provide for the physical and emotional needs of the adults and to procreate new people. The system parts are the family members themselves. These parts establish a certain working order—for example, communication patterns, rules, levels of self-esteem. Energy to keep the system going is supplied by food, water, housing, and so forth, plus certain beliefs regarding the emotional, intellectual, social, and spiritual lives of the family members and how one fits in with another (Satir, 1972, pp. 113–119).

Like all systems, each family system is bounded, in that family communication patterns have special forms and a special significance and purpose (for example, continuation of the family). However, the boundary around the family is permeable to varying degrees. In a healthy family system, new information flows into and out of the family through the boundary, and the family is thus characterized as an open system. In this open system, rules are related to communication, and change is considered normal. The members' self-worth is granted higher importance than the maintenance of a fixed power structure. In contrast, in a relatively closed system, family members cling to the familiar even when it is painful and does not foster growth. Where self-worth is low, pain is at least familiar and thus preferable to the unknown. Self-worth is relegated to a secondary position below fixed authority, change is resisted, and relationships are regulated by force (at the whim of the person on top). Information from outside the system is resisted, because there is just one "right way."

To repeat, when a family comes to therapy, they generally do so to have the therapist "fix" a particular family member so that their system can maintain itself as before, only without the stress that the identified client has been recently exerting. The perspective of the systems-oriented family therapist is, however, that the identified client developed problematic behavior to help maintain the family system in some way. Now the problematic behavior has become severe enough that the family views it as a problem. So when the referral for therapy is made by a family member or outside institution (for example, school), the therapist will insist on involving all family members, even very young children. The therapist will want to determine from direct observation and careful questioning what function the problematic behavior of the identified client plays in maintaining the family system, and how and why it has now become stressful.

Many family-oriented therapists will refuse services if the family will not participate in treatment. However, if a significant subsystem of the family agrees to involve itself (perhaps the mother and the child), the therapist may consider beginning therapy with this part of the system with the hope that the rest will enter in later. This decision is a delicate one, and every therapist gradually evolves criteria for choosing when to refer and when to start with a subsystem only.

Four Approaches to Family Therapy

Several noted family therapists have contributed to the growing theory and practice of family therapy. Here we briefly describe the theoretical frameworks of

CASE EXAMPLE

Using a Genogram: The Kull Family

Jim Kull is referred by Rock County District Attorney's Office to the Rock County Domestic Violence Program. He was arrested two nights ago for an incident in which his wife, Diane, received several severe bruises on her body and her face. Kris Koeffler, a social worker, has an intake interview with Mr. Kull. Mr. Kull is an involuntary client and is reluctant to discuss the incident. Ms. Koeffler informs Mr. Kull he has a right not to discuss it, but if he chooses not to, she is obligated to inform the district attorney that he refused services. She adds that in such cases the district attorney usually files a battery charge with the court, which may lead to jail time.

Mr. Kull reluctantly states he and his wife had a disagreement, which ended with her slapping him, and he defending himself by throwing a few punches. He adds that yesterday, when he was in jail, he was informed she left home with the children and is now staying at a women's shelter. He is further worried she may contact an attorney and seek a divorce.

Ms. Koeffler inquires about the specifics of the "disagreement." Mr. Kull indicates he came home after having a few beers, his dinner was cold, and he "got on" Mrs. Kull for not cleaning the house. He adds that Mrs. Kull then started "mouthing off," which eventually escalated into them pushing and hitting each other. Ms. Koeffler then inquires whether such incidents had occurred in the past. Mr. Kull indicates "a few times," and then adds that getting physical with his wife is the only way for him to "make her shape up." He indicates he works all day long as a carpenter while his wife sits home watching soap operas. He feels she is not doing her "fair share"; he states the house usually looks like a "pigpen."

Ms. Koeffler asks Mr. Kull if he feels getting physical with his wife is justifiable. He responds with "sure," and adds that his dad frequently told him "spare the rod, and spoil both the wife and the kids." Ms. Koeffler asks if his father was at times abusive to him when he was a child. He indicates that he was, and adds that to this day he detests his dad for being abusive to him and to his mother.

Ms. Koeffler then suggests that together they draw a "family tree," focusing on three areas: episodes of heavy drinking, episodes of physical abuse, and traditional versus modern gender stereotypes. Ms. Koeffler explains that a traditional gender stereotype includes the husband as the primary decision maker and the wife as submissive to him and primarily responsible for domestic tasks. The modern gender stereotype involves an equalitarian relationship between husband and wife. After an initial reluctance (related to his expressing confusion as to how such a "tree" would help get his wife back), Mr. Kull agrees to cooperate in drawing such a "tree." The resulting genogram is presented in Figure 8.5.

The genogram helps Mr. Kull see that he and his wife are products of family systems that have strikingly different values and customs. In his family the males drink heavily, have a traditional view of marriage, and use physical force in interactions with their spouse. (Mr. Kull further adds his father also physically abused his brother and sister when they were younger.) On questioning, Mr. Kull mentions he frequently spanks his children and has struck them "once or twice." Ms. Koeffler asks Mr. Kull how he feels about repeating the same patterns of abuse with his wife and children that he despises his father for using. Tears come to his eyes, and he says "not good."

Ms. Koeffler and Mr. Kull then discuss courses of action that he might take to change his family interactions, and how he might best approach his wife in requesting that she and the children return. Mr. Kull agrees to attend Alcoholics Anonymous (AA) meetings as well as a therapy group for batterers. After a month of attending these weekly meetings, he contacts his wife and asks her to return. Mrs. Kull agrees to return *if* he stops drinking (since most of the abuse occurred when he was intoxicated), *if* he agrees to continue to attend group therapy and AA meetings, and *if* he agrees to go to counseling with her. Mr. Kull readily agrees. (Mrs. Kull's parents, who have never liked her husband, express their disapproval.)

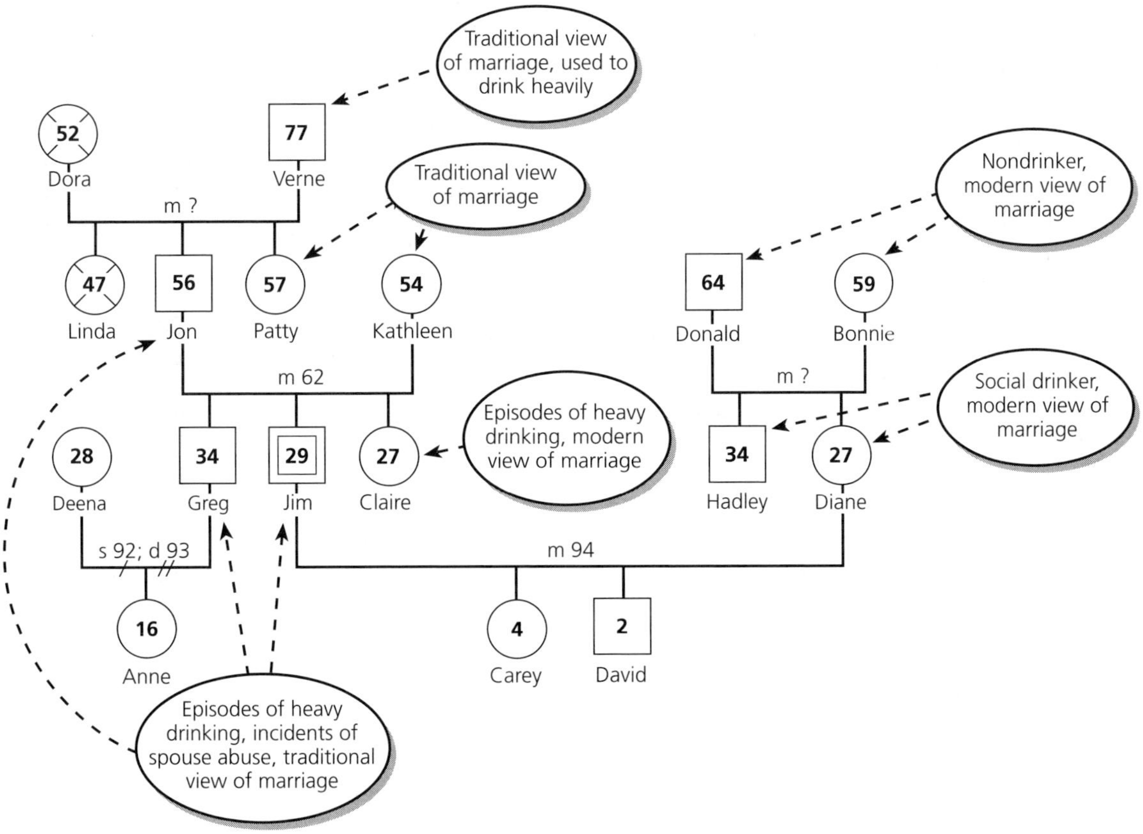

FIGURE 8.5 Sample genogram: The Jim and Diane Kull family

For the first few months, Mr. Kull is on his best behavior and there is considerable harmony in the family. Then one day, on his birthday, he decides to stop for a few beers after work. He drinks until he is intoxicated. When he finally arrives home, he starts to verbally and physically abuse Mrs. Kull and the children. For Mrs. Kull, this is the last straw. She takes the children to her parents' house, where they stay for several days, until they are able to find and move into an apartment. She also files for divorce and follows through in obtaining one.

At first glance, this case is not a "success." In reality, many social work cases are not successful. However, Mr. Kull now realizes that he has acquired, and acts out, certain dysfunctional family patterns. Unfortunately, he is not ready to make lasting changes. Perhaps in the future he will be more committed. At the present time he has returned to drinking heavily. Mrs. Kull and the children are safer and can now start to break the cycle of abuse.

Counseling Skills at Work in Generalist Practice

In the Kull family case example, the social worker used the following roles that, as described in Chapter 1, are components of generalist social work practice: brokering Mr. Kull to participate in AA meetings, educating Mrs. Kull to understand she needs to take action to stop the physical abuse, and brokering Mr. Kull to attend a therapy group for batterers.

Virginia Satir, Salvador Minuchin, Jay Haley, and Ivan Boszormenyi-Nagi. These theorists use a systems perspective, but they apply it in different ways.

Virginia Satir

Satir (a social worker, now deceased, who was a pioneer in family therapy) stressed clarification of family communication patterns in her work. She noted, in particular, that communication patterns among troubled families tend to be vague and indirect. In other words, rather than speaking clearly for themselves, the marital pair avoid talking with each other about their needs and desires; or they talk to each other through their children. Children are thus maneuvered into the stressful position of speaking for, and therefore allying with, one parent or another, precipitating fear of loss of the other.[2]

In Satir's view, indirect communication in the troubled family begins with the courtship process (if not before), due to the low self-esteem of the individuals involved. Each potential partner feels worthless, but hides the feeling of worthlessness by acting confident and strong. Neither person talks about these feelings of worthlessness for fear of driving the potential mate away. So each sees in the other a strong person who will take care of him or her, and essentially becomes part of a couple to gain an extension of the self, but a stronger self who will be able to meet all felt needs; in other words, each marries (or commits) to "get" (Satir, 1967, pp. 8–10).

Unfortunately, after marriage some of the illusions must fall away. Each partner realizes at some level that the other is not just an extension of the self. One insists on using a separate toothbrush, for example, and the other wants to share the same one. Such incidents force perceptions of difference, and difference is experienced as bad because it leads to arguments. A desire for fusion and to be cared for conflicts with the other's different felt needs. Facing difference feels frightening—it might lead to arguments and that could result in the other's leaving.

Hence, each frightened partner with low self-esteem and high need for the other masks differences as much as possible, attempting to please the other on one level to keep him or her, while fearing and resenting expressed needs from the other that may be experienced as undesirable. Because both partners are in the same uncomfortable position of resenting differences yet needing the other, interpersonal communication gradually becomes more and more indirect. Rather than risk a clear statement, such as "I'd like to get a dog," the partner desiring a pet might state something like "Aunt Matilda likes dogs." The hope is that the other will mind-read the intended message and then spontaneously agree to get a dog for the family. However, the receiver of this particular message will more likely communicate a return response dealing with Aunt Matilda, bringing disappointment to the speaker. The speaker isn't able to negotiate the desired dog with this type of communication and is left with angry feelings and a sense of unfulfilled needs, but this state of affairs is experienced as being preferable to risking a point-blank denial. Meanwhile, the receiver of the message becomes aware of the disappointment or anger of the speaker through nonverbal channels but has no idea what caused it. If the partner is also afraid to deal with conflict, he or she will not ask the reason for the apparent upset. So the misunderstanding and tension build.

Satir also notes that communicating involves far more than the literal meaning of the words used. First of all, she notes that much communication is nonverbal—gestures, facial expressions, voice tone, posture, and the like. If nonverbal communication matches the meaning of the words used (if, for example, "I am sad" is accompanied by tears and a downturned mouth), then Satir considers the communication *congruent*. The receiver is not likely to misunderstand the meaning of this message because the verbal and nonverbal components agree. However, messages sent are often *incongruent*. For example, "I am sad" may be accompanied by a grin. Which message should the receiver believe—the words or the facial expression? The receiver is likely to make a mistaken interpretation unless he or she explicitly asks the sender to explain. But the person who feels safe only with indirect communication is not likely to ask. Moreover, the sender who becomes skilled at sending incongruent communication for self-protection may even be unaware of the action and will be unable to explain if asked. Satir believes that incongruent communication leads to misunderstanding in troubled families. Mother, for example, says to her spouse, "I am angry with you." However, because she

[2]Use of traditional terms such as marital pair, spouse, or partner are used in this chapter for convenience, but should be understood to include other adult partners in committed relationships involving children (gay couples, stepparents, etc.).

CASE EXAMPLE

School Phobia

A system inherently attempts to maintain a dynamic balance, or homeostasis, to maintain the particular arrangement or ordering of parts that was successful in the past and resulted in establishment of the system. As an example of how problematic behavior in a family member may help maintain the family homeostasis (balance of the system so the system can continue), let us discuss a school phobia that arose in a little girl in a Jefferson County, Wisconsin, elementary school. The school phobia arose apparently spontaneously, but the school social worker discovered on her first home visit that the little girl was almost mute with strangers (at least with the social worker herself), and in fact ran out onto the yard rather than cope with a new person. The mother would not fetch the daughter ("she's too frightened of strangers") and offered only the most broad and general information about the child's development. However, the mother did want to talk about herself; she listed a variety of stresses in her life unrelated to the daughter, in particular her aloof husband and her boring job. It became increasingly clear that this mother resented the time and attention her daughter was receiving; she wanted some attention herself. Yet the only reason she was receiving any attention from her husband was due to the daughter's phobia. The husband had to talk to the lonely woman fairly often because of the little girl's problematic behaviors (in the home the child would often stay in her room, or refuse her supper, and so forth). Because of the girl's school phobia, the mother got to stay home from her disliked job and to talk with her husband.

A combination of family therapy to help create a genuine relationship between the marital pair without the assistance of the daughter's problematic behaviors, plus reduction in the mother's work hours, helped reduce this family's need for a problematic daughter. At school, during the initial stages of the family therapy, the little girl was placed in a special class with an empathic and firm teacher. The father was assigned the task of taking his daughter to school. The mother was to accompany them but not take responsibility. Fortunately, the father was a well-meaning person and faithfully carried out his responsibility, which strengthened his relationship with the child and thus his investment in the family system as a whole. After successfully getting the child to school, the father and the mother would discuss their success, strengthening their own communication and increasing their appreciation of one another. The school phobia disappeared within a few weeks.

fears rejection if she sends this message too forcefully, she smiles sweetly as she says it. The spouse chooses to believe the smile, not to take his spouse's words seriously, and continues the very behavior that made her use the word *angry.* This makes her angrier, but she doesn't feel safe enough to express the feeling more congruently, and the communication driving the spouses apart goes on.

Incongruent communication is one example of a double message; another type of double message places the receiver in a *double bind,* where no matter how he or she responds, the sender will criticize. This situation can occur where Father says, on the one hand, that all good children pick up their toys, and yet on the other, tells his son that all "real" boys are messy. The boy who receives these two messages will be unable to please his father whether he keeps his toys neat or messy. He may solve the problem by refusing to listen at all. At the extreme, he may pull away from reality to such a degree that he develops a severe emotional disturbance.

Satir's therapeutic goals and techniques are based on her assumption that people have the inherent ability (even drive) to grow and to mature. She felt that people can choose to take responsibility for their own lives and actions and that the mature person will

1. Manifest himself clearly to others.
2. Be in touch with signals from his internal self, thus letting himself know openly what he thinks and feels.
3. Be able to see and hear what is outside himself as differentiated from himself and as different from anything else.

4. Behave toward another person as someone who is separate and unique.
5. Treat the presence of differentness as an opportunity to learn and explore rather than as a threat or signal of conflict. (Satir, 1967, p. 92)

To help members of a troubled family differentiate from one another and learn to "own" their special unique beings, Satir patiently taught each person to speak for himself or herself and to send "I-messages."[3] She served as an active, directive, loving role model. She taught that differentness is normal and should be viewed as a catalyst for growth. She pointed out incongruent messages and double binds and taught family members to send clear, congruent messages. She used touch and other nonverbal means, such as family sculpting, to illustrate to families the unverbalized assumptions they operate by, and in this way took the burden of labeling off identified clients and revealed their symptomatic behavior as a product of the family system as a whole.

Family sculpting is used for both assessment and treatment purposes. It is a physical arrangement of the members of a family in space, with the placement of each person determined by an individual family member acting as "director." The resulting tableau represents that person's symbolic view of family relationships. Goldenberg and Goldenberg (1991) describe family sculpting as follows:

> The procedure calls for each member to arrange the bodies of all the other family members in a defined space, according to his or her perception of their relationships either at present or at a specific point in the past. Who the sculptor designates as domineering, meek and submissive, loving and touching, belligerent, benevolent, clinging, and so on, and how those people relate to each other becomes apparent to all who witness the tableau. The sculptor is invited to explain the creation, and a lively debate between members may follow. The adolescent boy who places his parents at opposite ends of the family group while he and his brothers and sisters are huddled together in the center conveys a great deal more about his views of the workings of the family system than he would probably be able to state in words. By the same token, his father's sculpture—placing himself apart from all others, including his wife—may reveal his sense of loneliness, isolation, and rejection by his family. The mother may present herself as a confidante of her daughter but ignored by the males in the family, and so forth. (p. 242)

[3]"I-messages" are described in Module 9.

Satir also analyzed rules in the family and helped clarify them in the context that some rules may be bad, but the people setting the rules or bound by them are not. She taught that bad rules can be changed and had the family members negotiate new ones as she insisted that each member be heard in her presence, thus teaching respect for each person and point of view.

Clearly, then, Satir viewed the family as a system and worked with the family as a whole as the means of relieving the distress of the identified client, or of the family itself due to the previous dysfunctional behavior of the identified client. Her major emphasis in intervention with the family as a system was to clarify the family communication patterns and to help them become direct and congruent. Basically, Satir's therapeutic goal of improving methods of communication involves three outcomes: (1) Members should be able to report congruently, completely, and obviously on what they see and hear, feel, and think about themselves and others. (2) Each person should be related to his or her uniqueness so that decisions are made in terms of exploration and negotiation rather than in terms of power. (3) Differentness should be openly acknowledged and used for growth (Okun & Rappaport, 1980, p. 93).

Salvador Minuchin

Like Satir, Minuchin is a pioneer in family therapy who operates from a systems perspective. In short, this means that if a particular person is referred for therapy due to certain undesirable symptoms, Minuchin assumes that this behavior is generated and maintained by needs of the family as a whole, so that intervention with the family will be necessary for effective alleviation of the problems of the identified client.

Unlike Satir, however, Minuchin's major emphasis in therapy is not clarification of communication patterns per se but restructuring of the major subsystems within the family (spouse, parental, sibling) so each can accomplish its appropriate functions. Because of this emphasis, Minuchin is considered to be a member of the *structural* school of family therapists. In restructuring the family, Minuchin works with communication patterns in the family, just as in clarifying communication patterns, Satir restructured the family subsystems into a more functional relationship. However, Minuchin's theoretical perspective on the importance of clear, direct communication versus a functional family structure is clearly different. Minuchin, for example, bypasses direct cognitive understanding by a family of its communication patterns to restructure the family subsystems; for example, he may use a paradoxical suggestion in working with a resistant family. However, he does so only in highly selected circumstances where direct explorations and clarifications of family communication patterns and behavior in therapy failed to change the dysfunctional aspects.

A *paradoxical suggestion* is a technique in which the therapist tells the family members to continue their symptomatic behavior and sometimes to "improve on it." This technique makes members more aware of the existence of the dysfunctional behavior and the dysfunctional consequences they derive from it. The ultimate goal of a paradoxical suggestion is to subtly encourage one or more family members to terminate engaging in the dysfunctional behavior. Minuchin provided the following illustration of the use of a paradoxical suggestion:

> A systemic paradox is used in treatment of the Allen family, in which an eight-year-old boy is failing in school. The therapist determines that the symptom serves the function of keeping the mother's disappointment focused on her son, Billy, rather than her husband. The husband is failing in business and, rather than redoubling his efforts, is sinking into apathy, leaving the mother to shoulder much of the financial burden. He gives off signals that he would collapse if confronted openly with this issue and the mother collaborates in protecting him. Whenever she becomes angry at his lack of ambition, she nags Billy to straighten out and make something of himself, do his homework, practice his violin, or clean up his room. The mother and Billy end up fighting, and the father retires to the den to watch television. Both parents deny there is a marital problem, the wife stating, "My husband doesn't like to fight and I've accepted this."
>
> The therapist tells the mother it is important for her to continue to express her disappointment in Billy, because otherwise she might begin to express her dissatisfaction with her husband. This would be risky, as her husband might become depressed, and since Billy is younger and more resilient than her husband, he can take it better. Billy is advised to continue to protect his father by keeping the mother's disappointment focused on him, and the father is commended for his cooperation. The mother has an immediate recoil, saying, "You're suggesting I fight with my eight-year-old son instead of my husband, a grown man? Why should I damage my son to protect my husband?" thus defining her own predicament. The husband supports the therapist, saying he thinks her suggestion is a good one "because Billy bounces right back. With him it doesn't last for a long period of time, and he doesn't get depressed as I do. Besides, we can't know for sure if it's doing him any damage." The mother is outraged at her husband and proceeds to fight with him. The conflict is refocused onto the parents, and Billy is released from his middle position. Defining and prescribing their system in a way that is both accurate and unacceptable makes it impossible for them to continue it. (Minuchin & Fishman, 1981, p. 247)

In this example, by the use of paradoxical suggestion Minuchin clarified the boundaries around the spouse subsystem in such a way that the son is appropriately excluded. Solving the problems of the spouse subsystem is squarely placed back within the boundaries of the spouse subsystem. The wife's disappointment with her husband is not "cured" nor is the apathetic behavior of the husband toward his failing business, but the wife's dissatisfaction with her spouse is now appropriately expressed within the boundaries of the spouse dyad, where it can be dealt with directly. Prior to use of this therapeutic technique, eight-year-old Billy was being pulled in between the spouses to divert them from fighting. Billy's inappropriate inclusion by the parents in their spouse subsystem might temporarily work to keep the family together for a longer period, but the cost to Billy is unacceptable. In the long run, using Billy this way will not work for the spouses either, for their problems obviously cannot be solved by Billy's failing in school.

In Minuchin's structural perspective, every family contains multiple interacting systems, including each particular individual and the various dyads, but three major subsystems are of particular importance in families with children. These are the spouse, the parental, and the sibling subsystems. Each has different major functions that must be fulfilled if the family is to survive as a healthy unit. The spouse subsystem must be able to protect itself as a unique entity with clear boundaries if the spouses' long-term psychological needs are to be met. This will involve certain rules of interaction with other significant subsystems, such as in-laws or children, that reinforce rather than interfere with the rights and needs of the spouses to interact as spouses. Once children are born, a parental subsystem then comes into being. The parental subsystem is likely to interfere with the spouse subsystem, because when one parent bonds closely with a newborn child, then the primacy of the relationship with the other spouse is threatened. Moreover, in-laws may demand parental rights that conflict with the wants and needs of the biological parents. Later on, older children may be asked to take on parental functions that interfere with their own needs to be nurtured and protected as they learn and grow. Finally, the sibling subsystem is of particular importance because this is the context in which children first learn what the world is all about for them: initially, how to interact and deal with peers and hierarchies. Minuchin points out that families continue to develop and change as children are added, grow, and leave home, so constant adaptational changes are required for every family. The family has both to maintain itself and to change with the changing conditions. Sometimes professional intervention is required to help troubled families cope successfully.

In working with a given family, Minuchin analyzes its structure to determine whether the boundaries of the major subsystems are clear and defined, or too enmeshed (too close, as when a parent and a child are emotionally closer than the two members of the spouse subsystem), or too disengaged (as when two spouses communicate with each other only through their children). Minuchin diagrams a hypothetical structure of the family, noting positions and types of boundaries as they exist when the family is referred. He then rediagrams the subsystem boundaries as new information emerges or as they change throughout the therapeutic process. His goal is to restructure the family so there is (1) a functioning spouse subsystem with a clear boundary differentiating it from other subsystems; (2) a parental subsystem with clear executive functions that may or may not involve other persons besides the spouses, but where at any rate the channels of authority are clear; and (3) a sibling subsystem that is free from enmeshment with both the spouse and the parental subsystems so the siblings may develop and grow under the protection, guidance, and appropriate authority of the parents.

To achieve these objectives, Minuchin developed a creative variety of techniques ranging from direct education of the family members all the way to the occasional use of paradoxical suggestion, where the family interactional patterns are restructured within appropriate subsystem boundaries without the members' conscious understanding of how it happened. Minuchin uses himself actively and directly within the therapy sessions according to his assessment of the requirements of the situation. He moves people physically around his office or out of the office, and himself physically as well, to demonstrate and enact appropriate and inappropriate subsystem boundaries.

Minuchin cautions against preoccupation with therapeutic techniques. He believes that they should be studied with care and then consciously forgotten, so the educated therapist can spontaneously meet the requirements of each unique therapeutic situation. He describes his own restructuring techniques in family therapy as belonging to three major categories: boundary making, unbalancing the current dysfunctional family structure, and complementarity (changing perceptions of hierarchical relationships within the family) (Minuchin & Fishman, 1981, p. 145).

Jay Haley

Like Satir, Jay Haley, a leading advocate for the approach generally known as *strategic,* was an early student of communication theory. He actively participated in the research that developed the concept of the double bind in interpersonal communication theory, described earlier in the discussion on Satir (Bateson, Jackson, Haley, & Weakland, 1956). Like both Satir and Minuchin, Haley was an adherent of the family systems approach. Rather than search for intrapsychic causes for behavioral symptoms, he looked instead for interpersonal meanings of symptomatic behavior. For example, Haley viewed symptoms (such as certain illnesses, alcoholism, or phobias) as creative means for the sufferer to exert control in a relationship. Such unhealthy means for control would surely arise as a last resort and outside of the consciousness of the sufferer. Nevertheless, these symptoms constitute important interpersonal tactics for control in a relationship; the sufferers would not be able to give them up without meeting the need for control in some other way.

For example, a woman whose husband engages in a series of affairs may develop a severe physical illness that eludes exact diagnosis, but which forces the husband to come home at night to take care of her physical needs. The philandering husband's time is now required for shopping, housecleaning, and meal preparation. He no longer has time to conduct extramarital affairs. Thus, the wife regains control in her marital relationship. The cost to her is her health, a price she may be more than willing to pay to reclaim her husband. However, both she and her husband will be puzzled about the nature of the illness and concerned that she doesn't seem to be getting well. Doctors may call her a hypochondriac.

In his strategic model of therapy, Haley was interested in family communication patterns, but his particular interest involved communication specifically in the present. How does current communication, both verbal and nonverbal, maintain the status quo (homeostasis) in the family? Haley consciously focused narrowly on the presenting problem as it was brought to him by the family. He felt that this is the most powerful point of entry for family therapy. He worked actively with the whole family to help them define the presenting problem clearly and distinctly. Then, he developed a specific plan to change the particular behavior that has been described as problematic. He used directives or tasks to get the family to move beyond the present functioning that is maintaining the problem behavior. For example, one family's presenting problem was bedwetting by a young daughter. The father sided with the daughter against the mother—he felt that the mother should be more understanding. So the therapist assigned the father the task of washing the sheets every time his daughter wet the bed (Haley, 1963, p. 60).

Many systems-oriented therapists argue against "just curing a symptom" in family therapy. They argue that after one symptom is cured, another will crop up to fill the same function that the first symptom served (maintaining the family homeostasis, or status quo). Haley's point of view, however, was that if the therapist can get a family to experience positive change, the family members will learn from the results of their actions. The learning can then be applied to further systems change. For example, in the case just mentioned, Haley's immediate strategy was to end the bed-wetting. But the reason Haley believed the intervention would work involved a structural perspective. According to Haley's observation of the current interactions within this family, the father and daughter formed a subsystem that was "tighter" than either the parental subsystem (father and mother) or the spousal subsystem (husband and wife). By assigning the father the task of washing wet sheets, Haley assumed that the father would soon tire of the daughter's symptomatic behavior and would join with the mother in defeating it. To do so, the father would have to disengage from the daughter. This disengagement could then become the basis for further work, in which different tasks could be assigned to help the father and mother strengthen their own subsystems (parental and spousal). Work with the marital pair could then remove the need for development of further symptomatic behavior by the daughter.

Even more than Minuchin's structural model, Haley's strategic therapy utilizes paradoxical directives (also called paradoxical suggestions) in helping families change symptomatic behavior. The paradoxical approach is normally used only with families who consciously wish to change but who resist control by the therapist. They resist because, unconsciously, the change they think they want is threatening to them in some way. Yet they have contracted for help. The therapist might find, for example, that for some apparently inexplicable reason a given family does not carry out the therapist's directives as assigned. In such a circumstance, Haley would experiment with paradoxical directives. Supposing, in the given case, the father forgets that his task is to wash his daughter's wet sheets, or the mother forgets that the father is supposed to do it and does the washing herself before he gets the chance. Haley would then *reframe* the bed-wetting to the family as something the daughter is doing to help the parents in some way. Reframing is a therapeutic technique in which the meaning of problem behavior is redefined as somehow good for the family system as a whole. (Reframing changes the conceptual and/or emotional setting or viewpoint in relation to which a situation is experienced and places it in another frame that fits the "facts" of the same concrete situation equally well, or even better, and thereby changes its entire meaning.)

In this case, the therapist might suggest that the daughter be encouraged to wet her bed because the bed-wetting might just be the most important thing the couple has to talk about at the end of the day. The therapist might even tactfully suggest that if the girl were cured, the couple might grow bored with each other and split apart. This would be a terrible thing, and so the parents should be advised not to do anything to change the bed-wetting behavior.

According to the theory behind paradoxical interventions such as these (actually, this is double-bind theory applied to the therapeutic intervention itself), if the family were to follow Haley's instructions as given, the bed-wetting would continue; yet the parents cannot consciously consent to this directive. The parents cannot consciously let themselves think that the daughter's bed-wetting is important to the preservation of their marriage. But to continue to resist the therapist's directives, as they have been doing so far, the parents have to cure the bed-wetting! When the bed-wetting is cured, the therapist must act puzzled and complimentary, saying that he doesn't know how the family has managed to bring about this important change. (This helps stabilize the results.)

Ivan Boszormenyi-Nagi

Ivan Boszormenyi-Nagi's influence as a family therapist has been growing in recent years. In his early practice, he was not a systems-oriented theorist. Born in Hungary, Boszormenyi-Nagi was educated as a psychiatrist and psychoanalyst. Because of their medical training, psychiatrists tend to look for biological origins for symptomatic behavior. Psychoanalysts are trained to look for intrapsychic origins of symptomatic behavior, believing that symptoms are manifestations of unconscious conflicts within the individual. Both models (medical and psychoanalytic) place heavy emphasis on the individual as the appropriate unit for analysis to understand symptomatic behavior.

Boszormenyi-Nagi emigrated to the United States in 1948. Several years later he began studying the origins of schizophrenia at the Eastern Pennsylvania Psychiatric Institute, which he founded in 1957. Given his medical background, Boszormenyi-Nagi originally searched for biological causes for the illness. When this research did not produce significant results, he gradually began to pay attention to the role of family dynamics in the development and maintenance of the disease.

Boszormenyi-Nagi was influenced by Erikson's (1963) emphasis on the importance of trust in normal human psychological development (Erikson's "trust versus mistrust" developmental stage) and Martin Buber's (1958) emphasis on accountability in human interaction (Buber's I–Thou relationship). He began paying attention not only to families in their various nuclear and extended forms but also to multigenerational issues and themes, particularly those dealing with trust and accountability.

Although remaining psychoanalytic in his basic orientation, Boszormenyi-Nagi began to view families from a systems perspective as well, appreciating the family as an organic whole composed of interacting parts, each one affecting all others—not only at a given time but over many generations.

Boszormenyi-Nagi (see Goldenberg & Goldenberg, 2000, pp. 187–192) identified a new dimension in family therapy that he believed was crucial to facilitate normal child development and healthy human behavior: the ethical dimension. He named his new approach *contextual therapy* to highlight that what happens in terms of ethical behavior in one generation affects the next. He believed that, whenever possible, therapy should be conducted with at least three generations present to help work out unaddressed issues of fairness and to reconcile family members of each generation.

From his research, Boszormenyi-Nagi believes that every family has a sense of who owes what to whom—a sort of multigenerational "family ledger." The family's bookkeeping system isn't strict or exact, but it does affect the "context" of daily life. For example, if the mother has put the father through medical school, there will be agreement in the family on some level that the father "owes" her. If he pays his debt via loyalty to the mother over the years, and perhaps even puts her through law school later, the ledger will be "balanced" and family members will have a sense of well-being. If he treats her badly, however—for example, abandons her emotionally on the excuse that she is no longer his intellectual equal—a sense of imbalance in the ledger may affect the next generation and beyond. Regardless of whether the source of psychological discomfort is known by later generations, Boszormenyi-Nagi believes that unresolved feelings of injustice may result in symptomatic behavior later.

Unresolved intergenerational issues may explain otherwise inexplicable incidents of symptomatic behavior. Boszormenyi-Nagi theorizes that every person experiences that family ledger as an assortment of unsettled accounts—accounts in which each individual owes or is owed. These accounts are fundamentally psychological in nature. Among important accounts to be settled (debts and entitlements) are issues of family loyalty and obligations to maintain significant relationships. Family legacies may include the obligation to mistrust significant others, to fail at one's work, or to excel at all costs. The purpose of therapy is to uncover these legacies and free oneself by consciously "balancing the ledger." All family relationships must be reassessed in the process.

Constructivist Approach—A Recent Trend

The early pioneers in family therapy, such as Virginia Satir and Salvador Minuchin, struggled to educate their peers in a systems perspective so that families would become a basic unit for intervention rather than the individual only. By the end of the 1970s, their efforts had succeeded to the point that family therapy had become an accepted practice. Then, as is common for established practices, some of the basic assumptions began to be reexamined.

One group of theorists who criticize the systems-oriented approach are known as constructivists (or constructionists). These theorists insist that reality is a mental creation of the observer. Therefore, family therapists must remain aware of what family members think they perceive in the therapy process, because it is a simply a product of their assumptions. Constructivists discard many of the assumptions of systems-based therapists, including the central hypothesis that symptomatic behaviors of family members are elicited to maintain family homeostasis or balance. They focus instead on exploring people's own assumptions about their problems, and the special meanings they assign to them. In the process of exploring the meaning families place on their own problems and experiences, they are encouraged to tell their own "stories." Then, through attentive conversation with an inquiring and respectful therapist, new and more empowering stories may unfold (Wells, 1998).

According to constructivist therapists, as people try to make sense of their lives, they develop stories that provide them with a sense of continuity and meaning. Each person's story (how my mother's alcoholism made me an alcoholic; how my illness as a child made me feel inferior, etc.) provides a framework upon which ongoing experience is structured. The stories we shape ourselves then shape our lives. The therapeutic process can make people aware of their stories and deliberately reshape them, helping redirect their lives in more positive directions (Goldenberg & Goldenberg, 2000).

An influential constructivist model, initially called "brief therapy" and later "solution focused therapy" has been developed by de Shazer and Berg. It is popular in today's managed-care environment because it provides effective short-term therapy. Clients are encouraged to tell their stories, and then asked to identify exceptions to the problems they identify, solutions that worked for them in the past, no matter how briefly. In this way people disentangle from their problems and recognize that they do not always exist. Clients are then encouraged to develop more hopeful stories than the ones initially presented. A major technique used for this purpose is the "miracle" question. Clients are asked to imagine that a miracle has occurred in which their problems have already been solved; they are then asked to imagine exactly what happened that permitted the miracle to take place. They are then helped to develop a step-by-step practical solution to their problems given their own ideas as prompted by the miracle question. This constructivist approach is short-term, pragmatic, and, as noted above, adapted to today's managed-care environment (Wells, 1998). (Solution-focused therapy is described in more detail in Module 9.)

Problem-Solving Stages

Family therapy can be viewed as a process of problem solving in a systems context, and from this perspective can be seen to consist of different stages, although in the actual interview session these stages may not appear to be distinct and may actually take place at the same time. However, for the best cognitive understanding of the process, distinguishing the stages is helpful. The stages of the problem-solving process can be conceptualized as follows:

1. Gathering information
2. Assessing information
3. Defining the problem
4. Planning for action
5. Developing an explicit contract for action
6. Carrying out the action plan
7. Evaluating results; modifying action plan if necessary
8. Terminating when appropriate

At the initial interview, the anxious family may spill out the entire problem as they see it; or, at the opposite extreme, they may be unable to speak coherently at all. (Recall the Whitlock family's first session.) The initial session may be spent largely in helping the family feel comfortable in this new environment so that they can function more or less in their own normal manner. Of primary importance is building a relationship between the therapist and family that will involve essential trust and goodwill. The therapist can help by making sure that the physical office and furnishings are comfortable and pleasing to the eye, eliminating frightening barriers such as the huge desk that some professionals seem to feel safer thrusting between themselves and their clients. A desk, if needed, can be pushed into a corner and chairs can be placed so that other physical objects do not come between them (unless used for the therapeutic purposes, for example, to demonstrate visibly the invisible barriers that may separate family members). The therapist can also help build a trusting relationship by modeling a reachable, personal, and informal style of communication. The beginning part of the initial interview is usually a social session in which all participants get a feel for each other. An atmosphere of hope and goodwill can make the therapy session much less threatening. Satir (1967) suggested taking a structured family history during the initial interview or interviews. Since questions on a family history are reasonably predictable, this procedure may help the family members feel safer and more in control, while they reveal important information about themselves. For example, Satir asked couples how and when they met, and how and why they decided to marry each other in particular. She asked each spouse what his/her family of origin was like, including parents, siblings, and lifestyle. She asked what each spouse expected to get from marriage, and what early married life was actually like. She asked each spouse how their expectations of marriage, gleaned from their respective families of origin, affected their present marriage in its early stages. Satir continued to question each spouse about his or her significant experiences in marriage up to the present, so a smooth transition to present problems was usually possible (Satir, 1967, p. 135). Tactics for building trusting relationships are not fixed, and different therapists develop their own techniques over time.

When a family therapist feels that the family is ready, she will ask for initial information regarding the family's perception of the problem and what brings them for help. Family members will frequently talk about their concern for or frustration with a particular member—the identified client. The therapist with a systems orientation will recognize that the problematic behavior of the identified client manifests strains throughout the family system.

Social workers as a profession, however, historically have taken the point of view that the most effective problem-solving interventive efforts can be achieved by "starting where the client is." If the family states that its problem is a particular child and wants help in "fixing" that child, a legitimate initial contract between family and therapist is working on that issue. The skilled therapist will, however, enlist the participation of other family members as consultants and helpers.

Regardless of the content of the therapeutic contract, it is important to take time to discuss and establish a contract in the problem-solving process. The contract specifies the respective roles of the participants in therapy and is an initial working agreement, which can be renegotiated later as new facts shed light on a need for new contract terms. The contract specifies the "problem for work" as well as more mundane agreements such as fees, frequency, place of interviews, and so forth.

It may become apparent with time that people outside the nuclear unit need to be included in some of the therapy sessions. A divorced spouse or a grandparent may wield strong influence that is not understood at the beginning of therapy. The therapist will strongly attempt to have all involved family members included in the sessions, although very young children may not be included by some therapists except at the initial sessions and then on occasion later.

Beginning the Counseling Process

Let's revisit the Whitlocks. Due to nonverbal cues of spatial position in the office, the family therapist has already formulated some initial hunches about family alliances. These hunches are based on visual data and hence are worth investigating, although only some will prove true. For example, the physical separation of the husband and wife, with the husband barely in the office, and the wife well inside, might indicate an emotional distance between the two as well as the relative positions of the marital pair within the family, one at the center and one on the way out, so to speak. The location of the older daughter (Pat, 14) close to the father and also near the door, might indicate that they form a coalition of some sort. The mother's holding the younger daughter's hand (Susan, 10) might indicate a similar close bond. Both sons maintain positions alone, and each further separates himself from family contact in a physical way—the younger son (George, 7) by staring at the floor and the older son (Lacey, 16) by looking out the window and whistling. These cues also signal family pain, felt in different ways and probably to different degrees by each member. It is likely that this family does not experience much closeness as a group; however, it is also possible that anxiety relating to this interview alone is precipitating the separation of various members of this family group.

An initial interview for family therapy is not a normal situation for the Whitlocks, and hence their behaviors will not be normal; most likely "company manners" or anxiety will be exhibited.

When the therapist seats the family and asks the members to introduce themselves, even though Mrs. Whitlock has already taken charge and done so for everyone, the therapist is structuring a new communication style that is important in family therapy to break old and unsatisfying patterns. Each family member needs to learn how to speak for himself or herself to minimize the amount of mind reading the other family members must do (and often inaccurately) and also to reduce the tendency of the Whitlock communication system to relegate a member to a fixed position in the family structure that is not necessarily the one he or she wants.

When Pat Whitlock attempted to introduce herself, she found *p* a difficult sound to pronounce. After a second or two of stuttering, Mrs. Whitlock broke in in a loud, impatient voice. "Now Pat, take a deep breath and speak slowly or you'll never learn to stop stuttering," She turned to the therapist and explained: "Pat doesn't need to stutter. She never stutters when she takes a deep breath first and slows down. She just tries to say everything so fast." "We'll come back to Pat when she's ready," the therapist commented. "Pat, you tell me when you are ready," the therapist continued.

And then the therapist went around to each member of the family and asked for names. The therapist checked with Pat visually and observed that Pat was not yet ready to speak. She had a hunch that Pat needed to feel safe. The therapist then turned to Mr. Whitlock. "Mr. Whitlock, I'm wondering what it is that you hope will change for you and your family." This statement contains an embedded question that assumes that the father has hopes for change that may not necessarily be the same as the mother's. The question is aimed intentionally at Mr. Whitlock because all too often in the American family the male is excluded from important family transactions, partly because his primary work is considered to take place outside the home. So much of many an American father's time is in fact spent outside the home that his sporadic presence can actually be experienced as uncomfortable by other family members. Systematic adjustments will be made to maintain the normal interactional system as if the father were in fact still absent, which socially "erases" him. However, a wife and an absent husband do not form an intact marital pair, and the stability of the family system is endangered. The family may fall apart unless primary contact between the marital pair can be re-established in some way. There is real danger that the father will continue his drift out of the mainstream of the family system until he formalizes the reality with desertion, divorce, alcoholism, or in some instances "accidental" death.

Mr. Whitlock responded that the problem as he saw it was out of the province of the therapist to help. His daughter was having problems in school as his wife said, but he knew that she was an intelligent girl and she was just a little lazy this year. Lots of children go through periods of being lazy. That was the same reason she was fat—she just lacked self-discipline. She'd outgrow it. He wasn't concerned. What did bother him was his health. His stomach constantly bothered him. But, he repeated, he certainly didn't expect a family therapist to be much help with that. Moreover, he hated his job, and the therapist couldn't do anything about that either. These children all had to get to college, and the first one would start in two years. Time was passing fast, and the savings account looked pretty inadequate to put four children through college. However, if his wife thought that therapy was important for Susan, and the agency said he had to come too, he wouldn't object. But he sure was upset about the cost. (Mr. Whitlock was already demonstrating potential for change—he was unhappy, he knew it, and when given an opportunity to express himself, words came flooding out. But his attitude, while overtly cooperative, came across like that of a self-perceived martyr, who was good enough to sacrifice himself but who would let his family know subtly that he was being wronged.)

"Now, Sam," interrupts Mrs. Whitlock, "you know you're just being a hypochondriac about your stomach. The doctor says there's nothing wrong with you. And you've got a good job. We can afford whatever is important. You always find something wrong with your boss, no matter who he is. And we're lucky all our children are bright and college material."

Mr. Whitlock spills out his words when elicited, the therapist notes, but Mrs. Whitlock has just cut him off. Is this by coincidence, or is it an ongoing pattern? This is something to check out over time.

The therapist now asks the oldest son Lacey what he experiences as a problem in the family. "We're OK," he responds, "only Dad's always afraid I'm going to screw my girlfriend, and Mom doesn't like her because of her religion . . ."

"And," interrupts Mrs. Whitlock, "she's skinny and she'll grow up to look worse. You can tell by what her own mother looks like. I can't imagine marrying a woman like that—that's why I keep my figure, so that the boys who date my girls can see that I'm . . ."

"But Mother," interrupts her son, "who says I'm going to marry her?"

"It's not a matter of wanting to marry her," Mrs. Whitlock retorts. "She's just the kind of girl who would try to trap you, just trap you—you're too young to understand . . ."

"I understand exactly what you mean," Lacey replies angrily. "You think she's going to get pregnant. That's crazy. Anything I do I'll do of my own choosing."

"Well," says Mother, looking vacant. Silence ensues.

The older son can stop Mother, the therapist notes. Father is silent and fidgeting.

Both parents are apparently worried about their older son's sexuality. How satisfactory is their own sexual relationship?

"How do you feel about Susan's problem?" the therapist asks Lacey. "She's OK, just a little too fat," he replies. "She'll be a knockout someday." "Anything else?" probes the therapist. "Nope," responds Lacey.

The therapist turns to Pat and asks how she feels about the family situation. Pat begins to respond, "Susan isn't v-very happy when k-k-kids t-tease her. K-kids are mean, and I tr-try to k-k- . . ."

"Now Pat, take a deep breath . . ." says Mother.

The therapist intervenes, "Let Pat keep going. I'm interested in what she has to say. You find that kids are mean sometimes, Pat, and what do you try to do about it?" "Tr-try to k-k-keep to myself a lot. The gym t-t-teacher lets me run on th-the t-track by m-m-myself whenever I want t-t-to, and I run alone during study halls and by m-myself a lot after school. I hate school." Pat has said that she hates school clearly and effectively.

"You hate school, but you stay there when school is out in the afternoon?"

"Well, M-M-Mom w-w-won't let us stay in the house . . ."

Mrs. Whitlock breaks in. "She drives me crazy when she's home. All she does is sit in her room with the door closed and the radio blaring. Children need fresh air to stay healthy. I make her go out in the afternoon for her own good. All of the children have to keep out of the house to get their air after school. That's my job, to keep them healthy until they know better. They'll thank me someday. A woman's place is in the home."

"I see," responds the therapist, noting to herself that Mother apparently holds a very traditional view of marriage. "But I don't believe that Pat is finished. Pat, go on."

"W-W-Well," says Pat, "th-th-that's ab-b-bout i-i-it."

Pat has been effectively silenced by Mother, notes the therapist. And she seems to stutter a little worse after each interruption.

"George," says the therapist, "please feel free to share with us what you think hurts in your family."

"Aw," says George looking at his toes, and then he starts to cry. "George," says Mr. Whitlock, "don't act like a baby." George drops his head and shoulders further.

Father has not scolded Pat, his apparent ally, for her stuttering. Mother has. But Father has ordered his youngest son to hide his feelings, just as Mother ordered Father to hide his feelings. Is it possible that Father tries to maintain his self-esteem by putting down his youngest son?

"He-he-he-he's n-n-not acting l-l-like a b-baby," says Pat. Interestingly, Pat, although apparently part of a coalition with the father, is now allying herself with George, with considerable personal effort.

George stops crying but continues to look at his toes with a theatrically tragic look on his face. Even with encouragement by the therapist, he won't say a word. He does look up at the therapist once or twice with big moist eyes, a pathetic, almost doglike expression warping his features.

"Susan," asks the therapist, "what makes you feel unhappy at times? I understand that sometimes you talk about being very unhappy, and that is why the family came here tonight." "Oh, not at home," gasps Susan. "I never say anything at home. My teacher told on me. I thought she wouldn't tell; she said she wouldn't ever get me in trouble with Mom. And then she went and called Mom and she must have told her everything I said. I'm not going to talk to anybody anymore. People can't keep a secret. Nothing's the matter with me except I wish I weren't so fat. But Mom says sometimes she's so upset she might as well commit suicide, and nobody cares."

At this point Mrs. Whitlock begins to cry loudly and insistently. "Now everybody's going to blame me for everything," she sobs, "and I'm only trying to help as best I know how. Here I work hard trying to get everybody in here for this appointment, and nobody here has even asked me what I think the problem is even though I tried to explain right when I got here. And now everybody's going to think everything is all my fault. Just listen to her, saying that I've threatened to commit suicide, like it was all my idea. Susan, you know I never meant it, and you are a very naughty child for talking about that here." (The session is overtaken by several minutes of loud sobbing by Mother. The therapist gets a box of tissues.)

Mother has now effectively shut off Susan, as she has shut off Father, George, and Pat. Only Lacey has been able to gain the upper hand with her in this session, but Lacey's life is clearly far from his own. Now is not the time to bring this communication pattern to the attention of Mother and the family. Mother, although she is effectively manipulating (controlling everyone's attention and silencing others), is genuinely hurting. At this time she will not be able to assimilate any information the therapist has already learned about the functioning of this family system and the roles the various members are playing that maintain rather than alleviate family pain. The communication pattern in this family system, which inhibits the growth of most of its members, will need to be demonstrated over time by a therapist who can remain outside of its control. The family will have to be taught how to change its pattern of communication and personal interaction, with opportunities for concrete practice of the new patterns.

The usual introductory social phase of an initial interview has been virtually omitted in this particular session, because Mother immediately attempted to control the input of information to the therapist. The therapist has had to intervene immediately to model and elicit new communication patterns, asking for information from each family member directly rather than permitting that information to come through Mother. However, the phase of problem exploration and family interaction has yielded rich data for the therapist. The therapist estimates that the family has already undergone as much stress as is a good idea in the initial interview (for the family may choose not to return to therapy if more fearful than hopeful); therefore she will use the pause precipitated by Mother's crying to decrease the situational stress. The therapist's goal at this point, in recognizing a genuinely troubled family, is to enable the family to decide to return. Kleenex tissues and reassurance of the mother that she is capable, having produced four admirable children, will mollify her and reestablish her position of family dominance, which will return the family to its normal homeostasis. In future interviews the task will be to upset this same homeostasis because it manifestly inhibits self-expression and personal growth in every member of the family. The therapeutic goal for the future will be to restructure the rules and interactional patterns of the family system into a more satisfying and growth-enhancing system, with high rather than low morale or self-esteem among the members.

The basic purpose of an initial session is beginning problem definition, at least to the stage of the presenting problem; basic fact finding related to the presenting problems, which one hopes will reveal clues about contributing underlying systemic factors; and helping the family to begin to trust the therapist. The therapist and family also need to work out a tentative initial contract, defining the initial "problem for work," the respective roles of the therapist and family, specification of who will be included in the interviews, fees, places of meeting, frequency and time of appointments, and so forth.

In the latter part of this initial interview, the therapist will endeavor to reduce the family's (particularly the mother's) fear of family therapy by helping them see the therapist's role as that of helper rather than judge. She can reassure the family that when pain is present, it is reasonable and normal to seek outside consultation to gain relief. Many families have indeed benefited from working on their problems together, she will point out, and she has noted many family strengths that make their particular situation look hopeful as far as potential for improvement is concerned. The therapist will list these strengths: intelligence, caring, ability to work hard, sense of responsibility, ability to present thoughts verbally (and the clear potential for those less comfortable with speaking, Pat and George, to develop the ability to do so).

The therapist will then help the family develop an initial commitment to therapy. Is the family willing to invest the time and effort necessary to make their family circumstances better? Can the family afford the fee (perhaps a sliding scale is available to alleviate worries about cost)? If the family is willing to enter into a contract to meet with the therapist for general improvement of family functioning, this is a useful and open-ended agreement. If the family is willing to meet with the therapist only on the more limited problem of learning how to help Susan, this is a valid contract also. If the entire family will agree to meet together regarding how to help Susan, then Susan becomes the key to working with the family. Later, the therapist may recontract with the parents: "It is becoming clearer that Susan's unhappiness has something to do with the fact that you, Mr. Whitlock, and you, Mrs. Whitlock, are not very happy yourselves, and that you sometimes are not happy about certain things concerning each other. I think it would be a good idea to talk about you and your relationship together. How about it?" When Mr. and Mrs. Whitlock have come to trust the therapist and her concern for them, they will more likely be willing to admit that they have a problem between themselves.

The Whitlocks clearly have the capacity for change, but there are indications that change will be difficult. For one thing, commitment to therapy is low. Mr. Whitlock indicates feelings of hopelessness, and he believes the important things that are stressing his life (the pain in his stomach, the endless need to earn money, his dissatisfaction with his job) cannot possibly be changed through family therapy. He believes therapy can only cause him more pain (it costs money). Mr. Whitlock has said that he isn't worried about Susan. From his point of view at the commencement of therapy, therapy is only an unnecessary new financial pressure.

Mrs. Whitlock is threatened by therapy, because already in the first interview her preferred patterns of family communication have been disturbed. She is the controlling member of the family. Yet she has felt a bigger threat from outside. That threat is her fear of loss of social standing if one of her products (her child Susan) should be labeled defective by a highly visible outside institution, the school. So Mrs. Whitlock's commitment to therapy does not initially involve a desire to bring about any change in herself or her lifestyle; rather, she wants to have her daughter straightened out.

Continuing the Counseling Process

For a therapist to work effectively with the Whitlocks (or any family), he or she will have to create a safe setting for interaction, a setting in which all members reduce their fearfulness and recognize that their attempts at communication will be received empathetically and nonjudgmentally. Reducing fear reduces the need for defensiveness. The therapist will need to structure the interviews with certain rules that help decrease the threat for all members, from very basic ones such as "no hitting," to more complex ones such as "each person here speaks for herself or himself."

The therapist needs to know how to ask for information in such a way that the person is enabled to answer. Questions that a family member may not feel safe to answer early in therapy may be necessary and possible later when trust is firmer. Techniques such as the use of embedded questions, which clearly verbalize the therapist's question without demanding or otherwise putting the client "on the spot," are helpful, as are questions that ask for a description or clarification rather than a simple yes or no answer.

A feeling of safety in the therapeutic setting can also be enhanced by therapists' demonstrating that they are not afraid to discuss or observe issues that are emotion laden and by offering support as family members experience the fears, stresses, and strains of life itself and of the experience of therapy. Therapists must also be able to demonstrate that they will not be sucked into the family system with its destructive operational patterns. Use of a co-therapist on occasion can be very helpful in avoiding the pitfall of becoming too intimate a part of the family system rather than a change agent for the system. Also useful is a one-way mirror through which a consultant watches the session. The interview can be taped or videotaped so that the therapist, the family, or both, can study it later.

Family interactional patterns and rules resist change. This is the nature of systems, as discussed earlier in this chapter. Merely "diagnosing" the nonfunctional behavior patterns and communication systems and telling family members about them will not be sufficient to create change. The family needs more than an intellectual grasp of their respective roles in maintaining dysfunctional family patterns. However, therapists must understand the patterns and rules of the ongoing family system if they are to select appropriate intervention techniques to change the system. Hence, therapists need to observe how the family interacts, so they will insist that family members talk with each other in the sessions. Where an identified client or scapegoat is present, therapists will try to understand the function of that individual in maintaining the system.

Often, the term *scapegoat* is used in a more limited sense than the term *identified client.* A child identified as a scapegoat is usually a child *blamed* by the family for a series of misdemeanors that make the family angry at him or her: bad behavior, instigating family arguments, and so forth. The term *identified client* includes the scapegoat, but can also include children whom the family do not apparently blame for creating problems for anybody except themselves. They merely see the child as having embarrassing or self-destructive problems, such as obesity, suicidal tendencies, or anorexia nervosa.

In the Whitlock family, Susan is clearly the identified client, but why Susan, and what function does she perform? Other persons in the family could have been presented as the identified client: Pat, for one, because of her stuttering and extreme social discomfort, and Father, for another, because of his feelings of hopelessness and his physical problems, which appear to be psychosomatic in origin (that is, largely caused by stress). It is probable that Susan became the identified client in this case because she is manifesting Mother's own fantasies, "committing suicide."

If the model used for therapy with this family were purely strategic, as in Haley's approach, in the first session Susan's symptoms would be highlighted more specifically as the immediate problem for work. Susan's presenting symptomatic behaviors would be explored more deeply and outlined in detail: staying at home during many school days, doing poor work at school, overeating, and talking about suicide. A specific plan to change these behaviors would be developed. For example, the therapist might direct Susan to stay home from school every day for the first week between sessions; Susan might have been directed to talk about suicide with Mother every day, but only between the hours of 9 and 10 A.M. The therapist would be acting on the theory that this would allow Susan to stay home. Then, as a part of expected behavior, she would thus practice obedience. The fearful pull of suicide would be reduced by getting that topic right out into the open, yet discussion of suicide would be confined to 1 hour per day. Mother, as a responsible parent, would feel constrained to tell Susan that she herself had no intention of committing suicide; Mother would come up with all sorts of reasons to persuade Susan that Mother wouldn't really do such a thing, and that Susan shouldn't consider doing such a thing either. Under close scrutiny, the "pull" of suicide as a means of problem solving (gaining attention) would be exposed as inadequate (the perpetrators wouldn't be around to enjoy the attention they would receive).

Under the strategic therapy model, how the task was carried out (and the results) would be discussed in detail at the next family therapy session. Further tasks would then be assigned as needed to interrupt Susan's symptomatic behaviors. The therapist would hope that this type of work would lead into therapy with the married couple, Mr. and Mrs. Whitlock.

The Whitlocks' therapist doesn't use a purely strategic model, however. She chooses to begin with a structural approach combined with techniques derived from the communication model. She studies patterns of interaction in the family as a whole to determine what factors maintain Susan's symptomatic behavior. Further interviews reveal that Mother feels stressed and unappreciated, even though she is clearly the dominant parent, and in that role is key to the family pain. Mother makes the decisions in this family. But what factors led to this situation?

Mrs. Whitlock, the only child of elderly parents, learned when she was young that she could get anything she wanted by making enough noise about it. When a direct request was ignored—because her parents were tired or involved in community issues—asking, insisting, tears, and finally temper tantrums always worked if carried on long enough. Hence, she learned to get the attention she needed by demanding it, and her demands were effective for her in that setting. Mr. Whitlock, however, was a middle child in a large family controlled by a very dominant male parent. He didn't get what he wanted, either materially or in terms of affection, no matter what he did, and so he withdrew and felt hopeless during much of his childhood. He made the most gains with his own father when he was visibly obedient, so Mr. Whitlock tended to repeat the role of the good child in his family of procreation because it worked best for him as a child. But it didn't meet his needs very well in either situation, and as an adult he still feels helpless and hopeless. From the perspective of Boszormenyi-Nagi's contextual approach, Mr. Whitlock feels he was short-changed as a child in terms of appreciation and nurturing, and that these are now owed him. Because they are not forthcoming, either from his parents or his wife, he plays the martyr role.

The combination of a demanding, blaming wife and a withdrawn, compliant, and placating husband developed into an increasingly rigid system. Mrs. Whitlock kept right on demanding, and on the surface of things, she got everything she wanted; Mr. Whitlock did her bidding. However, he was able to send effective messages to his wife that he did not appreciate how he was treated, that he did not deserve the treatment, and that he did not like Mrs. Whitlock very much because of how she treated him. Mr. Whitlock feels used and unappreciated, but Mrs. Whitlock feels lonely and misunderstood. The spousal subsystem is clearly stressed.

A new family system has developed in which everyone's self-esteem remains low and rules are rigid (set by the mother). In the new rules everything goes through Mother and must be approved by her before communication is considered valid. This type of system is "feminizing" family members (speaking in terms of the female gender role as culturally tending to be in the direction of impulse control, inhibition, passivity, and dependence on the parents, in this case the mother). All males in the Whitlock family, at the time of entrance to therapy, respond by withdrawing in one way or another, and, in fact, Pat is also. Only Susan is emotionally bonded with Mrs. Whitlock.

It is interesting to note how cultural norms for male and female gender roles affect the Whitlocks' life and emotions, helping produce some of the unhappiness and confusion of various family members. Mrs. Whitlock isn't happy, but she cannot openly admit her unhappiness to herself and thus examine the causes because she is doing exactly what she has been taught she should want to do: be a wife and a mother. She thinks she ought to feel happy and spends a lot of energy telling herself and everybody else how happy she is and what a fine family she has. However, when her children or husband try to defy her strong will, she feels desperate and deserted and breaks into tears, threatening to commit suicide because "nobody cares about me around here." As four children and one husband add up to five against one, even with Mother the very dominant and controlling personality, incidents of defiance do occur with reasonable regularity. However, Mother's tears, angry words, and accusations usually bring her the desired results. She wins each battle at the price of standing alone—nobody dares to get emotionally close to her. All defend themselves against her.

Mother's closest emotional bond is with her 10-year-old daughter, Susan, who feels her mother's loneliness. Susan becomes fearful of leaving Mother (does poorly in school, stays home from school a lot), talks about suicide with her teacher when she does attend school (the environment in which she consciously feels the most stressed), and overeats. Susan's problem then has the function of manifesting Mother's unhappiness as well as her own. Moreover, Susan does not feel especially wanted by her father. She doesn't think her father likes her very much and knows her existence is a financial burden to him.

Susan's problems are the ones recognized by the family quite simply because Mother is the parent with the power to recognize them. She is the dominant parent and thus can make the decision to take Susan to therapy when virtually nobody else wants to go. Mother will want to help Susan because she feels a bond with Susan. She will not necessarily recognize that Susan's problems reveal her own distress, although this realization comes very close to the surface in the first interview.

Further interviews reveal that Mr. Whitlock feels alienated from and angry with his wife. He feels she has put him in an impossible position. He hates his work but knows he has to work to support his family. His gender-role norm dictates that monetary support of the family is up to him, or he is a failure. He feels responsible to support his children now that they are born, but he wishes they hadn't been born, particularly Susan and George, because he felt overburdened already after the birth of the first two. He feels stuck, and because Mrs. Whitlock made him have a large family, everything is her fault. To do his duty to his family, he will have to continue to do work he dislikes forever. He is extremely resentful about it, toward his wife and the children too. He can't express his resentment toward his wife overtly because she is too powerful—she verbally puts him down whenever he expresses resentment, or she bursts into tears and threatens suicide. Besides, she can make him feel very guilty about his wish to have had fewer children. How can he not want George and Susan? Sometimes Mr. Whitlock expresses his resentment toward his children in subtle ways—by criticizing Lacey's relationship with his girlfriend or George's hypersensitivity. Mr. Whitlock is also developing somatic problems—taking out on his own body what he cannot express against the significant others in his life. This happens because his constant tension affects his body chemistry.

Continued therapy sessions reveal clear coalitions or subsystems within the family: Father and Pat, Mother and Susan, Mother and Lacey (not as strong), Pat and George, which occasionally conflicts with Pat and Father. Father has little or no relationship with Lacey, because of competition for influence with the mother. Lacey can get his way with Mother more than Father can. Mother respects Lacey more than Father as Lacey is a successful leader at school and a social success, although she disapproves of all the girls he dates. Father avoids George and Susan; he feels too tired to play with them when he comes home from work, and they are still little enough that at times they ask for his attention. Mother has little or no relationship with Pat, except to criticize her social awkwardness, her stuttering, and her appearance. Mother does not think Pat is a very good family showpiece. She is obviously awkward.

The normal *natural* subsystems do not manifest themselves in this family. The husband-wife, or spouse, subsystem exists only minimally—Father brings home the income and Mother takes care of the housework and the children. Emotionally they do not satisfy each other's basic needs, and each feels resentful about what he or she is not getting (appreciation, love, and so forth). To use Boszormenyi-Nagi's perspective, each feels unjustly treated, and the ledger is not balanced. However, Mr. and Mrs. Whitlock are also both fearful of completely losing each other, the only scrap of adult sustenance they have. Once Mother did run off with Susan to her father's home, terrifying Mr. Whitlock that he would be left having to hire a babysitter to take care of George. She came home, however, and no one spoke of the incident thereafter until it finally came up in therapy. Mrs. Whitlock had hoped that her leaving would make Mr. Whitlock more attentive, but after the first stir, nothing changed. Mr. Whitlock felt he was already doing more than could be reasonably expected of him in terms of holding up his end of the family bargain. Only Mr. Whitlock's fear of the unknown and his strong conservative values keep him from leaving his family. He feels he doesn't love Mrs. Whitlock any longer, although he doesn't admit it to her. He hasn't attempted a sexual relationship for years; she demeans him as being impotent. In fact, anger and fear of another pregnancy have created Mr. Whitlock's main sexual problem. Being ignored sexually, of course, effectively communicated to Mrs. Whitlock her husband's displeasure with her.

The children do not form a normal subsystem, either. Only Pat and George have even a minimal bond between them, and this is actually a substitute parent bond. Neither Mr. nor Mrs. Whitlock feels close to George—each has other favorites. George is alone except for Pat; their relationship has to be parental in nature as Pat is seven years older. However, she cannot provide George with much protection, since no one can stand up to Mother's anger except Lacey. The isolation is frightening for the little boy, and when he begins therapy he is effectively speechless. Mother's dominance has, in fact, kept all the children separate. She doesn't permit the children any sort of conflict in her presence, which creates an emotional separation among the children. Rather than help them solve problems of conflict together, so they can learn how to communicate and to resolve their differences constructively, she separates them and punishes them individually for quarreling. She also doesn't permit the children to stay inside the house during the day except to do chores, because they irritate her. The children actually don't have much time together. Mr. Whitlock, although he often disapproves of his wife's parenting when he is present to observe it, rarely offers any parenting of his own, corrective or otherwise. Lacey has no strong relationship with any sibling, nor does Susan. It is every child for himself or herself.

Restructuring the Family System

In this household full of isolated individuals, the family subsystems need restructuring. The husband-wife bond needs to be strengthened and made primary to provide the protection and nurturance the children need. The lopsided dominance relationship between Mr. and Mrs. Whitlock needs to be a relationship of equals. Even though their cultural mores call for the male to be dominant, and Mr. Whitlock's suffering in his subordinate position in this family is only increased due to the perceived gap in what he sees as his reality and the cultural ideal, the family need is not male dominance. What is needed is a relationship in which the needs of both parents are more nearly equally met. Each spouse needs to feel treated in a just, ethical manner by the other. By apparently meeting all the dominance needs of Mrs. Whitlock and none of those of the father, both parents are isolated and both are suffering, along with the children. Mr. Whitlock's essential feelings of suffering revolve around hopelessness and helplessness and being stuck as an overburdened economic provider. Mrs. Whitlock's essential feelings of suffering revolve around loneliness and the sense of not being loved or appreciated.

The parent subsystem has been truncated in this family so it effectively consists of Mother only. Father has withdrawn into depression and somatic complaints. The parent subsystem needs restructuring and strengthening so it includes both parents.

Moreover, the boundary between the spouse subsystem and the sibling subsystem is enmeshed. Mrs. Whitlock and Lacey, and Mr. Whitlock and Pat, are more involved emotionally than the two spouses are with each other. Such a lack of boundary between the spouse subsystem and the sibling subsystem can only be frightening and confusing to the children and to the marital pair as well.

The children could benefit by a strengthening of their subsystem as well. If the bonds among the children were stronger, or their bonds with peers outside the family were stronger, their dependence on the emotional situation between their parents would not be so profound.

Restructuring a family system is a difficult task. Certain techniques can help a family prepare for change, however. Family members can watch themselves interact on videotape, which can sensitize them to how they come across to other people. Even an audiotape recording can be very helpful for this purpose. Family members can also be separated from the rest of the family and allowed to observe family interaction patterns from behind a one-way mirror. Or, a subgroup can sit behind the rest of the family as they interact, in the role of observers. At the end of the specified interaction, the people in the subgroup can provide feedback to the family on the communication patterns they observe.

The therapist can have various members of the family group reenact conflicts through role play. Role play brings the conflicts right into the therapy room. But in role-play situations, there is opportunity to reconstruct the scenes. The therapist may choose to model more constructive ways of handling conflict, or may instruct the family members to reenact the scene but perform different or reversed roles. The therapist may have a child play the role of a parent in instances where discipline is an issue, may have the respective parent play the child, and so forth. Role play offers the possibility of practicing new and more constructive methods of conflict resolution and of developing empathy for the other person's point of view.

In the therapy sessions, the therapist may choose to escalate stress to break a nonproductive stalemate in a family conflict. Escalation of stress can temporarily break an unhealthy pattern of interaction. For example, in the Whitlock family situation, the therapist might side with Father on every issue until Mother explodes; the therapist can then deal with the function of tears and threats, and discuss and demonstrate other means of conflict resolution. Or, she may side with the mother on every issue until the father is goaded into changing his habitual pattern of placation and martyrdom and finally becomes angry enough to defend himself. The therapist can then observe his method of expressing angry feelings and learn why they are normally so ineffective in the particular family. New methods of self-assertion may be discussed, demonstrated, and practiced (Minuchin & Fishman, 1981, p. 179).

The therapist may take on an educator's role, explaining how apparent success at dominating and getting what a person wants in the short run can rob him or her of the goodwill of significant others, eventually resulting in isolation (no one left to dominate), as is happening between Mr. and Mrs. Whitlock. To fortify the intellectual understanding, simulation and role-play games can be used.

Satir (1972), for example, used family sculpting and communication games in which she had appropriate members of the family model the stance and nonverbal gestures of the placater, the blamer, the computer, and the distractor (Satir, 1972, pp. 59–79). Thus, Mrs. Whitlock would initially be assigned the role of the blamer. The therapist would help her position her body so that the nonverbal symbols of blaming would be highlighted and magnified—the pointed finger, twisted face, and so forth. Mr. Whitlock would be arranged as the placater, kneeling, open hand upward, and so forth. Lacey could be the distractor, looking off in an irrelevant direction, whistling, and so on, and Pat the computer (stiff body, upright spine). The next step is to act out the corresponding roles. Satir suggested role-playing the communication stereotypes in triads, keeping sessions to approximately 5 minutes in length. The family chooses the problem to communicate about, but each role player must stick to his or her role in a given role-play situation.

The very humor of some of the games, and the surprises revealed through observing themselves on audiotape or videotape, can loosen the rigid defenses of individual family members and break up the rigidity of the old communication patterns. Among the Whitlocks, a communication pattern exists in which Mrs. Whitlock plays blamer, Mr. Whitlock placater, and the children shift between the placater and the distractor roles in the real family situation. Through practice and demonstration, they can shift these patterns toward the more ideal interaction pattern that Satir called "leveling" or "telling it like it is."

Mrs. Whitlock also creates a typical double-bind situation for everyone. She insists that people shouldn't speak unless they have something pleasant to say. She also tells them people worth their salt are honest and should be frank, like herself. If she then asks a family member to express an opinion on something she has done ("Look at the new dress I made; what do you think of it?") to get some needed attention, but then uses a double bind if that person doesn't like the dress. If the person lies and says the dress is lovely, then that person is worthless. If the person is frank, Mother feels unappreciated and becomes angry. It is a "damned if you do, damned if you don't" communication system.

Because Mrs. Whitlock frequently places other family members in double-bind situations, they have learned to avoid real communication with her. They are experts at evasiveness ("I'm sure you must have worked hard on it, Mother") or at disappearing, either through silence, stuttering, or through activities away from home. Lacey generally chooses the latter by remaining as uninvolved as possible. The toll is great, even on Lacey, because he needs the nurturance and protection a family should provide. Moreover, Mrs. Whitlock is openly critical of all his friends, and Lacey can't always silence her. Mother recognizes that Lacey prefers his friends to her.

The toll is also great on Mrs. Whitlock. Nobody levels with her and she knows it, driving her to distress. She has no idea that she created the double binds and thus has no idea of her own role in driving her family away. She can learn to identify the setup, however, through audiotapes, videotapes, and role play, and she can then decide which she really wants most—a real relationship with her family or placation and rote obedience. She will need courage and persistence to break her patterns of relationship. It is hard to change, and besides, a dominant role provides a lot of immediate rewards.

The therapist identifies a destructive family communication "loop" involving Mother. Mother usually has to initiate verbal exchange if she wants verbal communication, due to the various types of withdrawal of the rest of the family. But then when she succeeds in eliciting responses, she criticizes them, precipitating a new withdrawal response. The new withdrawal response angers her, and she criticizes further, usually couched in language of "I'm only telling you this because I love you." Her words are of love, but her voice tone and facial expression are of anger. Family members generally believe the visual communication cues rather than the verbal, and respond as if attacked: Lacey by attacking in return, the others by further withdrawal, precipitating a new destructive communication loop, with Mother forcing a new response to try to maintain contact, being displeased with the response, and criticizing it. Pat and George effectively solve this problem by being unable to speak in their own various ways, so it is harder for Mother to "hook" them. Not surprisingly, Mrs. Whitlock feels closer to Lacey and Susan.

To break the loop, all family members have to recognize it intellectually. Then they have to practice new patterns of communication, using techniques of role play and modeling by the therapist. Mrs. Whitlock's control of the communication process has to be blocked. The process will take a great deal of energy and commitment from the family. The person for whom new self-assertion will be hardest is Mr. Whitlock, because he honestly feels he is being "a good guy" by letting Mrs. Whitlock run her show the way she thinks she wants it. He has to understand that she is in pain, too, before he can permit himself to alter his placater role. Moreover, he has never successfully attempted any other role in his life. He has to begin to believe that his own feelings are important, that he isn't being a good guy but is rather dishonest and lazy by withdrawing from the household, and that he isn't totally stuck with his unsatisfactory life. He can change. (He has to learn emotionally to understand that Mrs. Whitlock's control over him is not as invincible as his father's was when he was a small boy.)

The therapist assigns tasks to Mr. Whitlock and Mrs. Whitlock that they are to do together without the children to strengthen their marital bond. Lacey is old enough to baby-sit, so the parents are instructed to go away together on several different weekends, all by themselves, leaving Lacey in charge.

The therapist engages the couple in a discussion of their lengthy sexual abstinence, and brings the fear of pregnancy out into the open. Fear of pregnancy is discussed early in the therapeutic process, and Mr. and Mrs. Whitlock agree to share responsibility for birth control. Fortunately they don't have to cope with negative religious values in this area. Some sexual activity resumes. Later in the therapeutic process, as part of discussions of the functions of sex in the marriage as a means of communicating approval or disapproval, Mr. Whitlock will realize that he is equally responsible with his wife for procreating four children. Gradually he lets go of most of his resentment toward his wife for "insisting" on having the children. In fact, Mr. Whitlock had chosen to go along with her desires and could instead have exerted the energy to refuse to participate in conception. Mrs. Whitlock never deliberately deceived her husband through, for example, "forgetting" to use her means of contraception and "accidentally" conceiving children. She had been emotionally powerful enough to secure her husband's voluntary (if grudging) cooperation. It was only later on that Mr. Whitlock's growing resentment manifested itself in sexual abstinence. (In family therapy, some therapy sessions may be scheduled with particular family subsystems if there is a special purpose. Most of Mr. and Mrs. Whitlock's therapeutic sessions surrounding their sexual lives together will be conducted with the husband-wife subsystem.)

Lacey's baby-sitting responsibilities will involve him more closely with the sibling system without bringing him in competition with Mrs. Whitlock. Attention from Lacey pleases all the children and helps strengthen the sibling system. Another related task the therapist assigns is for Mrs. Whitlock to take time outside of her family system without her children, leaving Mr. Whitlock in charge, strengthening his bond with the children and weakening her total dependence on child-rearing as her only meaning in life. The therapist also meets with Susan and her teacher (as soon as possible after the commencement of the family counseling) to discuss ways to overcome her fear of school. A "big sister," who also acts as a tutor, is found for her. (A major and very important difference between social workers doing family therapy and professionals from other backgrounds such as psychology doing similar work is that social workers are much more likely to involve resources from the wider environment. That is because social workers are educated to use a "person-in-environment" perspective.)

An opening for working with the family "story" arises. Working with a family's story is a creative intervention suggested by constructivists, as discussed earlier in this chapter. As also mentioned earlier, Mrs. Whitlock openly verbalized that "a woman's place is in the home." Her family has accepted this pronouncement without challenge, although such a role description is certainly very traditional and conservative. Since the mother repeated it often, however, it had become a virtual "family story."

The therapist decides to explore the story. "Where did it come from?" she asked after repeating it during a session.

"Why, my mother told me," responds Mrs. Whitlock, obviously surprised at the question. "My mother always said a woman's place was in the home."

"Was your mother a full time homemaker?"

"Yes, of course she was. In her generation everybody was."

"How happy was your mother as a full time homemaker?"

"Very happy, of cour—" Mrs. Whitlock begins. And then she stops and begins to frown.

She continues slowly. "Actually, my mother had a beautiful contralto voice. She wanted to be a singer. She even began taking voice lessons, but her father made her stop. When I was a child Mother sang solos in church every Sunday, but I always knew she wanted to do more, to sing professionally. She died pretty young; her health was never very good, as I remember."

"Could your mother's health have been affected by frustration, perhaps frustration of her desire to be a singer?"

A vacant look comes over Mrs. Whitlock's face. This is difficult for her to think about. "I suppose so," she says at last.

After a lengthy pause, the therapist continues. "You know, times are changing. Many people today believe that a woman's place is anywhere she wants to be."

"But a mother must be available to supervise her children."

"Yes," agrees the therapist, validating the mother before challenging her. "That's a very important responsibility for any parent. But I'm not sure it's the sole responsibility of the mother. Today, fathers expect to pitch in, or other arrangements for child care can be made. People believe that women, like men, have dreams they wish to accomplish outside the home. I'm wondering if there's anything else you've wanted to do—a hobby, a profession, something like that."

"Oh," Mrs. Whitlock replies promptly. "I do have a hobby, right now. I love to sew, to make home decorations, curtains, draperies, that sort of thing."

"That's an impressive talent," responds the therapist seriously. "Have you ever thought of turning it into a paid profession?"

"But what about the children—"

"*Have* you ever thought of turning your talent at interior decoration into a paid profession? You know, that would relieve your husband from having to carry the entire burden of supporting this family. Your children are old enough now to spend some time by themselves."

Mr. Whitlock speaks without being specifically addressed, a rare offering. "I must admit, Elsie, it would be a relief to me. I might be able to look for a different job if we had another financial provider in the family."

Startled, Mrs. Whitlock asks her husband, "You mean, you would like me to work outside our home, Harry?"

While the therapist doesn't comment on it here, use of given names rather than titles such as "Mother" and "Daddy" indicate that these two are now functioning as members of a spousal subsystem, not just the parental.

"Yes," Mr. Whitlock replies simply. "If you would consider it, and if you could find a job you liked, of course."

"Maybe it's time to change the family story," suggests the therapist. "By that, I mean that I think you have been using 'a woman's place is in the home' as a sort of family story, and I'm not sure it fits any more. Can you think of something that might work better for you now?"

Again, it is Mr. Whitlock who speaks. "How about something like, 'a woman's place is anywhere in the human race.' " He grins and continues, "and that might include the rat race they call the job market."

Mrs. Whitlock looks hard at her husband. The children are amazed; they've rarely heard their father speak so frankly.

"A woman's place is anywhere in the human race," Mrs. Whitlock repeats slowly. "What would my mother think." Then she looks directly at her husband. "Why," she says with a smile that seems almost shy, "I think she would have liked it."

"Can we consider this your new family story?" asks the therapist. "A new story with an important new idea to think about?"

Both parents nod, and the children grin, pleased. "It's about time," says Lacey.

At this point, the therapist senses the entire family is ready to talk about change. In the next few sessions, she will invite each family member to discuss their hopes for the future.

It becomes clear that Pat in particular is not excited about going to college but would prefer to work in a music store for a while. She thinks she might want to go to college someday but is willing to save some money in advance for it. However, she is certain her parents would insist on college attendance right after high school and hence has resented rather than appreciated her parents' real financial sacrifice in her behalf as they tried to save for her college expenses. George and Susan are too young to know what they think about college, but Mr. and Mrs. Whitlock recognize that their preoccupation with college for their children is more their own expectation (reflecting a societal status symbol) than a necessity. Lacey does want to go to college right after high school but is willing to pay some of his own expenses.

None of the children want Mr. Whitlock to continue working at a job he hates. They feel responsible for his misery and helpless to change it. Mother also recognizes that Father's unhappiness more than cancels out the benefits of his reliable and adequate income. Moreover, Mrs. Whitlock recognizes that she doesn't enjoy being in the home all day herself, that maybe her place isn't totally in the home, and that perhaps she could better utilize her time and energy by providing part of the family income. Once Mrs. Whitlock recognizes her irritation with child-rearing without guilt, the family can make some shifts in its linkage with the economic market. Mr. Whitlock will change to a lesser paying job that allows him more freedom and personal creativity, which he craves. Mrs. Whitlock will take a part-time job with an interior decorating firm which demands emotional energy, thus reducing her demands on her children to supply her meaning in life. She will thus help reduce financial pressures. The family ledger will be more evenly balanced, each spouse clearly receiving as well as giving. The children will understand that seemingly hopeless circumstances can indeed be changed and that they can influence their own futures. They will take themselves seriously, and the family will pull together.

Maintenance of Gains and Termination of Counseling

Family therapy can often be effectively completed in a few weeks, but the problems of the Whitlocks required a longer time to resolve. Therapy for the family continued for approximately a year, until Mr. Whitlock was established in a new job and Mrs. Whitlock was working part-time and able to release her rigid control on the family system. Important changes have taken place and are being maintained. Lacey works part time, saving for college, and Pat seriously visits music stores with an eye toward future employment. She still stutters somewhat but is no longer reprimanded for it. Susan attends school regularly, doing average work scholastically, and no longer talks of suicide. George talks, at least occasionally. Mr. and Mrs. Whitlock regularly take time to do things as a couple, and even though they still disagree with each other frequently, they can talk with each other about their feelings and work out compromise solutions. At this point, termination of therapy became appropriate.

Termination itself requires preparation so that the family system won't revert to its old patterns of interaction, which can be brought on by distress precipitated by the withdrawal of the person (the therapist) who has been actively intervening to restructure the system. Discussion of termination must begin well in advance of its occurrence. Mutual evaluations by family members of where they came from at the beginning of therapy, where they are now, and where they would like to go ideally can be helpful. Assurance by the therapist of continued availability should the family feel the need is also helpful. A gradual tapering off of interview sessions—for example, from once a week to once every two weeks, with a final meeting a month or so later—may help reduce regression. (For further information on termination and evaluation, see Chapters 6, 7, and 11.)

Summary

This chapter describes social work practice with families. A wide diversity of family patterns exists in the world. Although the nuclear family is still the predominant family form in our society, it is a serious mistake for social workers to use the nuclear family as the ideal model that individuals should strive to form. Many other family forms also function well and deserve respect.

Family patterns and forms are substantially affected by the culture (larger system) in which they are located. Families in our society perform the following functions that help maintain continuity and stability in society: replacement of the population, care of the young, socialization of new members, regulation of sexual behavior, and provision of affection.

An infinite number of problems can occur in families. When there are problems in a family, social services are often needed. There is extensive variation in the types and forms of services social workers provide to troubled families.

The two areas in social work practice with families that have received the most attention are family assessment and family therapy. Two assessment techniques are described: eco-maps and genograms. An eco-map provides a snapshot view of important family interactions at a particular point in time. A genogram, essentially a family tree, is a graphic way of investigating the origins of family problems over at least three generations.

One of the many social services provided to families is family therapy. In this chapter family therapy is defined. Characteristics of open and closed family systems are described. Coalitions and alliances between subsystems and members of subsystems are discussed, as well as ideas of how and why certain subsystems are formed and how behaviors of particular subsystems affect behaviors in others. The role of the identified client and/or scapegoat in helping maintain unhealthy family homeostasis and in serving as somewhat socially acceptable tickets of admission to therapy is explored and discussed in detail.

Four system approaches to family therapy are described and compared: those of Satir, Minuchin, Haley, and Boszormenyi-Nagi. Satir stressed clarification of family communication patterns. Satir pointed out incongruent messages and double binds to family members and taught family members to send clear, congruent messages instead. She analyzed rules in the family and helped clarify them in the context that rules may be bad but the people setting or bound by them are not. She taught family members how to change bad rules and insisted each member be heard in her presence, thus teaching respect for each person and each point of view. She emphasized that differentness between family members should be openly acknowledged and used for growth.

Minuchin's major emphasis in therapy is restructuring the major subsystems (spouse, parental, and sibling) within the family so that each can accomplish its appropriate functions. Minuchin is considered to be a member of the structural approach to family therapy. According to Minuchin, the parental, the spouse, and the sibling subsystems have different major functions that must be fulfilled if the family is to survive as a healthy unit. In restructuring the family, Minuchin had members consciously understand and improve communication patterns. Or, he bypassed direct cognitive understanding by a family of its communication patterns and instead use a paradoxical suggestion.

Haley's approach involves clearly defining and describing the presenting problem and assigning specific tasks or directives to solve the presenting problem. With resistive families, paradoxical directives may be used, with the therapist choosing to act "puzzled" when the presenting problem is alleviated.

Boszormenyi-Nagi introduced an ethical dimension to family therapy, calling his approach contextual therapy. He believed that every family keeps a kind of "ledger" of debts and entitlements that must be reasonably well balanced within and across generations. If not, a sense of injustice may lead to symptomatic behavior by various family members.

Also described is the constructivist approach (a recent trend in family therapy), which asserts that reality is merely a product of our expectations and assumptions, and as such can be challenged and changed. Constructivist therapists work to identify family stories or narratives that actively shape their experiences, and then assist families to develop more hopeful stories that can shape lives in more satisfying directions.

The chapter also examines the role of the social worker as change agent in the guise of family counselor or therapist, using the perspective of family counseling and therapy as an example of the problem-solving process in the systems perspective.

EXERCISES

1. AN ECO-MAP OF MY FAMILY

Goal: To gain insight into the dynamics of families using eco-maps.

Step 1: Draw an eco-map of your family.

Step 2: Volunteers share and describe their eco-maps.

Step 3: Class discussion about problems encountered and the merits and shortcomings of eco-maps.

2. A GENOGRAM OF MY FAMILY

Goal: To gain insight into the dynamics of families using genograms.

Step 1: Draw a genogram of your family.

Step 2: Volunteers share and describe their genograms.

Step 3: Class discussion on the problems encountered and the merits and shortcomings of genograms.

3. *THE APPLICATION OF SYSTEMS THEORY CONCEPTS TO A FAMILY'S INTERACTION*[4]

Goal: To explore systems theory principles. Student volunteers are asked to assume specific roles in a family. The family is presented with various situations, and then family members are asked to describe their reactions. Following each situation is a brief class discussion focusing on the identification of various systems concepts to describe family interactions.

Objectives
1. Describe some systems theory concepts and apply them to a family's interactions.
2. Examine the effects of various problem and crisis situations on families.

Step 1: Role-play. Three groups of volunteers are needed. You can opt to role-play the situations noted below extemporaneously or rehearse them for next class.

Step 2: Class presentations of the role-play.

Step 3: Class discussion of how the family system might be affected in each of the three situations.

Rob: husband and father; age 41; calm, level-headed; makes most of the family's decisions; works as an accountant; makes an upper-middle-class income	Laura: wife and mother; age 35; pleasant, attractive, warm; typically follows Rob's lead; does not work outside the home	Benji: 15-year-old son; quiet, private, likes to spend time alone; has a few friends who tend to have a history of minor delinquencies; maintains a B– average in school	Susie: 10-year-old daughter; outgoing, personable; has numerous friends and interests; maintains an A average in school

Situation 1: Rob loses his job and the family is in serious financial difficulty.

Family members' reactions

a. Stress due to economic conditions may cause Rob and Laura to have marital conflict. The spouse subsystem may be weakened.
b. Benji and Susie may be confused and worried about the future.
c. All family members might be angry at the lack of funds for personal use.

Systems theory applications

a. Homeostasis within the system is disrupted.
b. Change affecting Rob affects the entire family system.
c. The system may change from being an open system with easy interchange of information across system boundaries to a closed system under stress. New information and input may no longer be easily assimilated.

[4]This exercise was written by Karen K. Kirst-Ashman, Ph.D., professor in the social work department, University of Wisconsin—Whitewater.

(continued)

EXERCISES
(continued)

Situation 2: Rob finds another comparable job. However, Laura finds a full-time job as a receptionist at a law firm. She decides she likes the additional income and the feeling of competence and independence that the job provides.

Family members' reactions

a. Rob may resent Laura's newfound sense of independence. The spouse subsystem may be further disrupted.
b. The children may resent not having a mother doing things for them at home more regularly.
c. All family members may feel more pressure to participate in household tasks when they are at home.

Systems theory applications

a. The parental subsystem may be disturbed as a result of the change in roles.
b. Boundaries within the system may change. Rob, Benji, and Susie may form a new subsystem in reaction to Laura's absence.

Situation 3: The school vice-principal calls and complains that Benji has fallen asleep in his class several times, and that a bottle of Southern Comfort was found in his school locker.

Family members' reactions

a. Rob and Laura are shocked and worried about what to do.
b. Benji may feel isolated and become even more withdrawn.
c. Susie may become very worried about Benji and approach him to offer any help she can give.

Systems theory applications

a. Homeostasis within the family system has been disturbed.
b. The parental subsystem may be strengthened to combat this newly defined problem.
c. The sibling subsystem may be strengthened if Benji and Susie form an alliance.
d. The entire family system may have to become a more open system to work with outside resources to solve the problem. The school, a counselor or therapist, or Alcoholics Anonymous may become involved in problem solving.

CHAPTER 9

Social Work with Organizations

An organization is defined here as a collectivity of individuals gathered together to serve a particular purpose. The purposes (or goals) that people organize to achieve are infinite in number, ranging from obtaining basic necessities to eliminating the threat of worldwide terrorism or attaining world peace. In each case an organization exists because people working together can better accomplish tasks and achieve goals than one individual can.

Etzioni (1964) described the importance of organizations in our lives:

> We are born in organizations, educated by organizations, and most of us spend much of our lives working for organizations. We spend much of our leisure time paying, playing, and praying in organizations. Most of us will die in an organization, and when the time comes for burial, the largest organization of all—the state—must grant official permission. (p. 1)

The importance of organizations for social work practice has been summarized by Netting, Kettner, and McMurtry (1998):

> As social workers, our roles within, interactions with, and attempts to manipulate organizations define much of what we do. Clients often come to us seeking help because they are not able to obtain help from organizations that are critical to their survival or quality of life. In turn, the resources we attempt to gain for these clients usually come from still other organizations. . . . Social workers with little or no idea of how organizations operate, how they interact, or how they can be influenced and changed from both outside and inside are likely to be severely limited in their effectiveness. (pp. 193–194)

Many disciplines (including business, psychology, political science, and sociology) have produced a prodigious amount of theory and research on organizations. However, in spite of the importance of organizations to social work practice, the amount of social work literature devoted to organizations is limited. One significant reference in this area is *Social Work Macro Practice* 2nd ed. (Netting, Kettner, & McMurtry, 1998). Another is *Generalist Practice with Organizations and Communities* (Kirst-Ashman & Hull, 1997).

One subcategory of organizations that is particularly relevant to social work is social agencies. Most social workers are employed by social agencies. According to Barker (2000), a social agency is:

> An organization or facility that delivers *social services* under the auspices of a board of directors and is usually staffed by human services personnel (including professional social workers, members of other professions, paraprofessionals, clerical personnel, and sometimes indigenous workers). It provides a specified range of social services for members of a population group that has or is vulnerable to a specific social problem. (p. 447)

This chapter will provide you with an introduction to social work practice with organizations. Several theories are presented, providing a variety of perspectives for viewing and analyzing organizations.

Models of Organizational Behavior

The Autocratic Model

The autocratic model has existed for thousands of years. During the Industrial Revolution, it was the prominent model of organizational function. The model depends on *power.* Those who are in power act autocratically. The message to employees is "You do this—or else," meaning that employees who don't follow orders are penalized, often severely.

The autocratic model uses one-way communication—from the top down to workers. Management believes that it knows best. The employees' obligation is to follow orders. The thinking is that employees have to be persuaded, directed, and pushed into performance; this is management's task. Management does the thinking, and the workers obey the directives. Under autocratic conditions, the workers' role is *obedience* to management.

The autocratic model is very effective in some settings. Military organizations throughout the world are formulated on this model. The model was also used during the Industrial Revolution—for example, in building great railroad systems and in operating giant steel mills. Today, it is a legitimate question to wonder whether modern models of organizational behavior might not have worked better in these historic endeavors.

The autocratic model has a number of disadvantages. Workers are often in the best position to identify shortcomings in the structure and technology of the organizational system, but one-way communication prevents feedback to management. The model also fails to generate commitment among workers to accomplish organizational goals. Finally, the model fails to motivate workers to further develop their skills (skills that often would be highly beneficial to the employer).

The Custodial Model

Many decades ago when the autocratic model was the predominant model of organizational behavior, some progressive managers began to study their employees and soon found that the autocratic model had disturbing side effects. Employees felt insecure about their continued employment, were frustrated, and had feelings of aggression toward management. Since they could not express their discontent directly, they expressed it indirectly. Among other things, employees sabotaged production. Davis and Newstrom (1989) described sabotage in a wood-processing plant:

> Managers treated workers crudely, sometimes even to the point of physical abuse. Since employees could not strike back directly for fear of losing their jobs, they found another way to do it. They *symbolically* fed their supervisor to a log-shredding machine! They did this by purposely destroying good sheets of veneer, which made the supervisor look bad when monthly efficiency reports were prepared. (p. 31)

In the 1890s and 1900s progressive employers thought that if these feelings could be alleviated, employees might work harder, which would increase productivity. To satisfy employees' security needs, a number of companies began to provide welfare programs, such as pension programs, child-care centers at the workplace, health insurance, and life insurance. However, researchers found that the custodial approach leads to dependence on the organization. According to Davis and Newstrom (1989, p. 31), "If employees have ten years of seniority under the union contract and a good pension program, they cannot afford to quit even if the grass looks greener somewhere else!"

Employees working under a custodial model tend to focus on economic rewards and benefits. They are happier and more content than under the autocratic model, but they don't have a high commitment to helping the organization accomplish its goals. They give *passive cooperation* to their employer. The model's most evident flaw is that most employees produce substantially below their capacities. They are not motivated to advance to higher capacities. Employees don't feel fulfilled or motivated. The point here is that contented employees are not necessarily the most productive employees.

The Scientific Management Model

One of the earliest and most important schools of thought on the management of workplace functions and tasks was based on the work of Frederick Taylor (1947). Taylor was a mechanical engineer, an American industrialist, and an educator. He focused primarily on management techniques that would increase productivity. He asserted that many organizational problems involved misunderstandings between managers and workers. Managers erroneously thought that workers were lazy and unemotional, and they mistakenly believed they understood workers' jobs. Workers mistakenly thought that managers only wanted to exploit them.

To solve these problems, Taylor developed the *scientific management model,* which focused on the need for managers to conduct scientific analyses of the workplace. One of the first steps was to conduct a careful study of how each job could best be accomplished. An excellent way to do this, according to Taylor, was to identify the best workers for each job and then carefully study how they effectively and efficiently did the work. The goal of this analysis was to discover the optimal way of doing the job—in Taylor's words, the "one best way." Once this best way was identified, tools could be modified to better complete the work, workers' abilities and interests could be fitted to particular job assignments, and the level of production that the average worker could sustain could be gauged.

Once the level of production for the average worker was determined, Taylor indicated the next step was to provide incentives to increase productivity. His favorite strategy for doing this was the piece-rate wage, in which workers were paid for each unit they produced. The goals were to produce more units, reduce unit cost, increase organizational productivity and profitability, and provide incentives for workers to produce more.

Taylor's work has been criticized as having a techniques bias, since it tends to treat workers as little more than cogs in a wheel. No two workers are exactly alike, so the "one best way" of doing a job is often unique to the person doing it. In fact, forcing the same work approach on different workers may actually decrease both productivity and worker satisfaction. In addition, Taylor's approach has limited application to human services. Since each client is unique—with unique needs, unique environmental impacting factors, and unique strengths and capacities—each human services case has to be individualized, and therefore it is difficult (if not impossible) to specify the "one best way" to proceed.

The Human Relations Model

In 1927, the Hawthorne Works of the Western Electric Company in Chicago began a series of experiments designed to discover ways to increase worker satisfaction and worker productivity (Roethlisberger & Dickson, 1939). Hawthorne Works manufactured telephones on an assembly-line basis. Workers needed no special skills and performed simple, repetitive tasks. The workers were not unionized, and management sought to find ways to increase productivity. If job satisfaction could be increased, employees would work more efficiently, and productivity would then increase.

The company tested the effects on productivity of a number of factors: rest breaks, better lighting, changes in the number of work hours, changes in the wages paid, improved food facilities, and so on. The results were surprising. Productivity increased, as expected, with improved working conditions; but it also increased when working conditions worsened. This latter finding was unexpected and led to additional study.

The investigators discovered that participation in the experiments was extremely attractive to the workers. They felt they had been selected by the management for their individual abilities, and so they worked harder, even when working conditions became less favorable. In addition, the workers' morale and general attitude toward work improved because they felt they were receiving special attention. By participating in this study, the workers were able to work in smaller groups and became involved in making decisions. Working in smaller groups developed a stronger sense of solidarity with their fellow workers. Being involved in decision making decreased their feelings of meaninglessness and powerlessness about their work.

In sociological and psychological research, the results of this study have become known as the "Hawthorne effect." In essence, when subjects know they are participants in a study, this awareness leads them to behave differently and substantially influences the results.

The results of this study, and of other similar studies, led some researchers to conclude that the key variables affecting productivity are social factors. Etzioni (1964, pp. 34–35) summarized some of the basic tenets of the human relations approach:

- The level of production is set by social norms, not by physiological capacities.

- Noneconomic rewards and sanctions significantly affect the behavior of the workers and largely limit the effect of economic incentive plans.
- Workers do not act or react as individuals but as members of groups.
- The role of leadership is important in understanding social factors in organizations, and this leadership may be either formal or informal.

Numerous studies provide evidence to support these tenets (Netting, Kettner, & McMurtry, 1998).

Workers who are capable of greater productivity often will not excel because they are unwilling to exceed the "average" level set by the norms of the group, even if this means earning less. Studies have also found that attempts by management to influence workers' behaviors are often more successful if targeted at the group as a whole, rather than at individuals. Finally, studies have documented the importance of informal leadership in influencing workers' behavior in ways that can either amplify or negate formal leadership directives. This model asserts that managers who succeed in increasing productivity are most likely responsive to the workers' social needs.

One criticism of the human relations model is (surprisingly) that it tends to manipulate, dehumanize, oppress, and exploit workers. The model leads to the conclusion that management can increase productivity by helping workers become content rather than by increasing economic rewards for higher productivity. It concentrates power and decision making at the top. It is not intended to empower employees in the decision-making process or to assist them in acquiring genuine participation in running the organization. The practice of dealing with people on the basis of their perceived social relationships in the workplace may also be a factor in perpetuating the "good old boys" network; this network has disadvantaged women and people of color over the years. Another criticism of the human relations approach is that a happy workforce is not necessarily a productive workforce, because the norms for worker production may be set well below the workers' levels of capability.

Theory X and Theory Y

Douglas McGregor (1960) developed two theories of management. He theorized that management thinking and behavior are based on two different sets of assumptions, which he labeled Theory X and Theory Y.

Theory X managers view employees as incapable of much growth. Employees are perceived as having an inherent dislike for work and as attempting to evade work whenever possible. Therefore, X-type managers believe they must control, direct, force, or threaten employees to make them work. Employees are also viewed as having relatively little ambition, wishing to avoid responsibilities, and preferring to be directed. Theory X managers therefore spell out job responsibilities carefully, set work goals without employee input, use external rewards (such as money) to force employees to work, and punish those who deviate from established rules. Because Theory X managers reduce responsibilities to a level at which few mistakes can be made, work usually becomes so structured that it is monotonous and distasteful. These assumptions, of course, are inconsistent with what behavioral scientists assert are effective principles for directing, influencing, and motivating people. (Theory X managers are, in essence, adhering to an autocratic model of organizational behavior.)

In contrast, *Theory Y managers* view employees as wanting to grow and develop by exerting physical and mental effort to accomplish work objectives to which they are committed. These managers believe that the promise of internal rewards, such as self-respect and personal improvement, are stronger motivators than external rewards (money) and punishment. They also believe that under proper conditions, employees will not only accept responsibility but seek it. Most employees are assumed to have considerable ingenuity, creativity, and imagination for problem solving. Therefore, they are given considerable responsibility to test the limits of their capabilities. Mistakes and errors are viewed as necessary phases of the learning process, and work is structured so employees have a sense of accomplishment and growth.

Employees who work for Y-type managers are generally more creative and productive, experience greater work satisfaction, and are more highly motivated than employees who work for X-type managers. Under both management styles, expectations often become self-fulfilling prophecies.

The Collegial Model

A useful extension of Theory Y is the collegial model, which emphasizes the team concept. It involves employees working closely together and feeling a commitment to achieve a common purpose. Some organizations—

such as university departments, research laboratories, and most human services organizations—have a goal of creating a collegial atmosphere to facilitate achieving their purposes. (Sadly, many such organizations are unsuccessful in creating such an atmosphere.)

Creating a collegial atmosphere is highly dependent on management building a feeling of partnership with employees. When such a partnership develops, employees feel needed and useful. Managers are then viewed as joint contributors rather than as bosses. Management is the *coach* who builds a better team. Davis and Newstrom (1989) described some of the approaches to developing a team concept:

> The feeling of partnerships can be built in many ways. Some organizations have abolished the use of reserved parking spaces for executives, so every employee has an equal chance of finding one close to the workplace. Some firms have tried to eliminate the use of terms like "bosses" and "subordinates," feeling that those terms simply create perceptions of psychological distance between managers and nonmanagers. Other employers have removed time clocks, set up "fun committees," sponsored company canoe trips, or required managers to spend a week or two annually working in field or factory locations. All of these approaches are designed to build a spirit of mutuality, in which every person makes contributions and appreciates those of others. (p. 34)

If the sense of partnership is developed, employees produce quality work and seek to cooperate with coworkers, not because management directs them to do so but because they feel an internal obligation to produce high-quality work. The collegial approach thus leads to a sense of *self-discipline.* In this environment, employees are more apt to have a sense of fulfillment, to feel self-actualized, and to produce higher quality work.

Theory Z

William Ouchi described the Japanese style of management in his 1981 best-seller *Theory Z.* In the late 1970s and early 1980s, the U.S. business world focused on the Japanese approach to management, as markets long dominated by American firms (such as the automobile industry) were taken over by Japanese industries. Japanese industrial organizations had rapidly overcome their earlier reputation for poor quality work and were setting worldwide standards for quality and durability.

Theory Z asserted that the theoretical principles underlying Japanese management went beyond Theory Y. According to Theory Z, a business organization in Japan is more than the profitability oriented entity that it is in the United States. It is a way of life. It provides lifetime employment. It is enmeshed with the nation's political, social, and economic network. Furthermore, its influence spills over into many other organizations, such as nursery schools, elementary and secondary schools, and universities.

The basic philosophy of Theory Z is that involved and committed workers are the key to increased productivity. Ideas and suggestions about how to improve the organization are routinely solicited and implemented, where feasible. One strategy for accomplishing this is the *quality circle,* where employees and management routinely meet to brainstorm about ways to improve productivity and quality.

In contrast to American organizations, Japanese organizations don't have written objectives or organizational charts. Most work is done in teams, and decisions are made by consensus. The teams tend to function without a designated leader. Cooperation within units, and between units, is emphasized. Loyalty to the organization is also emphasized, as is organizational loyalty to the employee.

Experiments designed to transplant Japanese-style management to the United States have met with mixed success. In most cases American organizations have concluded that Theory Z probably works quite well in a homogeneous culture that has Japan's societal values, but some components do not fit well with the more heterogeneous and individualistic character of the United States. In addition, some firms in volatile industries (such as electronics) have difficulty balancing their desire to provide lifetime employment with the need to adjust their workforces to meet rapidly changing market demands. And Japan's two-decade-long recession has shown that consensus can also foster paralysis.

Management by Objectives

Fundamental to the core of an organization is its purpose; that is, the commonly shared understanding of the reason for its existence.

Management theorist Peter Drucker (1954) proposed a strategy for making organizational goals and objectives the central construct around which organizational life is designed to function. In other words, instead of focusing on employee needs and wants, or on organizational structure, as the ways to increase efficiency and productivity, Drucker proposed beginning with the desired outcome and working backward. The strategy is first to identify the organizational objectives or goals, and then to adapt the organizational tasks, resources, and structure to meet those objectives. This management by objectives (MBO) approach is designed to focus the organization's efforts on meeting these objectives. Success is determined, then, by the degree to which stated objectives are reached.

This approach can be applied to the organization as a whole, as well as to internal divisions or departments. When the MBO approach is applied to internal divisions, the objectives set for each division should be consistent and supportive of the overall organizational objectives.

In many areas, including human services, the MBO approach can also be applied to the cases being serviced by each employee. Goals are set with each client, tasks to meet these goals are then determined, and deadlines are set for completion of these tasks. The degree of success of each case is then determined at a later date (often when a case is closed) by the extent to which stated goals were achieved.

An adaptation of the MBO approach, called strategic planning and budgeting (SPB), has become popular in the 1990s and early 2000s. The process involves first specifying the overall vision or mission of an organization, then identifying a variety of more specific objectives or plans for achieving that vision, and finally adapting the resources to meet the specific high-priority objectives or plans. Organizations now often hire outside consultants to oversee the SPB process.

One major advantage of the MBO approach for an organization (or its divisions) is that it produces clear statements (made available to all employees) about the objectives and the tasks that are expected to be accomplished in specified time periods. This type of activity tends to improve cooperation and collaboration. The MBO approach is also useful because it provides a guide for allocating resources and a focus for monitoring and evaluating organizational efforts.

An additional benefit of the MBO approach is in the area of diversity in the workplace. Prior to this approach, those responsible for hiring failed to employ women and people of color in significant numbers. As affirmative action programs were developed within organizations, the MBO approach was widely used to set specific hiring goals and objectives. The result has been significant changes in recruitment approaches that have enabled a number of women and other minorities to secure employment.

Total Quality Management

The theorist most closely associated with developing total quality management (TQM) is W. Edwards Deming (1986). Deming formed many of his theories during World War II when he developed statistical methods to speed up military production. Deming taught the Japanese his theories of quality control and continuous improvement following World War II, and he is now recognized, along with J. Juran (1989) and others, for laying the groundwork for Japan's industrial and economic boom.

Total quality management has been defined by Omachonu and Ross (1994) as:

> The integration of all functions and processes within an organization in order to achieve continuous improvement of the quality of goods and services. The goal is customer satisfaction. (p. 1)

TQM is based on a number of ideas. It means thinking about quality in terms of all functions of the enterprise and is a start-to-finish process that integrates interrelated functions at all levels. It is a systems approach that considers every interaction between the various elements of the organization. TQM asserts that the management of many businesses and organizations makes the mistake of blaming what goes wrong in an organization on individual people, not the system. TQM, instead, believes in the *85/15 rule,* which asserts that 85 percent of the problems can be corrected only by changing systems (structures, rules, practices, expectations, and traditions that are largely determined by management), and less than 15 percent of the problems can be resolved by correcting individual workers. When problems arise, TQM asserts that management should look for causes in the system and work to remove them before casting blame on workers.

TQM asserts that quality includes continuously improving all of the organization's processes that lead to customer satisfaction. Customer satisfaction is the main purpose of the organization. The customer is not the "point of sale"; the customer is part of the design and production process. Therefore, customers' needs must be monitored continuously.

In recent years numerous organizations have adopted a TQM approach to improve their goods and services. One of the reasons quality is being emphasized more is because consumers are increasingly shunning mass-produced, poorly made, disposable products. Companies are realizing that to remain competitive in global markets, quality of products and services is essential. Ford's motto of "Quality Is Job One" symbolizes this emphasis on quality.

There are a variety of approaches to TQM, largely because numerous theoreticians have advanced somewhat diverse approaches. A summary of these approaches is contained in *Principles of Total Quality* (Omachonu & Ross, 1994). A description of all of these approaches is beyond the scope of this text. However, Hower (1994, p. 10) provides a summary of many of the principles of TQM:

- Employees asking their external and internal customers what they need, and providing more of it
- Instilling pride into every employee
- Concentrating on information and data (a common language) to solve problems, instead of concentrating on opinions and egos
- Developing leaders, not managers, and knowing the difference
- Improving every process (everyone is in a process), checking this improvement at predetermined times, then improving it again if necessary
- Helping every employee enjoy his or her work while the organization continues to become more productive
- Providing a forum or open atmosphere so that employees at all levels feel free to voice their opinions when they think they have good ideas
- Receiving a continuous increase in those suggestions, and accepting and implementing the best ones
- Utilizing the teamwork concept, since teams often make better decisions than individuals
- Empowering these teams to implement their recommended solutions and learn from their failures
- Reducing the number of layers of authority to enhance this empowerment
- Recognizing complaints as opportunities for improvement

These principles give a "flavor" of TQM.

Summary Comments About Models of Organizational Behavior

Any of these models can be successfully applied in some situations. The question of which model to apply to obtain the highest productivity depends on the tasks to be completed and on employee needs and expectations. For example, the autocratic model works well in military operations, where quick decisions are needed to respond to rapidly changing crises. However, this model does not work well in human services organizations in which employees expect Theory Y management style.

In addition, some of these models or approaches can be applied simultaneously. For example, the management by objectives approach can be used at the same time that an organization is using any of the other models described.

Value Orientations in Organizational Decision Making

In theory, the task of making decisions (on objectives and goals) in organizations should follow a definite rational process, including identifying the problems, specifying resource limitations, weighing the advantages and disadvantages of proposed solutions, and selecting the resolution strategy with the fewest risks and the greatest chance of success. In practice, however, subjective influences (particularly on value orientations) can impede the rational process.

Most people tend to believe that decisions are made primarily on the basis of objective facts and figures. However, values and assumptions form the bases of most decisions, and facts and figures are used only in relation to these values and assumptions. Consider the following list of questions pertinent to providing social services. What do they indicate about how we make our most important decisions?

- Should abortions be permitted or prohibited during the first weeks following conception?
- Should homosexuality be viewed as a natural expression of sexuality?
- When does harsh discipline of a child become child abuse?
- Should the primary objective of imprisonment be rehabilitation or retribution?

Answers to these questions are usually not based on data uncovered after careful research; they are based on individual beliefs about the value of life, personal freedom, and protective social standards. Even everyday decisions are based largely on values.

Practically every decision is also based on certain assumptions. Without assumptions, nothing can be proved. Assumptions are made in every research study to test any hypothesis. For example, in a market survey analysts assume that the instruments they use (such as a questionnaire) will be valid and reliable. It cannot even be proved the sun will rise in the east tomorrow without assuming that its history provides the proof.

Decision makers bring not only their objective knowledge and expertise to the decision-making process but also their value orientations, unique attitudes, feelings, biases, and vested interests.

Value orientation means an individual's own ideas about what is desirable and worthwhile. Most values are acquired through prior learning experiences in interactions with family, friends, educators, organizations such as the church, and anyone else who has made an impression on a person's thinking.

The philosopher Edward Spranger (1928) believed that most people eventually come to rely on one of six possible value orientations. Although it is possible for a person to hold values in all six orientations, each person tends to lean more heavily toward one type in the decision-making process. The six value orientations are theoretical, economic, aesthetic, social, political, and religious.

Theoretical: A person with a theoretical orientation strives toward a rational, systematic ordering of knowledge. Personal preference does not count as much as being able to classify, compare, contrast, and interrelate various pieces of information. The theoretical person places value on simply knowing what is—and why.

Economic: An economic orientation places primary value on the utility of things, and practical uses of knowledge are given foremost attention. Proposed plans of action are assessed in terms of their costs and benefits. If the costs outweigh the benefits, the economic-oriented person is not likely to support the plan.

Aesthetic: An aesthetic orientation is grounded in an appreciation of artistic values, and personal preferences for form, harmony, and beauty are influential in making decisions. Because the experience of single events is considered an important end in itself, reactions to aesthetic qualities will frequently be expressed.

Social: A social orientation is an empathetic one that values other people as ends in themselves. Concern for the welfare of people pervades the behavior of the socially oriented decision maker, and primary consideration is given to the quality of human relationships.

Political: A political orientation involves a concern for identifying where power lies. Conflict and competition are seen as normal elements of group activity. Decisions and their outcomes are assessed in terms of how much power is obtained and by whom because influence over others is a valued goal.

Religious: A person with a religious orientation is directed by a desire to relate to the universe in some meaningful way. Personal beliefs about an "absolute good" or "higher order" are employed to determine the value of things, and decisions and their outcomes are placed into the context of such beliefs.

Liberalism versus Conservatism

With regard to value orientations, two diverse views that have major impacts on human services organizations are liberalism and conservatism. Politicians and decision makers often make their decisions on human service issues in terms of whether they adhere to a liberal philosophy or to a conservative one. The Republican party has been considered relatively conservative, and the Democratic party relatively liberal. (Today, however, party lines are blurring and shifting. Ironically, a liberal Democratic president recently presided over a huge dismantling of government, and the current Republican president is, due to the horrific events of September 11, advocating a huge expansion of government services.)

Conservatives (derived from the verb "to conserve") resist change. They emphasize tradition and believe that rapid change usually results in more negative consequences than positive ones. In economic matters, conservatives feel that government should not interfere with the workings of the marketplace. They encourage the government to support (for example, through tax incentives) rather than regulate business and industry in society. A free-market economy is thought to be the best way to ensure prosperity and fulfillment of individual needs. Conservatives embrace the old adage that "Government governs best which governs least." They believe that most government activities constitute grave threats to individual liberty and to the smooth functioning of the free market.

Conservatives generally advocate a residual approach to social welfare programs (see Chapter 2 for a fuller description of the residual and institutional approaches to social welfare programs). They believe that dependency is a result of personal failure and that it is natural for inequality to exist among humans. They assert that the family, the church, and gainful employment should be the primary defense against dependency. Social welfare should be a temporary function, they assert, that is used sparingly, because prolonged social welfare assistance leads recipients to become permanently dependent. Conservatives believe that charity is a moral virtue, and that the "fortunate" are obligated to help the "less fortunate" become productive, contributing citizens in a society. If governmental funds are provided for health and social welfare services, conservatives advocate that such funding should go to private organizations that are thought to be more effective and efficient than public agencies in providing services.

In contrast, liberals believe that change is generally good, as it brings progress. Moderate change is best. They view society as needing regulation to ensure fair competition among various interests. In particular, a free-market economy is viewed as needing regulation to ensure fairness. Government programs, including social welfare programs, are viewed as necessary to help meet basic human needs. Liberals advocate government action to remedy social deficiencies and to improve human welfare. They feel that government regulation and intervention is often necessary to safeguard human rights, to control the excesses of capitalism, and to provide equal chances for success. They emphasize egalitarianism and the rights of minorities.

Liberals generally adhere to an institutional view of social welfare. They assert that because modern society has become so fragmented and complex and because traditional institutions (such as the family) have been unable to meet emerging human needs, few individuals can now function without the help of social services (including work training, job location services, child care, health care, and counseling).

Surviving in a Bureaucracy

Basic structural conflicts exist between helping professionals and the bureaucratic systems in which they work. Helping professionals place a high value on creativeness and changing the system to serve clients. Bureaucracies resist change and are most efficient when no one "rocks the boat." Helping professionals seek to personalize services by conveying to each client that "you count as a person." Bureaucracies are highly depersonalized, emotionally detached systems that view every employee and every client as a tiny component of a large system. In a large bureaucracy, employees *don't* count as "persons" but only as functional parts of a system. Additional conflicting value orientations between helping professionals and bureaucratic systems are listed in Exhibit 9.1.

Any of these differences in value orientations can become an arena of conflict between helping professionals and the bureaucracies in which they function. Knopf (1979) summarized the potential areas of conflict between bureaucracies and helping professionals:

> The trademarks of a BS (bureaucratic system) are power, hierarchy, and specialization; that is, rules and roles. In essence, the result is depersonalization. The system itself is neither "good" nor "bad"; it is a system. I believe it to be amoral. It is efficient and effective, but in order to be so it must be impersonal in all of its functionings. This then is the location of the stress. The hallmark of the helping professional is a highly individualized, democratic, humanized, relationship-oriented service aimed at self-motivation. The hallmark of a bureaucratic system is a highly impersonalized, valueless (amoral), emotionally detached, hierarchical structure of organization. The dilemma of the HP (helping person) is how to give a personalized service to a client through a delivery system that is not set up in any way to do that. (pp. 21–22)

Numerous helping professionals respond to these orientation conflicts by erroneously projecting a "personality" onto the bureaucracy. The bureaucracy is characterized as "red tape," "officialism," "uncaring," "cruel," "the enemy." A negative personality is sometimes also projected onto officials—they are "paper shufflers," "rigid," "deadwood," "inefficient," and "unproductive." Knopf (1979) stated:

> The HP (helping person) . . . may deal with the impersonal nature of the system by projecting values onto it and thereby give the BS (bureaucratic system) a "personality." In this way, we fool ourselves into thinking that we can deal with it in a personal way. Unfortunately, projection is almost always negative and reflects the dark or negative aspects of ourselves. The BS then becomes a screen onto which we vent our anger, sadness, or fright, and while a lot of energy is generated, very little is accomplished. Since the BS is amoral, it is unproductive to place a personality on it. (p. 25)

Bureaucratic systems are neither good nor bad. They have neither a personality nor a value system.

EXHIBIT 9.1

Value conflicts between helping professionals and bureaucracies

Orientations of Helping Professionals	*Orientations of Bureaucratic Systems*
Desires democratic system for decision making.	Most decisions are made autocratically.
Desires that power be distributed equally among employees (horizontal structure).	Power is distributed vertically.
Desires that clients have considerable power in the system.	Power is held primarily by top executives.
Desires a flexible, changing system.	System is rigid and stable.
Desires that creativity and growth be emphasized.	Emphasis is on structure and the status quo.
Desires that focus be client-oriented.	System is organization-centered.
Desires that communication be on a personalized level from person to person.	Communication is from level to level.
Desires shared decision making and shared responsibility structure.	A hierarchical decision-making structure and a hierarchical responsibility structure are characteristic.
Desires that decisions be made by those having the most knowledge.	Decisions are made in terms of the decision-making authority assigned to each position in the hierarchy.
Desires shared leadership.	System uses autocratic leadership.
Believes feelings of clients and employees should be highly valued by the system.	Procedures and processes are highly valued.

They are simply structures developed to carry out various tasks.

Helping professionals have various emotional reactions to these conflicts in orientation with bureaucratic systems.[1] Common reactions are anger at the system, self-blame ("It's all my fault"), sadness and depression ("Poor me"; "Nobody appreciates all I've done"), and fright and paranoia ("They're out to get me"; "If I mess up I'm gone").

Knopf (1979) identified several behavior patterns that helping professionals use in dealing with bureaucracies. *Warriors* lead open campaigns to destroy and malign the system. They discount the value of the system and often enter into a win-lose conflict. Warriors generally lose and are dismissed.

Gossips are covert warriors who complain to others (including clients, politicians, and the news media) about how terrible the system is. Gossips frequently single out a few officials for criticism. Bureaucratic systems often make life very difficult for gossips by assigning them distasteful tasks, refusing to promote them, giving very low salary increases, and perhaps even dismissing them.

Complainers resemble gossips but confine their complaints to other helping persons, to in-house staff, and to family members. Complainers want people to agree in order to find comfort in shared misery. They want to stay with the system, and generally do.

Dancers are skillful at ignoring rules and procedures. They are frequently lonely, often reprimanded for incorrectly filling out forms, and have low investment in the system or in helping clients.

Defenders are scared, dislike conflict, and therefore defend the rules, the system, and bureaucratic officials. Defenders are often supervisors and are viewed by others as "bureaucrats."

Machines are "bureaucrats" who take on the orientation of the bureaucracy. Often a machine hasn't been involved in providing direct services for years. They are frequently named to head study committees and policy groups and to chair boards.

Executioners attack persons within an organization with enthusiasm and vigor. They usually have a high

[1]This description highlights a number of negatives about bureaucratic systems, particularly their impersonalization. In fairness, an advantage of being part of a large bureaucracy is that the potential is there for changing a powerful system to the clients' advantage. In tiny or nonbureaucratic systems, the social worker has lots of freedom but little opportunity or power to influence large systems or mobilize extensive resources on behalf of clients.

energy level and are impulsive. Executioners abuse power by indiscriminately attacking and dismissing not only employees but also services and programs. Executioners have power and are angry (although the anger is disguised and almost always denied). They are not committed to either the value orientation of helping professionals or to the bureaucracy.

These roles won't get you very far and may well destroy your career. There are alternatives, and they do work. Knopf (1979) listed 66 tips on how to survive in a bureaucracy. A number of the most useful suggestions are summarized here:

1. Whenever your needs, or the needs of your clients, are not met by the bureaucracy, use the following problem-solving approach: (a) Precisely identify your needs (or the needs of clients) that are in conflict with the bureaucracy; this step is defining the problem. (b) Generate a list of possible solutions. Be creative in generating a wide range of solutions. (c) Evaluate the merits and shortcomings of the possible solutions. (d) Select a solution. (e) Implement the solution. (f) Evaluate the solution.

2. Obtain a knowledge of how your bureaucracy is structured and how it functions. This knowledge will reduce fear of the unknown, make the system more predictable, and help in identifying rational ways to best meet your needs and those of your clients.

3. Remember that bureaucrats are people who have feelings. Communication gaps are often most effectively reduced if you treat them with as much respect and interest as you treat your clients.

4. If you are at war with the bureaucracy, declare a truce. The system will find a way to dismiss you if you remain at war. With a truce, you can identify and use the strengths of the bureaucracy as an ally, rather than having the strengths being used against you as an enemy.

5. Know your work contract and job expectations. If the expectations are unclear, seek clarity.

6. Continue to develop your knowledge and awareness of specific helping skills. Take advantage of continuing education opportunities (for example, workshops, conferences, courses). Among other advantages, your continued professional development will assist you in being able to contract from a position of competency and skill.

7. Identify your professional strengths and limitations. Knowing your limitations will increase your ability to avoid undertaking responsibilities that are beyond your competencies.

8. Be aware that you can't change everything, so stop trying. In a bureaucracy, focus your change efforts on those aspects that most need change and that you have a fair chance of changing. Stop thinking and complaining about those aspects you cannot change. It is irrational to complain about things that you cannot change or to complain about those things that you do not intend to make an effort to change.

9. Learn how to control your emotions in your interactions with the bureaucracy. Emotions that are counterproductive (such as most angry outbursts) particularly need to be controlled. Doing a rational self-analysis on unwanted emotions (Module 6) is one way of gaining control of your unwanted emotions. Learning how to respond to stress in your personal life will also prepare you to handle stress at work better.

10. Develop and use a sense of humor. Humor takes the edge off adverse conditions and reduces negative feelings.

11. Learn to accept your mistakes and perhaps even to laugh at some of them. No one is perfect.

12. Take time to enjoy and develop a support system with your co-workers.

13. Acknowledge your mistakes and give in sometimes on minor matters. You may not be right, and giving in sometimes allows other people to do the same.

14. Keep yourself physically fit and mentally alert. Learn to use approaches that will reduce stress and prevent burnout (see Chapter 14).

15. Leave your work at the office. If you have urgent unfinished bureaucratic business, do it before leaving work or don't leave.

16. Occasionally take your supervisor and other administrators to lunch. Socializing prevents isolation and facilitates your involvement with and understanding of the system.

17. Do not seek self-actualization or ego satisfaction from the bureaucracy. A depersonalized system is incapable of providing this. Only you can satisfy your ego and become self-actualized.

18. Make speeches to community groups that accentuate the positives about your agency. Do not hesitate to ask after speeches that a thank-you letter be sent to your supervisor or agency director.

19. If you have a problem involving the bureaucracy, discuss it with other employees; focus on problem solving rather than on complaining. Groups are much more powerful and productive than an individual working alone to make changes in a system.

20. No matter how high you rise in a hierarchy, maintain direct service contact. Direct contact keeps you abreast of changing client needs, prevents you from getting stale, and keeps you attuned to the concerns of employees in lower levels of the hierarchy.

21. Do not try to change everything in the system at once. Attacking too much will overextend you and lead to burnout. Start small and be selective and specific. Double-check your facts to make certain they accurately prove your position before confronting bureaucratic officials.

22. Identify your career goals and determine whether they can be met in this system. If the answer is no, then (a) change your goals, (b) change the bureaucracy, or (c) seek a position elsewhere in which your goals can be met.

Summary

An organization is a collection of individuals gathered together to serve a particular purpose. This chapter presents theories that provide a variety of perspectives for viewing and analyzing organizations. The theories covered include the autocratic model, the custodial model, the scientific management model, the human relations model, Theory X, Theory Y, the collegial model, Theory Z, management by objectives, and total quality management. These models are not exhaustive of the large number of models that have been developed. Any of these models can be applied successfully in some situations. Some of them can be applied to organizations while other models are being used.

Values and assumptions (rather than facts and figures) form the bases of most decisions in organizations. Spranger (1928) identified six value orientations that frequently have an impact on decision making: theoretical, economic, aesthetic, social, political, and religious.

Two diverse value orientations that have major impacts on human service organizations are liberalism and conservatism. Politicians and decision makers often make their decisions on human service issues in terms of whether they adhere to a liberal or conservative philosophy. Conservatives generally advocate a residual approach to social welfare programs, whereas liberals generally follow an institutional view of social welfare.

Knopf (1979) noted that there are numerous potential areas of conflict between bureaucracies and helping professionals. Helping professionals want bureaucratic systems to individualize interactions with clients and employees, to be humanized, to be democratic in decision making, to be relationship-oriented, and to quickly change to meet emerging needs. In contrast, bureaucratic systems are generally depersonalized, autocratic, procedures- and process-oriented, emotionally detached, and resistive of change. Such differences in orientations can become arenas of conflict between helping professionals and the systems in which they work. A number of suggestions are given on how to survive in a bureaucracy.

EXERCISES

1. HARD CHOICES—FUNDING SOCIAL PROGRAMS

Goals: To help students understand that most decisions are based on values and assumptions and to realize that setting budgets for social programs involves hard choices because of scarce resources.

Step 1: The instructor explains that funding sources (such as the federal, state, and local governments and United Way) have to make difficult choices about how much money to allocate to diverse social programs. Financial resources to fund all social programs are simply unavailable, and some people suffer greatly because they do not receive the needed services and funds.

Step 2: Students form subgroups of five or six members each. The instructor informs each subgroup that it is the funding source for human services in a local community and that it has $10 million to allocate for the following social programs, which need a total of $15 million. Each subgroup has the task of deciding how much money to allocate to each agency. No subgroup can go over the $10-million limit. Read the following material:

The Center for Developmental Disabilities needs $1.5 million to care for adults who have severe or profound cognitive disabilities. These adults have such severe cognitive disabilities that most are unable to walk. It costs $75,000 a year to care for each adult. If the center does not receive its requested funds, some of these clients may not receive necessary medical care and may die.

The Anti-Poverty Agency needs $3.5 million to maintain families at an income level of only 80 percent of that defined as the poverty line. It costs $14,000 per year to maintain a family of three (generally a single parent with two children). If the agency does not receive its requested funds, many of these families will go hungry, have inadequate shelter, and lack essential clothing for winter.

Protective Services needs $1 million to combat abuse, neglect, and incest. If the agency does not receive all of its needed funds, a number of children will continue to be exposed to abuse, neglect, or incest, which could severely affect them for the rest of their lives.

The Mental Health Center needs $2.5 million to help clients with severe emotional problems, some of whom are so depressed they are suicidal. If the center does not receive all of its needed funds, inadequate services will be provided to clients, and the problems of many clients will intensify. A few may even take their own lives.

The Alcohol and Drug Abuse Treatment Center needs $2 million to help chemically dependent clients and their families. If the center does not receive all of its needed funds, inadequate services will mean that the problems experienced by clients and their families are apt to intensify. Because alcohol and drug abuse is a contributing factor to many other problems (such as poverty, mental illness, and family violence), these problems will also intensify.

The Shelter for Battered Women, which is located in a house in a residential area, is requesting $500,000. If funds are cut back, the shelter staff assert they will have to turn away some of the battered wives and their children who request shelter and other services.

Group Homes for Youths runs four group homes: two for young women and two for young men. It needs $500,000. If needed funds are cut back, this agency will have to reduce the number of youths it is serving. Some will be transferred to more expensive residential treatment programs, some returned to an unhealthy home environment, and some will simply run away.

The Red Cross needs $1 million for its blood bank and for disaster relief. If funds are cut back, there will be an insufficient supply of blood available for transfusions, and many of the families who are hit by disasters (such as tornadoes and floods) will not be served.

The Rehabilitation Center provides work training and sheltered work to clients with a variety of physical or mental disabilities. It needs $2 million, or it will be forced to turn away clients. If clients are turned away, they will lose hope of becoming productive and perhaps self-supporting. Some of these clients may also end up requesting assistance from the Mental Health Center and from the Anti-Poverty Agency.

Equal Rights is an agency providing a wide range of services to people of color in the area: work training, job placement, and housing location. It also investigates and takes legal action against employers and landlords charged with racial discrimination. The agency needs $500,000. If funds are cut back, discrimination against people of color will increase.

(continued)

EXERCISES *(continued)*

Step 3: Each subgroup shares with the class its decisions for allocating funds. (The cuts that are made can be summarized on the chalkboard by having the instructor list the names of the agencies, and then having a representative from each subgroup list the amount of money that was cut—totaling $5 million—from the requested allocations.) Each subgroup states its reasons for making its cuts in funding. The instructor should help the students recognize that most of these reasons are based on values. The instructor asks the students to discuss how they felt making such funding decisions that would (in real life) have significant adverse impacts on potential recipients of services. The instructor asks the class if the exercise helps them understand that making funding decisions for human services involves hard choices caused by scarce resources.

2. *ANALYZING A HUMAN SERVICES ORGANIZATION*

Goals: To analyze a human services organization.

Visit (perhaps in groups of two or three) a human services agency and write a report covering the following information. (Some agencies may not have information or data on one or more questions. If the information is unavailable, indicate this in your reports.) Include in your report the name and telephone number of the person you met with.

a. What is the agency's mission statement?
b. What are its clients' major problems?
c. What services does the agency provide?
d. How are client needs determined?
e. What percentage of clients are people of color, women, gays or lesbians, elderly, or members of other at-risk populations?
f. What was the total cost of services for the past year?
g. How much money is spent on each program?
h. What are the agency's funding sources?
i. How much and what percentage of funds are received from each source?
j. What eligibility criteria must prospective clients meet before services will be provided?
k. What other agencies provide the same services in the community?
l. What is the organizational structure of the agency? For example, is there a formal chain of command?
m. Is there an informal organization (that is, people who exert a greater amount of influence on decision making than would be expected for their formal position in the bureaucracy)?
n. How much decision-making input do the direct service providers have on major policy decisions?
o. Does the agency have a board that oversees its operations? If yes, what are the backgrounds of the board members?
p. Do employees at every level feel valued?
q. What is the morale among employees?
r. What are the major unmet needs of the agency?
s. Does the agency have a handbook of personnel policies and procedures?
t. What is the public image of the agency in the community?
u. In recent years what has been the rate of turnover among staff at the agency? What were the major reasons for leaving?

v. Does the agency have a process for evaluating the outcomes of its services? If yes, what is the process, and what are the outcome results?
w. What is your overall impression of the agency? For example, if you needed services that this agency provides, would she or he want to apply at this agency? Why, or why not?

3. UNDERSTANDING AND APPLYING MODELS OF ORGANIZATIONS

Goal: To increase your knowledge of organizational models.

Step 1: The instructor summarizes the models of organization described in this chapter: the autocratic model, the custodial model, the scientific management model, the human relations model, Theory X, Theory Y, the collegial model, Theory Z, management by objectives, and total quality management. (As an alternative, students read this material in the text.)

Step 2: Form groups of about five members. Group discussion about which models currently apply to the organizational behavior of social work faculty.

Step 3: Class discussion of group conclusions. What models do you think would improve the efficiency and effectiveness of the department?

4. THEORY X AND THEORY Y

Goal: To analyze management styles in terms of Theory X and Theory Y.

Class discussion of employers you have worked under and their styles of management.

CHAPTER 10

Social Work Community Practice

In the first decades of the twentieth century, the emerging social work profession moved away from the reformist and total community perspective of the settlement house movement and embraced an individualistic view of practice, which was influenced by the popularity of the work of Sigmund Freud.[1] Focusing on an individual's pathologies and early childhood experience, the link between community/societal health and individual functioning was largely overlooked. Consequently, when the country was thrust into the Great Depression in 1929, the social work profession was not prepared to take a leadership role in designing and implementing the massive social welfare policy changes that were part of President Roosevelt's New Deal (Trattner, 1989).

Currently, the United States is experiencing social welfare changes as profound as those that occurred in the 1930s when the Social Security Act inaugurated federally funded public assistance programs. A "devolution revolution," is occurring in the United States with regard to the provision of social services (see Chapter 2). Political leaders view block grants as a means of transferring decision-making power about social programs and human services from the federal government to the state and local levels. A prime example, discussed in Chapter 2, is the replacement of the AFDC program (which provided financial assistance to poor parents until the youngest child reached 18 years of age) with the 1996 Welfare Reform legislation that transfers from the federal government to state and local governments most of the decision making about financial assistance to poor families with children. In addition, recipients of financial benefits will receive no more than two years of financial assistance without working, and there is a five-year lifetime limit of benefits for adults. While the number of families receiving public assistance declined in the first years of welfare reform, the number of people living in extreme poverty and homelessness has increased (National Monitoring and Advocacy Partnership, 2000).

It is clear that local communities will play an increasingly important role in developing programs and services for vulnerable populations, and social work will be one of the primary professions called upon in local communities to develop approaches to meet the needs of populations-at-risk. Social work faces extraor-

[1]This chapter was especially written for this text by James Winship, M.S.W., D.P.A. Dr. Winship is an associate professor in the social work department at the University of Wisconsin—Whitewater.

dinary challenges in the current era of diminishing federal responsibility. Social workers will be at the "front line" as they endeavor to respond to the needs of people in dire straits because of the dismantling of the federal safety net.

It is not clear how prepared social workers are to meet these challenges. For example, a study found that frontline child welfare workers in Canada, mostly BSW graduates, were rarely involved in change activities that would improve the situation of children. Neither as part of the workers' jobs nor in their activities outside their job roles were these social workers active in advocacy or community practice (Herbert & Mould, 1992).

In responding to the devolution revolution, social work practice will need to stress community building. This increased attention to community comes at a time when we are recognizing both the importance of community and the ways that recent societal changes make it more difficult to strengthen communities. Churches, civic clubs, and other institutions in the local community are being asked to "take up the slack" created by the federal government downsizing its support for social welfare programs. Healthy communities will be able to respond to social problems by providing a web of support for families and individuals to fill the holes in the social service safety net that are occurring due to the devolution revolution (Lyon, 1987). Amitai Etzioni, a respected commentator on civic life, states that "institutions, from local schools to community policing, from local churches to museums, are important for communities above and beyond the services they provide. Communities congeal around such institutions" (1993, p. 135).

Community building efforts face a number of recent challenges. The supportive power of communities has fragmented and declined (Pilisuk, McAllister, & Rothman, 1996). Middle-class communities are increasingly populated by adults who live in one locality and work in another, with reduced loyalty to the place they sleep at night. In addition, they don't stay there as long; the average U.S. household moves every six years (Lyon, 1987). Two-worker families are less involved in community life than families were a generation ago when a much higher percentage of women did not work outside the home. Putnam (2000) warns about the loss of social capital, as most Americans belong to fewer organizations and know their neighbors less than before. One indicator of this is the "bowling alone" phenomenon—more Americans bowl than ever before, but not in bowling leagues. In single-parent homes, the one adult's role as sole provider and caregiver for the children often leaves little time for community involvement.

Wilson (1996) has documented the impact of the loss of manufacturing jobs in the 1980s and 1990s on inner-city neighborhoods. The number of neighborhoods in which the majority of adults are not working has grown sharply. In those neighborhoods, distrust of one's neighbors, worries about safety in attending meetings, and widespread pessimism about the future are social forces that work against involvement in community life.

Frequently, local problems are manifestations of global decision making. Decisions that directly affect local communities are increasingly made by multinational corporations with no ties to the community. Citizens in communities perceive themselves as disempowered; government, business, and media/information decisions that affect their lives are made from afar (Pilisuk, McAllister, & Rothman, 1996). Given these realities, which community-practice models can guide us toward local solutions that strengthen our communities?

Models of Community Practice

A variety of approaches have been developed to bring about community change. In reviewing these approaches, Rothman and Tropman (1997) categorized them into three models: locality development, social planning, and social action. These models are "ideal types." Actual approaches to community change tend to blend characteristics of all three models. Advocates of the social planning model, for example, at times will use community change techniques (such as extensive discussion and participation by a variety of groups) that are characteristic of the other two models. For analytical purposes, however, we'll view the three models as "pure" forms. (Examples of the three models are found in Exhibits 10.1–10.3.)

Locality-Development Model

The locality-development (also called community development) model asserts that community change can best be brought about through broad-based participation by a wide spectrum of people at the local community level. The model seeks to involve a cross section of individuals (including the disadvantaged and the power structure) in identifying and solving problems.

EXHIBIT 10.1

The locality-development model

Robert McKearn, a social worker for a juvenile probation department, noticed in 1996 that an increasing number of school-age children were being referred to his office by the police department, school system, and parents from a small city of 11,000 people in the county served by his agency. The charges included status offenses (such as truancy) and delinquent offenses (such as shoplifting and burglary). He noted that most of these children were from single-parent families.

Mr. McKearn contacted the community mental health center, the self-help organization Parents Without Partners, the Pupil Services Department of the public school system, the county Social Services Department, and some members of the clergy in the area. Nearly everyone he talked with saw an emerging need to better serve children in single-parent families. The Pupil Services Department mentioned that these children performed less well academically in school and displayed more serious disciplinary problems.

Mr. McKearn arranged a meeting of representatives from all the groups and organizations he had contacted. At the initial meeting, a number of concerns were expressed about the problematic behaviors displayed by children with single parents. The school system considered these children to be at risk for high rates of truancy, dropping out of school, delinquent activities, suicide, emotional problems, and unwanted pregnancies. Although a number of problems were identified, no one at this initial meeting was able to suggest a viable strategy to better serve single parents and their children. The community was undergoing an economic recession; therefore, funds were unavailable for an expensive new program.

Three more meetings were held. At the first two, several suggestions for providing services were discussed, but all were viewed as too expensive or impractical. At the fourth meeting, a single mother representing Parents Without Partners mentioned that Big Brothers and Big Sisters programs in some communities appeared to benefit children from single-parent families substantially. This idea energized the group, and suggestions began to "piggyback." However, members determined that no funds were available to hire staff to run a Big Brothers and Big Sisters program. Then, Rhona Quinn, a social worker in the Public Services Department, offered to identify at-risk younger children in single-parent families and to supervise qualified volunteers in a Big Buddy program.

Mr. McKearn mentioned that he was currently supervising a student in an undergraduate field placement from an accredited social work program in a nearby college. He suggested that perhaps undergraduate social work students could be recruited to be Big Buddies to fulfill their required volunteer experience. Rhona Quinn said she would approve the suggestion if she could screen interested applicants. Arrangements were made over the next two months for social work students to be Big Buddies for at-risk younger children from single-parent families. After a two-year experimental period, the school system found the program to be sufficiently successful that it assigned Ms. Quinn to supervise it half time. Her duties include selecting at-risk children, screening volunteer applicants, matching children with Big Buddies, monitoring the progress of each matched pair, and conducting followup to ascertain the outcome of each pairing.

Some themes emphasized in this model are democratic procedures, a consensus approach, voluntary cooperation, development of indigenous leadership, and self-help.

In this model community practitioners function as enablers, catalysts, coordinators, and teachers of problem-solving skills and ethical values. It is assumed that conflicts among various groups can be creatively and constructively resolved. People are encouraged to express their differences freely but to put aside self-interests to further the interests of their community. The basic theme of this model is, "Together we can figure out what to do and then do it." The locality-development model uses discussion and communication among different factions to reach consensus on which problems to focus on and which strategies and actions to use to resolve these problems. A few examples of such efforts include neighborhood work programs conducted by community-based agencies; Volunteers in Service to America; village-level work in some overseas community-development programs, including the Peace Corps; and a variety of activities performed by self-help groups.

An analysis of locality-development efforts reveals that there is a greater likelihood of such efforts succeeding under the following conditions:

1. Leadership and organizational capacity within the community is sufficient.
2. Relatively simple tasks are adequate for the goal.
3. Small scale projects will accomplish the goal.
4. The community is sufficiently committed to the project.
5. There is a common interest and people in the community believe that they will benefit from the project.

EXHIBIT 10.2

The social-planning model

In 1995 the board of directors of Lincoln County Social Planning Agency authorized its staff to conduct a feasibility study on establishing a centralized information and referral center. Donald Levi (social planner on the staff) was assigned to direct the study. Mr. Levi collected data showing the following:

- Over 350 community service agencies and organizations existed in this largely metropolitan county of one-half million people. Not only clients but also service providers were confused about what services were available from this array of agencies.
- There was a confusing array of specialized information and referral (I&R) services being developed. (Specialized information and referral services provided I&R services in only one or two areas.) Specialized I&R services were developing in suicide prevention, mental health, cognitive disabilities, day care, adoption services, and alcohol and drug treatment.

Mr. Levi designed a program for providing a centralized information and referral service. The model described services that provided I&R services on *all* human and community services in the county. For example, I&R would provide information not only on what day-care services are available but also on where to find public tennis courts and whom to call to remove a stray cat killed in front of your house. The centralized information and referral service number would be widely publicized on television, radio, and billboards and in newspapers and telephone directories. Mr. Levi also developed a budget for program costs.

The board of directors of the Lincoln County Social Planning Agency concluded that a centralized information and referral service would be more efficient and economical than the current decentralized approach. The board therefore authorized Mr. Levi to pursue the development of this service.

Mr. Levi conducted a survey of all the human service agencies and clergy in the county. The results showed that both groups strongly supported the development of the centralized I&R service. In addition, the Easter Seal Society felt so strongly for the need of this service that they offered to donate funds for the new program. Mr. Levi was delighted, and an arrangement was worked out for the Easter Seal Society to fund the program for a three-year demonstration period.

Only one barrier remained. The proposal for this new service needed to be approved by the county board of supervisors, as the proposal required the county to fund the program (beginning three years in the future) if the service proved to be effecive during the demonstration phase. Mr. Levi and two members of the board of the Lincoln County Social Planning Agency presented the program proposal to the county board of supervisors. Their presentation included graphs showing the savings of a centralized I&R service over specialized services and contained written statements of support from varied sources, including city council members, the United Way, human service agencies, and members of the clergy. They also noted that there would be no cost to the county for the three-year demonstration period. At the end of the demonstration, the program's merits and shortcomings would be evaluated. Mr. Levi fully expected approval and was speechless when the county board of supervisors said "no." They turned the proposal down because (1) they felt a centralized I&R meant that more people would be referred to county social service agencies, which would raise costs to the county and (2) this board was opposed to funding new social welfare programs.

The county continues to be served by less effective specialized I&R services. Unfortunately, not all planning efforts are successful.

EXHIBIT 10.3

The social-action model

Saul Alinsky, a nationally noted social action strategist, provides an example of a creative social-action effort. His example also shows that social-action efforts are often enjoyable:

> I was lecturing at a college run by a very conservative, almost fundamentalist Protestant denomination. Afterward some of the students came to my motel to talk to me. Their problem was that they couldn't have any fun on campus. They weren't permitted to dance or smoke or have a can of beer. I had been talking about the strategy of effecting change in a society and they wanted to know what tactics they could use to change their situation. I reminded them that a tactic is doing what you can with what you've got. "Now, what have you got?" I asked. "What do they permit you to do?" "Practically nothing," they said, "except—you know—we can chew gum." I said, "Fine, Gum becomes the weapon. You get 200 or 300 students to get two packs of gum each, which is quite a wad. Then you have them drop it on the campus walks. This will cause absolute chaos. Why, with 500 wads of gum I could paralyze Chicago, stop all the traffic in the Loop." They looked at me as though I was some kind of nut. But about two weeks later I got an ecstatic letter saying, "It worked! It worked! Now we can do just about anything so long as we don't chew gum."

Source: Saul Alinsky, *Rules for Radicals* (New York: Random House, 1972), pp. 145–146.

6. Benefits are tangible and not too far off in the future.
7. Predicted benefits outweigh the costs (Rothman, 2000).

Community or locality development has expanded in recent years to include community economic development. One example of community economic development is Chicanos por la Causa in Phoenix, Arizona (Weil & Gamble, 1995, p. 585). This organization received funding from corporations and development groups to improve services and resources to Hispanics in the following areas: job development and training, housing, day care, and educational and training services for adolescent parents and disadvantaged youths.

Social-Planning Model

The social-planning model emphasizes problem solving. It assumes that community change in a complex industrial environment requires highly trained and skilled planners who can guide complex change processes. The expert is crucial to identifying and resolving social problems. The expert or planner is generally employed by a segment of the power structure, such as an area planning agency, city or county planning department, mental health center, United Way board, Community Welfare Council, and so on. Because social planners are employed by the power structure, they tend to serve the interests of that structure. Marshaling community resources and facilitating radical social change are generally not emphasized in this approach.

In this model planners gather facts, analyze data, and serve as program designers, implementers, and facilitators. Community participation varies from little to substantial, depending on the community's attitudes toward the problems being addressed. For example, an effort to design and fund a community center for the elderly may or may not generate participation by interested community groups, depending on the politics surrounding such a center. Much of the focus of the social-planning model is on identifying needs and on arranging and delivering goods and services to people who need them. In effect, the philosophy is, "Let's get the facts and take the next rational steps."

Social-Action Model

The social-action model assumes that a disadvantaged (often oppressed) segment of the population needs to be organized, perhaps in alliance with others, to pressure the power structure to increase resources or for social justice. Social-action models seek basic changes in major institutions or in basic policies of formal organizations. The objective is the redistribution of power and resources. Whereas locality developers envision a unified community, social-action advocates see the power structure as the opposition—the target of action. Perhaps the best-known social activist was Saul Alinsky (1972, p. 130), who advised: "Pick the target, freeze it, personalize it, and polarize it."

In this model community practitioners function as advocates, agitators, activists, partisans, brokers, and negotiators. Tactics used in social-action projects include protests, boycotts, confrontation, and negotiation. The change strategy is one of "Let's organize to overpower our oppressor" (Alinsky, 1969, p. 72). The client population is viewed as being "victimized" by the oppressive power structure. Examples of the social-action approach include boycotts during the civil rights movement of the 1960s, strikes by unions, protests by antiabortion groups, and protests by African American and Native American groups.

The social-action model is not widely used by social workers at present. Involvement in social-action activities can lead employing agencies to penalize those social workers with unpleasant work assignments, low merit increases, and withholding of promotions. Many agencies will accept minor and moderate changes in their service delivery systems but are threatened by the prospect of the radical changes that are often advocated by the social-action model.

Exhibit 10.4 summarizes the three models.

Generalist-Practice Skills and Macropractice

Macropractice is an integral part of social work practice, and many of the skills and much of the training for micro- and mezzopractice also apply to macropractice. Working on a scale larger than one-on-one or group still involves working with people, and the interpersonal and communication skills are indispensable in this area.

Especially in rural areas, the ability of social workers to communicate effectively with others and be accepted as a person can be as significant in getting approval or cooperation for a project as the worth of the project itself (Davenport & Davenport, 1982;

EXHIBIT 10.4

Comparison of the three models of community organization practice

Characteristic	*Locality Development*	*Social Planning*	*Social Action*
1. Goals	Self-help; improve community living; emphasis on process goals	Using problem solving to resolve community problems; emphasis on task goals	Shifting of power relationships and resources to an oppressed group; basic institutional change; emphasis on task and process goals
2. Assumptions concerning community	Everyone wants community living to improve and is willing to contribute to the improvement	Social problems in the community can be resolved through the efforts of planning experts	The community has a power structure and one or more oppressed groups; social injustice is a major problem
3. Basic change strategy	Broad cross section of people involved in identifying and solving their problems	Experts using fact gathering and the problem-solving approach	Members of oppressed groups organizing to take action against the power structure, which is the enemy
4. Characteristic change tactics and techniques	Consensus: communication among community groups and interests; group discussion	Consensus or conflict	Conflict or contest: confrontation, direct action, negotiation
5. Practitioner roles	Catalyst; facilitator; coordinator; teacher of problem-solving skills	Expert planner; fact gatherer; analyst; program developer and implementer	Activist; advocate; agitator; broker; negotiator; partisan
6. Views about power structure	Members of power structure as collaborators in a common venture	Power structure as employers and sponsors	Power structure as external target of action, oppressors to be coerced or overturned
7. Views about client population	Citizens	Consumers	Victims
8. Views about client role	Participants in a problem-solving process	Consumers or recipients	Employers, constituents

Falck, 1966). Showing empathy and respect are not confined to counseling sessions.

In their article on planning in social work, Googins, Capoccia, and Kaufman (1983) also stressed the importance of the interactive aspects of planning as well as the analytic or cognitive dimensions. The interactive skills of social workers are crucial in facilitating and integrating the efforts of all the people involved in the planning process.

Problem-solving skills are also as appropriate on the macro level as they are at the micro and mezzo levels. The ability to help people clarify issues and problems, decide which issues are the most important, set feasible goals, evaluate options for action, decide on appropriate actions, implement the plan, and then evaluate it are as important in working with citizen groups and community projects as in individual work.

It has been my experience that well over half the attempts by groups to address community problems (for example, a group concerned over the lack of recreational facilities for youth) are not successful. In many cases, people who come to meetings with an interest in doing something are stymied by unorganized discussions or fragmented planning. Thirty-three people may come to the first meeting, nineteen to the second, and only five to the third. These five complain about the apathy in the community, unaware that if someone had served as a facilitator in the meetings, the group might have made the kind of progress that would maintain interest.

Related to this is the need for skills in working with groups. In working to help people form self-help groups, social workers use group work skills, including those of the enabler and catalyst. At the beginning, to attract potential members, social workers may use information networks as well as the media. As the group becomes established, workers begin to focus on process-oriented issues that help group members express themselves, work out differences, question the movement of the group, and so on (King & Meyers, 1981).

The skills of relationship formation and communication, problem solving, and working with groups are as important in macropractice as they are in working with individuals and groups. However, just as there are specific intervention techniques and knowledge appropriate for these levels, there are also specific skills and knowledge useful in macropractice. The following sections emphasize the importance of knowing your community.

Knowledge for Macropractice

Know Your Community

Given your agency and client base, it is useful to know not only your community but also the community as it is perceived by newcomers to the area, by members of minority groups, by those with differing sexual orientations, and so on. Different groups have preferences for the kinds of help they seek or use. Farm families, according to one study, are more likely to turn to clergy, family, or friends when problems arise (Martinez-Brawley & Blundall, 1989). Pregnant teenagers in one urban area also demonstrated a preference for their informal supports (families and friends) over formal organizations (Bergman, 1989).

Too often social work educators talk in general terms about how social services and financial assistance programs meet human needs—for example, "home health care services can be started in communities, which will be useful in helping the elderly stay in their homes." Although this statement is an accurate reflection of the worth of that service, it also leaves the impression that all communities are essentially alike—what will work in Midland, Texas, will work in Midland, Michigan. In actuality, characteristics of regions and communities work for and against the success of projects. For this reason, it is essential that you know the services, governmental structure, values, and other characteristics of the community you serve.

In localities that are not ethnically homogeneous, you need to understand the values and economic and political realities of the ethnic communities. A lack of understanding can lead to your identifying erroneous concerns that are inappropriate for members of these groups (Rivera & Erlich, 1992). This lack of understanding can also lead to the development of programs or approaches that are not culturally sensitive. One study on patterns of family intimacy yielded wide variations in bathing practices, sleeping arrangements (where children slept), and physical intimacy between African Americans, Cambodians, Caucasians, Hispanics, Koreans, and Vietnamese. The authors of the study fault sexual abuse prevention programs that are not sensitive to the values and customs of the groups with which they are working (Ahn & Gilbert, 1992).

How do local governments, or departments therein, really function today? Who is to blame when they don't function well? What are common long-range problems? What are common short-term problems? Does failure to resolve problems result from the lack of money and capable people? Or is it because of conflicting or overlapping responsibilities? Does the problem need to be handled by the city or be treated regionally, or by the neighborhood? Is the system itself dysfunctional? Does it fail because of the people in charge, or because it doesn't have enough people?

Average citizens (if unable to get help with a problem) may want to change the system. But they can't make much of a start without knowing something about "the system," or at least about the part that needs to change. A little digging may show that it isn't the system but the people in charge who are at fault. Or citizens may find that the local government wants to do certain things but can't—because the state constitution or the state legislature won't let it raise the money or provide the services.

Citizens who want to bring about change in community government should first analyze how the existing apparatus is meant to work, the departmental limits that concern them, who imposes limits, and how each part fits the system.

Beyond correcting particular problems, social workers and other citizens have a tremendous stake in finding workable solutions to the ever-increasing demands on governments. Future problems as well as current ones need to be taken into account. If we are to make intelligent proposals for change, we must first analyze our present government, its structure, its functions, what it can do now, and what it cannot do. We should also analyze our neighborhood governments and the more comprehensive systems of which our local government is a part, because the actions of these systems affect our local communities.

The questionnaire in Exhibit 10.5 is a useful tool in obtaining the kind of specific information that is invaluable in planning for services (or just functioning as a social worker in the community).

A recent development that can help you gain an understanding of your community is Geographic Information Systems (GIS) software. This software has been widely used by social planners in the past decade to present community or county data in a graphical format so that the data are more understandable. Now, community groups are beginning to use these tools. For example, the New York Public Interest Group has a project that provides low-cost computer mapping services to grassroots organizations and non-profit organizations (www.nypirg.org).

Know the Organizations

Social workers who get involved in macropractice will need information on how organizations function in general, and specific knowledge on their employing organizations. For example, if you work in protective services and are interested in starting a Parents Anonymous group for single mothers, one important issue is that of permission and approval. Does your supervisor approve of this involvement? Does this approval extend to your being involved in this undertaking on agency time? Are you acting as a representative for the agency or as an individual? Does your supervisor (or other administrator) see potential conflicts as a result of this activity? These questions are best answered before you become too involved. Otherwise, you may find yourself in a position not unlike the cartoon character who walks out on a tree limb and hears the sound of the proverbial saw.

I was once employed by a private social services agency in a midwestern city. Not long after I was hired, the director asked me to represent him at a meeting of people interested in expanding area mental health services. After the meeting, I enthusiastically reported to the director that I was serving on one of the task forces. He became irate, informing me that my purpose was to go and observe and not to become involved in a project about which he had reservations. What I didn't know how to do at that time was to get clarification on my purpose and ask what behaviors would be supported.

Another important concept is that of organizational memory. Individually, each of us may have positive or negative associations with a particular object or event because of past experiences. A friend of mine doesn't eat bananas because he once was violently ill after eating them. Even though he knows that the bananas didn't cause the flu, the association is too powerful.

Similarly, some organizations or governing bodies may be unwilling to become active in certain areas if past efforts were unsuccessful. If you and others are interested in starting a program that would provide jobs or job training for teenagers, you need to know whether anything in this area has been attempted before. It may be that five years ago a program was funded but was poorly supervised. Youths were paid for standing around, and in some instances, even when they weren't there. Armed with this knowledge, you will not be surprised when people have reservations about new youth employment programs and would thus take this into account in your efforts to get approval.

Be cognizant about the realities of organizational change. As Pruger (1978) pointed out, much of the discussion of organizational change is not applicable or relevant to the situation of most social workers:

> Organizational change is an attractive subject to many students and faculty. Consequently, it is likely to come up in classroom discussions even where the formal curriculum seems to allow no place for any consideration of bureaucratic phenomena. The problem here is that most treatments are not helpful. They are ideological in character, rather than oriented to skill building. In class, as in the literature, the matter is too often addressed as if the central problem of change is to convince people to be for it. Though it is difficult to identify anyone who has directly opposed change, somehow there is an endless supply of able advocates seeking opportunities to cross swords with this invisible enemy. The results of these efforts are as morally satisfying as they are intellectually dulling. Through them, audiences regularly experience an invigorating, personal commitment to change. Unfortunately, such vicarious experience is no substitute for the patient observation, hard-headed analyses, and consistent behavior required to effect real change. (p. 161)

EXHIBIT 10.5

Your community—Its background

A. Community characteristics

1. What are the major population characteristics—for example, what percentage is white? Foreign-born? African American? Mexican American? Chinese American? Puerto Rican American? What are the principal ethnic and religious groups? What is the age composition? How do the population characteristics compare to state and national averages?
2. What are the principal economic characteristics of the community? Principal types of employment? Major industries? What other sources of wealth are there? Have there been recent changes in the economic life? (Moving in or out of industry? Substantial industrial or other expansions? Diversification?)
3. What is the unemployment rate? Its characteristics—that is, largely African American, Latino, young people, and so on? Have there been recent changes in this rate? If so, to what can the changes be attributed? Are there sections of your community where the rate is appreciably higher than the average?

   What is the median family income? If only average per capita income figures are available, assess in terms of these questions: Is the average skewed because of large numbers of wealthy people? Large numbers of poor? How does it compare to the national average? (*Caution:* Even if it is lower, or higher, it may not reflect, in either case, wide variations or a skewed range in your community.)
4. What are the housing patterns? Percentage of residential property that is high cost, moderate, low? Condition of housing—for example, mostly new? Well kept or maintained? Deteriorating? What is the pattern of rental property; that is, range of rents? Availability of moderate- and low-cost housing? Is the community dependent on a large metropolitan area for employment? For housing of those who work in your community?
5. To what degree are "outsiders" accepted by the "insiders" who have always lived there? To what degree do "newcomers" and "old-timers" use the same services and facilities?
6. What are the norms regarding the role of the church in helping? Do the churches help out their own members who are having difficulties or are in need? Do they help other community members who are not church members? If so, what kinds of persons are aided?
7. What are the norms on conformity to community values for individual conduct? Which norms seem to be strongest? How are people treated who violate these norms?

B. Community life

1. How many newspapers are there? (If more than one, are they independently owned?) Radio stations? Television stations? Are radio and/or television stations owned by newspapers? Is news of your community carried on a regular basis in a metropolitan newspaper? What are the principal out-of-town media influences? How does one learn about local government activities? Hearings? Meetings? Community cultural activities?
2. What are the voluntary welfare organizations? Is there a community welfare council? Joint fund-raising, such as United Way? If more than one overall fund-raising effort, why?
3. What are principal communitywide civic and service organizations? Fraternal groups? Labor organizations? Business organizations? Cultural groups? Do they work together on communitywide problems? Are there coalitions among these groups on common interests? Ad hoc? Of longer standing? Which groups are more likely to be aligned? On what kinds of issues? Are there neighborhood groups? If so, what are they organized around—cultural, school, political interests, other?
4. How successful is the community in resolving disputes among various groups or over issues such as schools and zoning? Is there high participation in local decision making (as measured by voter turnout)? Are the elected officials and local leaders committed to long-term local services, or are they "training" for statewide office?

Public Welfare/Social Services

A. Administration

1. What government agencies (town, county, state, federal) are involved in administration of public welfare or social services in your community?
2. Is there a public welfare board? If so, what is its composition? How are members selected? Are there legal

requirements for their selection? What are the terms of office? Salaries? Duties?

3. What employees are engaged in public welfare or social service activities? How are they selected? What qualifications are required? What are the salaries? Are any jobs available in public welfare or social service functions for those on public assistance?

B. Interagency cooperation

1. What cooperative programs exist between public welfare agencies and the juvenile court, probation officers, schools, day-care centers, nursing homes, public health, other agencies?
2. What cooperation is there with private social services agencies, if any exist? If there are any, what are they? Is there exchange of information? Joint planning?

C. Programs and facilities

1. Noninstitutional care
   a. What agency or agencies administer services for children—neglected, abandoned children without parents or relatives to care for them? Are foster homes used? What is the rate of pay to foster homes? How are such homes chosen? Supervised?
   b. What money is available for aid to families with dependent children? General assistance? How much comes from state? Federal government? Local sources? What is the average amount available for each child? What is the caseload per worker? What type of care is provided? Are there efforts to help parents find jobs? If so, what kind? Are there adequate day-care centers?
   c. Is there an adoption service?
2. Other public assistance programs
   a. What programs are there for needy blind persons? Permanently disabled? Partially disabled? Elderly who don't qualify for social security?
   b. What other assistance programs exist? Temporary assistance, special and corrective needs, exceptional needs (fares, emergencies, and so on), employment services, legal services, others? What money is available for such assistance? From what sources is it available? How do individuals apply for such assistance? How is information about such special assistance made available to the people?
   c. Are special assistance programs administered by a public department? If so, what agency or agencies?
3. Institutional care
   a. Are there public institutions for individuals with a physical or mental disability? The elderly? Orphaned? Delinquent? Emotionally disturbed? Needy persons? If private institutions are used, how? On a contracting-for-services basis? Cost sharing? Are county, regional, or state institutions used? If so, on what basis?
   b. How are public institutions administered? What are the procedures and requirements for admission?
   c. What kind of services (educational, recreational, training, and so on) are provided in each public institution? Do any community groups or individuals provide services? If so, what kinds?
   d. What is the cost per resident per day? What is the average stay? Do any of the users pay? On what basis? Do these institutions operate on a budget or a given amount per day per patient?
   e. Are there standards for public institutions—inspections, licensing, state supervision, and so on?
   f. How many persons from your community are in state institutions? What is the cost to your local government per patient? What is the procedure for admission? Average length of stay by case type?
   g. Do any of the local institutions provide outpatient services? What kinds?
4. Self-help groups and voluntary associations
   a. Are there self-help groups for persons seeking to work with others in similar situations? Are there local meetings of Alcoholics Anonymous, Narcotics Anonymous, and Recovery, Inc. (for persons with chronic mental illness), as well as of local (nonnationally affiliated) groups?
   b. Are there voluntary associations, such as churches and civic organizations, that are important sources of support and leadership, especially within neighborhoods or ethnic communities?

Source: This guide was adapted from League of Women Voters, *Know Your Community.* Copyright 1972, pp. 6, 7, 35–37. Adapted by permission of League of Women Voters of the United States.

For those of you interested in changing your employing organization or others in the community, the following organizational characteristics are relevant:

1. All organizations change. Just as individuals are not the same people they were a year ago, neither are organizations. Changes in funding or funding priorities, changes in societal values or trends, occurrences within the community, and changes in personnel all affect an organization's actions and policies.

2. The perceived risks and benefits of the proposed change to the organization need to be assessed and communicated to others in the organization as part of the change strategy. Identifying these can lead to understanding the sources of support and resistance to a proposed change (Frey, 1990).

3. Realize that change within an organization is a continuous process and be prepared to attempt to influence organizational policies and politics when the opportunity arises. The juvenile probation worker who believes that his or her agency does an inadequate job of working with clients who are ethnic minority members can develop documentation to support this. If the present director and staff don't share the concern, the case can then be made if a new director is hired, or new training funds become available, or if other changes in the organization or community occur that allow the issue to be raised again. To the organized go the spoils.

4. As change occurs slowly in organizations and communities, individuals who "stick around" are more likely to be able to contribute to change than persons who "parachute" into a community and then leave a year or two later. The image of a community organizer that many people have is that of a social justice activist who comes into a community, helps people right wrongs, and then rides off like the Lone Ranger. Although outside organizers can be useful in winning battles, wars are won and lost by the people who have staying power in organizations and communities.

Know Funding Sources and Funding Cycles

As noted earlier in this chapter, social workers often become involved in helping people or groups organize to develop services for unmet community needs. In some cases, such as self-help groups, money may not be needed. In many other cases, funds will be needed to put the ideas or plans into operation.

Three questions are important in this area:

1. *Where is the money?* Simply put: The person who has the gold rules.

Many times organizations and communities are able to do only what the state or federal government is funding at that time. A knowledge of those funding sources is crucial, as is an awareness of other sources of funding. In states where funding has been decentralized, county governments make most of the decisions on how mental health, mental retardation, and juvenile corrections services will be provided.

Additionally, local foundations in some areas will provide "seed" money for services or organizations in their first year or two of operation. United Way or United Givers may be another source of funds for new or expanded services.

Another option for securing money is fund-raising, which will be covered later in the chapter.

2. *What is the funding cycle of the government unit or organization with the money?* Every level of government—city, county, state, federal—and every formal organization has a defined fiscal year. For the federal government, it is October 1 to September 30. For many state and local governments, it is July 1 to June 30. Some organizations use the July 1 to June 30 fiscal year, and some use the standard calendar year. Depending on the fiscal year used, decisions on how money will be spent are made at different times by different government bodies. For example, a county government that might fund a Youth Diversion Project (to treat youthful offenders in their home community) may be on a July 1 to June 30 calendar. Budget hearings and deliberations are generally held in March and April for the coming year. By June 1 at the latest, all funding decisions for the coming year will be made. If a community group approaches the county on that date, the county's reply will most likely be "maybe next year."

3. *How "real" is the money?* At times there is an announcement of a new source of funds that gets people excited about the prospect of doing something about unmet needs. Often, it turns out that the "new program" is simply a relabeling of an already existing program that supports service programs, and no additional money is available. I was working in Georgia in 1976 when Title XX funding for social services was introduced. Public hearings were held all over the state to help the state government decide how the $300 million plus was to be spent. Hundreds of people came to hearings in rural counties, advocating their interest.

(In reality, the hearings measured the effectiveness of individual agencies' transportation systems in busing their clients to the meetings rather than measuring community opinion!) What people discovered at the hearings was that there would be no additional money, and if they wanted funding for new services, this would require reduced funding for the day-care centers, senior citizen programs, and so on, that had been funded in the past years.

Social work students generally learn about governments and the mechanisms by which they fund programs in social welfare policy courses. This information may seem dry and somewhat irrelevant at the time, but it becomes extremely useful when working in a community with unmet needs.

When you and the people you work with are familiar with the political process, you are more likely to see political change as possible; when you are unfamiliar with change processes, you will tend to avoid them (Rubin & Rubin, 1992). Social workers who get involved in political processes also need to be aware of the informal as well as the formal political processes. Individuals with economic or other kinds of power can have great influence in local or statewide decision making, although they never run for political office (Fellin, 1987).

Skills for Macropractice—Group Decision-Making Skills

In addition to specific information and knowledge applicable to macropractice, a number of skills and techniques are useful in certain situations. Some of these, like the decision-making techniques described later, are also used in group work. Others, such as fundraising and community awareness, are used primarily in macropractice.

Brainstorming

One excellent technique to use in groups that are looking for ways to accomplish a goal is brainstorming (Maier, 1970; Osborn, 1963). *Brainstorming* generates ideas about an issue. To use brainstorming effectively people try to identify as many different ways of achieving a goal as possible. Developed by Osborn (1963), here are the ground rules:

1. Time: anywhere from about one minute to half an hour.
2. Brainstorm as long as ideas are being generated.
3. Be freewheeling and open.
4. The *quantity* of ideas counts, not the quality. A greater number of ideas increases the likelihood that usable ideas will be suggested.
5. Build on the ideas of other members whenever possible, so that thoughts are expanded and new combinations of ideas emerge.
6. Focus is on a single issue or problem. Don't skip from problem to problem, or try to brainstorm a multiproblem situation.
7. Create a relaxed, congenial, cooperative atmosphere.
8. Encourage every member (no matter how shy and reluctant to participate) to contribute.
9. Limit members to one idea at a time so that less vocal individuals feel encouraged to say their ideas.
10. Explain the rationale and rules for brainstorming.
11. Seek members with some diversity of opinion and background.
12. After the brainstorming session is over, select the best ideas (or a synthesis of these ideas) related to the issue or problem.

Brainstorming has a number of advantages:

1. It increases involvement and participation by all members.
2. It reduces dependence on a single authority figure.
3. It provides a procedure for obtaining a large number of ideas in a relatively short period.
4. It reduces the pressure to say the "right things" to impress others in the group.
5. It makes the meeting more interesting, fun, and stimulating.
6. It encourages an open sharing of ideas.
7. It helps create a nonevaluative climate.
8. The ideas of one member can build on those of others so that creative and unique combinations are suggested.

Some shortcomings of brainstorming should be noted. For many people brainstorming is a strange experience and can cause some initial discomfort. For a restricted, self-conscious group, brainstorming may actually hinder participation because it forces members into new patterns of behavior. That said, in some situations brainstorming can also be effective as an icebreaker that opens up a stuffy and inhibited group. Whether brainstorming will have an inhibiting effect or an opening-up effect will depend partially on the leader's skills and timing.

Here is one example of a situation in which brainstorming was useful. A group of residents in a part of a town where there were no recreational facilities for children negotiated with the city to turn a city-owned lot in the area into a park. The city council agreed to let the residents use the area indefinitely as a park and to have city maintenance personnel keep the area mowed. However, the residents would have to raise the money for the playground equipment.

A social worker met with the group and acted as facilitator for a brainstorming session. The 23 neighborhood residents were initially skeptical about the process but "got into it" as the ideas started proliferating. A total of 46 ideas were generated and then categorized. The two major categories were fund-raising and looking for playground equipment not presently being used. After some discussion, the residents decided to hold a carnival on the proposed site and to use that as a focus for the fund-raising effort. One group worked on that project. Another group made inquiries into locating unused playground equipment.

Nominal-Group Technique

The process for using this technique was explained in Chapter 6. It can be a useful approach to help groups reach consensus or at least to give group members information on the thoughts of the other members.

Several years ago I was asked by an interagency council in a medium-sized southern county to help them define their priorities. The interagency council was well attended by representatives of health and social service agencies in that county, and the council leadership believed that the group could influence both the United Way and the county commission if they were to speak with one voice. The problem, as always with service providers, was that members tended to think that their area of concern (the elderly, juveniles, people with developmental disabilities, and so on) was most deserving of support.

I met with 40 or more human services professionals representative of all the service providers in a one-day planning session. I asked the participants at each step to identify *two* groups that they considered to be especially in need of services and at a later stage in the process to list *two* specific kinds of services that should be started or strengthened. By using the nominal-group technique, the individual biases of the participants toward their own services canceled out. By the end of the day, participants had agreed on two specific service areas that they later proposed to the funding bodies.

As this example indicates, nominal-group techniques can provide members of a task force or planning group with information about their own priorities. As such, it can also be considered a needs assessment technique. This concept is explained in the next section.

Needs Assessment

Needs assessment (NA) is a term that has acquired wide usage and a variety of meanings. It has been used to refer to a statewide comprehensive appraisal of problems and needs. It has also been used on a smaller scale to refer to assessment of a community's needs or an agency's assessment of its clients' needs. For example, a youth services agency in a community may conduct a needs assessment of its clientele. On a large or small scale, needs assessment refers to efforts of acquiring and making sense out of information so it can be used as an aid in making decisions.

DEFINING NEEDS. We can define needs by differentiating among four different kinds of needs: felt, expressed, proscribed, and comparative. *Felt needs* are those that are perceived by the person with the need. For example, you perceive your need for water when you are thirsty or for shelter if you are homeless. However, we also use the same term to refer to *wants:* "I need a red Porsche so people will notice me." Gerard Egan (1985) pointed out that people can also have unfelt needs; for example, they may need medical care or dental care without realizing it. *Expressed needs* are the felt needs that are communicated to others, because people don't automatically express the needs they feel. Part of the social worker's role is to help people voice their needs in a way that others will hear them. *Proscribed needs* or normative needs are those that some expert or formal organization perceives to be needed in a given situation. A professor may write on a student's paper, "You need to write more clearly," although the student may not feel that this is a need or problem. In a family, a protective services agency may see a need for the parents to reduce the intensity and frequency of harsh disciplining of their children, even though the parents feel the discipline is justified and appropriate. Similarly, in a community, those outside the community may see that there is a need for youth programs or parenting classes, even though the residents don't feel that need. *Comparative needs* arise when we compare one area or community or part of town to another and notice a discrepancy. If one section of town receives few police patrols and another more affluent area has more police cars patrolling the streets, we can speak of a comparative need. The capacity to distinguish among these kinds of needs is essential for good community practice. We must be clear about who is defining the need so that one set of values is not blindly imposed on community residents by others (Egan, 1985).

Social workers involved in macropractice can find themselves in situations where they have no information for making decisions, or at other times they will have an overabundance of data and have difficulty sorting out the pertinent information. When a needs assessment study is being designed, the following questions help sharpen its focus.

WHY DO WE WANT THE INFORMATION? An NA is conducted for various reasons. A sponsoring group knows that a need exists, but without documentation it will be difficult to convince decision makers and others of the necessity for action. In the same vein, an NA can increase the visibility of an issue, condition, or subpopulation (Center for Social Research and Development, 1974).

An agency or organization may conduct an NA to determine whether its efforts are addressing the most critical needs. Especially when new money is involved, NAs can be used to gain information about various problem areas to determine which area most needs attention.

NAs are frequently required by funding agencies. Various government and private funding organizations have policies that include a needs assessment as part of the proposal development process.

NAs can be used as consciousness-raising devices. Based on the work of Paolo Freire, who combined adult literacy with politicization in working with the poor in Latin American countries, NAs are designed with low-income community members in mind so the NA becomes a vehicle for discussing empowerment and community needs as well as a data collection and analysis technique (Marti-Costa & Serrano-Garcia, 1987).

One general rule: If you can't clearly answer the "why" question, you are probably better off not conducting an NA at this time. Information collected without a clear purpose is rarely used.

WHO WILL USE THE DATA? In the early stages of drawing up an NA, it is essential to identify and involve the decision makers who will eventually use the data. Allowing the potential consumers of the data to define the NA's scope, focus, and content is required if the findings are to have an impact on their concerns (Center for Social Research and Development, 1974, p. 58).

WHAT KIND OF INFORMATION DO WE WANT? Many different types of information can be appropriate for a given local needs assessment. Exhibit 10.6 summarizes some of the types of information used in needs assessments.

WHERE DO WE GET THE DATA? There are two broad categories of data used in NAs. One is already existent information, and the other is information that needs to be generated.

Sources of existing information for every community include census records, state labor department and health department statistics, and agency records and reports. These data can serve as statistical indicators of the extent of problems or conditions. Another potential source of existent information are studies conducted at some previous time for a different purpose.

One good source of information is the regional planning commission that serves the given geographical area. In addition to possessing certain statistical information, individuals on planning commissions can be helpful in directing one to other sources. City and county planning units can also be valuable sources of information.

There are times when information that is not presently available will need to be generated. This can be done in many ways—for example, community forums, or interviews with selected individuals, community leaders, frontline workers, or clients.

One common way to generate data is the survey. Three survey techniques used to gather information are (1) the telephone interview; (2) the mailed questionnaire; and (3) the person-to-person interview.

A survey can yield useful information that cannot be obtained in other ways. The obvious advantage of surveys is that information directly relevant to the problem under consideration is collected.

The drawbacks are that surveys require substantial time, substantial effort, survey research expertise, and

EXHIBIT 10.6

Types of information used in needs assessments

A. *Profile of community characteristics:* A profile gives an overview of the demographic characteristics of a community—for example, age structure, ethnic and racial composition, length of residence, and so on.

B. *Profiles of domains of living:* These profiles provide data on the incidence of a problem and the social patterns of the population. This can include the following:
   1. Economic data, including income levels, expenditures analysis, money management, and credit patterns.
   2. Employment data, including occupational levels, work history, occupational aspiration levels, and vocational needs.
   3. Family patterns, such as parent-child relationships, adjustment problems of children, marriage problems, and divorce rate.
   4. Educational patterns, including educational attainment and needs of adults, school adjustment of children, school dropout rate, and educational attainment.
   5. Housing, such as density, condition of dwelling units, and overcrowding.
   6. Physical and mental health, including long-term disability, causes of death, incidence of diseases, and environment conditions.
   7. Home management, including housekeeping problems, nutrition, home maintenance, and child care.
   8. Recreational patterns, including leisure activities, sports and athletics, and cultural activities.
   9. Criminal justice, including adult crime and juvenile delinquency rates, fear of crimes, and so on.
   10. Life satisfaction, such as community solidarity and self-appraisal.

C. *Knowledge and utilization of services:* Persons needing a service often are unaware of existing services or resources. Before making decisions, it is important to discover whether this lack of knowledge among those needing services is one cause of the problem's persistence.

D. *Barriers to service utilization:* Individuals who need services may be aware of them and still not use the services because of barriers to utilization. The following types of barriers can be identified in a needs assessment:
   1. Physical barriers, such as inadequate transportation or distance of the agency from target population.
   2. Negative attitudes of the staff, as perceived by the clients or potential clients.
   3. Feelings that a social stigma is attached to service usage.
   4. Fee for usage, which is beyond the means of those needing services.
   5. Actual or perceived restrictive eligibility criteria.

E. *Existing community information system:* Before a service can be utilized, the potential service recipients must be aware of its existence. A needs assessment can identify the formal and informal channels by which a given group is most likely to be reached.

F. *Resource assessment:* Identification of existing and potential resources should occur before planning or allocating decisions are made.

G. *Political resources assessment:* Mobilizing of political and community leaders and the population at large may be necessary because decisions are generally made in the political arena.

usually money. The way in which a survey is designed and conducted will influence the results. Although the question "When did you stop beating your wife?" is laughable, there are questions in surveys that produce results almost as slanted.

It is a good idea to bring in someone with expertise or special knowledge on surveys to assist with the preparation or implementation. Potential sources of expertise can be found in the state office of human services departments, local colleges, or the business community.

Agency frontline workers are often an excellent source of information for determining needs, especially for expanded services. In Hamilton County, Ohio (which includes Cincinnati), 90 case managers were asked to review the records of over 1,400 clients and report on what kinds of needs, met and unmet, their clients had. They determined that among the top priorities were unmet needs for ways to monitor medications and provide therapy, for socialization, and for subsidized apartments (Ford, Young, Perez, Obermeyer, & Rohmer, 1992).

WHO ELSE NEEDS TO BE INVOLVED? Besides involving the potential users of the data, it may also be appropriate to enlist the cooperation of other organizations, agencies, and prominent individuals in the needs assessment planning. This involvement may be advisable because the NA may indicate problem areas that the sponsoring agency is not involved in. Also, if other agencies help collect and prepare the data, they are more likely to use it in their planning and decision making. A third reason is that at times the information will be more favorably received in a community if key individuals are involved in the NA process.

WHAT INFORMATION IS NECESSARY ON AN ONGOING BASIS? Some of the NA information may become obsolete in a short time. One thing that agencies discover in conducting NAs is that certain types of information need to be updated periodically to be useful. Also, the NA process often indicates what information is not available; this in itself is an important finding.

An NA can be a long, complex, and costly process, or it may be relatively simple and straightforward. The process should mirror the NA's purpose and be designed to fully yield the information needed by those making decisions.

PR Skills

As social workers we are aware of the amount of misinformation "out there" about human services and those who use them. We also are keenly aware of the power of the media. Yet, we are often ill prepared to use the media to get our message across. Skills in public education and public relations are not generally a part of social work curricula.

Brawley (1983) believed that a number of barriers to effective use of the media exist:

> Many of the barriers that exist to the achievement of positive media treatment of human service topics are primarily psychological in nature. We think that the media are entirely out of sympathy with or disinterested in our causes; we think that prevailing "news values" that stress conflict, immediacy, sensationalism, personalities, and the like present hopeless obstacles to the proper understanding and reporting of human service issues; or we view the domain of radio, television, and newspapers as alien territory that we enter only at considerable risk.
>
> Other barriers are more concrete. The typical human service practitioner simply does not know enough about the workings of the news media to know what opportunities exist for positive action and does not possess the tools needed to undertake activities in this area with confidence that his or her efforts will be productive. (p. 13)

For social workers who want to use the media, either to publicize a new service on a one-time basis or to spotlight a community problem as part of a larger change process, it is necessary to develop relationships with the media and to acquire the skills to utilize them.

Know Your Media

The first step in getting coverage for your program is to get to know, personally, those who report the news in your community. Introduce yourself to the editor of a county weekly paper or the reporter for a daily paper that would cover your story. The persons in charge of news at local radio and television stations are also important to know. When working with the media, you should follow some basic rules.

1. Be honest at all times. This includes not only being truthful but also not leaving out important facts about a situation or issue. Media representatives will forgive mistakes if they trust you, so don't do anything to damage their trust.
2. Know the deadlines of newspapers and those of the radio and TV news shows. Nothing is as irritating for an editor as someone walking in with a news article two hours after the deadline or five minutes before the deadline.
3. Know the orientation of the newspaper. Are they pro–social services or do they have axes to grind?
4. Know the staff of the newspaper. To whom do you address your story?
5. Don't complain about a story unless a serious error has been made, and then first call the reporter who handled the story. Don't go to his or her boss unless it is absolutely necessary.
6. Don't heckle newspeople by constantly asking them why a story you submitted wasn't used. It is all right to ask your contact if there was something wrong that you can correct next time. But there are many reasons your story might have been thrown out at the last minute to make room for something the editor considered more newsworthy.
7. Don't forget to say "thank you." Letting members of the press know you appreciate their efforts pays big dividends. When someone does a particularly good job of reporting about your program, a short, simple thank-you note will always be appreciated and remembered. And if you are thanking a reporter, write to the editor with a copy to the reporter.

8. Every newspaper is run differently. General rules of how newspapers operate are just that—general. To know the specifics of each paper, ask for a copy of its *style sheet*. This is a list of news article rules that editors give to beginning reporters. If a small newspaper doesn't have a style sheet, the editor will probably refer you to a sample article or articles as a guide to how articles should be written.

9. There are distinct differences in the editorial content of a daily versus a weekly newspaper. Although a daily typically has a larger audience, a weekly places more stress on local issues and is therefore more closely targeted to the immediate needs of the readers. This is especially true in a rural area. Dailies usually have larger staffs than weeklies, so weekly editors may have a need for well-written news stories for their papers.

Use Media Skillfully

Familiarizing yourself with the rules of the media is one step toward getting good coverage, but this doesn't automatically get your story in print or on the air. If writing newspaper articles or public service announcements (PSA) for the radio is not your forte, try one of these approaches:

1. *Find out whether the media will do the actual work.* Some newspapers do all of their own writing. If you want a feature on a client who has established a self-help program for others, a feature writer will come out and do the story. Similarly, some radio and television stations have people on staff who will develop public service information.

2. *Find community volunteers to do publicity.* People enjoy doing what they do well. In all communities, there are people with expertise in drawing, writing, design and layout, and so on. Some of these people will be interested in helping your agency, either for one project or on an ongoing basis. Journalism and public relations classes at nearby colleges and universities are also a good resource.

3. *Develop the skills.* A number of excellent books on using the media have detailed explanations on writing news articles, getting your message on television, and so forth (Brawley, 1983; Church, 1980; MacShane, 1979). Writing or designing community awareness materials is a skill. Like leading a group or interviewing, the more you do it, the better you get.

Supports for carrying out public relations and community awareness efforts are also becoming more and more available on the Internet. One site that is particularly geared to people who work directly with homeless students but has broad application is the Community Awareness section of the website of the National Center for Homeless Education (www.serve.org/nche).

Fund-Raising

People who help others are keenly aware of the limitations of government funding. There is rarely enough money or the money must be used for certain purposes but not for others. Regulations on how dollars are to be spent are designed to prevent waste and target the money, but they also restrict flexibility on how program dollars can be spent.

For new or small agencies and community groups, it can be difficult to get any or sufficient government help. There may not be "new" money available, or the agency or group may not have the expertise or time to write a complicated, 250-page grant proposal. In all these cases, fund-raising can be an answer.

In addition to the obvious benefit of having the money when you do fund-raising, there are other advantages:

1. You gain credibility when you can show that local people support you.

> When Kate Bradley was raising money for the Petros, Tennessee, health clinic, she learned the railroad was going to sell the land around its unused tracks. She wrote the president of the railroad and asked for the first option to buy the land for the clinic building. Then the politicians in Morgan County learned the land was for sale and tried to outbid her. It was clear they could double or triple her offer. Coal companies in Tennessee are used to getting their own way by using county and state politicians. Kate drove 175 miles to Nashville to meet with the railroad president and the representatives of the coal companies. When she walked into the meeting, she was the only woman in the room.
>
> The president said, "You must be Mrs. Bradley."
>
> "I am," she said, looking him straight in the eye. Without waiting to be asked, Kate Bradley spoke her piece to the older man:
>
> "Sir, I know you are going to honor your letter giving the health clinic the right to buy your land in Petros. I know these politicians can give you a lot more money. But I just want you to know that our money comes from cupcakes. We've had a rummage sale every Saturday, and held dinners and bake sales. Everyone in the com-

munity has given me a quilt, or a jar of beans, or put up some preserves to sell for the clinic. That's where my bid comes from."

The railroad president sold her the land, and adjourned the meeting. (Flanagan, 1977, pp. 16–17)

2. It looks good to other funding sources if you have raised a significant amount of money. A women's center raised $2,500 its first year of operation through a raffle and solicitation of donations. They were able to use this as a demonstration of public support when they went to a United Way for support.

3. It creates favorable publicity for the agency or group. When people buy tickets for a raffle, attend a benefit concert, or buy a cupcake, they have some contact with the sponsoring organization. This can be a time for informing the public, one at a time, about the organization.

A number of excellent books and pamphlets explain the "how-to's" of fund-raising (Clifton & Dahms, 1980, chap. 3; Flanagan, 1977; Grubb & Zwick, 1976; Leibert & Sheldon, 1972). In deciding what to do and carrying it out, the following principles are useful:

1. *Be creative.* One shelter for abused women in Wisconsin created and copyrighted a logo with the phrase "Women—You Can't Beat Them." They sell T-shirts, bags, and other items with that logo locally and nationally and support most of their activities with the proceeds.

2. *Work on your fears, and the fears of those working with you, of asking people for money.*

> Money is like sex. Everyone thinks about it, but no one is supposed to discuss it in polite company. Everyone has a lot of inhibitions about money, especially asking for money; think of all the cartoons of the office worker afraid to ask for a raise. In our society fears about money are normal.
>
> Most people are afraid to ask someone else for money. They are afraid they will fail and afraid they will lose face. A few admit they are afraid, but others will give a lot of excuses: I can't make calls at the office; I don't know anyone rich; I can't get a baby-sitter. Or they postpone forever: I can't do it until after the kids are back in school, the holidays, the election, the tennis season, the vacation, the promotion. Volunteers often make asking for money sound like a bothersome chore, like taking out the garbage. It is not a chore; it is a challenge. Asking for money is like going out to beat up a bear. The larger the amount, the more frightening it becomes because you have to beat up a bigger bear.
>
> One of the jobs of a good fund-raiser is to teach volunteers how to conquer their fear of the unknown. The first step is understanding that each person comes complete with his or her own set of fears and hang-ups, and the package of inhibitions usually includes a fear of asking for money. The second step is realizing this is normal and nothing to be ashamed of. The third step is working with the volunteers so they can get control of their own fears.
>
> It is imperative that you understand and appreciate your volunteers' real feelings, because when members succeed at fund-raising they do more than bring in money for the organization. They have also overcome their own fear. When they raise money, they have won a personal victory, they have conquered the bear. When people can raise money, they can do anything. (Flanagan, 1977, p. 38)

3. *Make the fund-raising activity appropriate for your community.* A benefit concert may not work in a small town where few people go out at night to hear music. Some churches have admonitions against gambling, which includes raffles. In a community where many people attend such churches, a raffle may not work.

4. *Make it fun.* When people work together on a project, they develop camaraderie and make friends. An atmosphere that allows the social as well as the work aspect of a fund-raising project (coffee, doughnuts, and fruit at work meetings, for example) helps people feel good about what they're doing. After a fund-raising effort is finished, celebrate what you have accomplished with a party.

Political Activity and Lobbying

Alexander (1982) stated that "the social work profession, from its inception, has had a love-hate relationship with politics" (p. 15). Partly because their interests and much of their interaction is on a one-to-one basis, and partly because of a lack of skills in the area, social workers have shied away from the political arena. Yet, because of their work "in the trenches," social workers have a greater knowledge of inequities and inadequate legislation than most people.

Recently, in the social work profession there has been a growing acceptance of the need to understand the political process and to work with it. Social workers are now active in issues that affect the profession—such as lobbying—and that affect clients.

The whole arena of social work and politics is too large to cover here. Examples of the ways social workers can be politically active include writing and introducing legislation, guiding it through the legislative process, and helping elect candidates. At various times, social workers will be involved in these activities. On a regular basis, however, social workers and human services agencies can attempt to influence local, state, and federal elected officials.

Attempting to influence elected officials, or lobbying, is an activity that we usually associate with high-powered, high-paid lobbyists in expensive suits. Yet, it is something that all social workers can do effectively. The following principles are useful:

1. Get to know your legislators. Agencies can invite elected officials to meet with staff to share information and concerns at a time when the legislature is not in session. My experience has been that breakfast is a good time for this. It's before the elected official's schedule is too busy, and it can be more relaxed than a meeting sandwiched between other appointments. Often, legislators don't know much about the nuts and bolts of what social workers and human services agencies do, and they appreciate the knowledge.

2. Contact your legislators not only when you want them to do something but also when you approve of what they've done. Elected officials don't get a lot of fan mail. They appreciate it and will remember it.

3. Never write anyone off. A lobbyist I know says, "There are no permanent friends or permanent enemies, only permanent issues." People who oppose your position may change eventually, especially if you don't treat them as the enemy. The social work values of treating people as individuals worthy of respect applies to people in public life as well as to clients.

Community Practice—A Problem-Solving Process

One of the dilemmas of teaching social work practice is that reality is not always as sequential as we make it out to be. For example, in micropractice we talk of problem identification, followed by problem assessment or clarification, followed by goal setting. However, as you work with clients on one issue, they often reveal during goal setting that they have more urgent concerns.

Similarly, in macropractice, things don't always go as smoothly as the following process indicates. Yet, a knowledge of the ideal is helpful. Therefore, in this section, we examine how the problem-solving process can be used in macropractice.[2]

Planning, according to Ruoss (1970), is organized foresight. From the time a problem or opportunity arises until some action is taken, the people involved in the decision making will in some manner gather information, look at alternatives, and make a decision. This may be done in an organized fashion or the principals may just "muddle through."

Many efforts, such as involving citizens in an advisory committee or designing a telephone reassurance system, seem overwhelming at first sight. A man was once invited to dinner, and when he arrived was seated at a table where an immense elephant, cooked in its entirety, was laid out before him. When he asked in shock how he was supposed to eat something so big, the host calmly replied, "One bite at a time."

In this section, we look at the planning process "one bite at a time." The various steps are grouped into three stages:

Preplanning. Questions to ask:

- Why is the planning being done?
- Who is the sponsor?
- Who is to do the planning?
- Are varying points of view included?

Planning. Plans to make:

- Problem assessment
- Problem clarification
- Goal setting
- Objective setting
- Examination and decision among alternatives
- Determination of strategy

Impact. Steps to take:

- Implementation of strategy
- Monitoring
- Evaluation

Use this section as a guide for when you embark on a planning process. Be sure to consider all thirteen steps; just be aware that the amount of time and effort you spend on each step will vary depending on the situation.

[2]This section is adapted from James R. Shimkus and James P. Winship, *Human Service Development: Working Together in the Community,* Athens: University of Georgia Printing Department, 1977, pp. 8–17. Adapted by permission of the copyright owners.

The agency setting, the time frame, the resources to be utilized, and other factors will (and should) determine how much effort you expend in each step. You don't call the Army Corps of Engineers to build a sandbox. Similarly, an extensive needs assessment or prolonged search for all alternatives may be unnecessary if the outcome of the planning process is a relatively minor program change.

Preplanning: Questions to Ask

Preplanning includes all the activities that go on before a decision is made to confront actively a problem or opportunity.

Answer "Why is the planning being done?" first. Generally, planning is done because someone perceives a problem or an opportunity.

The existence of a problem or an opportunity is not in itself sufficient reason to begin planning. Before you begin to plan, ask the following questions to check the validity of the problem and the assumptions on which it is based:

1. Is this concern *our* concern, or is it some other individual's or group's concern?
2. Is this concern our concern *alone,* or should it be shared with others?
3. Is this a concern that is important to us *now,* or would it be better to postpone consideration to a later time?
4. Is the apparent concern the *real concern,* or is it a symptom of a deeper underlying problem—or of a different but related problem? DeBoer (1970, p. 75)

Sometimes the "why" is answered for you. Legislation or administrative mandates may indicate that you begin planning to comply with legislation or administrative policy by a certain date. Although there may be some latitude in these instances, thorough examination of these questions is important before you move on to the next step.

From the beginning, the agency or organization sponsoring the human services development effort must be clearly identified. The organizational base often influences the nature of the effort. For example, a task force composed of professionals from many agencies and cities looking at the needs of youth will likely come up with a plan that differs from one developed by a single agency.

Another reason to clarify sponsorship is to identify those individuals who have responsibilities for working on the effort. Planning on the local level is linked to service delivery, and if the agency involved is to deliver the service, the administrator may be the person doing the planning. If the administrator is not the chief planner, the planning manager still needs to have the active support of the administrator to conduct the planning and to ensure that the results are implemented.

There may be times in a planning process when the administrator is the appropriate person to initiate contacts; if the administrator is not "on board" with the process and is not willing to take appropriate actions, it may falter. At times, the administrator may also need to have the approval of his or her division or board before tackling a project.

The other component of the "who" question deals with the composition of the group doing the planning. A "planner" formulating a "plan" in an office separated from an agency's activities will produce a far different outcome than a task force composed of staff, representatives from other agencies, consumers, and other interested citizens.

Preplanning includes persuasion; the project should be formulated with regard to the known philosophies of those who must approve what is to be done. Involving key persons who have differences at an early stage affords them the opportunity to voice their ideas, and the final product is less likely to be rejected by those who participated in it.

At times, influential individuals will register initial opposition to an effort and refuse to participate in it. In these situations it is important that the planning group formulates its strategy in a way that recognizes and adjusts to the expected opposition.

Planning: Plans to Make

The first step in the planning sequence is the problem assessment. As used here, problem assessment includes needs assessment, problem identification, problem causal analysis, and resource assessment.

Needs assessment involves the gathering, ordering, and analyzing of information pertinent to the problem.

Bernanos (1970) once stated that "the worst, the most corrupting of lies, are problems poorly stated." Problem identification is concerned with ascertaining whether the problem under consideration is the appropriate problem, and how well the problem is stated.

The difficulty in problem identification lies in the subjective nature of "problems"—a problem is what somebody or something perceives as a problem. The nature of the problem is determined by the manner in which it is perceived (Cartwright, 1973).

The perceptions of what the problem is are shaped by data, attitudes, and value judgments. A merchant and a juvenile court worker may interpret the same data on juvenile delinquency quite differently.

Because of the difficulty in defining a problem, determining who is to do the planning is very important. If the problem under consideration is a controversial one, such as juvenile delinquency, conflict about what the problem is and what the solution should be is inevitable. If the planning process is carried out by relatively few people, when the results are released or the program is to be implemented, there likely will be considerable conflict. The proposed program may be rejected, or be so embroiled in controversy that it is not fully effective. This may be because the omission of certain persons in the planning process has caused the planning group to overlook vital information about conditions, resources, or attitudes.

Whenever the problem under consideration is controversial or affects a large number of people, conflict will arise. It can be postponed; it cannot be avoided. What *can* be done is to attempt to involve the principals in the planning process, starting with problem identification. If people can agree on the problem, there is more likelihood that they will be able to agree on goals, objectives, alternatives, and strategies. If a number of people are involved, they are more likely to advocate the action or plan in the larger community.

As the dimensions of the problem are revealed, the next step is to clarify them. Three measures that are helpful in this process relate to the problem's identity (exactly what is it?), its location (where is the problem under consideration?), and its magnitude (what is the extent of the problem?). For example, a group working on housing might define the problem as deteriorating housing (what) in a 14-block neighborhood, south of the downtown area (where), which has 37 percent substandard housing according to the last census, compared to 23 percent in the previous census (to what extent).

In clarifying a problem, it helps to identify what is *not* the problem. In the previous example, the problem is not the sidewalks, the streets, or the storm sewers.

After identifying the problem, the next component of problem assessment is to analyze its causes. In doing this, it is necessary to look at the forces that contribute to the problem—economic factors, political pressures, institutionalized values, and attitudes.

Another reason for conducting a causal analysis is that the analysis may reveal that the problem under consideration is not the "real problem," and it is necessary to backtrack and redefine the problem. Several decades ago it was thought that people who committed crimes did so because they were mentally retarded. This theory led to the notion that the crime problem could be solved by developing approaches to prevent and treat mental retardation. However, intelligence testing of prison inmates found that most inmates were of normal intelligence. The mental retardation theory of criminal behavior was then discarded. Discarding this theory forced criminologists to change their conceptualizations of criminal behavior.

An integral part of problem assessment is resource assessment. This involves cataloging all actual and potential resources for dealing with the problem. It may include a compilation of agencies and community groups involved in or sympathetic to the problem, a listing of potential funding sources, and a determination of the amount of advocacy around this problem present in the community. In the case of funding sources, it is important to ascertain the limitations under which the money may be spent. In many instances, "form follows financing."

The next step in the planning process is to establish goals. Goals are the long-term aims of the project and may be expressed in general terms. They are statements about a desired condition, and they may not be attainable. In the neighborhood housing example, the goal might be to bring every housing unit in the neighborhood up to code-enforcement standards, even though the project planners know there is little likelihood of this occurring.

In writing goals, it is helpful to express them in terms of generally accepted standards whenever possible. In the housing example, the state or local housing code regulations serve as a standard. In describing adequate or satisfactory conditions in other areas, such as child-care or homemaker services, state agencies or private accrediting groups will have standards against which to measure the adequacy of a program.

After establishing the goals, the next step is to set specific objectives. These should relate directly to the goals, but they are different in that they describe outcomes that the planners realistically expect to meet instead of expressing an ideal condition.

Objectives are quantifiable. An objective is measurable both in relation to what is to be done and within what time period it is to be done. The use of the standards and measures in the objectives should also reflect the quality desired.

In the housing example, specific objectives might be:

1. Conducting a housing inspection of every house in the neighborhood within the first three months.
2. Rehabilitating 20 housing units in the first year that are structurally sound but do not presently meet code regulations.
3. Beginning proceedings to condemn and demolish all vacant houses judged not structurally sound.

There are two types of objectives. Certain objectives must be reached if the project is to be a success. Other objectives are desirable but not essential. The three objectives mentioned above are essential objectives. A desirable objective might be:

4. Planting trees along four residential streets.

Clear, specific objectives are necessary for several reasons. The consideration of alternatives and the selection of the strategy are based on the objectives. As computer operators say, "garbage in, garbage out."

Furthermore, it is extremely difficult to evaluate a program if it does not have quantifiable objectives. Without good objectives, one can evaluate a program only by personal biases.

In the sport of archery there is one sure way for beginners to hit the bull's-eye on the side of the barn every time—paint the bull's-eye after the arrow has landed! A program that is launched without a clear statement of goals is just such an arrow; though wide of the mark intended by its launchers long ago, it may be dubbed on target by anyone who can paint a convincing bull's-eye (DeBoer, 1970, p. 108).

After objectives are set, the next step is to examine and choose among alternative approaches. In most cases there will be more than one way to meet the objectives.

The bases on which the alternatives are judged will vary with the circumstances. In selecting among alternative approaches, factors such as cost resources, technical feasibility, and political feasibility will be considered. The length of time in which a program has to prove itself is a consideration. If it is funded for only one year and then must find alternative sources of support, an approach that gives short-term results must be chosen.

When selecting among alternatives, guard against the practice of selecting the approach that seems most manageable or more interesting or convenient for the staff rather than the one that best meets the objectives.

When the approach that best meets the objectives has been selected, the next step is to determine strategy. The process of identifying the problem, setting the goals and objectives, and choosing among alternatives has indicated *what* needs to be done. In determining the course of action, the questions of *how* it is to be done and *who* will do it are addressed.

In this step, you are packaging the plan of action. Parts of the strategy will have become apparent in the previous steps, but you can easily ignore some important factors unless a thorough examination of the proposed course of action is undertaken.

Realism is imperative. Further refinements of the selected approach may be necessary. When considering who is to implement the plan and how it is to be done, the participants may discover that there are not sufficient resources to implement the approach fully, and some hard decisions about modifying the approach will need to be made.

In setting the strategy, it is also necessary to build in procedures that facilitate implementation, monitoring, and evaluation. If money is to be secured for a new program, and if there are civil service or state merit systems to work with, preparing the positions should be done before the money is received to cut down on the start-up time. Similarly, you can begin informally to look for staff before the hiring process can officially begin.

The mechanisms for monitoring and evaluation need to be decided on at this time. If an evaluation of the effects of the actions on a target population is desired, then data on that population's characteristics need to be gathered before the program is implemented.

Impact: Steps to Take

The final stage of the planning process is the impact stage, which covers implementing the strategy, monitoring it, and evaluating it. In all these steps, especially implementation, the actual situation will determine what actions need to be taken.

The last two steps are too often left out. Planning is done, a program is launched, and then there is an inclination to neglect monitoring (that is, the process of continually gaining information about the program's performance) and evaluation until such time as a review is called for.

The procedures and instruments for monitoring activities might include (1) reporting forms for fiscal transactions, personnel, training, and participant intake in a program; (2) site visits by the appropriate persons; and (3) mechanisms for permitting client feedback.

Monitoring serves many important purposes. It provides information for guidance while the program is in operation. If the administrator receives up-to-date information, he or she can make adjustments and correct program flaws before they become major.

Monitoring also provides information for periodic evaluations. Two requisites for effective evaluation are clear objectives against which to measure performance and accurate data that reflect the performance.

The importance of evaluation cannot be overstated. In the planning process itself, participants should continually check to see whether the objectives meet the problem and whether the strategy addresses the problem and objectives. Participants should also concern themselves with periodically evaluating how well they are working together.

Values and Macropractice

In Chapter 2, we discussed values in social work practice. In this section, we address values in macropractice. Exhibit 10.7 illustrates the importance of recognizing and adhering to community values.

Exhibit 10.7 illustrates the barriers to social workers' using natural helping networks; in this case, Sally's and Jim's attitudes hinder the effective involvement of Mrs. Worthington in meeting community needs. It also shows how disregard for community values can thwart the efforts of social workers to secure or improve services for their clients. Because Sally Meanwell has a reputation as a violator of community values, her reception from the board when she advocated expanded services was negative. (Incidentally, the authors state that although the dialogue is exaggerated, they have either committed or observed every ill-considered action in the account!)

Social workers in macropractice are also confronted with other value issues. One of these goes back to the assertion at the start of the chapter that the client is the community, and that the community benefits if human needs are met better than they were before. This assertion is a value statement that is not shared by everyone. Some people believe that social welfare benefits and services should be eliminated or severely curtailed, either because they believe that people should "make it on their own" or because they do not want to support government helping programs with their taxes. Others may not share these values when it comes to particular actions or programs. Public or community education efforts in sex education are opposed by people who believe that information on sexuality leads to increased promiscuity among teenagers. Within their value framework, the community would be worse off if such community education efforts were carried out.

Another value issue that can be raised is whether social work and social welfare institutions are "part of the problem or part of the solution." Galper (1980) stated that "conventional social work community organization practice is as likely to serve a co-optive role, or to function as a commonly based approach to social control, as it is to operate as a vehicle for progressive change" (p. 151). From the perspective of Galper and other radicals, much of what is advocated in community organization and other macropractice approaches has two basic aims. One is to give people who participate in planned change activities a sense of belonging, of not being powerless or isolated from society. In their opinion, the sense of power may not reflect reality. A second goal is to make minor changes in programs or practices that do not have an impact on the major societal forces that oppress the poor, persons of color, and others (Galper, 1975).

An important value to consider in community or macro practice is *beneficence*. This can be defined as doing good for others, and not doing harm (Netting, Kettner, & McMurty, 1998). It is essential that social workers in social planning and locality-development roles understand the life situations of those involved before setting up programs. For example, a group setting up a food pantry for low-income families needs to take into account the fact that most low-income adults work, and the hours of the food pantry need to accommodate the work schedules of both first- and second-shift workers. Otherwise, the service won't be of use to many people who could benefit from it.

All social workers in practice must question the goals of any effort they are involved in. They must also question the means they are using, especially in working with people who are culturally or ethnically different. It may be that what you envision as feasible may not seem so to the people you are working with.

EXHIBIT 10.7

Sally Meanwell and Jim Goodheart

(As you read this, try to identify which community values Sally and Jim are violating.)

Sally and Jim are employed by a small human services agency in Gusty, Wyoming, a ranching-farming community about 50 miles from Cultureville, a city of 100,000. Sally was unable to find a job in her native Chicago and accepted employment in Gusty a little over a year ago. Jim, a native of New York, plans to return to the East but views his present employment as a "good experience," akin to the Peace Corps. He has been in Gusty for two years. It is Friday afternoon and they are taking a coffee break.

Jim slumps back in his chair and exclaims, "What a week; I'll sure be glad to get into Cultureville!"

"What have you got planned?" asks Sally.

"Oh," Jim replies, "I think I'll take in a play at the university, but first I better get my hair cut and styled. It's getting pretty long again and people have made comments. And I sure don't want Johnson to butcher it again. These locals don't keep up with anything. Anyway, last time I was in there, I started talking about a beef boycott to protest high beef prices, and he and a couple of ranchers in there really got into it with me. I think one of them even tore my 'Question Authority' bumper sticker off when he left."

"I know what you mean," said Sally. "Johnson wouldn't even let me put up a family planning poster in there. He's a Mormon and you know how they are. Guess I'll be glad to escape Gusty too. I need to pick up some groceries at the new mall. They have a better selection than Bick's [the local grocer]. Anyway, I don't feel like supporting Bick. He butchers deer for hunters and I think hunting should be outlawed. At the very least, they should let the poor deer grow up to be elk."

"By the way," Jim interjected, "Worthington wants you to call her before five. I think it's about the O'Connell family."

"Oh, yeah," responded Sally, "the O'Connell kid has cancer and the family can't afford all the expenses. Mrs. Worthington has been trying to help them. She means well, but I think she's getting too involved."

"She doesn't have any education or training in helping people, does she?"

Sally shook her head, "No, she's done some volunteer work for us, but she didn't seem very sure of herself. Anyway, she's talking about getting some community groups to help the O'Connells. It sounds good, but I'm not sure she can pull it off. I'm willing to help if I can, but I don't know much about organizing."

"Neither do I," replied Jim. "My background is all clinical. I did have a course in c.o., but it was dry as hell and I cut it a lot. Say, wouldn't confidentiality be a problem here? You just can't tell the whole community a lot of personal stuff about the family."

"That is a problem," nodded Sally. "Perhaps I should tactfully discourage Mrs. Worthington."

"I meant to ask you," said Jim, "how did your board meeting go?"

"You would ask!" said Sally, with a negative countenance. "It was the pits. I had the new budget request all ready and I was ready to answer any possible questions. But most of them didn't seem to be all that interested in expanded services. Baldwin really gave me a rough time."

"Isn't Baldwin the guy with all the sheep?"

"Yeah," replied Sally, "I think he found out I signed that 'Save the Coyotes' petition. He claims they killed thirty-seven of his sheep in one day, but everyone knows they only kill for food. Hell, the coyotes were here first."

"Sure," said Jim, "anyway, people eat too much meat for their own good. Why don't you suggest that Baldwin go on a macrobiotic diet?"

"Don't kid, Jim. I was halfway joking once when I suggested a Marxist perspective on county problems. He's had it in for me ever since."

"Well, what about Reverend Gebhart? Wasn't he really pushing for extra services?"

"He sure was," said Sally, "but he's been a little cool lately. You know, he lives down the street from you, and he must know we sometimes spend the night together. He sure knows that neither one of us goes to church. He was lukewarm toward the new budget, and the board voted to table the request until further study. I'm not too optimistic about it."

"Too bad," said Jim, "it's a hell of a note when people don't separate our personal lives from professional ones. Not much we can do about that, though. It's a good excuse to have a few drinks in Cultureville, though."

"Sounds good, Jim. Why don't we take off now? I can call Mrs. Worthington Monday."

Source: This vignette is adapted from Judith Davenport and Joseph Davenport, III, "Utilizing the Social Network in Rural Communities," *Social Casework,* February 1982, pp. 109–110. Permission to use this material has been received from the publisher, Families International, Inc.

A number of the activities previously discussed (lobbying, publicity, fund-raising, group decision making) may not be within the range of behaviors of many people. For example, many Asian Americans come from a culture in which authority is not questioned, so pressuring a local official is not an activity in which they feel comfortable. It has been my experience that Appalachian whites do not participate easily in community meetings in which a variety of persons are present. Their cultural values discourage "opening up," especially in front of strangers.

What social workers need to do, in Saul Alinsky's words, is to "never go outside the experience of your people. When an action or tactic is outside the experience of the people, the result is—confusion, fear, and . . . a collapse of communication" (1972, p. 127).

Social workers can look for culturally sensitive or culturally acceptable methods of achieving goals. For example, one traditional Native American ritual, the Talking Circle, has been used with a number of Northwest tribes in the United States as a means for group decision making and communication (Stephenson, 1983).

A Focus on Assets

Paying attention to assets in a community is a new way of thinking about working with low-income communities or counties; its focus on resources rather than problems has much in common with the strengths perspective in social work practice (Page-Adams & Sherraden, 1998).

Traditional approaches to working with troubled neighborhoods and poor counties have focused on the deficits of the community—boarded-up houses, gang activity, lack of jobs—and have tried to "fix" these problems. An alternative path is capacity-focused or asset-focused development. When the assets or strengths of a community are mapped, block by block or area by area, a surprising array of activity, strong groups, and talents are found. Citizens' associations and churches are found to be doing good work (although often not cooperating with each other). There are institutions in the community that are doing good work, with the capacity for doing more. The talents and abilities of individuals, often underutilized, are discovered (Kretzmann & McKnight, 1993).

The term "asset building" also refers to efforts to help individuals and families build assets. Most policy efforts toward aiding the poor have focused on income support. Recently, there have been efforts to increase home ownership among the poor, to help low-income people with an enterprising business plan form small businesses or microenterprises, and to subsidize long-term savings among the poor with Individual Development Accounts (Sheradden & Sherraden, 2000). (An Individual Development Account is a program by the state or federal government to provide incentives for the working poor population to save money for specified purposes such as retirement or home ownership. In the program, the state or federal government helps the client set up the account in a financial institution and then matches the amount the client pays into the account. The program is modeled after the individual retirement account system that benefits more affluent citizens.) When individuals have equity in a house or in a business or have a viable savings account, they are more likely to both increase their financial well-being and weather economic crises. There also seems to be a relationship between asset holding and lower levels of marital violence. This may be significant in that research on domestic violence has concentrated on psychological rather than economic issues (Page-Adams & Sherraden, 1998).

Summary

Current models of community practice include locality development (also called community development), social planning, and social action.

Community practice (also called macropractice) describes social work activities in which the client is the community, where the focus of the change effort is larger than an individual, family, therapy group, or organization. Social workers are usually involved in this at some point in their careers and lives.

There are similarities between community practice and work with individuals, families, groups, and organizations. Skills in communicating and forming relationships, skills in working with groups, and problem-solving skills are as applicable in this realm of practice as in the others.

To be effective, however, social workers need to have knowledge of communities and organizations in general, and of the specific community and organization(s) they work in. For some efforts, knowledge of funding sources and funding cycles is essential.

Depending on the kind of macro effort in which the social worker is involved, the following techniques can be utilized: group decision-making techniques, community awareness or publicity approaches, fund-raising techniques, and lobbying strategies.

The problem-solving model can also be used to address community problems. The various steps in a community problem-solving model were summarized in the following three stages: preplanning (questions to ask), planning (plans to make), and impact (steps to take). In using this or other macro approaches, value issues such as community values, the role of social welfare in society, and ethnic or cultural sensitivity have to be considered.

In the coming years, social workers interested in community practice and community well-being will increasingly find that the Internet is a valuable source of knowledge and skill acquisition for their home communities.

EXERCISES

1. COMMUNITY NEEDS ASSESSMENT

Goal: To conduct a community needs assessment.

Step 1: Form groups of five.

Step 2: Select a community and use the questions in Exhibit 10.5 to conduct a community needs assessment.

Note: Alternatively, the entire class can assess one community, with groups focusing on different topics.

2. NEEDS ASSESSMENT AND PROPOSAL DEVELOPMENT

Goal: To conduct a needs assessment and develop proposals to meet the needs identified.

Step 1: Form groups of five or six. Your task will be to conduct a needs assessment of an issue on campus or in the surrounding community and then develop a proposal to meet the needs identified.

Note: This assignment may be a major course assignment. Alternatively, make as much progress as you can in a class period to conduct a needs assessment and develop a program proposal. For example, if the latter approach is used, ask the following questions:

a. What are the most urgent, unmet needs of our social work program?
b. What evidence or documentation is there that these are urgent, unmet needs?
c. What additional information needs to be sought to determine fully whether these needs are urgent and unmet?
d. What specific, realistic proposals do we have for meeting the needs that have been identified?

Step 2: The subgroups present their needs assessments and proposals in verbal or written form. The instructor provides feedback to the subgroups.

3. IDENTIFYING VIOLATIONS OF COMMUNITY VALUES

Goal: To recognize violations of community values.

Step 1: The instructor explains the purpose of the exercise. The instructor asks for a volunteer (who is of the opposite gender of the instructor) to read a vignette with the instructor. The instructor informs the class that a vignette will be read and that the task of each student is to identify the specific attitudes and specific behaviors that are apt to be violations of the values in a rural community in Wyoming.

(continued)

EXERCISES
(continued)

Step 2: The instructor and the volunteer read the Sally Meanwell and Jim Goodheart vignette presented in Exhibit 10.7.

Step 3: Students state the violations of community values that they have identified. The instructor ends the exercise by stating the importance of identifying community values, and discusses with students whether they are willing to make possible adjustments in their personal lives to live up to community expectations. The instructor indicates that a balance sometimes has to be found between living the way you want to live and meeting community expectations to maintain credibility.

4. *IDENTIFYING COMMUNITY VALUES*

Goal: To examine the values of your home communities.

Note: Community values influence the types of services that are publicly available and supported by a community.

Break into groups of three or four. Discuss your home communities' reactions to the following community activities.

a. High school students seek to establish a clinic in their school that dispenses contraceptive materials.
b. An avowedly lesbian woman launches a campaign to seek election to a local political office (such as to the city council).
c. A group of working parents requests the local school system to establish an all-day kindergarten, partially to meet the needs of working parents.
d. An AIDS support group seeks authorization to use the public meeting room of the library for its weekly meetings.
e. A local organization seeks the establishment of an additional (or the first) shelter for the homeless in your neighborhood.

5. *ANALYZING COMMUNITY-PRACTICE EFFORTS*

Goal: To analyze community-practice efforts.

Step 1: Form groups of three. Select a community-change or community-planning effort to report on to the class. An example of a planning effort is a project by the social work student organization to arrange an educational conference or workshop on a topic such as AIDS. Another example is the efforts of a community group to establish a homeless shelter.

Step 2: Research information on the questions that follow on your selected community-change effort. Try to interview at least one planner.

Questions

a. What are the goals of the planning effort? How many planners are involved? Who are the planners, and what are their planning credentials? Why is this planning effort being undertaken?
b. Which of the three community practice models is this planning group primarily using? What characteristics of this model are being displayed by the planners? Does this planning effort have some characteristics of the other models? If "yes," which models, and what characteristics of these models does it have?
c. What are the results of this planning effort; that is, to what extent are the goals being accomplished? What are the strengths and shortcomings of this planning effort?

Step 3: Class presentations of group reports.

CHAPTER 11

Evaluating Social Work Practice

Thus far in this course, you've learned about social work with individuals, families, groups, organizations, and communities.[1] You've studied systems analysis, and you will study psychoanalysis (Module 1) and transactional analysis (Module 3), and you will read about a number of other therapies. You're no doubt eager to try out your new knowledge, confident that you can help your prospective clients. But wait! How will you know if your choice of therapy is working?

As a professional social worker, you are accountable to your clients, to your agency, and to yourself. You'll want to know whether your clients achieve their goals and, if so, whether it is because of your interventions. In short, you'll want to evaluate your practice. That is what this chapter is all about.

Although most social workers evaluate their practice implicitly, few approach evaluation as systematically as they might. Systematic evaluation of your practice provides you with reliable information about the achievements of your clients and improves your practice (Slonim-Nevo & Anson, 1998). Good evaluation also helps you avoid jumping to unwarranted conclusions about your work.

[1]This chapter was especially written for this text by Wallace J. Gingerich, MSW, Ph.D. Dr. Gingerich is a professor in the Mandel School of Applied Social Sciences at Case Western Reserve University, Cleveland, Ohio.

What Is Evaluation?

Evaluation, as we shall use the term here, refers to the use of research techniques to assess the outcome of social work interventions. As Thomas (1984) has suggested, there are two types of evaluation: outcome evaluation and evaluative research. As you will see, these two types of evaluation address different but related objectives.

Outcome evaluation asks whether the intended outcome was achieved. Simply put, was the goal achieved? Outcome evaluation has a limited objective, and it is relatively easy to do. It requires minimal methodological know-how, and it doesn't impose rigid requirements on practice. Outcome evaluation should be part of normal practice. However, outcome evaluation does not provide a sound basis on which to conclude whether the intervention was effective.

Evaluative research also asks whether the outcome was achieved, but in addition it seeks to determine if the outcome can be attributed to your intervention. In other words, was treatment effective? Evaluative research is similar to traditional experimental research in that causal relationships are the focus of study. You might think of evaluative research as research applied to questions of practice effectiveness. Although it is relatively easy to determine whether the intended outcome was achieved (outcome evaluation), inferring that it was due to the intervention is considerably more difficult.

Evaluating the effectiveness of interventions is important. If we know that it was our intervention that produced the outcome, we will want to continue using it. Conversely, if we know the intervention had little or no impact, we should stop using it and look for something better. Good evaluative research enables us to contribute to the knowledge base of our profession and is mandated by our professional code of ethics.

Although both types of evaluation are important for social work practice, the main focus of this chapter is on outcome evaluation. Outcome evaluation is an essential part of ordinary practice; you and your client will always want to know if the desired outcome was achieved. Outcome evaluation does not interfere with practice but can enhance and improve it (Gingerich, 1983). In contrast, rigorous evaluative research is not a requirement of ordinary practice (Gingerich, 1990b). The additional controls and measurements needed to conduct evaluative research may conflict with service objectives (Thomas, 1978). We are required as a profession to conduct scientific research to improve our knowledge of practice effectiveness; however, in many instances evaluative research is best left to trained researchers who can implement the rigorous controls and measurements required for inferring causality.

Just as social work practice is carried out at various levels of intervention (individuals, groups, families, organizations, and communities), evaluation is also carried out at different levels. Evaluation at the level of individuals, families, and groups has sometimes been referred to as *clinical evaluation,* while evaluation at the level of program development and community practice has been called *program evaluation.* The main focus of this chapter is on evaluation at the level of individuals, families, and groups. Many of the concepts and methods underlying clinical evaluation apply to program evaluation as well.

Until recently, evaluating practice usually meant using some form of experimental control group research design (Bloom, 1983). Such designs assign subjects randomly to two groups: One group gets the intervention and the other does not (or gets a different intervention). After intervention, the groups are compared on some measure of the desired outcome. Assuming all else is equal, differences between the two groups are attributed to the intervention the experimental group received. Although experimental control group designs are a useful research strategy, they are often not practical for evaluating day-to-day social work practice.

During the 1970s a new approach to evaluating practice began to emerge, based on the earlier work of clinical psychologists who were trained in research (Bloom, 1983). This approach, known as *single-subject* or *single-system* research, took a rather different approach to evaluation, an approach that is much more compatible with clinical practice. Instead of comparing randomly assigned groups of clients on some outcome measure after intervention, the single-system approach observes a single client (or client system) repeatedly, before, during, and after intervention, and notes changes in the outcome measure that coincide with the intervention. In this way it is possible to determine whether the outcome was achieved and, perhaps, whether the change was due to the intervention.

Single-system designs are not as rigorous methodologically as classical control group designs, but they are much more compatible with most social work practice. Furthermore, they are adequate in most instances for purposes of outcome evaluation. Thus, the single-system approach to evaluation is the one taken here.

The Single-System Evaluation Approach

Much has been written about how to evaluate practice (Alter & Evens, 1990; Barlow, Hayes, & Nelson, 1984; Barlow & Hersen, 1984; Bloom, Fischer, & Orme, 1999; Blythe & Tripodi, 1989; Jayaratne & Levy, 1979; Tripodi, 1994). As a result, the procedures for evaluating practice are well defined. They are generally described as follows:

1. Specify the goal.
2. Select suitable measures.
3. Record baseline data.
4. Implement the intervention and continue monitoring.
5. Assess change.
6. Infer effectiveness.

If these steps sound familiar, that is because they parallel very closely the steps you follow in social work practice (Jayaratne & Levy, 1979). Evaluation is based on the problem-solving process, just as social work practice is. The difference is one of emphasis, and it is a slight difference at that. Whereas the main purpose of practice is to produce a desired outcome, the main purpose of evaluation is to assess whether in fact the outcome was achieved.

Specify the Goal

The first step in single-system evaluation is to specify the goal of your work with your client. The goal should reflect the information obtained in the social work assessment and should state in concrete terms what will be different at the end of treatment. Usually the goal involves a change in behaviors, thoughts, or feelings, or perhaps a change in social relationships or the environment. The goal should reflect the needs and wishes of your client and what is realistic to achieve, but it also must be an outcome that can be defined specifically and measured.

Specifying the goal is probably the single most important step in evaluating practice. It is essential that the behavior you select for the goal be the *same behavior* as the focus of intervention. Remember, when you evaluate your practice, you are evaluating whether the client changed, and whether your intervention was successful. Your evaluation can show success only if it is focused on the actual changes the client is making. As you move ahead to the next step in evaluation and select a suitable measure, you can lose sight of your original goal, particularly if it is a difficult one to measure. After you have designed your measurement package, it's always a good idea to review your goal statement to be sure that both are focused on the same thing.

Select Suitable Measures

Evaluation requires that the desired outcome be measurable in some reliable way. Measurement means that the outcome must be quantifiable. At a minimum you must be able to tell whether it has occurred or not; but you may also be able to rate the level of the outcome using a scale or some other procedure.

Although some outcomes seem to defy measurement, it would be irresponsible to intervene if you have no way to know if the outcome has occurred (Hudson, 1978). Neither you nor your client could tell if things were getting better. When workers say they cannot measure their clients' outcomes, they usually mean the outcomes are difficult to measure directly, or they are too complicated and multifaceted to measure quantitatively. Numerous advances have been made in the field of measurement in recent years, and many measuring instruments and procedures are available.

Measurement Methods

There are three main methods for measuring client outcomes: direct observation, self-anchored rating scales, and standardized measures (Bloom, Fischer, & Orme, 1999).

DIRECT OBSERVATION. Many client outcomes are behavioral. Simply put, clients want to *do* something different. When the outcome can be stated in behavioral terms, direct observation by the client or someone else is usually the measurement method of choice. Direct observation requires a clear, objective definition of the behavior. *Clear* means that two people using the definition agree on occurrences of the behavior. *Objective* means that the behavior is directly observable; that is, it requires little or no inference by the observer.

Examples of typical behavioral outcomes are playing cooperatively, completing assigned homework, having fewer headaches, or discussing disagreements calmly. Even some seemingly nonbehavioral outcomes, such as improved self-esteem or reduced depression, can be stated in behavioral terms. Clients can often give specific behavioral indicators of internal states when asked; for example, when asked what they will be doing (or not doing) when they have improved self-esteem, clients may indicate such behaviors as initiating conversations, making positive self-statements, or working more productively. Although it is not always possible to specify outcomes in behavioral terms, it is useful to attempt to do so. From a therapeutic standpoint, the client (and you) will have a more concrete idea of the actual desired outcome. From an evaluation standpoint, direct observation is generally considered the most reliable and direct measurement method. By the way, specifying behavioral outcomes does not imply that you must, or even should, use behaviorally based interventions. It simply means that the outcome you and the client are interested in is behavioral.

Behaviors may be observed and counted using a variety of methods (Barlow, Hayes, & Nelson, 1984). The most common method is a *frequency count.* Here, you simply record the number of times the behavior occurs during a specified time interval. For example, you might record the number of temper tantrums a child has each day, or the number of problems a child solves correctly during math class. Frequency counts work well for discrete behaviors (behaviors that have clear beginnings and endings) that do not occur too frequently to make counting impractical.

A related method of observation is counting *discriminated operants*. These behaviors occur only in the presence of clearly specified antecedents. For example, a child can comply only when the parent makes a request, or a husband and wife can resolve differences only when they have a disagreement. In such cases, rather than report the absolute frequency of occurrence, you would report the percentage of times the desired behavior occurred following the antecedent.

Continuous behaviors (no clear beginnings or endings) or high-frequency behaviors can be observed using *time-sampling* methods. In time-sampling the observation period is divided into short intervals (usually 5–15 seconds) during which you record the behavior as occurring or not. Usually this is done on an all-or-none basis, with the results presented as a percentage. For example, you might observe whether a psychiatric patient attends to the therapy group discussion during a 10-minute period using 15-second intervals. If the patient was observed to attend for 35 of the 40 intervals, you would report that she or he attended 88 percent of the time. Because of its nature, time-sampling is almost always done by someone other than the client, usually a staff member or perhaps a parent.

Several other observational methods are sometimes used. *Latency* measures the elapsed time between a particular event and the behavior; for example, the time it takes a child to get into bed after being told to do so. *Duration* measures how long the behavior lasts, such as how many minutes the child spends doing homework, or how long a headache lasts.

General procedures for observing behaviors, as well as specific definitions, codes, and recording systems for observing many predetermined behaviors, are described in detail by Bellack and Hersen (1998) and Ciminero, Calhoun, and Adams (1986).

SELF-ANCHORED RATING SCALES. Not all desired outcomes can be stated in behavioral terms. Sometimes the outcome is a change in an internal state (for example, thought, feeling, belief), such as becoming more self-confident, less anxious, or less depressed. In such cases, it would not make sense to try to define the outcome behaviorally if the client truly views the problem as an internal state. Accordingly, when the desired outcome is an internal state, the most direct method of measurement is of necessity some form of self-report.

One of the best methods of measuring internal states is to develop a self-anchored rating scale (Bloom, 1975). A self-anchored scale is a rating scale you and your client develop specifically to measure your client's outcome (Gingerich, 1979). To construct a self-anchored scale, begin with a 5- or 7-point rating scale (see Figure 11.1). Give the scale the name of the outcome you and your client have agreed on; for example, you might call it a "feeling good" scale.

Next, develop anchors for the low end of the scale by having your clients imagine a recent time when they did not feel good at all. After they have begun to visualize the situation, ask them to recall: (1) what they were doing, (2) any recurrent thoughts they were having, and (3) what they were feeling. Behaviors sometimes occur along with internal states; for example, your client may stay in bed all day, not answer the phone, cry frequently, and overeat on a bad day. Your client may also experience recurrent thoughts or self-statements such as "No one likes me," "I am ugly," or "Life is not worth living." Feelings are more difficult to elicit but often are expressed best in word pictures such as "feeling blue," "my stomach is tied up in knots," or "I'm down in the dumps." In any case, the behaviors, thoughts, and feelings the client experiences when at the low point on the scale become the anchors for that point.

Once you have anchored the low point, ask your clients to imagine a recent time when they were feeling very good. This time you will elicit anchors for the high end of the scale. You should proceed to develop anchors for other points of the scale as well; ideally, at least alternate points of the scale should be anchored.

If you have developed the anchors carefully, the completed scale should be a sensitive measure of your client's outcome as he or she uniquely experiences it. Because self-anchored scales are client-specific, you must develop a new one for each new client and each new outcome.

Because self-anchored scales are subjective (they measure the client's internal state), they have sometimes been criticized on methodological grounds. Their reliability cannot be assessed directly, and they are always potentially reactive (more about these measurement issues later). However, self-report measures are

FIGURE 11.1 Self-anchored scale

the most direct measure of internal states, and there is little evidence that self-reports are any less adequate methodologically than many other types of measures (Bloom, Fischer, & Orme, 1999). For purposes of outcome evaluation, self-anchored scales are often useful, and sometimes they are the only direct measure of the outcome.

STANDARDIZED MEASURES. In most cases the preferred method of measuring client outcomes is direct observation of behavior or self-anchored ratings of internal states. That is because these methods are likely to provide the most direct and sensitive measures of outcome. Occasionally, however, standardized measures may exist that would provide a suitable measure of outcome. Furthermore, it is often a good idea to use standardized measures, in addition to behavioral and self-report measures, to provide a basis of comparison with known groups, or to be sure that you are measuring what you think you are.

Standardized measures include tests, questionnaires, rating scales, inventories, and checklists. These measures have three characteristics. First, they have uniform procedures for administration and scoring, so everyone who uses the instrument uses it in the same way. Second, standardized measures must meet minimal standards of methodological adequacy (namely, reliability and validity). Third, most standardized measures have established norms; that is, they have guidelines for interpreting test scores based on the scores of known groups who have completed the measure or some independent standard of performance.

Standardized measures fall into two broad categories: published and unpublished. Published measures (commercially published) are described in *The Eleventh Mental Measurements Yearbook* (Kramer & Conoley, 1992). Published measures have met accepted standards of reliability and validity, so you can use them with assurance that they will in fact measure what you think they will. The publishers of these measures require a fee, however, and some of them are available only to psychologists or other qualified professionals.

Unpublished measures have been developed and used in research and practice situations but are not published commercially. There is no one source or listing of unpublished measures; however, several collections have particular value for social work practice. Hudson (1982) and Nurius and Hudson (1993) have developed more than 20 scales (known as the WALMYR scales) designed for use in social work practice. Sample scales include self-esteem, marital satisfaction, child's attitudes toward parents, and generalized contentment. All of these scales are scored and interpreted in the same way, making them easy to use in daily practice. Many of the more widely used WALMYR scales are reprinted in Bloom, Fischer, and Orme (1995, pp. 218–237), so you can review them and determine their suitability to your situation. The scales are copyrighted, however, which means you must purchase them from the publisher (available on the web at www.syspac.com/~walmyr) in order to use them in your work. Computerized versions of the scales are also available from the publisher.

Corcoran and Fischer (2000) have compiled a collection of several hundred measures that they refer to as *rapid assessment instruments*. Instruments are included for children, adults, and couples and cover a broad range of psychological, behavioral, and interpersonal problems. The sourcebook includes a description of each measure, its norms and scoring procedures, and reliability and validity data. In addition, each measure is reproduced in the book so you can decide for yourself whether it would be suitable for your clinical application.

In addition to these two collections, a wide range of standardized measures may be found in Bellack and Hersen (1998); Ciminero, Calhoun, and Adams (1986);

Freedman and Sherman (1987); Grotevant and Carlson (1987); Hersen and Bellack (1988); and Touliatos, Perlmutter, and Straus (1990).

General Issues in Measurement

At times we refer to the reliability and validity of measurement. These terms describe the methodological adequacy of measures. *Validity* refers to what the measure measures, and *reliability* refers to how well it measures it. If a measure is not reliable, it will not give consistent and accurate readings. Thus, when observing behavior, for example, it is important that the description of the behavior be clear and objective so the observer will record it consistently from day to day. If a measure is not valid, it will not measure what you think it measures. That is why, when developing self-anchored scales, for example, you should be sure that the anchors the client gives are real indicators of the outcome for each scale point.

In addition to reliability and validity, you also want a measure to be *sensitive* to the changes you expect a client to make. Direct observation of client behavior and self-anchored rating scales are sensitive measures of most client outcomes. Standardized scales frequently are not as sensitive, as these scales have been developed to measure personality traits that, by definition, are relatively fixed and are not likely to change significantly during intervention.

Another requirement of measurement in single-case evaluation is that the measure be suitable for *repeated use* (at least weekly) during treatment. This is true for most behavioral observation measures and self-anchored scales but is often not true for standardized scales. The rapid assessment scales described by Hudson (1982), Nurius and Hudson (1993), and Corcoran and Fischer (2000) are exceptions.

Finally, it is important to consider the *reactivity* of your measure. In most instances clients will be recording their own behavior, and the measurements process itself will likely have some impact on the behavior it is reporting. For example, if you ask a mother who complains of her child's temper tantrums to count the tantrums, it is likely that she will notice some new things about her child's behavior as well as her own, and her behavior and that of her child may change as a result.

Because reactivity influences the behavior the measure is meant to measure, it is difficult to sort out how much behavior change is due to the intervention and how much is due to reactivity. Researchers generally try to minimize this problem by using unobtrusive measures (having someone else observe the client, for example), so they can be more sure of the exact impact on the intervention. However, from a practice point of view, reactivity may actually benefit the client. This is especially true if you are helping someone learn problem-solving strategies in which observing and altering his or her own behavior are explicit goals of treatment.

Reactivity is a very complex process, and its effect is difficult to gauge. Generally, however, you should have your clients record *positive* behaviors or internal states rather than negative ones, because the effect of reactivity (all else being equal) is apt to increase response rates rather than decrease them. For example, rather than recording an unwanted behavior, such as eating snacks between meals, you could have your clients record the number of times they thought of snacking but refrained. Koop (1988) provided an excellent discussion of the factors involved in estimating the reactivity of self-monitoring and how you can use it for your client's benefit.

Measurement of client outcomes is a crucial step in evaluating practice. Conclusions about whether the outcome has been achieved will be valid and trustworthy only if appropriate measures are used, so care and thoughtfulness are advised. You have also probably noticed the parallels between measurement as we have talked about it here and assessment as it has been discussed in Chapter 3. We have been talking about the same process from different perspectives. In the present discussion of measurement, the emphasis has been on *how* to assess, whereas in Chapter 3 the emphasis was on *what* to assess. Clearly, you will want to pay careful attention to both aspects of assessment in your practice.

Record Baseline Data

After selection of the measure or measures, the next step is to collect data for a period of time before you implement the intervention. This is called *baselining,* meaning that you are establishing the rate of the outcome measure before intervention occurs and the expected change takes place. The main purpose for baselining is to provide a basis of comparison for data collected during and after treatment. If the treatment data show a different level or pattern from the baseline data, you may reasonably conclude there has been a change. If you collected data only after treatment, you would have no way of knowing whether there had been a change.

Because you may not implement treatment during the baseline period, an important question is, How long should you baseline? Barlow, Hayes, and Nelson (1984) made several recommendations. First, you should collect baseline data for a *minimum of three data points.* At least three points are required to begin to assess the level, trend, and stability of the data. (More about these properties later when we discuss assessing change.) Although three data points constitute a minimum, in normal practice baselines are often taken for a week or more. Some statistical aids for assessing change require a minimum of ten baseline observations. Second, you should continue baselining until the data form a *stable pattern.* Frequently there is some fluctuation or trend in evidence during baseline; for example, there may be four or five tantrums one day and none the next, or the number of tantrums may seem to be decreasing. The idea is to baseline long enough that the pattern of behaviors becomes clear and consistent and (ideally) there is no upward or downward trend.

To confirm the patterns contained in your data, you should always graph the data (see Figure 11.2). Not only is this helpful for you, but graphs are a very effective way to provide feedback to your clients (and others such as parents and third-party funders). Using lined graph paper, begin by drawing a vertical line on the left side and a horizontal line at the bottom. The vertical axis is always used to represent the outcome, and the horizontal dimension represents time units. Thus, you might record self-anchored ratings of "feeling good" on the vertical axis and days on the horizontal axis. Drawn in this way, the pattern of the client outcome over time can readily be seen. Other considerations in graphing are discussed in more detail in Bloom, Fischer, and Orme (1999) and Parsonson and Baer (1978).

Conceptually, baselining parallels the assessment phase of treatment when the worker gathers information about the level of the client's problem, and when and where it happens. Seen in this way, baselining usually does not require you to delay the start of intervention any longer than you normally would. From a practice standpoint, it is unwise to begin intervening until you have a clear description of the problem or desired outcome and have reliable information about its current level.

Occasionally you will find yourself in situations (crises, for example) where you must intervene immediately; that is, you cannot delay introduction of treatment to gather baseline information. In these situations you can gather baseline data *retrospectively* rather than *prospectively,* as has been described up to now. To construct a baseline retrospectively, develop a measure of the goal behavior as usual, then ask clients to recall from memory how they would have rated themselves each day for the past week or so. This process is analogous to what workers often do during assessments when asking clients to give them a history of the target behavior, except here workers are getting the information in a more systematic way so it can be used as a basis for evaluation. Retrospective baselines are not as reliable as prospective baselines, but experience shows that they often yield useful information and, in any case, are better than having no information at all. Without any baseline data whatsoever, you will be severely hampered in determining whether there has been change in the goal behavior.

Implement the Intervention and Continue Monitoring

Once you have established a baseline, it is time to implement the intervention. The most important consideration from the point of view of evaluating practice is to specify and describe clearly just what the intervention consists of. Assuming your client improves, you will want to know what you did so you can do it again and describe it to other professionals as well.

This step sounds easy, but it is perhaps the most difficult aspect of evaluation. In fact, there is ongoing debate in the literature regarding the extent to which interventions can be described and replicated (Frank, 1973). The helping process is a complex, multifaceted activity that can probably never be described completely. The practical goal, however, is to describe the intervention with sufficient clarity and completeness that someone else can replicate it and obtain similar results (Blythe & Tripodi, 1989). Furthermore, it is assumed that although your actions from the start may be generally therapeutic, you will implement a *specific intervention* at the conclusion of baseline.

In addition to describing your intervention, you should verify that you have actually implemented it. Planning to do something does not necessarily mean it will happen. Occasionally, research studies on practice effectiveness have failed to produce positive results but on closer examination reveal that the intervention was never implemented as planned. This is important to know because it prevents you from mistakenly concluding that the intervention was unsuccessful when in fact it was never implemented.

Once you have implemented intervention, you should continue the same measurement procedure established during baseline (Figure 11.2). It is important

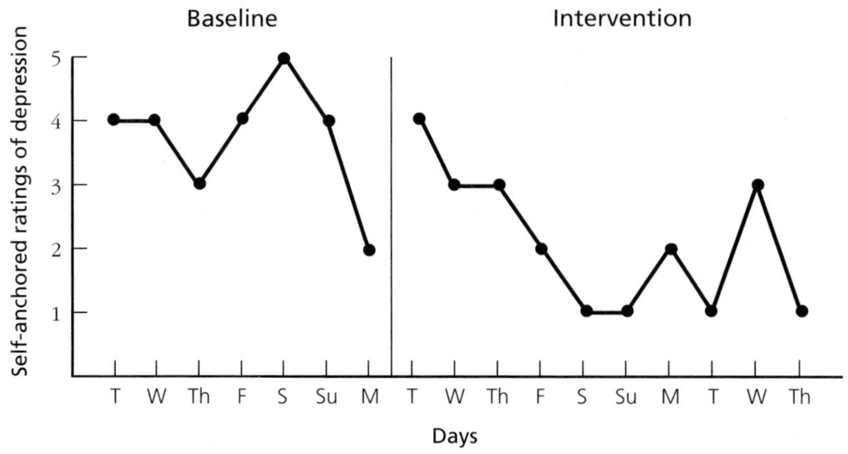

FIGURE 11.2 A simple graph

that there be no changes in the definitions, times of measurement, or measurement procedures because such changes could affect the data you obtain. If you keep the measurement procedure exactly the same as baseline, changes in the data during treatment will reflect changes in the outcome itself, not the measurement procedure.

Assess Change

After you have collected data on your outcome measure during the baseline and treatment phases, the next step is to assess whether there has been any change. Actually, the issue is whether any significant change has occurred from a statistical or clinical standpoint (Kazdin, 1977a). Statistical or *experimental* change refers to actual change in outcome between phases. It is assessed on purely statistical and logical grounds. Clinical or *applied* change refers to change that is sufficient, desirable, or meaningful from a clinical or practical standpoint.

The first task is to determine whether there has been experimental change; that is, whether there has been any real change in the outcome during intervention. This task is sometimes made difficult because of some of the unique characteristics of time-series data (Crosbie, 1993; Jones, Vaught, & Weinrott, 1977; Kratochwill, 1978; Rubin & Knox, 1996). Time-series data may be characterized by their level, trend, variability, and autocorrelation. *Level* refers to the central tendency or location of a set of data. When there is no trend, level is equivalent to the mean of observations in the baseline or treatment phase. *Trend* refers to a deterministic change in the level of the data over time—that is, a continuing upward or downward trend. *Variability* refers to the extent to which the data vary around the trend line. The more fluctuation around the trend line, the greater the variability of the data. Finally, *autocorrelation* refers to the possibility that the value of one observation may be related to previous observations. This is a complicated statistical phenomenon, which in practical terms means that most of the usual statistical techniques (which assume independence of observations) may not be suitable for assessing change in time-series data.

There are two general approaches for assessing change in time-series data: visual analysis and statistical analysis. We emphasize visual analysis because it is fairly straightforward and easy, and it is one procedure you should do routinely. The following discussion of visual analysis is based heavily on the work of Parsonson and Baer (1978).

Visual analysis simply means that you look at the graphed data and, applying rules of analysis, conclude whether there has been change in the client outcome from phase to phase. The standard of significance for visual analysis is "clearly evident and reliable"; that is, the change must be clear and unmistakable (Parsonson & Baer, 1978, p. 112).

The first step in visual analysis is to graph the baseline and treatment data following the suggestions noted earlier. The data within phases should be connected by a solid line, and the phases should be divided by a vertical line.

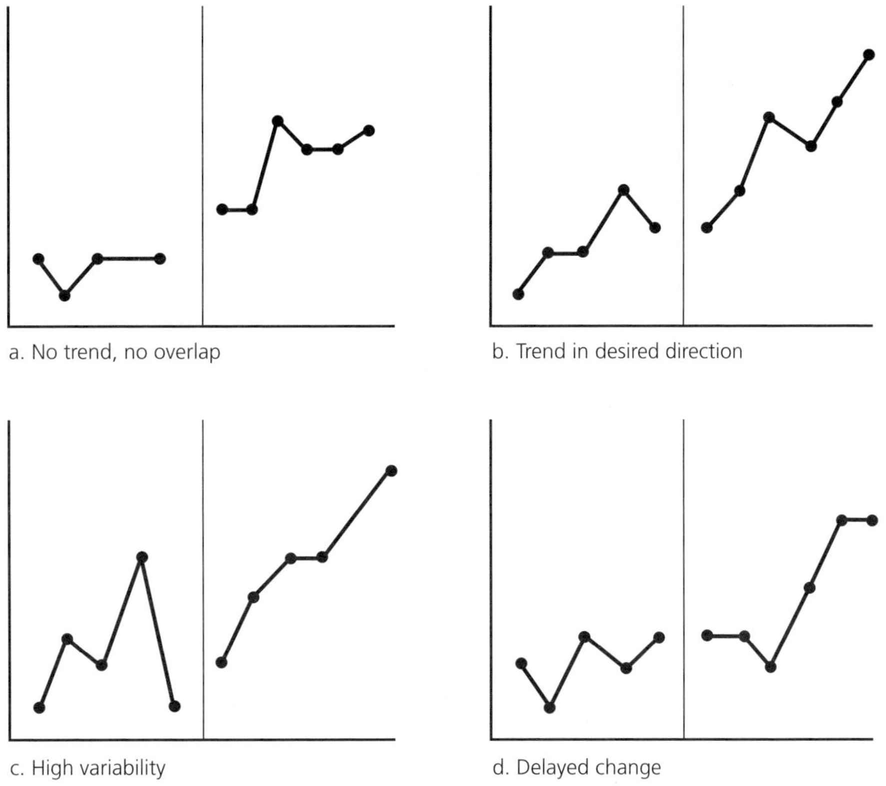

■ FIGURE 11.3 Visual analysis of graphed data

Ideally, in visual analysis you would want to see little or no overlap between phases, with no clear trend in the data (see Figure 11.3a). In such cases it is clear there has been a change. Also, the more immediate the change and the greater its magnitude, the easier it is to conclude there has been real change.

Sometimes the baseline data may contain a trend; that is, the outcome measure seems to be on a continuing increase or decrease. When this happens, you should make every effort to extend the period of baseline to see whether the trend tapers off and stabilizes around a constant level. If not, you must analyze change cautiously. If the trend is in the opposite direction of desired change, then it will have little impact on assessing change. However, if the trend is in the desired direction, assessment of change will be ambiguous (Figure 11.3b). From a practice standpoint, it may be wise not to intervene in such cases because the desired change appears to be happening already. If you must intervene, and if intervention produces a large and immediate increase in outcome or a change in slope, you might cautiously conclude there has been change. However, in most situations where there is a trend in the desired direction, it will be difficult if not impossible to conclude reliably that there has been change.

On occasion the baseline data may be highly variable such that they overlap with the treatment data (Figure 11.3c). Again, your first strategy should be to try to reduce the variability by extending the baseline period or observing extraneous events affecting your client's responses that can be controlled. If not, it will be difficult to conclude unequivocally there has been change. On rare occasions the goal of intervention may be to increase or decrease the variability of a client's behavior (for example, to help a person with mood swings maintain a steadier state). Unfortunately, there are no readily available techniques for assessing change in variability of time-series data.

It is not uncommon in social work practice for client change to be delayed or gradual (Figure 11.3d). Because the change is not immediate and phases overlap, it is difficult to reach a reliable conclusion (Gibson

CASE EXAMPLE

Treatment of Obsessive-Compulsive Disorder

This case example is based on a study by Cooper (1990), in which she used behavioral interventions to help a client reduce her ritualizing behavior. Cooper also noted improvement in depression and anxiety.

1. *Specify the goal.* This study involved a woman in her late twenties who displayed at intake pervasive ritualistic behavior, social isolation, depression, and anxiety. She had been in psychotherapy for the previous five years. The specific goals for this study were to reduce three behaviors: ritualistic opening and shutting of her makeup case, excessive rinsing in the shower, and ritualistic counting of belongings.

2. *Selecting suitable measures.* The measure used was client self-monitoring of the three behaviors on a 3 x 5 note card. The client recorded the number of times she opened and closed her makeup case, the minutes spent rinsing after soaping in the shower, and the percentage of time she counted her belongings when carrying them. In addition to these target behaviors, Cooper also asked her client to complete the Spielberger State-Trait Anxiety Inventory and the Beck Depression Inventory.

3. *Record baseline data.* Cooper implemented a modified form of the multiple baseline design in which each behavior was recorded for a variable period prior to the start of treatment. Baselines ranged from 13 days for opening and closing the makeup case to 6 weeks for counting belongings while carrying them.

4. *Implement intervention and continue monitoring.* The intervention consisted of behavior modification techniques (including modeling and response prevention). It was directed first toward the makeup case ritual, then the excessive rinsing, and finally the counting of belongings. The order of target behaviors was determined by client ratings of each on an anxiety hierarchy. Cooper continued to monitor each target behavior during the intervention period.

5. *Assess change.* Each target behavior was monitored during intervention (just as in baseline) and placed on a time-series graph. The results for the opening and closing of the makeup case are shown in Figure 11.4. It is clear from visual analysis that there was significant change during intervention—there was no overlap across phases, and behavior changed abruptly when treatment was started. Cooper did a celeration line test (that is, a trend line test) that confirmed her visual analysis. The other two target behaviors showed similar reductions. Pre and post measures on the State-Trait Anxiety Inventory and the Beck Depression Inventory showed no significant change. Anxiety scores began high and continued high, and depression scores began low and remained so throughout. Cooper did three-month and six-month follow-ups, which verified that changes the client made during treatment continued.

6. *Infer effectiveness.* This study used a modified multiple baseline design to evaluate the impact of behavioral intervention on three ritualistic behaviors. In each case, introduction of treatment was followed immediately by a reduction in the target behavior. These results were confirmed using the celeration line. The fact that treatment was begun at different points in time for the three different target behaviors and was followed by immediate change lends credibility to the hypothesis that treatment produced the change, not

& Ottenbacher, 1988). In such cases the best thing to do is continue the intervention and continue observing to see whether the behavior eventually stabilizes around a new level. If so, you can be relatively confident there has been change in the outcome.

Ideally, our interventions should be so effective that visual analysis of graphed data would be sufficient to reach reliable conclusions about change. Of course, we know that this doesn't always happen. Sometimes there appears to be some change, but the change doesn't strictly meet the criteria of "clearly evident and reliable." What then? Some writers suggest that if change is not clearly evident the intervention is simply not potent enough to be of interest, so we should abandon it altogether rather than try to sort out whether there was significant change. This argument is very persuasive from

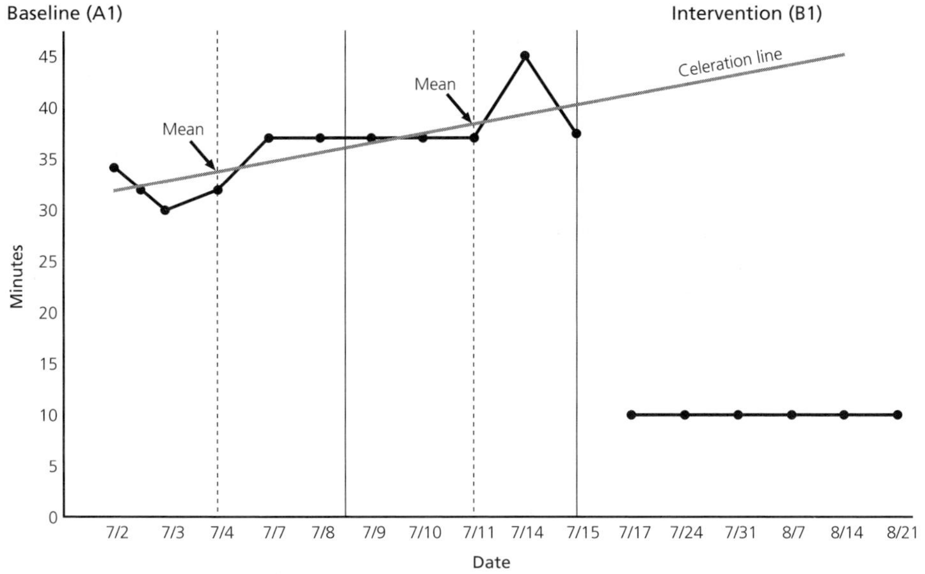

FIGURE 11.4 Number of twists, presses, and clicks of makeup case by client each morning at baseline (7/2 to 7/15) and after intervention (7/17 to 8/21)

historical events, maturation, or some other factor. Thus, we can be fairly safe in concluding that the intervention produced the observed changes in target behaviors. Intervention did not appear to influence general anxiety or depression.

This study is a good example of the extent to which a fairly rigorous single-subject evaluation design can be implemented in direct practice. It used clear, concrete measures of the target behaviors. The modified multiple baseline design is able to rule out most competing explanations for the observed change in target behavior. Although realities of the practice situation did not permit an exact implementation of the multiple baseline design, it could be closely approximated, which adds considerably to the therapist's ability to infer the effectiveness of the intervention. Even if the multiple baseline design could not have been implemented, a simple AB design (baseline-intervention) on any one of the target behaviors would have provided valuable information about change.

Source: Marlene Cooper, "Treatment of a Client with Obsessive-Compulsive Disorder," *Social Work Research and Abstracts,* 26 (1990), pp. 26–32.

a practical standpoint. However, some of the outcomes we are interested in change slowly, and change may not be very immediate or dramatic. Furthermore, when developing new interventions, it may be important to know whether there is even a small change, so we can improve and refine the intervention to the point that it may be of practical value. In cases such as these, statistical and quasi-statistical techniques may be needed to determine whether there has been a reliable change in outcome. Although such techniques are beyond the scope of this text, good discussions are available in Bloom, Fischer, and Orme (1999) and Gingerich (1983).

In contrast to experimental significance, applied (clinical) significance compares the amount of change that has occurred with the amount of change thought necessary or desirable. This is often a difficult judgment to make because individuals disagree on what is necessary or desirable.

Kazdin (1977a) discussed a number of approaches for assessing applied significance. One of these, the *aim-star technique,* simply places an *aim-star* on the graph at the level and day that represent the desired outcome. You then graph the treatment data to see if they are moving in the direction of the aim-star. If the data coincide with the aim-star, you have achieved applied significance. *Goal attainment scaling* offers a similar approach conceptually (Kiresuk & Lund, 1978). Both procedures are admittedly subjective, although they probably better reflect what our clients consider significant change than does experimental significance.

Kazdin discussed several additional ways to evaluate applied significance. One of these, *social comparison,* compares the client's performance in the target area with that of "normal" peers. For example, you decide what a reasonable standard of cooperative play is by observing "normal" children in the natural setting. Another approach for assessing applied significance is called *subjective evaluation.* Here you would poll qualified individuals such as teachers, social workers, or probation officers to determine what a reasonable standard of performance would be. For a more detailed discussion of applied significance, see the articles by Kazdin (1977a) and Gingerich (1983).

In practice you should always attempt to assess change using both experimental and applied criteria. At the minimum, you should perform visual analysis of graphed data, and perhaps use some of the statistical techniques available if visual analysis is ambiguous. In addition, you should always specify before intervention what the goal of intervention is. You may express this verbally or graphically using the aim-star technique.

These five steps constitute the necessary steps for carrying out outcome evaluation as defined earlier. Your measure should indicate in quantitative terms what the desired outcome is; data should show what the baseline level was and whether there was change during intervention; and finally, your analysis should tell you whether the change was significant. Practice evaluation should be a regular part of normal social work practice.

You may have noticed that so far almost nothing has been said about intervention effectiveness—that is, whether the intervention was responsible for producing the change. The question of effectiveness leads us into evaluation research per se, in which we must use research designs to develop a logical and empirical basis for making inferences about treatment effectiveness. Although it is not the goal of this text to make you a skilled researcher, a brief review of research designs and design issues will help you begin to think about effectiveness and, perhaps more important, deter you from making assertions about effectiveness that go beyond your data.

Infer Effectiveness

To infer that your intervention was effective, you must show logically and empirically that the intervention is the only plausible explanation for the observed change in client outcome. To put it a bit differently, you must rule out other possible explanations for the observed change.

The primary criterion for inferring causality is *concomitant variation;* that is, the observed change in client outcome must occur at (or soon after) the time the intervention is implemented. If change begins before intervention, logically we would have to conclude that something other than the intervention was responsible for the change. Likewise, if change occurs too long after intervention, other possible explanations take on more credence.

Threats to Validity

Concomitant variation alone is not sufficient to establish causality; it is only suggestive of a causal relationship. We must also rule out other possible (and plausible) explanations for why the client changed. These competing explanations fall into several categories, which have been called threats to validity (Cook & Campbell, 1979). *Validity,* as the term is used here, refers to the best available approximation of truth regarding the cause of client change. The following discussion includes several of the more important threats to validity.

HISTORY. History refers to any event that may have occurred during the time the intervention was implemented that could also account for the change. Examples are events such as getting a promotion, getting a new classroom teacher, or having a birthday. Observed improvements in the client's functioning may result from such historical events rather than the intervention. Simple baseline-intervention designs (AB designs) do not permit us to rule out the effects of history. Other more advanced designs are needed.

MATURATION. Maturation includes any processes within the client that operate as a function of the passage of time, such as growing up, becoming senile, or becoming tired. Maturation generally becomes more of a threat the longer it takes for the intervention to have an impact.

STATISTICAL REGRESSION. Usually clients come to social workers for help when things have gotten worse; that is, they are in an extreme state. However, chances are good that things will look better at the next observation simply because of the random fluctuations of the behavior. This threat to validity is called statistical regression. The best way to control statistical regression is to take an adequate baseline. If the baseline shows an upward or downward trend, or an unusual amount of variability, you should continue to baseline to see whether the data stabilize or the pattern of normal variability becomes clear. The point is to not mistake normal variation in your client's behavior for a real change in behavior.

MULTIPLE INTERVENTION INTERFERENCE. When a client receives more than one intervention at a time, there is no empirical basis for knowing which intervention produced the change. This is a common problem, particularly in institutional settings where clients may participate in a variety of groups, receive individual therapy, and perhaps take medication. Again, simple AB designs are inadequate to control for this threat. Other designs, such as multiple baseline designs, are useful in ruling out multiple intervention interference.

Although these are the most common and obvious threats to the validity of single-system evaluation, others are discussed by Cook and Campbell (1979) and Kratochwill (1978).

Single-System Designs

The Basic AB Design

Thus far we have discussed only the simplest of single-system designs, the baseline-intervention or AB design. It is the most basic design because it provides the information necessary for determining that there has been change, and it suggests the possibility that the intervention produced the change. Since AB designs are not able to control for many of the threats to validity mentioned earlier, they are generally not adequate for inferring causality or intervention effectiveness. More advanced single-system designs are needed to control for such threats.

Withdrawal Designs

Withdrawal designs are characterized by repeated occasions in which the intervention is implemented and then withdrawn. The rationale underlying withdrawal designs is that the causal inference is stronger when there are more occasions on which client outcome can be shown to vary concomitantly with intervention. Common examples are the ABA and ABAB designs (see Figure 11.5). In the former, treatment is withdrawn after it has been implemented, and in the latter treatment is implemented again. Withdrawal designs are useful for controlling threats due to history, maturation, and statistical regression, among others. Withdrawal designs are often difficult to implement in day-to-day practice, however, because they require withdrawal of intervention, even when it appears to be working. This is one example in which the goals of research (demonstrating causality) may conflict with the goals of service (providing effective treatment).

It is important to be careful to distinguish between withdrawal phases and follow-ups. In withdrawal designs the objective is for the client outcome to return to the pretreatment level to demonstrate repeatedly that it is under the control of the intervention. In follow-ups, however, the objective is to show that change is permanent and that it lasts even after treatment has been discontinued. You should be clear in your own mind about which objective you are addressing so you will know how to interpret the data.

MULTIPLE BASELINE DESIGNS. In multiple baseline designs several outcomes of interest are identified and baselined simultaneously. The intervention is then implemented on each outcome at staggered intervals (Figure 11.6). This type of design is stronger than simple AB designs because it provides for several occasions on which outcome can vary concomitantly with intervention. Further, it avoids the practical and ethical problems of withdrawing treatment as in ABA and ABAB designs.

Still other advanced single-system designs should be considered if the objective is to infer causality. The texts by Jayaratne and Levy (1979); Bloom, Fischer,

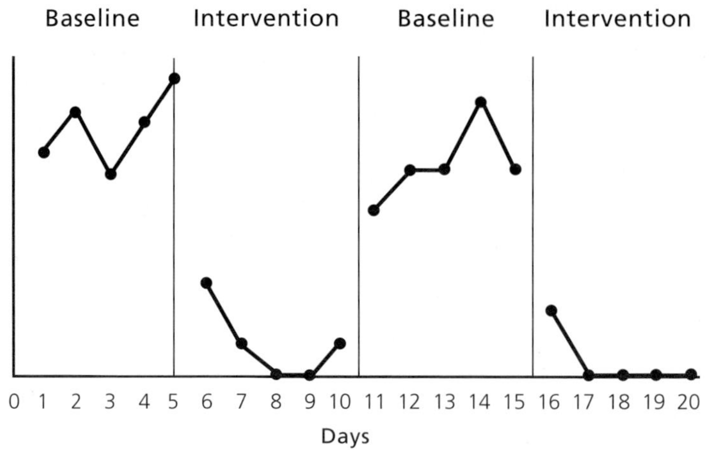

FIGURE 11.5 Withdrawal design

and Orme (1999); and Barlow and Hersen (1984) offer a more detailed discussion of single-system research designs.

Evaluating Programs

Most of the discussion thus far has assumed that we are evaluating social work practice with individuals, groups, and families. There is nothing inherent in the single-system approach that limits it to clinical evaluation, however. Some of the first applications of single-system designs were to evaluate the impact of policy, such as a change in speed limits or a change in monetary policy. Single-system designs can easily be applied to the evaluation of policy and program interventions. The basic designs are the same; the primary differences are the conceptualization of the intervention and outcome, and the selection of suitable measures.

In program evaluation, the policy or program becomes the intervention. Such interventions include providing incentives for able-bodied welfare recipients to obtain employment, instituting a token economy to reward good behavior in a group home, or starting a new procedure whereby staff ignore the obnoxious noises of children but give positive attention for appropriate talk.

Likewise, in program evaluation the desired outcome has to do with the behavior of the targets of the policy or program change, usually a group of people. Accordingly, the measures must be ones that are suitable for all individuals. This usually rules out client-specific measures such as self-anchored scales. Frequently, the desired outcomes are observable behaviors, such as getting a job, cooperative play in the cottage, or appropriate table conversation. In program evaluation you must be careful to define outcomes in sufficiently general terms so that the definitions will be relevant for all individuals in the target group. When the desired outcome is an internal state, you may need to use some of the standardized measures or rapid assessment instruments mentioned earlier.

Program evaluation, then, is no different conceptually from clinical evaluation. The distinction is that the intervention is a policy or program rather than a therapeutic technique, and the outcome is reflected in the behaviors of a target group of individuals rather than a single individual or therapy group.

The single-system approach to evaluation has much to recommend it. Single-system designs are compatible with most of social work practice, and they provide a beginning basis for inferring that our interventions are effective. Single-system designs, including the more advanced designs, are not always sufficient, however. They cannot always rule out all threats to validity. Some social work interventions, particularly policy and program changes, cannot be implemented abruptly, and other interventions sometimes have a delayed effect on outcome. In both cases it is difficult empirically to relate changes in outcome to the intervention. In such cases, traditional group designs may be justified.

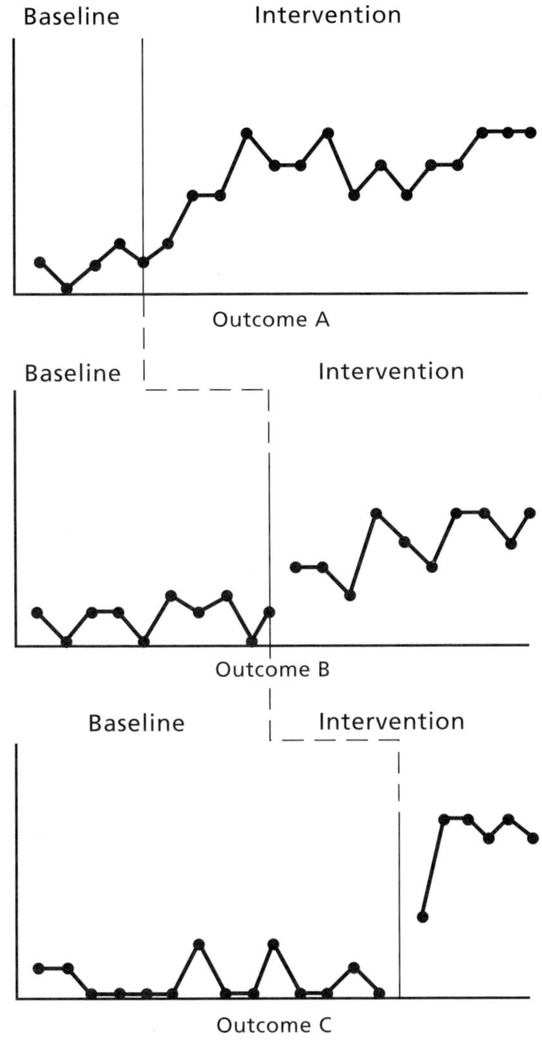

FIGURE 11.6 Multiple baseline design

The requirements of group designs—random assignment to groups, relatively large numbers of clients, and uniform treatment of all subjects within groups—make them costly and difficult to implement in normal practice settings. Frequently, the potential benefits of doing a group evaluation do not justify the costs involved. There are times, however, when group designs are warranted, particularly when single-system evaluation has provided cumulative evidence of effectiveness and a more rigorous test is desired. Group evaluation is a rather technical undertaking for which research expertise is advised. Texts by Weiss (1972); Rossi, Freeman, and Wright (1979); Posavac and Carey (1980); and Kaufman and Thomas (1980) are recommended for further reading in this area.

Evaluation in a Managed Care Environment

Systematic practice evaluation will help you know if your clients are improving, and it may also provide evidence that your interventions are effective. This is reason enough to make evaluation part of your ordinary practice activities. However, as managed care becomes more prevalent in social work settings, there is added reason to evaluate your practice. Managed care agencies, and others who fund social work services, will increasingly ask for "hard evidence" that clients are benefiting from your services (Mullen & Magnabosco, 1997). Hard evidence almost always means a standardized measure of some sort, and perhaps client-specific data also, such as the behavioral data or rating scales discussed earlier. Unstructured clinical impressions are not adequate for such purposes.

Increasingly, social workers will be required to use standardized measures to document client change, usually of the rapid assessment type described by Corcoran and Fischer (2000). The most widely used general purpose instrument is the Short-Form Health Survey (SF-36), which was designed for clinical use in health settings (Ware & Sherbourne, 1992). The SF-36 has well-established validity and reliability and includes subscales on general mental health and on limitations in role activities because of emotional problems. Another general-purpose measure is the Outcome Questionnaire (OQ™-45.2), which is specifically designed to measure client progress and can be used at every meeting with the client if desired (American Professional Credentialing Services, 1996). The Questionnaire OQ™-45.2 assesses three dimensions: intrapsychic functioning, interpersonal relationships, and social role performance. In addition, it includes screening items for suicidality, substance abuse, and physical violence. Depending on the setting, more specific measures such as the Beck Depression Inventory (Beck, Rush, Shaw, & Emery, 1979) or the Addiction Severity Index (McLellan, Luborsky, Woody, & O'Brien, 1992) may be used instead. In any case, it is advisable to identify one or more rapid assessment instruments relevant for your client population and administer them routinely at the beginning and end of treatment. Such a practice will help you accumulate evidence that your clients benefit from services. Make sure that the measure you use is relevant for the client goal you are working on, however, or it will likely show no change.

Rapid assessment instruments should not replace the repeated use of direct observations or rating scales as your primary measure of client change, however. Pre and post measures give no information on how your client is progressing during intervention. Further, because standardized measures are designed for use across many clients, usually they are not as sensitive to client change as are client-specific measures. Thus, a good procedure is to use a client-specific measure (behavioral observation or rating scale) on a repeated basis (daily, if possible) and supplement it with an appropriate rapid assessment instrument at the beginning and end of treatment.

The Ethics of Evaluation

Most of the discussion in this chapter has assumed that we are conducting outcome evaluation as part of normal practice. That is, we identify goals, select measures of them, and monitor change to verify that the desired goals have been achieved. Outcome evaluation is integral to practice because it tells us if we are making progress and when we can terminate the helping process. Because it is a part of normal practice, outcome evaluation as a process is treated no differently than any other aspect of practice. Accordingly, the usual ethical requirements of confidentiality, informed consent, and client access to records discussed in earlier chapters apply.

When we undertake evaluative research to infer causality and advance our knowledge of effective practice, however, additional ethical guidelines are required to protect our clients as research subjects. The distinction between evaluation as a practice activity and evaluative research as a knowledge-building activity is often ambiguous. As a general rule, however, if the primary purpose of your activity is to develop the knowledge base of the profession rather than deliver a service to your client, you are engaging in research. If you plan to present your results to a professional meeting or publish them in a journal, you are probably engaged in research rather than practice. If in doubt, consider the activity to be research.

When clients are asked to participate in research activities, additional ethical standards apply (see the NASW Code of Ethics, Section 5.02, Evaluation and Research, at: www.naswdc.org). We must be sure that clients will not be subjected to undue risk as a consequence of their participation in the research activity. Furthermore, clients must be fully informed of the nature of the activity, both the intervention itself and the measurement and design requirements of the research component. Finally, clients' participation must be completely voluntary, with no adverse consequence if they decide not to participate in the research. The principle of voluntary informed consent is a fundamental ethical requirement for all research activity and must be carefully followed and documented at all times.

Information Technology in Social Work Practice

Computers have been used for some time in evaluation and research, and they are beginning to have an impact in many other aspects of social work practice as well. This brief introduction reviews some of the ways information technology is currently being used and suggests how you may be using technology in your practice in the near future.

Although modern computer technology has been in existence for 50 years and is now essential in industries such as banking, travel reservations, and medical care, it has yet to make a serious impact on social work practice. That is about to change, however, due to developments in the technology that make it more useful in the less structured situations characteristic of social work practice, and due to the availability of extraordinary computing capability at steadily declining cost. Today it is possible to obtain a desktop computer for $1,000 that has the computing capacity of a large mainframe computer (costing hundreds of thousands of dollars) of a decade or two ago.

The most striking development in the past several years has been the rapidly increasing use of the World Wide Web. High-speed communications technology link computers around the world, giving a user at any point on the network access to all the information contained in the entire network. The Internet is opening up many new possibilities for social work practice and social work education, and we will discuss some of the more important ones later in this section.

EXHIBIT 11.1

*Resource materials on computer applications for social work practice**

Gingerich, W. J., & R. K. Green, 1996. Information technology: How social work is going digital. In P. R. Raffoul & C. A. McNeece (Eds.), *Future Issues for Social Work Practice* (pp. 19–28). Needham Heights, MA: Allyn & Bacon.
Grant, G. B., & L. M. Grobman, 1998. *The social worker's Internet handbook.* Harrisburg, PA: White Hat Communications.
Grohol, J. M. 2000. *The insider's guide to mental health resources online 2000/2001 Edition.* New York: Guilford Press.
Holden, G., G. Rosenberg, & A. Weissman, 1996. World Wide Web accessible resources related to research on social work practice. *Research on Social Work Practice, 6,* 236–262.
Journal of Technology in Human Services. New York: Haworth Press. A new journal devoted exclusively to computer applications in the human services.
Schoech, D. 1999. *Human services technology: Understanding, designing, and implementing computer and Internet applications in the social services* (2nd ed.). New York: Haworth Press.
Trabin, T. 1996. *The Computerization of Behavioral Healthcare.* San Francisco: Jossey-Bass.

*For more information on the computer programs in this chapter, write to:

Wallace J. Gingerich
Mandel School of Applied Social Sciences
Case Western Reserve University
10900 Euclid Avenue
Cleveland, OH 44106
E-mail: wjg4@po.cwru.edu

Today the most common use of information technology in social work practice is word processing. Increasingly, social workers use their computers to write assessments and progress notes and routine correspondence and reports. Some workers also use database programs to create electronic filing systems for their caseloads and to do reports and analyses of their caseload activities. Personal information managers (PIMs) help you keep track of your appointments, addresses and phone numbers, and business expenses. All of these applications are readily available in local computer stores at reasonable cost—many are included with the purchase of a new computer. With a little thought and effort, these applications can be customized to your particular setting and can be quite useful in your work. For additional information on computer applications in social work see the resources listed in Exhibit 11.1.

In this section we will look at applications that have been developed specifically for use in social work or, more broadly, human services practice.

Assessment and Testing

Assessment and testing applications constitute by far the largest number of computer applications in social work practice. There are more than 200 such programs currently available, most of them consisting of computer-administered testing, scoring, and interpretation packages. The MMPI and various depression inventories were among the first instruments to be computerized. Most of the commonly used assessment devices are now available in computerized versions, including DSM-IV interviewing and diagnostic programs. The Clinical Measurement Package developed by Walter Hudson provides for administration and scoring of all Hudson rapid-assessment scales, now numbering over 30 (Nurius & Hudson, 1993). In addition this package will maintain a history of assessment scores for individual clients, enabling the graphic representation of client change over time. Demonstration and educational versions of this package are available free of cost. Information on many of these applications is readily available on the Internet.

Computerized Clinical Records

Computerized clinical record keeping systems maintain the complete case record on the computer and usually incorporate case management and caseload management functions as well. Many of these systems also incorporate appointment scheduling, community resource directories, and billing and accounting functions. Typically, clinical record keeping systems operate on a network or large computer, and the individual worker accesses the system through a computer located in his or her office. Because of the complexities and idiosyncrasies of record keeping requirements, most of these systems have been custom designed for a particular agency and are not available on the open market. In other cases large software companies have developed packages that can be adapted for a particular agency's needs. In either case, these systems are very costly ($20,000 or more) and often require sophisticated equipment and trained systems staff to support them.

Other record keeping programs emphasize treatment planning and case management. These systems assist the practitioner in conducting the assessment and selecting treatment goals, and then help to monitor client change over time (Corcoran & Gingerich, 1994; Gingerich, 1995b). In addition, case management programs can remind the worker of tasks that need to be done and even identify which clients are not making progress so that their plans can be reviewed. Increasingly, case management programs will be able to use the information contained in the case record to assist workers in managing their caseload more efficiently, and may even reduce the amount of time spent on paperwork.

Practice Management and Billing

A number of psychotherapy practice management programs are now available commercially. Most of these systems are designed for small group practices and focus heavily on the clinical information needed to justify services (such as DSM diagnoses, target complaints, level of functioning, and service data) and maintain patient accounts (such as preparing insurance billings and tracking payments). Many of these programs are advertised both in professional publications such as the *NASW News* and on the Internet. Because these applications are intended for solo use, they typically cost only several hundred dollars per workstation.

Managed Care Applications

Computer technology is rapidly being applied in the field of managed behavioral health care, with many of the applications designed for use by practitioners (Gingerich & Broskowski, 1996). These systems generally aim to maximize the efficiency of behavioral health interventions by advising on the level of treatment to be provided, the type of treatment to be used, and the most cost-effective management of particular types of cases. Some systems are designed to improve consistency in diagnosing problems and authorizing services. Others are designed to guide the practitioner on what kind of intervention to use and for how long. Managed care applications basically use information technology to implement the managed care firm's approved authorization criteria and practice guidelines. Many of these are based in part on research data, but they also inevitably incorporate the company's own practice philosophy. Ironically, these applications may have the most value for practitioners interested in evaluating their practice because they are most focused on client change and the interventions that seem to produce client change.

Expert Systems

Expert systems are computer programs that contain the expertise of a human expert on a specified problem area and advise the user on the specified problem area (Gingerich, 1990a, 1995a). Expert systems grew out of research in artificial intelligence and have been implemented widely in industry, medicine, and computer software. Because of the newness of the technology and unresolved product liability issues, few if any clinical expert systems are in routine use in social work practice today. Experimental systems have been developed for assessing the risk of child abuse, advising on risk to women of domestic violence, advising on treatment interventions using a brief solution-focused therapy approach (see Module 9), or assessing suicide risk. Although expert-system applications have yet to be implemented in social work practice, the process of conceptualizing, designing, and testing an expert system can have valuable knowledge-building benefits and can be a useful educational experience. Inexpensive expert-system shells are available that perform the technical programming chores and allow the user to concentrate on developing the rules that go into the knowledge base and the inferencing strategy to be used.

Computer-Based Interventions

Computer programs have been used to administer cognitive therapy to patients experiencing anxiety and to provide sex therapy for couples. The systems carry out an assessment and assign homework. Based on the response of the client, the computer then provides additional advice and feedback. Another system has been developed for delivering exposure therapy to patients experiencing anxiety (see Module 4). This computer-administered program is available to patients via touch-

EXHIBIT 11.2

World Wide Web sites for social work

World Wide Web Resources for Social Workers
www.nyu.edu/socialwork/wwwrsw
Social Work Access Network
www.sc.edu/swan
Computer Use in Social Services Network
www2.uta.edu/cussn
New Social Worker Online
www.socialworker.com
Social Work Search–Social Work Web Ring
www.socialworksearch.com
National Association of Social Workers
www.naswdc.org
Association of Social Work Boards (licensing)
www.aasswb.org
Mental Help Net
mentalhelp.net
Computers in Mental Health–software listing
www.ex.ac.uk/cimh/software.htm
International Society for Mental Health Online
www.ismho.org
United States Government
www.fedworld.gov
The White House
www.whitehouse.gov
U.S. National Institute of Mental Health
www.nimh.nih.gov
U.S. Department of Health and Human Services
www.os.dhhs.gov
U.S. Census Bureau
www.census.gov

tone telephone, making it accessible for people anywhere to access it virtually anytime. Computer-administered interventions can produce results similar to those delivered by human practitioners and are preferred by some clients.

Graphing Packages

A number of packages have been developed that produce graphs or charts useful in assessment and intervention. Several packages are available that can draw family genograms or eco-maps (see Chapter 8) based on information the user enters into the computer. Some of these programs can maintain a database of the ecosystem over time and permit the user to graph these changes. Some of the record keeping and managed care systems previously mentioned also incorporate a variety of graphs. Increasingly we will see programs that can present the target behavior in the form of a graph, which will provide immediate visual feedback on progress to the client and the worker.

Internet and Online Services

The rapid growth of the Internet and readily available access to it has opened up a vast array of potential applications in social work practice. The Internet provides immediate access to a rich storehouse of information relevant to social work practice and this is probably the most common use of the Internet today. Information on many topics of interest to social workers can be accessed via web sites such as World Wide Web Resources for Social Workers and the Social Work Access Network (see Exhibit 11.2). These sites contain links to many sites of interest and are organized to make it easy for you to find what you are looking for. Government sites give access to informative reports, regulations, and statistical data of value to social workers (Exhibit 11.2). State and local governments, and increasingly many social service agencies also have their own web sites, which can be located through World Wide Web search engines such as Google.com. Some individual social workers have developed their own sites for professional use. Visit the author's site at gingerich.net and click on the Social Work Web Ring to visit many other social worker sites.

Unlike commercial and academic publishing houses who use rigorous review procedures to ensure the quality of the information they put out, the information on the Internet has passed no such test. Thus, it is important for you to think critically about the information you access over the Internet and judge for yourself whether it is reliable.

Another common use of the Internet is online support groups. These are discussion groups organized by users with a particular interest such as coping with depression, incest survivors, Alzheimers caregivers, parents of children who committed suicide, and hundreds of other topics. You can find information about these sites in books such as *Health Online* (Ferguson, 1996) and *The*

Insider's Guide to Mental Health Resources Online (Grohol, 2000). Web portals such as Yahoo (www.yahoo.com) also provide easy access to many support group sites and other informative health related sites.

The Internet is also used by many social workers (and social work students) for networking and professional development. You can join mailing lists organized around topics of particular interest, search for a graduate school or a job, or chat with other students or social workers about issues of mutual interest. The New Social Worker Online site (Exhibit 11.2) is a good place to start, as well as the *The Social Worker's Internet Handbook* (Exhibit 11.1).

Finally, the Internet is beginning to be used to deliver professional services. Recently, a researcher offered a smoking cessation program over the Internet, and 360,000 people subscribed! Some social workers are beginning to offer professional services such as counseling over the Internet, via email, chat rooms, or real-time voice and video. These services are called variously eTherapy, eHealth, TeleHealth, or simply online services. Types of services, mode of delivery, and payment mechanisms are still being developed, and it is impossible to tell now what form online services will eventually take. You should be aware, however, that difficult issues pertaining to legal liability, licensing, informed consent, and privacy and confidentiality have yet to be resolved. Social workers delivering services online place themselves at some risk until these issues can be clarified.

Summary

Outcome evaluation asks whether the desired client outcome was achieved, and evaluative research asks whether the observed change was due to the intervention. Because it is an inherent part of the problem-solving approach to interventions, outcome evaluation should be done with all clients. Evaluative research requires more rigorous controls. It is more difficult to carry out and often requires research expertise.

The single-system approach to evaluation consists of six steps. (1) Specify the outcome you and your client are interested in. (2) Select a suitable measure of the outcome, one that is adequate methodologically and is sensitive to the changes you expect your client to make. (3) Record baseline data on the outcome measure until the pattern of behavior before intervention is clear. (4) Implement your intervention and continue to monitor the outcome. (5) Analyze your data to decide whether there is significant change in the outcome. (6) If you have used an appropriate research design, you may be able to infer whether your intervention produced the change.

Although it uses research techniques to assess change and infer treatment effectiveness, the single-system approach to evaluation is compatible with most social work practice. In treatment you ordinarily make informal judgments about whether your client is getting better and whether your intervention is working. Evaluation simply makes the process more systematic and rigorous with a view to improving your information and making your conclusions more reliable. The goal of evaluation is to improve your information about outcomes and thereby improve your practice. Furthermore, several studies show that clients may actually prefer to work with practitioners who evaluate their practice (Campbell, 1988, 1990).

The chapter concludes with a summary of computer applications in social work practice. Not only are computers used in evaluation and research, they are beginning to have an impact on many other aspects of social work practice as well. The most common computer applications in social work fall into these areas: assessment and testing, record keeping, practice management, managed care, expert systems, clinical interventions, graphing packages, and Internet and online services.

EXERCISES

1. SELECTING A SUITABLE OUTCOME MEASURE

Goal: To measure client outcomes.

Step 1: Form groups of three or four. A volunteer "client" in your group decides on an outcome that will become your focus for this exercise. The outcome can be a real one or a hypothetical one.

Step 2: Group members interview the "client" to find out more about the desired outcome. How would the "client" like things to be? What will he or she be doing differently when the outcome is achieved?

Step 3: Identify at least two possible measurement strategies to evaluate the outcome. Describe each measure in detail. What will the anchors be on the self-anchored scale, for example? What specific behavior will you observe or ask your "client" to observe?

Step 4: Ask the "client" to estimate what data he or she would have collected during the past week had they used each measure. What would the data be like when the problem has been solved?

Step 5: Group discussion of the pros and cons of each measure developed. Consider these questions: (a) How reliable (accurate and consistent) will the measurement data be? (b) How valid will the data be—that is, would the behavior counts or self-ratings be good indicators of the outcome the "client" is hoping to achieve? (c) Will the measure be sensitive to changes the "client" would like to see? Do you really expect to see changes in the measures you have selected? (d) Which measure does your "client" think is best? Why?

Step 6: Class presentation of group findings.

2. THREATS TO INFERRING CAUSALITY

Goals: To experience some of the problems involved in inferring causality.

Step 1: Break into groups of five. You will conduct an evaluation of the following case: Your client, a mother of two children (ages 5 and 8), comes in complaining that her 8-year-old, Joey, clings to her too much and doesn't play with other children his age. You and she agree that the desired outcome is for Joey to play with neighbor children his own age. Mother agrees to record the number of 15-minute periods each evening after supper and before bedtime that Joey plays nicely with his peers. She dutifully collects baseline information, as shown below.

After a week of baselining, you instruct the mother to invite a neighbor child over to play with Joey each evening to get the children started in an activity appropriate to their age level. Once the activity has started, she is to give specific praise to the children for their play and to continue to praise every 5 or 10 minutes as it seems appropriate. Also, she is instructed to ignore Joey when he clings to her dress and whines. After role playing some situations in your office, you are convinced that she understands the intervention and is able to carry it out. Mother returns the next week for her appointment. You review the data and refine and rehearse again the intervention. The next week Mother reports the following data:

(continued)

E X E R C I S E S
(continued)

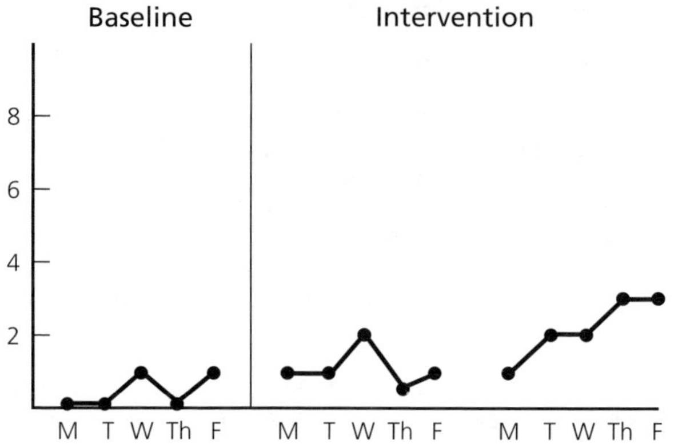

During the interview, she reports the following additional information. She has begun to think that Joey is a nice kid after all. Last week when she took him to the park to play they had a really good time. Joey seemed to get along well with the other children on the playground too. Mother also mentioned that Joey seemed to enjoy his last two weekend visits with his dad. In general, Joey seems to be getting back to his good old self.

Step 2: Decide first whether you agree with Mother that Joey's behavior has changed. Is the standard of "clearly evident and reliable" met? Is the change experimentally or clinically significant?

Step 3: Enumerate other possible explanations of Joey's behavior change. What is the likelihood of these explanations? Does the simple AB design used allow you to rule out these explanations?

Step 4: Class discussion of group findings. Has the intervention been successful? How confident are you of your conclusions? Does the intervention seem promising enough to continue using it and observing the results?

CHAPTER 12

Social Work Practice with Diverse Groups

The social work profession prides itself on its recognition of the importance of ethnic, cultural, racial, and sexual differences.[1] Social workers helped to establish the National Association for the Advancement of Colored People (NAACP) and the National Urban League (Garvin & Cox, 1995, p. 73). The National Association of Social Workers' (NASW) Code of Ethics specifically prohibits discrimination against others "on the basis of race, ethnicity, national origin, color, sex, sexual orientation, age, marital status, political belief, religion, or mental or physical disability." The 1990 Delegate Assembly of NASW adopted a resolution calling on the Council on Social Work Education to strengthen its standards on sexual orientation. On the basis of public pronouncements at least, one would expect that social workers would perform admirably when working with people from among these groups. Unfortunately, this benign view is not necessarily accurate. All of us were raised and socialized in a racist system. As a result, all of us are apt to have some racist stereotypes. In addition, Gilligan's (1982) work on gender underscored that much of what we have assumed about human development is based on a male perspective. Clearly, there is evidence that social workers face a difficult task understanding and working with clients whose backgrounds differ from their own.

In this chapter we consider barriers inherent in worker-client differences and point out reasons for the problematic nature of cross-cultural relationships. It is beyond the scope of this text to provide content on all populations-at-risk. Information covering a greater number of populations-at-risk can be found in *Social Work with Diverse Populations* (Harper & Lantz, 1996).

Problems and Barriers

Clearly, the social work profession needs to recognize the reality of practice in a culturally diverse environment. A variety of studies demonstrate that social workers and other helping persons share many of the prejudices and misperceptions of the general society (Harper & Lantz, 1996; Lum, 1996; Van Den Bergh, 1995).

[1]Most of this chapter was specially written for this text by Grafton H. Hull, Jr., Ed.D. Dr. Hull is Director, BSW Program, University of Utah. The section titled "Macro Strategies to Promote Social and Economic Justice" was written by Charles Zastrow.

Multiple examples of sexism can be found in the social work knowledge base. De Jong and Berg (1998), in summarizing the work of several other social work authors, note that "for too long, the helping professions have operated with built-in preferences for the traits and behaviors of middle-class white males. Such preferences have minimized or ignored the characteristics more common among poor people, women, and people of color" (p. 204). For example, males working with depressed women may simply re-create old relationships between the dependent woman and the controlling male, relationships counter to the goals of intervention.

The tendency to use our own cultural, social, or economic values as the norm poses additional dangers for well-meaning workers. The ease with which many workers confuse a healthy adaptation to a sick environment with pathology points up the difficulty. Both the habit of misreading strengths as deficits and the assumption that African Americans and other minorities are culturally deprived arise from the use of norms derived from the dominant white middle class. The problematic nature of cross-cultural counseling does not, however, preclude its effectiveness. Some white workers, for instance, can establish viable working relationships with minority clients, whereas in other instances, minority workers are less effective with others of the same race or culture (Logan, 1990; Proctor & Davis, 1994; Logan, 1990, p. 33) concluded that "ethnicity and class are important variables in service delivery and should not serve as barriers to effective client-worker relationships." Despite rather disparate backgrounds and experiences, many social workers and clients do develop productive relationships. This is not to say there are not difficulties in intercultural relationships. It is only natural that our life experiences affect how we view the world around us. It clearly can affect our ability to understand and assist others whose life experiences are markedly different from our own. It should not be surprising then that social workers don't always know how to respond when confronted with cultural or other differences. The problem becomes increasingly complex when we focus on some of the major barriers to effective cross-cultural social work practice. In the following sections we examine selected characteristics of a sample of diverse groups with whom social workers are likely to interact and will identify some of the potential dangers facing the unwary helper. These issues are intended only to sensitize you to your upcoming tasks and are not designed to cover all possible situations. They should be viewed accordingly.

Native American Clients

A social worker counseling a Native American client might readily assume that the client's quietness indicates either an uncooperative attitude or, conversely, that the worker and client are on the same wavelength (Green, 1999). Unfortunately neither assumption may be correct. In fact, Native Americans may not correct or challenge a worker who is off track because to do so violates a basic tenet of Native American culture: noninterference. Noninterference in practice is similar, but not identical, to the social work value of self-determination. It requires Native Americans to meet unwanted attempts at intervention or intrusion with withdrawal—emotional, physical, or both. In other cases, this may take the form of changing the subject or pretending not to hear the offending words. Even the most well-intentioned worker may be perceived as a coercive authority figure whose efforts are resisted passively but firmly. Consequently Native Americans are perhaps less likely to assert themselves than might be true of members of other protected classes. Assuming that clients will give feedback if you are off target is only one of several beliefs you must "unlearn" to practice effectively in a cross-cultural environment.

Another response pattern of social workers that frequently proves counterproductive is direct eye contact. Many Native Americans consider such face-to-face eye contact rude and intimidating. Ivey & Ivey (1999) and Kadushin (1990) noted that ethnic differences in eye contact have been acknowledged by other writers and that Native Americans in particular find eye contact disrespectful. Avoiding eye contact is a way of showing deference in this culture. Obviously, a white worker who plans to practice in a Native American community needs to be cognizant of these factors to avoid exacerbating the already tenuous relationship that exists between cultures. Lacking a thorough knowledge of Native American culture often results in a failure to recognize its complexity, and workers do this at their peril.

In the dominant white culture, a firm handshake generally means that a person may be trusted, but many Native Americans view a firm handshake as aggressive and disrespectful (Harper & Lantz, 1996). In addition, white social workers should not be surprised if Native Americans do not trust them in the initial stage of intervention, as Native Americans have a long history of being victimized by the dominant white group in our society.

Middle-class white social workers may also be surprised to discover that many Native Americans consider it a sign of disrespect to question a person in detail about his or her personal life. A social worker taking a social history on a Native American client may unknowingly be acting in a very disrespectful manner if the client does not share the worker's views of the value of full self-disclosure. Honest and direct questioning by the worker is apt to be experienced by the Native American client as interrogation (Harper & Lantz, 1996).

African American Clients

With African American clients the picture is somewhat similar; workers frequently misread the meaning of client behavior with resultant deleterious consequences. For example, the adaptive behavior of many African Americans, which includes "aloofness" or reserve can be mistaken by whites as hostile or rejecting (Green, 1999). Grier and Cobbs (1968) suggested that a certain level of cultural paranoia on the part of the African American client can intrude on the client-white worker relationship, and Gary (1996) found that African Americans in particular experience frequent racism from government agencies. With these factors in mind, it is easy to understand why some writers and others feel that only a worker from the client's cultural background can effectively work with minority clients. At times a non–African American worker may attempt to overcompensate for these differences by unrealistic empathy. A worker may ascribe all the emotional and social difficulties experienced by African American clients to a racist society. This, in effect, denies clients their individuality and similarities with other human beings, a result that is, of course, unintended.

Language differences serve as barriers to communication in subtle ways as well as the more obvious ones. African Americans use *Ebonics,* verbal communications that include not only rate and rhythm but also syntax, word choice, and nonverbal communication. The result is that words have different meanings to the speaker and to the listener. For example, "that is nasty" means "disgustingly filthy" to some of us, but others of us take it to mean "impressive." Such language differences can affect both oral communication and performance on psychological tests and pose difficulties for the novice social worker.

Some authors have argued that traditional Eurocentric views of human behavior provide additional barriers to understanding and helping African Americans (Schiele, 1996). For example, our tendency to focus on individuals rather than seeing a person as a part of a larger social group ignores the cooperative and sharing traditions that represent untapped client strengths. Our lack of attention to spirituality and the role it plays in understanding African American clients is also cited as a problem. Finally, we may fail to recognize the importance that emotions play when we tend only to the rational side of the person's life situation. An Africentric view recognizes that emotions and thoughts are not independent and that thoughts "are no more superior to emotions than emotions are to thoughts" (Schiele, 1996, p. 287). Adopting this perspective is consistent with the social work sensitivity to feelings but can challenge more rational approaches to helping. The theoretical concepts of the Africentric perspective and worldview are receiving increased attention and recognition. These concepts are described in Exhibit 12.1.

Another barrier is the tendency to rely on research findings not applicable to African Americans for our understanding of certain family dynamics. For example, there is substantial evidence that white women who are battered are much more likely to use community resources such as shelters than are African American women (Daly, Jennings, Beckett, & Leashore, 1995). Similarly, comparisons of homeless men and women show very different patterns depending on whether clients are white or nonwhite. Socioeconomic factors and lack of institutional resources are much more likely to account for the homeless state of African Americans, whereas white homeless individuals and families are more likely to suffer substance abuse and various psychiatric illnesses, which contribute to their present situation (North & Smith, 1994).

Latino Clients

As noted earlier, even workers who share common characteristics with minority clients sometimes experience comparable difficulties. Bilingual white practitioners, for example, who work in a Latino community don't necessarily possess the requisite skills to understand all aspects of the language. The special language of the barrio in particular is not easily understood unless one has some shared experience with the culture. Both the meaning of words and their usage differ, sometimes significantly. As a consequence, workers who speak Spanish must be acutely sensitive to the possibility that words can have other meanings.

Our ability to perceive communication accurately is enhanced by knowing the client's life experiences.

EXHIBIT 12.1

The Africentric perspective and worldview

African American culture includes elements from traditional African culture; from slavery, reconstruction, and subsequent exposure to racism and discrimination; and from "mainstream" white culture. The *Africentric perspective* (Devore & Schlesinger, 1996) acknowledges African culture and expressions of African beliefs, values, institutions, and behaviors. It recognizes that African Americans retain, to some degree, a number of elements of African life and values.

The Africentric perspective asserts that applying Eurocentric theories of human behavior to explain the behavior and ethos of African Americans is often inappropriate. Eurocentric theories of human behavior reflect concepts developed in European and Anglo-American cultures. Eurocentric theorists historically vilified people of African descent and other people of color. Such theorists explicitly or implicitly claimed that people of African descent were pathological or inferior in their social, personality, or moral development (Schiele, 1996). The origins of this denigration can be found in the slave trade, as slave traders and owners endeavored to justify the enslavement of Africans. Eurocentric theories portray the culture of people of African descent as "uncivilized" and as having contributed practically nothing of value to world development and human history.

The Africentric perspective seeks to dispel the negative distortions about people of African ancestry by legitimizing and disseminating a worldview that goes back thousands of years and that exists in the hearts and minds of many people of African descent today. (The concept of worldview involves perceptions of ourselves in relation to other people, objects, institutions, and nature. It focuses on our view of the world and our role and place in it.) The worldview of African Americans is shaped by unique and important experiences, such as racism and discrimination, an African heritage, traditional attributes of the African American family and community life, and a strong religious orientation.

The Africentric perspective also promotes a worldview that facilitates human and societal transformation toward moral, spiritual, and humanistic ends and that seeks to persuade people of different cultural and ethnic groups that they share a mutual interest in this regard. The Africentric perspective rejects the idea that individuals can be understood separately from others in their social group. Instead, it emphasizes a collective identity, which encourages sharing, cooperation, and social responsibility.

The Africentric perspective also emphasizes the importance of spirituality, which includes moral development and attaining meaning and identity in life. The Africentric perspective asserts that the major sources of human problems in the United States are oppression and alienation. Oppression and alienation are generated not only by prejudice and discrimination but also by the European worldview that teaches people to see themselves primarily as material, physical beings seeking immediate pleasure for their physical, material, or sexual desires. It is further asserted that the European worldview discourages spiritual and moral development.

The Africentric perspective has been used to explain the origins of specific social problems. For example, violent crimes by youths are thought to result from their limited options and choices for economic advancement. Black youths seek a life of street crime as a logical way to cope with, and protest against, a society that practices pervasive employment discrimination (associated with minimum wages, layoffs, lack of opportunities for education or training, and a wide gap between the rich and the poor). These youths understand that they can make more money from a life of street crime than from attending college or starting a legitimate business with little start-up capital. Choosing a life of crime is also thought more likely to occur in a society that uses the European worldview, which deemphasizes spiritual and moral development, because individuals have little or no awareness of collective social responsibility.

The Africentric perspective values a more holistic, spiritual, and optimistic view of human beings. It supports the "strengths perspective" and "empowerment" concepts of social work practice.

All groups have problems and characteristics that arise from longstanding value systems, ethnic backgrounds, socioeconomic factors, languages, and behavior patterns. Workers who are familiar with these variables will be more effective practitioners. In the case of Latinos, bilingualism is not a sufficient condition for successful practice but it is often necessary or helpful.

Lest you become discouraged at this point about the difficulties inherent in cross-cultural social work, even counselors of the same ethnic or cultural background are not guaranteed freedom from problems. Issues such as different life experiences, language fluency, and gender influence the worker-client relationship even when client and worker share the same ethnicity.

Gay and Lesbian Clients

It has been estimated that approximately 10 percent of the adult population is primarily homosexual (Berger, 1987, p. 797). This fact, combined with the usual family constellation, suggests that a large number of people are directly affected by the issue of homosexuality. Humphreys (1983, p. 60) estimated that the lives of almost half of all Americans are touched by homosexuality. Berger (1987, p. 797) concluded that "virtually everyone, whether self-identified as homosexual or heterosexual, has a close relationship with a gay man." Woodman (1987) suggested that the actual incidence of homosexuality may be greater than estimates.

Unfortunately, homosexuality traditionally has been viewed variously as deviant, criminal, an illness, an emotional disturbance, and, among some groups, a sin. The result has been an irrational fear of homosexuality—homophobia—that is as serious a problem as other forms of prejudice, such as sexism and racism.

Helping professionals are as likely to be affected by these prejudices as the general public. Lack of knowledge, acceptance of stereotypes, and fear of the unknown are not limited to the layperson. Many social workers may have been exposed to minority group members, but the stigma associated with gay and lesbian sexuality has kept a large number of homosexuals from sharing information with others. As a result, social workers who come in contact with gay and lesbian clients are often no better prepared to help these groups than is the general public. The tendency to stereotype homosexual clients flies in the face of what is known about the differences and similarities among human beings. Loewenstein (1980, p. 31) argued, for example, that "lesbian women are extremely diverse in personality, family constellation, and developmental experiences, and categorizing them as a group becomes as meaningless as categorizing all heterosexual women." The same can be said for gay men.

Social workers who work with gay and lesbian clients can start with the information on diversity and yet still recognize common difficulties experienced by homosexuals in our society. The barriers and discrimination encountered by gays and lesbians should be acknowledged for their impact on the client's life as well as for their effect on the relationship between worker and client.

As a beginning, it is helpful to recognize that debate over causation of homosexuality is irrelevant in efforts to help. A focus on etiology does not assist the client with present functioning and tends to obscure the multiple problems resulting from societal reaction to gays and lesbians. Attempts to focus on cause have not been beneficial in coping with stereotypes and in fact have led to homosexuals' being mistreated to correct for some presumed deficit in early life experiences. Furthermore, few gays and lesbians can be identified either by appearance or mannerisms. This, coupled with the risks in coming out (publicly identifying oneself as homosexual), has resulted in a lack of attention to the needs of gay and lesbian clients. As Berger (1982, p. 236) noted, "This has especially been true of older homosexuals who have been all but ignored by the social work profession." Moreover, recent research shows that homosexual youth are at much greater risk for suicide, resulting, in part, from the pain of being isolated and discriminated against (Proctor & Groze, 1994). Youth without adequate support systems are more likely to consider suicide as a coping mechanism. Later in this chapter we suggest several means by which social workers can assist lesbian and gay clients by recognizing and dealing with the specialized needs of this group.

Rural Settings

Like practitioners in a biracial environment, social workers who work predominantly with clients of their own race or ethnic group may not be spared the necessity of adjusting their practice style. For example, workers who practice in a basically rural environment must also be aware of a multiplicity of factors that impinge on effectiveness. The case example "Unwritten Community Value Prevails" illustrates ignorance of the norms of a rural area. Seemingly innocuous factors like style of dress, hair length, and model of car can set the social worker in a rural community apart. In addition, the worker in a rural area may discover that events of the past still affect the behavior of residents today. Long-standing family and church conflicts may exist and create barriers to getting community members together to work on a problem or issue. The fact that many rural social workers lack exposure to the rural environment before beginning their practice creates additional difficulties. The worker's attitudes and ideas regarding rural communities may be outdated or even quite negative. This can affect interactions with residents just as strongly as racial bias in a minority community. The struggle to survive in a rural setting under these conditions may explain the burnout commonly experienced by in-migrant practitioners.

CASE EXAMPLE

Unwritten Community Value Prevails

Marty Jacobsen has been an active member of the small community in a rural Midwestern state. She has served on several community committees, attended the customary volunteer fire fighters fund-raising chicken dinners, and was chair of her church's auxiliary. She is also a faculty member at Ravenswood University, a small institution which has over time become one of the largest employers in the area. When Marty decided to run for a seat on the Ravenwood City Council, she expected to receive strong support from her friends and acquaintances in the community. The current city council has seven members, three of whom are university employees. She has heard about an unwritten community value that university employees will never constitute a majority on the City Council. Regardless, she waged a vigorous campaign, posted signs in the yards of scores of her "friends," and explained carefully her well-thought-out positions on important community issues. On election day she was soundly beaten by her opponent, a retired Army Sergeant with no connection to the university who had campaigned very little. Once again, the norms of the community were maintained and power on the City Council maintained in the hands of the non-university population.

Feminist Social Work

Increasing sensitivity to the impact of gender on the development, definition, and amelioration of social and personal problems has helped identify another barrier to effective social work practice—sexism. There is greater recognition today that many of the difficulties experienced by both men and women in society are related to gender inequality, specifically in the areas of privileges, power, and access to resources. The enormous role played by gender limits the effectiveness of social work practice and suggests ways in which the worker's own sex can be a contributing problem. Van Den Bergh and Cooper (1987, p. 610) identified situations where a male worker may be less appropriate than a female practitioner:

1. All-female groups, which may reinforce stereotypic dependencies or set up competition for male attention.
2. Women who are hostile to men unless they work as a co-therapist in the therapeutic process.
3. Women who relate to male therapists primarily in a seductive manner.
4. Extremely dependent, inhibited women who equate femaleness with passivity and docility.
5. Women who are in the midst of a divorce crisis and who may, as a result of intense transference feelings, see the male therapist as a surrogate spouse.

As we shall see later, these limitations do not mean that gender must always be a limiting factor in social work practice. It does mean, however, that both male and female social workers must be aware of ways that gender shapes a client's problems and how help can and should be provided. The significant consideration is the extent to which gender-related oppression encompasses all aspects of society—economic, social, religious, and political—and the fact that gender itself plays no less a role in social work practice than race, sexual orientation, and location. The difficulty in overcoming the bondage of sexism provides a challenge as great as dealing with factors that perpetuate racism and homophobia. Some methods of providing effective intervention within the context of nonsexist practice will be described later. (See Module 7 for a discussion of the feminist perspective on therapy.)

Other Examples

Many elements can separate worker and client and undermine the empathic quality of the relationship. Cultural, racial, and sexual differences that create this gulf have been discussed, but Kadushin (1990) described additional worker-client characteristics that can also affect outcomes. The age difference between a younger worker and an older client, for instance, can be a barrier because of differences in values, perceptions, or physiological factors. At the same time, workers attempting to establish relationships with children will find that as adults they are potentially contaminated by their association with parents, a state of affairs that may have to be overcome if the child is to trust the counselor. Even a worker's preference for a particular type of intervention or treatment may be inappropriate when the client's environment provides no support. Similarly, some problems are chronic in nature due to social and economic injustices that are not alleviated by counseling no matter how competent the social worker.

Clearly, a social worker's role is complex. Critical and fundamental issues affecting the worker's practice, however, are generally categorized into four areas: ignorance of the culture or characteristics of clients, stereotypic perceptions of the target group, lack of self-knowledge, and reliance on standard counseling techniques and approaches without regard to their implications for the target group. Each of these areas can be overcome, providing you are willing and able to make the necessary adaptations. The task is not an easy one because, as Gross (1996) and others have noted, much of the research available to interested social workers paints an inaccurate picture of minority groups, misjudging such salient areas as family structure and lifestyle characteristics.

Part of the problem experienced in gathering factual data, of course, is that much of the research is based on the perceptions of middle-class white investigators. Despite this handicap, workers who have a significant intercultural practice must seek appropriate information on their client groups. However, knowledge is only the beginning. Cross-cultural social work demands a high degree of self-knowledge and self-awareness on the part of workers. Unlike sociological, psychological, and anthropological data, which is obtained with reasonable ease, self-knowledge is perhaps the most difficult to obtain because it can be anxiety-producing. Few of us want to acknowledge our own prejudices in part because to do so reflects badly on our self-perception. Understandably, we prefer to view ourselves as enlightened and nondiscriminatory. However, the route to effective cross-cultural social work practice requires examining our beliefs, attitudes, and values and perhaps changing them. Complete elimination of every vestige of prejudice is difficult, but the effort is valid. While we must expect to practice in a prejudiced world, our own interventions must be culturally appropriate and sensitive.

Knowledge You Will Need for Cross-Cultural Work

Knowledge of Self

There is no substitute for self-awareness. The ability to be responsive to your own senses, feelings, behavior, and thoughts is a prime requisite for effective practice in the helping professions. This includes a thorough recognition, knowledge, and acceptance of your value system. Workers need to understand how their own professional actions contribute to social and economic injustice in the world and especially for those who are at risk because of their culture.

In some cases, our feelings about racism and the plight of minorities or other groups suffering from discrimination can effectively block our functioning by generating guilt, depression, or a sense of being overwhelmed. This process can be averted by recognizing the likelihood we have grown up prejudiced and by being willing "to be more ready to listen, less ready to come to conclusions, more open to guidance and correction of . . . presuppositions" (Kadushin, 1990, p. 306). The ability to correct our own tendencies toward racist thinking obviously requires sensitivity and effort. We must be willing to make fundamental changes in our thinking patterns, attitudes, and behavior. Still, such growth in self-knowledge (of and by itself) is insufficient without a concomitant growth in awareness of the uniqueness of the client group.

Knowledge of Differences

It has long been asserted that similar needs exist in all cultures, but how those needs are molded and shaped is culturally relative. Thus, although a basic acceptance of the worth and dignity of each human being is important, workers who practice with diverse groups must enhance this acceptance with hard facts. We believe ourselves to be grounded in reality, but our reality is nevertheless only a function of our perception of the real world. An individual who comes to a counseling situation from a different cultural background, especially one who has experienced racist or sexist behavior, will have a different reality. Therefore, we must be aware of the ways in which cultural and other background factors affect perceptions and feelings and the expression of these qualities.

As an example, Kravetz (1982, p. 46) pointed out that "Women's personal concerns, experiences, and problems are intricately related to their social, economic, legal, and political condition." Institutionized prejudice against women presents workers with additional problems. Thus, workers must be aware of the unique vulnerabilities of women, the absence of certain coping resources, and the stereotyping tendencies of much of society.

Also beneficial is some knowledge of the history and language of the client group. Becoming familiar with common phrases and vocabulary will be helpful even if you are not bilingual. You should endeavor to build a solid knowledge base in minority lifestyles so your clients' strengths and ability to adapt are not ignored or branded as abnormal behavior. For example, minority clients who appear hostile or suspicious of a white worker may be expressing a quite reasonable reaction based on past experiences with well-meaning professionals or other representatives of "helping" agencies.

The growing incidence of ethnoviolence (conflict and violence motivated by prejudice) experienced in the United States over the past 15 years is testimony to the continued difficulties of members of minority groups (Harper & Lantz, 1996). It also underscores the earlier observation of Thomas and Sillen (1972, p. 63) that "to judge what is healthy or morbid in an individual's psychological functioning, one must be aware of what is appropriate within his cultural milieu." Living with racism, prejudice, discrimination, and violence have important consequences for clients' feelings, thoughts, and behaviors. Workers cannot ignore this reality.

Simple behaviors that we take for granted often carry radically different meanings to people from different cultures. Even something as "simple" as personal space varies dramatically across cultures. If your class is diverse, take a class survey of culturally acceptable ways to point fingers, for example. Thus, workers must consider family and cultural norms as well as community organizations and structures.

The knowledge of how a given group responds to authority, to stress, and to dependency is invaluable as a worker without a sound grasp of the culture can easily mistake a reaction as inappropriate. This grounding can come from living in a minority area and taking part in community activities such as council meetings, powwows, and neighborhood get-togethers. Certainly, these activities should be pursued by all social workers serving a given population. A background of direct experience with minorities is of course ideal, but most social workers who begin practice lack this base. As a result, it behooves you to take advantage of the excellent bibliographic material available on cultural diversity, some of which can be found in the reference list at the end of this text. Workers, for example, who intend to work with Native Americans should carefully study the unique cultural heritage of this group. There are many Native American cultures, and each tribe has its own history, traditions, customs, and environment. This makes it difficult to generalize from tribal group to tribal group. However, there are some important similarities. For example, the fact that some Native American fathers play a strong disciplinarian role in their families may suggest to the unknowing worker that child abuse is occurring, when in fact the Native American family is perhaps less dependent on corporal punishment than the average non–Native American family. The failure to recognize cultural factors such as this inevitably result in misunderstanding and frustrations for the erring worker. Awareness of the principal values of Native Americans and an understanding of the cultural context in which they exist will lessen this possibility.

The Native American tradition of sharing is another area that confuses white workers unaccustomed to this kind of hospitality. Even if resources are meager, the Native American is willing to allow other family and friends to partake of what there is. Although this may appear to be nonfunctional to many whites, the value is intrinsic to the Native American heritage. To do otherwise would be to ignore part of a value system that has helped the culture survive more than 400 years of racism.

Even the Native American use of time can be a subject of confusion to the non–Native American. Green (1999, pp. 32–33) noted that some Native Americans observe "social time" that is "person-centered" and focuses on family and personal needs. "White time" or clock time, which exists primarily for business, is less important specifically because it is not oriented to human beings. Arriving on time for an appointment with the social worker may be much less important than stopping to help a friend or talking with a family member. This does not mean that all Native Americans ignore "white time" but that the use of time should be taken into account when working with this group.

Although some might suggest otherwise, Native Americans are not unaware of time; however, they do not subject themselves to its tyranny as many whites have done. Punctuality is not a pressing concern, a fact that confounds many time-conscious helping professionals. The time-bound worker may also misperceive the related Native American value of patience as evidence of laziness or lack of motivation. Respect for and appreciation of the Native American culture is essential if the worker is to establish an effective relationship.

Similarly, the Latino experience will be sufficiently new to most workers that a dedicated effort must be made to replace ignorance with knowledge. As in the case of Native Americans, the family unit of Latinos is more likely to be characterized as extended. This expanded family network is another indication of the adaptability of Latinos. Workers therefore need to be alert for the boundaries of the family system so they do not exclude or overlook pertinent members. The fact that the elderly have an important role to play and must be included in planning places a special burden on workers. The significance of religion in Latino life is more commonly known to most non-Latinos, as is the importance of the male role. Although some evidence suggests that cross-cultural differences in these areas may be exaggerated in the literature, workers need to be aware of the significance of these factors in Latino life.

The diversity of cultural backgrounds in Native American culture is duplicated in Latino culture. The tendency to see any culture as unidimensional fails to recognize the diversity within cultures. For instance, the term *Latino* encompasses Mexican Americans, Puerto Ricans, Colombians, Brazilians, and others whose ancestry can be traced to Spanish or Portuguese beginnings. It is probably more helpful for social workers to learn how clients describe themselves (such as Puerto Rican or Cuban American) rather than using less specific terms such as Latino or Hispanic.

Like Latinos, Asian Americans are such an extraordinarily diverse group that it is difficult to characterize them by identifying commonalities. For example, comparisons among Hmong, Laotian, and Japanese clients are most difficult. The recent immigrant experiences of the Hmong and other Southeast Asian groups, coupled with cultural differences between these groups and others who have been here for several generations, make it unlikely that one set of guidelines would ever be helpful. In addition, the tendency to lump these groups together has been criticized, because it does not specifically address the unique needs of individual Asian cultures (Fong & Mokuau, 1996). Special programs involving interpreters, language classes, and other efforts aimed at helping new immigrants learn about American culture are needed for recent immigrant groups. Such programs are one way to promote social and economic justice for populations-at-risk.

The Hmong and Cambodians in the United States often speak little English, hold very low-paying jobs, and struggle with overt discrimination more often than third- or fourth-generation Asian Americans. In one sense, their experiences resemble those of immigrants in the nineteenth and early twentieth centuries. To be of help, one community used innovative school programs to ensure that Hmong students and their parents felt a part of the educational system. These included using bilingual aides to talk to parents about school programs, explain homework assignments, confirm parent-teacher conference times, and invite parents to participate in school programs (Alexander, 1993). The result of such programs has been almost 100 percent participation by parents in conferences and children in after-school programs. Such programs exemplify the kind of innovative efforts needed to reach at-risk populations.

Although the client group and community may not be ethnically or racially different from that of workers, those who serve in rural environments must also possess a certain knowledge base to be effective. They must be aware of the network of nontraditional services often available in these areas. Service clubs and church groups, for instance, assume greater importance than in larger, more metropolitan communities. Likewise, the existence of natural support systems can be a real asset, but workers must know about them before they can use them effectively. (Natural support systems include family and friendship groups, local informal caregivers, volunteer service groups, and mutual or self-help groups.) Knowledge of the local power structure is perhaps more crucial than for urban workers, because the effectiveness of rural workers may be seriously impaired without the necessary sanction and cooperation. As in the case of other diverse groups, ignorance of values, beliefs, and attitudes of the rural client system is inexcusable and counterproductive. If this need to be alert to, and operate within, local norms is seen as onerous by workers, then they should consider moving elsewhere.

As discussed earlier, age differences between worker and client can also affect practice. Kadushin (1990) suggested, for example, that workers must be aware of the effect that the physical condition of the elderly can have on the interview. Among other factors, lack of energy and hearing difficulties can impair the aged client's ability to participate in the relationship. Thus competent workers must have a firm foundation in human behavior and development as well as sensitivity to the nuances of communication in helping relationships.

It is common for social workers to identify and build on clients' strengths. Assessment of these strengths, however, requires recognizing their clients' vast and diverse experiences. Too often, a strength that is overlooked is the spiritual element. Spiritualism takes many forms, especially among the diverse groups in our society. Social workers might consider whether clients regularly attend church or belong to religious organizations. Such activities often serve as a source of support in tough times and can also be both an emotional and economic resource. Religious values may dictate appropriate behavior toward other family members and non-family members, as well as how clients express pain and suffering. In addition, in Caribbean, Hispanic, and some Asian cultures (Canda & Furman, 1999), spiritualism is used to explain a variety of physical and emotional problems. The importance of spirituality is relevant to understanding human behavior, affects social work practice, and has an impact on social policy and research.

Applying Your Knowledge: Techniques of Intervention

Once a sufficient knowledge base is acquired, you must incorporate this into practice to increase the effectiveness of your intervention activities. In this section we review specific intervention approaches and techniques designed to enhance your capabilities. The material presented is not intended to be exhaustive, and obviously there is no substitute for direct experience. Workers whose practice encompasses any of these areas must do more extensive reading (and, it is hoped, receive formal training) than is presented here.

Basic to any relationship, according to Ivey and Ivey (1999), is empathy, clearly communicated to clients, plus warmth and genuineness. Workers in a bicultural relationship must pay special heed to this advice because authenticity is even more crucial when differences are great between client and helper. Moreover, workers must use their own patterns of communication and avoid the temptation to adopt the client's vocabulary and speech. A worker who does not follow this stricture may find clients either withdrawing from the relationship or attacking the helper for lack of sincerity. In many cross-cultural relationships, there is a greater need on the part of the client to know the worker as a person (Kadushin, 1990). A helper who is uncomfortable stepping outside the professional role will have difficulty working with many minority clients or practicing in a rural environment where greater informality is expected in both settings.

There are clear limits to the time and place for informality in intercultural counseling. Generally the kind of informality that marks the effective relationship does not occur immediately. For example, in the initial interview, Kadushin (1990) and Kirst-Ashman and Hull (1999) recommend using all the formalities associated with culturally prescribed displays of respect. This should include use of the client's proper full name, title (Mr., Miss, Mrs., Ms., Dr.), greeting with a handshake, and the other courtesies usually extended. Workers must also be up front with clients about the reasons for their presence. For example, if the contact was worker-initiated, the worker should give identification, state the reasons for the meeting, and avoid placing the client in the position of having to guess the purpose.

> The helping relationship is in itself a power relationship in which the dynamics of power and lack of power are operating. The expertise of the worker and the neediness of the client place them in positions of power and lack of power, respectively. The cross-racial and cross-ethnic helping encounter compounds the consequences of this power differential. Power issues related to differences in ethnicity, class, sex, age, and other social markers may exaggerate the power inherent in the helping role in a way that causes the worker to misperceive the client. (Pinderhughes, 1979, p. 315)

Workers in an empathic relationship must be alert to the power differential engendered by race and other differences and strive to reduce or eliminate this differential. Proper protocol aids in this effort.

Awareness of these differences and a degree of sensitivity to the subtle impact of racial prejudice should help workers avoid the related trap of color blindness that often confuses the novice. To avoid appearing prejudiced, the new worker may decide to adopt the strategy of color blindness and ignore the client's race or ethnic background. Although well-intended, color blindness is ineffective because of the tendency it creates for separating "the black person's internal problems from his color" (Burgest, 1973, p. 23). According to Thomas and Sillen (1972), color blindness ceases to be a "virtue if it means denial of differences in the experience, culture and psychology of black Americans and other Americans (p. 58). . . . To gloss over race in a racist society may in itself be a capitulation to racism" (p. 143). It is understandable if on occasion the worker's feelings about racism get in the way of the relationship; guilt, depression, or a sense of being overwhelmed are not uncommon reactions, yet helpers must reject sympathy when empathy is required. Conversely, even though some impact of racism will almost always exist, its impact on the presenting problem may be greater or less. It may be a contributing factor in the client's problem, the cause of the problem, or entirely unrelated to the issues at hand. Workers should not automatically attribute all difficulties to racism.

Like the culturally sensitive worker, an agency can be equally dedicated to providing services to different client groups. The agency's responsiveness can be demonstrated through relatively simple measures such as establishing hours that coincide with the needs of the groups to be served. This may include evening hours to avoid the need for some clients, already economically marginal, to lose time from jobs, and it could extend to weekend hours and walk-in arrangements, as Kadushin (1990) suggested. The fact that the poor are frequently afflicted by crises requires that more flexible means of dealing with immediate client needs and greater accessibility to services for the here-and-now, present-oriented client. Logically, the immediacy of the situation coupled with the economic and political existence of many minority clients suggest that first-level needs must be attended to on a priority basis. This orientation is basic to the social work principle of starting where the client is. It is most unlikely that the client whose housing needs are urgent and tenuous will tolerate a worker who insists on focusing on the dynamics of the marital interactions. Clients from all cultures will reject an incompetent and insensitive social worker.

Within the relationship, workers will have to judge the need to be more or less active. As you shall see later, a high level of intervention on the part of the worker dealing with a Native American family may well prove less productive than with a client from another cultural or racial group. Kadushin (1990) recommended that the focus in the relationship be on specific problems and behaviors.

African American Client—White Worker

African Americans can easily be defined as a historically oppressed group. The patterns of discrimination they have encountered since colonial times and their history, intertwined with the institution of slavery, have combined to create a population-at-risk. For more than three centuries, racism and mistreatment have enveloped the experiences of individuals and families. Our society assigns African Americans to inferior roles (for example, in employment) and all too frequently erroneously views them as having lower status (Allen-Meares, 1999; Schaefer, 1993). This places African Americans in a disadvantaged position relative to community institutions, including social welfare agencies. Fortunately, most of the guides to practice discussed earlier are directly applicable to the relationship between the non–African American worker and the African American client. In addition, however, Lee (1999) stressed the need to avoid placing African American clients in a position of dependency. The power discrepancy described earlier often results when this is neglected. Both workers and agencies serving African American clients, according to Franklin (1999), must recognize the value of supporting African American manhood as well as efforts aimed at maintaining the male's role in the family. This may require that the agency arrange to have male social workers available in situations where a sex differential would be counterproductive to the goal of supporting African American males as males. Same-sex workers are by no means required in all cases, but agencies should be sensitive to the possibility that individual cases may necessitate using a same-gender worker.

In the area of group services to minority clients, Davis (1979) recommended that membership be selected so that no one race vastly outnumbers the others. Biracial leadership can have a benign effect if members are more open with workers of the same race. As always, if workers are alert and responsive to their client's feelings and reactions, needed adjustments in the intervention approach can be made and the use of standard formulas for success can be tempered by judgment.

Because the client's exposure to and experience with professional therapeutic relationships may be limited, Kadushin (1990) pointed out that workers may need to educate their clients about the processes of counseling. The use of unambiguous jargon is the best way to convey this information and, in fact, should be the rule for most worker-client interaction. Also suggested is the promotion of concrete activities by worker and client, including greater use of role playing, gaming, and simulations to supplant or supplement, as appropriate, more verbal techniques. Clients from lower socioeconomic backgrounds may better understand and appreciate direct action.

Some general guidelines for practice with African Americans include:

1. Assume nothing about your client. For example:
   a. Don't assume he or she wants to talk to someone of the same race.
   b. Don't assume you completely understand the experiences of African American clients.
   c. Don't assume that the client's beliefs, actions, behaviors, or speech will match those of other African Americans you have known.
2. Don't comment on the client's clothes, hair, or other personal characteristics.

3. When assessing client strengths, consider such often-overlooked resources as spiritual or religious values. For example, the church has played a major role in the African American community over the centuries and is a significant source of support for many individuals and families.
4. Become familiar with Ebonics so that you can better understand clients who use this form of English, and don't be afraid to ask the meaning of a term or phrase you don't understand. Seeking clarification shows clients that you are listening to them and trying to understand everything they say to you (Proctor & Davis, 1994). (Currently there is substantial controversy regarding the usefulness of identifying nonstandard English used by some African Americans as a separate language or language form. One question that arises is, "Do we use a different standard when correcting grammar and syntax with African American students?" If "yes," then do we also apply different standards with Hispanic students or other ethnic groups who may use something other than standard English?)
5. When assessing potential family strengths and resources, consider the possibility of "kinship care" when out-of-home placement of children is required (Scannapieco & Jackson, 1996). Kinship care uses relatives as primary caretakers of children when they cannot remain in their own homes.
6. Recognize that past experiences with white authority figures can lead African Americans to distrust white workers. Consider explaining the reasons behind your request for information to help reduce what Grier and Cobbs (1968) called "healthy paranoia."
7. Be particularly conscious of your nonverbal messages to ensure they are congruent with your verbal communications. Incongruence in this area may be seen as a sign of insincerity.
8. Orient clients to the helping process to facilitate trust between worker and clients.

These practice suggestions increase the likelihood that an intervention will not be marred by inappropriate or stereotyped behaviors on your part.

Latino Client—Non–Latino Worker

With Latino clients, as with other groups, the verbal tradition of social work may need to be supplemented by other means of communication. Workers must bear direct responsibility for communicating when language difficulties compound the situation and the need for an interpreter is apparent. Lest the worker err by commission, however, certain rules apply to the use of such individuals. First, bilingual children should not be used as family interpreters. Respect for the individual and for the family relationships dictates that children maintain their culturally established place. Serving as conduits for sensitive family information is not an acceptable role for children to play and places an unfair and unpleasant burden on them. In addition, children lack an adult's knowledge base, a fact that further reduces their value as interpreters. This prohibition on the use of children applies equally to other ethnic groups, including Asian Americans. Described in the following paragraphs is a situation in which a probation officer ignored some of the basic caveats of relationship building with unfortunate consequences for the client.

> The purposes in mind for this first interview were accomplished, to meet Mr. and Mrs. X personally and to establish a comfortable relationship that would lead to a partnership once they were able to share their problems with the social worker. The next step is to share a common purpose, in this case, helping Freddy.
>
> Mr. X was included in the helping process from the beginning. Had he been left out, it would have meant that Mrs. X was assuming an improper role, that Mr. X was being put down by her, and that his role as head of the household plus his macho role were being jeopardized.
>
> The following day Mr. and Mrs. X came a little late to the meeting and were reluctant to talk about their conference with the probation officer. Mr. X remained silent, looking down. Mrs. X, red-eyed, finally said, "I am very ashamed. You should have heard what the probation officer said about us. He blamed us for all the troubles with Freddy and said that if we were not able to speak English we should go back to Mexico. Perhaps worst of all, our daughter heard all of this because she had to translate for us."
>
> I suggested that they arrange to meet with the probation officer the next time at the center; there the social worker could translate for them and make the necessary interpretations. Thus the harmful effect of the probation officer's prejudices against them would be minimized. Mr. and Mrs. X were assured that they had certain legal and moral rights that had to be respected—among them the right to be treated as human beings. Major differences between the systems of law in the United States and Mexico were explained, as were the functions of the probation department and the role of its officers.
>
> Mr. and Mrs. X then seemed somewhat relieved and looked less tense and fearful. Mrs. X thanked the

social worker and, looking at her husband, said: "We are not ignorant and dumb. We just did not understand anything about what was happening." (Aguilar, 1972, p. 189)

A second guide to the use of interpreters is equally important. Workers must at all times relate and talk to their clients, not to the interpreter. Addressing the translator diverts attention from clients and places them in the position of a bystander to, rather than a central figure in, the relationship. The opportunity to enhance client dignity and individual autonomy should be vigorously pursued, as the same goal of helping clients to help themselves is applicable both between and within cultures.

Workers beginning a relationship with Latino clients should be prepared for a longer assessment period and should be more leisurely, warm, personal and informal, and more low key than otherwise might be the case (Aguilar, 1972). Directness is considered rude and should be minimized in these situations. Boulette (1975) suggested that a behavioral approach would be an appropriate methodology to employ in working with Mexican Americans from a low-income background, which coincides with Kadushin's (1980) belief. Aguilar (1972) noted that obstacles faced by Mexican American families include prejudice, ignorance, fear of formal social and legal systems, and a reluctance to deal with them. This would suggest some areas to which workers could direct their attention during the early stages of the relationship. Mexican Americans often make decisions more quickly than is typical of Anglo clients. Once alternatives have been explored, the worker should be prepared for a decisive response from the client.

Successful intervention with Latino families, however, requires greater knowledge of their culture. Ghali (1982) provided some helpful guidance in this matter, focusing on the Puerto Rican culture. She noted that close family ties exist in this culture and stressed that these ties are a source of pride. Anglo culture, in contrast, values independence from the family. She also pointed out that practices frowned on in American society are more readily accepted among many Puerto Ricans. Examples include common-law marriages among those with low incomes; the bearing of a child by a teenager, which often accords the mother the status of adulthood; and the relatively supreme position of the father in the family. Ghali acknowledged that many Puerto Rican values need to be changed to reflect the reality of living in the dominant culture, pointing to the subservient role of the woman as an example.

Ghali (1982) correctly identified the special dilemma of Puerto Ricans who have two countries, two languages, and two cultures. The role confusion this can entail, the resultant family problems, and the value conflicts inherent in this duality must be recognized. She suggested that workers keep these in mind during interviews. Other suggestions include the following:

- Determine how important the client's ethnic values are and whether the values are a source of conflict. (This could be ascertained by asking which, if any, of the old traditions, such as holidays, are still observed.)
- Focus on the short-term benefits and on strengthening the worker-client relationship.
- Recognize that some measure of client dependence is likely.
- Demonstrate competence, respect, and warmth toward the client.
- Share a personal experience.
- Respect the role of the father in the family.
- Ask "What do you see as the problem here?" rather than "How do you feel about this?"
- Be alert to nonverbal cues to feelings, such as facial expressions and tone.
- Be prepared to explain the therapeutic process to the client.
- Begin and end the session with a handshake (the man extends his hand to the woman first).
- Use formal greetings to convey respect.
- Accept food or drink offered in the client's home (not doing so may offend the host).
- Recognize that the client may verbally agree with the worker to show respect for authority but may not follow through.
- Remember that Puerto Rican culture does not look favorably on laughing at oneself, so humor must not be of the self-deprecatory type.
- Remember that strangers do not touch little girls, even to be friendly.
- Place signs in both Spanish and English in the agency.

Ghali's recommendations are very appropriate and serve as a model for effective practice with Puerto Rican families.

Delgado and Humm-Delgado (1982) suggested other ways to provide assistance to Latino families. The use of natural support systems is one recommendation. They identify four types of resource systems important for Latino clients: extended family, folk healers, religious institutions, and merchants' and social clubs. Included in the category of extended family are the family of origin, nuclear family members, others related by marriage or blood or custom including "adopted relatives" and *"como familia"* (nonfamily members who are considered to be like family) (Delgado & Humm-Delgado, 1982, p. 84). Godparents also become an important resource for Latino children in the event that anything befalls the natural parents.

Folk healers include a variety of individuals including spiritists and *santeros* who focus on emotional and interpersonal problems, herbalists and *santiguadors* who deal primarily with physical ailments, and the *curanderos* whose interventions include both emotional and physical realms. In Mexican American, Cuban, and Puerto Rican communities any one of the five, or a combination, may exist. The *santero* is more common in the Cuban community, and the *curandero* is found frequently in Mexican American communities (Delgado & Humm-Delgado, 1982, pp. 84–85). Some folk healers use treatments that blend natural healing methods with spiritual or religious beliefs. This is not surprising given the importance of religion, particularly Roman Catholicism, in Latino life.

Religious institutions that serve as a resource include the Roman Catholic church as well as such denominations as the Jehovah's Witness, Seventh-Day Adventist, and Pentecostal. Among the services offered are pastoral counseling, housing and job-locating assistance, emergency money, and specialized programs in areas such as drug abuse (Delgado & Humm-Delgado, 1982, p. 85).

Finally, merchants' and social clubs provide herbs and native foods, credit and information, referrals to other resources, recreation, prayer books, and the services of healers. Exhibit 12.2 identifies the types of needs served by these various resource systems in the Latino community.

Natural support systems are highly significant. They ensure "maintenance of the Hispanic tradition and language," provide "warm, personal helping relationships," and include acceptance of those who are emotionally disturbed without stigmatizing the person (Delgado & Humm-Delgado, 1982, pp. 85–87). Formal agencies that provide services to Latinos should benefit from the availability of these additional community resources. The reluctance of some clients to come to the formal agency could be reduced if the agency staff made greater use of the natural support system and increased attempts to reach the target population. Outreach can be done at merchants' and social clubs, at churches, through radio and newspaper ads or public service announcements, and through notices on barrio grocery bulletin boards (Watkins & Gonzales, 1982, pp. 68–73). Agencies should consider developing community resource directories in both English and Spanish and including nontraditional resources within the directory.

Workers who serve the Latino community must be much more alert to the unique resources available as well as to the many cultural issues that impinge on social work practice with what has become the fastest-growing minority group in the United States.

Native American Client—Non–Native American Worker

"Social agencies mandated to provide services to American Indian populations are staffed predominantly by non-Indian social workers whose professional education may not have provided the tools to deliver culturally appropriate services" (Williams & Ellison, 1996, p. 147). They may not know, for example, that "any kind of intervention is contrary to the Indian's strict adherence to the principle of self-determination" (Good Tracks, 1973, p. 30). With these statements in mind, the well-meaning worker might respond, "Well, how can I help if I can't intervene?" The difficulty of this dilemma is at the heart of the problems faced by many non–Native American social workers. Native Americans will request intervention only infrequently, and white workers must develop patience and wait for the necessary acceptance. How long this will take varies from client to client. During this period, the non–Native American should be available and may offer assistance as long as there is no hint of coercion accompanying the offer. Once help is accepted, the worker's competence will be tested and, if found wanting, the word will spread. Conversely, the worker's ability to do what he or she says will spread equally fast. The results of the former will be a cessation of clients; in the latter case, just the opposite is true. The situation described in the following extract indicates noninterference with a Native American family:

> The Redthunder family was brought to the school social worker's attention when teachers reported that both children had been tardy and absent frequently in the past weeks. Since the worker lived near Mr. Redthunder's neighborhood, she volunteered to transport the children back and forth to school. Through this regular but informal arrangement, the worker became acquainted with the entire family, especially with Mrs.

EXHIBIT 12.2

Needs served by latino natural support systems

	Natural Support Systems			
Needs Served	*Extended Family*	*Folk Healers*	*Religious Institutions*	*Merchants' and Social Clubs*
1. Accessibility to community	X	X	X	X
2. Communication in Spanish	X	X	X	X
3. Continuation of cultural traditions	X	X	X	X
4. Crisis intervention	X	X	X	X
5. Emotional support for interpersonal problems	X	X	X	X
6. Friendship, companionship, trust	X	X	X	X
7. Identification with Hispanic role models, leaders, or experts	X	X	X	X
8. Information and referral	X	X	X	X
9. Care and treatment of the disabled or aged	X	X	X	
10. Financial aid or credit	X		X	
11. Medical care and pharmaceutical products	X	X		X
12. Recreation	X		X	X
13. Translation or interpretation	X		X	
14. Advocacy	X		X	
15. Physical and emotional rehabilitation		X	X	
16. Religious or spiritual affiliation		X	X	
17. Baby-sitting, day care, respite care, foster care, or adoption	X			
18. Child-rearing and parent education	X			
19. Educational alternative to public school			X	
20. Housing	X			

Source: Reprinted from Melvin Delgado and Denise Humm-Delgado, "Natural Support Systems: Source of Strength in Hispanic Communities," *Social Work,* 27, no. 1 (January 1982). Table 1, p. 87. Copyright 1982, National Association of Social Workers, Inc. Reprinted with permission.

Redthunder, who expressed her gratitude to the worker by sharing her homegrown vegetables.

The worker sensed that there was much family discomfort and that a tumultuous relationship existed between Mr. and Mrs. Redthunder. Instead of probing into their personal and marital affairs, the worker let Mrs. Redthunder know that she was willing to listen should the woman need someone to talk to. After a few gifts of homegrown vegetables and Native American handicrafts, Mrs. Redthunder broke into tears one day and told the worker about her husband's problem of alcoholism and their deteriorating marital relationship.

Realizing Mr. Redthunder's position of respect in the family and his resistance to outside interference, the social worker advised Mrs. Redthunder to take her family to visit the minister, a man whom Mr. Redthunder admired. The Littleaxe family, who were mutual friends of the worker and the Redthunder family, agreed to visit the Redthunders more often. Through such frequent but informal family visits, Mr. Redthunder finally obtained a job, with the recommendation of Mr. Littleaxe, as recordkeeper in a storeroom. Mr. Redthunder enjoyed his work so much that he drank less and spent more time with his family. (Lewis & Ho, 1975, p. 381)

White workers who serve Native Americans can expect that the interview will also be a new experience. Periods of silence at the start of the interview, for example, are not uncommon. Neither is the practice of some clients of switching from English to their native tongue and back as they address other members of the family. The use of Native American languages is not necessarily meant to keep the message from the worker but rather indicates that this is the easiest way to translate a particular idea.

Establishing intervention objectives should also be consistent with the environment of the Native American client, as must the specific techniques to be used. Culturally repugnant approaches will not succeed regardless of the worker's good intentions. Transactional analysis is an example of one approach that will likely prove ineffective as it ignores "differences in culture and background between client and worker" (Lewis & Ho, 1975, p. 381). Any type of manipulation is likely to fail also, although providing alternative choices for the Native American client to choose from is generally acceptable. Lewis and Ho (1975, p. 380) emphasized that "techniques based on restating, clarifying, summarizing, reflecting and empathizing" are more likely to succeed with Native Americans. Certainly, a low-key, nondirective, permissive, and nonthreatening relationship can be effective and gratifying for both client and worker (Palmer & Pablo, 1978).

Lewis and Ho (1975) discuss the use of groups for treating Native Americans as a natural approach, although group composition needs to be more racially homogeneous than might be true for many other groups, notably Latinos (Boulette, 1975). The use of both indirect and extra-group means of influence is particularly recommended. For example, careful planning and implementation of program activities is preferred to more direct and unwelcome techniques. The use of group pressure on individuals is a tactic to avoid if the worker and setting are not to appear coercive. Also recommended are self-help groups and other family support networks that are group based and are consistent with the values and culture of Native American clients.

Williams and Ellison (1996) provide a number of useful suggestions for social workers who serve Native Americans. For example, during assessments workers would be wise to consider the recent literature that recognizes that most Native Americans exist on a "cultural continuum" that includes traditional, marginal, middle-class, and pan-Indian lifestyles. As might be expected, more traditional Native American clients observe the customs of their tribal group. This affects their view of problems they encounter, especially those involving health difficulties.

Native Americans who are marginal typically live between two worlds, sometimes fitting into neither. It is important to assess the clients' reliance on traditional approaches to problem solving and their willingness to work within the values of the dominant society. Middle-class Native Americans include those who have adopted mainstream middle-class values and beliefs. At the same time, their connections to more traditional patterns need to be considered. Acceptance of most middle-class attitudes and ways of behaving does not always rule out links to traditional patterns. Finally, pan-Indians are those who seek a return to more traditional Native American culture. They will not routinely access non–Native American health and social services because these services are not sensitive to traditional Native American values.

Female Client—Male Worker

Evidence shows that women continue to be at risk from a number of forces. Women's salaries continue to lag behind men's, and the concept of the "glass ceiling," which limits upward mobility of women, is discussed often in the media. Women constitute almost three-quarters of the elderly poor (Kornblum & Julian, 1998). The statistics for elderly women of color are even worse. Factors accounting for such discrepancies include family obligations (women as primary caregivers) and employment histories (often affected by job discrimination). If it were not for the success of the Social Security system, impoverishment among women would be much greater. Until 1983, even private pension plans were allowed to pay women lower retirement benefits than men.

Women are also more likely to shoulder the burden for caring for elderly family members. This can have devastating economic consequences when it comes at the expense of employment. When these factors are coupled with the concentration of women in low-paying jobs with few fringe benefits, women are clearly a population-at-risk. These factors reflect an institutional sexism, which can impede cross-sex social work interventions and challenge the worker-client relationship.

Although it is generally conceded that a difference in gender between client and worker is not an insurmountable barrier to an effective relationship, some issues should be considered when such differences exist.

According to Davenport and Reims (1978, p. 308), a clinician's sex has a decided influence on attitudes toward women's roles and, as a result, "anyone preferring a therapist with contemporary attitudes toward women would more likely be successful with a female therapist." Kravetz (1982, p. 44) has argued that most social workers hold "traditional and stereotypic views of women" and that such views have detrimental effects on women's health and their treatment by the systems of our society. Certainly, counselors of the same sex may be more of an aid in modeling new behaviors or when client identification with the worker is a major part of the change effort (Hook, 1979). Some authors feel that female social workers engage in more modeling for women clients and are more likely to take the client's problems seriously. Some topics may be more comfortably discussed with a counselor of the same sex, and workers and agencies must not overlook this possibility. However, as in many other situations where dissimilarities between client and worker exist, the relationship can usually transcend the differences.

Because the sexist nature of much of society in part contributes to the problems experienced by women, Thomas (1977) and Berlin (1976) provided a useful set of guides for work with women clients. First, the nature of the relationship between males and females in our society tends to be characterized by the same sort of power disparity noted in cross-cultural relationships; therefore, reducing this power differential should be one goal of the therapeutic process. The suggestions discussed earlier in regard to this issue are equally applicable here. Second, workers who can comfortably engage in greater levels of self-disclosure and use of self and of their own experiences should help reduce this power differential. Third, the use of contracts with specified goals involves the client in her own treatment effort. Fourth, a greater emphasis on problem solving and action should help achieve a degree of self-mastery for which the client can feel justifiably proud. Fifth, the assessment period should involve a thorough analysis of the client's "strengths, frustrations, wants and satisfactions" (Berlin, 1976, p. 493). This requires separating the client's needs, feelings, and beliefs from those of significant others, such as parents and husband. This can be accomplished through the use of a journal detailing the day's significant events, as illustrated in the following example:

> Since early childhood, Jill had tried hard to be what she thought people wanted her to be. Despite her efforts to be sweet and compliant, the stored-up resentment and anger sometimes emerged. Her parents strongly objected to these outbursts and shamed her for them. To be "good" in the eyes of her parents—and later her male friends—Jill suppressed her "selfishness," her own thoughts, views, and feelings, until she felt like a nonentity. When she came in for counseling, Jill said that she no longer knew what she liked and didn't like or who she was. She was living with a boyfriend but felt distant from him. At the age of twenty-four, her life had already taken on a bland, weary quality.
>
> At her counselor's suggestion, Jill began keeping a journal in which she recorded the events of her day and her different responses to them. During each counseling session these details were reviewed to reveal that Jill did indeed have specific likes and dislikes: she liked gardening; she liked being alone in the house; she liked to read, draw, and visit with a particular friend. She didn't like the routine nature of her job. Particularly, although she was afraid of standing up for herself, she didn't like herself to be closed or passive with her boyfriend, other friends, and her mother. She disliked not having a room of her own and resented it when her boyfriend pursued his own interests without telling her when he would be away. Jill found that there was a whole range of thoughts, talents, and behaviors that made her an identifiable and specific person. Moreover, she learned to pinpoint which of these aspects she wanted to capitalize on. Eventually Jill decided to move into her own apartment. She left her job and got a new one in a plant nursery. She began practicing more assertive, honest responses to the people in her life. (Berlin, 1976, pp. 493–494)

Sixth, help clients to recognize alternatives and to choose among them rather than feel limited or constrained unnecessarily. The following case example illustrates this guideline:

> Ellen has lived through an almost unendurable number of personal crises—the death of two children, the subsequent divorce from her husband, a second brutal marriage, financial problems, the loss of custody of her third child, and a second divorce. Her reaction to all these events was flight, the abuse of amphetamines, and just plain helplessness.
>
> As a girl, Ellen was brought up to sparkle and to make others laugh. It was assumed that she would find a clear-headed, stable man who could make the hard decisions and manage the details of living. Ellen didn't know how to take care of herself and didn't think she could. Her solution to loneliness—spending binges, reckless driving, instant intimacy with strangers—only brought more problems and more guilt. Each time she was called on to take a stand and protect herself, Ellen would capitulate. The situations were too much for her and she felt victimized by them.

> The counselor's approach to this situation was a relatively simple and basic one. She tried to help Ellen perceive different alternatives—to see that there were some things she could do differently if she wanted to. In addition to realizing that she had choices, Ellen needed to decide what she wanted to do and to acquire the skills and confidence to do it. She had to be made aware that she didn't lose control, but that she stopped exercising it; that she wasn't being punished for being a bad person, but that she associated with people who were disrespectful and abusive. Ellen is now finding what she can do to make her life less frantic and destructive. She wants to continue her education, to clear up her debts, and to achieve equality in her relationships with other people. (Berlin, 1976, p. 494)

Workers should encourage action on available options and can aid the client by posing questions such as: "What choices do you see yourself as having?" "Do you know what you like about this particular alternative?"

Seventh, the use of behavioral rehearsal and practice in decision making can be extremely effective in building the necessary skills essential for choosing and implementing choices. The following client illustrates this guideline:

> Cynthia came for counseling in a state of panic because the woman she loved and was living with was considering ending the relationship. Although there was little she could do to persuade her partner to stay, Cynthia did have considerable latitude in deciding how she wanted to behave and the way in which she could influence other facets of the terminating relationship.
>
> Realizing that she still had considerable choice was a partial antidote to Cynthia's sense of helplessness. Instead of waiting silently and miserably for her friend to leave, Cynthia practiced certain responses with the counselor until she felt able to cope with the reality of the situation. She explained to her partner her feelings regarding the relationship—that she valued it, was aware that both of them needed to make some specific changes in order for it to stay viable, and that she herself was willing to make certain accommodations. She acknowledged that her friend would be the one to decide whether to stay or leave, but Cynthia wanted the decision made within the week—she didn't want to be tortured by uncertainty. To this extent, Cynthia ceased to be the victim. She felt strengthened by her new position of influence and control over her circumstances. (Berlin, 1976, p. 495)

Eighth, a client who exhibits fears and a poor self-concept needs to be helped to evaluate these perceptions realistically. Workers must press the client for concrete examples she believes exemplifies her perceived self-worthlessness and expose them to a rigorous objective analysis. The likelihood is that under this sort of scrutiny the client's behavior will indicate more evidence of self-worth than she has been led (or has led herself) to believe. Simultaneously, workers should help the client identify successful experiences and personal competencies currently overlooked.

Workers who maintain a focus on assisting the client increase her control over her own life can be "profoundly helpful to . . . women by encouraging them to value their own ideas and interests, by helping them decide what they want, by urging them to develop the necessary skills and by letting them know they are not alone in their efforts" (Berlin, 1976, p. 497). Kravetz (1982, p. 46) has suggested additional guidelines:

> 1. Problem assessment and goals must not be based on culturally prescribed sex-role behaviors. Alternative lifestyles, lesbianism, and other behaviors that do not meet cultural expectations should not be viewed as pathological or deviant.
>
> 2. It is growth-producing for women to understand the influence of social factors on their personal lives. Therefore, work with women should incorporate a sex-role analysis, encouraging women to evaluate the ways in which social roles and norms and structural realities influence their personal experience, and to explore solutions that transcend traditional ones.
>
> 3. Women's lack of social power can generate passivity, dependence, and submissiveness. Therefore, intervening should encourage female clients to be assertive, autonomous, and self-directed.

Pro-feminist social work is practiced by both men and women. It requires a commitment to challenging the oppression that pervades much of our society and to empowering clients to act in their own behalf. It means being willing to alter everything from the client-worker relationship to the larger institutions of society. On a one-to-one basis, it includes reducing client-worker distance and power differentials and encouraging clients to redefine experiences to recognize oppression they have encountered. It also means recognizing sexist assumptions regarding appropriate gender behavior; encouraging assertive, independent client behavior; building on client strengths; encouraging woman-to-woman bonding rather than competition between women; and advocating equalitarian rights for women. This stance does not necessarily mean that workers must develop an entire new intervention model, but it does require a recognition that some traditional approaches are inconsistent with a pro-feminist stance. Psychoanalytic social work is largely inappropriate because of its focus on the intrapsychic and its failure to take into account environmental influences. Humanistic practice approaches, problem-solving interventions, and systems perspectives are largely functional if used by workers who also recognize that many problems develop precisely because of the systemic inequities structured in society (Van Den Bergh & Cooper, 1987, pp. 613–614).

In summary, pro-feminist workers will be more sensitive to ecological factors in the etiology of problems, oriented to prevention whenever possible, and supportive of client empowerment strategies. This approach is consistent with good social work practice, in keeping with the values of the profession, and will help ensure that workers do not perpetuate gender-based oppression of women. Additional material on intervening with female clients is presented in Module 7.

Gay and Lesbian Clients

The bigotry of some homophobic elements of society, in conjunction with the ignorance and fear of many Americans, produces another population-at-risk; namely, gay men and lesbian women. This perspective has been carefully documented by Hidalgo, Peterson, and Woodman (1985); Pierce (1993); and others. Some evidence suggests that social workers as a group may be as homophobic as other groups of helping professionals (DeCrescenzo, 1985). This evidence, coupled with the need to educate all social workers about sexual orientation, led the Council on Social Work Education to require content on gay and lesbian people in all social work programs (Council on Social Work Education, 1992a, 1992b).

Pierce (1993, p. 5) identified four person-in-environment issues that all gay men and lesbians must face in the workplace. These include the unusual situation of being part of a group yet remaining invisible in terms of sexual orientation, facing a potential of physical violence and harassment, dealing regularly with discrimination and prejudice, and living in a society that characterizes homosexuality as "bad." These experiences must be considered when you begin to work with lesbian and gay clients and recognized as affecting the lives of your colleagues as well.

Recent debates about gays and lesbians in the military are evidence of the high degree of ignorance and homophobia that exist. Arguments against allowing gay and lesbian persons in the military mirror similar arguments made against allowing African Americans to serve with whites several decades ago. Social workers have an obligation to help gay and lesbian clients with the same degree of professionalism accorded other clients and to work in the political process to overturn homophobia-based barriers that hinder gays and lesbians from enjoying the same rights and privileges as other Americans.

In individual worker-client relationships, the role of social work in providing assistance to gay and lesbian clients is clear. The worker's responsibility is to help clients meet their basic human needs and provide linkages with resources that further these goals. The problems of homosexual clients are often similar to those of heterosexuals. In other situations the problems are unique to gays and lesbians. For younger homosexuals, the stress associated with identity confusion regarding their sexuality is a source of difficulty that often requires intervention. Workers can assist here by "making the client aware of the incongruence between ways of acting, thinking, and feeling and the client's self-image" (Berger, 1983, p. 134). The goal of such help is self-acceptance by the client. Workers can also help with finding peer support if clients have decided to adopt or maintain their identity as a homosexual. Such a decision may also necessitate dealing with the client's parents, employers, and friends. Here again, social workers can be of help. Significant others can be worked with individually or in groups to assist them in dealing with their own feelings and reactions.

For older gays and lesbians, the tasks and problems are considerably different. Berger (1982) identified four problem areas facing the elderly homosexual: institutional, legal, emotional, and medical. The older gay may find that institutional rules prohibit visits to a hospitalized patient by anyone but a member of the immediate family, thus excluding a lover of many years. Similarly, medical decisions in case of emergency often require consent by next of kin, thus ignoring the gay or lesbian partner completely. Services to the grieving spouse are common, but almost no efforts are made to provide similar help to the partner of the deceased homosexual. The need for companionship and dealing with loneliness in old age are also problems confronting many gays and lesbians that can be ameliorated by professional assistance. Workers can help clients prepare relationship contracts and encourage them to make other arrangements, such as wills.

The difficulties of the older gay differs somewhat from those of younger homosexuals. For instance, the task of coming out may be easier when one is older because the most common problem of dealing with one's parents often no longer exists. At the same time, older gays may prefer not to address the issue of sexual orientation directly, and workers would be advised to follow suit. This requires workers who are open to their client's needs but who feel no compulsion to press the client into coming out or openly communicating his or her sexuality.

For some homosexual clients, homophobia is indeed a problem requiring assistance. The stigma associated with sexual orientation sometimes creates self-loathing among homosexuals themselves. Such a reaction is at odds with the goal of self-acceptance and can be dealt with accordingly. Social workers should be aware of local support groups and should encourage the development of such organizations when absent. Likewise, agencies that provide specialized services to gays or that are especially sensitive to their needs can be supported by referrals and by other means.

On another level, there are equally concrete activities in which social workers can engage. Support for legislation to decriminalize same-sex acts would help reduce the psychological risks of being gay or lesbian, and civil rights protection would help ensure that discrimination in employment and housing would be avoided. Currently, many cities and states have adopted such laws removing yet another unnecessary burden to those whose sexual orientation is gay or lesbian.

Adequate sex education in schools, churches, and within the family can also be encouraged (Gramick, 1983). In-service training for agency staff on the topic of homosexuality and multiagency efforts to combat prejudice and discrimination toward gays and lesbians can also be undertaken. Gramick (1983) also suggested refusing to accept homophobic behavior from colleagues and argued that such actions should be pointed out as a violation of the NASW Code of Ethics.

Certainly, to be of help to gay and lesbian clients, we must become more comfortable with the topic of homosexuality and begin to deal with our own homophobic tendencies. Just as in other areas of practice, ignorance and confusion about sexual orientation must be dealt with directly and openly.

Rural Settings

Social workers who elect to practice in rural settings are likely to discover that a multiplicity of differences exist in the way they conduct business. For example, social workers who comfortably assume the role of advocate in an urban setting will quickly find that this is more difficult in a rural setting. Rural advocates risk losing the trust of the community that they nurtured so carefully in such other roles as broker, mediator, and problem solver. The degree of risk must be assessed as one step in the problem-solving process (Kirst-Ashman & Hull, 2001). The fact that workers become more a part of the area they serve means that there is greater informality and less professional detachment than would be true in an urban setting. The need to have relationships with, and the support of, community power sources makes it more difficult to pursue changes that threaten those interests.

Workers, especially in-migrant practitioners, are often perceived as outsiders, and it takes time for the community to develop trust and confidence in their competence. Thus, to advocate strongly for anything under these conditions is not recommended if other effective alternatives can be pursued. The greater autonomy of rural workers is an asset, but it also carries additional responsibilities. Workers need to develop the ability to form relationships quickly because the geographical distance to be covered means less time can be devoted to long-term projects. Making each contact with a client count is essential as those contacts are more infrequent than would otherwise be the case.

Knowledge of natural and informal rather than formal support systems is crucial, as is the ability to work with other professionals and nonprofessionals in achieving change. Rural workers must also be patient, however, because changes, when they come, can be exceedingly slow. Any "attempt to change beliefs or practices can cause dislocations, anxiety, and resistance against the change agent" (Buxton, 1976, p. 37). Workers must be knowledgeable and compliant with local norms and etiquette. Workers may need to adjust their personal lifestyles to the community and to the job to be done. Clearly not every social worker will be willing or able to accomplish this. It follows from what we have indicated previously that existing cultural or ethnic differences can complicate understanding of, and practice in, the rural communities.

Social workers new to rural areas and small towns sometimes ignore the many ways their private actions affect the way they are seen as professionals. For example, workers finding higher prices in smaller communities have often resorted to shopping in nearby communities that are larger. Purchases of groceries, automobiles, clothes, and other items are often made without regard to how this affects the local community. This pattern of shopping may result in a lower price paid for goods and services, but the net result may be that the worker is not seen as a member of the community. Shopping in the community where you practice helps link you with that community, supports the local economy, and gives you an opportunity to talk regularly with businesspeople and leaders in the area. This entree makes it easier to approach community leaders later on when you are pursuing a macro change opportunity.

Similarly, participating in local community activities helps ensure that you are seen as a member of the community. Workers who serve a community but do not live there, shop there, or participate in community activities have greatly diminished ability to exert influence within that setting. In smaller communities, becoming part of the community is key to influencing local events. Workers are encouraged to attend the local chicken dinners sponsored by church or civic groups, participate in the volunteer fire department fund-raising effort, serve on the centennial committee, and accept membership in local service organizations. Other ways to become involved include volunteering to work on special projects (such as historical museum renovations, tree planting, and community beautification efforts). In the long run, the worker who is seen as part of the community will be better able to influence the course of events within that community.

Other Differences Affecting Practice

A variety of potential and actual differences between client and worker can impinge on the relationship and affect the outcome of interventive efforts. Age differences, as mentioned earlier, will dictate certain adaptations to your usual style. When serving older clients, for example, workers should exercise greater patience and understanding of the problems of the elderly, and if feasible, elect to conduct the interview out of the office, in a location more suitable to the client. Home interviews are suggested when possible.

Similar care should be used when workers are engaged in a practice with young children. As an adult, you may need to place some distance between yourself and the child's parents to gain the youngster's confidence. Although children are more open in many ways, they are also quick to tune out questions, thus reducing your reliance on standard verbal techniques. The child's medium is play, and workers would be advised to utilize such activities in the helping process. Adult rules of conversation are more strict, whereas an interview with a child may appear both random and disorganized (Kadushin, 1990). This places a special responsibility on workers to be sensitive to the unspoken aspects of the interview and to stay attuned to the bits and pieces of information that are generated in these situations. Although the process can be somewhat disjointed, the rewards are substantial.

Ethnic-Sensitive Practice

Traditionally, professional social work practice has used the medical model for the delivery of services. The medical model is a deficit model, which focuses on identifying problems or deficits in a person. The medical model largely ignores environmental factors that can have an impact on the person-in-situation. Also, with its focus on deficits, strengths and resources are ignored. (When only shortcomings are emphasized, a client's self-esteem is apt to be severely affected negatively. Defining oneself in terms of shortcomings overlooks strengths and resources.)

Ethnic-sensitive practice seeks to incorporate understanding of diverse ethnic, cultural, and minority groups into the theories and principles that guide social work practice (Devore & Schlesinger, 1996). Ethnic-sensitive practice is based on the view that practice must be attuned to the values and dispositions related to clients' ethnic group membership and social-class position. Ethnic-sensitive practice requires that social workers have an in-depth understanding of the effects of oppression on racial and ethnic groups.

Another important conceptual framework is that of the "dual perspective" (Norton, 1978). This concept is derived from the view that all people are part of two systems: (1) the dominant system (the society that one lives in), which is the source of power and economic resources; and (2) the nurturing system, composed of the physical and social environment of family and community. The dual perspective concept asserts that the adverse consequences of an oppressive society on the self-concept of a person of color can be partially offset by the nurturing system.

Ethnic-sensitive practice asserts that social workers have a special obligation to be aware of and to seek to redress the oppression experienced by ethnic groups. Ethnic-sensitive practice assumes that each ethnic group and its members have an ethnic history with roots in the past that have a bearing on the members' perceptions of current problems. For example, the individual and collective history of many African Americans leads to the expectation that family resources will be available in times of trouble (Devore & Schlesinger, 1996). Ethnic-sensitive practice, however, assumes that the present is most important. For example, many Mexican American and Puerto Rican women currently feel tension as they attempt to move beyond traditionally defined gender roles into mainstream society as students and paid employees (Devore & Schlesinger, 1996).

Ethnic-sensitive practice introduces no new practice principles or approaches. Instead, it urges adaptation of prevailing therapies, social work principles, and skills to take account of ethnic reality. Regardless of which practice approach is used, empowerment and the strengths perspective should be emphasized.

EMPOWERMENT. This concept has been defined as "the process of helping individuals, families, groups, and communities increase their personal, interpersonal, socioeconomic, and political strength and influence toward improving their circumstances" (Barker, 1999, p. 153). In working with an ethnic or racial group, empowerment counters the negative image or stereotypes of a group (rendered through a long history of discrimination) with a positive value or image and an emphasis on the ability of ethnic group members to influence the conditions of their lives. Empowerment counters hopelessness and powerlessness by emphasizing the ability of each person to address problems competently, beginning with a positive view of self. Empowerment counters oppression and poverty by helping ethnic groups and their members increase their ability to make and implement basic life decisions.

STRENGTHS PERSPECTIVE. The strengths perspective is closely related to empowerment. The strengths perspective seeks to identify, use, build, and reinforce individuals' abilities and strengths, emphasizing their interests, aspirations, resources, beliefs, and accomplishments. This is in contrast to the pathological perspective, which focuses on deficiencies.

For example, some strengths of African Americans in the United States include the following. There are more than 100 predominantly African American colleges and universities; fraternal and women's organizations; and social, political, and professional organizations. Many of the schools, businesses, churches, and organizations that are predominantly African American have developed social service programs—such as family support services, mentoring programs, food and shelter services, transportation services, and educational and scholarship programs. Through individual and organized efforts, self-help approaches and mutual aid traditions continue among African Americans. African Americans tend to have strong ties to immediate, extended family. They also tend to have a strong religious orientation, a strong work and achievement orientation, and egalitarian role sharing (Billingsley, 1993).

Some General Observations

In this chapter we have focused extensively on the unique differences of various groups, such as people of color, women, rural populations, and gay and lesbian individuals. Although the emphasis has been on characteristics that differentiate these groups and social work practice as it relates to the groups, there are some important commonalities that affect our efforts to help. In this section we will attempt to highlight some of these similarities.

Any intervention effort that is ethnically sensitive should take into account those individuals affected by the problem. Social workers, for example, who plan to work with minority families should be certain they understand "who the appropriate actors are" (Devore & Schlesinger, 1996, p. 187). This might include nuclear family members as well as other relatives and friends who are "like family." Most minorities of color evidence a sound respect for elders and seek their advice and opinion. In addition, most are also tolerant of other ethnic groups to a degree not found among the dominant majority. Even though religious orientations and spiritual beliefs may differ markedly among groups, each is likely to be characterized by some degree of religiosity or belief in a supreme being (Burgest, 1983).

People of color also share their commonality of color, their oppression, and their victimization by white society. Most have experienced conflict with this society ranging from colonization to slavery to economic bondage (Burgest, 1983). The result of this conflict is a distrust of traditional social service institutions, a pride of and reliance on one's own kind, and a sense of impotence when dealing with the typical government agency.

To provide competent social services within the framework outlined earlier, workers must attend to a variety of issues. First, it is helpful to keep in mind that feelings, emotions, and thoughts are all shared. Differences most often lie in how we choose to express them. Our own culture influences us to the extent that some say we are culture-bound. As a result, feelings, thoughts, and ideas we felt were firmly under control or previously resolved may become aroused during one-on-one encounters with those of a different race. It is healthier to recognize this possibility than to be surprised by it at an inopportune time. Our attempts to provide sensitive and effective social work intervention can be enhanced by observing the following guidelines:

1. Avoid color blindness.
2. Avoid jargon and clichés, such as referring to clients as culturally deprived.
3. Concentrate on building the relationship first and showing sensitivity to the client's culture and difficulty.
4. Consider client behavior as functional/dysfunctional rather than normal/abnormal based on an a priori standard.
5. Recognize and accept that client distrust is likely to be the norm.
6. Accept the limits of your own knowledge.
7. Acquire some familiarity with the clients' language whenever possible.
8. Recognize that culture is fluid, not static.
9. Acquire and maintain a sound working knowledge of programs, services, agencies, and workers providing specialized assistance to diverse groups.
10. Keep abreast of new rules and laws affecting diverse groups.
11. Support training and education for agency staff related to diverse groups.
12. Take active steps to combat discrimination within your own agency and programs.
13. Place greater emphasis in your practice on developing community-based alternatives to reduce the discriminatory reliance on institutional placements for people of color.
14. Recognize that all clients are individuals and may share all, some, or none of the customs, norms, values, or beliefs of their racial or ethnic group.

Macro Strategies to Promote Social and Economic Justice

Thus far, we have primarily focused on micro and mezzo strategies to promote social and economic justice for populations-at-risk. In this section we summarize a variety of macro strategies; it is not an exhaustive list of available strategies. (As noted in Chapter 1, social workers have an obligation to employ micro, mezzo, and macro strategies to promote social and economic justice for individuals and groups who are victimized by discrimination and oppression.)

Social Programs

Thousands of social programs have been enacted at national, state, and local levels to promote social and economic justice for a variety of populations-at-risk. A few examples are presented here.

The 1935 Social Security Act initiated a variety of programs for several populations-at-risk. Aid to the Blind provides financial assistance to low-income people of any age whose vision is 20/200 or less with correction. Aid to the Disabled provides financial assistance to low-income people, ages 18–65, who have a permanent disability. Old Age Assistance provides financial assistance to the low-income elderly (ages 65 and older). Aid to Dependent Children provides financial assistance to low-income mothers with children under age 18 and no father in the home.

In the 1960s Lyndon Johnson declared a War on Poverty. A variety of antipoverty programs were created, including Head Start, Medicare, and Medicaid. (Medicare helps the elderly pay the high cost of health care; Medicaid primarily provides medical care for recipients of public assistance.)

In 1975 the U.S. Congress passed the Education for All Handicapped Children Act. This legislation mandates that all school districts identify students with physical, developmental, learning, and social-emotional problems that hamper their education. Once the children are identified, school districts are then required to develop specialized programs to meet their needs.

In 1990 the U.S. Congress passed, and President Bush signed into law, the Americans with Disabilities Act. This act prohibits discrimination against persons with a disability either in employment or by limiting access to public accommodations (such as restaurants, stores, museums, and theaters). The law requires that new public buildings be accessible to persons with a disability and requires that barriers in existing public buildings be removed, if the changes can be accomplished without much difficulty or expense.

In 1996 the Personal Responsibility and Work Opportunity Reconciliation Act established the Temporary

Assistance for Needy Families (TANF) program. TANF replaced the Aid to Families with Dependent Children (AFDC) program originally created in 1935. Each state receives a block grant from the federal government and is allowed enormous flexibility in setting up and operating the TANF program. Program purposes include providing assistance to needy families so that children can remain in their own homes; reducing dependency by helping recipients acquire job skills, encouraging work and marriage; eliminating out-of-wedlock pregnancies; and encouraging two-parent families. Unlike AFDC, TANF sets time limits and work requirements for recipients.

Social workers have an obligation to be involved in enacting and implementing social programs to meet the needs of individuals and groups subjected to discrimination and oppression. Ways that social workers can participate in the enactment of needed social programs include running for political office, calling and writing to political officials to express their views about needed programs, campaigning for persons running for office who support the enactment of needed social programs, lobbying for needed programs, and joining and becoming active in groups that support the enactment of needed social programs. A more detailed list and discussion of macro-level strategies appears in Kirst-Ashman and Hull (2001).

Mass Media Appeals

Newspapers, radio, and television at times present programs designed to explain the nature and harmful effects of prejudice and to promote social and economic justice for populations-at-risk. Mass media reaches large numbers of people simultaneously. By expanding public awareness of the existence of discrimination and its consequences, the media can strengthen control over highly prejudiced people. But it has limitations in changing prejudiced attitudes and behaviors; it primarily provides information and seldom has a lasting effect in changing deep-seated prejudices through propaganda. Broadcasting platitudes like "all people are brothers and sisters" and "prejudice is un-American" is not very effective. Highly prejudiced people are often unaware of their own prejudices. Even if they are aware, however, they generally dismiss mass media appeals as irrelevant to them or as propaganda. Mass media has probably had a significant impact in reducing racial discrimination by showing nonwhites and whites working harmoniously in commercials, on news teams, and on TV shows.

Civil Rights Laws

In recent decades equal rights laws have been legislated in certain areas (such as employment, voting, housing, public accommodation, and education) for a variety of populations-at-risk. A few of these populations for which federal civil rights laws have been enacted include people of color, women, persons with disabilities, and the elderly. Civil rights laws prohibit overt discrimination in certain specified areas. For example, in 1986 the U.S. Congress outlawed most mandatory age retirement policies. Passage of this law prohibited overt discrimination of forced retirement against the elderly, which is age related.

The passage of a civil rights law protects the population-at-risk in only the area or areas that are specified in the law. It does not provide protection in areas that are unspecified. Subtle discrimination often continues to exist because it is hidden and therefore difficult to document.

A key question is, How effective are laws in curbing discrimination and reducing prejudice? Proponents of civil rights legislation make certain assumptions. The first is that new laws will reduce discriminatory behavioral patterns. The laws define what was once "normal" behavior (discrimination) as now being "deviant" behavior. Through time, it is expected that attitudes will change and become more consistent with the forced nondiscriminatory behavior patterns.

A second assumption is that the laws will be used. Civil rights laws enacted after the Civil War prohibited discriminatory behavior against African Americans. However, such laws were seldom enforced and gradually eroded. It is also unfortunately true that some officials will find ways to evade the intent of the law by eliminating only the extreme, overt symbols of discrimination without changing other practices. Thus, the enactment of a law is only the first step in the process of changing prejudiced attitudes and practices. However, as Martin Luther King, Jr., noted, "The law may not make a man love me, but it can restrain him from lynching me, and I think that's pretty important" (Cummings, 1977, p. 198).

Activism

The strategy of activism attempts to promote social and economic justice through direct confrontation of policies involving discrimination and oppression. Activism has three types of politics: the politics of creative disorder, the politics of disorder, and the politics of escape (Johnson, 1973, pp. 374–379).

The *politics of creative disorder* operates on the edge of the dominant social system and includes school boycotts, rent strikes, job blockades, sit-ins (for example, at segregated restaurants), public marches, and product boycotts. This type of activism is based on the concept of nonviolent resistance. A classic illustration of nonviolent resistance began on December 1, 1955, when Rosa Parks, an African American of Montgomery, Alabama, refused to give up her seat on a bus to a white person. (Exhibit 12.3 describes Rosa Parks' act of courage.)

The *politics of disorder* reflects alienation from the dominant culture and disillusionment with the political system. In this type of activism, those being discriminated against resort to mob uprisings, riots, and other forms of violence.

In 1969 the National Commission on Causes and Prevention of Violence reported that 200 riots had occurred in the previous five years, when our inner cities erupted (Johnson, 1973, p. 376). In the early 1980s, there were again some riots in Miami and in some of our other inner cities. In 1992 race riots devastated parts of Los Angeles, following the acquittal of four white police officers charged with using excessive force to arrest Rodney King, an African American; the brutal arrest had been videotaped. The focus of most of these riots has been aggression by people of color against white-owned property.

The *politics of escape* engages in passionate rhetoric about how oppressed populations are being victimized. But because the focus is not on arriving at solutions, the rhetoric is not productive, except perhaps for providing an emotional release.

The principal value of activism or social protest seems to be that it informs the public of the existence of certain problems. The civil rights protests in the 1960s made practically all Americans aware of the discrimination to which nonwhite groups were being subjected. With this awareness, at least some of the discrimination has ceased, and race relations have improved. Continued protest beyond a certain (although indeterminate) point, however, appears to have little additional value (Sullivan, Thompson, Wright, Gross, & Spady, 1980).

School Busing

School busing is a strategy that has been used to increase integration among whites and people of color. Housing patterns in many large metropolitan centers have led to "de facto" segregation; that is, African Americans and certain other people of color live in one area and whites live in another. This segregation has affected educational opportunities for people of color. Nonwhite areas have fewer financial resources, and as a result, the educational quality is often substantially lower than in white areas. In the past four decades, courts in a number of metropolitan areas have ordered that a certain proportion of nonwhites be bused to schools in white areas and that a certain proportion of whites be bused to schools in nonwhite areas. The objectives are twofold: to provide equal educational opportunities and to reduce racial prejudice through interaction. In some areas school busing has become accepted and appears to be meeting the stated objectives. In other areas, however, the approach is highly controversial and has exacerbated racial tensions. Busing in these areas is claimed (1) to be highly expensive; (2) to destroy the concept of the "neighborhood school" as a recreational, social, and educational center of the community; and (3) to result in lower quality education. A number of parents in these areas feel so strongly about busing that they send their children to private schools. In addition, some have argued that busing increases "white flight" from neighborhoods where busing has been ordered.

In certain communities, busing may also intensify racial tensions. For example, in Boston in 1975, a federal judge ordered school busing to counter housing segregation patterns. The Irish and Polish descendants of South Boston (who saw themselves as oppressed ethnic minorities) violently opposed the busing, and racial tensions intensified for several years. Sociologists also voice concern that school busing in an atmosphere of hostility may reduce the quality of education and increase racial prejudices and tensions.

Three decades of school busing have failed to deliver all the benefits its boosters hoped for and its critics demanded. Scores of studies generally agree that white students do not suffer academically from school integration via busing (Eddings, 1997). Integration via busing appears to improve the academic performance of African-American students, but mainly in the primary grades, not in junior high or high school (Eddings, 1997).

There have been other benefits of integration via busing. African Americans who attend elementary and high schools with whites are substantially more likely to attend white-majority colleges, get jobs in desegregated workplaces that offer higher pay, and have white friends as adults. Also, African-American students who go to integrated suburban schools rather than segregated city ones are less likely to drop out of high school, get in trouble with the police, drop out of college, or bear a child before age 18, and they are more likely to

EXHIBIT 12.3

Rosa Parks' act of courage sparked the civil rights movement

On December 1, 1955, Rosa Parks was in a hurry. She had a lot of things to do. When the bus came to the boarding area where she was standing in Montgomery, Alabama, she got on without paying attention to the driver. She rode the bus often and was aware of Montgomery's segregated seating laws, which required blacks to sit at the back of the bus.

In those days in the South, black people were expected to board the front of the bus, pay their fare, then get off and walk outside the bus to reboard on the back. But Rosa Parks noted the back was already crowded, standing room only, with black passengers even standing on the back steps of the bus. It was apparent to Rosa that it would be all but impossible to reboard at the back. Besides, bus drivers sometimes drove off and left black passengers behind, even after accepting their fares. Rosa Parks spontaneously decided to take her chances. She paid her fare in the front of the bus, then walked down the aisle, and took a seat toward the back of the bus that was still in the area reserved for whites. At the second stop after boarding, a white man got on and had to stand.

The bus driver saw the white man standing, and ordered Rosa Parks to move to the back. She refused, thinking, "I want to be treated like a human being." Two police officers were called and they arrested Rosa. She was taken to city hall, booked, fingerprinted, jailed, and fined. Her arrest and subsequent appeal all the way to the U.S. Supreme Court were the catalyst for a year-long boycott of the city buses by blacks, who composed 70 percent of the bus riders. The boycott inspired Martin Luther King, Jr., to become involved. The boycott ended when the Supreme Court declared Montgomery's segregated seating laws unconstitutional. Rosa Parks' unplanned defiance of the segregated seating law sparked the civil rights movement. This movement not only has promoted social and economic justice for African Americans, but also has served to inspire other groups to organize to advocate for their civil rights. These groups include other racial and ethnic groups, women, the elderly, persons with a disability, and gays and lesbians.

---

have white friends and live in integrated neighborhoods. Whites also benefit from attending school with African-American students because they learn more about diversity and tend to more thoroughly confront their racial stereotypes (Tye, 1992).

Are the benefits of school busing worth the costs? This is a complex issue, and as yet there is no definitive answer. The financial costs of busing children from one school district to another are high. Many authorities in both white and nonwhite neighborhoods increasingly argue it would be better to use the money currently spent on busing to improve school facilities. Critics assert that busing for integration purposes almost always becomes a major obstacle for parental involvement in the school system, due to the long distances created between the location of the schools and the residences of the parents. Extensive parental involvement is associated with higher educational achievement of students; parental involvement leads to teachers, parents, and school administrators working together to improve school facilities and to develop innovative programs to instruct students (Coleman & Cressey, 1995).

Surveys indicate a majority of Americans (including a large number of African Americans) oppose busing for integration purposes (Eddings, 1997). The main reason for the growing opposition to busing is that it often has not raised educational achievements of students of color (Eddings, 1997). As a result, it is unlikely there will be a resurgence of political support for expanding efforts to promote busing for integration purposes.

School busing to achieve integration was vigorously pursued by the court system and the Justice Department in the 1970s. In 1981 the Reagan administration stated it would be much less active in advocating busing as a vehicle to achieve integration. The Bush and Clinton administrations have also been fairly inactive in promoting school busing. In the past decade there has been less emphasis in many communities on using busing to achieve integration. In 1991 the U.S. Supreme Court ruled that busing to achieve integration, when ordered, need not be continued indefinitely. The ruling allows communities to end court-ordered busing by convincing a judge they have done everything reasonable to eliminate discrimination against African Americans.

Affirmative Action Programs

Affirmative action programs provide for preferential hiring and admission requirements (for example, admission to medical schools) for minority applicants. Affirmative action programs cover minority groups, including women, many groups of color, and persons with a disability. (Women—though in the majority in the United States—are considered a minority group because for generations they have been subjected to discrimination and have been denied equal opportunities.) Affirmative action programs also require that employers must (1) make active efforts to locate and recruit qualified minority applicants, and (2) in certain circumstances, have hard quotas under which specific numbers of minority members must be accepted to fill vacant positions (for example, a university with a high proportion of white, male faculty may be required to fill half of its faculty vacancies with women and members of other minority groups). Affirmative action programs require that employers must demonstrate, according to a checklist of positive measures, that they are not guilty of discrimination.

A major dilemma with affirmative action programs is that preferential hiring and quota programs involve reverse discrimination, in which qualified majority group members are sometimes arbitrarily excluded. Several successful lawsuits have claimed reverse discrimination. The best-known case to date has been that of Alan Bakke, who was initially denied admission to the medical school at the University of California, Davis in 1973. He alleged reverse discrimination because he had higher grades and higher scores on the Medical College Admissions Test than several minority applicants who were admitted under the university's minorities quota policy. In 1978 his claim was upheld by the U.S. Supreme Court in a precedent-setting decision (Sindler, 1978). The Court ruled that strict racial quotas were unconstitutional, but the Court did not rule out that race might be used as one among many criteria in making admissions decisions.

Supporters of affirmative action programs note that the majority group expressed little concern about discrimination when its members were the beneficiaries instead of the victims of discrimination. They also assert there is no other way to rapidly make up for past discrimination against minorities—many of whom may presently score slightly lower on qualification tests because they have not had the opportunities and the quality of training that the majority group members have had.

With affirmative action programs, some minority group members are given preferential treatment, which results in some whites being discriminated against. But minority group members still face more employment discrimination than whites do.

Affirmative action programs raise delicate and complex questions about achieving equality through giving preferences in hiring and admissions to minorities. Yet, no other means has been found to end subtle discrimination in hiring and admissions.

Admission to educational programs and well-paying jobs are crucial elements in working toward integration. The history of immigrant groups who have made it (such as the Irish, Japanese, and Italians) suggests equality will be achieved only when minority group members gain middle- and upper-class status. Once such status is achieved, the minority group members become an economic and political force to be reckoned with. Dominant groups are then pressured into modifying their norms, values, and stereotypes. For this reason, a number of authorities have noted that the elimination of economic discrimination is a prerequisite for achieving equality and harmonious race relations (Kornblum & Julian, 1998). Achieving educational equality between races is also crucial because lower educational attainments lead to less prestigious jobs, lower incomes, lower-living standards, and the perpetuation of racial inequalities from one generation to the next.

Critics of affirmative action assert that it is a highly politicized and painful remedy that stigmatizes many of those it was meant to help. Affirmative action is now perceived by many in our society as a system of preferences for the unqualified. Critics further assert that while affirmative action may have been necessary 30 years ago to make sure that minority candidates received fair treatment to counter the social barriers to hiring and admission that stemmed from centuries of unequal treatment, such programs are no longer needed. They assert that it is wrong to discriminate against white males for the sole purpose of making up for an injustice that somebody's great-grandfather may have done to somebody else's great-grandfather. They assert that it is wrong for the daughter of a wealthy African-American couple, for example, to be given preference in employment over the son of a homeless alcoholic who happens to be white.

In 1996 voters in the state of California passed Proposition 209, which explicitly rejects the idea that women and other minority group members should get special consideration when applying for jobs, government contracts, or university admission. This affirmative action ban became law in California in August 1997. In addition, a number of lawsuits have been filed objecting to reverse discrimination. If the courts rule in favor of those filing the lawsuits, the power of affirmative action programs will be sharply reduced. In November 1997 the U.S. Supreme Court rejected a challenge to the California law that ended racial and gender preferences in that state. This Supreme Court action clears the way for other states and cities to ban affirmative action.

Supporters of affirmative action believe that if we abandon affirmative action, we return to the old-boy network. They assert that affirmative action has helped a number of women and people of color to attain a good education and higher-paying positions, and thereby to remove themselves from the ranks of the poor. They assert that in a society in which racist and sexist attitudes remain, affirmative action is necessary in order to give women and people of color a fair opportunity at attaining a quality education and well-paying jobs.

Is there a middle ground for the future of affirmative action? Zuckerman (1995) recommends:

> The vast majority of Americans would probably accept a return to the original notion of affirmative action—an aggressive outreach to minorities to make sure they have a fair shot. They would probably see a social benefit in accepting that racial justice might be relevant in a tiebreaker case, or might even confer a slight advantage. The goal must be a return to policies based on evenhandedness for individuals rather than for groups. Then employers can concentrate on whether a minority applicant is the right person for the job rather than being moved by whether the applicant looks litigious. All employees could take it for granted that they had a fair shot. (p. 112)

Minority-Owned Businesses

Running one's own business is particularly attractive to many members of minority groups; it provides an opportunity to increase income and wealth while avoiding some of the racial and ethnic discrimination that occurs in the workplace (such as "glass ceilings" that block promotion of qualified minority workers).

Since the 1970s, federal, state, and local governments have attempted to assist minority-owned businesses in a variety of ways. Programs provide low-interest loans to minority-owned businesses. Set-aside programs stipulate that government contracts must be awarded to a minimum proportion, usually 10–30 percent, of minority-owned businesses. Some large urban areas have created enterprise zones that encourage employment and investment in blighted neighborhoods through the use of tax breaks. Minority-owned businesses have slowly been increasing in number, yet only a small fraction of the total number of people classified as members of minority groups have benefited from government support of minority-owned businesses (Schaefer, 1996).

Confrontation of Jokes and Discriminatory Actions

Jokes and sarcastic remarks related to people of color, women, persons with a disability, and other populations-at-risk perpetuate stereotypes and prejudices. It is important that we all seek to tactfully but assertively indicate that we do not view such remarks as humorous or appropriate. We must also tactfully and assertively point out the inappropriateness of discriminatory actions by others against populations-at-risk. Such confrontations make explicit that jokes and discriminatory actions involving populations-at-risk are harmful; this has a consciousness-raising effect. Gradually, such confrontations will help reduce prejudices and discriminatory actions.

Grassroots Approaches to Improving Inner Cities

Ghettos are a national disgrace. The United States is the richest and most powerful country in the world, yet we have been unable to improve living conditions in our inner cities.

Our country has tried a variety of approaches to improve ghetto living conditions. Programs and services provided include work training, job placement, financial assistance through public welfare, low-interest mortgages to start businesses, Head Start, drug and alcohol treatment, crime prevention, housing, rehabilitation, day-care services, health care services, and public health services.

One of the most comprehensive undertakings to assist inner cities was the Model Cities Program, which was part of the War on Poverty in the 1960s. Several inner cities were targeted for this massive intervention. The program tore down dilapidated housing and constructed comfortable living quarters. Salvageable buildings were renovated. In addition, these Model City projects had a variety of programs that provided job training and placement, health care services, social services, and educational opportunities. The results are more than depressing. The communities have again become slums, and living conditions are as bleak, or bleaker, than at the start of the Model City interventions (Schaefer, 1993).

To date, practically all programs that have endeavored to improve inner cities have had, at best, only short-term success. No other conclusion can be made. Ghettos continue to have abysmal living conditions. In the 1980s, and extending into the 1990s, the federal government appears to have given up trying to improve living conditions; federal programs for inner cities have either been eliminated or sharply cut back.

Our society, for better or worse, is materialistic. The two main legitimate avenues for acquiring material goods are by getting a good education and obtaining a high-paying job. It appears that many ghetto residents realize the prospects are bleak for them getting a good education (when only inferior schools exist in their areas) or obtaining a high-paying job (when they have few marketable job skills). As a result, many turn to illegitimate ways to get material goods (shoplifting, drug trafficking, robbery, and con games). Many also turn to immediate gratification (including sex and drug highs). A value system is developing that includes being resigned to being dependent on the government through welfare for a substandard lifestyle.

One promising approach to improving inner cities is grassroots organizations. These organizations can sometimes effect positive, long-lasting changes in a variety of settings, including inner cities. Grassroots organizations are community groups, composed of community residents who work together to improve their surroundings. (It may be that lasting changes can be made only in neighborhoods whose residents are inspired to improve their community.) The following is a description of a successful grassroots effort in Cochran Gardens in St. Louis, Missouri (Boyte, 1989).

Cochran Gardens was once a low-income housing project typical of many deteriorating housing projects in large urban areas. It was strewn with rubbish, graffiti, and broken windows, and its residents were plagued by frequent shootings, crime, and drug trafficking.

Bertha Gilkey grew up in this housing project. Had it not been for her, this neighborhood might have continued to deteriorate. As a youngster, Gilkey believed the neighborhood could improve if residents worked together. As a teenager she attended tenant meetings in a neighborhood church. When she was 20 years old, she was elected to chair this tenants' association. The neighborhood has since undergone gradual, yet dramatic, positive changes.

Gilkey and her group started with small projects. They asked tenants what realistically achievable things they really wanted. There was a consensus that the housing project needed a usable laundromat. The project's previous laundromats had all been vandalized, and the only working laundromat in the projects had no locks. In fact, the entry door had been stolen. Bertha and her group requested and received a door from the city housing authority. The organization then held a successful fund-raiser for a lock. The organization next held a fund-raiser for paint, and that too was a success. The organization then painted the laundromat. The residents were pleased to have an attractive, working laundromat, and its presence increased their interest in joining and supporting the tenants' association. The association then organized to paint the hallways, floor by floor, of the housing project. Everyone who lived on a floor was responsible for being involved in painting their hallway's floor. Gilkey stated:

> Kids who lived on the floor that hadn't been painted would come and look at the painted hallways and then go back and hassle their parents. The elderly who couldn't paint prepared lunch so they could feel like they were a part of it too. (Boyte, 1989, p. 5)

The organization continued to initiate and successfully complete new projects to spruce up the neighborhood. Each success inspired more and more residents to take pride in their neighborhood and to work toward making improvements. While improving the physical appearance of this housing project, Gilkey and the tenants' organization also reintroduced a conduct code for the project. A committee formulated rules of behavior and elected monitors on each floor. The rules included no loud disruptions, no throwing garbage out of the windows, and no fights. Slowly, residents got the message, and living conditions improved, one small step at a time.

The building was renamed Dr. Martin Luther King, Jr., Building. (Symbols are important in community-development efforts.) The organization also held a party and a celebration for each successfully completed project.

Another focus of Gilkey's efforts was to reach out to children and adolescents. The positives were highlighted. The young people wrote papers in school on "What I like about living here." In art class they built a cardboard model of the housing project that included the buildings, streets, and playground. Such efforts were designed to build the self-esteem of the young people and to instill a sense of pride in their community.

Today, Cochran Gardens is a public housing project with flower-lined paths, trees, and grass—a beautiful and clean neighborhood filled with trusting people who have a sense of pride in their community. The high-rise buildings have been completely renovated. There is a community center, and there are tennis courts, playgrounds, and townhouse apartments to reduce density in the complex. Cochran Gardens is managed by the tenants. The association (now named

Tenant Management Council) has ventured into owning and operating certain businesses: a catering service, day-care centers, health clinics, and a vocational training program.

The Cochran success has been based on the principles of self-help, empowerment, responsibility, and dignity. Gilkey stated:

> This goes against the grain, doesn't it? Poor people are to *be* managed. What we've done is cut through all the bullshit and said it doesn't take all that. People with degrees and credentials got us in this mess. All it takes is some basic skills. . . . If we can do it in public housing, it can happen anywhere. (Boyte, 1989, p. 5)

Such successes suggest that it is desirable for our federal, state, and city governments to improve inner-city conditions by encouraging and supporting (including financially) grassroots efforts. Social workers can use their macropractice skills as catalysts in the formation of grassroots organizations. Once such organizations are formed, social workers can provide invaluable assistance by helping them identify community needs and then plan and implement interventions to meet these needs.

Summary

This chapter reviews some of the barriers inherent in worker-client differences and discusses some of the obstacles to workers' forming relationships with clients who differ in terms of race, culture, age, gender, or sexual orientation. The chapter provides information on how such obstacles and barriers can be overcome. Another section provides specific techniques and approaches that can be used (or should be avoided) in social work practice with Native Americans, African Americans, Latinos, women, gays and lesbians, children, and rural clients.

Generally the difficulties workers experience can be attributed to four fundamental issues: (1) ignorance of the culture or characteristics of those with whom they are working; (2) retention of stereotypic perceptions of the target group; (3) insufficient knowledge of self; and (4) a tendency to rely on standard interventive techniques without regard to their appropriateness for the client group.

The existence of these barriers may give you the impression that client and worker differences present obstacles that only superhuman effort on the part of the helper can overcome. In actuality, the similarities between helper and client often outweigh the dissimilarities. Workers can deemphasize some of the differences that do exist through those mechanisms that are important to all relationships. A belief in (and practice consistent with) respect for the worth and dignity of the client is significant. A worker who is genuinely interested in the problems and situation of the client and who gives hope for improvement will assuage much of the division caused by racial, ethnic, cultural, or sexual orientation differences. Adhering to the values of the profession, although not a panacea, increases the likelihood that the worker in these situations will be accepted and accorded the status of a competent and sensitive professional. When coupled with a thorough knowledge of the client group, a depth of self-understanding, and a repertoire of culturally relevant techniques, the applied values of the profession provide an effective means to this end. Ethnic-sensitive practice seeks to incorporate understanding of diverse ethnic, cultural, and minority groups into the theories and principles that guide social work practice. Two concepts that are emphasized in ethnic-sensitive practice are empowerment and the strengths perspective.

The chapter concluded with a presentation of macro strategies to promote social and economic justice for populations-at-risk. The strategies included social programs, mass media appeals, civil rights laws, activism, school busing, affirmative action programs, minority-owned businesses, confrontation of jokes and discriminatory actions, and grassroots approaches to improving inner cities.

EXERCISES

1. DIVERSITY SELF-ASSESSMENT

Goal: To confront your own attitudes toward various groups.

Step 1: Look over the diversity checklist that your instructor has just handed out. (See page 305.)

Step 2: Take 10 minutes to complete the self-assessment guides. (See page 306.) *Do not* note your name on these.

Step 3: Break into groups of six to eight and discuss your findings, focusing on what you have learned about yourself.

Step 4: Class discussion of the class profile and its implications for social work practice.

Diversity Self-Assessment Checklist

The following table lists a number of individuals with whom you may come in contact in your role as a social worker. The questions should be answered with each of the individuals mentioned in mind. This exercise works best if you strive for honesty. Your responses will not be revealed to anyone in the class.

Instructions

a. Answer only one question at a time. Continue until you have answered the first question for each individual listed. Then proceed to question 2.
b. Place an X in the columns when your answer is no. Also place an X if you hesitate before answering yes.

Question 1: Can I greet this person warmly and sincerely?

Question 2: Am I comfortable interviewing this person? Can I really listen to his or her problems?

Question 3: Can I comfortably help this person deal with their problems?

	Question		
Individuals	1	2	3
1. Asian American			
2. Mexican American			
3. Jew			
4. Gay male			
5. Native American			
6. Senile senior citizen			
7. Ku Klux Klan member			
8. Prostitute			
9. Blind person			
10. Alcoholic			
11. Drug pusher			
12. Farmer			
13. African American			
14. Lesbian			
15. Puerto Rican			
16. Person in a wheelchair			
17. Person with cerebral palsy			
18. Jehovah's Witness			
19. Pimp			
20. Person with a badly disfigured face			

(continued)

EXERCISES
(continued)

Diversity Self-Assessment

This assessment will help you recognize areas of potential difficulty in working with various groups.

Be alert to any concentration of Xs under the categories given as they may indicate potential barriers to your efforts to work with certain groups. Transpose your answers from the Diversity Self-Assessment Checklist to this guide.

Question 1: Can I greet this person warmly and sincerely?

Question 2: Am I comfortable interviewing this person? Can I really listen to his or her problems?

Question 3: Can I comfortably help this person deal with their problems?

Categories	*Question* 1	2	3
Ethnic or Racial			
1. Asian American			
2. Mexican American			
5. Native American			
13. African American			
15. Puerto Rican			
Lifestyle			
4. Gay male			
8. Prostitute			
10. Alcoholic			
11. Drug pusher			
12. Farmer			
14. Lesbian			
19. Pimp			
Religious or Spiritual			
3. Jew			
18. Jehovah's Witness			
Mental or Physical Disability			
6. Senile senior citizen			
9. Blind person			
16. Person in a wheelchair			
17. Person with cerebral palsy			
20. Person with a badly disfigured face			
Political			
7. Ku Klux Klan member			

2. THE BILLY MARTIN CASE

Goal: Clarify your values toward gays and lesbians, and foster care.

Step 1: Form groups of five, and read the following vignette.

Billy Martin has been in foster care for the past three years. At age 14 he was thought too old to be adopted, and his worker expected he would remain with Julie and Ed Saunders until he turned 18. A typical teenager, Billy has begun to act up and assert his independence, challenging the Saunderses on almost every issue. Mrs. Saunders has a difficult time coping with Billy but is willing to try because Billy really has no other alternative.

Last week, Billy's older brother, Glenn, who is 24 and works as a repairman for the telephone company, offered to take Billy to live with him. Glenn is now living with another man and is active in the movement to have the city adopt an ordinance prohibiting discrimination against gays and lesbians. He is also involved with the Gay Task Force and a strong advocate for rights for homosexuals. Billy would miss the Saunderses but wants to live with his big brother. Glenn is economically able to care for Billy, but the case manager, Mr. Walton, has strong reservations.

Step 2: Group discussion of the following questions.

a. Would you let Billy live with his brother? Why, or why not?
b. Should Billy be moved to another foster home if the Saunders are no longer able to handle him?
c. How much should the sexual orientation of a person affect decisions on such issues as suitability for raising children?

Step 3: Class discussion of group conclusions.

3. THE MARY MILLS CASE

Goal: To clarify your values toward the roles of gender in our society.

Step 1: Form groups of five, and read the following vignette.

Mary Mills is angry. Her husband has been arguing with her about the time her new job takes and the fact that she is not home to vacuum and clean, as she was before. The Millses have been married for seven years and have no children. During the first years of marriage, Mary stayed home because her husband felt he should be the breadwinner. But she eventually got bored with this routine, so she got a part-time job as a clerk in the local supermarket. Although they don't need the money, Mary enjoys meeting people and doing something different. After six months on the job, the manager asks Mary to become her assistant. The new job is full time, and Mary is excited about the job possibilities. Mr. Mills is opposed to her taking the position. Her best friend, a social worker named Allison Goetz, suggests she shouldn't take the job because it would cause difficulties in the Mills's marriage. Instead, she suggests Mary do volunteer work at the local hospital. This would give her a chance to get out of the house and would not be opposed by her husband.

Step 2: Group discussion of the following questions.

a. Is Mary better off to stay at home and not risk her marriage?
b. Is Allison right in her opinion that Mary should quit her job and do volunteer work of which her husband approves?
c. Does it make any sense for Mary to take a full-time job with important responsibilities if her husband objects so strongly?
d. If you had been Allison, what would you have recommended?

Step 3: Class discussion of group conclusions.

(continued)

EXERCISES
(continued)

4. *RACIAL AND ETHNIC PREJUDICES*[2]

Goal: To identify your racial and ethnic prejudices and to demonstrate that every one of us has racial and ethnic stereotypes.

Step 1: Assume you are single. Place an X by the following groups that you would hesitate to marry into. Do not write your name on this sheet. Briefly note your reasons for your answers.

___ Russian
___ Cuban
___ French
___ Mexican
___ African American
___ Native American
___ Puerto Rican
___ Italian
___ German
___ Polish
___ Norwegian
___ Samoan
___ Arab
___ Israeli
___ Chinese
___ Japanese
___ Filipino
___ Eskimo
___ Brazilian
___ Hungarian
___ Vietnamese
___ Pakistani
___ Korean
___ Anglo-American

Step 2: Class tally of student answers. Which group is viewed as least "marriage-able"? Class discussion of reasons and the implications of profiling.

a. Do class results suggest that everyone has racial and ethnic stereotypes and prejudices?
b. How do stereotypes and prejudices develop in people?
c. How would you feel if you were a member of a racial or ethnic group being disparaged by others?
d. How can we eradicate stereotypes and prejudices?
e. Is such profiling ever justified? Why or why not?

[2]This exercise was written by Charles Zastrow.

CHAPTER 13

Spirituality and Religion in Social Work Practice

You are a social worker for the following clients. An older male client who displays manic-depressive symptoms informs you that he recently had an intense spiritual experience, and he now wants to quit his job, separate from his wife and grown children, and make pilgrimages to holy sites. How do you respond to his stated intentions?

A married mother of seven children who is a devout Roman Catholic is pregnant. Her husband and she both work full time, but their combined earnings are well below the poverty level for their family size. She and her husband come to see you about their options for this pregnancy. They ask whether you believe abortion is a morally acceptable option. How do you respond?

A 75-year-old male with a terminal degenerative illness is in intense pain that painkillers are unable to relieve. He asks you for a referral for physician-assisted suicide. How do you respond?

A married couple contacts you for advice about a plan to physically kidnap their son from a religious cult. The son dropped out of college after joining this cult and now lives in a distant state in a cult commune. How do you respond to their request for advice?

Such questions pose various moral, ethical, and value dilemmas. Bullis (1996) notes:

> The spiritual issues clients raise are as diverse as the clients themselves. For some, grief over the loss of a loved one, a job or career, a marriage, or a child is spiritual. For some, decisions over pregnancy, marriage, separation and divorce, disease, terminal illness, or debilitating illness are spiritual. For others, the experience of depression, alienation, isolation or ennui evokes spiritual issues. For still others, crises of war, immigration, child custody disputes, child abuse, or domestic violence trigger spiritual concerns. Spiritual questions deserve thoughtful, deliberate, and authentic responses. (p. 9)

Spirituality and Religion

A major thrust of social work education is to prepare students for culturally sensitive practice. Because religion and spirituality play important roles in all cultures, it is essential that social workers comprehend the influence of religion and spirituality in human lives. Educational Policy and Accreditation Standards of the Council on Social Work Education now requires that accredited baccalaureate and master's programs provide practice content in this area so that students will develop approaches and skills for working with clients with differing spiritual backgrounds.

Spirituality and religion are separate, though often related, dimensions. *Spirituality* can be defined as "the general human experience of developing a sense of meaning, purpose, and morality" (Miley, 1992, p. 2). The key components of spirituality include the personal search for meaning in life, having a sense of identity, and having a value system. In contrast, *religion* refers to the formal institutional contexts of spiritual beliefs and practices.

Note that social work has its historical roots in religious organizations. The philanthropic founders of social work were inspired in their endeavors in this area by Judeo-Christian religious traditions. Jewish scriptures and religious law requiring the emulation of God's creativity and caring have spurred social welfare activities for many centuries. Similarly, the Christian biblical command to love one's neighbor as oneself is interpreted as meaning a moral responsibility for social service. This idea drove the development of charity organizations and philanthropy in the United States during the 19th century. Social workers need to be trained for effective practice with religiously oriented clients. Many social issues today have religious dimensions—including abortion, use of contraceptives, acceptance of gays and lesbians, cloning, reproductive technology, roles of women, prayer in public schools, and physician-assisted suicide.

Social workers need to have an appreciation and respect for religious beliefs that differ from their own chosen beliefs. There is a danger that those who believe that their religion is the "one true religion" will tend to view people with divergent religious beliefs as being ill-guided, evil, mistaken, or in need of being "saved." More wars have been fought over religious differences than for any other cause. A major source of intolerance, discrimination, and oppression is the belief that "my religion is the one true religion; those who believe as I do will go to heaven, whereas those who believe in some other religion are heathens who will go to eternal damnation."

Furman (1994, p. 10) notes, "The goal of incorporating religious and spiritual beliefs in social work curricula should include a broad array of knowledge of many different religious and spiritual beliefs, primarily to expand students' understanding and sensitivity." As a beginning effort to move in this direction, Exhibit 13.1 summarizes information on four prominent religions: Judaism, Christianity, Islam, and Buddhism. These religions were selected because of their prominence, but there are hundreds of other religions in the world. Practicing social workers should have a knowledge and appreciation of the religious beliefs and value systems of their clients.

Rationale for the Use of Spirituality and Religion in Social Work Practice

Traditionally, social work literature has tended to ignore religion's or spirituality's impact on social work practice. Loewenberg (1988) identified the following reasons for this neglect. The psychoanalytic movement (which social work was involved with for many years) rejected religious approaches to furthering the personal and social well-being of people. An economic, political, and professional competition has at times existed between members of the clergy and secular social workers. In the United States the philosophy of separation of church and state led many social workers to avoid spiritual assessments and interventions with clients. Some social workers avoid spiritual aspects of human behavior because of their perception that spirituality and social work are totally distinct from one another. Spirituality has been viewed (erroneously) as having only heavenly concerns, whereas social work has been viewed (erroneously) as having only earthly concerns.

As noted in Chapter 1, the pioneers of the social work profession (like Jane Addams, who founded Hull House) often used interventions that had religious or spiritual components (such as initiating and leading Bible classes) in providing services to their communities. In addition, many religious organizations are heavily involved in providing social services—examples of such organizations include Jewish Social Services, Catholic Charities, Lutheran Social Services, YMCA (Young Men's Christian Association), and YWCA (Young Women's Christian Association). Twelve-step self-help groups also have a spiritual component, emphasizing the recognition of a "higher power." Examples of twelve-step self-help groups include: Alcoholics Anonymous, Emphysema Anonymous, Smokers Anonymous, Gamblers Anonymous, Narcotics Anonymous, Overeaters Anonymous, and Families Anonymous.

Social work, historically and philosophically, is connected to spirituality. Philosophically, social work and spirituality are natural allies in working for personal and social well-being. Social workers and the clergy have

EXHIBIT 13.1

Four prominent religions

JUDAISM. Judaism is the religion of the Jews. Jews believe in one God, the creator of the world who delivered the Israelites out of their bondage in Egypt. The Hebrew Bible is the primary source of Judaism. (The Hebrew Bible was adopted by Christians as part of their sacred writings, and they now call it the "Old Testament.") God is believed to have revealed his law (Torah) to the Israelites; part of this law was the Ten Commandments, which were given to Moses by God. The Israelites believe God chose them to be a light to all humankind.

Next in importance to the Hebrew Bible is the Talmud. The Talmud is an influential compilation of rabbinic traditions and discussions about Jewish life and law. The Talmud consists of the Mishnah (the codification of the oral Torah) and a collection of extensive early rabbinical commentary. Various later commentaries and the standard code of Jewish law and ritual (Halakhah) produced in the later Middle Ages have been important in shaping Jewish practice and thought.

Abraham (who lived roughly 2,000 years before Christ) is viewed as an ancestor or father of the Hebrew people. According to Genesis, he came from the Sumerian town of Ur (now part of modern Iraq) and migrated with his family and flocks via Haran (the ancient city of Nari on the Euphrates) to the "Promised Land" of Canaan, where he settled at Shechem (modern Nablus). After a sojourn in Egypt, he lived to be 175 years old, and was buried with his first wife Sarah. By Sarah he was the father of Isaac (whom he was prepared to sacrifice at the behest of the Lord) and grandfather of Jacob ("Israel"). By his second wife Hagar (Sarah's Egyptian handmaiden), he was the father of Ismael, the ancestor of 12 clans. By his third wife Keturah, he had six sons who became the ancestors of the Arab tribes. He was also the uncle of Lot. (Interestingly, Abraham is regarded as being an important ancestor or father in Judaism, Christianity, and Islam.)

All Jews see themselves as members of a community with origins around the time in which Abraham lived. This past lives on in its rituals. The family is the basic unit of Jewish ritual, although the synagogue plays an important role. The Sabbath, which begins at sunset on Friday and ends at sunset on Saturday, is the central religious ritual. The synagogue is the center for community worship and study. Its main feature is the "ark," a cupboard containing the handwritten scrolls of the Pentateuch (the five books of Moses in the Hebrew Bible, comprising Genesis, Exodus, Leviticus, Numbers, and Deuteronomy). Rabbis are primarily teachers and spiritual guides.

There is an annual cycle of religious festivals and days of fasting. The first of these is Rosh Hashanah, the Jewish New Year, which falls in September or October. During this New Year's Day service, a ram's horn is blown as a call to repentance and spiritual renewal. The holiest day in the Jewish year is Yom Kippur, the Day of Atonement, which comes at the end of ten days of penitence following Rosh Hashanah; Yom Kippur is a day devoted to fasting, prayer, and repentance for past sins. Another important festival is Hanukkah, held in December, commemorating the rededication of Jerusalem after the victory of Judas Maccabees over the Syrians. Pesach is the Passover festival, occurring in March or April, commemorating the exodus of the Israelites from Egypt; the festival is named after God's passing over the houses of Israelites when he killed the first-born children of Egyptian families.

CHRISTIANITY. Developed out of Judaism, Christianity is practiced in numerous countries and is centered on the life and work of Jesus of Nazareth in Israel. The earliest followers were Jews who, after the death and resurrection of Jesus, believed Jesus to be the Messiah or Christ promised by the prophets in the Old Testament. He was declared to be the Son of God. During his life he chose 12 men as disciples who formed the nucleus of the church. This communion of believers believed that Jesus would come again to inaugurate the "Kingdom of God." God is believed to be one in essence but threefold in person, comprising the Father, Son, and Holy Spirit or Holy Ghost (known as the Trinity). Jesus Christ is also wholly human because of his birth to Mary. The Holy Spirit is the touch or "breath" of God which inspires people to follow the Christian faith. The Bible is thought to have been written under the Holy Spirit's influence.

Jesus Christ was the son of Mary and Joseph, yet also the Son of God, created by a miraculous conception by the Spirit of God. He was born in Bethlehem (near Jerusalem) but began his ministry in Nazareth. The main records of his ministry are the New Testament Gospels, which show him proclaiming the coming of the Kingdom of God and, in particular, the acceptance of the oppressed and the poor into the kingdom. The duration of his public ministry is uncertain, but it is from John's Gospel that we get the impression of a three-year period of teaching. He was executed by crucifixion under the order of Pontius Pilate, a Roman ruler. The date of death is uncertain, but it is considered to be when Jesus was in his early thirties.

At the heart of the Christian faith is the conviction that through Jesus's death and resurrection, God has allowed humans to find salvation. Belief in Jesus as the Son of God, along with praying for forgiveness of sin, brings forgiveness of all sin. Many Christians believe that those who ask for forgiveness of

(continued)

EXHIBIT 13.1

Continued

their sins will join God in heaven, while unbelievers who do not ask for forgiveness of their sins will be consigned to hell. The Gospel of Jesus was proclaimed at first by word of mouth, but by the end of the first century A.D. it was written and became accepted as the authoritative scripture of the New Testament. Through the witness of the 12 earliest leaders (Apostles) and their successors, the Christian faith, despite sporadic persecution, spread through the Greek and Roman world, and in A.D. 315 it was declared by Emperor Constantine to be the official religion of the Roman Empire. Christianity survived the break-up of the Empire and the "Dark Ages," largely through the life and witness of groups of monks in monasteries. The religion helped form the basis of civilization in the Middle Ages in Europe. Since the Middle Ages, major divisions of Christianity have separated as a result of differences in doctrine and practice.

ISLAM. Islam is the Arabic word for "submission" to the will of God (Allah). Islam is also the name of the religion originating in Arabia during the seventh century through the prophet Muhammad. Followers of Islam are known as Muslims, or Moslems.

Muhammad was born in Mecca. He was the son of Abdallah, a poor merchant of the powerful tribe of Quaraysh, hereditary guardians of the shrine in Mecca. Muhammad was orphaned at age 6 and raised by his grandfather and uncle. His uncle Abu Talib trained him to be a merchant. At the age of 24 he entered the service of a rich widow, Khadijah, whom he eventually married. They had six children. While continuing as a trader, Muhammad became increasingly drawn to religious contemplation. Soon afterward he began to receive revelations of the word of Allah, the one and only God. These revelations given to Muhammad by the angel Gabriel over a period of 20 years were eventually codified into the Quran (Koran). The Quran commanded that the numerous idols of the shrine should be destroyed and that the rich should give to the poor. This simple message attracted some support but provoked a great deal of hostility from those who felt that their interests were threatened. When his wife and uncle died, Muhammad was reduced to poverty, but he began making a few converts amongst pilgrims to Mecca. Muhammad eventually migrated to Hegira. The name of this town was changed to Medina, "the city of the prophet." This migration marks the beginning of the Muslim era. After a series of battles with warring enemies of Islam, Muhammad was able to take control of Mecca, which recognized him as chief and prophet. By A.D. 360 he had control over all Arabia. Two years later he fell ill and died in the home of one of his nine wives. His tomb in the mosque at Medina is venerated throughout Islam.

The religion of Islam embraces every aspect of life. Muslims believe that individuals, societies, and governments should all be obedient to the will of God as set forth in the Quran. The Quran teaches that there is one God, who has no partners. He is the Creator of all things and has absolute power over them. All persons should commit themselves to lives of praise-giving and grateful obedience to God, as everyone will be judged on the Day of Resurrection. Those who have obeyed God's commandments will dwell forever in paradise, whereas those who have sinned against God and have not repented will be condemned eternally to the fires of hell. Since the beginning of time, God has sent prophets (including Abraham, Moses, and Jesus) to provide the guidance necessary for the attainment of eternal reward.

There are five essential religious duties, which are known as "the pillars of Islam." (1) The Shahadah (profession of faith) is the sincere recitation of the twofold creed: "There is no god but God" and "Muhammad is the Messenger of God." (2) The Salat (formal prayer) must be performed at fixed hours five times a day while facing toward the holy city of Mecca. (3) Alms-giving through the payment of Zakat ("purification") is regarded primarily as an act of worship and is the duty of sharing one's wealth out of gratitude for God's favor, according to the uses stated in the Quran. (4) There is a duty to fast (Saum) during the month of Ramadan. (Ramadan is the ninth month of the Muslim year during which Muslims abstain from eating and drinking between sunrise and sunset.) (5) The pilgrimage to Mecca is to be performed if at all possible at least once during one's lifetime.

Shariah is the sacred law of Islam and applies to all aspects of life, not just religious practices. This sacred law is found in the Quran and the sunnah (the sayings and acts of Muhammad).

BUDDHISM. Buddhism originated in India about 2,500 years ago and is derived from the teachings of Buddha (Siddharta Gautama). Buddha is regarded as one of a continuing series of enlightened beings.

Buddha was born the son of the rajah of the Sakya tribe in Kapilavastu, north of Benares. His personal name was Siddharta, but he was also known by his family name of Gautama. At about age 30 he left the luxuries of the court, his beautiful wife, and all earthly ambitions. He became an ascetic, practicing strict self-denial as a measure of personal and spiritual discipline. After several years of severe austerities, he saw in meditation and contemplation the way to enlightenment. For the next four decades he taught, gaining many followers and disciples. He died at Kusinagara in Oudh.

The teaching of Buddha is summarized in the four noble Truths, the last of which asserts the existence of a path leading to deliverance from the universal human experience of suffering. A central tenet of Buddhism is the law of Karma, by which good and evil deeds result in appropriate rewards or punishments in this life or in a succession of rebirths. It is believed that the sum of a person's actions is carried forward from one life to the next, leading to an improvement or deterioration in that person's fate. Through a proper understanding of the law of Karma, and by obedience to the right path, humans can break the chain of Karma.

The Buddha's path to deliverance is through morality (Sila), meditation (samadhi), and wisdom (panna). The goal is nirvana, which is the "blowing out" of the fires of all desires and absorption of the self into the infinite. All Buddhas are greatly revered, with a place of special accordance being given to Gautama.

There are two main branches of Buddhism, dating from its earliest history. Theravada Buddhism adheres to the strict and narrow teachings of the early Buddhist writings; in this branch salvation is possible for only the few who accept the severe discipline and effort to achieve it. Mahayana Buddhism is more liberal and makes concessions to popular piety; it teaches that salvation is possible for everyone. It introduced the doctrine of the bodhisattva (or personal saviour). A bodhisattva is one who has attained the enlightenment of a Buddha but chooses not to pass into nirvana. Rather, this person voluntarily remains in the world to help lesser beings attain enlightenment. This view emphasizes charity toward others. Mahayana Buddhism asserts that all living beings have the inner potential of Buddha nature. Buddha nature is a kind of spiritual embryo that holds out the promise to all people that they can eventually become Buddhas because they all have the potential for Buddhahood.

Source: From *Dictionary of Beliefs and Religions,* edited by Rosemary Goring, 1994, New York: Larousse.

numerous similar goals—both promote personal and community welfare, both urge the ending of interpersonal violence, and both are advocates for family values.

The spiritual aspects of a person's life should be an important area of assessment by both social workers and the clergy. To ignore this aspect is a serious error. As indicated earlier, a client's spiritual beliefs often are major determinants in their decisions in such areas as terminating a pregnancy, seeking a divorce, seeking physician-assisted suicide, entering the military (which may lead to deadly combat with an enemy), and using reproductive technology.

Spiritual and Religious Assessments of Clients

In the twentieth century many social workers (and psychologists and psychiatrists) ignored religious and spiritual aspects of clients in their assessments. However, today helping professions increasingly recognize the importance of attending to religious and spiritual aspects in assessments. The Curriculum Policy Statements of the Council on Social Work Education now identify spirituality as an important area for social workers to attend to in their work with individuals, groups, families, organizations, and communities. The newest version of the American Psychiatric Association's *Diagnostic and Statistical Manual-IV* (2000) recognizes spiritual and religious issues as an important area of assessment. For example, section V62.89 titled "Religious or Spiritual Problem" states:

> This category can be used when the focus of clinical attention is a religious or spiritual problem. Examples include distressing experiences that involve loss or questioning of faith, problems associated with conversion to a new faith, or questioning of spiritual values that may not necessarily be related to an organized church or religious institution.

What kinds of questions are useful in a spiritual/religious assessment with a client? Here are a few suggestions:

1. What are your main religious and spiritual beliefs?
2. What is your current religious or spiritual affiliation?
3. Would you describe yourself as strict or lenient (casual) in following the values and principles of your religious/spiritual affiliation?

4. What changes have occurred in your religious and spiritual orientation since your childhood years? What events or experiences were associated with these changes?
5. What was the religious or spiritual faith of your parents? Were they strict or casual in their beliefs?
6. How have your parents' beliefs influenced you in the past? Do their beliefs still influence you? If "yes," how?
7. What do you think are the most important spiritual beliefs held by your parents? Do you currently hold these same beliefs?
8. What are the main religious beliefs of the people closest to you (such as a spouse or partner)?
9. In what religious/spiritual orientation were they raised? Have they remained with this orientation? Why, or why not?
10. What, if any, religious or spiritual issues have caused problems with those you are closest to? Are there some current unresolved spiritual issues with your partner?
11. How comfortable are you with your current religious and spiritual beliefs?
12. Are you currently struggling with religious or spiritual issues? If "yes," what are those issues?

In conducting a spiritual assessment, clients may ask what your religious affiliation is. How should you respond to the question? If your spiritual/religious affiliation differs from that of your clients, they may erroneously believe that the difference will interfere with rapport, with your comprehension of their spiritual dilemmas, and with solutions you may suggest. Therefore, a useful response is, "Our agency has a policy that instructs us not to share our religious affiliation." (To ensure honesty, you may well want to request that your agency adopt such a policy.)

Nelson and Wilson (1984) identify an exception to the guideline that social workers generally should not share their religious beliefs with clients. In their view it is ethical for social workers to share their religious beliefs with a client if three conditions are met: (1) if there is a high probability that such sharing will assist in problem solving the client's issues, (2) if the discussions related to sharing are held within the client's own belief systems, and (3) if such sharing is defined within the intervention contract. (Note that at the present time few intervention contracts discuss such sharing.)

Spiritual and Religious Interventions with Clients

Which spiritually related interventions should social workers use, and which should not be used? This is an important question! Spiritually related interventions vary widely, from referring clients to twelve-step self-help groups, using or recommending religious literature in counseling, teaching spiritual meditation to clients, meditating spiritually with clients, praying privately for clients, praying with clients in counseling, using religious language or metaphors in counseling, touching clients for "healing" purposes, reading scripture with clients in counseling, helping clients clarify religious or spiritual values in counseling, referring clients to religious counselors or to members of the clergy, exploring religious elements in dreams, recommending religious penance or some other religious ritual in counseling, to performing exorcism. Which of these interventions are appropriate, and which are inappropriate? The social work profession and the judicial system have not established clear-cut guidelines, but a review of social work literature provides some ideas. However, many questions remain unanswered in this area.

Sherwood (1981) and Keith-Lucas (1985) provide some guidelines for social workers with strong religious beliefs. They note the following:

1. At times you may encounter major value conflicts between the values of the social work profession and their religion. Possible areas of conflict include abortion, rights to be accorded to gays and lesbians, military combat service, use of contraceptives, use of reproductive technology, and physician-assisted suicide. Integrating faith and practice involves difficult judgments and compromise because every choice will advance certain values at the expense of other values.

2. It is possible to work with clients whose values are at variance with yours. It is acceptable for you to express your own values, when appropriate, as long as they are clearly labeled as yours and as long as you emphasize that clients have the right and responsibility to make their own choices (and to then be accountable for the consequences).

3. A social agency, particularly a secular one, is not an appropriate setting for a social worker witnessing his or her religious beliefs.

4. When working in a social agency, you have an obligation to carry out the policy of the agency. For example, in a public health clinic you must adhere to the agency's policies on issues such as discussing the use of condoms with gays and with unmarried clients as a means of AIDS prevention, providing birth control information to teenagers, discussing abortion as an option to a problem pregnancy, and discussing strategies for obtaining clean needles with IV drug addicts. Keith-Lucas (1985, p. 32) notes: "One has no right to ignore policies or give them subtly some other meaning than that which the agency intends. Clients have a right to rely on an agency's consistency and Government or a Board of Trustees that its money be spent as it directs."

5. Should you be asked at the employing agency to do something that you cannot in good conscience do, there are three choices. One is to resign. The second is to refuse to carry out the policy (in which case you may be fired). The third is to advocate for a change in agency policy.

Many religiously affiliated agencies employ social workers who are themselves not very religious. What should you do when a religiously affiliated agency asks you to do something that runs counter to the values of your profession? For example, what should pro-choice social workers do when employed by a Catholic agency that has a strict policy against discussing abortion as an option for clients? Workers in such a setting certainly have an obligation to follow agency policy and to not discuss abortion—but they also have an obligation to follow the pro-choice position of the social work profession. Workers in such a setting can resign, request that the agency change its policy (which a Catholic affiliated agency in this situation will not do), adhere to the policy of the agency, or ask to be reassigned to another unit of the agency where they will not be serving pregnant clients. (It is perfectly ethical for a Catholic-affiliated agency to have a pro-life policy as long as clients know about it ahead of time. It is not ethical for an agency to call itself a "Pregnancy Counseling Center" (implying it offers all options) if it in fact does not offer abortion as an option.

The following guidelines may be useful in helping you decide which spiritual or religious interventions are appropriate (and inappropriate) to use:

1. Social workers should not use interventions that have the potential of resulting in harm to the client or to others whom a client interacts with. If you were to use such an intervention, you would be at risk of being sued for malpractice. For example, an intervention that is inappropriate for social workers to engage in with clients is a religious ritual involving the sacrifice of an animal.

2. Social workers should never engage in actions that can be construed as seeking to convert a client to the social worker's religious beliefs. Thus, encouraging a devout Buddhist to read the Bible is inappropriate.

3. Some interventions (such as leading a Bible class with clients that emphasizes adherence to Christian principles and values) may be appropriate in some sectarian (religiously affiliated) settings but will be inappropriate in most secular (not religiously affiliated) settings.

4. When you have questions about which spiritually related interventions are appropriate (or inappropriate), consult with your supervisor.

5. Social workers should use interventions with proven therapeutic value and generally avoid using techniques with no proven value.

6. Interventions that are clearly beyond the purview of social work should not be used. For example, administering sacraments (such as Communion) is the purview of designated members of the clergy and certainly beyond the purview of social workers.

7. Spiritually related interventions should generally be limited to those specifically identified in the intervention contract with the client—with such an intervention contract being approved by the worker's supervisor or agency director.

8. It is crucial that social workers gain an understanding of their clients' religious and spiritual beliefs, traditions, and rituals—and of the laws related to these religious and spiritual practices. Three examples will be presented. Members of the Native American Church, a religious organization, use peyote (a hallucinogenic drug derived from a cactus plant) for ceremonial purposes; 23 states have now passed statutes allowing this church to use this illegal drug for sacramental purposes (Bullis, 1996, p. 89). In a major 1993 U.S. Supreme Court decision, *Church of the Lukumi Babalu Aye v. City of Hialeah* (Bullis, 1996, pp. 89–92), the Court ruled that the City of Hialeah, Florida, could not prohibit members of the Santeria faith from sacrificing live animals (including chickens, pigeons, pigs, doves, ducks, goats, sheep, and turtles); this decision follows the precedent of other Supreme Court decisions that unusual or popularly distasteful spiritual practices are sometimes afforded First Amendment protection when the religious

practice is a central ritual component of spiritual importance for a religious organization. In another area Bullis (1996) notes several court decisions that have generally sided with cult members when their parents have sought to rescue or kidnap them from seemingly unusual and even bizarre spiritual groups. The courts have generally asserted that cult members' First Amendment rights and their ethical rights of self-determination outweigh the wishes of parents and other family members. Social workers who assist or even encourage parents in rescuing and deprogramming an adult son or daughter from an unpopular cult should be prepared to defend themselves against a suit for false imprisonment, intentional infliction of emotional distress, and other torts.

Bullis (1996) conducted a study to determine whether clinical social workers believe it is professionally ethical to use a variety of religious and spiritual interventions. Survey questions were sent to 294 clinical social workers in Virginia, with 116 (44%) responding. The results are compiled in Exhibit 13.2.

Most clinical social workers in this survey believe that it is professionally ethical to use a variety of religious and spiritual interventions. The study also found that these clinical social workers use a wide variety of such interventions in their practice. With the recent attention to spirituality by a variety of helping professionals (including social workers, psychologists, and psychiatrists), it is anticipated that ethical guidelines increasingly will be developed related to the use of spiritual and religious interventions.

In a review of court decisions involving which spiritual and religious interventions are appropriate (and inappropriate) to use in social work practice, Schoener (2000) concludes the following. Spiritual and religious interventions are appropriate to use if *all* of the following conditions exist: (1) there is no evidence the interventions physically or emotionally harm clients, (2) the helping professionals inform clients of the spiritual and religious interventions they use prior to contracting with clients for services, and (3) the helping professionals are *in no way* using the spiritual and religious interventions to persuade clients to join a particular religious faith.

Social Work and Religion in Limited Partnership

Ram Cnann in *The Newer Deal* (1999) indicates in the United States the "devolution revolution" (the federal government's surrender of its responsibility for the welfare of its citizens) has been gaining momentum since the 1980s (see Chapter 2). Devolution of social welfare is a broad national process that originated with the Reagan administration to shift responsibility for the administration of funding of social and health services to state and local governments and to nonprofit organizations. Devolution includes two complementary trends: privatization of service delivery, and the end of some entitlements (such as the replacement of the program Aid to Families with Dependent Children with the program Temporary Assistance to Needy Families). Cnaan (1999) notes:

> Devolution is the antithesis of the welfare state in which the central government assumes full responsibility for the social and health needs of individuals with low income. In the United States, the process of devolution has resulted in the replacement of federal allocations for social services by smaller block grants to states. The states, in turn, asked counties and cities to do more with less and to engage nonprofit organization in the provision of services. This process culminated in 1996 welfare reform legislation. This legislation not only substantially reduced the responsibility of the federal government for social welfare but also heightened both the visibility and the role of the religious-based services providers as a viable replacement. (pp. x and xi)

An important outcome of the devolution revolution is that the religious community (as it was in the 1800s) is again becoming a major provider of social services. The historical role of religious-based services provision in maintaining the local social services infrastructure is currently stronger than ever. Most religious groups now provide social and community services as a means to witness their faith, to fulfill religious teachings and beliefs, and to simply "do good" in providing for those in need in the community.

In regard to the principle of church and state separation in the United States, Cnann (1999) notes:

> Despite all the attempts to separate church and state in the United States, the two are quite interwoven.
>
> We would like to believe that church and state can be fully separated. However, this is not the case. In a country that calls upon the religious community to do more for the welfare of strangers and that willingly pays religious-based groups to do so, church-state separation is merely an ideal. Politicians recognize that the separation does not exist. Managers of religious-based social services also know it. After all, more than 50 percent of the budgets of Catholic Charities, Jewish Family and

EXHIBIT 13.2

Practitioners' report of professional ethics and personal comfort with the use of religious or spiritual interventions in practice*

Interventions	*% Reporting Professionally Ethical*	*% Reporting Personally Comfortable*
Explore Client's Religious Background	94.7% (*n* = 108)	97.3% (*n* = 110)
Explore Client's Spiritual Background	99.1% (*n* = 112)	96.4% (*n* = 108)
Use or Recommend Religious Books	55.0% (*n* = 60)	41.3% (*n* = 45)
Use or Recommend Spiritual Books	88.6% (*n* = 101)	83.3% (*n* = 95)
Teach Spiritual Meditation to Clients	71.8% (*n* = 74)	36.7% (*n* = 40)
Meditate Spiritually with Clients	45.1% (*n* = 46)	19.3% (*n* = 21)
Pray Privately for Client	83.5% (*n* = 91)	70.5% (*n* = 79)
Pray with Client in Session	37.1% (*n* = 39)	24.5% (*n* = 27)
Use Religious Language or Metaphors	66.4% (*n* = 71)	54.1% (*n* = 59)
Use Spiritual Language Metaphors	88.4% (*n* = 99)	81.6% (*n* = 93)
Touch Client for "Healing" Purposes	13.5% (*n* = 14)	10.9% (*n* = 12)
Read Scripture with Client	32.4% (*n* = 35)	21.4% (*n* = 24)
Recommend Participation in Religious Program (Sunday school, religious education)	72.1% (*n* = 80)	65.5% (*n* = 74)
Recommend Participation in Spiritual Programs (Meditation groups, 12-step programs, men's/women's groups)	95.4% (*n* = 104)	91.8% (*n* = 101)
Help Clients Clarify Religious Values	78.2% (*n* = 86)	72.3% (*n* = 81)
Help Clients Clarify Spiritual Values	95.6% (*n* = 108)	94.7% (*n* = 107)
Refer Clients to Religious Counselors	90.0% (*n* = 99)	87.3% (*n* = 96)
Refer Clients to Spiritual Counselors	85.2% (*n* = 92)	80.9% (*n* = 89)
Help Clients Develop Ritual as a Clinical Intervention (House blessings, visiting graves of relatives, etc.)	90.9% (*n* = 100)	86.5% (*n* = 96)
Participate in Client's Rituals as a Clinical Intervention	57.1% (*n* = 60)	38.0% (*n* = 41)
Explore Religious Elements in Dreams	82.6% (*n* = 90)	61.5% (*n* = 67)
Explore Spiritual Elements in Dreams	93.6% (*n* = 103)	82.6% (*n* = 90)
Recommend Religious/Spiritual, Forgiveness, Penance, or Amends	65.1% (*n* = 71)	57.7% (*n* = 64)
Perform Exorcism	5.7% (*n* = 6)	3.6% (*n* = 4)
Share Your Own Religious/Spiritual Beliefs or Views	60.9% (*n* = 67)	60.2% (*n* = 68)

Source: Copyright 1996 from Table 5.1 on page 102 from *Spirituality in Social Work Practice* by Ronald K. Bollis. Reproduced by permission of Taylor & Francis, Inc., http://www.routledge=ny.com.

*Clinical social workers in Virginia were asked if they believed it was professionally ethical to use, and whether they were personally comfortable in using, these interventions in social work practice.

Children's Services, and Lutheran Social Ministries, to name just a few agencies, comes from the public coffers. It is now time for the profession of social work, its leaders, its scholars, and its practitioners to acknowledge the same: the church-social work separation is unwarranted.

If the religious community is to be even more deeply involved in social services provision, then we must learn how to cooperate with organized religion to improve the lot of those whom we serve and whose interests we represent. We must apply a more pluralistic model, one that enables both sides to maintain their ideological and value stances while collaborating where possible and when beneficial for both. (pp. 300–301)

Congregations and church-affiliated organizations provide a wide range of social services, which are frequently partly financed by purchase of care arrangements with federal, state, and local governmental units.

Examples of social services provided by congregations and church-affiliated organizations include counseling; telephone reassurance; free use of church buildings for meetings by self-help groups, such as Alcoholics Anonymous, Narcotics Anonymous, Al-Anon, Alateen, and Overeaters Anonymous; emergency food assistance; congregate meals; soup kitchens; emergency shelter; mobile meals; cash assistance; housework for elderly and those with a disability; food preparations; legal help; brokering services; child care; after-school care; adult daycare; tutoring; employment help; pregnancy counseling; foster care; housing for health clinics; food banks; housing rehabilitation; adoption services; and refugee resettlement.

Religious congregations and organizations are not solely "member-serving" organizations, but also are "other-serving" organizations that are committed to improving the quality of life in their communities. Clearly, a limited partnership is emerging between social work and the religious community. Cnaan (1999) recommends:

1. That baccalaureate and masters programs in social work teach students about the increasing role of the religious community in the provision of local social services, which would include field placements that prepare their graduates to work more effectively within religious-based social service organizations.

2. That social work professionals form coalitions with religious-based social services and other religious groups when planning and implementing community projects as a means of increasing both the legitimacy and resource base of the projects, because religious organizations have the trust and support of many local residents.

3. That social work professionals offer consultative services to religious congregations to assist them in expanding or reorganizing the programs they provide to the community.

4. That baccalaureate and masters programs in social work educate their students on the boundary issues between social work and religious organizations. At time the values and principles of the profession of social work and those of religious organizations will conflict. When conflicts occur (for example, between the pro-choice position of social work and the pro-life position of some religious organizations), social work professionals need strategies for resolving such conflicts.

Summary

A major thrust of social work education is to prepare students for culturally sensitive practice, including helping social workers comprehend the influence of religion and spirituality in human lives. The philanthropic founders of social work were inspired by Judeo-Christian traditions to pursue social work. Social workers need to have an appreciation and respect for religious beliefs that differ from their own chosen beliefs. Although social work literature has largely ignored religion's or spirituality's impact on social work practice, there has been a resurgence in recent years to attend to the spiritual aspects of clients' lives. Philosophically, social work and spirituality are natural allies in working for personal and social well-being. Clients' spiritual beliefs are major determinants in a wide variety of their decisions.

This chapter summarizes the kinds of questions that are useful in a spiritual/religious assessment of clients. Some guidelines with regard to appropriate and inappropriate interventions were also provided. However, many questions remain unanswered in this area. It is crucial that social workers gain an understanding of their clients' religious and spiritual beliefs, traditions, and rituals—and of the laws and court decisions related to these religious and spiritual practices.

A limited partnership between social work and religion is emerging in the provision of social services in communities.

EXERCISES

1. RESPECTING SPIRITUAL AND RELIGIOUS BELIEFS AND PRACTICES OF CLIENTS

Goals: To gain background information about diverse religions, learn to respect religious beliefs that differ from your own, and become more comfortable with your own religious beliefs.

Step 1: Read Exhibit 13.1.

Step 2: Form groups of three and discuss the following questions:

a. Some religions assert that God is all good, all knowing, and all powerful. If God has these three characteristics, why would she or he allow diseases like AIDS or send people to eternal damnation?
b. What evidence is there that God existed and that she or he currently exists?
c. Most prominent religions in the world have a "bible"—that is, a book of sacred scriptures. Is one of these bibles more accurate in being the word of God than the others? If your answer is "yes," what is it, and what evidence do you have?
d. Is there "one true religion"? If your answer is "yes," what is it, and what evidence do you have?
e. If a social worker believes strongly that his or her religion is the one true religion, can that worker fully accept clients who adhere to other religious faiths?

Step 3: Class discussion of group thoughts.

Step 4: How does intolerance of others' religious beliefs contribute to other forms of prejudice, such as racism? Sexism? Homophobia?

2. TIMELINE OF YOUR RELIGIOUS AND SPIRITUAL JOURNEY

Goal: To describe the chronology of your religious and spiritual journey.

Step 1: You are to draw a timeline of your religious and spiritual experiences. Begin by drawing a straight line at the bottom of a sheet of paper and numbering the line with numbers corresponding to your current age; a 22-year-old student would have 22 numbers. Note significant religious and spiritual events that occurred at various ages. These events can include significant experiences with people, places, ideas, books, movies, churches, and so on. End with a summary of your current religious and spiritual beliefs and values.

Step 2: Form groups of three or four and share your timelines. (You may also choose not to share.)

3. USING RELIGIOUS AND SPIRITUAL INTERVENTIONS

Goal: To explore the ethics of using religious and spiritual interventions in practice.

Step 1: You are a social worker at a *secular* (not religiously affiliated) agency. For each intervention in the following table, mark on a separate sheet of paper whether you believe the intervention is professionally ethical for you to use, and whether you personally would be comfortable using this intervention at your agency.

Step 2: Group discussion of student responses.

(continued)

EXERCISES
(continued)

Interventions	*Professionally Ethical to Use*		*Personally Comfortable Using*	
	Yes	No	Yes	No
1. Lead a Bible class				
2. Explore client's spiritual background				
3. Help clients clarify spiritual values				
4. Recommend participation in spiritual programs (meditation groups, twelve-step programs, men's/women's groups)				
5. Explore client's religious background				
6. Explore spiritual elements in dreams				
7. Help clients develop ritual as a clinical intervention (house blessings, visiting graves of relatives, and so forth)				
8. Refer clients to religious counselors				
9. Use or recommend spiritual books				
10. Use spiritual language metaphors				
11. Refer clients to spiritual counselors				
12. Pray privately for client				
13. Explore religious elements in dreams				
14. Help clients clarify religious values				
15. Recommend participation in religious programs (Sunday school, religious education)				
16. Teach spiritual meditation to clients				
17. Use religious language or metaphors				
18. Recommend religious/spiritual forgiveness, penance, or amends				
19. Share your own religious/spiritual beliefs or views				
20. Participate in client's rituals as a clinical intervention				
21. Use or recommend religious books				
22. Meditate spiritually with clients				
23. Pray with client in session				
24. Read scripture with client				
25. Touch client for "healing" purposes				
26. Perform exorcism				

4. *PROVIDING SERVICES TO CASES WITH RELIGIOUS OR SPIRITUAL ISSUES*

Goal: To see how social workers can set goals and objectives in cases that involve religious or spiritual issues.

Step 1: Form groups of five. Arrive at a consensus as to the goals and objectives you would set for the following scenarios.

a. You work at a secular agency. A married couple asks your help in rescuing (kidnapping) their 19-year-old daughter from a religious cult. The daughter has dropped out of college and joined this cult. She lives in a distant state in a commune sponsored by this cult. Her parents ask for a referral to an organization that rescues adult children from such cults and also asks your help in deprogramming her once she is rescued (kidnapped). How do you respond?

b. You work at a secular agency in a community where a religious group that practices voodoo wants to locate (voodooism includes the practice of witchcraft). A citizen's group forms to stop this religious group from locating in your community. The organization contacts your agency requesting any help you can provide. How do you respond?

c. You are a hospital social worker, and a nurse approaches you for help. A Haitian patient has requested that his spiritual adviser conduct a healing ceremony in his hospital room. The patient and his spiritual adviser practice voodooism. The nurse is concerned that the ceremony may be inappropriate in a hospital that is loosely affiliated with the Catholic church and that the ceremony may upset other patients. How do you respond to this nurse's concerns?

d. You work in protective services. A teacher at an elementary school reports that an 8-year-old boy is being emotionally abused. His parents practice the Santeria religion and require that their son attend ritual slaughters of lambs, pigs, and turtles. The teacher asserts that forcing the child to attend such sacrifices is upsetting to him and therefore constitutes emotional abuse. You investigate and find that the child does become upset after attending such ceremonies but does not appear to be unduly traumatized. How would you proceed with this case? What would be your goals?

Step 2: Class discussion of group conclusions.

PART 3

Taking Care of Self

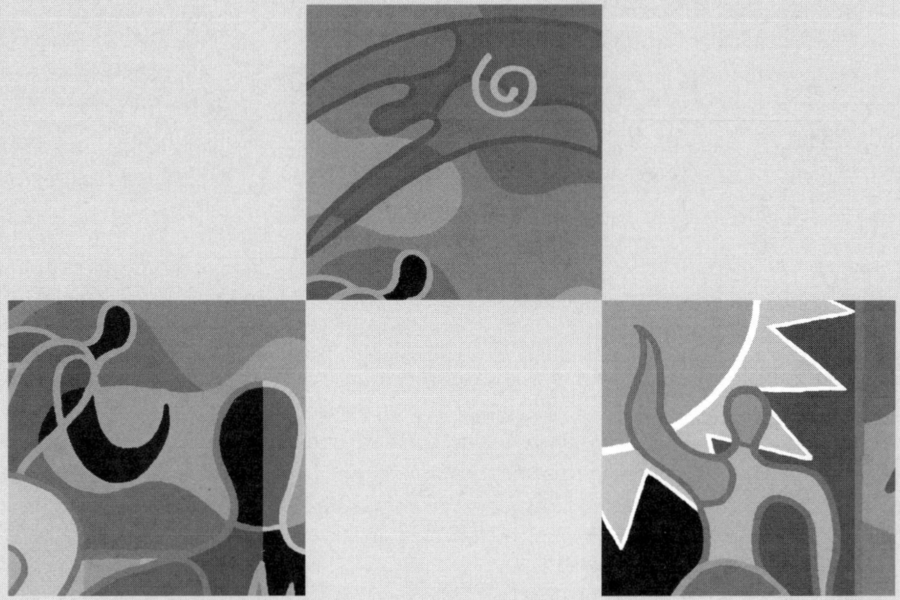

CHAPTER 14

Surviving and Enjoying Social Work

To be of help to others, helping professionals must first take care of themselves. Good emotional and physical health are internal resources that helping professionals need to be able to help others. In this chapter we focus on how to survive and enjoy a career in social work.

Students' Common Concerns

One of the surprises I found in teaching social work students is that although they have a number of common concerns, they believe their concerns are so unique and "secret" that they are reluctant to share and discuss them with others. In this section we examine a number of these concerns and offer some suggestions for resolving them.

Will I Be Able to Make It in Field Placement?

Associated with this concern are a number of specific concerns. Will I be accepted and liked by the agency staff? Will I be accepted and liked by the clients who are assigned to me? Will I be able to help clients? Will the clothes I wear be acceptable? Will my shortcomings do me in? (*Every* student perceives a number of personal shortcomings—such as unusual tone of voice, inability to speak clearly, a low level of interviewing skills, questionable personal appearance, or inability to start and maintain a conversation, and so on; students by far are their own harshest critics.) Am I emotionally stable enough to handle field placement? Will I be able to speak on the telephone? Will I be able to learn to do all the paperwork? Will I be attacked by clients? Will my car hold up, or will I be able to get where I'm supposed to be? Will I become too anxious and get stage fright when I'm assigned certain tasks?

In 30 years of supervising students in field placement, I have heard these and many similar concerns from practically every student. The students I worry about in arranging field placements are those who deny having such concerns; I have found that they generally are not perceptive about themselves. If people are not perceptive about personal concerns and emotions, it generally means they won't be perceptive about the thoughts and emotions of clients and therefore won't make a skillful counselor.

Practically every student is anxious before field placement and during at least the first few weeks at placement. This anxiety is to be expected. You will find in field placement that your moderate level of anxiety will drain your energy, and you may be exhausted when you leave in the evening.

Although such anxiety and concerns are normal, there are ways of reducing some of these concerns.

1. In many social work programs, students have considerable input in choosing their field placement setting. If you have such input, use this opportunity to visit the agency you are considering for a placement. Meet with agency staff, ask them to describe the agency's programs, and also discuss the expected tasks for student interns. Certain other concerns, such as expected dress code, can also be discussed. If after the visit you have serious reservations about taking a placement at that agency, discuss your reservations with the faculty who coordinate field placements. If your concerns are not allayed after this discussion, many programs allow you to visit another agency to explore doing a field placement there.
2. Ask other students currently in field placement, or who have completed field placement, to share and discuss their experiences and concerns. This will give you a better idea of what placement is like and may also provide you with answers to some of your concerns. It is particularly useful to talk with students who have worked at the agency you are considering.
3. Discuss your concerns with faculty who coordinate field placements at your school. They will be able to answer some of your concerns and provide additional information about the agency.
4. Volunteer in your classes to role-play simulated counseling situations. Videotaping these sessions is particularly useful. Reviewing the tapes will enable you to assess and further develop your interviewing skills. Zastrow and Navarre (1979) found that videotaped role playing of counseling situations also develops students' confidence in their counseling capacities.
5. Express any concerns you have to your agency supervisor. Make sure you understand agency procedures and policies, and expectations for student interns. Open communication between you and your agency supervisor is an important key to making it in field placement.

These suggestions will reduce some, but certainly not all, of your concerns about whether you will make it in field placement. It is normal to be anxious at the beginning. As the weeks pass, and you receive feedback that you are doing well, you will become more relaxed.

Will I Conduct a Satisfactory Interview with My First Client?

Concerns that relate to this question include How will I know what to say? How will I keep the conversation going? If I say the wrong thing, won't it be a calamity for the client? How will I introduce myself? Will clients discover that I am only a student and therefore feel they are being used as guinea pigs to train me? What if I become tongue-tied and am unable to say anything? Am I really ready to assume the awesome responsibility of counseling others? I've got personal problems that are unresolved—how can I possibly help others?

Some students become so concerned before seeing their first client that they can't sleep the night before; others develop tension headaches. A few students have told me they couldn't eat or developed diarrhea or were nauseated. It happens. If you have severe reactions, you are not alone. Just remember, it is highly unlikely that you will "bomb" during your first interview. Most anxious students report once the interview began they relaxed and the interview went fairly well.

Here are suggestions for reducing your concerns:

1. Role-play simulated counseling situations, ideally playing the roles of both counselor and client. Videotaping and reviewing the tape is particularly helpful. Such role playing will give you practice in counseling.
2. To prepare for the interview, identify your objectives, and think about the kinds of questions you will need to ask to accomplish them. Review the material in Chapters 4 and 5 on how to begin and end interviews, how to build a relationship, and how to begin to explore the client's problems.
3. Clients are much less fragile than beginning counselors believe they are. If you fail to cover something, you can probably do that at some future interview. If you fail to phrase a question properly, you won't cause a calamity in the client's life. It is irrational to expect that if you make some mistakes in this first interview that you will cause a disaster for the client—no one has that kind of power. Clients have been exposed to much more trauma and chaotic situations than talking to you; they survived those experiences; they will survive talking to you.
4. Review the interview with your agency supervisor or your faculty supervisor to identify which aspects you did well, and which ones you need to improve. Don't expect perfection—in your first interview, or in *any* interview. You *will* make mistakes; everyone does.

Remember, the main purpose of field placement is *training*—helping you test and further develop your social work skills and techniques. Therefore, agency staff expect you to make mistakes. Students who generally do best in placement are those who test out and develop their social work skills. It is a serious mistake to "hang back" in field placement for fear of making mistakes. Focusing on making few errors so that you can get a high grade usually leads student interns to "hang back," and this usually *lowers* your grade.

5. If you have specific questions prior to this first interview, ask your agency supervisor. Perhaps you are wondering whether you should inform the client that you are a student. Different agencies handle this question differently. Your agency supervisor wants to hear your questions and concerns. Only by hearing your questions can your agency supervisor determine "where you are" and how to be most helpful to you. Agency supervisors were once in training themselves. They are fully aware of the pressures and anxieties of being in field placement and are committed to helping you. Many have told me that the questions students ask frequently add a fresh, new perspective to their practice, which leads them to make improvements in their counseling and interviewing approaches.

My Supervisor Interviews Much Better Than I—Will I Ever Be Able to Do That Well?

When student interns observe the interviewing and counseling skills of their agency or faculty supervisor, many become disheartened because they realize their skills are not as highly developed. They tend to "awfulize" and erroneously conclude they never will do well at interviewing and counseling. *Of course* your skills are not as good as your supervisor's; you haven't had 30 years in the field! Rome was not built in a day, and neither are interviewing skills. You *will* get better. Be patient, observe carefully, and *don't* think negatively!

How Do I Separate the Roles of Counselor and Friend?

Students generally have a small caseload in field placement, which allows them to spend considerable time with clients. It is not uncommon for clients to begin to become attracted to their worker because sharing personal concerns fosters an attachment. Students are also generally young and physically attractive, which also fosters attachments. Frequent questions students in field placement have include, "Is this client beginning to see me as someone he wants to get socially involved with—how do I handle this?" "This client has invited me to her home—should I go?" "This client has suggested we have a cup of coffee (or dinner) together—should I go?" "This client has suggested we go to a park (or play golf, or go to a bar, or play cards)—should I go?"

There are no yes or no answers to these questions. Most agencies frown on, and some prohibit, fraternizing with clients. For example, if you as a probation officer socialize extensively with a probationee, problems may arise. The probationee might violate some conditions of probation and then try to use the friendship with you to avoid the consequences. In addition, other probationees and parolees are apt to become aware of the friendship and conclude they no longer have to rigidly adhere to the conditions of probation or of parole because you are "a nice guy" and "a soft touch." In addition, administrative officials will view the friendship as a conflict of interest situation and will disapprove highly of such a relationship.

In addition, if you become socially involved with a client, it is difficult to counsel that person effectively. The client, for example, may no longer be willing to accept suggestions from you—he may misinterpret the suggestions as being "put-downs." Counseling someone you are socially involved with elicits clashes, not unlike when you tried to teach your sister how to drive a car.

All this said, the attraction of client to counselor *can* be a component of a helping relationship, and one that can occasionally be used positively. I've seen elderly, apathetic, depressed male clients in nursing homes become attracted to female student interns. These interns then used this attraction to motivate these elderly men to become involved in programs at the nursing homes (such as hobbies and craft activities). Once involved in the programs, they started to enjoy them, and as a result became more energetic, happier, and more active.

How then should counselors decide whether to accept social invitations from clients? The guideline is simple. *If* you believe doing something with your client will help you develop a working relationship and would be constructive for the client, then do it. For some clients, going to a park and talking helps them relax and develops the kind of atmosphere in which they will feel free to share and discuss their secret personal concerns. However, *if* you believe that accepting an invitation has the potential for being destructive to the helping process, then don't do it. If you believe going to a park will lead the client to conclude that you want to become romantically involved, then tactfully decline the invitation. (Establishing professional boundaries with clients is discussed at greater length in Chapter 2.)

It is useful for beginning workers to understand the essential difference between a friendship and a professional relationship. Friendship is for *both* of you to *give* and *receive;* a professional relationship involves the helping person *giving* and the client *receiving*.

Beginning counselors often wonder how, in practice, to separate their roles of counselor and friend. With experience, this problem usually disappears. Experienced counselors become more perceptive in determining the intents behind invitations from clients and more skillful in conveying the boundaries of the professional relationship. Experienced counselors also have more cases; this reduces the amount of time spent per client, which reduces socializing opportunities.

How Do I Avoid Becoming Too Emotionally Involved?

Every counselor has, at one time or another, become overly emotionally involved in a case.

I recently supervised a student in a child welfare unit at a public welfare department. One case assigned to this student involved a 14-year-old girl who had been in a series of foster homes since she was 3. The student, Linda H., became fairly attached to the girl. This client wanted to date, which her conservative foster parents could not accept. Considerable friction developed, and the foster parents suggested to the agency that it would be best for the girl to be placed in a different foster home. Linda H. arranged a meeting between the foster parents and the girl to try to work out a compromise because the girl felt rejected, but the meeting resolved nothing. So Linda H., after considerable effort, found another foster home, and a trial visit was attempted. Linda H. indicated that she "felt like a nervous mother" about this visit. (Right away this statement led me to believe she was becoming overly involved.) The trial visit went fairly well, but after a day of reflecting, these foster parents decided they did not want to take a foster child at this time. Not only did the girl feel rejected, unloved, and depressed, Linda H. became so depressed that she had to take two days off from her placement. She sympathized, rather than empathized, with the girl. Fortunately she realized she was too emotionally involved at this point to search for another foster family. (She did ask the foster parents to keep the girl for a few more days until a new placement could be found, which they consented to do.)

As Linda H.'s example indicates, counselors who are too emotionally involved have a reduced capacity to help clients discuss their problems and to explore alternative solutions objectively with clients.

Several types of irrational thinking lead to overinvolvement. Exhibit 14.1 lists these types of irrational thinking and presents rational self-challenges to counter them.

Beginning counselors are much more apt to become overly involved than experienced counselors, because with experience, counselors increasingly learn that clients own their problems, that clients are the primary problem solvers, and that to be of optimal assistance counselors need to remain objective rather than exaggerating the consequences of resolution approaches that don't work out. (The main reason counselors are less successful in counseling close friends and relatives is because they are too involved to be objective.)

Yet even experienced counselors at times become involved. I speak from experience. A few years ago I was asked to provide professional help for a number of personal problems to a client—including burnout, grief over her husband's death, drinking problems, insomnia, depression, and lack of meaning in work or in living. She was highly respected in her profession. I realized I was giving myself the following irrational thinking that was leading to over-involvement: "I must solve her problems. If she resigns her position this will be tragic, as several thousand people will be adversely affected. If this person resigns, it will be awful." By countering my thinking with rational self-challenges, I was able to help her explore her problems, one at a time, and we developed strategies to handle each.

When you feel emotionally involved in a case (for example, taking it home with you by thinking about it for several hours),

1. Discuss it with others, particularly your supervisor. Other people are often able to offer suggestions on alternatives and may be able to suggest ways to become more objective and less emotionally involved.

2. Do a rational self-analysis (described in Module 6) on your unwanted emotions about a case. This will help you identify your irrational thinking so that you can counter it with rational self-challenges.

3. Seriously consider transferring the case to another worker if your involvement is simply too intense. It is irrational to expect to be able to handle all cases optimally. You will handle some cases better than your

EXHIBIT 14.1

Irrational thinking leads to emotional overinvolvement, which can be changed by rational self-challenges

Irrational Thinking	*Rational Self-Challenges*
1. "This client has shared his problems, and therefore I must help this client resolve these problems." (Such thinking leads to taking ownership of the client's problems.)	1. "Clients own their problems and have the responsibility for resolving them. I do not have the power to resolve them. All I can do is help clients explore their problems, explore alternative solutions, and encourage clients to select a resolution approach."
2. "If things (events) don't work out for clients, I have failed. I am at fault for their problems. I am a failure."	2. "Everyone has ups and downs. We are all fallible, and we all have problems. If one resolution approach does not work out for a client, it only means that approach failed. It in no way means I am a failure. What the client and I need to do is to examine why that approach did not work out, explore other alternatives, select one, and try that."
3. "If things don't work out for clients, it is *awful, terrible, overwhelming, unbearable.*"	3. "As Ellis and Harper (1977) pointed out, it is irrational to conclude that a problem is awful, overwhelming, or unbearable. Adverse events are often inconvenient and problematic, but assigning labels such as awful only leads to unwanted emotions. Instead of viewing problems as being overwhelming, I need to take each problem one at a time, and in a step-by-step fashion develop strategies to deal with each."
4. "If I don't solve the client's problems, the consequences for the client, the client's family, and others close to the client will be tragic, unbearable." (Overly involved counselors often view the consequences as being more tragic than the clients themselves view the consequences.)	4. "Clients own their problems and have the responsibility to resolve them. I am not God; I have no miracle power to resolve problems. All I can ever do is 'give it my best shot' in counseling. It is irrational and counterproductive to overexaggerate consequences. If the selected approach doesn't work, the client needs to select and try another."
5. "I've tried the only approach that there is, and that failed. There is no hope. Things are certainly bleak for this client. I feel overwhelmed—I give up!"	5. "There is always hope. Even though I am unaware of other alternatives, there may well be others. I need to talk to an authority in this area to learn about other alternatives."

fellow workers, and they will handle other cases better than you. Intense emotional involvement with a case for an extended period lessens your objectivity and indicates a transfer is necessary.

Do I Really Want a Career in Social Work?

Related concerns include the following: Do I have capacities to be a competent social worker? What area of social work (for example, mental health, corrections) should I pursue? Will a career in social work pay me enough money to live the way I want to live? What do I really want to do with my life? What will my parents, friends, and relatives think of me if I become a social worker? Is there a profession or vocation that I would find more enjoyable and gratifying?

Most of these questions can only be answered by you. As far as the money question goes, faculty members in your social work department will be able to tell you about average starting salaries in your area for graduates of baccalaureate and master's programs in social work. Starting salaries vary considerably in different regions, and in different positions. Pay increases are largely determined by you—your skills, your efforts to obtain advanced degrees, and your efforts to seek administrative and supervisory positions that generally pay more than direct services. Psychotherapists in private practice (who have an M.S.W. degree and two or more years of counseling experience) can earn over $100,000 per year. Skills at grant writing, consultation, public speaking, and developing new programs are also often financially rewarded.

But how do you determine whether social work is the right career for you and, if so, which area of social work to pursue? Only you can decide. Here are some suggestions that may help you:

1. Relax, don't be in a hurry to make a final career decision. Some social work students think they have to make such decisions within a few weeks. Thinking about the pros and cons makes them so anxious they can't make any decision. In one sense you've got the rest of your life to make career decisions. Today people routinely start new careers in their forties, fifties, sixties, and even seventies.

2. Try a trial-and-error approach. If you find one area of social work unsatisfying, try another. Skills learned in one area won't be wasted. You may find one area fulfilling for a while, but then find you need new challenges. If you really don't think you want a career in social work, fine; try something else—you may like it. Perhaps someday you'll change your mind and want to try social work again. No problem. You can take refresher or continuing education courses or attend workshops to polish your skills and learn new techniques and revised procedures. We have students in our undergraduate courses in their forties, fifties, and sixties who are just now pursuing a career in social work. Do not think that this is your *final* career decision. Times change, agencies change, our interests and values change, and—yes, our careers change too.

All this said, however, does not mean you should idly sit back and wait for some unknown force to decide your career path for you. You are in the driver's seat, and it's up to you to decide on the *first* destination on your journey and then to drive yourself there.

Safety Guidelines for Social Workers

The social work perspective views violence as erupting in context rather than residing within the "violent individual." Rather than viewing some people as inherently violent, social workers understand that most violent behavior occurs because of interactions between the environmental context, the worker's interaction with the potentially violent client, and the client's internal dynamics. People differ in both their tendency toward and the speed with which they convert emotions into violent behavior. The immediate context tempers whether a person with a shorter fuse (that is, more prone to violence) gets further agitated. Violent behavior is often a defensive reaction—the person expects harm or perceives a threat. Because the immediate environmental context is important, social workers are often able to use their skills to deter potentially violent behavior.

Environmental Signals of Danger

The context—the environment—may signal a violent situation. Certain situations have more potential for violence than others. Consider these scenarios. A protective service worker decides to remove a child from a home in which one, or both, of his parents are abusing him. A social worker at a battered women's shelter takes a resident to her home (where the batterer may be present) to pick up her belongings. A social worker at a police department goes with a police officer to a home where domestic violence is reportedly occurring. A social worker at a neighborhood center works with juvenile gang members to curb criminal activity. In assessing risk in these and other potentially violent situations, social workers need to determine the following:

- Are there people present who are inciting the situation?
- Are colleagues present who can assist me?
- Are there obvious weapons present, or objects that can be used as weapons?

Client Signals of Danger

Weinger (2001), in a review of the literature on social worker safety, has identified client signals that indicate an increased risk of violence; these are listed in Exhibit 14.2.

The best predictor of violent outbursts is a history of violent expressions. Clients who have a history of violent reactions stand a greater chance of becoming violent again. Therefore, if at all possible, workers should read clients' records prior to meeting with them. Diagnoses of antisocial personality disorder, borderline personality, and schizophrenia are also associated with proneness to violence.

EXHIBIT 14.2

Client signals of danger

Signal Type	*Behavior*
Angry verbalizations	Swearing, threatening statements, complaining, sarcasm
Emotional distress	Suspicious, hostile, irritable, unhappy, angry
Thinking difficulties	Confused, disoriented, hallucinations, paranoid ideas
Bodily changes	Trembling, heavy breathing, shakes, sweating
Speech	Sharp, loud, pressured speech
Signs of intoxication	Slurred speech, flushed face, unsteady gait, dilated pupils, lack of coordination
Body movements	Exaggerated movements, pacing, shifting positions, flailing arms, threatening gestures, clenched fists, pounding of fists on objects, wringing of hands, tense muscles
Facial cues	Muscle tension in face and neck, pale, gritting teeth, dilated pupils, glaring, scowling
Agitation	Hyperactive, tenseness, ill at ease, overly anxious

Another indicator is a history of substance abuse. Alcohol intoxication lowers inhibitions, and it interferes with a client's judgment. Use of such drugs as cocaine, PCP, and amphetamines increase the risk of violence because they increase the potential for agitation, suspicion, grandiosity, and delusional beliefs.

Yet another indicator is a history of child abuse, or witnessing repeated abuse at home when growing up. Sadly, children who have been abused are more prone to violence as adults. Other indicators of an increased risk of violence include fitting these categories: male, military combat experience, and having been incarcerated. In regard to these warning signals, Weinger (2001) astutely notes three caveats:

> First, although knowing the predictive factors may increase awareness, there are many false positives. Persons who do not resort to violence may also have these risk factors . . . Second, in fueling the flames of racism we have often linked violence and crime to race. Although research has demonstrated that when different groups live in the same social, economic, and political environment their rate of violence is comparable, we have not always absorbed these findings into our mindsets. Because of these distortions, for example, a social worker may too readily suspect an African American client and may overlook the warning signs exhibited in contact with a White client. . . .
>
> Finally, there is a potential to use predictors of violence in a way that will create more risk to the clinician. If clinicians forsake their level of alertness because a client doesn't meet the criteria for potential risk factors, they may overlook important signals. It is important to realize that a client who presents or does not present risk factors can exhibit assaultive behaviors. (p. 37)

Worker Signals of Danger

Listen to your gut-feelings. This is crucial. You are already in social work because of your inherent ability to empathize and understand people—you pick up on signals probably a lot better than the proverbial "man on the street." *Use this ability here as well.* This doesn't always mean you will be correct in your assessment. You can also be misled by your personal biases, cultural biases, and by misinformation. Always remember that gestures, body language, and verbal expressions have different meanings in different cultures.

Assault Cycle

Kaplan and Wheeler (1983) note that most assaults follow a predictable pattern of five phases:

1. *Triggering phase:* Everyone has a baseline of normative behaviors. In the triggering phase, an event occurs that ignites the first deviation from the baseline demeanor. The event can be infinitely varied—such as receiving criticism, or receiving a speeding ticket.

2. *Escalation phase:* Clients become increasingly emotionally aroused. Their speech, behavior, and emotions move away from their normative expressions. The best time to intervene is early in this cycle. Interventions can involve active listening, nonjudgmental lis-

tening, and problem solving, to prevent the agitation from escalating further.

3. *Crisis phase:* Clients are so aroused physiologically and psychologically that they are unable (or at least not inclined) to control angry and hostile feelings. They become verbally or physically aggressive. At this point, interventions like active listening and problem solving are no longer effective. It is time to attend to your own safety, the safety of others, and the safety of the aggressive client.

4. *Recovery phase:* Clients begin to return to baseline behaviors, but are still in a precarious state. If further events upset them they can rapidly return to the crisis phase. To support the recovery, pace your interventions in response to clients' cues, and perhaps reassure them that they will be safe. Avoid disapproving comments, and do not explore the reasons for, and consequences of, the behavior.

5. *Postcrisis depression phase:* At this point clients have calmed down and returned to baseline behaviors. They may even be more subdued than their normal baseline behaviors. They may be mentally and physically exhausted. They are likely to feel remorse and shame, which then make them more receptive to social work interventions. In this phase, Weinger (2001) notes:

> It may be appropriate to reflect on the assaultive episode with the client . . . to help the client discuss the consequences of the behavior and deal with feelings of fear or guilt that someone got hurt . . . to understand the dynamics or events that preceded her or his losing control, and to consider appropriate choices and behavioral options for the future when she or he becomes anxious or angry. (p. 35)

This progression of reactions provides clues on when and how interventions can deescalate the situation. Thus, during the crisis and recovery phases, active listening and problem solving probably won't be helpful; yet, these same techniques may be more than usually effective during the postcrisis phase.

Preventing Violence

The best way to deal with violence, of course, is to prevent it from happening in the first place. Usually the most constructive way to do this is to lessen perceived threats and feelings of helplessness. Fortunately, a variety of options help do just this.

Deescalate verbal communication. Help clients express their feelings and thoughts—that is, let them vent. To do this, use your skills of active listening and reflecting feelings. This helps clients feel worthy. Use disarming (Chapter 7)—that is, find some truth in what the client is saying, and then express this "agreement." Disarming also helps the client feel understood and validated, and hopefully more open to examining another point of view. Use empathy (Chapter 7)—paraphrase what clients say. Restating their thoughts and feelings helps them reflect and move to problem solving.

Encourage clients to problem-solve. This can also help deescalate verbal communication. Weinger (2001, p. 38) notes that violence-prone clients have difficulty generating nonviolent solutions. They may need help thinking of nonviolent options.

It may be time for small talk. Sometimes redirecting clients' attention to less emotionally charged subjects deescalates verbal communication. For example, say, "It's really getting warm in here. Let's take a walk. We'll come back to this later."

Avoid aggressive, confrontational, or macho responses when a potentially violent client is emotionally upset. Such responses increase the likelihood of violence.

Deescalate nonverbal communication. Weinger (2001, p. 39) recommends approaching the client from an angle (rather than head-on or from the back) in order to convey a nonconfrontational approach. Approach the client casually and gradually, so as not to appear aggressive. Maintain some distance, so that the client doesn't feel his personal space is being violated. Individuals with a history of violence often require a wider personal space than do less violent individuals (Weinger, 2001, p. 39). Avoid touching the client (other than shaking hands), because touching can be perceived as a challenge, or it may arouse emotionally charged memories of past physical abuse.

Some eye contact with potentially violent clients may be useful; it conveys interest and it enables you to be watchful. However, sustained eye contact (and definitely glaring) should be avoided.

If your client's body language is agitated, mirror their body language, but do so at a somewhat slower and softer pace. This conveys that you are "in sync" with the client, that you are an ally. Once the client feels in sync with you, gradually reduce the intensity of your movements; the client will often unconsciously model this reduced level of activity. With this approach, you are literally leading the client to a more relaxed state.

Set limits. Many angry clients fear losing control. For such clients (Weinger, 2001, p. 40) recommends that you say something like, "It's OK to be angry, but it's not OK to strike out. What can I do to help you feel more in control right now?" This statement clarifies that physical aggression is not acceptable. The tone and wording should support the client's worth, and should not increase feelings of powerlessness. Don't come across as a parent. Don't be nonassertive. Both can trigger additional arousal. Set limits in a confident, assertive, but neutral, tone.

Stay calm and generate options. As much as possible, remain calm. Communicate calmness, both verbally and nonverbally, even if you are agitated and frightened. An even, slow, soft-toned voice and a confident nonjudgmental, nonauthoritarian approach reassures an agitated person and doesn't pressure them. Conveying your agitation can provoke aggression.

Remaining calm also helps you figure out constructive options (including escape strategies). Fear and anxiety interferes with generating and assessing appropriate options. Use relaxation techniques (Module 9) and self-talk (Module 6) to get to calm.

Safeguards in the Workplace

The nature of your work setting can increase or decrease the risk of violence. Disorganization, cold-appearing surroundings, staff conflict, isolated offices, overcrowding, and lack of an alarm system can contribute to the likelihood of client violence.

Safety accommodations in the workplace vary according to the field of social work practice, and the type of clients. Different settings need different safeguards. Typical workplace safeguards include the following:

1. Metal detectors. Some settings (such as some schools and courthouses) now use metal detectors that screen for weapons. There should also be a dependable planned-response system when a weapon is detected.

2. Alarm systems and other security devices include cellular phones, intercoms, panic buttons, and hand-held or mounted buzzers. Again, when using these systems, have a dependable, planned, and *rehearsed* response system in place.

3. Possible weapons. Be aware of items in the workplace that can be used as weapons. Limit the presence of potential weapons such as soda bottles, pens, ashtrays, vases, pictures, and radios. When interviewing potentially violent clients, remove your clothing accessories that can be used in harmful ways, such as neckties, dangling earrings, and necklaces.

4. Interview rooms should be in view and have two exits (for escape purposes). The agency may also choose to have a special interview room with a large window that other staff can view into, or have a one-way mirror for viewing from the outside.

5. Furniture should be arranged so that staff (and clients) can make quick exits. Chairs that are light in weight can be picked up by workers and used as shields.

6. Pleasant surroundings. Waiting rooms and interview rooms should be designed for comfort and for stress reduction. Try to have soft lighting, comfortable chairs, current magazines, and calming color schemes (such as pastel colors).

Response Planning

Planning for "what if" scenarios needs to be an ongoing part of staff training and meetings. The following guidelines are useful:

1. Report and record all violent incidents. Agency administration should keep records.
2. Have a policy that informs clients and workers that violence will not be tolerated.
3. Schedule initial interviews with clients at times when other staff are present. Workers should never be alone in the office or building with clients who are identified as potentially violent.
4. Have strategies in place for summoning immediate help from other staff—such as cell phones or panic buttons.
5. Plan how the agency will respond to agitated clients—including when and how police should be called, and how other staff are expected to respond.
6. Role-play and rehearse what staff will say and do when clients are verbally combative and/or physically combative.
7. Keep each other informed of potentially violent clients.
8. Keep waiting time to a minimum. Clients waiting for service should be treated in a respectful, courteous manner, and given an approximate estimate of the length of time they will have to wait.

Home Visits

Specific safety precautions need to be tailored to the individual situation. However, the following are some safety guidelines for home visits.

If possible, have clients come to the office, where safety is more easily achieved. If the meeting cannot be held in the office, try to hold it in some other public place, such as a library or restaurant.

If the visit must be held in the home, arrange for two workers (or a worker and a supervisor) to attend. If the potential for violence is especially high, (as in helping a woman at a battered women's shelter retrieve belongings from home when the batterer is present), arrange for a police officer to accompany you.

Obtain as much information as possible on your clients, prior to home visits. Review the file for evidence of a history of violence, and for risk factors (such as alcohol or other drug abuse). Determine whether others in the household present a risk. Also, find out whether there is an aggressive dog in the home or yard.

At the beginning of the visit, note exit routes. Wear shoes that facilitate a rapid exit. Don't wear expensive jewelry and clothes in deteriorating neighborhoods. Not only do such items underscore that you are from a different socioeconomic class and thus unlikely to relate to the client's circumstances, they also tempt muggers and others in the neighborhood. Wear professional attire that presents you as a nonthreatening person. Make certain your agency knows your itinerary and location. Have a staff "partner"—you know their location and approximate departure times, and they know yours. Carry a cell phone and have it on. (Workers should also call the agency if they anticipate being late.) Cellular phones should be programmed with agency and emergency numbers for quick dialing.

Present yourself as a confident, assertive person. Timid or aggressive behavior can elicit aggressive responses. If other people are present and appear threatening near your destination, you may choose to return another time or day—and perhaps take another staff member along.

Park your vehicle in a place that allows for a quick escape. If a noisy argument is occurring at your destination, consider returning at another time.

As you enter a house, do a quick visual scan looking for signs of danger, such as weapons or drugs. Be watchful of *all* persons in the home. Ask who else besides your client is at home. If there are signs of danger, promptly and politely postpone the visit, saying something like, "I'm sorry, you're going to have to excuse me. I just remembered I'm supposed to be at another meeting. I'll call you this afternoon to arrange another time when we can meet." It's best, at least at first, to stay near the entrance door, in case a quick exit is needed. The bottom line when conducting a home visit—*remain calm*. "Calm" helps you generate and assess your options. And always trust your "gut feelings." If it feels dangerous, it probably is.

Burnout

Ron Pakenham is ten days behind in his paperwork. He has been a juvenile probation and parole officer for the past 3½ years. Both his agency director and the juvenile judge are pressuring him to do his paperwork. Mr. Pakenham also has problems at home. His mother has emphysema, and he and his wife are going through a divorce. While working on his paperwork, he receives a call from a houseparent at a group home for adolescent youths, inquiring when high school is starting in fall. (Mr. Pakenham supervises two teenage boys at this home.) Mr. Pakenham replies, "Hey, I don't know. You'll have to call the school system. I'm not your errand boy. Don't you know I have more important things to do than to hunt information for you?" Moments later, Mr. Pakenham regrets his response. Pondering his family problems and his mountain of paperwork, Mr. Pakenham realizes he is nearing burnout.

Definitions and Symptoms of Burnout

Burnout is a serious problem for helping professionals. Pines and Aronson (1981) defined burnout as being

> a state of mind . . . accompanied by an array of symptoms that indicate a general malaise: emotional, physical, and psychological fatigue; feelings of helplessness, hopelessness, and a lack of enthusiasm about work and even about life in general. (p. 3)

Maslach and Pines (1977) studied burnout extensively among social workers, psychiatrists, psychologists, prison personnel, psychiatric nurses, legal aid attorneys, physicians, child care workers, teachers, ministers, and counselors. They summarized a number of symptoms:

> Burnout involves the loss of concern for the people with whom one is working. In addition to physical exhaustion (and sometimes even illness), burnout is characterized by an emotional exhaustion in which the professional no longer has any positive feelings, sympathy, or respect for clients or patients. A very cynical and dehumanized perception of these people often develops, in which they are labeled in derogatory ways and treated accordingly. As a result of this dehumanizing process, these people are viewed as somehow deserving of their problems and are blamed for their own victimization, and thus there is a deterioration of the quality of care or service that they receive. The professional who burns out is unable to deal successfully with the

> overwhelming emotional stresses of the job, and this failure to cope can be manifested in a number of ways, ranging from impaired performance and absenteeism to various types of personal problems (such as alcohol and drug abuse, marital conflict, and mental illness). People who burn out often quit their jobs or even change professions, while some seek psychiatric treatment for what they believe to be their personal failings. (pp. 100–101)

Freudenberger (1977) described burnout as follows:

> Briefly described, burnout includes such symptoms as cynicism and negativism and a tendency to be inflexible and almost rigid in thinking, which often leads to a closed mind about change or innovation. The worker may begin to discuss the client in intellectual and jargon terms and thereby distance himself from any emotional involvement. Along with this, a form of paranoia may set in whereby the worker feels that his peers and administration are out to make life more difficult. (pp. 90–91)

Burnout Is a Reaction to High Stress

We don't always differentiate burnout from *alienated, indifferent, apathetic, cynical, discouraged, mentally or physically exhausted,* and *overwhelmed by stress.* To better understand the nature of burnout, it is useful to conceptualize it as one reaction to high levels of stress. This suggests that stress management strategies can be used to prevent and treat burnout.

Stress is a contributing factor in most illnesses, including heart attacks, migraine headaches, diabetes, allergies, colds, cancer, arthritis, insomnia, emphysema, hypertension, and alcoholism (Seaward, 1994). It is also a contributing factor in numerous emotional and behavioral difficulties, including depression, anxiety, suicide attempts, spouse abuse, child abuse, physical assaults, irritability, and stuttering (Seaward, 1994). Becoming skillful in reducing stress is an effective way to prevent emotional and physical disorders, and it is also an effective adjunct to treatment for emotional and physical disorders (Seaward, 1994).

Stress can be defined as our emotional and physiological reaction to stressors. A stressor is a demand, situation, or circumstance that disrupts our equilibrium and initiates the stress response. Possible stressors include crowding, noise, death of a friend, excessive cold, loss of a job, toxic substances, arguments—the list is infinite.

Hans Selye (1956), one of the first authorities on stress, found that we have a three-stage reaction to stress: the alarm stage, the resistance stage, and the exhaustion stage. Selye called this three-stage response the General Adaptation Syndrome.

In the alarm stage our body recognizes the stressor, such as an argument, then reacts to it by preparing to fight or flee. Our physiological reactions are complex and numerous and will be summarized only briefly here (for an extended discussion, see Seaward, 1994). The body sends messages from the brain (hypothalamus) to the pituitary gland to release its hormones. These hormones trigger the adrenal glands to release adrenaline. Adrenaline increases the rate of breathing and heartbeat, increases perspiration, raises blood sugar level, dilates the pupils, and slows digestion. This results in a huge burst of energy, better hearing and vision, and greater muscular strength—all reactions that increase our capacity to cope with the situation. During the alarm stage the body's immune system functions at a sharply reduced level. (The immune system fights germs, bacteria, and viruses, and facilitates healing within the body.)

In stage 2, resistance, the body becomes relaxed. When relaxed, our immune system functions at its optimal capacities. During this stage the body (and the immune system) repairs any damage caused during the alarm stage. Most stressors cause the body to go through only the stages of alarm and resistance. During our lifetimes we go through these two stages innumerable times.

Note that stress can be beneficial. It increases concentration and enhances our capacities to accomplish physical tasks. A life without stress is, well, boring and may even be impossible—even dreaming produces some stress.

Stress that causes long-term damage results when the body remains in a stage of high stress for an extended period. When this happens, the body is unable to repair the damage and eventually the third stage, exhaustion, occurs. Exhaustion is characterized by the development of one or more stress-related illnesses, such as ulcers, hypertension, or arthritis.

A number of authorities on stress note two components in stressors: the events or experiences encountered and our thoughts and perceptions about these events. This conceptualization of stressors, stress, and stress-related illnesses (Exhibit 14.3), suggests two general approaches for reducing stress: Change the distressing events or change your thoughts and perceptions about the events.

As noted earlier, burnout is one reaction to high stress levels (see Exhibit 14.4 on page 336). Burnout is

EXHIBIT 14.3

Conceptualizing stressors, stress, and stress-related illnesses

Stressor
- Events or experiences (for example, backing into another car in a parking lot)
  ↓
- Certain kinds of thinking ("What have I done! I'm going to get a ticket and maybe even get kicked out of my insurance company. What a hassle this is going to be!")

↓

Stress
- Emotional reaction (tenseness, anxiety, worry, alarm)
  ↓
- Physiological reactions (alarm stage of General Adaptation Syndrome)
  The body prepares for fight or flight. Adrenaline and other hormones increase heartbeat and rate of breathing, increase perspiration, raise blood sugar levels, dilate the pupils, and slow digestion. The process results in greater muscular strength, a huge burst of energy, and better vision and hearing. The body's immune system functions at a sharply reduced level.

↓

Stress-related illness
- If the body remains at a high level of stress for a prolonged period, stress-related disorders such as ulcers, insomnia, or heart or digestive problems develop.

caused primarily by what we tell ourselves about events or experiences. "I've had it." "What's the use, whatever I try won't work." "I'm going to give up—am no longer going to make an effort." Avoiding these self-defeating thoughts reduces burnout.

Structural Causes of Stress That May Lead to Burnout

Because burnout is one possible reaction to, or consequence of, high stress levels, it therefore follows that events (structural factors) that contribute to high stress levels also contribute to burnout. Edelwich (1980) identified structural factors associated with work that contribute to high stress levels and lead to burnout:

- Too many work hours
- Career dead end
- Too much paperwork
- Insufficient training
- Not appreciated by clients
- Not appreciated by supervisor
- Not paid enough money
- No support for important decisions
- Powerlessness
- System not responsive to clients' needs
- Bad office politics
- Sexism
- Too much travel
- Isolation from peers
- No social life

Edelwich added that people who seek careers in the helping professions are particularly vulnerable to burnout because many enter this field with unrealistic expectations. Such expectations include the beliefs that (1) the services they provide will decisively improve the lives of practically all their clients; (2) they will be highly appreciated by the employing agency and practically all clients; (3) they will be able to substantially change bureaucracies to be more responsive to clients' needs; and (4) there will be many opportunities for rapid advancement and high status. The frustrations experienced at work and the gradual recognition that many of these expectations are unrealistic are contributing factors to stress and to burnout.

Maslach (1976) found that high caseloads in the helping professions are a major cause of stress and burnout:

> Burnout often becomes inevitable when the professional is forced to provide care for too many people. As the ratio increases, the result is higher and higher emotional overload until, like a wire that has too much electricity flowing through it, the worker just burns out and emotionally disconnects. (p. 19)

A lack of approved *time-outs* at work is another source of stress and may be a factor in burnout. Time-outs

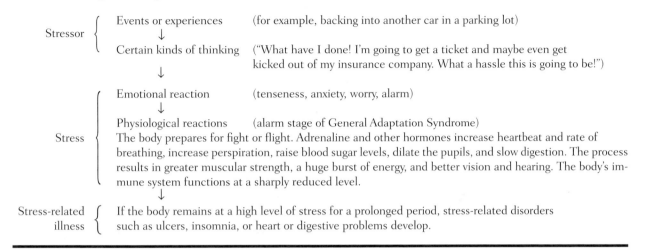

EXHIBIT 14.4

Burnout is a reaction to high levels of stress

Stressors	Events or experiences	(for example, extensive paperwork or considerable turmoil in family life)
	↓	
	Certain kinds of stressful thinking that leads to Burnout	(for example, "This is overwhelming. I've had it. Just leave me alone. This is more than I can take!")
	↓	
Stress	Emotions	(the emotions identified with burnout—anxiety, frustration, anger, apathy, and so on)
	↓	
	Physiological reactions	(the alarm and exhaustion stages of the General Adaptation Syndrome)
	↓	
	Actions	(the actions characteristic of burnout; lack of respect for others; cynical toward life; less attention to work and family life; absenteeism, change of jobs, and so on)

These thinking processes, emotions, physiological reactions, and actions constitute BURNOUT.

are not merely short coffee breaks from work; they are opportunities for professionals having a stressful day to switch to less stressful tasks. Time-outs are possible in large agencies that have shared work responsibilities.

Additional causes of burnout include poor time management, inability to work effectively with other people, lack of purpose or undefined goals in life, and inability to handle effectively emergencies that arise (Pines & Aronson, 1981).

Clients can add to staff burnout (Maslach, 1978). Some clients cause high levels of stress, particularly those with depressing or emotionally draining problems (such as terminally ill clients, belligerent clients, suicidal clients, obnoxious clients, incest cases, and severe abuse cases). Chronic clients who show no improvement (such as an alcoholic family in which the problem drinker denies a drinking problem) can lead to frustration and high stress levels for workers. So can clients who remind workers of personal difficulties they presently face, such as providing marriage counseling services when workers are having marital difficulties at home. Extensive home responsibilities, such as taking care of a terminally ill parent, can also drain energy needed at home and at work.

Taking "ownership" of clients' problems contributes to burnout. When a client tells you his or her innermost secrets and problems, you may want to rescue that person. Helping professionals, especially in their early years of practice, often fall victim to the "white knight" fantasy. You cannot slay your client's dragons. They must slay their own dragons. Remember, we are called helping professionals, *not* rescuing professionals!

Approaches to Manage Stress and Prevent Burnout

OK, you ask, so what can I do to avoid burnout? Lots of things, it turns out. What follows is a small sampling of strategies. The key is to select strategies you will be most motivated to use. These strategies parallel healthy diet plans—they work for those who put forth effort to make them work. (The references provide expanded reading of these strategies.)

Goal Setting and Time Management

Not knowing what you want out of life is distressing and even depressing. Many people muddle through life without ever setting goals. The result? Frustration and boredom. (Boredom, by the way, is highly stressful.) The solution? Realistic goal setting. What do you get? Increased self-confidence, improved decision making, a greater sense of purpose, and an improved sense of security. Do you set goals, or do you muddle?

Time is life; and to waste time is to waste life. Managing your time well is empowering.

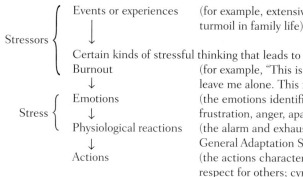

Time management approaches help you set goals and use your time effectively to reach short-term and lifetime goals. Time management has users first set lifetime and short-term goals (Lakein, 1973). (Admittedly this can be a lengthy process. But failure to set goals almost guarantees feeling unfulfilled and dissatisfied.) For high-priority goals (both short-term and lifetime goals), write down tasks that will help you accomplish these goals. Then prioritize tasks according to what is most important to do to accomplish each goal. Do the high-priority tasks first and—generally—ignore doing the low-priority (low payoff) tasks. Low-priority tasks bog down your time and interfere with high-priority tasks.

Positive Thinking

Is your cup half full or half empty? You and you alone choose how you view your "cup of life." Negative self-talk ("I've had it. I'm no longer going to try. I'm just going to go through the motions. I'm giving in.") becomes self-fulfilling.

Choose positive thinking. Taking a positive view and positive action not only leads to others' liking you, you will also feel worthwhile, you will like yourself, you will be productive and creative, and good things will happen. (Positive thinking is discussed more fully later in this chapter.)

Travel through life at a "relaxed cruising speed." Look at the scenery with enjoyment, remain calm during crises and emergencies, approach work thoughtfully and strive to be creative, and enjoy your leisure.

Changing "Burnout Thoughts"

Rational therapy (Module 6) demonstrates that what we tell ourselves about our experiences causes our emotions and shapes future actions. Burnout is thus primarily determined by our thinking processes.

Although we cannot change events that happen to us, we can think rationally and positively about the events. Challenge your "burnout thoughts." "I am *not* going to give up. I've handled challenges in the past, and I can handle this one. One step at a time, that's what I have to do. When the going gets tough, I get going."

Keys to changing "burnout thoughts": (1) Recognize when you are thinking them. (2) Select positive thoughts that challenge burnout ones. And (3) every time you start thinking burnout thoughts, replace them with positive thoughts.

Relaxation Techniques

Burnout doesn't happen in a day. But it does happen one day at a time. The days accumulate, and bingo, you're in burnout. So you challenge burnout one day at a time. How? By taking the time to relax. The relaxation response is a powerful challenge to burnout. Use it. You have many techniques to choose from: deep-breathing relaxation, imagery relaxation, progressive muscle relaxation, meditation, self-hypnosis, and biofeedback. (See Module 9.)

Exercise

Regular exercise reduces stress (period). Choose an exercise program that you enjoy (be it softball or belly-dancing). Not only will you get fit (which of course we feel good about) you will also have increased energy to meet crises and emergencies. Negative aspects of your job and home life won't seem so bad. Exercising uses up fuel, reduces heart rate and blood pressure, and sets off numerous physiological changes that reduce stress and induce the relaxation response (Seaward, 1994).

And don't forget to eat properly, get sufficient sleep, and get appropriate medical care.

Outside Activities

Have a life. Family and friends, church and meditation, hobbies and travel, fun—find the mixture that makes you healthy. These are your antidotes to stress and burnout and the source of your inner strengths.

Reward yourself for tasks done well. We don't hesitate to compliment others for jobs done well; don't forget to take pride in your own work well done and a life well lived. Take a mental health day. In periods of extended stress, take a day off and do only the things you want to do. (Some agencies now allow a certain number of mental health days with pay.) You will return to work more effective and ready to charge.

Social Support Systems

Develop trusting and mutually caring relationships at work. We all need a "lifeline." Maslach (1976) noted:

> Our findings show that burnout rates are lower for those professionals who actively express, analyze and share their personal feelings with their colleagues. Not only do they consciously get things off their chest, but they have an opportunity to receive constructive feedback from other people and to develop new perspectives of their relationship with patients/clients. This process is greatly enhanced if the institution sets up some social outlets such as support groups, special staff meetings or workshops. (p. 19)

Social support groups (at work or outside work) let us let our hair down, help us "kid around," share our lives, keep in touch, and give us a source of security that helps when crises arise. Support groups have several essential features: (1) the group meets regularly, (2) the same people attend, (3) a feeling of closeness has developed, and (4) there is an opportunity for spontaneity and informality (Greenberg, 1980). Possible support groups come in many "shapes and sizes": co-workers, friends, sport or hobby groups, family, church groups, and community organizations such as Parents Without Partners.

Variety at Work

No doubt about it—doing the same thing day in and day out becomes exhausting. The simple fact is, emotionally draining work (like suicide counseling or hospice work) can be done only for limited periods, or burnout will rear its ugly head. Therefore, it is important to structure your practice so that you have a variety of job tasks during the week. "Variety is the spice of life." Also, participating in workshops, conferences, continuing education courses, and in-service training programs adds variety and helps you grow professionally.

Humor

We cannot say enough about laughter as a coping mechanism. Humor relaxes us, makes work more enjoyable, and "takes the edge off." Humor at work and at home relieves stress and helps prevent burnout.

Distressing Events

Bad things happen—to us, to friends and family we care about, and to clients we care about. Competent people lose their jobs, friends die, romantic relationships end, we question our faith, the list is endless.

When distressing events arise, what can you do? Actually, many things. It is important to confront events head-on to attempt to improve the situation. Power is always better than helplessness. For example, if you feel beginning burnout, identify what is frustrating and exhausting you at work and then develop new approaches for handling these responsibilities. One worker finds incest cases particularly exhausting, whereas another finds working with the terminally ill more draining—consider exchanging these cases. If you are frustrated because program objectives and job expectations are unclear, get clarification from your supervisor.

Many distressing events get less distressing when we confront them head-on and take positive action. Not all events or situations can be changed. For example, you may not be able to change certain distasteful aspects of your job. In such situations, the only constructive remaining alternative is to "bite the bullet" and accept them. It is counterproductive to spend time complaining about a situation you cannot change.

Enjoying Social Work and Your Life

To gather material to write this section, I asked friends who have practiced social work for several years to summarize their satisfactions and frustrations about pursuing a career in social work. Here is one reply.

> It is difficult to find the right words to describe my satisfaction with having made a decision to be a social worker. I have worked in a protective services unit of a public welfare department for two years, as a probation and parole officer for three years, and now am a director of a group home for teenage males who have conflicts with their parents.
>
> One of the satisfying aspects of social work is that there are a wide variety of areas where a person can work. When I found myself becoming stale as a probation officer, it was inspiring to look forward to moving on to something else. If this job becomes routine and no longer something I would look forward to doing, I would again move on to some other social work position.
>
> I truly find it gratifying to work with people. If you don't like working with people, then certainly this is the wrong job to have. I know this sounds "naive," but when I feel I've been of some help in assisting someone to better handle a personal or social problem, it really makes me feel good. It should be noted I'm no longer as idealistic as I was when I was going to college and thought I would be able to help the vast majority of my clients. I've learned that most clients simply aren't sufficiently motivated to put forth the time and effort needed to improve their lives—it's like exercising; we all know exercising will improve our health and keep us trim, but only a few people are willing to put forth the time and effort.
>
> Social work is a challenging profession. Every client's problem is unique. For that matter every client's personality is unique. Interacting with new people, and developing somewhat different treatment strategies with each client is a challenge. Through helping clients I also grow as a person and learn more about myself. Also challenging, and often learning experiences, are speaking to groups in the community, and seeking to develop new services when a need arises. Also educational (and a way of seeing old friends) are in-service training sessions that are held at the agencies I've worked at.
>
> I don't want to give an ever-glowing picture of social work. There are also frustrations. At every agency there seem to be occasional personality conflicts between staff. (Such conflicts are furthered by staff members being pitted against each other for merit increases, for desired task assignments, and for who will get to go to conferences.)
>
> Another frustration is the amount of paperwork. At the three agencies I've worked at, 10 to 15 hours per week are spent on paperwork.

Some social workers complain this profession doesn't pay enough. I've found that in social work there are some jobs that pay a lot more than others. When I first started out, my annual salary was pretty low, but now that I'm a director of this group home I have no complaints.

Another thing that is frustrating is being aware that there are a few workers who are cynical, who always look at the negative side of things, and who really appear to be only interested in drawing their paycheck, rather than helping people. With their negative attitude, I frankly don't see how they can ever help anyone. If I was a client of theirs, I would become even more discouraged and apathetic. To me, these social workers are "deadwood" and are on "welfare" themselves as they are drawing a check without doing anything productive. These people either burned out years ago or were never "encouraging" persons who were motivated to help others.

All in all I really am delighted I chose a career in social work. I enjoy working with most clients (certainly not all of my clients as some I do find obnoxious) and with most of the other staff. I hope this information will be useful to you, and if you ever want someone to speak in your classes, give me a "jingle."

Become a Positive Thinker

One factor identified by this social worker is the importance of being an "encouraging" person. Chapter 5 noted this as a crucial characteristic of effective counselors. Closely related to this is positive thinking, which is not only important in working with clients but also in enjoying life.

In *A Treasury of Success Unlimited,* W. Clement Stone (1966) presented some of the basic principles of positive thinking:

> Your most precious, valued possessions and your greatest powers are invisible and intangible. No one can take them. You, and you alone, can give them. You will receive abundance for your giving. The more you give—the more you will have!
>
> Give a smile to everyone you meet (smile with your eyes)—and you'll smile and receive smiles. . . .
> Give a kind word (with a kindly thought behind the word)—you will be kind and receive kind words. . . .
> Give appreciation (warmth from the heart)—you will appreciate and be appreciated. . . .
> Give honor, credit and applause (the victor's wreath)—you will be honorable and receive credit and applause. . . .
> Give time for a worthy cause (with eagerness)—you will be worthy and richly rewarded. . . .
> Give hope (the magic ingredient for success)—you will have hope and be made hopeful. . . .
> Give happiness (a most treasured state of mind)—you will be happy and be made happy. . . .
> Give encouragement (the incentive to action)—you will have courage and be encouraged. . . .
> Give cheer (the verbal sunshine)—you'll be cheerful and cheered. . . .
> Give a pleasant response (the neutralizer of irritants)—you will be pleasant and receive pleasant responses. . . .
> Give good thoughts (nature's character builder)—you will be good and the world will have good thoughts for you. . . . (pp. 9–10)

Few living Americans can write or speak on the power of positive thinking with more authority than W. Clement Stone. Beginning as a newsboy on the streets of Chicago, Mr. Stone applied the principles of positive thinking to amass, and share with others, a fortune that is in excess of $160 million (Mandino, 1966).

Harold Sherman (1966), in "The Surest Way in the World to Attract Success—or Failure," further elaborated on positive thinking:

> "You might know this would happen to me!" Is this a comment you have made, not once, but many times, when things have gone wrong? . . . Certainly—you *knew* it was going to happen—and it did. Your *faith* in "things going wrong" caused the "power of TNT" [thinking negative thoughts] within you to work *against* you instead of for you. There is a great law of mind by which your thinking and your conduct should always be guided: "Like attracts like."
>
> Think good thoughts; you will eventually attract good things. Think bad thoughts, you will ultimately attract bad things.
>
> Simple—easy to remember—but also easy to forget. . . .
>
> Get this point clearly in mind: *you* supply the material (by the nature of your thoughts) out of which your creative power builds your future. If the material is inferior, comprised of mental pictures of failure, despair, defeat and the like, you can readily see that only unhappy results can be materialized from them. . . .
>
> Whatever conditions you are facing at the moment are the result of your past thinking—good and bad. These conditions cannot change until you have first changed your thinking. . . .
>
> Things first happen in your mind before they can happen in this outer world. What are you picturing? Do you want it to happen? If not, you are the only one who can prevent it. Your future success or failure is in your hands—where it should be. (pp. 111–113)

Numerous books have been written on positive thinking philosophy (*Looking Out for No. 1,* by Robert Ringer, 1977; *Move Ahead with Possibility Thinking,* by Robert Schuller, 1973; *Positive Thinking Everyday,* by

Norman Vincent Peale, 1993; and *Positive Thinking*, by Vera Pfeiffer, 1993, to name but a few). Positive thinking certainly has considerable merit. However, there is a potential danger. Every accomplishment requires certain abilities. For those who set goals above their capacities, positive thinking creates a false sense of hope. When people (particularly those suffering from emotional problems like anxiety or depression), fail to achieve unrealistic goals, they are headed for a downturn. Authorities now suggest replacing *positive thinking* with *optimal thinking* to avoid the pitfall noted above. In optimal thinking we look for all *realistic* options for a situation. Then we assess the merits and shortcomings of those options, and finally, we select the option that appears to be most constructive. (The optimal thinking approach utilizes the principles of the problem-solving process described in Chapter 1.)

Positive thinking usually gets people started on a project. Many people don't realize their own potential, and a bright outlook and positive action helps them achieve their goals. It is your choice. You can think and act negatively about events that happen to you, or you can think and act positively about those same events. Positive thinking helps you enjoy your career and your life.

Develop an Identity[1]

What kind of a person are you? What do you want out of life? What kind of person do you want to be? These questions are among the most important ones you will ever face. Without answers, you are prepared to make major life decisions. Unfortunately, many people muddle through life and never contemplate these questions. Those who don't have a clue about these questions may find themselves depressed, indecisive, anxious, and unfulfilled. All too often, their lives are carbon copies of Stan Sinclair's.

At age 18, Stan graduated from high school. Unable to find a job, he enlisted in the army for a three-year hitch. At 20, he started dating Julia Johnson while he was stationed in Illinois. He liked Julia. She became pregnant, and they decided to get married. Money was tight, and Julia wanted to live near her relatives. Two months after his discharge, Stan became a father. Needing a job in the area, he became a gas station attendant because it was the only employment he could find. Two and one-half years later, an opening occurred in an auto assembly plant. The pay was better, so Stan applied and was hired. The job was relatively easy but monotonous. Stan faithfully attached mufflers to new cars, over and over for 40 hours a week. During the next eight years, Stan and Julia had three more children. The pay and fringe benefits, combined with his family and financial responsibilities, locked Stan into this assembly line job until he retired at age 65. The morning after he retired, he looked into the mirror and began asking, finally, the key questions. Was it all worth it? Why did he feel empty and unfulfilled? What did he want out of the future? Never having in the past figured out what he wanted out of life, his only answer was a frown.

Identity is our sense of who we are, a knowledge and a feeling of the ways in which we are separate, distinct persons.

Identity Development

Identity development is a lifelong process, and our identity changes throughout our lifetime. During the early years our sense of who we are is largely determined by the reactions of others. A long time ago Cooley (1902) suggested that this labeling process results in the *looking-glass self;* that is, people who experience their self-concept in terms of their perceptions of how others relate to them. For example, if a neighborhood identifies a male youth as a "troublemaker" (a delinquent), the neighbors will not trust him, may accuse him of delinquent acts, and will label his semi-delinquent and aggressive behaviors as *delinquent*. The youth begins to realize that this label gives him prestige and status, at least from his peers. In the absence of objective ways to gauge whether he is, in fact, a delinquent, the youth will rely on the subjective evaluations of others. Thus, gradually, as people relate to him as a delinquent, he begins to perceive himself in that way and begins to become a delinquent in earnest.

Fortunately, identity development is a lifetime process, and positive changes are possible even for those with negative self-concepts. In identity formation, a key principle to remember is that although we cannot change the past, what we want out of the future, along with our motivation to achieve what we want, is more important (than our past experiences) in determining our future.

[1]This section is adapted from Charles Zastro, "Who Am I? The Quest for Identity," in *The Personal Problem Solver,* edited by Charles Zastrow and Dae H. Chang, © 1977, pp. 365–370. Adapted by permission of Prentice-Hall, Inc., Englewood Cliffs, New Jersey.

How to Determine Who You Are

Forming an identity involves thinking about, and arriving at, answers to these questions: (1) What do I want out of life? (2) What kind of person am I? (3) What kind of person do I want to be?

The most important decisions you make in your life may well depend on your answers to these questions.

This is not to say these questions are easy to answer. They require considerable contemplation and trial and error. But if you are to lead a gratifying, fulfilling life, it is imperative to find a direction in order to live the kind of life you find meaningful.

So, here are some questions to consider:

1. What is satisfying/meaningful/enjoyable to me? (Only after you know this will you be able to consciously seek activities that make your life fulfilling, and avoid those activities that are meaningless or stifling.)
2. What is my moral code? (One possible code is to seek to fulfill your needs and to do what you find enjoyable, doing so in a way that does not deprive others of the ability to fulfill their needs.)
3. What are my religious beliefs?
4. What kind of a career do I want? (Ideally, you should choose work that you find stimulating and satisfying, that you are skilled at, and that earns you enough money to support the lifestyle you want.)
5. What are my sexual mores? (Find a code that you are comfortable with and that helps you meet your needs without exploiting others. There is no one right code—what works for one may not work for another because of differences in lifestyles, life goals, and personal values.)
6. Do I want to marry? (If yes, to what type of person and when; how consistent are your answers here with your other life goals?)
7. Do I want to have children? (If yes, how many, when, and how consistent are your answers here with your other life goals?)
8. What area of the country/world do I want to live in? (Climate, geography, type of dwelling, rural or urban setting, closeness to relatives or friends, and characteristics of the neighborhood.)
9. What do I enjoy doing with my leisure time?
10. What kind of image do I want to project to others? (Your image will be composed of your dressing style and grooming habits, your emotions, personality, degree of assertiveness, capacity to communicate, material possessions, moral code, physical features, and voice patterns. You need to assess your strengths and shortcomings honestly in this area and seek to make improvements.)
11. What type of people do I enjoy being with and why?
12. Do I desire to improve the quality of my life and that of others? (If yes, in what ways, and how do you hope to achieve these goals?)
13. What types of relationships do I want to have with relatives, friends, neighbors, with people I meet for the first time?
14. What are my thoughts about death and dying?
15. What do I hope to be doing 5 years from now? 10 years? 20 years?
16. How can I achieve the goals that I identified above?

To have a well-developed sense of identity, you will at some time need answers to most, but not all, of these questions. Very few of us arrive at rational, consistent answers to all the questions. But having at least contemplated these questions will provide a reference for you as you embark on life after college.

Note that these questions are simple to state, but arriving at answers is a complicated, ongoing process. In addition, expect some changes in your life goals as time goes on. Your circumstances will change in unexpected ways. Activities and friends you enjoy in the future may not be what you enjoy now. Be flexible as life throws you curves. Rigid adherence to a certain path is a sure prescription for failure.

Use Rational Challenges to Develop a Success Identity

Some people muddle through without a clear sense of what they want or who they are, but others wallow in self-pity, seeing themselves as failures. In another publication (Zastrow, 1979) I compared people who have a success identity with those who have a failure identity:

> Success identities are characterized by the following kinds of self-talk. "I have accomplished many of the things I have tried in the past." "I am a competent, worthwhile person." "I, similar to other people, have certain special talents." "Trying something new is challenging and stimulating." "I look forward to trying something more complicated that has the opportunity for substantial payoffs, and which will test and further develop my special talents." "Trying new things helps me grow as a person, and helps provide meaning to living." "I look forward to each new day with its opportunities for involvement in activities that will be gratifying and fulfilling."

CASE EXAMPLE

Developing a Positive Self-Concept

Since her early teenage years Sarah had viewed herself as a failure.[2] Her sense of being a failure was temporarily alleviated during her junior and senior years in high school, when she steadily dated and became overly dependent on Tom. However, her failure concept returned shortly after Tom left to attend the Air Force Academy. In this case example Sarah describes her deep sense of being a failure and how she used rational self-challenges to develop a more positive self-concept.

An excerpt from Sarah's journal:

Breakfast at the airport appeared cheerful enough. His parents, full of optimistic talk of his future, kept the conversation light and promising. And I, my real feelings hidden by a facade of carefully planned cheerfulness, made attempts at bright small talk, which seemed to add to the somehow phony color and splendor of the day.

At that point, after all of the months of waiting and preparation, all was ready. Every last detail had been checked, and it was time. Tom was ready to embark on a new and challenging lifestyle—without me!

Later, as I recall that first painful goodbye, our words edged with emotion, full of promises for the future, and yet our every thought charged with the upcoming agony of being apart from one another, I do not once remember thinking of how I was going to adjust to his absence. Tom was the most significant person in my life to that date, and yet I had not realized the powerful effect our new "separateness" would take in relation to my life from there on.

The sequence(s) of events and emotions that followed seemed to me to be normal or what I thought as being normal reactions for a person to feel when a loved one is away for a prolonged period of time. That is when I began my "Poor Me" syndrome!

It was summer, and I was very lonely and didn't have enough to keep me busy. I worked at a local restaurant as much as I possibly could to pass the time, but it didn't seem to be enough—I still had those lonely nights to myself.

"Poor me," I'd say to myself. "I'm alone and no one cares enough to spend time with me, I must be worthless, boring, etc." This became repetitious with me to the point that whenever I felt a bit depressed I would reinforce those feelings with other intense feelings of worthlessness. I could really bring myself down, you see, because I truly felt that I could never be happy, feel my personal worth, expand myself unless Tom was with me. I guess that was a rather natural feeling for me to have because while he was home I allowed myself to be dependent upon him to fill my every need and whim. And gladly he filled them. Call it "ego" or whatever, but it somehow filled a need in him to have me need him so desperately. It seemed to be a very workable arrangement while he was home with me. My belief was that we were "in love" and it was a very positive point to "need" someone I loved. What I hadn't considered was how my dependency upon him was, in fact, setting me up for a lifetime of unhappiness. Time progressed, and I felt myself more and more alone. I walled myself off from my "helpful friends," people who did in fact care for me and who wanted to include me in their activities. I did join them on occasion, but generally if I did, I'd begin to feel sorry for myself and bring out my tale of woe. Of course they listened, but one can listen to the same negative thoughts only so many times. I remember having feelings of bitterness and hostility toward these friends, people who had things going their way. I was jealous.

It seemed as though everything was going wrong. I began to drink more and to experience the effects of drugs. At times this seemed to be a haven for me, an escape from what seemed to be insurmountable problems.

I took an apartment with an acquaintance who was pregnant. (It created many problems.) I overextended myself financially, knowing full well that I was. I was enrolled in classes but had neither the motivation nor goal to attend all of them.

[2]Names and other identifying information in this case example have been changed.

All around I began to see myself as a failure. Whenever I'd receive a poor grade on a test, paper, or quiz, I'd tell myself that I was stupid. If it came time to pay the bills and I did not have the money, I'd tell myself that I was a failure at supporting myself. Then, to pay those same bills for which I spent the money on extravagances, I'd have to work doubly hard.

Well, eventually I became tired of feeling negative all the time. After all, if I could feel good about myself when I was with Tom, then somehow I should be able to feel good about myself at other times. I had to—either that, suicide, or stay miserable. Neither of the latter two sounded too appealing, so I decided to make the best of it and give myself a positive try. Many times, over tears on the telephone, I would explain to Tom my fears and anxieties and it would hurt him some, as he felt a bit responsible. He is a person whom I genuinely care for, and I began to have my doubts as to what I should and shouldn't tell him. After all, I really don't intend to make those I care for feel responsible for my feelings and actions. I'm responsible for myself.

Fortunately, it was at this point in my life that I enrolled in a course on counseling, which exposed me to the concepts of rational therapy, and I proceeded to write the following rational self-analysis (RSA) on my personal concerns.

A *Event*	*D*[1] *Camera Check*
In August my boyfriend left for the Air Force Academy. At his leave-taking the two of us promised to wait until the end of his education and then to marry. I had little confidence in myself as a person to begin with. When he left, I became less confident and began to discount myself as a person having no worth or value. As time progressed, I began to do poorly in several aspects of life: poor grades, too much financial responsibility (too many extravagances), poor organization of my life's plans (work or school, which has priority?), hostile attitude toward friends, etc. I generally felt worthless and sad because Tom left.	This is all factual.

B *Self-Talk*	*D*[2] *Rational Self-Challenges to the Self-Talk in Section B*
1. "I am able to be happy only if Tom is with me." (bad)	1. False. If I hope to be a self-sufficient and satisfied person in my lifetime, I know that I must do it alone—for myself. Others may make it easier for me, but essentially, I have to make myself happy.
2. "I'm dependent upon Tom in all ways if I allow his leaving to affect me this way." (bad)	2. True. But I'm not allowing myself my own rights as a person. I realize that I could never mold my life around another's wants and likes. I've got to have my own identity.

(continued)

CASE EXAMPLE
Positive Self-Concept
(continued)

B *Self-Talk*	*D²* *Rational Self-Challenges to the Self-Talk in Section B*
3. "I'm a failure in my studies." (bad)	3. False. I'm not a failure and never have been. At my lowest point, I still received C's for grades. I received those C's with a minimal amount of effort; so if I really tried, I could do better.
4. "I'm worthless." (bad)	4. False. Every person has some worth. I do too. At times when I'm depressed I may like to tell myself I'm worthless, but I really know that I'm not. Every human being has some worth. I'm as valuable as any other person, just because I'm human.
5. "My friends won't like me if I react to them in a hostile manner." (bad)	5. True. My friends don't like to spend time with me when I react to them in a negative, hostile way. It doesn't do much for the friendship, which was built of positive, mutual concern to begin with. I really don't like to treat them in this way, and from now on I will make a conscious effort to be more pleasant.
6. "I can't support myself sufficiently. I buy extravagant items." (bad)	6. False. In the past I've done quite well. It is when I take trips to visit Tom or buy a new wardrobe that I feel depleted financially. At other times I manage quite well, and even if I overextend myself—I still work to pay for my expenses.
7. "Because Tom has left me, all things go wrong in my life." (bad)	7. False. Things do not go wrong because Tom left me but because of circumstances or something I do to allow things to go wrong. Tom is away; there is no possible way he can control what happens to me here.
8. "The only thing I can look forward to is becoming Tom's wife and then I will hopefully feel better." (bad)	8. False. I intend to become a counselor if I really put forth an effort. If I do decide to become Tom's wife, that will be a major event to look forward to—a life together —but that is not all I'm looking forward to. For two and a half years I've struggled with college—certainly not for nothing!
9. "Tom is responsible for my feeling so rotten. It's all his fault!" (bad)	9. False. Tom is away and has no control over my life. He never did. In the past I felt the way I wanted to, did what I liked because that is the power that I have as a person. When Tom left, it was an unfortunate circumstance. I allowed myself to blame him for all the "wrongs" and unhappiness in my life when actually he had nothing to do with it. I'm the person living my life—choosing my own feelings, situations, etc., over which Tom has no control.

C *My Emotions*	E *Emotional and Behavioral Goals*
Depression, sadness, insecurity, inferiority, and loneliness. I had nine "bad" self-talk statements. That doesn't say much for my ability to adjust well to a given situation.	In the future I'd like to try to build my self-image so that I will be capable of accepting and utilizing change in my life in a positive way. A way in which I can do this is through my self-talk—what I tell myself about occurrences. The given (A) situation is a continuing occurrence—it happens at least once every summer. Having worked on the problem since September, I've begun to realize what I need to do in this situation to make myself happy. I need to see myself happy. I need to see myself as a strong, self-sufficient, happily functioning person—with a "separate" life and identity from Tom. These qualities (strength, independence, self-sufficiency) have been hidden in me for some time, and I've yet to cultivate them totally, but instead I'm working on them slowly. This, I expect, will make me a more satisfied person, and for others more pleasant and satisfying to be with.

(Sarah also wrote the following summary of the usefulness of this approach.)

I used rational therapy with the belief that I really did have the power to control my emotions and then, in turn, to control my life. I have always been a person of a negative nature—I had too much to say about all the "bads" and "wrongs" in my life that happened, and too little to say of the good.

I saw myself as a worthless, weak, submissive, and stupid person who really didn't matter in the course of this big world. There was one person who made me feel valuable, and when he left I allowed myself to feel useless again. This was followed by a succession of negative thoughts about myself, and fears.

A strong point of doing an RSA is what I found to be my ability to look at myself objectively on paper. What is written on paper looks factual and truthful. I found myself debating those facts and truths and actually finding out more of how I really felt inside. I had an outsider's view of myself on the objective side. This allowed me to weigh the pros and cons of my behavior, emotions, etc., and to take positive, realistic means to change what I didn't like.

Also doing a rational self-analysis on my emotional and behavioral problems helped me to become more rational and realistic in regard to living my everyday life. In a world that is so disproportionate in itself, I find it easy to stretch many aspects of my personal life out of proportion. A rational self-analysis doesn't allow me to do that. A person must face the facts, debate the thoughts underlying his dysfunctional behaviors and unwanted emotions, and determine what he chooses to feel from there on. A rational self-analysis allows only honesty and a willingness to change those feelings that one is not comfortable with. A person who does his rational self-analysis dishonestly will get nowhere.

(continued)

CASE EXAMPLE
Positive Self-Concept
(continued)

Ultimately, rational therapy taught me the power of control. A human person is a complex, highly intelligent organism. Then why should he not have the power of controlling what could turn out to be his own destiny in life?

An excerpt from Sarah's journal two years later:

Inside myself, I guess that I'm really satisfied with the person I'm becoming. Sure, it can be a long, hard struggle at times, and often frustrating, but it is a part of my life. That is how things become important and significant in life—through the living of such experiences. Sometimes I'm amazed when I think that I was born a person in my own right, with potential emotional growth, strength, and abilities, to become what I choose to become.

Source: This case example is reprinted from Charles Zastrow, *Talk to Yourself: Using the Power of Self-Talk,* © 1979, pp. 99–105. Reprinted by permission of Prentice-Hall, Inc., Englewood Cliffs, New Jersey.

Do you give yourself these types of positive self-talk, or do you give yourself the following negative kinds of self-talk, . . . characteristic of those with a "failure identity"?: "I can't accomplish anything I try." "I'm inferior to other people." "Why can't I be as competent, capable, or attractive as others?" "I'm a failure." "I can't afford to risk trying anything new as it will reveal my weaknesses to others." "I wish people would stop picking on me, and making cutting comments about my shortcomings." "I've got a number of personal problems that are overwhelming me, and draining my energy." "There just is no hope for a brighter tomorrow." "My problems are certainly more confusing and unresolvable than those that other people have." "Life is certainly the 'pits' and really not worth living." "I wish I was someone else." "I wonder why such and such hurt me so badly—I just can't stop thinking about it." "What did I do wrong to deserve all this misery?"

Such self-talk by people with failure orientations generates a variety of negative emotions, including excessive worry, fatigue, anxiety, boredom, depression, loneliness, and/or general feelings of misery. (pp. 92–93)

Merlin Manley (1977) also noted:

A sense of failure becomes a further problem since it limits the amount of risk-taking behavior in which we are willing to engage. If we feel that we are failures, we will feel threatened by any new behavior patterns that we perceive as risky. Accordingly, we will be very reluctant to try any such behaviors. This means that we will continue to operate as we have in the past, thereby creating somewhat of a "rut." To the degree that we follow this practice, we are precluded from growing psychologically or expanding our behavioral responses. We are stultifying ourselves from greater use of our potential and becoming a more complete individual. We learn and grow by our experiences. If we limit ourselves to only the "tried and true" modes of behavior, we are putting disabling constraints on ourselves and seriously limiting our growth potential. (p. 38)

To be an "encouraging" person as you work with clients and to feel good about yourself, it is essential that you have a positive, success self-concept. A very simple formula helps people who view themselves as failures improve their lives; they shift their thinking from focusing on negative items to focusing on positive items.

One way to change a failure identity into a success identity is to identify the failure self-talk, and then challenge this with rational self-talk (see Module 6 for how to write a rational self-analysis). A feeling of failure is an emotion similar to any other emotion. This feeling results mainly from negative self-talk, and this emotion can be changed by rational self-challenges.

Summary

To be of help to others, social workers must first take care of themselves. Good emotional and physical health are internal resources that social workers need to have to be of help to others. This chapter presents material on how to survive and enjoy social work and, in a broader sense, how to enjoy living.

Although social work students have a number of common concerns, often they are reluctant to share them with others. The following concerns are discussed, with suggestions given for resolving them: Will I be able to make it in field placement? Will I be able to handle my first interview with my first client? I'm really depressed because my supervisor is able to handle an interview much better than I—will I ever be able to do that well? How should I separate the role of counselor from that of friend? How can I avoid becoming too emotionally involved with clients' problems? Do I really want to pursue a career in social work?

Safety guidelines for social workers are presented. In the social work perspective, violence erupts in context, rather than residing within the "violent individual." Since the immediate environmental context is important, social workers are often able to use their skills to deter potentially violent behavior. Social workers need to be aware of the following signals of danger: environmental cues, client cues, and worker cues.

Most assaults follow a predictable pattern of five phases: triggering, escalation, crisis, recovery, and post-crisis depression.

A number of strategies to preventing violence are summarized. Techniques to deescalate verbal communication, and nonverbal communication are discussed. In some situations it is important for social workers to state acceptable limits for clients to express their discontent. Agencies need environmental safeguards (such as workers having cellular phones) and response systems to deter potential violence. Guidelines were presented to increase worker safety during home visits.

Burnout is a major problem encountered by helping professionals. The symptoms and causes of burnout are discussed and suggestions given for reducing stress and preventing burnout. Because burnout is one reaction to high levels of stress, it follows that stress management techniques are also useful in preventing burnout.

The chapter ends by providing tips on how to enjoy social work and life. The value of positive thinking is described. Also, the importance of developing a sense of who you are and what you want out of life is discussed, and suggestions are given for developing such an identity. Having a failure identity is contrasted with having a success identity, and a rational self-analysis is presented as one approach that is useful in challenging and changing a failure identity.

E X E R C I S E S

1. *COMMON CONCERNS OF SOCIAL WORK STUDENTS*

Goal: To become more comfortable with your concerns about field placement.

Step 1: On a note card or a sheet of paper, list a few concerns you have about field placement or about pursuing social work as a career. Do not sign your name. Turn these in at the end of class.

Step 2: Next class session: Class discussion of student concerns.

2. *REDUCING STRESS AND PREVENTING BURNOUT*

Goal: To practice reducing stress and burnout.

Step 1: On a separate sheet of paper, fill in the following blanks:

a. A few problematic situations that are presently causing high levels of stress in my life are __________.
b. My current ways of handling these high levels of stress are __________.
c. Ways in which I could better handle these situations and become more relaxed are __________.

Step 2: Form groups of three and share what you wrote. Brainstorm suggestions on how to handle the stress-producing situations and on how to relax. (*Note:* You can choose not to self-disclose.)

Step 3: Group presentation of their most promising solutions.

Step 4: Class discussion.

(continued)

EXERCISES
(continued)

3. *ESTABLISHING A SENSE OF IDENTITY*

Goal: To establish a better sense of self and to determine what you want out of life.

Step 1: Answer the 16 questions listed on page 341 on identity formation in this chapter.

Step 2: Form groups of three and share the questions you don't have answers to.

Step 3: Class questions and comments.

4. *SELF-FULFILLING PROPHECIES*

Goal: To understand how positive and negative thinking often become self-fulfilling prophecies.

Step 1: On a sheet of paper describe a situation in your own life (or that of someone you know well) in which positive thinking led to a self-fulfilling prophecy. Do the same for negative thinking.

Step 2: Class discussion of student experiences.

5. *ASSESSING RISKS OF VIOLENCE BY CLIENTS*

Goal: To practice assessing the risk of violence from clients.

Step 1: Break into groups of five. For each scenario, discuss (a) what risk factors are present, and (b) what precautionary measures should be taken.

SCENARIO 1: As a protective service worker, you are investigating a complaint of child abuse phoned in by a neighbor. The neighbor states the abuse has been recurrent. Arriving at the home of the alleged victim, you find a 5-year-old child, and she is crying. She has severe bruises on her arm and her forehead. The only adult at home is the father. He is intoxicated, and he acknowledges that he lost emotional control when his daughter continued to cry after he ordered her to stop. He indicates that he hit his daughter a few times "to shape her up." The more the father talks, the more agitated he becomes. The father further adds his wife is in another state, helping her mother move to a nursing home. You conclude that the child must be removed from the home immediately. As you make this removal, what risk factors are present and what precautionary measures should you take?

SCENARIO 2: You work at a shelter for battered women. A woman who has been physically abused by her husband over an 11-year period came to the shelter two nights ago with her three children. The woman asks you to go with her to her home to pick up clothes and other items that she and her children need. The woman is unsure whether her husband will be home. In going to this home, what risk factors of violence are present, and what precautionary measures should be taken?

SCENARIO 3: In your duties at a neighborhood center, you work with a juvenile gang. Your purpose is to curb their criminal activity. Several members of the gang are currently under supervision for illegal possession of weapons and for illegal drug possession. A member of the gang was shot and severely wounded about an hour ago. You discover the gang is currently meeting to discuss how to respond to the shooting. You decide you need to attend this meeting. What risk factors of violence are present, and what precautionary measures should you take?

SCENARIO 4: You are a social worker in a middle school where for the past several months two brothers have been "bullying" many of the other students. Their father is incarcerated. They live with their mother, who divorced the father a few years ago. The mother works full time, and is overwhelmed by the dual responsibilities of work and caring for two boys who are frequently in trouble. Both boys have committed several delinquent offenses, and are under juvenile court supervision. After the older boy assaults another student with a pocket knife, you advocate for the boy to be placed at a residential treatment facility, and he is. However, a few days later, the younger brother, age 11, walks into your office and states, "You'll be sorry you ever got involved in this," and then stomps out. What risk factors of violence are present, and what precautionary measures should you take?

Step 2: Group presentation of their strategies.

Step 3: Class discussion.

Counseling Theories Resource Manual (CTRM)

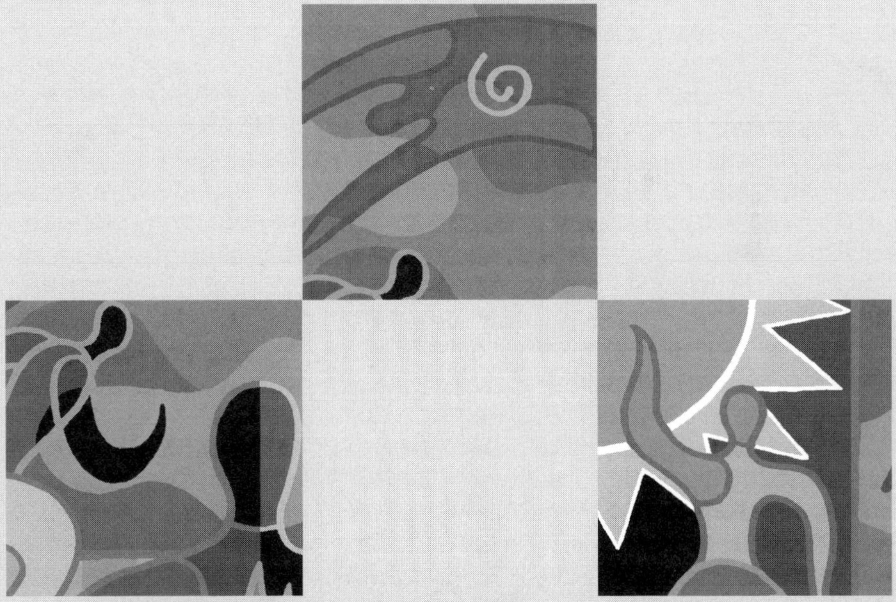

In this manual you will find the prominent theories of counseling summarized and critiqued. Use it as a reference guide in your future practice, and as a primer in your current coursework.

An effective social worker needs a knowledge of comprehensive counseling theories[1] and specialized treatment techniques to determine precisely what problems exist and how to intervene effectively. There are a number of contemporary comprehensive counseling theories, including psychoanalysis, client-centered therapy, rational therapy, behavior modification, feminist intervention, reality therapy, and transactional analysis. These theories typically present material on (1) personality theory, or how normal psychosocial development occurs; (2) behavior pathology, or how emotional and behavioral problems arise; and (3) therapy, or how to change emotional and behavioral problems.

An effective counselor generally knows several treatment approaches and, depending on the problems being presented by the client, is able to pick and choose from a "bag of tricks" an intervention strategy likely to have the highest probability of success. In addition to comprehensive counseling theories, social workers also use a number of specialized treatment techniques for specific problems: assertiveness training for people who are shy or overly aggressive; muscle relaxation training for people under stress or suffering from stress-related problems; and parent effectiveness training for parent-child relationship difficulties. A conscientious worker strives to gain a working knowledge of a wide variety of treatment techniques to increase their effectiveness with clients.

It is near impossible for social workers to acquire a working knowledge of all the comprehensive and specialized intervention approaches that are available. The material in this CTRM summarizes contemporary approaches to counseling that social workers commonly use. Case examples illustrate how each is used.

[1] In a comprehensive counseling theory, the theorist proposes a certain counseling approach that can be used to treat practically all personal problems.

MODULE 1

Psychoanalysis

Sigmund Freud

The theories of psychoanalysis proposed and developed by Sigmund Freud (1924) have had an immense impact on the helping professions, including psychiatry, psychology, and social work.

Freud was born in Moravia on May 6, 1856, and died in London on September 23, 1939. For over 70 years, however, he lived in Vienna and left that city only when the Nazis overran Austria. He developed his theories primarily between 1895 and 1925, which was the end of the Victorian age (an era of sexual oppression). Every personality theorist's hypotheses (and definitely Freud's) relate to societal concerns and to internal concerns. Freud's emphasis on sexuality reflects Europe's sexual oppression at this time and also some of Freud's personal struggles.

Freud graduated from the medical school of Vienna, was married, and had six children. He conducted a searching self-analysis that began in the 1890s and continued throughout his life, had personal conflicts with his parents, and suffered in his later years from cancer of the jaw. Freud had considerable charisma, which enabled him to "market" and gain adherents to his views. However, he had trouble interacting with colleagues who questioned aspects of his theories; these interactions often resulted in intense disagreements and a discontinuance of further communication.

A number of authorities have recognized Freud as being one of the great contributors to humanity in the 20th century. Although adherence to psychoanalysis is now waning, between 1920 and 1950 social workers, psychiatrists, and certain psychologists largely believed and adopted Freud's approach to therapy.

The Mind

Freud's conception of the mind was two-dimensional, as indicated in CTRM Figure 1.1. One dimension consisted of the conscious, the preconscious, and the unconscious. The second dimension consisted of the id, the superego, and the ego.

Emphasis on the Unconscious

In Freud's theory the mind is composed of thoughts (ideas), feelings, instincts, drives, conflicts, and motives; these elements are located in the unconscious or preconscious. Elements in the preconscious area have a fair chance of becoming conscious, whereas elements in the unconscious are unlikely to rise to a person's conscious mind. The small "conscious cap" at the top of CTRM Figure 1.1 shows how in Freud's theory a person is aware of only a fraction of the total thoughts, drives, conflicts, motives, and feelings in the mind.

The "repressed" area is a barrier behind which disturbing material (primarily thoughts and feelings) is placed by the defense mechanism of repression. Freud thought that repression is the defense mechanism that causes the most problems psychologically. Thus repression causes unacceptable desires, memories, and thoughts to be excluded from consciousness by sending the material into the unconscious. Repressed material has energy and acts as an unconscious irritant, producing unwanted emotions and bizarre behavior, such as anger, nightmares, hallucinations, and enuresis.

The Id, Superego, and Ego

The *id* is the primitive psychic force in the unconscious. At birth a child's mind is thought to be entirely composed of the id. As the child grows older, the ego and superego develop out of, and become differentiated from, the id. The id contains biological instincts. Many

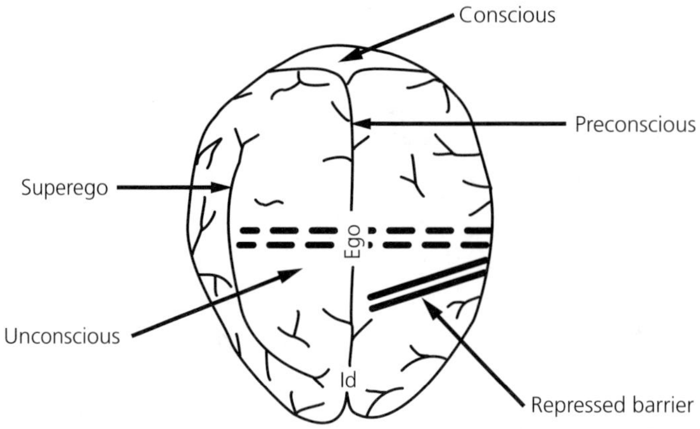

CTRM FIGURE 1.1 Freud's conception of the mind

of these instincts are viewed as immoral or asocial and need to be controlled by the individual and the larger society. The id is governed by the pleasure principle; that is, the instincts within the id seek to be expressed regardless of the consequences.

The *superego* normally develops sometime between the ages of 3 and 5 and consists of the traditional values and mores of society that are interpreted to a child by the parents. The superego's main function is to decide whether something is right or wrong. The superego is considered to contain a person's conscience and also his or her self-ideal (what that person wants to become). When an instinctual demand strives for expression and the superego disapproves, the superego sends a signal of anxiety to the ego as a warning to prevent the expression of the instinct. The emotion of guilt is said to originate from the superego.

The *ego* begins to develop from the id through experience shortly after birth. The ego acts as the coordinator of the personality, its major function being to find the least painful balance between meeting the desires or demands of the id, the superego, and the outside world. It operates on the basis of the reality principle, and endeavors to achieve a balance between id instincts, the demands of the superego, and the demands of society.

To illustrate how the id, superego, and ego function, suppose a sex instinct seeks expression from the id of a teenager. The superego notes the instinct is seeking to be expressed and sends a signal of anxiety to the ego to inform it that an "evil" instinct is seeking expression. This alerts the ego that such expression will lead to condemnation from the superego. The ego is then in a crisis and functions defensively to handle the instinct. On one hand, the ego has severe pressure from the id to allow the instinct to be expressed; on the other, it is aware that a direct expression will lead to condemnation from the superego and probably also from the outside world. The ego must thus choose between various options: One option, letting the instinct be directly expressed (for example, through intercourse or self-stimulation), will probably lead to condemnation from the superego and society. In another option, do nothing, the energy from the sexual instinct (which in this case is not allowed to be expressed) is transformed into anxiety. (Freud thought anxious people were generally sexually frustrated.) A third option uses a defense mechanism (CTRM Exhibit 1.1 lists common defense mechanisms). The ego might *sublimate*—that is, consciously channel unacceptable instinctual demands into acceptable forms for gratification like athletic activity. Alternatively, the ego might repress the sexual instinct.

THE LIBIDO. The energy of the biological instincts is called the *libido,* which is conceived as being primarily sexual energy. The libido gives energy to an individual's personality. In various writings Freud vacillated between locating the libido in the ego and locating it in the id. For Freud the location of the libido was a vexing dilemma: if he claimed the libido was located in the ego, he could not explain where the id obtained its energy, and vice versa.

EROS AND THANATOS. In his early writings Freud thought that humans primarily have only sexual instincts (also called Eros). Unable to explain sadism

CTRM Exhibit 1.1

Definitions of common defense mechanisms postulated by psychoanalytic theory

Defense mechanism: Any *unconscious* attempt to adjust to painful conditions, such as anxiety, frustration, or guilt. Defense mechanisms are measures through which a person preserves self-esteem and softens the blow of failure, deprivation, or feelings of guilt.

Compensation: Making up for a real or fancied defect or inferiority by creating a real or fancied achievement or superiority. A common example is an effort to achieve success in one field after failure in another.

Repression: Mechanism through which unacceptable desires, feelings, memories, and thoughts are excluded from consciousness by being sent down deep into the unconscious.

Sublimation: Mechanism whereby consciously unacceptable instinctual demands are channeled into acceptable forms for gratification. For example, aggression can be converted into athletic activity.

Denial: Mechanism whereby a person escapes psychic pain associated with reality by unconsciously rejecting reality. For example, a mother may persistently deny that her child has died.

Identification: Mechanism through which a person takes on the attitudes, behavior, or personal attributes of another person whom he or she has idealized (parent, relative, popular hero).

Reaction formation: Development of socially acceptable behavior or attitudes that are the opposite of repressed unconscious impulses. For example, a social worker who has an unconscious dislike for children might specialize in working with children and be an advocate for more stringent legal measures against child abuse.

Regression: Acting in a more childish fashion. This mechanism involves a person's falling back to an earlier phase of development in which he or she felt secure. Some adults when ill, for example, will act more childish and demanding with the unconscious goal of having others around them give them more care and attention.

Projection: Mechanism through which a person unconsciously attributes his or her own unacceptable ideas or impulses to another. For example, a person who has an urge to hurt others may turn it around and consciously feel that others are trying to hurt him.

Rationalization: Mechanism by which an individual, faced with frustrations or with criticism of her actions, finds justification for them by disguising from herself (as she hopes to disguise from others) her true motivations. Often this is accomplished by a series of excuses that the person believes. For example, a student who fails an exam may blame it on poor teaching, having to work, and so on, rather than consciously acknowledging the real reason—that he or she simply decided to study very little for the exam.

Undoing: Mechanism whereby when a person feels guilty about some act or wish, he or she acts or speaks in a manner reflecting the reverse of some act or wish. For example, a spouse who has been unfaithful may react by being overly attentive to his or her mate.

Isolation: The separation of an object (idea, experience, or memory) from the emotions associated with it, resulting in the person's showing no emotion to the object. This mechanism makes it possible for an individual to avoid the pain of anxiety, shame, or guilt. For example, a person is using this mechanism when discussing a violent act he or she has committed without showing any emotion.

Fantasy formation: Involves using fantasy to dull the pain of reality. For example, an unhappy child in an adopted family may fantasize that his natural parents are exalted, loving people who will one day rescue him.

(pleasure from hurting others) and masochism (pleasure from being hurt), in his later writings Freud identified a second type of instinct (Thanatos), which he indicated was the death instinct. He was then able to explain masochistic and sadistic behavior in terms of fulfilling the death instinct's focus on seeking to return to an inorganic state, either by hurting oneself or by seeing others hurt.

EMPHASIS ON SEXUALITY. Influenced no doubt in part by the sexual attitudes of his time, Freud concluded that many people had sexual conflicts. He therefore made sexuality a focus of his theories and defined most emotions and behaviors as being primarily sexual in nature. Freud defined sexuality as including physical love, affectionate impulses, self-love, love for parents and children, and friendship associations. Freud believed sexual excitement originates from diverse sources: stimulation of an erogenous zone (which can be located on any part of the body—for example, "tingling sensations" on an ear), expression of an impulse (such as laughing), muscular activity (like running), emotional excitement (such as fear or happiness), and intellectual work. As can be seen from these examples, Freud had an exceedingly broad definition of the components of human sexuality.

Psychosexual Development

Freud's theory of psychosexual, or personality, development includes five stages: oral, anal, phallic, latency, and genital.

Oral Stage

This phase, which extends from birth to approximately 18 months, is called *oral* because the child's primary activities are centered around feeding and the organs (mouth, lips, and tongue) connected with that function. Feeding is considered an important area of conflict, and a child's attention is focused on receiving and taking. People fixated at this stage are thought to have the most severe personality disorders, such as schizophrenia or psychotic depression. (By the term fixated, Freud meant that an individual's personality development is largely, though not completely, halted at the specified stage.)

Anal Stage

From ages 18 months to 3 years, a child's activities are mainly focused on giving and withholding, primarily connected with retaining and passing feces. Bowel training is an important area of conflict. People fixated at this stage have such character traits as messiness, stubbornness, rebelliousness; or they may have a *reaction formation* and exhibit opposite traits such as being meticulously clean and excessively punctual.

Phallic Stage

From 3 to 5 years the child's attention shifts to the genitals. Prominent activities of the child are pleasurable sensations from genital stimulation, showing off one's body, and looking at the bodies of others. Also, a child's personality becomes more complex during this stage. Although still self-centered, the child wants to possess those who give him or her pleasure. The child becomes more curious, wants to love and be loved, and seeks to be admired. Character traits that can develop from fixation at this stage include pride, promiscuity, and self-hatred.

Boys and girls experience separate complexes during this stage. Boys encounter an Oedipus complex. (Freud took many of his terms from Greek mythology. *Oedipus Rex* was a Greek drama in which Oedipus, raised by foster parents, unwittingly kills his father, marries his mother, and then undergoes severe psychological trauma when he discovers what he has done.)

The *Oedipus complex* refers to the dilemma faced by every son at this stage when he falls sexually in love with his mother and has antagonism toward his father, whom he views as a rival for her affections. As the intensity of these relationships mounts, the son increasingly suffers from castration anxiety; that is, he fears his father will discover his "affair" with his mother and then remove his genitals. Successful resolution of the Oedipus complex occurs through defense mechanisms. A typical resolution is for the son to first repress his feelings of love for his mother and his hostile feelings toward his father. Next, the son has a reaction formation in which he stops viewing his father negatively, but now turns this around and has positive feelings toward his father. The final step is for the son to *identify* with his father and thereby take on his attitudes, values, and behavior patterns. Freud also asserted that the resolution of this complex results in the formation of the superego. (Precisely how the resolution of this complex results in the formation of the superego has not been clarified.)

Girls undergo an *Electra complex* during this phallic stage. (Freud, as you will see, would not be very popular with the feminist movement if he were advancing his theories today.) In the Greek drama *Electra,* Electra assisted her brother in avenging their father's death by slaying their mother—this mother had conspired with her lover to murder her husband.

Freud believed girls fall sexually in love with their fathers during this stage and view their mothers with antagonism. Because of these relationships, girls also suffer from castration anxiety, but the nature of this anxiety differs from that for boys. Castration anxiety in a girl results from the awareness that she lacks a penis. She then concludes she was castrated in infancy and blames her mother for this. Freud went on to theorize that because girls believe they have been castrated they come to regard themselves as inferior to boys (have penis envy). From this point on, they perceive their role in life to be submissive and supportive of males. Freud never identified how the Electra complex is resolved.

Latency Stage

This stage usually begins when the Oedipus/Electra complexes are resolved, and ends with puberty. The sexual instinct is relatively unaroused during this stage. The child can now be socialized and becomes involved in the educational process and in learning skills.

Genital Stage

This stage occurs from puberty to death. It involves mature sexuality, and a person reaching this stage is fully able to love and to work. Again, we see Freud's emphasis on sexuality and on the work ethic, which was part of the Protestant ethic and highly valued in Freud's era.

Psychopathological Development

In his analysis of psychopathological development, or the development of emotional and behavioral problems, Freud theorized that disturbances arise from several sources. One source is traumatic experiences that a person's ego is unable to cope with directly and thus strives to resolve using such defense mechanisms as repression. However, the energy associated with the repressed material then unconsciously acts as an irritant. Breuer and Freud (1895) provide an example through Anna O., who developed a psychosomatic paralysis in her right arm. Anna O. was sitting by her father's bedside (her father was gravely ill) when she dozed off and had a nightmare that a big black snake was attacking her father. She awoke terrified and hastily repressed her thoughts and feelings about this nightmare for fear of alarming her father. While she was asleep, her right arm was resting over the back of a chair and became "numb." Freud theorized that the energy connected with the repressed material then took over physiological control of her arm, resulting in psychological paralysis.

In addition to unresolved traumatic events, Freud thought that internal unconscious processes can also cause disturbances. A range of sources exists. An unresolved Electra or Oedipus complex can lead to a malformed superego or to a variety of sexual problems—such as frigidity, promiscuity, sexual dysfunctions, excessive sexual fantasies, and nightmares with sexual content. Unresolved internal conflicts (for example, an unconscious liking and hatred of one's parents) can be another source of behavioral problems such as hostile and aggressive behavior and emotional problems such as temper tantrums. Fixations at early stages of development are additional sources that can prevent development at later stages and lead the person to display undesirable personality traits such as messiness or stubbornness. (Freud thought that traumatic experiences are important contributing factors leading to internal conflicts and fixations.)

As indicated earlier, the main source of anxiety is thought to be sexual frustration. Freud believed that anxiety arises when a sexual instinct seeks expression but the ego blocks its expression. If the instinct is not diverted through defense mechanisms, the energy connected with sexual instincts is transformed into anxiety.

Obsessions (a recurring thought such as a song repeatedly on one's mind) and compulsions (such as an urge to step on every crack of a sidewalk) are thought to be mechanisms through which a person works off energy connected with disturbing unconscious material.

For all types of mental disorders, unconscious processes (including fixations, internal conflicts, and defense mechanisms) are thought to be the causes. These disturbing unconscious processes are almost always connected with traumatic experiences, particularly traumatic experiences during childhood that are repressed.

Psychoanalysis

The goal of Freud's psychoanalysis is to discover the disturbing unconscious processes and bring them into the conscious part of the patient's mind so that the unconscious emotion (or energy) can be expressed (and thereby dissipated) and the disturbing unconscious ideas (now conscious) can be "worked through" (dealt with). Freud thought that emotional disturbances often result from pent-up, undischarged emotional tension connected with the repressed memory of a traumatic childhood sexual experience.

Psychoanalysis is a long process, generally because the chain of traumatic events from deep in the past is believed to be the determinant of each symptom. To treat a patient, the memory of these traumatic experiences must be brought to the conscious part of the patient's mind to trigger an emotional catharsis (release of pent-up energy) and to allow the person to consciously handle the disturbing ideas connected with the trauma.

For example, in the case of Anna O., Freud (Breuer & Freud, 1895) asserted that her arm became psychologically paralyzed due to her repression of her nightmare of the snake attacking her father. The paralyzed right arm was viewed as a *symptom* of unconscious processes that buried deep in Anna O.'s past. Freud asserted that the paralysis disappeared when Anna, through psychoanalysis, remembered the nightmare, had an emotional catharsis, and was then able to deal consciously with the nightmare. However, Freud asserted that only the symptom (paralyzed arm) of her emotional disturbance was treated by remembering this event. Freud believed Anna was still severely disturbed because the underlying unconscious processes that caused this symptom remained. Therefore, psychoanalysis treats not only the symptoms but also the unconscious processes that cause the symptoms. The goal then is to bring the unconscious memory of each traumatic event to the conscious mind so an emotional catharsis could occur and, through such an awareness or insight, the patient can consciously handle the disturbing ideas. In Anna's case, Freud believed that her nightmare indicated an unresolved Electra complex. Freud theorized that snakes in dreams symbolize the male sex organ. Anna's snake nightmare suggested to Freud that she had sexual conflicts stemming from repressed childhood sexual traumas. Freud thus sought with all his patients to help them become aware of (gain insight into) these traumatic experiences. The case example on page 000 discusses treating multiple personality with psychoanalysis.

To discover such unconscious processes, Freud (1924) used four main techniques: hypnosis, free association, dream analysis, and transference.

Hypnosis

Freud used *hypnosis* early in his career; however, he soon discarded it because many of his patients could not be hypnotized. Also, even for those patients who could be hypnotized, Freud usually did not know the exact date and time a traumatic event had occurred so he did not know where to direct a patient's attention. (Hypnosis is described in Module 9.)

Free Association

Freud also used *free association,* in which a patient is instructed to say whatever comes to mind, no matter how trivial. The thinking is that if patients let their minds associate while relaxed, their defenses will also relax and disturbing unconscious material will have a much greater chance of coming into the conscious mind. To facilitate this relaxed state, patients usually lie on a couch without looking at the analyst. They then make free associations with dreams, traumatic experiences, thoughts, feelings, fantasies, anything that comes to mind. At times patients remember traumatic events that occurred far back in their past, have an emotional catharsis, and then "work through" the disturbing ideas with the analyst. Usually after about 45 minutes of associating, and occasionally during this time, the analyst helps the patient gain insight into the meaning of some associations by interpreting the significance in terms of the psychoanalytic framework of what is being said—for example, pointing out that clambering out of water symbolizes the birth process (Freud, 1924, p. 160). During the association, the analyst also watches for emotional reactions such as signs of distress or resistance to the treatment.

Dream Analysis

A third Freudian technique is *dream analysis.* Freud believed that dreams center around unfulfilled wishes. (If you receive a grade on an exam that you are satisfied with, you probably won't dream about it; but if you strongly desired a higher grade, you probably would dream about it.) Freud thought dreams are a direct route to the unconscious, because a person's defenses are relaxed while dreaming. Freud believed there are two distinct types of dreams content: manifest content and latent content. What we remember on awakening is the manifest content. It is not the psychologically significant portion of the dream, because in the process of becoming conscious, it undergoes considerable distortion to make it more acceptable to our conscious self. The latent or hidden content is much more important and must be discovered by searching deep below the surface of the manifest content.

This analysis is accomplished in one of two ways. One, the patient can free-associate around elements of the dream. Presumably the elements have some hidden significance that may be uncovered as the patient free-associates about thoughts and feelings related to these elements.

Two, the latent content can be uncovered through symbol analysis. The meaning of many symbols in dreams varies from individual to individual, and this individual meaning must be determined. Yet certain symbols have similar meanings for nearly everyone. The majority of symbols in dreams are sexual. Parents appear in dreams as king and queen, or as other exalted personages. Clothes and uniforms stand for nakedness. Male sex organs appear in the form of poles, sticks, steeples, snakes, or other pointed objects. Female genitals appear as trunks, caves, enclosed places, or pocketbooks. Children and sisters and brothers are symbolized by little animals or vermin. Dying is indicated by setting out on a journey or traveling by train (Freud, 1924).

Transference

Freud also used *transference* to discover disturbing unconscious processes. In psychoanalysis, analysts seek to be unobtrusive and neutral; they do not reveal themselves. Freud noted that when patients are in analysis, they often transfer to the analyst feelings and thoughts about significant people (usually parent figures) in their lives. The patient may react as if he is a small child and the analyst is his father. Transference came to be recognized as an important area of insight. The analyst observes the transfer and gains an awareness of the patient's unconscious feelings and thoughts about significant people in their life. This insight is interpreted to the patient and further discussed.

Gaining insight into the patient's traumatic events, unconscious conflicts, and fixations allows the process of "working through" to begin. Working through involves interpreting the patient's difficulties and is a long process involving repetition, elaboration, and amplification. One or two experiences of insight into one's conflicts are usually not sufficient to bring about changes. The analysis is continued many times and in many different ways so the patient increasingly gains insight into the disturbing unconscious. Once insight is achieved, it is expected that the patient will be able to function better.

Evaluation

Freud was instrumental in developing a worldwide recognition that people with emotional problems are in need of psychological help. Before his time, many disturbed people were looked on as "malingerers" and given little support or understanding. Freud also formulated a comprehensive theory of personality development that is still widely used in assessing human behavior. When Freud began formulating his theories, there was little interest in psychological understanding or help for people with personal problems. Freud demonstrated the importance of helping people through "talk" therapy and inspired a wide range of theorists.

Freud's theories paved the way for the medical model of mental disorders. (The medical model was contrasted with the ecological model in Chapter 1.) CTRM Exhibit 1.2 summarizes the current classification of mental disorders by the American Psychiatric Association.

There are, however, a number of shortcomings in his theories:

1. Most of his concepts are difficult to operationalize (test out), so his hypotheses are difficult to prove or disprove. For example, there is no way to determine scientifically whether the concepts of the death instinct, Oedipus complex, penis envy, castration anxiety, Electra complex, superego, libido, fixation at the phallic stage of development, and unconscious conflict even exist.
2. Research has shown that patients undergoing psychoanalysis have a *lower* rate of improving than people with comparable problems who receive no treatment (Eysenck, 1965)! This startling result has been found in a number of reviews of outcome studies on psychoanalysis (Arlow, 1989; Stuart, 1970). The reason for these discouraging results may be that when a person with a problem such as depression undergoes psychoanalysis, the treatment does not focus the person's attention on how to better handle the problem; the analysis may instead lead them to worry, say, about an anal fixation or an unresolved Electra complex and thus become even more disturbed (Stuart, 1970).
3. Freud gives little attention to personality development beyond puberty. Other authorities note that personality development and changes occur throughout life (Hall & Lindzey, 1957). Theorists also note that conscience development occurs throughout life, rather than only between the third and fifth year as Freud suggests (Maddi, 1968).
4. Psychoanalytic theory is culture bound, particularly Freud's emphasis on sexuality. He lived in an era of sexual repression, a time when many people had sexual concerns. Other theorists note that factors other than sexual instincts also drive personality development. Rogers (1951), for example, discusses a self-actualization motive that strives to develop one's capacities to the fullest. Glasser (1972) indicates that the need to form an identity is a primary factor in personality development.
5. Psychoanalysis is time-consuming and expensive. A complete analysis takes several years, with the patient seeing the analyst once or twice a week. Who can afford the time and the money (usually over $150 per hour) to see an analyst?

CTRM Exhibit 1.2

Major mental disorders according to the American Psychiatric Association

DISORDERS USUALLY FIRST DIAGNOSED IN INFANCY, CHILDHOOD, OR ADOLESCENCE include, but are not limited to, mental retardation, learning disorders, communication disorders (such as stuttering), autism, attention-deficit/hyperactivity disorders, and separation anxiety disorder.

DELIRIUM, DEMENTIA, AND AMNESTIC AND OTHER COGNITIVE DISORDERS include delirium due to alcohol and other drug intoxication, dementia due to Alzheimer's disease or Parkinson's disease, dementia due to head trauma, and amnestic disorder.

SUBSTANCE-RELATED DISORDERS include mental disorders related to abuse of alcohol, caffeine, amphetamines, cocaine, hallucinogens, nicotine, and other mind- altering substances.

SCHIZOPHRENIA AND OTHER PSYCHOTIC DISORDERS include delusional disorders and all forms of schizophrenia (such as paranoid, disorganized, and catatonic).

MOOD DISORDERS—emotional disorders such as depression and bipolar disorders.

ANXIETY DISORDERS include phobias, post- traumatic stress disorder, and anxiety disorders.

SOMATOFORM DISORDERS—psychological problems that manifest themselves as symptoms of physical disease (for example, hypochondria).

DISSOCIATIVE DISORDERS—problems in which part of the personality is dissociated from the rest (for example, dissociative identity disorder, formerly called multiple personality disorder).

SEXUAL AND GENDER IDENTITY DISORDERS include sexual dysfunctions (such as hypoactive sexual desire, premature ejaculation, male erectile disorder, male and female orgasmic disorders, and vaginismus), exhibitionism, fetishism, pedophilia (child molestation), sexual masochism, sexual sadism, voyeurism, and gender identity disorders (such as cross-gender identification).

EATING DISORDERS include anorexia nervosa and bulimia nervosa.

SLEEP DISORDERS—insomnia and other problems with sleep (such as nightmares and sleepwalking).

IMPULSE-CONTROL DISORDERS—the inability to control certain undesirable impulses (for example, kleptomania, pyromania, and pathological gambling).

ADJUSTMENT DISORDERS—difficulty in adjusting to the stress created by such common events as unemployment or divorce.

PERSONALITY DISORDERS—an enduring pattern of inner experience and behavior that deviates markedly from the expectations of the individual's culture, is pervasive and inflexible, has an onset in adolescence or early adulthood, is stable over time, and leads to distress or impairment. examples include paranoid personality disorder, antisocial personality disorder, and obsessive-compulsive personality disorder.

OTHER CONDITIONS cover a variety of disorders including parent-child relational problems; partner relational problems; sibling relational problems; child victims of physical abuse, sexual abuse, and neglect; adult victims of physical abuse and sexual abuse; malingering; bereavement; academic problems; occupational problems; identity problems; and religious or spiritual problems.

Source: Diagnostic and Statistical Manual of Mental Disorders–IV, Text: Revision, by the American Psychiatric Association, 2000, Washington, DC: American Psychiatric Association.

A few final comments about the case of Sybil:[2] Multiple personality cases are very rare. Sybil's life was indeed startling, and the book and the TV movie that followed were engrossing. The psychoanalytic interpretation was fascinating. But is it accurate? And is it the only interpretation of the case that we can make? Certainly other interpretations are possible. Sybil was in analysis for 11 years, a very long time. Being in analysis for such a long time certainly gave Sybil considerable emotional support for her concerns. Perhaps Sybil developed some of her different personalities in an attempt to keep her analyst interested and to continue her therapy. I wondered whether Sybil was not in fact aware of the other personalities, but played these

[2]I present this alternative explanation of Sybil's problematic behavior to convey that the same facts can often be explained in very different ways. Which explanation is more accurate—the psychoanalytic or mine—is unknown. In fact, other explanations could probably be presented. Research is needed on counseling theories to determine which framework is more accurate. As can be seen in this case example, different explanations suggest radically different intervention approaches by therapists.

CASE EXAMPLE

Sybil

The most widely known case treated by psychoanalysis in recent years is that of Sybil Dorsett (a pseudonym) (Schreiber, 1973). Sybil was a young woman living in New York City who exhibited 16 different personalities, most of whom were unaware the other personalities existed. The main personality, "Sybil," was depressed, quiet, nonassertive, and plain-looking. "Vicky" was a self-assured, sophisticated, attractive blonde. "Peggy Lou" was an assertive, enthusiastic, and often angry pixie with a pug nose and a Dutch haircut. "Vanessa" was a very attractive, intensely dramatic redhead. "Mike," one of Sybil's two male selves, had dark hair and was a builder and carpenter. "Clara" was intensely religious and highly critical of Sybil. A total of 15 personalities were observed.

Sybil's development of multiple personalities was explained as being the only way she could give expression during her childhood years to different aspects of herself. The analyst theorized that had Sybil not developed these personalities, she would simply have exhibited some other mental disorder.

Sybil had a traumatic childhood. Born and raised in a small midwestern town, her parents were prominent and wealthy. Her father was described as religious, weak, and nonassertive. Sybil's problems mainly stemmed from her mother, Hattie. In outward appearance Hattie appeared to be deeply religious and proper. But her private life and her interactions with Sybil were bizarre and deeply disturbed. For example, Hattie would take Sybil for a walk and defecate with perverse pleasure on the lawns of neighbors. Hattie baby-sat children and sometimes played "horsey" by putting her finger in the girls' vaginas while yelling, "giddyap." She held and moved young boys between her hips stimulating her genitals. She tortured Sybil in numerous ways on numerous occasions. She forced objects such as a flashlight and a dinner knife into Sybil's genitals. She filled her rectum with water, and pressed a hot flatiron on Sybil's hand. At other times Hattie was warm and loving toward Sybil and gave the impression she was a model mother. Hattie often preached to Sybil and admonished her to behave in a prudish and puritanical manner. Such an environment, the analyst hypothesized, caused Sybil to develop multiple personalities as a way to cope with the abuse, to give expression to her wishes and desires and to different aspects of herself, to develop and grow, and to avoid total mental and emotional breakdown.

Sybil was in analysis for 11 years. The analyst used hypnosis, dream analysis, free association, and transference to assist Sybil in recollecting these traumatic experiences that had been repressed. She also used sodium pentothal (a barbiturate drug) to help Sybil remember the experiences. The aim of analysis was to help Sybil relive these traumas. Reliving these experiences released the energy or emotion of each experience and led to increased insights. Delving into the past in this manner enabled the analyst, Dr. Cornelia Wilbur, to understand why each personality emerged. The process of reintegrating all the personalities into one personality (the new Sybil) was largely accomplished through hypnosis. Dr. Wilbur first gradually suggested to each personality, individually, that they were growing older and older until each became 37 years old (Sybil's age at that time). Then Sybil was placed in a deep hypnotic sleep, and each personality (over several months) was introduced to her. She was given the suggestion that she would remember each one and that they would become part of her. The reintegration process was fraught with resistance from some of the personalities and required several more years of analysis. Gradually a new, integrated Sybil emerged. After the integration of her personalities, Sybil continued her education, graduated from college, and eventually secured a college teaching position.

different *roles* to get attention. (I have worked with a number of people who developed elaborate contrived stories—and if they received positive responses from enacting these roles, they continued to play these roles.) Also, if Sybil was truly unaware of the other personalities within her, would not a more effective treatment approach have been to videotape the different personalities and then play it back to her? Such an approach would have confronted her directly with the other personalities.

It is difficult to believe that Sybil was not aware of the other personalities within her. Each personality dressed differently. Sybil must have had an apartment full of different clothes and wigs. How could she not be aware there were other personalities when she could see all these clothes and wigs? Perhaps Sybil intentionally played different roles and knew exactly what she was doing.

In reviewing this case I question whether Sybil had a loss of memory of her other personalities. A student I supervised in a probation and parole setting was assigned a woman arrested for theft. The woman claimed to have no memory of taking things, and added that she occasionally "blanked out," and when she "reconnected with reality," she would at times have additional possessions. The student asked me for advice, and I suggested the woman's so-called loss of memory might be a "con act" to have people feel sorry for her. My suggestion was to inform this woman that if she claimed she didn't remember taking things the judge would probably find her "mentally ill" and send her to a mental hospital for an indefinite period. The student intern tried this, and within a few minutes the woman admitted she knew she had taken the items and that she initially denied it because she thought the court might go "easier" on her if she pretended to be a split personality.

Summary

Psychoanalysis is a long process. To treat a patient it is necessary to bring the memory of traumatic experiences to the conscious part of the patient's mind, thus causing an emotional catharsis, and then to allow the person consciously to work through the disturbing thoughts connected with the trauma. To do this, psychoanalysis uses hypnosis, free association, dream analysis, and transference.

Although Freud's concepts and theories about human behavior are still frequently used by some social workers, very few social workers now use psychoanalysis to counsel clients. The description here was included because of its historical significance.

EXERCISES

1. *ANALYZING UNUSUAL BEHAVIOR*

Goal: To demonstrate how unusual human behavior is analyzed in terms of psychoanalytic concepts.

Step 1: Read a book or watch a TV program or movie that seeks to explain why someone does something unusual. (The movie *Sybil* is a good choice or review newspaper articles about the Lorena Bobbitt case.)

Step 2: Class discussion using psychoanalytic concepts of why the selected character did something unusual.

2. *WORD ASSOCIATION*

Goal: To experience one form of free association.

Step 1: Break into groups of five to six students.

Step 2: Role play. Using the following list, one student "counselor" speaks each word (neutrally, with disinterest) and one student "client" responds with the first word that comes to mind.

chair	mother	death	sky
room	brother	vacation	table
grave	marriage	college	pencil
blue	pepper	grief	money
window	spoon	grandmother	stress
book	love	sister	plant
sex	red	salt	car
green	fire	fork	summer
picture	lamp	mountain	winter
gift	relationship	romance	

Step 3: As the association continues, "counselor" starts to insert words that have emotional connotations, like death, midterms, boyfriend.

Step 4: The group notes how the "client" responds. Do they hesitate? Give an unusual response (for example, say "death" in response to "vacation")? Exhibit nonverbal cues that indicate a sensitivity?

Step 5: Entire group proposes underlying motives to responses using Freudian concepts.

Step 6: Class discussion of the pros and cons of this technique. What do you think of the subjectivity of this technique? How much training do you think you would need to use it effectively. In what situations do you think it would have value?

Step 7: Discuss student thoughts about word association. (*Note:* Do *not* try to psychoanalyze the volunteer's responses.)

3. DREAM REVIEW

Goal: To show how dreams may have themes of unfulfilled wishes and personal concerns.

Step 1: A volunteer shares a recurring dream. Students explore what may be unfulfilled wishes or personal concerns in the dream. (*Note:* There is no way to determine the "real" focus.) If the volunteer becomes visibly upset while the other students are giving their interpretations, the instructor should end the discussion of this dream and ask the sharer of the dream to meet with him or her after class to further discuss the dream.

Step 2: The exercise may be continued in the same manner with other students sharing recurring dreams.

4. HYPNOSIS

Goal: To understand hypnosis.

Step 1: Listen to an audiotape of a hypnosis session.

Step 2: Class discussion.
- How would you use hypnosis in counseling?
- What are its strengths and weaknesses?

Step 3: Search the Internet for training requirements and liability issues.

MODULE 2

Client-Centered Therapy

Central Concepts

Carl Rogers (1902–1987), the founder of client-centered therapy,[1] received a doctorate in clinical psychology from Columbia University (New York City) in a highly Freudian atmosphere. He then worked 12 years in a community guidance clinic in Rochester, New York, where he diagnosed and treated delinquent and underprivileged children. During these years Rogers was exposed to a variety of therapy approaches, including psychoanalysis and Otto Rank's functional approach. In 1940 he accepted a full professorship at Ohio State University where he remained for five years. During this time he developed a distinctive point of view in psychotherapy, and in 1942 he published *Counseling and Psychotherapy,* which brought the term *nondirective* (later replaced by *client-centered*) into wide use. He published a number of other books and taught at the University of Chicago and the University of Wisconsin. In 1968 Rogers and some colleagues established a Center for the Studies of the Person in La Jolla, California.

Rogers's views have found wide applications in psychiatry, psychology, social work, and guidance counseling. His contributions in delineating the type of therapist-client relationship that is conducive to positive therapeutic changes are especially noteworthy. His emphasis on such concepts as empathy, nonjudgmental attitude, acceptance, and nonthreatening atmosphere is now prevalent in social work literature.

[1]Rogers and his colleagues now prefer the term *person-centered* therapy to *client-centered;* they believe this term more accurately describes the human values their way of working incorporates.

Rogers was a world leader in humanistic approaches to therapy. (*Humanism* is a philosophy that emphasizes the dignity and worth of people and their capacity for self-realization through reason.) His work inspired humanistic changes in business, education, and marriage.

The central hypothesis of client-centered therapy, as stated by Meador and Rogers (1979), is that

> the growth potential of any individual will tend to be released in a relationship in which the helping person is experiencing and communicating realness, caring, and a deeply sensitive nonjudgmental understanding. (p. 131)

Meador and Rogers (1979) further add:

> The basic theory of person-centered therapy can be stated simply in the form of an "if-then" hypothesis. If certain conditions are present in the attitudes of the person designated "therapist" in a relationship, namely, congruence, positive regard, and empathetic understanding, then growthful change will take place in the person designated "client." (p. 131)

To understand client-centered therapy, it is essential to understand certain terms. Client-centered therapy assumes that everyone has a *self-actualization motive,* defined as the inherent tendency of every person (and all organisms) to develop their capacities in ways that maintain or enhance the person (Rogers, 1959). Rogers believed a therapist should not make suggestions or interpretations in therapy, because the actualizing motive will best guide a client. If this motive does not exist, then there is no rationale for a therapist to be nondirective.

In contrast to Freud, who viewed our basic nature as "evil" (having immoral, asocial instincts), Rogers viewed our basic nature as inherently good. Rogers further believed that if a person remains relatively free of influence attempts from others, that person's self-actualization motive will lead them to become a sociable, cooperative, creative, and self-directed person.

Here are the key concepts in client-centered therapy:

Self-concept—Our conception of who we are.

Ideal self—What we would like to be.

Incongruence between self and experience—The discrepancy between our self-concept and what we experience. Example: Kathy perceives herself as outgoing, attractive, and sociable; but when she is with others, she feels ignored. This discrepancy causes her to feel tension, internal confusion, and anxiety.

Psychological maladjustment—Condition in which a person denies or distorts to awareness, significant experiences. A psychologically maladjusted person has an incongruence between self and experience.

Congruence, congruence of self and experience—Condition in which our concept of self is consistent with what we experience.

Need for positive regard—Our need to be valued and held in esteem by others.

Need for self-regard—Need to value ourself.

Conditions of worth—The result of the introjection of others' values that are inconsistent with our self-actualization motive. A person has conditions of worth when he feels his worth as a person is judged conditionally on certain behaviors. Those behaviors that are valued low will be avoided. The result? Behaviors not actually experienced as satisfying are regarded positively; behaviors not actually experienced as *un*satisfying are regarded negatively. Contrary to what the term *conditions of worth* may connote, Rogers asserted that it is psychologically unhealthy to have conditions of worth.)

Empathy—Our capacity to perceive the internal frame of reference of another with accuracy *as if* we were the other person. Example: To sense the hurt or the pleasure of another as that person senses it.

Unconditional positive regard—To value another, irrespective of the different values that we might place on his or her specific behaviors. The therapist thus believes in the inner wisdom of the self-actualization motive—that the client is best able to decide what courses of action are most advantageous. Showing unconditional positive regard means to communicate respect, warmth, acceptance, liking, caring, and concern for a client, all of which are *not* conditional on what the client says or does.

Genuineness or congruence of the therapist—To be genuine or congruent, therapists read their own inner experiencing and allow the quality of this inner experiencing to be apparent in the therapeutic relationship. Meador and Rogers (1979) stated:

> Congruence in the therapist's own inner self is his sensing of and reporting his own felt experiencing as he interacts in the relationship. The therapist trusts his own organismic responses in the situation and conveys those feelings of his that he intuitively believes have relevance in the relationship. (p. 153)

Being genuine or congruent is being "real" in a relationship; it is the absence of phoniness and defensiveness. Being genuine means the therapist does not put up a professional front or personal facade.

Theory of Personality Development and Psychopathology

Developing a theory of personality has not been a primary focus of client-centered theorists. Rogers was more interested in investigating the manner in which personality *changes* come about than in identifying the *causes* of present personality characteristics.

The driving force in personality development is the "self-actualization motive." As an infant grows, the infant's self-concept starts to form. Our self-concept is highly dependent on our *perceptions* of our experiences, which is influenced by our "need for positive regard" (to be valued by others). Positive regard is seen as a universal need in every person (Rogers, 1959). We thus base our sense of self on the perception of the regard we receive from others.

Emotional and behavioral problems develop when the child *introjects* (takes on) values of others that are inconsistent with his or her self-actualizing motive. Introjecting values inconsistent with one's self-actualizing motive results in "conditions of worth." Example: a child introjects values from his parents that sex is dirty or that dancing is bad.

When a person has conditions of worth, the result is that some behaviors are regarded positively (for example, avoiding all sexual activity) by the person even when they are not internally experienced as unsatisfying. Meador and Rogers (1979) stated:

> What happens to the actualizing tendency as conditions of worth develop in the self-regard system? The actualizing tendency remains the basic motivation for the individual. However, a conflict develops between his organismic needs and his self-regard needs, now containing conditions of worth. The individual, in effect, is faced with the choice between acting in accord with his organismic sense or censoring the organismic urging and

acting in accord with the condition of worth he has learned. (p. 144)

Conditions of worth lead to an "incongruence between self and experience." For example, Maria feels morally righteous and views herself as a value setter for refusing to dance or date; however, her peers consider her a prude with archaic values. When a discrepancy exists between our self-concept and our experiences, we feel tension, anxiety, and internal confusion.

We respond to this "incongruence" in a variety of ways. We may use various defense mechanisms. A person thus *denies* that experiences are in conflict with their self-concept. Or the person *distorts* or *rationalizes* the experiences that are then perceived as being consistent with their self-concept. If we cannot reduce the inconsistency through such defense mechanisms, we are forced to face the fact directly that incongruencies exist between our self and our experiences, which can lead us to feel unwanted emotions (such as anxiety, tension, depression, guilt, or shame).

A large or significant degree of incongruence between self and experiences can cause "disorganization of self" (that is, a "psychotic" breakdown).

Theory of Therapy

Client-centered therapy asserts that three therapist attitudes are necessary and sufficient conditions to effect positive change in the client: empathy, positive regard, and genuineness or congruence. That is, whenever therapists display these three attitudes toward a client, the actualizing potential of the client will begin to change and grow.

Empathy is the capacity of therapists to "put themselves in the shoes" of the client so they can understand what the client is thinking and feeling. Empathy also involves communicating this understanding to the client.

Unconditional positive regard means that therapists fully accept the client and convey a genuine caring for the client. A nonjudgmental attitude is key here. Also, therapists do not express approval or disapproval, do not make interpretations, and do not probe unnecessarily. Therapists convey that they fully trust the client's resources for increased self-understanding and positive change. With this attitude the client concludes (Meador & Rogers, 1979, p. 152): "Here is someone who repeatedly tells me in one way or another that he believes in my ability to find my way in the process of growth. Perhaps I can begin to believe in myself."

Genuineness or *congruence* is therapists' capacity to "trust their gut reactions," and then convey those feelings or reactions that they believe have relevance in the relationship. This willingness to be real and to express what they are thinking and feeling provides the client with a reality base that the client can trust. It also takes away some of the risk of sharing hidden secrets with another.

For Rogers the *nature* of the client-therapist relationship is *the* key variable in producing positive changes.

Rogers indicated that two conditions are necessary before therapy can occur. First, the client needs to be uncomfortable or anxious because of incongruencies between self and experiences. (Client-centered therapy will not work well with clients who deny that a problem exists or who are unmotivated to change.) Second, therapists must create a nonthreatening atmosphere in which the client feels fully accepted and understood and that the therapist genuinely cares for the client.

In such a relationship a client feels free (perhaps for the first time) to explore incongruencies between self and experiences. (Example: Paul begins to examine the inconsistency between believing that sex is sinful even though his experiences do not support this view.) The client then comes face-to-face with an awareness of the incongruence, and thus begins to examine it and to think about what would happen if other values were held (such as a value that responsible sexual experiences are desirable). During this process the client usually experiences feelings that have in the past been denied, repressed, or otherwise kept from consciousness. (Similar to Freud, Rogers believed the person in therapy should become aware of unconscious feelings and ideas and deal with them in the conscious part of the mind.) If and when this occurs, the concept of self is reorganized to include those experiences that have been kept from consciousness, and the concept of self becomes increasingly congruent with one's experiences and more consistent with the self-actualizing processes.

The therapist's role is best characterized as *nondirective*. Therapists create a permissive, nonthreatening atmosphere in which clients feel accepted and feel free to explore their defenses and the incongruencies between self and experiences. If growth is to occur, each person must assume responsibility for their actions, decisions, and behavior. Significant and enduring change must be self-initiated. Therefore, complete responsibility for the direction of treatment rests with the client. Client-centered therapists do *not* bring up subjects to discuss, give advice, make interpretations, or provide suggestions. A person's self-actualization motive best knows what courses of action they should take, and therefore client-centered therapy focuses on helping the client gain insight into inconsistent values and then allowing the self-actualizing processes to determine future directions.

During therapy a client-centered therapist seeks to help the client clarify personal thoughts and feelings. Three types of statements are primarily, and continually, used in the interview: clarification or reflection of feeling, restatement of content, and simple acceptance.

CLARIFICATION OR REFLECTION OF FEELING. Example: A client begins an interview by making critical statements about his boss, his wife, and the weather. The therapist then helps the client better understand what he is feeling by reflecting: "You seem angry today" or "You're really upset about something today."

Client-centered therapists sometimes add to the reflection by expressing their own feelings at the moment:

Client: I think I'm beyond help.

Therapist: Huh? Feel as though you're beyond help. I know. You feel just completely hopeless about yourself. I can understand that. I don't feel hopeless, but I can realize that you do. Just feel as though nobody can help you and you're really beyond help. (Meador & Rogers, 1979, p. 157)

The focus of a therapist in reflecting feelings is not simply to repeat the feelings expressed by the client but to reflect their intensity and meanings (that is, how the client feels) about the feelings he or she is expressing.

RESTATEMENT OF CONTENT. Example: A wife goes on a 20-minute outburst about how her husband is not supporting the family, is not affectionate, and frequently comes home drunk. The therapist says, "You're pretty unhappy with the way your husband is treating you and the children"—the intent here is to help the wife take an overall look at her marriage. In restating content therapists express their view of the meanings of the content being expressed by the client.

SIMPLE ACCEPTANCE. Example: The therapist responds with "I see" or "M-hm" to something the client has said, the tone conveying that the therapist understands and fully accepts what the client has said.

The objective of therapy is for the client to become fully functioning. A fully functioning person is a mature individual who has achieved complete congruence and hence is psychologically adjusted. This is not a static state but is a process, the person is continually changing (Rogers, 1959). Client-centered therapy frees clients of their faulty learning so they can be what they are innately meant to be. Therapy may not produce an optimally adjusted person, but the experience can promote the development of a new pattern of adjustment.

The fully functioning person is an ideal that Rogers believed the vast majority of people do not fully become—even with the benefit of extensive therapy. Fully functioning people

- Are open to all experiences
- Do not use defenses to distort or deny experiences
- Have a self-concept congruent with experiences
- Have a locus of evaluation—they determine what choices are best (These decisions are based on their judgments of what is desirable or undesirable rather than on what others say.)
- Have unconditional positive regard for self
- Enjoy others because of the reciprocal positive regard
- Are generally socially effective and approved by significant others

Evaluation

Rogers is to be praised for the outstanding contributions he has made in articulating the components of a therapeutic relationship. He emphasized the importance of these central concepts in building a helping relationship: nonthreatening atmosphere, nonjudgmental attitude, empathy, genuineness, unconditional positive regard, and client as problem solver. Rogers also developed therapist response techniques that facilitate development of a constructive relationship: clarification (or reflection) of feeling, restatement of content, and simple acceptance. The relationship between the social worker and the client, partly due to Rogers's emphasis, is now recognized as the cornerstone of social work practice (Simon, 1970).

Fischer (1978) reviewed a large number of studies conducted on the three attitudes hypothesized by Rogers as necessary and sufficient conditions for producing positive changes in clients—the three attitudes of empathy, genuineness, and positive regard or warmth. He concluded:

> The findings from these studies have been remarkably consistent. Taken together, this research strongly supports the view that the level of therapist or helper empathy, warmth, and genuineness and associated interpersonal skills is related to positive change in client

> personal and social functioning. Practitioners who are relatively high on these core conditions of interpersonal helping tend to be effective practitioners. These findings hold with a wide variety of types of practitioners regardless of training, background, or theoretical orientation. (p. 207)

These findings dramatically suggest that, regardless of a counselor's theoretical orientation, a successful outcome of counseling is highly dependent on conveying empathy, warmth, and genuineness!

Rogers is also to be credited for emphasizing the importance of evaluation studies. Client-centered therapy is one of the most extensively researched approaches to counseling in existence (Prochaska, 1979).

In spite of these strengths there are some limitations of client-centered therapy.

1. Eysenck (1965) reviewed outcome studies conducted on the effectiveness of contemporary psychotherapy approaches, including that of client-centered therapy. The results are not encouraging for client-centered therapy, because the studies of this approach *fail* to demonstrate that clients receiving this therapy improve at a higher rate than control groups of people with similar problems. Although the results are complex and subject to different interpretations, studies generally show that about two-thirds of clients receiving "insight" counseling improve, which is the same rate of improvement for people with personal problems who receive no counseling. (Client-centered therapy is an "insight" approach to counseling. Insight approaches seek to increase the client's awareness and understanding of his or her problems, without focusing on ways to resolve those problems. (See Module 10.)

Why these rather discouraging results? It would seem that even though developing a helping relationship and helping clients gain insight into their problems are essential parts of counseling, these elements do not constitute the total healing process. As indicated in Chapter 5, clients need to understand the nature and causes of their problems, but they also need to know what courses of action they can take to resolve the problem. Client-centered therapists do not inform clients of available resolution strategies, because they believe it is the clients' responsibility to figure this out for themselves. Many therapists, such as Glasser (1965), point out the importance of having the counselor suggest various alternatives, of helping clients explore the merits and consequences of these alternatives, and then having clients make commitments (contracts) to try one of these alternatives.

Examples of the importance of exploring alternatives are easily found. People who are depressed may understand why they are depressed (for example, a broken romance) but may not know how to resolve the depression. A person who knows he has a drinking problem may be unaware of the various programs and approaches to resolve his addiction. A mother who knows she is an ineffective parent may be unaware of what she can do to be more effective. A person who knows he is shy or aggressive may not know about assertiveness training techniques that he can use to express himself more effectively. A person who has a phobia knows a problem exists but is often unaware of how to resolve the fear and anxiety.

Although empathy, warmth, and genuineness may well be essential parts of counseling, Prochaska (1979, p. 137) noted that Rogers "seems to have gone too far and concluded that what may be necessary conditions for therapy to proceed are also sufficient conditions for therapy to succeed."

2. Rogers claimed to be nondirective. He indicated that a therapist should not bring up topics to discuss, or make suggestions or interpretations. Rogers believed that the direction an interview takes should be the sole responsibility of the client. Truax (1966) has, however, shown that client-centered therapists do in fact subtly direct clients with nonverbal communication (for example, by showing greater interest in certain topics) and by selectively choosing which topics to respond to (discouraging further communication by not saying anything when a client talks about his job, and encouraging further communication by reflecting feelings when a client talks about how she feels about her spouse).

3. Client-centered therapy does not provide much useful material on personality development, or on how emotional and behavioral problems arise. For example, the theory does not help very much in explaining why depression, grief, and shyness occur, or why an individual displays behavioral problems like enuresis, problem drinking, aggressive behavior, and acts of crime and violence.

4. Rogers assumed with his emphasis on therapists being "genuine" with clients, that therapists will like all their clients. (It would not be very therapeutic for a therapist to say, "You know, I really don't like you.") In reality, therapists do not like all clients.

5. Prochaska (1979) provided an intriguing interpretation of client-centered therapy from a learning theory perspective. Prochaska asserted that whatever positive effects occur from this therapy occur due to extinction—that is, by gradually reducing the client's

CASE EXAMPLE

Gloria

In 1964, Carl Rogers interviewed a client named "Gloria" for a film series, *Three Approaches to Psychotherapy.* This film is available for purchase or rental (Rogers, 1965). Rogers believed this film was an excellent example of client-centered therapy. Meador and Rogers (1979, p. 180) stated: "The quality of this interview is like a piece of music, which begins on a thin persistent note and gradually adds dimension and levels until the whole orchestra is playing."

Gloria is a 30-year-old divorcée. Her presenting problem involves how she recently responded to her 9-year-old daughter, Pammy, when Pammy asked whether she had made love with any man since her divorce. She indicated to Rogers she lied by telling her daughter no. She feels guilty about this, because she feels she has always been honest with Pammy. She also wonders whether she should tell Pammy the truth—that she lied. Furthermore, she wonders how she should respond in the future if Pammy again raises this question and whether the truth will affect Pammy adversely.

At the beginning of this interview Gloria asks, "I want you to tell me if it would affect her wrong if I told her the truth, or what?" On two later occasions, Gloria directly asks for Rogers's opinion to this question. On all three occasions Rogers's responses convey that he understands her dilemma and that he feels this is a question she can best answer by herself. At one point Gloria shows her frustration with his response by saying, "You're just going to sit there and let me stew in it, and I want more." Rogers replies, "No, I don't want to let you just stew in your feelings, but on the other hand, I also feel this is the kind of very private thing that I couldn't possibly answer for you. But I sure as anything will try to help you work toward your own answer."

Throughout the interview Rogers uses the three types of statements mentioned earlier: clarification or reflection of feeling, restatement of content, and simple acceptance. He also conveys empathy, positive regard, and congruence. The main focus of the interview is to help Gloria examine the dilemma of what to tell her daughter, while conveying that she has the resources to decide what to do, and then to carry out her decisions. After a while Gloria realizes that Rogers is not going to give his opinion or suggestions on how to handle this. She further realizes that Rogers believes she has the ability to find the answer herself. Gloria goes on to discuss some other concerns, including the fact that she has never felt very close to her father.

Rogers is able to form a very close relationship with Gloria in this interview. Near the end Gloria says:

> All of a sudden while I was talking to you, I thought, Gee, how nice I can talk to you and I want you to approve of me and I respect you, but I miss that my father couldn't talk to me like you are. I mean, I'd like to say, Gee I'd like you for my father. I don't even know why that came to me.

Rogers responds:

> You look to me like a pretty nice daughter. But you really do miss that fact that you couldn't be open with your own father.

Since making this film, Rogers (1984) noted that Gloria continued to write to him, once or twice a year for 15 years until her untimely death. Rogers (1984) added:

> I am awed by the fact that this fifteen-year association grew out of the quality of the relationship we formed in one thirty-minute period in which we truly met as persons. It is good to know that even one half-hour can make a difference in a life. (pp. 423–425)

concerns through having clients repeatedly talk about their concerns in an environment free of positive or negative consequences. Prochaska (1979) noted:

> Beneath all the rhetoric, Rogers is advocating a treatment that is apparently based on a fuzzy form of extinction. Theoretically, troubled responses are assumed to have been conditioned by the contingent love and regard of parents. The therapist is supposed to reverse the process by establishing a social learning environment in which there are no contingencies, no conditions for positive regard. The client is allowed to talk on and on

about troubled behavior without being reinforced or punished. Eventually the absence of contingencies leads to an extinction of talking about troubles. Of course, we cannot determine from this verbal extinction paradigm alone whether the client's troubled behavior itself has changed or whether the client has just quit talking about such problems.

But why rely on extinction when it is unnecessarily lengthy and can lead to complications such as the spontaneous recovery of the extinguished responses? Furthermore, when only extinction is used, there is no way of telling which new behaviors will be learned in place of the maladaptive responses that are being extinguished. (p. 136)

Summary

Client-centered therapy postulates that every person has a self-actualization motive. The driving force in personality development is the self-actualization motive, which seeks to optimally develop a person's capacities. Emotional and behavioral problems develop in childhood when the child *introjects* (takes on) those values of others that are inconsistent with his or her self-actualizing motive. Introjecting values inconsistent with one's self-actualizing motive cause "incongruencies" between one's self-concept and one's experiences. Such incongruencies cause a person to feel tension, anxiety, and internal confusion. A person can respond to this "incongruence" through a variety of defense mechanisms: denial, distortion, and rationalization. If the defense mechanisms do not work, the person is forced to directly face the fact that incongruencies exist that are leading the person to feel unwanted emotions. A significant degree of incongruence between self and experiences can cause "disorganization of self."

The focus in therapy is to help clients become aware of incongruencies between their self-concept and their experiences. Once this insight is achieved, the self-actualizing motive fosters a reorganization of the self-concept to be more congruent with experiences. Client-centered therapists are nondirective. They do not even suggest possible resolution approaches to clients.

Client-centered therapy asserts that three therapist attitudes are necessary and sufficient conditions to effect positive changes in clients: empathy, positive regard, and genuineness or congruence. Whenever a therapist displays these three attitudes toward a client, the actualizing potential of the client will begin to change and grow. During therapy, a client-centered therapist seeks to help clients clarify their thoughts and feelings primarily by using three types of statements: clarification or reflection of feeling, restatement of content, and simple acceptance.

Client-centered therapy has made outstanding contributions in identifying the components of a therapeutic relationship. A shortcoming of the approach appears to be that client-centered therapists do not suggest viable alternatives when clients are unaware of strategies to resolve their difficulties.

EXERCISE

UNDERSTANDING CLIENT-CENTERED THERAPY

Goal: To gain an understanding of the merits and shortcomings of client-centered therapy.

Step 1: Two volunteers select and develop a contrived problem that they share (for example, a "wife" wants to become a surrogate mother, and her "husband" doesn't want her to) out of hearing from two volunteer "counselors."

Step 2: "Counselors" counsel the "clients" using these client-centered therapy techniques: reflection, restatement, acceptance. "Counselors" must not ask questions, interpret, or suggest.

Step 3: "Counselors" share with class their feelings about the restrictions. "Clients" share their impressions.

Step 4: Class discussion of the pros and cons of this therapy approach.

MODULE 3

Transactional Analysis

The founder of transactional analysis was Eric Berne (1910–1970). Like many psychotherapy innovators, Berne was formally trained in classical psychoanalysis. He began his training as a psychoanalytic candidate in New York, but his training was interrupted by World War II. In the army he became interested in group therapy and began to move away from the strict one-to-one format of psychoanalysis.

After the war he resumed his psychoanalytic studies and in 1956 applied for membership in the Psychoanalytic Institute. He was turned down on the basis that he was not doing orthodox analysis. Berne then disassociated himself from psychoanalysis. A year later he presented his first paper on transactional analysis (TA), which he had been developing for several years. Beginning in the early 1950s, he began to present his emerging theory and have it critiqued by professionals.

In 1964 he published *Games People Play,* which was written primarily for professionals interested in TA and which became a national best-seller. The popularity of TA grew dramatically. Several books written by other TA authors, such as *I'm OK—You're OK* (Harris, 1969), have also become best-sellers.

Theory of Personality Development

Personality Structure

The basic premise of transactional analysis is that human personality is structured as three separate ego states: Parent, Adult, and Child. The definition of these ego states varies somewhat among TA authorities. Dusay and Dusay's (1979) definitions, which are consistent and easily understood, are presented here. TA authorities assert that these ego states are not theoretical constructs but are realities that are readily identified by anyone trained in TA concepts.

Our Parent ego state is composed of attitudes and behaviors that we copy through identification with parents and other authority figures. Although much of the Parent is learned during childhood, it can be modified throughout life as we copy new authority figures. The Parent is the limit-setting, controlling, and rigid rule maker of our personality. It expresses our morals, value systems, and beliefs, and uses such words as *ought, should, must,* and *you'll be sorry.* Certain gestures, like pointing a finger, also characterize the Parent. The Parent's attitudes and behaviors may promote growth in others, as well as being critical and controlling. The Parent can be judgmental and opinionated, as well as protective and nurturing.

The *Parent* ego state has two forms: the Critical Parent and the Nurturing Parent. The *Critical Parent* is the part of our personality that finds fault and criticizes. It also is directing and assertive; it sets rules, enforces our value system, and stands up for our rights. Too much Critical Parent is dictatorial. The *Nurturing Parent* is empathic, acts out of genuine concern for others, and is warm, supportive, and protective. It usually promotes growth in others, but too much Nurturing Parent leads to overprotection, overinvolvement, and can be smothering. A classic example of a Nurturing Parent is a warm, friendly, parental, yet firm, police officer.

The *Child* ego state is considered the best part of our personality, because it is the only part that can truly enjoy life. People in the Child state speak, stand, think, perceive, and feel as they did in childhood. Behavior is impulsive rather than restrained by reason. Typical expressions include daydreaming, fantasizing, throwing temper tantrums, being irrational or irresponsible, having fun, and being creative.

The Child has two types: Free Child and Adapted Child. Our *Free Child* is impulsive, creative, curious, playful, fun-loving, free, and eager. Too much Free Child leads to the person's becoming uncontrollable. Our *Adapted Child* is compromising, conforming, adapting, compliant, and easy to get along with. A person with too much Adapted Child may display a variety of personal problems: depression, guilt, robotlike behavior, or temper tantrums.

Our *Adult* ego state is factual, nonemotional, precise, nonjudgmental, and accurate. Our Adult essentially acts like a computer, an unfeeling aspect of our personality that gathers and processes information for making predictions and decisions. The Adult accurately evaluates the environment and assesses the demands and emotions of the Parent and of the Child.

Each of these ego states has adaptive functions—when used in the appropriate situation.[1] The Parent is ideally suited when control is needed, for example, in disciplining children. The Child is best when creative solutions to problems are required. The Child is also most adaptive for parties, celebrations, and other fun situations. The Adult is best suited for making important decisions like career or marriage decisions. The well-adapted personality, then, switches from one ego state to another depending on the circumstances.

Harris (1969) described "a great moment in psychotherapy" involving a client in therapy, which was significant in leading Berne to conclude the existence of the Parent, Adult, and Child ego states:

> A thirty-five-year-old lawyer, whom he was treating said, "I'm not really a lawyer, I'm just a little boy." Away from the psychiatrist's office he was, in fact, a successful lawyer, but in treatment he felt and acted like a little boy. Sometimes during the hour he would ask, "Are you talking to the lawyer or to the little boy?" Both Berne and his patient became intrigued at the existence and appearance of these two real people, or states of being, and began talking about them as "the adult" and "the child." Treatment centered around separating the two. Later another state began to become apparent as a state distinct from "adult" and "child." This was "the parent" and was identified by behavior which was a reproduction of what the patient saw and heard his parents do when he was a little boy. (p. 39)

[1]Berne appears to have been influenced by Freud in developing his Child, Adult, and Parent ego states. The Child resembles the id; the Adult the ego; and the Parent the superego.

Psychosocial Drives

Although ego states provide the structure of the personality, the motivation for behavior comes from fulfilling basic human needs (food, shelter, sex) and from psychosocial drives. Berne (1966) identified the following psychosocial drives: stimulus hunger, recognition hunger, structure hunger, and excitement hunger.

Stimulus hunger is the need to be stimulated. Stimulus deprivation studies show that people become highly disturbed when they are deprived of adequate amounts of physical stimulation (Hebb, Held, Riesen, & Teuber, 1961; Solomon et al., 1961; Spitz, 1945). One of the most important forms of stimulation is "receiving strokes." The basic motivating force for all human social behavior is our lifelong hunger for human recognition, which TA terms as "seeking strokes." Spitz (1945) demonstrated that young children need direct physical contact that comes from being cuddled, held, and soothed. Without such contact, their emotional and physical development is severely stunted.

Although direct physical contact is the most nourishing form of stimulation, adults generally fulfill their *recognition hunger* by being recognized or attended to by others. Thus, strokes such as greetings, smiles, approval, cheers, and applause are highly valued. However, if such strokes are not received, negative strokes are then sought because they are considered better than no strokes. Negative strokes include cold looks, disapproval, criticism, and frowns. Dusay and Dusay (1979, p. 388) noted, "Habitual criminals with high recidivism rates illustrate that negative strokes are better than no strokes at all." This principle is illustrated by battered women who choose to continue to live with their abusive husbands rather than living alone and receiving no strokes. As can be seen by this discussion, stimulus hunger is closely related to recognition hunger. Stimulus hunger is a broader term that encompasses recognition hunger. It is possible to receive stimulation from the environment (for example, being caught in a thunderstorm) that is not a form of recognition.

Structural hunger is the need to structure time and develops out of our dilemma of what to do with 24 hours a day, 168 hours per week, 8,736 hours per year. This dilemma is heightened in societies such as ours in which people have surplus time. Preferred ways of structuring times are those that are most exciting.

Excitement hunger is our desire to avoid boredom and to have interesting and exciting things to do. The most interesting ways of structuring time involve getting strokes from others and exchanging strokes with others.

Types of Transactions

A "transaction" is a unit of social intercourse, and is composed of a transactional stimulus (verbal and nonverbal messages from one person) and a transactional response (verbal and nonverbal messages from another person reacting to the transactional stimulus). Here is an example of a transaction:

Husband: What are we going to have for dinner tonight?

Wife: I don't know—whatever you'd like to make.

Structure hunger, excitement hunger, and recognition hunger motivate humans to participate in transactions. TA identifies five types of transactions:

1. *Ritual:* This is the safest form of interaction; it is a stereotyped transaction programmed by external social forces. Informal rituals include casual social greetings and exchanges. Formal rituals include weddings and funerals, which are highly structured and predictable. Rituals indicate mutual recognition and result in very little sharing of information between the persons involved in the transaction.

2. *Activity:* Activities structure time. Activities (studying, yardwork, office work) can be satisfying in and of themselves, or they can lead to satisfactions in the future through receiving strokes. During the activity there may or may not be involvement with another person. Some people use their work activity to avoid intimate involvement with others. (Critics of TA have questioned whether activities are transactions.)

3. *Pastime:* Pastimes are semiritualistic and are usually shared with people who have mutual interests. Pastimes allow people to structure their time in fairly interesting ways but that minimize the possibility of incidents that are threatening or too emotional. Small talk at social gatherings is a typical example of a pastime.

4. *Intimacy:* These are entirely spontaneous and direct. Intimate transactions can be exciting but can also be threatening and overwhelming. Such free and unstructured exchanges are generally avoided in favor of structured and safer interactions.

5. *Game:* This is a set of transactions with a "gimmick" (that is, a hidden scheme for attaining an end). In a game one or more participants consciously or unconsciously strive to achieve an ulterior outcome by using a hidden scheme.

Two levels of communication are involved in games: social and psychological. The social level is the overt or manifest; the psychological level is the covert or latent. Prochaska (1979) gave an example of these two levels of communication in a game that is diagrammed in CTRM Figure 3.1.

> For example, if a woman asks a man, "Why don't you come by my place to see my collection of sculpture?" and the man responds "I'd love to. I'm really interested in art," they may be having a simple, candid interchange between two adults beginning to share a pastime. In a game, however, both players are also communicating a message at a different level, such as Child-to-Child messages like "Boy, I'd really like to get you alone in my apartment" and "I'd sure love to look at your curves." (pp. 237–238)

For the game to progress, at least one of the participants has to pull a switch, as further described in Prochaska's (1979) example:

> For the payoff to occur, one of the players has to pull a switch. In this case, after fixing drinks and sitting close on the couch examining a reproduction of Rodin's *The Kiss,* the woman still seems to be sending a seductive communication. The man's vanity convinces him to proceed, and he puts his hand on her leg, only to be rebuffed by a slap on the face and an irate "What kind of a woman do you think I am?"
>
> The couple has just completed a heavy hand of RAPO.[2] Besides gaining mutual recognition, excitement, and some structured time together, there is also a strong emotional payoff for each. The woman is able to proudly affirm her position in life that she is OK, while feeling angry toward men for not being OK, just as her mother always said. The payoff for the man is to feel depressed and thereby reaffirm his conviction that he is not OK. (p. 238)

People who are attempting to achieve a hidden outcome may or may not be aware of their intentions—or aware of the gimmick they are using. Although some games can lead to substantial financial loss or mental anguish for participants, not all games are necessarily undesirable. For instance, an individual with a strong need for social approval may perform many "altruistic" and "charitable" deeds.

[2]Berne (1964) defined RAPO as being "Kiss Off" or "indignation."

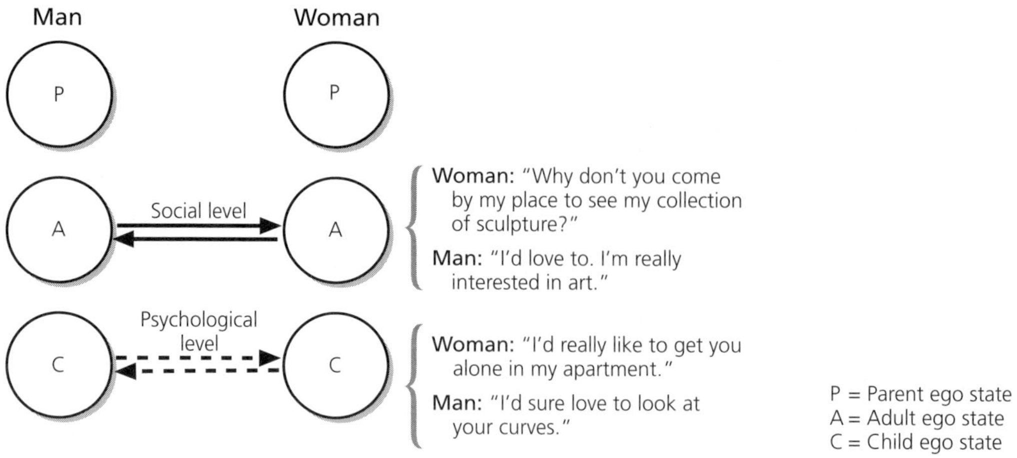

Man
Woman
P
P
A
Social level
A
Woman: "Why don't you come by my place to see my collection of sculpture?"
Man: "I'd love to. I'm really interested in art."
C
Psychological level
C
Woman: "I'd really like to get you alone in my apartment."
Man: "I'd sure love to look at your curves."
P = Parent ego state
A = Adult ego state
C = Child ego state

CTRM FIGURE 3.1 A game diagram

A game may be repeated over and over. For some, playing a certain game becomes so much a part of their personality that it can aptly be called their style of life. An alcoholic who denies to himself and to others that he has a drinking problem is an example of this. (His payoffs are the rewards he receives from drinking—feeling high and temporarily escaping his problems.)

The "alcoholic" game also illustrates another aspect of games—several people may be involved. In the traditional alcoholic game described by Berne (1964), the alcoholic may have companions who frequently invite him to "Let's go have a drink—a drink will be good for you." Their payoff is the fun and partying they have. There may also be a sympathetic listener—perhaps a bartender who listens in order to get the alcoholic to spend his money.

Some people play games that have destructive outcomes. They are often unaware that a destructive game is being played. For example, family members may go to elaborate lengths to hide the drinking problem from others without realizing they are enabling the alcoholic to continue to drink.

Common Games

Eric Berne listed numerous psychological games in *Games People Play* (1964). People often have a repertoire of favorite games, and many base their social relationships on finding partners to play the corroborating roles. Here are some common ones.

"Why Don't You? Yes, But . . . ." A person consistently asks for suggestions or advice and then consistently rejects what is offered. The other participants assume that the principal player is attempting to solve a real problem in a concrete manner so they offer suggestions. The principal player gets at least two payoffs—attention from other people, and putting others down by implying "That's really a dumb suggestion." The other participants may get a payoff through telling themselves "I must be a warm, caring person, because this person respects and trusts me enough to share this problem with me."

"One Up." One person seeks to top whatever someone else says. If the conversation is about big fish, the One Upper has a story about how he caught this mammoth fish. If the topic is about bad grades, the One Upper amazes everyone with how bad her grades are.

"Wooden Leg." People attempt to manipulate others to not expect too much from them because of handicaps like being raised in a ghetto, a tragic romance, or emotional problems. Closely related, *"If it weren't for . . ."* is a cop-out game in which players seek to rationalize failure.

"Poor Me." A person continually seeks sympathy and may at times try to get others to do things for him. Closely related is *"Ain't It Awful"* where the person takes a negative view of events. Such a person is usually seeking attention and sympathy. In *"There I Go Again,"* the player excuses away her ineffective behavior without taking responsibility.

Some clients enjoy playing "Confession" when they tell all their personal and interpersonal troubles in the hopes of receiving recognition and help from others. Some unhappily married men get together and enjoy discussing "Wives Are a Pain" as a way of venting their unhappiness. Some unhappily married wives enjoy discussing "Men Aren't Worth It" as a way of venting their frustrations. Parents enjoy discussing "Look How Hard I've Tried" when a home situation is particularly uproarious and hostile as a way to relieve their frustrations that the goals for their family have not been achieved. Many people avoid assuming responsibility for their failures and shortcomings by playing "It's All Them."

Some individuals who have received few positive strokes end up seeking a lot of negative strokes, which to them is better than receiving no strokes. One game that is played to receive negative strokes is "Kick Me," in which the player does things that elicit negative reactions from others.

People who enjoy creating trouble for others are apt to play "Let's You and Him Fight."

People who receive psychological rewards in analyzing others and in giving advice often play "Psychiatry." A person trying to have as many different sexual relationships as possible may be playing "Love 'Em and Leave 'Em." Men are socialized in our society to play "Mr. Macho," and women are socialized to play "Miss America."

"Monday Morning Quarterbacks" make themselves feel important by telling you what you should have done differently *after* things have not turned out well for you.

The number of different games that can be played is best described as infinite.

Life Scripts

A life script and a theatrical script have many similarities. Each has a cast of characters, dialogue, themes and plots, acts and scenes; generally both move toward a climax. Often, however, a person is unaware or only vaguely aware of the life scripts he or she is acting out. Public stages on which people act out their scripts include home, social gatherings, church, school, office, and factory. As Shakespeare noted, "All the world's a stage."

We all have "life scripts" (plans) that we form during childhood that are based on early beliefs about ourselves and others. These plans are developed from early interactions with parents and others and are largely determined by the pattern of strokes that are received. These scripts enable us to conceptualize where we are in our activities and direct what we need to do to complete our activities and to accomplish our goals. Scripts help us remember what we have done in the past.

Parental opinions, suggestions, and encouragements supply much of the life script. Examples include "She's such a cute girl, everyone loves her." "He's stupid and will never amount to much." Fairy tales, myths, TV shows, early life experiences, and children's stories are all important sources of life scripts. However, the life script is still the creation of the person holding the script. Our life script may be about winning or losing, being a success or a failure, being exciting or banal. Each script also includes specific roles. For example, at a young age Dan Kull comes to believe his roles in life include: being the breadwinner in his family, finding a wife who will be submissive, partying with his male friends, and going hunting or fishing whenever the opportunity arises.

Harris (1969) identified four general life scripts that people choose based on how they view themselves in comparison with others. These four positions are (1) I'm OK—You're OK; (2) I'm OK—You're not OK; (3) I'm not OK—You're OK; and (4) I'm not OK—You're not OK.

"I'm OK—You're OK" people tend to be productive, law-abiding people who are successful and who have positive, meaningful relationships with others.

"I'm OK—You're not OK" people predispose themselves to exploit, cheat, and rob others or succeed at the expense of others. Criminals, ruthless business executives, and destructive lovers exemplify this script.

"I'm not OK—You're OK" people feel inferior in the presence of those they judge as superior. This can lead to withdrawal to avoid being reminded of not being OK, but it is not the only alternative. The person may write a counterscript based on lines from early authority figures: "You can be OK if . . ." The person is then driven to achieve the "if" contingencies.

"I'm not OK—You're not OK" people tend to be the most unhappy and disturbed. Prochaska (1979) stated:

> The extreme withdrawal of schizophrenia or psychotic depression is their most common fate. They may regress to an infantile state in the primitive hope that they may once again receive the strokes of being held and fed. Without intervention from caring others, these individuals will live out a self-destructive life of institutionalization, irreversible alcoholism, senseless homicide, or suicide. (p. 241)

Decisions about life scripts are generally made early in childhood. James and Jongeward (1971) provide an incident in the life of a 43-year-old client that led her to conclude "I'm not OK, and men are not OK either."

> My father was a brutal alcoholic. When he was drunk he would hit me and scream at me. I would try to hide. One day when he came home, the door flew open and he was drunker than usual. He picked up a butcher knife and started running through the house. I hid in a coat closet. I was almost four years old. I was so scared in the closet. It was dark and spooky, and things kept hitting me in the face. That day I decided who men were—beasts, who would only try to hurt me. I was a large child and I remember thinking, "If I were smaller, he'd love me" or "If I were prettier, he'd love me." I always thought I wasn't worth anything. (p. 35)

Based on this script, she married an alcoholic at age 23, and for the next 20 years lived her life drama of feeling worthless and living with a "beast."

One area where our behavior is largely guided by scripts is sexual behavior. Sexual scripts result from elaborate prior learning in which we acquire an etiquette of sexual behavior. Scripts tell us who are appropriate sexual partners, what sexual activity is expected, where and when the sexual activity should occur, and what should be the sequence of the different sexual behaviors.

Scripts vary greatly from one culture to another. Powdermaker (1933) provided the following description of a script about female masturbation generally held by the Lesu of the South Pacific:

> A woman will masturbate if she is sexually excited and there is no man to satisfy her. A couple may be having intercourse in the same house, or near enough for her to see them, and she may thus become aroused. She then sits down and bends her right leg so that her heel presses against her genitalia. Even young girls of about six years may do this quite casually as they sit on the ground. The women and men talk about it freely, and there is no shame attached to it. It is a customary position for women to take, and they learn it in childhood. They never use their hands for manipulation. (p. 241)

Most life scripts are learned at an early age. As children grow they learn to play roles—villains, law enforcers, heroes, heroines, victims, and rescuers—and seek others to play complementary roles. Through playing roles, children integrate new themes and parts into their roles and gradually develop their life scripts. The particular scripts that are developed are substantially influenced by the reactions they receive from significant people in their lives.

Individuals follow scripts, and so do families and cultures. Cultural scripts are expected patterns of behavior within a society. In regard to cultural scripts, James and Jongeward (1971) noted:

> Script themes differ from one culture to another. The script can contain themes of suffering, persecution, and hardship (historically the Jews); it can contain themes of building empires and making conquests (as the Romans once did). Throughout history some nations have acted from a "top-dog" position of the conqueror; some from an "under-dog" position of the conquered. In early America, where people came to escape oppression, to exploit the situation, and to explore the unknown, a basic theme was "struggling for survival." In many cases this struggle was acted out by pioneering and settling. (p. 70)

Historically, women were socialized in our society to have life scripts that were different from those of men. American women traditionally were expected to be affectionate, passive, conforming, sensitive, intuitive, dependent, and "sugar and spice and everything nice." They were supposed to be concerned primarily with domestic life, to be nurturing, to instinctively love to care for babies and young children, to be deeply concerned about their personal appearance, and to be self-sacrificing for their family. They were socialized to not appear to be ambitious, aggressive, competitive, or more intelligent than men. They were expected to be ignorant and uninterested in sports, economics, or politics. In relationships with men they were socialized to not initiate forming a relationship and were expected to be tender, feminine, emotional, and appreciative.

There were also a number of traditional sex-role expectations for males in our society. A male was expected to be tough, fearless, logical, self-reliant, independent, and aggressive. He was expected to have definite opinions on the major issues of the day and was expected to make authoritative decisions at work and at home. He was expected to be strong, to be a sturdy oak, never to be depressed, vulnerable, or anxious. He was not supposed to be "sissy" or feminine. He was expected not to cry or openly display so-called feminine emotions. He was expected to be the provider, the breadwinner, to be competent in all situations. He was supposed to be physically strong, self-reliant, athletic; to have a manly air of confidence and toughness; to be daring and aggressive; to be brave and forceful; always to be in a position to dominate any situation. He was supposed to initiate relationships with women and was expected to be dominant in relationships with them. (The women's movement has now made changes in these sex-role scripts.)

American society is amazingly diverse today, and each of our subcultures has its own scripts. Street gangs, Hispanics, Texans, Presbyterians, Jews, professional baseball players, dentists, farmers, and college students each have their own subcultural scripts. For example, common aspects of college student scripts include last-minute cramming for exams, procrastination, partying, idealism, shortage of money, and expectations of success and happiness following graduation.

Families have scripts. These scripts provide a set of directions for family members. Examples include the following:

We Winships have always been pillars of the community.
We Navarres have always been rowdy.
The men in our family have always held political offices in our community, and the women have always been active in the church.
We Hubbards have always been in trouble with the police.
We Schomakers have always been gamblers.
We Collinses have always taken a long vacation each year.
We Hepps have never had to ask for a handout from anyone.
We Watsons have all gone to college.
We Rices have always been Democrats.
The men in our family have all been coal miners who are active in union activities.

If a family member does not live up to the script expectation, he or she is often viewed as a "deviant" or as a "black sheep."

Berne (1966) emphasized the importance of scripts in determining human behavior:

> Nearly all human activity is programmed by an ongoing script dating from early childhood, so that the feeling of autonomy is nearly always an illusion—an illusion which is the greatest affliction of the human race because it makes awareness, honesty, creativity, and intimacy possible for only a few fortunate individuals. For the rest of humanity, other people are seen mainly as objects to be manipulated. They must be invited, persuaded, seduced, bribed or forced into playing the proper roles to reinforce the protagonist's position and fulfill his script. (p. 310)

The number of script themes is infinite. A few of the more common themes are:

I must be loved by everyone.
I've got to be perfect.
I've got to be the best at what I do.
My purpose in life is to save sinners.
When people tell me their problems, I have to rescue them.
I will take my life some day.
To be noticed I must play tricks on people.
People will only love me if I make them laugh.
I'll also be a victim.
I'm a martyr.
I can always get what I want by being pushy.
I'll eventually go crazy.
My life will always be one big party.
I'm cut out to be a leader.
I'm a failure and always will be.
I'll never get anywhere.
I've got to save for a rainy day.
If I acquire a lot of money, I'll be popular.
I'm always the life of a party.
I'm always miserable.
Life has always shortchanged me.
I should always be silent; it is wrong to rock the boat.
Men are assholes.
I will never let anyone get the best of me.
I'm headed for fame and fortune.

James and Jongeward (1971) provided the following example of how a life script is played:

> A woman who had taken the position, "Men are bums," marries a sequence of "bums." Part of her script is based on "Men are not OK." She fulfills her own prophecy by nagging, pushing, complaining, and generally making life miserable for her husband (who has his part to play). Eventually, she manipulates him into leaving. Then she can say, "See, I told you. Men are bums who leave you when the going gets rough." (pp. 84–85)

Often people play games as part of their life scripts. A person whose script requires him to be Casanova plays the game "Love 'Em and Leave 'Em." A person whose script requires "I won't let anyone get the best of me" is apt to play "One Up."

Theory of Psychopathology

According to transactional analysis, personal problems involve personality problems (intrapsychic) or interpersonal problems, or both.

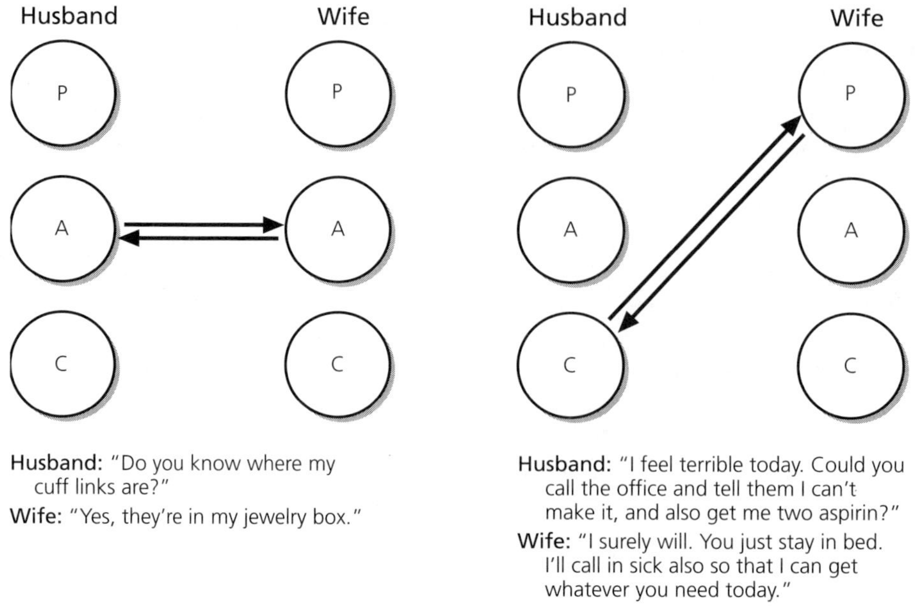

Husband
Wife
P
A
C
Husband
Wife
P
A
C
Husband: "Do you know where my cuff links are?"
Wife: "Yes, they're in my jewelry box."
Husband: "I feel terrible today. Could you call the office and tell them I can't make it, and also get me two aspirin?"
Wife: "I surely will. You just stay in bed. I'll call in sick also so that I can get whatever you need today."

CTRM FIGURE 3.2 Two examples of complementary transactions

Intrapsychic problems result from several sources. Besides the self-defeating life script described previously, a person can rigidly hold to one ego state and shut out the other two. A balance of the three ego states is healthy. "Workaholics" spend too much time in the Adult ego state and thereby cannot enjoy their family or have fun. People who are too much the "Parent" in romantic relationships constantly give advice and smother their partner by trying to do things for, rather than with, them.

In another intrapsychic problem, the person is in an inappropriate ego state for what the circumstances warrant—for example, clowning around (being in the Child) when one should be studying for an exam or completing an urgent project at work.

In interpersonal problems, TA focuses on how different individuals communicate (both verbally and nonverbally) with one another. There are three rules of communication:

1. "Communication will proceed smoothly as long as transactions are *complementary*." Complementary transactions are those in which the arrows are parallel (see CTRM Figure 3.2).

2. "Communication on the specific topic ceases immediately whenever a crossed transaction occurs." A *crossed transaction* is one in which the arrows are not parallel, as illustrated in CTRM Figure 3.3.

3. "Behavior cannot be predicted by attention to the social message alone; the psychological message is key to understanding the meaning and to predicting behavior." Examples of psychological games are presented in CTRM Figure 3.4.

Psychological games can be constructive or destructive. If the payoffs help people, then they are constructive. For example, people who volunteer to give their time and resources at social services agencies sometimes are volunteering for some hidden personal reasons and usually receive such payoffs as feeling worthwhile and good about themselves. In some cases boredom and loneliness are also curbed. At the same time such volunteers perform useful services for others. Other games, because of the payoff, are undesirable. Some people continually play "One-Upmanship," where they are overly competitive, even to the point of continually disparaging others and trying to top every story that others tell them.

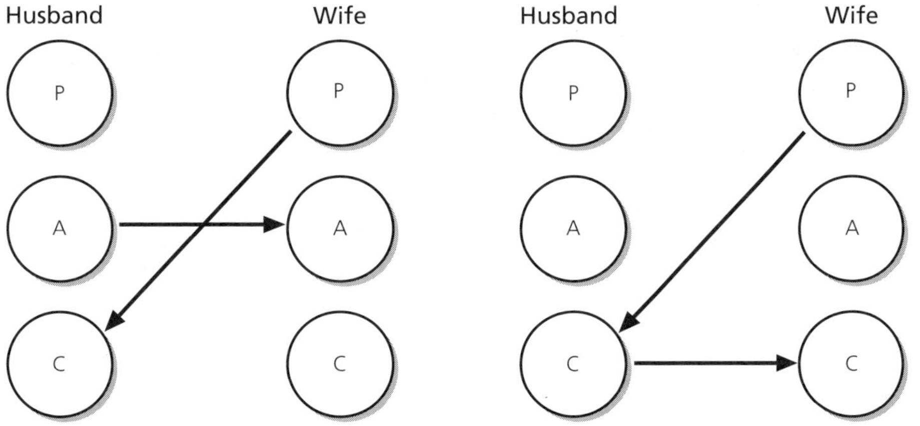

Husband: "Do you know where my cuff links are?"

Wife: "When are you ever going to learn to take care of your things—you lose everything."

Husband: "Let's call in sick to work today and go fishing."

Wife: "You're so irresponsible. You know it isn't right to do that."

CTRM FIGURE 3.3 Two examples of crossed transactions

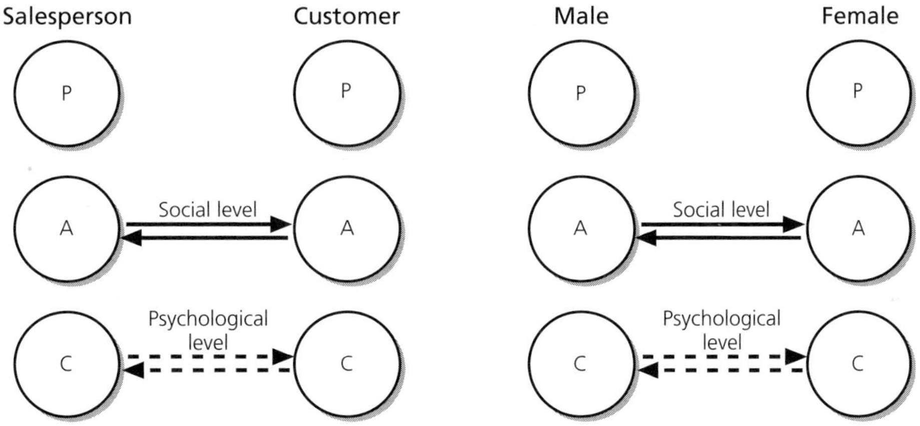

Social level

Salesperson: "This is a better product, but I don't think you can afford it."

Customer: "I'll take it!"

Psychological level

Salesperson: "I'll motivate this person to buy the expensive item."

Customer: "I'll show this salesperson I'm as good as anyone else."

Social level

Male: "That dress really looks attractive on you."

Female: "Well, thank you. I like people who notice positive things about me."

Psychological level

Male: "If I say something nice, maybe I'll find out if she's interested in getting something going between us."

Female: "This fellow appears interested in me, and I'll indirectly indicate that I'm interested in him."

CTRM FIGURE 3.4 Two examples of psychological games

Theory of Therapy

Transactional therapy seeks to have clients first become aware of the intrapsychic and interpersonal problems they face. To help clients gain insight into their problems, therapists teach them the terms of TA. This instruction occurs in therapy (either one-to-one or in groups) and by giving clients reading such as *Games People Play* (Berne, 1964), *I'm OK—You're OK* (Harris, 1969), and *Born to Win* (James & Jongeward, 1971). Early in this instructional process, clients are taught *structural analysis;* that is, how to identify their Parent, Adult, and Child ego states. They also learn to analyze problematic transactions by diagramming them, and they learn to analyze games and life scripts. If TA classes are offered in the client's community, clients may be urged to take a course in TA before or during therapy. As clients learn about the TA approach and become more aware of their own ego states, they often are able to teach others how to analyze themselves. Prochaska (1979, p. 243) stated: "The client's work is usually a pattern of going from student to self-analyzer to teacher of others."

To encourage clients to analyze their communications in terms of the TA format, therapists frequently ask, "Which ego state is talking now?" If clients are confused or disagree with the therapist's or group's analysis of their ego states, the therapist may audiotape or videotape the clients' interactions and then play the tape back to let them see and hear how they are interacting.

Clients' problems are then analyzed in terms of TA concepts so clients gain insight into their personal problems. Much of the therapist's work is helping clients to become aware, often through confronting them, of the ways in which they contribute to their intrapsychic and interpersonal problems.

Game Analysis

Two treatment techniques increasingly used in transactional analysis are game analysis and script analysis. In *game analysis* therapists help clients gain insight into some of their interactions through game concepts. Game analysis focuses on games that lead to undesirable outcomes for the client or for others.

The therapist has several roles in analyzing games: (1) Teach clients the terminology of game analysis. This perhaps can best be accomplished at the first occasion in which a therapist helps a client gain insight into a game. (2) Point out that playing games is not necessarily undesirable. This may be therapeutically valuable; some clients may feel it is wrong to play games because games have an exploitative connotation. This feeling may cause resistances to examining games. These resistances can be reduced by informing clients that everyone plays games; some games have beneficial outcomes, whereas others have undesirable outcomes. (3) Help clients recognize destructive games, and gain insight into how these games are being played. (4) Encourage clients to explore new ways of responding after they understand how their role leads to undesirable consequences. (5) Help clients assign names to undesirable games they are playing. Using colloquial names for games is often acceptable and advantageous, because they are memorable and have more meaning for clients. (6) Teach people what games they need to play to achieve their goals. Some people have goals considered beneficial for themselves and society but do not know how to achieve these goals. Often such people can be instructed on what to do using game concepts. For example, a person seeking a job may need to learn how to play "How to Get an Interview" and "How to Sell Yourself in an Interview." A couple who feud frequently may need to learn "How to Fight Fairly" and "How to Give in a Relationship to Get What You Want."

Game analysis appears to be a useful therapeutic approach for three reasons: (1) Naming a behavior pattern (in this case a game) increases clients' capacities to recognize similar transactions when they occur in the future. Once clients recognize that a game is causing them difficulty, they are in a better position to cease their destructive behavior and to explore alternative modes of behavior. (2) Analyzing behavior in terms of games intrigues clients and, therefore, can lead to greater involvement in therapy and increase their motivation to resolve their difficulties. (3) Game analysis provides clients with a way to analyze problematic interactions.

Script Analysis

Script analysis can be defined as a treatment technique in which a therapist enables clients to gain insight into the scripts they are acting out through the use of script concepts. The types of scripts that are the primary focus of script analysis are those that lead to undesirable outcomes for clients or for others.

CASE EXAMPLE

Game Analysis and Script Analysis

James and Jongeward (1971) described the life scripts of Persecutor, Victim, and Rescuer. Often a person will play a variety of games in conjunction with one of these life scripts. Victims may also be persecuting those around them, and occasionally shift directly to Persecutor. In the following example, James and Jongeward (1971) show how transactions between a married couple can be analyzed in terms of games and life script concerns:

> Ted and Mary came into counseling complaining about the failure of their second honeymoon. Each claimed to have been victimized by the other. He shouted, "You had the gall to take your mother along. She even shared our motel room." She retorted, "And you were very rude and embarrassed me." After a number of hostile exchanges, they were asked to tell about their first honeymoon. Ted challenged, "What does that have to do with us now?" Mary retorted, "I'll tell you what. You took your parents along on our honeymoon fifteen years ago. You said, 'They never get a chance to go anywhere.' You've been taking advantage of me ever since." (p. 89)

Mary had assumed the role of Victim all these years. She had played the games of "Poor Me" and "See How Hard I Tried," and finally got even by assuming the role of Persecutor herself. Her favorite game became "Now I've Got You, You S.O.B." For 15 years the theme of their marriage drama had been "Getting Even."

The therapist has the following roles in analyzing scripts: (1) Teach clients the terminology of script analysis. (2) Point out that everyone is playing a variety of scripts, and that scripts largely determine human behavior. Indicate that some scripts have beneficial outcomes and others have undesirable outcomes. (3) Help clients recognize scripts with undesirable outcomes. (4) Help clients assign names to scripts they are playing, so they can easily identify the script when they encounter it in the future. (5) Help clients develop new, desirable scripts, and encourage and teach them more effective responses.

Game and script analysis can be used with families and with small-sized groups as well as with individuals.

TA therapists emphasize personal responsibility. They believe, as does Ellis (1962), that clients are responsible for their emotions, their thoughts, and their behaviors (this concept is more fully described in Module 6). If a client says "I can't think today," the TA therapist will confront him with "You mean you have decided not to think today." Or if a client says "She makes me feel bad," the TA therapist will say "You know that you are choosing to feel bad—in response to her." Or if a client says "He made me steal," the therapist will say "You mean you chose to steal."

As clients become aware of their personal problems and of their own contributions, various courses of resolution are explored. Clients then make a contract specifying what they will do (and perhaps also what the therapist will do) to attempt to resolve the problem. Workaholics, for example, might make a contract limiting the number of hours per day they will spend on work. They may also be given homework assignments that involve them in fun activities.

TA therapies differ widely. Berne originally used TA as an adjunct to psychoanalysis. TA has also been combined with reality therapy and rational therapy. Other TA therapists restrict their practice to the TA approach. Transactional analysis is used individually, with groups, with families, with couples, in marathons, in prison, in outpatient and inpatient wards, and in business and industry settings.

TA group therapy uses a variety of techniques. One approach in game analysis involves psychodrama, originally developed by Moreno (1946). Dusay and Dusay (1979) described a psychodrama in which the client plays the director and instructs other group members in how he or she is playing a destructive game. Dusay and Dusay (1979) noted that with psychodrama, clients can step outside their own game:

> . . . in this view he can view, think and direct his own part in the game. . . . Through these maneuvers, the client will gain a new awareness and experiment with corrective procedures. (p. 403)

Psychodrama is further described in Module 9.

Evaluation

Transactional analysis has grown remarkably in acceptance and popularity since its formulation by Eric Berne in the 1950s. Dusay and Dusay (1989) provided reasons for its popularity:

> Because of its easily understood vocabulary and because of the willingness of therapists to share ideas with clients, TA rapidly became a popular psychotherapy. As such, TA has been used not only by psychiatrists, psychologists, social workers, and other traditional therapists, but also by paraprofessionals who found that the theoretical aspects of TA were easy to learn and had direct applicability to their concerns. Indeed, street workers and prison inmates have become outstanding TA therapists. Effort for the TA therapist is in practical applications rather than in decoding mystical jargon. (p. 448)

The widespread popularity of TA books suggests that readers find TA concepts helpful in resolving numerous personal problems.

Another positive feature of TA is to borrow techniques (such as psychodrama) from other therapy approaches that are useful in producing therapeutic change. Transactional analysis is an "open" therapeutic approach that actively encourages experimentation with new techniques. In contrast to other approaches, participation in TA is even enjoyable for both clients and therapists. The approach uses a number of experimental exercises, such as role playing. In addition, analyzing personal problems in terms of games and life scripts has a game mystique that facilitates interest.

However, some criticisms can also be made:

1. There have been very few studies on the outcome of transactional analysis. In a review of TA, Merkel (1975) was able to locate only two studies, and the results were inconclusive regarding whether TA is effective. In a review of research conducted on TA, Dusay and Dusay (1989, pp. 438–439) cite only a few outcome studies—none of which provides convincing evidence that TA is effective.

2. The concepts of TA explain some aspects of human behavior but certainly not all. For example, what causes grief, depression, anger, love, happiness, and other emotions? How are such emotions perpetuated? What causes burglaries, alcoholism, crimes of violence, or such positive actions as helping others in need? Game analysis and script analysis provide some reasons but not all of them.

3. There is a danger in analyzing the personality as the separate ego states of Parent, Adult, and Child. Most authorities on human behavior emphasize the importance of the personality's functioning as an integrated "whole." The danger of a tripartite personality approach is that it may encourage clients to function in separate roles as a Parent, Adult, and Child rather than as an integrated individual. For example, TA indicates the Adult ego state is best suited for work activities. But being a rational computer at work will lead a person to miss out on the "fun" activities at work and probably lead to ostracism by fellow employees who will find an Adult to be boring, especially during slack times. Even when times are hectic, humor is often useful in relieving tension.

4. I have participated in some TA groups and have found it difficult at times to determine which ego state a transaction is coming from. I have asked leaders of groups to identify the ego state producing certain communications and have gotten different answers. For example, in response to "If a male student intern in field placement decides to greet his first client as his father greets a stranger, and the father is very effective in interacting with people, which ego state is such a transaction coming from?" TA group leaders gave three different answers. My concern is that the counseling process can get bogged down in a long, fruitless discussion of which ego state is the source of a transaction rather than focusing on exploring and resolving clients' problems.

In raising this concern I am aware that Thompson (1972) found in a study that ego states are observable, that trained TA experts have a high degree of agreement in rating which ego state is in operation in a given client, and that naive observers can be trained to correctly identify ego states. (Thompson is an advocate of TA.)

Part of my concern results from the observation that there are *substantial* differences among TA authorities in defining the PAC ego states. Berne (1964) stated the Parent ego state has two forms, Direct Parent and Indirect Parent, and the Child has two forms, Adapted Child and Natural Child. Dusay and Dusay (1979) stated that the Parent ego state has two forms, the Critical Parent and the Nurturing Parent, and the Child's two forms are Adapted Child and Free Child. James and Jongeward (1971) stated the two Parent forms are the Nurturing Parent and the Prejudicial Parent, and the Child ego state has three forms, Natural Child, Adapted Child, and Little Professor. Steiner (1974) divided the PAC states into 27 forms!

Summary

In transactional analysis the human personality is structured into three separate ego states: Parent, Adult, and Child. Basic human needs and psychosocial drives (for example, recognition hunger) are motivational forces.

Intrapsychic problems arise because clients adopt self-defeating life scripts, rigidly hold to one ego state and shut out the other two, and operate in inappropriate ego states. Interpersonal problems arise because clients play destructive psychological games and cross transactions while communicating.

In TA analysis clients strive to become aware of their intrapsychic and interpersonal problems. TA therapists then analyzed and interpreted problems in terms of TA concepts. Once their problems are analyzed, clients contract to pursue specific courses of resolution. TA emphasizes the importance of clients' taking personal responsibility for their thoughts, emotions, and actions and uses a number of experiential techniques (such as psychodrama) to help clients understand and work out their problems. Two treatment techniques increasingly being used are game and script analysis.

Especially useful TA concepts include game analysis, script analysis, complementary transactions and crossed transactions, seeking strokes, and personal responsibility for emotions and actions. TA theorists need to work toward consistent definitions of the Parent, Adult, and Child ego states. There is also a need for outcome studies on the effectiveness of this approach.

EXERCISES

1. *LIFE SCRIPT ANALYSIS*

Goal: To identify and describe destructive life scripts and to explore changing scripts.

Step 1: Read the following life script.

Mrs. H has been married for 22 years. She was brought up to believe that a woman's role was to be supportive of her husband and to do the domestic tasks involved in raising children. She and her husband, Paul, have two children. The oldest, Kelly, is a senior in college, and Jason is a freshman. Both children no longer live at home.

The first several years of their marriage were fairly happy but a financial struggle. Paul was a life insurance salesman, so it took several years to get a large enough number of clients to make a decent standard of living. Mrs. H helped out by doing paperwork and answering the phone at home.

As they became more financially secure, they took an occasional vacation and traveled some. About seven years ago, Mrs. H discovered that for the previous five years Paul occasionally had extramarital affairs. When Mrs. H confronted him, there was considerable conflict. Mrs. H considered a divorce, but she was afraid she wouldn't be able to support herself and the children. She decided to stay with her husband, particularly after he apologized and stated he would never stray again.

Paul, as Mrs. H discovered 18 months later, did not live up to his word. He continued to have occasional affairs. Mrs. H has tried to make the best of it. She has not been sexually involved with her husband since the time she first discovered his philandering. Their marriage has become an empty shell. The children have now left home, and Mrs. H has little to do. Increasingly depressed, she has felt considerable tension in recent years. Her husband and her doctor note that her medical concerns border on hypochondria. Her role of raising children is complete. Her life plans of having a satisfying, happy marriage have long since disappeared. Her husband now earns enough that if she stays in the marriage she can live comfortably financially. But she is increasingly depressed about her circumstances. With

(continued)

EXERCISES
(continued)

few job skills, she believes living independently from her husband would be very difficult. Being a strict Catholic, she is morally opposed to a divorce. She is in a severe dilemma about what she should do.

Step 2: Construct a destructive life script using someone you know, but code his or her name for confidentiality reasons.

Step 3: Form groups of three and share your scripts. Discuss what might be done to help your client.

Step 4: Class discussion of the strengths and potential pitfalls of this technique for social work practice.

2. *GAME ANALYSIS*

Goal: To identify and describe destructive games and to explore how to prevent them from being replayed.

Step 1: Class brainstorms a list of games people play.

Step 2: Think about your family, friends, fellow students, and professors. What games do they play? Select a particularly destructive one or one that really annoys you and analyze it using TA concepts and terminology. For confidentiality reasons, code the names of the persons you write about.

Step 3: Break into groups of five and share your games. Do "universal" games emerge from your analyses—that is, do people tend to play similar games? Brainstorm some contracts "clients" in your scripts could pursue to resolve their problems.

Step 4: Class discussion of the effectiveness of game analysis and social contracts in social work practice.

Step 5: Food for thought: Consider your own way of relating to people. What games do you play?

3. *ANALYZING YOUR OWN LIFE SCRIPTS*

Goal: To identify and reflect on some of your own life scripts.

Step 1: As you learned in this module, life scripts are generally formed at a young age. To discover your own life script, think back to your childhood. What attitudes did your parents convey to you through comments about the following aspects of your life?

Your health	Your friends
Your worth	Your gender roles
Your intelligence	Your abilities
Your morals and values	Your future
Your looks	Your race

Step 2: Reflect on whether your current assessment of yourself is consistent or inconsistent with what your parents conveyed to you.

Step 3: Class discussion of the merits and shortcomings of this exercise.

MODULE 4

Behavior Therapy

No one person is credited with developing behavioral approaches to psychotherapy. Behavior therapists vary considerably in both theory and technique. The main assumption in this therapy is that maladaptive behaviors are acquired primarily through learning and can be modified through additional learning.

Founders

Historically, learning theory has been the philosophical foundation for behavior therapy even though there has never been agreement as to which learning theory is the core of behavior therapy. A number of authorities have advanced somewhat different theories of how people learn. Pavlov, a Russian who lived between 1849 and 1936, was one of the earliest. Other prominent learning theorists include E. L. Thorndike (1913), E. R. Guthrie (1935), C. L. Hull (1943), E. C. Tolman (1932), and B. F. Skinner (1938). Behavior therapists who have achieved international recognition for developing therapies based on learning principles include R. E. Alberti and M. L. Emmons (1970), A. Bandura (1969), B. F. Skinner (1948), J. B. Watson and R. Rayner (1920), and J. Wolpe (1958).

In spite of the wide variation in behavioral therapy approaches and techniques, there are some common emphases. One is that the maladaptive behavior (such as bed-wetting) is the problem and needs to be changed. This approach is in sharp contrast to the psychoanalytic approach that views the problematic behavior as a *symptom* of some underlying, unconscious causes. Psychoanalysts assert that the underlying causes must be treated to prevent the substitution of new symptoms or the return of old symptoms, but behavior therapists assert that treating the problematic behavior will not result in symptom substitution.

Behavior therapists assert that therapies must be tested and validated by rigorous experimental procedures. This focus requires that the goals of therapy be articulated in behavioral terms that can be measured. Baseline levels of problematic behaviors are established before therapy to measure whether the approach is producing the desired change in the rate or intensity of responding.

The use of behavior modification therapy in counseling has increased dramatically in the past 30 years. Behavior therapy intervention techniques are now among the most widely used techniques in counseling and psychotherapy (Wilson, 1989).

Behavior therapists have devoted little attention to developing a behavioral model of personality. Behaviorists generally believe that environmental conditions or experiences are of much greater influence in controlling behavior than are internal personality traits.

Types of Learning Processes

Before we examine the prominent behavioral therapy techniques, it behooves us to discuss the three major types of learning processes—operant conditioning, respondent conditioning, and modeling.

Operant Conditioning

According to learning theory, much of human behavior is determined by positive and negative reinforcers. A *positive reinforcer* is any stimulus that, when applied following a behavior, increases or strengthens that behavior. Common examples include food, water, sex, attention, affection, and approval. The list of positive reinforcers is inexhaustible and highly individualized. Praise, for example, is a positive reinforcer when, and only when, it maintains or increases the behavior with which it is associated (for example, efforts to improve one's writing skills).

A synonym for negative reinforcer is aversive stimulus. A *negative reinforcer* (or aversive stimulus) is any stimulus that a person will terminate or avoid if given the opportunity. Common examples include frowns, electric shock, and criticism. (The same stimulus—for example, the smell of Limburger cheese—can be a positive reinforcer for one person and a negative reinforcer for another.)

There are four basic learning principles involving positive reinforcers and aversive stimuli:

1. If a positive reinforcer (for example, food) is presented to a person following a response, the result is positive reinforcement. With positive reinforcement, the occurrence of a given behavior is strengthened or increased.
2. If a positive reinforcer is withdrawn following a person's response, the result is punishment.
3. If an aversive stimulus (for example, an electric shock) is presented to a person following a response, the result is punishment. (As can be seen, there are two types of punishment.)
4. If an aversive stimulus is withdrawn following a person's response, the result is negative reinforcement. In negative reinforcement, a response (behavior) is increased by removing an aversive stimulus (for example, fastening one's seat belt to turn off the obnoxiously loud and annoying buzzer).

In sum, positive and negative reinforcements increase behavior, and punishment decreases behavior. Principles of operant conditioning are used in several behavioral techniques described in this module, including assertiveness training, token economies, contingency contracting, and aversive techniques.

Respondent Conditioning

Respondent learning has also been called classical or Pavlovian conditioning. A wide range of everyday behaviors are considered respondent behaviors—perspiring, salivating, and, more important, many anxieties, fears, and phobias. A key concept in respondent learning is "pairing"; that is, behaviors are learned by being consistently paired over time with other behaviors or events. To explain respondent conditioning, let's first define the following key terms:

- *Neutral stimulus (NS):* One that elicits little or no response.
- *Unconditioned stimulus (UCS):* One that elicits an unlearned or innate response.
- *Unlearned response (UR):* A response that is innate; for example, salivating because of food in the mouth.
- *Conditioned response (CR):* A new response that has been learned.
- *Conditioned stimulus (CS):* An original neutral stimulus that, through pairing with an unconditioned stimulus, now begins to elicit a conditioned response.

Respondent learning asserts that when a neutral stimulus (NS) is paired with an unconditioned stimulus (UCS), the neutral stimulus will also come to elicit a response similar to that being elicited by the UCS. That new response is called a conditioned response (CR) because it has been learned; the originally neutral stimulus, once it begins to elicit the response, becomes the conditioned stimulus (CS). Thus, it is possible for an event that originally elicited no fear whatsoever (for example, being in the dark) to elicit fear when it is paired with a stimulus that does elicit fear (for example, horrifying stories about being in the dark). This learning process is indicated in the following paradigm:

1. *UCS* (horrifying stories about being in the dark) → elicits *UR* (fear)
2. *NS* (being in the dark) paired with *UCS* → elicits *CR* (fear)
3. *NS* becomes *CS* → elicits *CR* (fear)

The *CS-CR* bond can be broken by respondent extinction or by counterconditioning. *Respondent extinction* involves continuing presentation of the conditioned stimulus without any further pairing with the unconditioned stimulus. Respondent extinction gradually weakens, and eventually eliminates, the CS-CR bond. Implosive therapy, soon to be discussed, is based on this principle.

Counterconditioning is based on the principle that the CS-CR bond can be broken by using new responses that are stronger than, and incompatible with, old responses that are elicited by the same stimulus. For example, it is possible to teach a person to relax (new response) instead of becoming anxious (old response) when confronted with a particular stimulus (for example, the prospect of flying in a small plane). Systematic desensitization and in vivo desensitization (to be discussed later in this module) are based on counterconditioning. Another technique to be discussed, covert sensitization, is based on establishing new CS-CR connections to eliminate problematic behavior.

Modeling

Modeling refers to a change in behavior as a result of the observation of another's behavior—that is, learning by vicarious experience or imitation. Much of everyday learning is thought to take place through modeling—using both live models and symbolic models (such as films). Modeling has been used in behavior modification to develop new behaviors that are not in a person's repertoire—for example, showing a youngster how to swing a bat. Modeling has also been used to eliminate anxieties and fears—for example, using a model in assertiveness training. Anxieties and fears are reduced or eliminated through modeling by exposing fearful observers to modeled events in which the model performs the feared activity without experiencing any adverse effects and even enjoys the process.

Theory of Psychotherapy

Behavior therapy is based on the assumption that all behavior occurs in response to stimulation, internal or external. The first task of the behavior therapist is to identify the probable stimulus-response (S-R) connections that are occurring for the client. This part of the therapy process is called the behavioral or functional analysis. The following illustrates an S-R connection: For a person who fears heights, the stimulus (S) of flying in a small plane elicits the response (R) of intense anxiety and avoidance of the stimulus.

Prior to and during the time therapists perform the behavioral analysis, they also attempt to establish a working relationship. (The characteristics of a working relationship have been described in Chapter 5.) In regard to this emphasis on establishing a working relationship, Chambless and Goldstein (1979) stated:

> Although behaviorists are often portrayed as cold and mechanical, a study of recordings of therapy sessions yields a different picture. When measured on variables used in the study of client-centered therapy, behavior therapists showed high warmth and positive regard for their clients (equal to other psychotherapists in the study) and higher empathy and self-congruence than the other therapists. (p. 243)

During the behavioral analysis, therapists attempt to determine the stimuli associated with the maladaptive responses. Through this analysis, both client and therapist arrive at an understanding of the problem and generally how it developed. This insight, although it does not treat the problem, is useful because it reduces client anxiety, and they no longer feel possessed or overwhelmed by unknown, mysterious forces. Errors about hypothesized S-R connections at this diagnostic stage usually lead to ineffective treatment because the treatment will then be focused on treating S-R connections that are *not* involved in perpetuating the maladaptive behavior.

A behavioral analysis begins with the therapist taking a detailed history of the presenting problem, its course, and particularly its association with current experiences. In making such an analysis, it is crucial to obtain specific, concrete details about the circumstances in which the presenting problem arises. If, for example, clients are shy in some situations, it is important to identify the specific interactions in which they are shy. Furthermore, it is important to determine the reasons they are shy: Is it because they do not know how to express themselves, or is it because they have certain fears? The treatment chosen depends on such information. If clients do not know how to express themselves, a *modeling* approach through role playing might be used. However, if they have the response potential but are inhibited by certain fears, a desensitization procedure (described later in this module) to reduce these fears might be used.

The objective in the behavioral analysis is to identify the antecedent stimuli that are generating the maladaptive responses. Once therapists identify these connections, they discuss them with their clients to help the clients gain insight and to obtain their feedback on possible erroneous connections. Client and therapist then agree on the goals for the treatment. The process of how therapy will proceed (along with the techniques to be used) are described to clients. This provides them with an idea of their role in treatment. Orne and Wender (1968) found that this knowledge fosters positive outcomes and reduces the dropout rate.

Chambless and Goldstein (1979) described the sources of information for making a behavioral analysis:

> The behavior therapist may base the functional analysis on interviews with the client and important people in

the client's life or on information gained by having the client keep a journal. Questionnaire data are often useful. Interpersonal problems may be more clearly defined if the therapist and client role play interactions with which the client reports difficulty. When the therapist has a difficult time making the analysis, observing the client in the situation where the problem occurs may lead to a wealth of information. Obviously, there are times when this would be impossible or in poor taste, but direct observation is used much less frequently than it should be. (pp. 244–245)

Assertiveness Training

Assertiveness training has become the most frequently used method in modifying unadaptive interpersonal behavior. It is particularly effective in changing both timid behavior and aggressive behavior. Wolpe (1958) originally developed this approach, and it has been further developed by a variety of authors, including Alberti and Emmons (1970) and Fensterheim and Baer (1975).

In recent years interest has grown enormously, sparked by the recognition that sex-role stereotyping has led to a general lack of assertiveness in women. Assertiveness training groups are now widely offered. During the past several years an increasing number of men are also getting involved, either individually or through groups, in assertiveness training. Outcome research on assertiveness training has found the approach to be effective in assisting participants to become more assertive (Cormier & Cormier, 1991).

Overview of Assertiveness Training[1]

Do you handle put-down comments well? Are you reluctant to express your feelings and opinions openly and honestly in a group? Are you frequently timid in interacting with people in authority? Do you react well to criticism? Do you sometimes explode in anger when things go wrong, or are you able to remain calm? Do you find it difficult to maintain eye contact when talking? If you are uncomfortable with someone smoking near you, do you express your feelings? Are you timid in arranging a date or social event? If you have trouble in any of these situations, there is, fortunately, a useful technique—assertiveness training—that helps people become more effective in such interpersonal interactions.

Assertiveness problems range from extreme shyness, introversion, and withdrawal to inappropriately flying into a rage that results in alienating others. A nonassertive person is often acquiescent, fearful, and afraid of expressing his or her real, spontaneous feelings in a variety of situations. Frequently, resentment and anxiety build up, which may result in general discomfort, feelings of low self-esteem, tension headaches, fatigue, and perhaps a destructive explosion of temper, anger, and aggression. Some people are overly shy and timid in nearly all interactions. Most of us, however, encounter occasional problems in isolated areas in which it would be to our benefit to be more assertive. For example, a bachelor may be quite effective and assertive in his job as store manager but still awkward and timid when attempting to arrange a date.

There are three basic styles of interacting with others: *nonassertive, aggressive,* and *assertive*. Characteristics of these styles have been summarized by Alberti and Emmons (1975):

> In the *nonassertive* style, you are likely to hesitate, speak softly, look away, avoid the issue, agree regardless of your own feelings, not express opinions, value yourself "below" others, and hurt yourself to avoid any chance of hurting others.
>
> In the *aggressive* style, you typically answer before the other person is through talking, speak loudly and abusively, glare at the other person, speak "past" the issue (accusing, blaming, demeaning), vehemently expound your feelings and opinions, value yourself "above" others, and hurt others to avoid hurting yourself.
>
> In the *assertive* style, you will answer spontaneously, speak with a conversational tone and volume, and look at the other person, speak to the issue, openly express your personal feelings and opinions (anger, love, disagreement, sorrow), value yourself equal to others, and hurt neither yourself or others. (p. 24)

Simply stated, *assertive behavior* is being able to express yourself without hurting or stepping on others.

Assertiveness training is designed to lead people to realize, feel, and act on the assumption that they have the right to be themselves and to express feelings freely. Assertive responses generally are not aggressive responses. The distinction between these two types of interactions is important.

[1]This material on assertiveness training is adapted from Charles Zastrow, "How to Become More Assertive," in *The Personal Problem Solver*, edited by Charles Zastrow and Dae H. Chang © 1977, pp. 236–243. Adapted by permission of Prentice-Hall, Inc., Englewood Cliffs, New Jersey.

Let's look at two examples of nonassertive, aggressive, and assertive behavior. You are a social worker driving in a car with an associate to a conference in another city. The associate lights up a pipe; you soon find the smoke irritating and the odor somewhat stifling. What are your choices?

1. *Nonassertive response:* You attempt to carry on a "cheery" conversation for the 3-hour trip without commenting about the smoke.
2. *Aggressive response:* You increasingly become irritated until exploding, "Either you put out that pipe or I'll put it out for you—the odor is sickening."
3. *Assertive response:* In a firm, conversational tone, you look directly at the associate and state, "The smoke from your pipe is irritating me. I'd appreciate it if you put it away."

At a party with friends, during small-talk conversation, your husband gives you a subtle "put-down" by stating, "Wives always talk too much." What do you do?

1. *Nonassertive response:* You don't say anything, but feel hurt and become quiet.
2. *Aggressive response:* You glare at him and angrily ask, "John, why are you always criticizing me?"
3. *Assertive response:* You carry on as usual. On the drive home, you calmly look at him and say, "When we were at the party tonight, you said that wives always talk too much. I felt you were putting me down when you said that. What did you mean by that comment?"

Steps in Assertiveness Training[2]

This section contains 12 self-training steps.

Step 1: Examine your interactions. Are there situations that you need to handle more assertively? Do you at times hold back your opinions and feelings for fear of what would happen if you expressed them? Do you occasionally lose control and lash out angrily at others? To study your interactions, keep a diary for a week or longer, recording the situations in which you acted timidly, aggressively, and assertively.

[2]These self-training steps are a modification of assertiveness training programs developed by Robert E. Alberti and Michael L. Emmons, *Your Perfect Right* (San Luis Obispo, CA: Impact Publishers, 1995), and by Herbert Fensterheim and Jean Baer, *Don't Say Yes When You Want to Say No* (New York: Dell Publishing Co., 1975).

Step 2: Select those interactions in which it would be to your benefit to be more assertive. They may include situations in which you were overly polite, overly apologetic, timid, or allowed others to take advantage of you while you were harboring feelings of resentment, anger, embarrassment, fear of others, or self-criticism for not having the courage to express yourself. Overly aggressive interactions in which you exploded in anger or walked over others also need to be dealt with. For each set of nonassertive or aggressive interactions, you can become more assertive, as shown in the next steps.

Step 3: Concentrate on a specific incident in the past in which you were either nonassertive or aggressive when you wanted to be assertive. Close your eyes for a few minutes and vividly imagine the details, including what you and the other person said, and how you felt at the time and afterward.

Step 4: Write down and review your responses. Ask yourself the following questions to determine how you presented yourself:

a. Eye contact—did you look directly at the other person in a relaxed, steady gaze? Looking down or away suggests a lack of self-confidence. Glaring is an aggressive response.
b. Gestures—were your gestures appropriate, free flowing, relaxed, and used effectively to emphasize your messages? Awkward stiffness suggests nervousness; other gestures (such as an angry fist) signal an aggressive reaction.
c. Body posture—did you show the importance of your message by directly facing the other person, by leaning toward that person, by holding your head erect, and by sitting or standing appropriately close?
d. Facial expression—did your facial expression show a stern, firm pose consistent with an assertive response?
e. Voice tone and volume—was your response stated in a firm, conversational tone? Shouting may suggest anger. Speaking softly suggests shyness, and a cracking voice suggests nervousness. Tape recording and listening to one's voice is a way to practice increasing or decreasing the volume.
f. Speech fluency—did your speech flow smoothly, clearly, and slowly? Rapid speech or hesitation in speaking suggests nervousness. Tape recording assertive responses that you try out in problem situations is a way to improve fluency.

g. Timing—were your verbal reactions to a problem situation stated at a time closest to the incident that would appropriately permit you and the other person time to review the incident? Generally, spontaneous expressions are the best, but certain situations should be handled at a later time—for example, a challenge to some of your boss's erroneous statements should be made in private rather than in front of a group in which he or she is making a presentation.

h. Message content—for a problem situation, which of your responses were nonassertive or aggressive and which were assertive? Study the content and consider why you responded in a nonassertive or aggressive style. (At this point it is very helpful to identify the self-talk that led you to act nonassertively or aggressively, and to challenge this self-talk with rational, assertive self-challenges—see Module 6.)

Step 5: Observe one or more effective models. Watch the verbal and nonverbal approaches that are assertively used to handle the types of interactions with which you are having problems. Compare the consequences between their approach and yours. If possible, discuss their approach and their feelings about using it.

Step 6: Make a list of alternative approaches for being more assertive.

Step 7: Close your eyes and visualize yourself using each approach. For each one, think through what the full set of interactions would be, along with the consequences. Select one, or a combination of approaches, that you believe will be most effective for you to use. Through imagery, practice using this approach until you feel comfortable with it.

Step 8: Role-play the approach with a friend or counselor. If certain segments of your approach appear clumsy, awkward, timid, or aggressive, practice modifications until you become comfortable with the approach. Obtain feedback from the other person on the strengths and shortcomings of your approach. Compare your interactions to the verbal and nonverbal guidelines for assertive behavior in step 4. It may be useful for the other person to role-play one or more assertive strategies that you could then practice using.

Step 9: Repeat steps 7 and 8 until you develop an assertive approach that you believe will work best for you and that you are comfortable with.

Step 10: Use your approach in a real-life situation. The previous steps are designed to prepare you for the real event. Expect to be somewhat anxious when first trying to be assertive. If you are still too fearful of attempting to be assertive, repeat steps 5–8. For those few individuals who fail to develop the needed confidence to try being assertive, professional counseling is advised—expressing yourself and effective interactions with others are essential for personal happiness.

Step 11: Reflect on the effectiveness of your effort. Did you remain calm?[3] Considering the nonverbal guidelines for assertive behavior discussed in step 4, what components of your responses were assertive, aggressive, and nonassertive? What were the consequences of your effort? How did you feel after trying out this new set of interactions? If possible, discuss how you did in regard to these questions with a friend who observed the interactions.

Step 12: Expect some success, but not complete personal satisfaction, with your initial efforts. Personal growth and interacting more effectively with others is a continual learning process. Quite appropriately "pat yourself on the back" for what you did well—you earned it. But also note the areas in which you need to improve, and use these steps for improving your assertive efforts. These steps are not to be followed rigidly. You need to develop a process that works best for you.

Helping Others Become More Assertive

Either as a friend or as a social worker, you can be very helpful in assisting another person, your "client," to become more assertive. The following guidelines are suggested.

1. Together identify the situations or interactions in which your client needs to be more assertive. Get information about such interactions from your observations and knowledge about the person, and from discussing in depth the interactions in which they feel a need to be more assertive. You may also ask them to keep a diary of interactions in which they feel resentment over being nonassertive, and those interactions in which they were overly aggressive.

[3]Getting angry at times is a normal human emotion, and it needs to be expressed. However, the anger should be expressed in a constructive, assertive fashion.

2. Develop together some strategies for the person to be more assertive. Small assignments with a high probability of successful outcomes should be given first. A great deal of discussion and preparation should take place between the two of you in preparing for the "real event." For a person who is generally shy, introverted, and nonassertive in all interpersonal relationships, it may be necessary to explore in great detail the connection between nonassertive behavior and feelings of resentment or low self-esteem. In addition, for very shy people, certain attitudes, such as "don't make waves" or the "meek will inherit the earth," may need to be dealt with before developing strategies for the person to be more assertive.

3. Role playing is a very useful technique in preparing for being assertive. The helper first models an assertive strategy by taking the shy person's role. Shy clients concurrently role-play the role of the person with whom they want to be more assertive. Then the roles are reversed; clients role-play themselves and the helper plays the other role. Besides the above-mentioned benefits of modeling and practice experience, role playing has the added advantage of reducing the anxiety that the shy person has about attempting to be assertive. For feedback purposes, if possible, record the role playing on audio- or videotape.

4. Explain the 12 steps described earlier that your client can use on his or her own to handle future problem situations involving assertiveness. If possible, provide reading material on these steps.

Although individuals must be able to express themselves in their own unique style, an additional guideline is often useful. A good rule is to start sentences with "I feel" rather than making threatening or aggressive statements. (I-messages are further described in Module 9.) Frequently, in our fast-paced society we simply don't take the time to express our real feelings to others; as a result we end up creating serious misunderstandings, hurt feelings, and verbal fights that take ten times as long to work through. Consider the following example of two busy people, a working mother and her 15-year-old son.

Mother: John, please do the dishes for me tonight.

John: I can't, I'll do them tomorrow.

Mother: [*Getting angry*] You never do anything for me.

John: I said I'll do the dishes tomorrow.

Mother: And you always forget. I asked you to clean your room two weeks ago, and you still haven't done that. [*Now angry*] I just don't know what I'm going to do with you. Just for that you can't go camping this weekend.

And the argument has ignited. Contrast this to the following approach:

Mother: John, I feel very tired this evening. I had a bad day at work, and I still have to do all the washing and ironing tonight. Could you please help me out by doing the dishes?

John: I'm sorry you had a bad day. I'm supposed to be at basketball practice in five minutes. I'll be back at eight-thirty, would it be all right if I did them then?

Mother: Yes, if you don't forget.

John: I won't.

Assertiveness training is relatively simple to comprehend. Considerable skill, common sense, and ingenuity, however, is needed to create an effective strategy for a real-life situation. The joy and pride obtained from being able fully to express oneself assertively is nearly unequaled.

Behavior Rehearsal

This technique enlarges the client's repertoire of coping behaviors. Behavior rehearsal has four stages. First, therapists prepare their clients by explaining the importance of acquiring new behaviors (for example, to express anger assertively rather than aggressively), getting them to accept behavior rehearsal as a useful device, and reducing any initial anxiety over the prospect of role-playing. The second stage involves selecting target situations. Together, therapists and clients select one or more rehearsal situations that relate directly to those situations in which the client is having difficulty (for example, learning to respond assertively rather than aggressively when the client is being criticized by his co-workers). The third stage is the actual behavior rehearsal. Therapists sometimes model an appropriate response pattern first. For example, the client may take on the role of being a critical co-worker while the therapist role-plays an assertive response to receiving criticism from a co-worker. Frequently, then, the roles are reversed and the client role-plays responding assertively to being criticized by a co-worker (with the therapist as co-worker). The fourth and final stage is the client's actual use of the newly acquired skills in real-life situations, after which client and therapist review the client's performance and feelings about the experiences. Sometimes clients are asked to keep diaries describing the real-life situations they encounter, their behavior, its consequences, and so on.

Token Economies

Tokens are symbolic reinforcers, not unlike poker chips or points on a tally sheet, that can later be exchanged for reinforcement rewards, such as candy or increased privileges. An exchange system, an "economy," is set up that specifies exactly what the tokens can be exchanged for and how many tokens it takes to get particular items or privileges. Target behaviors (such as going to school or making a bed) are specified. These earn tokens; a certain response rate earns a particular number of tokens. For example, attending school every day for two weeks earns ten tokens at an adolescent group home, and ten tokens can be exchanged for attending a sports event.

Token economies have been successfully used in a wide variety of institutional settings, including mental hospitals, training schools for delinquents, classrooms for students with emotional problems, schools for individuals with cognitive disabilities, sheltered workshops, and group homes for adolescents. Considerable evidence supports the effectiveness of token economies (Kazdin, 1977b), which have been used to effect positive changes in a wide variety of behaviors, including personal hygiene, social interactions, job attendance and performance, academic performance, domestic tasks such as cleaning, and personal appearance. At times, token economies are arranged so that clients not only earn tokens for desired behaviors but also lose tokens for undesired behaviors (for example, instigating a fight).

Effective token economies are, however, more difficult to establish than it appears at first glance. Prochaska (1979) summarized important factors that need to be given attention in establishing a successful token economy:

> Some of the more important considerations include staff cooperation and coordination, since the staff must be more observant and more systematic in their responses to clients than in a noncontingent system. A variety of attempts at establishing token economies have failed because the staff did not cooperate adequately in monitoring the behavior of residents. Effective token economies must also have adequate control over reinforcements, since an economy becomes ineffective if residents have access to reinforcements by having money from home or being able to bum a cigarette from a less cooperative staff member. Problems must be clearly defined in terms of specific behaviors to be changed in order to avoid conflicts among staff or patients. Improving personal hygiene, for example, is too open to interpretation by individuals, and patients may insist that they are improving their hygiene even though staff members may disagree. There is much less room for misunderstandings if personal hygiene is defined as clean fingernails, no evidence of body odor, clean underwear, and other clear-cut rules. Specifying behaviors that are positive alternatives to problem behavior is very critical in teaching residents what positive actions they can take to help themselves rather than relying on just a negative set of eliminating responses. Perhaps most important for more lasting effectiveness of token economies is that they be gradually faded out as problem behaviors are reduced and more adaptive responses become well established. Obviously the outside world does not run according to an institution's internal economy, and it is important that clients be prepared to make the transition to the larger society. Using an abundance of social reinforcers along with token reinforcers helps prepare clients for the fading out of tokens, so that positive behaviors can be maintained by praise or recognition rather than by tokens. Also encouraging patients to reinforce themselves, such as by learning to take pride in their appearance, is an important step in fading out tokens. Some institutions use transitional wards where clients go from token economies and learn to maintain adaptive behaviors through more naturalistic contingencies, such as praise from a fellow patient. In such transitional settings, backup reinforcers are available if needed, but they are used much more sparingly than in the token economies. Without the use of fading, token economies can become nothing more than hospital management procedures that make the care of patients more efficient without preparing patients to live effectively in the larger society.[4]

Contingency Contracting

Closely related to token economies is contingency contracting. Contingency contracts provide clients with a set of rules that govern the change process. Contracts may be unilateral; that is, clients may make a contract

[4]James O. Prochaska, *Systems of Psychotherapy* (Pacific Grove, CA: Brooks/Cole, 1979), pp. 324–325.

with themselves. For example, a person with a weight problem may limit himself to a certain calorie intake, using a system of rewards for staying within the calorie limit and negative consequences for going over the calorie limit. Contracts can be bilateral and specify the obligations and the mutual reinforcements for each party.

Kanfer (1975, p. 321) noted that a good contingency contract contains the following seven elements:

1. A clear and detailed description of the required instrumental behavior.
2. Criterion for the time or frequency limitations that constitute the goal of the contract.
3. Specified positive reinforcements, contingent on fulfillment of the criterion.
4. Aversive consequence(s), contingent on nonfulfillment of the contract within the specified time or with the specified frequency.
5. Bonus clause with additional positive reinforcements obtainable if the person exceeds the minimal demands of the contract.
6. Specified means by which the contracted response is observed, measured, and recorded; and a procedure for informing clients of their achievements during the contract's duration.
7. Delivery of reinforcement contingencies to follow the response as quickly as possible.

Helping professionals increasingly find contingency contracts useful. Such contracts specify desired goals, tasks to be performed to meet these goals, tasks for the client and those for the therapist, and the deadline for completing them.

Kanfer (1975) indicated that marriage counseling is one area in which contingency contracts are especially effective. In these contracts each spouse agrees to change behaviors that irritate the other, with a specified system of reinforcements and consequences depending on the extent to which the contract provisions are met.

Formulating contracts with clients in both one-to-one settings and in group settings has a number of advantages. Contracts guide clients in terms of specific actions they need to take to improve their situations. Contracts have a motivational effect because when people commit to the terms of a contract, they usually feel a moral obligation to follow through. In addition, reviewing whether commitments made in contracts are being met provides therapists and clients with a method for measuring progress.

Systematic Desensitization[5]

A useful technique for a person who is unduly anxious about a specific stimulus is systematic desensitization. Most of us have anxiety reactions (phobias) to some of the following stimuli: taking exams, snakes, rats, making love, being alone, fire, heights, walking alone, injections, medications, being in a small place or a crowded place, locked doors, steep stairways, the unknown, death, nightmares, traffic, thunder and lightning, talking to authority figures, sexual dysfunctions, speaking in public, criticism, and losing one's mind.

Systematic desensitization was developed by Joseph Wolpe (1969). The basis for this approach is the scientific fact that a person cannot be simultaneously anxious and relaxed. Wolpe used "relaxation" as a counterconditioner to the feared stimulus. *Systematic desensitization* involves three phases: training in deep muscle relaxation, constructing anxiety hierarchies, and counterposing through imagery the anxiety-evoking stimuli and relaxation.

For training in deep muscle relaxation, a modification of Jacobson's (1934) procedures is used. The client, under the instruction of a therapist, is taught how to relax by tensing and then relaxing progressive groups of muscles. This phase is completed when the client is able to relax the muscles through imagery.[6]

The second phase is the construction of anxiety hierarchies. In a series of interviews the therapist seeks to discover the stimulus situations that elicit fear or anxiety. Suppose a woman has an unreasonable fear of heights. Her fear arises in these scenarios—"themes": being in tall buildings, high-altitude driving, flying in a small plane, amusement park rides. For each theme, a set of stimuli are ranked according to how fear-producing they are, from the least frightening to the most. For example, rankings of stimuli about flying in a small plane might be the following:

Thinking about having to fly in a small plane some time in the future.

Knowing that in two weeks you have to fly in a small plane.

[5]This material on systematic desensitization is excerpted from Charles Zastrow, "Systematic Desensitization," in *Talk to Yourself: Using the Power of Self-Talk*, © 1979, pp. 190–193. Reprinted by permission of Prentice-Hall, Inc., Englewood Cliffs, New Jersey.
[6]Muscle relaxation approaches are more fully described in Module 9.

Knowing that next week you will have to fly in a small plane.

⋮

Encountering a thunderstorm while flying.
Looking out the window during a thunderstorm.

Wolpe indicated that constructing the anxiety hierarchies is the most difficult phase of the desensitization technique.

The third phase is the counterposing, with imagery, of relaxation and anxiety-evoking stimuli from the hierarchies. The objective of this phase is to replace the fear of each stimulus with relaxation. This is done by having the client imagine each fear-producing stimulus while in a relaxed state.

1. The client is told that she will be asked to imagine (think about) various scenes from her anxiety hierarchies. The themes are worked on separately, beginning with the least-frightening stimulus situation in each theme.

2. The client is told that if she becomes anxious while imagining a stimulus situation, she should raise an index finger.

3. Taking a theme, the client is then asked to imagine the least-frightening stimulus situation in that theme. She is asked to think about it, then told to relax, then asked to think about it, then told to relax, and so on. The scene and relaxation are counterposed several times.

4. If the client indicates no anxiety arises, the next scene in the anxiety hierarchy is presented and counterposed with relaxation. Gradually the client and therapist work their way up the anxiety hierarchy in this manner. If the client indicates anxiety with any stimulus, the therapist instructs her to relax. After she is relaxed, a scene lower in the hierarchy is presented and the therapist and she gradually work their way up the anxiety hierarchy again.

The advantage of desensitization through imagination is that the appearance of the feared stimulus can be regulated. The client, by encountering the feared stimuli in a stepwise hierarchy in her imagination, will be unlikely to become overly anxious.

As a clinical technique, systematic desensitization has been found to be highly effective in substantially reducing anxieties, fears, and phobias that are attached to specific conditions (Paul, 1969).

There is also some evidence that systematic desensitization can be used as a self-modification procedure—that is, by a person who is not under the supervision of a therapist (Kahn & Baker, 1968; Migler, 1968; Rardin, 1969). Watson and Tharp (1972) cautioned that self-desensitization "should be discontinued if the course of anxiety-reduction is not relatively smooth and *it should be immediately discontinued if any increase in anxiety is noted*" (p. 179).

Self-desensitization involves the same stages as systematic desensitization: learning to relax through imagery after learning a muscle relaxation technique, constructing anxiety hierarchies, and counterposing the anxiety-evoking stimuli with relaxation. (Learning to relax with muscle relaxation techniques is described in Module 9.)

In constructing anxiety hierarchies, Watson and Tharp (1972) advised that each feared situation be listed on a separate card, and then hierarchies with themes be constructed. For example, phobias of certain animals may include themes of snakes, rats, and dogs. In constructing the themes, various types of hierarchies may be used. For example, if a person has a fear of taking exams, hierarchy types might include amount of time before the feared event occurs, importance of the exam, and the exam taker's acquaintance or comfortableness with the anticipated content of the exam.

Desensitization occurs through counterposing the anxiety-eliciting stimuli with relaxation. A theme is selected and, while deeply relaxed, you present to yourself the lowest fear-producing item in the theme by looking at the card on which it has been written. Keep counterposing through imagery the item and relaxation. When you feel completely relaxed while imagining the item, you are ready to go on to the next.

In Vivo Desensitization[7]

In vivo (from the Latin "in life") desensitization refers to a real-life desensitization process in which a person gradually approaches an actual feared event or stimulus while being in a relaxed state. To carry out in vivo desensitization, the following three steps should be taken:

1. Make a ranked list of fear-producing situations, arranging items from least to most anxiety-producing. (This step is identical to the construction of anxiety hierarchies in systematic desensitization.)

[7]This material on in vivo desensitization is excerpted from Charles Zastrow, "In Vivo Desensitization," in *Talk to Yourself: Using The Power of Self-Talk,* © 1979, pp. 195–196. Reprinted by permission of Prentice-Hall, Inc., Englewood Cliffs, New Jersey.

2. Learn to produce or achieve relaxation, perhaps by meditation, muscle relaxation, deep breathing relaxation, or imagery relaxation.[8]
3. Gradually approach an actual feared event while remaining relaxed.

A 22-year-old male college student used this approach to overcome several situations (themes) connected with a fear of heights. He first became skilled at producing the relaxation response by imagery of his ideal relaxation place. (His ideal relaxation place was lying on the beach in Acapulco. With practice he became skilled at relaxing himself by fully focusing his thinking on relaxing in Acapulco.) He then gradually approached feared situations while remaining in a relaxed state with his imagery of Acapulco. For example, he countered his fear of tall buildings by looking out the window in the lower floors and gradually moving upward while thinking about being relaxed in Acapulco. He also used this approach to overcome his fears of taking amusement park rides and of flying in small planes.

Watson and Tharp (1972) indicated that in vivo desensitization is an effective method in eliminating fear and anxiety reactions associated with specific stimuli (events).

Implosive Therapy

Like systematic desensitization, implosive therapy has the client imagine (think about) anxiety-provoking material. Unlike systematic desensitization, relaxation training is not required or used.

Implosive therapy was developed by Stampfl and Levis (1967). The approach is based on *extinction.* As used by Stampfl and Levis, extinction refers to the gradual reduction in the occurrence of an anxiety response as a result of the continuous presentation of the fear-producing stimulus situation in the absence of the reinforcement that perpetuates the fear.

In using implosive therapy, the therapist first constructs an Avoidance Serial Cue Hierarchy. On the basis of interviews with the client, the therapist develops a ranking of important cues involved in the client's fear. For example, if a person has a fear of flying, a cue low on the hierarchy might be driving to the airport, whereas a cue high on the hierarchy might be taking off in a plane during a thunderstorm. In developing the hierarchy the therapist seeks primarily to include cues thought to be capable of producing a *maximum* level of anxiety in the client. An example of this type of hierarchy is described by Hogan and Kirchner (1967):

> Fear of rats
>
> Imagine that you are touching a rat in the laboratory. . . . It begins nibbling at your finger . . . and then runs across your arm. The rat suddenly bites you on your arm, and then you feel it run rapidly over your body. . . . It begins biting your neck and swishing its tail in your face . . . then it claws up your face into your hair . . . clawing in your hair . . . you try to get it out with your bloody arm, but you can't. It then goes for your eyes . . . you open your mouth and it jumps in and you swallow it. . . . It then begins to eat away at various internal organs—like your stomach and intestines, causing you great discomfort and pain . . . , etc. (p. 109)

After the hierarchy is developed, the therapist describes implosive therapy to the client. The client is then presented with the scenes and asked to make every effort to imagine the scenes as vividly as possible. The client is encouraged to "live" the scenes with emotion.

The objective of implosive therapy is to extinguish fears through having clients produce in their minds frightening experiences of such magnitude that, in the absence of reinforcement, they will *lessen* the fear of the particular situation. Stampfl and Levis (1967) stated:

> An attempt is made by the therapist to attain a maximal level of anxiety evocation from the patient. When a high level of anxiety is achieved, the patient is held on this level until some sign of spontaneous reduction in the anxiety-inducing value of the cues appears . . . the process is repeated, and again, at the first sign of spontaneous reduction of fear, new variations are introduced to elicit an intense anxiety response. This response is repeated until a significant diminution in anxiety has resulted. (p. 500)

Sessions end after 30–60 minutes, generally after clients experience a reduction in anxiety to the implosive scenes. Between sessions clients are encouraged to practice imagining the implosive scenes at home to help them realize they can effectively handle the fears.

Morris (1986) indicated that few outcome studies have been conducted on implosive therapy, with the studies showing mixed results. There is a danger that implosive therapy may *increase,* rather than lessen, the fear of the particular situation (Morris, 1986). Because

[8]All of these techniques are described in Module 9.

of this possibility, the technique should be used only by clinicians with extensive training.

Exposure Therapy

Exposure therapy is a refinement of implosive therapy. Exposure therapy is also based on the principle of *extinction.* In exposure therapy clients expose themselves to those stimuli or situations that were previously feared and avoided. The "exposure" can be in real life (in vivo) or in fantasy (in imagino). In the latter case, clients are asked to imagine themselves in the presence of the feared stimulus (for example, a snake) or in the anxiety-producing situation (for example, giving a presentation in class). The theory behind exposure therapy is that the occurrence of an anxiety response will gradually lessen as a result of continuously presenting the fear-producing stimulus situation in the absence of the reinforcement that perpetuates the fear.

Exposure therapy has been found by researchers to be effective in treating panic disorders, specified phobias, agoraphobia (abnormal fear of crossing or being in open spaces), social phobia, posttraumatic stress disorder, and obsessive-compulsive disorder (Emmelkamp, 1994). Exposure therapy differs from implosive therapy in three distinct ways:

1. The anxiety hierarchies constructed in exposure therapy are based on actual anxiety cues that elicit fear or anxiety in the client (in implosive therapy the therapist creates an anxiety hierarchy of cues that produce a maximal level of anxiety in the client).

2. In exposure treatment the client is only exposed to those cues that have in the past elicited anxiety or fear (in implosive therapy the client is exposed to cues that are designed to produce a maximal level of anxiety).

3. Exposure therapy exposes the client to the anxiety cues in real life or through visualization (only visualization is used in implosive therapy).

Several researchers suggest that the following features must be present in exposure treatments for the client to achieve maximum benefits (Barlow & Cerny, 1988):

1. Exposure should be of long duration.
2. Exposure should be repeated until all fear and anxiety is eliminated.
3. Exposure should be graduated, starting with low-anxiety stimuli or situations and progressing to high-anxiety stimuli or situations.
4. Clients must attend to the feared stimulus and interact with it as much as possible.
5. Exposure must produce anxiety.

Exposure therapy asserts that panic attacks or phobias are essentially "false alarms" issued by the body in response to a cue or signal that the client has learned to associate with danger or threat. Through the process of extinction, it is theorized that the anxiety or fear elicited in reaction to the false alarm will gradually subside as the client learns that there is no basis for the fear associated with the false alarm.

A recent innovation with exposure therapy is the use of "virtual reality" computer-simulated environments. For example, at the University of Washington in Seattle, people with serious fear of spiders are treated by using virtual reality in which they simulate entering a kitchen, chasing a tarantula around a countertop, and flushing it down a sink (Ritter, 2000). At the Department of Veterans Affairs medical centers in Atlanta and Boston, some Vietnam veterans with posttraumatic stress disorder are visiting "Virtual Vietnam," a re-creation of the wartime environment that still haunts them (Ritter, 2000). Virtual reality is also being used to treat a wide variety of other phobias—including fear of flying, fear of public speaking, and fear of heights (Ritter, 2000).

The idea is to teach people how to manage fears, and then (through virtual reality) take them to whatever situations terrify them. There they learn they can control their emotions and that these situations are not so scary after all. The advantage of virtual reality is that it can provide the feared environment in the therapist's office. No more driving to the airport for fear-of-flying treatment, for example, which of course saves time and money.

Covert Sensitization

Covert sensitization is an aversive counterconditioning approach first developed by J. R. Cautela (1967). Instead of inhibiting anxiety with relaxation as in systematic desensitization, covert sensitization is used to elicit anxiety in certain problematic situations. The technique is claimed to be particularly appropriate for treating such behavioral excesses as sexual deviations, alcoholism, stealing, overeating, and drug addiction (Anant, 1967, 1968; Ashem & Donner, 1968; Sundel & Sundel, 1975).

The first step in covert sensitization is to instruct the client in how to relax—for example, by using a muscle relaxation technique. (Relaxation techniques are described in Module 9.) In the next step clients visualize becoming involved in their problematic behavior while imagining extremely distasteful consequences.

Jehu (1972) described how covert sensitization is used with people who have a drinking problem:

> The patient is relaxed and asked to imagine a sequence of scenes leading up to the performance of the problem behavior; for example, looking at a glass containing his favorite alcoholic drink, holding the glass in his hand and bringing it to his lips. At this point he signals and the therapist tells the patient to imagine that he begins to feel sick and is vomiting in his drink and all over himself and his companions. He is then asked to visualize the whole sequence and final scene by himself, and to actually feel nauseous as he prepares to drink. Alternate scenes are presented in which the patient imagines himself abstaining from drinking and then "rushing out into the fresh clean air," or "home to a clean invigorating shower." The presentation of such relief scenes constitutes an escape and avoidance training component in the procedure. After several trials with the therapist, the patient is instructed to repeat the whole procedure on his own and immediately to imagine the vomiting scene whenever he is tempted to drink alcohol. (pp. 57–58)

Prochaska (1979) described using covert sensitization with a man who was having homosexual relationships with children:

> A thirty-year-old pedophiliac was asked to imagine approaching a ten-year-old boy to whom he was attracted. As he approaches the boy to ask him to come up to his apartment, he feels his stomach become nauseous. He feels his lunch coming up into his esophagus, and just as he goes to speak to the boy he vomits all over himself and the boy. People on the street are staring at him and he turns away from the boy and immediately begins to feel better. He begins walking back to his apartment feeling better and better with each step he takes. He gets back to his apartment, washes up, and feels great. After teaching this man the covert scene we had him practice it overtly, including making vomiting noises and gestures. To make the scene even more vivid we had him sit in his apartment window, and when he saw a boy on the street that he would like to approach sexually, we had him go to the bathroom and stick his finger down his throat and vomit as he imagined propositioning the young boy. Within two months this chronic offender was no longer feeling the urge to approach young boys and he had followed through on our assertiveness techniques for forming adult homosexual relationships. (p. 30)

A word of caution—covert sensitization should be used only by skilled therapists with extensive training in this technique. Improper application of this approach can create anxiety reactions in clients (and perhaps lead to other adverse side effects) without eliminating the problematic behavior.

Aversive Techniques

An aversive stimulus is any stimulus that an organism (person) will avoid or terminate if given the opportunity. Examples include electric shock, unpleasant imagery, holding one's breath, stale cigarette smoke, vile-smelling substances, white noise, and shame. Covert sensitization is an aversive technique in which the client imagines unpleasant consequences in conjunction with the maladaptive behavior. This technique results in diminished interest in the formerly desirable stimuli.

In a review of aversive methods, Sandler (1986) found aversive therapy has been used to treat self-injurious behavior (such as head banging and self-biting), enuresis, sneezing, stuttering, alcoholism, cigarette smoking, overeating, gambling, sexual deviations (for example, fetishes and transvestism), and aggressive behavior. The following are some illustrations of aversive techniques.

Vogler, Lunde, Johnson, and Martin (1970) served cocktails to alcoholic clients in a simulated lounge arrangement. Each time clients took a drink, they were given an electric shock, and the shock was maintained until they spat out the drink. The investigators did a follow-up and concluded the treatment led to abstinence. Alcoholic clients have also been treated using adversive therapy by giving them an emetic drug (for example, Antabuse) that produces nausea or vomiting when they take a drink. Sometimes the emetic drug is mixed with the drink. This combination of alcohol and emetic is usually given for a week to ten days. Eventually, just the sight of a drink is sufficient to induce nausea and discomfort in many clients (Phares & Trull, 1997, p. 390).

In regard to the use of aversive techniques, Chambless and Goldstein (1979) cautioned:

> When reporting on behavior therapy, the popular press emphasizes such techniques and often gives the impression that punishment is the behaviorist's major tool. On the contrary, punishment is used quite infrequently by behavior modifiers even though many clients initially ask for help via punishment in curbing unwanted behavior. To begin with, no behavior should be punished if no alternative behavior is available. For example, if a client complains of sexually deviant behavior, the first therapeutic intervention is usually directed toward reducing any inhibitions about normal sexual contact. This may be accomplished by a combination of desensitization procedures and training in appropriate expression. Generally the unwanted urges decrease when anxieties about "normal" sex, that is, sex with a consenting partner, diminish.
>
> Such an approach is dictated not only by the moral imperative to employ the least painful method when there is a choice but also by the experimentally demonstrated futility of eliminating behavior through punishment when no alternative modes of satisfaction are available. Opening up alternatives is important in most cases in which punishment might otherwise be used. (p. 252)

Phares and Trull (1997) add:

> Many critics, both within and without the behavior therapy movement, have been highly critical of aversion therapy. The concentration of punishment and the use of what are sometimes terrifying stimuli often seem totally incompatible with human dignity. Whether or not patients present themselves voluntarily for treatment is beside the point. Such techniques as inducing vomiting, using a curare-like drug so that the patient will experience the sensation of suffocating, or injecting stale smoke into the nostrils seem better relegated to the status of torture than dignified as treatment. (p. 391)

Positive reinforcement approaches are generally more effective than those based on punishment. Punishment is often counterproductive as it can lead to the client's becoming hostile about the treatment procedures. Also, punishment may have only temporary effects. When clients realize they are no longer under surveillance, they may engage in the dysfunctional behavior again. Aversive techniques probably should only be used when all other therapeutic approaches have failed. In general, aversive procedures should be applied only to people with seriously debilitating problems (such as alcoholism or sexual deviations) and who are in despair because nothing else has worked.

Cognitive Behavior-Modification Techniques

A major trend in behavior therapy in the past three decades has been toward recognizing the role of cognition (thinking processes) in human behavior. Following the observations of cognitive therapists such as Albert Ellis (1962) and A. T. Beck (1976), cognitive behavior therapists have accepted the notion that changing one's thoughts often changes one's feelings and behavior.

The traditional paradigm of behavior therapy has been *S* (stimulus) → *R* (response). Cognitive behavior therapists insert an additional step in this paradigm:[9]

S	→	O	→	R
(stimulus)		(cognitions of organism)		(response)

The following techniques have been developed to change cognitions: thought stopping and covert assertion, diversion techniques, and reframing.

Thought Stopping and Covert Assertion

Thought stopping is used for clients whose major problems involve obsessive thinking and ruminations about events that are very unlikely to occur (such as worrying that a plane they will be taking in two weeks will crash or that they are becoming mentally ill).

In thought stopping, the client is first asked to concentrate on and express aloud her obsessive, anxiety-inducing thoughts. As she begins to express those thoughts, the therapist suddenly and emphatically shouts "Stop." This procedure is repeated several times until the client reports that her thoughts are being successfully interrupted. Then the responsibility for the intervention is shifted to the client, so that the client now tells herself "Stop" out loud when she begins to think about the troubling thoughts. Once the overt shouting is effective in stopping the troubling thoughts, the client begins to practice saying "Stop" silently to herself whenever the troubling thoughts begin.

Rimm and Masters (1974) supplemented the thought-stopping technique with a *covert assertion* pro-

[9]This paradigm is similar to the paradigm of rational therapists [Events → Self-talk → Emotions and Actions]. See Module 6 on rational therapy.

cedure. In addition to having the client learn to interrupt the obsessive thoughts with saying "Stop," the client is encouraged to produce a positive, assertive statement that is incompatible with the content of the obsession. For example, a client who worries about becoming mentally ill (when there is no basis for such thinking) may be encouraged to add the covert assertion "Screw it! I'm perfectly normal" whenever he interrupts the obsessive thinking with "Stop."

Mahoney (1973) successfully used thought stopping and covert assertion as part of a comprehensive program for overweight clients. Mahoney first instructed clients to become aware of such self-statements as, "I just don't have the willpower" and "I sure can taste eating a strawberry sundae." Clients were then trained to use thought stopping and covert assertion to combat these thoughts.

Diversion Techniques

Diversion techniques are used to treat clients with strong unwanted emotions such as loneliness, bitterness, depression, frustration, and anger. As indicated in Module 6, unwanted emotions stem primarily from negative and irrational thinking. When clients with unwanted emotions become involved in physical activity, work, social interactions, or play, they will usually switch their negative cognitions to different cognitions related to their new diversion activities. Once they focus their thinking on the diversion activities that they are finding meaningful and enjoyable, they experience more pleasing emotions.

Diversion techniques are used in both rational therapy (see Module 6) and cognitive behavior therapy, which are closely related. In fact, rational therapy is often classified as a cognitive behavioral approach.

Reframing

Reframing involves assisting a client to change those cognitions that are causing unwanted emotions or dysfunctional behaviors. Several categories of cognitions can be reframed; we describe six here.

Positive thinking. When unpleasant events occur (such as receiving a lower grade on an exam than anticipated), we always have the choice of thinking positively or negatively. If we take a positive view and focus on problem solving, we are apt to identify and initiate actions to improve the circumstances. However, if we think negatively, we often develop unwanted emotions (such as depression and frustration) and fail to focus on how to solve the problem. With negative thinking, we may not do anything constructive and may even engage in destructive behavior.

When a client is thinking negatively, a therapist can use reframing to help the client realize he is thinking negatively. At times it is helpful to remind clients that both negative and positive thinking become self-fulfilling prophecies (see Module 6). Then, by asking clients to identify some positive aspects of the situation, therapists assist clients in thinking more positively. (If clients are unable to identify any positives, therapists suggest some.) Clients may then be encouraged to tell themselves "Stop" whenever they begin to think negatively and instead to focus on telling themselves positive aspects of the situation. Some people take a negative view of most events; for such people, reframing through using positive cognitions is more difficult and time-consuming. However, if they succeed in learning to think positively, they often make substantial gains.

Deawfulizing. When distressing events occur, most of us tend to "awfulize"—we exaggerate the negatives. When we awfulize, we focus only on the negatives and do not identify constructive actions to improve the situation. When clients are awfulizing, therapists can usually help them identify such thought processes by simply inquiring, "I wonder if you're awfulizing?" Therapists can then assist their clients to give themselves positive cognitions oriented toward problem solving.

When clients awfulize about distressing events that occurred, it is also helpful for the counselor to reframe the awfulizing by relating stories such as "Good luck? Bad luck? Who knows?" (De Mello, 1978):

> There is a Chinese story of an old farmer who had an old horse for tilling his fields. One day the horse escaped into the hills and when all the farmer's neighbors sympathized with the old man over his bad luck, the farmer replied, "Bad luck? Good luck? Who knows?" A week later the horse returned with a herd of wild horses from the hills and this time the neighbors congratulated the farmer on his good luck. His reply was, "Good luck? Bad luck? Who knows?" Then, when the farmer's son was attempting to tame one of the wild horses, he fell off its back and broke his leg. Everyone thought this very bad luck. Not the farmer, whose only reaction was, "Bad luck? Good luck? Who knows?" Some weeks later the army marched into the village and conscripted every able-bodied youth they found there. When they saw the farmer's son with his broken leg, they let him off. Now was that good luck? Bad luck? Who knows? (p. 140)

The point here is, distressing events often are crises, but they also frequently lead those involved to make positive changes in their lives.

Decatastrophizing (Beck & Weishaar, 1989). This technique is used when clients are "catastrophizing" over anticipated feared events. Decatastrophizing involves continually asking clients "what if" an anticipated, undesired consequence occurs. The following is a dialogue with a 21-year-old college student who fears expressing his thoughts and feelings in class:

Therapist: What do you think will happen if you begin expressing your views in your classes?

Client: My voice may crack and the others may laugh at me.

Therapist: It is unlikely that your voice will crack. But even if it does, and the students happen to laugh a little, is that really worse than your anger and frustration over not sharing your thoughts?

Client: I don't know.

Therapist: Which is worse when you're asked a question in class? Shrugging your shoulders and appearing tongue-tied, or responding as well as you can even though your voice may crack?

Client: I hear what you're saying.

Therapist: What other negative consequences might occur if you begin expressing yourself in class?

Client: (*pause*) None that I can think of.

Therapist: What positives may come from your speaking up in class?

Client: I'd probably get more out of the class and feel better about myself. Enough of this. I get the message loud and clear. I will commit myself to speaking up at least once a week in each of my classes.

People who catastrophize usually exaggerate the feared consequences. Decatastrophizing demonstrates that even if such consequences occur (which they seldom do), they aren't as severe as feared.

Separating positive intents from negative behaviors. The intent here is that the positive intents become linked to new positive behaviors. A physically abusive parent has the positive intent of raising her child well, but when she is under stress and the child is misbehaving, that parent may not be aware of other, much more constructive options. A therapist can assist such a parent by helping her reframe her thinking so that when the child misbehaves in the future she focuses her thinking processes on alternative responses, such as asking her husband to handle the child's misbehavior when she is under stress or by punishing the child with a time-out. (This type of reframing is described further in Module 8.)

Redefining. This is used for clients who believe a problem is beyond their personal control (Beck & Weishaar, 1989). A person who believes "Life is boring" may be encouraged to think, "The only reason I'm bored is because I don't have special interests and because I'm not initiating activities. It's not life that is boring; it's my thinking processes that make me feel bored. I need to get involved in activities I enjoy and initiate interactions with people I like." Redefining is accomplished by therapists first demonstrating that emotions, such as boredom, stem primarily from thoughts (see Module 6). Next, therapists demonstrate that if clients think more positively and realistically, they will feel better. Together, client and therapist then identify the negative thinking patterns that are causing clients to believe the problem is beyond their personal control. Finally, they identify cognitions that the client commits to using to counter cognitions that are causing unwanted emotions and ineffective behaviors.

Decentering. This is used with anxious clients who erroneously believe they are the focus of everyone's attention (Beck & Weishaar, 1989). Clients are asked to observe the behaviors of others rather than focusing on their own anxiety; thereby they come to realize they are not the center of attention. Beck and Weishaar (1989) gave an example:

> One student who was reluctant to speak in class believed his classmates watched him constantly and noticed his anxiety. By observing them instead of focusing on his own discomfort, he saw some students taking notes, some looking at the professor, and some daydreaming. He concluded his classmates had other concerns. (p. 310)

Additional cognitive change methods are being developed and hold considerable promise for behavior therapists to become increasingly involved in changing unwanted emotions and maladaptive behaviors of clients by changing their troubling thoughts (Hepworth, Rooney, & Larson, 1997).

It is somewhat difficult to specify what is and is not a cognitive behavioral technique. In addition to techniques described here, Cormier and Cormier (1991) identified the following as cognitive behavioral techniques: role playing, problem-solving efforts, meditation, muscle relaxation, and paradoxical suggestions (see Chapter 8). Module 6 notes that changing irrational and negative cognitions may be the key psychotherapeutic change agent. Because practically all effective psychotherapeutic techniques change cognitions, then, in a broad sense, practically all psychotherapeutic techniques can be considered cognitive behavioral techniques.

Evaluation

Behavior therapy is composed of a wide range of therapy techniques, some of which are more effective than others. Also, behavior therapy is based on a variety of different learning theories, and behaviorists have never agreed on which learning theory should be the main focus of behavior therapy. Particularly controversial among behavior therapists is the learning approach advocated by cognitive behavior therapists that states that emotions and actions are largely determined by our thoughts. Cognitive techniques are incompatible with the traditional principles of behaviorism, which has ignored cognitive processes because these thought processes cannot be measured and tested. Traditional behaviorism has endeavored to explain all behavior in terms of stimuli-response connections.

In the past 45 years behavior therapy has experienced a dramatic growth in new treatment techniques and in their adoption by members of the helping professions. Two pivotal books that inspired this development were *Science and Human Behavior* (Skinner, 1953) and *Psychotherapy by Reciprocal Inhibition* (Wolpe, 1958). Behavior therapists have developed, and are continuing to develop, more treatment techniques than any other psychotherapeutic area. One area we haven't yet examined, but which uses behavior therapy techniques heavily, is sex therapy. (Module 10 describes sexual counseling and sex therapy in considerable detail.)

Behavior therapy is to be highly commended for its emphasis on testing the effectiveness of its treatment techniques. This is consistent with the demand by the public that human services be accountable. Approaches shown to be effective that are widely being used include assertiveness training, behavior rehearsal, contingency contracting, token economies, and systematic desensitization and exposure therapy.

The future for behavior therapy is indeed bright. Helping professionals (psychologists, psychiatrists, social workers, guidance counselors, psychiatric nurses) are increasingly being trained in behavior techniques.

Some criticisms can be made of behavior therapy:

1. Research has focused on applying the techniques to problems that are readily tested in laboratory situations, with successful results. However, these problems are not the kinds of problems that clients commonly face. As Prochaska (1979) noted:

> So what if desensitization can reduce a college coed's fear of white rats? Does that have anything to do with the devastating problems that therapists are confronted with daily in their clinical practices? Whoever sees a snake phobic in a clinic? Most behaviorists would do themselves justice when planning a study if they asked the key clinical question for any outcome research—the so-what question. So what if having college students imagine vomiting in their lunches leads to a loss of a pound a week? So what if some of the loss lasts for four months? There is plenty of evidence that eighty-five percent of the people who lose weight through any means regain it within two years. How come only a tiny fraction of their studies use a two-year follow-up? Are the authors more concerned with completing a thesis quickly or rushing to publish than with establishing a really useful therapy? (p. 354)

2. Problems that clients face in the real world often involve arriving at some decision. Should a pregnant 17-year-old teenager have an abortion or carry the pregnancy to full term? How do you get a person with a drinking problem to admit he has a problem and make a decision to seek help? Should sons and daughters of an elderly parent seek to place him in a nursing home? How do you help a teenager who has run away from home make future plans about where to live? Behavior therapy does not help clients arrive at such decisions. The focus of behavior therapy is on changing maladaptive behavior, not at arriving at decisions.

3. Behavior therapy is an amalgam of techniques, which leads to the potential for theoretical chaos. Some techniques are based on operant conditioning; others on classical conditioning and modeling principles; still others on cognitive theories. Phares and Trull (1997) note:

> Without an integrating theoretical framework, individual clinicians may find themselves flailing about in a morass of competing techniques, each claiming to be forms of behavior therapy. What is needed is a systematic theoretical position that will incorporate the techniques, classify them, and help the clinician decide when and under what conditions to employ one technique over another.

Such a theoretical framework would be infinitely more efficient than multiple rules of thumb. (p. 404)

Summary

Behavior therapy is based on learning theory. Behavior therapists assume that maladaptive behaviors are acquired primarily through learning and can be modified through additional learning. A number of different learning theories have been developed, and no consensus exists about which learning theory should be the basis of behavior therapy.

The main trend in behavior therapy is the growing recognition of the role of cognition in human behavior. Some behavior therapists now identify themselves as cognitive behavior therapists and accept the notion that changing thoughts often changes feelings and behaviors. These theorists use techniques such as thought stopping, covert assertion, and reframing.

Common focuses include the following: (1) Maladaptive behavior is the problem and attention should be directed at changing the behavior, not the underlying causes. (2) Therapy techniques are tested using rigorous experimental procedures.

Behavior therapy assumes that all behavior occurs in response to stimulation, internal or external. Therapists first do a behavioral analysis, which involves identifying the probable stimulus-response connections of the maladaptive behavior. Therapists also attempt to establish a working relationship. Once the behavioral analysis is completed, the findings are discussed with the client, and client and therapist agree on treatment goals.

EXERCISES

1. CONTINGENCY CONTRACTING

Goal: To demonstrate the principles of contingency contracting.

Step 1: Choose a behavior that you would like to change, such as eating less, drinking less, exercising more, ending procrastination, studying more, or increasing contact with parents and other relatives.

Step 2: Prepare a contract, answering the following:

a. What behavior do you want to change? (Be as specific as possible.)
b. What is your goal?
c. Construct a "treatment path" for achieving this goal, giving deadlines for each task.
d. How will you reward yourself for adhering to your contract?
e. What adverse consequences have you set up for failure to adhere to the contract?

Step 3: Class discussion of the merits and shortcomings of contingency contracts.

Step 4: (Optional) Decide as a class whether you want to attempt to fulfill the conditions in your contracts. If the class decides to do this, set a date (such as four weeks later) to describe successes and failures.

2. LEARNING TO BE ASSERTIVE

Goal: To learn to be assertive in problematic interactions.

Step 1: Identify a situation in the past in which you wished you had been assertive.

Step 2: The instructor leads the class in a visualization exercise that goes as follows.

"We will now do a visualization exercise that is designed to help you learn to be more assertive in the situation you identified. There will be no tricks in this exercise. Close your eyes and keep them closed during this exercise. Get as comfortable as possible in your chair, and slowly take a couple of deep breaths to become relaxed.

"Focus on a specific incident in your past when you wanted to be assertive, but instead were either nonassertive or aggressive. Visualize all the details of what happened. *(Pause a few seconds after asking each of the following questions.)* What was said to you? What did you fail to say that you wanted to say? What did you say that you didn't want to say? How did you feel about what was said? How do you now feel about this incident? Your nonverbal communication is as important in being assertive as is verbal communication. Think about your nonverbal communication. What did you communicate with your facial expressions? What did you communicate with your body posture? Did you look down or away from the other person? Did you glare at the other person? What did your gestures communicate? What was your voice tone and volume like? Did your voice crack? Did you yell or speak softly? Did you speak rapidly or with hesitation? During this incident which of your verbal and nonverbal communications were nonassertive? which were aggressive? which were assertive?

"Now, let's turn to focus on how to handle this situation more assertively when it arises again. Continue to keep your eyes closed. What might you say that would assertively handle this situation? *(Pause.)* What changes do you need to make in your nonverbal communication to present yourself more assertively? *(Pause.)* Is there someone you know who would be good at handling this situation assertively? *(Pause.)* If there is someone, what would this person say or do? *(Pause.)* Does this assertive model give you some ideas on how you might assertively handle this situation? *(Pause.)*

"Continue to visualize various approaches that might work for you. Also, visualize yourself using each of these approaches. For each approach, imagine the full set of interactions that would occur if you were to use the approach. *(Pause.)*

"Now select an assertive approach that you believe would best work for you when the nonassertive or aggressive situation arises again in the future. Are you now sufficiently prepared and confident to use this approach in a real-life situation? If not, you may want to visualize further what you might say or do to increase your confidence. Or you may want to select another approach that you would be more comfortable in using. Or you may want to role-play your approach with a friend so that you become more comfortable using the approach. *(Pause.)*

"The real test will come when you try out your assertive approach in a real-life situation. The next time your problematic situation arises, use your assertive approach. After trying it out, analyze how it turned out. Pat yourself on the back for what you did well. Identify aspects of your nonverbal and verbal communication that you need to improve to express yourself more assertively. Visualize ways in which you might more assertively express yourself in the areas you need to work on.

"Above all, congratulate yourself on your efforts to become more assertive. You've earned feeling good about yourself. Learning to express yourself in situations that you're comfortable in is one of the greatest thrills you'll ever experience. OK, gradually open your eyes, and take a little while to relax."

Step 3: Class discussion, questions, and comments.

(continued)

EXERCISES
(continued)

Step 4: Break into groups of three. Decide on a situation to role-play. One of you will role-play the person practicing assertive behavior, one of you will be the antagonist, the third person will be the coach.

Step 5: Change roles and role-play the same situation, or a different one. Your group decides.

3. EXPRESSING ANGER ASSERTIVELY

Goal: To learn constructive ways to express anger.

Step 1: Class discussion of ways we express anger, both appropriately and inappropriately. What are the consequences of each?

Step 2: Brainstorm ways people could express anger toward *you* that would not put you on the defensive, ways you think would be constructive.

Step 3: Complete these statements:

a. Three or four things that make me angry are
b. I usually express my anger by
c. Things that I can do to better handle and express my anger are

Step 4: Break into groups of three to share what you wrote in step 3. Brainstorm additional suggestions on how anger can be expressed more effectively.

Step 5: Class discussion of questions and comments brought up in the groups.

4. REFRAMING

Goal: To reframe cognitions involving "awfulizing."

Step 1: Private responses:

a. Briefly describe a distressing event that occurred to you over which you awfulized.
b. Specify the awfulizing cognitions you gave yourself about this event.
c. For each awfulizing cognition, specify a positive and realistic cognition that you could give yourself. (Ideally, countering cognitions should facilitate problem solving.)
d. Indicate the approximate length of time that you awfulized over this event. Are you still awfulizing about this event?
e. Do you think countering cognitions would have shortened the time you spent awfulizing?

Step 2: Break into groups of four. Two of you will construct a distressing event and then awfulize about it. Two of you will devise countering cognitions.

Step 3: Reverse the roles of step 2.

Step 4: Class discussion of their group experiences, including difficulties encountered. What are the merits and shortcomings of reframing therapy?

MODULE 5

Reality Therapy

The founder of reality therapy, William Glasser (1925–1995), graduated from Western Reserve Medical School in Cleveland, Ohio, in 1953. In 1956 he became a consulting psychiatrist to the Ventura School for Girls, a California state institution for the treatment of delinquent girls.

Glasser had grown skeptical of the value of orthodox psychoanalysis. At the Ventura School for Girls, he set up a new treatment program based on the principles of his *reality therapy.* The program showed promise, and participants expressed enthusiasm.

Successes with this new approach at the University of California at Los Angeles and the Veteran's Hospital in Los Angeles led to the publication of *Reality Therapy* (Glasser, 1965). In 1966 Glasser began consulting in the California school system and applied the concepts of reality therapy to education. His emphasis on the need for schools to highlight involvement, relevance, and thinking continues to have a profound impact on the educational system.

Theories of Personality Development and Psychopathology

Glasser developed two theories of personality development and psychopathology: an identity theory in the 1960s, and a control theory in the 1980s. Both are summarized here; each has considerable merit in conceptualizing human behavior. The two theories are quite distinct; Glasser died before he could integrate them.

Control Theory

A major thrust of control theory is that we carry around pictures in our heads both of what reality is like and of how we would like it to be. Glasser (1984, p. 32) asserted, "All our behavior is our constant attempt to reduce the difference between what we want (the pictures in our heads) and what we have (the way we see situations in the world)."

Some examples will illustrate this idea. Each of us has a detailed idea of the type of person we would like to date or form a relationship with; when we find someone who closely matches these characteristics, we seek to form a relationship. Each of us carries around a picture album of our favorite foods; when we're hungry, we select an item and go about obtaining that food.

How do we develop these pictures/albums/ideas that we believe will satisfy our needs? Glasser asserted that we begin to create our albums at an early age (perhaps even before birth) and that we spend our whole life enlarging them. Essentially, whenever what we do gets us something that satisfies a need, we store the picture of it in our personal albums. Glasser (1984) gave the following example of this process by describing how a hungry child added chocolate-chip cookies to his picture album:

> Suppose you had a grandson and your daughter left you in charge while he was taking a nap. She said she would be right back, because he would be ravenous when he awoke and she knew you had no idea what to feed an eleven-month-old child. She was right. As soon as she left, he awoke screaming his head off, obviously starved. You tried a bottle, but he rejected it—he had something more substantial in mind. But what? Being unused to a howling baby, and desperate, you tried a chocolate-chip cookie and it worked wonders. At first, he did not seem to know what it was, but he was a quick learner. He quickly polished off three cookies. She returned and almost polished you off for being so stupid as to give a baby chocolate. "Now," she said, "he will be yelling all day for those cookies." She was right. If he is like most of us, he will probably have chocolate on his mind for the rest of his life. (p. 19)

When this child learned how satisfying chocolate-chip cookies are, he placed the picture of these cookies in his personal picture album.

By the term *pictures,* Glasser meant *perceptions* from our five senses of sight, hearing, touch, smell, and taste. The pictures in our albums do not have to be rational. Anorexics picture themselves as too fat and starve themselves to come closer to their irrational picture of unhealthy thinness. Rapists have pictures of satisfying their power needs and perhaps sexual needs through sexual assault. To change a picture, we must replace it with one that will at least reasonably satisfy the need in question. People who are unable to replace a picture may endure a lifetime of misery. Some battered women, for example, endure brutal beatings and humiliations in marriage because they cannot picture themselves as worthy of a loving relationship.

Glasser noted that whenever the picture we see and the one we want to see differ, a *signal* generated by this difference leads us to behave in a way that will obtain the picture we want. We examine our behavior and select one or more that we believe will help us reduce this difference. These behaviors not only include straightforward problem-solving efforts but also manipulative strategies like anger, pouting, and guilt. People who act irresponsibly or ineffectually have either failed to select responsible behaviors from their repertoires or have not yet learned responsible courses of action.

Glasser believed we are driven by five basic, innate needs. As soon as one need is satisfied, another need (or perhaps more than one acting together) pushes for satisfaction. Our first need is *to survive and reproduce.* This includes such vital functions as breathing, digesting food, sweating, regulating blood pressure, and meeting the demands of hunger, thirst, and sex.

Our second need is *to belong—to love, share, and cooperate.* We generally meet this need through family, friends, pets, plans, and material possessions.

Our third need is *power.* Glasser said this need involves getting others to obey us and to then receive the esteem and recognition that accompanies power. Our drive for power is sometimes in conflict with our need to belong. Two people in a relationship may struggle to control it rather than create an equalitarian relationship.

Our fourth need is *freedom.* People want the freedom to choose how they live their lives, to express themselves, to read and write what they choose, to associate with whom they select, and to worship or not worship as they believe.

Our fifth need is *fun.* Glasser believed learning is often fun; this gives us a great incentive to assimilate what we need to satisfy our needs. Classes that are grim and boring are major failings of our educational system. Laughing and humor help fulfill our needs for fun. Fun is such a vital part of living that most of us have trouble conceiving of life without it.

Glasser added that there may be other yet unidentified needs. He also noted that individuals differ in the intensity of their needs. Not everyone wants to be a CEO, for example.

Glasser also asserted that any theory that contends our behavior is solely a response to outside stimuli or events is wrong. He rejected behaviorism's stimulus-response system; people in his view are in control of what they do.

Identity Theory

Reality therapy is based on the premise that we all face a single basic psychological need: the need for an identity. Glasser and Zunin (1979, p. 302) defined this need as "the need to feel that each of us is somehow separate and distinct from every other living being on the face of this earth and that no other person thinks, looks, acts, and talks exactly as we do."

Although identity can be viewed from several viewpoints, Glasser believed that from a therapeutic vantage point it is most useful to conceptualize identity in terms of people who develop a *success identity* versus those who develop a *failure identity.*

People who develop a success identity do so through pathways of *love* and *worth.* People who view themselves as successes must feel that at least one other person loves them, and that they also love at least one other person. They also believe that at least one other person feels they are worthwhile, and that they themselves are worthwhile (Glasser & Zunin, 1979).

> In reality therapy, we see *worth* and *love* as two very different elements; consider, for example, the extreme case of the "spoiled" child. One may fantasize that a child, if showered with "pure love," whose parents' "goal" was never to frustrate or stress or strain this child in any way, and when he was faced with a task or difficulty always had his parents to perform this task for him, this child always relieved of responsibility would develop into an individual who would feel loved but would not experience worth. Worth comes through accomplishing tasks and achieving success in the accomplishment of those tasks. (p. 312)

A person can also feel worthwhile through accomplishing tasks (for example, a successful businessperson), but believe he or she is unloved. Experiencing only one of these elements (worth or love) without the other can lead to a failure identity.

A failure identity can develop when a child receives inadequate love or is made to feel worthless. People with failure identities express their sense of failure by becoming mentally ill, by delinquency, or by withdrawal. Almost everyone with a failure identity is lonely.

Why do some people become "mentally ill"? Glasser indicated such people often deny or distort reality. They change the world in their minds to feel important, significant, and meaningful. A failure identity is experienced as intensely discomforting, and changing reality through fantasizing is one way to deal with this discomfort. Glasser and Zunin (1979) elaborated further:

> The person who is mentally ill has distorted the real world in his own fantasy to make himself feel more comfortable. He denies reality to protect himself from facing the feeling of being meaningless and insignificant in the world around him. For example, both the grandiose delusion and the persecutory delusion of the so-called schizophrenic provide support or solace for him. (p. 313)

Glasser (1976) described the *choice* aspect of those who decide to become "crazy":

> Crazy, psychotic, nuts, loony, bonkers, schizophrenic. There are a dozen popular, as well as pseudoscientific, words for this condition. I happen to prefer "crazy" because it is understandable; it doesn't have the pseudoscientific connotation of schizophrenia, it is not technical, and it emphasizes much better than any of the other terms *the choice aspect* of this category. Schizophrenia sounds so much like a disease that prominent scientists delude themselves into searching for its cure, when the "cure" is within each crazy person who has chosen it. If he can find love or worth he will give up the choice readily—a big "if," I will admit, but hundreds do each day as they are discharged from good hospitals and clinics. With adequate treatment they learn to become strong enough to stop choosing to be crazy. Becoming crazy is actually a fairly sensible choice of the weak because no one expects a crazy person to fulfill his needs in the real world for the obvious reason that he is no longer in it. He now lives in the world of his mind, and there within his own mind, crazy as it may be, he tries to find, and to some extent usually succeeds in finding, a substitute for the adequacy he can't find in reality. Within his own mind, within his own imagination, out of his own thought processes, he may be able to reduce the pain of his failure and find a little relief. For inadequacy he provides delusions of grandeur; for loneliness, hallucinations to keep him company. He may have a delusion that everybody loves him or that he is an overwhelmingly omnipotent person, which does relieve his pain. Every mental hospital has one or two Jesus Christs, the acme of omnipotence and power. When all of this is created within a person's own mind we call it crazy, but it makes sense to him because it doesn't hurt as much as being lucid but miserably inadequate. (pp. 19–20)

Other individuals handle the discomfort of a failure identity by withdrawal or ignoring reality, even though they are aware of the real world. Glasser and Zunin (1979, p. 313) described these people: "These individuals are referred to as delinquents, criminals, 'sociopaths,' 'personality disorders,' and so on. They are basically the anti-social individuals who choose to break the rules and regulations of society on a regular basis, thereby ignoring reality."

Success or failure identities are not measured by finances or labels but rather in terms of how people perceive themselves. It is possible for individuals to regard themselves as failures even though others view them as successful. Failure identities begin to form about the time when children first enter school. At about this age (5 or 6) children develop the social and verbal skills and the thinking capacities to define themselves as successful or unsuccessful. As they grow, children tend to associate with others with similar identities; those with failure identities associate with others who have failure identities, and success identities associate with other successful people. As the years pass the two groups associate less and less with each other. Glasser and Zunin (1979, p. 312) noted, "for example, it is indeed rare for a person with a success identity to have, as a close and personal friend, someone who is a known criminal, felon, heroin addict, and so forth." People with success identities tend to compete constructively, meeting and seeking new challenges. Also, they tend to reinforce one another's successes. Conversely, people with failure identities find facing the real world to be uncomfortable and anxiety producing and therefore choose either to withdraw, to distort reality, or to ignore reality.

Theory of Therapy

In counseling clients, reality therapy advances 14 principles.

1. Encourage Responsible Behavior

The main goal of reality therapy is to help clients reject irresponsible behavior and to learn improved ways of functioning. A responsible person has the ability to fulfill personal needs in a way that does not deprive others of the ability to fulfill their needs.

Reality therapists confront clients with their cop-outs. They do not excuse clients' irresponsible behavior by blaming personal problems on the past actions of parents or on other excuses. Responsibility is emphasized, because for clients to feel worthwhile they must feel they are maintaining a satisfactory standard of behavior.

2. Recognize Mental Illness Labels as Destructive

Glasser agreed with Szasz (1961) that mental illness is a myth. Glasser (1965) presented his view:

> In consonance with our emphasis on responsibility and irresponsibility, we who practice reality therapy advocate dispensing with the common psychiatric labels, such as neurosis and psychosis, which tend to categorize and stereotype people. Limiting our descriptions to the behavior which the patient manifests, we would, for example, describe a man who believes that he is President Johnson as irresponsible, followed by a brief description of his unrealistic behavior and thinking. Calling him psychotic or schizophrenic immediately places him in a mental illness category which separates him from most of us, the label thereby serving to compound his problem. Through our description it can immediately be understood that he is unsuccessful in fulfilling his needs. He has given up trying to do so as John Jones and is now trying as President Johnson, a logical delusion for a man who feels isolated and inadequate. The description *irresponsible* is much more precise, indicating our job is to help him to become more responsible so that he will be able to satisfy his needs as himself. (pp. 15–16)

Glasser urged that the word *irresponsible* be used in place of medical model labels of neurotic, psychotic, schizophrenic, and so on.

Glasser raised the question, "If we relate to people who have emotional problems as if they are insane and lock them up in a mental institution, how can we expect them to learn to be responsible and productive?" Those who adjust to the routine in a mental hospital are in no way learning how to make it in the real world, because a mental institution is an artificial environment in which dysfunctional behavior is expected and excused. Glasser asserted that labeling people as mentally ill sidetracks them onto dwelling on the erroneous notion that they have a "disease of the mind," which no one as yet knows how to treat. Instead, it would be far better to relate to people with emotional and behavioral problems as people with excellent potential to improve and resolve their personal problems. It is well known that how people are treated is how they come to perceive themselves. If people are treated as mentally ill, they perceive themselves as mentally ill, and they may play that role for the rest of their life. However, if they are treated as sane, with a high potential to solve their problems, they are much more likely to become responsible and productive (see CTRM Exhibit 5.1).

3. Foster Involved Relationships

The identity we develop is largely dependent on our involvement with others. Therefore, therapists need to help clients clarify and understand themselves, including their beliefs, values, opinions, and self-concepts.

Therapist involvement is also important; we all need at least one person who cares about our wellbeing. Detachment and aloofness are not helpful. Reality therapists thus convey warmth, understanding, and concern.

Reality therapists are *personal* in therapy; that is, they present themselves as real people. They do not project an image of omnipotence but reveal themselves, including their strengths and frailties. When doing so is appropriate and constructive, reality therapists will personalize the counseling by self-disclosing their own experiences.

Glasser and Zunin (1979) further elaborated on being personal and involved:

> The purpose of becoming personal in reality therapy is to help people become involved with someone who can help them understand that there is more to life than focusing on misery or symptoms or irresponsible behavior. However, it is an important part of the caring relationship to define the limits of involvement. It is not possible for a therapist to become deeply involved with everyone who comes for help. He becomes involved only within the context of the office. The therapist must be honest about this. . . .

CTRM EXHIBIT 5.1

Two approaches to mental illness

Much of the language relating to emotional disturbances is a familiar part of our lexicon. We use *crazy, psychotic, neurotic, nervous breakdown, insane, sick, uptight, mad* to express judgments (often unfavorable) about unusual behavior or unusual emotions. Whatever terms we use, we often have only a vague idea of its technical meaning. Amazingly, though, we act as if the label is completely accurate and then relate to the person as if the label is absolutely correct. However, we all know it is impossible to define these terms precisely.

Helping professionals use two approaches to diagnose people who display emotional disturbances and abnormal behaviors: the medical model and the interactional model.

Medical Model

This model presents emotional and behavioral problems as illnesses, comparable to physical illness. Mental illness labels use medical terminology (for example, schizophrenia, paranoia, psychosis, or insanity) to describe emotional problems. Adherents of this approach believe the disturbed person's mind is affected by an internal condition. This condition, they assert, results from genetic endowment, metabolic disorders, infectious diseases, internal conflicts, chemical imbalances, unconscious use of defense mechanisms, or traumatic early experiences.

The medical model has a lengthy classification of mental disorders defined by the American Psychiatric Association. (See Chapter 1 for a summary of the numerous specific mental disorders that are classified in DSM-IV [1994].)

The medical model arose in reaction to the historical notion that the emotionally disturbed were possessed by demons and could therefore be blamed for their disturbances. The medical model treats the disturbed as in need of help and has stimulated enormous amounts of research into the nature of emotional problems. Therapeutic approaches owe their development to the medical model.

Interactional Model

Critics of the medical model assert that medical labels have no diagnostic or treatment value and may actually have an adverse effect. Thomas Szasz (1961) was one of the first authorities to assert that mental illness is a myth—that it does not exist. Szasz's theory is interactional; it focuses on the processes of everyday social interaction and the effects of labeling.

Beginning with the assumption that the term *mental* illness implies a "disease of the mind," Szasz categorized all so-called mental illnesses into three types of emotional and behavioral disorders and discussed the inappropriateness of calling them "mental illnesses":

1. *Personal disabilities,* such as excessive anxiety, depression, fears, and feelings of inadequacy. Szasz said such so-called mental illnesses may be appropriately considered "mental" (in the sense that thinking and feeling are "mental" activities), but he asserts that they are not diseases.

2. *Antisocial acts,* such as bizarre homicides and social deviations. (Homosexuality used to be listed in this category but was removed from the American Psychiatric Association's list of mental illnesses in 1974.) Szasz said such antisocial acts are actually social deviations, and not "mental" or "diseases."

3. *Deterioration of the brain with associated personality changes.* This category includes the "mental illnesses" in which personality changes result from brain deterioration caused by arteriosclerosis, chronic alcoholism, AIDS, general paresis, or serious brain injury. Common symptoms are loss of memory, listlessness, apathy, and deterioration of personal grooming habits. Szasz says these disorders can appropriately be considered "diseases" but are diseases of the brain rather than of the *mind.*

Szasz (1961) asserted that calling people with emotional problems "mentally ill" is as absurd as calling the emotionally disturbed "possessed":

> The belief in mental illness as something other than man's trouble in getting along with his fellow man is the proper heir to the belief in demonology and witchcraft. Mental illness exists or is "real" in exactly the same sense in which witches existed or were "real." (p. 84)

In reality, being labeled "mentally ill" occurs in three steps: the person displays some deviant behavior; the behavior is not tolerated by the family or community; and the professional labeler, usually a psychiatrist, believes in the medical model and assigns a mental illness label. Scheff (1966) and Mechanic (1962) offered evidence that family and community intolerance of deviant behavior and the professional labeler's belief in the medical model are more crucial than the behavior itself in determining whether someone will be labeled "mentally ill."

The point here is that people have emotional problems, not mystic "mental illnesses." Thus, reality therapists use the following terms to describe behavior: depression, anxiety, obsession, compulsive, excessive fear, feelings of failure. These are personal problems, not illnesses. Medical terms (for example, schizophrenia or psychosis) are not useful because no distinguishing symptom indicates whether a person has, or does not have, the "illness." In addition, Rosenhan and Seligman (1995) pointed out that considerable variation exists among cultures regarding what is mental illness. Indeed,

(continued)

CTRM EXHIBIT 5.1

Continued

psychiatrists themselves frequently disagree in their "medical" diagnoses.

In a dramatic study, psychologist David Rosenhan (1973) demonstrated that professional staff in mental hospitals could not distinguish between "sane" and "insane" people. Rosenhan and seven "normal" associates went to 12 mental hospitals in five different states and claimed to hear voices. After they were admitted, these pseudopatients said they had stopped hearing the voices. Although they then began to behave completely normally, the hospital personnel were unable to recognize the difference between their sanity and the "insanity" of the other patients. The pseudopatients were confined to the hospitals for an average of 19 days and then discharged with a diagnosis of "schizophrenia in remission."

Medical labels have several adverse labeling effects. People who are labeled mentally ill (and frequently their therapists) believe that they have a disease for which unfortunately there is no known "cure." The label gives them an excuse for not taking responsibility for their actions (for example, innocent by reason by insanity). Because there is no known "cure," the disturbed frequently idle away their time waiting for someone to discover a cure rather than assuming responsibility for their behavior, examining the reasons for their problems, and making efforts to improve. Other undesirable consequences of the label mentally ill are that those so labeled lose legal rights; can be stigmatized as dangerous, unpredictable, untrustworthy, or of "weak" character; and find it more difficult to secure employment or receive a promotion (Rosenhan & Seligman, 1995).

An even more harmful effect is that "mentally ill" people view themselves as different and therefore play the role of the "sick" person. Everyone needs to evaluate feelings, opinions, and abilities. In the absence of objective, nonsocial criteria, people rely on other people to gauge the validity of their beliefs and feelings. If others define us as mentally ill and react to us accordingly, we may begin to say, "I must be crazy, because other people treat me as if I were insane."

Authorities who adhere to the interactional model raise a key question, because expectations generally guide behavior: "If we relate to people with emotional problems as mentally ill, how can we expect them to act in emotionally healthy and responsible ways?" Also, a diagnosis of mental illness carries a greater stigma than physical illness.

Szasz (1967) also argued that the mental model is used (perhaps unintentionally) to control people who do not conform to social expectations. The former Soviet Union had a long history of labeling dissenters (including poets, writers, and intellectuals who would be respected in this country) as mentally ill and sending them to concentration camps or to insane asylums. In the past, psychiatrists in Russia often concluded that people who did not accept Marxist-Leninist philosophy were psychologically impaired. Are some psychiatrists using the mental illness label to control the behavior of nonconformists in our country? Szasz (1967) asserted that they are. As an example, he cites listing homosexuality as a mental disorder by the American Psychiatric Association. As another example, Szasz (1963) quoted Dana L. Farnsworth, a Harvard psychiatrist and an authority on college psychiatric services:

> Library vandalism, cheating and plagiarism, stealing in the college or community stores or in the dormitories, unacceptable or antisocial sexual practices (overt homosexuality, exhibitionism, promiscuity), and the unwise and unregulated use of harmful drugs are examples of behavior that suggest the presence of emotionally unstable persons. (p. 76)

Mental illness labels have a "boundary" effect, defining what behaviors a society considers "sick" and pressuring citizens to avoid such behaviors. Szasz's point is that nonconformists can be adversely affected by the use of the medical model.

Labeling as the Primary Cause of Chronic "Mental Illness"

We must, of course, ask "If mental illness does not exist, why do some people go through life as if they were mentally ill?" Scheff's theory (1966) provides an answer. He hypothesizes that labeling is the most important determinant of chronic functional "mental illness."

Scheff began by first arriving at a definition of mental illness.

> One source of immediate embarrassment to any social theory of "mental illness" is that the terms used in referring to these phenomena in our society prejudge the issue. The medical metaphor "mental illness" suggests a determinant process which occurs within the individual: the unfolding and development of disease. In order to avoid this assumption, we will utilize sociological, rather than medical concepts to formulate the problem. (p. 31)

The symptoms of mental illness can thus be viewed as violations of social norms; for Scheff's purposes the term *mental illness* refers to those assigned this label by professionals.

Literally thousands of studies have been conducted to identify the origins of long-term mental disorders. Practically all of these studies identified the causes as somewhere inside a person (for example, metabolic disorders, unconscious conflicts, heredity factors). These research efforts are based on medical and psychological models of human behavior. Yet, amazingly, in spite of this extensive research, the determinants of chronic mental disorders (such as schizophrenia) are largely unknown. Scheff suggested that the major determinants are not medical but are our social processes (that is, our interactions with others).

Scheff's theory is summarized here. Everyone, at times, violates social norms and commits acts that could be labeled symptoms of mental illness. For example, a person may on occasion angrily engage in fights with others, or experience intense depression or grief, or be highly anxious, or use drugs or alcohol to excess, or have a fetish, or be an exhibitionist, or commit a highly unusual and bizarre act.

Usually the person who has unwanted emotions or who commits deviant acts is not identified (labeled) as being mentally ill. In such cases, the unwanted emotions and deviant actions are usually not classified as symptoms of a mental illness but instead are ignored, unrecognized, or rationalized in some other manner.

Occasionally, however, such norm violations are perceived by others as being "abnormal." The offenders are then labeled mentally ill and consequently related to as if they are mentally ill. When people are publicly labeled, they are highly suggestible to cues from others. They realize they have done something unusual and turn to others to obtain an assessment of who they really are. In the absence of objective measures of their sanity, they rely on others for this assessment. If others relate to them as if they are mentally ill, they begin to define and perceive themselves as being mentally ill.

Traditional stereotypes of mental illness define the mentally ill role, both for those who are labeled mentally ill and for people they interact with. Frequently people they interact with reward them for enacting the social role of being mentally ill. The rewards may be sympathy and attention, not having to hold a job, not being held responsible for wrongdoing, or they fulfill the requirements of other roles.

In addition, the "mentally ill" are punished for attempting to return to conventional roles. They are viewed with suspicion and have considerable difficulty obtaining employment.

The effect of all this is a gradual change in one's self-concept; people thus labeled begin to view themselves as different—as insane, and a vicious circle is created. The more one enacts the role of being mentally ill, the more one is defined and treated as mentally ill, and so on. Unless interrupted, the cycle leads to a "career" of long-term mental illness. Scheff concluded that with this process labeling is the single most important determinant of chronic mental illness.

If labeling is an important determinant of chronic functional mental illness, significant changes are suggested in certain diagnostic and treatment practices. Mental health personnel are frequently faced with uncertainty in deciding whether a person has a mental disorder. An informal norm has been developed to handle this uncertainty; when in doubt, it is better to judge a well person ill than to judge an ill person well. This norm is based on two assumptions taken from treating physical illness: (1) a diagnosis of illness results in only minimal damage to the status and reputation of a person, and (2) unless the illness is treated, the illness will become progressively worse. However, both of these assumptions are questionable. Unlike medical treatment, psychiatric treatment can drastically change a person's status in the community; for example, it can remove rights that are difficult to regain. Furthermore, if Scheff is right that labeling is the key determinant in leading to long-term mental illness, the exact opposite norm should be established to handle uncertainty; namely, when in doubt, do not label a person mentally ill. This would be in accord with the legal approach that follows the norm, "When in doubt, acquit," or "A person is innocent until proven guilty."

If labeling is indeed a major determinant of mental illness, certain changes are also suggested in treating violators of social norms. One is to attempt to maintain people with problems in their local community without labeling them mentally ill or sending them to a mental hospital where their playing the role of the mentally ill is apt to be reinforced. In the past several years, the field of mental hygiene has been moving in this direction. Another outgrowth of Scheff's theory would be increasing public education efforts to inform the general public of the nature of emotional and behavioral problems and the adverse effects that result from inappropriate labeling.

The adverse effects of labeling ultimately raise the issue of the value of labeling anyone mentally ill.

Source: This material is adapted from the following articles: (1) Charles Zastrow, "When Labeled Mentally Ill," in *The Personal Problem Solver,* edited by Charles Zastrow and Dae H. Chang, © 1977, pp. 163–169. Adapted by permission of Prentice-Hall, Inc., Englewood Cliffs, New Jersey; (2) Charles Zastrow, "Understanding Deviant Behavior," in *Talk to Yourself: Using the Power of Self-Talk,* © 1979, pp. 117–124. Adapted by permission of Prentice-Hall, Inc., Englewood Cliffs, New Jersey.

> The therapist must define the situation so the patient understands exactly what the relationship is, where it is, and where it is going. (p. 317)

4. Focus on Present and Future

Reality therapists believe that what we want now and in the future, along with our motivation to achieve what we want, is more important than our past experiences in determining our future. The past is fixed; it cannot be changed. But we can change the present and the future. Dwelling on the past is a waste of time. If the past is discussed, it is always related to current behavior.

5. Focus on Behavior Rather Than on Feelings

Feelings and actions are interrelated and mutually reinforcing. Reality therapists assume that we have only limited control over our feelings. Changing actions is therefore the most productive way to feel better. Glasser and Zunin (1979, p. 317) noted, "We cannot order ourselves to *feel* better but we can always order ourselves to *do* better, and so *doing better* makes us *feel better.*"

Reality therapists believe clients need to figure out what they are doing that is causing them difficulty. If a client states, "I really feel sad and miserable" a reality therapist will say, "What are you doing to make yourself depressed?" Or if a client indicates at some length that he is unhappily married, the reality therapist will ask "What are you doing that contributes to the unhappiness?" or "What are you planning to do about your unhappiness?"

6. Encourage Value Judgments

A major task for reality therapists is to help clients face the morality of their behavior. Reality therapists help clients judge whether their behavior is irresponsible. Clients are assisted in seeing that their behavior is irresponsible whenever they hurt themselves or hurt others—and this judgment is to be made by clients. Therapists generally do not make value judgments for clients as this would prevent them from accepting responsibility for their behavior.

7. Encourage Planning

Reality therapists examine problems in depth with clients and then explore alternative solutions and their consequences. If clients cannot develop a personal plan for future action, the therapist helps them develop one. Once the plan is worked out, a contract is drawn up and signed by client and therapist. The plan is usually a realistic one for behaving differently in situations where the client admits to acting irresponsibly. If the contract is broken, a new one is designed and agreed on.

Commitment is a keystone in reality therapy. Making and following through with plans helps people gain a sense of self-worth and maturity.

8. Reject Excuses

Of course, not all client plans and commitments will be achieved. Glasser did not encourage searching for reasons to justify irresponsible behavior; doing so supports a belief that clients have acceptable reasons for meeting their commitments. Excuses let people off the hook, but they eventually lead to more failure and to a failure identity.

When a client fails to meet a commitment, the therapist simply asks, "Are you planning to meet your commitment?" If the answer is in the affirmative, the therapist asks, "When?" If the client says he has changed his mind and indicates he does not want to meet the commitment, the therapist may suggest working together to develop a new contract.

In not accepting excuses, the therapist does not seek to deprecate or demean the client for failing but seeks to convey that a reasonable plan for improvement is always possible.

9. Eliminate Punishment

Punishment for failing to meet a commitment reinforces a failure identity. It serves only as a temporary means of forcing different behavior. When clients no longer believe they are under surveillance, they often return to exhibiting irresponsible behavior.

Eliminating punishment is quite different, Glasser notes, from following through on the natural consequences of not meeting one's obligations.[1] For example, if a runaway youth contracts to receive shelter at a runaway center on the condition that she will remain drug free and then is caught smoking pot, the center must follow through on the consequences spelled out in the contract, which may include removal from the shelter. Not following through on such consequences only reinforces the irresponsible behavior.

10. Do Not Offer Sympathy

Sympathy does little more than convey the therapist's lack of confidence in the client's ability to act responsibly. Listening to long, sad stories about the client's

[1] Glasser has a minor conceptual problem in this area because learning theory defines following through on consequences as a form of punishment.

CASE EXAMPLE

A Reality Therapy Group

A number of years ago when I was employed as a social worker at a maximum security hospital for the criminally insane, my supervisor requested that I develop and lead a therapy group. When I asked "What should be the objectives of such a group?" and "Who shall be selected to join?" my supervisor indicated those decisions would be mine. He added that no one else was doing any group therapy at this hospital, and the hospital administration thought it would be desirable to develop group therapy programs for accountability reasons.

I was wary because I was newly employed and had never led a group before. I asked myself, "Who is in the greatest need of group therapy?" and "If the group members do not improve, or if they deteriorate, how will I explain this—that is, cover my tracks?" I concluded that I should invite those identified as the "sickest" (chronic schizophrenics) to join the group. Chronic schizophrenics are generally expected to show little improvement. With such an expectation, if they did not improve, I felt I would not be blamed. However, if they did improve, it would be viewed as a substantial accomplishment. Having been trained in reality therapy in graduate school, I decided to use this approach.

I read the case records of all the residents (11) diagnosed as chronic schizophrenic and then met with each person to invite them to join the group. (To my surprise, each resident appeared very different from what I was expecting from their case records.) I explained the purpose of the group and the topics we would cover. Eight people decided to join, some mainly because it would look good on their record and increase their chances for an early release.

I began the first meeting by stating that I knew what the "key" was to their being discharged from the hospital, and I asked if they knew what that might be. This got their attention right away. The key, I said, is very simple: "learn to act sane, so the medical staff will think you have recovered."

At the first meeting, I explained that the purpose was not to review their past but to help them make their present life more enjoyable and meaningful and to help them plan for the future. We would cover how to convince the hospital staff they no longer needed to be hospitalized; how to prepare themselves for returning to their community; what to do when they felt depressed or had some other unwanted emotion; and, following their release, what to do if and when they had an urge to do something that would get them in trouble again.

This focus on improving their current circumstances stimulated their interest, but soon they found it uncomfortable and anxiety producing to examine what the future might hold for them. The idea they had some responsibility and control over that future also made them anxious. They reacted to this discomfort by stating they were labeled mentally ill and therefore some internal condition caused their strange behavior. A cure for schizophrenia had not yet been found, so they could do little to improve their situation.

I retorted that their excuses were "garbage" (stronger terms were used) and spent a few sessions getting them to understand that the label "chronic schizophrenic" was meaningless. I explained that mental illness was a myth (that is, people do not have a "disease of the mind," even though they have emotional problems). Thus what had gotten them locked up was their deviant behavior. I continued to stress that they held the key for getting released—"act sane."

Their next set of excuses revolved around their broken homes, or ghetto schools, or broken romances—in short, anything that had "messed them up," the bottom line being they could do little about their situation. They were again informed that such excuses were "garbage." Yes, their past experiences were important in getting them here, but what they wanted out of the future and their motivation were much more important in determining what their future held.

Finally, after working through a series of excuses, we began to focus on how they could better handle specific problems. Yes, they could handle being depressed. Yes, they could stop acting "strange." Yes, they could present themselves as being "sane," and so the list went. We examined what they wanted out of the future and the specific steps they would have to take to achieve their goals.

(continued)

CASE EXAMPLE
Reality Therapy
(continued)

The results were very encouraging. Instead of idly spending much of the time brooding about their situation, they became motivated to improve it. At the end of the 12 weeks (when I had to return to school), the eight members spontaneously stated that the meetings were making a positive change in their lives and requested that another social worker from the hospital be assigned to continue the group. This was arranged. Three years later I was told that five of the eight group members had been released to their home communities; two were considered to have shown improvement; while the final member's condition was described as "unchanged."

Counseling Skills at Work in Generalist Practice

This case example illustrates the social worker used the following roles that, as described in Chapter 1, are components of generalist social work practice: group facilitator, educating clients to understand they are largely responsible for their future, brokering clients to use resources of the mental hospital, helping clients to problem-solve, and being an encouraging role model.

Source: This case example is adapted from an illustration of a therapy group presented in Charles Zastrow's *Introduction to Social Work and Social Welfare,* 7th ed. (Pacific Grove, CA: Brooks/Cole, 2000), pp. 86–87.

past or sympathizing with a person's misery does nothing to improve their ability to live responsibly.

11. Rarely Ask Why

Asking a client the reasons for irresponsible actions implies that such explanations make a difference. Reality therapists believe that irresponsible behavior is just that, regardless of the reasons. Listening to the "reasons" for irresponsible behavior is not only time-consuming it is also counterproductive because clients may conclude that the behavior can continue as long as they can come up with excuses for it. By giving little attention to such explanations, the reality therapist conveys that responsible behavior is expected.

12. Praise Responsible Behavior

People need recognition for their positive accomplishments and for *trying* to accomplish something even though they may not succeed. Reality therapists reinforce and praise responsible behavior. They also convey their belief that people are capable of changing their irresponsible behavior. It is easier to do things well when others are encouraging and realistically optimistic.

13. Question Traditional Case Histories

Traditional case histories emphasize the client's failures, shortcomings, problems, and traumas. These histories are often tragic and notorious misrepresentations. They usually tell more about the paradigms of the writer than about the client. Rarely do case histories assess the person's successes and strengths, which are at least as important as their shortcomings and failures.

14. Foster Success Experiences

As clients develop plans to improve their circumstances, reality therapists foster *realistic* goals and mastering the tasks involved in accomplishing the goals. To counteract failure identities, clients must take risks and experience successes. Gradually, such successes lead clients to perceive themselves more positively.

Evaluation

Reality therapy is a commonsense approach to therapy. It affirms the dignity of humans and their ability to improve their situations. The concept of personal responsibility for one's behavior has broad applications. It fosters meaningful personal growth. It helps clients identify their irresponsible behavior and helps them learn to be more responsible. It provides a useful focus for counseling people. The concepts of this approach are relatively simple to learn and apply, which is a distinct advantage.

Reality therapy differs substantially from psychoanalysis. Glasser (1965) discussed these differences, which are briefly summarized in CTRM Exhibit 5.2.

Research shows that reality therapy is substantially more effective than psychoanalysis in producing posi-

CTRM EXHIBIT 5.2

Psychoanalysis versus reality therapy

Psychoanalysis	*Reality Therapy*
1. Mental illness exists.	1. The concept of mental illness is not accepted.
2. Therapist probes deep into client's past life.	2. Focus is on the present and the future.
3. Therapist should relate to patients as a neutral figure to further transference.	3. Therapist should relate as a genuine, real person.
4. Unconscious processes and conflicts are emphasized.	4. Unconscious processes and conflicts are deemphasized.
5. Patients are not responsible for their deviant behaviors, which are caused by unconscious motivations or mental illness.	5. Clients are responsible for their actions.
6. Patients will spontaneously learn better behavior through insight into the historical and unconscious sources of their problems.	6. Insight into problems will not of itself produce change; clients need to learn to act more responsibly.

tive therapeutic changes (Eysenck, 1965; Glasser & Wubbolding, 1995; Stuart, 1970). It has been successfully applied in a variety of settings, including corrections, mental health, education, unemployment, public welfare, and in treating delinquency.

Some criticisms of reality therapy can also be made:

1. Although meaningful activity may be one way to alleviate unwanted emotions, it is not the only way. Ellis (1962) demonstrated that all emotions, including unwanted emotions, are primarily caused by our thoughts; changing our thoughts is also a very useful way to alleviate unwanted emotions. (See *rational therapy* in Module 9.)

2. Glasser's theory fails to explain why some people become depressed while others become highly anxious, or explode in anger, or are shy, or experience guilt and shame. Neither does his theory explain why some people commit robbery whereas others commit murder or white-collar crimes or neglect their children and so on.

3. Glasser did not specify how his two theories, identity and control, relate to each other.

Summary

Control theory asserts that all human behavior is an attempt to reduce the differences between the pictures in our head of what we want and how we perceive the world.

Identity theory asserts that our most important psychological need is our need for identity. People who develop a success identity do so through the pathways of love and worth. A failure identity can develop when a child receives inadequate love or is made to feel worthless. People with failure identities express their discomfort in facing reality by distorting reality (becoming "mentally ill"), by withdrawal, or by ignoring reality (engaging in antisocial activities).

Reality therapy seeks to help clients reject irresponsible behavior and learn improved ways of functioning.

The question regarding whether mental illness exists is examined. Szasz (1961) and other authorities asserted that mental illness labels have no diagnostic or treatment value and may complicate therapy efforts due to labeling effects. These authorities assert that people certainly do have emotional and behavioral problems, but they do not have a disease of the mind as implied by the term *mental illness.*

Scheff's (1966) theory hypothesized that labeling is the single most important determinant of longterm mental illness. If the theory is accurate, significant changes are suggested in diagnostic and treatment practices—for example, attempting to maintain people with problems in their local community without labeling them mentally ill or sending them to a mental hospital.

Reality therapy is increasingly being used by social workers in a wide variety of settings. It is a commonsense approach to therapy that research has found to be effective.

EXERCISES

1. COUNSELING WITH REALITY THERAPY

Goal: To use reality therapy in a counseling situation.

Step 1: Set up counseling situations. Break into groups of ten. Three of you will develop two problem scenarios for which a husband and wife (or two gay partners) are seeking counseling. Two of you will role-play the "clients." The rest of you will develop counseling strategies using reality therapy concepts. Select one person to role-play the "counselor."

Step 2: Now switch roles and role-play the counseling sessions again. How does this therapy feel for the "counselor"? How does this therapy feel for the "clients"? How could you improve the counseling sessions?

Step 3: Class discussion: Would you as counselors use this approach? If so, why and in what situations? When would this approach not be a good choice?

2. DOES MENTAL ILLNESS EXIST?

Goal: To explore the question, "Is mental illness a myth?"

Step 1: Form two debate teams and assign sides. Set a date for the class debate. Elect judges to score the debate.

Step 2: Meet with your team, brainstorm arguments for and against your stance, then divvy up the research topics. If your team deems it necessary, set dates for meetings in which you will assemble your material and develop the arguments—points and counterpoints—you will use. Select the presenters, who may wish to rehearse.

Step 3: The debate. Judges will score points according to agreed upon rules.

Step 4: Class discussion: Did this debate change your viewpoint?

MODULE 6

Rational Therapy

The founder of rational therapy, Albert Ellis (1913–) practiced psychoanalytic approaches to therapy during the late 1940s and early 1950s, but became disenchanted with both the results and the approach. Ellis observed that even when patients achieved incredible insight into their childhood and unconscious processes, they continued to experience emotional difficulties.

Ellis developed a new approach, *rational therapy* (also called *rational-emotive therapy*), in which he treated clients by challenging and changing their irrational beliefs. Ellis (1957) was able to demonstrate significant effectiveness using this new approach.

In 1959 Ellis established the Institute for Rational Living in New York City, which provides adult education courses in rational living and a moderate-cost psychotherapy clinic for clients. In 1968 Ellis founded the Institute for Advanced Study in Rational Psychotherapy, which provides helping professionals with extensive training in rational therapy and also provides seminars and workshops throughout the country. Ellis is also recognized nationally as an authority on sexuality. In addition to running workshops and seminars and being a practicing psychotherapist, he has written nearly 40 books and 400 articles!

Rational therapy has had an enormous impact on both professionals and the public. The principles of rational therapy have been applied to such areas as assertiveness training, sexuality, adolescence, law and criminality, religion, executive leadership, children's literature, music, feminism, philosophy, personal problems, alcoholism, marriage and the family, and sex adjustment and therapy.

Theory of Personality Development and Psychopathology

Self-Talk Determines Our Feelings and Actions

Most people believe that our emotions and our actions are determined primarily by the events that happen to us. Rational therapists assert (Ellis, 2000) that the primary cause of all our emotions and actions is what we *tell* ourselves about the events that happen to us.

All feelings and actions occur according to the following format:

Events
↓
Self-talk (Our evaluating thoughts about facts and events that happen to us.)
↓
Emotion
↓
Actions

This is not a new idea. As the stoic philosopher Epictetus wrote in the first century A.D., "Men are disturbed not by things, but by the view which they take of them" (Ellis, 2000).

CTRM Exhibit 6.1 illustrates this process. The most important point here is that our self-talk determines how we feel and act; by changing our self-talk, we can change how we feel and act. We cannot always control events that happen to us, but do we have the power to think rationally about them and thereby change our unwanted emotions and ineffective actions.

Maultsby (1977) indicated that thinking and behavior is rational if it is based on objective reality (it

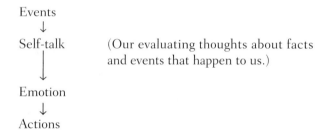

CTRM EXHIBIT 6.1

How self-talk determines events

Event: A husband unexpectedly arrives home early and on walking into his living room sees his wife and an acquaintance embracing.
↓
Self-talk: "My wife and this guy are having an affair—this is awful."
"This guy is threatening my personal life."
"This is morally wrong—this is the worst thing that could happen to me."
"This guy is violating my rights—I've got to forcefully protect my rights."
↓
Emotion: Anger, rage, and a vengeful feeling.
↓
Action: Running at the acquaintance and physically getting into a fight.

If, however, the husband remembers that his wife and the acquaintance are preparing to put on a romantic play at a nearby college, the following may occur:

Event: A husband unexpectedly arrives home early and on walking into his living room sees his wife and an acquaintance embracing.
↓
Self-talk: "Well, apparently they're only practicing for the play."
"I'll watch closely, but I don't think there is anything romantic occurring."
"There is no reason for me to get upset and make a fool of myself."
↓
Emotion: More emotionally relaxed and calm, although somewhat wary.
↓
Action: Casually making small talk with his wife and the acquaintance while observing their interactions.

---

fits the facts) and helps us

- protect our lives
- achieve our short- and long-term goals most quickly
- avoid significant trouble with other people
- feel the emotions we want to feel

If our thoughts or our actions conflict with any of these criteria, they are considered irrational.

We cannot always control events. However, we can tell ourselves rational thoughts about each experience. Lembo (1974) notes:

> We can think rationally or irrationally about *the things that will happen to us* and insist that we will not be a failure if our boss fires us or that we will be a worthless no-account if we are dismissed from our job; that nothing catastrophic will happen if our parents die or that it will be horrible and unbearable if they do die. (p. 9)

Because we determine our feelings and our behaviors via self-talk, we truly are in control of our lives. If we are unhappy, unfulfilled, unsatisfied, frustrated, depressed, grief-stricken, or whatever, it is primarily our doing. Lembo (1974, p. 10) notes, "We have the ability to create a satisfying life for ourselves, and we will succeed in doing so if we rationally manage the thoughts we tell ourselves."

Personality Development and Self-Concept Formations[1]

Our personality is composed of our emotions and our behaviors. Therefore, it is our self-talk that primarily controls our personality.

Most personality theorists focus on outside events in describing how our personality develops. Sigmund Freud, for example, focused on early traumatic childhood experiences, and on the nature of the relationships between parents and the child. Relatively few personality theorists have addressed how our thinking processes develop.

Our sense of identity (who and what we are) incorporates the ongoing sets of self-talk. (Other writers refer to the sense of identity as our self-concept of our self-image.) Our sense of identity is therefore *the* key element of our personality.

[1]This section is adapted from Charles Zastrow, *Talk to Yourself: Using the Power of Self-Talk*, © 1979, pp. 85–88. Adapted by permission of Prentice-Hall, Inc., Englewood Cliffs, New Jersey.

How our personality develops involves how our self-concept develops, and is a lifetime process. It begins during the early years and continues to change throughout our lifetime. During the early years, our sense of identity is largely determined by the reactions of others.

A long time ago, Cooley (1902) discussed this early labeling process as resulting in the "looking-glass self"; that is, we develop our self-concept in terms of how we perceive that others relate to us; others are our looking-glass or mirror. For example, if we receive respect from others and are praised for our positive qualities, we are apt to feel good about ourselves, will gradually develop a positive sense of worth, will generally be happy, and will seek responsible and socially acceptable ways to continue to maintain the respect of others. Conversely, if others relate to us as if we are irresponsible, we are likely to begin to view ourselves as irresponsible and gradually develop a negative self-concept. Such a view causes us to reduce our efforts to act responsibly. How others relate to a person becomes a self-fulfilling prophecy.

The labeling process undoubtedly substantially shapes behavior. Yet it fails to explain why children treated essentially the same engage in very different behavior and develop different self-concepts. We all know stories about people raised in similar circumstances who follow vastly different paths, one of crime or one of productive leadership. Why? Rational therapy may have some answers to this question.

The following theory of self-concept development is adapted from the work of the Soviet psychologists Luria (1961) and Vygotsky (1962).

Phase I: Child's behavior determined by physical needs (hunger) and outside events (parental actions).

Phase II: The child learns to control behavior through verbal instructions and reactions of others (parents).

Phase III: Verbal instructions and reactions of others shape elementary beliefs; the child begins to regulate some actions through self-talk.

Phase IV: Future behavior patterns develop through an interaction of events and self-talk about those events. Self-talk becomes covert (that is, *goes underground,* to use Vygotsky's term) and becomes attitudes, beliefs, and values.

Phase V: These attitudes, beliefs, and values form our sense of identity. Our self-talk about events then largely controls our emotions and actions.

CTRM Exhibit 6.2 shows how events and self-talk interact to form our self-concepts and our personalities.

Given this, why, when two children have essentially the same experiences, do they develop very different personalities? Because their self-talk about their experiences varies. For example, if an 8-year-old child is caught for shoplifting candy and is spanked by her parents, a wide range of self-talk is possible. If she says, "I have done wrong. Stealing is wrong. Somehow I have got to restore my parents' trust in me," her inclinations to steal will be sharply reduced. However, if she says the following, shoplifting attempts are apt to continue: "Shoplifting is exciting. It's a way for me to get what I want. This is the first time I've been caught. Guess I was careless. I'll have to be more careful the next time." Thus, self-talk varies because (1) the values, beliefs, attitudes, and desires on which self-talk is based varies among individuals; and (2) we have thousands of different values and beliefs, and in a particular situation, each of us somewhat haphazardly selects only a few of those beliefs and values to base our self-talk on.

In summary, two components largely determine our personality: (1) our experiences, and (2) our self-talk about the experiences. Of these two components, self-talk is the key element in developing and perpetuating personality.

Additional Aspects of Self-Talk

With repeated occurrences of an event, our emotional reactions to it become nearly automatic because we rapidly give ourselves a set of self-talk responses, which we gradually acquired over time. For example, a few years ago I counseled a woman who became intensely emotionally upset every time her husband (who had a drinking problem) came home intoxicated. In examining this situation, it became clear that because of repeated occurrences she routinely gave herself the following self-talk on seeing him inebriated:

Self-talk: "He's foolishly spending the money we desperately need in this family."
"He's making a fool of himself and me in that condition."
"He's setting a terrible example for our children."
"One of these days he's going to have a serious accident, get hurt, and then what will we do?"
↓
Emotions: Anger, frustration, some depression, general unhappiness.

CTRM Exhibit 6.2

Formation of our self-concept and our personality

Events (experiences)
↓
Self-talk → Ongoing, repeated sets of self-talk become attitudes, values, and beliefs. (Beliefs about who and what we are form our *self-concept*.) → Self-talk (which is based on our attitudes, beliefs, and needs) about our experiences determines all of our emotions and behaviors (namely, our *personality*, which is composed of our emotions and behaviors).
↓
Immediate emotions
↓
Immediate actions

We are often unaware of how self-talk affects us, and it behooves counselors to discover this self-talk. Several years ago I counseled a married woman who expressed a strong desire to continue having extramarital affairs but was afraid her husband would discover them and end the marriage. Although she was fully aware of her emotional desire for having affairs, she was unaware of the self-talk that generated this feeling. I got her to look at the self-talk that was driving her desire to have extramarital sex, and she gradually discovered the underlying self-talk, "I enjoy the feeling of being able to seduce someone to whom I am attracted," "The people I seduce then feel somewhat obligated to me," and "The conquest of someone who is very attractive is three-quarters of the thrill."

Another aspect of self-talk is *layering,* in which the emotional reaction (*C*) becomes a new event (*A*) by "Tom" giving himself additional self-talk (*B*) about his initial reaction. Ellis (1973) described layering as follows:

> Once the individual becomes emotionally upset—or, rather, upsets himself—another startling human thing frequently occurs. Most of the time, he *knows* that he is anxious, depressed, enraged, or otherwise agitated; and he also generally knows that his symptoms are undesirable and (in our culture) socially disapproved. For who approves or respects highly agitated or "crazy" people? He therefore makes his emotional Consequence (*C*) or symptom into another Activating Event (*A*).
>
> Thus, he originally starts with something like "(*A*) I did poorly on my job today; (*B*) Isn't that horrible! What a worm I am for failing!" and he winds up with (*C*) feelings of anxiety, worthlessness, and depression. He now starts all over: "(*A*) I feel anxious and depressed, and worthless. (*B*) Isn't *that* horrible! What a worm I am for feeling anxious, depressed, and worthless!" Now he winds up with (*C*) even greater feelings of anxiety, worthlessness, and depression. Or, in other words, once he becomes anxious, he frequently makes himself anxious about being anxious. Once he becomes depressed, he makes himself depressed about *being* depressed. Et cetera! He now has two consequences or symptoms for the price of one; and he often goes around and around in a vicious cycle of (1) condemning himself for doing poorly at some task; (2) feeling guilty or depressed because of his self-condemnation; (3) condemning himself for his feelings of guilt and depression; (4) condemning himself for condemning himself; (5) condemning himself for seeing that he condemns himself and for still not stopping condemning himself; (6) condemning himself for going for psychotherapeutic help and still not getting better; (7) condemning himself for being more disturbed than other individuals; (8) concluding that he is indubitably hopelessly disturbed and that nothing can be done about it; and so on, and so forth. (p. 178)

Although self-talk is often based on our attitudes, beliefs, and values, self-talk is a distinct entity. It has a here-and-now quality; it represents those thoughts we tell ourselves in the present. Although we hold thousands of beliefs, attitudes, and values, our self-talk at a given time is based on only a fraction of them. Our self-talk is also driven by our needs, wants, and motives.

Understanding Deviant Behavior

Rational therapy maintains that the reasons for any deviant act can be determined by examining the offender's thoughts before and during the act.

The Charles Manson case illustrates this idea. In 1969 Charles Manson and several followers murdered actress Sharon Tate and four other people in her home. The next night they brutally stabbed to death a wealthy businessman and his wife. Why did Manson and his followers commit these bizarre murders? The prosecuting attorney documented the following reasons (Bugliosi & Gentry, 1974). Manson hoped that these brutal murders would create fear and panic among white people. Manson thought that whites, unable to determine who actually did the killing, would conclude these murders were committed by African Americans and that out of fear, whites would go into inner cities and start killing African Americans, causing a race war. Such a war would lead to a split between liberals and conservatives, who would then begin killing each other. Manson also thought the "true black race" (identified by Manson as the "Black Panthers" or the "Black Muslims"[2]) would go into hiding and thus be unaffected. After almost all whites had perished, the "true black race" would come out and kill the remaining whites, except for Manson and his followers who would be in hiding in Death Valley. Manson further thought the remaining African Americans would not have the capacities to govern the nation, and that after failing to govern they would turn to him to be the leader of the nation.

Thus, it appears that this unrealistic belief system led Manson and his followers to murder seven people. All the defendants in this case were judged sane. While living together in isolation in a commune, the members gave mutual support to each other for the accurateness of Manson's beliefs, probably partly because objective evidence was unavailable to refute Manson's interpretations. (Throughout history, erroneous beliefs have been held at one time or another: the earth was flat; blood-letting was therapeutic; thunder was a god; criminals were possessed by demons. We no doubt hold beliefs today that will one day be found to be wrong. However, having an unrealistic belief system does not make a person "crazy.")

Theory of Therapy

The initial focus of therapy is to help clients become aware of the irrational and negative self-talk that is the primary source of their unwanted emotions and irresponsible behaviors. (Unwanted emotions are those emotions that clients want to change.) After clients grow aware of their irrational self-talk, they are encouraged to challenge such irrational self-talk with more rational and positive self-talk. Developing rational self-challenges to irrational self-talk is done by the client, either through discussions with the therapist or by writing a "rational self-analysis."

CTRM Exhibit 6.3

Format for RSA

A Facts and Events	D(a) Camera Check of A
B Self-Talk	D(b) Rational Debate of B
1. ____________	1. ____________
2. ____________	2. ____________
and so on	and so on
C Emotional Consequences of B	E Emotional Goals and Behavioral Goals for Similar Future Events

Rational Self-Analysis[3]

Maultsby (1977) developed *rational self-analysis* (RSA), which is very useful in alleviating undesirable emotions. An RSA has six parts, as shown in CTRM Exhibit 6.3.

The goal in RSA is to change unwanted emotions (such as anger, guilt, depression, or shyness). An RSA is done by recording the event and self-talk on paper.

Part A (facts and events): Simply state the facts or events that occurred.

Part B (self-talk): Write all of your thoughts about A. Number each statement (1, 2, 3, 4, and so on). Write either "good," "bad," or "neutral" after each self-talk statement to show how you believe each B section statement reflects on you as a person. (The RSA case example on page 000 illustrates the mechanics of an RSA.)

Part C (emotional consequences): Write simple statements describing your gut reactions/emotions stemming from your self-talk in B.

Part D(a) is written *only* after you have written sections A–C, and *only* after you have reviewed the five guidelines for rational thinking (pages 417–418). Part D(a) is a "camera check" of part A. Reread part A and ask yourself, "If I had had a video of what happened, would it verify what I wrote as 'fact'?" Videos record facts, not personal beliefs or opinions.

[2]The Black Panthers and Black Muslims were African American organizations active in the civil rights movement in the 1960s and 1970s. Sometimes these organizations advocated the use of physical force to achieve racial equality.

[3]This description of rational self-analysis is adapted from Charles Zastrow, *Talk to Yourself: Using the Power of Self-Talk,* © 1979, pp. 32–36. Adapted by permission of Prentice-Hall, Inc., Englewood Cliffs, New Jersey.

An example in part B of a personal opinion is mistaken as a fact is, "Karen made me look like a fool when she laughed while I was trying to make a point." Under D(a) (video check of A), the opinion part of this statement is corrected by writing only the factual part: "I was attempting to make a serious point when Karen laughed." Then add the personal opinion part of the statement to B ("Karen made me look like a fool").

Part D(b) challenges and thus may change negative and irrational thinking. Take each B statement separately. Read B–1 first and ask yourself whether it is inconsistent with any of the five questions for rational thinking. It will be irrational if it does one or more of the following:

1. Is not based on objective reality.
2. Hampers you in protecting your life.
3. Hampers you in achieving your short- and long-term goals.
4. Causes significant trouble with other people.
5. Leads you to feel emotions that you do not want to feel.

If the self-talk statement is consistent with the five questions for rational thinking, merely write "that's rational." If, however, the self-talk statement meets one or more of the guidelines for irrational thinking, then think of an alternative "self-talk" to that B statement. This new self-talk statement is of crucial importance in changing your undesirable emotion and needs to (1) be rational and (2) be a self-talk statement you are willing to accept as a new opinion for yourself. After writing down this D(b–1) self-talk in the D(b) section, then consider B–2, B–3, and so on, in the same way.

Under Part E, write down the new emotions you want to have in similar future A situations. In writing these new emotions that you desire, keep in mind that they will follow from your self-talk statements in your D(b) section. This section may also contain a description of certain actions you intend to take to help you achieve your emotional goals when you encounter future As.

Rational self-challenges will work only if clients actively practice using the rational self-challenges they develop. Self-challenges work best when used by clients every time they start the original negative, irrational self-talk.

Therapy Is an Educational Process

Learning how to think rationally and to counter irrational and negative self-talk is a process. Clients can learn to analyze and change irrational self-talk in a variety of ways: instruction by their therapist; viewing videotapes and films; reading books and pamphlets; and attending workshops or seminars on rational therapy. Ellis has demonstrated that the basic principles of analyzing irrational self-talk and thinking rationally can be successfully taught both to adults and to elementary and secondary school students.

Therapists teach clients how to analyze irrational self-talk using probes, confrontation, explanations, interpretations, humor, and suggestions that help clients discover their irrational thinking. Once clients become aware of their irrational self-talk, rational therapists use a variety of techniques to help them change.

An Eclectic Approach

Rational therapists use whatever approaches show promise in changing irrational self-talk. Ellis (1979, p. 186) noted, "The rational therapist uses role playing, assertion training, desensitization, humor, operant conditioning, suggestion, support, and a whole bag of other 'tricks.'"

Rational self-challenges (including RSAs) are often used to change unwanted emotions. For certain unwanted emotions, such as depression, rational therapists may attempt to get clients involved in meaningful or enjoyable activities (for example, playing golf, joining a social club). (Reality therapists, Module 5, use this approach to change unwanted emotions.) Rational therapists theorize that getting clients involved in enjoyable activities works because it switches their negative focus to a positive one, which then changes their emotions.

For people who are shy or prone to temper outbursts, rational therapists may use assertiveness training techniques (Module 4). For clients with drinking problems, rational therapists may supplement therapy by getting clients involved in Alcoholics Anonymous. For clients with sexual dysfunctions, rational therapists use techniques such as sensate focus and other techniques (see Module 10) developed by Masters and Johnson (Belliveau & Richter, 1970).

Homework assignments are frequently given. Shy clients try out assertive approaches that they role-played in therapy. They may write an RSA in which they identify and challenge the negative and irrational self-talk that makes them feel shy. A male client who states he can't stand to be rejected by the opposite sex might ask three different females out on dates to test the hypothesis that he can indeed survive rejection. Clients also read books to help them learn and apply the basic concepts.

Rational therapists often disclose their own foibles to dispute the client's irrational belief that anyone, even a therapist, can be more than human.

Common Irrational Beliefs

Rational therapy seeks to refute clients' irrational beliefs. Clients are confronted with their irrational beliefs. Therapists ask "Show me where it is written that you must succeed at everything you try to feel good about yourself?" or "What evidence do you have that your girlfriend *must* treat you fairly?"

Several writers (Criddle, 1974; Ellis, 1958; Ellis & Harper, 1977; Hauck, 1972; Raimy, 1977; Zastrow, 1979, 1993) have identified common beliefs that generate negative or irrational self-talk; see CTRM Exhibit 6.4.

Thinking in terms of "needs," "shoulds," "musts," "awful," and "unbearable" distorts reality and frequently leads us to overact. A more rational philosophy is "I would like to be treated reasonably well by people and life."

What Really Causes Change?

Client-centered therapy, psychoanalysis, rational therapy, feminist intervention, behavior therapy, transactional analysis, reality therapy, hypnosis, meditation, and crisis intervention are all used to treat a wide range of emotional and behavioral problems: people who are depressed, or lonely, or have marital or other interpersonal relationship problems; or who have disabling fears and phobias, or are overly aggressive, or have drinking problems; or who suffer from grief, shame, or guilt. Each of these therapies differs substantially in terms of explaining why therapeutic change occurs.

How can all these distinct and diverse therapies produce positive change in clients?[4] What produces changes in therapy? Is there a single explanation?

Practically every theory postulates a different view for why change occurs. In reviewing this dilemma, Raimy (1977) stated:

> Psychotherapists today are faced with an insistent, nagging problem: since widely diverse methods of treatment for similar problems have their successes as well as their failures, how can one defend a given set of treatment procedures as superior to others? Clearly, since quite different, even contradictory, methods of treatment produce similar results, explanations for the success of treatment must be sought outside the realm of method or technique. (p. 1)

[4]This section tentatively assumes that all the above-mentioned therapies produce positive changes. Module 11 questions whether a few of these therapies do in fact produce positive changes.

What Causes Disturbing Emotions and Ineffective Actions?

Before attempting to provide an explanation of what produces positive changes in therapy, it is important to identify the primary determinants of emotional and behavior problems.

The most important point about the rational therapy formula (Events → Self-Talk → Emotions → Action) is that our self-talk determines how we act; by changing our self-talk, we can change how we act. Generally we cannot control events that happen to us, but we have the power to think rationally and thereby change *all* of our unwanted emotions and dysfunctional behaviors. Self-talk is hypothesized as the primary determinant of all actions and all emotions, including love, fear, anger, grief, depression, anxiety, shame, happiness, hate, and frustration. Zastrow (1979, 1993) has also shown that self-talk is the primary determinant of our self-concept, sense of success or failure, our personality, and stress-related illnesses.

Restructuring Thinking: Is This the Key Therapeutic Agent?

Rational therapy asserts that discomforting emotions and dysfunctional actions arise primarily from negative or irrational self-talk. If this conceptualization is accurate, an important corollary is that any therapy technique that succeeds in changing emotions or actions is effective primarily because it changes self-talk. In other words, self-talk appears to be the key therapeutic agent in all approaches that produce positive changes. Practically all the contemporary approaches to psychotherapy can be reinterpreted to be consistent with the basic therapeutic principle of restructuring thinking. A few examples are presented in the following paragraphs.

PSYCHOANALYSIS. Freud (1924) saw the basic goal of therapy as bringing disturbing, suppressed ideas and emotions to the conscious part of the mind so the ideas (now conscious) could be dealt with and the unconscious emotion (energy) could be expressed. Is not

CTRM Exhibit 6.4

Common beliefs that generate negative self-talk

1. *Irrational:* Everyone must approve of everything I do.
   Rational: I cannot please everyone, so I will do what *I* think is best.
2. *Irrational:* To be a worthy person, I must be perfect in all my skills and competencies.
   Rational: Perfection is impossible, maybe even unhealthy; I can—and will—fail sometimes. So what. There's always tomorrow. I'll do better tomorrow.
3. *Irrational:* When things don't go my way, it's the end of the world. (*Note:* this is awfulizing.)
   Rational: Life happens; I am strong so I can—and will—go on.
4. *Irrational:* Life is just.
   Rational: Life is unfair. I can deal.
5. *Irrational:* I can't help how I feel.
   Rational: Events don't cause happiness; my responses to events cause me to feel happy or unhappy.
6. *Irrational:* Worry prevents problems, really.
   Rational: I can't change event X, so I'm not going to worry about it.
7. *Irrational:* Others are responsible for my happiness.
   Rational: I am responsible for my happiness. I believe in myself, in my judgment, in my ability to create a happy life.
8. *Irrational:* My past made me this way, and therefore I can't do anything about it.
   Rational: Of course I can change. I own my future.
9. *Irrational:* If only so-and-so would change, then I could be happy.
   Rational: So-and-so owns his problems. I own mine, he has a right to run his life his way.
10. *Irrational:* So-and-so's problems are my problems.
    Rational: As in 9, so-and-so owns his problems.
11. *Irrational:* People that are different from me are weird.
    Rational: That's a lot of people, like several billion. They are just as normal as I am, just different.
12. *Irrational:* Happiness is going to just happen to me because . . .
    Rational: We get out of life what we put in.
13. *Irrational:* I *must* get what I *want.*
    Rational: I don't always get what I *want,* but I generally get what I *need.*
14. *Irrational:* For me to be happy, everything in my life must be perfect. Or, I am entitled to a perfect life.
    Rational: Life *is* imperfect; the world does not revolve around me.

Freud, in essence, seeking to help clients become aware of their disturbing ideas (self-talk) so they can then change this disturbing self-talk? Once such disturbing self-talk is changed, the format presented here suggests that the unwanted emotions generated by the original self-talk (now changed) will be alleviated.[5]

Psychoanalysis asserts that these disturbing ideas are usually unconscious. Rational therapists partially agree as it appears that clients occasionally may not be fully aware of the "disturbing ideas" that are getting them into trouble. Sometimes considerable probing is needed to identify such "self-talk."

BEHAVIOR THERAPY. Originally, behavior modification therapists conceptualized their efforts as being *S* (stimulus) $\rightarrow$ *R* (response) in nature. Their efforts were focused on identifying and applying stimuli that would change unwanted responses (behaviors). In the past 30 years, there has been an increasingly large group of behavior therapists who emphasize the importance of changing cognitions to modify human behavior (Beck, 1976; Cautela & Upper, 1975; Craighead, Mahoney, & Kazdin, 1976; Goldfried & Merbaum, 1973; Lazarus, 1971; Mahoney, 1974; Meichenbaum, 1975). These authorities on behavior therapy are now calling themselves *cognitive behaviorists.* Their approach is focused on changing the person's thinking to change the behavior. Instead of the old $S \rightarrow R$ conceptualization, they emphasize that behavior changes are best conceptualized as involving a change in a person's thinking, as illustrated in the following format: $S \rightarrow O$ (organism's thinking) $\rightarrow R$. Thought-stopping and reframing, which are described in Module 4, are good examples of techniques used to change irrational thoughts to alle-

[5]Module 11 presents research suggesting that psychoanalysis, overall, appears to be less effective than receiving no treatment. How is this explainable? One explanation is that when the therapist suggests the client may be suffering from a variety of maladies (such as being psychotic, being fixated at the oral stage of development, or having an oedipal complex) the client is apt to be side tracked from focusing his or her thinking on resolving real problems and instead focuses on irrational self-talk connected with worrying about having (and trying to resolve) mystical problems that do not exist. Such irrational self-talk, it is hypothesized, may then lead to deterioration.

CASE EXAMPLE

Rational Self-Analysis: Coping with a Sexual Affair

Cindy sought counseling after her boyfriend Jim told her that a few months earlier he had become sexually involved with Linda. Jim and Cindy had dated for two years. But they began to argue frequently and so decided not to see each other during the summer. In the fall, they again felt strongly about each other and resumed their relationship. A few weeks later, Jim (after Cindy questioned him) informed her about Linda.

Cindy told the counselor that she wanted to better handle her unwanted feelings about this affair. After discussing them in some depth, the counselor informed her that she could counter her undesirable emotions with a rational self-analysis, and Cindy wrote the following RSA.

A (Facts and Events)	*D(a) Video Check of A*
My boyfriend, Jim, informed me that he had sex with Linda, after a party where they had both been drinking.	This is all factual. I know this because Jim told me himself. Jim and I are very close, and I know he wouldn't lie to me.

B (Self-Talk)		*D(b) Cindy's Rational Debate of B*	
B–1	It's not fair! How could Jim do such a thing to me? (bad)	D(b–1)	Jim had sex with Linda. I'll just have to accept that. People are human and fallible, I can't expect to always be treated with fairness. Besides, Jim and I had broken up, so I'm sure they didn't have me in mind when they did it. At the time they were sexually involved, neither Jim nor I had any commitment to each other. Truth be told, I also considered having a fling this summer and would have had I met the right guy.
B–2	That creep just had sex with Linda because he wanted a piece of ________. (bad)	D(b–2)	Jim probably had sex with Linda for other reasons. I know he's not the type who uses a woman merely for relief of his sexual tensions. It is also a mistake to label him a creep. No one is a creep. People are humans. If I mislabel him a creep, it may lead me to view him in terms of an inaccurate label.
B–3	Jim and Linda had no good reasons for doing what they did. They only did it because they were both drunk. What a couple of jerks! (bad)	D(b–3)	Alcohol obviously had something to do with their having sex. I know that Jim is much less inhibited when he has had a few drinks. I don't know about Linda, though. The drinking can't be the only reason they had sex. Maybe they felt attracted to each other and wanted to have sex. I've got to remember that this summer Jim and I had no commitments to each

(continued)

CASE EXAMPLE

Rational Self-Analysis:

(continued)

	B (Self-Talk)		*D(b) Cindy's Rational Debate of B*
			other, and therefore I do not have the right to expect that he would be celibate to please me. Also, it is a mistake for me to refer to Jim or Linda as being a "jerk." People are people.
B–4	Linda must be some kind of cheap tramp. Only a tramp would have sex with a guy she didn't love. (bad)	D(b–4)	I don't even know Linda so I shouldn't judge her like this. Furthermore, I have no way of knowing how Linda felt about Jim. Maybe she felt she loved him at the time. A woman isn't necessarily loose if she has sex with a guy.
B–5	Jim must think he's some kind of stud now. (bad)	D(b–5)	Jim has told me that he has had sex with only two women. My idea of a "stud" is a guy who thinks he can have sex with any woman who comes along. I know Jim better than that. He doesn't think he could, nor would he try to, conquer just any woman.
B–6	Jim and I will never again be able to have a good sexual relationship of our own now that he has someone else to compare me to. I just know that he'll be thinking of Linda from now on. (bad)	D(b–6)	Jim and I love each other. Jim told me that he does not love Linda. Just because Jim had sex with Linda does not mean our relationship will always be adversely affected. We can communicate easily during sex, and it has always been satisfying so far. It would be silly for Jim to compare our entire relationship to the one night he spent with Linda.
B–7	This is the worst thing that Jim could have done. (bad)	D(b–7)	This is not the worst thing that Jim could have done. What he did was not a crime, like murder or rape, which would have been worse. The situation would be worse if Jim had slept with Linda while he was still seeing me. I'm glad to know that he would never do that.
B–8	Now that I know Jim had sex with Linda, our whole relationship will be ruined. (bad)	D(b–8)	The fact that Jim had sex with Linda does not have to ruin our relationship. The event occurred in the past. It's over. Past sexual experiences should have no bearing on the future of our relationship. I want the relationship to continue, and I don't want to see it ruined.

B (Self-Talk)		D(b) Cindy's Rational Debate of B	
B–9	I should never have broken up with Jim. Then he would never have slept with Linda. It's all my fault. (bad)	D(b–9)	It's not my fault at all. I broke up with Jim because I felt it was the best thing to do at the time. I know Jim would not have been unfaithful to me had we still been dating, but we weren't dating at the time this happened. I had no way of knowing he would some day go to bed with Linda, and knowing would not have changed my decision to break up with him. It's not my fault because I wasn't even involved.
B–10	From now on, whenever I hear Linda's name mentioned I'm going to have a fit! I won't be able to handle it! (bad)	D(b–10)	When I hear Linda's name mentioned, I don't have to respond by having a fit. I can handle my feelings by being calm and not letting the mention of her name bother me.

C *My Emotions*	*E* *My Emotional and Behavioral Goals*
I feel guilty, hurt, angry, upset, and jealous. (very bad)	I want to get over my unwanted emotions that I have had about this affair. I want to put this affair in our past. At the time it happened, Jim and I had no commitments to each other. What is important to Jim and me is our present and future relationship and not what happened one evening when Jim and I had broken up.

viate unwanted emotions and to change dysfunctional behaviors.

One of the most popular applications of behavior therapy is assertiveness training. All of us are shy or timid in some situations, perhaps in arranging a date, in talking to an authority figure, or in asking someone to put out a cigarette. Authorities on assertiveness training have pointed out that we are shy, or aggressive, because of what we tell ourselves about these situations and that it is necessary to change our cognitions to be able to express ourselves assertively (Alberti & Emmons, 1975).

CLIENT-CENTERED THERAPY. The goal of this approach is to help clients gain insight into the inconsistencies between their ideas about self and their experiences, so they can then reorganize their self-concept to be more consistent with what they experience. Isn't Carl Rogers saying that clients need to identify the thoughts (self-talk) about themselves that are inconsistent with reality and then reorganize these thoughts to become more consistent with reality?

OTHER COMPREHENSIVE THERAPY APPROACHES. In *Misunderstandings of the Self,* Raimy (1977) proposed a theory to explain positive changes in counseling that is nearly identical to the self-talk approach presented here. Raimy's main hypothesis was "If those ideas or conceptions of a client or patient that are relevant to his psychological problems can be changed in the direction of greater accuracy where his reality is concerned, his maladjustments are likely to be eliminated." Raimy called his hypothesis the *misconception hypothesis* (Raimy, 1977, p. 7). He then provided a rationale that positive changes obtained

CASE EXAMPLE

Using Rational Therapy to Change Irresponsible Behavior

Dan Barber, age 4½, was taken to the emergency room of St. Mary's Hospital in a midwestern city. He was unconscious, severely bruised, and had a broken arm. Dan was brought in by neighbors after Mr. Barber telephoned them. Dan had a concussion, sustained from what appeared to be several blows. Seven weeks earlier Dan had been rushed to the hospital for a broken leg. That time Mr. Barber stated Dan fell down a stairway. Protective services was contacted by the hospital, and in the initial interview Mr. Barber acknowledged that he beat Dan on both of these occasions. Why? The following is Mr. Barber's account of the thinking processes (self-talk) that led him to abuse his son.

> Dan is my only son. His mother and I got a divorce eight months ago. I'm an accountant and up until about a year ago I really thought I had it made. Mary is very attractive and we got along well. We had a nice house, and I had a good income—many days I worked 11 or 12 hours, getting overtime pay. Mary primarily took care of our son.
>
> One day I arrived home and there was a note from my wife saying she was leaving me. I was shocked and couldn't believe it. A few weeks later I received papers indicating she had gotten a divorce in Mexico. Shortly afterward I heard she married a person from the same church I used to go to. I really don't understand how she could leave both Dan and me, without even talking about it. I guess I've been so involved with my work that I didn't realize how she felt.
>
> As time went by after she left I discussed my problems with some of our neighbors. A few indicated that several men over the years visited with my wife during the day when I was at work. Apparently she had been having affairs for a long time.
>
> My mother moved in after Mary left, to help take care of Dan.
>
> In the past few months, I have been wondering if Dan is really my own son. (At this point Mr. Barber was asked to indicate what he was thinking during the last time he abused Dan. The events and self-talk are put into the format presented earlier.)

through correcting "misconceptions" account for the changes in the following therapies: Adlerian, rational-emotive, psychoanalysis, transactional analysis, Gestalt therapy, client-centered therapy, and certain behavior modification techniques.

Nontraditional Psychotherapy Techniques

Zastrow (1979, 1993) presented a rationale that changing self-talk primarily accounts for the positive changes produced with hypnosis, systematic desensitization, bio-feedback, meditation, muscle relaxation, deep-breathing relaxation, imagery relaxation, in vivo desensitization, acupuncture, electroshock therapy, covert sensitization, sex therapy for sexual dysfunctions, assertiveness training, diet counseling, and therapy for alcoholics (Zastrow, 1979). The rationale for a few of these approaches is summarized as follows:

MEDITATION. Daniel Goleman (1977) summarized contemporary approaches to meditation and described how each attempts to accomplish its goal. Practically all the approaches seek to achieve a meditative state by having a person concentrate on an object (such as breathing or ideal relaxation place) or repeat a mantra (such as a sound, a word, a phrase, a chant, a prayer, or a spiritual value). As described in Module 9, deep-breathing relaxation, imagery relaxation, and repeating the word *relax* are all forms of meditation.

Herbert Benson (1975) noted that the key element in inducing the relaxation response via meditation is having a passive attitude in which the meditator lets go of the thoughts underlying daily concerns. Maultsby (1975) showed that feelings of stress and anxiety arise primarily from negative and irrational self-talk about day-to-day problems. Meditation, it is hypothesized here, reduces the feelings of stress and anxiety by having the meditator switch his or her think-

Event: That evening I came home from work feeling exhausted. I wanted just to relax and have a peaceful evening. My mother went grocery shopping, and I guess I was feeling sorry for myself. Dan was quite noisy, and I told him to stop making so much noise. But he continued.

↓

Self-Talk: "I can't take any more of this."
"Here I have to take care of a kid who may not even be my own."
"This kid reminds me of the hurt that Mary has caused me. I have a right to even the score."
"I can't stand this! I've got to shut this brat up!"
"My father beat me when I did wrong—that's the best way to show kids who's the boss."

↓

Emotions: Anger, revenge, hostility, frustration.

↓

Actions: Hitting Dan, knocking him down several times. (Mr. Barber added, "Once I started hitting Dan, I thought I was evening the score with Mary, and didn't want to stop.")

At first, Mr. Barber indicated he couldn't understand how he could lose control and abuse his son. He appeared remorseful and desirous of changing his actions. Through therapy he gradually came to understand that he controlled his emotions and actions and that he could change his unwanted emotions and actions by changing his self-talk. He knew he had severely hurt his son and that he could lose him if the abuse was not curbed.

Mr. Barber's concerns about being Dan's biological fathers were relieved by the results of DNA testing, and he learned through rational therapy how to challenge and change the self-talk that led him to abuse his son. Mr. Barber was also instructed to leave Dan in the care of his mother whenever he felt an urge to abuse Dan. If the mother wasn't available, Mr. Barber agreed to call the protective service worker to ventilate his feelings over the phone rather than at Dan. Mr. Barber also received counseling about his feelings toward his wife and about the importance of focusing his thoughts and energies on the present and future rather than wallowing in self-pity and dwelling on the past.

ing from focusing on day-to-day problems to focusing on the mantra or meditative object. This process can be diagrammed as follows:

A. Event: Concentrating and repeating a mantra while great care is taken to prevent interruptions or distractions.

↓

B. Self-talk: "This is relaxing." (At the same time the person stops thinking about day-to-day concerns.)

↓

C. Emotion: Feeling of being relaxed.

HYPNOSIS. Hypnosis essentially involves two processes: (1) becoming relaxed so that a person goes into what is called a hypnotic trance; and (2) while in a trance, giving oneself hypnotic suggestions. The hypnotic trance state can be induced by a variety of relaxation techniques, including deep-breathing relaxation, imagery relaxation, and other forms of meditation. The hypnotic trance state can best be understood as a state of deep relaxation. As explained in the previous section on meditation, this relaxed state is induced by the meditator's letting go of thinking about everyday concerns.

The second process of hypnosis involves hypnotic suggestions. The therapeutic power of self-talk is dramatically demonstrated by hypnotic suggestions. While in a trance, a person can be given a wide variety of instructions or suggestions, many of which are increasingly being used for therapeutic reasons. Nearly all of these hypnotic suggestions are, in actuality, self-talk statements, as the following illustrates:

"I will feel no pain," for those with arthritis or undergoing surgery, for those with terminal cancer, for childbirth, and for practically any type of pain.

"I will relax," for those who are very anxious or tense.

"I will fall asleep after going to bed and counting to ten," for those suffering from insomnia.

"My menstrual period will now be regular," for those with irregular periods.

MUSCLE RELAXATION. Deep muscle relaxation is a technique that people can use to become more relaxed when they are tense or anxious (Paul, 1966). The technique is learned by having a person first tighten and then relax a set of muscles. When relaxing the muscles, the person is instructed to think about the relaxed feeling, while noting that the muscles are more relaxed than before they were tensed. The following excerpt (Watson & Tharp, 1972) gives a brief illustration of the procedure.

> Make a fist with your dominant hand (usually right). Make a fist and tense the muscles of your (right) hand and forearm; tense it until it trembles. Feel the muscles pull across your fingers and the lower part of your forearm. . . . Hold this position for 5 to 7 seconds, then . . . relax. . . . Just let your hand go. Pay attention to the muscles of your (right) hand and forearm as they relax. Note how those muscles feel as relaxation flows through them (20 to 30 seconds). (pp. 182–183)

After a person learns to relax one set of muscles, he or she learns to relax other sets (for example, muscles of the arms, neck, shoulders, chest, stomach, lower back, hips, thighs, and so forth).

Applying the principles of *rational therapy,* it appears that self-talk is a key to achieving a relaxed state:

Event:	A person relaxes a set of muscles after having tensed the muscles.
↓	
Self-talk:	"This is relaxing." "Feels good." "This is calming."
↓	
Emotional consequence:	Relaxation.

Advocates of muscle relaxation point out that, with practice, a person can achieve deep relaxation without having to tense muscles—that is, by imagery (Watson & Tharp, 1972). Apparently the following is occurring:

Event:	I am imagining my arm (thigh, and so on) muscles first tensing and then becoming very relaxed.
↓	
Self-talk:	"This feels good, is relaxing."
↓	
Emotional consequence:	Relaxation.

Muscle relaxation, it is hypothesized here, also reduces the feelings of stress and anxiety by helping a person switch thinking from focusing on day-to-day problems to focusing on the relaxation exercises.

Consistent with the belief of a number of authorities, it is asserted that discomforting emotions and dysfunctional actions arise primarily from our self-talk, generally self-talk that is negative or irrational. If this conceptualization is accurate, an important corollary is that any therapy technique that is successful in changing emotions or actions is effective primarily because it changes a person's thinking from negative or irrational self-talk to more rational and positive self-talk.

At this point there is some support (although more research is needed) for the notion that changing negative or irrational self-talk is the key therapeutic agent in psychotherapy approaches. If accurate, the old argument of which therapy approaches are effective and which are not (Eysenck, 1952; Stuart, 1970) may be refocused to "Which therapy approaches are most effective in changing negative and irrational self-talk?" and "How can present therapy approaches be refined, and new approaches developed, to change negative and irrational self-talk more effectively?"

Explaining Mental Illness from a Rational Therapy Perspective

While working at a mental hospital, I was assigned a case of a 22-year-old male who decapitated his 17-year-old girlfriend. Two psychiatrists diagnosed him as being schizophrenic, and a court found him to be "innocent by reason of insanity." He was then committed to a mental hospital. Why did he do it? Labeling him as insane provides an explanation. But does such a label explain *why* he committed this act rather than doing something else bizarre? Does it suggest what treatment would cure him? The answer to all these questions is, of course, "no."

What Is Schizophrenia?

Schizophrenia is commonly defined as a psychotic condition that usually occurs during or shortly after adolescence that is characterized by disorientation, loss of contact with reality, and disorganized patterns of thinking and feeling. Let's examine this definition. People who are intoxicated, or stoned on drugs, or who are asleep, or who have not slept for over a day experience a loss of contact with reality and their feelings and thinking patterns become disorganized. Are they schizophrenic? No. What about those adults who have such a severe cognitive disability that their mental age is less than 2 years? They have these symptoms but are not considered schizophrenic. What about people who go into a coma following a serious accident? They also fit the definition but are not considered schizophrenic. The young man who committed the bizarre homicide knew the act was wrong, was aware of what he was doing, was in contact with reality, and told me why he did it. Then why was he labeled schizophrenic? Could it be that *there is no definition of symptoms that separates people who have this "disease" from those who do not?* Module 5 presents the interactional model, which asserts that mental illness is a myth.

A Perspective from Rational Therapy

People are labeled mentally ill in our society because they either display bizarre behavior or have serious discomforting emotions. Why do bizarre acts and discomforting emotions occur?

Rational therapy asserts that bizarre acts can be understood by discovering the person's self-talk that led to the "strange act." In almost all cases the reasons for deviant acts can be determined by examining what offenders told themselves before and during the act.

Furthermore, identifying the self-talk that leads to deviant acts generally provides information on what services are needed to prevent the deviant behavior from recurring.

Committing deviant acts or displaying deviant behavior are not the only reasons people are labeled mentally ill. Mental illness labels are also applied to people who have serious, discomforting emotions such as severe or chronic depression, anxiety, grief, or feelings of inferiority.

Discomforting emotions range in severity from mild to extreme. Labelers who adhere to the medical model must draw a line on this continuum to separate the "insane" from the "sane."

Rational therapy asserts there is no need to attach a medical label (like labeling a severe depression "psychotic") to a severe, discomforting emotion. Such medical labels have no diagnostic or treatment value and may well complicate therapy efforts due to labeling effects.

A Bizarre Murder

Let's return to the young man who was labeled *schizophrenic* for murdering his girlfriend. A medical diagnosis should identify the general causes of the medical condition and suggest a treatment approach. In this case the label does not tell us why the murder occurred, nor does it suggest what type of rehabilitation is needed. (Incidentally, this young man was seen by a psychiatrist a few months before the slaying and was viewed as sane.)

However, after he described what happened, it was understandable (even though bizarre) why he did what he did, and his account also identified the specific problems he needed help with. He described himself as an isolated person who, except for his girlfriend, had no close relatives or friends. He came from a broken home and was raised by a variety of relatives and foster parents. Because of frequent moves, he attended a number of different schools and made no lasting friends. At age 20 he met the victim and dated her periodically for two years. She provided the only real meaning that he had in life. He held the traditional vision of marrying her and living happily together thereafter.

However, a few months before the fatal day, he became very alarmed that he was going to "lose her." She encouraged him to date others, mentioned that she wanted to date others, and suggested that they no longer see as much of each other.

He thought intensely about how he could preserve the relationship. He also realized he had rather intense sexual tensions with no outlet. Putting the two together he naively concluded, "If I'm the first person to have sexual relations with her, she will forever feel tied to me." He therefore tried on several occasions to have coitus, but she always managed to dissuade him. Finally, one afternoon during the summer when he knew they would be alone together, he arrived at the following self-talk decision, "I *will* have sex with her this afternoon, even if I have to knock her unconscious." He stated he knew such action was wrong, but said, "It was my last hope of saving our relationship. Without her, life would not be worth living."

He again tried to have sexual relations with her that afternoon, but she continued to dissuade him. Being emotionally excited, he then took a soda bottle and knocked her unconscious. He again attempted to have coitus, but was still unsuccessful for reasons related to her physical structure. In an intense state of emotional and sexual excitement, he was unable rationally to consider the consequences of his actions. (All of us, at times, act dysfunctionally while angry or in a state of intense emotional excitement.) At this point he felt his whole world was caving in. When asked during an interview what he was thinking at this point, he stated, "I felt that if I couldn't have her, no one else would either." He found a knife, became further carried away with emotions, and ended up slaying her. He knew it was wrong, and he was aware of what he was doing.

These conversations (and identification of the self-talk before and during the murder) pinpoint factors that help explain why the murder took place. Such reasons help explain why the bizarre behavior took place; the label *schizophrenia* does not.

If the above problems had been known before the murder, the slaying might have been prevented. What he needed was to find other sources of interest and other meaningful relationships in his life. Joining groups or developing hobbies may well have helped. An appropriate sexual outlet for his passions also probably would have been helpful. Better control of his passions and other sources of finding meaning might have prevented him from losing control of his emotions that afternoon, as would reducing the intensity of his jealous and possessive feelings, along with developing more mature attitudes toward romance and sexuality. These specific problems are the areas that he needs help with while in a mental hospital rather than with finding a cure for schizophrenia. In no way do I feel that he should be excused for his actions, as implied by the term *innocent by reason of insanity.* But he does need help for the specific problems identified. (In 10 or 15 years, he will probably be released and return to society.)

In summary, when a deviant act occurs, asserting that the behavior is due to a "mental illness" does not provide a useful explanation for why it occurred. All deviant behaviors are understandable, however, when viewed from the actor's perspective.

If you wonder how someone could arrive at a point of doing something bizarre, remember it is necessary to attempt to view the situation from the person's perspective. To understand such a perspective, it is essential to try to consider all the circumstances, pressures, values, and belief systems of the person. An unusual true example may help you become aware that practically anyone will do something bizarre when circumstances become desperate. Some years ago a passenger plane crashed in the Andes mountains in the wintertime. A number of people were killed, but there were nearly 30 survivors. Rescue efforts initially failed to locate the survivors, who took shelter from the cold in the wreckage of the plane. The survivors were without food for over 40 days until they were finally rescued. During this time the survivors were faced with the choice of dying of starvation or cannibalism of those who had died. It was a very desperate, difficult decision. (Psychologically, many people who commit a bizarre act feel they face a comparable decision.) In this situation, all but one of the initial plane crash survivors chose cannibalism. The one who refused died of starvation.

Evaluation

Rational therapy is one of the most widely used therapy approaches. DiGiuseppe, Miller, and Trexler (1977) summarized a large number of outcome studies conducted on rational therapy and found over 90 percent of these studies supported its claims. Ellis (2000) noted that more than 400 outcome studies have been published showing that rational therapy is effective in changing the thoughts, feelings, and behaviors of individuals with various kinds of disturbances. DiGiuseppe et al. (1998) stated that the studies conducted on rational therapy show that the approach usually works better than no therapy, and that rational therapy is often more effective than other methods of psychotherapy.

Rational therapy has been used successfully to treat clients with a wide range of problems, including unwanted emotions (depression, anxiety, fears and phobias, guilt, shame), sexual problems and sexual dysfunctions, worrying, marital problems, interaction problems, alcoholism, shyness, and such irresponsible actions as committing crimes, procrastination, and jealous actions. Its major hypotheses are also useful in child-rearing, education, and executive management.

By asserting that we primarily cause our unwanted emotions and irresponsible behaviors by what we think, the approach squarely puts the responsibility on us for improving our lives. We are in charge of our lives and have the power to alleviate unwanted emotions and change ineffective actions. Zastrow (1979, 1993) theorized that our self-talk has immense effects on our lives that we only now are beginning to understand. Self-talk, for example, plays a major part in chronic stress; and chronic stress causes a wide range of stress-related illnesses, including ulcers, migraine headaches, insomnia, diarrhea, heart problems, digestive problems, cancer, hypertension, and obesity. It is also hypothesized that success at any competitive game is substantially determined by the kind of self-talk we give ourselves.

Rational therapy has made a substantial contribution to psychotherapy. Yet there are some important unanswered questions:

1. *Physiology of self-talk and emotions.* As yet we do not precisely know the physiological components of thinking or of emotions. Our brain, of course, is important in enabling us to think. But what precisely takes place in the brain that leads us to conceptualize our thoughts? Are other parts of the body involved in thinking? Thinking is related to memory. But what precisely is memory, and how do we "store" and "recall" experiences that we have? And how are memory and thinking physiologically related?

If self-talk primarily causes our emotions, what are the physiological processes involved? What different physiological processes occur for such varied emotions as love, depression, happiness, anger, sorrow, and so on? And how, physiologically, do certain types of self-talk and certain kinds of emotional states influence our health?

2. *Separating the effects of self-talk from the effects of physiological factors.* For people with injuries or abnormal conditions in the brain, it is at times extremely difficult to separate the effects of their medical conditions from those of self-talk. Injuries in different areas of the brain cause changes in the person's emotions and behaviors (Rosenhan & Seligman, 1995). Abnormal conditions of the brain result from a wide range of factors, including brain tumors, disorders such as cerebral palsy, chronic alcoholic intoxication, Alzheimer's disease, general paresis, AIDS, and cerebral arteriosclerosis. Such medical conditions are a factor in causing confusion, incoherence, clouding of consciousness, loss of recent or past memory, reduction in reasoning capacities, listlessness, apathy, reduction in intellectual capacities, and sometimes perceptual changes. Although these conditions can have permanent or long-lasting effects on thinking patterns and emotional reactions, other factors also change mental activity—such as high fever, toxins or poisons, and the intake of drugs and alcohol.

Even with the presence of these factors, one's self-talk about these conditions also affects one's emotions and behaviors. Separating which effects result from other factors and which from self-talk often is difficult.

3. *Nature versus nurture.* Nurture can be defined as the sum of the influences modifying the expression of the genetic potentialities of a person. The theory of human behavior presented in this module focuses on nurture determinants, as it states human behavior is determined by events and self-talk. This theory fails to include genetic factors, which obviously influence human behavior.

4. *The importance of experiences or events themselves.* Critics of rational therapy assert the events that happen to a person are as important (and perhaps even more important) in determining behavior than the self-talk about such experiences. These critics point out that events such as poverty, discrimination, child abuse, overprotective parents, inadequate education, and being victimized by crime are major determinants of human behavior.

5. *Boundaries of self-talk.* Rational therapy theorizes that self-talk has immense effects on our lives, and many of these effects have been summarized in this module. But what are the limits of the effects of self-talk? In reference to this question, Zastrow (1979) presented the following example:

> A college student recently asked if her mother's long-time concern about giving birth to a child with a "dwarf" arm might have led to her youngest being born with a malformed arm.
>
> The student mentioned that her mother had been mildly concerned for a number of years that she would give birth to a child with a malformed arm. This young woman and her older brother were born without having such a malformation. However, shortly after the mother became pregnant the third time, a neighbor woman gave birth to a child with a malformed arm. This led the mother to have intense concerns that the child she was carrying would be born with a "dwarf" arm. When the child was born, it in fact was born with a "dwarf" arm.
>
> After I had given several lectures on the effects of self-talk in one of my classes, the student asked whether I thought this malformation was partly caused by self-talk or was just a matter of coincidence.
>
> In truth, I answered I didn't know—and I still don't know. We know certain drugs (such as thalidomide and excessive drinking) can cause malformations. So can having certain illnesses, such as German measles, during the time when the mother is pregnant. There is also speculation that the mother's emotional state while pregnant can influence the emotional and physiological development of the unborn child (Ainsworth, 1966; Dunn, 1977). Is it possible that this mother's thoughts and fears about having a malformed child might have been a factor in the child's being born with a malformed arm? . . .
>
> Daily I become aware of new ways in which my life, and that of others, is being influenced by self-talk. And,

as I discuss the concept with others, the discussion usually ignites their relating to me specific incidents in which their self-talk has had a powerful effect on them.

At this point I frankly do not know what the boundaries are for the effects of self-talk. It may well be that we are only at the "tip of the iceberg" in understanding all its effects. (pp. 327–328)

Summary

Rational therapy asserts that the primary cause of all our emotions and actions is not our experiences but rather what we tell ourselves about events that happen to us. Generally we cannot control events, but we can think rationally and thereby change unwanted emotions and dysfunctional actions. Self-talk has a here-and-now quality because it represents our present thoughts. Self-talk is frequently based on our attitudes, beliefs, values, wants, needs, drives, and motives.

Rational therapy maintains that the reasons for deviant acts can be determined by examining what offenders tell themselves prior to and during the act.

The initial focus of therapy is to help clients become aware of the irrational and negative self-talk that is the primary source of their unwanted emotions and dysfunctional actions. Once the irrational self-talk is identified, a wide range of techniques is used to change the irrational self-talk. A frequently used technique is to have the client develop and practice using rational self-challenges to counter the irrational self-talk. Clients also write rational self-analyses.

Rational therapy has a wide variety of applications. It is used to reduce stress, change negative self-concepts, improve negative aspects of personalities, help clients become more assertive, and treat sexual dysfunctions.

The question "What really causes therapeutic change?" is raised. Proponents of rational therapy assert that therapy techniques that succeed in changing emotions or actions are effective primarily because they change negative or irrational self-talk.

Unanswered questions remain about rational therapy, including how does self-talk physiologically lead to emotions, and what are the limits of the effects of self-talk?

EXERCISES

1. CHANGING UNWANTED EMOTIONS

Goal: To conduct a rational self-analysis.

Step 1: Using the discussion on RSAs (pages 421–422 and 425–427) as a guide, choose a recent event in your life that made you sad or angry and conduct an RSA of it.

Step 2: Use your new self-talk for a week.

Step 3: Class discussion of class experiences with their RSA. Did it work?

2. POSITIVE AFFIRMATIONS

Goal: To use another approach to change negative and irrational thinking.

Step 1: Writing a rational self-analysis can be time-consuming and cumbersome. An alternative is to use positive affirmations. A positive affirmation is a positive assertion that helps in achieving emotional and behavioral goals. Writing a positive affirmation also enables one to identify negative and irrational thinking that one may be unaware of.

Step 2: Select a realistic emotional or behavioral personal goal that you are currently struggling with. The following are examples:

"I believe I am a person of worth."
"I will no longer be depressed about ________."
"I will no longer get angry and aggressive when ________ occurs."
"I will lose five pounds in two months."

"I will stop smoking today."
"I will limit my drinking of alcoholic beverages to two drinks when I go out."
"I will no longer feel guilty about ________."
"I believe I am an attractive person."
"I will assertively express myself when ________ occurs."

Step 3: Write your selected positive affirmation. When negative thoughts enter your mind, record them and continue writing for 10–15 minutes the positive affirmation according to the following format:

Positive Affirmation	*Negative Thoughts*
"I will lose five pounds in two months."	
"I will lose five pounds in two months."	
"I will lose five pounds in two months."	"I overeat when I'm bored, depressed, or lonely."
"I will lose five pounds in two months."	
"I will lose five pounds in two months."	"I will need to develop an exercise program, which I hate to do."
"I will lose five pounds in two months."	"One reason I'm fat is because I snack between meals."
"I will lose five pounds in two months."	"I will have to limit the number of beers that I have when I go out—beer is putting a lot of weight on me."
"I will lose five pounds in two months."	"I wonder if I really want to make all the changes that I will have to make to lose five pounds."
"I will lose five pounds in two months."	
"I will lose five pounds in two months."	
"I will lose five pounds in two months."	

Step 4: Class discussion of the merits and shortcomings of writing positive affirmations.

3. *ASSESSING AND CHANGING DYSFUNCTIONAL BEHAVIORS*

Goal: To evaluate the merits and shortcomings of focusing on cognitions in assessing and changing dysfunctional behaviors.

Step 1: Divide into groups of 3–6 students. Choose one of the following problematic behaviors: (a) alcoholism, (b) child abuse, (c) bulimia, (d) date rape, (e) suicide attempt, and (f) compulsive gambling.

Step 2: (10 minutes.) Identify *thinking processes* that could lead a person to engage in this dysfunctional behavior, and (b) identify intervention strategies for changing the thinking patterns.

Step 3: Presentation of your results to the class.

Step 4: Class critique of the strategies.

Step 5: Class discussion of the merits and shortcomings of rational therapy.

MODULE 7

A Feminist Perspective on Therapy

A History of Sex Roles and Sexism

In almost every known society women have had a lower status than men.[1] Women have been bound by more social restrictions and have consistently received less recognition for their work. They have also been regarded differently, not only biologically but also emotionally, intellectually, and psychologically. Double standards have often existed for dating, marriage, and social and sexual conduct.

The traditional doctrines of most religions (including Judeo-Christian, Hindu, and Islam) ascribe an inferior status to women. This tradition continues to exist today in most countries, even though women attend church more often, hold firmer religious beliefs, pray more often, and are more active in church programs (Kornblum & Julian, 1998). Many societies have concluded that it is divinely ordained that women shall play a secondary and supportive role to men. In many Christian religions, women cannot become ministers or priests. Some orthodox Jewish men offer a daily prayer of thanks to God for not having made them women. In almost all churches, God is referred to as "he."

Historically, in hunting and gathering societies women spent much of their adult lives being pregnant, nursing infants, and raising children. Because they were forced to remain close to home, women were also assigned the less prestigious "domestic tasks" of cooking, serving, and washing. Once these sex roles became established, these distinctions were recognized not only as a practical means of doing the necessary work but also as the "natural" way for men and women to behave.

Before the Industrial Revolution practically all societies assigned distinct roles to men and to women. Women were generally involved in domestic and child-rearing activities, whereas men were involved in what were then considered to be the productive and protective functions for the family. In preindustrial societies women were also often involved in food producing and economic support, such as making clothes, growing and harvesting garden crops, and helping on the farm. But their specific responsibilities were often viewed as inferior and as requiring fewer skills.

The 19th-century Industrial Revolution brought dramatic changes in sex roles. Instead of working on a small farm, men went outside the home to work in factories or other settings. The economic role of women declined as they were less likely to be performing economically productive tasks. Women's roles were increasingly defined as child-rearing and housework, despite the fact that the amount of time required to perform these roles was declining for several reasons. Families had fewer children. With mass education, older children went to school. Gradually, labor-saving devices reduced the need for women to perform time-consuming domestic tasks such as baking bread, canning vegetables, and handwashing clothes. As traditional roles began to change, some women began to pursue activities (for example, outside employment) that had traditionally been limited to men. With these changes, sex roles began to blur and to become less clear-cut.

The struggle for women's rights in the United States has been going on for nearly two centuries. In

[1] Heidi J. Pendleton, M.S.W., collaborated in writing this chapter. Ms. Pendleton is employed with Juneau County Department of Human Services (Wisconsin) as a social worker in Juneau County Alternative Needs (JCAN), which is an alternative school for severely and emotionally disturbed adolescents.

the early part of the 19th century, women who were working for the abolition of slavery became aware that they too were denied rights such as voting. (An 1840 antislavery conference even refused to seat women while the male delegates gave impassioned speeches about the moral right of ending slavery.)

In 1848 two feminists, Susan B. Anthony and Elizabeth Cady Stanton, organized the first women's rights caucus, which was held in Seneca Falls, New York. These early leaders demanded suffrage (the vote for women) and the reform of many laws that were openly discriminatory toward women. It took more than 70 years (until 1920) to pass the 19th Amendment to the Constitution, which gave the vote to women. The suffrage movement was marked by jailing of feminists and fierce controversy. The enormous struggles and the number of years spent in getting this amendment passed led many women leaders to believe that the right to vote went hand in hand with sexual equality. After the 1920 passage, the "women's movement" was nearly dormant for the next 40 years.

In 1912, modern birth control techniques became available. Margaret Sanger helped women by providing them with information about safe, effective birth control methods. Through this advance, women gained greater freedom from the traditional roles of child-rearing and housework.

During World War II, large numbers of women were employed outside the home for the first time, taking the places of men who had been drafted into the military. At this time more than 38 percent of all women 16 years of age and over were employed, causing a further blurring of traditional sex roles (Blaire, 1979, p. 272).

The 1960s saw a resurgence of interest in sex-role inequality, for a variety of reasons. The civil rights movement had a consciousness-raising effect, and people became more aware of and concerned about inequalities. The civil rights movement to curb racial discrimination also served as a model, suggesting to a number of concerned women that sexual discrimination could also be alleviated through social action. More women attended college and thereby became more informed about inequalities. As women moved into new occupations, they became increasingly aware of discriminatory practices. Finally, there was an explosion of research suggesting that sex-role differences were not innately determined but were in fact the result of socialization patterns and that the effects of such sex roles were often discriminatory toward women.

Betty Friedan, in her 1963 book *The Feminine Mystique,* provided the ideological base for the resurgence of the women's movement. With the term *feminine mystique,* Friedan referred to the negative self-concept, lack of direction, and low sense of self-worth among women. The book served as a rallying point for women and led Friedan and others to form the National Organization for Women (NOW) in 1966. Today NOW is the largest women's rights group in the country and an influential political force. NOW and other women's groups have been working to end sexual discrimination, to achieve sexual equality, to end sexual double standards, and to improve the self-identity of women.

The Civil Rights Act of 1964, primarily intended to end racial discrimination, also prohibited discrimination on the basis of sex. A variety of statutes designed to prevent sex discrimination have been passed. The federal Equal Pay Act of 1963 and a number of similar state laws require equal pay for equal work. As mentioned earlier, the Civil Rights Act of 1964 outlaws discrimination on the basis of race, color, sex, or religion. Executive Order 11246, as amended by Executive Order 11375 on October 13, 1967, forbids sex discrimination by federal suppliers and contractors and provides procedures for enforcement. In addition, numerous court decisions have set precedents establishing the illegality of sex discrimination in hiring, promotions, and rates of pay. The Equal Credit Act of 1974 bars discrimination on the basis of marital status or sex in credit operations. A number of states have passed laws prohibiting discrimination against pregnant women in hiring, training, and promotion.

Affirmative action programs apply to women as well as to ethnic minorities. Women are considered a minority group because for generations they have been subjected to discrimination and have been denied equal opportunities. Employers must demonstrate active efforts to locate and recruit minority applicants (defined to include women) and demonstrate positive efforts to increase the pool of qualified applicants (for example, special training programs for minorities).

A major dilemma with affirmative action programs is that preferential hiring and quota programs create reverse discrimination, in which qualified majority group members are sometimes arbitrarily excluded. Affirmative action programs raise delicate and complex questions about achieving equality through preferential hiring and admissions policies for minorities. Yet no other means has been found to end obvious discrimination in hiring and admissions. Critics of affirmative action assert the program is now a highly politicized and painful remedy that has stigmatized many of those it was meant to help. Affirmative action is now perceived by many in our society as a system of preferences for the unqualified. Critics further assert that affirmative action may have been necessary 30 years ago to ensure that minority candidates received fair treatment to counter the social barriers to hiring and admission that stemmed from centuries of unequal treatment. But today such programs are no longer needed. They maintain it is wrong to discriminate against White males for the sole reason of making up for the injustices that somebody's great-grandfather may have done to somebody else's great-grandmother. They believe it is wrong for the daughter of a wealthy African American couple to be given preference in employment over the son of a homeless alcoholic who happens to be White.

Supporters of affirmative action assert, "If we abandon affirmative action, we return to the old-boys' network." They believe affirmative action has helped a number of women and people of color to attain a good education and higher-paying positions, and thereby to remove themselves from the ranks of the poor. They maintain that, in a society where racist and sexist attitudes remain, it is necessary to have affirmative action to give women and people of color a fair opportunity at attaining a quality education and well-paying jobs.

In 1996 voters in the state of California passed Proposition 209, which explicitly rejects the idea that women and other minority group members receive special consideration when applying for jobs, government contracts, or university admission. This affirmative action ban became law in California in August 1997. In addition, a number of lawsuits have been filed objecting to reverse discrimination. If the courts rule in favor of those filing the lawsuits, the power of affirmative action programs will be sharply reduced. In November 1997, the U.S. Supreme Court rejected a challenge to the California law that ended racial and gender preferences in that state. This Supreme Court action clears the way for other states and cities to ban affirmative action.

Contemporary Women's Issues

Women have been the victims of sexism in numerous ways. Among the current issues that impact women are welfare reform, economic inequality and comparable worth, sexual harassment, sexist language, battered women, rape, and special counseling needs of women.

WELFARE REFORM. Chapter 2 indicated that a "devolution revolution" is occurring in the United States in the provision of social services. Many political leaders now view block grants as a means of transferring decision-making power about social programs from the federal government to the state and local levels. Perhaps the most prominent example of this is replacement of the AFDC program (which provided financial assistance to poor parents, primarily single mothers, until the youngest child reached 18 years of age) with the 1996 Welfare Reform Act, which transferred from the federal government to state and local governments most of the decision making about financial assistance to poor families with children. (Recipients of financial benefits now receive no more than two years of financial assistance without working, and there is a five-year lifetime limit of benefits for adults.)

The program that has replaced AFDC is Temporary Assistance to Needy Families (TANF). Many politicians believe this program has been successful as they note there have been dramatic decreases in the number of families (usually a mother with children) receiving TANF benefits compared to families who received AFDC benefits. Critics of TANF assert the program places many children (along with the parent or parents) in poor families at risk, because many of these families are plunged deeper into poverty—with accompanying dangers of living in deteriorated neighborhoods; homelessness; less access to education; and being even more victimized by crime, family violence, stress-related illnesses, and drug and alcohol abuse.

ECONOMIC INEQUALITY AND COMPARABLE WORTH. Even today women generally earn less than men; women who work full time earn about 75 percent of what men earn (U.S. Bureau of the Census, 2000). A variety of explanations have been given for gender-based salary differences. One prominent explanation is that men and women are clustered in different kinds of occupations, with the occupations held by men generally paying higher wages and salaries.

Questions are being raised about why men are paid substantially more money than women doing work that requires similar levels of preparation and skill. Why, for example, are male janitors generally paid more than female secretaries? The concept of *comparable worth* has therefore arisen. It calls for equal pay for males and females doing work that requires comparable skill, effort, and responsibility under similar working conditions (Bellak, 1984, p. 75). Comparable worth advocates assert that women have the right to receive equal pay for doing work comparable to that which men traditionally do. Comparable worth is increasingly being used as a basis for pay discrimination lawsuits.

Comparable worth is not a simple concept. Advocates of comparable worth assert the need for equal pay for comparable work. Opponents focus on the cost of implementation and on the complexities of determining what is "comparable work."

SEXUAL HARASSMENT. Sexual harassment is *not* flirtation, flattery, request for a date, and other acceptable behaviors that occur in workplaces and classrooms (see CTRM Exhibit 7.1). It is also distinct from other forms of harassment that do not involve conduct of a sexual nature. Sexual harassment is sexual coercion that relies on the power of the perpetrator to affect the victim's economic or academic status; it does not necessarily involve physical force. Sexual harassment is a form of discrimination in employment and education and is prohibited by Title VII of the Civil Rights Act of 1964. It is defined as:

> Unwelcome sexual advances, requests for sexual favors, and other verbal or physical conduct of a sexual nature constitute sexual harassment when 1.) submission to such conduct is made either explicitly or implicitly a term or condition of an individual's employment; 2.) submission to or rejection of such conduct by an individual is used as a basis for employment decisions affecting such individual; or 3.) such conduct has the purpose or effect of unreasonably interfering with an individual's work performance or creating an intimidating, hostile, or offensive working environment. (Charney & Russell, 1994, p. 11)

Sexual harassment almost always involves elements of unequal power and coercion. Although most victims are women, males can also experience sexual harassment. Repeated incidents of sexual harassment result in hostile, intimidating, or anxiety-producing work or educational environments.

SEXIST LANGUAGE. The words we choose greatly influence our interpretation of what reality is. Sexist language in our society has been a significant factor in defining and maintaining the dominant position of males in our society, with females assigned a supportive or submissive role. Here are some words and phrases that portray men as dominant: *chairman, policeman, congressman, best man for the job, mankind,* and *man and wife.*

There are other examples of how sexism has infiltrated the English language. In the past (there has been considerable improvement in recent years), books tended to use the pronoun "he" to refer, in a generic sense, to a person when gender was unspecified. On reaching adulthood, a man becomes a "Mr." for the remainder of his life; this is a polite term that makes no reference to the status of a man's personal life. A woman, however, begins as a "Miss" but becomes a "Mrs." upon marriage, which clearly identifies her marital status. In addition, traditionally a woman will, upon marriage, use her husband's last name instead of her own birth name. Language is a powerful tool for shaping our perceptions, and sexist language has clearly played a part in defining women in our society.

BATTERED WOMEN. Spouse abuse has become a national concern only relatively recently. Spouse abuse received extensive national attention in 1994 following the death of Nicole Simpson. Her former husband, O. J. Simpson, was charged with the murder. At least eight times prior to her death, police were called to the Simpson home for alleged battering (Roberts, 1994).

Nearly 11 percent of all murder victims are killed by their spouses (Kornblum & Julian, 1998). Women tend to endure cruelty and abuse much longer than men, perhaps because they feel trapped by financial insecurity. The dominant theme is the systematic use of violence and the threat of violence by men to "keep their wives in line." That is to say, some segments of our society believe husbands have a right to control their wives and to force them to be submissive.

Domestic violence is the major cause of injury to women (Kornblum & Julian, 1998). Injuries from battering are more common than rape, mugging, and auto accidents. Every 15 seconds another American woman is victimized by domestic violence (Kornblum & Julian, 1998). Incidents of physical abuse between spouses are not widely isolated but tend to recur frequently in a marriage. Spouse abuse occurs as often among the well educated as among those less educated. A sizable number of both men and women believe it is appropriate for a husband to hit his wife "every now and then" (Kornblum & Julian, 1998).

There are a variety of other reasons why men batter women. Many have a poor self-image and are insecure about their worth as breadwinners, fathers, and sexual partners. They have a stereotyped view of their wives as submissive and in need of control. Many abuse alcohol and other drugs and are much more apt to be violent when intoxicated or high.

CTRM EXHIBIT 7.1

Types of sexual harassment

Sexual harassment falls into three categories: verbal, nonverbal, and physical. The following examples can be considered sexual harassment if the behavior is clearly unwelcomed and not reciprocated.

Verbal

- Sexual innuendos ("So you're majoring in packaging? I love your packaging.")
- Suggestive comments ("Those jeans really fit you well.")
- Sexual remarks about a person's clothing, body, or sexual activities ("I noticed you lost weight; I'm glad you didn't lose your gorgeous chest too.")
- Sexist insults or jokes or remarks that are stereotypical or derogatory to members of the opposite sex ("Women should be kept barefoot, pregnant, and at the edge of town.")
- Implied or verbal threats concerning one's grades or job ("It's simple. If you want to pass this course, you have to be nice to me, and sex is the nicest thing I can think of.")
- Sexual proposition, invitations, or other pressures for sex ("My office hours are too limited; why don't you drop by my house tonight? We'll have more privacy and time to get to know each other.")
- Using employment position to request dates or sexual favors

Nonverbal

- Visual sexual displays; unwanted display of pornographic pictures, posters, cartoons, or other materials
- Body language (such as leering at one's body or standing too close)
- Whistling suggestively
- Mooning or flashing
- Obscene gestures
- Actions that involve gender-directed favoritism or disparate treatment

Physical

- Patting, pinching, and any other inappropriate touching or feeling
- Bra-snapping
- Brushing against the body
- Grabbing or groping
- Attempted or actual kissing or fondling
- Coerced sexual intercourse
- Attempted or actual sexual assault

In battered spouse families a cycle of violence is set up. A battering incident occurs, and the wife sustains injuries. The husband feels remorse, and fears his wife may leave or report the incident to the police, so he tries to "honeymoon" his wife into thinking he won't abuse her again. Gradually the "honeymoon" efforts on his part cease, and tensions about his work or family matters begin to build again. A minor incident then sets him off, often while he's intoxicated, and he again batters his wife. The battering–honeymoon–tension building–battering cycle is repeated again and again.

Abusive husbands often isolate their spouses; and wives become even more dependent after ties are severed with relatives and friends. The men ridicule their wives' friends and relatives, and they usually create an embarrassing scene when the wife is with her friends or relatives. The husband seeks to have her end contact with them to "keep peace." Abusive husbands also continually ridicule them, which lowers the women's self-esteem and leads them to play a submissive role. Financial dependence is often created by having children and by creating barriers that prevent wives from seeking high-paying employment.

A surprising number of battered women do not permanently leave their husbands. Many are socialized to play a subordinate role to their husbands, and their husbands use violence and psychological abuse to make them feel too inadequate to live on their own. Some women believe it is their moral duty to stick it out to the end—that marriage is forever, for better or for worse. Many hope (in spite of the continuing violence) that their husbands will change. Some fear that if they leave their husbands will retaliate with even more severe beatings. A fair number do not view leaving as a viable alternative because they feel financially dependent on their husbands. Many have young children and do not believe they have the resources to raise children on their own. Some believe that occasional beatings are better than the loneliness and insecurity connected with leaving. Some dread the stigma associated with separation or divorce. These women are captives in their own homes.

Fortunately, in recent years new services have been developed for battered women. Shelter homes for battered women have been established in many communities. These shelters give abused women an opportunity to flee the abusive situation. Such women often receive counseling, assistance in finding a job, and legal help. Some areas have programs for the husbands, which include group therapy for batterers, marriage counseling for both spouses, and 24-hour "hot lines" that encourage potential spouse abusers to call when they are angry. (Unfortunately, many batterers refuse to participate in such programs.) Many communities also have public information programs to inform battered women of their legal rights and of available resources for help.

RAPE. Forced intercourse is a common violent crime in the United States. More than 90,000 cases are reported annually, and many more cases go unreported (Kornblum & Julian, 1998). Victims of rape are hesitant to report cases because they fear (1) that reporting the case will do them no good because they already have been victimized; (2) being humiliated by the questions the officer will ask; (3) the reactions of the general public and of people close to them, including their husband or partner; and (4) reporting the offense may make the attacker more likely to attack them again. Some try to forget about it. Others fail to report it because they do not want to testify in court. But perhaps the most common reason women fail to report sexual assault victimization is because they feel—usually wrongly—that they somehow contributed to the rape's occurrence. This is especially true in the most frequent type of rape—that between acquaintances.

No one profile fits all rapists. Rapists vary considerably in terms of motivations for committing the rape, prior criminal record, education, occupation, marital status, and so on. In a majority of cases the rapist and his victim know each other on a first-name basis. A significant proportion of rapes are date rapes.

Rape is first an aggressive and second a sexual act. Rape is a sexual expression of aggression, not an aggressive expression of sexuality. Many people wrongly believe rape occurs because the rapist manages his sexual arousal poorly or because he is "oversexed." Rape is, instead, the mismanagement of aggression in which the rapist's gratification (if any) comes not from the sexual act but rather from the expression of anger or control through the extreme violation of another's body.

A number of typologies classify rapists. One straightforward model was developed by A. Nicholas Groth (1979), who describes rapists as falling into one of three categories: the anger rapist, the power rapist, and the sadistic rapist.

The *anger rapist* performs his act to discharge feelings of pent-up anger and rage. He is brutal in the commission of his assault, using far more force than is necessary to gain sexual access to his victim. His aim is to hurt and debase his victim; forced sex is his ultimate weapon in degrading his victim.

The *power rapist* is interested in possessing his victim sexually, not harming her. He acts out of underlying feelings of inadequacy and is interested in controlling his victim. He uses only the amount of force necessary to gain her compliance. He may kidnap his victim and hold her under his control for a long period of time, perhaps engaging in sexual intercourse with her numerous times.

The *sadistic rapist* eroticizes aggression; that is, aggressive force creates sexual arousal in him. He is enormously gratified by his victim's torment, pain, and suffering. His offenses often are ritualistic and involve bondage and torture, particularly to the sexual organs.

We live in a society that promotes aggression and represses sexuality. In the United States males are socialized to be aggressive, including in seeking sexual gratification. Men, for example, are often expected to play the "aggressive" role in sex. In our culture sex and aggression are frequently confused and combined. In Swedish culture, where sexual information is readily available in the media but depictions of aggression are not, the rate of rape is low. According to Janet Hyde (1994), the confusion of sex and aggression in socialization practices can lead males to commit rape.

> It may be, then, that rape is a means of proving masculinity for the male who is insecure in his role. For this reason, the statistics on the youthfulness of rapists make sense; youthful rapists may simply be young men who are trying to adopt the adult male role, who feel insecure about doing this, and who commit a rape as proof of their manhood. Further, heterosexuality is an important part of manliness. Raping a woman is a flagrant way to prove that one is a heterosexual. (p. 49)

DATE RAPE. Date rape is not a rare occurrence. In some cases date rape occurs because the man believes that if he spends money on the woman he is entitled to (or she is implicitly giving consent to) sexual behavior. One view of dating holds that if the woman says "no," she really means "yes." Unfortunately, media depictions of this misinformation abound, from John Wayne movies to such classics as *Gone With the Wind.* For example, there's the old John Wayne movie, *The Quiet Man,* in which Wayne plays a macho, quiet Irishman. He courts a feisty woman played by Maureen O'Hara, but to no avail. Only after beating up a mean rival, spanking the woman in front of the townspeople, and literally dragging her home does he win her compliance and cooperation. The underlying message can be that "real men" obtain power, status, and sexual gratification by violating women sexually—a very dangerous message indeed!

The vast majority of date rapes go unreported. In fact, many of the female victims of sexual assault do not interpret the assault as such (Hyde & DeLamater, 1997). Because many of the victims view themselves as being "in love" with the perpetrator, they view the rape as within the realm of acceptable behavior.

Kanin (1985) studied 71 unmarried college men who were self-disclosed date rapists and compared them to a control group of unmarried college men. The date rapists tended to be sexually predatory. When asked how frequently they attempted to seduce a new date, 62 percent of the date rapists said "most of the time," compared with 19 percent of the controls. The date rapists were also much more likely to use a variety of manipulative techniques on their dates, including falsely professing love, getting them high on alcohol or other drugs, and falsely promising going steady or marriage.

Men need to learn that "no" means "no." Date rape educational programs are needed in elementary, secondary, and higher education settings. Laws against date rape need to be more vigorously enforced. The entertainment industry and our society need to stop glamorizing rape and instead convey that it is a serious crime that has devastating effects on victims.

EFFECTS ON VICTIMS. Rape is a severe crisis for the victim, and adjustment effects often persist for six months or longer. Victims undergo a series of emotional changes that have been identified as the *rape trauma syndrome* (Burgess & Holmstrom, 1974; Hyde & DeLamater, 1997). This syndrome occurs in two phases: The *acute phase* begins immediately after the rape (or attempted rape) and may last for several weeks. Victims have an expressive reaction in which they cry and have feelings of anger, fear, humiliation, tension, anxiety, and a desire for revenge. During this phase victims often have periods of controlled reaction in which they mask or deny their feelings and appear calm, composed, or subdued. Victims also experience many physical reactions during this phase, such as stomach pains, nausea, headaches, insomnia, and jumpiness. In addition, women forced to have oral sex report irritation or damage to the throat. Those forced to have anal intercourse report rectal pain and bleeding. Two feelings are especially common: fear and self-blame. Many women fear future physical violence or continued to suffer from the fear of being murdered during the attack. The self-blame is related to the tendency on the part of the victim and others to "blame the victim." Victims often spend hours agonizing over what they think they could have done to bring on the attack or to fight off the attacker. Common self-criticisms are, "If only I hadn't walked alone," "If only I had bolt-locked the door," "If only I hadn't worn that tight sweater," "If only I hadn't been dumb enough to trust that guy."

In the *long-term reorganization phase* victims experience a variety of major disruptions. Women raped outdoors may develop fears about going outdoors; those raped indoors may develop fears about being indoors. Some are unable to return to work, particularly if the rape occurred at work. Some quit their jobs and remain unemployed for a long time. Many fear the rapist will find them and assault them again. To attempt to avoid an assault by the same rapist, some move (sometimes several times), change their telephone number, or get an unlisted number. Others develop sexual phobias and have severe difficulties in returning to their regular sexual lifestyle. It can take several years for the victim to return to her previous lifestyle.

In addition, if the victim reports the rape, the police investigation and the trial (if it occurs) are further crises. Police and the courts have a history of abusive and callous treatment of rape victims, although this is changing. The police have, at times, conveyed the idea that the victim is fabricating the assault or that she willingly agreed to have sex but then changed her mind. The police must ask embarrassing questions about the details of the assault, and they don't always show understanding and sympathy. In court it is common for defense attorneys to imply that the victim seduced the defendant, and then decided to call it rape. Victims are made to feel as if they are the ones who are on trial.

Fortunately, many police departments now have sensitive crime units with specially trained officers who handle rape and child sexual assault. A number of states have also enacted "shield" evidence laws, which prohibit defense attorneys from asking questions about the victim's previous sexual experiences (except with the alleged rapist) during trial.

Rape and its aftereffects are extremely traumatic. Therefore, counseling to victims should (1) provide support and allow victims to ventilate their feelings, (2) lend support and guidance during the medical tests and while police are questioning them, (3) be similarly supportive during the trial, and (4) provide follow-up counseling for emotional reactions to the rape.

Because a majority of rapes are not reported, many of the nonreporters have a *silent rape reaction.* Nonreporters not only fail to report the rape to the police but often tell no one about it. Nonreporters experience the same adjustment problems as victims who report the rape experience. However, their trauma is often intensified because they have no way to express or vent their feelings. Some eventually seek professional counseling for other problems such as depression, anxiety, or inability to have orgasms. Often, the problems are then found to stem from the rape. Women who have had secret rape experiences should be helped to talk about the rape experience so they can gradually learn to deal with it. A number of communities now have rape crisis centers that provide counseling, medical services, and legal services to victims.

SPECIAL COUNSELING NEEDS OF WOMEN. Collier (1982, pp. 57–77) has identified eight personal issues that women frequently bring to counseling situations:

Sense of powerlessness: Women who have been socialized to be passive and dependent often feel that no matter what they do they cannot improve their life situation.

Limited behavioral and emotional options: Because of gender-role expectations, women often do not see the variety of alternatives open to them. For example, a battered wife who has been raised to believe that marriage is a permanent commitment may not view leaving her husband as an option.

Anger: Many women experience deep-seated anger because of the way they are treated at work or at home. Some women turn their anger inward, blaming themselves for their predicaments; this results in depression.

Failure to nurture self: Women who have devoted themselves to nurturing and caring for others may feel unfulfilled and unsure of who they are.

Inability to balance independence with interdependence: Many women struggle with being overly dependent on someone else. Others struggle with finding a balance between being independent (not needing anyone for anything, including emotional support) and interdependent (feeling confident enough to function autonomously, yet acknowledging that interactions with other people are important).

Lack of trust in self-direction: Women with low self-esteem and little experience in taking independent action have difficulty trusting their own judgment on how to proceed.

Inadequate communication skills: Some women feel they do not have the right to express their thoughts and feelings, due largely to traditional gender-role expectations. Others raised to be passive may not know how to express themselves assertively.

Old rules and expectations: A woman who is seeking an egalitarian relationship with a man will encounter conflict if she becomes romantically involved with a man with traditional gender-role expectations. Conflicts are likely to arise in a variety of areas, including her choice of careers, division of domestic tasks, and decision making.

Social Work's Response to Women's Issues

The social work profession has responded to women's issues in numerous ways. In 1973 the Delegate Assembly of NASW added sexism to poverty and racism as basic concerns and priorities for the profession. The Council on Social Work Education (CSWE) requires in its accreditation standards for baccalaureate and master's programs that content on women's issues be included throughout the curriculum. CSWE also has an accreditation standard that prohibits gender discrimination in social work educational programs and mandates affirmative action programs for women administrators, faculty, students, and staff in social work educational programs.

The NASW Legal Defense Fund provides financial support in sex discrimination cases. In addition, NASW is working on other issues related to sexism.

In practice there is some truth that social work has an emphasis on serving women because a majority of social work clients are women. About three-fourths of all people receiving public assistance and welfare payments are females (U.S. Bureau of the Census, 2000). Because women still primarily care for children, they are the main users of child welfare services. They are more likely to seek and receive counseling, and they are the major consumers of services for the aged. In addition, females are the primary consumers of family planning, pregnancy counseling, abortion services, rape crisis services, services from shelters for battered wives, and displaced homemaker services.

There are a number of other reasons why more women are social work clients. For one thing, women outnumber men in the United States. Rauch (1989, p. 342) identifies another reason: "Most women in this country are socialized to accept weakness and dependence with more ease than men. The role of client is compatible with behaviors expected of women but is not congruent with men's expectations of themselves." Women tend to need more services because poverty disproportionately affects them; women who work full time are paid substantially less than men who work full time. Women have higher rates of unemployment and are much more likely to be single heads of households.

Rauch (1989) summarizes a number of additional reasons why women are more likely to be social work clients:

> . . . teenage and unwanted pregnancies, postpartum depression, and sexual dysfunction; the need, resulting from the concentration of parenting functions in women's hands, for services for mothers who abuse or neglect their children and for the mothers of emotionally disturbed, learning disabled, mentally retarded, blind, or otherwise handicapped children; women's vulnerability to wife abuse and rape; the limitations of the wife-mother role and the "empty nest" syndrome; the practical and emotional stresses for women of separation or divorce and the difficulties of raising children alone; and the norm that women marry older men, which, in combination with women's longer life expectancy leads to widowhood and the stresses of bereavement, loss of the role of wife, and loneliness. (pp. 343–344)

It is important that social workers understand that the traditional socialization process and the sex-role stereotypes in our society account for many of the problems that confront female, as well as male, clients. Workers should be skilled in helping clients to actualize themselves and to overcome rigid sex-role stereotypes. Many interaction problems between males and females in our society are consequences of sex-role stereotyping. One therapy approach widely used to help both men and women express themselves more effectively and gain skills in countering sex-role stereotypes is assertiveness training (see Module 4). Women's consciousness-raising groups help clients become more aware of sex-role stereotypes, establish a better self-concept, and foster contact with others who are also working to end sexism.

The growing awareness of sexism and women's issues has led to improved services for groups that were once largely ignored: victims of rape, battered wives, women seeking abortions, husbands and wives with marital concerns, people with sexual dysfunctions, single-parent households headed by women, and displaced homemakers.

The Feminist Perspective

Women have been highly involved in the development of social work and social welfare programs. One of the founders of modern social work was Jane Addams (see CTRM Exhibit 7.2). Approximately two-thirds of current social workers are female (U.S. Bureau of the Census, 2000). Female social workers hold numerous leadership positions as deans of graduate schools, chairs of undergraduate social work programs, and directors of agencies. Women also write a vast number of social work texts and professional journal articles.

The feminist perspective on social work intervention has been developed by a number of authors; no one is specifically recognized as being its founder. Miller and Stiver (1993, pp. 421–431) present a number of central themes for working with women:

1. Social workers must recognize the powerful impact of cultural context on women's lives. In a patriarchal culture where women have less power than men, women are always attempting to adapt to relationships that are unequal, essentially nonmutual. As a result, women often do not feel sufficiently empowered to have an impact on the important relationships in their lives or, by extension, on society. In such settings, the ways in which the less powerful group (women) adapts and differs from the dominant group (men) are apt to go unnoticed and be misunderstood. This dynamic perpetuates the disempowered status of the subordinate group.

2. It is essential that social workers understand the importance of relationships as the central organizing feature in women's development. Instead of struggling toward independence and autonomy, which is how most developmental models of growth and maturity are characterized, women more often are searching for connections with others. Traditionally, these

CTRM EXHIBIT 7.2

Jane Addams: A prominent founder of social work

Born in 1860 in Cedarville, Illinois, Jane Addams was the daughter of a successful couple who owned a flour mill and a wood mill. Addams graduated from Rockford Seminary (a college in Rockford, Illinois) and briefly attended medical school but was forced to leave because of illness. She then traveled for a few years in Europe, perplexed about what to undertake as her life work. At the age of 25 she joined the Presbyterian Church, which helped her find a focus for her life—religion and humanitarianism and, in particular, serving the poor. (Later in her life she joined the Congregational Church, now known as the United Church of Christ.) Addams heard about Toynbee Hall in England and returned to Europe to study its approach. Its staff was composed of college students and graduates, mainly from Oxford, who lived in the slums of London to learn conditions firsthand and to help improve life in the slums with their own financial and personal resources.

Addams returned to the United States and rented a two-story house (later called Hull House) in an impoverished neighborhood in Chicago. With a few friends, she initiated a variety of group and individual activities for the community. Group activities included a literature reading group for young women, a kindergarten, and groups with the following foci: social relationships, sports, music, painting, art, and discussion of current affairs. Hull House also provided services to individuals who came asking for immediate help, such as food and shelter and information and referral for other services. A Hull House Social Science Club was formed, which studied social problems in a scientific manner and then became involved in social action efforts to improve living conditions. One of its successful efforts was to work for passage of Illinois legislation to prevent the employment of children in area sweatshops. Addams also became interested in the various nationality groups in the neighborhood. She was fairly successful in bringing the various nationalities together at Hull House, where they could interact and interchange cultural values.

The success of Hull House served as a model for the establishment of settlement houses in other areas of Chicago and in many other large cities in the United States. Settlement house leaders believed that by changing neighborhoods they would improve communities, and by altering communities they would develop a better society. For her extraordinary contributions, Jane Addams received the Nobel Peace Prize in 1931.

Source: Herbert Stroup, "Jane Addams," in *Social Welfare Pioneers* (Chicago: Nelson-Hall, 1986), pp. 1–29.

---

relationships have been directed toward fostering the development of others—children certainly but also other adults. Women's relational style is increasingly apparent in other arenas. For example, in the workplace the collaborative approach of women managers is drawing considerable attention.

3. An appreciation of women's relational qualities and activities as potential strengths and as providing a new pathway for healthy growth and development is necessary when working with women. This stands in stark contrast to the prevailing view that had misinterpreted many of women's most valuable qualities as defects or deficiencies. In traditional theory, women's ability to express emotions more freely and their attention to relationships often led to pathological labeling like "hysterical" or "too dependent."

Feminism is a multifaceted concept. In *The Social Work Dictionary* Barker (1999) defines *feminism* as "the social movement and doctrine advocating legal and socioeconomic equality for women" (p. 173). He then defines *feminist social work* as "the integration of the values, skills, and knowledge of social work with a feminist orientation to help individuals and society overcome the emotional and social problems that result from *sex discrimination*" (p. 173). He defines *feminist therapy* as follows:

> A psychosocial treatment orientation in which the professional (usually a woman) helps the client (usually a woman) in individual or group settings to overcome the psychological and social problems largely encountered as a result of *sex discrimination* and sex-role stereotyping. Feminist therapists help clients maximize potential, especially through *consciousness-raising,* eliminating sex stereotyping, and helping them become aware of the commonalities shared by all women. (p. 173)

Collins (1986) defined feminist theory as "a philosophical perspective or way of visualizing and thinking about situations and an evolving set of theories attempting to explain the various phenomena of women's oppression" (p. 217). Kirst-Ashman and Hull (1999) defined feminism as follows:

> The *philosophy of equality* between women and men that involves *both attitudes and actions,* which infiltrates

> virtually *all aspects of life,* which often necessitates providing *education and advocacy* on the behalf of women, and which appreciates the existence of *individual differences* and personal accomplishments regardless of gender. (p. 495)

Let's discuss the five components of this definition. The philosophy of equality between men and women does not mean that women should adopt behaviors that are typically masculine. It means that women and men should have equal or identical rights to opportunities and choices and that neither women nor men should be discriminated against on the basis of gender.

The second component embodies both *attitudes and actions.* By attitudes, feminism emphasizes the importance of viewing other people in a fair, objective perspective and of avoiding stereotyping. By actions, feminism involves a commitment to act on one's beliefs involving gender equality. For example, a supervisor who asserts that he or she believes in feminism has an obligation to confront a supervisee who tells sexist jokes or who treats women according to traditional gender-based stereotypes (for example, by making demeaning comments about female social workers being too emotionally involved with their clients).

In the third component, *all aspects of life,* equality does not apply only to equal opportunity to attain a specific job or promotion, it also involves many other aspects of life: freedom to ask another person out for a date; freedom to decide what to do with leisure time; freedom to choose to become involved in competitive sports; freedom to choose to have a sexual encounter; and so on.

The fourth component is the frequent need to *provide education and advocacy* on behalf of women. Feminism involves valuing equal opportunities for both women and men. Because women have been subjected to sex-role stereotyping and gender-based discrimination, a person who values feminism has an obligation to provide education and advocacy on behalf of women. For example, the male employee who is telling sexist jokes at work needs to be educated about sexual harassment. He also needs to be informed about the negative impact such jokes have on women and that adverse consequences will result if he continues to make sexist remarks. Feminist advocacy involves speaking out for (or championing the rights of) those women who need help. These women are usually in positions of lesser power and opportunity.

The fifth component is appreciation of *individual differences.* The feminist perspective places a high value on empowering women by emphasizing individual qualities and strengths.

Principles of Feminist Therapy

The emphasis of feminist therapy is on equality for women. Feminist therapists strive to behave in ways that reflect these values with clients, in professional relationships, and in their daily lives. There is great diversity among feminist therapists in their philosophical influences and preferences, training, background, and implementation in practice. Feminist therapists tend to be liberal, cultural, and radical.

Kanuha (1990, pp. 30–33) describes four necessary components of ethical feminist therapy philosophy and practice:

1. Directly address the concept of an "integrated analysis of oppression" (which means the conceptualization of feminist therapy must address and integrate the many facets of oppression relating to women).
2. Include an integrated analysis of oppression in policies and position papers.
3. Education and training in antiracism, homophobia, class issues, anti-Semitism, and all other forms of oppression that affect the lives of women not only in the United States but internationally.
4. Develop specific strategies to actively recruit and support non-White, non–middle-class, nonheterosexual women into the feminist therapy profession.

Van Den Bergh and Cooper (1987), Van Den Bergh (1992), and Kirst-Ashman and Hull (1999) identify nine principles of feminist intervention.

1. A client's problems should be viewed "within a sociopolitical framework" (Kirst-Ashman & Hull, 1999, p. 496). Feminist intervention is concerned with the inequitable power relationship between women and men and is opposed to all "power-over" relationships, regardless of gender, race, class, age, and so on. Such relationships lead to oppression and domination. Feminism is concerned with changing all social, economic, and political structures based on the relationships between the haves and the have-nots. The problems of the have-nots are often rooted in a sexist social and political structure. Another way of stating this principle is that "personal is political." According to Van Den Bergh (1992):

> This principle maintains that what a woman experiences in her personal life is directly related to societal dynamics that affect other women. In other words, an individual woman's experiences of pejorative comments based on sex and of blocked opportunities are directly related to societal sexism. For ethnic minority women, racism and classism also are factors that affect well-being. (p. 103)

A primary distinguishing characteristic of feminist treatment is to help the client analyze how her problems are related to systematic difficulties experienced by women in a sexist, classist, and racist society.

2. Traditional sex roles are pathological, and clients need encouragement to free themselves from traditional gender-role bonds. Traditionally, American women are expected to be affectionate, passive, conforming, sensitive, intuitive, dependent; in other words, "sugar and spice and everything nice." They are supposed to be primarily concerned about their personal appearance and to be self-sacrificing for their family. They are raised to not appear to be ambitious, aggressive, competitive, or more intelligent than men. They are expected to be ignorant about and uninterested in sports, economics, or politics. They are not supposed to initiate relationships with men and are expected to be tender, feminine, emotional, and appreciative in these relationships.

Women are put in a double bind due to *femininity achievement incompatibility;* there is a traditional view in our society that a woman cannot be both feminine and an achiever. Achievement is erroneously thought to reduce a woman's femininity, and the truly feminine female is thought to be someone who does not seek to be an achiever. Traditionally, women have been socialized to fill a "learned helplessness" role. Van Den Bergh (1992) described the effects of such sex-role stereotyping:

> Sex-role stereotypes suggest that women should be submissive, docile, receptive, and dependent. The message is one of helplessness; that women cannot take care of themselves and are dependent upon others for their well-being. This sets up a dynamic in which a woman's locus of control is external to her self, preventing her from believing that she can acquire what she needs on her own in order to develop and self-actualize. In other words, oversubscription to sex-role stereotypes engenders a state of powerlessness in which a woman is likely to become involved in situations where she becomes victimized. . . . For example, because young girls are socialized to be helpless, when they become women they tend to have a limited repertoire of responses when under stress; e.g., they respond passively. (p. 101)

In feminist treatment, clients are helped to see how their difficulties may be related to oversubscription to traditional sex-role stereotypes. They are shown that by internalizing traditional sex roles women are inevitably set up to play passive, submissive roles and to experience low self-esteem and self-hatred. The feminist approach asserts that clients need encouragement to make their own choices and to pursue the tasks and achievements they desire, rather than being constrained by traditional sex roles.

3. Intervention should focus on client empowerment. Van Den Bergh (1992) described the empowerment process:

> Helping women to acquire a sense of power, or the ability to affect outcome in their lives, is a crucial component of feminist practice. Empowerment means acquiring knowledge, skills, and resources that enhance an individual's ability to control her own life and to influence others. Traditionally, women have used indirect, overt techniques to get what they want, such as helplessness, dependency, coyness, and demureness. (p. 104)

Empowerment is fostered in a variety of ways: (1) by helping the client define her own needs and clarify her personal goals so she can derive a sense of purposefulness, (2) by providing the client with education and access to resources, (3) by helping the client see that the direction and ability to change lies within herself (that is, alterations in her life will result only from her own undertakings), and (4) by focusing on the identification and enhancement of the client's strengths rather than on her pathologies. Women need to be empowered so they can increase their ability to control their environments to get what they need.

4. Clients' self-esteem should be enhanced. Self-esteem and self-confidence are essential for empowerment. Self-esteem can be enhanced in a variety of ways. The worker should try to be an encouraging person, as described in Chapter 5. The worker should help clients identify and recognize their unique qualities and strengths. Many clients with low self-esteem blame themselves for everything that is wrong. For example, battered women typically blame themselves for being battered. These clients need to look more realistically at these areas. They need to distinguish where their responsibility for dysfunctional interactions ends and other individuals' responsibility begins.

5. Clients should be encouraged to develop their identity (sense of self) on the basis of their own strengths, attributes, qualities, and achievements. It is a

serious mistake for a woman to develop her identity in terms of her spouse or dating partner. Women need to develop an independent identity that is based on their relationships with others.

6. Clients need to value and develop social support systems with other women. In a society that devalues women, it is all too easy for some women to view other women as insignificant. With social support systems women can ventilate their concerns and share their experiences and the solutions they've found to similar problems. They can serve as brokers in identifying resources and can provide emotional support and nurturance to one another.

7. Clients need to find an effective balance between work and personal relationships. Feminist intervention encourages both women and men to share in the nurturant aspects of their lives and in providing economic resources.

8. The nature of the relationship between practitioner and client should approach equality as much as possible. Feminist practitioners do not view themselves as experts in resolving clients' problems but as catalysts whose role is helping clients empower themselves. Feminist practitioners try to eliminate dominant-submissive relationships. In regard to an egalitarian relationship, Van Den Bergh (1992) noted:

> Obviously, there is an innate power differential between practitioner and client because the former has expertise and training as an "authority." However, the feminist admonition is to avoid abusing that status; "abuse" in this sense might be, for example, taking all credit for client change, or using terminology and nomenclature that are difficult for the client to understand. (p. 104)

9. Many clients can benefit from learning to express themselves assertively. The steps in assertiveness training are described in Module 4. Because many women are socialized to be passive and nonassertive, they have difficulty expressing themselves assertively. Clients can be helped through individual and group counseling. Clients who learn to express themselves assertively will experience increased self-confidence and self-esteem. They will be better able to communicate their thoughts, feelings, and opinions. Also, learning to express oneself assertively is an important component of empowerment.

Many women feel considerable anger over being victimized by sex discrimination and gender stereotyping. Some of these women turn these feelings inward, resulting in depression. Assertiveness training can help these women recognize their right to be angry and also help them identify and practice constructive ways to express their anger (for example, expressing their anger assertively rather than aggressively).

Evaluation

Feminist therapy can be (and usually is) used in conjunction with other theoretical approaches. Therapists with a feminist perspective almost always have training in and use psychotherapeutic approaches such as behavior therapy, reality therapy, rational therapy, and transactional analysis. They also often use a number of specific treatment approaches such as assertiveness training, parent effectiveness training, mediation, meditation, sex therapy, and relaxation techniques.

Because feminist therapy is almost always used in conjunction with other approaches, it is extremely difficult to conduct evaluative studies that test its effectiveness.

Van Den Bergh and Cooper (1987) emphasized that the feminist perspective is consistent with the core values of social work practice, including equality, respect for individuals, and promotion of social and economic justice for populations-at-risk. They concluded that "a feminist social work practice is a viable way to accomplish the unique mission of social work to improve the quality of life by facilitating social change" (p. 617).

Most contemporary approaches to psychotherapy look for the causes of a client's problems inside the client (for example, internal conflicts, repressed feelings, and early childhood traumas), but the feminist perspective views a client's problems in terms of social work's emphasis on the person-in-environment, a systems approach and an ecological approach.

The feminist perspective has been helpful in identifying and conceptualizing numerous structural problems in our society. For example, feminists who practiced in the mental health field in the early 1970s began to view traditional psychotherapy as an agent of social control that maintained traditional sex roles by encouraging women to "adapt" (Van Den Bergh, 1992). Feminists assert that women need to be recognized as having the right to their reproductive capacities (including the right to choose to terminate a pregnancy); otherwise their lives will be largely controlled by the men who impregnate them as raising a child requires a commitment of at least two decades. Feminists have also drawn

CASE EXAMPLE

Marge Corcoran

Marge Corcoran came into therapy feeling hopeless and helpless. She indicated she had been mildly depressed for many years. She was brought up to believe that a marriage vow should never be broken, no matter how difficult the situation may become. Ms. Corcoran has a number of life scripts (a term from transactional analysis; see Module 3) associated with this view: (1) wives do the domestic tasks around the home, (2) wives have the main responsibility for raising children, (3) wives cover up for her husband's drinking, (4) God will reward her in the afterlife for her trials and tribulations in this present life, (5) wives can work outside the home to meet financial needs, and (6) wives should put up with the abuse that husbands dish out. Ms. Corcoran is now in her sixties and has been married for 34 years. She has raised three children and has worked as a nurse all the years of her marriage. Her husband is an alcoholic. He was a construction worker but has not worked for the past 19 years because he has cirrhosis and has had one stroke.

He continues to drink. Throughout their marriage, he has been verbally and physically abusive. She recently retired. The three children moved away from home several years ago and now have families of their own. The husband comes home drunk three or four times a week and is now incontinent. Ms. Corcoran is becoming increasingly frustrated, angry, and depressed about having to nurse her husband who continues to berate her. He has been in numerous alcoholic treatment programs, including Alcoholics Anonymous, but nothing has curbed his drinking. He now needs extensive health attention, currently provided by his wife. She does not want to place him in a nursing home because this expense would wipe out the money that she has worked so hard to save for retirement. She is at her wit's end.

The social worker, Nicole Felber, began by establishing rapport with Ms. Corcoran. She complimented Ms. Corcoran on a number of her strengths: raising three children, having a career in an important profession, being the main breadwinner, going to unbelievable lengths to try to make her marriage work, and doing most of the domestic tasks.

Then Ms. Felber began asking a number of probing questions.

Ms. Felber: Do you still love your husband?

Ms. Corcoran: No, not for many years.

Ms. Felber: Do you feel marriage entitles a husband to abuse his wife?

Ms. Corcoran: Certainly not.

Ms. Felber: Do you feel you have a right not to be abused?

Ms. Corcoran: Yes.

Ms. Felber: Then why are you continuing to live in an abusive relationship?

Ms. Corcoran: That's a good question. I don't have a good answer.

Ms. Felber: Are you feeling fulfilled and contented in your retirement?

Ms. Corcoran: No, not at all. My feelings are better described as being angry for having to take care of an abusive alcoholic. At times I am depressed and have a feeling of being trapped in a situation I can't get out of.

Ms. Felber: Are you really trapped?

Ms. Corcoran: Yes, I think so. I don't see any other options.

Ms. Felber: Are you aware there are other options?

Ms. Corcoran: No.

Ms. Felber explained that one option was divorce. Ms. Felber mentioned she was aware that Ms. Corcoran had a value that a marriage commitment was forever. Ms. Felber asked Ms. Corcoran to speculate what her life would be like if she continued to remain married to Mr. Corcoran. Ms. Corcoran rambled for a while and finally concluded that her husband's health would continue to deteriorate, her "living hell" of a life would only get worse, and her husband would eventually have to be placed in a nursing home, which

(continued)

CASE EXAMPLE
Marge Corcoran
(continued)

would deplete all her savings. She added that an even worse scenario would be her dying first from a stress-related illness.

Ms. Felber asked Ms. Corcoran to think about, until they next met, what her life might be like if she pursued getting a divorce. Ms. Felber added that as far as finances were concerned, the divorce laws in their state would require equal splitting of any assets. Ms. Corcoran replied, "Unreal—if I stay married, all my assets will probably go to paying for his care in a nursing home. If I get a divorce, he immediately gets half of the assets I acquired." Ms. Felber indicated that was a fairly accurate summary. Ms. Corcoran remarked that she might be judged harshly in the afterlife if she divorced her husband. Ms. Felber suggested she discuss this with her pastor (a Lutheran minister), whom she has known for years.

Ms. Corcoran came back the next week. She indicated that she had thought for hours about what life might be like if she sought a divorce. She said she had also talked to her minister, who had informed her that in his view God probably sees her as being a saint for all the abuse she has taken; that God is "all-good" and "all-knowing," and such a God would want her to have her remaining years be as enjoyable and contented as possible. She said she had made her decision to get a divorce last night when her husband came home intoxicated again and became verbally and physically abusive. She showed Ms. Felber a big bruise on her shoulder where he had hit her. Ms. Felber complimented her on making a responsible decision and asked if she had an attorney to process the divorce. Ms. Corcoran indicated she had contacted one earlier in the day.

Ms. Felber continued to see Ms. Corcoran biweekly for several months. She did secure a divorce, and Mr. Corcoran moved in with his brother, who lived alone. Ms. Corcoran became more active in her church and, at Ms. Felber's suggestions, she began doing volunteer work at a local shelter for battered women. Her sharing of the course of her domestic relationship has helped a number of women at the shelter decide to get out of their abusive relationships.

Counseling Skills at Work in Generalist Practice

This case example illustrates the social worker used the following roles that, as described in Chapter 1, are components of generalist social work practice: educating Ms. Corcoran to understand she needed to divorce her verbally and physically abusive husband, brokering Ms. Corcoran to do volunteer work at a local shelter for battered women, and helping Ms. Corcoran problem-solve her dilemmas.

attention to the sociopolitical forces that have led to an increase in the feminization of poverty in our society.

An extremely positive aspect of the feminist perspective is the view that all social workers have an obligation to identify inequalities in our social, economic, and political systems and then use macropractice techniques to confront these inequalities. According to Collins (1986):

> The social work profession must realize that feminism is more than a list of problems relevant to women. It is also much more than an effort to gain females an equal role in what feminists regard as an oppressive society. The social work profession needs to understand and incorporate feminist perspectives and theories—not solely as these pertain to the personal lives and problems as females as clients or as social workers—but as paradigmatic ways of understanding our patriarchal culture, its masculine ethos, and the inevitable conflict between it and what social workers and feminists want for humanity and society. (p. 214)

Sometimes feminist social workers involve clients in changing systems. Van Den Bergh (1992) noted:

> The social worker should model her concern for changed societal conditions that eliminate institutionalized inequalities by working on some social change projects, such as abortion rights, comparable worth, anti-apartheid activism, or environmental protection. Clients can be encouraged to engage in social activism themselves, as the experience of collective action can help to validate one's sense of self, personal worth, and power to change. However, judgment will have to be used as to whether this is appropriate, based on the

> client's current level of functioning and willingness to take risks. (p. 105)

Feminism is concerned with ending oppression and discrimination in our society and throughout the world.

The women's movement has and is continuing to bring about a gender-role revolution in our society. Men and women are more aware of the negative effects of gender-role distinctions. More women are entering the labor force. More women are involved in athletics. Women now pursue a number of professions and careers that previously were all male. Women are more assertive, and many seek equalitarian relationships with men. Men are also beginning to realize the negative effects of gender-role distinctions. They are gradually realizing that stereotypical "male" roles limit their opportunities in terms of emotional expression, interpersonal relationships, occupations, and domestic activities.

A limitation of the feminist perspective is that certain segments of society reject feminism. In this regard, Kirst-Ashman and Hull (1999) stated:

> Some people have extremely negative reactions to the word "feminism." The emotional barriers they forge and the resulting resistance they foster makes it very difficult even to approach the concept with them. Others consider feminism a radical ideology which emphasizes separatism and fanaticism. In other words, they think feminism involves the philosophy adopted by women who spurn men, resent past inequalities, and strive violently to overthrow male supremacists. Still, others think of feminism as an outmoded tradition that is no longer relevant. (p. 495)

Summary

Sexism, sexual discrimination, and gender-role stereotyping are serious problems. Additional contemporary issues for women include welfare reform, economic inequality and comparable worth, sexual harassment, sexist language, battered women, rape, and special counseling needs of women.

Women have been highly involved in the development of social work and social welfare programs. The feminist perspective on social work intervention has been developed by numerous authors.

Feminism is the philosophy of equality between women and men that involves both attitudes and actions, that infiltrates virtually all aspects of life, that often necessitates providing education and advocacy on behalf of women, and that appreciates the existence of individual differences and personal accomplishments of gender (Kirst-Ashman & Hull, 1999, p. 495).

Principles of feminist intervention in social work include the following. A client's problems should be viewed within a sociopolitical framework. Traditional sex roles are pathological, and clients need encouragement to free themselves from these gender-role bonds. Intervention should focus on client empowerment. Clients' self-esteem should be enhanced. Clients should be encouraged to develop their identity based on their strengths, attributes, qualities, and achievements. Clients need to value and develop social support systems with other women. Clients need to find a balance between work and personal relationships. The nature of the relationship between practitioner and client should approach equality as much as possible. Many clients can benefit from learning to express themselves assertively.

The feminist perspective to intervention is often used in conjunction with other intervention approaches. The feminist perspective is consistent with the core values of social work practice. An extremely positive aspect of this perspective is the view that all social workers have an obligation to identify inequalities in our social, economic, and political systems and then use macropractice techniques to confront them.

EXERCISES

1. THE FEMINIST PERSPECTIVE IN COUNSELING

Goal: To apply the feminist perspective to counseling.

Step 1: Break into groups of five and choose one of the following scenarios.

a. A woman discovers her partner has had three affairs since they began dating four years ago.
b. A woman is frequently verbally abused by her partner.
c. A wife is physically abused by an alcoholic husband; she feels she cannot leave him because she has three young children and is not employed outside the home.
d. A female employee is being sexually harassed by her male employer; for financial reasons, she needs to continue working.

Step 2: Take turns role-playing the feminist perspective in the scenario.

Step 3: Group critique of the role play.

Step 4: Class discussion on how to apply the feminist perspective to counseling.

2. SEXIST WORDS

Goal: To explore the pervasiveness and power of sexist language in our society. The words we use greatly affect our perception of reality. Sexist words are a significant factor in defining and maintaining the dominant position of males. Many English words reflect an aura of sexism. For instance, the following words and phrases can be considered to be sexist:

mankind	man and wife
chairman	he (when referring to someone who may be a male or a female)
salesman	man of God
congressman	man-made
policeman	
man-to-man	
best man for the job	

Yet a number of other words also have *man, men,* or *male* as a component.

female	manner	menstruate
human	mantle	menstruation
manage	mantra	mental
management	manual	mentality
manager	manufacture	mention
mandate	menarche	mentor
mandatory	menopause	menu
man hole	menorrhagia	woman
manicure	mense	women
manifest	menses	
manifold	menstrual	

Step 1: Class discussion of sexist words. Why do words that relate primarily to female biological functioning (menses, menstruation, and menopause) have "men" as a component?

Step 2: *(Optional)* Research some linguist texts for the origin of sexist words.

3. DOUBLE STANDARDS

Goal: To examine double standards in male and female interactions.

Step 1: Form groups of four to five students of male-only and female-only.

Step 2: Brainstorm and list double standards in dating relationships, marital relationships, and sexual behaviors. For example, society generally allows males to be more aggressive and to use more vulgar language; and males are expected to ask females for dates; but females traditionally have been raised to believe they should not ask males for dates. For each double standard, the group should decide whether the double standard is desirable or undesirable. (Males are separated from females in this exercise because they may have differing views about the desirability of the double standards that are identified.)

Step 3: Present your conclusions.

Step 4: Class discussion of the lists. Do any of these standards surprise you? How many double standards operate favorably for men? For women?

MODULE 8

Neuro-Linguistic Programming

Neuro-linguistic programming (NLP), developed by John Grinder, Richard Bandler, and several other authorities (Lankton, 1980), is a recently developed model of communication that promises to have substantial application in assessing human behavior, in developing rapport, in influencing others (in education, public speaking, and sales), and in changing behavior (psychotherapy).[1]

Practically all the psychotherapeutic treatment approaches we've examined were developed by psychiatrists and clinical psychologists. In contrast, NLP was developed primarily by specialists in communication and linguistics. The roots of NLP can be traced to Gregory Bateson, an anthropologist, who conducted a broad range of research projects, including studies in anthropology, psychiatry, and communication patterns among dolphins. Bateson synthesized cybernetic ideas with anthropology. *Cybernetics* is the science of communication and control theory; it focuses primarily on the comparative study of automatic control systems—such as comparing the human central nervous system with mechanical-electrical systems. Bateson investigated communication in hypnosis, ventriloquism, animal training, popular moving pictures, the nature of play, humor, schizophrenia, neurotic communication, psychotherapy, family systems, and family therapy.

In the 1970s Grinder and Bandler, specialists in communication and linguistics, studied the nonverbal and verbal communication patterns between prominent therapists and their clients. The therapists included Salvador Minuchin (Chapter 8), Virginia Satir (Chapter 8), and Milton Erickson (a leading practitioner of medical hypnosis, which is described in Module 9).

By observing the communication patterns of prominent psychotherapists and then detailing what they do, what cues they respond to, and how they go about helping clients, it was thought that others could learn how to use the same procedures and get similar results.

Numerous texts describe application of the NLP communication model to business, sales, education, and psychotherapy (Bandler & Grinder, 1975, 1976b, 1979, 1982; Haley, 1973; Laborde, 1984; Lankton, 1980). Primarily a model of communication, NLP does not provide a theory of personality development or of psychopathology.

NLP Defined

Neuro-linguistic programming is the study of the structure of subjective experience (Lankton, 1980, p. 13). It makes explicit patterns of behavior and change that we understood only intuitively. The term *neuro-linguistic programming* refers to the following:

neuro: nervous system through which experience is received and processed via the five senses
linguistic: language and nonverbal communication systems through which neural representations are coded, ordered, and given meaning
programming: ability to organize our communication and neurological systems to achieve specific desired outcomes

NLP is a model, not a theory of human behavior. A theory attempts to explain or interpret why things relate as they do. A model, in contrast, is a copy or pattern of already existing phenomena, which, as de-

[1]Material in this chapter is adapted from Charles Zastrow, Virginia Dotson, and Michael Koch, "The Neuro-Linguistic Programming Treatment Approach," *Journal of Independent Social Work,* 1 (Fall 1986), pp. 29–38. Permission to adapt this material was received from The Haworth Press, Inc.

CASE EXAMPLE

Sensory Representational Systems

A married couple sought counseling because their sexual relationship was deteriorating. After rapport had been established, the counselor asked each, "What turns you on sexually?" The husband mentioned hearing romantic things said to him, whereas the wife mentioned being softly touched in a variety of areas. Not too surprisingly, the husband was trying to excite his wife by saying romantic things (without touching her much), and the wife was seeking to excite her husband by touching him while remaining silent. A simple description of the importance of "joining" with the other's representational system greatly enhanced their love life.

signed, can be imitated or re-created. A model deals only with what can be observed. For example, a theory of what causes psychotherapeutic changes seeks to specify key variables that lead to positive changes. A model, in contrast, focuses on formulating a framework. The framework described by NLP represents verbal and nonverbal communication between people. Factors specified in the framework determine the kinds of verbal and nonverbal messages from a therapist that lead to improved or desired responses from clients.

Representational Systems

Before reading further, take a few minutes to identify what you remember most about the following:

The last grocery store you were in.
What you did on your last birthday.
Your high school days.
Your most enjoyable sexual experience.
Your most enjoyable vacation.

Everyone has, at most, five sensory systems through which we connect with physical reality: the eyes (visual), ears (auditory), skin (kinesthetic), nose (smell), and tongue (taste). For each situation, your memories involved only one or two senses. Perhaps you recalled an *image* of fresh fruits and vegetables, or *heard* the hustle and bustle of the activity, or *smelled* the fresh flowers.

Whenever we interact with the external world, we do so through sensory representations. Your sensory connection with a grocery store is apt to be quite different from your friend's. The same applies for everyone. Your most enjoyable sexual experience may be a visual one; your partner's may be auditory or kinesthetic.

We operate out of our sensory representations of the world, and not in "reality" itself. Our sensory representations provide us with a *map* of the territory. But the map is *not* the territory.

According to NLP, to assess another's actions accurately, it is important to identify the sensory representational system used by that person. If we are able to identify the other's representational system and "join with" that system in our interactions with the person, communication is apt to flow much more smoothly and rapport is enhanced. Conversely, if two people are unable to "join" together with the same representational system, communication may be tangential, and rapport will be adversely affected. The implications of this point are immense. Successful salespersons, educators, and therapists identify and "join" with the representational systems of the people they seek to influence. Once a person (customer, student, or client) has joined with the influencer, the influencer is able to lead the person in the direction she or he chooses. To a large extent the process of therapy, education, and sales can be defined as involving two steps: (1) the influencer's finding a way to join with the person to be influenced, and (2) the influencer then leading the person in a new (and, one hopes, positive) direction. It is intriguing to note that there are some remarkable similarities between social workers and salespeople (see CTRM Exhibit 8.1).

There are several ways for an influencer to join with the person to be influenced. These include (1) joining with the person's representational system, (2) talking knowledgeably with them about subjects that interest them, and (3) mirroring (without their being consciously aware of the mirroring) their nonverbal communication—such as posture, gestures, and breathing patterns.

Representational System Predicates

The adverbs, adjectives, and verbs we use reveal the sensory system we are most conscious of at that point in time. NLP calls these words *predicates*.

CTRM Exhibit 8.1

Social workers and salesworkers: Similarities and differences

The essential characteristics of competent social workers and successful salesworkers are strikingly similar. I am aware that some social work purists will find it degrading to compare the characteristics of social workers (who seek to empower people to achieve self-fulfillment and social well-being) to the characteristics of salesworkers (who are viewed as being guided primarily to sell more for personal financial gain). In response to such criticism, I urge that such purists reflect on the similarities and differences between these two endeavors. Note that social workers frequently need to "sell" themselves and the services they provide (Lankton, 1980). It appears that competent social workers possess extensive selling skills.

Contrasting Goals of Sales and Social Work

The goals of salesworkers and social workers differ substantially. Salesworkers sell products and services. Successful ones receive high salaries and substantial commissions. Social workers are "change agents"—helpers employed specifically to create planned change. As change agents, social workers are expected to be skilled at working with individuals, groups, organizations, and families to bring about community changes.

Capacity to Influence

In spite of the differences in goals, successful social workers and salesworkers share a key characteristic: they have the capacity to influence others.

Steps in Influencing

According to NLP, the first step in influencing someone involves establishing rapport.

A number of guidelines have been developed for social workers to use in establishing rapport with clients. Social workers should:

- Seek to establish a nonthreatening, comfortable atmosphere in which clients feel safe to communicate their needs or wants while feeling accepted as a person.
- Observe nonverbal and verbal communication closely to identify better the client's needs and wants.
- "Sell" themselves in initial contacts—not arrogantly but as a knowledgeable, understanding person who may be able to help and who seeks to find ways to meet the client's needs or wants.
- Not laugh or express shock when clients talk about their needs or wants. Emotional outbursts, even if subtle, will lead clients to believe the social worker is not going to understand their problems.
- Generally be nonjudgmental, not moralistic; show respect for the client's values and should not try to sell his or her values to the client.
- Engage in small talk with the client. Such informal conversation sometimes provides information to the social worker about the needs and wants of the client.
- Not seek to establish a superior-inferior relationship with the client. Instead, the social worker should convey that the client is a worthy, "equal" person in the relationship. If the client feels he or she is being treated as an inferior, he or she will be less motivated to reveal wants and needs.
- Generally not use high-pressure techniques designed to force clients to choose an option they may not want. Instead, the social worker should make a variety of options available, help clients assess the merits and shortcomings of each option, and convey that clients have the right and responsibility to make their own decisions.
- Use a "shared vocabulary" with clients. This does not mean that the social worker should use the same slang words and the same accent. If clients perceive the social worker's speech as artificial, they may be seriously offended. The social worker should use words that clients readily understand and that are not offensive.
- Convey through tone of voice and nonverbal communication that the social worker empathetically understands the clients' wants and needs and cares about their feelings.
- Convey that clients are important, worthwhile people.
- Have good listening skills.

Note that salesworkers also need to "join with" customers. It is interesting that guidelines for establishing rapport with sales customers are remarkably similar to those guidelines for social workers and their clients.

Social workers must be skilled at working with individuals, groups, families, organizations, and communities. They function as counselors, brokers, advocates, and consultants. They work with administrators, public officials, board members of funding sources, and helping professionals at other agencies. In practically all this work, bringing about positive change requires that the social workers establish rapport and then seek to lead people in a new direction.

Differences Between Social Workers and Salesworkers

It would be a serious mistake, however, to conclude that because of these similarities social workers can also be viewed as salesworkers. There are substantial differences between social workers and salesworkers:

- Social workers have the responsibility of helping people find ways to meet their social, financial, recreational, and health needs. Salesworkers sell products and services. Salesworkers are guided by profit motives.
- Social workers receive substantially more training in human behavior, intervention techniques, research, social policy, social problems, and social services. Salesworkers re-

ceive more training in product knowledge and sales techniques. Certain sales techniques are practically never used by social workers, such as lavishly entertaining clients.

- One of the highest rewards and satisfactions in social work comes from seeing people grow and develop. A major reward for salesworkers is to sell more and earn more money.
- Laborde (1984), in *Influencing with Integrity,* made an important distinction between "influencing with integrity" and manipulating. In manipulating, the influencer leads a person in a direction that is in the influencer's self-interest. "Influencing with integrity" involves leading influences in directions in their best interests. Salesworkers by definition seek to influence customers in the salesworker's self-interests (that is, they seek to sell products from which they benefit financially). Social workers have a strong ethical obligation to influence with integrity.
- Social workers focus on helping clients assess and identify their personal, social, emotional, health, and financial needs. Once such needs are identified, social workers then help clients explore alternatives for meeting these needs. Salesworkers rarely assess and identify their clients' social-emotional needs. Their focus is on identifying the customers' purchase desires and to stimulate purchase desires in customers.
- The focus of the relationship between social workers and clients is to create a nonthreatening atmosphere in which clients can communicate their personal concerns, some of which are highly charged emotionally. In a salesworker-customer relationship, customers share purchase desires, not highly charged personal concerns.

Why is it important to compare the nature of social work and saleswork? In order to emphasize that in establishing relationships with clients social workers must nonarrogantly "sell" themselves as warm, caring people who have expertise and who may be able to assist clients with their difficulties. In the process of establishing a relationship, social workers need to present themselves in ways that are remarkably similar to how successful salesworkers present themselves to customers.

Social workers have an ethical obligation to influence clients with integrity rather than for personal gain. Some of you may dislike viewing social workers as influencers and indeed may even assert that clients have a right to self-determination and that we therefore should not seek to influence them.

In reality, social workers *must* seek to influence clients in constructive directions. Conceptualizing social workers as influencers is *not* inconsistent with clients' rights to self-determination. Of course, clients retain the right to express their opinions, and to make their own decisions. Social workers act as influencers by using a problem-solving process. The steps in this process include helping clients:

1. Identify their problems and needs
2. Identify alternatives for meeting these difficulties and needs
3. Assess the merits and shortcomings of these alternatives
4. Select and implement one or more of these alternatives
5. Evaluate outcomes after the strategies have been implemented for a reasonable length of time

Source: This material is adapted from Charles Zastrow, "Social Workers and Salesworkers: Similarities and Differences," *Journal of Independent Social Work,* 4, no. 3, 1990, pp. 7–16.

In our culture people primarily use the visual, auditory, and kinesthetic (touch) systems. (A few other cultures place greater emphasis on smell and taste.) Unless the listener is aware of the sensory representational system the speaker is using, the listener may misinterpret what the speaker is intending. For example, when a client says "I understand you," the intended message depends on the representational system he or she is in:

Visual: "That looks really good to me."
Auditory: "I hear you clearly."
Kinesthetic: "What you are saying feels right to me."

In the course of growing up, people learn to favor particular representational systems for particular events. We are not only visual or auditory or kinesthetic. The sense in use depends on the situation, the context. It appears, though, that we tend to have a primary mode, in that we use more of one mode (Laborde, 1984, p. 57).

CTRM Exhibit 8.2 identifies a number of visual, auditory, and kinesthetic "predicates." Mismatched predicates interfere with communication and rapport, as indicated by the following example:

Client: I *feel* so awful! The IRS has just audited me, and I just can't *handle* it!

Counselor: I *hear* you. It *sounds bad, but tell* me what it is that's so bad.

Client: I just can't *lift* this *feeling.* It's so *heavy!*

Counselor: Yes, but I don't *hear* what the problem is. *Listen* to me, and *tell* me what's so bad!

CTRM EXHIBIT 8.2

Predicates to identify sensory representational systems

Visual	*Auditory*	*Kinesthetic*
Appear	Audible	Back away
Clear	Buzz	Break down
Colors	Double talk	Bounce
Farsighted	Earshot	Caress
Foresee	Echo	Catch
Glance	Hear	Cold
Hindsight	Hear from	Dig in
Horizon	In tune with	Feel
Illustrate	Listen	Firm
Image	Loud	Grasp
In the dark	Muffled	Handle
Look	Noisy	Hard
Observe	Pronounced	Hold
Overview	Quiet	Iron out
Picture	Resound	Press
Resemble	Rings a bell	Rack your brains
Scan	Roar	Run through
See	Rumbling	Sensitive
Show	Screech	Sensuous
Tint	Sound	Stumble upon
Vague	Sound off	Toss around
Vision	Thundering	Touch
Watch	Whispering	Vibes

This client may end up viewing the counselor as insensitive. Now let's match predicates:

Client: I *feel* so awful! The IRS has just audited me and I just can't *handle* it!

Counselor: You *feel* as if you're *breaking down* because of the *heaviness* of the audit.

Client: That's exactly it. I'm *stumbling*, but yet *grasping to hold on*.

Counselor: What do you *feel* you need to *hold* on?

Client: *Support* and understanding from my wife, my tax accountant, and you.

Note that the counselor phrases her responses to be consistent with the client's representational system; this leads to better understanding and increased trust and rapport.

Eye-Accessing Cues

Eye-accessing cues is another reliable way to determine which representational system is dominant at a given time. Note the cues displayed in CTRM Figure 8.1. As always with rules, there are exceptions: For example, left-handers' kinesthetic representation system often has eyes down and to the left, with eyes down and to the right their auditory representational system. To test this information, ask your friends or acquaintances questions such as "What do you remember most about your last vacation?" and observe whether their eye-accessing cues are consistent with visual, kinesthetic, or auditory responses.

A simple example illustrates the importance of recognizing eye-accessing cues. In our society, when parents scold their children, they often become additionally angry when the children look down. Such parents erroneously assume their children are ignoring what they are saying. They may even yell, "Look at me when I'm talking to you!" In actuality, the eyes being down signals that the children feel bad about their misbehavior.

The Four-Tuple

The four-tuple represents a person's sensory experience at a moment in time. (A *tuple* is a set of elements, which in this instance consists of sensory channels.) Its general form is V, K, A, O. These capital letters are abbreviations for the major sensory channels: Visual, Kinesthetic, Auditory, and Olfactory/ Gustatory.

It is also useful to distinguish between experiences that are internally generated (remembering or imagining a visual image, feeling, sound, or smell) and those that are externally generated (sights, sensations, sounds, or smells from the external world). Therefore, the superscript *e* refers to external cues and the superscript *i* to internal cues. The experience of someone whose senses are fully turned outward is V^e, K^e, A^e, O^e. Someone attending fully to an internal event, oblivious of the immediate surroundings, is V^i, K^i, A^i, O^i.

Most of us, at any point in time, are generally in a mixed state in which some of our senses are outwardly attending and some of our experiences are remembered or imagined. Also, one or more of the sensory systems may not be in use. The following example shows how this notational system is used. Whenever Mrs. Worth *hears* about the Christmas season, she *visualizes* being

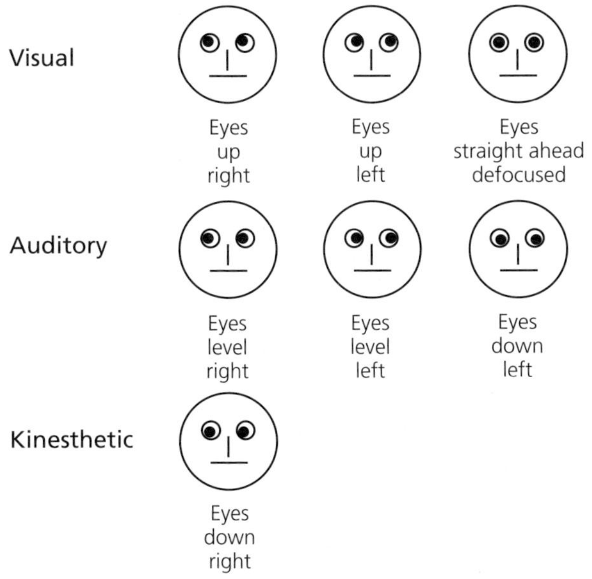

CTRM FIGURE 8.1 Eye-accessing cues

at her husband's funeral several years ago, two days before Christmas day. (He was killed in an automobile accident.) She remembers how depressed she *felt* afterward. These cues in sequence are: A^e, V^i, K^i.

The usefulness of this concept can be readily demonstrated. Think about the last time you said something to someone and received an unusual response. Undoubtedly what happened was that your intended message led the listener to remember auditory, visual, kinesthetic, or olfactory events from the past, which then led them to respond primarily in terms of the internal cues. NLP makes an important point: *The meaning of a communication is the response it elicits, regardless of the intent.*

In therapy an NLP counselor frequently seeks to identify the patterns of destructive or disturbing thought processes, and then seeks directly or indirectly to change their patterns. Two techniques used in this process are metaphors and reframing.

Causing Change by Communicating in Metaphor

NLP uses the term *metaphor* to refer to the use of anecdotes, puns, analogies, and stories in therapy. Metaphors are particularly useful for clients who tend to resist direct suggestions. Metaphors also stimulate the interest of clients. One of the most recognized experts in the use of metaphors was Dr. Milton Erickson, a psychiatrist. (Grinder and Bandler studied Erickson's techniques extensively while developing the NLP approach.)

Haley (1973) provided the following example of Erickson's use of metaphors in working with a married couple who are embarrassed about discussing directly a conflict over their sexual relationship.

> He will choose some aspect of their lives that is analogous to sexual relations and change that as a way of changing the sexual behavior. He might, for example, talk to them about having dinner together and draw them out on their preferences. He will discuss with them how the wife likes appetizers before dinner, while the husband prefers to dive right into the meat and potatoes. Or the wife might prefer a quiet and leisurely dinner, while the husband, who is quick and direct, just wants the meal over with. . . . He might end such a conversation with a directive that the couple arrange a pleasant dinner on a particular evening that is satisfactory to both of them. When successful, this approach shifts the couple from a more pleasant dinner to more pleasant sexual relations without their being aware that he has deliberately set this goal. (pp. 27–28)

I have used storytelling (with some real and others contrived to fit the clients' circumstances) with a variety of clients. Here is an example. A male college student was thinking of taking his life because his woman friend had left him to date someone else, he was not receiving the grades he desired, and he did not know what he wanted to major in. I asked him to visualize the following scene.

> Let's assume you slit your wrists this evening and no one discovers you until you're dead. There will be blood all over. Tomorrow morning your younger brother or someone else will discover you in this pool of blood. For months and years afterward, this person will have nightmares about this scene. Eventually he may seek to end his nightmares in the same way you did—that happens! After they find you, a funeral director will be called, and he will embalm you, which involves a variety of unpleasant procedures. Your parents will be shocked and will forevermore be searching for why you did what you did—and feeling guilty that they had failed you. Your former woman friend will be temporarily shocked, but she will experience a sense of relief that you will no longer be able to manipulate her by threatening suicide. She'll move on with her life and eventually marry

someone else. People will come to your funeral and say a variety of things, including the statement that you didn't have the courage to face life's problems. In this funeral scene of mental anguish and confusion, the cover of the coffin will then be closed. You will be taken to the cemetery. Perhaps it's raining and chilly. You will be lowered into the ground, and slowly your body will deteriorate. If there is an air leak in the coffin, you will deteriorate much faster—perhaps worms may enter. Is this what you want?

Most people contemplating suicide think only about the pain and difficulties they are facing. The preceding story helps them see that what happens after suicide may be worse than their present agony. In this case the male student stopped thinking about taking his life and started focusing on resolving the problems he faced.

For a 21-year-old woman who was dating a married man (the married man refused to come into counseling), I vividly told a detailed story about another client who had a miserable life for seven years while dating a married man; that man refused to leave his wife for financial reasons and because he did not want to disappoint his children. This story helped the woman give her male friend an ultimatum—either you leave your wife in 30 days or our relationship is over. In this case the man refused to leave his wife and the woman ended the relationship.

For a 15-year-old adolescent female who thought her life would improve if she became pregnant and then had a child who would love her, I arranged for a single working mother (in her twenties) to talk about the following: young children *take* love and affection and *give* very little in return; the financial costs of raising a child are enormous; and being a mother is a full-time job that interferes with dating, partying, forming a relationship with a male, and developing a career. After this talk, the 15-year-old decided to wait for several years before wanting to again try to become a parent.

Reframing

Reframing involves turning clients' negative behavior, thoughts, and feelings into resources. The function of the problem part is simply altered for the clients' benefit to get them what they want more effectively. (See the case example on reframing.)

NLP asserts that it is enduringly useful to presuppose a positive intent behind all behavior. The focus of reframing is to separate the positive *intent* from the negative *behavior* so that the positive intent then becomes linked to new positive behavior.

According to NLP "The cure lies within" the client. Clients already have the resources they need to resolve their difficulties. Clients in problematic situations are generally making undesirable choices. Reframing helps clients make more constructive choices. (Reframing is also described in Module 4.)

Therapeutic Change Often Occurs Without Knowing the Cause of the Problem

Counselors who use traditional psychotherapeutic approaches spend considerable time trying to assess the causes of the problematic behavior. NLP asserts that positive changes can occur without intense attention being directed at the causes. Instead, the focus is on first identifying what clients want and then on helping them identify the ways and the resources they already have to achieve these goals. Here is an example:

A college student walked into my office at the start of spring semester. She stated she was very depressed, and her slumped posture, downcast eyes, and sad facial expressions verified this assessment. She started rambling on about how she had received a speeding ticket over vacation and that she was also sad about seeing a former male friend dating someone else.

The following transactions then occurred:

Counselor: Can you now do anything constructive about these two situations?

Client: No.

Counselor: Do you realize that dwelling on them will only make you more depressed?

Client: Yes.

Counselor: We need instead to focus on what you now want. Do you know what you now want?

Client: Yes, to be happy and face this semester with an optimistic outlook.

Counselor: Good, now we're getting someplace. Tell me about some of the things you could do in the next few hours that are enjoyable for you and that will also get your mind off upsetting things that you can't change.

CASE EXAMPLE

Reframing

A 28-year-old woman was in treatment because she wanted her husband to stop drinking so much. She indicated that one or two nights a week her husband stopped off at a bar with other construction workers. She added that he was usually 2 or 3 hours late for dinner and quite intoxicated when he arrived home. She would then often chastise him for being late, for spending their scarce money on alcohol, and for ruining her evening by his "foolish talk." The husband often reacted by calling her names and verbally abusing her in other ways. The wife added that there were generally problems in the marriage only when her husband was drinking. She also stated that her husband denies he has a drinking problem and refuses to join her in counseling. The counselor reframed the positive intent of her behavior in the following manner:

> It appears that both you and your husband get along well except when he's been drinking. When he comes home drunk, you definitely want to make the best of the situation. Up until now, your wanting to do so has led you to respond by verbally getting on his case for drinking. At that point he probably feels a need to defend himself, and a "blow-up" occurs. Since you want to avoid the heated exchanges with him when he's drunk, I'm wondering if there aren't other actions you can take—such as taking a walk by yourself, going shopping, or going to visit someone when he is intoxicated?

The wife thought about this and concluded that such suggestions might well work. A month later she reported that the strategy of leaving home when her husband came home intoxicated was working well. Since she realized she did not have the capacity to stop her husband from drinking, she stated that reducing the difficulties the drinking created was her next best choice.

The client at this point began talking about a variety of things she could do—taking a walk, calling some friends to get together for lunch, and listening to her stereo. The more she talked about these things, the more relaxed she became. After about 10 more minutes of talking, she smiled, said good-bye, and proceeded to get involved in her enjoyable activities.

Evaluation

Neuro-linguistic programming is rich in new concepts. Those described here are some of the more prominent NLP principles but are only a small subset of the tenets of NLP. The interested reader is encouraged to read further in texts (such as those referenced in this module) and attend NLP training institutes (such institutes exist in various regions of the country).

Studying the verbal and nonverbal communication patterns between prominent therapists and their clients to identify what causes positive changes has considerable merit. NLP includes numerous concepts that help in explaining how a person (therapist, teacher, salesperson, public speaker) can influence another.

The concepts advanced by NLP have considerable power in helping influencers to influence more effectively. There are also criticisms that can be made about NLP:

1. Little research has been conducted on NLP to test its principles and concepts.
2. NLP is not a theory of human behavior, and therefore does not have concepts that can be used independently to assess the causes of emotional and behavioral difficulties. The principles and concepts of NLP are perhaps best viewed as being useful adjuncts to other theories in assessing and changing human behavior.
3. A stated NLP goal is to identify key change agents that result in positive changes for clients undergoing therapy. NLP includes a number of concepts in this area, including the therapist's finding a way to "join" with the client and then "leading" the client in a positive direction. "Joining" and "leading" may well be essential components in the process of influencing. However, I question whether "joining" and "leading" are the key psychotherapeutic change agents for treating emotional and behavioral problems. (Module 6 presents an alternative explanation, which asserts that restructuring thinking patterns is the key psychotherapeutic change agent.) With its focus on only what is

observable, NLP largely ignores thinking patterns—and thereby may fail to focus on a key component in change (see Module 6 for an elaboration).

Summary

NLP is a model of communication that has substantial application in assessing human behavior, in influencing others (in education, sales, and public speaking), and in psychotherapy. NLP is the study of the structure of subjective experience. It makes explicit patterns of behavior and change that have previously been only intuitively understandable. NLP has advanced a number of concepts and techniques that are useful in assessment, building rapport, and treating clients. These concepts and techniques include sensory representational systems; the map is not the territory; joining with the client's representational system builds rapport; influencing someone involves the influencer joining and then leading the influencee; predicates identify representational systems; eye-accessing cues; four-tuples; using metaphors in counseling; reframing; and therapeutic change often occurs without knowing the cause of the problem. The principles and concepts of NLP appear to be useful ideas that can be used as adjuncts to other theories in assessing and treating emotional difficulties and dysfunctional behavior.

EXERCISES

1. *EYE-ACCESSING CUES*

Goal: To demonstrate that visual, auditory, and kinesthetic representational systems can be identified by eye-accessing cues.

Step 1: Break into groups of ten. Have two volunteers in each group step outside for 10 minutes.

Step 2: While volunteers are gone, review the eye positions of CTRM Figure 8.1.

Step 3: Volunteers return and are asked to *think* about, but not respond to, the following questions. What do you remember most about

a. the last grocery store you were in?
b. what you did on your last birthday?
c. the last time you were really angry?
d. what you did on New Year's Eve?
e. your most romantic experience?

Record eye positions as volunteers think about each question. (It is permissible to record two or more positions.)

Step 4: For each identifiable eye position, ask the volunteers whether they experienced the accompanying representation system as they considered the question, for example:

a. Visual eye position—Did you have a visual image or picture of your answer to question ____?
b. Auditory—Did you hear some sounds in your answer to questions ____?
c. Kinesthetic—Did you have a feeling experience in your answer to question ____?

Step 5: Record how many eye position cues signaled the correct internal thinking process.

2. *JOINING*

Goal: To learn to build better rapport with strangers (and future clients).

Step 1: Start conversations with three people you don't know very well. Try to use predicates during these conversations that are consistent with the strangers' representational systems and to mirror their gestures, posture, and breathing patterns in a nonnoticeable manner.

Step 2: Class discussion of student result. Did you have difficulty using predicates that were consistent with the strangers' representational systems? Did you have difficulty mirroring behavior? Are these techniques useful in building rapport?

MODULE 9

Prominent Specific Treatment Techniques

Earlier modules presented treatment techniques that are components of comprehensive theories of psychotherapy. This module summarizes a variety of other treatment techniques that are used to treat clients. Because these treatment approaches were developed independently of a comprehensive theory of psychotherapy, we'll call them *specific treatment approaches.*

This module covers milieu therapy, psychodrama, play therapy, parental education, crisis intervention, task-centered practice, solution-focused therapy, meditation, relaxation, deep breathing and imagery, mediation, hypnosis, and biofeedback. Social workers have used crisis intervention, milieu therapy, play therapy, parental education, and psychodrama for many years. Mediation is a technique that has existed for some time, but only a few social workers used the technique until recently. The approach is being used increasingly to help resolve conflicts between two or more people. Relaxation approaches, meditation, hypnosis, and biofeedback have been around for a long time but have been used infrequently by social workers. With the recognition that stress (and resulting stress-related illnesses) is our nation's number one health problem (Seaward, 1994), there has been a rising interest in training social workers to use these approaches.

Milieu Therapy

In milieu therapy a learning/ living environment is created that systematically uses the events that occur in day-to-day living as formats for treating emotional and behavior problems. The idea is that our environment has an immense impact on our behavior and can therefore be structured to change deviant behavior and antisocial norms and values.

There are several models of milieu treatment. Milieu programs have been based on a wide variety of intervention approaches, including reality therapy, behavior therapy, rational therapy, client-centered therapy, and psychoanalysis. Some milieu programs emphasize individual therapy as part of the milieu; others emphasize changing behavioral and emotional problems in a group context. A token economy (described in Module 4) is a milieu treatment program. Milieu programs typically use a team of professional staff members that may include social workers, psychiatrists, psychologists, special education teachers, occupational and physical therapists, and psychiatric nurses.

Although the components of milieu programs vary widely, there are some common focuses. Programs stress being democratic, permissive, and humanistic, and having reality-oriented living experiences. Milieu programs assume that lasting changes are more likely to take place through group interactional experiences. The community (including the professional staff, nonprofessional staff, and residents) meets and interacts regularly, often discussing common problems. An underlying philosophy is that personal problems primarily involve faulty interactions with others and that examining these difficulties through discussion can lead to understanding and resolution. Usually the traditional pyramid of authority is flattened in milieu programs, staff roles and ways of functioning are frequently reevaluated (Black, 1977).

Milieu programs have been used with a variety of client populations, including juvenile delinquents, persons with mental illness, children and adults with cognitive disabilities, the elderly, alcoholics and drug abusers, emotionally disturbed children, and correctional clients. These programs have been used in mental hospitals, day hospitals for the emotionally disturbed, halfway houses, residential treatment centers, day-care programs for disturbed children, nursing homes, group homes, correctional institutions, therapeutic communities for alcohol and drug abusers, and sheltered workshops.

The therapeutic community is one of the treatment programs that is often selected in treating drug addiction in this country. The theory is that drug addiction is a form of behavior that is encouraged by a particular subculture and that therapeutic communities can provide group support to help people give up the drug subculture and also pressure them to replace previous norms and values with those acceptable to the general society.

Psychodrama

The primary developer of psychodrama was J. L. Moreno (1946). Its objective is to assist a client or client group to overcome personal problems through role-playing, drama, or action therapy. Through these media, clients are helped to express feelings of conflict, anger, aggression, guilt, and sadness. Moreno thought, as did Freud, that the expression of pent-up emotions has a cathartic effect (eliminates emotional complexes by bringing them to consciousness and allowing the emotional energy to be expressed). Role playing is a direct outgrowth of psychodrama (Blatner, 1995).

Moreno also thought psychodrama is therapeutic because people who want to change maladaptive behavior are presented with feedback about their behavior and allowed to try out and practice new behaviors. Psychodramas can be arranged to have other people model alternative behaviors and then to have clients practice new behaviors in a particular sequence to ensure success. Thus, clients can practice new behaviors in small bits until they incorporate them into their repertoire and gain mastery through practice.

Psychodrama is a group therapy approach. Whittaker (1974) provided a brief description of psychodrama:

> Psychodrama uses four major instruments: the stage, which is both the psychological and physical living space for the subject or client; the director, or worker; the staff of "auxiliary egos," or therapeutic aides; and the audience. Both the auxiliary egos and the audience are made up of other group members. The strategy is to enable the subject to project himself into his own world and draw responses from fellow group members. Below are several commonly used techniques:
>
> 1. Self-presentation. The client presents himself or a figure who is significant in his life.
> 2. Direct soliloquy. The client steps out of the drama and speaks to herself or to the group.
> 3. Double technique. An auxiliary ego acts with the client and does everything the client does and at the same time.
> 4. Mirror technique. An auxiliary ego acts in place of the client as clearly as he can. The client watches from the audience to see himself as others see him.
> 5. Role reversal. The client assumes the role of her antagonist and an auxiliary ego plays the client's part. (p. 230)

The director or worker functions as the producer and as the therapist. As the producer, the social worker selects and arranges the scenes and also directs the psychodrama action. The scenes are selected to reflect the client's problem—which is apt to be an emotionally charged situation for clients or one in which they behave ineffectively or inappropriately. As the therapist, the worker provides the actors with support and clarification; at times the worker makes interpretations (often with the help of the other group members) of the play action.

Psychodrama is presently used by practitioners who subscribe to a variety of psychotherapeutic theories. Psychodrama has been used in marital therapy, with children, with drug and alcohol abusers, with people having emotional problems, in prison settings, to train psychiatric residents, to train people with physical and mental impairments, in business and industry, and in education and decision making. Fine (1979) noted:

> We have all had experience with psychodrama. As children, one way we tested and mastered the world was to play roles. Lori put a coronet in her hair and became a queen and her girlfriend became her lady-in-waiting. Gary built satellites and took elaborate interstellar space explorations in his room. Children's play is an enactment of their fantasies in which they practice the social roles of their culture. The action and enacting world of the child is full of energy, excitement, and social learning. . . .
>
> Modern psychodrama is an extension of life in which catharsis and insight are available not only to the audience but to the players as well. (p. 487)

Barocas (1972) used psychodrama to train police officers to handle family crises more effectively. Domestic fights are a serious hazard for police officers; the "family disturbance call" is now the single most frequent source of officer injury and death. Barocas hired trained actors and actresses to perform skits developed from actual family fights reported by police officers. Actors developed the basic fight, and the police officer trainees practiced interventions. The skits were videotaped and other police officer trainees observed the intervention approach, which was then discussed in a group. The trainees who role-played were also shown the videotape, and their performance was then critiqued further. Barocas concluded that this approach was effective in improving how police officers handled family disputes.

Play Therapy

Play therapy is used with young children. Play is seen as a young child's most natural vehicle for self-expression and is therefore viewed by play therapists as a method for relating to, and communicating with, young children. Play therapy serves many purposes: making a diagnosis, forming a relationship, ventilating feelings, working through unwanted emotions, teaching desired new behaviors, or modeling alternative behavior.

Play therapists vary on a continuum from almost totally nondirective to highly directive. Play therapy is used by therapists with widely diverging orientations, including psychoanalysis, client-centered therapy, reality therapy, rational therapy, transactional analysis, and behavior therapy.

Whittaker (1974) described play therapy as follows:

> The therapist may use initial play sessions for diagnostic purposes to observe such things as relationship, attention span, areas of preoccupation, areas of inhibition, direction of aggression, wishes and fantasies, and self-perception. Depending upon orientation, the therapist typically encourages free play with a variety of available materials (paints, dolls, punching bags, puzzles, clay), interprets the child's affect to him ("You seem to be angry at the doll"), and finally offers insights into the child's behavior. The child may experience some regression to earlier levels of functioning while in the play situation and also may practice newly acquired skills and try on new behaviors. A central notion of play therapy is that the child is expressing symbolically through play the conflicts he is experiencing in the outside world. In the relative safety of the play situation, these conflicts can be worked through and—so the theory goes—transferred to the child's real-life situation. (pp. 225–226)

Play therapy generally takes place in a playroom, with only the child and the therapist present. At times other children are present, which helps the child learn to interact more effectively with others. Occasionally parents attend the play therapy sessions, which helps them better understand their child and learn more effective interaction approaches with their child. Play materials include such items as dolls (usually composing a doll family), puppets, clay and finger paints, crayons, a sandbox, toy animals, soldiers and weapons, and cutting-out materials. In play therapy children are generally allowed to express themselves as freely as they desire. Usually minimal limits are set: establishing the duration of the play sessions, forbidding the willful destruction of play materials, and forbidding the child from physically attacking others in the playroom.

In recent years a number of protective services programs have used anatomically correct dolls to gather information from young children who are suspected victims of sexual abuse. A worker first forms a relationship with a child and then asks the child to show, with the dolls, what the alleged perpetrator did. In some jurisdictions this process is videotaped and is available for court use if formal charges are brought against the alleged perpetrator.

Parental Education: Parent Effectiveness Training

The primary goal of parental education programs is to help parents understand child behavior and develop child-rearing skills. Most programs are based on the assumption that rearing children is a difficult and complex task for which society ill prepares young people. A number of theoreticians have developed somewhat different educational programs: Dreikurs (1964), Ginott (1965), Gordon (1970), Patterson (1971), and Spock (1957). These programs use a variety of educational formats: short courses, small discussion groups, and programmed self-instruction.

CASE EXAMPLE

Play Therapy

Dawn, age 7, was a second-grader who was referred by her teacher to a school social worker. Academically and socially she was functioning far behind her peers, even though tests showed she was of normal intelligence. The social worker observed her in her play interactions with peers. She was withdrawn and tried to avoid competitive game situations. Forced to participate, she would quit whenever she fell behind. When the social worker discussed Dawn's behavior with her teacher, the teacher indicated that Dawn shied away from doing her assignments and seldom completed any. Dawn was observed for a few sessions in a playroom at school. At one point Dawn held the mother doll and called the baby girl "stupid" and stated, "You'll never be able to do what your brother does." The social worker felt that Dawn's academic and social problems were resulting from Dawn's having such a low self-concept that she had virtually given up trying. Dawn's interactions with the dolls suggested her mother might be contributing to her low self-concept by disparaging her. Several meetings were then held with Dawn's parents, with Dawn present for two of these. The social worker observed that the mother was highly critical of Dawn without ever praising her. Dawn was placed in a special educational program for the next 18 months; here she received close attention and considerable praise for her academic and social efforts. The worker also counseled the parents on how they were contributing to her low self-concept and how they needed to praise Dawn for her efforts and to get her more involved in interests she had. On three separate occasions Dawn, her parents, Dawn's brother, and the social worker met in a playroom. The family members were encouraged to play together in various games, and the parents were instructed to praise Dawn whenever she made efforts to participate positively. Also, Dawn's mother was encouraged to refrain from disparaging Dawn. After this intensive program, Dawn was able to rejoin her class at the start of the fourth grade and had become much more outgoing and self-confident.

Source: In the classic *Play Therapy,* Axline (1947) provided a number of other case examples in which play therapy has been used for diagnostic purposes, for helping children to understand themselves and their problems better and to resolve their problems.

Probably the most popular program is Parent Effectiveness Training (PET), developed by Thomas Gordon (1970). The basic concepts of this approach are presented here, partly because some of the techniques, such as active listening, I-messages, and no-lose problem solving, can be used by any person to interact more effectively with others.

Parent Effectiveness Training (PET) courses are now offered in hundreds of communities throughout this country and have been endorsed by numerous public and private agencies serving parents and youth. The PET system has been found to work effectively with children of all ages. It fosters warmer and more harmonious relationships between parents and their children, and children learn to become more responsible. The principles are applicable not only for parents and parent surrogates (such as teachers, principals, counselors, and youth leaders) but for anyone who wants to improve their interactions with others.

Parents Are People, Not Gods

Gordon urges parents to be "real" in their relationships with children. "Realness" is much more important than the impossible guidelines of always being consistent in displaying feelings, putting up a "united front," and being unconditionally tolerant and accepting. In a close relationship, it is impossible to hide our true feelings, so it is normal and real for parents to be accepting of some behaviors of their children and nonaccepting of other behaviors. Parents should recognize their true feelings and not attempt to convey false acceptance when they dislike what their children are doing. It is normal and real for one parent to be more accepting than the other, and one parent may feel accepting and the other nonaccepting of the same behavior. Being honest and human in interacting with children will improve a relationship substantially more than conveying false acceptance or trying to always be consistent.

Who Owns the Problem?

PET asserts that appropriate parental responses depend on the answer to the question "Who owns the problem?" We own a problem only when the situation affects our ability to get our needs met in a concrete and tangible way. If the *child* owns a problem, then *active listening* is an appropriate technique for a parent to use. If the *parent* owns the problem, then *I-messages* are appropriate for the parent to use. If the situation involves a conflict between the parent and the child in meeting the needs of both, then *no-lose problem solving* is an appropriate technique. If the situation involves a conflict in values between the parent and the child, Gordon provides guidelines for *resolving collisions of values.*

PET Techniques

Active Listening

When a 16-year-old son announces "I hate school and I'm going to drop out," parents can respond in a variety of ways: ordering him to stay in school, warning him that he'll be sorry if he drops out, moralizing by saying it would not be proper or right, giving advice by saying he should discuss it with the high school counselor, and so forth. Such approaches are generally not effective or productive in helping children express their feelings, explore their problems, and arrive at a comfortable solution.

Active listening is a much more effective way of interacting. The following steps are involved in active listening: (1) the receiver of a message tries to understand what the sender's message means or what the sender is feeling; and (2) the receiver then puts this understanding into her own words and returns this understanding for the sender's verification. In using this approach, the receiver does *not* send a message of her own—such as a question, advice, her feelings, or an opinion. The aim is to feed back only what she feels the sender's message meant. Active listening is a difficult skill to learn and takes practice to master.

This approach is illustrated here in a set of interactions, with the parent consistently using the active listening technique.

Youth: I hate school, and I'm going to drop out.

Parent: You're fed up with school and thinking about leaving.

Youth: Yes I am! My teachers are real bummers this year.

Parent: You're disappointed with your current teachers.

Youth: Especially my Spanish teacher. He asks us questions in Spanish and expects us to understand what he's saying. All I hear is words that I can't understand.

Parent: You're having trouble understanding your Spanish teacher when he speaks in Spanish.

Youth: I've been getting As and Bs on tests, but the other students appear to understand Spanish better when it is spoken.

Parent: Your grades show that you are doing well in Spanish, but you have trouble understanding Spanish when it is spoken.

Youth: Yeah, I wonder what I could do to learn to understand people better when they speak Spanish.

Parent: You're wondering how you can better learn to hear and speak in Spanish.

Youth: Maybe I could talk to my teacher. He'd know. He might have some ideas.

Gordon listed a number of advantages for using the active listening technique. It facilitates problem solving by the child, which fosters the development of responsibility. By talking a problem through, a person is more apt to identify the root of the problem and arrive at a solution than by merely thinking about a problem. When a child feels that his parents are listening to him, a by-product is that he will be more likely to listen to their point of view. In addition, the relationship between parent and child is likely to improve, because when the child feels he is being heard and understood by another person, he is apt to feel warmth toward the listener. Finally, the approach helps the child explore, recognize, and express personal feelings.

Gordon noted that parents need to have certain attitudes to use the technique effectively. Parents must view the child as a separate person with their own feelings. Parents must be able to accept the child's feelings, whatever they may be. Parents should genuinely want to be helpful and must want to hear what the child has to say. And parents must trust the child's capacities to handle personal problems and feelings.

Parents initially make some common mistakes as they use the technique: (1) They guide the child's behavior or thinking toward what the parents think the child should do. If parents have this intention, children are likely to feel they are being manipulated and the approach may be counterproductive. (2) They parrot back the words rather than the intended meaning or feeling.

For instance, if a daughter yells at her father "You stupid jerk," an appropriate response geared to the message would be "You're angry with me," rather than parroting the words "You think I'm a jerk." (3) They use active listening at the wrong time. If a child does not want to talk about her feelings, or is simply too tired, the parent should respect the child's right and need for privacy.

I-Messages

Active listening is used when the child has the problem. However, many occasions arise when the child causes a problem for the parent; for example, a child talks loudly in church, or gets too close to a precious glass vase, or is about to walk on a new carpet with muddy shoes, or is driving recklessly. In such cases entirely different communication skills are required. Confronted with such situations, many parents send either a *solution message* (they order, direct, command, warn, threaten, preach, moralize, or advise) or a *put-down message* (they blame, judge, criticize, ridicule, or name-call). Solution and put-down messages can have devastating effects on a child's self-concept and are generally counterproductive in helping a child become responsible.

Solution and put-down messages are primarily you-messages: "You do what I say," "Don't you do that," "Why don't you be good," "You're lazy," "You should know better."

PET advocates that parents should instead send *I-messages* for those occasions when a child is causing a problem for the parent. For example, if a child is walking on a clean carpet with dirty shoes, instead of saying, "John, get off that carpet, you're a pig!" PET urges parents to use an I-message: "I shampooed the living room rug today and want to keep it clean as long as possible."

I-messages are nonblaming messages that communicate only how the sender of the message believes the receiver is adversely affecting the sender. I-messages do not provide a solution nor are they put-down messages. It is possible to send an I-message without using the word *I,* as the essence of I-messages involves sending a nonblaming message of how the parent feels the child's behavior is affecting the parent. For example, a parent riding in a car driven by the 17-year-old son, who is exceeding the speed limit, may say, "Driving fast really terrifies me."

You-messages are generally put-down messages that convey to children either that they should do something or that they are bad. In contrast, I-messages communicate to children much more honestly the effect of the behavior on the parent. I-messages are also more effective because they help children learn to assume responsibility for their own behavior. An I-message tells children that the parent trusts them to respect the parent's needs, that the parent is leaving the responsibility with them, and that the parent is trusting them to handle the situation constructively.

You-messages frequently end up in a struggle between parent and child, whereas I-messages are much less likely to produce an argument. I-messages lead to honesty and openness in a relationship and generally foster intimacy. Children, as well as adults, often do not know how their behavior affects others. I-messages produce startling results as parents frequently report that their children express surprise on learning how their parents really feel.

The following are examples of you-messages and I-messages:

You-Messages	*I-Messages*
1. Don't you ever kick me again; you're real pain.	Ouch! That kick really hurt me.
2. John, you stop pestering me now!	John, I am very tired today, and I just do not have the energy to play with you this evening.
3. You're a reckless driver and someday you'll kill someone.	I'm afraid to drive with you when you drive so fast.

I-messages work only if the child does not want his actions to adversely affect his parent. If the child does not want to cause discomfort in his parent, the child will seek to change his adversive behavior when an I-message is used. However, if the child enjoys causing discomfort in his parent, then I-messages may result in an *increase* in the adversive behavior as the child is now more fully aware of how to cause discomfort in his parent.

No-Lose Problem Solving

In every parent-child relationship, situations inevitably arise in which the child continues to behave in a way that interferes with the needs of the parent. Conflict is part of life and is not necessarily bad. Conflict occurs because people are different and have different needs and wants, which at times do not match. What is important is not how frequently conflicts arise but how they get resolved. Generally conflicts create a power struggle.

In many families the power struggle is resolved by one of two *win-lose* approaches. Most parents try to resolve the conflict by having the parent win and the child lose. Parents generally have the greater authority. When the parent wins, the child resents the parent, the child is less motivated to carry out the solution, and the child has no opportunity to develop self-discipline and self-responsibility. Such children may rebel or become dependent and withdrawn.

Alternatively, the win-lose conflict is resolved when parents give in to their children out of fear of frustrating their children or fear of conflict. These children come to believe their needs are more important than anyone else's, and they generally become self-centered, selfish, demanding, impulsive, and uncontrollable. They are viewed by others as being spoiled, they have difficulty interacting with peers, and they do not respect the property or feelings of others.

Of course, few parents use either approach exclusively. Oscillating between the two approaches is common. There is evidence that both approaches lead to development of emotional problems in children (Gordon, 1970, p. 161).

The two win-lose approaches are illustrated in the following situation:

Parent wins—child loses:

Mother: Since I'm now working, we need to divide the work tasks around the house. I'll continue to do most of the work, but from now on I'd like you to wash the dishes in the evening.

John: But I don't like washing dishes.

Mother: Well, I don't like cooking, and washing and ironing clothes, but I have to do them. We all have to do things we don't like to do.

John: Washing dishes is for girls.

Mother: Look, I'm not going to argue with you about this. You're now old enough to help out. In this family we all have to contribute. If you don't do the dishes you won't receive your allowance. In fact, from now on, every evening you do not wash dishes, fifty cents will be deducted from your weekly allowance.

Child wins—parent loses:

Mother: Since I'm now working, we need to divide the work tasks around the house. I'll continue to do most of the work, but from now on I'd like you to wash the dishes in the evening.

John: But I don't like washing dishes.

Mother: Why?

John: Washing dishes is for girls.

Mother: But many boys help their mothers with the dishes.

John: Tom and Gary don't help their mothers. What would they say about me washing dishes?

Mother: You may be right. Could you instead help me with washing clothes, or dusting, or cleaning your room?

John: Aw—Mom, those things are for girls, too.

Mother: (*Dejectedly*) Well, OK, I'll try to do these things while also working.

Gordon seriously questioned whether power is necessary or justified in a parent-child relationship. As children grow older, they become less dependent and parents gradually lose their power. Rewards and punishments that worked in younger years are less effective. Children resent those with power over them, and parents frequently feel guilty after using power. Gordon believed that parents continue to use power because they have little experience in using nonpower methods of influence.

PET suggests a new approach, the *no-lose approach,* to resolve conflicts. In this approach, parent and children resolve their conflicts by finding their own unique solutions acceptable to both.

The following example illustrates this approach:

Mother: Since I'm now working, I will have less time to do the work that needs to be done around the house. I would appreciate it if you would help me out with some of the things that need to be done.

John: I suppose I could help—what needs to be done?

Mother: The meals need to be cooked, dishes washed, the house cleaned, grocery shopping done, and the garbage taken out.

John: Let's see. I'd be willing to vacuum the floor and dust. Will my allowance be increased? I'd like to get a new bike.

Mother: Yes, since we'll have some more money now that I'm working, we could increase your allowance, with the increase dependent on how much additional work you do.

John: In addition to helping to clean the house, I'd be willing to wash the clothes if you show me what to do. I also could carry out the garbage.

The no-lose approach is simple to state: Each person in the conflict treats the other with respect, neither person tries to win by using power, and a creative solution acceptable to both parties is sought. There are two basic premises to no-lose problem solving: (1) All people have the right to have their needs met, and (2) what is in conflict is not *needs* but *solutions* to those needs.

Gordon (1970, p. 237) listed six steps for the no-lose method:

1: Identify and define the needs of each person.
2. Generate possible alternative solutions.
3. Evaluate the alternative solutions.
4. Decide on the best acceptable solution.
5. Work out ways of implementing the solution.
6. Follow up to evaluate how it worked.

There are several advantages to this approach. It motivates children to carry out the solution because they participated in the decision. It develops children's thinking skills and responsibility. It requires less enforcement, eliminates the need for power, and improves relationships with parents.

Resolving Collisions of Values

Collisions of values are common between parents and their children, particularly as the children become adolescents and young adults. Likely areas of conflict include values about sexual behavior, clothing, religion, choice of friends, education, plans for the future, use of drugs, hairstyles, and eating habits. In these areas emotions run strong and parents generally seek to influence their offspring to follow the values the parents hold as important. Teenagers, however, often think their parents' values are old fashioned and stupid and declare that they want to make their own decisions about these matters.

Gordon describes three constructive ways in which parents and teenagers can seek to resolve these conflicts. (For the sake of simplicity, I will use the term *mother* here—a father or teenager can also use these techniques.)

First, the mother models the values she holds important. If she values honesty, she should be honest. If she values responsible use of drugs, she should not get drunk or drink and drive, for example. If she values openness, she should be open. She asks herself if she is living according to the values she professes. If her values and behaviors are incongruent in certain areas, she needs to change either her values or her behavior in the direction of congruency. Congruence between behavior and values is important if she wants to be an effective model.

Second, she acts as a consultant to her teen. There are some do's and don'ts of a good consultant. A good consultant finds out whether the teen would like her consultation. If the answer is yes, she makes sure she has all the available pertinent facts. She then shares these facts—once—so the teen understands them. She leaves the teen the responsibility of deciding whether to follow the advice. A good consultant is neither uninformed nor a nag; otherwise she may not be used as a consultant again.

Third, a mother can reduce tensions by modifying her own values. By examining her teen's values, she may realize they have merit, and she can then move toward their values or at least toward understanding why the teen holds them.

In summary, PET concepts are designed to improve relationships between parents and children and to develop responsibility in children. A large number of parents who have participated in PET courses, or read Gordon's *Parent Effectiveness Training,* find them to be effective. In recent years, these PET concepts have been found useful not only in improving relationships between parents and children but also in improving interactions and communication between people in all manner of transactions.

PET techniques work if influencees respect influencers and want a positive relationship with them. If the influencee neither respects nor wants a positive relationship with the influencer, then these techniques don't work.

Crisis Intervention

Crisis intervention (CI) postulates that in a crisis situation current levels of functioning are disrupted and previously manageable internal psychological difficulties stirred up. CI views the emotional disturbances presented by people facing crisis as the result of (1) the stressful situation they face, and (2) underlying emotional dispositions that come to the surface only in crisis situations. CI postulates that underlying emotional difficulties are ingredients of all personalities. People are viewed as being fairly normal in their general adjustment, with the crisis being a major cause of a person's emotional difficulties.

CASE EXAMPLE

Crisis Intervention

John Franzene (age 28) went to work intoxicated one day and was promptly fired. John became incensed and yelled obscenities at his supervisor. He then went to a local tavern and drank until he passed out. A friend took him home. When his wife found out that John had been fired from his job as a janitor, she packed her bags that evening and took the two children to live with her mother. She indicated that this was the "last straw."

John is an alcoholic and drinks an average of eight bottles of beer and a pint of whiskey every day. He has been drinking excessively for the past decade. Three years ago his wife separated from him because he was abusive to her and the children, both physically and verbally, when intoxicated. At that time John promised to stop drinking if his wife would only return; she did, and three weeks later he again began drinking. Five years ago he lost his position as an elementary schoolteacher because of his drinking and his frequent absenteeism. Two years ago he lost his driver's license for driving while intoxicated. In the past five years, he has lost three other jobs.

The next day John went to his mother-in-law's home to try to talk his wife into returning. She refused to speak to him. John, feeling sorry for himself, went to a local tavern and again got drunk. He blamed his supervisor for his current difficulties. While intoxicated he decided to "straighten this matter out." He went to the office where he had been fired and got into a fight with his supervisor. He was arrested. While in jail he got the "DTs" (delirium tremens), which really scared him. He was transferred to a hospital. The doctor at the hospital explored his interest in receiving help for his drinking problem. John indicated he was willing to talk about it to someone, and he was referred to Tom Halaska, the hospital social worker.

For the first time in his life, John acknowledged that he had a drinking problem and needed help. Mr. Halaska met with John on several occasions during the next four days. The ways that alcohol was affecting his life (including his job and his family life) were traced, and John gained an awareness that he got into trouble only when he was drinking. Mr. Halaska explored the reasons John drank, and it became clear that he drank excessively either when he was with male friends in a tavern or when he sought to relieve unwanted emotions of feeling tense, moody, or depressed. John appeared at this time to be sincerely committed to giving up drinking. Mr. Halaska suggested that one thing he would have to do to give up drinking was to stop meeting his friends at a tavern. John indicated that saving his marriage meant more to him than hanging out with his friends. Mr. Halaska arranged a meeting between John and his wife. His wife agreed to return if John would first go one month without drinking, promise never to drink again, and actively participate in AA meetings. John agreed. Mr. Halaska referred him to an AA group and also referred him to the outpatient treatment unit of the mental health center. Among other services, this outpatient treatment service provided marriage counseling services to John and his wife and helped him explore job opportunities.

John occasionally stops by the hospital to visit Mr. Halaska briefly. It has now been 14 months since he had a drink. He is a sales clerk at a clothing store and is seeking a teaching position. He reports that he and his wife are getting along better than they ever have.

Counseling Skills at Work in Generalist Practice

This case example illustrates the social worker used the following roles that, as described in Chapter 1, are components of generalist social work practice: helping Mr. Franzene to acknowledge he had a drinking problem, mediating some of the issues between Mr. Halaska and his wife, encouraging him to attend AA meetings and to receive outpatient treatment at a mental health center, and brokering marriage counseling for Mr. and Mrs. Franzene.

Note: Additional case examples using crisis intervention are presented in Parad (1965).

Ell (1995) notes that there are an infinite number of crisis situations in which CI is appropriate. These crises include serious illness or trauma, death of a loved one, disasters, violent crimes, moving away from home, and unplanned pregnancy.

Because people are often in a frozen position when a crisis arises, CI services often have two tasks: to resolve the current crisis and to resolve problems the people have previously been denying or ignoring. For example, if a person is fired from a job because of drinking problems, services might focus not only on helping them find another job but also on breaking down their denial of their drinking problem. Golan (1979, p. 500) noted that at the point of crisis "a minimal effort . . . can produce a maximal effect; a small amount of help, appropriately focused, can prove more effective than extensive help at a period of less emotional accessibility."

Crisis intervention services are generally brief and provided primarily when the client is in desperate need emotionally. The specific treatment techniques are borrowed from other approaches. Here are a few examples: Role playing helps a pregnant single woman gather her nerve to inform her parents and her sexual partner. Confrontation helps a person arrested three times for drunken driving acknowledge that he has a drinking problem. A person whose engagement has been broken learns to counter unwanted emotions with a rational self-analysis. A young woman who has been raped is given immediate medical attention and counseling on both legal implications and on her thoughts and feelings about the assault. A counselor uses the active listening technique in counseling someone who is suicidal.

Whittaker (1974) provided a summary of crisis counseling services:

> Requisite worker skills include the ability to function effectively and efficiently in an emotionally tense atmosphere and to give support and direction while at the same time helping the client to develop autonomous coping skills.
>
> Crisis intervention generally progresses in the following manner: (1) An attempt is made to alleviate the disabling tension through ventilation and the creation of a climate of trust and hope. (2) Next the worker attempts to understand the dynamics of the event that precipitated the crisis. (3) The worker gives his impressions and understanding of the crisis and checks out these perceptions with the client. (4) Client and worker attempt to determine specific remedial measures that can be taken to restore equilibrium. (5) New methods of coping may be introduced. (6) Finally, termination occurs—often after a predetermined number of interviews—when the agreed-upon goals have been realized. (p. 212)

Crisis intervention services are provided in a wide variety of traditional and nontraditional settings, including runaway centers, rape crisis centers, "hot lines," hospital emergency rooms, mental health clinics, suicide prevention services, neighborhood centers, crisis hostels, halfway houses, detention facilities, and self-help groups such as Parents Anonymous. Crisis intervention services are provided by both professionals and paraprofessionals and volunteers.

Task-Centered Practice

The primary developers of task-centered practice are William J. Reid and Laura Epstein, social work faculty members of the School of Social Service Administration at the University of Chicago. Task-centered practice is described in Reid and Epstein (1977).

In the initial interview with clients, counselors seek to elicit, explore, and clarify clients' problems. During this interview counselors may point out problems clients have not recognized, or the consequences of allowing significant problems to go unattended. In the first or second interview, counselor and client explicitly agree on the problems to be dealt with. The problems are defined in terms of specific circumstances to be changed. Counselor and client also agree on the duration and amount of service to be given. There are usually 6–12 interviews over a two- to four-month period. The kinds of services agreed on and the number of interviews to be held form the basis of the service contract, which can be modified by additional agreements as service proceeds.

Counselors and clients then identify tasks that clients can undertake to alleviate specific problems. These tasks may be general in nature in that they give the client a direction for action but do not precisely specify the expected behavior—for example, client Jim K will seek to establish a better relationship with his parents. Or, tasks may be very specific—for example, Jim K will inform his parents how much he appreciates their financial support in sending him to college.

During the discussion of the tasks, counselors help clients structure the tasks to increase their chances of being accomplished. If clients are unable to arrive at alternatives for resolving the problems, counselors may suggest various possibilities. The counselor's primary roles in this change process are to help clients identify target problems, to help them identify tasks for resolving these problems, and to then carry out agreed-on tasks together with the client. The general tasks of clients, in this model, become the clients' own goals for change. In this change process counselors use relationship skills (discussed in Chapter 5) and a variety of resolution approaches, such as contingency contracting, assertiveness training, and game analysis.

During the treatment process, a substantial amount of the counselor's efforts goes into structuring communication during interviews to keep clients' attention and efforts focused on the tasks. A number of efforts are made to enhance clients' awareness of their problems and to help them understand obstacles to task performance. Clients are given substantial encouragement about constructive actions they are contemplating or are undertaking. Clients may also be given suggestions or directions on how to proceed with the task.

Usually in the treatment process there is an emphasis on counselors helping clients break down general tasks into more specific, operational tasks that they are then expected to carry out before the next treatment session. Incentives for task accomplishment are usually identified. Actions called for by the tasks are rehearsed or practiced (for example, through role playing). This task-centered approach has been used not only with individual clients but also with families and with groups (Reid & Epstein, 1977).

Treatment is short term by plan. It is theorized that when a contract is made with clients for a set number of interviews (usually 6–12), clients will work hard to resolve their problems during this brief time period.

Another emphasis is to focus treatment sharply on target problems and resolution tasks—that is, to specify problems and tasks in operational and measurable terms. Thus, both counselor and client are more aware of precisely what needs to be done and what progress is being made during the treatment process in resolving the problems.

A final emphasis is the use of explicit agreements or contracts. These specify problems, goals, and tasks to be worked on during the treatment process. The contract is formed in the first or second interview and guides the treatment process. This contract may be oral or written; it may be modified later if both parties agree to changing it.

A number of case examples of task-centered practice are given in Reid and Epstein (1977). The task-centered approach has many similarities to the counseling process described in Chapter 5 and to reality therapy described in Module 5.

Solution-Focused Therapy

Solution-focused therapy is also called "solution-oriented therapy" and "strategic therapy." Solution-focused therapists ask clients *what* is happening now and *how* it should be changed. They do not ask *why.* This approach does not focus on pathology (the approach of fixing what is wrong) but on identifying clients' requests. This shift in focus results in an entirely different set of assumptions about therapy and has a profound effect on what interventions are used. For clients to learn to be the person they want to be is quite different (and often less time-consuming) than learning why they are the way they are. Solution-focused therapy has been developed by a variety of researchers, including Berg and Miller (1992), de Shazer (1988), and DeJong and Miller (1995).

Solution-focused therapy emphasizes two intervention techniques: (1) developing *well-formed goals* with clients that are within their frame of reference, and (2) developing solutions with the client based on *"exceptions."*

WELL-FORMED GOALS. Berg and Miller (1992) identify seven characteristics of well-formed goals in solution-focused therapy:

1. Goals that are important to clients. Clients should want to achieve these goals, and the goals should be expressed in the clients' language. The only time the worker should object to the desired goals of the client is when the stated goals will result in danger to the client (like a goal of terminating his life) or to others (like a goal of physical retaliation for a perceived wrong).
2. Small goals are easier to achieve than larger goals.
3. Goals are concrete, specific, and behavioral. This allows both client and worker to observe when progress is being made. For example, "going out to lunch with a friend three times a week" is concrete, specific, and behavioral.
4. Goals describe the presence of something (for example, "taking walks") rather than the absence of something (for example, "no longer feeling discouraged").
5. Goals have beginnings ("arranging a pleasant vacation with my spouse for this summer") rather than endings ("having a happy marriage"). Stating goals as a beginning process helps clients conceptualize

the first steps they need to take to achieve their desired ends.
6. Goals are realistic—clients can achieve them within the context of their lives.
7. Goals are perceived by clients as involving "hard work." Goals call for changes in what clients do, and change is difficult. Clients are generally motivated to work hard to achieve highly desired goals.

Setting well-formed goals assumes that goals are negotiated between the worker and client. Articulating goals in such a way that they are consistent with these guidelines often requires considerable effort.

DeJong and Miller (1995) assert that a "miracle" question is often a superb way to assist clients formulate goals:

> Suppose while you are sleeping tonight a miracle happens. The miracle is that the problem that has you here talking to me is somehow solved. Only you don't know that because you are asleep. What will you notice different tomorrow morning that will tell you that a miracle has happened? (p. 731)

Additional questions asked in this vein include:

> What is the very first thing you notice after the miracle happens?
> What will your husband (child, friend) notice about you that gives him the idea that things are better for you?
> When he notices that, what might he do differently?
> When he does that, what will you do?
> And when you do that, what will be different around your house? (p. 731)

These questions shift clients' attention from their difficulties and pathologies to imagining a future where their problems are resolved. The questions provide an opportunity for workers to help clients formulate goals consistent with the guidelines.

EXCEPTIONS. "Exceptions" in solution-focused therapy are those occasions in clients' lives when their problems could have occurred, but did not. For example, a married couple characterize their recent years as "continual fighting"; the worker asks the couple to describe times when they weren't fighting. Workers focus on the who, what, when, and where of exception times (rather than the problem times), and an in-depth exploration of client problems is avoided. The result is a growing awareness in both worker and client of the client's strengths relative to his goals rather than his deficiencies relative to his problems. Once these strengths are brought to clients' awareness, they can mobilize them to move in the direction of achieving their miracle.

In another example of the exceptions strategy a worker asks a depressed client to do this homework assignment: "Pay attention to the times when you are not depressed or when the depression is less of a problem. What is different about those times?" During the next session, the worker asks the client what she did differently during those times when she noticed the depression was not a problem or was less of a problem. Such a question implies that clients already have the skills to function in a more satisfying manner.

Solution-focused therapy involves a different set of stages from those used in problem solving. The well-known stages of problem solving include: specifying the problem; generating resolution strategies; evaluating the merits and shortcomings of the strategies; selecting and implementing a strategy; and evaluating at some later date how well the selected strategy is working. In contrast, the stages of solution-focused therapy are: briefly describing the concern or problem in the client's words; developing well-formed goals; exploring for exceptions (successes or times in the clients' life when problems do not happen or are less severe); evaluating client progress as they define it; and ending the session with feedback comprising affirmations of the client's goals and strengths. Homework assignments are often given in solution-focused therapy.

In a study of 275 clients, Berg and DeJong (1996) found a 77 percent success rate using solution-focused therapy. Forty-five percent of the clients indicated that their treatment goal was met, and another 32 percent indicated some progress in attaining their treatment goal.

Solution-focused therapy is highly consistent with the strengths perspective in social work, which is described in Chapter 3. Solution-focused therapy, task-centered therapy, and some forms of cognitive-behavior therapy (see Module 4) are examples of brief therapies. Brief therapies are becoming increasingly popular with clients and with funding sources, as our society and individuals are clamoring for approaches that result in significant therapeutic change in a short time at a reasonable cost.

Mediation

In the past three decades, mediation has been used increasingly to resolve conflicts between disputing groups. As far back as 1913, the federal government established the use of federal mediators to help resolve issues between employers and employees (Moore,

1986, p. 21). Mediated settlements were expected to prevent costly strikes or lockouts and to protect the welfare and safety of Americans. Federal use of mediation in labor disputes has set a precedent, encouraging many states to pass laws and to train a cadre of mediators to handle intrastate labor conflicts.

Mediation is currently used in a variety of ways. The Civil Rights Act of 1964 created the Community Relations Service of the U.S. Department of Justice to use mediation to resolve disputes relating to discriminatory practices based on race, color, or national origin (Moore, 1986, pp. 21–22). Diverse private agencies, civil rights commissions, and state agencies now use mediation to handle charges of sex, race, and ethnic discrimination. The federal government funds Neighborhood Justice Centers that provide free or low-cost mediation services to the public to resolve disputes, informally, inexpensively, and efficiently (Mayer, 1995, pp. 618–620). Disputes settled through mediation are resolved much more efficiently and creatively than those resolved in court. Mediation is also used in schools to resolve issues between students, between students and faculty, between faculty members, and between faculty and administration. The criminal justice system uses mediation to resolve disputes in correctional facilities—for example, for prison riots, hostage negotiations, and institutionalized grievance procedures.

Mediation is also used extensively in family disputes involving child custody and divorce proceedings, disputes between parents and children, conflicts involving adoption and the termination of parental rights, and domestic violence situations. Moore (1986, p. 23) stated: "In family disputes, mediated and consensual settlements are often more appropriate and satisfying than litigated or imposed court outcomes."

Mediation is used to settle disputes between business partners, private individuals, government agencies and individuals, landlords and tenants, businesses and customers, and disputants in personal injury cases.

Many professionals now occasionally act as mediators to help people or groups in conflict resolve their concerns. Such professionals include attorneys, social workers, psychologists, and guidance counselors. A few social workers, attorneys, and other professionals work full time as mediators—often in public or private mediation agencies.

Moore (1986) defined mediation as follows:

> Mediation involves the intervention of an acceptable impartial and neutral third party who has no authoritative decision-making power to assist contending parties in voluntarily reaching their own mutually acceptable settlement of issues in dispute. . . . Mediation leaves the decision-making power in the hands of the people in conflict. Mediation is a voluntary process in that the participants must be willing to accept the assistance of the intervenor if the dispute is to be resolved. Mediation is usually initiated when the partners no longer believe that they can handle the conflict on their own and when the only means of resolution appears to involve impartial third-party assistance. (p. 6)

Various models describe the mediation process (Moore, 1986). The one developed by Blades (1985) is summarized here. Blades viewed the mediation process as involving five stages:

1. *Introduction/commitment:* This stage usually is accomplished in a one- to two-hour session. The mediator sets ground rules, describes mediation, answers questions, discusses fees, and seeks to gain a commitment to the process from the two parties. The mediator also seeks to develop an understanding of the more pressing issues, gains a sense of the personal dynamics of the two parties, and tries to ascertain whether they are ready and willing to mediate. If one or both parties are unwilling to mediate, then the mediation probably should not proceed. If one or both parties are hesitant to proceed, the mediator usually describes the alternatives to mediation—such as a lengthy and expensive court battle.

2. *Definition:* The two parties, with the mediator's assistance, define the areas in which they already agree and disagree. At this stage certain disputes, such as divorce mediation, require a considerable amount of information.

3. *Negotiation:* Once the two parties agree on the issues in conflict and relevant factual information on these issues is obtained, the two parties are ready to begin negotiating. At this stage the mediator seeks to have the parties focus on one issue at a time. A problem-solving approach is used in which the needs of each party are first identified and alternatives are generated. The mediator recedes into the background when discussions are proceeding well and steps in when emotions intensify or when the two parties are overlooking creative solutions that will meet their needs.

4. *Agreement:* Once alternatives are generated and related facts are evaluated, the two parties are ready to begin making agreements on the issues. The role of the mediator is to maintain a cooperative atmosphere and to keep the two parties focused on a manageable number of issues. The mediator summarizes areas of agreement and provides legal or other infor-

mation necessary to a discussion. The mediator helps the two parties examine the merits and shortcomings of the options. During this stage the mediator praises the parties for the progress they are making and gets them to praise themselves for progress made. The mediator seeks to create a positive atmosphere.

5. *Contracting:* In this final stage of mediation the two parties review the agreements and clarify any ambiguities. The agreements are almost always written in the form of a contract, which is available for future reference. Either party, the mediator, or everyone together may write the contract. The contract expresses what each party agrees to do, may set deadlines for the diverse tasks to be completed, and may specify consequences if either party fails to meet the terms of the contract. Mediators seek to have specific agreements stated in concrete form to prevent future controversies. The ultimate goal of mediation is a contract in which no one is a loser and by which both parties willingly abide.

One of the major techniques mediators use is a caucus (Moore, 1986). At times a mediator, or either party, may stop the mediation and request a caucus. In a caucus the two parties are physically separated from each other and there is no direct communication between them. The mediator meets with one of the parties or with both parties individually. Caucuses are called for many reasons: to vent intense emotions privately, to clarify misperceptions, to reduce unproductive or repetitive negative behavior, to clarify a party's interests, to provide a pause for each party to consider an alternative, to convince an uncompromising party that the mediation process is better than going to court, to uncover confidential information, to educate an inexperienced disputant about the processes of mediation, or to design alternatives that will later be brought to a joint session.

Caucuses allow parties to express in private concessions they are willing to make. Usually such concessions are conditional on the other party's making certain concessions. In caucuses, mediators go back and forth relaying information from one party to the other in order to develop a consensus.

Relaxation Approaches

The relaxation response can be achieved by muscle relaxation approaches, deep-breathing techniques, and by imagery relaxation methods.

Muscle Relaxation Approaches[1]

A number of muscle relaxation programs are available; Bernstein and Borkovec (1973) review them in detail. Muscle relaxation approaches stem from Jacobson's (1934) pioneering work in teaching people to help themselves deal with stress and anxiety. *Stress* is a state of bodily and mental tension that results from physical, chemical, or emotional stressors; for example, stress can result from having a high-pressure job. (See Chapter 14 for a fuller description of stress and its effects.)

Anxiety has long been recognized as an emotion that accompanies stress. Anxiety is generally described as uncomfortable feelings of tension, apprehension, and dread.

Jacobson's investigations led him to the well-established fact that people are able to regulate certain effects of the automatic nervous system through their own efforts. Specifically, he discovered that anxiety is associated with the sensation of tension experienced when muscle fibers are shortened or contracted as they are during stress. Jacobson developed muscle relaxation to counteract anxiety. He demonstrated that anxiety can be sharply reduced by relaxing muscles. His approach is an elaborate system that teaches people to progressively tighten and then relax the major muscles of their body. He also demonstrated that anxiety will not exist in the presence of complete muscle relaxation (Jacobson, 1938a).

Jacobson (1934, 1938b, 1959, 1964, 1973) published many popular books on how to relax, how to handle fatigue, how to sleep well, how to relax while having a baby, and how to help schoolchildren relax in the classroom.

His approach to relaxation consists of teaching people to relax 20 major muscle groups. Each group is tensed and relaxed in several different ways during a 60-minute period, practiced every day until the person becomes skilled in the procedure. Jacobson's method is thorough but time-consuming.

Muscle relaxation is very effective in reducing and eliminating both stress and anxiety (Brown, 1977). Practically anyone can learn to reduce both anxiety and stress using muscle relaxation. In recent years shorter programs of muscle relaxation have been developed (Seaward, 1994).

[1]This material on muscle relaxation approaches is adapted from Charles Zastrow, "Muscle Relaxation Approaches," in *Talk to Yourself: Using the Power of Self-Talk*, © 1979, pp. 179–183. Adapted by permission of Prentice-Hall, Inc., Englewood Cliffs, New Jersey.

Learning to relax via muscle relaxation is accomplished by having people first tighten and then relax a set of muscles. When relaxing muscle groups, they are instructed to think about the relaxed feeling while noting that the muscles are more relaxed than before they were tensed. The instructions for muscle relaxation is given in CTRM Exhibit 9.1.

With continued practice, people can generally relax whenever anxious simply by *visualizing* (that is, thinking about) muscles relaxing. The procedure is to think about the tension progressively leaving the various muscle groups. A brief example of this procedure is given in Brown (1977):

> Think of your lower arm, elbow, and upper arm, all the way up to your shoulders. Picture all the tension just melting away. . . . Think about your stomach and chest, up to your throat and neck. As you continue breathing more deeply, just imagine all the tension flowing out and you are relaxing more and more.
>
> Now think about your throat, neck, and head, feeling limp and relaxed. Relax your facial muscles. Drop the jaw, parting the lips and teeth. Picture yourself completely relaxed. (pp. 261–262)

In recent years physicians, psychiatrists, psychologists, social workers, and other counselors have increasingly explored and used muscle relaxation approaches to reduce both stress and anxiety (Seaward, 1994). Muscle relaxation is also used to relieve tension and migraine headaches (Seaward, 1994). Suinn (1976) demonstrated that relaxation helps athletes and others reduce stress before important events. It is useful in reducing hypertension (Seaward, 1994). Relaxation training is used as a technique in its own right and is used in conjunction with other therapy approaches such as self-hypnosis, biofeedback, and systematic desensitization.

Deep-Breathing and Imagery Relaxation Approaches

In addition to muscle relaxation approaches, the relaxation response can be achieved by deep-breathing techniques and using the imagery of being in a relaxing place. Brown (1977) described the deep-breathing technique:

> *Relaxation technique: deep breathing (five minutes)*
>
> 1. Select a comfortable sitting position.
> 2. Close your eyes and direct your attention to your own breathing process.
> 3. Think about nothing but your breath, as it flows in and out of your body.
> 4. Say to yourself something like this: "I am relaxing, breathing smoothly and rhythmically. Fresh oxygen flows in and out of my body. I feel calm, renewed and refreshed."
> 5. Continue to focus on your breathing as it flows in and out, in and out, thinking of nothing but the smooth, rhythmical process of your own breathing.
> 6. After five minutes, stand up, stretch, smile, and continue with your daily activities.[2] (p. 259)

This example uses imagery (Brown, 1977):

> *Relaxation technique: mental relaxation place (five to ten minutes)*
>
> 1. Select a comfortable sitting or reclining position.
> 2. Close your eyes, and think about a place that you have been before that represents your ideal place for physical and mental relaxation. (It should be a quiet environment, perhaps the seashore, the mountains, or even your own backyard. If you can't think of an ideal relaxation place, then create one in your mind.)
> 3. Now imagine that you are actually in your ideal relaxation place. Imagine that you are seeing all the colors, hearing the sounds, smelling the aromas. Just lie back, and enjoy your soothing, rejuvenating environment.
> 4. Feel the peacefulness, the calmness, and imagine your whole body and mind being renewed and refreshed.
> 5. After five to ten minutes, slowly open your eyes and stretch. You have the realization that you may instantly return to your relaxation place whenever you desire, and experience a peacefulness and calmness in body and mind.[3] (pp. 259–260)

Practice gradually increases the proficiency of achieving the relaxation response. Developing the capacity to achieve the relaxation response is highly effective in alleviating anxiety and stress, and thereby experiencing more pleasing emotions, maintaining health, preventing or coping better with stress-related disorders, and probably also extending life expectancy. Counselors are increasingly using relaxation approaches to help clients reduce anxiety and stress.

[2]From *Stress and the Art of Biofeedback,* by Barbara B. Brown. Copyright © 1977 by Barbara B. Brown. By permission of Bantam Books, New York. All rights reserved.
[3]Ibid.

CTRM Exhibit 9.1

Instructions for muscle relaxation exercise

PREPARATION. Spend a little time getting as comfortable as you can. While you are finding a good position, you will also want to loosen any tight clothing. Loosen your belt or tie if they are not already loose. If your shoes feel tight, you may wish to take them off. Your legs and arms should be slightly apart.

Slowly open your mouth and move your jaw gently from side to side. . . . Now let your mouth close, keeping your teeth slightly apart. As you do, take a deep breath . . . and slowly let the air slip out.

While you tighten one part of your body, try to leave every other part limp and loose. Keep the tensed part of your body tight for a few seconds and then relax and let it go. Then take a deep breath, hold it, and as you breathe out, silently say, "Relax and let go." In time, this will be a technique you can use to produce rapid relaxation. Now begin your relaxation practice.

TOTAL BODY TENSION. First, tense every muscle in your body. Tense the muscles of your jaws, eyes, arms, hands, chest, back, stomach, legs, and feet. Feel the tension all over your body. . . . Hold the tension briefly and then silently say, "Relax and let go" as you breathe out. . . . Let your whole body relax. . . . Feel a wave of calm come over you as you stop tensing. Feel the relief.

Gently close your eyes and take another deep breath. . . . Study the tension as you hold your breath. . . . Slowly breathe out and silently say, "Relax and let go." Feel the deepening relaxation. Allow yourself to drift more and more with this relaxation. . . . As you continue, you will exercise different parts of your body. Become aware of your body and its tension and relaxation. This will help you to become deeply relaxed on command.

HEAD AND FACE. Keeping the rest of your body relaxed, wrinkle up your forehead. Do you feel the tension? Your forehead is very tight. Briefly pause and be aware of it. . . . Now, relax and let go. Feel the tension slipping out. Smooth out your forehead and take a deep breath. Hold it. (Briefly pause.) As you breathe out, silently say, "Relax and let go."

Squint your eyes as if you are in a dust storm. Keep the rest of your body relaxed. Briefly pause and feel the tension around your eyes. . . . Now, relax and let go. Take a deep breath and hold it. (Briefly pause.) Silently say, "Relax and let go" as you breathe out.

Open your mouth as wide as you can. Feel the tension in your jaw and chin. Briefly hold the tension. . . . Now, let your mouth gently close. As you do, silently say, "Relax and let go." Take a deep breath. Hold it. (Briefly pause.) As you breathe out say, "Relax and let go."

Close your mouth. Push your tongue against the roof of your mouth. Study the tension in your mouth and chin. Briefly hold the tension. . . . Relax and let go. Take a deep breath. Hold it. (Briefly pause.) Now, silently say, "Relax and let go" as you breathe out. When you breathe out, let your tongue rest comfortably in your mouth, and let your lips be slightly apart.

Keep the rest of your body relaxed, but clench your jaw tightly. Feel the tension in your jaw muscles. Briefly hold the tension. . . . Now relax and let go, and take a deep breath. Hold it. (Briefly pause.) Silently say, "Relax and let go" as you breathe out.

Think about the top of your head, your forehead, eyes, jaws, and cheeks. Make sure these muscles are relaxed. . . . Have you let go of all the tension? Continue to let the tension slip away and feel the relaxation replace the tension. Feel your face becoming very smooth and soft as all the tension slips away. . . . Your eyes are relaxed. . . . Your tongue is relaxed. . . . Your jaws are loose and limp. . . . All of your neck muscles are also very, very relaxed.

All of the muscles of your face and head are relaxing more and more. . . . Your head feels as though it could roll from side to side, and your face feels soft and smooth. Allow your face to continue becoming more and more relaxed as you now move to the other areas of your body.

SHOULDERS. Now shrug your shoulders up and try to touch your ears with your shoulders. Feel the tension in the shoulders and neck. Hold the tension. . . . Now, relax and let go. As you do, feel your shoulders joining the relaxed parts of your body. Take a deep breath. Hold it. (Briefly pause.) Silently say, "Relax and let go" as you slowly breathe out.

Notice the difference, how the tension is giving way to relaxation. Shrug your right shoulder up and try to touch your right ear. Feel the tension in your right shoulder and along the right side of your neck. Hold the tension. . . . Now, relax and let go. Take a deep breath. Hold it. (Briefly pause.) Silently say, "Relax and let go" as you slowly breathe out.

Next, shrug your left shoulder up and try to touch your left ear. Feel the tension in your left shoulder and along the left side of your neck. Hold the tension. . . . Now, relax and let go. Take a deep breath. Hold it. (Briefly pause.) Silently say, "Relax and let go" as you slowly breathe out. Feel the relaxation seeping into the shoulders. As you continue, you will become loose, limp, and relaxed as an old rag doll.

(continued)

CTRM EXHIBIT 9.1

Continued

ARMS AND HANDS. Stretch your arms out and make a fist with your hands. Feel the tension in your hands and forearms. Hold the tension. . . . Now, relax and let go. Take a deep breath. Hold it. (Briefly pause.) Silently say, "Relax and let go" as you slowly breathe out.

Push your right hand down into the surface it is resting on. Feel the tension in your arm and shoulder. Hold the tension. . . . Now, relax and let go. Take a deep breath. Hold it. (Briefly pause.) Silently say, "Relax and let go" as you slowly breathe out.

Next, push your left hand down into whatever it is resting on. Feel the tension in your arm and shoulder. Hold the tension. . . . Now, relax and let go. Take a deep breath. Hold it. (Briefly pause.) Silently say, "Relax and let go" as you slowly breathe out.

Bend your arms toward your shoulders and double them up as you might to show off your muscles. Feel the tension. Hold the tension. . . . Now, relax and let go. Take a deep breath. Hold it. (Briefly pause.) Silently say, "Relax and let go" as you slowly breathe out.

CHEST AND LUNGS. Move on to the relaxation of your chest. Begin by taking a deep breath that totally fills your lungs. As you hold your breath, notice the tension. Be aware of the tension around your ribs. . . . Silently say, "Relax and let go" as you slowly breathe out. Feel the deepening relaxation as you continue breathing easily, freely, and gently. (Briefly pause.)

Take in another deep breath. Hold it again and again. Feel the contrast between tension and relaxation. As you do, tighten your chest muscles. Hold the tension. . . . Silently say, "Relax and let go" as you slowly breathe out. Feel the relief as you breathe out and continue to breathe gently, naturally, and rhythmically. Breathe as smoothly as you can. You will become more and more relaxed with every breath.

BACK. Keep your face, neck, arms, and chest as relaxed as possible, arch your back up (or forward if you are sitting). Arch it as if you had a pillow under the middle and low part of your back. Observe the tension along both sides of your back. Briefly hold that position. . . . Now, relax and let go. Take a deep breath. Hold it. (Briefly pause.) Silently say, "Relax and let go" as you breathe out. Let that relaxation spread deep into your shoulders and down into your back muscles.

Feel the slow relaxation developing and spreading all over. Feel it going deeper and deeper. Allow your entire body to relax. Face and head relaxed. . . . Neck relaxed. . . . Shoulders relaxed. . . . Arms relaxed. . . . Chest relaxed. . . . Back relaxed. . . . All these areas are relaxing more and more, becoming more deeply relaxed than you thought possible.

STOMACH. Now, begin the relaxation of the stomach area. Tighten up this area. Briefly hold the tension. . . . Relax and let go. Feel the relaxation pour into your stomach area. All the tension is being replaced with relaxation, and you feel the general well-being that comes with relaxation. Take a deep breath. Hold it. (Briefly pause.) Silently say, "Relax and let go" as you slowly breathe out.

Now, experience a different type of tension in the stomach area. Push your stomach out as far as you can. Briefly hold the tension. . . . Now, relax and let go. Take a deep breath. Hold it. (Briefly pause.) Silently say, "Relax and let go" as you slowly breathe out.

Now, pull your stomach in. Try to pull your stomach in and touch your backbone. Hold it. . . . Now relax and let go. Take a deep breath. Hold it. (Briefly pause.) Silently say, "Relax and let go" as you breathe out.

You are becoming more and more relaxed. Each time you breathe out, feel the gentle relaxation in your lungs and in your body. As you continue to do these exercises, your chest and stomach area will relax more and more. Check the muscles of your face, neck, shoulders, arms, chest, and stomach. Make sure they are still relaxed. If they are not, then tense and release them again. Whatever part is still less than fully relaxed is starting to relax more and more. Soon you will be able to tell when you have tension in any part of your body. You will learn that you can always relax and let go of the tension you may find in any part of your body.

HIPS, LEGS, AND FEET. Now, begin the relaxation of your hips and legs. Tighten your hips and legs by pressing down the heels of your feet into the surface they are resting on. Tighten these muscles. Keep the rest of your body as relaxed as you can and press your heels down. . . . Now, hold the tension. . . . Relax and let go. Feel your legs float up. Take a deep breath. Hold it. (Briefly pause.) Silently say, "Relax and let go" as you breathe out. Feel the relaxation pouring in. Notice the difference between tension and relaxation. Let the relaxation become deeper and deeper. Enjoy the relaxation.

Next, tighten your lower leg muscles. Feel the tension. Briefly hold the tension. . . . Now, relax and let go. Take a deep breath. Hold it. (Briefly pause.) Silently say, "Relax and let go" as you breathe out.

Now, curl your toes downward. Curl them down and try to touch the bottom of your feet with your toes. Hold them and feel the tension. . . . Relax and let go. Wiggle your toes gently as you let go of the tension. Let the tension be replaced with relaxation. Take a deep breath. Hold it. (Briefly pause.) Silently say, "Relax and let go" as you breathe out.

Now, bend your toes back the other way. Bend your toes right up toward your knees. Feel the tension. Try to touch your knees with your toes. Feel the tension. Hold the tension. . . . Relax and let go. Feel all the tension slip right out. Take a deep breath. Hold it. (Briefly pause.) Silently say, "Relax and let go" as you slowly breathe out. Feel the tension leaving your body and the relaxation seeping in.

BODY REVIEW. You have progressed through all the major muscles of your body. Now, let them become more and more relaxed. Continue to feel yourself becoming more and more relaxed each time you breathe out. Each time you breathe out, think about a muscle and silently say, "Relax and let go," . . . Face relax. . . . Shoulders relax. . . . Arms relax. . . . Hands relax. . . . Chest relax. . . . Back relax. . . . Stomach relax. . . . Hips relax. . . . Legs relax. . . . Feet relax. . . . Your whole body is becoming more and more relaxed with each breath.

Spend a few more minutes relaxing, if you would like. If, during your day, you find yourself getting upset about something, remember the relaxation you have just experienced. Before you get upset, take a deep breath, hold it, and as you breathe out, silently say, "Relax and let go." With practice, you will be able to use this technique to relax whenever you begin to feel the stress of everyday living.

Source: Reprinted with the permission of Scribner, a Division of Simon & Schuster, from *Stress Management: A Comprehensive Guide to Wellness,* by Edward A. Charlesworth and Ronald G. Nathan. Copyright © 1984 Edward A. Charlesworth and Ronald G. Nathan.

Meditation[4]

Recorded accounts of meditative practice date back over 2,000 years among Zen monks, Indian yogis, Judaic spiritual leaders, and Christian monks. The earliest known Christian meditators were hermits who lived during the fourth century A.D. in the most isolated areas of the Egyptian desert. Like present-day Indian yogis in the Himalaya mountains, they sought isolation to communicate with God, free from worldly distractions. The meditative practices of these earliest Christian monks are strikingly similar to practices of Hindu and Buddhist meditators in India at that time (suggesting a cultural exchange). These Christian meditators repeated quietly or silently a selected phrase from the Scriptures. The most popular phrase or *mantra* was "Lord Jesus Christ, Son of God, have mercy on me, a sinner." Many of these monks repeated the short form of this mantra, "Kyrie eleison," silently for hours each day. Today, this form of meditation is no longer practiced among Christians in the West but still survives in some Eastern orthodox monasteries (Goleman, 1977).

Numerous meditation approaches are practiced today. Goleman (1977) described the following:

Hesychasm: Christianity's Yoga
Kabbalah: Hidden Judaism
Sufism: Muslim Mysticism
Transcendental Meditation: Hinduism for Americans
Patanjali's Yoga Sutras
Bhakti: The Hindu Path of Devotion
Swami Muktananda's Kundalini Yoga
Tantra's Left-Handed Path
The Buddha's Middle Way
Tibetan Buddhism
Zen
Gurdjieff
J. Krisnamurti's Methodless Method

Practically all the approaches achieve a meditative state by having the person concentrate on or repeat an object: word, phrase, chant, sound, spiritual value, imagery of an exquisite painting, and so forth. Different approaches use different rituals, different objects, have somewhat different goals, and produce somewhat different meditative experiences.

[4]This material on meditation is adapted from Charles Zastrow, "Meditation," in *Talk to Yourself: Using the Power of Self-Talk,* © 1979, pp. 185–189. Adapted by permission of Prentice-Hall, Inc., Englewood Cliffs, New Jersey.

There is considerable evidence that meditation reduces stress and anxiety through a simple set of general procedures that can be learned without elaborate rituals or large expense (Goleman, 1976). A strong advocate of this view is Herbert Benson, a Harvard cardiologist who carefully reviewed contemporary meditation approaches. Benson (1975) identified the following four elements as key to eliciting the relaxation response in any meditation approach:

1. *Being in a quiet environment* that facilitates tuning out external distractions and internal stimuli.

2. *Being in a comfortable position,* such as sitting or lying down. The position should be one in which the meditator can feel comfortable for at least 20 minutes.

3. *Having an object to dwell on,* which also facilitates tuning out thoughts about day-to-day concerns. Examples of suitable objects include one's breathing, a word or phrase chanted to oneself, an audiotape of ocean waves, a symbol to be gazed at steadily, or the sights and sounds of a relaxing place, visualized with one's eyes closed.

4. *Having a passive attitude,* in which the meditator "lets go" of day-to-day concerns. A passive attitude appears to be key to eliciting the relaxation response; people become relaxed when they focus their cognitions on relaxing thoughts and stop thinking about everyday problems. If day-to-day concerns drift into the meditator's awareness, he or she should allow them to pass on as effortlessly as possible.

An example of a simplified, nonreligious meditation approach is as follows:

1. Find a quiet environment, such as a quiet room, where you will not be interrupted.

2. Sit quietly in a comfortable position.

3. Close your eyes.

4. Breathe in and out through your nose at a relaxed, natural pace. As you breathe out, silently say the word *relax* slowly to yourself.

5. Continue this process for 10–20 minutes: Slowly breathe in, as you exhale slowly say "relax" to yourself.

6. Do not focus your thoughts on day-to-day concerns, and do not worry whether you will achieve a deep level of relaxation. Deep levels of relaxation are gradually achieved with continued practice. The state of being relaxed comes slowly as you let go of your worries and concerns. When distracting thoughts enter your mind, allow them to drift away as effortlessly as possible. Focusing your thoughts on your breathing and on silently saying "relax" as you exhale facilitates your "letting go" of worries and concerns.

7. When you finish, sit quietly for several minutes, first with your eyes closed and then with your eyes open. Practice this technique once or twice daily. With practice, you will gradually achieve more rapid and deeper levels of relaxation. A word of caution: walk around for 15 or more minutes before driving, as you are apt to be lethargic, with your response reaction time being lengthened considerably.

Note that meditation and relaxation approaches are closely related. Both techniques are therapeutic because they produce the relaxation response. In addition, certain components of the muscle relaxation and deep-breathing relaxation approaches are used by some meditation approaches to aid in producing the relaxation response. Finally, imagery relaxation resembles those of meditation and can in fact be considered a meditation approach.

Research has demonstrated that meditation is physiologically and psychologically more refreshing and energy-restoring than deep sleep (Wallace, 1973). Many meditators, in fact, have reported that they needed less sleep after they began meditating, which suggests that a regenerative process occurs during meditation (Bloomfield, Cain, & Jaffe, 1975). Meditation has been used successfully in the treatment of many stress-related disorders including hypertension (Benson, Rosner, & Marzetta, 1973) and asthma (Honsberger & Wilson, 1973). It has also been effective in decreasing the use of drugs, alcohol, and cigarette smoking (Seaward, 1994); alleviating sleep disorders; and accelerating the bodily healing process (Seaward, 1994).

Meditation has also been found to have a number of other positive effects. It is useful in treating phobias (Boudreau, 1972) and in treating people with emotional problems (Bloomfield, Cain, & Jaffe, 1975). Regular practice of the technique improves learning ability (Abrams, 1974), perceptual motor performance (Blasdell, 1974), ability to recover from stress (Seaward, 1994), perceptual acuity (Pelletier, 1974), work productivity and job satisfaction (Frew, 1974), and creativity (Seaward, 1994). Meditation improves psychological health (Shelly, 1973); heightens self-awareness (Bloomfield, Cain, & Jaffe, 1975); increases self-actualization (Ferguson & Gowan, 1974); reduces anxiety, depression, and aggression (Ferguson & Gowan, 1974); reduces reaction time (Shaw & Kolb, 1974); increases recall ability (Abrams, 1974); and improves academic performance (Seaward, 1994).

Meditation's potential medical value in eliciting the relaxation response is dramatically described by Benson (1975):

> The prevention of stress-related diseases carries with it enormous significance, certainly for the individual and his family in terms of their own physical and mental well-being, and for society as a whole through huge dollar savings in health expenditures. It is possible that the regular elicitation of the Relaxation Response will prevent the huge personal suffering and social costs now being inflicted on us by high blood pressure and its related ailments. (pp. 156–157)

A word of caution. If and when you use meditation (or any relaxation technique) you should walk around for several minutes before driving because you may be so relaxed you will have difficulty concentrating for a short period.

Hypnosis and Self-Hypnosis[5]

Many people erroneously believe that the effects produced by hypnotism are the result of some mystical, magical power of the hypnotist. Authorities on hypnotism, however, are in full agreement that the effects result from the thinking processes and imaginative processes of the hypnotized person (Caprio & Berger, 1963; Freese, 1976; Lecron, 1964; White & Watt, 1973).

Being hypnotized involves entering a mental state of aroused concentration so intense that everything else is ignored and the hypnotized person goes into a trance. Freese (1976) defined hypnosis as follows:

> To understand hypnosis, the trance state, one must always keep in mind this picture of aroused intense concentration. When we concentrate deeply on a book and become completely absorbed in its contents, we're not asleep even though we don't move a muscle, don't hear a thing going on about us. . . . In short, hypnosis is a normal state into which we will slip readily during our everyday lives. It's what happens to us every time we become entranced (note that word) by a movie or mind-blowing experience, a TV show or a work of art or even a conversation. It's the daydreamer lost in her or his vivid imagery. (pp. 37–38)

Caprio and Berger (1963) noted that all hypnosis is self-hypnosis. People who become hypnotized, hypnotize themselves by thinking and concentration. If a person does not wish to be hypnotized, it is almost impossible for a hypnotist to put that person in a hypnotic state. According to Caprio and Berger:

> Hypnotists do not possess any unusual or mystic powers. A hypnotist is a person who knows that his subject actually hypnotizes himself. The hypnotist is merely a person who has learned or perhaps mastered the science and art of *effective suggestion*. He teaches the subject how to bring about or self-induce the hypnotic state. Hypnotism has sometimes been called the "manipulation of the imagination." . . . The hypnotic state is similar to becoming completely absorbed in a movie or a book. In other words, it represents a concentration of attention. (pp. 15–16)

Almost anyone can be hypnotized. It takes imagination, a willingness to cooperate with the hypnotist, and a willingness to accept suggestions. Caprio and Berger (1963) added:

> To be hypnotized, (1) you must *want* to be hypnotized; (2) you must have confidence in the hypnotist; (3) you must train your mind to *accept* suggestion. (p. 17)

While under hypnosis a person will not do anything contrary to his or her moral code. Those hypnotized have the power to select the suggestions they are willing to accept, and they will reject improper or unethical suggestions. The hypnotized person also has the power to terminate the hypnotic state at will. There has never been a case in which the hypnotized person did not return to the waking state. Hypnotized people are never in anybody else's power. They won't go into a trance unless they want to. They won't do anything unless they want to. They have the power to come out of a trance whenever they want to (Caprio & Berger, 1963). Caprio and Berger further described hypnosis and its medical value:

> All hypnosis is self-hypnosis. In hypnosis the subject responds to the suggestions of the hypnotist. The subject *permits* the hypnotist to bring about a state of calmness and relaxation because he, the subject, *desires* this mental state.
>
> Hypnosis involves (1) motivation, (2) relaxation and (3) suggestion.
>
> In self-hypnosis, the relaxation is self-induced, followed by the hypnotic state. It is the influence of our own minds over our bodies. By including our own hypnotic

[5]The material on hypnosis is adapted from Charles Zastrow, "Hypnosis and Self-Hypnosis," in *Talk to Yourself: Using the Power of Self-Talk,* © 1979, pp. 197–203. Adapted by permission of Prentice-Hall, Inc., Englewood Cliffs, New Jersey.

> state, we heighten our suggestibility and are then capable of influencing our body functions. . . .
>
> The phenomena of hypnosis and self-hypnosis explain many of our publicized miracles of faith cures. Self-hypnosis is really a form of *psychic healing* accomplished through the voluntary *acceptance and application of one's own suggestions.* (p. 19)

Hypnotists use many techniques to induce a trance. One technique is relaxation: the hypnotist's voice gradually becomes monotonous (like a lullaby) as he or she keeps suggesting relaxation until the hypnotic state is reached.

Freese (1976) documented that over the centuries thousands of different rituals have been used for trance induction. Such rituals include chants or dances of witch doctors, a simple flashing light or a swinging pendulum, or a monotonous beat of a *metronome* (an instrument designed to mark exact time by a regularly repeated tick).

Whatever technique is used to induce a trance, all hypnosis is self-hypnosis in which a state of aroused intense concentration is achieved because the hypnotized person cooperates with the hypnotist and desires to enter this mental state.

The mechanics of how to induce self-hypnosis and how to help yourself with self-hypnotic suggestions will now be briefly described. The first step is to decide what you would like to use self-hypnosis for: losing weight, cutting back on drinking alcoholic beverages, overcoming anger, eliminating jealousy, combating insomnia, relieving a pain, stopping smoking, reducing a phobia, learning to relax in certain anxiety-producing situations—whatever.

The next step is to become very relaxed. Such relaxation can be achieved using one of the approaches described earlier: muscle relaxation, deep-breathing relaxation, imagery relaxation, or meditation. Such relaxation approaches are effective if (and only if) they shift your thinking from focusing on day-to-day problems to focusing on calming, monotonous, or relaxing thoughts. This relaxation phase of hypnosis and self-hypnosis is very important because it facilitates the hypnotized person's capacity to accept and follow through on hypnotic suggestions.

The final key component of hypnosis and self-hypnosis is a suggestion (or a set of suggestions) that you give yourself while in a relaxed state. All such suggestions are simply statements in which you tell yourself that you must, can, and will be able to achieve a certain goal: for example, "I can and will stop smoking"; "I will feel no pain"; "I am able to relax myself and fall asleep whenever I need to"; "I am able to relax and reduce my blood pressure"; "I can control my drinking and will never ever take more than two drinks when I go out with friends."

For self-hypnotic suggestions to work, it is essential to give yourself these suggestions daily to keep your attention focused on achieving your goal (for example, telling yourself that you can and will follow a certain diet to lose weight).

This phase assumes that what the mind causes, it can cure; or, as Caprio and Berger (1963) noted, it is based on the power of telling yourself

> I can—I must—I will achieve my goal—that I have the mind-power to accept and carry out certain self-given suggestions which will enable me to overcome almost any handicap, to improve my personality and acquire a healthier philosophy of life. (p. 34)

After giving yourself a hypnotic suggestion, you can arouse yourself from the self-hypnotic trance by telling yourself that you will "come out" as you slowly count to ten. It is needless to worry that in the event of an emergency you will not be able to arouse yourself rapidly from the trance. Under hypnosis you are always able to arouse yourself immediately from the hypnotic state and are rapidly able to respond to the given emergency situation.

Caprio and Berger (1963) provided a number of case examples of hypnosis being successfully used. One involved a noted scientist in his seventies who was hesitant to address audiences because of stage fright. He generally declined invitations to speak. On one speaking engagement he became so frightened that he nearly fainted, and he experienced heart palpitations. This scientist was aware that his fear was largely caused by his thoughts and deduced that if he could learn to control his thoughts he would in turn control his fear. He practiced a relaxation technique and repeatedly gave himself the following suggestions: "I have nothing to fear—I am going to concentrate on the message I wish to pass on to my audience and not on myself—I have confidence in the power of my mind" (p. 126). He reduced his fear with this approach and subsequently used this self-hypnosis approach before future lectures. He reportedly was able to deliver many talks with this approach and experienced little fear.

Hypnotic and self-hypnotic suggestions have been used for a wide variety of medical and psychological purposes:

- To control weight
- To alleviate emotional problems
- To reduce stress and anxiety
- To stop drinking or smoking
- To alleviate insomnia
- To improve one's sex life
- To treat sexual dysfunctions
- To alleviate pain
- To reduce tension
- To relax
- To alleviate depression
- To improve memory
- To increase self-confidence
- To improve interpersonal relationships
- To improve one's self-image
- To reduce fatigue
- To treat stress-related illnesses
- To reduce hostility and anger
- To reduce jealousy and guilt
- To overcome feelings of inferiority
- To conquer fears and phobias
- To treat migraine headaches, asthma, arthritis, backaches, bursitis, and allergies
- To treat gynecological problems
- To anesthetize
- To treat stuttering, by reducing anxiety and tension
- To alleviate pain during dentistry
- To treat hypertension

A more extensive review of the uses of hypnosis is contained in Caprio and Berger (1963), Freese (1976), Lecron (1964), and Blonna (1996).

Biofeedback[6]

Biofeedback is simply a mirror reflecting some aspect of your physiology. Learning takes place only when there is feedback. In the same way your eyes give you feedback when you throw a ball, a biofeedback machine gives you feedback about what you are doing with your body. Biofeedback machines are able to gauge levels of arousal or physical change that we usually do not become aware of until a markedly high level of arousal is reached. During an hour interview, for example, your hand temperature is apt to vary by 5–7 degrees. A higher hand temperature represents a more relaxed state, whereas a lower hand temperature indicates a higher level of tension or anxiety (when you are tense, blood flows inward, away from the skin, which lowers skin temperature). It is unlikely that you will be aware of these gradual changes, even though they are graphic indicators of your emotional state.

There are certain things biofeedback can and cannot do. Biofeedback does not alter our physiological processes, nor does it solve personal or emotional problems, and it definitely does not reveal our hidden thoughts or fantasies. What it does by meters, lights, or sounds is indicate what is happening in our body at that moment.

A wide range of biofeedback measures exist. Some common ones that we generally don't associate with biofeedback are mirrors to reveal how we look, bathroom scales to measure our weight, tape measures to show our height, and fever thermometers to gauge our body temperature. A lie detector test is another common biofeedback machine that measures levels of arousal. Here are some other ones:

- A thermometer to measure hand temperature
- Muscle feedback units to measure muscle tension and anxiety
- Equipment to measure pulse rate
- Galvanic skin response equipment to measure levels of arousal and anxiety
- Auditory feedback (using an amplified stethoscope) to measure peristaltic activity in the intestinal tract
- Equipment to measure blood pressure levels
- Electroencephalogram to measure brain wave activity
- Electrocardiograph to record changes in electrical potential occurring during the heartbeat

Basically, all of these devices gauge stress (levels of anxiety or arousal) in various parts of the body. The problem that biofeedback training seeks to alleviate is stress and its long-term effects on our feelings, bodies, and thinking processes. Stress is an intense state of physical and emotional arousal that results from our perception of being threatened or endangered. The body prepares itself on the basis of the perception, not on whether the perception is realistic or unrealistic. If the perception is realistic, the physiological and emotional arousal prepares us better to handle the danger. If the perception is unrealistic, we needlessly expend our adaptive energy. Furthermore, prolonged stress plays a key role in the development and severity of a wide variety of stress-related illnesses.

[6]This material on biofeedback is adapted from Charles Zastrow, "Biofeedback," in *Talk to Yourself: Using the Power of Self-Talk,* © 1979, pp. 204–210. Adapted by permission of Prentice-Hall, Inc., Englewood Cliffs, New Jersey.

There are three basic ways to cope with high levels of stress and tension:

1. You can change the events that contribute to your high stress level. For example, if you are dating someone and feel considerable anxiety over whether your partner is committed to the relationship, you can arrange a time to talk with your partner about commitment to the relationship. Often, however, events that cause your stress cannot be changed.

2. You can reassess whether you are realistically assessing situations. A rational self-analysis (see Module 6) is one structured way to examine stress-producing self-talk and to challenge irrational self-talk that may be prolonging high levels of stress.

3. You can get involved in meaningful activities that will stop you from thinking about the distressing event. Instead, you will think about the enjoyable and meaningful activity that you are involved in, which will reduce your stress level. Many activities can help shift your mental focus: hobbies, exercising, going to a movie, relaxation techniques, meditation, hypnosis, biofeedback, and any other activity that you find enjoyable.

Conceptually, biofeedback is based on two basic principles: (1) Any biological function that can be monitored and amplified by electronic instrumentation and fed back to us through one of our five senses can be regulated by us. (2) "Every change in the physiological state is accompanied by an appropriate change in the mental emotional state, conscious or unconscious, and conversely, every change in the mental emotional state, conscious or unconscious, is accompanied by an appropriate change in the physiological state" (Pelletier, 1977, pp. 264–265).

Biofeedback research has demonstrated that many *autonomic* (that is, involuntary) nervous system processes can be brought under conscious control if a person obtains information about these processes. Such processes include heart rate, muscle tension, brain waves, body temperature, and stomach acidity level.

The following example described by Pelletier (1977) illustrates how it is possible to regulate heart rate via biofeedback.

> During the initial stages of electrocardiogram (ECG) or heart-rate feedback, patients are surprised to see how volatile their heart rates really are. At first the pattern seems random. . . . After a relatively short time the patient realizes that minor changes in his physical posture—even flexing an index finger, or changes in his breathing pattern—have a profound effect upon the heart. Breathing in a slow or regular manner or sitting in an upright posture helps to decelerate the heart rate, whereas slouching or breathing shallowly and quickly tends to accelerate it. . . . When thinking of a pleasant or relaxing vacation, he notes that his heart rate begins to decelerate. Conversely, when he thinks about a perplexing or stress-inducing situation, like his income tax or an argument with a close friend, heart rate accelerates. . . . Once this link between internal sensations and their effects upon the cardiovascular system is established, the individual has a means of regulating this critical autonomic function. (pp. 265–266)

The basic principles of learning how to regulate your heart rate, which are described in this example, provide a model of how biofeedback can be used to regulate practically all autonomic processes.

Brown (1977) provided another illustration of biofeedback:

> The average person can demonstrate to himself the biofeedback phenomenon by using an ordinary thermometer purchased from the drugstore or hardware store. One six to eight inches long and filled with fluid is best. He can tape the thermometer bulb to the fat pad of the middle finger with masking tape, making sure of good contact, but no constriction of circulation. After five or so minutes of quiet sitting, preferably with the eyes closed, note the temperature of the finger. Then, while still sitting quietly, repeat a few autosuggestion phrases to yourself slowly, such as, "I feel relaxed and warm," "My hands feel warm and relaxed," "I feel calm and relaxed." Repeat the phrases slowly, allowing the suggestion to take effect, then go on to the next one, and then repeat the series. Every five or ten minutes, take a reading of the finger temperature. Most people will show a rise in finger temperature three to five or even ten degrees, some only a degree. Only a few may not change or may even show a small fall in finger temperature. With repeated practice, everyone can learn to increase finger temperature by using mental activity. (pp. 4–5)

An increase in finger temperature indicates that a person is becoming more relaxed.

Clinical biofeedback can be integrated with other therapy techniques or used as a technique in and of itself. Clinical biofeedback has been successfully used in conjunction with traditional psychotherapy, rational therapy, behavior modification, hypnosis, meditation, and relaxation techniques. (Techniques such as relaxation approaches, meditation, and hypnosis are used at times together with biofeedback to help a person learn how to relax.)

Although biofeedback achieves the same relaxation response as meditation, hypnosis, and relaxation techniques, the essential difference is that biofeedback amplifies biological signals. Pelletier (1977) described an advantage of being able to amplify biological signals:

> An advantage of biofeedback over nonfeedback techniques is that the physiological information tells an individual precisely how he is functioning. Interpreting the feedback, a person knows exactly how tense he is in certain muscles, and through trial and error he can discover the means of relaxing those muscles. When he is successful, the feedback lets him know immediately. (p. 260)

Most people are unaware when their body is under moderate stress. Only when they are highly anxious or highly aroused do they consciously become aware of their level of stress. Yet, moderately high levels of stress over extended periods can be damaging to physiological functioning and result in breakdown (that is, a stress-related illness). Biofeedback shows people their level of stress precisely. It also provides immediate feedback when that level is increased or reduced. Increases or decreases in stress are caused primarily by our thinking processes, and biofeedback immediately provides feedback to a person on the kinds of thoughts that lead to a reduction in stress. Thus, through trial and error, with biofeedback, people can identify what kind of thinking (such as meditating or visualizing being in a relaxing place) will work for them in reducing stress.

Another advantage of biofeedback is that it provides instantaneous feedback on the particular area of affliction. An overall relaxation response usually induces all neurophysiological functions to move toward a state of deep relaxation. Yet the movement toward relaxation may vary considerably in various systems of the body. At times most systems become relaxed, while a few remain tensed. An additional advantage of biofeedback is that a specific physiological process (for example, high blood pressure of a hypertensive person) that needs to be corrected can be monitored, feeding information to the person to help evaluate progress in alleviating this dysfunction.

Brown (1977) described the therapeutic value of biofeedback:

> There are more than fifty major medical and psychological problems in which biofeedback has been used with either greater success than conventional treatments or at least with equal benefits. The mind and body ailments that respond to biofeedback treatment span the entire spectrum of illnesses human beings suffer: emotional, psychosomatic, and physical disabilities. (pp. 3–4)

Biofeedback can be used to exert voluntary control over heart rate, skin temperature, blood pressure, muscle tension, brain waves, or any other internal biological function capable of being monitored. Biofeedback is radically altering the doctor-patient relationship in that it requires doctors to instruct patients in being active participants in the healing process.

Brown (1977) and Blonna (1996) provide summaries of disorders that have been reported to respond to biofeedback: problems that are primarily emotional—anxiety, phobias, chronic headaches, tension headaches, hyperactivity, stage fright, insomnia, alcoholism, drug abuse, depression with anxiety; problems that are primarily stress-related—asthma, essential hypertension, bruxism (grinding of the teeth), menstrual distress, ulcers, colitis, functional diarrhea; and problems that are primarily physical—muscle spasms with pain, strokes, paralysis, spasticity, cerebral palsy, migraine headaches, and epilepsy.

Summary

This module presents a variety of treatment approaches for people with personal problems: milieu therapy, psychodrama, play therapy, parent effectiveness training, crisis intervention, task-centered practice, solution-focused therapy, mediation, muscle relaxation approaches, deep-breathing relaxation, imagery relaxation, meditation, hypnosis, and biofeedback. These approaches were developed independently of a comprehensive theory of psychotherapy.

Parent effectiveness training has four techniques that anyone can use to improve interactions with others: active listening, I-messages, no-lose problem solving, and resolving collisions of values. Task-centered therapy focuses on helping clients identify and carry out specific tasks that will help them resolve their problems. Solution-focused therapy emphasizes the strengths of clients in achieving their goals.

Mediation is used by a variety of professions to resolve conflicts between two or more people. Social workers have used the following treatment approaches for a number of years: crisis intervention, milieu therapy, play therapy, and psychodrama.

Relaxation approaches, meditation, hypnosis, and biofeedback have been around a long time, but only recently have social workers begun to use these approaches. With the recognition that stress (and resulting stress-related problems) is our nation's number one health problem, social workers are using these approaches more and more to induce the relaxation response and thereby reduce anxiety and stress (among other objectives).

EXERCISES

1. USING I-MESSAGES

Goal: To phrase I-messages.

Step 1: As a class, brainstorm I-messages in response to typical situations and list them on the blackboard:

a. Someone is smoking a cigarette near you and the smoke is bothering you.
b. You're riding in a car that a friend is driving dangerously fast.
c. Someone is playing a stereo loudly in your dorm; it is interfering with your studying.
d. A friend has just made another snide remark about your being overweight.
e. A person you're dating continues to write to someone he or she has dated in the past.

Step 2: Indicate which responses are you-messages and which are I-messages, and why.

Step 3: Restate each you-message as an I-message.

Step 4: Class discussion of the merits and shortcomings of this approach.

2. ACTIVE LISTENING

Goal: To develop active listening skills.

Step 1: Review the discussion for active listening techniques on pages 468–469.

Step 2: Break into pairs. Choose a topic (a philosophical or moral issue such as abortion, a problem with a roommate, or a problem at school).

Step 3: One person discusses the topic; the other person responds with active listening statements.

Step 4: Self-critique in pairs. Assess the quality of your active listening statements. Did you make suggestions, ask questions, or talk about your own experiences?

Step 5: Reverse roles and discuss the same topic or a different one. Self-critique again.

Step 6: Class discussion of their experiences. Did active listening motivate the speakers to continue talking? Did this process feel natural or artificial?

3. MEDITATION AND RELAXATION

Goal: To use a relaxation technique. Deep-breathing relaxation, meditation, imagery relaxation, and muscle relaxation.

Step 1: Your instructor will lead you in a meditation exercise of his or her choosing. Here is one possible meditation:

I will now lead you in a meditation exercise. The purpose is to show you that through meditating you can reduce stress and anxiety. You can do this exercise by yourself whenever you are anxious or want to relax. You can do it, for example, before giving a speech in class, before taking a crucial exam, or before going to bed at night.

Herbert Benson, who wrote *The Relaxation Response* (1975), identified four key elements common to meditative approaches that help people relax. These four elements are (1) being in a quiet place; (2) getting in a comfortable position; (3) having an object to dwell on, such as your breathing or thinking about your ideal relaxation place, or a neutral word or phrase that you can continually repeat silently to yourself; and (4) having a passive attitude in which you let go of your day-to-day concerns by no longer thinking about them. Having a passive attitude is the key element in helping you relax.

Now, I want you to form a circle. [*Wait until a circle is formed.*] I will lead you in three types of meditation. First, we will do a deep-breathing exercise. Then, we will move into repeating the word relax silently to ourselves. Third, I'll have you focus on visualizing your most relaxing place. We will move directly from the first to the second, and then from the second to the third, without stopping. When we do this exercise, don't worry about anything unusual happening. There will be no tricks. Concentrate on what I'm telling you to focus on, while taking a passive attitude where you let go of your everyday thoughts and concerns. Everyday thoughts and concerns may occasionally enter your mind, but try to let go of them when they do.

Before we start, I want each of you to identify one of your most relaxing scenes. It may be lying in the sun on a beach or by a lake. It may be sitting in warm water in a bathtub reading a book. It may be sitting by a warm fireplace. Is there anyone who hasn't identified a relaxing scene? [*Wait until everyone has identified one.*]

OK, we're ready to start. [If possible, dim the lights, or turn out some of them.] First, I want you to close your eyes and keep them closed for the entire exercise. Next, get in a comfortable position. If you want, you can sit or lie on the floor. [*Take 5 or 6 minutes for each of the three meditative exercises. Speak softly and slowly. Pause frequently, sometimes for 20 seconds or more without saying anything. Feel free to add material to the following instructions.*]

First, I want you to focus only on your breathing. Breathe in and out slowly and deeply. . . . Breathe in and out slowly. . . . As you breathe out feel how relaxing it feels. . . . While exhaling, imagine your concerns are leaving you . . . as you're breathing in and out, feel how you're becoming more calm, more relaxed, more refreshed. . . . Just keep focusing on breathing slowly in and out. . . . Don't try to be in sync when I'm talking about breathing in and out. . . . Find a breathing rhythm that's comfortable for you. . . . Breathe in slowly and deeply, and then slowly breathe out. . . . You've got the power within you to get more and more relaxed. . . . All you have to do is focus on your breathing. . . . Breathe in slowly and deeply, and then slowly breathe out. . . . If other thoughts happen to enter your mind, just let them drift away as effortlessly as possible. . . . The key to becoming more relaxed is to let go of your day-to-day concerns. . . . To do this, all you need to do is simply focus on your breathing. . . . Breathe in slowly and deeply, and then breathe out.

Now, we will switch to repeating silently to yourself the word relax. Keep your eyes closed. . . . Just keep repeating to yourself the word relax. . . . Keep repeating "relax" to yourself silently and slowly. . . . If day-to-day thoughts enter your mind, let them drift away. . . . Keep repeating "relax" to yourself. . . . All of us encounter daily stressors. . . . It is impossible to avoid daily stressors. . . . The important thing to remember about stress management is not to seek to avoid daily stressors but to find ways to relax when we are under high levels of stress. . . . An excellent and very simple way to learn to relax is to sit in a quiet place, in a comfortable position, and silently repeat to yourself the word relax . . . "relax" . . . "relax." . . . By simply repeating the word relax to yourself, you have the power within you to become more and more relaxed. . . . Find a nice comfortable pace for repeating the word relax to yourself. . . . The pace should be slow enough that you can relax. . . . But not be so slow that thoughts about your day-to-day concerns enter your mind. . . . Remember, the key to relaxing is letting go of your day-to-day concerns. . . . If such concerns begin to enter your mind, focus more of your attention on repeating "relax" silently and slowly

(continued)

EXERCISES
(continued)

to yourself. . . . By repeating "relax" to yourself, you will find it will appear to have magical powers for you, as you will find yourself becoming more and more relaxed and refreshed. . . . [*Have the students repeat "relax" for 5 or 6 minutes.*]

Now, we will switch to focusing on your most relaxing scene. Don't open your eyes. . . . Focus on being in your most relaxing place. . . . Feel how good and relaxing it feels. . . . Just dwell on how relaxing it feels. . . . Enjoy everything about how calm and relaxing this place is. . . . Feel yourself becoming calmer, more relaxed. . . . Enjoy the peacefulness of this place. . . . Feel yourself becoming more relaxed, more renewed and refreshed. . . . Enjoy all the sights and sounds of this special place for you. . . . Notice and cherish the pleasant smells and aromas. . . . Feel the warmth, peacefulness, and serenity of this very special place for you. . . . Whenever you want to become more relaxed, all you have to do is close your eyes, sit quietly, and visualize yourself in this very relaxing place. . . . The more you practice visualizing being in your relaxing place, the quicker you will find yourself becoming relaxed. . . . It will appear to you that your relaxing place has magical, relaxing powers for you, but in reality you are simply relaxing yourself by letting go of your day-to-day concerns and instead focusing on enjoying the peacefulness of your most relaxing place. . . . If you have to give a speech, or are facing some other stressful situation, you can learn to reduce your level of anxiety by simply closing your eyes for a short time and focusing your thoughts on being in your most relaxing place. . . . You always have the power within you to reduce your level of anxiety. . . . All you have to do is close your eyes and visualize being in your very special relaxing place. . . . Feel yourself becoming more relaxed, refreshed, and calm. . . . If you're feeling drowsy, that's fine. . . . Feeling drowsy is an indication that you're becoming more and more relaxed. . . . You're doing fine. . . . Just keep on visualizing being in your very relaxing place. . . . You will become more and more relaxed by simply letting go of your day-to-day concerns and by enjoying this very special relaxing place. . . . [*Continue this imagery relaxation exercise for 5 or 6 minutes.*]

Unfortunately, in a minute or so it will be time to return to this class. But there is no hurry. I will slowly count backward from five to one, and then ask you to open your eyes shortly after we reach the number "one". . . . Five, enjoy how relaxed you feel. You may now feel warmer, drowsy, and so relaxed that you feel you don't want to move a muscle. . . . Enjoy this very special feeling. . . . It is healthy to become this relaxed as your immune system functions best when you are relaxed. . . . Four, slowly begin to return to this class. . . . There is no rush. . . . There is no hurry. . . . Take your time to become more alert. Any time you want to relax, all you need to do is use one of these three meditative approaches. With practice you will gradually get better at relaxing by using these approaches. . . . Three, you should now focus on returning in a short time to this class. . . . Take your time . . . we still have a half-minute or so. . . . Examine whether you want to make a commitment to using relaxation exercises to reduce the daily stress you encounter. . . . Two, we are nearly at the time to return to this class. . . . You should now work toward becoming more and more alert. . . . One, slowly open your eyes. . . . There is no hurry. . . . Take your time to get oriented. A word of caution: If you have to drive some place soon, please walk around for several minutes before trying to drive a car, as you may be so relaxed now that you may not be alert enough to drive safely.

Step 2: Class discussion of their experiences.

MODULE **10**

Sex Counseling and Therapy

What is sexuality?[1] To many people, this word connotes a man and a woman, preferably married to each other, having intercourse. To professionals who specialize in sexuality, the word describes many things:

- How we feel about ourselves as boys or girls, men or women—or as a combination of both genders
- Masturbation
- Having a baby
- Affection
- Deciding to terminate a pregnancy
- Deciding to continue a pregnancy
- People in parental roles using children for their own sexual arousal
- Romantic love
- People being biologically of one gender and psychologically of the other gender
- "Dirty old men"
- Using condoms to avoid transmitting HIV
- Babies touching their genitals to get pleasure
- Rape
- Pornography
- The wedding night
- Erectile dysfunction
- Intimacy
- A 17-year-old male realizing he is sexually attracted to other males
- Jealousy
- Getting sexually aroused by erotic thoughts
- Predictable physiological responses
- That warm, goosey feeling we get when we're touched by someone who arouses us
- An 85-year-old man making love with an 81-year-old woman
- Spending countless hours in sexually oriented websites
- And many, many more thoughts, feelings, and experiences

Very few social workers become sex therapists, but most of those with counseling responsibilities are frequently presented with clients' sexual concerns. Remember a simple adage, "The answers you get depend on the questions you ask." If you're perceived as "askable"[2] by your clients—that is, you are comfortable talking about sex, have some knowledge, are sensitive and receptive to clients' sexuality—you will be asked questions about sex. Clients are both perceptive and self-protective. If you're uncomfortable, don't worry; nobody will bring up sexual issues.

Social workers who specialize in sexual issues are often told by many clients suffering from sexual problems that in dozens of sessions of previous psychotherapy therapists *never* asked them any questions about sex. Or, following a serious injury or illness, the subject of resuming one's sex life was never addressed by helping professionals. These clients were eager to talk about sex, but "it never came up."

The goals of this module are (1) to encourage you to see the legitimacy of professional intervention in the sexual area of people's lives; (2) to teach you some basic sex counseling skills; (3) to help you examine and broaden your own comfort and knowledge in this sensitive area; and (4) to teach you some evaluation

[1]This chapter was especially written for this text by Lloyd G. Sinclair, A.C.S.W. Mr. Sinclair is a Certified Sex Educator, Sex Therapist, and Sex Therapy Supervisor at Midwest Center for Psychotherapy and Sex Therapy in Madison, Wisconsin.

[2]The concept of "askable" was developed by Sol Gordon, Ph.D., an Emeritus Professor at Syracuse University, Syracuse, New York. Dr. Gordon has written numerous books and articles on various aspects of adolescence and sexuality.

techniques that can be helpful in determining when it might be appropriate to intervene and when referral to a specialist is indicated.

Why is it so important and necessary for social workers to be able to intervene in this area? The most compelling reasons are (1) because sexuality is a significant and pervasive aspect of the human personality, indeed a driving biological force; and (2) because many other professionals who *should* be helpful to people with sexual concerns, such as physicians and psychotherapists, often are not. The legitimacy of scientific study of, and professional intervention in, people's sexual lives has received widespread recognition only in the fairly recent past. Consequently, only professionals who were trained in the last 20 years or so (either toward a degree or as continuing education) are likely to have acquired skills to assess, treat, or refer persons with sexual problems. The others are sexuality "experts" based solely on their personal experiences, which, even if the professionals are pretty "experienced," is woefully inadequate. Society's historical discomfort with sexuality has had countless effects. Within the profession, it has resulted in professionals not always being taught necessary information and skills.

Let's turn our attention now to some important concerns specific to counseling people on sex-related matters.

Knowledge

The first prerequisite to effective counseling in sexuality, as well as in any area, is knowledge. The information necessary to help people with sexual problems goes well beyond the scope of this text. In addition to other resources listed in the footnotes of this module, an excellent comprehensive overview and guide to treating clients with sexual problems is Sandra R. Leiblum and Raymond C. Rosen (eds.), *Principles and Practice of Sex Therapy* (2000).

Assumptions

Perhaps more than in any other area, counselors should be extremely careful to avoid making assumptions when clients raise issues about sex. Because people express their sexuality in a wide variety of ways, because people tend not to talk about their sexual experiences, and because so many people have deficits in their sexual knowledge, it is easy to assume that everyone expresses their sexuality like you express yours.

There are basically two dangers in making assumptions. The first is that you can easily draw the wrong conclusions if you don't persevere to determine that your understanding is correct. For example, if your client talks about masturbation, don't assume every man pleasures himself sexually by rubbing his penis with his hand, and every woman by rubbing her clitoris. Some people masturbate by rubbing against objects, with vibrators, or under streams of water. Some people tie themselves up when they masturbate. Others cross-dress (dressing in clothes of the other gender) or exhibit their genitals to strangers to feel aroused. If you assume everyone masturbates the same way, you counsel in ways that are unhelpful or even dangerous. If you reassure a client that masturbation is healthy and normal without learning that he risks harming himself by his particular method of self-stimulation, you are providing misinformation.

The second reason for avoiding assumptions is that your client may not view you as "safe" to ask questions of. If a man comes to you and says, "Lately I've had trouble getting an erection with my partner," and you ask, "How does *she* feel about it?" you have effectively slammed the door on that client if he is gay. This client may smooth it over nicely, and you'll never know of your mistake because gays and lesbians are used to dealing with heterosexual assumptions. But you won't be perceived as someone who is sensitive to the range of human sexual expression. And you will, consequently, counsel only those people who fit *your* stereotypes.

Words

Another important consideration is the vocabulary used by the counselors. Most counselors develop a vocabulary that is most comfortable for them. It is important to know the scientific words (*coitus, fellatio*) to understand much of the technical information about sexual response. But the English language contains many more "street" words for sexual expression than any other variety. Many clients are familiar only with those words. You will want to know the meaning of these terms (for example, *gettin' it on, going down on*) so that you understand what clients are talking about and you won't express shock when you hear them.

You probably will want to find words that describe in a straightforward manner (for example, does "sleeping together" mean having intercourse, or just sleeping?), in as value-free a way as possible, what you are trying to say (for example, intercourse, oral-genital sex).

Many counselors hide their discomfort with this subject by using medical language. The greatest danger in using unnecessarily scientific words is that you won't be understood. Clients are often embarrassed to admit they don't know the meaning of certain words, so they pretend they do. And if you're not communicating, you're not helping.

Some counselors hide their discomfort by going to the other extreme—by overusing street terms to appear "hip." The problem here is that street terms are often value-laden. To some people, the word *fuck* simply means intercourse. But to others, it is demeaning, sexist, aggressive, and repugnant.

Another extremely important concept to remember is that, in all likelihood, people with cognitive disabilities do not use language that we use routinely. When working with these clients, you may need to be especially graphic to be understood. Sensitive counselors try their vocabulary first, but when the client signals a lack of comprehension, they stop talking about "masturbation" and instead talk about "rubbing your penis 'til the white stuff comes out," or "rubbing your privates 'til you feel extra good."

One way to become more comfortable with words that clients might use is to practice saying "street" words out loud, either by yourself or with a friend. If you blush when you say words you were taught to feel uncomfortable about, your client is likely to feel embarrassed too. With practice at desensitizing yourself, you can learn to use these words comfortably.

Levels of Intervention

When clients express a sexual concern to social workers, it is important for the professional to make some preliminary evaluation regarding what their clients need to resolve the problem: a sentence or two of reassurance, or 12 weeks of intensive sex therapy?

Jack S. Annon has developed a useful conceptual scheme to help professionals make this determination.[3] He noted that very few persons with sexual problems need intensive sex therapy. Rather, they need intervention at the levels he identifies as permission, limited information, and specific suggestions.

Permission is the process of professional reassurance, letting clients know they are normal. The client reports, "My wife and I hear a lot about anal sex. We just aren't interested in doing that. Do you think there's something wrong with us?" The counselor can give permission: "Sex is best when you're doing things you *both* want to do, not because of somebody else's expectations. I would encourage you to do what you both like, and if at some point you want to try anal sex, fine. But if you don't, that's fine too. Enjoy."

Although the largest number of people with sexual issues would benefit from intervention at the level of permission, a significant but smaller number need *limited information* to alleviate their sexual concern. A client reports, "I'm happily married, we have a good sex life, but I still find I masturbate a couple of times a week. Do you think there's something wrong with me?" The counselor might respond with limited information:

> You might be interested in knowing a couple of things. First, it's a myth that masturbating indicates there's something wrong with you sexually. In fact, studies show that people who feel good about themselves sexually usually engage in a larger number of sexual activities, including partner sex *and* masturbation, than people who have a lower sexual self-image. And studies also show that most people masturbate in varying frequencies throughout their lives. It's simply not true that being in a sexual relationship means all your sexual needs and desires will automatically be met. If you enjoy masturbation, and it's not used as a weapon in your relationship to try to coerce your partner into being sexual with you, then it can do you no harm. Enjoy![4]

The third level of psychotherapeutic intervention is *specific suggestions*. Annon suggested that to make responsible and potentially helpful suggestions the counselor should take a sexual problem history. This is not a full social-sexual history but rather information related solely to the specific problem.

First, the counselor must obtain a *description of the current problem:*

Counselor: Juanita, what brings you to the office today?

[3]Jack S. Annon, *Behavioral Treatment of Sexual Problems: Brief Therapy* (New York: Harper & Row, 1976); *Behavioral Treatment of Sexual Problems: Volume 2, Intensive Therapy* (Honolulu: Enabling Systems, Inc., 1975).

[4]The counselor might also want to suggest some reading about male sexuality to this client. An excellent book is Bernie Zilbergeld's *The New Male Sexuality* (1999).

Juanita: I'm concerned because when Enrique and I have intercourse, it hurts me.

Counselor: Can you describe the pain more specifically for me? Is it sharp or dull, shallow or deep?

Juanita: It's more like a chafing pain—not really sharp, but it's sure uncomfortable. And sometimes it's deep, too, almost like he's banging into something deep inside me.

The counselor then asks about the *onset and course of the problem:*

Counselor: Has intercourse always been painful to you?

Juanita: No, not always. At first it was a little, but I think that was just because we were new at it. But then for a few years, I wasn't having any pain. But in the past several months, it's hurt.

Counselor: Has it been painful every time you've had intercourse in the past few months?

Juanita: No, and that confuses me. Sometimes, particularly when I initiate sex, it doesn't hurt.

Next, the counselor inquires about the *client's concept of the cause and maintenance of the problem:*

Counselor: Do you have any ideas about why you're having this problem?

Juanita: Well, not really. I thought for a while that maybe I was just overtired, or maybe I was making the pain up because sometimes Enrique is much more interested in intercourse than I am, but I don't think so. I really don't know.

The counselor explores with the client any *past treatment and outcome:*

Counselor: Have you tried anything to alleviate the pain besides coming to see me to talk about it?

Juanita: Yes. I asked my gynecologist about it during my last pelvic exam. He said I was fine. And I've talked with Enrique about it a lot, but neither of us knows what to do.

Finally, the counselor is interested in learning the client's *current expectancies and goals of treatment:*

Counselor: What would you consider to be a satisfactory resolution of this problem, Juanita?

Juanita: I just want intercourse to stop hurting. I used to enjoy it a lot more, and I'm starting to avoid it 'cause it hurts.

The counselor determines from this sexual problem history that intervention at the level of permission alone, or even at the level of limited information, would probably not alleviate the problem. She decides to give some permission, some limited information, and follow up with some specific suggestions:

Counselor (permission): I'm really glad, Juanita, that you had the courage to come in here today to explore this with me. I know that sex is difficult for most people to talk about, and it's especially difficult when you're having a problem with it. And you know, lots of women believe that it's natural for intercourse to hurt, almost as if that's a woman's lot in life. I'm sure glad you're not of that opinion.

Let me ask you one more question. Do you feel aroused, turned on, ready for intercourse when Enrique is ready?

Juanita: No, he seems to be ready for intercourse much more quickly than I am. I could never be as fast as he is.

Counselor (limited information): That's a pattern I hear from lots of couples. For whatever reason, the man often gets an erection and is ready for intercourse to begin long before the woman is adequately aroused. When you're turned on, your vagina will lubricate and your cervix, at the base of your uterus, will move up and out of the way of the penis. If you're not sufficiently aroused, Enrique's penis doesn't slide in easily and it bumps your cervix, which may be that deeper, sharper pain you talked about.

Juanita: So would an artificial lubricant help?

Counselor: Oh, it might help a little, but it wouldn't really solve the problem. What needs to happen is for you to be adequately turned on before you attempt intercourse. It's just as problematic for the two of you to be having intercourse if you're not lubricated as it is to attempt to have intercourse when Enrique doesn't have an erection.

Juanita: What can we do about this?

Counselor (specific suggestions): I would suggest that you spend more time concentrating on what *you* like in the sex play prior to intercourse. Maybe you could tell Enrique more about what is particularly arousing to you. Try to stay away from hurrying sex—lots of women need a good deal of time before they're adequately aroused and therefore lubricated, and there's nothing wrong with that. Perhaps if you take more initiative in directing the sexual encounter, you can do the things that are most arousing to you. I suspect one of the reasons you tend *not* to experience pain when you initiate sex is because you are likely to be more aroused at those times instead of being sexual according to Enrique's rhythms. And most important, don't go ahead with intercourse until you're really ready.[5]

The final level of therapeutic intervention described by Annon is *intensive therapy.* Intensive sex therapy is discussed later in this module under "Sexual Problems."

Sex Offender Counseling[6]

As indicated in the following case example, sexual assault is a public mental health problem due to its prevalence and victim's trauma. Historically, sex offenders have been incarcerated, which addresses society's need to punish them, but the mental health aspects of their problem often have been ignored. Social workers have been in the forefront of developing innovative and effective treatment methods that have proven effective in reducing sex offending. These methods significantly depart from typical treatments for other mental health problems. They include:

1. Breaking confidentiality between the client and the counselor in many circumstances (for example, counselors typically collaborate with client's probation officers to promote community safety) because confidentiality colludes with the secrecy frequently abused by sex offenders.
2. Increasing victimization awareness to assist clients in recognizing the full extent of harm their sexual assaults have caused to victims, families, and society.
3. Implementing behavioral interventions to reduce deviant sexual arousal while promoting nondeviant (adult, consenting) arousal and helping clients pair inappropriate sexual impulses with consequences.
4. Providing assertiveness training to reduce anger (a motivation for rape) and passivity (a motivation for seeking children as sexual targets), and to increase self-esteem.
5. Clarifying sexual values to address confusion clients have about sexual thoughts and behavior.
6. Giving information on preventing sexual dysfunction to help clients feel more confident in appropriate sexual encounters.
7. Reducing the rationalizations sex offenders use to justify their behaviors.
8. Preventing relapse by helping clients understand the thoughts and behaviors that preceded their offenses so they can recognize these patterns and avoid future assaults.

Recent studies have advanced our knowledge of which sex offenders are most likely to reoffend. These data are critical in determining which clients need sex offender treatment, which require incarceration and treatment, and in the most extreme cases, which are so dangerous that they may never be able to live unsupervised in society. An excellent review of the literature on factors associated with reoffense can be found in Anita Schlank and Fred Cohen, *The Sexual Predator* (1999).

AIDS[7]

AIDS and the Sexual Revolution

Sexual conservatism that emphasizes heterosexuality, marriage, and monogamy gave way to the sexual revolution of the 1970s. During this period many people questioned traditional values and experimented with various behaviors and lifestyles. Some found the sexual revolution liberating, but others were distressed by it.

By the 1980s, however, a sexual revolution of a far greater scope began to slowly emerge—the fear of contracting a sexually transmitted disease. Sexually transmitted diseases cause infertility, cancer, and especially in the case of acquired immunodeficiency syndrome (AIDS), death. AIDS is an infectious disease in which the human immunodeficiency virus (HIV) attacks the body's immune system, leaving victims susceptible to a wide variety of cancers and other diseases. Although new drug "cocktails" have been effective in alleviating many of the debilitating symptoms of the disease

[5]The counselor might also want to suggest two books to this client to help her understand more about women's sexuality. They are *For Yourself: The Fulfillment of Female Sexuality* (1975), by Lonnie Garfield Barbach; and *The New Vibrations Guide to Sex* (1997) by Cathy Winks & Anne Semans.

[6]Many of the ideas presented in this section are based on the author's clinical experience and are amplified in William L. Marshall, Dana Anderson, and Yolanda Fernandez, *Cognitive Behavioural Treatment of Sexual Offenders* (1999).

[7]The author wishes to acknowledge Amy Miller, M.S., APNP, Coordinator, HIV Counseling and Testing Service, University of Wisconsin-Madison Health Services, for her assistance with this section.

CASE EXAMPLE

Patty—Counseling for Sexual Abuse

Incest is increasingly being recognized as a major problem in our society. Usually when incest becomes known, the family breaks up. The following case example was selected because it illustrates a recent trend to keep such families intact.

Fourteen-year-old Patty was referred by her teacher to the school social worker because her grades and interest had fallen below her abilities and previous academic record. The social worker, Ms. White, discussed these concerns one morning with Patty. Patty alluded vaguely to "pressure at home," and after a good deal of gentle probing, she finally revealed to Ms. White that her father had been having intercourse with her since she was 11.

Patty was understandably very upset, and yet relieved. She had considered telling someone but had not been able to bring herself to talk about it before. Her father had told her many times not to tell anyone, yet she felt the situation had become intolerable.

Ms. White assured Patty that she would help her and her family. Since they lived in a state with a mandatory reporting law for suspected cases of child abuse and neglect, Ms. White telephoned the County Social Service Agency, which in turn notified the police. Social Services sent a social worker, Ms. Fox, their agency specialist in this area, to talk with Patty. Ms. Fox and Ms. White spoke with Patty together.

Both social workers were fully aware that, until a short time ago, incest was considered extremely rare in American society. Most people believed that such abuse occurred only in large, rural, economically deprived families. We now know this stereotype is very inaccurate. Sexual abuse is *not* a rare phenomenon, and more people now seek help, perhaps because of media attention, and perhaps because there are many more "blended" families. Current studies suggest that between one-fourth and one-third of adult women in the United States were sexually abused as children by someone in an authority position. Whether it is technically incest (a biological tie) or not often makes little difference. The critical issue is that the parent or parent surrogate is using his or her authority to engage in sexual acts *for the gratification of the adult.* By emotional and legal definition, no child can give consent for sexual contact with an adult because of the differences in power between them.

Ms. Fox and Ms. White also were aware that sexual abuse in families almost invariably results in severe trauma for the victims, including the inability to trust others or themselves. Violating this important sexual boundary destroys normal family roles. When father and daughter cease to be father and daughter, and the child is made to become a sexual object, how can they functionally switch back and forth? What about the mother? What about the other children, who feel the favoritism from Dad to daughter, or who may be being sexually abused by him as well?

Until recently, the typical scenario with such cases was to place the daughter or son in a foster home "for protection." Dad, whose reputation in the community plummets, generally was jailed briefly and released (pending trial), and was prohibited from seeing his family; the legal process often took months. Mother tried to hold the family together under tremendous economic, social, and emotional strain. And the son or daughter ended up feeling responsible and therefore terribly guilty for destroying the family—"If only I had kept my mouth shut, stayed 'til I was eighteen, and left." With this sequence of events, it is easy to comprehend why child sexual abuse often remained "the family secret," sometimes even known or at least suspected by the mother, for years.

Patty told Ms. Fox and Ms. White that she was extremely scared, mostly of what her father might do now. She said she had tried to tell her mother, but she just couldn't come right out and say it, so the secret was never broken. Ms. Fox explained that they would do what they could to protect her, to help her father, and to keep the family together—as long as the sexual abuse stopped. Ms. Fox arranged to meet with Patty's father shortly after he had been arrested. This collaboration of the law (represented by police, the courts, prosecuting and defense attorneys—with an emphasis on guilt or innocence) and the helping professions (represented by social workers and psychotherapists—with an emphasis on mental health) comprises a powerful combination of legal enforcement of mental health improvement. Outcome studies indicate that without the clout of legal sanctions, termination of sexually assaultive behavior is less likely to occur. Most enlightened police officers, judges, and district attorneys are aware that conviction leading solely to incarceration in prison often is not the most helpful course for the parties involved. Imprisonment takes the father away from the children so further sexual abuse doesn't occur, but it also takes him and all his *positive* contributions away as well. Sexual assault is a criminal violation; thus a legal response is appropriate. However, the behavior often does not change from punishment alone; specific sex offender treatment is also required.

Mr. Reed, Patty's father, retained an attorney. He acknowledged having intercourse with Patty ("for a few months"), but he denied having forced or even encouraged her. She had asked him questions about sex, and, he reasoned, "It was better for her to learn about sex at home, the right way, from a man who's had a vasectomy so she won't get pregnant, than from some kid on the street who doesn't care about her. So we went progressively from touching to fondling to intercourse. But now I've decided to stop and not do it anymore."

Once the legal charges were filed, the district attorney met with Mr. Reed, his attorney, and Ms. Fox. The district attorney agreed to recommend probation, with 90 days in jail with work release privileges, to the sentencing judge if the following conditions were met: (1) Mr. Reed would plead guilty to one count of sexual assault of a child (a felony); (2) Mr. Reed would move out of the family home until his therapist indicated he could safely return, and he was not to be alone with Patty (or any other minor children) under any circumstances until treatment had occurred. (The purpose of this is to protect Patty, of course, but also to support Patty's mother's role as parent in the household.) (3) Mr. Reed would participate in individual, couple, and family therapy over a period of not less than one year. If any of these conditions were not met, Mr. Reed's probation could be revoked (which would result in him being sent to prison).

Mr. Reed was evaluated by a social worker who specializes in the treatment of sex offenders, Mr. Salas. He knew that some people who molest children are pedophiles; that is, persons, generally men, whose primary and often exclusive sexual interest is in prepubescent (under the age of 14) children. Pedophiles often go to great lengths to place themselves with young children, most often boys, by pursuing occupations or hobbies, such as being newspaper carrier supervisors or baseball team coaches, to gain sexual access to them. But many child molesters are heterosexually oriented men who are married and are sexually aroused by children as well as adults. These men sometimes seek to replace a conflictual adult relationship with involvement with a child.

Mr. Salas believed Mr. Reed was this latter type of offender. He suggested the following goals in the treatment that ensued from the revelation of sexual abuse: (1) Mr. Reed was to take full and complete responsibility for all his deviant sexual behavior; (2) he was to end all sexual abuse; (3) he must understand the emotional and environmental precursors to his sexual assaults and begin to view them as warning signals, thereby changing his thoughts and behaviors early in his abusive cycle; (4) he must strengthen the marital relationship between himself and his wife; (5) he must participate in a forum for Patty to express her feelings honestly to her parents; (6) Mr. Reed must make the necessary lifestyle changes to promote his developing relationships with people based on mutuality and reciprocity, not manipulation and deception; (7) he must manage the compulsive aspect of his sexual assaults of Patty; and (8) he must assist in rebuilding the family with each family member assuming her or his appropriate role.

The issue of seductiveness often comes up in these cases. In an effort to reduce guilt feelings on the part of the perpetrator of sexual abuse, he can easily deceive himself by placing the blame on the victim. Children *are* seductive—for attention, not sexual interaction. Most children learn to attract the attention of significant adults by whatever means is effective. An adult who interprets these behaviors as *sexual* can project blame onto the child. Most counselors believe that it is absolutely necessary for the adult to acknowledge

(continued)

CASE EXAMPLE

Patty—Counseling for Sexual Abuse

(continued)

this deception, take full responsibility for his behavior, and say so to the child. This is seen as important primarily to (1) encourage the adult to see himself as in control, not a victim of circumstances, and therefore in control of *stopping* the behavior; and (2) unburden the child of her guilt for not stopping the sexual abuse and perhaps becoming aroused by the sexual interactions.

Mr. Reed was seen in group sex offender treatment and in various therapy combinations of father-daughter, husband-wife, and family treatment. Therapy occurred twice weekly for several months, then once weekly, and eventually monthly. Patty saw her own therapist to help her resolve feelings of guilt, anger, and confusion. Mr.Reed also participated in a self-help group of sexual abusers and their families to encourage mutual sharing and growth. No further incidents of sexual abuse were reported.

Counseling Skills at Work in Generalist Practice

This case example also illustrates that Mr. Salas (one of the social workers in this case) used the following roles that, as described in Chapter 1, are components of generalist social work practice: brokering Mr. Reed to receive group sex offender treatment, brokering treatment for Mr. Reed's daughter and wife, brokering family therapy for Mr. and Mrs. Reed and their daughter, and being a group facilitator in a self-help group of sexual abusers and their families.

(thereby greatly prolonging and improving the quality of life for people with AIDS who are fortunate enough to have access to these medications), there is no cure nor immediate hope of one. The social, economic, medical, and political consequences of this disease pose an unprecedented challenge to social workers worldwide.

The 1984 National Association of Social Workers' Delegate Assembly adopted a policy statement indicating how social workers can pursue action in six areas related to AIDS (Leukenfield & Fimbres, 1987, p. ix):

1. Basic epidemiological and clinical research on AIDS.
2. Distribution of accurate information on treatment available medical, financial, and psychosocial resources.
3. Provision of comprehensive psychological and social support to help persons with AIDS, their families, children, spouses, and loved ones.
4. Development of a comprehensive service delivery system to respond to the AIDS crisis, including suitable housing, home health care, and transportation services.
5. Protection of the civil rights and right to confidentiality of people with AIDS or AIDS-related complex (ARC).
6. Protection by helping professionals and appropriate licensing authorities of the eligibility for and receipt of benefits by people with AIDS.

There is a great deal of misunderstanding about AIDS. As misunderstanding combined with fear often results in prejudice and even panic, it is incumbent on social workers to be informed about AIDS. The basic facts about AIDS are listed in CTRM Exhibit 10.1. Share these facts often; they are the first line of defense against unreasonable fear.

Transmission of HIV

AIDS is caused by the human immunodeficiency virus. The first known death from AIDS occurred in England in 1959, and the disease is believed to have entered the United States in 1977. The only way to contract AIDS is for the virus to enter one's bloodstream. The four main ways this occurs are (1) through sexual contact, (2) by sharing an infected hypodermic needle (including ear piercing and tattooing with contaminated equipment), (3) by receiving AIDS-infected blood through transfusion or injection, or (4) by an infected mother transmitting it to her baby before or at birth or through breast milk. Although low levels of HIV have been found in saliva, "dry" kissing has not been demonstrated to transmit the virus. Less intimate contact will not result in transmission of the virus.

Medical experts have developed guidelines designed to minimize the likelihood of transmitting HIV. They include using safer sex practices and refraining

CTRM EXHIBIT 10.1

Basic facts about AIDS

- Once infected with the AIDS virus (HIV), you are infected *for life*. There is no cure, as yet, for the disease.
- Anyone infected with the AIDS virus can transmit the virus to a partner via anal, oral, or vaginal intercourse, or by sharing drug needles.
- It takes between three weeks and three months for the HIV to be detectable in one's blood. This means you can carry the virus even though your blood test is negative (that is, okay). On rare occasions, it can take up to six months for the HIV to be detectable in blood.
- Even though the HIV antibodies are not yet detectable in his or her blood, an infected person can transmit HIV to someone else.
- Latex rubber condoms are very effective in preventing the spread of HIV. They should be worn prior to any sexual activity. A space should be left at the tip to accommodate ejaculation, and water-based lubricants and spermicides should be used as well. Condoms, however, are not a foolproof method.
- You cannot get AIDS by donating blood.
- It is extremely unlikely that you could become infected with the AIDS virus by receiving a blood transfusion in the United States today. You cannot get AIDS by casual contact such as by working or attending school with persons with AIDS, or by sharing eating utensils, toilets, or towels.
- Two people who do not have the HIV virus and who do not use intravenous drugs have *no* risk of contracting AIDS through sexual contact with each other.

from illicit, injected drug use. Safer sex practices involve the following:

- No exchanging of body fluids. Do not allow another person's semen, blood (including menstrual blood), urine, feces, or vaginal secretions to come in contact with your body.
- Use latex condoms for all types of intercourse (oral, anal, vaginal), but be aware that condom failure with HIV may be as high as 17 percent. Therefore, condoms will not eliminate the risk of transmission and must be viewed as a secondary strategy.
- Use water-based, never oil-based, lubricants with condoms to reduce the risk of breakage.
- Never mix alcohol or other drugs with sexual activity; drugs impair your judgment and reduce your ability to make prudent decisions.
- Develop a relationship of trust with any person with whom you are going to have sexual contact, and learn as much as you can about his or her sexual history.
- Avoid having sex with multiple partners.
- Choose lower-risk sexual activities.

Symptoms

There may be no overt symptoms of AIDS for several years or more after HIV infection. Typical symptoms resemble influenza ("flu") and include recurrent fever and night sweats; persistent swollen glands in the neck, armpits, and groin; unexplained weight loss; recurrent diarrhea; persistent coughing; persistent debilitating fatigue; loss of appetite; unusual oral sores; blotches and bruised areas on the skin that do not go away; and a series of infections and illnesses.

Testing for AIDS

Screenings for HIV test for the presence of HIV antibodies, which the body produces in response to the presence of HIV antibodies. This indicates exposure to the virus that causes AIDS. Therefore, a positive result on the HIV antibody test indicates infection, not AIDS, and that the person is likely, at some time in the future, to develop AIDS. A diagnosis of AIDS is made when a person's constellation of symptoms reaches a defined medical level.

A person who is HIV-positive can infect others with the virus. The average time between HIV infection and the onset of AIDS symptoms has been approximately 10 years. However, this period is highly variable from person to person and can be affected by lifestyle and medical interventions. The HIV antibodies generally take 3–12 weeks to develop, and sometimes up to 6 months following infection. This means that a person recently infected with HIV may show an inaccurate "false negative" test result.

People seek testing for a number of reasons: knowing if you are HIV infected allows you to seek medical care that can delay the onset of AIDS or other life-threatening illnesses: knowing your HIV status can help you protect a partner(s) from becoming infected; knowing your HIV test result can help you decide the safety of having a child; and for some people, knowing the result of an HIV test, even if positive, can reduce the stress and anxiety that arises from worrying about the possibility of infection. In fact, many couples routinely seek HIV testing prior to sexual intimacy and again at a later point in the relationship when contemplating whether to discontinue the use of condoms.

A great deal of controversy surrounds the testing for HIV antibodies. Some states require HIV testing in order to obtain a marriage license, and the Centers for Disease Control recommends universal screening of pregnant women, but only with their consent. Others believe that for certain populations, such as prison inmates, the test should be mandatory. Many feel that such widespread compulsory testing will lead to discrimination if results are not kept secret, as well as great emotional upheaval in the lives of individuals who are fearful and confused about the meaning of their test results. Some states require health care providers to report the names of those who test positive for the virus, in part to facilitate identifying and notifying contacts who have been exposed. Although states maintain a high degree of confidentiality surrounding such reports, people's fears of discrimination and their inability to control the release of a positive HIV test prompt some to seek anonymous testing. The Center for Disease Control now is seeking name-associated reporting of positive HIV infections to more accurately determine the incidence of HIV and to avoid duplicitous reports. This presents a serious public policy issue: How can the public health and well-being be protected while still maintaining individual rights?

Who Has AIDS?

Seven hundred thousand people in the United States have been diagnosed with AIDS, and 58 percent of them have died. Almost half of those diagnosed with AIDS are African Americans and Hispanic Americans. AIDS clearly is not a gay disease, but the majority of people with AIDS in the United States have been homosexual or bisexual males or intravenous drug users. Some have confused this fact by viewing homosexuality as somehow causing AIDS. Worldwide, the greatest transmission of the HIV virus is through heterosexual contact. In the United States, women and adolescents are the groups with the largest incidence of new infections. Heterosexual intercourse is especially hazardous for women; one study found women who have sexual intercourse with HIV-infected men are 14 times more likely to contract the virus than are men who have sex with infected women (see Turner, Miller, & Moses, 1989).

Perhaps most tragically in the United States AIDS is increasingly striking groups who already benefit the least from this society and are the most difficult to help: the poor, minorities, drug users, and those with little education.

The health care costs for each individual AIDS patient from the time of diagnosis to death are, on average, about $120,000 (Watson, 1997). Understandably, a diagnosis of AIDS quickly plunges many sufferers into poverty. AIDS thereby presents a challenge of unprecedented magnitude to the U.S. health care system. It has been said that the measure of a society is determined by how well it cares for its least-advantaged members. Social workers have been, and will continue to be, advocates for these very disadvantaged members of our society.

AIDS has changed the social and sexual habits of many people. There has been an increased focus in sex education in institutions as well as at home. The use of condoms is more widely accepted, and they are being advertised and distributed in places where previously they were banned. Legislation requiring travelers to certify that they do not carry HIV antibodies is being passed in some countries. There are indications that monogamy and celibacy have increased, particularly in the gay community, and the divorce rate is expected to continue to decline in the heterosexual community.

Social workers have many significant roles to play in the challenges posed by AIDS: developing services; conducting research about social consequences; individual, group, couple, and family counseling; serving the needs of orphans whose parents have died from AIDS; training; educating; planning curricula—the list goes on. Indeed, AIDS raises every relevant social issue social workers have been taught to face. The values of the profession—respect for all people, the importance of self-determination, the commitment to community service, ethical responsibility to society, an individual's right to confidentiality, freedom from bigotry and discrimination, and the rights of all persons to adequate physical and mental health care—will serve social workers well as they endeavor to alleviate the effects of AIDS.[8]

[8]For further reading about AIDS, the most up-to-date information is available via the Internet. Recommended sites for accurate and current information include *www.hivinsite.ucsf.edu*; *www.gmhc.org*; *www.ashastd.org*; *www.poz.com*; *www.thebody.com/index.shtml*; *www.sfaf.org*; and *www.aids.org/immunet/home.nsf/page/homepage*. Recent books on HIV and AIDS include *HIV/AIDS at Year 2000: A Sourcebook for Social Workers* (2000), Vincent J. Lynch (ed.), Allyn & Bacon, Boston; *Understanding AIDS: Advances in Research and Treatment* (1999), Seth Kalichman, American Psychological Association, Washington, DC; *AIDS and Mental Health Practice* (1999), Michael Shernoff (ed.), Haworth, New York, NY; *AIDS Update 2000* (2000), Gerald J. Stine, Prentice Hall, Upper Saddle River, NJ; and *The AmFAR Complete Guide to Understanding HIV and AIDS* (1999), Darrel E. Ward, W. W. Norton & Co., New York, NY.

Sexual Problems

Why do people develop sexual dysfunctions? Typical patterns of child-rearing in America virtually guarantee sexual problems in adulthood. In other words, if you grew up in the United States and learned your lessons well, you'll likely have some sexual problems in adulthood. A little farfetched? Let's look at the evidence.

Young girls in America are encouraged to be sexy (become a cheerleader, attract boys) but certainly not sexual (nice girls don't . . .). They are taught that boys are naturally interested in sex (studs) but girls shouldn't be (because if you are, you're a slut, or at least "easy"). They are taught to attract boys but always to maintain a safe distance, giving sexual favors in a safe progression, always maintaining control.

A woman telephones the sex therapist, stating:

> I've been married for five years, I love my husband, we have a delightful child and a happy home. But when we get together sexually I turn on to a point and then, I just go numb. I don't feel anything.

This woman learned to control her sexual feelings so effectively in her earlier experiences that later, when it was no longer functional for her to maintain such control, her body responded, almost reflexively, by shutting down.

In contrast, boys are often taught to "sow their wild oats," to have many sexual experiences. Adolescent boys often view their virginity as a curse, a condition that must never be admitted. They too are given a contradictory message: Don't get caught, by the police, her parents, a pregnancy, or a sexually transmitted disease. And not incidentally, if you don't "perform" at all (if you don't get an erection), you'll be safe.

A man tells the sex therapist:

> I love my wife. We've been happily married now for ten years. But my problems don't go away. Oh, at first I thought we just needed to get to know each other better. But even now, after all this time, I sometimes don't get an erection and when I do and enter her vagina, I come to orgasm right away. We're both pretty frustrated by that.

This man learned to associate anxiety with sex and to reach orgasm quickly. He later became a victim of his own, previously functional, pattern.

Under normal circumstances, two people who are sexually attracted to each other will, if they pursue sexual contact, respond well together. This means they will experience erotic feelings that will cause many physiological changes in their bodies and eventually move to high levels of arousal culminating in orgasm for each. But this is the ideal. What happens if:

The man is so concerned about his partner's performance that he watches himself and therefore blocks incoming sexual stimulation?

The woman doesn't like her partner, and her sexual value system requires liking someone as a prerequisite to sexual feelings?

The man wants to have intercourse but doesn't know how it is done, nor does his partner?

The woman is with a man, but her sexual orientation is toward women—she is not aroused by men?

The only way the man can be aroused is when he is physically violent with his partner?

The only people the man is aroused by are children?

The woman is so angry at the man's insensitivity to her needs that she withholds sexual feelings to punish him and maintain her self-esteem?

Medication side effects practically eliminate sexual interest?

So you can see that normal, ideal circumstances often are not a couple's norm at all. And just as nothing succeeds like success in sex, nothing fails like failure. In other words, a sexual experience seen by the couple as a failure often causes them to watch themselves, fearing the worst. And the worst can rapidly become a self-fulfilling prophecy.

Sexual Dysfunctions Defined

Sexual dysfunctions can be defined on two levels: specific, behaviorally measurable functional disorders; and general, often relationship-oriented problems. Problems often occur on both levels.

The specific functional disorders for men are: (1) premature ejaculation, the "persistent or recurrent onset of orgasm and ejaculation with minimal sexual stimulation before, on, or shortly after penetration and before the person wishes it" (American Psychiatric Association, 2000, p. 552); (2) male erectile disorder, "persistent or recurrent inability to attain, or to maintain until the completion of the sexual activity, an adequate erection" (American Psychiatric Association, 2000, p. 545); (3) male orgasmic disorder, "a persistent or recurrent delay in, or absence of, orgasm following a normal sexual excitement phase" (American Psychiatric Association, 2000, p. 550); and (4) dyspareunia, "genital pain associated with sexual intercourse" (American Psychiatric Association, 2000, p. 554).

CASE EXAMPLE

Sex Therapy

Steve telephoned the sex therapy clinic and spoke with a male therapist. Steve explained that lately he had become increasingly upset about his marital and sexual problems and, after a particularly heated argument with his wife the previous evening, he realized something must be done. He first talked with his physician, who suggested he call the sex therapy clinic.

The therapist arranged to see Steve and his wife, Joan, together with his co-therapist. A principle subscribed to at this clinic is that because women and men grow up with such different messages about sex, and because there are obvious physical differences, women can best relate therapeutically to women and men to men. Thus, couples seen at the clinic are seen by a male-female, co-therapy team.

The Intake

At the initial appointment, the therapists asked each person about the nature of the problems occurring in the marriage.

Joan described her general dissatisfaction with the relationship as well as her specific sexual complaints. She found Steve to be preoccupied with his work and generally insensitive to her needs. She felt frustrated at her inability to get him to share his feelings with her. In the past couple of years, she admitted to basically "shutting down" to him and had given up trying to draw him out. She sought and received most of her intimacy needs from their two children. Their sex life had suffered greatly; she professed very little interest in sexual activities with Steve or by herself.

Steve was angry at Joan because he felt he fulfilled what he considered his principal role in the relationship—that of breadwinner—and increasingly was being asked to participate in duties around the house and with the children. At the same time, Joan was denying him a sexual relationship. He felt she was unfair in her expectations of him, and he increasingly had become more withdrawn.

The therapists learned further that sex early in the relationship had been good for Steve and Joan. Lately, however, their lives had become more complicated: by having children, by additional stresses from Steve's job, and by Joan's increasing lack of satisfaction in her role as housewife. Therefore, the quality and quantity of their sexual intimacy had progressively deteriorated. Intercourse occurred about twice a month now, and there was little physical affection in the relationship outside the sexual encounters.

The therapists found the couple was motivated to change. Each was frightened by the intensity of their dissatisfactions, but they were committed to each other and seemed eager to learn ways to improve their relationship.

The therapists discussed with Steve and Joan what their entering therapy would mean. They would meet once a week for therapy sessions and additionally would be expected to get together, in the privacy of their own home, three times a week for home experiences prescribed by the therapists. Sex therapy generally lasts for 12–18 sessions. The focus would be on intimacy—how to rebuild, through sexually intimate interactions, the strength of the marriage. There would be no demonstration or observation of sexual behavior in the sex therapy clinic.

Some areas of emphasis for Steve and Joan would be (1) improving verbal communication skills; (2) increasing their knowledge about sex; (3) helping each person individuate, or learn and act on what each wants rather than largely reacting to the other; (4) exploring both their histories to help them understand themselves better, with particular emphasis on parental role models; and (5) exploring the history of the relationship to better understand how the problems developed as they did and to discourage problems from developing again.

The therapists encouraged Joan and Steve to discuss, after this initial session, whether they wanted to enter therapy.

The "chicken and egg" question often comes up with sexual problems—that is, has the sexual relationship deteriorated because the marriage is in trouble, or is the marriage in trouble because the sexual relationship has deteriorated? The answer probably makes little difference. If successful intervention is made in the sexual area—the couple learns to talk honestly about their needs and desires, they learn to cooperate, and so on—improvement in the remainder of the relationship generally occurs. This is because, for most people, sexual intimacy is a microcosm of their entire relationship. They often play out their power struggles, their fears of getting close, and their anger in bed. Intervening in sexuality, furthermore, can be very focused. When a couple is given an assignment to get together for an experience touching each other, the therapists can learn a great deal about motivation, cooperation, communication, ability to give and receive pleasure, and so forth. This promotes the efficiency of therapy by giving a rather concrete focus.

Joan telephoned the therapists two days later to say they had discussed therapy and decided to get started. They scheduled the next appointment.

At the next treatment session, the therapists separated the couple, the male therapist meeting with Steve and the female therapist meeting with Joan.* This was for history taking and would be the only time they would meet separately. Each therapist took an extensive, 2-hour social/sexual history.**

The History

The history-taking session enables each therapist to develop rapport with and understand as effectively as possible the client they will represent in subsequent treatment sessions. It also gives the same-gender therapists and clients a better opportunity to get to know each other, facilitating openness and trust.

The therapists probed each client for their goals of therapy, childhood and adolescent experiences (including sexual assault victimization), sexual value systems, the history of the sexual problems, strengths and weaknesses in the marriage, descriptions of typical sexual experiences, and a great deal of other information that would help the therapists represent their client accurately and also in order to develop the treatment plan. Both clients were referred for medical evaluation to rule out physical causes.

During the history-taking session, the therapists were particularly careful to ask specific questions and press for specific, detailed answers. A very important rule for sex counselors and therapists to observe is to avoid *assuming* anything. Because specific, personal sexual experiences are not something people tend to talk about, particularly if there is a sexual problem involved, persons often assume their behaviors are similar to everyone else's. The thorough, careful therapists avoid serious pitfalls that can sabotage the success of therapy if they are not noticed.

The Roundtable

After medical evaluation confirmed that Joan and Steve had no physical impairments to sexual functioning, they met with the therapists for the subsequent therapy session, the roundtable. In this meeting, each therapist reviewed the significant contributions each partner makes to the strengths and weaknesses of their relationship. The areas of misunderstanding resulting from patterns of faulty communication were especially emphasized. The focus was not on whose fault the problems were, or who should feel guilty, but rather what was *dysfunctional* in their unique interactions with each other.

*This case history illustrates the method used most commonly by the author when seeing a couple in intensive sex therapy. Many sex therapists use similar treatment methods based on principles and techniques originally introduced by Masters and Johnson, *Human Sexual Inadequacy* (1970). The most common difference from the methods described here is the decline in the use of co-therapy teams, often because managed-care and health maintenance organizations will not pay for two therapists seeing one couple.

**Outlines of sexual histories can be found in Joseph LoPiccolo and Leslie LoPiccolo, eds., *Handbook of Sex Therapy* (1978), pp. 103–113.

(continued)

CASE EXAMPLE
Sex Therapy
(continued)

Sexual problems almost never develop in relationships because of conscious, malicious intent. Instead, they are due to patterns of interaction that, as a whole, are dysfunctional. Each interaction, taken out of context, may occur with the best of intentions. For example, Steve and Joan had fallen into a pattern of quick sex. This was largely because Steve knew Joan was not particularly enjoying their sexual experiences, so he hurried to complete them. Unfortunately, this exacerbated the problem because Joan was less likely to become aroused, and thus less likely to enjoy sex. The therapists pointed this out, along with many other patterns.

At the end of the roundtable session, they were asked to abstain from intercourse and were given the instructions in CTRM Exhibit 10.2 verbally and as a handout. Steve and Joan also were given the instructions shown in CTRM Exhibit 10.3 to improve their verbal interactions. Finally, Steve and Joan were instructed to take some time, each by himself/herself, to explore their bodies through whole-body touching and masturbation. Since masturbation to orgasms was something each of them had done many times before, this was not expected to be difficult. However, talking about masturbation had previously been awkward, and each felt some relief to get permission from the therapists and each other to self-pleasure.

The Physiology Session

The next therapy session focused on Steve and Joan's feedback about their touching experiences.

Both reported feeling awkward at first, but after they got over the feeling that they were touching solely as an assignment, they enjoyed each session a great deal. Joan felt much more relaxed than she had for some time. Because she wasn't expected to get aroused, she felt unburdened by expectations and was able to enjoy the sessions unencumbered by performance demands. Steve was encouraged; Joan initiated two of the three touching experiences they had that week. He had stated, when giving his history, his belief that if *he* never initiated sex, it wouldn't ever happen.

Both had used some "I-language" in discussing issues that came up throughout the week. Steve, particularly, said he needed to remind himself to use it more frequently.

The therapists explored, very specifically, the touching experiences with Joan and Steve, encouraging them to give each other as much feedback as possible. The emphasis on touching for the pleasure of the active partner, rather than to "turn her/him on," was further emphasized. The assignment for the next week was the same, except touching breasts and genitals was now permitted. Joan and Steve were instructed not to place too much emphasis on genital touching, however. They were to integrate genital touching with other touching, to learn and explore, not to arouse. If arousal took place, that was fine; it was *not,* however, the purpose of the experience.

Joan and Steve were further encouraged to continue their private self-stimulation sessions.

In the second half of this therapy session, the therapists reviewed significant information about the physiology of human sexual response, described as follows:

> The male therapist explained the genital response in the male, using slides and models to illustrate the physical changes. In the first stage of sexual response, excitement, blood flows into the erectile tissue of the penis (vasocongestion), resulting in erection. The scrotum (the sac surrounding the testicles) becomes thicker, more wrinkled, and the testicles move up closer to the body.
>
> The plateau stage of sexual response is characterized by the continuation of erection, although it often waxes and wanes during sex play with a partner. The testicles become fully elevated, rotate toward the front, and become blood-engorged, causing expansion in their size. The Cowper's gland secretes a small amount of clear fluid which comes out of the tip of the penis. The purpose of this fluid is generally thought to be to cleanse the urethra of urine, thereby neutralizing the chemical environment for the passage of sperm.

The orgasm stage in men consists of two phases. The first is ejaculatory inevitability, a short period during which stimulation sufficient to trigger orgasm has occurred, and the resulting ejaculation becomes inevitable. The second phase, ejaculation, results from rhythmic contractions forcing sperm and semen through the urethra. Simultaneous with this is the very pleasant physical sensation of orgasm.

The final stage, resolution, represents a return to the unstimulated state. In resolution, the penis loses its erection, and the testicles lose their engorgement and elevation.

In women, the excitement stage of sexual response ushers in many changes. The process of vaginal lubrication begins. This response is analogous to the male erection; it is caused by sexual stimulation and is, physiologically, a blood engorgement response. The uterus and cervix begin to move up and away from the vagina. The clitoris and labia minora enlarge and the labia majora spread. Breast size increases slightly and the nipples may become erect.

In the plateau stage, the uterus continues in its movement up and back, the vagina lengthens and balloons at the rear, and the outer third of the vagina contracts, causing a gripping effect. The clitoris retracts under its hood, making it seem to disappear as it increases in sensitivity.

At orgasm, the uterus and vagina become involved in wavelike muscular contractions. This response, as well as the subjective pleasure of orgasm, are very similar to the experience of the male.

In resolution, the cervix and uterus return to their normal positions, the outer third of the vagina returns to normal, followed by the inner two thirds. The clitoris and the breasts also return to normal.

The therapists also discussed the many involuntary extragenital physical responses in men and women. These include muscle tension responses such as facial grimace, spastic contractions of the hands and feet, and pelvic thrusting. Extragenital blood engorgement responses include sex flush, blood pressure and heart rate increases, and perspiration on soles of feet and palms of hands.

Finally, the therapists discussed how aging affects sexual response. They emphasized that persons are capable of experiencing pleasurable sexual response throughout life; while their bodies may slow down, they do not need to stop. (Sinclair & Zastrow, 1993, pp. 237–238)*

Subsequent Treatment Sessions

Joan and Steve saw the therapists weekly for nine more sessions. They were gradually instructed to try new sexual behaviors and to proceed at their own pace. Therapy progressed well until the fifth week.

The fifth, sixth, and seventh therapy sessions saw Joan reporting sexual interest and sexual arousal, but her progress faltered. At first the therapists interpreted the lack of progress as simply rough spots in the process of change. However, after three weeks, deeper exploration was indicated.

During a very intense seventh treatment session, the therapists identified a power struggle existing in the relationship that was hampering further progress. Basically, Joan felt *she* was being asked to change for Steve much more than he for her. Since being sexual was what he wanted more than anything from her, and sharing his feelings was what she wanted from him—something she felt he was doing very little of—she was not willing to give further. This was probably an unconscious choice, a way for Joan to protect herself from being fully dominated by Steve. The therapists tested this hypothesis by explaining this power relationship to Steve and working with him to open his feelings more to Joan. Subsequent weeks saw great improvement in this area and in the sexual relationship in general.

Therapy was terminated by agreement of clients and therapists when the couple found that the sexual relationship, as well as the relationship in general, had improved greatly. In addition, they had learned skills to foster further improvement in the months and years to come.

*A book that summarizes the effects of aging on sexuality is *Sex Over 40,* Saul M. Rosenthal (1999).

CTRM Exhibit 10.2

The therapists' instructions to Steve and Joan

Touching Experiences

For many persons, the idea of body touching is thought of only as a preliminary to orgasm. Thinking of touching in this way often causes the touching to become less valued for its own sake. Although the entire body may be pleasant to touch and to have touched, emphasis is usually placed on the breasts and vaginal area or on the penis and testicles. Touching need not be explicitly genital or goal-oriented to be pleasurable. Touching, by yourself or with a partner, can be a joyful expression of discovery and exploration, of giving and getting.

Plan ahead and prepare, together, a quiet and private, warm and comfortable place. Create an atmosphere that is pleasant for you. It may include soft, even colored lights or candles and music or other things that help you relax. Remove your clothing and assume positions that will permit comfort during long periods of touching. Give yourselves a lot of time. Slowly become very familiar with your partner's entire body. Remember, this experience is not one of trying to sexually arouse one's partner. It is designed to give you time to explore your own feelings about touching and being touched. Touch, stroke, squeeze, and caress your partner to explore what you feel. The feeling you receive need not be an arousing one. You will feel something; get in touch with whatever that feeling is.

You may wish to shower together, using pleasant soaps on one another's body, or try a shower in the dark (you must then rely on touch). Try a pleasant tasting, nonalcohol based lotion or oil, or a baby powder. These facilitate the movement of skin on skin and reduce friction. Oils or lotions should first be poured in your hands to be warmed or otherwise warmed beforehand.

Use your fingers, fingertips, your palms, and your full hand to touch and caress in different ways. This is not a massage. Massage is designed primarily to give pleasure to the other person. Remember, the major purpose of this touching experience is to discover feelings for yourself through touching your partner. It may be helpful to close your eyes while touching so you can focus on your own feelings without observing your partner's response. Try a joyful fantasy, if you like; or pretend you've lost the use of your sight for a while and must rely on touch alone. The person being touched has only to concentrate on his or her own feelings of being touched. Sometimes, too, you may want to explore your partner's body visually while you are touching and would feel more comfortable if your partner were to close his or her eyes. If so, ask your partner to do so. If you would like to comb your partner's hair, do so.

Since you are touching your partner for yourself, you need not concern yourself about your partner's reaction, unless it is one of discomfort or pain (if so, your partner must tell you). After each touching experience discuss your feelings with one another; not in a directive or accusatory fashion but with an effort toward understanding each other's feelings about touching and being touched. Do not make assumptions about your partner's feelings. Use "I" language to express your feelings. (See CTRM Exhibit 10.3.)

We ask you to have "nongenital touching experiences" a minimum of three times during the first week to reinforce comfortable feelings. We will discuss with you which partner should initiate the first touching experience. After the "initiator" has fully explored his or her feelings from touching the partner's body, change off, the person who was touching will then become the one who is touched. During this first week we do not want the man to touch his partner's breasts, nipples, or vaginal area; nor do we want the woman to touch her partner's nipples, penis, or testicles. Touching should be done only with the hands during this week period. (Much later you may wish to try touching your partner with other parts of your body: your feet, lips, face, etc.) (Midwest Therapy Center; Sinclair & Zastrow, 1993, p. 235)

The specific functional disorders for women are: (1) female sexual arousal disorder, "a persistent or recurrent inability to attain, or to maintain until completion of the sexual activity, an adequate lubrication-swelling response of sexual excitement" (American Psychiatric Association, 2000, p. 543); (2) dyspareunia, painful intercourse; (3) vaginismus, "the recurrent or persistent involuntary contraction of the perineal muscles surrounding the outer third of the vagina when vaginal penetration with penis, finger, tampon, or speculum is attempted" (American Psychiatric Association, 2000, p. 556).

The general sexual dysfunctions that pertain to men and women include: (1) hypoactive sexual desire disorder, "a deficiency or absence of sexual fantasies and desire for sexual activity" (American Psychiatric Association, 2000, p. 539); (2) sexual aversion disorder, "the aversion to and active avoidance of genital sexual contact with a sexual partner" (American Psychiatric Association, 2000, p. 541); (3) sexual dysfunction due to a general medical condition, "the presence of clinically significant sexual dysfunction that is judged to be due exclusively to the direct physiological effects of a

CTRM Exhibit 10.3

Improving verbal interaction

Self-Representation: The Use of "I-Language"*

Most sexually intimate couples think they know considerably more about each other's feelings, attitudes, and behaviors than they, in fact, really do know. They take pride in "outguessing" and in "predicting" their partner's responses without ever really communicating with each other. They believe "since he/she loves me—he/she *knows* how I feel."

Responsibility for self. We are each responsible for our own sexuality. We should not wait for someone else to discover it for us. We need to explore, discover, and understand our own sexual responses. We are then free to share or not to share our sexuality with another person. If we decide to share our sexuality, we need to be willing to communicate with our partner what we have learned about ourselves . . . to be open . . . to be vulnerable . . . to risk. We also need to be willing to learn about our partner's sexuality *from our partner.* We cannot make assumptions about his/her needs, feelings, etc., without asking. Too often our guesses are wrong. In order to share a sexual experience on an equal basis we must both have and express knowledge, comfort, and responsibility for our own sexuality. This "responsibility" is necessary to take ownership for our own feelings, attitudes, and ideas as well as our behaviors.

Representation of self. Once we are responsible for our own sexuality and have made a decision to share our sexuality with another person, we need to learn the best way of representing ourselves clearly to our partner.

"I-language." It begins with "I," taking responsibility for ourselves, and is followed by a feeling. "I appreciate your tenderness." "I'm upset because you're late, and I've had to delay a fine meal." "I would like to go to that new movie tonight and wonder if you would like to go with me." "I wonder what it would feel like if you touched me like this."

The purpose of "I" language is not to promote agreement but rather to encourage accurate communication and understanding. Only with accurate understanding can you ever know whether you agree or disagree. When you use "I" language you must first be aware of your own feeling, attitude, idea, before you can clearly state it to your partner. Thus, the use of "I" language helps you to identify your own feelings first. All feelings are real for you; they may not always be rational, yet you have them. It is your responsibility to represent your feelings—not your partner's feelings. Do not expect your partner to know your feelings clearly unless you represent them clearly. Through the use of "I" language you minimize putting your partner in a defensive position. You also optimize opening further communication. You speak for *you,* not for someone else. By openly expressing your feelings you encourage your partner to do the same. Openness often seems risky when used with someone we care about, but the alternative may be years of misinformation. The following are examples of "you" language, succeeded by more effective "I" language:

a. "You make me so angry when you don't pick up your clothes." (An accusatory statement that is most likely to place your partner on the defensive.)
b. "I'm angry because in addition to picking up my own clothes I feel I have to pick your clothes up too." (Permits further communication and represents your feelings.)

a. "Let's go out to dinner." (A confused message that takes over your partner's response.)
b. "I'd like to go out to dinner and wonder if you would like to also." (Much better.)

a. "You're too clumsy when you touch my breasts." (Another accusatory message likely to shut down communication—not open it up.)
b. "I get turned off when you touch my breasts that way because it hurts; I'd like to show you what kind of touch feels good."

a. "Do you want to go to the movies tonight?" (Answer: "I don't know, do you?" Next response—"I don't know, I asked you first." Result: confusion.)
b. "I would like to see __________ tonight, and wonder if you would also like to see that film." (Midwest Therapy Center; Sinclair & Zastrow, 1993, p. 236)

*"I-language" is a verbal communication technique suggested by many therapists. It was developed by Thomas Gordon, *Parent Effectiveness Training* (1970). I-language, also called I-messages, is further described in Module 9.

---

general medical condition" (American Psychiatric Association, 2000, p. 558); (4) substance-induced sexual dysfunction, "a clinically significant sexual dysfunction judged to be fully explained by the direct physiological effects of a substance (i.e., a drug of abuse, a medication, or toxin exposure)" (American Psychiatric Association, 2000, p. 562).

Treatment of Sexual Dysfunction

Historically, our understanding of sexuality and sexual problems was largely based on the ideas of Sigmund Freud (Strachey, 1962). (Freudian theory is also described in Module 1.) Freud believed that sexuality was an extremely important life force and that sexual problems occurred because one's personality development was incomplete at some life stage. Intervention, therefore, involved the therapist's guiding clients back into that incomplete life stage, gaining *insight* into themselves, thereby completing the development of the personality. And with a fully developed personality, full sexual function would occur.

Perhaps because the theory is faulty, or it accounts for only some people's problems, or it doesn't adequately account for all problems, including sexual problems, this "traditional" intervention method often failed to help people resolve their sexual problems. So the paradigm shifted.

An alternative view of treating sexual problems was first introduced by William Masters, M.D., and Virginia Johnson in 1970.[9] They suggested that sexual problems can be just sexual problems—that they may have nothing to do with incomplete life stages or other personality defect. Instead, sexual problems may be solely the result of faulty learning about sex and consequent poor experiences, repeated over and over again. So the intervention dictated by their theory was oriented to the present (as opposed to the past). They therefore departed from the traditional focus on the *individual* and instead defined and treated the *relationship* as the client, to help people (1) understand their sexual histories, sexual values, and physical responses more fully; (2) learn what is more interesting and arousing to them sexually and to communicate this information to their partner; (3) reduce goal- and performance-oriented sexual expression, concentrating more fully on the pleasure of the experience rather than on the goal of intercourse and orgasm; and (4) reduce their anxiety during sexual experiences.

Masters and Johnson treated people, often with long-standing sexual problems, in a two-week intensive therapy program. This was the beginning of *sex therapy* as a mental health specialty.

By definition, "sex therapy differs from other forms of treatment for sexual dysfunctions in two respects: first, its goals are essentially limited to the relief of the patient's sexual symptom and second, it departs from traditional techniques by employing a combination of prescribed sexual experiences and psychotherapy" (Kaplan, 1974, p. 187).

[9]An excellent synopsis of this medical text, written in laypersons' language, is Fred Belliveau and Lin Richter, *Understanding Human Sexual Inadequacy* (1970).

More than 30 years have passed since Masters and Johnson revolutionized the treatment of sexual dysfunctions, and the treatment pendulum appears to be swinging back toward the center. In the past, the pendulum initially swung from treating sexual problems by "traditional" methods (that is, by helping clients gain insight into their personality and not directly talking about sex) to using a programmed, behavioral approach. The former method was generally unsuccessful, whereas the latter frequently led to improvement—but sometimes only to a point. Some people started to "get better" and then their improvement plateaued short of their goals. To help clients progress beyond this plateau, sex therapists increasingly have borrowed other methods of intervention frequently used in relationship therapy.[10] Further, breakthroughs in medication and medical interventions, such as the use of sildenafil citrate (Viagra) to treat male erectile disorder, offer additional alternatives for treating sexual dysfunctions.

Summary

Any social worker who interacts with clients is presented with opportunities to be helpful in the area of sexuality. Because sex typically elicits concern and anxiety in people in this society, it is incumbent on social workers to examine their own feelings in this area and to become knowledgeable. Furthermore, they need to recognize the legitimacy and importance of their professional intervention in this area.

The first prerequisite to effective sex counseling is knowledge, and therefore social workers need to acquire accurate information. Counselors cannot assume that everyone expresses sexuality in the same way. Social workers also need to learn the technical words involving sexuality and to become desensitized to the expression of "street" words in counseling.

A useful conceptual scheme of intervention levels includes permission, limited information, specific suggestions, and intensive therapy. The largest number of clients benefit from intervention at the level of permission.

[10]Sex therapists have also become much more knowledgeable about diagnosing and treating sexual disorders. A book that summarizes this information is *Principles and Practice of Sex Therapy* (2000), Sandra R. Leiblum and Raymond C. Rosen (eds.).

Intensive sex therapy differs from other forms of treatment for sexual dysfunctions in two respects. First, it endeavors to relieve the patient's sexual symptom only. Second, it departs from traditional techniques by employing a combination of prescribed sexual experiences and psychotherapy. The stages of intensive sex therapy include problem definition, history gathering, physical examination, information dissemination, prescribed sexual and communication experiences, and ongoing evaluation.

In exploring some basic counseling skills that are helpful in working with clients, we hope that we have encouraged you to think about, recognize, and explore your own areas of discomfort. The challenge is yours. Will you further the age-old "conspiracy of silence" in this sensitive area, or will you learn, explore, and help your future clients enrich this important area of their lives?

EXERCISES

1. TELL YOUR NEIGHBOR

Goal: To acquire experiential appreciation for the difficulty people have in talking about their sexuality, even for those who can easily talk about sex in general.

Step 1: Break into groups of two.

Step 2: Tell your partner about a sexual problem *you* have.

Step 3: (30 seconds.) Your instructor says "stop." *Note:* The purpose here is *not* to elicit class members' sexual problems but rather to have you experience your own uneasiness in revealing some sexual vulnerability of your own.

Step 4: Class discussion of people's responses to steps 2 and 3.

2. THE WORD GAME

Goals: (a) To desensitize students to words they are uncomfortable with so this discomfort doesn't block their helpfulness with a client. (b) To identify a functional language that is comfortable and acceptable to use in a professional setting. (c) To learn new words that may be part of a client's vocabulary and hence should be familiar.

Step 1: Break into two groups, by making an aisle down the middle of the room.

Step 2: (3 minutes.) As your instructor writes a word on the blackboard, Group 1 calls out as many alternative words (from childhood, science, slang, etc.) as they can think of.

Step 3: (60 seconds.) Group 2 tries to generate a larger number of words than Group 1.

Step 4: Class discussion. Organize the words by gender bias, scientific, childhood, street slang, and any other category you can think of.

Step 5: Break into groups to practice using these words.

3. ANSWER THE QUESTION

Goals: (a) To experience the difficulty in answering a client's questions about sex, even when you know the answer. (b) To confront sexual values as you attempt to respond to the needs of a young person. (c) To realize that the

(continued)

EXERCISES
(continued)

commonly asked questions by adolescents about sex are about values and are therefore open to many answers.

Step 1: Break into groups of five. One of you will role-play an adolescent, and one of you will role-play the social worker. This teenager trusts you.

Step 2: Ask a question of your "counselor" along the lines of the following:

Why do you sometimes get a hard-on when you're not thinking about sex?
How tough is that hymen thing?
Will playing with yourself cause problems in intercourse?
How old should you be to have intercourse?
How many boys do it? How often? Do girls ever? How would they do it?
Do you automatically know how to have intercourse when you marry?
How do two females have sex together?
Can I use tampons if I'm a virgin?
How do you know if your girlfriend says no when she really means yes?
Why do boys like intercourse more than girls?
If you don't want to have sex before marriage, how far should you go?
Do people have control over their type of sexual behavior, and over how they feel? Is it biological or in your mind?
What does an orgasm feel like?
Will looking at pornography on the Internet hurt me?

Step 3: "Counselor" responds to the questions. Group members help the "counselor" respond.

Step 4: Class discussion: What was difficult? Where did class members differ with each other on how to handle sensitive matters? How were values dealt with? What reluctances did people have to discuss certain specific areas?

Step 5: Repeat the exercise with a new question, switching roles.

MODULE 11

Analysis of Therapy Approaches

Comparison of Counseling Theories

In this module we see how the theories we've examined in the preceding modules would treat a 46-year-old woman seeking treatment for depression.[1]

In the following descriptions, treatment is simplified; therapists with any of these treatment orientations would always look at broad range of possible causes and perhaps consider using a wider range of treatment approaches than shown here.

Psychoanalysts would consider the woman's depression a symptom of a more serious underlying problem and would seek to identify unconscious processes (including defense mechanisms) that underlie her depression. Psychoanalysts would explore possible causative factors such as unresolved, traumatic early childhood experiences that are probably sexual in nature. They would use hypnosis, dream analysis, free association, and transference to identify the unresolved unconscious processes that are causing the depression. In treatment, psychoanalysts would seek to bring the memory of the traumatic experiences to the conscious part of the woman's mind to release her pent-up emotions and to allow her to consciously work through the disturbing thoughts connected with the trauma. Once the pent-up emotions are released and she gains insight into her disturbing thoughts, it is theorized that her personality will be reorganized and the symptom of depression will disappear.

Person-centered therapists would consider the depression to be caused by incongruencies between the client's self-concept and her experiences. Their focus would be to help her become aware of these incongruencies. Once this insight is achieved, person-centered therapy postulates that the client's self-actualizing motive will foster a reorganization of her self-concept to be more congruent with her experiences. Because person-centered therapy asserts that the self-actualizing motive is the best guide for directing the client, person-centered therapists are nondirective. They seek to convey empathy, positive regard, and genuineness or congruence to clients. It is theorized that if therapists convey these three attitudes, the client will feel free to examine her incongruencies. Person-centered therapists would help the client gain insight into her thoughts and feelings using three types of statements: clarification or reflection of feeling, restatement of content, and simple acceptance.

Transactional analysis (TA) would view the causes of the woman's depression as stemming from a variety of factors. The client may have a self-defeating life script or be a victim of destructive psychological games that she or others are playing. She may have communication or interaction difficulties. She may be in an inappropriate ego state for the circumstances. TA therapists would seek first to identify and make the client aware of her intrapsychic and interpersonal problems. These problems would be analyzed and interpreted in terms of TA concepts (like game concepts or life script concepts). Once analyzed, TA therapists would make a contract with her that specifies courses of action she would take to alleviate her depression. If the client is depressed because her husband wants a divorce, TA therapists would help her understand how defective communication and interaction patterns contributed to the divorce, and also

[1]There are other comprehensive psychotherapy theories (for example, see Corsini & Wedding, 2000; or Prochaska, 1979), but the theories reviewed in this text are the primary ones used by social workers. The neuro-linguistic programming approach is not reviewed here, because NLP is not designed to be a theoretical framework for assessing unwanted emotions or dysfunctional behavior.

help her examine possible games and life scripts involved. They would then make a contract with her to take specific actions to improve problematic areas and to make constructive plans for the future.

Behavior therapists would focus on identifying the stimuli that are eliciting the woman's depression. They would seek to identify environmental pressures or stimuli rather than look "inside" the client for internal stimuli. Behavior therapists believe that numerous environmental stimuli can elicit the response of depression—a monotonous job, an unhappy relationship, pressure from relatives or in-laws, and so on. They would therefore try to identify as precisely as possible the stimuli associated with the response of depression. They would then choose from a variety of behavioral intervention techniques ones with the best promise of breaking the stimulus-response connection. If the client is being taken advantage of by a colleague at work, therapists might use role playing to teach her to be more assertive. If she is in an unhappy marriage, her husband may be brought in, and therapists would work to develop contingency contracts by which the client and her husband would do specific things that please the other and would stop doing the things that displease the other. Cognitive behavior therapists would identify the cognitions that are leading the client to be depressed and then use techniques like "thought stopping" and "reframing" to change these thoughts.

Feminist intervention therapists view women's personal problems, such as depression, as due to the constraints they experience in attempting to survive in a politically, economically, and socially oppressive society. Feminist intervention maintains that what women experience in their personal lives is directly related to societal dynamics. An immense number of societal dynamics have a negative impact on women. A depressed female's distress may be related to oversubscription to sex-role stereotypes, which suggest that a woman should be docile, submissive, and dependent. The message is one of helplessness—she is unable to take care of herself and must depend on others for her well-being. Oversubscription to sex-role stereotypes engenders a state of powerlessness in which women are likely to become involved in situations where they can be victimized. Because young girls are socialized to be helpless, as women they have a limited repertoire of resources when under stress. Oversubscription to sex-role stereotypes leads to a sense of diminished self-worth, which leads to depressive symptomology. Feminist intervention would first help the depressed client analyze how her problem is related to systematic difficulties experienced by women in a sexist, racist, and classist society. Is she in an abusive relationship? Is she being victimized by sex discrimination or sexual harassment at work? Is she so engrossed in providing care to others (such as her children or an elderly parent) that she hasn't been able to establish a positive sense of self? Is she an adult incest survivor?

Once the nature of the personal and societal dynamics of the client's problems are analyzed and she gains an understanding of them, the next stage is empowerment. In this stage therapists help clients recognize that they have choices. Therapist and client identify the alternatives together. During this stage, the client is encouraged to free herself from traditional gender-role expectations. Intervention focuses on identification and enhancing her client's strengths rather than on her problems. She is encouraged to develop an independent, positive identity, to view other women as valuable, and to establish social support systems with other women. She is helped to express herself assertively. Once the client selects some strategies to implement to improve her circumstances, she is given support by her therapist (perhaps through role playing, modeling, and other similar techniques) in implementing her courses of action. The client is also given support in taking responsibility for her personal change. Therapists may encourage her to become involved in social change efforts to combat oppression and discrimination in society.

Reality therapists would consider the depression as being related to the client's view of herself as a failure in some area of her life. They would focus on the present and future, because the past cannot be changed. Therapists would seek to have the client understand that what she wants now and in the future, and her motivation to achieve what she wants, is more important than her past experiences in determining her future. Therapists would form a working relationship with the woman, explore the nature of her depression in some depth, explore alternative actions she could take to alleviate the depression, and finally make a contract with her to take certain courses of action by specific deadlines. Reality therapists would convey that she is responsible for her behaviors through such questions as, "What are you doing that contributes to the depression?" and "What do you intend to do to improve the situation?" If the client is depressed because she is unhappily married, they would ask

"What are you doing to contribute to the unhappiness in the marriage?" and "What can you do to reduce your unhappiness?"

Rational therapists theorize that the woman's depression results primarily from her self-talk about events she is facing. They would inform her that unwanted emotions arise from negative and irrational self-talk rather than from events. The initial focus of therapy would be to help the client identify the irrational self-talk that is the primary source of her depression. Reality therapists would next inform her of three different constructive approaches for resolving the depression: (1) Change the events associated with her depression; (2) get involved in meaningful activities to shift her negative and irrational self-talk about problematic events to positive and rational self-talk; and (3) counter her negative and irrational self-talk with rational self-challenges. She would then be encouraged to make a verbal contract to try one or more of these alternatives. If the third alternative is selected, the client would be instructed in how to write a rational self-analysis.

Insight versus Resolution Approaches

A useful way to categorize therapies is as approaches that emphasize "insight" and those that emphasize "resolution strategies." This categorization is based on a framework originally developed by London (1964). Insight approaches assert that clients can resolve their problems through gaining an understanding or awareness of them. Resolution approaches assert that although it is helpful for clients to understand their problems, insight in and of itself will not resolve them; clients must also learn specific ways to resolve their problems once insight is achieved. The resolution category is also called "learning approaches" (Eysenck, 1961).

These categories represent *ideal types.* Most therapies do not really fit neatly into either of these two categories; they have some characteristics of both.

CTRM Exhibit 11.1 lists the characteristics of these two types and which therapy approaches adhere to each. Psychoanalysis and person-centered therapy are classified as being insight approaches. Reality therapy, rational therapy, transactional analysis, feminist intervention, and behavior therapy are classified as being resolution approaches. The purest approach (the one that has nearly all the characteristics) in the insight category is psychoanalysis, whereas behavior therapy is perhaps the purest example in the resolution category.

Is Counseling Effective?

In the future, some historian studying our era may amusingly label it "The Age of Psychotherapy." Hundreds of thousands of people in our country seek counseling or psychotherapy every year. Millions of dollars are spent annually to educate and train therapists and to pay for their services. The entertainment world routinely portrays the lives of people receiving psychotherapy. Every year dozens of books are written on the different theories and techniques of psychotherapy. Certainly, many Americans now believe that psychotherapy is a magical and effective way to change one's personality for the better, to relieve tensions, to resolve personal problems, and to lead a happier life. But is it really effective? Does psychotherapy actually help people?

Most people, including helping professionals, think this is an absurd question. They point out that many people do improve after receiving psychotherapy. But is psychotherapy the cause of their improvement, or is it simply coincidental with their improvement? Perhaps people who improve while undergoing therapy would improve just as much without having therapy. The only way to discover the effects of psychotherapy is to study the process and the outcome of psychotherapy experimentally; ideally this would involve taking two matched groups of people with personal problems, treating one group by giving them therapy, and then testing both groups to see how much they improved. If the therapy group improves more than the control group, then psychotherapy is probably effective; if both groups improve equally, then psychotherapy is probably ineffective.

At first thought, we would expect therapists to have conducted many studies on the effectiveness of psychotherapy for several reasons. First, from the beginning psychotherapy has been strongly criticized. Experimental studies to prove its effectiveness would go a long way toward answering this criticism. Second, clinical psychologists, most of whom at least are part-time therapists, strongly emphasize the necessity of research and have carried out numerous studies. Surely this profession has done many studies. Third, because there are so many different theories and techniques, the best way for therapists to show that they have the most effective method would be to test the method experimentally.

CTRM Exhibit 11.1

Comparison of insight and resolution approaches to therapy

Characteristics of Insight Category	*Characteristics of Resolution Category*
1. Behavior is largely determined by internal underlying unconscious processes. Therapies identify the cause of a person's actions by looking at internal factors. (Psychoanalysis, person-centered therapy)	1. Behavior is determined primarily by the environment. Therapies identify the causes of a person's actions by looking at environmental or external factors. (Transactional analysis, reality therapy, behavior therapy, feminist intervention)
2. The problematic behavior is a *symptom* of an internal, unresolved, and unconscious conflict or fixation. (Psychoanalysis, person-centered therapy)	2. Only the problematic behavior needs to be resolved. (Transactional analysis, reality therapy, rational therapy, behavior therapy, feminist intervention)
3. If only symptoms are treated, the underlying conflicts will cause another symptom. (Psychoanalysis, person-centered therapy)	3. If the behavior is resolved, symptom substitution will not occur. (Transactional analysis, reality therapy, rational therapy, behavior therapy, feminist intervention)
4. The goal: Resolve underlying conflicts or disturbing unconscious processes. (Psychoanalysis, person-centered therapy)	4. The goal: Eliminate the problematic behavior. (Transactional analysis, reality therapy, rational therapy, behavior therapy, feminist intervention)
5. Counselees are "patients." (Psychoanalysis)	5. People with emotional and behavioral problems are clients or consumers of services, not patients. (Practically all therapy approaches except psychoanalysis)
6. To resolve the underlying conflict, it is necessary to probe deeply into patients' past. (Psychoanalysis)	6. The "here-and-now" is important; it is not necessary to probe the past. (Practically all therapy approaches except psychoanalysis)
7. The goal: Bring the underlying conflict or the disturbing unconscious processes to the patients' awareness so (a) the unexpressed energy can be released and (b) the person can then consciously deal with the disabling ideas. (Psychoanalysis, client-centered therapy)	7. Specific resolution approaches are explored, with clients selecting and contracting approaches. (Transactional analysis, reality therapy, rational therapy, behavior therapy, feminist intervention)
8. Insight into problems is curative in and of itself. (Psychoanalysis, client-centered therapy)	8. Insight by itself is not curative; clients need to become aware of available resolution strategies to try. (Transactional analysis, reality therapy, rational therapy, behavior therapy, feminist intervention)
9. Therapy lasts for a long time, often a year or more. (Psychoanalysis, client-centered therapy)	9. Therapy is considerably shorter in duration. (Reality therapy, rational therapy, transactional analysis, behavior therapy, feminist intervention)
10. Mental illness exists. (Psychoanalysis, client-centered therapy, some advocates of transactional analysis, rational therapy, and behavior therapy)	10. Mental illness is a myth. (Reality therapy and some advocates of transactional analysis, rational therapy, and behavior therapy)
11. Mental illness results from internal unconscious processes, such as conflicts, fixations, and use of defense mechanisms. (Psychoanalysis, client-centered therapy)	11. Behavior, including abnormal behavior, is learned. (Reality therapy, rational therapy, transactional analysis, behavior therapy)
12. Unconscious processes cause emotional and behavioral problems. (Psychoanalysis, client-centered therapy)	12. Unconscious processes are deemphasized. (Reality therapy, rational therapy, transactional analysis, behavior therapy, feminist intervention)

Fourth, because Americans spend so much money on psychotherapy, we would naturally expect that there would be good proof to show that therapy deserves its high position in our society.

However, when we examine the research literature on the effects of psychotherapy, we find few well-designed studies on this subject. There are numerous reasons for this lack. Many therapists are so convinced of psychotherapy's effectiveness that they feel no need to actually demonstrate that it is effective. In addition, it is very difficult to design and carry out studies on this subject. Problems in designing outcome studies on psychotherapeutic approaches is beyond the scope of this text. However, an excellent discussion can be found in Sundberg and Tyler (1962) and in Phares and Trull (1997). The problems mentioned here illustrate the difficulties involved in this type of research.

Problem 1: Set up criteria to evaluate the success of treatment. One way to do this is simply to compare clients' report of their problems before and after therapy. But this is a very subjective method. We encounter what Hathaway (1948) has called the "Hello-Goodbye" effect; that is, when clients first ask for help, they try to convince the therapist that they have serious problems and need help; at the termination of therapy they give the impression that they have been helped—perhaps because they feel obliged to be courteous.

Alternatively, therapists could rate the progress of their clients. Obviously, this brings with it the danger of bias. Personality tests could be given before and after therapy to those clients for whom personality change is a goal of treatment. However, the validity of most personality tests is low (Phares & Trull, 1997). Perhaps the best way to solve the criterion problem is to use several different criteria to rate the improvement.

Problem 2: Set up an adequate control group. It is very difficult to match every person in the experimental group with one in the control group on variables that influence therapeutic change, such as social status, age, intelligence, sex, motivation for improving, and problems they're having. Researchers must also address the *placebo effect* (that is, when some people actually do improve just because they believe they are being treated). Thus, the experimental group may show improvement over the control group, but this improvement may be entirely due to the placebo effect and not to psychotherapy at all.

Problem 3: Length of therapy, which can run two or three years. Research, including follow-ups, may thus take five years or longer. With such a long time comes cost issues, tracking issues (subjects can die or move away). Also, it is hard to motivate researchers to do research on something that takes so long to obtain results.

These problems in research on psychotherapy are indeed serious, but with ingenuity and perseverance they can be overcome. To show the kind of ingenuity that is needed, H. J. Eysenck (1961) described how to get around the ethical problem of withholding treatment from the control group when an experimental study is being designed:

> There are several answers to this point. In the first place, the benefits are merely putative, and consequently nothing is being withheld which is known to be of assistance to the patient. The argument assumes that we have already proved what is in fact the point at issue. In the second place it is a universal practice in medicine, whenever a new method of treatment is put forward, that this new method must receive clinical trials, including a control group not treated by means of the new method. If this is ethically admissible in the whole of medicine, even when the most serious disorders are involved and where the a priori probability of effectiveness in favour of the new cure may be rather high, then it is difficult to see why a different set of ethical ideals should apply in psychiatry where disorders are rather less serious. . . . In the third place it is quite untrue that psychotherapy would have to be withdrawn from certain people in order to provide a control group. Of all those who are said to be able to benefit from psychotherapy only a very small number have in fact received it. In the United States, at least, there is a high correlation between the income of the patient and the choice of therapy; middle-class patients by and large get psychotherapy, working-class patients get physical treatment. It would be very easy indeed to get together large groups of patients who would not in the normal way obtain psychotherapy and to form an experimental and control group from these patients. If this were done the outcome would not be that psychotherapy was withheld, because of the experiment, from people who might otherwise benefit from it; rather, the experiment would be instrumental in bringing psychotherapy to people who would not otherwise have received it. (p. 701)

Today, well designed and well executed studies prove that we can do good outcome studies on psychotherapy. The Cambridge-Somerville Youth Study (Teuber & Powers, 1953) is a good example. For approximately eight years, from 1937 to 1945, this large-scale treatment effort was directed at the prevention of delinquency—by guidance, counseling, and therapy—in a group of over 600 delinquent boys. The surprising result of this study was that this treatment did not reduce the incidence of delinquency in the treatment group when compared to the control group. But what is important for our present purposes is that this study (1) used a control group that was properly chosen and had a large enough number of subjects in each group (control and experimental) to make the results statistically meaningful; (2) carried on the treatment and the follow-up over a long period to obtain meaningful results; (3) used objective criteria to evaluate the treatment; and (4) investigated the process of therapy in a properly controlled and unbiased fashion. Because this study was able to solve the problems of doing good outcome research on psychotherapy, it demonstrated that the effects of psychotherapy can be researched.

When we turn to studies on the effectiveness of psychotherapy, we find some very startling results!

In 1952 H. J. Eysenck first asked the question "Is psychotherapy effective?" Eysenck wanted to learn whether psychotherapy increased the rate of recovery from neurosis for adults over what might be expected if they received no psychotherapy. To set up his baseline of recovery from neurosis (the rate of recovery of those not receiving therapy), he used two sources of information: (1) Landis, in his study of New York State hospitals from 1917 to 1934, found that the recovery rate of the neurotic patients in these hospitals was 72 percent. This rate of recovery is probably even lower than that of all neurotic people because only severe neurotics are sent to state hospitals, and because at that time the patients in state hospitals received very little treatment besides custodial care. (2) Denker found that the rate of recovery of 500 disability claimants of the Equitable Life Assurance Society was also 72 percent. These 500 patients were under a physician's care but received no psychotherapy. Thus, Eysenck chose 72 percent as his baseline of recovery from neurosis.

Eysenck then examined the research literature on the effectiveness of psychotherapy and found 19 studies, covering over 7,000 cases, in which a wide variety of psychotherapeutic techniques were used. The studies were divided according to whether the treatment was psychoanalytic or less intensive therapy. The percentage of cured or much improved by psychoanalysis was 44 percent if all cases are considered. (If only completed cases are used, the rate was 66 percent.) The percentage of cured or much improved for other kinds of therapy was 66 percent. These percentages differ significantly from the baseline recovery rate of 72 percent for neurotic people *without* any therapy—but the differences are not in the predicted direction!

Eysenck (1952) summed up this study by stating:

> In general, certain conclusions are possible from these data. They fail to prove that psychotherapy, Freudian or otherwise, facilitates the recovery of neurotic patients. They show that roughly two-thirds of a group of neurotic patients will recover or improve to a marked extent within about two years of the onset of their illness, whether they are treated by means of psychotherapy or not. This figure appears to be remarkably stable from one investigation to another, regardless of type of patient treated, standard of recovery employed, or method of therapy used. From the point of view of the neurotic, these figures are encouraging: from the point of view of the psychotherapist, they can hardly be called very favourable to his claims. (p. 324)

These are startling results. They were reaffirmed by E. E. Levitt in 1957, who summarized a large number of unpublished and published studies in which children were treated with psychotherapy. He concluded:

> The therapeutic eclecticism, the number of subjects, the results, and the conclusions of this paper are markedly similar to that of Eysenck's study. Two-thirds of the patients examined at close, and about three-quarters seen in follow-up have improved. Approximately the same percentages of improvement are found for comparable groups of untreated children. . . . It now appears that Eysenck's conclusion concerning the data for adult psychotherapy is applicable to children as well; the results do not support the hypotheses that recovery from neurotic disorder is facilitated by psychotherapy. (p. 196)

Eysenck's results stimulated more research on this subject. However, the increase in research was not as great as might have been expected from such startling results—perhaps therapists thought that Eysenck's results were so erroneous that many just ignored them, or maybe research in this area was so threatening to therapists that they did not want to research something that could show they were providing little or no useful service. Anyway, Eysenck in 1961 examined the studies in this area that had been done since 1952. He found only three studies showing an increase in the rate of recovery from neurosis for those receiving therapy that was higher than the 72 percent baseline recovery rate for those not receiving therapy. These three studies were done by J. Wolpe, Lakin Phillips, and Albert Ellis. All three of these therapists base their treatment on learning theory. Eysenck (1961) concluded:

> With the single exception of the psychotherapeutic methods based on learning theory, results of published research with military and civilian neurotics, and with

> both adults and children, suggest that the therapeutic effects of psychotherapy are small or nonexistent, and do not in any demonstrable way add to the nonspecific effects of routine medical treatment, or to such events as occur in the patient's everyday experience.
>
> The writer must admit to being somewhat surprised at the uniformly negative results issuing from all this work. In advancing his rather challenging conclusion in the 1952 report the main motive was one of stimulating better and more worthwhile research in this important but somewhat neglected field; there was an underlying belief that while results to date had not disproved the null hypothesis, improved methods of research would undoubtedly do so. Such a belief does not seem to be tenable any longer in this easy optimistic form, and it would rather seem that psychologists and psychiatrists will have to acknowledge the fact that current psychotherapeutic procedures have not lived up to the hopes which greeted their emergence fifty years ago. (p. 720)

A little later in his summary, Eysenck (1961) went so far as to recommend the following:

> It would appear advisable, therefore, to discard the psychoanalytic model, which both on the theoretical and practical plane fails to be useful in mediating verifiable predictions, and to adopt, provisionally at least, the learning theory model which, to date, appears to be much more promising theoretically and also with regard to application. (p. 721)

In 1965 Eysenck again reviewed all the studies conducted on psychotherapy and concluded:

> Neurotic patients treated by means of psychotherapeutic procedures based on learning theory improve significantly more quickly than do patients treated by means of psychoanalytic or eclectic psychotherapy or not treated by psychotherapy at all.
>
> Neurotic patients treated by psychoanalytic psychotherapy do not improve more quickly than patients treated by means of eclectic psychotherapy, and may improve less quickly when account is taken of the large proportion of patients breaking off treatment.
>
> With the single exception of the psychotherapeutic methods based on learning theory, results of published research with military and civilian neurotics, and with both adults and children, suggest that the therapeutic effects of psychotherapy are small or nonexistent. (pp. 135–136)

A number of other authorities have reviewed the outcome studies conducted on psychotherapy and have arrived at similar conclusions. Stuart (1970), for example, concluded that only therapy approaches based on what we earlier categorized in this chapter as *resolution approaches* appear to be effective; outcome studies generally show that around 90 percent of clients treated by these approaches improve. Also, Stuart concluded that for clients treated by most insight approaches (such as client-centered therapy), the rate of improvement is about the same as for disturbed persons receiving no treatment.

Finally, for clients receiving therapy from the psychoanalytic approach, the rate of improvement is somewhat lower than for people with problems who receive no treatment. Stuart suggested that the reason for this deterioration is the assignment of nondescriptive medical labels (labels such as schizophrenia, unresolved Oedipus complex, psychosis) by psychoanalysts, even though they do not know the causes of these supposed disorders and even though these labels do not describe specific behavior. Stuart suggested that such labels have a negative effect; they do not suggest a treatment approach and instead lead patients, and often those who interact with the patients, to try to resolve some unknown, nonexistent illness rather than focusing on resolving their personal problems. Also, such labels lead patients to view themselves as different, as having an illness, which leads them to lose their self-esteem and self-confidence and sidetracks them from seeking to be responsible and productive. (More material on the effects of mental illness labels is presented in Module 5.)

A review of outcome studies by Lambert, Shapiro, and Bergin (1986) concluded that there is some psychotherapies that have beneficial results:

> Many psychotherapies that have been subjected to empirical study have been shown to have demonstrable effects on a variety of clients. These effects are not only statistically significant but clinically meaningful. Psychotherapy facilitates the remission of symptoms. It not only speeds up the natural healing process but often provides additional coping strategies and methods for dealing with future problems. Psychologists, psychiatrists, social workers, and marriage and family therapists as well as patients can be assured that a broad range of therapies, when offered by skillful, wise, and stable therapists, are likely to result in appreciable gains for the client. . . . Behavior therapy, cognitive therapy, and eclectic mixtures of these show superior outcomes to traditional verbal therapies in several studies on specific disorders. (p. 201)

As noted earlier, behavior therapy and cognitive therapy (an example is rational therapy) are resolution approaches. A recent review of outcome studies by Phares and Trull (1997) found similar results—evidence for the effectiveness of resolution approaches to therapy, but not for insight approaches.

Fischer (1973) asked the question, "Is casework effective?" He then reviewed 11 outcome studies on casework that used both an experimental group and a control group. The findings are similar to the findings of outcome studies on insight approaches to psychotherapy. Fischer (1973) reported:

> Of all the controlled studies of the effectiveness of casework that could be located, nine out of eleven clearly showed that professional caseworkers were unable to bring about any positive, significant, measurable changes in their clients beyond those that would have occurred without the specific intervention program or that could have been induced by nonprofessionals dealing with similar clients, often in less intensive service programs. In the two additional studies, the results were obfuscated by deficiencies in the design or the statistical analysis. Thus not only has professional casework failed to demonstrate that it is effective, but lack of effectiveness appears to be the rule rather than the exception across several categories of clients, problems, situations, and types of casework. (pp. 13–14)

Fischer (1979) raised the question "Isn't casework effective yet?" and concluded (p. 245), "There is still no evidence that MSW-level social workers can produce better results with their clients than would occur with no treatment at all."

What do such research findings mean? We can draw the following conclusions from reviews of outcome studies:

1. The effectiveness of casework, psychotherapy, and counseling can no longer be assumed. Additional research is needed to determine which therapeutic approaches are effective, and why.

2. Available evidence suggests that the psychoanalytic approach should either be discarded or at least tested extensively to determine why patients have a lower rate of improvement than people who receive no treatment.

3. Approaches that only seek to have clients gain insight into their problems appear to have no higher rate of improvement than people with problems who receive no treatment. (It appears that therapy techniques based on the insight model were largely used by caseworkers in the 11 studies reviewed by Fischer.) These research findings suggest that even though insight into a problem may be useful, it is not in and of itself sufficient to bring about positive changes.

4. Therapies based on learning theory are generally being found to be effective in outcome studies. A crucial component of learning theory appears to be exploring resolution strategies and having clients contract to use a specific resolution approach.

5. Module 6 speculates that therapeutic techniques that succeed in changing unwanted emotions and dysfunctional actions are effective primarily because they change a person's negative or irrational self-talk to rational and positive self-talk. If this is the key therapeutic agent, then the controversy over which therapy approaches are effective and which are not should be refocused to address "Which therapy approaches are most effective in changing negative and irrational self-talk?" and "How can present therapy approaches be refined, and new approaches developed, to change negative and irrational self-talk more effectively?"

Summary

This module categorizes comprehensive psychotherapy theories in terms of whether they have characteristics of the insight approach or the resolution approach to therapy. *Insight approaches* assert that clients will be able to resolve their problems by gaining an understanding or awareness of their problems. *Resolution approaches* assert that clients must be taught, or must learn, specific ways of resolving their problems once insight is achieved. Psychoanalysis is the purest insight approach, and client-centered therapy adheres to most of the principles of the insight approach. Transactional analysis, rational therapy, reality therapy, feminist intervention, and behavior therapy adhere to most of the principles of the resolution approach.

It is difficult to design outcome studies on psychotherapeutic approaches for a variety of reasons. There are difficulties in setting up criteria to evaluate the success of treatment. Controlling for the "Hello-Goodbye" effect is difficult. Setting up an adequate control group is often problematic. Finally, doing follow-up research on clients who are in therapy for several years takes a lot of time and resources.

The outcome studies that have been conducted on the effectiveness of psychotherapy generally show that clients treated by insight approaches have no higher rate of improvement than people with problems who receive no treatment. Studies have shown that patients treated by psychoanalysis have a lower rate of improvement than people with problems who receive no treatment. Therapies that are based on a resolution or learning approach have generally been found to be effective in outcome studies.

A final word of caution is given in ending this chapter. Many of the therapy techniques described in this text (psychoanalysis, implosive therapy, intensive sex therapy, aversive techniques, hypnosis, covert sensitization, and systematic desensitization) should be used only by skilled therapists with extensive training because there is a danger that improper utilization may intensify the problematic behavior or create undesired side effects.

EXERCISES

1. *WHAT CAUSES POSITIVE CHANGE IN THERAPY?*

Goal: To explore what comprises the key psychotherapeutic element in counseling.

Step 1: The instructor explains the purpose of the exercise, and indicates that at the present time there is no widely accepted theory about why such diverse therapies as behavior therapy, rational therapy, meditation, task-centered practice, reality therapy, hypnosis, transactional analysis, and feminist intervention are therapeutic.

Step 2: The instructor asks the class if they know of a key psychotherapeutic element that will explain why all these therapies lead to positive changes in clients. The instructor indicates that this question is crucial because if such an element is identified, greater attention can be given in therapy to make certain this element is fully incorporated into the therapeutic process.

Step 3: The instructor should indicate that the author of this text asserts that any therapy technique that is successful in changing unwanted emotions or dysfunctional actions is effective primarily because it changes a person's thinking from negative or irrational self-talk to self-talk that is more rational and positive. The instructor gives some examples (as described in this module) that such approaches as behavior therapy, psychoanalysis, client-centered therapy, and meditation can be "reinterpreted" to suggest that restructuring thinking is the key psychotherapeutic element in counseling.

Step 4: The instructor asks the students to discuss whether they believe restructuring thinking is the key psychotherapeutic element. Those who disagree should be asked to state what they believe the key psychotherapeutic element is.

2. *TREATING DEPRESSION*

Goal: To identify merits and shortcomings of therapeutic approaches used to treat depression.

Step 1: Break into groups of three or four.

Step 2: In your group rate on a scale of 1–7 your opinion of the effectiveness of the following therapies in treating depression: psychoanalysis, client-centered therapy, transactional analysis, behavior therapy, feminist intervention, reality therapy, and rational therapy.

Step 3: Research the literature for recent outcome studies of the approaches your group rates as most effective and least effective.

Step 4: Class discussion of group conclusions.

APPENDIX

Suggested Counselor's Responses to Client's Statements

The following are suggested responses to the client's statements in Exercise 3, Chapter 5:

1. "I sense that you feel strongly about this and that you've given this a lot of thought. I'd like to explore this further with you, as I care very much about you as a person. It makes me uncomfortable if you think that the only reason I meet with you is because I'm getting paid. Working with you and with the other clients I have is personally very gratifying. Perhaps I have miscommunicated with you, verbally or nonverbally. I'd like to hear more about why you've reached the conclusion that I don't care about you as a person."

2. "You're really feeling as if you're caught in a dilemma. Obviously in this situation, as in many situations, you can't please everyone. But are you aware that the most important person to please is yourself? You're the one who has to live with your decisions. I'm wondering what your feelings are toward Kent, and what your feelings are about getting married at this time in your life. I'm also wondering why your parents dislike Kent. Let's examine these one at a time. What are your feelings toward Kent?"

3. "Yes, I did. I took them two summers ago when I was vacationing in the Colorado Rockies. But we're here to talk about you and how your life is going. Let's begin by discussing how you're doing in school. Could you please tell me your midterm grades for each of your classes?"

4. "I sense this is extremely difficult for you to reveal. You are probably feeling very vulnerable at this point. I'm pleased that you shared this with me, and I want you to know that I have an open mind about sexual orientation. It took real courage for you to talk about this, and I now believe we are in a much better position to help you make some decisions about your future. Can you tell me more about this person you're involved with?"

5. "It's true that I am neither black, nor have I lived in an inner city. But I'm interested in you and in working with you. Just because I'm white doesn't mean we can't work together. Everyone, including me, has personal problems. You, too, have some personal problems. By taking each one, one at a time, and examining them and then coming up with some realistic ways of resolving them, I firmly believe we can make progress. Just as a teacher doesn't have to be blind to teach students with a visual disability, a counselor doesn't need to have the same color of skin to work with people who have personal problems. Have I said or done anything to lead you to believe that I am prejudiced against people of color?"

6. "I'm sorry you're still involved with drugs, especially since you were using drugs when you committed the offenses that resulted in your being sent here. I don't like to see you get into trouble, but I have no choice. I have to report this. I made it crystal clear to you at our first meeting that the consequences of drug involvement would probably be an extension of the time you spend here. As you know, we do have a drug treatment program. I suggest you seriously consider participating in this program. Participation in this program, now, may not only lead to an earlier release but may also help you become drug free. Are you interested in participating in this program?"

REFERENCES

Abrams, A. I. 1974. "Paired Associate Learning and Recall." In *Scientific Research on Transcendental Meditation: Collected Papers,* eds. D. W. Orme-Johnson, L. H. Domash, & J. T. Fallow. Los Angeles: MIU Press.

Addams, J. 1959. *Twenty Years of Hull House.* New York: Macmillan (original publication, 1910).

Aguilar, I. 1972. "Initial Contacts with Mexican-American Families." *Social Work 17* (May), pp. 186–189.

Ahn, H. N., & N. Gilbert. 1992. "Cultural Diversity and Sexual Abuse Prevention." *Social Science Review 66,* no. 3, pp. 410–427.

Ainsworth, M. D., et al. 1966. *Deprivation of Maternal Care.* New York: Schocken Books.

Alberti, R. E., & M. L. Emmons. 1975. *Stand Up, Speak Out, Talk Back!* New York: Pocket Books.

———. **1995.** *Your Perfect Right: A Guide to Assertive Behavior,* 7th ed. San Luis Obispo, CA: Impact Publishers.

Alexander, C. A. 1982. "Professional Social Work and Political Responsibility." In *Practical Politics: Social Work and Political Responsibility,* eds. M. Mahaffey & J. W. Hanks. Silver Spring, MD: National Association of Social Workers.

Alexander, K. 1993. "Changes in Delivery of Services for Students with Limited English." *The Advocate 1*(2), p. 1.

Alinsky, S. D. 1969. *Reveille for Radicals.* New York: Basic Books.

———. **1972.** *Rules for Radicals.* New York: Random House.

Allen-Meares, P. 1999. "African American Males: Their Status, Educational Plight, and the Possibilities for Their Future." In *Working with African American Males,* L. E. Davis, ed., Thousand Oaks, CA: Sage, pp. 117–128.

Alter, C., & W. Evens. 1990. *Evaluating Your Practice: A Guide to Self-Assessment.* New York: Springer.

American Professional Credentialing Services. 1996. *Administration and Scoring Manual for the OQ® 45.2.* Wharton, NJ: American Professional Credentialing Services, September.

American Psychiatric Association. 2000. *Diagnostic and Statistical Manual of Mental Disorders, Fourth Edition Text Revision.* Washington, DC: Author.

Anant, S. S. 1967. "A Note on the Treatment of Alcoholics by a Verbal Aversion Technique." *Canadian Psychologist 8,* pp. 19–22.

———. **1968.** "Verbal Aversion Therapy with a Promiscuous Girl: Case Report." *Psychological Reports 22,* pp. 795–796.

Anderson, J. 1981. *Social Work Methods and Processes.* Belmont, CA: Wadsworth.

Andreasen, N. 1985. *The Broken Brain.* New York: Harper & Row.

Annon, J. S. 1975. *Behavioral Treatment of Sexual Problems.* Vol. 2, *Intensive Therapy.* Honolulu: Enabling Systems.

———. **1976.** *Behavioral Treatment of Sexual Problems, Brief Therapy.* New York: Harper & Row.

Arlow, J. A. 1989. "Psychoanalysis." In *Current Psychotherapies,* 4th ed., eds. R. J. Corsini & D. Wedding, pp. 18–59. Itasca, IL: Peacock.

Asch, S. E. 1955. "Opinions and Social Pressure." *Scientific American 193,* no. 5, pp. 31–35.

Ashem, B., & L. Donner. 1968. "Covert Sensitization with Alcoholics: A Controlled Replication." *Behaviour Research and Therapy 6,* pp. 7–12.

Axline, V. 1947. *Play Therapy.* New York: Ballantine Books.

Bach, G., & P. Wyden. 1981. *The Intimate Enemy.* New York: Avon.

Baer, B. L. 1979. "Developing a New Curriculum for Social Work Education." In *The Pursuit of Competence in Social Work,* eds. F. Clark & M. Arkava, pp. 96–109. San Francisco: Jossey-Bass.

Baer, B. L., & R. Federico. 1978. *Educating the Baccalaureate Social Worker.* Cambridge, MA: Ballinger.

Bales, R. F. 1965. "The Equilibrium Problem in Small Groups." In *Small Groups: Studies in Social Interaction,* eds. A. Hare, E. Borgatta, & R. Bales, pp. 444–476. New York: Knopf.

Bandler, R., & J. Grinder. 1975. *The Structure of Magic,* vol. 1. Palo Alto, CA: Science and Behavior Books.

———. **1976a.** *Patterns of the Hypnotic Techniques of Milton H. Erickson, M.D.,* vol. 1. Cupertino, CA: Meta Publications.

———. **1976b.** *The Structure of Magic,* vol. 2. Palo Alto, CA: Science and Behavior Books.

———. **1979.** *Frogs into Princes.* Moab, UT: Real People Press.

———. **1982.** *Reframing.* Moab, UT: Real People Press.

Bandler, R., J. Grinder, & V. Satir. 1976. *Changing with Families,* vol. 1. Palo Alto, CA: Science and Behavior Books.

Bandura, A. 1969. *Principles of Behavior Modification.* New York: Holt, Rinehart & Winston.

Barbach, L. G. 1975. *For Yourself: The Fulfillment of Female Sexuality.* New York: New American Library.

———. **1982.** *For Each Other: Sharing Sexual Intimacy.* Garden City, NY: Doubleday.

———. **1984.** *Pleasures.* New York: Harper & Row.

Barker, R. L. 1999. *The Social Work Dictionary.* 4th ed. Washington, DC: National Association of Social Workers.

Barlow, D. H., & J. A. Cerny. 1988. *Psychological Treatment of Panic.* New York: Guilford.

Barlow, D. H., & M. Hersen. 1984. *Single Case Experimental Designs.* 2nd ed. Elmsford, NY: Pergamon Press.

Barlow, D. H., S. C. Hayes, & R. O. Nelson. 1984. *The Scientist Practitioner.* Elmsford, NY: Pergamon Press.

Barocas, H. A. 1972. "Psychodrama Techniques in Training Police in Family Crisis Intervention." *Group Psychotherapy and Psychodrama 25,* pp. 30–31.

Bartless, H. M. 1970. *The Common Base of Social Work Practice.* New York: National Association of Social Workers.

Bateson, G., D. Jackson, J. Haley, & J. Weakland. 1956. "Toward a Communication Theory of Schizophrenia." *Behavior Science.* Reprinted in *Communication, Family and Marriage* I, ed. D. Jackson. Palo Alto, CA: Science and Behavior Books, 1968.

Bays, L., & R. Freeman-Longo. 1989. *Why Did I Do It Again: Understanding My Cycle of Problem Behaviors.* Workbook 2. Brandon, VT: The Safer Society Press.

Beck, A. T. 1976. *Cognitive Theory and the Emotional Disorders.* New York: International Universities Press.

Beck, A. T., A. J. Rush, B. F. Shaw, & G. Emery. 1979. *Cognitive Therapy of Depression.* New York: Guilford.

Beck, A. T., & M. E. Weishaar. 1989. "Cognitive Therapy." In *Current Psychotherapies.* 4th ed., eds. R. J. Corsini & D. Wedding, pp. 284–320. Itasca, IL: Peacock.

Becker, D. G. 1968. "Social Welfare Leaders as Spokesmen for the Poor." *Social Casework 49,* no. 2 (Feb.), p. 85.

Bellack, A. S., & M. Hersen, eds. 1998. *Behavioral Assessment: A Practical Handbook.* 4th ed. Boston: Allyn & Bacon.

Bellak, A. O. 1984. "Comparable Worth: A Practitioner's View." In *Comparative Worth: Issues for the 80's.* Vol. 1. Washington, DC: U.S. Commission on Civil Rights.

Belliveau, F., & L. Richter. 1970. *Understanding Human Sexual Inadequacy.* New York: Bantam Books.

Bemner, R. M. 1962. "The Rediscovery of Pauperism," *Current Issues in Social Work Seen in Historical Perspective.* New York: Council on Social Work Education.

Benjamin, A. 1974. *The Helping Interview.* 2nd ed. Boston: Houghton Mifflin.

Benson, H. 1975. *The Relaxation Response.* New York: Morrow.

Benson, H., B. A. Rosner, & B. R. Marzetta. 1973. "Decreased Systolic Blood Pressure in Hypertensive Subjects Who Practice Meditation." *Journal of Clinical Investigation 52,* p. 80.

Benson, P., J. Galbraith, & P. Espeland. 1998. *What Kids Need to Succeed.* Minneapolis, MN: Free Spirit.

Berg, I. K., & P. DeJong. 1996. "Solution-Building Conversations: Co-Constructing a Sense of Competence with Clients." *Families in Society* (June), pp. 376–391.

Berg, I. K., & S. D. Miller. 1992. *Working with the Problem Drinker: A Solution-Focused Approach.* New York: W. W. Norton.

Berger, R. 1982. "The Unseen Minority: Older Gays and Lesbians." *Social Work 27,* no. 3 (May), pp. 236–242.

———. **1983.** "What Is a Homosexual? A Definitional Model." *Social Work 28,* no. 2 (March–April), pp. 132–135.

———. **1987.** "Homosexuality: Gay Men." *The Encyclopedia of Social Work,* pp. 795–805. Silver Spring, MD: National Association of Social Workers.

Bergman, A. 1989. "Informal Support Systems for Pregnant Teenagers." *Social Casework 70,* no. 9, pp. 526–533.

Berlin, S. B. 1976. "Better Work with Women Clients." *Social Work 21* (Nov.), pp. 492–497.

Bernanos, G. 1970. As quoted in J. C. DeBoer, *Let's Plan: A Guide to the Planning Process for Voluntary Organizations.* New York: United Church Press.

Berne, E. 1964. *Games People Play.* New York: Grove Press.

———. **1966.** *Principles of Group Treatment.* New York: Oxford University Press.

Bernstein, B. E. 1975. "The Social Worker as a Courtroom Witness." *Social Casework 56,* no. 9 (Nov.), pp. 521–525.

Bernstein, D., & T. Borkovec. 1973. *Progressive Relaxation Training: A Manual for the Helping Professions.* Champaign, IL: Research Press.

Berwick, D. 1980. "Nonorganic Failure to Thrive." *Pediatrics in Review 1,* pp. 265–270.

Billingsley, A. 1993. *Climbing Jacob's Ladder: The Enduring Legacy of African-American Families.* New York: Simon & Schuster.

Black, B. J. 1977. "Milieu Therapy." In *Encyclopedia of Social Work,* 17th ed., pp. 919–927. New York: National Association of Social Workers.

Blades, J. 1985. *Mediate Your Divorce.* Englewood Cliffs, NY: Prentice-Hall.

Blaire, F. D. 1979. "Women in the Labor Force: An Overview." In *Women: A Feminist Perspective.* ed. J. Freeman. Palo Alto, CA: Mayfield.

Blasdell, K. 1974. "The Effect of Transcendental Meditation upon a Complex Perceptual Motor Test." In *Scientific Research on Transcendental Meditation: Collected Papers,* eds. D. W. Orme-Johnson, L. H. Domash, & J. T. Farrow. Los Angeles: MIU Press.

Blatner, A. 1995. "Psychodrama." In *Current Psychotherapies,* 5th ed., eds. R. J. Corsini & D. Wedding. Itasca, IL: F. E. Peacock.

Blonna, R. 1996. *Coping with Stress.* St. Louis: Mosby.

Bloom, M. 1975. *The Paradox of Helping: Introduction to the Philosophy of Scientific Practice.* New York: Wiley.

———. **1983.** "Empirically Based Clinical Research." In *Handbook of Clinical Social Work,* eds. A. Rosenblatt & D. Waldfogel, pp. 560–582. San Francisco: Jossey-Bass.

Bloom, M., J. Fischer, & J. G. Orme. 1995. *Evaluating Practice Guidelines for the Accountable Professional.* 2nd ed. Boston: Allyn & Bacon.

———. **1999.** *Evaluating Practice: Guidelines for the Accountable Professional.* 3rd ed. Boston: Allyn & Bacon.

Bloomfield, H., M. Cain, & R. Jaffe. 1975. *TM: Discovering Inner Energy and Overcoming Stress.* New York: Delacourte Press.

Blythe, B. J., & T. Tripodi. 1989. *Measurement in Direct Practice.* Newbury Park, CA: Sage.

Boudreau, L. 1972. "Transcendental Meditation and Yoga as Reciprocal Inhibitors." *Journal of Behavior Therapy and Experimental Psychiatry* 3, pp. 97–98.

Boulette, T. R. 1975. "Group Therapy with Low Income Mexican Americans." *Social Work 20* (Sept.), pp. 403–405.

Boyte, H. C. 1989. "People Power Transforms a St. Louis Housing Project," *Occasional Papers* (Jan.) Chicago: Community Renewable Society, pp. 1–5.

Brawley, E. A. 1983. *Mass Media and Human Services: Getting the Message Across.* Beverly Hills, CA: Sage.

Brecher, E. M. 1984. *Love, Sex and Aging.* Boston: Little, Brown.

Breuer, J., & S. Freud. 1895. *Studies in Hysteria.* London: Hogarth Press.

Brieland, D., L. B. Costin, & C. R. Atherton. 1985. *Contemporary Social Work: An Introduction to Social Work and Social Welfare.* 3rd ed. New York: McGraw-Hill.

Brown, B. B. 1977. *Stress and the Art of Biofeedback.* New York: Bantam Books.

Browne, A., and D. Finkelhor. 1986. "Impact of Child Sexual Abuse: A Review of the Literature." *Psychological Bulletin 99,* pp. 66–77.

Buber, M. 1958. *I and Thou.* New York: Scribner.

Bugliosi, V., & C. Gentry. 1974. *Helter Skelter.* New York: Norton.

Bullis, R. K. 1996. *Spirituality in Social Work Practice.* Washington, DC: Taylor & Francis.

Burgess, A. W., & L. Holmstrom. 1974. *Rape: Victims of Crisis.* Bowie, MD: Robert J. Brady.

Burgest, D. R. 1973. "Racism in Everyday Speech and Social Work Jargon." *Social Work 18* (July), pp. 20–25.

Burgest, M. D. R. 1983. "Education and Skills for Multi-Racial and Multi-Ethnic Direct Practice." Presented at the Annual Program Meeting, Council on Social Work Education, New York.

Buxton, E. 1976. "Delivering Social Services in Rural Areas." In *Social Work in Rural Communities,* by Leon Ginsberg, pp. 28–38. New York: Council on Social Work Education.

Campbell, J. A. 1988. "Client Acceptance of Single-System Evaluation Procedures." *Social Work Research & Abstracts 24,* pp. 21–22.

———. **1990.** "Ability of Practitioners to Estimate Client Acceptance of Single-Subject Evaluation Procedures." *Social Work* 35, pp. 9–14.

Canadian Association of Social Workers. 1994 and 1983. *Social Work Code of Ethics.* Ottawa: Canadian Association of Social Workers.

Canda, E. R., & L. D. Furman. 1999. *Spiritual Diversity in Social Work Practice.* New York: Free Press.

Caprio, F. S., & J. R. Berger. 1963. *Helping Yourself with Self-Hypnosis.* Englewood Cliffs, NJ: Prentice-Hall.

Cartwright, T. J. 1973. "Problems, Solutions and Strategies: A Contribution to the Theory and Practice of Planning." *AIP Examination Readings.* Washington, DC: American Institute of Planners.

Cautela, J. R. 1967. "Covert Sensitization." *Psychological Reports 20,* pp. 459–468.

Cautela, J. R., & D. Upper. 1975. "The Process of Individual Behavior Therapy." In *Progress in Behavior Modification,* eds. M. Hersen, R. M. Eisler, & R. M. Miller, pp. 276–306. New York: Academic Press.

Center for Social Research and Development. 1974. *Analysis and Synthesis of Needs Assessment Research in the Field of Human Services.* Denver: University of Denver.

Chambless, D. L., & A. J. Goldstein. 1979. "Behavioral Psychotherapy." In *Current Psychotherapies,* 2nd ed., ed. R. Corsini. Itasca, IL: Peacock.

Charlesworth, E. A., & R. G. Nathan. 1984. *Stress Management.* New York: Ballantine Books.

Charney, D. A., & R. C. Russell. 1994. "An Overview of Sexual Harassment." *American Journal of Psychiatry 151,* no. 1 (Jan.), pp. 10–17.

Christie, R., & F. Geis. 1970. *Studios in Machiavellianism.* New York: Academic Press.

Church, D. 1980. *It's Time to Tell: A Media Handbook for Human Services Personnel.* Washington, DC: U.S. Department of Health and Human Services.

Ciminero, A. R., K. S. Calhoun, & H. E. Adams, eds. 1986. *Handbook of Behavioral Assessment.* 2nd ed. New York: Wiley.

Clifton, R. L., & A. M. Dahms. 1980. *Grassroots Administration: A Handbook for Staff and Directors of Small Community-Based Social-Service Agencies.* Belmont, CA: Wadsworth.

Cnaan, R. A. 1999. *The Newer Deal: Social Work and Religion in Partnership.* New York: Columbia University Press.

Cohen, N. E. 1958. *Social Work in the American Tradition.* Hinsdale, IL: Dryden Press.

Coleman, J. W., & D. R. Cressey. 1995. *Social Problems,* 8th ed. Englewood Cliffs, NJ: Prentice-Hall.

Collier, H. V. 1982. *Counseling Women: A Guide for Therapists.* New York: Free Press.

Collins, B. G. 1986. "Defining Feminist Social Work." *Social Work 31,* pp. 214–219.

Comfort, A. 1978. *Sexual Consequences of Disability.* Philadelphia: Stickley.

Commission on Accreditation. 1988. "Curriculum Policy for the Master's Degree and Baccalaureate Degree Program in Social Work Education." In *Handbook of Standards and Procedures, 1988.* Washington, DC: Council on Social Work Education.

Compton, B., & B. Galaway. 1999. *Social Work Processes.* 6th ed. Pacific Grove, CA: Brooks/Cole.

Computers in Human Services. New York: Haworth Press. A new journal devoted exclusively to computer applications in the human services.

"Conceptual Frameworks II." 1981. *Social Work 26* (Jan.), pp. 1–96.

Cook, T. D., & D. T. Campbell. 1979. *Quasi-Experimentation: Design and Analysis Issues for Field Settings.* Chicago: Rand McNally.

Cooley, C. H. 1902. *Human Nature and the Social Order.* New York: Scribner.

Cooper, M. 1990. "Treatment of a Client with Obsessive-Compulsive Disorder." *Social Work Research & Abstracts 26,* pp. 26–32.

Corcoran, K., & J. Fischer. 2000. *Measures for Clinical Practice: A Sourcebook.* 3rd ed. New York.

Corcoran, K., & W. J. Gingerich. 1994. "Practice Evaluation in the Context of Managed Care: Case-Recording Methods for Quality Assurance Reviews." *Research on Social Work Practice 4,* pp. 326–337.

Cormier, W. H., & L. S. Cormier. 1991. *Interviewing Strategies for Helpers.* Pacific Grove, CA: Brooks/Cole.

Corsini, R. J., & D. Wedding, eds. 2000. *Current Psychotherapies.* 6th ed. Itasca, IL: Peacock.

Coryell, W., J. Endicott, N. C. Andreasen, et al. 1988. *American Journal of Psychiatry, 145,* pp. 293–300.

Council on Social Work Education. 1968. *Working with the Poor: Cultural Differences—Worker and Community.* New York: Council on Social Work Education.

———. **1982.** "Curriculum Policy for the Master's Degree & Baccalaureate Degree Programs in Social Work Education." 1982. New York: Council on Social Work Education, adopted May 24.

———. **1992a.** *Curriculum Policy Statement for Baccalaureate Degree Programs in Social Work Education.* Alexandria, VA: Council on Social Work Education.

———. **1992b.** *Curriculum Policy Statement for Master's Degree Programs in Social Work Education.* Alexandria, VA: Council on Social Work Education.

———. **2001.** *Educational Policy and Accreditation Standards.* Alexandria, VA: Council on Social Work Education.

Craighead, W. W., M. J. Mahoney, & A. R. Kazdin. 1976. *Behavior Modification: Principles, Issues and Applications.* Boston: Houghton Mifflin.

Criddle, W. D. 1974. "Guidelines for Challenging Irrational Beliefs." *Rational Living* (Spring), pp. 8–13.

Crosbie, J. 1993. "Interrupted Time-Series Analysis with Brief Single-Subject Data." *Journal of Consulting and Clinical Psychology 61,* pp. 966–974.

Cummings, M. 1977. "How to Handle Incidents of Racial Discrimination." In *The Personal Problem Solver,* eds. C. Zastrow & D. H. Chang. Englewood Cliffs, NJ: Prentice-Hall.

Cunningham, C., & K. MacFarlane. 1991. *When Children Molest Children.* Orwell, VT: Safer Society Press.

Cutler, J. P. 1995. *Third Party Reimbursement for Clinical Social Work Services.* Washington, DC: National Association of Social Workers.

Cwikel, J. G., & R. A. Cnaan. 1991. "Ethical Dilemmas in Applying Second-Wave Information Technology to Social Work Practice." *Social Work 36,* pp. 114–120.

Daly, A., J. Jennings, J. O. Beckett, & B. R. Leashore. 1995. "Effective Coping Strategies of African Americans." *Social Work 2,* pp. 240–248.

Davenport, J., & J. Davenport. 1982. "Utilizing the Social Network in Rural Communities." *Social Casework 63* (Feb.), pp. 106–112.

Davenport, J., & N. Reims. 1978. "Theoretical Orientation and Attitudes toward Women." *Social Work 23* (July), pp. 306–309.

Davie, J. S., & A. P. Hare. 1956. "Button-Down Collar Culture: A Study of Undergraduate Life at a Men's College." *Human Organization 14,* pp. 13–20.

Davis, K., & W. Newstrom. 1989. *Human Behavior at Work.* 8th ed. New York: McGraw-Hill.

Davis, L. E. 1979. "Racial Composition of Groups." *Social Work 24* (May), pp. 208–213.

DeBoer, J. C. 1970. *Let's Plan: A Guide to the Planning Process for Voluntary Organizations.* New York: United Church Press.

DeCrescenzo, T. A. 1985. "Homophobia: A Study of the Attitudes of Mental Health Professionals Toward Homosexuality." In *With Compassion Toward Some: Homosexuality and Social Work in America,* by R. Schoenberg & R. S. Goldberg, with D. A. Shod. New York: Harrington Park Press.

Deitel, H. M., & B. Deitel. 1985. *Computers and Data Processing.* Orlando, FL: Academic Press.

DeJong, P., & I. K. Berg. 1998. *Interviewing for Solutions.* Pacific Grove, CA: Brooks/Cole.

DeJong, P., & S. D. Miller. 1995. "How to Interview for Client Strengths." *Social Work 40,* no. 6 (Nov.), pp. 729–736.

Delbecq, A. L., & A. Van de Ven. 1971. "A Group Process Model for Problem Identification and Program Planning." *Journal of Applied Behavioral Science* (July–Aug.).

Delgado, M., & D. Humm-Delgado. 1982. "Natural Support Systems: Source of Strength in Hispanic Communities." *Social Work 27,* no. 1 (Jan.), pp. 83–89.

DeMello, A. 1978. *Sadhana: A Way to God.* Garden City, NY: Image Books.

Deming, W. E. 1986. *Out of the Crisis.* Cambridge, MA: Massachusetts Institute of Technology, Center for Advanced Engineering Study.

DeMoya, A., D. DeMoya, M. E. Lewis, & H. R. Lewis. 1983. *Sex and Health.* New York: Stein & Day.

de Shazer, S. 1988. "The Death of Resistance." *Family Process 23,* pp. 79–93.

Deutsch, M. 1949. "A Theory of Cooperation and Competition." *Human Relations 2,* pp. 129–152.

Devore, W., & E. G. Schlesinger. 1981. *Ethnic-Sensitive Social Work Practice.* St. Louis: Mosby.

Devore, W., & E. G. Schlesinger. 1996. *Ethnic-Sensitive Social Work Practice.* 4th ed. Needham Heights, MA: Allyn & Bacon.

Dickson, D. T. 1998. *Confidentiality and Privacy in Social Work.* New York: Free Press.

DiGiussepe, R., N. Miller , & L. Trexler. 1977. "A Review of Rational Emotive Psychotherapy Outcome Studies." *Counseling Psychologist 7,* no. 1.

DiGiuseppe, R. A., M. Terjesen, R. Rose, K. Doyle, & N. Vadalakis. 1998. *Selective Abstractions Errors in Reviewing REBT Outcome Studies: A Review of Reviews.* Poster presented at the 106th Annual Convention of the American Psychological Association, San Francisco (August).

Dilts, R., L. Cameron-Bandler, R. Bandler, J. Grinder, & J. DeLozier. 1980. *Neuro-Linguistic Programming,* vol. 1, Cupertino, CA: Meta Publications.

Dolgoff, R., & D. Feldstein. 1980. *Understanding Social Welfare.* New York: Harper & Row.

Douglas, P. H., & L. Pinsky. 1996. *The Essential AIDS Fact Book.* New York: Pocket Books.

Dreikurs, R. 1964. *Children: The Challenge.* New York: Hawthorn Books.

Drucker, P. F. 1954. *The Practice of Management.* New York: Harper.

Dumont, M. 1968. *The Absurd Healer.* New York: Viking Press.

Dunn, J. 1977. *Distress and Comfort.* Cambridge, MA: Harvard University Press.

Dusay, J. M., & K. M. Dusay. 1979. "Transactional Analysis." In *Current Psychotherapies,* 2nd ed., ed. R. Corsini. Itasca, IL: Peacock.

———. **1989.** "Transactional Analysis." In *Current Psychotherapies,* 4th ed., ed. R. Corsini & D. Wedding. Itasca, IL: Peacock.

Eddings, J. 1997. "Second Thoughts About Integration," *U.S. News & World Report.* July 28, p. 32.

Edelwich, J. 1980. *Burn-Out.* New York: Human Sciences Press.

Egan, G. 1985. *Change Agent Skills in Helping and Human Service Settings.* Pacific Grove, CA: Brooks/Cole.

Eidson, T., ed. 1993. *The AIDS Caregiver's Handbook.* New York: St. Martin's Press.

Ell, K. 1995. "Crisis Intervention: Research Needs." In *Encyclopedia of Social Work,* 19th ed. Washington, DC: National Association of Social Workers.

Ellis, A. 1957. "Outcome of Employing Three Techniques of Psychotherapy." *Journal of Clinical Psychology 13,* pp. 344–350.

———. **1958.** "Rational Psychotherapy." *Journal of General Psychology* 58 (Jan.), pp. 35–49.

———. **1962.** *Reason and Emotion in Psychotherapy.* New York: Lyle Stuart.

———. **1973.** "Rational-Emotive Therapy." In *Current Psychotherapies,* ed. R. Corsini, pp. 167–206. Itasca, IL: Peacock.

———. **2000.** "Rational Emotive Behavior Therapy" in *Current Psychotherapies,* 6th ed. Edited by R. J. Corsini & D. Wedding. Itasca, IL: Peacock, pp. 168–204.

Ellis, A., & R. Harper. 1977. *A New Guide to Rational Living.* North Hollywood, CA: Wilshire Books.

Emmelkamp, P. M. G. 1994. "Behavior Therapy with Adults." In *Handbook of Psychotherapy and Behavior Change,* 4th ed., eds. A. E. Bergin & S. L. Garfield, pp. 379–427. New York: Wiley.

Eriksen, K. 1979. *Communication Skills for the Human Services.* Reston, VA: Reston Publishing.

Erikson, E. 1963. *Childhood and Society.* 2nd ed. New York: Norton.

Etzioni, A. 1964. *Modern Organizations.* Englewood Cliffs, NJ: Prentice-Hall.

———. **1993.** *The Spirit of Community: Rights, Responsibilities, and the Communitarian Agenda.* New York: Crown.

Eysenck, H. J. 1952. "The Effects of Psychotherapy: An Evaluation." *Journal of Consulting Psychology 11,* pp. 319–324.

———. **1961.** "The Effects of Psychotherapy." In *Handbook of Abnormal Psychology.* New York: Basic Books, pp. 697–725.

———. **1965.** "The Effects of Psychotherapy." *International Journal of Psychiatry 1,* pp. 97–144.

Falck, H. E. 1966. "Integrating the Rural Welfare Department into the Community." In *Can Welfare Keep Pace?,* ed. M. Morton. New York: Columbia University Press.

Federal Register. 1992. *Glass Ceiling Commission.* Washington, DC: U.S. Government Printing Office.

Federico, R. 1973. *The Social Welfare Institution.* Lexington, MA: Heath.

Fellin, P. 1987. *The Social Worker and the Community.* Itasca, IL: Peacock.

Fensterheim, H., & J. Baer. 1975. *Don't Say Yes When You Want to Say No.* New York: Dell.

Ferguson, P. C., & J. Gowan. 1974. "The Influence of Transcendental Meditation on Anxiety, Depression, Aggression, Neuroticism and Self-Actualization." *Journal of Humanistic Psychology,* pp. 51–60.

Ferguson, T. 1996. *Health Online.* Reading, MA: Addison-Wesley.

Findlay, S. 1991. "AIDS: The Second Decade." *U.S. News & World Report* (June 17), p. 66.

Fine, L. J. 1979. "Psychodrama." In *Current Psychotherapies,* 2nd ed., ed. R. J. Corsini. Itasca, IL: Peacock.

Finkelhor, D. 1979. *Sexually Abused Children.* New York: Free Press.

Fischer, J. 1973. "Is Casework Effective? A Review." *Social Work 18* (Jan.), pp. 5–20.

———. **1978.** *Effective Casework Practice.* New York: McGraw-Hill.

———. **1979.** "Isn't Casework Effective Yet?" *Social Work 24* (May), pp. 245–247.

Flanagan, J. 1977. *The Grass Roots Fundraising Book: How to Raise Money in Your Community.* Chicago: Swallow Press.

Fong, R., & N. Mokuau. 1996. "Not Simply 'Asian Americans': Periodical Literature on Asians and Pacific Islanders." In P. L. Ewalt, E. M. Freeman, S. A. Kirk, & D. L. Poole, eds. *Multicultural Issues in Social Work,* Washington, DC: NASW Press, pp. 2269–2281.

Ford, J., D. Young, B. Perez, R. Obermeyer, & D. Rohmer. 1992. "Needs Assessment for Persons with Severe Mental Illness: What Services Are Needed for Successful Community Living?" *Community Mental Health Journal 28,* no. 6, pp. 491–503.

Frank, J. D. 1973. *Persuasion and Healing.* 2nd ed. Baltimore: Johns Hopkins University Press.

Franklin, A. J. 1999. "Therapeutic Support Groups for African American Men." In *Working with African American Males,* L. E. Davis, ed. Thousand Oaks, CA: Sage, pp. 5–14.

Freedman, N., & R. Sherman. 1987. *Handbook of Measurements for Marriage and Family Therapy.* New York: Brunner/Mazel.

Freese, A. S. 1976. *How Hypnosis Can Help You.* New York: Popular Library.

French, J. R. P., & B. Raven. 1968. "The Bases of Social Power." In *Group Dynamics: Research and Theory,* 3rd ed., eds. D. Cartwright & A. Zander. New York: Harper & Row.

Freud, S. 1924. *A General Introduction to Psychoanalysis.* New York: Boni & Liveright.

Freudenberger, H. J. 1977. "Burn-Out: Occupational Hazard of the Child Care Worker." *Child Care Quarterly 6,* pp. 90–99.

Frew, D. R. 1974. "Transcendental Meditation and Productivity." *Academy of Management Journal 17,* no. 2 (June), pp. 362–368.

Frey, G. A. 1990. "A Framework for Promoting Organizational Change." *Families in Society 71,* no. 3, pp. 142–147.

Friedan, B. 1963. *The Feminine Mystique.* New York: Dell.

Furman, L. E. 1994. "Religion and Spirituality in Social Work Education: Preparing the Culturally-Sensitive Practitioner for the Future." Paper presented at Midwest Biennial Conference on Social Work, April 28–29, St. Paul, MN.

Gabriel, M. A. 1996. *AIDS Trauma and Support Group Therapy.* New York: Free Press.

Galper, J. H. 1975. *The Politics of Social Services.* Englewood Cliffs, NJ: Prentice-Hall.

———. **1980.** *Social Work Practice: A Radical Perspective.* Englewood Cliffs, NJ: Prentice-Hall.

Garland, J. A., & L. A. Frey. 1973. "Application of Stages of Group Development to Groups in Psychiatric Settings." In *Further Explorations in Group Work,* ed. S. Bernstein, pp. 1–33. Boston: Milford House.

Garland, J. A., H. Jones, & R. Kolodny. 1965. "A Model for Stages of Development in Social Work Groups." In *Explorations in Group Work,* ed. S. Bernstein. Boston: Milford House.

Garvin, C. D., & F. M. Cox. 1995. "A History of Community Organizing Since the Civil War with Special Reference to Oppressed Communities." In J. Rothman, J. L. Erlich, & J. E. Tropman, *Strategies of Community Intervention.* Itasca, IL: Peacock, pp. 64–99.

Gary, L. E. 1996. "African American Men's Perceptions of Racial Discrimination: A Sociocultural Analysis." In *Multicultural Issues in Social Work,* eds. P. L. Ewalt, E. M. Freeman, S. A. Kirk, & D. L. Poole. Washington, DC: NASW Press, pp. 218–240.

Germain, C. B., & A. Gitterman. 1980. *The Life Model of Social Work Practice.* New York: Columbia University Press.

Ghali, S. B. 1982. "Understanding Puerto Rican Traditions." Social Work 27, no. 1 (Jan.), pp. 98–102.

Gibson, G., & K. Ottenbacher. 1988. "Characteristics influencing the Visual Analysis of Single-Subject Data: An Empirical Investigation." *Journal of Applied Behavioral Science 24,* pp. 298–314.

Gil, E., & T. C. Johnson. 1993. *Sexualized Children: Assessment and Treatment of Sexualized Children and Children Who Molest.* Rockville, MD: Lauch Press.

Gilbert, G. C. 1974. "Counseling Black Adolescent Parents." *Social Work 19* (Jan.), pp. 88–95.

Gilligan, C. 1982. *In a Different Voice: Psychological Theory and Women's Development.* Cambridge: Harvard University Press.

Gingerich, W. J. 1979. "Procedure for Evaluating Clinical Practice." *Health and Social Work 4,* pp. 105–130.

———. **1983.** "Significance Testing in Single-Case Research." In *Handbook of Clinical Social Work,* eds. A. Rosenblatt & D. Waldfogel, pp. 694–720. San Francisco: Jossey-Bass.

———. **1990a.** "Expert Systems and Their Potential Uses in Social Work." *Families in Society 71,* pp. 220–228.

———. **1990b.** "Rethinking Single-Case Evaluation." In *Advances in Clinical Social Work Research,* eds. L. Videka-Sherman &

W. J. Reid. Silver Spring, MD: National Association of Social Workers.

———. **1995a.** "Expert Systems." In *Encyclopedia of Social Work,* 19th ed., ed. R. L. Edwards, pp. 917–925. Washington, DC: NASW Press.

———. **1995b.** *MY ASSISTANT: Computer-Assisted Record-Keeping for the Case Manager.* Poster session at the Nineteenth Annual Symposium on Computer Applications in Medical Care, New Orleans, LA.

Gingerich, W. J., & A. Broskowski. 1996. "Clinical Decision Support Systems." In *The Computerization of Behavioral Healthcare,* ed. T. Trabin, pp. 11–38. San Francisco: Jossey-Bass.

Gingerich, W. J., & R. K. Green. 1996. "Information Technology: How Social Work is Going Digital." In *Future Issues for Social Work Practice,* eds. P. R. Raffoul & C. A. McNeece. Needham Heights, MA: Allyn & Bacon.

Ginott, H. G. 1965. *Between Parent and Child.* New York: Macmillan.

Glasser, W., ed. 1989. *Control Theory in the Practice of Reality Therapy: Case Studies.* New York: HarperCollins.

Glasser, W. 1965. *Reality Therapy.* New York: Harper & Row.

———. **1972.** *The Identity Society.* New York: Harper & Row.

———. **1976.** *Positive Addiction.* New York: Harper & Row.

———. **1984.** *Control Theory.* New York: Harper & Row.

Glasser, W., & R. Wubbolding. 1995. "Reality Therapy." In *Current Psychotherapies,* 5th ed., eds. R. J. Corsini & D. Wedding, pp. 293–321. Itasca, IL: F. E. Peacock.

Glasser, W., & L. Zunin. 1979. "Reality Therapy." In *Current Psychotherapies,* 2nd ed., ed. R. Corsini, pp. 302–339. Itasca, IL: Peacock.

Golan, N. 1979. "Crisis Theory." In *Social Work Treatment,* 2nd ed., ed. F. J. Turner, pp. 499–531. London: Free Press.

Goldenberg, I., & H. Goldenberg. 1991. *Family Therapy, An Overview.* 3rd ed. Pacific Grove, CA: Brooks/Cole.

———. **2000.** *Family Therapy, An Overview.* 5th ed. Belmont, CA: Brooks/Cole.

Goldfried, M. R., & M. Merbaum, eds. 1973. *Behavior Change Through Self Control.* New York: Holt, Rinehart & Winston.

Goleman, D. 1976. "Meditation Helps Break the Stress Spiral." *Psychology Today 9* (Feb.), pp. 82–93.

———. **1977.** "Meditation Without Mystery." *Psychology Today 10* (March), pp. 55–67.

Good Tracks, J. G. 1973. "Native American Noninterference." *Social Work 18* (Nov.), pp. 30–34.

Googins, B., V. A. Capoccia, & N. Kaufman. 1983. "The Interactional Dimension of Planning: A Framework for Practice." *Social Work 18* (July–Aug.), pp. 273–278.

Gordon, T. 1970. *Parent Effectiveness Training.* New York: Wyden.

Goring, R., ed. 1994. *Dictionary of Beliefs and Religions.* New York: Larousse.

Gramick, J. 1983. "Homophobia: A New Challenge." *Social Work 28,* no. 2 (March–April), pp. 137–141.

Grant, G. B., & L. M. Grobman. 1998. *The Social Worker's Internet Handbook.* Harrisburg, PA: White Hat Communications.

Green, J. W. 1999. *Cultural Awareness in the Human Services.* Boston: Allyn & Bacon.

Greenberg, H. M. 1980. *Coping with Job Stress.* Englewood Cliffs, NJ: Spectrum.

Greene, L. J. 1969. *The Negro in Colonial New England.* New York: Atheneum.

Grier, W. H., & P. M. Cobbs. 1968. *Black Rage.* New York: Basic Books.

Grohol, J. M. 2000. *The Insider's Guide to Mental Health Resources Online, 2000/2001 Edition.* New York: Guilford Press.

Gross, E. R. 1996. "Deconstructing Politically Correct Practice Literature: The American Indian Case." In P. L. Ewalt et al., eds. *Multicultural Issues in Social Work.* Washington DC: NASW Press, pp. 241–254.

Grosser, C. F. 1973. *New Directions in Community Organization.* New York: Praeger.

Grotevant, H. D., & C. I. Carlson. 1987. "Family Interaction Coding Systems: A Descriptiive Review." *Family Process 26,* p. 49.

Groth, A. N. 1979. *Men Who Rape.* New York: Plenum Press.

Groth, A. N., R. E. Longo, & J. B. McFadin. 1982. "Undetected Recidivism Among Rapists and Child Molesters." *Crime and Delinquency 28,* pp. 450–458.

Grubb, D. L., & D. R. Zwick. 1976. *Fundraising in the Public Interest.* Washington, DC: Public Citizen.

Guthrie, E. R. 1935. *The Psychology of Learning.* New York: Harper & Row.

Gutman, H. G. 1976. *The Black Family in Slavery and Freedom: 1750–1925.* New York: Pantheon.

Haley, J. 1963. *Strategies of Psychotherapy.* New York: Grune & Stratton.

———. **1973.** *Uncommon Therapy.* New York: Norton.

Hall, C. S., & G. Lindzey. 1957. *Theories of Personality.* New York: Wiley.

Hall, E. T. 1959. *The Silent Language.* Greenwich, CT: Fawcett Books.

Hare, A. 1962. *Handbook of Small Group Research.* New York: Free Press.

Harper, K. V., & J. Lantz. 1996. *Cross-Cultural Practice: Social Work with Diverse Populations.* Chicago: Lyceum Books.

Harris, T. 1969. *I'm OK—You're OK.* New York: Harper & Row.

Hartman, A. 1978. "Diagrammatic Assessment of Family Relationships." *Social Casework* 59 (Oct.), pp. 465–476.

Hathaway, S. R. 1948. "Some Considerations Relative to Nondirective Counseling as Therapy." *Journal of Clinical Psychology 4,* pp. 226–231.

Hauck, P. A. 1972. *The Rational Management of Children.* New York: Libra Publishers.

Hebb, D. O., R. Held, A. Riesen, & H. Teuber. 1961. "Sensory Deprivation: Facts in Search of a Theory." *Journal of Nervous and Mental Disorders 132,* 17–43.

Hepworth, D. H., & J. Larsen. 1986. *Direct Social Work Practice: Theory and Skills.* 2nd ed. Pacific Grove, CA: Brooks/Cole.

———. **1993.** *Direct Social Work Practice.* 4th ed. Pacific Grove, CA: Brooks/Cole.

Hepworth, D. H., R. H. Rooney, & J. A. Larson. 1997. *Direct Social Work Practice,* 5th ed. Pacific Grove, CA: Brooks/Cole.

Herbert, M. D., & J. W. Mould. 1992. "The Advocate Role in Public Child Welfare." *Child Welfare 71,* no. 2 (March/April), pp. 114–130.

Hersen, M., & A. S. Bellack, eds. 1988. *Dictionary of Behavioral Assessment Techniques.* Elmsford, NY: Pergamon Press.

Hersey, P., & K. Blanchard. 1977. *Management of Organizational Behavior: Utilizing Human Resources.* 3rd ed. Englewood Cliffs, NJ: Prentice-Hall.

Hidalgo, H., T. Peterson, & N. H. Woodman. 1985. *Lesbian and Gay Issues: A Resource Manual.* Silver Spring, MD: National Association of Social Workers.

Hoffman, M. A. 1996. *Counseling Clients with HIV Disease.* New York: Guilford Press.

Hogan, R. A., & J. H. Kirchner. 1967. "A Preliminary Report of the Extinction of Learned Fears via Short-Term Implosive Therapy." *Journal of Abnormal Psychology 72,* pp. 106–111.

Holden, G., G. Rosenberg, & A. Weissman. 1996. "World Wide Web Accessible Resources Related to Research on Social Work Practice." *Research on Social Work Practice 6,* pp. 236–262.

Hollander, E. P. 1958. "Conformity, Status, and Idiosyncrasy Credit." *Psychological Review,* pp. 117–127.

Hollis, F. 1972. *Casework: A Psychosocial Theory.* New York: Random House.

Honsberger, R., & A. F. Wilson. 1973. "Transcendental Mediation in Treating Asthma." *Respiratory Therapy: The Journal of Inhalation Technology* 3, pp. 79–81.

Hook, M. V. 1979. "Female Clients, Female Counselors: Combating Learned Helplessness." *Social Work 24* (Jan.), pp. 63–65.

Hopkins, T. J. 1973. "The Role of the Agency in Supporting Black Manhood." *Social Work 18* (Jan.), pp. 53–58.

Hopps, J. G., & P. M. Collins. 1995. "Social Work Profession Overview." In *Encyclopedia of Social Work,* 19th ed. Washington, DC: National Association of Social Workers.

Howard, J. 1970. *Please Touch: A Guided Tour of Human Potential Movement.* New York: McGraw-Hill.

Hower, D. 1994. "David Hower's Definition of Total Quality." *Reporter* (Aug. 29), p. 10. Whitewater, WI: University of Wisconsin—Whitewater.

Hudson, W. W. 1978. "First Axioms of Treatment." *Social Work 23,* pp. 65–66.

———. **1982.** *The Clinical Measurement Package: A Field Manual.* Pacific Grove, CA: Brooks/Cole.

———. **1992.** *Walmyr Assessment Scales.* Tempe, AZ: Walmyr.

Hull, C. L. 1943. *Principles of Behavior.* New York: Appleton-Century-Crofts.

Hull, G. H. 1978. "The Parents' Anonymous Sponsor: A Professional Helping Role." Paper presented at the Child Welfare League of America Regional Conference, Omaha.

———. **1990.** *Social Work Internship Manual.* Eau Claire: University of Wisconsin—Eau Claire. Department of Social Work.

Humphreys, G. E. 1983. "Inclusion of Content on Homosexuality in the Social Work Curriculum." *Journal of Education for Social Work 19* (Winter), pp. 55–60.

Hyde, J. S. 1990. *Understanding Human Sexuality.* 4th ed. New York: McGraw-Hill.

———. **1994.** *Understanding Human Sexuality.* 5th ed. New York: McGraw-Hill.

Hyde, J. S., & J. DeLamater. 1997. *Understanding Human Sexuality.* 6th ed. New York: McGraw-Hill.

Ivey, A. E., & M. B. Ivey. 1999. *Intentional Interviewing and Counseling.* Pacific Grove, CA: Brooks/Cole.

Jackson, D. D. 1965. "The Study of the Family." *Family Process 4,* pp. 1–20.

Jacobson, E. 1934. *You Must Relax: A Practical Method of Reducing the Stress of Modern Life.* New York: McGraw-Hill.

———. **1938a.** *Progressive Relaxation.* 2nd ed. Chicago: University of Chicago Press.

———. **1938b.** *You Can Sleep Well: The ABC's of Restful Sleep for the Average Person.* New York: McGraw-Hill.

———. **1959.** *How to Relax and Have Your Baby: Scientific Relaxation in Childbirth.* New York: McGraw-Hill.

———. **1964.** *Anxiety and Tension Control: A Physiologic Approach.* Philadelphia: Lippincott.

———. **1973.** *Teaching and Learning New Methods for Old Arts.* Chicago: National Foundation for Progressive Relaxation.

James, M., & D. Jongeward. 1971. *Born to Win; Transactional Analysis with Gestalt Experiments.* Reading, MA: Addison-Wesley.

Janis, I. 1971. "Group Think." *Psychology Today 15,* no. 6. (Nov.), pp. 43–46, 74–76

Jayaratne, S., & R. L. Levy. 1979. *Empirical Clinical Practice.* New York: Columbia University Press.

Jehu, D. 1972. *Behavior Modification in Social Work.* New York: Wiley.

Johnson, D. W., & F. P. Johnson. 1975. *Joining Together.* Englewood Cliffs, NJ: Prentice-Hall.

———. **2000.** *Joining Together.* 7th ed. Boston: Allyn & Bacon.

Johnson, E. H. 1973. *Social Problems of Urban Man.* Pacific Grove, CA: Brooks/Cole.

Johnson, L. C. 1986. *Social Work Practice: A Generalist Approach.* 2nd ed. Boston: Allyn & Bacon.

Johnson, T. C. 1995. *Treatment Exercises for Child Abuse Victims and Children with Sexual Behavior Problems.* S. Pasadena, CA: Author.

Jones, R. R., R. S. Vaught, & M. R. A. Weinrott. 1977. "Time-Series Analysis in Operant Research." *Journal of Applied Behavior Analysis 10,* pp. 151–166.

Juran, J. M. 1989. *Juran on Leadership for Quality: An Executive Handbook.* New York: Free Press.

Kadushin, A. 1972. *The Social Work Interview.* New York: Columbia University Press.

———. **1980.** *Child Welfare Services.* 3rd ed. New York: Macmillan.

———. **1983.** *The Social Work Interview.* 2nd ed. New York: Columbia University Press.

———. **1990.** *The Social Work Interview.* 3rd ed. New York: Columbia University Press.

Kahn, M., & B. Baker. 1968. "Desensitization with Minimal Therapist Contact." *Journal of Abnormal Psychology 73,* pp. 198–200.

Kahn, T. J. 1992. *Pathways: A Guided Workbook for Youth Beginning Treatment.* Brandon, VT: The Safer Society Press.

———. **1996.** *Pathways: A Guided Workbook for Youth Beginning Treatment.* 2nd ed. Brandon, VT: The Safer Society Press.

Kalichman, S. 1999. *Understanding AIDS: Advances in Research and Treatment.* Washington, DC: American Psychological Association.

Kanfer, F. 1975. "Self-Management Methods." In *Helping People Change,* ed. F. H. Kanfer & A. P. Goldstein, pp. 309–355. Elmsford, NY: Pergamon Press.

Kanin, E. J. 1985. "Date Rapists: Differential Sexual Socialization and Relative Deprivation." *Archives of Sexual Behavior 14,* pp. 219–232.

Kanuha, V. 1990. "The Need for an Integrated Analysis of Oppression in Feminist Therapy Ethics." In *Feminist Ethics in Psychotherapy,* eds. H. Lerman & N. Porter. New York: Springer.

Kaplan, H. S. 1974. *The New Sex Therapy.* New York: Brunner/Mazel.

———. **1983.** *The Evaluation of Sexual Disorders.* New York: Brunner/Mazel.

Kaplan, S. G., & E. G. Wheeler. 1983. "Survival Skills for Working with Potentially Violent Clients." *Social Casework.* 64(6), June, pp. 339–346.

Katz, A. H., & E. I. Bender. 1976. *The Strength in Us: Self-Help Groups in the Modern World.* New York: Franklin-Watts.

Kaufman, R., & S. Thomas. 1980. *Evaluation Without Fear.* New York: New Viewpoints.

Kazdin, A. E. 1977a. "Assessing the Clinical or Applied Importance of Behavior Change Through Social Validation." *Behavior Modification 1,* pp. 427–452.

———. **1977b.** *The Token Economy.* Plenum.

Keith-Lucas, A. 1972. *The Giving and Taking of Help.* Chapel Hill: University of North Carolina Press.

———. **1985.** *So You Want to Be a Social Worker: A Primer for the Christian Student.* St. Davids, PA: North American Association of Christians in Social Work.

Kelly, H. H., & A. J. Stahelski. 1970. "Social Interaction Basis of Cooperators' and Competitors' Beliefs About Others." *Journal of Personality and Social Psychology 16,* pp. 66–91.

Kelman, H. C. 1965. "Manipulation of Human Behavior: An Ethical Dilemma for the Social Scientist." *Journal of Social Issues 21,* no. 2, pp. 31–46.

Kerr, M. E., & M. Bowen. 1988. *Family Evaluation: An Approach Based on Brown's Theory.* New York: Norton.

King, S. W., & R. S. Meyers. 1981. "Developing Self-Help Groups: Integrating Group Work and Community Organization Strategies." *Social Development Issues 5,* pp. 33–46.

Kiresuk, T. J., & S. H. Lund. 1978. "Goal Attainment Scaling." In *Evaluation of Human Service Programs,* eds. C. C. Attkisson, W. A. Hargreaves, M. J. Horowitz, & J. E. Sorensen, pp. 341–370. New York: Academic Press.

Kirst-Ashman, K. K., & G. H. Hull, Jr. 1997. *Generalist Practice with Organizations and Communities.* Chicago: Nelson-Hall.

———. **1999.** *Understanding Generalist Practice,* 2nd ed. Chicago: Nelson-Hall.

———. **2001.** *Generalist Practice with Organizations and Communities,* 2nd ed. Pacific Grove, CA: Brooks/Cole.

Klein, D., & P. Wender. 1993. *Understanding Depression.* DuPage County, IL: National Alliance for the Mentally Ill.

Knopf, R. 1979. *Surviving the BS (Bureaucratic System).* Wilmington, NC: Mandala Press.

Koop, J. 1988. "Self-Monitoring: A Literature Review of Research and Practice." *Social Work Research & Abstracts 24,* pp. 8–20.

Kornblum, W., & J. Julian. 1988. *Social Problems.* 9th ed. Upper Saddle River, NJ: Prentice-Hall.

Kramer, J. J., & J. C. Conoley. 1992. *The Eleventh Mental Measurements Yearbook.* Lincoln: University of Nebraska Press.

Kratochwill, T. R., ed. 1978. *Single Subject Research: Strategies for Evaluating Change.* New York: Academic Press.

Kravetz, D. 1982. "An Overview of Content on Women for the Social Work Curriculum." *Journal of Education for Social Work 18* (Winter), pp. 42–49.

Krech, D., R. S. Crutchfield, & E. L. Ballachey. 1962. *Individual in Society.* New York: McGraw-Hill.

Kretzmann, J. P., & J. L. McKnight. 1993. *Building Communities from the Inside Out.* Chicago: Acta Publications.

Kübler-Ross, E. 1969. *On Death and Dying.* New York: Macmillan.

Laborde, G. 1984. *Influencing with Integrity.* Palo Alto, CA: Syntony Publishing.

Lakein, A. 1973. *How to Get Control of Your Time and Your Life.* New York: Signet.

Lambert, M. J., D. A. Shapiro, & A. E. Bergin. 1986. "The Effectiveness of Psychotherapy." In *Handbook of Psychotherapy and Behavior Change,* 3rd ed., eds. S. L. Garfield & A. E. Bergin, pp. 157–211. New York: Wiley.

Landers, S. 1993. "AIDS Deepens Duty-to-Warn Dilemma." *NASW News* (Jan.), p. 3.

Lankton, S. 1980. *Practical Magic.* Cupertino, CA: Meta Publications.

Lazarus, A. A. 1971. *Behavior Therapy and Beyond.* New York: McGraw-Hill.

League of Women Voters. 1972. *Know Your Community.* Washington, DC: Author.

Levitt, J. E. 1974. *The Battered Child.* Morristown, NJ: General Learning Press.

Lecron, L. M. 1964. *Self-Hypnotism.* Englewood Cliffs, NJ: Prentice-Hall.

Lee, C. C. 1999. "Counseling African American Men." In L. E. Davis, ed., *Working with African American Males.* Thousand Oaks, CA: Sage, pp. 39–44.

Leibert, E. R., & B. E. Sheldon. 1972. *Handbook of Special Events for Nonprofit Organizations: Tested Ideas for Fund Raising and Public Relations.* Washington, DC: Taft Corp.

Leiblum, S. R., & R. C. Rosen. 2000. *Principles and Practice of Sex Therapy.* New York: Guilford Press.

Lembo, J. 1974. *Help Yourself.* Niles, IL: Argus Communications.

Leukenfield, C. G., & M. Fimbres, eds. 1987. *Responding to AIDS: Psychosocial Initiatives.* Silver Spring, MD: National Association of Social Workers.

Levitt, E. E. 1957. "The Results of Psychotherapy with Children: An Evaluation." *Journal of Consulting Psychology 21,* pp. 189–196.

Lewin, K., R. Lippitt, & R. K. White. 1939. "Patterns of Aggressive Behavior in Experimentally Created Social Climates." *Journal of Social Psychology 10,* pp. 271–299.

Lewis, R. G., & M. Keung Ho. 1975. "Social Work with Native Americans." *Social Work 20* (Sept.), pp. 378–382.

Leiberman, M. A., E. D. Yalom, & M. B. Miles. 1973. "Encounter: The Leader Makes the Difference." *Psychology Today 6,* pp. 69–76.

Lloyd, G. A. 1995. "HIV/AIDS Overview." In *Encyclopedia of Social Work,* 19th ed., pp. 1257–1290. Washington, DC: NASW Press.

Locklear, H. H. 1972. "American Indian Myths." *Social Work 17* (May), pp. 72–80.

Loewenberg, F. 1988. *Religion and Social Work Practice in Contemporary American Society.* New York: Columbia University Press.

Loewenberg, F., & R. Dolgoff. 1971. *Teaching of Practice Skills in Undergraduate Programs in Social Welfare and Other Helping Services.* New York: Council on Social Work Education.

———. **1988.** *Ethical Decisions for Social Work Practice.* 3rd ed. Itasca, IL: Peacock.

Loewenstein, S. 1980. "Understanding Lesbian Women." *Social Casework 61* (Jan.), p. 31.

Logan, S. 1990. "Black Families; Race Ethnicity, Culture Social Class, and Gender Issues." In *Social Work Practice with Black*

Families, eds. S. Logan, E. Freeman, & R. McRoy. New York: Longman.

London, P. 1964. *The Modes and Morals of Psychotherapy.* New York: Holt, Rinehart & Winston.

LoPiccolo, J., & L. LoPiccolo, eds. 1978. *Handbook of Sex Therapy.* New York: Plenum Press.

Loredo, C. 1982. *Sibling Incest.* Ontario: Penguin Books.

Losoncy, L. 1977. *Turning People On.* Englewood Cliffs, NJ: Prentice-Hall.

Lum, D. 1996. *Social Work Practice & People of Color.* 3rd ed. Pacific Grove, CA: Brooks/Cole.

Luria, A. 1961. *The Role of Speech in the Regulation of Normal and Abnormal Behavior.* New York: Liveright Publishing.

Lynch, V. J., ed. 2000. *HIV/AIDS at Year 2000: A Sourcebook for Social Workers.* Boston: Allyn & Bacon.

Lyon, L. 1987. *The Community in Urban Society.* Philadelphia: Temple University Press.

McGregor, D. 1960. *The Human Side of Enterprise.* New York: McGraw-Hill.

McMahon, F. B. 1971. *The Forty-Eight Item Counseling Evaluation Test; Revised.* Los Angeles: Western Psychological Services.

MacShane, D. 1979. *Using the Media: How to Deal with the Press, Radio, Television.* London: Pluto.

Maddi, S. 1968. *Personality Theories.* Pacific Grove, CA: Brooks/Cole.

Magner, D. K. 1993. "Colleges Faulted for Not Considering Differences in Asian-American Groups." *Chronicle of Higher Education* (Feb. 10), pp. A33–34.

Mahoney, M. J. 1973. "Clinical Issues in Self-Control Training." Paper presented at the meeting of the American Psychological Association, Montreal.

———. **1974.** *Cognition and Behavior Modification.* Cambridge, MA: Ballinger.

Maier, N. R. F. 1970. *Problem Solving and Creativity in Individuals and Groups.* Pacific Grove, CA: Brooks/Cole.

Maluccio, A. 1979. "Perspectives of Social Workers and Clients on Treatment Outcome." *Social Casework 60,* pp. 394–401.

Mandino, O., ed. 1966. *A Treasury of Success Unlimited.* New York: Hawthorn Books.

Manley, M. J. 1977. "How to Cope with a Sense of Failure." In *The Personal Problem Solver,* eds. C. Zastrow & D. Chang. Englewood Cliffs, NJ: Prentice-Hall.

March, J. G. 1956. "Influence Measurement in Experimental and Semi-Experimental Groups." *Sociometry 19,* no. 4 (Dec.), pp. 260–271.

Marshall, W. L., D. Anderson, & Y. Fernandez. 1999. *Cognitive Behavioural Treatment of Sexual Offenders.* Chichester, United Kingdom: Wiley.

Marti-Costa, S., & I. Serrano-Garcia. 1987. "Needs Assessment and Community Development: An Ideological Perspective" In *Strategies of Community Organization: Macro Practice,* eds. F. M. Cox, et al. Itasca, IL: Peacock.

Martinez-Brawley, E., & J. Blundall. 1989. "Farm Families' Preference toward the Personal Social Services." *Social Work 34,* no. 6, pp. 513–522.

Maslach, C. 1976. "Burned-Out." *Human Behavior* 5 (Sept.), pp. 16–22.

———. **1978.** "The Client Role in Staff Burn-Out." *Journal of Social Issues 34,* pp. 11–24.

Maslach, C., & A. Pines. 1977. "The Burn-Out Syndrome in the Day Care Setting." *Child Care Quarterly 6,* pp. 100–113.

Masters, W. H., & V. E. Johnson. 1970. *Human Sexual Inadequacy.* Boston: Little, Brown.

Mauksch, H. O. 1975. "The Organizational Context of Dying." In *Death: The Final Stage of Growth,* ed. E. Kübler-Ross, pp. 7–26. Englewood Cliffs, NJ: Prentice-Hall.

Maultsby, M. C., Jr. 1977. "The ABC's of Better Emotional Self-Control." In *The Personal Problem Solver,* eds. C. Zastrow & D. Chang, pp. 3–18. Englewood Cliffs, NJ: Prentice-Hall.

Mayer, B. S. 1995. "Conflict Resolution." In *Encyclopedia of Social Work,* 19th ed., pp. 613–621. Washington, DC: National Association of Social Workers.

McGregor, D. 1960. *The Human Side of Enterprise.* New York: McGraw-Hill.

McLellan, A. T., L. Luborsky, G. E. Woody, & G. P. O'Brien. 1992. "An Improved Diagnostic Evaluation Instrument for Substance Abuse Patients: The Addiction Severity Index." *Journal of Nervous and Mental Diseases, 168,* pp. 26–33.

McMahon, F. B. 1971. *The Forty-Eight Item Counseling Evaluation Test: Revised.* Los Angeles: Western Psychological Services.

Mead, M. 1935. *Sex and Temperament in Three Primitive Societies.* New York: Morrow.

Meador, B. D., & C. Rogers. 1979. "Person-Centered Therapy." In *Current Psychotherapies,* 2nd ed., ed. R. J. Corsini. Itasca, IL: Peacock.

Mechanic, D. 1962. "Some Factors in Identifying and Defining Mental Illness." *Mental Hygiene 46,* pp. 66–74.

Medina, C., & M. R. Reyes. 1976. "Dilemmas of Chicano Counselors." *Social Work 21* (Nov.), pp. 515–517.

Meichenbaum, D. 1975. "Self-Instructional Methods." In *Helping People Change,* eds. F. H. Kanfer & A. P. Goldstein, pp. 357–392. Elmsford, NY: Pergamon Press.

Meinig, M. B., & B. E. Saunders. 1994. "Offender's Family Contact Rules List." Presented as a handout at the 11th Annual Midwest Conference on Child Sexual Abuse and Incest, Nov. 6–9, 1995, in Madison, WI.

Merkel, W. 1975. "Controlled Research in Transactional Analysis." Unpublished manuscript. Kingston: University of Rhode Island.

Migler, B. 1968. "A Supplementary Note on Automated Self-Desensitization." *Behavioral Research and Therapy 6,* p. 243.

Milgram, S. 1963. "Behavioral Study of Obedience." *Journal of Abnormal and Social Psychology,* pp. 371–378.

Miley, K. 1992. "Religion and Spirituality as Central Social Work Concerns." Paper presented at the Midwest Biennial Conference on Social Work, April 9–10, LaCrosse, WI.

Miller, J. B., & J. P. Stiver. 1993. "A Relational Approach to Understanding Women's Lives and Problems." *Psychiatric Annals 23,* no. 8 (Aug.), pp. 424–431.

Minuchin, S., & H. C. Fishman. 1981. *Family Therapy Techniques.* Cambridge: Harvard University Press.

Mizrahi, T., & B. Rosenthal. 1993. "Managing Dynamic Tensions in Social Change Coalitions." In *Community Organization and Social Administration,* eds. T. Mizrahi & J. D. Morrison, pp. 11–40. New York: Haworth Press.

Money, J. 1986. *Venuses Penises.* Buffalo, NY: Prometheus Books.

Montiel, M. 1973. "The Chicano Family: A Review of Research." *Social Work 18* (March), pp. 22–31.

Moore, C. W. 1986. *The Mediation Process.* San Francisco: Jossey-Bass.

Moreno, J. L. 1946. *Psychodrama: Vol. 1.* Boston: Beacon House.

Morris, R. 1986. "Fear Reduction Methods." In *Helping People Change,* 3rd ed., eds. F. H. Kanfer & A. P. Goldstein, pp. 145–190. Elmsford, NY: Pergamon Press.

Mullen, E. J., & H. L. Mognabosco, eds. 1997. *Outcomes Measurement in the Human Services.* Washington, DC: NASW Press.

National Association of Social Workers. 1973. *Standards for Social Service Manpower.* Washington, DC: Author.

———. **1976.** *Standards for the Regulation of Social Work Practice.* Washington, DC: Author.

———. **1981.** *Classification Processes for Social Service Positions: Parts I–IV.* Washington, DC: Author.

———. **1982.** *Standards for the Classification of Social Work Practice.* Washington, DC: Author.

———. **1996.** *Code of Ethics.* Revised and adopted by the 1996 Delegate Assembly of NASW.

National Welfare Monitoring and Advocacy Partnerships. 2000. *Welfare to What, Part II: Trapped by Welfare to Imprisoned by Poverty.* Washington, DC: National Welfare Monitoring Advocacy Partnerships.

Nelson, A., & W. Wilson. 1984. "The Ethics of Sharing Religious Faith in Psychotherapy." *Journal of Psychology and Theology 12* (1), pp. 15–23.

Netting, F. E., P. M. Kettner, & S. L. McMurtry. 1998. *Social Work Macro Practice.* 2nd ed. New York: Longman.

North, C. S., & E. M. Smith. 1994. "Comparison of White and Nonwhite Homeless Men and Women." *Social Work* 39 (6), pp. 639–647.

Norton, D. G. 1978. "Incorporating Content on Minority Groups into Social Work Practice Courses." In *The Dual Perspective.* New York: Council on Social Work Education.

Nurius, P. S., & W. W. Hudson. 1993a. *Computer Assisted Practice: Theory, Methods, and Software.* Belmont, CA: Wadsworth.

———. **1993.** *Human Services Practice, Evaluation, and Computers.* Pacific Grove, CA: Brooks/Cole.

O'Connor, G. 1972. "Toward a New Policy in Adult Corrections." *Social Service Review 46* (Dec.), pp. 482–493.

Okun, B., & L. Rappaport. 1980. *Working with Families: An Introduction to Family Therapy.* North Scituate, MA: Duxbury Press.

Omachonu, V. K., & J. E. Ross. 1994. *Principles of Total Quality.* Delray Beach, FL: St. Lucie Press.

Orne, M. T., and P. H. Wender. 1968. "Anticipatory Socialization for Psychotherapy: Method and Rationale." *American Journal of Psychiatry 124,* pp. 1202–1212.

Ortiz, L. 1993. "Bibliography: Culture and Spirituality:" Paper presented at the CSWE Annual Program Meeting. New York, Feb.

Osborn, A. F. 1963. *Applied Imagination: Principles and Procedures of Creative Problem Solving.* 3rd ed. New York: Scribner.

Ouchi, W. 1981. *Theory Z: How American Business Can Meet the Japanese Challenge.* Reading, MA: Addison-Wesley.

Page-Adams, D., & M. Sherraden. 1998. "Asset Building as a Community Revitalization Strategy." In P. Ewalt, E. Freeman, & D. L. Poole, eds. *Community Building: Renewal, Well-Being, and Shared Responsibility.* Washington, DC: NASW Press.

Palmer, B., & S. Pablo. 1978. "Community Development Possibilities for Effective Indian Reservation and Child Abuse and Neglect Efforts." In *Child Abuse and Neglect: Issues on Innovation and Implementation,* vol. 1, eds. M. Lauderdale, R. Anderson, & S. Cramer, pp. 111–115. Washington, DC: U.S. Department of Health, Education and Welfare.

Parad, H. J., ed. 1965. *Crisis Intervention: Selected Readings.* New York: Family Service Association of America.

Parsonson, B. S., & D. M. Baer. 1978. "The Analysis and Presentation of Graphic Data. In *Single Subject Research: Strategies for Evaluation Change,* ed. T. R. Kratochwill, pp. 101–165. New York: Academic Press.

Patterson, G. R. 1971. *Families.* Champaign, IL: Research Press Co.

Paul, G. 1966. *Insight versus Desensitization in Psychotherapy.* Stanford: Stanford University Press.

———. **1969.** "Outcome of Systematic Desensitization." In *Behavior Therapy: Appraisal and Status,* pp. 63–159. New York: McGraw-Hill.

Peale, N. V. 1993. *Positive Thinking Everyday.* New York: Fireside.

Pelletier, K. R. 1974. "Altered Attention Deployment in Meditation." In *The Psychobiology of Transcendental Meditation,* eds. D. Kannellakos & J. Lucas. Hunter, NY: Benjamin.

———. **1977.** *Mind as Healer, Mind as Slayer.* New York: Dell.

Pfeiffer, J. W., & J. E. Jones. 1976. "Role Functions in a Group." In *1976 Annual Handbook for Group Facilitators,* by J. W. Pfeiffer & J. E. Jones, pp. 136–138. La Jolla, CA: University Associates.

Pfeiffer, V. 1993. *Positive Thinking.* Rockport, MA: Element Books.

Phares, E. J., & T. J. Trull. 1997. *Clinical Psychology.* 5th ed. Pacific Grove, CA: Brooks/Cole.

Pierce, D. 1993. "Developing a Framework for Social Work Practice with Lesbian Women and Gay Men." Paper presented at CSWE Annual Program Meeting. New York, Feb.

Piers, E. V., & D. B. Harris. 1969. *The Piers-Harris Children's Self-Concept Scale.* Los Angeles: Western Psychological Services.

Pilisuk, M., J. McAllister, & J. Rothman. 1996. "Coming Together for Action: The Challenge of Community Grassroots Organizing." *Journal of Social Issues* 52 (1), pp. 15–37.

Pincus, A., & A. Minahan. 1973. *Social Work Practice: Model and Method.* Itasca, IL: Peacock.

Pinderhughes, E. B. 1979. "Teaching Empathy in Cross Cultural Social Work." *Social Work 24* (July), pp. 312–316.

Pines, A., & E. Aronson. 1981. *Burnout: From Tedium to Personal Growth.* New York: Free Press.

Pope, H. B., & J. I. Hudson. 1992. "Is Childhood Sexual Abuse a Risk Factor for Bulimia Nervosa?" *American Journal of Psychiatry 4,* p. 460.

Posavac, E. J., & R. G. Carey. 1980. *Program Evaluation: Methods and Case Studies.* Englewood Cliffs, NJ: Prentice-Hall.

Powdermaker, H. 1933. *Life in Lesu.* New York: Norton.

Powell, J. 1996. *AIDS and HIV-Related Diseases.* New York: Plenum Press.

Powell, T. J. 1987. *Self-Help Organizations and Professional Practice.* Silver Spring, MD: National Association of Social Workers.

Prochaska, J. O. 1979. *Systems of Psychotherapy.* Pacific Grove, CA: Brooks/Cole.

Proctor, C. D., & V. K. Groze. 1994. "Risk Factors for Suicide Among Gay, Lesbian, and Bisexual Youths." *Social Work* 39 (5), pp. 504–513.

Proctor, E. K., & L. E. Davis. 1994. "The Challenge of Racial Difference; Skills for Clinical Practice." *Social Work* 39 (3), pp. 314–323.

Pruger, R. 1978. "Bureaucratic Functioning as a Social Work Skill." In *Educating the Baccalaureate Social Worker: Report of the Undergraduate Social Work Curriculum Development Project,* by B. L. Baer & R. Federico. Cambridge, MA: Ballinger.

Putnam, R. D. 2000. *Bowling Alone: The Collapse and Revival of American Community.* New York: Simon and Schuster.

Quinsey, V. L., M. L. Lalumiere, M. E. Rice, & G. T. Harris. 1995. "Predicting Sexual Offenses." In *Assessing Dangerousness,* ed. J. C. Campbell. Thousand Oaks, CA: Sage.

Raimy, V. 1977. *Misunderstandings of the Self.* San Francisco: Jossey-Bass.

Rardin, M. 1969. "Treatment of a Phobia by Partial Self-Desensitization." *Journal of Consulting and Clinical Psychology 33,* pp. 125–126.

Ramussen, S. A., & M. T. Tsuang. 1986. *American Journal of Psychiatry 143,* pp. 317–322.

Rauch, J. B. 1989. "Gender as a Factor in Practice" in *Social Work: A Profession of Many Faces,* eds. A. Morales & B. W. Sheafor. Boston: Allyn & Bacon, pp. 340–344.

Reid, W., & L. Epstein. 1972. *Task-Centered Casework.* New York: Columbia University Press.

———. **1977.** *Task-Centered Practice.* New York: Columbia University Press.

Reid, W., & A. Shyne. 1969. *Brief and Extended Casework.* New York: Columbia University Press.

Richmond, M. E. 1917. *Social Diagnosis.* New York: Russell Sage Foundation.

Riessman, F. 1965. "The 'Helper Therapy' Principle." *Journal of Social Work 10,* no. 2 (April), pp. 27–34.

———. **1987.** "Foreword." In *Self-Help Organizations and Professional Practice,* ed. T. J. Powell. Silver Spring, MD: National Association of Social Workers.

Rimm, D., & J. Masters. 1974. *Behavior Therapy.* New York: Academic Press.

Ringer, R. J. 1977. *Looking Out for No. 1.* New York: Fawcett Books.

Ritter, M. 2000. "Virtual Reality Coming Into Vogue as Therapy," in *Wisconsin State Journal,* July 2, pp. 1A & 10A.

Rivera, F. G., & J. L. Erlich. 1992. *Community Organizing in a Diverse Society.* Boston: Allyn & Bacon.

Roberts, S. V. 1994. "Simpson and Sudden Death." *U.S. News & World Report* (June 27), pp. 26–32.

———. **1995.** "Affirmative Action on the Edge." *U.S. News & World Report* (Feb. 13), pp. 32–39.

Roethlisberger, F. J., & W. J. Dickson. 1939. *Management and the Worker.* Cambridge: Harvard University Press.

Roehlkepartain, J., & N. Leffert. 1999. *What Young Children Need to Succeed.* Minneapolis, MN: Search Institute.

Rogers, C. R. 1942. *Counseling and Psychotherapy.* Boston: Houghton Mifflin.

———. **1951.** *Client-Centered Therapy.* Boston: Houghton Mifflin.

———. **1959.** "A Theory of Therapy, Personality, and Interpersonal Relationships as Developed in the Client-Centered Framework." In *Psychology: A Study of a Science,* ed. S. Koch, vol. 3, pp. 184–256. New York: McGraw-Hill.

———. **1965.** Client-Centered Therapy, film no. 1. In *Three Approaches to Psychotherapy,* ed. E. Shostrom. (Three 16mm color motion pictures) Santa Ana, CA: Psychological Films.

———. **1970.** *Carl Rogers on Encounter Groups.* New York: Harper & Row.

———. **1984.** "A Historic Note—Gloria." In *Client-Centered Therapy and the Person-Centered Approach,* pp. 423–425. New York: Praeger.

Romero, D. P. 1977. "Biases in Gender-Role Research." *Social Work 22* (May), pp. 214–218.

Rosenhan, D. 1973. "On Being Sane in Insane Places." *Science 179,* pp. 250–257.

Rosenhan, D. L., & M. E. Seligman. 1995. *Abnormal Psychology.* 3rd ed. New York: Norton.

Rosenthal, S. M. 1999. *Sex Over 40.* New York: Putnam Books.

Rossi, P. H., H. E. Freeman, & S. R. Wright. 1979. *Evaluation: A Systematic Approach.* Newbury Park, CA: Sage.

Rotella, E. J. 1995. "Women and the American Economy." In *Issues in Feminism,* ed. S. Ruth. Mountain View, CA: Mayfield.

Rothman, J. 1979. "Three Models of Community Organization Practice, Their Mixing and Phasing." In *Strategies of Community Organization,* 3rd ed., eds. F. M. Cox, J. L. Erlich, J. Rothman, & J. E. Tropman. Itasca, IL: Peacock.

Rothman, J. 2000. "Collaborative Self-Help Community Development: When Is the Strategy Warranted?" *Journal of Community Practice,* 7 (2), pp. 89–105.

Rothman, J., & J. E. Tropman. 1995. *Strategies of Community Intervention,* 5th ed., Itasca, IL: F. E. Peacock.

Rubin, A., & K. S. Knox. 1996. "Data Analysis Problems in Single-Case Evaluation: Issues for Research on Social Work Practice." In *Research on Social Work Practice, 6,* pp. 40–65.

Rubin, H. J., & I. S. Rubin. 1992. *Community Organizing and Development.* New York: Macmillan.

Ruoss, M. 1970. As quoted in J. C. DeBoer. *Let's Plan: A Guide to the Planning Process for Voluntary Organizations.* Princeton, NJ: Pilgrim Press.

Sager, C. J., T. L. Brayboy, & B. R. Waxenberg. 1970. *Black Ghetto Family in Therapy: A Laboratory Experience.* New York: Grove Press.

Saleeby, D. 1997. *The Strengths of Perspective in Social Work Practice.* 2nd ed. New York: Longman.

Salter, A. C. 1995. *Transforming Trauma.* Thousand Oaks, CA: Sage.

Sandler, J. 1986. "Aversion Methods." In *Helping People Change,* 3rd ed., eds. F. H. Kanfer & A. P. Goldstein, pp. 191–235. Elmsford, NY: Pergamon Press.

Satir, V. 1967. *Conjoint Family Therapy.* Rev. ed. Palo Alto, CA: Science & Behavior Books.

———. **1972.** *Peoplemaking.* Palo Alto, CA: Science & Behavior Books.

Scannapieco, M., & S. Jackson. 1996. "Kinship Care: The African-American Response to Family Preservation." *Social Work 41* (2), pp. 190–194.

Schachter, S. 1959. *The Psychology of Affiliation.* Stanford: Stanford University Press.

Schaefer, R. T. 1993. *Racial & Ethnic Groups.* 5th ed. New York: HarperCollins.

Scheft, I. 1966. *Being Mentally Ill.* Hawthorne, NY: Aldine.

Schernoff, M., ed. 1999. *AIDS and Mental Health Practice.* New York: Haworth Press.

Schiele, J. H. 1996. "Afrocentricity: An Emerging Pardigm in Social Work Practice." *Social Work 41* (May), pp. 284–294.

Schinka, J. A. 1985. *Personal Problems Checklist for Adolescents.* Odessa, FL: Psychological Assessment Resources.

Schlank, A., & F. Cohen. 1999. *The Sexual Predator.* Kingston, NJ: Civic Research Institute.

Schnarch, D. M. 1991. *Constructing the Sexual Crucible.* New York: Norton.

———. **1997.** *Passionate Marriage.* New York: Norton.

Schoech, D. 1999. *Human Services Technology: Understanding, Designing, and Implementing Computer and Internet Applications in the Social Services.* 2nd ed. New York: Haworth Press.

Schoech, R. J. 1990. *Human Service Computing: Concepts and Applications.* New York: Haworth Press.

Schoener, G. R. 2000. "Duty to Warn or Protect," paper presented at Professional At Risk: Ethical Dilemmas Workshop at the University of Wisconsin—Madison, Nov. 13.

Schreiber, F. R. 1973. *Sybil.* New York: Warner Books.

Schwartz, B. K., & H. R. Cellini, eds. 1995. *The Sex Offender.* Kingston, NJ: Civic Research Institute, Inc.

Schwartz, G.1989. "Confidentiality Revisited." *Social Work* (May), pp. 223–226.

Schuller, R., II. 1973. *Move Ahead with Possibility Thinking.* Moonachie, NJ: Pyramid Publications.

Seaward, B. L. 1994. *Managing Stress.* Boston: Jones & Bartlett.

Selye, H. 1956. *The Stress of Life.* New York: McGraw-Hill.

Shaw, R., & D. Kolb. 1974. "One-Point Reaction Time Involving Mediators and Non-Mediators." In *Scientific Research on Transcendental Meditation: Collected Papers,* vol. 1, eds. D. W. Orme-Johnson, L. G. Domash, & J. T. Farrow. Los Angeles: MIU Press.

Sheafor, B. W., C. R. Horejsi, & C. A. Horejsi. 1988. *Techniques and Guidelines for Social Work Practice.* Boston: Allyn & Bacon.

Shelly, M. W. 1973. *Sources of Satisfaction.* Lawrence: University of Kansas Press.

Sherif, M. 1936. *The Psychology of Social Norms.* New York: Harper & Row.

Sherman, H. 1966. "The Surest Way in the World to Attract Success—or Failure." In *A Treasury of Success Unlimited,* ed. O. Mandino, pp. 111–113. New York: Hawthorn Books.

Shernoff, ed. 1999. *AIDS and Mental Health Practice.* New York: Haworth.

Sherraden, M., & M. Sherradan. 2000. "Asset Building: Incorporating Research, Education, and Practice." *Advances in Social Work.* 1(1), pp. 71–77.

Sherwood, D. A. 1981. "Add to Your Faith Virtue: The Integration of Christian Values and Social Work Practice." *Social Work and Christianity* 8 (Spring–Fall), pp. 41–54.

Shimkus, J. R., & J. P. Winship. 1977. *Human Service Development: Working Together in the Community.* Athens: University of Georgia Printing Department.

Shostrom, E. L. 1969. "Group Therapy: Let the Buyer Beware." *Psychology Today 2,* no. 12 (May), pp. 36–40.

Simon, B. K. 1970. "Social Casework Theory: An Overview." In *Theories of Social Casework,* eds. R. Roberts & R. Nee, pp. 353–396. Chicago: University of Chicago Press.

Simos, B. G. 1977. "Grief Therapy to Facilitate Healthy Restitution." *Social Casework* (June), pp. 337–342.

Sinclair, L., & C. Zastrow. 1993. "Human Sexuality Variations, Sex Counseling, and Sex Therapy." In *Introduction to Social Work and Social Welfare,* 5th ed., by C. Zastrow, pp. 193–243. Pacific Grove, CA: Brooks/Cole.

Sindler, A. P. 1978. *Bakke, DeFunis and Minority Admissions: The Quest for Equal Opportunity.* New York: Longmans, Green.

Skinner, B. F. 1938. *The Behavior of Organisms.* New York: Appleton-Century-Crofts.

———. **1948.** *Walden Two.* New York: Macmillan.

———. **1953.** *Science and Human Behavior.* New York: Free Press.

Slater, P. E. 1958. "Contrasting Correlates of Group Size." *Sociometry 21,* no. 2 (June), pp. 129–139.

Sloane, R. B., F. R. Staples, A. H. Cristol, N. J. Yorkston, & K. Whipple. 1975. *Psychotherapy versus Behavior Therapy.* Cambridge: Harvard University Press.

Slonim-Nevo, V., & Y. Anson. 1998. "Evaluating Practice: Does it Improve Treatment Outcome?" *Social Work Research, 22,* pp. 66–74.

Smith, L. L. 1978. "A Review of Crisis Intervention Theory." *Social Casework* 59, no. 7 (July), pp. 396–405.

Solomon, B. 1987. "Human Development: Socio-cultural Perspectives." In *The Encyclopedia of Social Work,* pp. 856–866. Silver Spring, MD: National Association of Social Workers.

Solomon, P., P. Kubzansky, P. Leiderman, J. Menderson, R. Trumbull, & D. Wexler, eds. 1961. *Sensory Deprivation.* Cambridge: Harvard University Press.

"Special Issue on Conceptual Frameworks." 1977. *Social Work* 22 (Sept.), pp. 338–444.

Spitz, R. 1945. "Hospitalism: Genesis of Psychiatric Conditions in Early Childhood." *Psychoanalytic Study of the Child 1,* p. 53.

Spock, B. 1957. *The Common-Sense Book of Baby and Child Care.* New York: Duell, Sloan & Pierce.

Spranger, E. 1928. *Types of Men.* New York: Hafner.

Stampfl, T. G., & D. J. Levis. 1967. "Essentials of Implosive Therapy: A Learning-Based Psychodynamic Behavioral Therapy." *Journal of Abnormal Psychology 72,* pp. 496–503.

Starkweather, C. L., & S. M. Turner. 1975. "Parents Anonymous: Reflections on the Development of a Self-Help Group." In *Child Abuse Interventions and Treatment,* eds. N. C. Ebeling & D. A. Hill. Littleton, MA: PSG.

Steiner, C. 1974. *Scripts People Live.* New York: Grove Press.

Stephenson, M. M. 1983. "The Talking Circle: A Resource for Personal and Community Development." Paper presented at the Eighth Annual Institute on Social Work in Rural Areas, July, Cheney, WA.

Stine, G. J. 1996. *Acquired Immune Deficiency Syndrome.* Englewood Cliffs, NJ: Prentice-Hall.

Stine, G. J. 2000. *AIDS Update 2000,* Upper Saddle River, NJ: Prentice-Hall.

Stone, W. C. 1966. "Be Generous." In *A Treasury of Success Unlimited,* ed. O. Mandino, pp. 9–10. New York: Hawthorn Books.

Strachey, J. 1962. *Sigmund Freud: Three Essays on the Theory of Sexuality.* New York: Basic Books.

Stroup, H. 1986. *Social Welfare Pioneers.* Chicago: Nelson-Hall.

Stuart, R. B. 1970. *Trick or Treatment.* Champaign, IL: Research Press Co.

Suinn, R. M. 1976. "Body Thinking: Psychology for Olympic Champs." *Psychology Today 10* (July), pp. 38–43.

Sullivan, T., K. Thompson, R. Wright, G. Gross, & D. Spady. 1980. *Social Problems.* New York: Wiley.

Sundberg, N. D., & L. E. Tyler. 1962. *Clinical Psychology.* New York: Appleton-Century-Crofts.

Sundel, M., & S. S. Sundel. 1975. *Behavior Modification in the Human Services.* New York: Wiley.

Suppes, M. A., & C. Wells. 2000. *The Social Work Experience, an Introduction to Social Work and Social Welfare.* 3rd ed. New York: McGraw-Hill.

Szasz, T. 1961. "The Myth of Mental Illness." In *Clinical Psychology in Transition,* comp. J. R. Braun. Cleveland: Howard Allen.

———. **1963.** *Law, Liberty and Psychiatry.* New York: Macmillan.

———. **1967.** "The Psychiatrist as Double Agent." *Trans-Action 4,* pp. 3–25.

Taylor, F. W. 1947. *Scientific Management.* New York: Harper & Row.

Teuber, H. L., & E. Powers. 1953. "Evaluating Therapy in a Delinquency Prevention Program." *Psychiatric Treatment 21,* pp. 138–147.

Thomas, A., & S. Sillen. 1972. *Racism and Psychiatry.* New York: Brunner/Mazel.

Thomas, E. J. 1978. "Research and Service in Single-Case Experimentation: Conflicts and Choices." *Social Work Research and Abstracts 14,* pp. 20–31.

———. **1984.** *Designing Interventions for the Helping Professions.* New York: Sage.

Thomas, S. A. 1977. "Theory and Practice in Feminine Therapy." *Social Work* 22 (Nov.), pp. 447–454.

Thompson, G. 1972. "The Identification of Ego States." *Transactional Analysis Journal* 2, pp. 196–211.

Thorndike, E. L. 1913. *The Psychology of Learning.* New York: Teachers College Press.

Thorpe, L. P., & B. Katz. 1948. *The Psychology of Abnormal Behavior.* New York: Ronald Press.

Toch, H. 1970. "The Care and Feeding of Typologies and Labels." *Federal Probation 34* (Sept.), pp. 46–57.

Tolman, E. C. 1932. *Purposive Behavior in Animals and Men.* New York: Appleton-Century-Crofts.

Touliatos, J., B. F. Perlmutter, & M. A. Straus, eds. 1990. *Handbook of Family Measurement Techniques.* Newbury Park, CA: Sage.

Trabin, T. 1996. *The Computerization of Behavioral Healthcare.* San Francisco: Jossey-Bass.

Trattner, W. I. 1989. *From Poor Law to Welfare State: A History of Social Welfare in America.* 4th ed. New York: Free Press.

Tripodi, T. 1994. *A Primer on Single-Subject Design for Clinical Social Workers.* Washington, DC: NASW Press.

Truax, C. 1966. "Reinforcement and Non-reinforcement in Rogerian Psychotherapy." *Journal of Abnormal Psychology 71,* pp. 11–19.

Truax, C., & K. M. Mitchell. 1971. "Research on Certain Therapists' Interpersonal Skills in Relation to Process and Outcome." In *Handbook of Psychotherapy and Behavior Change,* eds. A. E. Bergin & S. L. Garfield, pp. 299–344. New York: Wiley.

Tubbs, S. I., & J. W. Baird. 1976. *The Open Person.* Columbus, OH: Merrill.

Tuckman, B. 1965. "Developmental Sequence in Small Groups." *Psychological Bulletin 63,* pp. 384–399.

Turner, C., H. Miller, & L. Moses, eds. 1989. *AIDS: Sexual Behavior and Intravenous Drug Use.* Washington, DC: The National Academy Press.

Turner, J. B. 1972. "Education for Practice with Minorities." *Social Work 17* (May), pp. 112–118.

Tye, L. 1992. "Study: U.S. Retreats on Integration." *Wisconsin State Journal.* January 12, pp. 1A, 8A–9A.

U.S. Bureau of the Census. 2000. *Statistical Abstract of the United States, 2000.* Washington DC: U.S. Government Printing Office.

U.S. Bureau of Justice Statistics. 1994. "Child Rape Victims, 1992." In *Crime Data Brief,* by P. A. Langan & C. W. Harlow, BJS Statisticians, U.S. Department of Justice, June, Washington DC: Office of Justice Programs.

———. **1997.** "Sex Offenses and Offenders: An Analysis of Data on Rape and Sexual Assault," by L. A. Greenfeld, Statistician, U.S. Department of Justice, February, Washington DC: Office of Justice Programs.

***University of Pittsburgh Law Review.* 1975.** "Tarasoff v. Regents of University of California: *The Psychotherapist's Peril*" 37, pp. 159–164.

Van De Ven, A., & A. L. Delbecq. 1971. "Nominal versus Interacting Group Processes for Committee Decision-Making Effectiveness." *Academy of Management Journal 14,* no. 2 (June), pp. 203–212.

Van Den Bergh, N. 1992. "Feminist Treatment for People with Depression." In *Structuring Change,* ed. K. Corcoran, pp. 95–110. Chicago: Lyceum Books.

———. **1995.** *Feminist Practice in the 21st Century.* Washington, DC: NASW Press.

Van Den Bergh, N., & L. B. Cooper. 1987. "Feminist Social Work." In *The Encyclopedia of Social Work,* pp. 610–618. Washington, DC: National Association of Social Workers.

Vogler, R. E., S. E. Lunde, G. R. Johnson, & P. L. Martin. 1970. "Electrical Aversion Conditioning with Chronic Alcoholics." *Journal of Consulting and Clinical Psychology 34,* pp. 302–307.

Vygotsky, L. 1962. *Thoughts and Language.* Cambridge, MA: MIT Press.

Walker, R. 1996. *The Family Guide to Sex and Relationships.* New York: Macmillan.

Wallace, R. K. 1973. "Physiological Effects of Transcendental Meditation." *Science 167,* pp. 1751–1754.

Walz, T. H., & N. Blum. 1987. *Sexual Health in Later Life.* Lexington, MA: Lexington Books.

Ward, D. E. 1999. *The AmFAR Complete Guide to Understanding HIV and AIDS.* New York: Norton.

Ware, J. E., & C. D. Sherbourne. 1992. "The MOS 36-Item Short-Form Health Survey (SF-36)." *Medical Care 30,* pp. 473–483.

Watkins, T. R., & R. Gonzales. 1982. "Outreach to Mexican-Americans." *Social Work 27,* no. 1 (Jan.), pp. 68–73.

Watson, D. L., & R. G. Tharp. 1972. *Self-Directed Behavior: Self-Modification for Personal Adjustment.* Pacific Grove, CA: Brooks/Cole.

Watson, J. B., & R. Rayner. 1920. "Conditioned Emotional Reaction." *Journal of Experimental Psychology 3,* no. 1, pp. 1–14.

Watson, T. 1997. "Fighting AIDS the Morning After." *U.S. News & World Report,* April 21, p. 52.

Weick, A., C. Rapp, W. P. Sullivan, & W. Kisthardt. 1989. "A Strengths Perspective for Social Work Practice." *Social Work 34,* pp. 350–354.

Weil, M., & D. N. Gamble. 1995. "Community Practice Models." In *Encyclopedia of Social Work,* 19th ed., Vol. 1, pp. 577–594. Washington, DC: NASW Press.

Weinger, S. 2001. *Security Risk: Preventing Violence Against Social Workers,* Washington, DC: NASW Press.

Weiss, C. H. 1972. *Evaluation Research.* Englewood Cliffs, NJ: Prentice-Hall.

Wells, C. 1998. *Stepping to the Dance, the Training of a Family Therapist.* Pacific Grove, CA: Brooks/Cole.

Wender, P., & D. Klein. 1968. *Mind, Mood and Medicine.* New York: Meridian.

White, B., & E. J. Madara. 1998. *The Self-Help Sourcebook,* 6th ed. Denville, NJ: American Self-Help Clearinghouse.

White, M., & D. Epstein. 1990. *Narrative Means to Therapeutic Ends.* New York: Norton.

White, R. W., & N. F. Watt. 1973. *The Abnormal Personality.* 4th ed. New York: Ronald Press.

Whitman, D., & D. Friedman. 1992. "Busing's Unheralded Legacy." *U.S. News & World Report,* April 13, pp. 63–65.

Whittaker, J. K. 1974. *Social Treatment.* Hawthorne, NY: Aldine.

Wigmore, J. H. 1961. *Evidence in Trials at Common Law,* vol. 8 (rev.), ed. J. T. McNaughton. Boston: Little, Brown.

Wilensky, H., & C. Lebeaux. 1965. *Industrial Society & Social Welfare.* New York: Free Press.

Williams, D. A., T. Jackson, D. Weathers, N. Joseph, & M. Anderson. 1975. "Roots III: Souls on Ice: A Post-Civil Rights Generation Struggle for Identity." *Newsweek,* pp. 82–84.

Williams, E. E., & F. Ellison. 1996. "Culturally Informed Social Work Practice with American Indian Clients: Guidelines for Non-Indian Social Workers." *Social Work 41* (2), pp. 147–151.

Wilson, S. J. 1978. *Confidentiality in Social Work: Issues and Principles.* New York: Free Press.

Wilson, T. G. 1989. "Behavior Therapy." In *Current Psychotherapies,* 4th ed., eds. R. J. Corsini & D. Wedding, pp. 241–282. Itasca, IL: Peacock.

Wilson, W. J. 1996. *When Work Disappears: The World of the New American Poor.* New York: Knopf.

Winks, C., & A. Semans. 1997. *The New Good Vibrations Guide to Sex.* San Francisco: Cleis Press.

Wiseman, R. S. 1975. "Crisis Theory and the Process of Divorce." *Social Casework 56,* no. 4 (April), pp. 205–212.

Wolpe, J. 1958. *Psychotherapy by Reciprocal Inhibition.* Stanford, CA: Stanford University Press.

———. **1969.** *The Practice of Behavior Therapy.* Elmsford, NY: Pergamon Press.

Woodman, N. J. 1987. "Homosexuality: Lesbian Women." In *The Encyclopedia of Social Work,* pp. 805–812. Silver Spring, MD: National Association of Social Workers.

Wright, B. J., & V. R. Isenstein. 1975. *Psychological Tests and Minorities.* Rockville, MD: National Institute of Mental Health.

Yochelson, S., & S. E. Samenow. 1977. *The Criminal Personality,* vols. I & II. Dunmore, PA: Jason Aronson, Inc.

Zastrow, C. 1973. "The Nominal Group: A New Approach to Designing Programs for Curbing Delinquency." *Canadian Journal of Criminology and Corrections* (Jan.), pp. 109–117.

———. **1979.** *Talk to Yourself: Using the Power of Self-Talk.* Englewood Cliffs, NJ: Prentice-Hall.

———. **1990a.** "Social Workers and Salesworkers: Similarities and Differences." *Journal of Independent Social Work 4,* no. 3, pp. 7–16.

———. **1990b.** "Starting and Leading Therapy Groups: A Beginner's Guide." *Journal of Independent Social Work 4,* no. 4, pp. 7–26.

———. **1993.** *You Are What You Think: A Guide to Self-Realization.* Chicago: Nelson-Hall.

———. **2001.** *Social Work with Groups,* 5th ed. Pacific Grove, CA: Brooks/Cole.

Zastrow, C., & D. Chang, eds. 1977. *The Personal Problem Solver.* Englewood Cliffs, NJ: Prentice-Hall.

Zastrow, C., & R. Navarre. 1977. "The Nominal Group: A New Tool for Making Social Work Education Relevant." *Journal of Education for Social Work 13* (Winter), pp. 112–118.

———. **1979.** "Using Videotaped Role Playing to Assess and Develop Competence." In *The Pursuit of Competence in Social Work,* eds. F. Clark & M. Arkava, pp. 193–204. San Francisco: Jossey-Bass.

Zastrow, C., V. Dotson, & M. Koch. 1986. "The Neuro-Linguistic Programming Treatment Approach." *Journal of Independent Social Work 1* (Fall), pp. 29–38.

Zauner, P. 1974. "Mothers Anonymous: The Last Resort." In *The Battered Child,* ed. J. E. Leavitt. Morristown, NJ: General Learning Press.

Zilbergeld, B. 1999. *The New Male Sexuality,* 2nd ed. New York: Bantam Press.

Zuckerman, M. B. 1995. "Fixing Affirmative Action." *U.S. News & World Report,* March 20, p. 112.

INDEX

C R E D I T S

This page constitutes an extension of the copyright page. We have made every effort to trace the ownership of all copyrighted material and to secure permission from copyright holders. In the event of any question arising as to the use of any material, we will be pleased to make the necessary corrections in future printings. Thanks are due to the following authors, publishers, and agents for permission to use the material indicated.

Chapter 1: page 2 © Michael Newman/PhotoEdit
Chapter 2: page 33 © Robert Brenner/PhotoEdit
Chapter 3: page 58 © Spencer Grant/PhotoEdit
Chapter 4: page 82 © Gale Zucker/Stock, Boston
Chapter 5: page 94 © Rhoda Sidney/PhotoEdit
Chapter 6: page 116 © Mary Kate Denny/PhotoEdit
Chapter 7: page 143 © Michael Newman/PhotoEdit
Chapter 8: page 174 © Tony Freeman/PhotoEdit
Chapter 9: page 211 © Davis Barber/PhotoEdit
Chapter 10: page 226 © Joseph Sohm/CORBIS
Chapter 11: page 253 © Michael Newman/PhotoEdit
Chapter 12: page 275 © Bob Daemmrich/The Image Works
Chapter 13: page 309 © Dean Conger/CORBIS
Chapter 14: page 323 © Kevin Fleming/CORBIS

TO THE OWNER OF THIS BOOK:

We hope that you have found *Practice of Social Work, Seventh Edition* useful. So that this book can be improved in a future edition, would you take the time to complete this sheet and return it? Thank you.

School and address: ____

Department: ____

Instructor's name: ____

1. What I like most about this book is: ______________________________

____

____

2. What I like least about this book is: ______________________________

____

____

3. My general reaction to this book is: ______________________________

____

4. The name of the course in which I used this book is: ____________________

____

5. Were all of the chapters of the book assigned for you to read? ______________

If not, which ones weren't? ______________________________

6. In the space below, or on a separate sheet of paper, please write specific suggestions for improving this book and anything else you'd care to share about your experience in using the book.

____

____

____

____

____

Optional:

Your name:_____________________________ Date:____________________

May Brooks/Cole quote you, either in promotion for *The Practice of Social Work, 7th Edition,* or in future publishing ventures?

Yes: ___________ No:___________

Sincerely,

Charles Zastrow

FOLD HERE

NO POSTAGE NECESSARY IF MAILED IN THE UNITED STATES

BUSINESS REPLY MAIL

FIRST CLASS PERMIT NO. 358 PACIFIC GROVE, CA

POSTAGE WILL BE PAID BY ADDRESSEE

ATT: *Charles Zastrow*

Brooks/Cole-Thomson Learning
511 Forest Lodge Road
Pacific Grove, CA 93950-9968

FOLD HERE

Attention Professors:
Brooks/Cole is dedicated to publishing quality publications for education in the social work, counseling, and human services fields. If you are interested in learning more about our publications, please fill in your name and address and request our latest catalogue, using this prepaid mailer. Please choose one of the following:

☐ social work ☐ counseling ☐ human services

Name: ______________________________

Street Address: ______________________________

City, State, and Zip: ______________________________

FOLD HERE

NO POSTAGE
NECESSARY
IF MAILED
IN THE
UNITED STATES

BUSINESS REPLY MAIL
FIRST CLASS PERMIT NO. 358 PACIFIC GROVE, CA

POSTAGE WILL BE PAID BY ADDRESSEE

ATT: *Marketing*

The Wadsworth Group
10 Davis Drive
Belmont, CA 94002

FOLD HERE

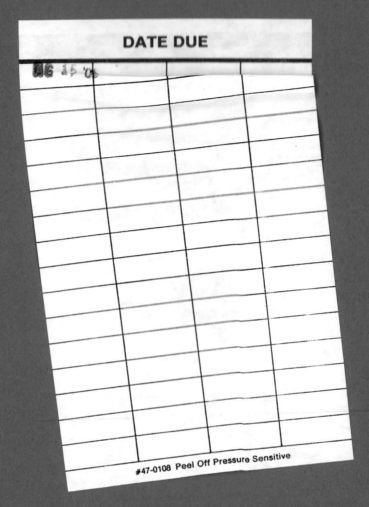